International Directory of
COMPANY
HISTORIES

International Directory of
COMPANY
HISTORIES

VOLUME 40

Editor
Jay P. Pederson

ST. JAMES PRESS

AN IMPRINT OF THE GALE GROUP

DETROIT • NEW YORK • SAN FRANCISCO
LONDON • BOSTON • WOODBRIDGE, CT

STAFF

Jay P. Pederson, *Editor*

Miranda H. Ferrara, *Project Manager*

Erin Bealmear, Christa Brelin, Joann Cerrito, Steve Cusack,
Kristin Hart, Melissa Hill, Margaret Mazurkiewicz, Carol Schwartz,
Christine Tomassini, Michael J. Tyrkus, *St. James Press Editorial Staff*

Peter M. Gareffa, *Managing Editor, St. James Press*

Library of Congress Catalog Number: 89-190943

British Library Cataloguing in Publication Data

International directory of company histories. Vol. 40
I. Jay P. Pederson
338.7409

ISBN 1-55862-445-7

Printed in the United States of America
Published simultaneously in the United Kingdom

St. James Press is an imprint of The Gale Group

Cover photograph: Minneapolis Grain Exchange
(courtesy: Minneapolis Grain Exchange)

10 9 8 7 6 5 4 3 2 1

CONTENTS

Company Histories

PREFACE _____

The St. James Press series *The International Directory of Company Histories (IDCH)* is intended for reference use by students, business people, librarians, historians, economists, investors, job candidates, and others who seek to learn more about the historical development of the world's most important companies. To date, *IDCH* has covered over 5,050 companies in 40 volumes.

Inclusion Criteria

Most companies chosen for inclusion in *IDCH* have achieved a minimum of US$25 million in annual sales and are leading influences in their industries or geographical locations. Companies may be publicly held, private, or nonprofit. State-owned companies that are important in their industries and that may operate much like public or private companies also are included. Wholly owned subsidiaries and divisions are profiled if they meet the requirements for inclusion. Entries on companies that have had major changes since they were last profiled may be selected for updating.

The *IDCH* series highlights 10% private and nonprofit companies, and features updated entries on approximately 45 companies per volume.

Entry Format

Each entry begins with the company's legal name, the address of its headquarters, its telephone, toll-free, and fax numbers, and its web site. A statement of public, private, state, or parent ownership follows. A company with a legal name in both English and the language of its headquarters country is listed by the English name, with the native-language name in parentheses.

The company's founding or earliest incorporation date, the number of employees, and the most recent available sales figures follow. Sales figures are given in local currencies with equivalents in U.S. dollars. For some private companies, sales figures are estimates and indicated by the abbreviation *est.* The entry lists the exchanges on which a company's stock is traded and its ticker symbol, as well as the company's NAIC codes.

Entries generally contain a *Company Perspectives* box which provides a short summary of the company's mission, goals, and ideals, a *Key Dates* box highlighting milestones in the company's history, lists of *Principal Subsidiaries, Principal Divisions, Principal Operating Units, Principal Competitors,* and articles for *Further Reading.*

American spelling is used throughout *IDCH*, and the word "billion" is used in its U.S. sense of one thousand million.

Sources

Entries have been compiled from publicly accessible sources both in print and on the Internet such as general and academic periodicals, books, annual reports, and material supplied by the companies themselves.

Cumulative Indexes

IDCH contains three indexes: the **Index to Companies**, which provides an alphabetical index to companies discussed in the text as well as to companies profiled, the **Index to Industries**, which allows researchers to locate companies by their principal industry, and the **Geographic Index**, which lists companies alphabetically by the country of their headquarters. The indexes are cumulative and specific instructions for using them are found immediately preceding each index.

Suggestions Welcome

Comments and suggestions from users of *IDCH* on any aspect of the product as well as suggestions for companies to be included or updated are cordially invited. Please write:

The Editor
International Directory of Company Histories
St. James Press
27500 Drake Rd.
Farmington Hills, Michigan 48331-3535

A.D.	Aktiebolaget (Sweden)
A.G.	Aktiengesellschaft (Germany, Switzerland)
A.S.	Aksjeselskap (Denmark, Norway)
A.S.	Atieselskab (Denmark)
A.Ş.	Anomin Şirket (Turkey)
B.V.	Besloten Vennootschap met beperkte, Aansprakelijkheid (The Netherlands)
Co.	Company (United Kingdom, United States)
Corp.	Corporation (United States)
G.I.E.	Groupement d'Intérêt Economique (France)
GmbH	Gesellschaft mit beschränkter Haftung (Germany)
H.B.	Handelsbolaget (Sweden)
Inc.	Incorporated (United States)
KGaA	Kommanditgesellschaft auf Aktien (Germany)
K.K.	Kabushiki Kaisha (Japan)
LLC	Limited Liability Company (Middle East)
Ltd.	Limited (Canada, Japan, United Kingdom, United States)
N.V.	Naamloze Vennootschap (The Netherlands)
OY	Osakeyhtiöt (Finland)
PLC	Public Limited Company (United Kingdom)
PTY.	Proprietary (Australia, Hong Kong, South Africa)
S.A.	Société Anonyme (Belgium, France, Switzerland)
SpA	Società per Azioni (Italy)

ABBREVIATIONS FOR CURRENCY _____

$	United States dollar	KD	Kuwaiti dinar
£	United Kingdom pound	L	Italian lira
¥	Japanese yen	LuxFr	Luxembourgian franc
A$	Australian dollar	M$	Malaysian ringgit
AED	United Arab Emirates dirham	N	Nigerian naira
		Nfl	Netherlands florin
B	Thai baht	NKr	Norwegian krone
B	Venezuelan bolivar	NT$	Taiwanese dollar
BFr	Belgian franc	NZ$	New Zealand dollar
C$	Canadian dollar	P	Philippine peso
CHF	Switzerland franc	PLN	Polish zloty
COL	Colombian peso	Pta	Spanish peseta
Cr	Brazilian cruzado	R	Brazilian real
CZK	Czech Republic koruny	R	South African rand
DA	Algerian dinar	RMB	Chinese renminbi
Dfl	Netherlands florin	RO	Omani rial
DKr	Danish krone	Rp	Indonesian rupiah
DM	German mark	Rs	Indian rupee
E£	Egyptian pound	Ru	Russian ruble
Esc	Portuguese escudo	S$	Singapore dollar
EUR	Euro dollars	Sch	Austrian schilling
FFr	French franc	SFr	Swiss franc
Fmk	Finnish markka	SKr	Swedish krona
HK$	Hong Kong dollar	SRls	Saudi Arabian riyal
HUF	Hungarian forint	W	Korean won
IR£	Irish pound	W	South Korean won
K	Zambian kwacha		

International Directory of

COMPANY
HISTORIES

A.O. Smith Corporation

11270 West Park Place
P.O. Box 245008
Milwaukee, Wisconsin 53224-9508
U.S.A.
Telephone: (414) 359-4000
Fax: (414) 359-4064
Web site: http://www.aosmith.com

Public Company
Incorporated: 1904 as A.O. Smith Company
Employees: 13,800
Sales: $1.21 billion (2000)
Stock Exchanges: New York
Ticker Symbol: AOS
NAIC: 333319 Other Commercial and Service Industry
    Machinery Manufacturing; 335228 Other Major
    Household Appliance Manufacturing; 335312 Motor
    and Generator Manufacturing; 333996 Fluid Power
    Pump and Motor Manufacturing

A.O. Smith Corporation is a manufacturer specializing in electric motors, water heaters, and boilers. The company's Electrical Products unit accounts for more than two-thirds of revenues and makes motors for air conditioners, refrigerators, furnaces, garage door openers, and pumps used in home water systems, swimming pools, and hot tubs. The remaining sales are generated by the Water Products unit, which makes both residential and commercial water heaters, as well as large-volume copper-tube boilers. Over its long history, A.O. Smith has evolved from a small bicycle parts factory to a specialized manufacturer of motors and water heating products. For a long period the company was a much more diversified manufacturer, with such additional product lines as automotive structural components, fiberglass piping systems, livestock feed storage systems, and storage tanks. Most of these businesses were divested in the late 20th century.

Early Decades: From Baby Carriage Parts to Auto Frames

Although A.O. Smith was founded in 1904, the company traces its history back to the mid-19th century, when Charles Jeremiah (C. J.) Smith emigrated from England to the United States. The journeyman metal tradesman ventured all the way to Milwaukee, Wisconsin, and, after being self-employed for a decade, went to work for the Milwaukee Railroad Shop. As a highly skilled workman, he made a good living, but went back into business for himself in 1874, when he opened a machine shop and began manufacturing baby carriage parts. Two of Smith's four sons, Charles S. and George H., joined the family firm in the mid-1880s.

As bicycles became popular in the last decade of the century, C.J. Smith and Sons branched out. By 1895, it was the largest manufacturer of steel bicycle parts in the United States. The patriarch called in his eldest son, Arthur O. (A. O.), an architectural engineer specializing in large buildings, to help build a five-story factory for the growing family business. After two years of close work with his father, A.O. decided to join the company permanently as treasurer. By then, C.J. Smith and Sons had declared itself the largest manufacturer of component bicycle parts in the world.

Increasing overcapacity in that industry and the advent of the automobile brought another change to C.J. Smith and Sons. In 1899 the family sold its business to the Federal Bicycle Corporation of America, a then-legal monopoly known as the "Bicycle Trust." A.O. retained management of the Milwaukee (or "Smith Parts") Branch of the Trust. Arthur Smith indulged his personal interest in the composition and manufacture of automobile frames with two years of "tinkering" that culminated in the sale of his first automotive frame to the Peerless Motor Car Co. in 1902. Word of his frame, which was lighter, stronger, more flexible, and cheaper than conventional ones, spread quickly: by the following year, Smith had contracts with six major automobile manufacturers.

A.O. Smith quit Federal in 1903, bought the Smith Parts Co. from his former employer, and incorporated it as A.O. Smith

Company in 1904. The company's sales totaled $375,733 and profits topped $100,000 that first year. Unfortunately, patriarch C.J. Smith also passed away in 1904.

In April 1906, Henry Ford contracted with A.O. Smith for frames. At the time, the company was producing only ten pressed steel frames a day. Ford needed 10,000 frames in four months, a tenfold increase in the prevailing production rate. Realizing that adding workers and space would only consume valuable time in training and construction, Smith looked for ways to increase efficiency through technological improvements. He and his team of engineers retooled existing presses to produce two corresponding halves of an auto frame simultaneously and arranged the presses to form a continuous assembly line. The delivery of 10,000 A.O. Smith frames that August helped Ford introduce his popularly priced Model N late in 1906 and attracted more automobile manufacturers to the supplier. Because A.O. Smith soon found itself turning away business, it built a new, larger headquarters on 135 acres on the outskirts of Milwaukee to accommodate demand. By the end of the decade, A.O. Smith was manufacturing 110,000 frames per year, over 60 percent of the auto industry's requirements.

Three years later, when A.O. Smith died, his son Lloyd Raymond (Ray) was made president. Ray's was not just a dynastic leadership, however. Both A.O. and L.R. Smith were later inducted into the Automotive Hall of Fame and the Wisconsin Business Hall of Fame. The 23-year-old former company secretary had previously proposed manufacturing improvements that multiplied A.O. Smith's production rate seven times: by 1916, the company was manufacturing 800,000 frames per year—half the auto industry's needs. Called "decisive, restless and a profound thinker" by corporate historians, Ray Smith also propelled the family company into new ventures. Smith bought a license to manufacture "The Motor Wheel," a small gas engine that could be attached to a bicycle's rear wheel to make a "motorbike." The company sold 25,000 of the vehicles nationwide from 1914 to 1919, and even applied the technology to a small wooden "sports car" called the Smith Flyer.

L.R. Smith's reluctance to pay for the marketing support necessary to maintain such products' popularity, combined with the fact that the United States was thoroughly embroiled in World War I, brought diversification to a halt in 1919. A.O. Smith manufactured hollow-steel artillery vehicle poles and bomb casings for the war effort. By war's end, the company was producing 6,500 bomb casings per day, thanks to a welding breakthrough that produced stronger bonds in less time.

1920s: The Mechanical Marvel

Throughout the war years, a team of Smith's best engineers formulated a revolutionary plan to automate the company's frame production process. Although expensive—construction consumed $6 million by 1920—the "Mechanical Marvel" they created produced 7,200 frames on two 180-man shifts per day. The machines performed 552 separate functions, including forming, trimming, and riveting. It took A.O. Smith 15 years to recoup its investment in the Mechanical Marvel (which was designated a National Historic Mechanical Engineering Landmark in 1979), but the plant ran practically without stop until 1958.

The Mechanical Marvel marked only the beginning of an enterprising decade, during which the company's 500-person engineering department developed new applications for the welding process formulated during World War I. A welded coupling designed to link seamless steel casings for oil drilling rigs soon became a petroleum industry standard. High pressure tanks for gasoline refineries developed by A.O. Smith could withstand three times the pressure of customary tanks. Engineers also modified those tanks for use in the paper, chemical refining, and other industries by adding an anticorrosive, stainless steel liner to the tanks. During the 1920s, A.O. Smith also originated the large-diameter, high-pressure pipe that launched the natural gas transmission industry and made natural gas a viable alternative to coal and oil. The company captured every order for large diameter pipe in the country. As the authority in this industry, Smith had to send its own employees out to weld pipeline installations around the world.

A.O. Smith was thus well positioned when the stock market crash of October 1929 ushered in the Great Depression. It had a two-year backlog of pipe orders and a dominant position in its other markets. As auto sales fell from 4.4 million in 1929 to less than two million in 1931, however, the company was forced to cut employment by 10 percent at its main plant. In 1930, sales plummeted from $57 million to $9 million and the company suffered an operating loss of $5 million the following year. L.R. brought in an outsider, William C. Heath, to play "bad cop." Heath cut executive salaries by 50 percent and reduced the operating staff by one-fourth, but even these measures did not bring the company into the black. In May 1932, 3,000 employees—almost half the total company's payroll—were laid off. Corporate historians noted that "Demand for frames was so low, supervisors painted them by hand to save the expense of starting the automatic equipment."

Mid-Century Diversification

A.O. Smith's "savior" came from a highly unlikely source—the December 1933 repeal of Prohibition. The end of that "noble experiment" brought America's brewing capital, Milwaukee, back to life, and A.O. Smith utilized its technical creativity to profit from the rebirth. The company quickly introduced a steel beer barrel with a special liner that protected the beer from metallic migration. The new keg's quick acceptance enabled A.O. Smith to recall 450 laid-off workers. The company also developed an innovative process to fuse glass to the

Key Dates:

1874: Charles Jeremiah Smith opens a machine shop in Milwaukee to make baby carriage parts.
1895: C.J. Smith and Sons is the largest maker of steel bicycle parts in the United States.
1899: Company is sold to Federal Bicycle Corporation and operates as the Smith Parts branch.
1902: Arthur O. Smith, son of C.J., sells his first automotive frame.
1904: A.O. Smith buys Smith Parts and incorporates it as A.O. Smith Company.
1910: Company has grown to become the largest auto frame maker in North America.
1921: Company's frame production process is automated through the construction of the Mechanical Marvel.
1936: A.O. Smith develops an affordable, durable, glass-lined water heater.
1940: Company diversifies into electric motors through the purchase of Sawyer Electrical Manufacturing Company.
1949: Harvestore glass-lined silos are introduced.
1959: A.O. Smith establishes glass fiber division, which begins making fiberglass pipe and fittings.
1972: Water heater division begins its first European operation in the Netherlands.
1986: Small motor division of Westinghouse is acquired.
1997: UPPCO, Incorporated, maker of electric motors, is acquired; automotive products business is sold to Tower Automotive Inc.
1998: A.O. Smith acquires the domestic compressor motor business of General Electric Company.
1999: The fractional horsepower motors business of MagneTek, Inc. is acquired.
2000: Fiberglass pipe business is sold to Varco International Inc.
2001: Company sells its storage tank unit to CST Industries, Inc. A.O. Smith now concentrates solely on electric motors and water heaters.

interior of 35,000 gallon tanks that resulted in the superior cleanliness demanded by the brewing industry.

Ray Smith left day-to-day management of the company to Heath after suffering a heart attack in 1934. Heath led the company to apply its glass-and-steel fusing process in A.O. Smith's first mass consumer product, the water heater. Before the product's introduction, most homeowners had to replace their all-steel water heaters often due to corrosion, or spend prohibitive amounts on stainless-steel ones. Although A.O. Smith developed its affordable, durable, glass-lined model in 1936 and was able to mass-produce it by 1939, world war interrupted the company's plans a second time.

Smith began to expand through acquisitions before World War II, purchasing Smith Meter Co., a Los Angeles firm that produced petroleum line measuring devices in 1937. The company diversified into electric motors with the 1940 acquisition of Los Angeles-based Sawyer Electrical Manufacturing Company and Whirl-A-Way Motors in Dayton, Ohio. By the end of

the 1950s, electric motors, especially hermetically sealed ones, were A.O. Smith's best-selling product.

By the time the United States entered World War II in 1941, A.O. Smith had already submitted proposals for aerial bombs made of welded pipe, won the government contracts, and built a factory to produce them. The company's engineers developed better, cheaper propeller blades and manufactured landing gear for B-17 "Flying Fortress" and B-29 "Super Fortress" fighter bombers. The company was such a vital wartime supplier that Adolf Hitler targeted it in an unexecuted invasion of the United States.

The investment of over $50 million in new plants and equipment before 1950 propelled A.O. Smith to unprecedented success in the booming postwar American economy. As new housing starts jumped to 4,000 per day and auto production soared to one million a month, the company was poised to prosper. Volume at the centrally located Kankakee water heater plant built in 1947 doubled twice before 1950, with the help of retail giant Sears, Roebuck & Co., which sold A.O. Smith water heaters under a private label. Monthly production approached 50,000 units by the mid-1950s. A.O. Smith had also entered the commercial water heater market in 1948 through the acquisition of Toledo, Ohio-based Burkay Company. In addition, A.O. Smith supplied all of Chevrolet's automotive frames during the 1950s, when that make was the most popular in the United States. The contract helped establish A.O. Smith as the largest independent supplier of chassis frames to the auto industry in the postwar era. Petroleum pipeline sales also recovered quickly and Smith formed a joint venture with steelmaker ARMCO to create a pipe factory in Texas close to customers.

Diversification continued under Heath in the postwar era, with the development in 1949 of Harvestore glass-lined silos that were filled from the top, emptied from the bottom, and were dark-colored to prevent wintertime freezing of the feed stored inside. After a slow start, the silos were well accepted by U.S. farmers, and the company offered them overseas in Germany and the United Kingdom beginning in the 1960s. A.O. Smith started exploring the fiberglass industry in 1953 in cooperation with Dow, forming a glass fiber division in 1959 (forerunner of Smith Fiberglass Products). The company soon developed fiberglass pipe and fittings for special niche applications in oil fields, and later made fiberglass Corvette Sting Ray bodies.

Diversification was accompanied by rationalization. When A.O. Smith's patent on the glass-lined water heater expired in 1955 and competition was opened, Smith eased out of the private-label segment, and scaled back efforts in the residential market to concentrate on the commercial segment with its leading Burkay brand. The company also phased out pressure containers such as beer and petroleum tanks in the late 1950s. A.O. Smith's own success thwarted some of its business interests. The completion of the U.S. Transcontinental Pipeline System significantly reduced the demand for pipe, eventually forcing the company to sell its steel pipe business in Texas to its partner, ARMCO. Despite these withdrawals from certain markets, sales at A.O. Smith increased from $190 million in 1946 to $280 million by 1960.

A.O. Smith's automotive division endured several upheavals throughout the 1960s and 1970s that threatened its existence. The proliferation of car models in the 1960s challenged Smith's adaptive ability and compelled it to retool from riveted frames to more adaptable welded frames. At the same time, 45 percent of U.S. auto production converted to unitized frame construction, effectively eliminating the need for a conventional frame. General Motors' decision to stick with the tried-and-true isolated frame construction kept the automotive division afloat for the time being.

L.B. "Ted" Smith was elected chairman and chief executive officer and Urban Kuechle became president in 1967. The team sought out new businesses to replace the ones that had been eliminated. In 1969 alone, A.O. Smith acquired Layne & Bowler Pump company in Los Angeles, Bull Motors of the United Kingdom, and a majority interest in Armor Elevator, the sixth largest elevator manufacturer in the United States. The company also pushed its international growth, forming a Mexican affiliate to manufacture auto frames, Canadian and Dutch water heater subsidiaries, and a consumer products division in Japan. Successive earnings records in 1968 and 1969 seemed to affirm the acquisition spree; sales climbed as well, from $355 million in 1969 to $600 million in 1973.

Overcoming Numerous Difficulties in the 1970s and 1980s

Unfortunately, the ensuing decade ushered in a myriad of problems that impaired A.O. Smith. The government wage and price freeze mandated in 1971 squeezed profit margins, and the Arab oil embargo that started in 1973 forever harmed sales of full-size, gas-consuming cars, which constituted the majority of Smith's remaining frame market. Labor unrest also plagued many Smith divisions. A ten-month strike at Armor Elevator, which had just completed two years of acquisitions, crippled that subsidiary in 1972. The following year saw strikes at plants in Pennsylvania and Kentucky and the first labor halt at the Milwaukee factory in its 100-year history.

In 1972 the water heater division began its first European operation, in Veldhoven, the Netherlands. L.B. Smith and President Jack Parker divested Armor Elevator, Bull Motors, and Meter Systems in 1975. After the strikes were settled and the government lifted the wage and price freeze, inflation set in. Still, A.O. Smith began to recover in the last half of the decade, winning a new contract with General Motors and expanding the Harvestore and Electrical Products divisions. Sales increased $100 million from 1976 to 1977 and profits were also on the rise.

However, General Motors' 1980 announcement that it would convert all of its production to front-wheel drive, unitized body autos threatened the survival of the $270 million automotive segment of A.O. Smith's $836 million business. Luckily, the massive automaker took more than eight years to phase out full-framed vehicles (A.O. Smith delivered its last Cadillac frame in 1990), and A.O. Smith used that time to transform its automotive division. Automotive, which had made truck frames since 1905, shifted its primary focus to the expanding market for trucks, vans, and sport utility vehicles, winning contracts with Ford, Chrysler, and General Motors in 1980 alone. By 1985, light truck frames were the corporation's single largest product line. Smith also won a contract to produce components for the critically acclaimed and top-selling Ford Taurus in the early 1980s.

The company would meet other challenges under the leadership of Tom Dolan, who became president in 1982 and advanced to chairman and chief executive officer upon the retirement of L.B. Smith. Pressures from auto manufacturers, who were themselves influenced by intense foreign competition, spurred A.O. Smith to simultaneously reduce costs and increase quality. It was no simple task for the automotive division, which was then characterized by hostility between labor and management and 20 percent defect rates. Management embarked on a three-stage strategy to increase employee involvement through quality circles, labor-management task forces, and cooperative work teams. Although the plan initially met resistance from union leaders, six years of gradual change yielded impressive results: the productivity growth rate doubled in 1988 and defects were reduced to 3 percent. The work teams also enabled A.O. Smith to save money by drastically reducing the ratio of foremen to workers from 1-to-10 in 1987 to 1-to-34 in 1988.

During this period of cultural revolution, A.O. Smith was hit hard by recessions in 1980 and 1982. Hundreds of workers were laid off as auto sales fell to their lowest levels in 20 years. The company slashed capital spending and expenses, cut officer salaries by 10 percent, and let one-fourth of the corporate staff go. Even more layoffs were necessary later in the decade, as the company trimmed net employment from a high of 12,300 in 1986 to 9,400 in 1990.

The farming crisis that occurred at this same time reduced the Harvestore subsidiary's sales from $140 million in 1979 to $21 million by 1984. The division shuttered two plants and consolidated all operations at the main DeKalb, Illinois, plant. A.O. Smith eventually shifted the subsidiary's focus to municipal water storage tanks and sold Harvestore's U.K. subsidiary. Although its revenues remained small, Harvestore did eventually return to profitability.

A.O. Smith's problems compounded in the early 1980s, as competition in the water heater industry exposed internal problems. Inefficient plants cost the Water Products Division $10 million in 1981 alone. The subsidiary closed one factory and opened a more efficient one, and other cost-cutting measures helped it achieve profitability in 1983 after four successive years of losses. Continuing efforts helped the division become one of A.O. Smith's most consistently profitable divisions, setting profit records in 1986, 1988, and 1990.

A.O. Smith's electric motors division was one of the corporation's few consistently bright spots in the 1980s. Despite fairly intense competition, the subsidiary was able to establish operations in Mexico and Texas and even acquire a primary competitor's small motor business (that of Westinghouse, purchased in 1986). The unit set a profit record of $45 million in 1985. Smith's fiberglass business had also recovered from the shocks of the previous decade to set four successive years of record profits beginning in 1987.

1990s and Beyond: Concentrating on Motors and Water Heaters

Despite an inconsistent earnings record in the 1980s—the company achieved only two successive profitable years during the decade—A. O. Smith had managed to pay cash dividends on its common stock every year since 1940. Having endured a grueling six years at the company's helm and achieving several of his goals, Tom Dolan retired from the chief executive office in 1988. Robert J. O'Toole assumed that office, adding the chairmanship in 1991. He directed the company's implementation of ''just-in-time'' delivery of automotive products through the construction of five regional assembly plants in close proximity to customers. Although the firm recorded a net loss in 1992, its return to profitability the following year coincided with a general economic recovery in the United States.

Sales rose steadily into the mid-1990s as the company was well-positioned to benefit from the explosive growth in sales of SUVs and light trucks in the 1990s. The company's automotive operation also sought new business with Japanese automakers, opening a sales and engineering office in Yokohama in 1993 and landing a major contract with Nissan for the manufacture of components for the sides of pickup trucks. In December 1995 A.O. Smith doubled the revenues of its storage tank business and entered the bulk dry storage market through the acquisition of Parsons, Kansas-based Peabody TecTank Inc. That same year, the company launched three joint ventures in China, one of which would make A.O. Smith the first U.S. company to manufacture water heaters in that rapidly developing country. Overall company revenues increased from $915.8 million in 1991 to $1.54 billion in 1995.

Despite the sales gains and steady profitability enjoyed by A.O. Smith in the mid-1990s, the company's automotive unit was under pressure to further ratchet up investments to maintain a competitive position. The difficulty was that every time an automaker began work on a new car or truck model, manufacturers of the frames had to spend $30 million to $50 million to retool their plants. A.O. Smith also did not have the financial resources to grow its automotive unit through acquisitions. After reviewing its strategic options, the company decided to make the dramatic move of selling off the automotive unit, which had the additional disadvantage of operating in a low-growth, cyclical industry. In April 1997 the unit was sold to Tower Automotive Inc. of Minneapolis for $710 million. The deal allowed A.O. Smith to virtually extinguish its long-term debt, buy back some of its stock, and concentrate on its key remaining units: electric motors, water heaters, industrial storage tanks, and fiberglass pipe. The company also still had its agricultural storage tank operation, Harvestore, but had decided, in the face of numerous lawsuits and class-action suits alleging that Harvestore had sold farmers defective silos, to sell the unit. A sale did not immediately materialize, however, and Harvestore was eventually merged back with the industrial storage tank unit.

Part of the proceeds from the automotive divestment were slated for acquisitions to build up the remaining units. Before the deal with Tower Automotive had even been completed, in fact, A.O. Smith had finished its first such acquisition, a $60.9 million deal for UPPCO, Incorporated, a manufacturer of subfractional horsepower electric motors based in Monticello, Indiana. Such motors were used in a variety of applications, including bathroom and range hood fans, microwave ovens, frost-free refrigerators, dishwashers, and humidifiers. In July 1998 A.O. Smith paid $125.6 million for the domestic compressor motor business of General Electric Company. Based in

Scottsville, Kentucky, the GE unit had annual sales of about $130 million for its compressors that were used primarily in residential and commercial air conditioning units and in commercial refrigeration units. This acquisition made the electric motors unit the largest A.O. Smith unit in terms of revenues. Then in August 1999, A.O. Smith made its third motor acquisition in as many years when it bought the electric motors unit of Nashville-based MagneTek, Inc. for $244.6 million, the largest acquisition in company history. The MagneTek unit, which had 1998 revenues of about $367 million, produced fractional horsepower motors for pools, spas, and air conditioners. Through this series of acquisitions, A.O. Smith was able to increase its sales of electric motors from the $340 million level of 1996 to $884.2 million by 2000. Meantime, the company began manufacturing residential water heaters in Nanjing, China, in 1998, having bought out its joint venture partner. By 1999 it had achieved $13 million in sales of A.O. Smith brand water heaters in that country.

Rounding out the company's whirlwind transformation were the divestments of the fiberglass pipe and storage tank businesses. In December 2000 A.O. Smith sold the fiberglass business to Varco International Inc., while the storage tank unit was sold to the newly formed CST Industries, Inc. in January 2001. Cash proceeds from the sales were about $63 million. These latest divestments were designed to allow the company to concentrate on its two main businesses—electric motors and water heaters—and to serve as a consolidator within those industries. The company seemed certain to grow these businesses through acquisitions as well as by expanding internationally. Under the continued leadership of O'Connor, A.O. Smith was beginning a new century as a radically different company from what it had been less than a decade earlier, and as a much stronger company as well.

Principal Subsidiaries

AOS Holding Company; A.O. Smith International Corporation; A.O. Smith Export, Ltd. (Barbados); A.O. Smith Electrical Products Canada Limited; A.O. Smith Enterprises Ltd. (Canada); A.O. Smith (China) Water Heater Co., Ltd.; A.O. Smith L'eau Chaude S.a.r.l. (France); A.O. Smith Warmwasser-Systemtechnik GmbH (Germany); A.O. Smith Electrical Products Limited Liability Company (Hungary); A.O. Smith Electric Motors (Ireland) Ltd.; A.O. Smith Holding (Ireland) Ltd.; IG-Mex, S.A. de C.V. (Mexico); Motores Electricos de Juarez, S.A. de C.V. (Mexico); Motores Electricos de Monterrey, S.A. de C.V. (Mexico); Productos de Agua, S.A. de C.V. (Mexico); Productos Electricos Aplicados, S.A. de C.V. (Mexico); A.O. Smith Electrical Products B.V. (Netherlands); A.O. Smith Water Products Company B.V. (Netherlands); A.O. Smith Electrical Products (S.E.A) Pte Ltd (Singapore); A.O. Smith Electrical Products Limited (U.K.).

Principal Operating Units

Electrical Products Company; Water Products Company.

Principal Competitors

American Water Heater Group Inc.; AMTROL Inc.; Baldor Electric Company; Bradford-White Corp.; Emerson; Fasco;

General Electric Company; Hayward Industries; Jakel Inc.; Paloma Industries Limited; State Industries, Inc.

Further Reading

A.O. Smith: ''Safe'' Diversification That Is Endangering Profits,'' *Business Week,* September 21, 1981, pp. 82+.

Fauber, John, ''Analysts Question A.O. Smith Cost Cuts,'' *Milwaukee Journal,* May 22, 1991, p. C8.

Gallagher, Kathleen, ''A.O. Smith's Motor Business Starting to Purr,'' *Milwaukee Journal Sentinel,* June 18, 2000, p. 45D.

Gores, Paul, ''A.O. Smith Sells Off Fiberglass Pipe Division,'' *Milwaukee Journal Sentinel,* December 12, 2000, p. 2D.

Hawkins, Lee, Jr., ''A.O. Smith Plans to Buy MagneTek Motor Business,'' *Milwaukee Journal Sentinel,* June 29, 1999.

——, ''A.O. Smith to Sell Off Division,'' *Milwaukee Journal Sentinel,* January 22, 2000, p. 1D.

——, ''Unit of A.O. Smith Divested,'' *Milwaukee Journal Sentinel,* December 19, 2000, p. 1D.

Hoerr, John, ''The Cultural Revolution at A.O. Smith,'' *Business Week,* May 29, 1989, pp. 66, 68.

Johnson, Robert, ''The Rust Bowl: A.O. Smith Sets Diversity As New Goal,'' *Wall Street Journal,* June 27, 1984.

Lazo, Shirley A., ''Revived A.O. Smith Rewards Its Holders,'' *Barron's,* April 4, 1994, p. 47.

Mullins, Robert, '' 'New' Smith Seeks Wall Street Attention,'' *Business Journal-Milwaukee,* September 19, 1997, pp. 23+.

Savage, Mark, ''A.O. Smith Buys Motor Unit from General Electric,'' *Milwaukee Journal Sentinel,* May 14, 1998.

Spivak, Cary, ''A.O. Smith to Use Cash from Deal for Acquisitions,'' *Milwaukee Journal Sentinel,* February 2, 1997.

Spivak, Cary, and Lee Hawkins, Jr., ''A.O. Smith Sells Unit Here,'' *Milwaukee Journal Sentinel,* January 28, 1997.

Stavro, Barry, ''Framed,'' *Forbes,* June 4, 1984, pp. 66+.

''Tower Automotive to Pay $625 Million for A.O. Smith Unit,'' *Wall Street Journal,* January 28, 1997, p. A6.

Wright, Charles S., and Roger S. Smith, *''A Better Way'': The History of A.O. Smith Corporation,* Milwaukee: A.O. Smith Corporation, 1992.

—April Dougal Gasbarre
—update: David E. Salamie

Abbott Laboratories

100 Abbott Park Road
Abbott Park, Illinois 60064-6400
U.S.A.
Telephone: (847) 937-6100
Fax: (847) 937-9555
Web site: http://www.abbott.com

Public Company
Incorporated: 1900 as Abbott Alkaloidal Company
Employees: 60,000
Sales: $13.75 billion (2000)
Stock Exchanges: New York Chicago Pacific Boston
   Cincinnati Philadelphia London Swiss
Ticker Symbol: ABT
NAIC: 325412 Pharmaceutical Preparation
   Manufacturing; 325413 In-Vitro Diagnostic Substance
   Manufacturing; 334516 Analytical Laboratory
   Instrument Manufacturing; 311514 Dry, Condensed,
   and Evaporated Dairy Product Manufacturing; 541710
   Research and Development in the Physical,
   Engineering, and Life Sciences

Abbott Laboratories is one of the oldest and most successful pharmaceutical companies in the United States. While about 30 percent of annual revenues come from the sale of pharmaceuticals—including Abbott's flagship drug, the antibiotic Biaxin—the company has a higher profile in the area of nutritionals, where its products include leading infant formula brands Similac and Isomil and a leading adult nutritional brand, Ensure. Abbott is also a top manufacturer of medical diagnostic equipment, with an emphasis on blood analyzers and the detection and monitoring of infections and diseases. The firm's hospital products unit produces electronic and injectable drug-delivery systems, intravenous solutions and supplies, anesthetics, and products used in critical care settings. Abbott's annual research and development budget exceeds $1 billion, with areas of emphasis including AIDS/antivirals, anti-infectives, diabetes, neuroscience, oncology, pediatric pharmaceuticals, urology, and vascular medicine.

Early Decades

Abbott Laboratories has its origin in the late 19th century in a small pharmaceutical operation run from the kitchen of a Chicago physician named Wallace Calvin Abbott. As did other physicians of the time, Dr. Abbott commonly prescribed morphine, quinine, strychnine, and codeine—all of which were liquid alkaloid extracts—for his patients. Because they existed only in a liquid form, these drugs were prone to spoilage over time, mitigating their effectiveness as treatments. In 1888, Dr. Abbott heard that a Belgian surgeon had developed alkaloids in solid form. Alkaloid pills soon became available in Chicago, but Dr. Abbott was dissatisfied with their quality, and he decided to manufacture his own.

Dr. Abbott began to advertise his products to other doctors in 1891. So successful was his business that he eventually sold shares to other doctors and incorporated his operation in 1900 as the Abbott Alkaloidal Company. By 1905, annual sales had grown to $200,000. Ten years later, the company changed its name to Abbott Laboratories. During World War I, Abbott's company was essential to the medical community, as several important drugs, manufactured exclusively by German companies, were no longer available in the United States. Abbott developed procaine, a substitute for the German novocaine, and barbital, a replacement for veneral.

After the war, Abbott continued to concentrate on the research and development of new drugs. In 1921, the company established a laboratory in Rocky Mount, North Carolina, which developed a number of new drugs, including sedatives, tranquilizers, and vitamins. Even after Dr. Abbott's death that year, the company continued to invest heavily in new product development and aggressive marketing campaigns. The company went public in 1929 with a listing on the Chicago Stock Exchange. Two years later, Abbott expanded outside the United States for the first time with the establishment of an affiliate in Montreal, Canada.

DeWitt Clough was named president of the company in 1933, ending a period of somewhat stale communal leadership. A more dynamic character than any since Dr. Abbott, Clough is best remembered for the inauguration of the company magazine, *What's New?* The publication had such a positive impact on worker morale and public opinion that several of Abbott's competitors started similar publications. In 1936 Abbott began its long-term association with anesthetics when it introduced sodium pentothal, which had been developed by Abbott scientists Ernest Volwiler and Donalee Tabern (who in 1986 were named to the U.S. Inventors Hall of Fame for this discovery).

During World War II, Abbott once again played an important role in battlefield and hospital healthcare. By this time, American pharmaceutical companies such as Abbott were much less dependent on Germany's companies, particularly the IG Farben—a conglomeration of the world's most advanced drug manufacturers. After the war, much of the IG Farben's research was turned over to American manufacturers. Abbott, however, had little to gain from this information; it was already a worthy competitor on its own.

After the departure of DeWitt Clough in 1945, Abbott shifted its attention to the development of antibiotics. The company developed the antibiotic erythromycin, which, introduced under the brand names Erythrocin and E.E.S. in 1952, constituted a significant portion of Abbott's prescription drug sales for several decades—even after the expiration of its 17-year patent. Sales of the drug increased dramatically when it was found to be an effective treatment for Legionnaire's disease.

Abbott stumbled onto a lucrative new product when one of its researchers accidentally discovered that a chemical with which he had been working had a sweet taste. The chemical, a cyclamate, could be used as an artificial sweetener. Initially, from 1950, it was marketed to diabetics, but in the 1960s, as Americans became more health and diet conscious, it was increasingly used as a sugar substitute in a wide variety of foods.

In 1964 Abbott completed the first major acquisition in company history when it purchased Columbus, Ohio-based M&R Dietetic Laboratories. M&R was the manufacturer of Similac baby formula and over the succeeding decades, as the company's Ross Products Division, formed the basis for Abbott's market-leading infant and adult nutritionals business.

Late 1960s and Early 1970s: Diversification and Crises

By the mid-1960s, Abbott had gone several years without a major breakthrough in research, and none was projected at any time in the immediate future. Then, in 1967, Edward J. Ledder was named president of the company. He advocated a reduction in Abbott's emphasis on pharmaceuticals by diversifying into other fields. In the years that followed, Abbott introduced an array of consumer products, including Pream nondairy creamer, Glad Hands rubber gloves, Faultless golf balls, and Sucaryl, the cyclamate sugar substitute. In an effort to ensure the success of Abbott's consumer product line, Ledder placed Melvin Birnbaum, a highly experienced and able manager he had hired away from Revlon, in charge of the division. Ledder's policy of diversification laid the groundwork for more flexible corporate strategies. No longer exposed exclusively within the pharmaceuticals market, Abbott was able to cross-subsidize failing operations until they could be rehabilitated.

Despite this flexibility, Abbott soon realized new obstacles to its growth. The company's hospital products competed in a limited, institutional market. New drugs had greater profit margins but were subject to government approval procedures that kept companies waiting for several years before they could market their discoveries. Consumer products, on the other hand, involved more expensive marketing and generated less profit than pharmaceuticals. Unable to increase profits without substantial risk, Abbott's management decided to maintain the strategies that were in place.

Cyclamate sales had grown so dramatically that by 1969 they accounted for one-third of Abbott's consumer product revenues—or about $50 million. The increasing popularity of cyclamates as an ingredient in diet foods, however, led the Food and Drug Administration (FDA) to conduct an investigation of possible side effects from their overuse. The FDA's research was widely criticized as "fragmentary" and "fatally flawed," but it was nonetheless used as evidence that cyclamates were carcinogenic. The market collapsed in August 1970 when the FDA banned domestic sales of cyclamates. Abbott, which overnight had suffered the loss of one of its most profitable operations, protested the ban, but was unable to reverse the decision. Although the company continued to petition the FDA, subsequent studies confirmed that metabolization of cyclamates can lead to chromosome breakage and bladder cancer.

Less than a year after cyclamates were banned, Abbott was forced to recall 3.4 million bottles of intravenous solution. The bottles were sealed with a varnished paper called Gilsonite, which, it was discovered, harbored bacteria. The contamination was discovered only when healthcare workers noticed and then investigated the high incidence of infection in patients who had been administered Abbott's intravenous solutions. The Center for Disease Control linked the contaminated solutions to at least 434 infections and 49 deaths. With sales down from $17.9 million to $3 million, Abbott's share price began to fall. Abbott moved quickly to replace its Gilsonite seals with synthetic rubber, but the company was unable to regain its leadership of the intravenous market. Litigation resulted in the company eventually pleading no contest to a charge of conspiracy and paying a $1,000 fine.

Late 1970s Through 1980s: Emphasizing R&D, Nutritionals, Diagnostic Equipment

The crises of the early 1970s left the company's upper echelon of management weakened and vulnerable to criticism. Although Edward Ledder was recognized for the success of his diversifica-

Key Dates:

1888: Dr. Wallace Calvin Abbott begins manufacturing alkaloid pills.

1900: Abbott incorporates his firm as Abbott Alkaloidal Company.

1915: Company changes its name to Abbott Laboratories.

1929: Abbott goes public with a listing on the Chicago Stock Exchange.

1936: Company introduces the anesthetic sodium pentothal.

1952: Company launches a new antibiotic, Erythrocin.

1964: Abbott acquires M&R Dietetic Laboratories, maker of Similac baby formula.

1967: New president Edward J. Ledder begins a diversification into consumer products, including Sucaryl, a cyclamate sugar substitute.

1970: FDA bans the sale of cyclamates.

1971: Abbott is forced to recall 3.4 million bottles of intravenous solution.

1977: Company forms joint venture with Takeda Chemical Industries, Ltd. of Japan called TAP Pharmaceuticals Inc.

1985: Abbott develops the first diagnostic test for AIDS.

1987: Abbott's Hytrin is approved by the FDA for the treatment of hypertension.

1991: Clorithromycin, an antibiotic, is introduced.

1996: Abbott acquires MediSense, Inc., a maker of blood-testing devices for diabetics.

1999: Abbott agrees to acquire ALZA Corporation for $7.3 billion but the deal later collapses; Abbott agrees to pay a $100 million fine relating to quality control problems at its medical test kit plants; suture maker Perclose, Inc. is acquired.

2000: FDA approves the AIDS drug Kaletra; Abbott agrees to acquire the Knoll Pharmaceutical Co. unit of BASF AG for $6.9 billion in cash.

tion program (and largely excused for his inability to prevent either the cyclamate ban or the intravenous solution crisis), conditions were obviously ripe for the expression of talent by a new manager. Robert Schoellhorn, a veteran of the chemical industry, was just such a manager. His efforts as a vice-president in the hospital products division at Abbott resulted in a revenue increase of 139 percent for that division between 1974 and 1979. He correctly predicted that the next most profitable trend in health-care would be toward cost-effective analysis and treatment. Schoellhorn was later promoted to president and chief operating officer of the company. Meantime, in 1977 Abbott entered into a joint venture with Takeda Chemical Industries, Ltd. of Japan called TAP Pharmaceuticals Inc. for the codevelopment and comarketing of pharmaceuticals.

Abbott Laboratories registered an annual sales growth rate of 15.5 percent and an earnings growth rate of 16.5 percent by 1979. This expansion was attributed by financial analysts to the company's increased productivity, reduced costs, expansion into foreign markets, and greater involvement in hospital nutritionals and diagnostic testing equipment. The company also

introduced three new drugs in 1979: Depakene, an anticonvulsant; Tranxene, a mild tranquilizer; and Abbokinase, a treatment for blood clots in the lungs. All three products were the direct result of the company's increased investment in research and development in the mid 1970s.

Utilizing its knowledge of intravenous solution production, vitamin therapy, and infant formula, Abbott developed a comprehensive nutritional therapy program to speed the recovery of hospital patients and thereby reduce medical care costs. In the 1980s, as many as 65 percent of all hospital patients suffered from some form of malnutrition, so Abbott was highly successful in marketing their program. Another advantage of adult nutritional products was that they had a place in the growing home care market.

Abbott had similar success marketing its lines of diagnostic equipment. Electronic testing devices developed by Abbott proved more accurate than manual procedures. In order to strengthen the technical end of its diagnostic equipment research, Abbott hired two top executives away from Texas Instruments to head the division.

Robert Schoellhorn, who advanced to chairperson and chief executive officer in 1979, continued to emphasize investment in pharmaceutical research and development in the 1980s. Seven new drugs introduced in 1982 accounted for 17 percent of sales in 1985. Foreign operations also remained extremely important to Abbott, and the company had more than 75 foreign subsidiaries and manufacturing facilities in more than 30 countries. Schoellhorn continued to support Ledder's original diversification policy. The introduction of Murine eye-care products and Selsun Blue dandruff shampoo served to expand the domestic consumer product line and promised to provide earning stability in the event of a downturn in any of the company's other markets.

Schoellhorn was also credited with promoting Abbott's emphasis on diagnostic equipment, especially blood analyzers. These devices were increasingly used to detect legal and illegal substances in the bloodstream. Abbott led the trend, developing the first diagnostic tests for Acquired Immune Deficiency Syndrome (AIDS), in 1985, and hepatitis. The company's "Vision" blood analyzer fit on a desktop and performed 90 percent of typical blood tests within eight minutes. By the end of the 1980s, sales of blood analysis devices represented a billion-dollar business, and medical diagnostic products (at $2.3 billion per year) constituted nearly half of Abbott's annual sales. Meanwhile, in the pharmaceuticals arena, Abbott in 1987 received FDA approval for a new drug called Hytrin for the treatment of hypertension. Hytrin was approved in 1993 for the treatment of noncancerous enlarged prostate.

Schoellhorn was widely praised as the driving force behind Abbott's phenomenal growth during the 1980s—sales nearly tripled, profits doubled, and the pharmaceutical company rose to 90th from 197th on *Fortune*'s list of the world's top 500 companies. The leader's aggressive management style, however, often led to conflict. Over the course of the 1980s, three presidents—James L. Vincent (1981); Kirk Raab (1985); and Jack W. Schuler (1989)—quit. In December 1989, Abbott's board of directors unseated Schoellhorn, who in turn sued the company for his job. Abbott accused Schoellhorn of misappropriation of company assets and "fraudulent conduct," adding that the former CEO exercised stock options worth $9.3 million within days of his release. Schoellhorn was succeeded by Vice-Chairman Duane L. Burnham.

1990s and Beyond: New Drug Introductions and Acquisitions

Unlike many of its competitors (including Merck, SmithKline Beecham, and Eli Lilly), Abbott did not acquire a drug distribution manager in the early 1990s. Instead, the company plowed funds into research and development. R&D outlays rose from 5.2 percent of sales in 1982 to more than 10 percent of sales by 1994—by the latter year, R&D expenditures neared $1 billion. That year marked the company's 23rd consecutive earnings lift and helped Abbott's stock hold its value better than most competitors in the uncertain healthcare environment of the early 1990s.

Among key developments in the early 1990s was the introduction in 1991 of clorithromycin, an antibiotic developed as a successor to Abbott's erythromycin. Marketed in the United States under the name Biaxin, clorithromycin was useful in the treatment of common upper respiratory ailments such as the flu as well as other types of infections. It quickly became Abbott's flagship pharmaceutical—eventually achieving $1 billion in annual sales—remaining so into the early 21st century.

New product introductions continued in the middle years of the decade. In 1994 Abbott introduced sevoflurane, an inhalation anesthetic that soon gained popularity because of its wide range of uses. The following year, TAP, the joint venture with Takeda Chemical, received FDA approval for Prevacid, an ulcer treatment (sales of Prevacid reached $1.3 billion by 1998). In 1996 FDA clearance was granted for Norvir, a protease inhibitor for the treatment of HIV and AIDS.

Despite these R&D successes, Abbott's earnings were failing to increase at the high-double-digit rate that they had in the 1980s, and the company was beginning to face the risk of being gobbled up by a larger rival in the rapidly consolidating healthcare industry of the 1990s. Shrugging off the conservative management of the early 1990s, Abbott moved aggressively in the second half of the decade to expand via acquisition and thereby stave off being acquired itself. In 1996 Abbott bolstered its diagnostics division through the $867 million purchase of MediSense, Inc., a Waltham, Massachusetts-based maker of blood-testing devices for diabetics. This was the company's first major deal since the 1964 acquisition of M&R Dietetic Laboratories. In 1997 Abbott spent about $200 million for certain intravenous product lines of Sanofi Pharmaceuticals, Inc., the U.S. unit of France's Sanofi S.A. Included in this deal was Carpujet, an injectable drug-delivery system based on preloaded, single-dose syringes. Also in 1997, Abbott suffered a potential setback when Takeda Chemical did not renew a ten-year contract that gave Abbott the right of first refusal to distribute Takeda's new drugs in the United States via the TAP venture. Takeda had decided to set up its own sales and marketing organization in the United States. By this time TAP was generating annual sales in excess of $2 billion, primarily from the marketing of Prevacid and Lupron, a prostate-cancer drug.

By 1997 Abbott had doubled its sales and earnings since Burnham had taken over from the ousted Schoellhorn. In early 1998 Burnham announced that he would retire in 1999. At the begin-

ning of that year, Miles D. White, who had been a senior vice-president in charge of the diagnostics division, took over as CEO. Later in 1999, White was named chairman as well. During the leadership transition period in 1998, Abbott acquired Murex Technologies Corporation, a maker of diagnostics products, for $234 million. During 1999, Abbott's appetite for growth increased exponentially with the announcement in June of a deal to acquire ALZA Corporation for $7.3 billion in stock. ALZA was a leading producer of advanced drug-delivery systems and had a solid pipeline of new pharmaceuticals under development. The Federal Trade Commission (FTC), however, raised antitrust concerns about the merger, and when the two sides were unable to reach an agreement with the FTC, they called off the merger in December. Another possible factor in the collapse of the deal was the decline in Abbott's stock price following the company's agreement in November to pull 125 types of medical-diagnostic test kits off the U.S. market and to pay a $100 million civil penalty to the U.S. government. Since 1993 the FDA had been issuing warnings to Abbott regarding quality control deficiencies at its test kit plants, with the market withdrawal and payment of the fine being the outcome of this process. The FDA also cited poor manufacturing controls as the reason for its halting the sales of Abbott's clot-dissolving agent Abbokinase in early 1999.

In the meantime, Abbott managed to complete two smaller acquisitions in 1999. It acquired Perclose, Inc., a maker of sutures used to close arteries during angioplasty procedures, for about $600 million in stock. Abbott also paid $217 million in cash to Glaxo Wellcome Inc. for five anesthesia products. In January 2000 Abbott sold its agricultural products business to Sumitomo Chemical Co., Ltd. Abbott was now for the first time in decades a pure healthcare firm. Abbott in April of that year began marketing Biaxin XL, a new once-daily formulation of its flagship Biaxin antibiotic. The FDA in September 2000 granted expedited approval to Kaletra, a second-generation AIDS medication developed by Abbott. Kaletra had the potential to overtake the top AIDS drug, Pfizer Inc.'s Viracept, because it had fewer side effects. It also appeared that patients did not develop resistance to Kaletra over time, as happened with most other AIDS drugs, including Viracept. Then in December 2000 Abbott launched another attempt at a major acquisition when it reached an agreement to acquire the Knoll Pharmaceutical Co. unit of German chemical giant BASF AG for $6.9 billion in cash. Once again, Abbott's aim was to bolster its product pipeline, and Knoll had at least one potential blockbuster in a drug called D2E7, an experimental rheumatoid arthritis treatment. Knoll's existing products included Meridia, an obesity drug with annual sales of about $400 million, and Synthroid, a $150 million thyroid drug. The acquisition would also boost Abbott's pharmaceutical R&D budget to nearly $1 billion.

Principal Subsidiaries

Abbott Chemicals Plant, Inc.; Abbott Fermentation Products de Puerto Rico, Inc.; Abbott Health Products, Inc.; Abbott Home Infusion Services of New York, Inc.; Abbott International Ltd.; Abbott International Ltd. of Puerto Rico; Abbott Laboratories Inc.; Abbott Laboratories International Co.; Abbott Laboratories Pacific Ltd.; Abbott Laboratories (Puerto Rico) Incorporated; Abbott Laboratories Residential Development Fund, Inc.; Abbott Laboratories Services Corp.; Abbott Trading Company, Inc.; Abbott Universal Ltd.; AC Merger Sub Inc.; CMM Transportation, Inc.; Corporate Alliance, Inc.; IMTC Technologies, Inc.; Murex Diagnostics, Inc.; North Shore Properties, Inc.; Oximetrix de Puerto Rico, Inc.; Perclose, Inc.; Solartek Products, Inc.; Sorenson Research Co., Inc.; Swan Myers, Incorporated; TAP Finance Inc.; Tobal Products Incorporated, Abbott Laboratorios Argentina, S.A.; Abbott Australasia Pty. Limited (Australia); MediSense Australia Pty. Ltd.; Abbott Gesellschaft m.b.H. (Austria); Abbott Hospitals Limited (Bahamas); Murex Diagnostics International, Inc. (Barbados); Abbott, S.A. (Belgium); Abbott Laboratorios do Brasil Ltda. (Brazil); Abbott Laboratories Limited (Canada); International Murex Technologies Corporation (Canada); Abbott Laboratories de Chile Limitada (Chile); Abbott Laboratories de Colombia, S.A.; Abbott Laboratories s.r.o. (Czech Republic); Murex Diagnostica, Spol. s.r.o. (Czech Republic); Abbott Laboratories A/S (Denmark); Murex Diagnostics A/S (Denmark); Abbott Laboratorios del Ecuador, S.A.; Abbott, S.A. de C.V. (El Salvador); Abbott OY (Finland); Abbott France S.A.; Alcyon Analyzer S.A.; MediSense France SARL; Murex Diagnostics (France) S.A.; Abbott G.m.b.H. (Germany); Abbott Diagnostics G.m.b.H. (Germany); Murex Diagnostica GmbH (Germany); Abbott Laboratories (Hellas) S.A. (Greece); Abbott Laboratorios, S.A. (Guatemala); Abbott Laboratories Limited (Hong Kong); Abbott Laboratories (Hungary) Ltd.; Abbott Laboratories (India) Ltd. (51%); Abind Healthcare Private Limited (India); P.T. Abbott Indonesia (97%); Abbott Laboratories, Ireland, Limited; Abbott Ireland Ltd.; Abbott S.p.A. (Italy); Murex Diagnostici S.p.A. (Italy); Abbott Japan K.K. (Japan); Dainabot Co., Ltd. (Japan; 73%); Abbott Korea Limited; Abbott Middle East S.A.R.L. (Lebanon); Abbott Laboratories (Malaysia) Sdn. Bhd.; Abbott Laboratories de Mexico, S.A. de C.V.; Abbott Laboratories (Mozambique) Limitada; Edisco B.V. (Netherlands); Abbott B.V. (Netherlands); Abbott Laboratories B.V. (Netherlands); Abbott Finance B.V. (Netherlands); Abbott Holdings B.V. (Netherlands); MediSense Europe B.V. (Netherlands); MediSense Netherlands, B.V.; IMTC Holdings B.V. (Netherlands); IMTC Finance B.V. (Netherlands); Murex Diagnostics Benelux B.V. (Netherlands); Abbott Laboratories (N.Z.) Limited (New Zealand); Abbott Norge A S (Norway); Abbott Laboratories (Pakistan) Limited (83.42%); Abbott Laboratories, C.A. (Panama); Abbott Overseas, S.A. (Panama); Abbott Laboratorios S.A. (Peru); Abbott Laboratories (Philippines); Abbott Laboratories Sp. z.o.o. (Poland); Abbott Laboratorios, Limitada (Portugal); Abbott Laboratories (Singapore) Private Limited; Abbott Laboratories South Africa (Pty.) Limited; Abbott Laboratories, S.A. (Spain); Abbott Cientifica, S.A. (Spain); Abbott Scandinavia A.B. (Sweden); Abbott A.G. (Switzerland); Abbott Laboratories S.A. (Switzerland); Abbott Finance Company S.A. (Switzerland); Abbott Laboratories Taiwan Limited; Abbott Laboratories Limited (Thailand); Abbott Laboratuarlari Ithalat Ihracat Ve Tecaret Limited Sirketi (Turkey); Abbott Investments Limited (U.K.); Abbott Laboratories Limited (U.K.); Abbott (UK) Holdings Limited; Abbott Laboratories Trustee Company Limited (U.K.); IMTC Holdings (UK) Limited; MediSense Britain, Ltd. (U.K.); MediSense UK Ltd.; Murex Biotech Limited (U.K.); Specialist Diagnostica Limited (U.K.); Abbott Laboratories Uruguay Limitada; Abbott Laboratories, C.A. (Venezuela); Medicamentos M & R, S.A. (Venezuela).

Principal Divisions

Pharmaceutical Products; Ross Products; Hospital Products; Abbott International; Diagnostics; Specialty Products.

Principal Competitors

Merck & Co., Inc.; Eli Lilly and Company; Pfizer Inc.; Bristol-Myers Squibb Company; American Home Products Corporation; Johnson & Johnson, AstraZeneca PLC; Aventis; Bayer AG; GlaxoSmithKline plc; Schering-Plough Corporation, Novartis AG; Roche Holding Ltd.

Further Reading

"Abbott: Profiting from Products That Cut Costs," *Business Week,* June 18, 1984, pp. 56+.

"Baby Bottle Battle," *Forbes,* November 28, 1988, pp. 222+.

Barrett, Amy, and Richard A. Melcher, "Drugmaker, Heal Thyself," *Business Week,* October 11, 1999, pp. 88+.

Benoit, Ellen, "Abbott Laboratories: Room at the Top," *Financial World,* October 17, 1989, p. 28.

Berss, Marcia, "Aloof But Not Asleep," *Forbes,* August 29, 1994, pp. 43–44.

Bleiberg, Robert M., "Abbott and Costello: The Ban on Cyclamates Is a Comedy—or Tragedy—of Errors," *Barron's,* October 9, 1978, p. 7.

"Bob Schoellhorn Is Refusing to Go Quietly," *Business Week,* March 26, 1990, pp. 34+.

Burton, Thomas M., "Abbott Laboratories and Alza Call Off Their Deal," *Wall Street Journal,* December 17, 1999, p. B10.

——, "Abbott Labs to Buy BASF Unit for $6.9 Billion," *Wall Street Journal,* December 15, 2000, pp. A3, A12.

——, "Abbott's White Wins CEO Job," *Wall Street Journal,* September 16, 1998, p. A3.

——, "Abbott to Pay $100 Million in Fine to United States," *Wall Street Journal,* November 3, 1999, p. A3.

——, "Federal Judge Clears Abbott in Formula Case: Bid Process for Infant Food Is Called 'Questionable,' but Oversight Is Faulted," *Wall Street Journal,* June 1, 1994, p. A3.

Carter, Kim, "Abbott Laboratories Betting Its Future on the Development of New Products," *Modern Healthcare,* November 7, 1986, pp. 138+.

Klein, Sarah A., "Abbott's Biotech Biz Gets a Booster Shot: Picking Up Keys to State-of-the-Art Lab in BASF Deal," *Crain's Chicago Business,* January 1, 2001, p. 4.

——, "Restocked Product Pipeline Invigorating Abbott," *Crain's Chicago Business,* September 4, 2000, p. 4.

Kogan, Herman, *The Long White Line: The Story of Abbott Laboratories,* New York: Random House, 1963, 309 p.

Merrion, Paul, "Nestlé Sours Baby Formula for Abbott," *Crain's Chicago Business,* June 13, 1988.

Miller, James P., "Abbott Labs Agrees to Purchase Alza," *Wall Street Journal,* June 22, 1999, p. A3.

——, "Abbott Ousts Schoellhorn As Chairman, Drawing Lawsuit by Embattled Official," *Wall Street Journal,* March 12, 1990, p. B6.

Oloroso, Arsenio, Jr., "Abbott's Prescription for Sluggish Drug Biz Pays Off," *Crain's Chicago Business,* October 21, 1991, p. 3.

——, "Abbott's Tough Rx: Buy or Risk Being Bought," *Crain's Chicago Business,* March 2, 1998, p. 3.

——, "Abbott Tries Costly Growth Drug: M&A," *Crain's Chicago Business,* April 8, 1996, p. 4.

——, "New CEO Poised to Rev Up Sleepy Abbott's Strategy," *Crain's Chicago Business,* September 21, 1998, p. 4.

Salwan, Kevin G., "Infant-Formula Firms Rigged Bids, U.S. Says," *Wall Street Journal,* June 12, 1992, p. A3.

Somasundaram, Meera, "Abbott Set to Stock Medicine Cabinet: Drug Giant Expected to Shop for Mid-Sized Rivals," *Crain's Chicago Business,* February 1, 1999, p. 1.

—April Dougal Gasbarre
—update: David E. Salamie

AB ALEXANDER & BALDWIN, INC.

Alexander & Baldwin, Inc.

822 Bishop Street
P.O. Box 3440
Honolulu, Hawaii 96801-3440
U.S.A.
Telephone: (808) 525-6611
Fax: (808) 525-6652
Web site: http://www.alexanderbaldwin.com

Public Company
Incorporated: 1900 as Alexander & Baldwin, Limited
Employees: 2,029
Sales: $1.07 billion (2000)
Stock Exchanges: NASDAQ
Ticker Symbol: ALEX
NAIC: 111339 Other Noncitrus Fruit Farming; 111930 Sugarcane Farming; 221111 Hydroelectric Power Generation; 221119 Other Electric Power Generation; 221310 Water Supply and Irrigation Systems; 233110 Land Subdivision and Land Development; 311311 Sugarcane Mills; 311920 Coffee and Tea Manufacturing; 422490 Other Grocery and Related Products Wholesalers; 483113 Coastal and Great Lakes Freight Transportation; 484220 Specialized Freight (Except Used Goods) Trucking, Local; 488320 Marine Cargo Handling; 488330 Navigational Services to Shipping; 488510 Freight Transportation Arrangement; 493190 Other Warehousing and Storage; 531110 Lessors of Residential Buildings and Dwellings; 531120 Lessors of Nonresidential Buildings (Except Miniwarehouses); 531190 Lessors of Other Real Estate Property

Alexander & Baldwin, Inc., one of the original "Big Five" Hawaiian companies, is a diversified corporation with operations in ocean transportation, food products, and property development and management. Ocean transportation, overseen by Matson Navigation Company, Inc., a wholly owned subsidiary, accounts for about 80 percent of the company's revenue.

Through Matson, Alexander & Baldwin (A&B) is a leading carrier of containerized cargo and automobiles between Hawaii and the U.S. Pacific Coast. Matson's fleet of 19 ships and barges also provides service to several islands in the South Pacific and to Guam. Matson also provides terminal services, such as cargo handling, in Hawaii, and arranges intermodal transportation in North America for shippers and carriers, which involves the ground and rail transport of cargo from Pacific Coast ports to interior U.S. locations. A&B's property development and management segment provides about 10 percent of the company's revenues. With some 91,000 acres of land in Hawaii, the majority of it on the island of Maui, A&B is the fifth largest landowner in the state. The company develops residential, commercial, and light industrial properties and has about 1.2 million square feet of income-generating properties. A&B's food products business is involved in sugarcane and coffee. The company's Hawaiian Commercial & Sugar Company division had 37,000 acres of sugarcane fields and is Hawaii's largest producer of raw sugar. The company processes the cane into raw sugar at its mill on Maui, and most of the raw sugar is then sold to C&H Sugar Company, Inc., which refines it in California and markets it throughout the western United States. A&B holds about a 36 percent stake in C&H Sugar, whose C&H brand is the leading sugar brand in the western United States. The coffee operations are conducted through Kauai Coffee Company, Inc., a subsidiary of A&B. Kauai operates the largest coffee estate in the United States, with approximately 3,800 acres, and is responsible for about 60 percent of the coffee grown in the country. Kauai markets most of its crop in the United States and Asia as premium-priced, green (unroasted) coffee. Food products, A&B's founding business, now generate less than 10 percent of the company's revenues.

Sugarcane Roots

Although A&B was not incorporated until 1900, the company was founded 30 years earlier by the two men whose names it bears, Samuel T. Alexander and Henry P. Baldwin, both sons of missionaries living in Hawaii. Longtime friends, the two men began working together in the mid-1860s, when Alexander hired the younger Baldwin as his assistant in managing a sugar plantation in Waihee on the island of Maui. In 1869 the pair purchased 12 acres of land in central Maui; the following year, with an additional 559 acres, they established their own sugarcane plantation, marketing sugar on the mainland through such exporting firms as Castle & Cooke. Alexander and Baldwin became in-laws that year when Baldwin married Emily Alexander, his partner's sister.

By 1876, the volume of sugarcane growing on the plantation had increased so much that the readily available supply of water could not support it. To address this problem, Alexander devised a sophisticated irrigation plan that involved the construction of a gigantic ditch through rain forest terrain. The resulting Hamakua ditch, 17 miles long and capable of carrying 60 million gallons of water a day from the waters of East Maui, was completed in 1878 and served as the model for many other such irrigation projects throughout Hawaii.

The partnership of Alexander and Baldwin was incorporated in 1883 under the name Paia Plantation. That year, Alexander resigned as manager of the neighboring Haiku Sugar Company, a position he had held since before the opening of Paia, and moved to California, leaving Baldwin to manage both plantations. Over the next few years, Paia acquired controlling interest in Haiku, as the partners continued to acquire land and expand their sugar production.

In 1894, A&B launched its own sugar agency, based in San Francisco. The agency was headed by Alexander's son, Wallace, and Joseph P. Cooke, son of Castle & Cooke cofounder Amos S. Cooke. In its first year of operation, the Alexander & Baldwin agency turned a profit of $2,670. By 1899, A&B was serving as agent for a formidable collection of companies, including the Paia and Haiku plantations, the Hawaiian Sugar Company, and the Hawaiian Commercial & Sugar Company (HC&S) and its subsidiary, Kahului Railroad Company. A&B had in fact purchased a controlling interest in HC&S in 1898.

Expanding in the Early 20th Century

By 1900, the company had outgrown its partnership structure, and a new corporation, Alexander & Baldwin, Limited, was formed. In addition to the company's Honolulu headquarters, a branch office was maintained in San Francisco; Baldwin served as president. That year, the corporation reported its first annual profit, $150,000. A&B went into the insurance business the following year, establishing a division overseen by Alexander's son-in-law, John Waterhouse. By 1920, the division was acting as agent for several established insurance companies, including Home Insurance Company, German Alliance Insurance Association, and the Commonwealth Insurance Company, all based in New York. The insurance division thrived for several decades before it was sold off in 1967.

Another new entity, the Maui Agricultural Company (MA Co.), was founded in 1903, in order to offset the effects of the Organic Act, which limited the amount of land a new corporation could hold to 1,000 acres. In response, A&B formed five companies with less than 1,000 acres each. These five companies were then combined with the Paia and Haiku plantations to form MA Co. Through MA Co. and HC&S, A&B now controlled the operations of two of Maui's most important plantations.

Samuel Alexander died in 1904. In 1906, Henry Baldwin was succeeded as manager of HC&S by his son Frank, and when Henry died five years later, Frank became HC&S president, a position he would retain until his death in 1960. Both MA Co. and HC&S prospered during the first part of the 20th century. In 1908, the two companies jointly formed the East Maui Irrigation Company (EMI) to manage the extensive system of irrigation ditches that was in development. In 1917, MA Co. built a distillery for producing alcohol from molasses, the first such facility in the United States. HC&S completed several other major projects during this time, including the construction of the new Waihee ditch and the modernization of its power plant and other equipment. Another plantation, Kihei, was merged into HC&S during this period as well.

A&B's cargo shipping business was developed to complement its sugar operations. In 1908 the company became a minority shareholder in Matson Navigation Company, which had been handling most of A&B's shipping between Hawaii and San Francisco for years. A&B continued to increase its investment in Matson, and the company eventually became a wholly owned subsidiary of A&B in 1969.

Wallace Alexander served as CEO of A&B from 1918 to 1930. During this time, the company began marketing pineapples, EMI completed construction of the Wailoa ditch, its final major ditch project, and A&B's headquarters building in Honolulu was completed. The following year, John Waterhouse succeeded Wallace Alexander as company president.

The 1930s were a period of technological advancement in A&B's sugar operations. In 1932, the company completed construction on the Alexander Dam, one of the largest hydraulic fill earth dams in the world. The Alexander Dam, located at the company's McBryde plantation, cost over $360,000 to build and was the site of a 1930 mud slide that killed several people. Both HC&S and MA Co. switched from steam plows to tractors around this time, and HC&S began mechanical harvesting on a large scale in 1937.

Venturing into Property Development in the 1940s

A&B sold its Hawaiian Sugar Company plantation in 1941. Although this plantation remained productive and profitable, it was situated on leased land, and A&B was unable to negotiate favorable lease terms or a purchase agreement. In 1945 Waterhouse was replaced as president of A&B by J. Platt Cooke, who served for a year before turning over the office to Frank Baldwin. In 1948, the HC&S and MA Co. plantations merged, creating one

Key Dates:

1870: Samuel T. Alexander and Henry P. Baldwin establish a sugarcane plantation on the Hawaiian island of Maui.

1878: An irrigation project called Hamakua ditch is completed, bringing much needed water to the growing plantation.

1898: Company purchases controlling interest in Hawaiian Commercial & Sugar Company (HC&S).

1900: Company is reorganized under a new corporation, Alexander & Baldwin, Limited (A&B).

1908: A&B acquires a minority interest in Matson Navigation Company, a cargo shipping firm.

1949: Company moves into property development with formation of a subsidiary called Kahului Development Co., Ltd.

1950: Kahului Development begins building a new residential community on Maui that will eventually evolve into the city of Kahului.

1962: A&B takes full control of HC&S, which becomes a division of the company; A&B changes the "Limited" in its name to "Inc."

1964: A&B acquires a 94 percent controlling interest in Matson.

1969: A&B increases its holding in Matson to 100 percent.

1987: Joint venture is formed with Hills Brothers to grow coffee on Kauai, a venture that will eventually be 100 percent owned by A&B and be called Kauai Coffee Company; Matson forms Matson Intermodal System, Inc.

1989: Matson forms Matson Leasing Company, Inc.; A&B creates A&B-Hawaii, Inc. (ABHI) as its main subsidiary for its food products and property development and management operations.

1993: A&B takes full control of California and Hawaiian Sugar Company, Inc. (C&H), the main purchaser and marketer of A&B's sugar.

1995: Matson Leasing is sold to Xtra Corp. for about $362 million.

1996: Matson Navigation begins ten-year trans-Pacific shipping alliance with American President Lines, Ltd.

1998: A&B sells a 64 percent stake in C&H to an investment group.

1999: ABHI is merged into the parent company.

large plantation operating under the HC&S name. The two plantations produced more than 100,000 tons of sugar during the first year of the merger. Soon thereafter, the plantation began to phase out its railroad distribution system in favor of trucking.

A&B began to move into property development in 1949, forming Kahului Development Co., Ltd. as a subsidiary of HC&S. In response to the complaints of plantation employees regarding the inadequate housing available to them, Kahului Development built a new residential community, which was opened in 1950 and became known as Dream City. This development gradually evolved into the city of Kahului, Maui's most populous community.

A&B operated several general stores on plantations and railroad sites. In 1950, its stores and equipment manufacturing concerns, as well as the lumberyard and mill operations of the Kahului Railroad Company, were organized under the A&B Commercial Company. The following year, A&B opened the first A&B Super Market, as well as the Kahului Store, Maui's first complete department store.

The company made several technological strides in its sugar operations during the 1950s. In 1951, HC&S's two factories combined to produce a record 151,000 tons of sugar. Several improvements in machinery for weed control and harvesting were introduced during this time, and, in 1957, HC&S put the world's largest bagasse (cane residue) burning boiler into operation at its Paia sugar factory.

Taking Full Control of HC&S and Matson in the 1960s

Up until the 1960s, A&B had remained essentially a sales agent that held substantial interest in the companies it represented. Its income came from agency fees and dividends on the stock it owned in its client companies. This began to change, however, as A&B started turning many of its clients into subsidiaries. Much of this shift took place under C.C. Cadagan, who was named president of A&B in 1960, becoming the first chief executive from outside the founding families. In 1962, HC&S was merged into A&B, becoming a division of the company. HC&S's three subsidiaries, Kahului Railroad Company (KRR), East Maui Irrigation Company, and Kahului Development Company, all became subsidiaries of A&B. A&B Commercial Company, which ran the HC&S plantation stores, was made a division. At the same time, the last word of the company's name was changed from "Limited" to "Inc."

Using funds it had received from the liquidation of Honolulu Oil Corporation, a company in which it had initially invested in 1911, A&B acquired a 94 percent controlling interest in Matson Navigation Company in 1964. The following year, the company eliminated what remained of KRR's unprofitable railroad operations, and that subsidiary was later renamed Kahului Trucking & Storage, Inc. By the end of the decade, the company had terminated its pineapple business and had increased its holding in Matson to 100 percent. The McBryde and Kahuke plantations had become wholly owned subsidiaries as well.

The 1970s were a frustrating period of stalled expansion plans for A&B. In 1970, Allen Wilcox was named CEO, replacing Stanley Powell, Cadagan's successor four years earlier. Under Wilcox, A&B abandoned its plans to expand its Far East shipping operations, choosing instead to concentrate on its business closer to home, such as developing some of its Maui land for resort use. Another change in leadership took place in 1972, when Lawrence Pricher was named CEO. Under Pricher, the company launched another expansion push, which included investments in oil refiner Pacific Resources, Inc. and Teakwood Holdings Ltd. (a Hong Kong furniture company), the purchase of Rogers Brothers Co. (an Idaho potato business), and the formation of a consulting firm called A&B Agribusiness Corporation. None of these ventures proved particularly fruitful, and, at the same time, some earlier investments that also proved unprofitable were sold off, including Edward R. Bacon Company and Acme Fast Freight, Inc. With the price of sugar falling, and profits at Matson unimpressive, A&B's net income remained sluggish through the mid-1970s.

Yet another change in command took place in 1978, when Gilbert Cox left Amfac Inc., Hawaii's biggest sugar producer, to assume the presidency of A&B. Cox's strategy for growth involved selling off most of Pricher's small acquisitions, such as the potato company, and using the money for a major acquisition. In 1979, an agreement was reached under which A&B would acquire the 80 percent of Pacific Resources it did not already own. This deal fell through, however, following opposition from a group of stockholders led by well-known investor Harry Weinberg.

The rapid succession of new presidents at A&B finally slowed in 1980 with the arrival of Robert Pfeiffer, formerly the CEO at Matson. An upward swing in sugar prices helped boost the company's profits that year, and, by 1983, sugar accounted for 21 percent of A&B's $395 million in sales. As the company again considered diversification, Harry Weinberg, Hawaii's largest individual landowner, increased his holding in A&B to 25 percent. In 1984, Weinberg forced a proxy battle for control of the company, arguing that A&B's land holdings were worth far more than its books indicated and that property development should be the company's top priority. Unlike most of his boardroom conflicts with large Hawaiian companies, however, this one ended with Weinberg and his associates forced off the A&B board of directors.

In January 1987, A&B got rid of its merchandising division, selling A&B Commercial Company to Monarch Building Supply, Inc., a Honolulu-based company. By this time, A&B had revenues of $655 million, the bulk of which was generated by Matson, which controlled about 75 percent of the container cargo shipping market between Hawaii and the West Coast. Between 1983 and 1987, profits more than doubled to $120 million, and about three-fourths of that total came from Matson. In 1987 A&B began preparing to grow coffee on Kauai through a joint venture between its McBryde subsidiary and Hills Brothers. Another development in 1987 was Matson's formation of a new subsidiary, Matson Intermodal System, Inc., whose specialty was arranging for the transport by rail and truck of cargo containers from Pacific Coast ports to destinations in the U.S. interior.

Several key events occurred in 1989. A&B sold off its remaining shares of Pacific Resources to Australia's Broken Hill Proprietary Company for $123 million, pocketing a substantial profit. The company made another tidy sum on the sale of the Wailea resort community on Maui to Shinwa Golf Group for about $198 million. A&B had been developing the beachfront resort since 1970. Some of the proceeds from these sales were used to purchase development property on the U.S. mainland, most notably in California, Washington state, Colorado, and Texas. Matson formed another subsidiary in 1989, this one called Matson Leasing Company, Inc. Matson Leasing quickly grew into one of the largest lessors of marine cargo containers in the world, establishing 12 offices in the Americas, Europe, Asia, and Australia and operating from 98 depot locations across the globe. A final key development in 1989 was a company restructuring in which there would now be two main subsidiaries of A&B: Matson Navigation and the newly created

A&B-Hawaii, Inc. (ABHI). The latter took over management of all of A&B's food products and property development and management subsidiaries and operations. A&B recorded net income of $199 million on revenue of $846 million in 1989. Two years later Pfeiffer passed the reins of the company to John C. Couch, who became president and CEO. Couch had served A&B for 15 years, initially with Matson Navigation Company.

1990s and Beyond

A&B's revenues stagnated and net income slumped during the first part of the 1990s, as the Hawaiian economy was battered from both the recession in the United States and the bursting of the late 1980s bubble economy in Japan. With sales hovering around the $750 million mark from 1990 to 1992, company earnings dipped to under $19 million in 1992, the lowest level in over a decade. That figure included a $15.8 million charge to cover losses from Hurricane Iniki, which devastated Kauai in 1992. Nevertheless, A&B mounted a successful comeback the following year. The company reported major increases in both profit and revenue, up to $67 million and $979 million, respectively. Moreover, in June 1993, A&B's $63 million purchase of the 72 percent of California and Hawaiian Sugar Company, Inc. (C&H) that it did not already own helped bolster revenues and profits. For most of the 20th century, C&H had bought the bulk of the raw sugar produced by A&B and had been cooperatively owned by all of Hawaii's sugar producers. A&B took full control of C&H in order to fund needed improvements at the company's huge refinery in Crockett, California. C&H, which had annual revenues of about $500 million, was the leading brand of sugar west of the Mississippi. Also in 1993, Nestlé Beverage Co., successor to Hills Brothers, pulled out of the Kauai coffee joint venture following the devastation of Hurricane Iniki, leaving A&B in full control of what would eventually be called Kauai Coffee Company, Inc.

The takeover of C&H helped propel revenues past the $1 billion mark in 1994, to $1.14 billion. Earnings grew only slightly, however, totaling $74.6 million. That year, Matson launched a Pacific Coast shipping service linking the ports of Los Angeles, Seattle, and Vancouver, British Columbia. This "shuttle" service offered shippers an alternative to rail and truck transport along the coast. In April of the following year, Pfeiffer retired and Couch was named to the additional post of chairman. Two months later A&B sold Matson Leasing for about $362 million to Xtra Corporation, a Boston-based transportation services firm that had approached A&B with an unsolicited offer. A&B had built Matson Leasing into the world's seventh largest marine container leasing company and would have needed to make additional investments in the subsidiary to maintain its rapid growth rate. Most analysts applauded the sale for both its timing and its price. Other developments in 1995 included a restructuring of C&H, which was operating in the red. About one-fourth of the jobs at C&H's refinery in Crockett, California, were eliminated. A&B also phased out its unprofitable sugar operations on Kauai.

In early 1996 came the start of a planned ten-year transPacific shipping alliance between Matson Navigation and American President Lines, Ltd. (APL). The first step involved APL selling six container ships and some assets in Guam to

Matson for $164 million. Matson would use five of the vessels on westbound voyages from the Pacific Coast to Hawaii and Guam. Then APL would charter the ships for excursions to the Far East. Meantime, A&B continued to battle the effects of the prolonged economic malaise afflicting Hawaii, managing in spite of this operating environment to post record revenues of $1.28 billion in 1997 and earnings of $81.4 million, the latter the company's best performance in six years. Aiding in these positives were A&B's income-generating properties on the mainland, which by this time included three million square feet in six western states. Although the Maui sugar plantation performed poorly that year, Kauai Coffee produced a record harvest of more than four million pounds, a 70 percent increase over the previous year and a total that represented nearly 60 percent of the coffee grown in the entire United States. Unfortunately, the coffee subsidiary had yet to make a profit.

In July 1998 Couch took an indefinite medical leave after he began receiving treatment for liver cancer. Pfeiffer was brought back as chairman temporarily, with Charles M. Stockholm taking over as chairman in August 1999. In October 1998 W. Allen Doane was promoted from executive vice-president to president and CEO of A&B, having joined the company in 1991 as executive vice-president and COO of ABHI. A&B made a strategic shift in December 1998 when it sold a 64 percent stake in C&H to an investment group headed by Citicorp Venture Capital Ltd. The company received about $80 million in proceeds but still posted a nearly $20 million loss on the sale. In December 1999 A&B's subsidiary structure was altered when ABHI was eliminated through its merger into the parent company. The former subsidiaries of ABHI were now direct subsidiaries of A&B. Another significant change to the food operations came in 2000 when the company decided to close one of its two sugar mills on Maui.

On the transport side, Matson in September 1998 entered into a joint venture with Saltchuk Resources, Inc. and International Shipping Agency, Inc. to operate an ocean shipping service between Florida and Puerto Rico. Matson Logistics Solutions, Inc. was formed in 1998 to begin offering supply and distribution services. In July of the following year, Matson formed a joint venture with Stevedoring Services of America that combined the companies' terminal and cargo handling services operations in Los Angeles, Long Beach, Oakland, and Seattle. At the same time, Matson Intermodal was being rapidly expanded, including through the acquisition in 2000 of Paragon Transportation Group, an intermodal marketing firm based in Dublin, California, that was particularly strong in the California, Nevada, Montana, Oklahoma, and Michigan markets and was therefore able to bolster Matson's national coverage. In late 2000 the Pacific Coast shuttle service that was launched by Matson in 1994 was replaced by regular rail and truck service between Los Angeles and Seattle operated by Matson Intermodal.

The Hawaiian economy finally appeared to be entering into at least a period of moderate growth by 2000, and A&B's results reflected the better times. Revenues increased 7 percent, while earnings before exceptional items increased 15 percent. With the sale of the majority interest in C&H, the ocean transportation operations now dwarfed both the real estate and food sectors, having generated about 80 percent of 2000 revenues. A&B planned to continue to expand its transport operations and

launched a $32 million program to substantially improve its main terminal in Honolulu at Sand Island. In real estate, a key initiative was the company's 1,045-acre residential-resort community in Poipu, Kauai, the plans of which called for more than 200 hotel rooms, 700 time-share vacation units, and as many as 3,000 residential units. A&B's troubled food operations received some good news in 2000 in the form of the first year of profitability for Kauai Coffee. The company was also investing $11 million into a new plant where sugarcane bagasse would be made into environmentally friendly composite panelboard. A&B was the last of Hawaii's Big Five companies to remain independent and based on the islands; its durability over more than 130 years of operation proved that a mainland address was not a prerequisite for long-term success.

Principal Subsidiaries

A&B Development Company; A&B Properties, Inc.; East Maui Irrigation Company, Limited; Hawaiian Duragreen, Inc.; Kukui'ula Development Company, Inc.; Matson Navigation Company, Inc.; Matson Intermodal System, Inc.; Matson Logistics Solutions, Inc.; Matson Services Company, Inc.; Matson Terminals, Inc.; McBryde Sugar Company, Limited; Kauai Coffee Company, Inc.; Kahului Trucking & Storage, Inc.; Kauai Commercial Company, Incorporated.

Principal Divisions

Hawaiian Commercial & Sugar Company.

Principal Competitors

CSX Corporation; Sauce Bros., Inc.; Aloha Cargo Transport, Inc.; Pasha Hawaii Transport Lines LLC.

Further Reading

"A&B, Land & Sea: One Hundred and Twenty-Five Years Strong," *Ampersand* (special issue), Honolulu: Alexander & Baldwin, Inc., 1995.

"Alexander & Baldwin: Cutting Sugar's Role with Big Acquisitions," *Business Week,* February 12, 1979, pp. 88–91.

"Alexander & Baldwin: Will It Put Its Money Where Its Mouth Is?" *Business Week,* March 19, 1984, pp. 92–93.

Baldwin, Arthur D., *A Memoir of Henry Perrine Baldwin, 1842 to 1911,* Cleveland: [privately printed], 1915.

Beauchamp, Marc, "Hunkering Down Is No Strategy," *Forbes,* October 31, 1988, pp. 54–62.

"Can Alexander & Baldwin Do It Again?" *Financial World,* May 15, 1981, pp. 27–28.

Christensen, Kathryn, "After Years of Turmoil, a Hawaii Sugar Firm Returns to Stability," *Wall Street Journal,* August 20, 1981 p. 1.

Cieply, Michael, "East of Eden," *Forbes,* January 31, 1983, pp. 34–36.

Davies, John, "Coffee Replaces Sugar in Some Hawaiian Fields," *Journal of Commerce,* July 9, 1990, p. 1A.

Fuller, Larry, "Kauai Coffee Grows into Next Millennium," *Pacific Business News,* March 12, 1999, p. 3.

Garcia, Art, "Spotlight on Alexander & Baldwin," *Journal of Commerce,* April 7, 1980, p. 3.

Gillis, Curis, "Matson Makes Tracks," *American Shipper,* September 2000, p. 60.

"An Hawaiian Company Invests Its Sugar Profits," *Business Week,* April 14, 1975, pp. 80–81.

Kamhis, Jacob, "Doane Replaces Couch As A&B Head," *Pacific Business News,* November 2, 1998, p. A2.

——, "W. Allen Doane: A&B Exec's Biggest Early Goal Was Owning a Car," *Pacific Business News,* September 21, 1998, p. A18.

Lynch, Russ, "A&B Picks Doane to Lead Company," *Honolulu Star-Bulletin,* October 23, 1998, p. B1.

Roig, Suzanne, "Matson Sells Container Lease Firm," *Honolulu Advertiser,* May 3, 1995.

Smith, Christopher, and Cynthia Green, "A Seasoned Raider Loses His Touch," *Business Week,* May 13, 1985, p. 31.

Stindt, Fred A., *Matson's Century of Ships,* Kelseyville, Calif.: F.A. Stindt, 1982, 319 p.

"A Sweet Stock from the Islands," *Fortune,* November 25, 1985, pp. 161–68.

Trifonovitch, Kelli Abe, "From Big Five to Top Five," *Hawaii Business,* August 2000, p. 36.

Wastler, Allen R., "Accounting Changes, Iniki Fallout Depress Alexander & Baldwin Profit," *Journal of Commerce,* February 3, 1993, p. 1B.

Whitehead, John S., "Western Progressives, Old South Planters, or Colonial Oppressors: The Enigma of Hawaii's 'Big Five,' 1898–1940," *Western Historical Quarterly,* Autumn 1999, pp. 295–326.

Wood, Bill, "Alexander & Baldwin Fights Battle to Grow," *Pacific Business News,* July 18, 1994.

Worden, William L., *Cargoes: Matson's First Century in the Pacific,* Honolulu: University Press of Hawaii, 1981, 192 p.

Zipser, Andy, "When Its Ship Comes In," *Barron's,* pp. 28–29.

—Robert R. Jacobson
—update: David E. Salamie

Amdahl Corporation

1250 East Arques Avenue
Sunnyvale, California 94088-3470
U.S.A.
Telephone: (408) 746-6000
Fax: (408) 746-3243
Web site: http://www.amdahl.com

Wholly Owned Subsidiary of Fujitsu Limited
Incorporated: 1970
Employees: 10,000
NAIC: 541511 Custom Computer Programming Services;
541512 Computer Systems Design Services; 541519
Other Computer Related Services; 541610
Management Consulting Services; 511210 Software
Publishers; 421430 Computer and Computer
Peripheral Equipment and Software Wholesalers

Having abandoned its founding business of manufacturing mainframe computers, Amdahl Corporation has positioned itself in the early 21st century as a developer and implementer of information technology systems and services, and enterprise-level software, and as a provider of professional and consulting services. As an adjunct to its services businesses, the company, a wholly owned subsidiary of Japan's Fujitsu Limited, continues to offer its customers computer servers and storage systems. Among Amdahl's subsidiary operations are DMR Consulting Group, Inc., which focuses on e-consulting services and business solutions for both large corporations and Internet startups; Fujitsu Software Technology Corporation, which provides comprehensive software solutions in various areas of data storage; Fujitsu Technology Solutions, Inc., the unit that handles the company's operations in the areas of servers and storage systems; and trustedanswer.com, a provider of outsourced customer service and customer support services.

Prehistory and the Startup Stage

Amdahl Corporation was founded on October 19, 1970, in Sunnyvale, California, by Gene M. Amdahl. Born in 1922 in South Dakota, Amdahl left his home state to pursue a doctoral degree in theoretical physics. With a knowledge of electronics gained in the Navy and a familiarity with computer programming garnered from a brief course, Amdahl designed and helped construct an early computer known as the WISC (Wisconsin Integrally Synchronized Computer).

In 1952 Amdahl joined IBM and became chief designer of the IBM 704 computer, which was released in 1954. In 1955 Amdahl and other systems designers began conceptualizing a new computer for IBM, which they christened the Datatron. IBM's Stretch, also known as the IBM 7030, was an outgrowth of the Datatron, a computer using new transistor technology. The name Stretch was not an acronym, but rather stood for ''stretching the limits of computer technology development.'' Although Stretch was a financial failure for IBM, it was valuable as the precursor to the successful IBM System 360. In 1956 Amdahl left IBM; he worked at two other high-technology firms before returning to IBM four years later. Amdahl later became the principal architect for the phenomenally successful System 360, which was introduced in 1964.

Amdahl was appointed an IBM fellow, and was thus free to pursue his own research projects. In early 1969, while director of IBM's Advanced Computing Systems Laboratory in Menlo Park, California, he began to investigate the company's cost-pricing cycle as it applied to a large computer they were developing. His team concluded that to make the computer pay for itself, IBM would also have to market two scaled-down versions of the advanced technology. IBM management insisted that Amdahl stay with the original plan to create only one large processor, while Amdahl recommended that they shut down the laboratory. The laboratory was closed in the spring of 1969.

Over the following few months, Amdahl reviewed the policies that prevented IBM from aiming at the high end of computer development and presented his analysis to IBM's top three executives. Although the officers agreed with his analysis, they maintained that it would not be in IBM's best interest to change direction. Amdahl decided to strike out on his own.

Amdahl submitted his resignation to IBM for the second time in September 1970 and founded Amdahl Corporation just a few

Company Perspectives:

With more than 30 years of experience delivering large-scale computing and client/server technology, the Amdahl mission is to deliver innovative systems, services and support to lead customers to the most complete and powerful data centers of the 21st century.

weeks later. Amdahl took none of IBM's technical personnel with him when he left; he was joined only by young financial specialist Ray Williams and two secretaries. Amdahl and Williams determined that they would need between $33 million and $44 million to see a product to completion (in fact, it took $47.5 million). They had chosen a difficult year for raising money, as new capital gains taxes and an advancing recession made venture capital scarce. Amdahl and Williams first took their business plan to investment bankers, who rejected their proposal because they felt that Amdahl Corporation could not effectively challenge IBM. The pair eventually received $2 million from Heizer Corporation, venture capitalists in Chicago, the day after spending the last of their own investment.

At the same time, three other young California computer companies—MASCOR (Multiple Access Systems Corporation, which was started by staff members who left IBM after the closing of the Advanced Computing Systems Laboratory), Berkeley Computers, and Gemini Computers—had gone bankrupt. Many of their employees joined Amdahl Corporation, forming an impressive technical team.

During Amdahl Corporation's first eight months, it continued the search for more capital. The needed funds came from Fujitsu Limited, a leading Japanese computer manufacturer, which suggested a joint development program and licensing under Amdahl's patents. This 1971 agreement was accompanied by the $5 million investment that Amdahl needed to complete its second phase of development.

In 1972 Nixdorf Computers, a leading German computer manufacturer, agreed to invest $6 million if Nixdorf could represent Amdahl in Europe. Fujitsu also increased its investment, and U.S. investors began to appear. Amdahl amassed a total of $20 million to build a prototype computer and a production facility.

Also in 1972, IBM announced the debut of the 370, its first computer with virtual memory, a flexible, advanced memory technology. Amdahl had been developing a computer like the IBM 370, but without virtual memory, and IBM's introduction forced Amdahl to scrap its initial design.

Amdahl Corporation decided to offer stock publicly in early 1973, but could not find an underwriter. The company then experienced delays with the Securities and Exchange Commission until 1974, by which time the stock market had declined, so Amdahl returned to the private market.

In August 1974 Eugene R. White, a vice-president at Fairchild Camera and Instrument Corporation, was appointed president of Amdahl Corporation. Effecting changes that helped save the company, White laid off almost half the employees and concentrated on marketing efforts and field support services. He was also instrumental in negotiations with Fujitsu and Heizer to get the funding necessary to complete the company's first product.

Delivery of First Computer: 1975

In June 1975 Amdahl shipped its first computer, the Amdahl 470 V/6, to NASA's Goddard Spaceflight Center in New York. The computer competed directly with IBM's System 370 Model 168. The initial sale was followed by sales to the University of Michigan, Texas A & M University, and the University of Alberta. Massachusetts Mutual Life, Amdahl's first commercial customer, chose Amdahl's 470 V/6 over the IBM 370 when IBM raised its prices and delayed delivery. Other customers followed, including AT&T.

Determined to best IBM, Amdahl was the first truly plug-compatible manufacturer, or manufacturer whose products were compatible with both IBM hardware and software. Critics maintained that the Amdahl machines provided better performance for less money. IBM's machines were water-cooled, while Amdahl's were air-cooled, which decreased installation costs by $50,000 to $250,000. The use of LSI (large-scale-integration), many integrated circuits on each chip, meant the Amdahl 470 V/6 was one-third the size of IBM's 360/168; the V/6 also performed more than twice as fast and sold for about 10 percent less. Machine sales remained slow because of concerns over the company's survival, but by the spring of 1977 Amdahl had 50 units in place, seriously challenging IBM in large-scale computer placements. To improve its cash position, Amdahl decided to sell rather than lease its equipment. IBM responded by slashing prices, forcing Amdahl to follow suit.

In 1976 Amdahl successfully went public with its stock. With the new funds, the company converted its debt to equity, created substantial cash reserves, and found itself operating at a profit. Revenues climbed from less than $14 million in 1975 to $321 million in 1977, with net income of $48.2 million.

In response to the challenge from Amdahl, IBM announced several machine enhancements. Not until the announcement of its 3033 in 1977, however, did IBM come up with a competitor for the price/performance ratio of Amdahl's 470 V/6. Amdahl responded by announcing a new computer: the 470 V/7. About one-and-a-half times faster than IBM's 3033, it would cost only 3 percent more. A year later Amdahl had installed 100 of the machines.

Amdahl's loosely organized corporate structure was very unusual for such a high-revenue organization. Even after two years of full operation, Gene Amdahl and Gene White still spent much of their time in high-level sales—in fact, many customers insisted on meeting Amdahl personally before closing the deal. Any mention of a chief executive officer was intentionally omitted from the corporate bylaws, but in 1977 Amdahl did hire John C. Lewis as president. Lewis had previously served as president of the business systems and data systems divisions of Xerox Corporation, and had spent ten years in management at IBM. Gene White became deputy chairman.

In early 1979, IBM introduced a line of medium-sized computers called the 4300 series. This line, coupled with reports that

Key Dates:

1970: Gene M. Amdahl founds Amdahl Corporation as a developer of mainframe computers.
1971: Fujitsu Limited makes its first investment into the company.
1975: Company ships its first computer, the Amdahl 470 V/6.
1976: Amdahl Corporation goes public.
1979: Proposed merger with Memorex Corporation is blocked by Fujitsu, Amdahl's largest shareholder.
1980: Another merger proposal, with Storage Technology Corporation, is also blocked by Fujitsu.
1982: Company introduces the 580 series; branches out into storage devices.
1984: Fujitsu increases its stake in Amdahl to 49 percent.
1985: Amdahl's model 5890 debuts.
1988: Company introduces the 5990 processor.
1993: Collapse of mainframe market leads to 33 percent decline in revenues and a net loss of more than $575 million.
1995: DMR Group Inc., an information technology services firm, is acquired.
1996: Another technology services company, Trecom Business Systems Inc., is acquired.
1997: Fujitsu purchases the 58 percent of Amdahl it does not already own for $878 million, making Amdahl a wholly owned subsidiary.
2000: Amdahl announces that it will exit from the mainframe market.

IBM would soon be announcing the H-Series of large computers, prompted many Amdahl customers to lease rather than buy equipment in order to be able to shift to an IBM product later. This development created serious cash flow problems at Amdahl. Revenues dropped by $21 million in 1979, with a 64 percent drop in net income.

On September 1, 1979, Gene Amdahl resigned as chairman, a post he had held since 1970. Deputy Chairman Eugene R. White became chairman of the board and CEO, a post that had never before been filled. Staying on the board as chairman emeritus, Amdahl led a new technical excellence committee and focused on strategic development. Less than a year later he resigned from the board to form Trilogy Corporation, a computer company that would compete directly with Amdahl and IBM. Recognized as one of the world's leading innovators in computer design, Amdahl again put his creativity to work on a new venture.

In 1979 and 1980 Amdahl Corporation failed in two attempted mergers, first with Memorex Corporation, a manufacturer of computer data-storage equipment, and then with Storage Technology Corporation, a maker of printers and tape and disc storage subsystems. The failures were attributed to Fujitsu, Amdahl's largest shareholder with a 34 percent holding, which feared losing its influence in a merger and sought to keep tight reins on proprietary technology. Fujitsu's demands were rejected by the merger partners.

1980s: 580 Series, 5990 Processor, Branching Out

In November 1980, IBM announced the 3081 processor, previously labeled the H-Series, which would offer twice the performance of IBM's top model, the 3033, upon its completion in late 1981. The industry waited for Amdahl's response. Six days later Gene White announced the 580 series, a computer with processors twice as powerful as the Amdahl 470 series and still compatible with it, which also featured a more compact body and greater energy efficiency. Amdahl's new product was not slated for shipment until April 1982, however, and did not actually ship until August 1982, causing a drop in net income. In addition, Amdahl's early 580 series processor had significant reliability problems and was lacking in some of the features of the new IBM product. Amdahl's competitive advantage was further eroded by a U.S. Justice Department decision to dismiss a 13-year-old antitrust suit against IBM, enabling the giant computer manufacturer to price its products more aggressively and move faster with new technologies.

To expand its market, in 1980 Amdahl completed the successful acquisition of Tran Telecommunications Corporation, a maker of digital data communication networks. In 1982 Amdahl branched into storage devices by offering a direct-access storage device supplied by Fujitsu. This enabled Amdahl to broaden its product base and provided a buffer against the vicissitudes of direct competition with IBM's large-scale computers. By 1988 Amdahl's sales of storage devices had grown to about 20 percent of total sales. To remain competitive in its fierce battle with IBM, Amdahl was spending 13 percent of total sales on research and development in 1983, while IBM spent only 6.3 percent.

In 1984 Amdahl developed UTS, its version of UNIX, the operating system developed by AT&T. Amdahl claimed that UTS, which was compatible with UNIX, operated 25 percent faster run on the Amdahl 580 than on IBM's product, and did so for a lower licensing fee. The developers of the operating system ensured its complete compatibility with IBM's control programs.

Amdahl introduced multiple domain feature (MDF) in late 1984. MDF enabled a computer to run two or more different operating systems concurrently, while also performing multiple tasks. In just over two years, 30 percent of the Amdahl 580 series sites used this feature, cutting costs on software, hardware, and personnel.

In 1984 Heizer decided to liquidate its Amdahl stock. Fujitsu bought the offering, expanding its holdings to about 49 percent. The Japanese firm was prohibited by mutual agreement from owning more than 49.5 percent of Amdahl's shares, and in 1990 Fujitsu held about 43 percent of the company's stock.

Over the years Fujitsu provided important components and subassemblies for Amdahl processors, including LSI logic chips and very large-scale integration emitter-coupled logic chips, which were essential to Amdahl products. Fujitsu also played an important role in the design and manufacture of peripheral products. The two companies worked closely in supporting each other in their respective technological developments.

In May 1985 a former IBM executive, E. Joseph Zemke, joined Amdahl as COO, sharing the office of the president with

President and CEO John C. Lewis. Zemke had most recently been president and CEO of Auto-Trol Technology of Denver, Colorado, and had been corporate director of marketing at IBM.

Amdahl's model 5890, introduced in October 1985 to compete directly with IBM's Sierra-class CPU, stood up against its IBM counterpart in reliability and technology and offered multiprocessor capabilities that enhanced the performance range of Amdahl processors. In late 1986, Amdahl began shipping its new model. The computers performed even better than advertised, and final quarter sales boosted revenues to nearly $1 billion. The success of the model 5890 was reflected in Amdahl's increased customer base. Between 1980 and 1985 its customer sites in the United States grew from 450 to 1,350, and it expanded internationally from 14 to 19 countries. The company also increased sales of its large-scale disc-storage products made by Fujitsu.

Continued shipment of its successful product lines during 1987 catapulted Amdahl's revenues to $1.5 billion, an increase of almost 56 percent over the previous year, and earnings jumped nearly 250 percent. The company upgraded its successful 5890 to keep abreast of improvements in IBM's 3090 computer. Its further commitment to UTS enhanced its strength.

John C. Lewis was elected chairman of Amdahl in May 1987, retaining the title of CEO. Joseph Zemke became president, but continued his duties as COO. Gene White, formerly chairman, again became vice-chairman.

For most of its existence, Amdahl had played catch-up to IBM's product announcements, but in May 1988, it took the initiative and announced a new product line, the 5990 processor. Orders poured in. IBM reacted quickly to defend its 69 percent of the U.S. large-scale computer market share, but the new processor—acknowledged as the fastest in the industry—not only outperformed IBM by almost 50 percent, but was also more compact and less costly. By the end of 1988, Amdahl had shipped more than 40 of its new mainframes. The price and performance features of Amdahl's products raised sales nearly 17 percent to $2.1 billion. IBM responded by discounting its systems. Amdahl announced its own discounts, and the decreased profit margin caused earnings to fall by 30 percent in 1989.

Amdahl's consistent ability to produce computers with a superior price/performance ratio helped keep the company competitive in a market dominated by IBM. Staying on the leading edge of technology and catering to its customers' needs launched Amdahl to more than $2 billion in revenues in 1989. In February, Amdahl acquired Key Computer Laboratories, Inc., a company specializing in scalar computing that was expanding globally, with 33 percent of its revenues coming from Europe and 8 percent from Asia and the Pacific region in 1989. In 1991 Amdahl introduced Huron, a successful new application development software, and established the Canadian Software Development Centre. The center was run by Huron's creator, Helge Knudsen.

1990s: Shrinking Mainframe Market, Focusing on Services

As the 1990s progressed, the major threat to Amdahl's viability no longer appeared to be IBM, but the shrinking main-

frame computer market. As smaller, cheaper, and more powerful machines became available, Amdahl found its sales slipping. Excessive costs forced the company to stop work on a mainframe Unix product that had long been underway. By September 1993, sales had collapsed. Amdahl's Zemke (who became CEO in 1992) was quoted in *Business Week* as saying, "It was like Death Valley." Amdahl shut down factory lines and cut back the workforce three times that year. The company reported a net loss of more than $575 million for 1993 and revenues fell to $1.68 billion, a 33 percent drop from the record revenues of $2.52 billion the previous year.

Analysts predicted that Amdahl's continued success would require stronger innovation. Amdahl's strategy was to offer its customers integrated packages combining its hardware technology with the industry's most advanced software, as well as stellar support and consulting services. Amdahl's maintenance, support, and consulting services made up 28 percent of revenues in 1993 and increased another 11 percent in the first quarter of 1994. Margins on those services were almost double the hardware margins, and Amdahl's service businesses were consistently given the highest ratings in the industry.

In the following year, Amdahl entered into new partnerships with three computer firms: Electronic Data Systems, nCube, and Sun Microsystems. The agreement with Electronic Data Systems spawned the Antares Alliance Group, a joint software development group 80 percent owned by Amdahl. Antares was formed to market Amdahl's Huron and research new software ideas and prototypes for business analysis and modeling programs. Helge Knudsen became director of the Antares Research Institute.

In 1994 Amdahl introduced the Xplorer 2000 series. The new product was the result of an alliance between Amdahl, Oracle, and Information Builders, Inc. The partnership was formed, according to *Software Magazine,* to explore opportunities to create "massively parallel database servers and software that will let customers process thousands of transactions per second and share data between MVS and Unix systems."

Later that year, Amdahl and Sun Microsystems introduced A + Edition, a group of extensions that allowed Sun's symmetrical multiprocessing servers to perform more efficiently when a higher number of total possible servers were working. The software accomplished this by providing tuning for database applications with a large number of users and more evenly distributing the workload among the processors in the servers. While the new product was well received, some potential customers expressed concern about the cost for the value.

Expanding on its position as a provider of integrated services, Amdahl won a bidding war for DMR Group Inc., acquiring the Canadian firm in November 1995 for about $140 million. DMR provided information technology consulting services as well as systems development, systems integration, and outsourcing services on a worldwide basis. The firm had annual revenues of nearly $220 million, which boosted the share of Amdahl revenue that came from software and services to 40 percent. DMR was combined with Amdahl's Business Solutions Group to form DMR Consulting Group, Inc., which operated as a subsidiary.

Zemke resigned as CEO in March 1996 for "personal reasons." The move came in the wake of rather dismal results for 1995: net income of only $28.5 million and a further decline in revenues to $1.52 billion. Lewis became CEO once again. Soon thereafter, Amdahl acquired another services-oriented company, Trecom Business Systems Inc., for $145 million. Based in Edison, New Jersey, Trecom focused mainly on designing and providing client-server networks for corporations. Its geographic presence in the eastern and southern United States meshed well with DMR's strength in the West and in Canada. The firm had annual revenues of $140 million. Trecom was eventually merged into DMR.

Amdahl returned to the red for 1996, reporting a $326 million net loss on revenues of $1.63 billion, partly due to costs related to the integration of its acquisitions. An even larger factor was a $130 million writeoff of outmoded water-cooled mainframe inventory. Amdahl's mainframes were hurt by IBM's 1995 introduction of CMOS-based mainframes, which were air-cooled and less costly to operate. Amdahl had to play catch-up in introducing its own CMOS-based models, the Millennium Global Servers, in late 1996. The later months of 1996 also saw Amdahl begin selling a line of Windows NT-based servers called EnVista. Amdahl packaged the servers with software and services related to the Internet, intracompany communications and data sharing, and database applications. In the area of open systems, the company added new storage systems to its product line and began reselling Sun Microsystems' SPARC servers. Meantime, nearly two-thirds of revenues for 1996 were generated by Amdahl's software and services operations.

By mid-1997, with Amdahl having posted six straight quarterly losses, there was much skepticism about the future viability of the company. Those concerns were laid to rest in September of that year when Fujitsu purchased the 58 percent of Amdahl it did not already own for $878 million. Amdahl was now a wholly owned subsidiary of Fujitsu and could tap into the very deep pockets of the Japanese electronics giant. In the immediate wake of the buyout, David B. Wright was named to succeed Lewis as CEO. Wright had been executive vice-president of the company's hardware and systems support operations, and his background in services was a key factor in his selection as Amdahl continued to increase its emphasis on software, services, and consulting. DMR in particular was growing at the rapid rate of 30 percent per year and its revenues reached $700 million in 1997. Part of this surge came from the accelerating demand for services related to the fixing or replacement of systems affected by the year 2000 computer bug.

In early 1998 Amdahl entered into an alliance with Microsoft Corporation to provide products and services designed to integrate Microsoft's Windows NT and BackOffice products with mainframe systems. The following year the company acquired Sentryl Software, which developed software for automated storage management systems.

In October 2000 Wright resigned as CEO, with Yasushi Tajiri named interim CEO. Just a few weeks later, the company announced that it was exiting from its founding mainframe business. On the hardware side, Amdahl would now be involved only in the server and storage sectors. The company's future, in any event, clearly lay in the world of services and consulting. In December 2000 Amdahl announced that it would eliminate nearly one-fifth of its California workforce in connection with its exit from mainframes. At the same time, Fujitsu turned Amdahl into a holding company for several businesses: Amdahl Software; DMR Consulting; Amdahl IT Services, which focused on information technology infrastructure services for large-scale enterprises; and Fujitsu Technology Solutions, which was the company's hardware arm, selling servers and storage systems. In March 2001 Amdahl Software was relaunched as Fujitsu Software Technology Corporation (Fujitsu Softek), with a mission of providing comprehensive software solutions in various areas of data storage. These moves early in the new millennium continued Amdahl's transformation from mainframe manufacturer to provider of information technology software, services, and consulting.

Principal Subsidiaries

Amdahl Federal Service Corporation; Amdahl IT Services; Amdahl Region Sales and Service; DMR Consulting Group, Inc.; Fujitsu Software Technology Corporation; Fujitsu Technology Solutions, Inc.; trustedanswer.com; Amdahl Deutschland GmbH (Germany); Amdahl Ireland Ltd.; Amdahl (Schweiz) AG (Switzerland); Amdahl (U.K.) Ltd.

Principal Competitors

NEC Corporation; International Business Machines Corporation; Electronic Data Systems Corporation; Unisys Corporation; Computer Sciences Corporation; Getronics NV; Compaq Computer Corporation; Hewlett-Packard Company; Cap Gemini Ernst & Young; Bull; Silicon Graphics, Inc.; Accenture Ltd.; Computer Associates International, Inc.

Further Reading

Amdahl, Gene M., "The Early Chapters of the PCM Story," *Datamation,* February 1979.

Barker, Paul, "Developer of Huron Goes Back to His Roots," *Computing Canada,* March 30, 1994, p. 13.

Barret, Larry, "Amdahl Shifts to Services As the Millennium Nears," *San Jose Business Journal,* June 10, 1996, p. 3.

Bozman, Jean S., "Amdahl, Sun Honor Promise with A+," *ComputerWorld,* October 3, 1994, p. 77.

Cancilla, Susan, "Amdahl, IBM Awake to Mainframe Revival," *Info Canada,* March 1995, p. IC2.

Clark, Don, "Fujitsu's Amdahl Plans to Stop Making IBM Compatibles, Seeing Little to Gain," *Wall Street Journal,* October 19, 2000.

DePompa, Barbara, "Amdahl Buys into Services: Mainframe Maker Announces Acquisition of DMR in Bid to Speed Diversification," *InformationWeek,* October 2, 1995, p. 102.

Goldberg, Michael, "Amdahl Ventures Out of Glass House," *Computer World,* September 30, 1996.

Gomes, Lee, "Amdahl's Autonomy Fades As Fujitsu Offers $850 Million for Remaining Stake," *Wall Street Journal,* July 31, 1997, p. A3.

Haber, Carol, "Fujitsu to Buy Rest of Amdahl," *Electronic News,* August 4, 1997, pp. 4, 53.

Hof, Robert D., "Amdahl Escapes 'Death Valley,' but Now What?" *Business Week,* May 16, 1994, p. 88.

Kelley, Bill, "Amdahl Jumps Out of the Box," *Journal of Business Strategy,* May/June 1995, pp. 22–29.

McGee, Marianne Kalbasuk, "Services Driven: Amdahl Sees DMR Consulting Unit As Engine of Growth Beyond Mainframes," *InformationWeek*, February 16, 1998, p. 117.

Rodengen, Jeffrey L., *The Legend of Amdahl*, Fort Lauderdale, Fla.: Write Stuff Syndicate, 2000, 144 p.

Schmedel, Scott, "Taking on the Industry Giant," *Harvard Business Review*, March-April 1980.

Swartz, Jon, "Fujitsu to Absorb Amdahl," *San Francisco Chronicle*, July 31, 1997, p. D1.

Ubois, Jeff, and Jack Vaughan, "Parallelizing DBs Come to Town," *Software Magazine*, June 1994, p. 24.

Uttal, Bro, "Gene Amdahl Takes Aim at I.B.M.," *Fortune*, September 1977.

Vijayan, Jaikumar, "Amdahl Gives Up on Mainframe Business," *ComputerWorld*, October 23, 2000, pp. 1, 83.

Vizard, Michael, and Ted Smalley Bowen, "Amdahl to Reinvent Itself in E-Services Push," *InfoWorld*, December 20, 1999, p. 3.

—Ann T. Russell
—updates: Katherine Smethurst, David E. Salamie

American Red Cross

American Red Cross

430 17th Street NW
Washington, D.C. 20006
U.S.A.
Telephone: (202) 737-8300
Fax: (703) 248-4256
Web site: http://www.redcross.org

Nonprofit Company
Incorporated: 1881
Employees: 32,000
Sales: $2.4 billion (1999)
NAIC: 621991 Blood and Organ Banks; 62423
    Emergency and Other Relief Services

The American Red Cross is a nonprofit agency with a long history of providing relief to individuals affected by war and natural disaster. It was first formed in order to aid men wounded on the battlefield. It evolved into a network of approximately 1,300 local chapters of volunteers who respond to flood, fire, earthquake, and drought. The American Red Cross has played an enormously important historical role in supporting American troops in the two world wars and in ensuing conflicts. It has also been instrumental in organizing relief in countless natural disasters, from the Johnstown Flood to the Great San Francisco Earthquake to many more recent catastrophes. The organization's national presence and prestige allow it to spearhead fundraising drives to benefit stricken communities, and it also often serves as the distribution network for funds or goods raised by other organizations or donated by the government. Though the Red Cross was formed in response to war and disaster, it also developed a coherent peacetime mission, including teaching first aid and life-saving, and running blood banks. The Red Cross controls about 50 percent of the blood services market in the United States. About half the organization's revenue comes from the sale of its blood products. The rest comes from charitable donations from individuals and corporations. It also receives money through the charitable fundraising organization United Way.

Inspiration of Clara Barton

The American Red Cross dates its formal beginning to 1881, but it was active before that. Its roots lie in Europe, where the International Red Cross was founded in Geneva in 1864. The impetus for the founding of the international group was a book published in 1862 by a Swiss businessman, Jean Henri Dunant. Dunant witnessed the horrific aftermath of a battle between Austrian and French forces near the Italian village of Solferino when he was traveling in the vicinity for business. Some 30,000 to 40,000 dead and wounded men lay on the battlefield, with no one to care for them. Dunant was so struck by the carnage that he wrote a book about what he had seen, and pleaded for the formation of volunteer civilian groups to aid wounded soldiers. Dunant spearheaded a group that soon formed the International Committee of the Red Cross. Though the United States sent an observer to the inaugural Red Cross conference, the U.S. did not at that time ratify what became known as the Geneva Convention. The United States was in the midst of its own Civil War, and paid little attention to this event in Switzerland. Yet battlefield relief for the wounded was vitally important. Clara Barton, a former schoolteacher and patent office clerk, became a one-woman force behind the Red Cross in the United States. Though she was not trained as a nurse and was a single woman of modest means, Barton had friends in high places in Washington, through her Patent Office work. She began a crusade to bring supplies and aid to the Civil War wounded, and went herself to the front lines, driving a mule-wagon of supplies, serving hot soup, and nursing, all as needed. After the war, she organized a search for missing prisoners of war. When ill health sent her to Europe for a rest, she became acquainted with the work of the Red Cross there. When she returned to the United States, she lobbied for a Red Cross in her home country, becoming a noted speaker all across the nation. With the war over in the United States, Barton had the idea of instituting the Red Cross as a disaster relief organization. Nothing like this existed at the time. Barton became the American representative of the International Red Cross in 1881, and in 1882, Congress finally ratified the Geneva Convention.

In its earliest years, the American Red Cross existed almost solely through the energy of Clara Barton. She shaped its mission, and it was her political connections that made things work. She was an extraordinarily driven and hands-on person. The Red Cross did little without her direct involvement. One of the organization's first major disaster relief efforts was the Johnstown Flood of 1889, which drowned over 2,000 people and displaced most of Johnstown, Pennsylvania's 30,000 residents. Barton and her small staff went to Johnstown immediately, and stayed for five months. The Red Cross raised cash, disbursed goods, and oversaw the building of temporary housing with donated lumber. The Red Cross became increasingly skilled at handling this kind of disaster, and the organization won great praise for its domestic work. The limits of the organization's duties were not clearly spelled out, however, and the Red Cross extended itself to wherever Clara Barton felt called. The Red Cross sent wheat to Russia to aid starving peasants in 1892, and Barton sailed to Turkey in 1896 to negotiate aid for the violently oppressed Armenians. During the Spanish-American War of 1898, the exact duties of the American Red Cross were not clear, leading to conflict with the Army Medical Corps. Though the Red Cross was usually seen as ultimately helpful, it was also criticized for overstepping bounds and sometimes for its accounting practices. Congress officially chartered the American Red Cross in 1900, but the group was nevertheless plagued with factionalism and lack of focus. Clara Barton was elected president-for-life of the Red Cross in 1901, but resigned in 1904 after an aborted investigation into diversion of funds.

Role in Peace and War

The group reincorporated under a new Congressional charter in 1905, which made it a semi-governmental agency with some of its governors appointed by the President of the United States. The Red Cross developed a "peacetime" program around this time, defining a role for itself when neither war nor natural disaster threatened. It began training people in first aid and running courses in water safety. By 1917, the Red Cross had spread to 267 chapters across the United States. It had working funds of about $200,000 and a paid staff nationwide of 167 people. The group was exceedingly active in World War I, enrolling millions of volunteers to sew and knit clothing, roll bandages, and package food and supplies. The Red Cross sent thousands of nurses and ambulance drivers into the war, and raised millions of dollars in donations. After the war, the group was criticized for allegedly mismanaging funds and for taking on duties that properly belonged to the government. The Red Cross restated its mission in 1922, dedicating itself first to military welfare and to disaster relief. Promotion of public health was its third area of concern. In addition, the group spelled out its intention not to duplicate the work of other agencies. Membership grew and spread through the 1920s and

1930s, though the size of chapters and their level of funding varied considerably from place to place. By 1941, total American Red Cross membership had grown to over nine million people. During World War II, membership swelled dramatically. Members were counted as anyone who donated a dollar or more to the organization. There were over 36.6 million members by 1945, which was more than 25 percent of the U.S. population. The group had close to 4,000 chapters, and during World War II the Red Cross raised more than $666.5 million.

Rise of Blood Banking

The Red Cross began operating blood banks in 1937. In 1940 it began a "Plasma for Britain" project to send blood to British soldiers. This was the first mass blood donation campaign, and the first mass production of blood products. The plasma campaign was overseen by a pioneer of blood bank science, Dr. Charles Drew. Drew, an African American, was a noted founder of blood storage technology. The U.S. military asked the Red Cross to provide blood for battlefield transfusion when the United States entered the war. Drew directed the Red Cross program for eight months, but resigned in outrage because the Red Cross continued to comply with the military's request that the blood of black and white donors be segregated. The Red Cross continued to segregate blood by race until 1950. During World War II, the Red Cross collected blood from over six million donors. Running blood banks became one of the most important missions of the Red Cross over the next 50 years. In 1948, with the war behind it, the Red Cross established a National Blood Donor Program to provide blood to hospitals. Blood was collected by local chapters, and processed through 28 regional blood centers. Over the next decades, Red Cross researchers pioneered key aspects of blood bank technology. A Red Cross researcher discovered how to process blood for an anti-hemorrhaging agent, and Red Cross scientists also crafted a method to process the clotting agent needed by hemophiliacs. The Red Cross's donated blood was at first given without charge to hospitals, but in the 1950s it began charging enough to recoup its costs. By the end of the 1970s, the Red Cross managed about half the nation's blood supply. It continued to hold this market share. By the early 2000s, sale of blood products accounted for about half the group's operating revenue, and the Red Cross provided just over half the blood products used in the United States.

The Red Cross continued its services to soldiers during the Korean War and after. Besides running blood banks, its peacetime mission largely consisted of disaster relief. Each year the organization set aside a specific sum in its budget to pay for its disaster relief work. Extra money was put in a reserve fund. Then, in case of extreme need on the heels of a particularly devastating disaster, the group mounted fundraising drives. Chains of disasters often spelled financial peril for the organization. For example, hurricanes, floods, and tornados of unprecedented strength in 1955, 1956, and 1957 all but wiped out the Red Cross's reserves. The group relied on extra fundraising campaigns to make up its losses. In 1985, the group budgeted $17 million annually for disaster relief. A succession of hurricanes that year forced the Red Cross to spend about $48 million, putting it severely over budget. In the mid-1980s, the Red Cross ran fundraising campaigns by mailing out so-called "disastergrams,'' which asked for money for victims of the latest catastrophe. Much of the charity's money came from the umbrella fundraising organization United Way. Money brought in by disastergram went to a general disaster fund. After the earthquake in San Francisco in 1989, the Red Cross allowed donors to specify that they wanted their money to go only to victims of a specific incident. This helped fend off allegations, which had been raised since Clara Barton's time, that money raised for a specific cause might end up being spent elsewhere.

Revamping Programs in the 1990s

The Red Cross spent an increasing amount of money on disaster relief through the 1980s. It started the decade spending about $50 million, and by 1989 was spending over $100 million. This spiked to over $224 million in 1990. Although the organization provided relief on a massive scale, it was often criticized for the way it carried out its duties. By the early 1990s, the group considered cutting back its services, since so much of its budget was taken up with extraordinary disaster expenses. In 1991, Elizabeth Dole, who had held cabinet posts as Secretary of Labor and Secretary of Transportation, became president of the American Red Cross. Dole vowed to turn the organization around. The Red Cross was financially troubled because of its recent massive spending on disaster relief. In addition, the Red Cross had been plagued since the mid-1980s with questions about the safety of its blood supply. The Red Cross used a test manufactured by Abbott Laboratories in the mid-1980s to test donated blood for the AIDS virus. Despite known problems with the Abbott test, it continued to use it into 1986. People who contracted AIDS through tainted blood transfusions later sued both Abbott and the Red Cross. The biomedical services division, as the Red Cross's blood bank operations were called, was cited repeatedly in the 1980s and early 1990s for problems with its record-keeping. A report by a Food and Drug Administration (FDA) investigator made public in 1990 recorded dozens of incidents of sloppy record-keeping and computer errors. The FDA investigator told a Congressional committee that ensuring the safety of the nation's blood supply was made difficult by the Red Cross's problems. The investigator also found Red Cross officials insufficiently concerned about mending its ways. When Dole took over the Red Cross, she announced a $120 million overhaul of the biomedical division's record-keeping, and scheduled improvements to staff training and blood testing. Eventually the revamping of the Red Cross's

blood banks cost around $287 million. But the changes apparently did not go quickly enough. In 1993, the FDA filed suit against the Red Cross to force it to agree to make reforms. The Red Cross and the FDA settled the suit with a court-ordered consent decree outlining what the organization would do to improve. The Red Cross spent some $170 million to $180 million on computer systems, and built eight regional blood testing laboratories in a move to centralize its operations. The cost of these changes put the biomedical services division in the red. By the late 1990s, the division was in debt by about $300 million.

During this period, the Red Cross was nearing completion of its expensive overhaul of its biomedical services division. The division had evolved from a string of mainly autonomous regional blood centers to a much more centralized organization. An article in *Modern Healthcare* from June 22, 1998 averred that the division "looks and feels more like a drug company." The Red Cross had remade its blood banks, significantly improving the safety of its products. But the makeover had been very expensive. By 1998 the Red Cross was said to have about 46 percent of the nation's blood supply market share, or almost half of the $2 billion industry. The Red Cross vowed to increase its market share, aiming for 65 percent over the next three years. This move was made specifically to enhance the blood division's finances. In 1995, the division brought in $937 million, but was in the red by $113 million. For 1997, the division brought in $1.1 billion, but still ran a deficit. The Red Cross began a campaign of tough competition, moving into markets that had traditionally been served by other companies. Its main competitor was a loose network of community blood banks that operated under the umbrella of America's Blood Centers, or ABC. Blood banks had operated as virtual local monopolies since the 1970s, so that either the Red Cross, an ABC clinic, or a hospital blood bank, would serve a particular community. In the mid-1990s the Red Cross began moving into towns where it had been shut out of before, such as Kansas City, Dallas, and Phoenix. It was often only able to secure a tiny market share, for example 5 percent in Kansas City within two years of entering that market. But the Red Cross had changed the way blood products were marketed by introducing such direct competition. Some doctors and hospitals found that the new competitiveness brought prices down, while others worried that organizations vying for donors would ultimately scare the donors away. The new relationship between the Red Cross and its competitors became so acrimonious that the charity, ABC, and two other blood banking societies engaged a professional mediator to allow them to talk about their differences. The industry leaders formed a working group called the Blood Forum, and hoped to come up with rules that would allow them to compete gracefully. But the level of hostility was so high that an ABC official quoted in *Modern Healthcare* (June 22, 1998) claimed the Blood Forum was "... as bad as putting the Arabs and Israelis in the same room."

Aside from its problems with its biomedical services division, the Red Cross continued to strain to respond to unusual catastrophes in the 1990s. Flooding in the Midwest in 1993 led to the organization's largest relief effort ever, when over 20,000 workers assembled to combat the water damage. The Red Cross's most expensive disaster relief operation came just five years later, when Hurricane George in 1998 cost the charity over $100 million.

Elizabeth Dole left the Red Cross in 1999 to pursue a run for president of the United States. Her successor was the first physician to head the agency in a hundred years, Bernadine Healy. Dr. Healy had been director of the National Institute of Health, had taught at Johns Hopkins University, and had unsuccessfully run for the Senate. On taking over the Red Cross, Healy had to deal with the organization's ongoing fiscal and regulatory problems. She aimed to cut administrative positions to contain costs and streamline management. She also wanted the group to spend more money on research and development. At the end of 2000, the FDA again announced that the Red Cross was not doing enough to ensure the safety of its blood products, and Healy moved to borrow $100 million to fund improvements. But the FDA acted more aggressively than it had in the past, and asked to be allowed to fine the Red Cross, which it said had been out of compliance with FDA regulations since 1985. Healy claimed to be amazed at the seriousness of the FDA's allegations of sloppiness, since the Red Cross was supposed to have made drastic improvements in its blood operations after 1993. Healy was also faced with the ongoing problem of sour relationships with its competitors. In 2001 a California blood bank brought an antitrust suit against the Red Cross, alleging that the group artificially lowered prices in its region in order to drive other blood banks out of business. Into the 2000s the charity seemed to be facing the same difficulties that had beset it since the 1980s.

Principal Divisions

Biomedical Services; Disaster Services; Armed Forces Emergency Services; Health and Safety Services; International Services; Community Services.

Principal Competitors

America's Blood Centers.

Further Reading

Babcock, Charles R., and Judith Havemann, ''Managing an Agency and Image,'' *Washington Post*, February 16, 1999, p. A01.

Burton, Thomas, ''Panel Probes Early Abbott AIDS Test; Decision by Red Cross Is Questioned,'' *Wall Street Journal*, June 28, 1993, p. A11C.

Hensley, Scott, ''Out for Blood,'' *Modern Healthcare*, June 22, 1998, p. 26.

——, ''Rising to the Challenge,'' *Modern Healthcare*, May 1, 2000, p. 80.

Hurd, Charles, *The Compact History of the American Red Cross*, New York: Hawthorn Books, 1959.

Jones, Laurie, ''FDA: Red Cross Record-Keeping May Hurt Blood Safety,'' *American Medical News*, July 27, 1990, p. 1.

Kaufman, Marc, ''FDA Finds Problems with Red Cross Blood,'' *Washington Post*, December 2, 2000, p. A04.

Mulvihill, Kathleen, ''Hectic Year Drains Red Cross's Fund for Disaster Relief,'' *Christian Science Monitor*, December 3, 1985, pp. 3, 4.

Reitman, Judith, *Bad Blood: Crisis in the American Red Cross,* New York: Kensington Publishing Corp., 1996.

Sebastian, Pamela, ''Red Cross Is Strained By Disasters Even As It Revamps Its Programs,'' *Wall Street Journal*, September 15, 1992, pp. A1, A10.

Tanner, Lisa, ''Battling for Blood Business,'' *Dallas Business Journal*, March 21, 1997, p. 3.

Taylor, Mark, ''Red Cross Faces Antitrust Lawsuit,'' *Modern Healthcare*, January 1, 2001, p. 20.

—A. Woodward

AMF Bowling, Inc.

8100 AMF Drive
Richmond, Virginia 23111
U.S.A.
Telephone: (804) 730-4000
Toll Free: (800) 342-5263
Fax: (804) 730-1313
Web site: http://www.amf.com

Public Company
Incorporated: 1900 as American Machine Foundry Co.
Employees: 15,683
Sales: $732.7 million (1999)
Stock Exchanges: OTC
Ticker Symbol: AMBW
NAIC: 71395 Bowling Centers; 33992 Sporting and
    Athletic Goods Manufacturing; 42191 Sporting and
    Recreational Goods and Supplies Wholesalers

AMF Bowling, Inc. is the leading bowling company in the world. It manufactures a complete line of equipment including automated lanes, pins, balls, and shoes; operates more than 500 bowling centers in the United States and nine other countries; and also makes billiard tables and runs golfing facilities through subsidiaries. Expanding rapidly in the late 1990s, AMF suffered huge losses due to both the Asian economic downturn and the company's own overly ambitious business plan. The debt-ridden company has subsequently instituted cost-cutting and quality improvement measures in an effort to remain viable. Investment banking firm Goldman, Sachs & Co. owns a majority interest in AMF Bowling.

Beginnings

The roots of AMF Bowling date to March 16, 1900 when the American Machine Foundry Co. was formed by Moorehead Patterson. The New Jersey-based concern began as a manufacturer of equipment for the tobacco industry, and continued to ply its trade in this field over the next several decades. In the late 1930s an inventor named Fred Schmidt patented a method for picking up and re-setting bowling pins through the use of mechanical suction cups. Schmidt initially approached Brunswick Corporation, a leading bowling products manufacturer, but his appeal for financial backing was turned down. Brunswick itself had earlier attempted to create a pin-setting device, but had abandoned the concept as unworkable. Without backing, Schmidt sold the rights to his invention, at which point American Machine picked up the scent. They bought the patents, and then spent six years fine-tuning the idea. In 1946, at the American Bowling Congress's annual tournament in Buffalo, New York, the first fully automated ''Pinspotter'' was unveiled. Although many in attendance were impressed, the two-ton prototype proved unreliable, and another five years were spent refining the machine.

Reintroduced in 1951, the perfected Pinspotter was greatly improved, reliable, and accurate. The ingenious device's operation began when a bowling ball rolled through the pins and off the end of the lane into a cushion. This triggered a suction cup-equipped rack to descend toward the pins that remained standing, lifting them out of the way while a bar dropped to the lane and raked away the fallen pins. Finally, the lifted pins were lowered back into place. The total cycle took less than 20 seconds. After the second and last ball of the bowling ''frame'' had been rolled, the bar would drop again and remove any remaining pins, and a fresh set would be lowered from above for the next player. The Pinspotter would then reload the original ten pins into their rack. Other devices were created to complement the Pinspotter, including an under-lane ball return, the ''Pindicator'' lighted pin indicator (to aid in scoring), and an electric-eye foul line violation detector.

The Pinspotter, which American Machine leased to alley owners for a fee of 12 cents per game, caused a revolution in the bowling industry. Prior to its availability, all pins had to be reset by hand, with stereotypically surly and unkempt teenage boys the usual workers, earning five to ten cents a game. Noisy, male-dominated bowling alleys had a reputation similar to billiard parlors as places of drinking, smoking, and gambling, where upstanding women and children dared not go. With the efficient new Pinspotter and its quieter, more user-friendly accouterments, alleys began to take on a less seedy ambience, and the bowling industry began to promote the sport heavily to families and women. Business picked up industry-wide in the wake of the Pinspotter, which was joined by the competing Brunswick "Pinsetter" in 1956. By 1960 an estimated 90 percent of American lanes had been outfitted with automatic pin-setting machines. American Machine's headquarters, which had been in Manhattan for some time, were moved to Westbury, Long Island, that same year.

Diversification

In the wake of this success American Machine began to diversify away from the tobacco machinery it had previously concentrated on. The company's offerings came to include Hatteras brand boats, Head skis, and Harley-Davidson motorcycles, the latter acquired in 1968. Officially shortening its name in 1971, the company became known simply as AMF, Inc.

At the start of the 1980s, AMF's corporate makeup began changing again through divestiture of some of its leisure and consumer goods operations, including lawnmower, boat, and bicycle manufacturing. Harley-Davidson was also sold, purchased by its management in June 1981 for $81.5 million. At the same time, investments were made in a number of energy-related and scientific businesses. Though early results were positive, the changes soon backfired, with energy operations racking up $24 million in losses by 1983. With bowling still profitable, the company began a campaign of expansion in this area, spending nearly $100 million on acquisitions of bowling centers in 1984 and 1985.

By this time AMF chief Thomas York was becoming a controversial figure, both for his reputation as an autocrat and for the lavish perks he and other top executives enjoyed. In early 1985 the company's board applied pressure for change. One hundred staffers were laid off, the company moved to smaller quarters, and York even relinquished his limousine.

In April 1985 AMF became the subject of a hostile takeover bid from corporate raider Irwin L. Jacobs's Minstar, Inc. Despite adoption of a "poison pill" clause and other tactics, the company was sold to Minstar in June for $563.8 million. AMF's president, all but one of the company's directors, and CEO York resigned or were fired shortly afterwards. By that fall, Jacobs was making plans to sell 13 of AMF's subsidiaries, which accounted for more than half of the company's revenues. These were primarily the company's energy, scientific products, and foodservice ventures, with the majority of the sporting and leisure goods companies being retained. Jacobs also fired most

of the conglomerate's 400 corporate employees, leaving only a skeletal staff remaining.

Sale of Bowling Companies

In early 1986 several unsolicited offers came in to purchase the company's bowling division, which Jacobs had not put on the market. It was still AMF's most profitable business, making an impressive $13.6 million in profits on revenues of $109 million. However, an agreement was reached for its acquisition by New York investment firm Clayton & Dubilier, Inc. The deal fell through at the 11th hour, but then Commonwealth Venture Partners of Richmond, Virginia, stepped in with an identical offer of $223 million. Headed by William Goodwin, Jr., and Beverley Armstrong, the partners included executives of Major League Bowling Corp., which ran a chain of 22 southeastern U.S. bowling centers, and AMF-Union Machinery, which had been acquired from Minstar the previous year. AMF-Union President Frank Genovese was called on to run the newly independent company, which was renamed AMF Bowling Companies, Inc. At the time of its sale, AMF owned 110 bowling centers in the United States and abroad, and supplied almost half the pinsetting equipment worldwide.

Following the divestiture, AMF Bowling's headquarters were moved from Long Island, New York, to Richmond, home of its new owners. Over the next several years a successful campaign was launched to improve AMF's market share of bowling ball sales, with print and television ads for the company's Cobra and Sumo lines featuring real snakes and a Sumo wrestler rolling down a lane. AMF's AccuScore automatic scoring system was also being installed in increasing numbers of alleys nationwide. The computerized system displayed the results of each roll on a video screen above the lane, eliminating the need to rely on the traditional method of scoring by hand. During the early years of Commonwealth ownership several bowling center chains were also acquired, bringing the company's total holdings to 114 centers in the United States and 85 abroad.

By the 1980s the number of Americans who bowled regularly was declining as leisure time shrank, and new measures were needed to put the fizz back in the company's business. AMF Bowling Centers, Inc., the domestic bowling center arm, installed former PepsiCo executive Mark Willoughby as division head in 1991, and he rolled out a series of promotions intended to increase attendance among younger bowlers. Declaring that AMF would become "The McDonald's of bowling," Willoughby talked of building a chain of nationwide, lookalike centers and offering branded food from such names as Pizza Hut and Taco Bell.

Acquisitions continued in the early 1990s, with new subsidiaries including Bowler's Tape, Inc., billiard table maker Play Master-Renaissance, Inc., cue stick manufacturer Legendary Billiards, boating company Pompanette, Inc., industrial sewing company AMF Reece, Inc., the Ben Hogan Golf Co., and baking firm AMF Bakery Systems. In 1995 AMF became the largest bowling chain in the United States when it acquired control of Fair Lanes, Inc., owner of 106 centers. The purchase gave AMF more than 200 locations, easily topping Brunswick's 125. The company was continuing to seek new ways to draw in bowlers and, following Brunswick's example, introduced "Xtreme" bowling which featured day-glo balls, ultraviolet lighting, and loud rock music to create an otherworldly environment.

In 1996 AMF's owners approached New York investment banking giant Goldman, Sachs & Co., seeking advice on selling the bowling operations. After examining AMF's business, the investment firm made an offer of $1.37 billion itself, which was accepted. A new entity, AMF Group, Inc., was formed which owned AMF Bowling Centers, Inc., AMF Bowling, Inc., and related businesses. Goldman, Sachs held 65 percent of the company. AMF Bowling's former owners, Michael Goodwin and Beverley Armstrong, caused a sensation when they distributed $50 million of their profits to 3,400 company employees, giving each the equivalent of 10 percent of his or her salary for every year they had been with the firm.

An Aggressive Expansion Plan

The new corporation, headed by former bowling center division head Douglas Stanard, set out on a course of rapid expansion, and by year's end had picked up the 50-center Bowling Corporation of America chain for $106 million and the 43-unit American Recreation Centers chain for $70 million. Plans were also announced to create a $5 million, 40-lane bowling and entertainment center in Manhattan's Chelsea Piers, and to build a series of centers in India. CEO Stanard was also ramping up the company's marketing and modernization ef-

forts, which were intended to solidify the company's position as a familiar, consistent global brand.

In early 1997 a $40 million joint venture to build 20 bowling centers in Southeast Asia was launched with Hong Leong Corporation of Singapore. In the spring, another was formed with Playcenter of Sao Paolo, Brazil, to build as many as 39 centers in South America. Acquisitions of several small U.S. chains followed these moves, as did the purchase of Michael Jordan Golf Co., which operated several practice ranges. Gaining access to Jordan's services as an AMF spokesperson was a major part of the deal.

In November 1997 AMF Bowling Co. went public with an IPO on the New York Stock Exchange, offering 13.5 million shares at an opening price of $19.50. Goldman, Sachs retained more than 50 percent ownership. To celebrate, and to push the offering, the company set up a bowling lane in front of the exchange for six hours on opening day, during which time the price rose by more than 10 percent. Plans to acquire an additional 100 to 150 bowling centers during 1998 were announced soon thereafter.

Looking for a Strike, but Rolling a Gutter Ball Instead

By mid-1998 the corporation's numbers began to show signs of trouble. Earnings figures were considerably lower than expected, and revenues per existing center dropped by 3 percent instead of rising as anticipated. The most disappointing results came from the Bowling Products division, which reported downward revenue spikes of more than 20 percent two quarters in a row. This was attributed to the financial turmoil enveloping much of Southeast Asia, where AMF had been counting on a lucrative campaign of expansion. When the losses were calculated, they amounted to 60 cents per share for the second quarter, compared with a loss of 29 cents per share for the same quarter the previous year. The share price immediately tumbled, then continued to work its way down to less than $5 by year's end.

Although a few additional bowling centers were still being purchased, the company's expansion was put on hold, and a reorganization was effected, with the U.S. bowling center operation consolidated into six regional divisions from ten. The company also developed plans to move its Golden, Colorado lane-machine manufacturing and supply operation to Richmond. Some of the plant's 50 workers lost their jobs in the process.

When the third quarter results were announced in October, the company reported even bleaker figures. Losses for the period totaled $35.7 million, with bowling products sales down more than 36 percent. Soon after the information was released, CEO Stanard gave notice that he would be leaving by the end of the year.

His replacement was found in April 1999, when Roland C. Smith was recruited from Triarc Companies, where he had served as head of a restaurant group that ran the Arby's chain. Smith, a West Point graduate, announced that he wanted to learn the bowling business from the ground up, and did a stint as manager of a bowling center to get acquainted with his new employer.

In the fall of 1999, with losses continuing unabated, AMF downsized its bowling products operations. The company closed several plants and warehouses, and also began taking steps to recapitalize. Final figures for the year were not encouraging, as the company posted a net loss of $226 million on revenues of $733 million. By the summer of 2000, AMF stock was trading at less than a dollar per share, and a few months later it was delisted by the New York Stock Exchange, moving to the over-the-counter (OTC) market. Bankruptcy plans were reportedly under serious consideration after the company failed to make a September interest payment of $13.6 million. AMF now faced over $1.3 billion in debt, almost exactly the amount it had cost when purchased some five years earlier.

Though it was a leading bowling equipment manufacturer and the top operator of bowling centers around the world, debt-ridden AMF faced a difficult business environment and appeared down for the count. While it was still possible to prevail amidst these circumstances, the near future looked bleak, with only the courage and vision of the company's management and a much hoped for turnaround in the world bowling products market likely to bring the company back from the brink.

Principal Subsidiaries

AMF Group Holdings Inc.; AMF Bowling Worldwide, Inc; AMF Bowling Holdings Inc.; AMF Bowling Centers Holdings; AMF Bowling Products, Inc.; AMF Bowling Products International, B.V. (Netherlands); AMF Bowling India Private Ltd. (India); AMF Bowling Poland Sp.zo.o. (Poland); AMF Worldwide Bowling Centers Holdings Inc.; AMF Bowling Centers, Inc.; AMF Beverage Company of Oregon, Inc.; AMF Beverage Company of W. VA, Inc.; Bush River Corporation; King Louie Lenexa, Inc.; 300, Inc.; The 400 Club, Inc.; American Recreation Centers, Inc.; Michael Jordan Golf Company, Inc.; MJG-O'Hare, Inc.; Michael Jordan Golf Youth Program, Inc.; AMF Catering Services Pty. Ltd. (New South Wales); AMF Bowling Centers (Canada) International Inc.; AMF Bowling Centers (Hong Kong) International Inc.; AMF Bowling Centers International Inc.; AMF BCO-UK One, Inc.; AMF BCO-UK Two, Inc.; AMF BCO-France One, Inc.; AMF BCO-France Two, Inc.; AMF Bowling Centers Spain Inc.; AMF Bowling Mexico Holding, Inc.; AMF International BCO Holdings B.V. (Netherlands); AMF Bowling (U.K.); Worthing North Properties, Ltd. (U.K.); AMF Bowling France SNC (France); AMF Bowling de Paris SNC (France); AMF Bowling de Lyon la Part Dieu SNC (France); Boliches AMF y Compania (Mexico); Operadora Mexicano de Boliches, SA (Mexico); Promotora de Boliches SA de CV (Mexico); Inmuebles Minerva, SA (Mexico); Inmuebles Obispado SA (Mexico); Boliches Mexicanos SA (Mexico).

Principal Competitors

Bowl America, Inc.; Brunswick Corporation; Dave and Buster's, Inc.; Haw Par Corp. Ltd.; Jillian's Entertainment Holdings, Inc.

Further Reading

Berkowitz, Harry, "AMF Bowling Looks for Reset Button," *Newsday*, April 7, 1986, p. 5.

——, "The Waiting Is Over at AMF Bowling," *Newsday*, May 20, 1986, p. 45.

Blackwell, John Reid, "AMF Reorganizing, Cutting Jobs," *Richmond Times-Dispatch*, November 17, 2000, p. B8.

Breznick, Alan, "Bosses Bowl for Dollars by Funding AMF Face-Lifts," *Crain's New York Business*, May 26, 1986, p. 3.

Crews, Ed, "Sumo, Snakes and Bobcats—AMF Scores a Strike with Offbeat Campaigns," *Richmond Times-Dispatch*, May 11, 1992, p. B16.

Ehrlich, Elizabeth, "Behind the AMF Takeover," *Business Week*, August 12, 1985, p. 50.

Gibson, Richard, "Minstar's Jacobs to Sell AMF's Businesses," *Wall Street Journal*, August 30, 1985.

Gibson, Richard, and Johnnie L. Roberts, "AMF Agrees to Be Acquired by Minstar, Inc.," *Wall Street Journal*, June 17, 1985.

Hingley, Audrey, "AMF Wants to Be the McDonald's of Sports," *Richmond Times-Dispatch*, December 14, 1992, p. E7.

Hurley, Andrew, *Diners, Bowling Alleys and Trailer Parks,* New York: Basic Books, 2001.

Jones, Chip, "AMF Buyout Talks Are Confirmed," *Richmond Times-Dispatch*, February 7, 1996, p. C1.

Knight, Jerry, "AMF Bowling Strikes a Deal with Basketball's Jordan," *Washington Post*, October 27, 1997, p. F27.

Kushner, David, "Where All Lanes Are Fast Lanes: The High-Tech Bowling Alley," *New York Times*, January 7, 1999, p. 9.

McGeehan, Patrick, "Tale of Bad Timing at AMF: Silk Stockings and Bowling Shoes," *New York Times*, August 1, 2000, p. 1A.

Pinkston, Will, and Karby Keggett, "After Rolling a Few Gutter Balls AMF Needs a Strike," *Wall Street Journal*, December 18, 2000, p. B6.

Prial, Dunstan, "AMF Bowling Introduces Shares, with Eye on Overseas Growth," *Dow Jones Online News*, November 4, 1997.

Rayner, Bob, "AMF Chief Sees 'Great Opportunity'—New CEO Emphasizes Strong Leadership," *Richmond Times-Dispatch*, June 1, 1999, p. B6.

——, "AMF Rolls for a Strike on NYSE," *Richmond Times-Dispatch*, November 5, 1997, p. C1.

——, "On a Roll—AMF Bowling Worldwide Brings New Life to an Old Sport," *Richmond Times-Dispatch*, June 9, 1997, p. D14.

Silvestri, Thomas A., "Head of AMF Bowling Worldwide Needs to Roll Strikes Amid Change," *Richmond Times-Dispatch*, May 26, 1997, p. D5.

Weatherford, Greg, "AMF Bowling Gets Initial View of Pains, Joys in Stock Market Ride," *Richmond Times-Dispatch*, August 10, 1998, p. D14.

——, "AMF Chief Planning to Leave Company," *Richmond Times-Dispatch*, November 3, 1998, p. C1.

——, "Hoping to Bowl 'Em Over, AMF Clears Lanes in Effort to Consolidate Fragmented Industry," *Richmond Times-Dispatch*, June 20, 1998, p. C1.

Yost, Mark, "AMF Bowling Chief Will Go to Lanes to Learn Business," *Wall Street Journal*, May 4, 1999, p. B9.

——, "How a Bout of the Asian Flu Put AMF Bowling on Its Back," *Dow Jones News Service*, November 18, 1998.

—Frank Uhle

Amphenol Corporation

385 Hall Avenue
Wallingford, Connecticut 06492
U.S.A.
Telephone: (203) 265-8900
Fax: (203) 265-8793
Web site: http://www.amphenol.com

Public Company
Incorporated: 1942 as Amphenol Electronics Corporation
Employees: 11,600
Sales: $1.36 billion (2000)
Stock Exchanges: New York
Ticker Symbol: APH
NAIC: 334417 Electronic Connector Manufacturing;
335921 Fiber Optic Cable Manufacturing; 335929
Other Communication and Energy Wire
Manufacturing

Amphenol Corporation manufactures interconnect products—cable and connectors. Its fortunes have risen along with those of the electronics industry. Over the decades, Amphenol has been a prime target for corporate takeover attempts as it has itself acquired numerous companies in expanding markets. Venture capital firm Kohlberg Kravis Roberts & Company (KKR) owned half of Amphenol's stock in 2001. More than half of Amphenol's products end up in communications applications (voice, video, and data); about 20 percent go to the aerospace industry; and another 20 percent are used in other industrial, transportation, and miscellaneous enterprises.

Origins

Amphenol Electronics Corporation was founded in 1942. The Chicago-based company produced components for the nascent electronics industry; it had plants in Illinois, Connecticut, and California. By 1956, annual sales had reached $27.3 million (profits were $1.3 million). After selling shares over the counter, Amphenol began trading on the New York Stock Exchange in May 1957. The next month, Amphenol acquired Gas Purification and Chemical Company, which it renamed Amphenol Great Britain Ltd.

Amphenol merged with the George W. Borg Corp. in December 1958, forming Amphenol-Borg Electronics Corp. Based in Wisconsin, Borg manufactured electronic instruments, automobile clocks, and textiles. Meanwhile, the growth of electronics had Amphenol supplying the aircraft, telephone, computer, and television industries, and winning million-dollar military contracts. In 1959, the new company posted income of $3 million on sales of $55 million.

Matthew L. Devine was elected president of Amphenol-Borg in January 1960. Sales were $60 million for the year; they continued to climb until 1963.

Amphenol-Borg merged with another electronics concern, FXR, Inc., in May 1961. This boosted Amphenol's microwave technology. A Canadian subsidiary was added in November 1964. The buying spree continued, though a merger with Federal Sign fell through. Amphenol did manage to acquire Jefferson Electronics, Cadre Industries, and Micromega. By this time, the word ''Borg'' had been trimmed from the corporate name. Sales were rising again, to $80 million for 1965, which produced income of $2.5 million.

Other electronics companies were bought, new plants were built, and a French affiliate was licensed in the next two years. In 1967, another company launched a dramatic takeover attempt against Amphenol that culminated in allegations of corporate espionage.

Indeed, the entire year was filled with speculation about who would land what Wall Street considered a most attractive takeover candidate due to its strong earnings. Early in the year, Solitron Devices, Inc. began targeting the company. Solitron made transistors, semiconductors, and other electronic components.

In early October 1967, Amphenol worked out a hurried deal to merge with Sangamo Electric Co.; however, the continued rise in Amphenol's share price soon scuttled that arrangement. At the height of the takeover drama, Amphenol President

> ## Company Perspectives:
>
> *We have spent much effort in the past few years in moving our product lines to growth areas, especially in the communications market, and we have aggressively developed new products to address the rapid deployment of digital and fiber optic technology and the converging markets of voice, video and data communications. We have also made significant investments in new equipment and processes that allow us to keep pace with the growth, enhance quality and manufacture at a very competitive cost.*

Matthew Devine informed the press that an eavesdropping device (or ''bug'') had been placed inside one of his home telephones.

Solitron ultimately built up a 25 percent shareholding in Amphenol. By the end of 1967, however, Amphenol had agreed to merge with Bunker-Ramo Corp., a maker of specialized computers controlled by Martin Marietta Corporation.

Using the Name ''Bunker Ramo'' in the 1970s

The new company took the Bunker Ramo name. Amphenol Chairman Matthew Devine was named president and CEO, while John E. Parker remained in his position as chairman at the new Bunker Ramo.

The Amphenol Components group provided up to 70 percent of Bunker Ramo's income in the 1970s. The unit's income was $23.6 million in 1974, but slipped to just $3.7 million in 1975. According to *Electronics* magazine, innovative connectors from competitors such as AMP Inc. helped eat away at market share.

A comprehensive reorganization was begun in 1975 by Bunker Ramo President George S. Trimble. Amphenol Components had been divided into Industrial, Cadre, Connector, RF, Instruments, and Sales divisions. After the restructuring, there was a single Amphenol group for all Bunker Ramo connectors. (Bunker Ramo's other four divisions were Information Systems, Instruments, Electronics Systems, and Borg Textiles.) The Amphenol group was divided into Amphenol North America and Amphenol International in 1977.

Bunker Ramo also cut unprofitable operations making automobile clocks and certain textiles. By the late 1970s, the company had recovered from its earnings slump, thanks to a new emphasis on marketing and R&D. Electrical and electronic connectors remained Bunker Ramo's most important line of business.

Bunker Ramo Corp. earned $27.2 million on revenues of $467.6 million in 1980. Again, rising sales made the company an attractive takeover target; a relatively low debt load of $74 million added luster. Fairchild Industries Inc. bought 21 percent of Bunker Ramo stock from Martin Marietta Corporation in 1979 but was ultimately not successful in effecting a merger, in spite of offering $96 million for the rest of the shares. United States Filter Corporation also had made acquisition overtures.

Allied Control in 1981

Duane L. Burnham replaced George Trimble as president and CEO of Bunker Ramo in October 1980. Under Burnham, the company began seeking acquisitions that would give it more leverage in impending merger discussions. Finally, diversified chemical maker Allied Corp. agreed to pay $358 million for the company in May 1981.

Amphenol continued as an operating unit of Allied, later Allied-Signal Inc., under the name Amphenol Products. By the mid-1980s, Amphenol had manufacturing facilities in France, West Germany, Great Britain, Italy, and Canada as well as affiliates in Japan and India. It also boasted the world's largest network of electronics distributors.

Amphenol bought Thomson-CSF's Socapex S.A. connector subsidiary in December 1985 for FFr 199 million ($26 million). Socapex already had been licensed to manufacture Amphenol's line of Bendix connectors (taken on during the Allied acquisition) since 1960. The purchase brought Amphenol expertise in high technology connectors.

Amphenol posted an operating income of $33 million on sales of $487 million for 1986. In December of that year, Allied-Signal placed Amphenol on the market, as well as six other operating units in its electronics and instrumentation sector.

A total of 30 firms bid to buy Amphenol, including Litton Industries, Emerson Electric, Cooper Industries, and Siemens. In April 1987, Amphenol Acquisition Company, a newly formed subsidiary of the LPL Investment Group of Wallingford, Connecticut, beat them out with an offer of $430 million. LPL was a publicly traded investment company that had been formed only two years earlier to make acquisitions in the electronics and communications fields. Its sales were less than $100 million a year before the Amphenol purchase. In December 1985, LPL had acquired Times Fiber Communications, Inc., which would become part of the Amphenol empire.

LPL president Lawrence J. DeGeorge told the *New York Times* that Amphenol was so attractive because it would take 20 years to build a market leader in the industry. ''We serve the same marketplaces,'' he added, ''so the products are extremely complementary to the businesses we're already in.''

However attractive Amphenol may have seemed at the time, net sales fell from $442 million in 1988 to $421 million in 1990. Losses peaked at $14.5 million in 1989. This, and the junk bond financing that allowed LPL to buy it, left Amphenol teetering on the edge of bankruptcy by the early 1990s. It had debts of $373 million in 1991 versus $19.5 million of equity, reported the *Wall Street Journal.* The Persian Gulf War, however, was stimulating demand for its connectors.

Public Again in 1991

In August 1991, Amphenol announced an initial public offering (IPO), part of a restructuring plan. Before the offering was announced, Shearson Lehman bought $50 million of the company's $215 million in junk bonds for 70 cents on the dollar, according to the *Wall Street Journal;* the subsequent IPO

Key Dates:

1942: Amphenol is founded.
1957: Shares begins trading on the New York Stock Exchange.
1958: Company merges with George W. Borg Corp.
1967: Company merges with Bunker-Ramo Corp.
1981: Allied Corp. buys Amphenol Components division.
1987: LPL Investment Group acquires Amphenol in an LBO.
1991: Amphenol launches an IPO.
1992: LPL buys coaxial cable supplier Times Fiber.
1997: KKR buys Amphenol for $1.2 billion.

---

reportedly angered these bondholders, who had taken a loss on their investment.

The IPO was expected to net $160 million; there would be a concurrent offering of $100 million in senior secured notes. Amphenol was approved for listing on the New York Stock Exchange. Difficulties in obtaining financing forced Amphenol to delay its offering for two consecutive weeks in August 1991.

Amphenol parent LPL recently had been taken private in a management-led leveraged buyout of its own. As part of its IPO, Amphenol would issue LPL $65 million in stock for its sister connector companies Pyle-National Inc. and Amphenol Interconnect Products Corp. The three combined companies had 1990 sales of $497 million.

In May 1992, the company announced that it was cutting 5 percent of its 3,800 North American jobs and 10 percent of the 1,700 in Europe. Company President Martin H. Loeffler estimated the cost savings would exceed $11 million a year. As part of the restructuring program, Amphenol was shifting more of its manufacturing to its Bendix and Pyle units.

LPL acquired Times Fiber Communications, Inc. (TFC) in late 1992. Amphenol merged with LPL and TFC as part of the same transaction. TFC was a leading supplier of the coaxial cable used by the cable television industry, with annual sales of $78 million, mostly from the United States. The company was expanding aggressively overseas; a joint venture in China was announced in late 1993. Thanks to its overseas success, TFC was contributing a third of Amphenol's total sales by 1995.

By October 1995, however, Amphenol was suffering the discontent of a thousand workers who went on strike at the company's connector manufacturing facility in Sidney, New York. This one plant produced 80 percent of Amphenol's output of aerospace connectors; the strike threatened to delay a number of military and commercial aviation programs.

Chairman Lawrence DeGeorge handed over the duties of CEO to President Martin Loeffler in June 1996. Amphenol announced that it was buying the Sine Companies in the same month. Sine produced connectors for industrial markets and had annual sales exceeding $30 million. Amphenol's own sales for 1995 were $783 million.

Amphenol established R&D facilities in Hong Kong, Japan, and India during the 1990s. It bought a 51 percent interest in Taiwanese RF products provider Kai-Jack Industrial Co. Ltd. in January 1997.

Purchase by KKR in 1997

Kohlberg Kravis Roberts & Company (KKR) agreed to buy Amphenol (via KKR's NXS Acquisition Corporation affiliate) for $1.2 billion in January 1997. Amphenol's position in the expanding communications, aerospace, industrial, and automotive industries again made it an attractive takeover candidate.

KKR bought Amphenol during a bit of a slump for the electronics industry. Some shareholders sued to prevent the sale, feeling that the company was undervalued at $26 per share. In 1996, Amphenol posted a record net income of $17.5 million on sales of $211.7 million. Sales were up across Amphenol's geographic range.

Amphenol bought AMP Inc.'s Matrix Sciences line of military circular connectors in October 1997. In July 1998, it sold its Italian manufacturing operations to VEAM S.p.A., a division in Litton Industries Inc. The next month, Amphenol bought Advanced Circuit Technology Inc., a privately owned producer of interconnect products.

The company continued its expansion via acquisition in 2000, as annual sales passed $1 billion. T&M Antennas Inc. (cell phone antennas), Korean Air Electronics (cell phone system-connect switches), and Confektion E Gmbh (automotive cable assemblies) were all acquired in the first five months of the year. At the same time, Amphenol was expanding its manufacturing operations in China, the Czech Republic, Mexico, and Brazil. Future acquisitions seemed likely to come outside the communications industry, on which Amphenol was becoming increasingly dependent.

Principal Subsidiaries

Advanced Circuit Technology, Inc.; Advanced Circuit Technology; Amphenol Aerospace France, Inc. (U.S.A.); Amphenol Australia Pty Ltd.; Amphenol Benelux B.V. (Netherlands); Amphenol Borg Limited (U.K.); Amphenol do Brasil Ltda.; Amphenol Canada Corp.; Amphenol Commercial & Industrial France, L.L.C. (U.S.A.); Amphenol Commercial and Industrial UK, Limited; Amphenol Connexus AB (Sweden); Amphenol-Daeshin Electronics and Precision Co., Ltd. (Korea); Amphenol East Asia Limited (Hong Kong); Amphenol Foreign Sales Corporation (Barbados); Amphenol Funding Corp.; Amphenol Germany GmbH; Amphenol Gesellschaft m.b.H. (Austria); Amphenol Holdings Pty. Ltd. (Australia); Amphenol Holding UK, Limited; Amphenol Interconnect Products Corporation; Amphenol International Ltd.; Amphenol Italia, S.p.A. (Italy); Amphenol Japan K.K.; Amphenol-Kai Jack, Inc. (British Virgin Islands); Amphenol-Kai Jack Industrial Co., Ltd. (Taiwan); Amphenol-Kai Jack (Shenzhen), Inc. (China); Amphenol Limited (U.K.); Amphenol Optimize Manufacturing Co.; Amphenol Optimize Mexico S.A. de C.V.; Amphenol Socapex S.A.S. (France); Amphenol T&M Antennas, Inc.; Amphenol-TFC (Changzhou) Communications Equipment Co., Ltd. (China); Amphenol Taiwan Corporation; Amphenol Technical

Products International Co. (Canada); Amphenol-Tuchel Electronics GmbH (Germany); Amphenol USHoldco Inc.; Amphetronix Limited (India); Connex Connector Corporation, Guangzhou Amphenol Electronics Communication Co., Ltd. (China); Konfektion E Elektronik GmbH (Germany), Korea Air Electronic Co., Ltd.; LPL Technologies Holding GmbH (Germany); Lonef Svenska, AB; Matir, S.A. (Uruguay); Pyle-National Ltd. (U.K.); Pyle-National of Canada Inc.; Sine Systems*Pyle Connectors Corporation; Spectra Strip Limited (U.K.); TFC South America S.A. (Argentina); Times Fiber Canada Limited; Times Fiber Communications, Inc.

Principal Divisions

Advanced Circuit; Amphenol Aerospace; Amphenol Air LB; Amphenol Argentina; Amphenol Australia; Amphenol Brazil; Amphenol Canada; Amphenol DaeShin; Amphenol East Asia; Amphenol Fiber Optics; Amphenol Interconnect; Amphenol Japan; Amphenol RF; Amphenol RF Asia; Amphenol SINE Systems; Amphenol Socapex; Amphenol South Africa; Amphenol Spectra Strip; Amphenol T&M Antennas; Amphenol Tuchel Electronics; Amphenol UK Operations; Times Fiber Communications.

Principal Operating Units

Interconnect Products and Assemblies; Cable Products.

Principal Competitors

CommScope, Inc.; Molex Incorporated; Tyco International Ltd.

Further Reading

"Amphenol Begins a Cost-Cutting Plan," *Wall Street Journal*, May 26, 1992, p. A11.

"Amphenol, Bunker-Ramo Complete Their Merger; New Officers Are Named," *Wall Street Journal*, June 4, 1968, p. 4.

"Amphenol Corp. Says Several Firms Propose Merger Transactions," *Wall Street Journal*, December 12, 1967, p. 14.

"Amphenol Has Troubles But Gets Positive Review," *Junk Bond Reporter*, February 4, 1991, p. 3.

Anders, George, "Amphenol, Plagued by Debt, Maps Comeback That Places It Squarely on 'Going Public' Trail," *Wall Street Journal*, September 17, 1991, p. C2.

Armstrong, Larry, "Amphenol Picks Up Pieces," *Electronics*, July 22, 1976, p. 87.

Baljko, Jennifer L., "Another Buy for Amphenol," *Electronic Buyers News*, August 17, 1998, p. 8.

"Bunker-Ramo, Amphenol Set Plan to Merge," *Wall Street Journal*, December 14, 1967, p. 10.

Cowan, Alison Leigh, "Allied's Amphenol to Be Sold to LPL," *New York Times*, Sec. 2, Financial Desk, April 4, 1987, p. 34.

Donnelly, Christopher, and Betsy Treitler, "Rumors Swirl on Delay of Troubled Amphenol IPO," *Mergers & Acquisitions Report*, October 21, 1991, p. 1.

"Equipment Companies Decry Telecom Import Policy," *Economic Times of India*, October 23, 1999.

Goodwin, William, "Amphenol Corp.'s Lenders Win Sweetened Recap Terms," *American Banker*, October 21, 1991, p. 24.

Jasen, Georgette, "Allied Corp. Says It Agreed to Buy Bunker Ramo," *Wall Street Journal*, May 12, 1991, p. 4.

Jorgensen, Barbara, "Amphenol RF to Bolster Channel Services," *Electronic Buyers News*, September 27, 1999, p. 48.

Liotta, Bettyann, "Amphenol Shareholders File Suit," *Electronic Buyers News*, April 28, 1997, p. 10.

——, "Amphenol's Megadeal: Sold to KKR for $1.5 Billion," *Electronic Buyers News*, January 27, 1997, p. 1.

Maresca, Stephen, "No More Whipsaws? Bunker Ramo Hopes Earnings Growth Is Here to Stay," *Barron's*, April 9, 1979, pp. 31–32.

Norman, Diane, "Connectors: Amphenol Corp.," *Electronic Buyers News*, November 3, 1997, p. E27.

——, "Strikers Hit Amphenol; Military Connector Supply Uncertain," *Electronic Buyers News*, October 30, 1995, p. 1.

Robards, Terry, "Match-Makers See Solitron Take-Over of Amphenol Likely," *New York Times*, October 11, 1967, pp. 61, 72.

Schiesel, Seth, "Kohlberg Kravis Set to Offer $1.2 Billion for Cable Maker," *New York Times*, January 24, 1997, p. D2.

Schmedel, Scott R., "Solitron to Make Direct Offer for Amphenol," *Wall Street Journal*, November 10, 1967, p. 6.

Schuyten, Peter J., "Bunker Sought for a Merger," *New York Times*, September 11, 1980, p. D4.

Scouras, Ismini, "Amphenol Scouting Acquisitions," *Electronic Buyers News*, May 22, 2000, p. 40.

Sinakin, Yvonne D., "Early Involvement: Making a Global Connection," *Electronic Buyers News*, August 19, 1996, p. E36.

Smithers, K. Ames, "Corporate Espionage Claimed by Amphenol; Chairman Says Home Phone Was Bugged," *Wall Street Journal*, November 10, 1967, p. 6.

Treitler, Betsy, "Amphenol's Grand Plan Only Starts with Its IPO," *Mergers & Acquisitions Report*, August 26, 1991, p. 1.

Waurzyniak, Patrick, "Amphenol Picks Up Matrix from AMP," *Electronic Buyers News*, October 20, 1997, p. 4.

Williams, Winston, "Bunker Ramo Changes Its Tune; Still a Target, Company Is Now a Suitor," *New York Times*, December 2, 1980, pp. D1, D7.

Wright, Robert A., "Two Competing Plans Given to Amphenol," *New York Times*, January 25, 1968, pp. 51, 56.

—Frederick C. Ingram

Andrews McMeel Universal

4520 Main Street
Kansas City, Missouri 64111
U.S.A.
Telephone: (816) 932-6600
Toll Free: (800) 255-6734
Fax: (816) 932-6684
Web site: http://www.uexpress.com

Private Company
Incorporated: 1970 as Universal Press Syndicate
Employees: 350
Sales: $250 million (1999 est.)
NAIC: 51113 Book Publishers; 51111 Newspaper
   Publishers

Andrews McMeel Universal is a diversified publishing and media company that includes under its umbrella one of the nation's largest syndicators of newspaper comics and features, a leading humor book publishing company, and a gift, card, and calendar division. The company's Universal Press Syndicate division handles the work of over 125 writers and cartoonists, including Garry Trudeau, creator of the "Doonesbury" comic; Jim Davis, of "Garfield"; the advice columnist Abigail Van Buren; political cartoonist Oliphant; and columnists such as Garry Wills, William F. Buckley, and Erma Bombeck. Universal was the leading light of comics syndicates in the 1980s, when it also included on its roster Gary Larson's "The Far Side" and Bill Watterson's "Calvin & Hobbes." Andrews McMeel Publishing puts out a number of humor books, especially collections of comics by its syndicated artists, as well as general trade books, gift books, and children's books. The publishing division markets around 300 titles annually. It also sells over 11.5 million calendars each year. Andrews McMeel Universal also runs an electronic media division, Universal New Media, for electronic distribution of its properties. The company also markets gift items such as mugs and tee shirts, usually with a humor tie-in. The company is privately owned by founder John McMeel and Kathleen Andrews, widow of co-founder Jim Andrews.

Winning with "Doonesbury" in the 1970s

The company that became Andrews McMeel Universal started as a moonlighting alternative career of two firm friends, John P. McMeel and James F. Andrews. McMeel was a native of South Bend, Indiana, who majored in business at Notre Dame University. In 1960 James Andrews rented a room in the home of McMeel's mother, and the two young men became friends. They shared similar interests in humor, and soon they began a small business together, syndicating material for Catholic newspapers. McMeel eventually went to work for the Hall Syndicate, which distributed "Dennis the Menace" and "Pogo." Andrews found a job with Sheed & Ward, a religious publishing house that printed serious theological works. They continued to run their syndicate, called A/M Publication Services, as a sideline. Then sometime in the late 1960s, their wives jointly convinced them to take the risk of making the syndicate a serious, full-time venture. In 1970, McMeel and Andrews quit their other jobs and incorporated Universal Press Syndicate, choosing the name because it sounded large and impressive. Actually the company was far from impressive at the time. McMeel rented an office in Manhattan, but it was a fifth floor walk-up over a bar. Andrews worked out of his home in Kansas City. The young company's first coup was getting the serial rights to investigative reporter Seymour Hersh's *My Lai Massacre*. Universal paid $20,000 for the rights from Random House, and then sold excerpts of the book to about 50 newspapers. Universal gambled on the quality of Hersh's groundbreaking book, signing a deal with some papers to double its fee if Hersh won the Pulitzer Prize. He did indeed win the prize. Yet that was not enough to get the syndicate out of red ink. Its next move was to promote an obscure college cartoonist whose work had already been turned down by 40 papers. "Bull Tales," by Garry Trudeau, was running in the *Yale Daily News* when McMeel first spotted it in 1968. Despite its success with Hersh's book, Universal was close to bankruptcy before its first year was out. Consequently, McMeel contacted Trudeau about doing a more general interest strip than "Bull Tales." This became "Doonesbury." The controversial strip, which satirized current political figures, was turned down by many papers, but it slowly caught on. By the end of 1970, McMeel had peddled the strip to 28 newspapers, and "Doonesbury" took off from there. By

Company Perspectives:

The caretakers of a nation's culture are its storytellers. What is a culture, after all, but the collection of stories people tell about themselves through their music, art, dance and literature? Through the stories they tell, people remember their history and envision their future. They entertain and enlighten themselves. Since ancient times, the role of the bard has been to preserve and perpetuate a culture by telling its stories. For more than a quarter of a century, Andrews McMeel Universal and its divisions, Universal Press Syndicate, Andrews McMeel Publishing and uclick, have helped define American popular culture by giving a voice to storytellers of our age. Through comic strips, newspaper columns, books, calendars, greeting cards, gift items and Web sites, this quiet Kansas City company has discovered, nurtured and promoted many of the bards of our time.

1973, Universal Press Syndicate managed to turn a profit, and in 1975, Trudeau won the Pulitzer Prize.

Another early Universal success was ''Ziggy,'' by Tom Wilson. Kathleen Andrews, wife of Jim Andrews, saw a ''Ziggy'' cartoon in a book in an airport, and had the company call the artist to negotiate syndication. Wilson had been rejected by other syndicates, and apparently had little hope left, as he had stuck his ''Ziggy'' drawings away in his garage. ''Ziggy,'' through Universal, became a ubiquitous 1970s comic. Another comic hit was ''Herman,'' by Jim Unger. This was an obliquely humorous one-panel strip, unusual for comics at the time. But Universal was becoming known by picking up offbeat artists that other, larger syndicates would not touch. In 1976 Universal was the first syndicate to pick up ''Cathy'' by Cathy Guisewite, a comic about a single working woman. Nothing like it existed at the time, and the strip went on to great success, one of the first hits by a woman cartoonist. In 1979 Universal picked up another woman cartoonist, the Canadian Lynn Johnston. Her ''For Better or For Worse'' daily comic strip became another Universal best-seller.

The company made some other changes in the 1970s. In 1973, Universal Press Syndicate bought Sheed & Ward, the religious publisher Andrews had worked for. Universal wanted to get into book publishing, so it took over the small press. Eventually the publisher was renamed Andrews and McMeel, and it printed mostly humor books by Universal's syndicated cartoonists and columnists. Another move was to shut down McMeel's New York office in 1975. The rent and overhead were too much, and the company thought it gained by being out of the New York publishing loop. Hence, McMeel and his family moved to Kansas City and all the company's operations were consolidated there. Then in 1979, Universal bought the Washington Star Syndicate from Time, Inc. This brought Universal a stable of political writers, including William F. Buckley, Mary McGrory, and James J. Kilpatrick. Universal was instantly a presence on the editorial pages of papers across the country. When Universal negotiated the deal with Time, that company offered to take over the small syndicate. Universal's officers rejected the deal, but did allow Time to buy a 20 percent stake in the company. Universal eventually bought back its stake, however, valuing its independence.

Success with Comics in the 1980s

By 1980, Universal Press Syndicate seemed to warrant its impressive name. It had a growing list of prominent cartoonists and some of the best-known names in political commentary. Its reputation was such that it attracted one of the most recognizable names in the newspaper world, Abigail Van Buren, writer of the advice column ''Dear Abby.'' Van Buren was under contract with Tribune Media Services, but she was unhappy and wanted to switch. She called Universal one day in 1980 and McMeel, who took the call, first suspected it was practical joke. But McMeel was soon convinced it was really Abigail Van Buren on the line, and agreed to meet. Within days, Universal signed up the advice columnist. Also in 1980, the company signed one of the leading political cartoonists of the day, Patrick Oliphant. Everything seemed to have come together for the company that had once been more of a hobby than a business for Jim Andrews and John McMeel. Unfortunately, Andrews died of a heart attack in 1980, at the age of 44. His loss was a shock to the company. Yet his widow, Kathleen Andrews, increased her role at the company, and became vice-president in 1987, and later CEO.

Universal Press Syndicate prospered in the 1980s, snapping up some of the most popular cartoonists in the United States. In 1985, the syndicate picked up two cartoonists, one a novice and one an already established star. Bill Watterson had tried to sell his strip ''Calvin and Hobbes'' to Universal's rival syndicate United, but that company turned it down. Universal offered Watterson a contract, and within a few years ''Calvin and Hobbes'' was ''the hottest comic in syndication'' according to an *Editor & Publisher* article from March 17, 1990. Another hot comic artist was Gary Larson. His one-panel cartoon ''The Far Side'' was distributed by Chronicle Features, but Larson published books through Universal's Andrews and McMeel Publishing division. The book division had done very well publishing collections of work by Universal's syndicated artists. In 1983 it sold off Sheed & Ward, the Catholic book publisher, and continued under the Andrews and McMeel name mainly as a humor publisher. It also produced books by Abigail Van Buren and film reviewer Roger Ebert. After completing a book for Andrews and McMeel, Ebert moved his column to Universal. Gary Larson did the same thing. He signed on with Universal in 1985 and became one of the syndicate's best-selling artists. His cartoon was carried in more than 800 newspapers by the late 1980s, and he sold 12 books of his collected comics through Andrews and McMeel. By 1989, the books had sold over 12 million copies. Universal also opened a division called Oz in the 1980s to handle gift items, greeting cards, and calendars. This was an obvious way to extend the marketing of Universal's cartoonists. By the end of the 1980s, Oz had a line of 99 Gary Larson greeting cards, 96 Larson post cards, 20 different coffee mugs, and a hugely successful line of ''Far Side'' calendars. In 1988 Oz sold more than four million Larson calendars.

Universal was ranked the syndicate with the highest comic success rate in the 1980s, according to *Cartoonist Profiles* magazine. Not only did it have some of the biggest hits in American comics, but its strips had longevity. Over 40 percent of Universal's strips that debuted between 1980 and 1988 were

---

Key Dates:

1970: Firm incorporates, begins syndicating "Doonesbury."
1973: Company enters book publishing industry with acquisition of Catholic publisher Sheed & Ward.
1980: Cofounder Jim Andrews dies.
1985: Company begins syndicating Gary Larson and Bill Watterson.
1994: Jim Davis moves syndication of "Garfield" comic to Universal.
1997: Company name is changed to Andrews McMeel Universal.

---

still in syndication by the end of the decade, a higher rate than any other syndicate, including the larger King Features Syndicate and United Features Syndicate. Though the private company did not release financial details, industry estimates seemed to indicate Universal was doing well, with revenue of perhaps $55 million in 1987 rising to about $88 million in 1991.

Multimedia in the 1990s

By the end of the 1980s, Universal Press Syndicate was one of the three largest newspaper syndicates in the United States, and its publishing arm, Andrews and McMeel, was one of the largest humor publishers. Firmly grounded in these two areas, the company began to turn increasingly to other media segments. Universal bought three weekly papers and a daily in California in the late 1980s, and then entered a joint agreement with a television studio to develop programming based on Universal's syndicated properties. This was Universal Belo Productions, formed by Universal and A.H. Belo Corporation. Belo also owned the *Dallas Morning News*, and as part of its agreement with Universal, it asked the syndicate to drop its features from the rival *Dallas Times Herald*. This action resulted in a lawsuit by the *Times Herald* against Belo and Universal. Universal was later dropped from the suit, and the *Herald* eventually lost. Universal Belo went on to produce a show called *Beakman's World,* which was nominated for an Emmy award. Universal entered other marketing arrangements in the 1990s, leading it into new areas. The company signed up to distribute books for Turner Publishing, a venture owned by the media magnate Ted Turner. Universal's publishing division also entered the children's book market in the early 1990s, signing a contract with children's publisher Ariel Books in 1991 to distribute 32 Ariel titles. The children's book category was particularly hot in the early 1990s, and Andrews and McMeel also began producing its own children's books, which were packaged with toys or other products. Universal also started a 900-number, or pay-per-call telephone service designed to boost newspaper subscriptions.

Universal continued to be a big player in comics syndication in the 1990s. Though it lost some of its earlier stars, it gained one of the biggest names in syndication. Lynn Johnston, for example, moved her "For Better or For Worse" comic to United Media in the mid-1990s. In addition, both Bill Watterson, creator of "Calvin and Hobbes," and Gary Larson, of

"The Far Side," retired from cartooning. However, in 1994 Universal Press Syndicate announced that it would be handling the cartoon "Garfield," created by Jim Davis. United Media had previously syndicated Davis's comic, which appeared in over 2,400 newspapers worldwide at the time of the switch. Davis also had a slew of licensed products. He spent an estimated $15 million to $20 million to buy the rights to "Garfield" back from United. He handled licensed products through his own company, called Paws, but he wanted Universal to take care of the newspaper syndication of his comic strip. Apparently Davis had been unhappy with United for some time, and he was charmed by what he knew of John McMeel. They had met at publishing conventions, and McMeel used to jokingly try to get the cartoonist to sign a contract. Like Abigail Van Buren, Davis himself ultimately approached Universal about switching. "Garfield" was a huge coup for Universal. Though the strip was already a giant in the syndication world, Universal managed to add "Garfield" to over 100 additional papers within a few years. The company also marketed a "Garfield" calendar, though much "Garfield" licensing was tied up in Davis's other arrangements.

Universal's Andrews and McMeel publishing division continued to grow in the 1990s. It had a strong presence in humor, selling as many as 25 million books each by Gary Larson and Bill Watterson. It also published nonfiction books by its columnists. Beginning in 1995, the company moved to expand its nonfiction list, acquiring trade titles such as a book on the O.J. Simpson trial, self-help books, and a book about Bill Clinton. Its typical trade list ran to 20 titles in the early 1990s. The company planned 60 books for 1996. By 2000, the company was publishing 300 titles a year.

Because the company had grown more diversified and complex, it changed its name in 1997 from Universal Press Syndicate to Andrews McMeel Universal. The new name reflected the strength of the publishing division, which was renamed Andrews McMeel Publishing. The publishing division employed roughly 170 people by the time of the name change, and was the major contributor to the firm's annual revenues. Estimates put revenue in the late 1990s at around $175 million annually. The company also launched a division called Universal New Media in 1997, to handle electronic distribution of its properties.

By the close of the 1990s, Andrews McMeel Universal handled more than 125 syndicated features, including leading comics such as "Foxtrot," "Garfield," "Cathy," and "Doonesbury," and columns by Erma Bombeck and Abigail Van Buren. Its book division reached out into new areas, forming for example a unit specifically to handle the works of popular columnist Mary Engelbreit, and arranging to take over distribution for trade publisher Longstreet Press in 1998. The company also laid off over 30 employees that year, in what was announced as a cost-cutting move. Andrews McMeel Publishing also entered an agreement with major publisher Simon & Schuster to develop and market calendars, an area in which Andrews McMeel had particular expertise. The company had considerable talent to draw on from its pool of syndicated writers and artists. With its three principal divisions working in sync, the firm seemed adept at finding multiple ways to market that talent, from books to calendars to coffee mugs to web sites.

Principal Divisions

Universal Press Syndicate; Andrews McMeel Publishing; uclick.

Principal Competitors

King Features Syndicate; United Features Syndicate, Inc.; The E.W. Scripps Company.

Further Reading

"Andrews McMeel Forms New Division, Strikes Alliances," *Publishers Weekly*, January 26, 1998, p. 14.

Astor, David, "From 'Doonesbury' to 'Abby' to 'Calvin'," *Editor & Publisher*, March 17, 1990, pp. 54–57.

——, " 'Momentous' Event in the Syndicate Biz," *Editor & Publisher*, April 16, 1994, p. 46.

——, "Universal Birthday Celebrated in K.C.," *Editor & Publisher*, February 18, 1995, pp. 42–43.

——, "Universal Parent Lays Off over 30," *Editor & Publisher*, October 24, 1998, p. 35.

Butcher, Lola, "Andrews & McMeel Flourishes by Being Smart, Not Intelligentsia," *Kansas City Business Journal*, June 28, 1991, p. 1.

Davis, Mark, "Universal Press Syndicate of Kansas City, Mo., Changes Its Name," *Knight-Ridder/Tribune Business News*, June 13, 1997, p. 613B0968.

Kinsella, Bridget, "Andrews & McMeel Expands Trade Publishing," *Publishers Weekly*, June 10, 1996, p. 31.

Milliot, Jim, "Name Change for Andrews McMeel," *Publishers Weekly*, June 16, 1997, p. 24.

Musser, R.S., "Deals McMeel," *Ingram's*, February 1995, p. 28.

Unsworth, Tim, "Andrews & McMeel: A Hit with Syndicated Satire," *Publishers Weekly*, February 10, 1989, p. 45.

—A. Woodward

The Antioch Company

888 Dayton Street, P.O. Box 28
Yellow Springs, Ohio 45387
U.S.A.
Telephone: (800) 543-2397
Fax: (800) 542-7749
Web site: http:/www.antioch.com

Private Company
Incorporated: 1946 as Antioch Bookplate Company
Employees: 750
Sales: $200 million (2000 est.)
NAIC: 511191 Greeting Card Publishers; 511199 All
    Other Publishing

The Antioch Company is one of the largest manufacturers of book-related products, producing and distributing diaries, journals, bookmarks, bookplates, and address books. The company distributes gift and novelty items through bookstores in the United States, the United Kingdom, and Canada. Antioch Publishing holds licensing agreements with many prominent artists and cartoonists including Anne Geddes, and produces products with such notable cartoon names as Garfield, Peace Frogs, Looney Tunes, and Pokemon. Its wholly owned subsidiary Creative Memories is a direct sales scrapbook company which produces photo albums and related supplies. Creative Memories is the largest scrapbook company in the world and has expanded its operations to Australia, New Zealand, the United Kingdom, Taiwan, and Germany.

Enterprising Students: 1926

The earliest beginnings of The Antioch Company were forged in the halls of Antioch College of Yellow Springs, Ohio—a college well known for its free thinkers and liberal learning environment. Ernest Morgan and Walter Kahoe were students who worked part-time in the college print shop. Urged on by ingenuity, an aversion to waste, and a propensity for hard work, the two created bookplates from recycled scrap material and launched what was to come to be known as The Antioch Bookplate Company (ABC) in 1926.

Bookplates had their origin in the 15th century, and served the purpose of identifying ownership of a book. Many bookplates went beyond the basic function of reminding the borrower to whom the book belonged and served as a decorative label with the identifying crest or armorial devices of its owner. Often bookplates were embellished with artistry or clever poetry designed to warn the borrower to treat the book with care and return it to its rightful owner.

Ernest Morgan and Walter Kahoe had become interested in fine printing while interning with the famous printing house of W.E. Rudge in New York, and found bookplates to be an alternative way to start out in the printing business. Beginning with artwork done by students at the college and scrap material, it seemed to be an enterprising way to make a living.

Morgan was interested in finding a product that could be prepackaged and allowed a different printer's lifestyle than the one he saw during his internship. Many print shops at the time experienced very irregular schedules, the work was either slow or extremely intense. As Morgan related years later in his autobiography, *Dealing Creatively with Life,* "There was a method in my madness in joining up with Walter in the bookplate project. I liked printing—especially beautiful printing—but it was always feast or famine—overtime or idleness. Then, too, it seemed to me that if you bid high enough to make money, you lost the order, and if you bid low enough to get the order you lost money. Far better to design a beautiful product, put a reasonable price on it, and merchandise it. Bookplates seemed to offer possibilities in that direction.''

In its first year of operation, ABC had 20 sales agreements with bookstores throughout Ohio, Michigan, and Indiana. Morgan had taken to the road hitchhiking his way to bookstores and book dealers in the region, choosing those dealers he found most desirable, but it was not long before the business's future was tested. During its first year, Kahoe was offered a position off campus as manager of the local, unaffiliated Antioch Press, and he found the offer too good to pass up, so he decided to sell his interest in the company to Morgan. The settlement was a mere $200.

The company's beginnings were humble. Utilizing the Antioch Press, an independent press next door to the college, the company continued to print and sell bookplates but was more strongly committed to its progressive, people-centered philosophy of life and work, than profits and growth.

Morgan managed the company and formed a short-lived partnership with another former Antioch student, Jesse Shelton. Morgan's bother Griscom and his sister Frances helped keep operations running smoothly, doing everything from reassembling a new second hand press to printing bookplates to keep up with orders. By the end of 1927 sales had risen to an encouraging $700. By 1928, short on space, the company moved to a small building next door. It was at this time that Morgan and Shelton dissolved their partnership. Shelton sold his partnership to Morgan in exchange for Morgan covering his debts.

In 1928 Ernest Morgan refused an offer from McGraw-Hill Publishing in order to continue to grow his fledgling business. Faced with the Great Depression in the 1930s, Morgan was able to reach an agreement with his employees by introducing a pay scale that included profit sharing at year's end. Morgan agreed to pay his employees 80 percent of their pay and, if the company proved profitable at the end of each year, the employees would receive their 20 percent contingent pay as well as a share of the profits.

The company was able to stay afloat, and by 1934 ABC was selling its products in all 48 states. In 1935 Ernest Morgan joined the typesetter's union. Morgan had cultivated a sensitivity to worker's issues and became actively interested in Socialist party politics. At the time his affiliations with what were seen as fringe groups sometimes worked against him, but the company also ended up with a lot of new accounts because of its liberal leanings and union ties. Labor groups and socialist organizations used the Bookplate Company for much of their printing, though such work was often donated at cost by the company.

In 1937 Antioch Bookplate Company was faced with increasing competition. It seemed as though every small printer was capitalizing on the scrap in their shops and producing bookplates and bookmarks of some kind. ABC concentrated its efforts on exposing pirated merchandise and producing quality and innovative products. The company also bought out many competitors along the way, one of the first was Louis Silver, a Chicago printer. Morgan liked Silver's designs for bookplates and offered to purchase them. Silver agreed to give ABC its designs for bookplates if ABC would help distribute Silver's line of bookmarks. Morgan had limited success with the bookmarks and went to Silver with some suggestions to improve the product and its packaging, Silver suggested that ABC buy the

bookmark line and make the improvements themselves. Morgan agreed and the bookplate company began its bookmark business.

In 1941 perhaps the most significant early company growth occurred when fellow Antioch alumnus Dick Steinbeck proposed that ABC hire him as its full-time salesperson. Morgan tried to convince Steinbeck that he could not possibly make a living selling bookplates, but the deal was made with Steinbeck offering to keep expenses down by living in his car. Business took off, doubling in a year, and sales continued at a steady pace for some time.

In 1943, having begun printing and selling bookmarks, ABC produced its own line of bookmarks with religious text. The bookmarks proved very successful but some initial problems resulted when the company attempted to print on the plastic. The ink was not permanent and the text could be easily wiped off. Morgan remedied this by seeking out a chemical additive that rendered the ink unerasable. With the new "Morgan Ink" in hand the company produced many printed plastic products as part of its inventory.

Ernest Morgan was a fan of beautiful art and woodcuts and for years he had admired the work of a well-known artist by the name of Rockwell Kent. An eastern company had pirated some of his designs for its bookplates and when Morgan originally approached Kent about using his designs, Kent responded by asking Morgan why he was asking for permission now when he had been stealing his stuff in the past. Morgan explained that Kent was confusing ABC with another company. The two became friends and Kent produced many bookplate designs for ABC. The company throughout its history continued the tradition of seeking out popular artists and cartoonists for its materials.

It took until 1946 for the company to officially incorporate. At the time, the Walt Disney Company signed an exclusive agreement allowing ABC to produce products with Disney characters on them.

Beginning in 1958 Morgan's son Lee began working part-time in the family-run business. Lee had graduated from college and had decided to work at Antioch. By 1959 ABC was producing 90 percent of the world's bookplates and Lee Morgan was taking a more active role in the company, becoming a sales representative in 1962.

During the next decade the company expanded its print shop capabilities by purchasing new equipment that allowed Antioch to do innovative types of printing, including lithography and all forms of color printing, and to produce specialized leather bookmarks.

In 1968 sales figures for bookplates stood at 15 million a year, distributed through 5,000 dealers nationwide. At the end of the 1960s the nation was going through its own social experimentation and The Antioch Bookplate Company sought like-minded individuals for employment with the rapidly growing company. ABC advertised in alternative journals throughout the country. Ads appeals ran as follows: "Idealists wanted by printing business in unusual, well integrated, progressive college community. Staff includes persons of varied backgrounds, some with special interests in peace, human relations, economic democracy. . . ." Indeed, Morgan assembled a

---

Key Dates:

1926: Ernest Morgan and Walter Kahoe found The Antioch Bookplate Company (ABC) while students at Antioch College.

1927: Operations move off campus to the neighboring Antioch Press; Jesse Shelton joins the partnership.

1930: Antioch Bookplate Company introduces prepackaged bookplates.

1931: Company moves operations to 220 Xenia Ave.

1934: ABC supplies stores in all 48 continental states.

1936: ABC buys bookmark line of rival Louis J. Silver; acquires competitor Alfred Stenzel; sales increase by 75 percent.

1939: The company publishes its first children's co-op book.

1940: ABC hires its first full-time salesperson and sales soon double in volume.

1941: ABC introduces the first line of colored bookplates.

1943: Paper storeroom fire occurs at the press.

1945: Company purchases bookplate designs from notable artist Rockwell Kent; ABC invests in die press for engraving.

1946: Antioch Bookplate Company officially incorporates; ABC obtains exclusive bookmark license from Walt Disney Company.

1970: Ernest Morgan retires; Lee Morgan becomes executive vice-president, then president a year later.

1975: Sales exceed $1 million.

1977: Company starts its own community foundation, The Antioch Bookplate Foundation.

1981: Company changes its name to Antioch Publishing Company; sales surpass $5 million.

1984: Antioch UK Ltd. is established; company acquires Holes-Webway Company of St. Cloud, Minnesota.

1986: Sales exceed $10 million.

1987: Company forms Creative Memories division.

1993: Company expands Webway facility; Ernest Morgan resigns as chairman.

1995: Antioch opens production and distribution facility in Sparks, Nevada, for Creative Memories.

1997: Creative Memories division expands into Australia and Taiwan.

1999: Sales reach $200 million.

2000: Creative Memories opens Richmond, Virginia production and distribution facility and launches operations in New Zealand, Japan, and Germany; founder Ernest Morgan dies.

---

multicultural mix of coworkers for what looked more at times like an experimental workers' commune than a print shop.

Leadership Under Lee Morgan: 1970s

In 1970 Lee Morgan officially took over first as executive vice-president and then the following year as president. Morgan updated production by using offset technology to run the business. He also increased wages within the company, offering pay

that was more in keeping with industry standards; the changes took a toll on the company profit margin for some time. Although sales were up, profits lagged. In 1970 sales had reached $418,000, yet ABC recorded loses of $25,677. Some employee owners doubted Morgan's leadership, but the modernization and growth paid off over time.

ABC was outgrowing its building by this time and in 1974 it moved its operations to a newly constructed building at 888 Dayton St. Under Lee Morgan's leadership Antioch Bookplate Company experienced rapid growth and expansion. The company continued to develop new products including tasseled bookmarks, calendars, diaries, and novelty items with psychedelic designs. In 1975, the growth was starting to yield results and sales surpassed $1 million for the first time. Distribution was expanded to include Canada, England, and Australia.

Under Morgan's care ABC maintained its founding philosophy and its commitment to justice issues and workers' rights. Several examples throughout the 1970s stand out. In 1977 The Antioch Bookplate Foundation was formed. The Foundation enabled the company to give a portion of company profits back to the community.

In 1978 ABC was among the earliest of companies to discontinue sales in South Africa. The company employees voted to suspend all business with the country due to its racist system of apartheid. An employee stock ownership plan (ESOP) instituted in 1979 also exemplified ABC's commitment to its 50-plus workers. The company had long had a history of creatively paying its employees and the ESOP was another tribute to the way the Morgans valued their workers.

In 1980 ABC launched its first wholly owned subsidiary, Antioch Canada Ltd. The company was now manufacturing Advent calendars and religious greeting cards. ABC also had a licensing agreement with Jim Davis, creator of the comic "Garfield," for the production of bookmarks.

With the ever expanding merchandise the company was now producing and distributing, ABC made the decision to change its name officially to Antioch Publishing Company in 1981. Once again the company was outgrowing its space, so in 1981 it added 25,000 square feet to its main facility. Sales were now around the $5 million mark.

In 1982 Antioch Publishing acquired Sullivan Printing Works Co. The company now had over 100 employees and Antioch set up another wholly owned subsidiary, Antioch UK Ltd.

Outgrowing its production space once again, the company expanded its facility by 24,000 square feet in 1984.

Perhaps one of the most significant turns of events in the company history happened in 1985 when Antioch Publishing, eager to get into the photo album business, purchased Holes-Webway Company, based in Minnesota. Holes-Webway was a financially struggling producer of photo albums and social books. Unbeknownst to the company at the time, in 1987 Holes-Webway became an opportunity for Antioch Publishing Company to create its most successful sales division ever, Creative Memories.

Birth of Creative Memories: 1987

Creative Memories, a wholly owned subsidiary of The Antioch Company, came to be when a high-level employee at Holes-Webway, Marketing Vice-President Cheryl Lightle, answered the phone after the office had closed for the day. A Montana woman by the name of Rhonda Anderson had called to order 40 scrapbook albums. Anderson had been keeping scrapbooks of her family for years and a local women's group took notice of the beautiful memory books and asked her to present a workshop on her scrapbooking method. Inspired by her designs the group wanted to begin scrapbooks of their own.

When Anderson related her story to Lightle, the two immediately saw the possibilities for a direct sales scrapbook company. Anderson and Lightle spent time talking about the content of the presentation and Lightle began developing a business plan.

Lightle and Anderson's chance phone meeting started what was to become the largest scrapbook company in the world. Anderson and her family moved to St. Cloud, Minnesota, where Creative Memories was to be based, and Lightle became president of the new company.

In 1989 Antioch sold Sullivan Printing to Patented Printing and concentrated its production on albums, scrapbooks, journals, and gourmet giftbooks. The company was continually improving its printing abilities by adding technological advances to its print shops. Computer-assisted graphics and other technologies gave Antioch a greater range of production capabilities.

By 1992, 55 percent of the company's sales were in photo albums, and Creative Memories demonstrations and products were the first to set off a scrapbooking frenzy among crafters worldwide. The company also added a press capable of printing stickers and labels used in scrapbook design in 1995.

By 1997 Creative Memories, with thousands of consultants worldwide, was selling $1 million a day in products through home demonstrations and had expanded its operations into Australia and Taiwan. A production facility built in Sparks, Nevada, helped the company keep up with manufacturing and allowed for better distribution.

In 2000 demand for scrapbooks and scrapbook accessories continued to rise and Creative Memories opened a new manufacturing facility in Richmond, Virginia. The new facility also served as a distribution center to new markets in New Zealand, Japan, and Germany.

The Antioch Company from its humble beginnings to its tremendous success with Creative Memories stayed true to its corporate spirit of innovation and risk-taking. The company had developed beautiful products and creative ways to market them to the public, and in turn it had grown exponentially, more so than anyone might have imagined for a business that began in a college print shop. The company stood as a tribute to the creative spirit of its founder, Ernest Morgan, and the boldness, ingenuity, and management of his son and successor, Lee Morgan.

Principal Subsidiaries

Creative Memories; Webway; Antioch North America; Antioch UK Ltd.

Principal Competitors

Hallmark Cards, Inc.

Further Reading

"Carolyn-Bean Announces Agreement with Antioch Publishing Co for distribution to Waldenbooks," *Business Wire,* August 12, 1986.

Fischer, Meredith, "Minnesota-Based Direct Sales Company Plans Center in Walthall, Va.," *Richmond Times-Dispatch,* March 9, 2000.

Gebolys, Debbie, "Scrapbooking Industry Cropping up in Columbus," *Columbus Dispatch,* November 9, 1998, p.10.

"Holson Burnes Group to Purchase Heritage Springfield Photo Album Company," *Business Wire,* March 17, 1995.

LaFrance, Siona, "Storing Memories Scrapbooking Is a Newly Popular Phenomenon Apparently Fueled by Nostalgia, Concern About Photo Preservation and Good-Old Fashioned Commercialism," *Times-Picayune,* November 29,1998, p. E1.

Milliot, Jim, "Antioch Acquires Largely Literary Sidelines," *Publishers Weekly,* February 27, 1995, p. 18.

Morgan, Ernest, *Dealing Creatively with Life,* New York: Barclay House, 1999.

Reyes, Sonia, "Preserving the Past—in Photos," *Daily News* (New York), July 3, 1995, p. 39.

Zipkin, Amy, "You Can't Judge a Book by Its Cover," *Advertising Age,* May 16, 1998, p. S9.

—Susan B. Culligan

Arctic Cat Inc.

600 Brooks Avenue South
Thief River Falls, Minnesota 56701
U.S.A.
Telephone: (218) 681-8558
Fax: (218) 681-3162
Web site: http://www.arctic-cat.com

Public Company
Incorporated: 1983 as Arctco, Inc.
Employees: 1,700
Sales: $484.01 million (2000)
Stock Exchanges: NASDAQ
Ticker Symbol: ACAT
NAIC: 336999 All Other Transportation Equipment;
315211 Men's and Boys Cut and Sew Apparel
Contractors; 315239 Women and Girls Cut and Sew
Other Outwear

One of the pioneers as well as leaders in its field, Arctic Cat Inc. designs, manufactures, and sells Arctic Cat snowmobiles, all-terrain vehicles (ATVs), and generators, as well as related parts, accessories, and garments. Based in Thief River Falls, Minnesota, Arctic Cat was formed in 1983 under the name Arctco, Inc. to continue the legacy of snowmobile manufacturer Arctic Enterprises, Inc., which went bankrupt in 1981. In August 1996 Arctic Cat officially renamed itself after its most widely known product, the Arctic Cat snowmobile. Arctic Cat has firmly established itself as a leading producer of snowmobiles and ATVs, ranking third in market share in snowmobile sales and fifth in market share in ATV sales. Arctic Cat maintains production facilities in Thief River Falls, Minnesota, and Madison, South Dakota. In early 1996, the company entered the market for ATVs and has steadily become an industry leader, predicting that by the end of fiscal 2001 ATV sales will be equal to the company's snowmobile sales. Arctic Cat closed its Personal Watercraft Division in 1999 after steadily declining sales. The company manufactured the Tigershark brand of personal watercraft and despite discontinuing the production of new units, it still provides Tigershark parts, accessories, and service

through its 1,200 North American dealerships and its 40 distributors worldwide.

Origins

When Edgar Hetteen saw his first snowmobile, his reaction was immediate, leaving no question about his feelings. "I wouldn't have anything to do with the thing at first," he later recalled, "I told my brother-in-law, David [Johnson], he had wasted our time and money building it and I wanted no more of it." For someone who would spend nearly every waking hour for the next ten years trying to arouse widespread enthusiasm in snowmobiles, Hetteen's words marked a decidedly chilly beginning to what would become a lifelong love affair. Hetteen, who would go on to found the predecessor company to Arctic Cat and, by doing so, position himself among the handful of pioneers in the U.S. snowmobile industry, was more concerned at the time about his farming equipment fabrication company than the curious sled that greeted him upon his arrival in Roseau, Minnesota. The year was 1955 and Hetteen had just returned from a sales trip, his latest effort at turning his company, Hetteen Hoist and Derrick, into a flourishing concern. It was proving to be a difficult task. Far removed from more populated, lucrative markets, Hetteen Hoist and Derrick was struggling in its eighth year of business, scoring only a modicum of success as a custom fabricator of specialized farm implements and tools. Hetteen's latest business trip had achieved lackluster results, and he initially was unimpressed with Johnson's snowmobile. Before long, however, one of the world's preeminent snowmobile manufacturers was established, spawning the creation of Arctic Cat snowmobiles and a new form of winter recreation for millions of people.

Johnson's prototype had been built at the request of a local resident, Pete Peterson, who asked the manufacturer to fabricate a "gas-powered sled." The proceeds from the sale of Peterson's snowmobile enabled Hetteen Hoist and Derrick to make payroll, tempering Hetteen's view considerably, and shortly thereafter another Roseau local placed an order for a gas-powered sled, as demand for the novel snow machines began to build. By the end of the winter of 1955–56, Hetteen's company had constructed five snowmobiles; the following winter 75 machines were built, and during the winter of 1957–58, more

Company Perspectives:

The Arctic Cat brand name has existed for more than 30 years and is among the most widely recognized and respected names in the snowmobile industry.

than 300 snowmobiles were produced by Hetteen and his workers. In the space of a few short years, the primary business of Hetteen's company had switched from fabricating farm equipment to building and testing machines designed for snow travel. Hetteen, by this point, was hooked.

For years, Hetteen had endeavored to sell the straw cutters, post setters, and other equipment his company made to markets outside Roseau, but had found little success. With snowmobiles, he sensed the opportunity to achieve the success that had eluded him with agricultural machinery. Early on he realized that to make his new product a success in distant markets it would have to be marketed as a recreational device, but during the late 1950s public interest in snowmobiles was essentially nonexistent, a hurdle Hetteen would overcome by launching an ambitious public relations campaign. In March 1960, Hetteen and three of his cohorts took their snowmobiles to Alaska and completed an 1,100-mile trek from Bethel to Fairbanks in 18 days, drawing the attention of newspaper reporters, magazine writers, and ham radio operators.

Hetteen returned to Roseau pleased by his success in piquing public interest in snowmobiles, but his arrival home did not meet with applause or congratulatory pats on the back. Hetteen Hoist and Derrick had since been renamed Polaris Industries, Inc. and capitalized by local investors, who were somewhat miffed that Hetteen had abandoned his duties at Polaris and gone to Alaska. As this dispute over the future course of the company was being played out, Hetteen was approached by a group of investors from Thief River Falls, Minnesota. Led by L.B. Hartz, a successful food broker and supermarket owner, the group offered to financially back Hetteen if he moved his company to Thief River Falls; Hetteen declined, and in May 1960, two months after completing his successful trek in Alaska, Hetteen sold his controlling interest in Polaris and returned to Alaska, where he hoped to start a new career as a bush pilot and frontiersman.

Hetteen's second visit to Alaska was not as successful as his first. After several months of working at isolated airstrips as a pilot and mechanic, Hetteen decided to accept Hartz's offer and renew his interest in designing, building, and testing snowmobiles. By Christmas 1960, when Hetteen arrived in Thief River Falls, financial arrangements already had been made to provide him with a co-signed note for $10,000, which he used to rent a vacant 30- by 70-foot grocery warehouse and start his new business, Polar Manufacturing Company.

1962: Birth of Arctic Cat

Polar Manufacturing opened its doors on January 2, 1961, and initially manufactured electric steam cleaners and a device to kill insects called "Bug-O-Vac" to raise enough money to begin snowmobile production in earnest. The first snowmobile,

the "New Polar 500," was completed by the end of the year and marketed as a utility model for use by forestry, power and light, telephone, and oil exploration companies. Although Hetteen had wanted to develop snowmobiles as a recreational product nearly from the outset of his involvement with the machines, he knew he needed to develop a need for snowmobiles before he could begin to inspire a desire for them. In 1962, after its inaugural year of business, Polar Manufacturing was renamed Arctic Enterprises, Inc.. That year it introduced the red "Arctic Cat 100," the first front-engined sport sled in the United States, which Hetteen referred to as the "Tin Lizzie." Concurrent with the introduction of the Arctic Cat 100, a distribution network was established to carry the machine to distant markets, as Hetteen had always hoped. Although the New Polar 500 had been the first model produced, the Arctic Cat 100 represented the beginning of an era for both Arctic Enterprises and snowmobile enthusiasts across the country, ushering in a new winter sport and launching the Arctic Cat tradition.

Distributor relationships were forged throughout a wide territory ranging from New York to Idaho, as the fledgling company sought to secure a foothold in distant markets. There were 19 distributors signed up for the 1963–64 winter season and 13 Arctic Cat models, up from the six offered the previous year. During the first half of the decade, the company's sales climbed encouragingly, propelled by the increasing number of models produced each year and supported by a steadily growing distribution network, but annual profits were not demonstrating the same vibrancy. This inability to post consistent profit growth— the company lost $20,000 in 1964 on $750,000 in sales—was part of the reason Hetteen decided to step down from his leadership position in 1965 and hand the reins of command to Lowell Swenson. Hetteen, literally, had spent nearly all of his time during the previous decade trying to make a successful snowmobile manufacturing company; now as his company was on the brink of success he decided that a new leader was required to push Arctic Enterprises over the edge. Hetteen receded from the bustling activity pervading Arctic Enterprises but he did not disappear altogether. Years later, Hetteen would return, but during the interim, Arctic Enterprises would grow into the flourishing concern he had long sought.

When Swenson became president of Arctic Enterprises in 1966 he made one goal of the company's future clear: "We [will] concentrate on one machine," he vowed, "and make it a damn good one." True to his word, Swenson spearheaded the effort toward designing a snowmobile that could carry the company into the future, putting to an end the era of the red Arctic Cats after the 1965–66 winter season to make room for the black "Panther." Debuting in 1966, the Panther possessed technological breakthroughs that drove sales and, most importantly, profits upward for the remainder of the 1960s.

In 1968, Arctic Enterprises generated $7.5 million in sales, three times the amount collected the year before, and posted $379,000 in net income or eight times the figure recorded in 1967, ending the nagging worries about profitability. In 1969, annual sales continued their exponential march upward, reaching $21.7 million, while net income eclipsed the $1 million plateau, climbing to $1.2 million. Business was booming, with the company holding a firm grip on nearly 12 percent of the U.S. market for snowmobiles, a percentage that perhaps could have

Key Dates:

1955: Pete Peterson commissions "gas-powered" sled from Hetteen Hoist and Derrick.

1958: Snowmobiles become primary business of Hetteen Hoist and Derrick, later renamed Polaris Industries.

1960: Hetteen sells controlling interest in Polaris Industries.

1961: Hetteen moves operations to Thief River Falls, Minnesota, and founds Polar Manufacturing Company.

1962: Polar Manufacturing is renamed Arctic Enterprises, Inc.; Arctic Cat 100, the first front-engined sport sled, is introduced.

1969: Annual sales reach $21.7 million.

1970: Arctic Enterprises acquires Silverline Inc. of Moorhead, Minnesota.

1977: Lund Boat Company is acquired.

1981: Sales plummet and bankers call Arctic Enterprises' $48.5 million in loans; company files for bankruptcy.

1983: Arctco, Inc. is founded by Edgar Hetteen and investors.

1990: Arctco, Inc. goes public.

1993: Company enters personal watercraft industry.

1996: Company produces the first of its all-terrain vehicles (ATVs); Arctco changes its name to Arctic Cat Inc.

1997: Arctic Cat opens a distribution center in Bucyrus, Ohio.

1999: Arctic Cat closes its Personal Watercraft Division.

been higher, but the two shifts working the production lines at the Thief River Falls facilities were not enough to satisfy the mounting demand for Panther snowmobiles. As the company prepared for the 1970s, it exited the 1960s with a full head of steam and high expectations for future growth. Production facilities were expanded greatly in anticipation of rising demand and a line of snowmobile clothing was introduced to give the company a more diversified footing in the rapidly expanding snowmobile industry.

1970s Collapse

The 1970s began as expected, with the company's annual sales soaring 113 percent to reach $46.5 million, its market share rising to 13 percent, and its net income jumping to $2.9 million. Prosperous times gave Arctic Enterprises the ability to diversify further, providing the financial means to acquire boat manufacturer Silverline, Inc. of Moorhead, Minnesota, the company's first major cross-seasonal acquisition, and to introduce mini-bikes on the market, both of which became part of the company's operations in 1970. The following year, Arctic Enterprises moved farther afield, acquiring lawn and garden manufacturer General Leisure, and then, in 1973, introducing a line of French-made bicycles. By this point, however, the luster of Arctic Enterprises operations had dulled considerably. The years of robust growth were over as quickly as they started.

The line of bicycles proved to be unsuccessful and General Leisure proved to be a costly mistake, leading to its divestiture

in 1973. But these ancillary businesses were the least of Arctic Enterprises' problems. The demand for snowmobiles tapered off during the early years of the 1970s, beginning their downward path in 1971 and resulting in Arctic Enterprises' most disastrous year in 1974. If it was any consolation for the employees and management in Thief River Falls, who in the space of a few months had watched their prolific rise screech to a halt, Arctic Enterprises was not alone in its downward free-fall. Across the country, snowmobile manufacturers were reeling from the debilitative effects of depressed demand, with many going out of business. In 1970, when the snowmobile industry was thriving, there were more than 100 brands of snowmobiles on the market; by 1976, when the worst of the harsh economic times was over, the number of brands on the market had plunged precipitously to a mere 13.

As harmful as waning snowmobile demand had been to Arctic Enterprises' business, however, conditions in the industry after the shakeout was completed placed the Thief River Falls concern in what could be regarded as a stronger position. Much of the competition in the United States had been weeded out, and Arctic Enterprises continued to reign as the largest producer of snowmobiles in the country. Recovery was quick in the late 1970s, sufficient enough to enable the company to finance the acquisition of its second boat manufacturer in 1977, when Arctic Enterprises purchased the Lund Boat Company and gained control of its manufacturing facilities in Minnesota, Wisconsin, and Manitoba, Canada. Sales by the end of the year flirted with $100 million, reaching $99 million, while the company's market share had been bolstered by the departure of many of its competitors, rising to an impressive 25 percent. The following year, in 1979, sales soared 61 percent to $175 million, by which point the number of snowmobile manufacturers in the country had been whittled down to six. Once again business was booming, and the company was exiting the 1970s much as it had ended the 1960s, with its business interests moving forward on all fronts.

1980s: Reincarnation of Arctic Cat

To the chagrin of the workers and management at Thief River Falls, history continued to repeat itself in the decade ahead, as the early 1980s paralleled the early 1970s and rampant growth quickly disappeared. This time, however, the effects were much more devastating. Sales in 1980 climbed to $185 million, despite a decline in snowmobile sales throughout the country, but by far the most telling and most depressing financial figure for the year was the company's profit total. Arctic Enterprises lost $11.5 million during the year, a staggering blow that was followed by another $10 million loss the following year. As production totals in 1981 fell to their lowest levels since 1969, the bankers who had granted the company loans over the years became disgruntled and alarmed. Worried that the company would not be able to make good on its financial promises, the bankers called for the payment of $48.5 million in loans on February 6, 1981. Eleven days later, Arctic Enterprises filed for protection under Chapter 11 of the U.S. Bankruptcy Act. In a year that otherwise would have been celebrated as the company's 20th anniversary year, Arctic Enterprises was ruined financially.

The news could not have been worse, but even as steps were being taken to liquidate the snowmobile operations and the rest of the company was being sold piecemeal, there were some encouraging reports that at least seemed to underscore the strength of the Arctic Cat name in snowmobile circles across the country. Even though the company's production facilities had been shuttered, the demand for Arctic Cat snowmobiles had increased. Remarkably, sales were up high enough for the company to capture 38 percent of the U.S. market one year after production had stopped, providing ample evidence that loyalty to and confidence in Arctic Enterprises' products remained high.

Dead but not forgotten, Arctic Enterprises was etched in the memories of its loyal customers, some of whom vowed never to ride a snowmobile again. The memory of the company also was etched in the hearts of its former employees, the pangs of which led a small group of former managers to attend the auction of Arctic Enterprises' various properties. Included in this group was Edgar Hetteen, who returned to witness the dismemberment of the company he had left nearly 20 years earlier; by the end of the day the group had acquired enough of Arctic Enterprises' properties to establish a new snowmobile manufacturing company, which was incorporated as Arctco, Inc. in 1983. As company advertisements would soon announce, the Cat was back, and for the legions of faithful customers the return of the popular Arctic Cat snowmobiles was welcome news.

After acquiring the production rights and the exclusive use of the Arctic Cat brand name, Arctco made preparations to get its product to market, beginning production of its snowmobiles in August 1983. The less than 3,000 snowmobiles made for the 1984 model year sold out quickly, enabling the company to generate $7.3 million in sales and post $600,000 in profit. All of Arctic Cat's trademarks, equipment, and manufacturing properties were acquired subsequently in 1986 and 1987, restoring much of the luster formerly radiated by Arctic Enterprises. Sales and profits rose energetically throughout the remainder of the decade, reaching an encouraging $138.8 million and $12.5 million, respectively, by the end of 1990, the year Arctco became a publicly traded company.

During the first half of the 1990s, Arctco continued to enjoy impressive success, making its entry into the personal watercraft market and recording 21.5 percent annual growth in sales and 21.7 percent annual growth in net income. By 1994, when the company generated $268.1 million in sales, Arctco had surpassed the revenue volume recorded by Arctic Enterprises before its death knell had reverberated throughout Thief River Falls in 1981. As the company planned for the late 1990s and the new century ahead, prospects for future growth were encouraging, bolstering confidence that the coming years would bring continued success to the thriving company.

During the mid-1990s the North American snowmobile industry was expanding at a 20 percent annual clip, while the market for personal watercraft (PWC), the company's other primary business area, was recording annual gains in excess of 30 percent. In 1993 when Arctco began its PWC division by introducing its Tigershark brand, earnings remained strong and the company infrastructure looked very solid once again. In addition, Arctco had established a new company presence in the South, where dealers agreed to carry the Tigershark brand of PWC and its line of accessories. The next few years, however, found the PWC division unable to establish a solid foothold in the industry and by 1998 PWC earnings were down by 7 percent and the company's watercraft future appeared uncertain.

While Arctco's watercraft division was floundering, further opportunities for financial growth were opened to the company when it made its first foray into the market for all-terrain vehicles, a $1.2 billion industry during the mid-1990s that was recording nearly 20 percent annual growth. In January 1996, Arctco's first four-wheel-drive recreational and utility vehicle, the Bearcat 454, rolled off the company's production line, giving Arctco a diversified, cross-seasonal product line to drive its growth in the years ahead. Although finding it difficult to assert itself in the competitive field of PWC, Arctco seemed to have found its niche in the ATV arena. Following an aggressive marketing campaign targeted at its ATV products, Arctco posted a net earnings figure up 39 percent for 1997.

By the end of 1998 PWC sales for the company were significantly down and, faced with increasing competition and a significant loss of market share, Arctco announced its plans to exit the watercraft industry beginning in September 1999. The company's decision to pull out of PWC manufacturing came at the high pretax cost of $26.2 million, or $0.66 per share; the total cost amounted to a hefty $16.9 million after taxes.

In the midst of its expansion from snowmobiles into cross-seasonal products such as PWC and ATVs, Arctco changed its name in August 1996 to Arctic Cat Inc. The company had been urged by its dealers to rename itself. The more than 1,200 independent dealers nationwide were convinced that the Arctic Cat brand name had stronger name recognition with both customers and potential shareholders than did the previously used Arctco. With high customer brand loyalty in recreational and utility vehicles, the dealers reasoned that products produced by Arctic Cat Inc. would meet with greater enthusiasm than those manufactured by the little known Arctco.

In 1997 the newly named Arctic Cat continued its strong push into the ATV market. The company attributed its success to producing vehicles with competitive features while maintaining the lowest sticker price in each class. Arctic Cat continued to produce significant numbers of new ATV models and in 1997 it produced its line of 300s, offering both two-wheel-drive and four-wheel-drive vehicles. When asked about the company's plans to expand production for the ATV market, company spokesperson Mark Blackwell told *Dealernews,* "The new 300's are not the last of it. We will introduce additional new models . . . even during the next year. We are a market driven company and will respond to what the customers are asking for."

In keeping with its market-driven approach Arctic Cat surveyed ATV consumers and its research indicated that the primary uses of ATVs were for general recreation. The company's own figures from the D.J Brown Composite Index and Arctic Cat Inc. indicated that 41 percent of ATV buyers used their vehicles for recreation, 23 percent for hunting or fishing, 12 percent for farm or ranch use, 7 percent for hauling and towing, 7 percent for transportation, and 1 percent for commercial use. The numbers further indicated that the typical buying cycle was 3.6 years. Arctic Cat continued to diversify its line of vehicles accordingly, manufacturing ATVs and snowmobiles to meet the diverse needs of its customers.

In 1997 Arctic Cat reconfigured its means of supplying dealers by establishing a new distribution center in Bucyrus, Ohio. The new distribution center's location was chosen in part because it was located near a United Parcel Service (UPS) hub in Columbus, Ohio. The new 225,000-square-foot center allowed the company to move its products out quickly and efficiently and also to free up much needed production space at its Thief River Falls manufacturing facility.

In 1997 Arctic Cat faced litigation. Injection Research Specialists Inc. and Pacer Industries filed suit against the snowmobile manufacturer, maintaining that Arctic Cat, in purchasing engines from Fuji Heavy Industries, a Japanese supplier of a two-stroke electronic fuel injection system, had violated trade secrets. A similar suit had been filed against Arctic Cat's major competitor Polaris a year earlier but with differing results. The suit against Arctic Cat was dismissed in December 1998, whereas the suit against Polaris resulted in the defendant being ordered to pay $33.8 million, with a total pretax litigation cost to Polaris of $61.4 million.

Although fortunate in its legal battle Arctic Cat suffered big losses toward the end of the 1990s. Snowfall was significantly down in 1998 and 1999 and company earnings fell from $25 million in 1998 to $7.6 million in 2000.

Despite heavy losses Arctic Cat invested in new manufacturing technology in 2000. The CAD/CAM/CAE technology was as sophisticated as those technologies used by aerospace and automotive companies and allowed Arctic Cat to make major improvements in design and manufacturing. Company engineers could now achieve greater precision when building a machine and the company saved money in producing its pre-production molds. The result was that the company improved its design ability, its production capability, and, therefore, customer satisfaction.

While working on better technology for the snowmobile division, Arctic Cat launched a million-dollar safety campaign for young riders of ATVs. According to the U.S. Consumer Product Safety Commission (CPSC), more than 3,400 ATV-related deaths had occurred since 1982. "Four out of every 10 involved children under the age of 16." The new safety campaign utilized an interactive CD-ROM game and was sent free of charge to schools and libraries and was available to families who purchased ATVs.

With early snowfall in the closing months of 2000, Arctic Cat's quarterly net income quintupled to $21 million. The new century saw Arctic Cat introducing a new line of four-stroke snowmobiles to meet with consumer and government interest in snowmobiles that were quieter and more environmentally friendly. The top-of-the-line sleds were given a trial at Yellowstone National Park during the 2000–01 season. The U.S. Department of the Interior announced that snowmobiles would be banned from use in Yellowstone starting in 2003. The four-stroke technology was aimed to address the environmental concerns and put Arctic Cat Inc. once more on the cutting edge of product development.

Principal Subsidiaries

Arctco FSC, Inc. (U.S. Virgin Islands).

Principal Competitors

Polaris Industries, Inc.; Bombardier, Inc.; Yamaha Motor Corp.; Kawasaki Motors Corp.

Further Reading

Autry, Ret, "Arctco," *Fortune,* November 19, 1990, p. 174.

Campbell, Erin, "Shareholders of Minnesota Based Arctco Inc. Approve Name Change to Arctic Cat," *Knight-Ridder/Tribune Business News,* Dec. 18, 1998.

Copeland, Julie, "Lawsuit Against Minnesota Based Snowmobile Maker Dismissed," *Knight-Ridder/Tribune Business News,* December 18, 1998.

Cory, Matt, "Firms Advised to Rethink Ways to Address Labor Shortage," *Knight-Ridder/Tribune Business News,* May 20, 1999.

Davis, Ricardo A., "Minnesota's Arctco Leaps into All-Terrain Vehicle Market," *Knight-Ridder/Tribune Business News,* April 9, 1996, p. 40.

Farrell, Michael, "Arctic Cat Buys Back Shares," *Boating Industry,* June 1998, p. 20.

——, "Snowmobiles, ATV's Drive Sales," *Boating Industry,* July 1998, p. 18.

"Gas Assisted Molding Produces Lightweight Bumper," *Design News,* August 25, 1997, p. 29.

Harfiel, Robin, "Arctic Cat," *Dealernews,* August 1997, p. 30.

——, "Arctic Cat's 250 2+4: Carving Out a Niche in the ATV Market," *Dealernews,* October 1998, p. 28.

——, "Bear Market?," *Dealernews,* July 1997, p. 36.

Malmange, Paul, "CAD Got Your Model?," *Tooling and Production,* February 2000, p. 42.

Martyka, Jim, "Safety Is No Game for ATV Firms," *Minneapolis St. Paul City Business,* April 28, 2000, p. 7.

"New Powder or Ice Ahead," *Business Week,* February 17, 1992, p. 123.

Ramstad, C.J., *Legend: Arctic Cat's First Quarter Century,* Deephaven, Minn.: PPM Books, 1987.

"Year 2000 Report Card, Cigna, Western Wireless, G&K Services, Arctic Cat," *Forbes,* February 5, 2001, p. 192.

—Jeffrey L. Covell
—update: Susan B. Culligan

B&G Foods, Inc.

4 Gatehall Drive, Suite 110
Parsippany, New Jersey 07054
U.S.A.
Telephone: (979) 630-6400
Fax: (973) 364-1037
Web site: http://www.bgfoods.com

Private Company
Incorporated: 1996
Employees: 712
Sales: $351.4 million (2000)
NAIC: 311421 Fruit and Vegetable Canning; 311422
Specialty Canning

Established in 1996 by a coalition of New York investment firms, B&G Foods, Inc. has gathered together a number of well-known food brands, including B&G pickles, B&M baked beans, Louisiana Hot Sauce, Red Devil sauces, Underwood meat spreads, Ac'cent flavor enhancer, Los Palmas Mexican foods, the Polaner line of jams and jellies, Joan of Arc beans, Brer Rabbit molasses, Regina wine vinegars and cooking wines, Wright's liquid smoke hickory flavoring, Vermont Maid syrup, and the product line of Maple Grove Farms of Vermont. Already with major market shares on a regional basis, many of these brands have expanded their reach under B&G management. In 2000, B&G Foods also introduced an original product line with seasonings, salad dressings, marinades, and pepper sauces created by well-known chef and television personality Emeril Lagasse. B&G Foods is privately held, with more than 75 percent of its stock owned by the investment firm of Bruckman, Rosser, Sherrill & Co.

Creation of Specialty Foods in 1993: Forerunner of B&G Foods

Although B&G Foods is a young company, many of its brands have long and rich histories, with ownership changing hands a number of times over the years. The roots of B&G Foods as a collection of brands reaches back only to the mid-1980s, when Dutch conglomerate Artal NV began to buy a number of North American food businesses that included Bloch

& Guggenheimer, Inc., makers of B&G pickles, and M. Polaner, Inc. Leonard S. Polaner, who had run his family's 100-year-old business before Artal gained control, now served as a president under Artal. In 1989 he hired David Wenner, an executive at Johnson & Johnson for 13 years, to serve as assistant to the president, responsible for the management of the Bloch & Guggenheimer subsidiary.

After several years Artal began to divest itself of its food products. First to go in March 1993 was the Polaner line, sold to American Home Products for $67.5 million. Then in June a group of investors led by Texas billionaire Robert Bass created Specialty Foods, which subsequently bought eight of Artal's remaining food businesses in a $1.1 billion leveraged buyout. Polaner and Wenner also joined Specialty Foods as executives.

The high debt incurred in the deal, however, proved onerous for Specialty Foods. Moreover, commodity price swings, in particular a decline in the price of meat and an increase in the price of grain, had a devastating effect on the bottom line. Operating profits of $83 million in 1994 were followed by a loss of $165 million in 1995. By June 1996 Specialty Foods hired Merrill Lynch & Co. to sell off noncore holdings, as the company opted to focus on its bread and cheese businesses.

In November 1996 New York investors, led by the firm of Bruckman, Rosser, Sherrill & Co. and aided by Polaner and Wenner, created B&G Foods to acquire Specialty Foods subsidiaries Bloch & Guggenheimer and Burns & Ricker, Inc. (makers of bagel chips, pita crisps, biscotti, and crispini). On December 27, 1996, B&G Foods purchased the stock of the two holding companies that controlled Bloch & Guggenheimer and Burns & Ricker. Polaner assumed the role of chairman of B&G Foods, with Wenner serving as president and chief executive officer.

Although an entirely new corporate entity, B&G Foods drew its name from the more storied of its two acquisitions, Bloch & Guggenheimer, well known for B&G pickles. Bloch and Guggenheimer were immigrants who sold pickles in the streets of Manhattan. In 1889 they founded B&G to produce pickles and relish, as well as other condiments. Their company would grow into a large retail and foodservice business and produce the top condiment brand in the New York City area.

```
┌─────────────────────────────────────────┐
│         Company Perspectives:           │
│                                         │
│  We here at B&G have achieved our       │
│  enviable position through strict       │
│  adherence to good manufacturing        │
│  practices and efficient stock          │
│  rotation. We're dedicated to providing │
│  our customers with the highest level   │
│  of service found in the industry. And, │
│  as always, we regard quality to be our │
│  most important ingredient.             │
└─────────────────────────────────────────┘
```

In its first year of operations, B&G Foods quickly began to add to its business. On June 17, 1997, the company purchased four brands from Nabisco: Regina wine vinegars; Brer Rabbit, makers of molasses and syrups; Wright's, makers of liquid smoke hickory flavoring for use in marinades, sauces, soups, and stews; and Vermont Maid Syrup. On August 15, 1997, B&G Foods purchased Trappey's Fine Foods from the Louisiana-based McIlhenny Co., best known for its Tabasco products. Established in 1898 in the bayou country, and owned by McIlhenny since 1991, Trappey's produced Red Devil sauces, other lines of hot sauces, and a variety of pickled peppers.

B&G Foods Beginning to Grow Its Brands in 1997

The businesses B&G acquired in 1997 had established regional prominence over many years but had experienced a recent decline in sales. B&G Foods hoped not only to reverse that trend, through the introduction of new products, but also to extend the reach of the brands to the New York City area and to new regions through fresh distribution channels, such as mass merchants, nonfood outlets, and warehouse clubs. Financial results for 1997 indicated that the company was already showing signs of success. The Nabisco brands since July showed a 9 percent improvement over the prior year. Declining sales for Trappey products were halted in August and by the end of the year were up over the prior year. Furthermore, sales for B&G pickles and peppers grew by 8 percent, and foodservice sales of B&G products were up 18 percent. In all, annual revenues for the first full year of operations for B&G Foods stood at $151.6 million, compared with the 1996 total of $129.3 million for the same product lines under different management.

B&G Foods made yet another acquisition in July 1998 when it purchased privately held Maple Grove Farms of Vermont, Inc., makers of maple syrup and salad dressing under the Maple Grove Farm label, private-label maple syrup products, and natural foods under its Up Country Naturals label. With $37 million in 1997 sales, Maple Grove Farms was another brand with a rich history. The company was founded by Katharine Ide Gray, a member of one of the leading families of Vermont and an unlikely candidate to become a pioneer woman chief executive. In 1915 she began experimenting with maple sugar with her daughter, home for the summer from Columbia University where she studied Home Economics. Together with her daughter's friend, they created recipes for maple candy. A neighbor bought the first box of candy, and before long the women converted a back shed of Mrs. Gray's farm into a candy kitchen. The little business grew to the point that within four years it became a corporation and Mrs. Gray purchased an old mansion to convert into a factory. To lower overhead the mansion also became the Maple Grove Inn. As Maple Grove Candies expanded its offerings to include maple syrup and maple cream, as well as chocolates, Mrs. Gray purchased a maple reconditioning plant that became the basis of a second corporation, Maple Grove Products Vermont. To improve sales in New York City, Mrs. Gray would then open a restaurant and sales room on 57th Street, incorporated under the name of Maple Grove Products. Thus a kitchen operation would grow into an established business that by the end of the century would become part of a major food products company.

Financial results for 1998 showed an 18.6 percent increase in sales, from $151.6 million the previous year to $179.8 million. Maple Grove sales improved by $19.4 million, the Nabisco acquisitions by $10.3 million, and Trappey's by $10.2 million. Sales for B&G pickle and pepper products were relatively flat, increasing just 1.7 percent, or $.9 million. Sales for the Burns & Ricker snack food products, however, were disappointing, posting a loss of 11.2 percent, or $3.3 million.

Early in 1999, B&G Foods acquired the Polaner line of products, the family business of the B&G chairman with a history similar to that of Maple Grove Farms and Bloch & Guggenheimer. Polaner dates back to the 1800s when Max Polaner and his wife preserved fruit and pickled vegetables in a room next to the fruit and vegetable store they operated in Newark, New Jersey. Soon they were selling their products through other area stores, then across the Hudson River into New York City. As Polaner extended its reach over the years, it expanded its manufacturing facilities, especially after the increase in demand for its products caused by the post–World War II baby boom. Leonard Polaner joined the family business in 1956 after earning a master's degree from Harvard Business School. Almost 50 years later he would again be associated with the company that bears his name.

Whereas American Home Products had purchased Polaner in 1993 for $67.5 million, B&G foods paid only $30 million for the business six years later. American Home Products had little success with its food products holdings and in the face of declining sales opted to unload its brands in favor of concentrating on its core pharmaceutical and healthcare lines. The foods businesses were operated by a subsidiary, International Home Foods Inc., of which 80 percent was acquired in 1996 by the Dallas-based leveraged buyout firm of Hicks, Muse, Tate & Furst. B&G Foods hoped to use its expertise in operating smaller, specialty brands to revitalize the fortunes of Polaner.

Heritage Brands Acquisition: 1991

B&G Foods made its largest acquisition in 1999 with a $192 million purchase of the six ''Heritage'' brands from the Pillsbury Company, which deemed them to be nonstrategic. Pillsbury elected to focus on international megabrands, such as Green Giant and Häagen-Dazs, and U.S. brands, such as Progresso and Hungry Jack. Generating $140 million in 1998 sales, the Heritage brands included B&M Baked Beans, Ac'cent flavor enhancer, Las Palmas Mexican food, Joan of Arc canned beans, and Underwood meat spreads.

The Heritage brands were similar in many ways to the other product lines of B&G Foods, in that they were specialty brands with rich histories. The roots of Las Palmas reach back to a Mexican housewife named Rosa Ramirez in 1920s Ventura, California. Working out of her home she began selling enchilada sauce made from a family recipe to friends and neighbors and, eventually, opened the Ramirez & Feraud Chili Company. In 1923 Las Palmas was established and began to offer a number of canned Mexican foods and sauces.

The origins of Ac'cent flavor enhancer actually can be traced back 2,000 years to the Far East, where the use of glutamate, discovered in the process that converted soya bean meal to soya sauce, was first introduced. During World War I, potash, used in munitions, was in great demand and manufactured from the byproducts of the beet sugar industry. According to legend, a Detroit beet sugar mill owner searched for a new use of beet sugar after the war and discovered that it could provide a plentiful supply of glutamate. A factory to manufacture glutamate opened in 1936, and by 1949 the flavor enhancer began to be sold in grocery stores. Created from glutamate, Ac'cent has no flavor of its own; rather, it compensates for the loss of glutamate in processed food, thus restoring flavor.

The ancestor of B&M Baked Beans was a Portland, Maine canning company established in 1867 by George Burnham and George B. Morrill. Products included canned meat and fish as well as vegetables. The company became particularly known for its canned corn, but as corn-growing shifted from the Northeast to the Midwest in the early 1900s, the corn canning industry moved as well, relegating B&M's product to regional status. To make up for the loss of income, B&M in the 1920s began to experiment with baked beans, which until that time had not been canned successfully. Using the traditional New England brick oven method, B&M introduced its Brick Oven Baked Beans in 1927 and soon began advertising on a national basis. As the company discontinued its fish packing and chowder products following World War II, baked beans became B&M's main product. In 1965 the company was sold to Wm. Underwood Company, and the two became part of the Heritage brands that B&G Foods acquired in 1999.

Underwood's history reaches even further back than B&M's, dating to 1822 when an Englishman named William Underwood started a small condiment business in Boston. Beginning with mustard, Underwood soon began selling ketchup, marmalade, cranberries, and pickles, which were stored in bottles and glass jars produced by Boston glassmakers. Underwood shipped his products all over the world, and by 1836 he had outgrown the production capacity of the local glassmakers and was forced to turn to canisters. Underwood's canned goods were sold to the pioneers traveling westward as well as the Union Army during the Civil War. He died in 1864, and his sons took over the business. They experimented with a process they called "devilling," which mixed ground ham with special seasonings. A signature product resulted, as did the Underwood Devil logo, which was trademarked in 1870, the oldest still in use in the United States. A hundred years later, after it purchased B&M, the Underwood Company was acquired in 1968 by Piermont Foods of Montreal. Pet Inc. acquired both companies in 1982; they were then inherited by the Pillsbury Company in a 1995 acquisition of Pet. Just four years later B&M and Underwood would become part of the B&G family of specialty brands.

With recent acquisitions making a partial contribution, B&G saw its annual sales increase by 87 percent in 1999, reaching $336.1 million. With the exception of B&G foodservice, all of the company's product lines showed some measure of increased sales. In 2000 B&G continued to absorb its acquired brands; at the same time it launched a completely new line of business: Emeril's Original, 14 products created by chef Emeril Lagasse, including seasonings, salad dressings, basting sauce marinades, and pepper sauces.

Lagasse was both a well-respected chef and a television personality with a mass following. In 1982, while still in his early 20s, he was chosen to succeed Paul Prudhomme as chef at the legendary Commander's Palace in New Orleans. In 1990 he opened his first restaurant, followed by a second venture in 1992. With the advent of cable TV's Food Network in 1993, Lagasse, through his cooking show, grew into a famous personality, as well known for loading up his food with butter, oil, cheese, cream, and his special spice mixture called Essence, as he was for his over-the-top personality and trademark utterances such as "Kick it up a notch!" and "Bam!" With four cookbooks in print and two television shows that aired twice daily, Lagasse was a prize catch for B&G Foods.

In the first year, Emeril's Original branded products produced $4 million in sales. Overall results for the company in 2000, however, were somewhat disappointing. Net sales increased just 4.6 percent, or $15.3 million, to $351.4 million over the previous year. Showing a decrease in sales were Polaner, Las Palmas, Underwood, B&M Baked Beans, and Burns & Ricker.

In January 2001, B&G Foods elected to sell its Burns & Ricker subsidiary to Nonnie's Food Company, Inc., with the proceeds going toward paying down debt. Although B&G Foods had success in revitalizing a number of specialty brands in a short period of time and appeared to have established a profitable franchise with its Emeril's Originals, its many acquisitions left the company highly leveraged. Entering 2001, B&G Food's long-term debt stood at $329.3 million compared with stockholder's equity of just $56.8 million, leaving the company somewhat vulnerable in the foreseeable future.

Principal Subsidiaries

Ac'cent; B&G Pickle and Pepper Products; B&M Baked Beans; Brer Rabbit; Joan of Arc; Las Palmas; Maple Grove Farms of

Vermont, Inc.; M. Polaner, Inc.; Regina; Wm. Underwood Company; Vermont Maid Syrup; Wright's.

Principal Competitors

Aurora Foods Inc.; The J.M. Smucker Company; Vlasic Foods International Inc.

Further Reading

Burns, Greg, "Too Much on Bob Bass's Plate?," *Business Week,* July 15, 1996, p. 80.

Cohen, Laurie P., "Bass to Acquire Food Companies for $1 Billion," *Wall Street Journal,* July 27, 1993, p. A3.

Greer, Lois Goodwin, "Katharine Ide Gray," *Vermonter,* 1927.

Hayes, Jack, "Emeril Lagasse: Bam! This Top-Notch Chef Kicks His Career Up to the Highest Rung of Culinary Fame," *Nation's Restaurant News,* January 2000, pp. 108–10.

Topping, Dana C., "Foodie Call," *Us,* February 1999, pp. 84–87.

—Ed Dinger

Baker & Hostetler LLP

1900 East 9th Street, National City Center, Suite 3200
Cleveland, Ohio 44114-3485
U.S.A.
Telephone: (216) 621-0200
Fax: (216) 696-0740
Web site: http://www.bakerlaw.com

Partnership
Founded: 1916 as Baker, Hostetler & Sidlo
Employees: 1,400
Sales: $191 million (1999 est.)
NAIC: 54111 Offices of Lawyers

Headquartered in Cleveland, Baker & Hostetler LLP is one of the nation's largest law firms. It provides counsel in virtually all legal specialties to large corporate clients such as Ford and Boeing, small startup firms, and also foreign governments such as Peru. It serves traditional industries and also more recently created companies in such cutting edge areas as computers and biotechnology. The Baker law firm remained a modest operation until multiple mergers in the 1970s and 1980s added hundreds of attorneys and new branch offices in several states.

Origins and Early History

The law firm of Baker, Hostetler & Sidlo was started by three of Cleveland's top lawyers during the Progressive movement. Newton Diehl Baker (1871–1937) graduated from Johns Hopkins University and then the Washington and Lee University Law School in 1894. In 1901 Cleveland Mayor Tom L. Johnson recruited Baker to work for the city, and in 1902 Baker became the head of the city's new law department. There he helped Johnson push for various reforms and from 1912 to 1915 served as Cleveland's mayor. Mayor Baker soon recruited Joe Hostetler and Thomas Leon Sidlo, two graduates of Cleveland's Western Reserve University.

When his second mayoral term ended, Baker decided to form a law firm with his two aides as his fellow partners. Shortly after the partnership of Baker, Hostetler & Sidlo was

formed, Baker became President Woodrow Wilson's secretary of the War Department. The other two partners in 1916 served two main clients: the National One Cent Letter Postage Association and the International Molders Union of North America.

While Baker remained in the Wilson cabinet until early 1921, the firm added many new clients, including the Toledo Street Railway Commission and also the publisher of the *Plain Dealer*, which remained a client into the 1990s. E.W. Scripps hired the firm to write his will and trust, which led to representing the Scripps Howard newspaper chain for decades. In 1920 the Baker firm helped incorporate the Midland Bank, which remained a client until it merged with The Cleveland Trust Company in 1946. Other new clients in the 1920s included General Electric, Goodyear, the Federal Reserve Board, American League of Professional Baseball Clubs, the Federal Reserve Board, and the Hydraulic Steel Company. They began representing the owners of the Cleveland Indians baseball team, and in 1927 lawyers Baker and Hostetler became minor owners of the team.

In the 1920s and 1930s the firm represented the state of Ohio in a lawsuit called the Chicago Water Steal Case. Ohio and several other states objected to the depletion of Lake Michigan when its waters were diverted to flush sewage out of the Chicago River. A 1929 U.S. Supreme Court ruling prevented the uncontrolled diversion but also resulted in the construction of locks that regulated the water flow into the Chicago River. This case helped build the Baker firm's national reputation.

Another 1920s case ended up having widespread ramifications. The Baker firm represented The Ambler Realty Company and other landowners who objected to the Village of Euclid's zoning law that limited their development to just residential use. According to the Baker firm's history, in 1924 the U.S. Supreme Court "ruled in favor of the Euclid ordinance in a landmark decision that opened the way nationally for widespread zoning."

During the Great Depression, the federal government created the Tennessee Valley Authority (TVA) as a public power entity. The Baker firm represented a group of private electrical power companies headed by the Commonwealth and Southern

---

Company Perspectives:

Baker & Hostetler LLP was founded on the belief that we would strive to create successful, long-term relationships with clients, dedicate ourselves to the profession and be good corporate citizens in the communities where we live and work. That belief has helped us grow into one of the nation's largest law firms with 500 attorneys operating from nine offices coast to coast and in every time zone.

Our firm has been shaped by the strategic integration of skilled attorneys who have a strong work ethic and a dedication to client service. We have developed the people, the experience, the resources and the technologies to provide legal services worldwide.

Through our multidisciplinary approach, we help clients meet their business, professional and personal objectives. Whether our work is a corporation's complex multi-district litigation or an individual's financial and estate planning, clients receive comprehensive legal services.

We add value to the services we provide by listening to clients, learning their businesses and counseling them as advisors, confidants and, in many cases, friends.

Corporation that sued the government over what some critics said was an unconstitutional and socialistic program. However, the TVA survived the challenge and remained long after the Depression ended.

Although several Baker lawyers left for military or government service during World War II, the firm continued to provide services. Probably its most significant litigation was United States v. Cold Metal Process Company (Baker's client) filed in 1943. Although the government appealed this case all the way to the U.S. Supreme Court, it ultimately failed to cancel two Cold Metal patents used in making steel. The Baker firm continued to represent Cold Metal in other litigation filed during the 1950s.

Practice in the Post-World War II Era

In 1947 the Baker firm's clients, a group of plumbing supply companies, were granted an acquittal by the trial judge in a case where the federal government tried in vain to prove a general distribution antitrust conspiracy. Filed in 1940, United States of America vs. Central Supply Association was "the largest mass trial in the history of the U.S. District Court for the Northern District of Ohio," according to the Baker firm's history.

The firm prospered in the immediate postwar period. In 1949 it brought in over $1 million in fees for the first time in its history. During the 1950s, the partnership successfully represented major league baseball in several important lawsuits that challenged baseball's exemption from antitrust laws, its farm system, and the so-called "reserve clause." Baseball also used the firm to help it preserve the rights of individual teams to control broadcasts of their games.

In the 1970s and mainly the 1980s the Baker law firm grew rapidly through multiple mergers and the addition of its first

permanent branch offices. This expansion was led by Managing Partner John Deaver Drinko, a West Virginia native who had joined the firm in 1945. In 1971 the firm acquired the 12 lawyers of Cleveland's Falsgraf, Reidy, Shoup & Ault, whose clients included Continental Products Company, Newbury Industries, and the business interests of Cleveland's Frohring family and Cincinnati's Schott family. Two years later the firm added its first office outside of Cleveland when it merged with Washington, D.C.'s Frost, Towers, Hayes & Beck, a five-lawyer practice that dated back to 1923. The Frost firm represented Sperry Rand, Textron, and other *Fortune* 500 firms.

In 1979 the firm took several major steps. First, it adopted the permanent name of Baker & Hostetler. Second, it strengthened the Washington, D.C. office by merging with that city's Morison, Murphy, Abrams & Haddock, a ten-lawyer firm that had been started in 1952. Morison, Murphy specialized in antitrust and administrative law for clients such as Frontier Airlines and Sperry & Hutchinson.

The Baker law firm played a role in resolving Ohio's savings and loan (S&L) crisis that began in 1985 when Cincinnati's Home State Savings Bank collapsed after losing $144 million. Andrew Welsh-Huggins wrote, "Home State took down the Ohio Deposit Guarantee Fund and started a run that eventually led to the closing of 69 other thrifts insured by the private deposit insurance fund." Under the direction of Robert B. McAlister, a Baker lawyer appointed to head Ohio's Commerce Department's Division of Savings and Loan, eventually all the closed S&L's were allowed to reopen.

M&As, IPOs, and Other High-Profile Work: 1990s–2001

In the mid-1990s Baker & Hostetler's work in mergers and acquisitions (M&A) increased, which led the firm to add to the 50 lawyers in its Business Practice Group in Cleveland. Most of them worked on M&A, plus securities and debt and equity financing. For example, the Baker firm assisted McDonald & Co. Investments Inc. when it helped Qualitech Steel Corp. raise $500 million. The law firm also backed Boykin Management Co.'s initial public offering and represented Key Equity Capital Corp. when it bought CSM Industries Inc. for $50 million.

The firm in 1997 opened a new office in Cincinnati to cover southern Ohio, since it already had offices in Cleveland and Columbus in northern and central Ohio. The firm's clients in the Cincinnati area included E.W. Scripps Co., which owned the *Post* newspapers and WCPO-TV.

Genetically engineered foods became a major controversy in the 1990s, so in early 2000 the U.S. Department of Agriculture set up a committee to make suggestions concerning health and trade issues involving biotechnology. The department appointed Baker & Hostetler's Dennis Eckart, a former Democratic senator from Ohio, as the committee chairman.

Baker & Hostetler represented the government of Peru in a case with possible widespread consequences for other nations. The Second Circuit U.S. Court of Appeals in October 2000 ruled that Elliott Associates, a New York hedge fund, was entitled to all of Banco de la Nacion's assets in New York State

Key Dates:

1916: The partnership of Baker, Hostetler & Sidlo begins in Cleveland on January 1

1924: The firm moves to larger facilities in the Union Trust Building.

1931: The firm is renamed Baker, Hostetler, Sidlo & Patterson.

1938: The firm becomes Baker, Hostetler & Patterson after Tom Sidlo retires.

1939: A Washington, D.C. office is opened but then is closed in 1943.

1971: The firm's first merger is with Cleveland's Falsgraf, Reidy, Shoup and Ault.

1973: The firm reestablishes a Washington, D.C. office.

1979: The firm adopts its permanent name of Baker & Hostetler; merges with the Washington, D.C. firm of Morison, Murphy, Abrams & Haddock; begins offices in Orlando, Florida, and Columbus, Ohio, through mergers with local firms.

1980: Merger with Orlando's Johnson, Motsinger, Trismen & Sharp adds a Winter Park satellite office; merger with Clark, Martin & Pringle leads to Baker & Hostetler's first Denver office; Cleveland office relocates to the National City Center; merger with Columbus firm Moritz, McClure, Hughes & Kersher adds ten lawyers.

1986: Seventeen lawyers are added from merger with Columbus firm of Gingher & Christgensen.

1988: The firm closes its Winter Park office and moves its Orlando office to the SunBank Center.

1990: Merger with McCutchen, Black, Verleger & Shea adds offices in Los Angeles, Long Beach, and Houston.

1997: Firm opens a Cincinnati office.

2000: Formal affiliation with Brazil-based Franca Ribeiro Advocacia, is announced.

Amendment rights, but the prosecution decided to drop its requests.

After several years of working together on various projects, in 2000 Baker & Hostetler strengthened its international practice by starting a formal affiliation with Sao Paulo, Brazil's Franca Ribeiro Advocacia. Started in 1951, the Brazilian firm of 36 lawyers served mainly corporate client based in Latin America, the United States, and Europe.

As of August 31, 2000, Baker & Hostetler had 166 lawyers in its Cleveland home office. Its largest branch office, in Washington, D.C., had 80 lawyers, followed by 76 in Columbus, 48 in Orlando, 45 in Houston, 41 in Denver, 31 in Los Angeles, ten in Cincinnati, and five in Long Beach. Its litigation practice of 190 lawyers and its business practice with 156 lawyers were by far its two main concentrations.

At the end of the 1990s, Baker & Hostetler increased its gross revenues but declined in the *American Lawyer*'s annual ranking of the largest U.S. law firms. It went from 53rd in 1997 (based on gross revenue of $162 million), to 54th ($180 million) in 1998, to 63rd in 1999 ($191 million). The partnership of over 500 lawyers had come a long way from its original three lawyers but faced stiff competition from other large law firms. For example, its 1999 profits per equity partner of $340,000 was less than that of 90 of the other elite American firms in the annual survey. Baker & Hostetler was also not listed in the world's 50 largest law firms in a survey in the November 1998 issue of the *American Lawyer*.

At the start of the new millennium, Baker & Hostetler faced stiff competition from numerous large law firms, including some with many more lawyers. The United Kingdom's Clifford Chance and Chicago's Baker & McKenzie each had about 3,000 lawyers. New laws and international pacts, such as the North American Free Trade Agreement, presented other challenges to the law firm's clients. While Baker & Hostetler had no overseas offices, many of its rival law firms maintained at least a few such branches in order to cope with an increasingly globalized economy. These were just a few of the situations that would impact the future of Baker & Hostetler.

Principal Competitors

Akin, Gump, Strauss, Hauer & Feld, L.L.P.; Paul, Weiss, Rifkind; Skadden, Arps, Slate, Meagher & Flom.

Further Reading

D'Allegro, Joseph, "Collecting on Peru's Sovereign Debt," *Global Finance*, January 2001, p. 63.

Franz, Neil, "USDA Names Chemical Reps to Biotech Panel," *Chemical Week*, February 2, 2000, p. 18.

Gleisser, Marcus, "Law Newton Baker," *Plain Dealer* (Cleveland), December 31, 1999, p. 13S.

Hagan, John F., "Prosecutor Abandons Effort to Get Author's Notes," *Plain Dealer* (Cleveland), February 4, 2000, p. 3B.

Johnston, David Cay, "Writer Fights Subpoena in Sheppard Case," *New York Times*, January 10, 2000, p. C13.

Kelly, Katherine, *Foundations for the Future: A Commemorative Volume in Honor of Our 75th Anniversary: Baker & Hostetler, Coun-*

to pay off a debt guaranteed by Peru, which ended up settling out of court for $58 million. Peru, with the law firm's counsel, had tried to pay a reduced amount under the Brady Plan that allowed for creditors to partially forgive developing nations' debt under certain terms, but Elliott refused the offer. The appeals court decision could encourage other creditors to seek full repayment of loans and thus make it more difficult for debtor nations to restructure their debt.

The Cleveland law firm in 2000 also was involved in a sensational case concerning the murder of Marilyn Sheppard about 45 years earlier. Her husband, Dr. Sam Sheppard, served ten years in prison before the Supreme Court overturned the murder conviction that led to the television series and movie *The Fugitive*. The follow-up trial, for wrongful imprisonment, would ultimately determine if the estate of Dr. Sheppard, who died in 1970, would be entitled to compensation for lost wages. Baker & Hostetler represented James Neff, who was writing a book on the case. Neff's research files initially were sought as evidence in this case that pitted the search for truth against First *sellors at Law, LXXV, 1916–1991,* Cleveland: Baker & Hostetler, 1991.

Larkin, Patrick, "National Law Firm Opens Office," *Cincinnati Post,* September 11, 1997, p. 6C.

Schiller, Zach, "Baker & Hostetler Growing in Mergers, Acquisitions," *Plain Dealer* (Cleveland), January 1, 1997, p. 2C.

Segal, David, "In the Business of Billing? Lawyers Say a Rush for Money Is Shaking Profession's Standards Series: The Ethics Squeeze: Law Series Number: 2/3," *Washington Post,* March 22, 1998, p. H01.

Welsh-Huggins, Andrew, "Robert McAlister, Who Helped Pull Ohio from S&L Crisis, Dies," *Cincinnati Enquirer,* December 11, 1999, p. C8.

—David M. Walden

Bâloise-Holding

Aeschengraben 21
CH-4002 Basel
Switzerland
Telephone: (+41) 61-285-85-85
Fax: (+41) 61-285-70-70
Web site: http://www.baloise.com

Public Company
Incorporated: 1863 as La Bâloise, Compagnie
    d'Assurance contre l'Incendie
Employees: 8,425
Sales: SFr 6.6 billion ($4.4 billion) (2000)
Stock Exchanges: Switzerland
Ticker Symbol: BALN
NAIC: 524113 Direct Life Insurance Carriers; 524298 All
    Other Insurance Related Activities; 52599 Other
    Financial Vehicles; 523930 Financial Planning
    Services

Bâloise-Holding is positioning itself as a leading European integrated financial services provider. Expanding beyond its traditional core of life and non-life insurance products, Bâloise-Holding has been adding such banking and financial services as retirement and pension funds and investment and asset management activities, primarily through acquisition of existing European banks. In keeping with its new strategy, Bâloise, which formerly operated on a worldwide scale, has been refocusing its operations on the key markets of Switzerland, Germany, Austria, Belgium, and Luxembourg. This focus has led the company to exit such European markets as Italy, France, and Spain, where it held less than 1 percent of each market, and the United States, where the company had not succeeded in gaining any significant market share. The company remains a modest-sized player in global and local markets dominated by such giants as Prudential, Winterthur Swiss Insurance, Aegon, and Zurich Financial Services. The latter owns approximately 30 percent of Bâloise, which Zurich claims remains a financial investment and not the prelude to an eventual takeover of its smaller, Basel-based rival. In any event, Bâloise (Basel is known as Bâle to Swiss francophones) has taken steps to secure its lasting independence, including establishing shareholding provisions that limit to just 3 percent the voting rights allowed to be held by any single shareholder. Bâloise is led by Chairman and President Rolf Schäuble, who has been orchestrating the change in the company's strategy since the mid-1990s. Bâloise-Holding's shares are traded on the Swiss stock exchange. The company posted more than SFr 6.6 billion in revenues from premiums in the year 2000. Switzerland remains its largest market, representing some 55 percent of total premium sales.

Fired Up in the Mid-19th Century

When fire swept through the Swiss town of Glaris in 1861, more than 84 percent of the town was destroyed. The lack of insurance among the large majority of the population left the city destitute and dependent on charity. This spectacle inspired a group of 15 Basel-based businessmen to create an insurance company providing fire insurance policies to protect Swiss citizens from such losses in the future. In 1863, the group of 15 created La Bâloise, Compagnie d'Assurance contre l'Incendie (alternatively known as Die Basler, Versicherungs-Gesellschaft). The following year, the group expanded its range of insurance products to include transport and life insurance policies. These activities were brought under two new independently operating companies, La Bâloise Transport and La Bâloise Vie.

La Bâloise also quickly extended its operations beyond Switzerland, with both La Bâloise Incendie and La Bâloise Vie moving into the German markets, and La Bâloise Vie entering the French and Italian markets in 1864. In that same year, La Bâloise Vie made the group's first attempt to enter the far-off U.S. market. Meanwhile, La Bâloise Transport had extended its operations to include a network of agents in more than 15 European port cities, while forming a reinsurance subsidiary for its own activities. War between France and Germany, which lasted from 1870 to 1871, cut short La Bâloise's growth and, especially, hurt the Transport arm. Nonetheless, by 1874, the Bâloise companies were once again growing and were to enjoy steady growth, amidst the relative calm of the European continent, through the end of the century. The Bâloise companies

Company Perspectives:

Strategy: We have successfully completed the consolidation phase ushered in in 1993. The defining characteristics of this phase were the drive to focus on our core European markets and the disposal of unprofitable companies. Today, we are on the threshold of a new strategic phase, the main feature of which will be growth in our markets. As in the past, our main aim is still steady, significant earnings growth. The cornerstones of this strategy are: Shift from a non-life insurer to a provider of standardized insurance brands. Essentially, this strategy is based on cost leadership, proactive risk selection, innovative branding and multi-channel sales. Shift from a life insurer to a provider of individual pension solutions: this involves an innovative product concept and country-specific sales concepts; as well as a professional team of asset managers with broad international capital market know-how. Penetration strategy: we also see market penetration as a matter of developing new distribution channels and designing a new valued-added architecture in our sales operations through "loyalty group marketing." Acquisitions and partnerships: we reject alliances which either fail to generate such strategic benefits, or do so only inadequately. We see good chances of realizing the added value inherent in the Bâloise group ourselves and of creating a successful future even on our own.

expanded into new European markets, including Transport's entry into Austria-Hungary in 1874, followed by Bâloise Vie's move into Luxembourg in 1876 and then into Belgium in 1883.

The Swiss insurance industry was placed under government oversight in 1885, giving it a greater measure of respectability. Bâloise Vie moved into the provision of accident insurance in that year, while, in 1890, Bâloise Incendie received authorization to begin marketing its own life insurance products. The Swiss insurance industry was formalized further when the country's imperial government created an official agency overseeing the activities of private insurance companies. At the same time, the Swiss market was tightened up for foreign insurance companies. Meanwhile, Bâloise Vie was forced to retreat from the United States, where it had been posting losses. The company's exit in 1901 nonetheless protected it from the devastation caused by the San Francisco fire of 1906.

Bâloise was nonetheless to bear the full brunt of the outbreak of World War I. By then, the three Bâloise branches had continued their separate expansions across the European continent, each establishing offices and subsidiaries in the Italian, French, German, and Belgium markets. Although Bâloise's Swiss operations remained relatively protected by Swiss neutrality, its foreign operations were, in large part, crippled. The situation forced the company to transfer direction of its German subsidiaries to Berlin. During the war, Bâloise's international growth was restricted to new operations opened in Spain.

The end of World War I found Bâloise, like much of the continent's insurance industry, devastated. Bâloise Vie, more than the Transport and Fire arms, had been hard hit, especially

by the outbreak of a continent-wide flu epidemic that caused many thousands of deaths. Meanwhile, the German defeat and resulting hyperinflation wiped out Bâloise's customers and in turn the company's portfolio of policies.

The outbreak of World War II brought new troubles to the company. Its French and Italian operations were forced to shut down, as were its operations in the countries created out of the breakup of the Austro-Hungarian empire. The company's Luxembourg and Swiss operations were able to continue business despite the crisis in the rest of Europe. La Bâloise, together with much of Switzerland's insurance agency, later faced worldwide criticism for defrauding survivors and families of victims of the Holocaust. Not until the end of the century did the company agree to make reparations.

Postwar Fusions

La Bâloise slowly rebuilt its international operations after the end of the war, reestablishing itself in France, Austria, and Germany. The 1950s and 1960s were to transform the company from several independent—and overlapping—operations into a single insurance entity. This process began in 1959, when La Bâloise expanded its operations to become a general insurance issuer. The following year, the company was bought up by Rudolf Oetker, who changed the company's name to Bâloise-Holding, beginning a process of consolidation of the various Bâloise arms.

That process was formally begun in 1962. Yet merging the three operations—Fire, Transport, and Vie—was to require nearly a decade. The final merger of the separate companies into Bâloise-Holding was not officially completed until 1971. A number of factors contributed to the lengthy process, including tax laws that placed the merged company at a disadvantage, foreign policies and business that threatened to be lost as a result of a hasty merger, and the overlap of the three main branches, which, despite their names, each carried a more or less full range of insurance products. By 1971, the merger process had been completed, with the three arms now fused into a new single entity, La Bâloise, Compagnie d'Assurance (BCA).

The 1980s saw Bâloise enter a new period of growth. After going public in 1983, Bâloise began a long series of acquisitions that enabled it to strengthen its position in its core European market. In 1984, the company acquired a shareholding in Belgian insurer Mercator, one of the leading insurance companies dedicated to the Flemish market. Originally named Flandria when it was founded in 1919, the company had taken on the Mercator name in 1920. Bâloise became Mercator's majority shareholder in 1986. By then, Bâloise had made a new attempt to enter the U.S. market, establishing Bâloise Insurance Company of America in 1985. The company boosted its U.S. presence with the acquisition of Providence Washington Insurance Company in 1989. Yet Bâloise was unsuccessful in imposing itself on the U.S. market, and in 1998, after describing its share of the U.S. market as "insignificant," the company pulled out of that market.

Bâloise was more successful in its European expansion. The company had acquired German insurance specialist Deutscher

Key Dates:

1863: La Bâloise, Compagnie d'Assurance contre l'Incendie is founded.
1864: Bâloise Vie and Bâloise Transport are launched; company expands into Germany, France, Italy, and the United States.
1869: Reinsurance subsidiary is launched.
1874: Company enters Austria.
1876: Company enters Luxembourg.
1883: Company enters Belgium.
1962: Bâloise-Holding is created; company begins fusion of separate Bâloise companies.
1971: Merger is completed as La Bâloise.
1984: Company acquires share in Mercator, a leading Belgian insurer.
1985: Bâloise Insurance Company of America is established; Deutscher Ring is acquired.
1986: Company becomes majority shareholder of Mercator.
1988: Norditalia and Vita Nuova are acquired.
1989: Providence Washington Insurance Company is acquired.
1996: Mercator and Noordstar merge.
2000: BHK Spaarbank and Solothurner Bank are acquired.

Italian sales representing less than 1 percent of the company's total sales at the turn of the century, Bâloise decided to exit that country. A similar move was made in Spain, where, despite the acquisitions of Vascongada, based in San Sebastien, and Elpin, based in Madrid, and others, Bâloise remained only a minor player. The company exited the Italian market in 1997, selling its operations there to Banca Carige SpA. France also represented only a minor share of Bâloise's total sales—less than 1 percent—and the company exited this market too in 1997, selling its French subsidiaries to Rentenanstalt/Swisslife.

These moves were in keeping with a new strategy adopted by Bâloise, now led by Chairman and President Rolf Schäuble, in 1993. This strategy called for Bâloise to refocus its activities on a smaller number of core European markets—Switzerland, Germany, Belgium, Austria, and Luxembourg. The company also sought to recreate itself, moving beyond its concentration on the insurance market to become a full-range financial services company focused on what the company called "individual pension solutions."

The reorganization involved with Bâloise's new strategy was to keep the company occupied through much of the 1990s. By 1999, however, the reorganization was, in large part, completed and Bâloise once again turned toward external growth. In that year, the company increased its position in Mercator & Noordstar to more than 95 percent, placing it in position to take all of Mercator & Noordstar's shares. Bâloise itself found a new majority shareholder, when rival Swiss insurer Zurich Financial Services boosted its position to 30 percent of Bâloise's shares. Yet Zurich described its acquisition as a purely financial investment; Bâloise, meanwhile, which was protected by shareholding limits that restricted shareholders to no more than 3 percent of voting rights, continued to assert its intention to remain independent. A devastating storm that swept through much of Europe and proved especially damaging in Germany caused the company sharp losses in that year.

With a large war chest, Bâloise went shopping in 2000. The company acquired the remaining 50 percent of a joint venture initially set up by Mercator in 1992, giving Bâloise Amazon Insurance, a Volvo automobile financing company. Belgium proved a continued target of Bâloise's growth interests, when it announced its acquisition of HBK Spaarbank in April 2000. The company also had taken a 37.5 percent share of another Belgian bank, Bank Corluy. These acquisitions fit well not only with Bâloise's intention to boost its positions in its core European market—Belgium represented its third largest area of operations, behind Switzerland and Germany—but also its move into financial services.

Ring in 1985. That company had been founded in 1913 as Volkversicherungs AG, originally concentrating on small life insurance policies for its predominantly unionized clientele. That company's merger with other insurance firms created Deutscher Ring, which featured an expanded portfolio of life, fire, transportation, and health insurance policies. Deutscher Ring was appropriated by the Nazis in 1933; after the war, the company was not to return to business under the Deutscher Ring name until 1953.

An alliance formed between Mercator and fellow Flemish insurer Noordstar led the way toward Bâloise becoming a major player in that market. Noordstar had been founded in 1919, and, like Mercator, focused wholly on the Flemish-speaking part of Belgium. The company added fire, life, and reassurance activities in 1925; in the late 1930s, Noordstar expanded into the Walloon region, buying up Société Générale d'Assurances and Credit Foncier. Flemish-speaking Belgium remained, however, the company's major center of operations. The alliance between Mercator and Noordstar in 1991 gave way to a full-scale merger of the two companies, creating the Mercator & Noordstar subsidiary of Bâloise in 1996. With 95 percent of its activity taking place in Flemish Belgium, Mercator & Noordstar gave Bâloise not only a leading share of that market but placed it among the leaders in the entire Belgian market.

Refocusing for the New Century

Bâloise made a number of acquisitions to reinforce its Italian presence, including that of Tirenna, based in Rome, in 1986, and both Norditalia and Vita Nuova in 1988. Yet the company retained only a limited share of the Italian market. With its

That wing was further strengthened at the end of 2000, with the acquisition of Solothurner Bank, the second largest regional bank in Switzerland. The move was expected to enable Bâloise to roll out a range of retirement products in its home country. Although Solothurner had been primarily focused on the Solothurn canton, Bâloise promised to begin expanding it across the whole of Switzerland. Entering 2001, the company continued to boast a healthy war chest and promised that its acquisition drive had only just begun. Bâloise seemed poised to stake a claim for itself among Europe's top ten financial services and insurance groups in the new century.

Principal Subsidiaries

Amazon Insurance N.V. (Belgium); Bâloise (España) Seguros y Reaseguros, S.A. (Spain); Bâloise Finance (Jersey) Ltd. (Channel Islands); Bâloise Insurance Co. (Bermuda) Ltd.; Bâloise Insurance Co. (I.O.M.) Ltd. (Channel Islands); The Bâloise Insurance Company Limited; The Bâloise Life Insurance Company Ltd; La Bâloise Vie (Luxembourg) S.A.; Basler Immobilien GmbH (Austria); Basler Versicherungs-Aktiengsellschaft in Österreich (Austria); Compañía Vascongada Inversión S.A. (Spain); Deutscher Ring, Anlagenvermittlung GmbH (Germany); Deutscher Ring, Bausparkasse AG (Germany); Deutscher Ring, Lebens-Versicherungs-AG (Germany); Deutscher Ring, Sachversicherungs-AG (Germany); Euromex N.V. (Belgium); Haakon AG; HBK Spaarbank (Belgium); Mercator & Noordstar N.V. (Belgium); Merno Immo N.V. (Belgium); OVB Allfinanzvermittlungs-GmbH & Co. KG (Germany); Pylon Unternehmensberatungen GmbH (Germany).

Principal Competitors

AEGON N.V.; American International Group, Inc.; Eureko B.V.; Fortis (B); Hannover Rückversicherungs-Aktiengesellschaft; ING Groep N.V.; Münchener Rückversicherungs-Gesellschaft Aktiengesellschaft; Prudential plc; Swiss Life Insurance and Pension Company; Winterthur Swiss Insurance Company; Zurich Financial Services.

Further Reading

Ammerlaan, Nieck, "Zurich Ups Bâloise Stake to 23 Pct.," *Reuters,* November 8, 1999.
"La Bâloise au XXe siècle," *La Bâloise Corporate Publication,* 2000.
"La Bâloise 2000 Net Seen Up Over 20 Pct.," *Reuters,* February 15, 2001.
"Overnamehonger Bâloise niet gestild met HBK," *De Financieel Ekonomische Tijd,* November 13, 2000.

—M. L. Cohen

Belco Oil & Gas Corp.

767 Fifth Ave., 46th Floor
New York, New York 10153
U.S.A.
Telephone: (212) 644-2200
Fax: (212) 644-2230
Web site: http://www.belcooil-gas.com

Public Company
Incorporated: 1996
Employees: 181
Sales: $139.2 million (1999)
Stock Exchanges: New York
Ticker Symbol: BOG
NAIC: 211111 Crude Petroleum and Natural Gas
   Extraction

Belco Oil & Gas Corp. is an independent energy company that since its creation in 1992 has been primarily engaged in the exploration of natural gas and oil in the United States. Using state-of-the-art technology, Belco has been particularly successful at extracting oil in areas once considered unprofitable. The company, headquartered in midtown Manhattan, focuses its operations in four major geological regions: the Rocky Mountains, in particular the Green River Basin of Wyoming; the Permain Basin of West Texas; the Mid-Continent region in Oklahoma, north Texas, and southwest Kansas; and the Austin Chalk Trend in Texas as well as the formation's extension into Louisiana. Involved in oil exploration since the mid-1950s, Robert A. Belfer returned to the business with his son Laurence by starting up Belco, then taking the company public in 1996. The Belfer family maintains a controlling interest in Belco stock, which is traded on the New York Stock Exchange. Although committed primarily to growth through its drilling program, Belco also pursues a strategy of selective acquisition.

Birth of Two Family Businesses: 1950s–90s

Robert Belfer was born in Poland in 1935. When Germany invaded the country, he and his immediate family fled, making

their way to the United States in 1942. Belfer graduated from Columbia College in 1955 with an engineering degree, then earned a law degree from Harvard University. His father, Arthur Belfer, established Belco Petroleum Corporation in 1954. After a few years of exploring for oil on his own, Belfer joined Belco Petroleum in 1958. In 1965 he became president of the company, which had become one of the largest independent oil and gas companies in the United States, listed among the *Fortune* 500. In 1983 it merged with InterNorth, Inc., and Belfer became chief operating officer of the resulting BelNorth Petroleum Corp. In 1985 BelNorth merged with Houston Natural Gas and changed its name to Enron Corp. A year later Belfer, unwilling to move to the new Houston headquarters, resigned to pursue other business interests, although he remained a major stockholder in Enron and a board member.

Laurence Belfer graduated from Harvard University in 1988, then earned a degree from Columbia Law School. In a 1998 interview for *Oil & Gas Investor*, Robert Belfer recalled, "When my son finished law school, he had heard about all of the good times we had in the oil and gas patch and thought it would be nice to start another company; so we did in 1992. We went back to Wyoming where the old Belco had its roots, and started a successful drilling program along the Moxa Arch." Also joining them were several employees from the old Belfer Petroleum Corporation.

Although Belfer was only several years removed from the business of oil and gas exploration, the technologies for locating and drilling for resources, enhanced greatly by new computer capabilities, were in the process of dramatic change. Most of the elements had been around for decades, after the science of petroleum exploration expanded beyond the primitive methods of the 19th century that consisted of looking for surface oil seepages, or perhaps the use of a divining rod, then digging a hole with a pick and shovel. Cable-tool drills were developed to bore through hard rock formations, followed by faster rotary drills. In the 1930s horizontal drilling was developed to augment strictly vertical shafts, and seismic imaging was first used as a way to detect oil-bearing formations below the earth's surface. The oil industry was also an early advocate of computer technology. In fact, today's Texas Instruments was originally

Geophysical Service, created in 1930 to work with seismographic data for the oil industry. For decades, computers were only robust enough to provide crude two-dimensional pictures of geological formations. By 1975 three-dimensional seismic imaging came into commercial use, but it was too expensive and too slow. The method continued to evolve, however. In 1985 to process a square kilometer's worth of data required 800 minutes. Ten years later it would take only ten minutes. A 50-square-mile survey that cost $8 million in 1980 would cost $1 million in 1990 and less than $100,000 ten years later.

It was advances in horizontal drilling that had a major effect on Belco in its early years. From a single vertical shaft, new horizontal drilling capabilities allowed companies to create a network of shafts reaching out in all directions. This technique was particularly useful in certain geological conditions, such as those found in a limestone formation called the Austin Chalk Trend that cuts across southern Texas into Louisiana. Technological advances in the 1930s had led to the first cycle of extraction of oil in the region. When oil prices rose in the 1970s the area was again drilled, almost recklessly, only to be virtually abandoned when prices fell. The Austin Chalk was a difficult region to understand. A well would deliver generous amounts of oil then suddenly lose pressure and drop to a trickle. It rightly earned the nickname of "Heartbreak Field." Belfer called it a graveyard when Belco began working the area.

Using 3-D seismic imaging, engineers discovered that oil deposits in the Austin Chalk were to be found in thin horizontal strata, permeated with vertical cracks within which the oil pooled from the surrounding impermeable rock. If a vertical well intersected a crack it would strike oil, which would then be quickly drained. In the early 1990s, energy companies like Belco learned to drill a horizontal shaft that would intersect with a number of vertical cracks filled with oil, drawing several times the amount of oil that vertical shaft wells could produce in the area. Furthermore, energy companies could then repeat the process by drilling lower, reaching into another oil-bearing strata to drill another horizontal shaft to link up more vertical cracks containing oil. By employing this method companies now drew four times the amount of oil from the Austin Chalk than the region's previous peak.

Going Public: 1996

Belco's business thrived in the Austin Chalk. According to Belfer, "We recognized that we had a rather sizable company on our hands and decided to go public in March of 1996 with Goldman Sachs and Smith Barney as our managers." The sale of 6.5 million shares of common stock resulted in net proceeds of $113 million after expenses. The company's stated intention was to continue to pursue a core area concept, focusing on the Giddings Field of east central Texas, the Moxa Arch Trend of southwest Wyoming, and to a smaller extent the Golden Trend of southern Oklahoma. The core concept allowed Belco to achieve economies of scale with vendors, and it helped to keep down overhead. Furthermore, when the company discovered a new procedure that was successful with one well, it had other similar locations in which to apply it. The overall plan in 1996 was to continue to grow "through the drill bit" rather than acquisitions. Belco looked to keep costs down and manage the risk of price swings in oil and gas through a hedging program.

Belco's first year as a publicly traded company was successful on a number of levels. Revenues reached $116.4 million, an increase over the previous year of 48 percent. Operating profit and net income also showed healthy gains. Average daily production of natural gas was up 31 percent, and the company's reserves of natural gas increased 39 percent. During the course of the year, Belco began new drilling operations in Texas, Louisiana, and Michigan. It continued to apply the latest technology available. Belco participated in drilling the world's then deepest horizontal well. The company also teamed with Edge Petroleum Corporation to commission a 3-D seismic shoot of a 750-square-mile region of Texas; after interpreting the data, point targets could be identified and drilling could commence. Belco also prepared itself for future growth by hiring additional technical and nontechnical personnel, and by spending more than $60 million to add 868,000 net undeveloped acres of land in Louisiana, Michigan, Texas, and Wyoming. The company looked to build on its existing core areas, in particular the Austin Chalk Trend extension into Louisiana, as well as a possible new core area in the Central Basin of Michigan.

Belco went into 1997 looking to stay the course, but instead underwent some significant changes. For one, the prices of oil and natural gas went through a year of volatility that proved challenging for Belco and the industry as a whole. More importantly, in the first part of 1997 the company was unable to match the growth it had achieved in previous years. Many of its newer projects were still in the developmental stage, and the Austin Chalk now required deeper, more expensive wells that were also taking longer to begin producing. Thus, Belco decided to modify its growth strategy. In November 1997 it acquired Coda Energy, Inc. for $149 million in stock and the assumption of $175 million of debt.

Coda was a good fit for Belco on a number of levels. Coda added to the company's reserves of both oil and gas, and provided a better balance between the two commodities. Reserve life increased from 5.3 years to approximately nine years, and the reserve mix now stood at 51 percent oil and 49 percent natural gas. Coda's property also complemented Belco's core holdings, allowing the company to continue to exploit its economies of scale in these areas. Furthermore, Coda brought with it an organization and expertise in acquisition that could then be utilized for future transactions.

Because of the Coda acquisition, Belco incurred tax liabilities that resulted in an after-tax loss of $56.9 million in 1997. Nevertheless, underlying factors remained healthy for the company. Revenues increased by 9 percent to $126.8 million; and earnings before the costs of the Coda transaction were up 4.4 percent to $110.1 million. Overall, the benefits of the deal greatly outweighed the short-term hit.

Key Dates:

1992: Company is started by Robert Belfer and son Laurence.
1996: Belco goes public.
1997: Company acquires Coda Energy.

Drilling Cutbacks Due to Dropping Oil Prices: 1998

The economics of drilling in 1998 would be complicated by a fall in oil prices, which caused Belco to cut back on drilling as the year progressed. Belco would be significantly insulated from lower prices, however, because of its hedging program that placed contracts in the futures market and provided it with a more secure cash flow stream than other oil and gas companies. Coupled with low interest rates, the difficult financial environment of the industry actually presented Belco with opportunities to purchase the assets of weaker companies. After reviewing some $4 billion of potential acquisitions, the company would spend $53 million on new land.

On the surface, 1998 was an unsuccessful year for Belco. It reported a loss of $225.7 million before income tax benefits, but this result was mostly due to accounting requirements. Nevertheless, average daily production was up; Belco's reserve life increased to ten years; and pretax profitability stood at $47.3 million. The former Coda organization was moved from Houston and incorporated into the Dallas office. Building for the future, Belco generated and supervised a 145-square-mile 3-D seismic shoot in Texas, the results of which promised to provide the company with a significant number of targets for drilling. Furthermore, Belco employed advanced technology in other parts of its core region. In the Rocky Mountains it used innovative fracturing techniques to shatter rocks at the bottom of wells. In parts of Texas and Oklahoma it operated sophisticated enhanced recovery projects, flooding wells with water to force more oil to the surface. Less successful for Belco in 1998, however, were its investments in other companies. The company liquidated its position in Hugoton Energy. A major purchase of stock in Canada-based Big Bear Exploration also proved disappointing, but Belco remained hopeful about its future prospects.

Market conditions continued to be difficult in 1999 but improved through the course of the year. Belco remained a viable independent company, although it continued to labor through a transition from energetic small upstart to a steady mid-size company. Oil and gas revenues increased 12 percent to $139.2 million and Belco's reserve life stood at 10.6 years. Concentrating on gas projects, Belco spent $57 million on drilling-related expenditures, and its operating costs remained among the lowest in the industry. Although the company spent $18 million acquiring new assets, it was not able to strike as many deals with cash-strapped companies as it had hoped. Nevertheless, Belco retained $108 million of a $150 million credit line and looked to continue its strategy of selective acquisitions.

Belco entered the new century with some financial issues to resolve. In December 2000 it canceled a public offering of four million additional shares of stock, the proceeds of which it had planned to use to pay down debt and attract new institutional investors. The company blamed the cancellation on poor market conditions. The potential for Belco, however, remained strong. It boasted seasoned leadership and a firm grasp of the latest technology that continued to change the nature of the oil and gas business. Although the United States remained the most mature hydrocarbon region of the world, it had added impressively to its reserves, almost 90 percent of which came from old fields. There appeared to be a significant amount of U.S. resources yet to be extracted by savvy companies such as Belco.

Principal Subsidiaries

Belco Energy Corp.; Electra Resources, Inc.; Fortune Corp.; Belco Finance Co.

Principal Competitors

Barrett Resources; KCS Energy; Mitchell Energy & Development.

Further Reading

"Belco Oil & Gas," *Wall Street Transcript,* December 16, 1998.
Haines, Leslie, "All in the Family," *Oil & Gas Investor,* April 1998, pp. 46–48.
Rauch, Jonathan, "The New Old Economy: Oil, Computers, and the Reinvention of the Earth," *Atlantic Monthly,* January 2001.
Revkin, Andrew C., "Hunting for Oil: New Precision, Less Pollution," *New York Times,* January 30, 2001, p. F1.

—Ed Dinger

Benchmark Electronics

Benchmark Electronics, Inc.

3000 Technology Drive
Angleton, Texas 77515
U.S.A.
Telephone: (979) 849-6550
Fax: (979) 848-5270
Web site: http://www.bench.com

Public Company
Incorporated: 1981 as Electronics, Inc.
Employees: 5,856
Sales: $1.7 billion (2000)
Stock Exchanges: New York
Ticker Symbol: BHE
NAIC: 334412 Bare Printed Circuit Board; 421610
    Electrical Apparatus and Equipment, Wiring Supplies,
    and Construction Material Wholesalers

Benchmark Electronics, Inc., based in Angleton, Texas, provides electronic manufacturing services to original equipment manufacturers (OEMs) for a variety of products, including medical equipment, computers and peripherals, high-end audio and video equipment, and telecommunications products. As OEMs turned to contract manufacturers more and more during the 1990s, Benchmark expanded its operations, and the services it could offer, through a series of strategic acquisitions that made it one of the largest contract electronic manufacturers (CEMs) in a rapidly consolidating industry. With 14 manufacturing facilities in eight countries, and a vital presence in North America, South America, Europe, and Asia, Benchmark offers a full range of services to OEMs—from product design to post-production testing. In some cases Benchmark ships products directly into the client's distribution channels or directly to the end user. Its major customers are Lucent and EMC, which together account for a third of Benchmark's business.

Contract Manufacturing Gaining Momentum in the 1990s

Traditionally, technology companies developed products, then heavily invested in plant equipment in order to use manufac-

turing volume as a way to discourage rivals from entering the market. In the swiftly evolving world of electronics, however, the dynamics of the business changed significantly in the 1990s. If consumer demand shifted, companies could face massive re-tooling costs. Generally, OEMs had only contracted outside companies to manufacture their products when they were unable to keep up with orders. As CEMs proved they could produce quality products and deliver them in a timely fashion, the relationship between OEMs and CEMs underwent a fundamental change. Because of the volume of units a CEM manufactured for multiple customers, it became cheaper for a CEM to produce a product than for an OEM. Furthermore, if an OEM outsourced its manufacturing, it would no longer have to worry about the costs of retooling. Rather than a matter of necessity, OEMs now began to outsource manufacturing as a matter of policy. In fact, many companies began to question whether doing their own manufacturing provided any real competitive advantage. An increasing number of OEMs in the 1990s sold off their manufacturing facilities to CEMs, often with long-term manufacturing agreements. Not only did such divestitures save money, OEMs now were able to concentrate on what they viewed as their core strengths: product development and marketing. By the end of the decade, many CEMs became involved in the designing stage, working hand in hand with OEMs to gear up for cost-effective production. Of the $772 billion of electronic goods sold in 2000, 13 percent were outsourced, leaving plenty of room for growth in contracting. CEMs either looked to expand into global concerns, with manufacturing facilities located on the four major continents, or to find a niche with low-volume, high-quality products.

Benchmark Electronics evolved into a major CEM after it broke away from Intermedics, a pacemaker company that was run by a notorious chief executive named G. Russell Chambers. An engineer by training, Chambers ran a Louisiana television station before he became an investor in Intermedics through the advice of his son, a physician working in the medical equipment industry. Albert Beutel II created Intermedics in 1973. The company grew quickly after its 1976 introduction of the first small lithium battery-operated pacemaker, a major innovation that tripled the life of heart implants. When Beutel died in a helicopter crash in 1979, Chambers used the help of his son's employer, who was a member of Intermedics' board, to win control of the company.

Company Perspectives:

The mission of Benchmark Electronics, Inc. is to maintain a global leadership position in the high technology electronics manufacturing services industry. We will accomplish this through customer satisfaction as measured by our customers' expectations for the following: world class quality, flexible manufacturing, product diversity, leading edge technology, financial strength, managerial integrity.

Under Chambers, Intermedics branched out in a number of directions. It was in 1979 that the predecessor to Benchmark—Electronics, Inc.—was created by Intermedics to produce patient monitoring equipment, with production facilities in Texas. It would be incorporated in 1981 as a wholly owned subsidiary. For a time, Intermedics enjoyed tremendous success. Sales jumped from $79.6 million in 1979 to $164.2 million in 1981. Chambers hoped to reach $500 million in annual sales by 1985, with less than half coming from pacemakers. He went on a spending spree, running the company as if it were his own private enterprise. He invested in, or bought outright, companies that provided carbon coatings for artificial heart valves, materials for dental and oral surgery, orthopedic implants, nerve stimulators, implantable pumps for chemotherapy, as well as swimming pool filters and semiconductors. Chambers also liked to wine and dine potential customers. He spent freely on a hunting lodge and on a fishing boat (which he and his son owned and leased back to the company), in addition to three jets and two jet helicopters.

Aside from his extravagance, Chambers was reported to exhibit a secretive and abrasive management style. He insisted on making most of the decisions, was reluctant to delegate responsibility, yet would take off on personal business for weeks at a time without providing notice. To make up for rising costs, however, he could simply raise the price on pacemakers, which would be paid by Medicare's cost-plus reimbursement policy. When Medicare changed to a flat fee system as part of a cost containment effort, hospitals elected to purchase less expensive, less sophisticated pacemakers. Nevertheless, Chambers continued to overengineer his company's products, making them impossible to price competitively, no matter how superior they may have been. Compounding Chambers's problems was a 1982 congressional hearing on alleged bribes and kickbacks by pacemaker manufacturers that centered on Intermedics. Although five federal agencies would investigate the company, Intermedics was never found guilty of any charges. Nevertheless, Chambers's reputation was severely tarnished, while at the same time his company continued to hemorrhage money. Then in 1984 banks declared that Intermedics was in technical default on a $100 million loan. Chambers tried to renegotiate a new credit line, but was rebuffed. He was then forced to sell off assets, one of which was Electronics, Inc. Eventually, Chambers would be forced out at Intermedics, then turn his attention to the courts, suing the company over a severance agreement and holding up a possible merger deal through litigation. He also became involved in a bizarre legal skirmish over the sale of a television station, a case that would become a matter for the U.S. Supreme Court, which would render a major decision upholding the right of federal judges to punish litigants who abused the legal system.

Intermedics' Subsidiary Becoming Benchmark in 1986

It was in 1986 that Intermedics sold 90 percent of Electronics, Inc. to Electronic Investors Corp. (EIC), which was created by former Intermedics executives Donald Nigbor, Steven Barton, and Cary Fu. Nigbor would serve as president and chief executive officer, Fu as executive vice-president and the company's principal financial and accounting officer, and Barton as executive vice-president of marketing and sales. In 1988 Electronics, Inc. and EIC would merge to become Benchmark Electronics. Recognizing that many electronics manufacturers were increasingly outsourcing assembly work, Benchmark transformed itself into a CEM, catching the wave early. In July 1990 the company made an initial public offering of its stock, raising approximately $9 million, of which $2 million paid off long-term debt and the rest contributed to working capital. Benchmark upgraded its Houston manufacturing facility and purchased new equipment for a Beaverton, Oregon plant that it opened in 1991. In 1990 Benchmark generated $21.3 million in sales, earning $2 million, up from $1.4 million the year before. Rather than paying a dividend on its stock, Benchmark opted to invest its profits into research and development.

As early as 1992 Benchmark began to shop for possible acquisitions to grow the company. In the meantime it moved its headquarters from Clute, Texas, to a larger facility in nearby Angleton. Sales rose steadily until they reached $98.2 million in 1994 before sagging to $97.4 million in 1995, although profits increased from $5.8 million in 1994 to $6.1 million in 1995. The number of employees grew from 205 in 1990 to 568 in 1995.

In March 1996 Benchmark made an acquisition that would accelerate its growth. For $51 million in cash and stock, Benchmark purchased privately held EMD Technologies of Winona, Minnesota. EMD was established in 1974 and in addition to manufacturing facilities offered product design services, with sales and engineering offices in Madison, Wisconsin; St. Paul, Minnesota; and Cupertino, California. Rather than taking EMD public, its cofounders elected to join forces with Benchmark, which also found the deal highly advantageous on a number of levels. EMD, with sales of $160 million in 1995, would more than double Benchmark's volume and add 19 new customers. It also gave Benchmark a midwestern manufacturing presence. In addition, EMD's design, engineering, and testing services opened new markets for Benchmark.

As it absorbed EMD, Benchmark saw its sales top $200 million in 1996 while posting a net income of $8.9 million. The number of employees almost tripled, reaching 1,445. The following year, Benchmark would generate $325 million in sales with more than $15 million in net income. By 1998 Benchmark was utilizing most of its manufacturing capacity and was ready to make another acquisition to continue its growth. In January of that year it acquired the electronics manufacturing arm of Lockheed Martin Corporation, with its plant located in Hudson, New Hampshire, for $70 million in cash. A major defense contractor, Lockheed Martin elected to get out of electronics manufacturing to focus on its core business.

Not only did the Lockheed purchase provide Benchmark with another plant, capable management, and new customers, it also lent the company a presence in the Northeast, thus giving Benchmark coast-to-coast coverage in the United States. Nigbor indicated at the time of the purchase that Benchmark would now look to expand to Europe, followed by Asia, and possibly Mexico or South America after that. The company's goal was to reach $1 billion in sales before the new millennium. By the end of 1998 Benchmark would be halfway toward reaching the mark, generating $524 million in sales.

In September 1998 Benchmark gained a toehold in Europe when it agreed to lease a 45,000-square-foot manufacturing plant in Dublin, Ireland. Shortly after the facility was opened in 1999, Benchmark acquired certain assets from the Dublin plant owned by Stratus Computer Holdings of Marlboro, Massachusetts. Test and integration equipment, along with 200 employees, would be transferred to Benchmark's Dublin plant. As part of the transaction, Benchmark signed a three-year agreement to manufacture and test Stratus' fault-tolerant systems that served the banking, gaming, and telecommunications industries. Stratus recently had been purchased by Ascend Communications Inc. of Alameda, California, which elected to outsource the assembly of Stratus systems. Ascend was purchased subsequently by Lucent Technologies, a deal that would take several months to finalize. Nevertheless, Nigbor did not expect the Lucent transaction to affect the Stratus agreement. In fact, Lucent would become one of Benchmark's major customers. Aside from bolstering its European presence, Stratus helped Benchmark to expand into manufacturing complete systems, so-called box-build. Only 10 percent of its business to that time was box-build contracts.

The 1999 Acquisition of Avex: Largest-Ever CEM Deal

As the contract electronics manufacturing sector continued to expand in 1999, with an increasing number of OEMs electing to divest themselves of their manufacturing units, the pace of CEM mergers and acquisitions picked up dramatically. In June, Benchmark made another offering of stock, raising a net total of $93.6 million with the purpose of paying down debt as well as financing further acquisitions. Less than a month later, after just two weeks of negotiations, Benchmark announced the largest-ever CEM acquisition, one that had the potential of making the company one of the top five contract manufacturers in the world. For $289.1 million in cash and stock Benchmark ac-

quired Avex Electronics Inc. from the privately held J.M. Huber Corporation, a conglomerate with a stronger interest in oil and gas, chemicals, and timber than in contract manufacturing. Avex had been a top three CEM in 1994, but because it was controlled by a private company without access to the markets to raise the level of funding required in the heated environment of the CEM industry of the late 1990s, it sank to seventh in size by 1998.

While Huber gained capital with which it could grow its other businesses, in one stroke Benchmark accomplished a number of goals, not least of which was boosting annual sales well beyond the $1 billion target for 2000. With the addition of 4,440 Avex employees, Benchmark's workforce nearly tripled. The acquisition also gave Benchmark a global footprint, adding nine manufacturing plants in Alabama, Tennessee, Hungary, Mexico, Brazil, Ireland, Scotland, Singapore, and Sweden. Other than Ireland, the foreign facilities did not overlap, and Benchmark was able to gain much needed presence in the Far East, South America, and Europe. Furthermore, the Avex deal provided access to new customers. With its roots in the medical equipment business, Benchmark had mostly worked on high-cost, low-volume products, whereas Avex focused on low-cost, high-volume products, such as circuit board assemblies for personal computers.

The reaction on Wall Street to the Avex deal was generally positive. Benchmark already had experience in digesting large acquisitions that greatly increased its size, but there were still some reservations about how management would assimilate a multisite, international acquisition. Although analysts predicted continued strong growth for the CEM industry as a whole, many investors began to question whether the desire of CEMs to expand might lead to overpaying for assets and whether intense competition might lead to even thinner margins than were already common in the industry.

In October 1999, when Benchmark reported disappointing third quarter earnings, after delaying the announcement for a week, the acquisition of Avex would come under severe criticism. Nigbor blamed the poor financial results on defective components, the failure of suppliers to deliver on time, and lower than expected contributions from Avex. Analysts generally concluded that Benchmark had bitten off more than it could chew with Avex. Investor reaction was swift and harsh. The delay in reporting had itself caused a 22 percent drop in the price of Benchmark stock. The results themselves precipitated another 48 percent drop. In short order, the price tumbled from $35 per share to just $15.

Benchmark also found itself involved in litigation on two fronts. It was sued by shareholders who contended that the company's delay in releasing third quarter results had violated federal securities laws. At the same time, Benchmark sued Huber for breach of contract and fraud over the Avex transaction. In essence, Benchmark charged that the Avex financial statements were false, that Huber had failed to disclose that key customers had decided to either cut back on their contracts or discontinue them entirely, and that Huber had exaggerated the true value of Avex by tens of millions of dollars. Subsequently, Huber would countersue Benchmark.

As the various suits made their torturous journey through the legal system, Benchmark carried on with the job of absorbing Avex into its operations. Results for 1999 were less than anticipated, falling well short of the $1 billion mark in sales, coming in at $877.8 million. Benchmark's fortunes, however, would improve in 2000, as the company began to take advantage of underutilized Avex facilities and sign up new customers. Sales for 2000 would almost double, reaching more than $1.7 billion by the end of the year. The company's stock also rebounded and reached new heights, as did the stock of other contract manufacturers in general. As soon as one of the major CEMs announced that it would miss its quarterly earnings estimate, however, all of the stocks in the sector would tumble. Benchmark and the other large CEMs found themselves incurring debt through further stock offerings or loans in order to keep growing, lest they fall by the wayside. Everyone in 2000 was scrambling to bolster their performance in China and the Far East.

When judged in terms of operating margins and return on equity, CEMs were panned by critics, who contended that no matter how big these companies became, they were actually not very profitable. Yet, the continued move of OEMs to outsource manufacturing and unload facilities was indisputable. How Benchmark responded to the uncertainties of its volatile industry, and how financially sound it would be when everything settled, remained to be seen.

Principal Subsidiaries

AVEX Holdings; Benchmark Electronics AB (Sweden); Benchmark Electronics FSC; Benchmark Electronics UK; Benchmark BV Holdings.

Principal Competitors

ACT Manufacturing; Celestica; Flextronics Inc.; Jabil Circuit, Inc.; SCI Systems, Inc.; Solectron Corporation.

Further Reading

Barker, Robert, "No Trail of Broken Hearts: But Intermedics' Ex-Chief Left Behind Controversy," *Barron's National Business and Financial Weekly,* November 10, 1986, p. 13.

Carbone, James, "High-Tech Buyers See Tidal Wave of Opportunity," *Purchasing,* June 17, 1999, pp. 36–37.

Dunn, Darrell, "Benchmark, with Avex, a Billion-Dollar Player," *Electronic Buyers' News,* August 30, 1999, p. 49.

Engardio, Pete, "Year of the Outsourcer," *Business Week,* January 8, 2001, p. 95.

Ivey, Mark, "Will Radical Surgery Be Enough to Save Intermedics?," *Business Week,* August 19, 1985, p. 70.

Robert, Bill, "Contract Manufacturing: Ties That Bind," *Electronic Business Asia,* October 1998.

—Ed Dinger

Birmingham Steel Corporation

1000 Urban Center Drive, Suite 300
Birmingham, Alabama 35242-2516
U.S.A.
Telephone: (205) 970-1200
Toll Free: (800) 888-9290
Fax: (205) 970-1353
Web site: http://www.birminghamsteel.com

Public Company
Incorporated: 1983
Employees: 2,100
Sales: $932.55 million (2000)
Stock Exchanges: New York
Ticker Symbol: BIR
NAIC: 331111 Iron and Steel Mills

Birmingham Steel Corporation (BSC) operates seven steel production facilities across the United States. Its mill products are made from recycled scrap metal and include reinforcement bars (used in the construction of concrete buildings and highways) and steel rounds, flats, squares, angles, strips, and channels (used in the manufacture of a variety of products including farm equipment, safety walks, ornamental furniture, and fences). Although the company pays considerable attention to keeping its plants up-to-date and efficient, excess capacity both at home and abroad have made it difficult for Birmingham Steel to turn a consistent profit. After seven years of losing money in the special bar quality market, Birmingham Steel sold off its American Steel & Wire Corp. unit in 2000.

1983 Incorporation

The New York-based venture capital group AEA Investors Inc. incorporated Birmingham Steel in 1983. At that time, the U.S. steel industry was suffering financially from declining construction start-ups and intense competition from newer, more efficient European and Japanese mills. Encumbered by outdated technology, many mills were unable to compete. Throughout the 1970s and into the 1980s, both large and smaller mills eliminated jobs and many mills closed. Birmingham Steel was founded on the belief that some of these smaller mills were greatly undervalued, and if they were purchased and renovated, they could turn a profit. Birmingham Steel was to operate under the "market mill" concept, a manufacturing and marketing strategy developed as an alternative to that of the large U.S. steel mills. Also known as mini-mills, these new operations were smaller, more efficient, and more specialized than traditional U.S. mills, and were designed to be flexible and responsive to changing market demands.

Birmingham Steel's first acquisition was that of the Birmingham Bolt Co., which operated a pair of rebar and merchant product mini-mills in Birmingham, Alabama, and in Kankakee, Illinois. The investment was risky, saddling the company with $45 million in debt and two mills that were outdated and inefficient. "We had two of the oldest, meanest, most terrible mills in the nation," Birmingham Chairman and CEO James A. Todd (formerly chief of Birmingham Bolt) told *Iron Age* in 1993.

Todd, however, knew how to gain the confidence of investors. He met regularly with Wall Street analysts to apprise them of the progress of his company, and in early 1985 he negotiated a deal in which AEA Investors converted Birmingham Steel's $4 million in bonds to equity and put up another $12 million to fund the acquisition of the Mississippi Steel division of Magna Corp. With the acquisition of Mississippi Steel, Birmingham Steel was able to close its environmentally unsound melt shop in Kankakee and supply the mill with billets from its Alabama and Mississippi plants. Several months later, Birmingham Steel went public on the New York Stock Exchange, raising $28 million, which was used to pay down debt from the Mississippi Steel and Birmingham Bolt purchases and to upgrade existing facilities. In May 1986 the company made a convertible debenture offering that netted another $30 million.

Within three years, Birmingham Steel found itself in a comfortable position to further pay down debt, renovate existing mini-mills, and begin shopping for others. In the summer of 1986, the company acquired Intercostal Steel Corp., a privately held mini-mill located in Chesapeake, Virginia, for $6.5 million in cash. Birmingham Steel began operating the company under the name Norfolk Steel Corp. and announced its intent to capture some of the Northeastern rebar market segment that opened when industry giant Bethlehem Steel Corporation decided to close its Pennsylvania rebar plants. The market looked promising. The new Norfolk Steel had already captured two former Bethlehem accounts, and Birmingham Steel planned to renovate the facilities to increase production fourfold.

Not content to remain a regional producer, Birmingham Steel began searching for other mini-mills to acquire. "We're still hungry and we still have money," Todd told *American Metals Market* after the Norfolk purchase. Birmingham Steel next acquired Northwest Steel Rolling Mills Inc. of Seattle, a mini-mill with a 150,000-ton capacity and annual sales of $40 million. Less than two weeks later, Birmingham Steel purchased Judson Steel Corp. of Emeryville, California. The two mills provided Birmingham Steel with a foothold in the West Coast rebar and merchant markets, generating a total capacity of 300,000 tons per year. The Judson purchase was solidly in keeping with Birmingham Steel's strategy of acquiring undervalued mills: the entire operation had been slated for demolition by its Australian parent company, Peko-Wallsend Ltd., and the land had been earmarked for commercial development.

In the two years after it went public, Birmingham Steel's sales increased fivefold, reaching $218 million in 1987. Its annual steel output hit 648,000 tons, up 49 percent from the 436,000 tons shipped in 1986. Sales of roof support systems also grew at a steady rate, and Birmingham Steel held more than 50 percent of the market.

Modernization of its milling equipment was essential to maintain Birmingham Steel's competitiveness in an industry plagued by overproduction, and the company strove to continuously upgrade its production facilities. A new melt shop furnace was installed in its Birmingham plant that increased billet capacity to 275,000 tons; new casters and reheat furnaces in the company's Kankakee plant greatly improved productivity there; and the addition of more efficient rolling equipment at the company's Jackson plant led that operation to ship a record 1,100 tons per employee. More troublesome was Birmingham Steel's Norfolk operation. Production was expanded from 80 hours per week to a full 24-hour cycle in 1987, and management soon realized that the plant's efficiency was greatly in need of improvement. The company made some initial improvements that year and allocated $5 million for new rolling mill equipment in 1988.

Shipments, sales, and earnings reached record levels in 1988, fueled primarily by efficient operation of the Seattle, Jackson, and Birmingham plants. More than one million tons of steel were shipped in 1988, sales grew by 59 percent to $344 million, and earnings reached $24.7 million. The company streamlined operations by selling outdated steel fabricating facilities at its Seattle and Norfolk plants and a rebar coating facility that was part of its Kankakee operations. Capital improvements begun at its Kankakee and Norfolk mills also were completed.

Tough Times in 1989

The next year, 1989, was a difficult one for Birmingham Steel. Share prices rose to $29 on the strength of plans to take the company private through a merger with Harbert Corporation, then plummeted to $14.50 when the merger fell through. Per-share earnings dropped by 58 percent as steel prices slipped and scrap prices remained high. Earnings were further deteriorated by losses due to the troublesome start-up of a new melt shop at the Kankakee plant, costly repairs at the Norfolk plant, and an aborted joint venture to manufacture flat-rolled steel with Proler International Corp. and Danieli & C. officine Meccaniche of Italy. Regarding the decision to terminate the proposed joint venture (which cost Birmingham Steel $1.5 million), Todd reported to *Financial World* in 1990, "We'd better take care of what we know how to run before we try to run something that is a new business for us."

Management regrouped in 1990 and focused on expanding existing facilities. Its Jackson melt shop received a $40 million expansion and plans were made to relocate Salmon Bay's downtown Seattle rolling mill to the site of its suburban melt shop, freeing the Seattle real estate for sale or development. Birmingham Steel began planning the construction of a $125 million mini-mill near Phoenix. The Phoenix plant would replace the company's aging Emeryville mini-mill, the land under the Emeryville plant would be sold, and profits would go toward the construction of the new mini-mill.

For the first time in Birmingham Steel's history, net sales declined over the previous year, from $442.5 million in 1990 to $407.6 million in 1991. The sales drop was caused by recessions in both the West Coast and Northeast markets. This led to a 2 percent decline in steel shipments and a 5 percent drop in the selling price of steel. Earnings were eroded as the company closed its Emeryville and Norfolk plants and a melt shop near Seattle. "We probably made a mistake when we bought the mill at Norfolk," Todd conceded to *Iron Age* in 1993. The northeastern rebar market remained slow throughout the late 1980s, and this factor, combined with ongoing mechanical problems, squeezed profits. "Economic conditions dictated that the company could not tolerate unprofitable operations," Todd reported in the company's 1991 letter to stockholders.

Birmingham Steel boosted production at its four remaining mini-mills and opened steel distribution centers on both the East and West Coasts to serve clients who previously had been served by the closed operations. The company also purchased Seattle Steel Inc. and by late 1993 had consolidated its Seattle operations in a new $50 million mill. Plans continued for the new mini-mill to be built near Phoenix, but a site had not been chosen.

Despite strong competition in the steel market, per-share earnings improved greatly in 1992 as Birmingham Steel's continuous modernization program substantially lowered operating costs. The company netted $133 million in a common stock offering, invested $56 million in capital improvements, and reduced its debt by $51 million. By 1992 Birmingham Steel had also begun to sell steel abroad, exporting $24 million worth of steel overseas. In 1993 the company shipped a record 1.6 million tons of steel, 233,000 of which was exported overseas, and sales grew to $442.3 million, but earnings dropped 43 percent from the previous year.

In November 1993, Birmingham Steel purchased American Steel & Wire Corp., an Ohio-based producer of wire and steel rods, for $134 million. American Steel & Wire (ASW), which enjoyed a reputation as the nation's highest-quality producer of steel rods and wire products, provided Birmingham Steel with an entry into the coiled rod and wire (or SBQ—special bar quality) markets of the automotive, appliance, and aerospace industries and also greatly reduced its dependency on the highly competitive rebar market. Birmingham Steel began construction of a $110 million, state-of-the-art rolling mill that would boost ASW's annual output from 500,000 tons to approximately 1.1 million tons upon its completion in late 1996.

Birmingham Steel had much to celebrate as it entered its second decade of operation. Sales in 1994 jumped by 59 percent to $702.8 million. Common equity stood at $439 million, and the debt-to-capital ratio was lower than at any time in the company's history. In early 1995, Birmingham Steel sold its mine roof support business to Excel Mining Systems, Inc., a move that permitted the company to focus exclusively on steel production and sales. Birmingham remained committed to capital improvements, outlining a $650 million renovation program through the year 2000. The company was also well positioned to diversify into other markets and continued to investigate potential joint ventures into the flat rolled steel segment.

Upgrading in 1995

In 1995, Birmingham Steel Corporation had almost a dozen construction projects underway, all part of a $675 million plan to make the company more productive by 1999. The company built a new $175 million melt shop in Memphis to make the American Steel & Wire unit self-sufficient in raw steel, which had amounted to 70 percent of ASW's costs. Birmingham Steel's existing melt shop in Birmingham could not provide the quality required by ASW's automotive clients.

Birmingham Steel also decided to build a new rolling mill next to its existing rod mill in Ohio. The new mill would consume the excess capacity of the new melt shop. Sumitomo

Metal Industries was brought in from Japan to help design the state-of-the-art mill. Two U.S. firms, Morgan Construction and Kocks Pittsburgh Co., teamed to build it.

Several other existing facilities were slated for renovations. Birmingham Steel aimed to be the lowest cost producer in its market, with a goal of converting steel scrap metal to product for $100 a ton, according to *Metal Center News*. Other major mini-mills, including Nucor, North Star, Ipsco, and Oregon Steel Mills, also were expanding, laying out a combined $1 billion a year in capital expenditures in the mid-1990s.

Some of Birmingham Steel's units had a banner year in 1996. Nonresidential construction, agriculture, and road construction were some of the best performing areas. Total revenues were $832 million, compared with $442 million in 1990. The company employed 1,600 workers, twice as many as it had ten years earlier.

Robert Garvey, president of North Star Steel, replaced James Todd as CEO in January 1996. Both Todd and the board felt that a younger leader was required to carry out the expansion program Todd had started. Garvey aimed to make Birmingham Steel a $2 billion-a-year company by 2001, even in the face of an excess of capacity in many product lines. While expanding, Birmingham Steel had to become the most efficient provider possible. It soon bought a Georgia mill from Atlantic Steel for $43 million and expanded its raw materials operations. It fired most of the workers at the new mill—the company "didn't have the luxury of waiting three to four years to change the culture," Garvey told *New Steel*. The company also retired a significant amount of obsolescent equipment there.

By the fall of 1999, however, a dissident shareholder group led by two prominent steel executives, former Birmingham Steel Chairman Jim Todd and former Nucor Corp. CEO John Correnti, was attempting to oust Garvey. Stockholders, who had seen the company's share price fall from $17 to $4 in three years, voted Correnti CEO that December. Correnti himself had been forced to resign from Nucor only six months earlier.

Correnti immediately acted to improve the company's cash flow and reduce its debt. Its main problem was its SBQ operations in Cleveland and Memphis, which supplied the automotive industry. Correnti told shareholders an investment of $100 million was required to make them competitive. One of Birmingham's most solid performers was its mill at Kankakee, Illinois; it was slated for expansion in 2001. Even this plant was forced to reduce work hours due to a drop in the price of rebar; American steel mills alleged dumping on the part of several countries.

Birmingham finally sold off its SBQ operations in Cleveland and Memphis in November 2000. The buyer, North American Metals Ltd., had recently been formed to acquire niche companies in the steel industry. Birmingham Steel had conducted its SBQ operations under the American Steel & Wire name.

Principal Subsidiaries

American Iron Reduction, LLC (50%); Birmingham East Coast Holdings; Birmingham Recycling Investment Company; Birmingham Southeast, LLC (85%); Birmingham Steel Overseas,

Ltd. (Barbados); Port Everglades Steel Corporation; Richmond Steel Recycling, Ltd. (50%).

Principal Operating Units

Birmingham; Cartersville; Jackson; Joliet; Kankakee; Seattle.

Principal Competitors

Commercial Metals Company; Co-Steel Inc.; Nucor Corporation.

Further Reading

"Amtrak Crash Near Birmingham Steel Mill Kills 11," *Iron Age New Steel,* April 1999, pp. 14–18.

Barrett, Amy, "Outlasting Murphy's Law," *Financial World,* October 2, 1990, p. 46.

Berry, Bryan, "Steady in Kankakee," *Iron Age New Steel,* September 2000, p. 2.

"Birmingham Finds Billets, Hires Nucor Managers," *Iron Age New Steel,* May 2000, pp. 10–11.

"Birmingham Sells SBQ Business," *Metal Center News,* November 2000, pp. 84–85.

"Birmingham Steel: A Mini-Mill Powerhouse," *Institutional Investor,* January 1995, p. 4.

"Birmingham Steel Plans to Buy Facility from USX Corp.," *Wall Street Journal,* December 29, 1989, p. B5.

"Correnti New CEO of Birmingham," *Iron Age New Steel,* January 2000, p. 8.

Lamb, Michele R., "Birmingham Steel: Gearing Up for the 21st Century with Sweeping Modernization, Expansion Plans," *Metal Center News,* August 1995, p. 44.

Matthews, Robert Guy, "At Midlife, an Executive Battles with Steel Stigma—Ousted from Nucor, Correnti Forces a Showdown Over Top Job at a Minimill," *Wall Street Journal,* November 15, 1999, p. B1.

——, "Birmingham Steel CEO Considers Cuts in Staff and Temporary Plant Closings," *Wall Street Journal,* December 27, 1999, p. A4.

——, "In Birmingham Steel Bid for Control, Group Claims Victory After Proxy Battle," *Wall Street Journal,* December 2, 1999, p. B20.

McManus, George J., "A Whiz at Marketing," *Iron Age: The Management Magazine for Metal Producers,* August 1993.

"The Mill Scene," *Metal Center News,* 37, Issue 3, 1997, pp. 7-34.

Ninneman, Patrick, "From Sea to Shining Sea: The Growth of Birmingham Steel," *New Steel,* April 1997, http://www.newsteel.com/features/ns9704f9.htm.

Ritt, Adam, "The Battle for Birmingham," *Iron Age New Steel,* October 1999, p. 19.

——, "Major Minimills Broaden Their Reach," *Iron Age New Steel,* September 1995, pp. 30ff.

Swasy, Alecia, "Harbert Offer for Birmingham Steel Collapses As Bank Rejects Financing," *Wall Street Journal,* January 24, 1990, p. A4.

"Why a Big Steelmaker Is Mimicking the Mini-Mills," *Business Week,* March 27, 1989, p. 92.

Wocjik, Joanne, "Reclamation Firms See Profit, Not Risk in Pollution Sites," *Business Insurance,* February 5, 2001, pp. 3, 6.

—Maura Troester
—update: Frederick C. Ingram

C&A

Senneberg
Jean Monnetlaan
Vilvoorde
Belgium
Telephone: (+32) 22576864
Fax: (+32) 22576512
Web site: http://www.c-and-a.com

Private Company
Incorporated: 1841
Employees: 35,000
Sales: EUR 5 billion ($5.7 billion) (1999)
NAIC: 448120 Women's Clothing Stores; 448130
Children's and Infants' Clothing Stores; 448110
Men's Clothing Stores

C&A is a paradox. It operates nearly 450 highly visible retail clothing stores throughout Europe, but the company itself, controlled by the Brenninkmeijer family, has long been a highly secretive, privately owned corporation. Little has been published on the organization and it is hard to get information from the company on its operations beyond publicity for its fashions. Nonetheless, since the late 1990s the company has attempted to open up a bit, adding its first non-family members to the board of directors and publishing financial data for the first time. Moreover, C&A certainly wants customers to know all about its range of company-owned brands, including Clockhouse—itself being transformed into a retail chain at the beginning of the new century—Here & There, Kid's World, Signé Incognito, Westbury, Yessica, Canda, and others. In 2000, C&A pulled out of the United Kingdom, shutting down 113 stores. The company has focused its attention instead on entering the Latin American market, launching its first stores in Mexico, with plans to open 30 stores in that market by 2009.

Peddling a Clothing Empire in the 19th Century

The Brenninkmeijer family had its roots in Mettingen, a small community in the Tecklenburg area of today's northwest Germany, not far from the present border with the Netherlands, a country with which the area has strong links. Originally, Tecklenburg natives spoke a dialect of Low German with some resemblance to Dutch. Especially in the 17th century, Holland's golden age, much of the area's commerce focused on Holland's international ports and rich trading markets. The Rhine River and canals still link much of northwest Germany to the ports of Rotterdam and Amsterdam.

The first trading Brenninkmeijers left the family farm in Mettingen in 1671 to become traveling linen sellers in Holland. Even then the family was said to be secretive about their business. At this time, secrecy gave them a commercial advantage and permitted the avoidance of customs charges.

In 1841, the brothers Clemens and August Brenninkmeijer abandoned the itinerant life and laid the groundwork for the C&A chain when they opened their first store in the small Dutch town of Sneek. The store pioneered sales of affordable ready-to-wear clothing. The small firm of textile sellers was very successful, and within the next few years further stores were opened in the Dutch cities of Leeuwarden, Amsterdam, Utrecht, Rotterdam, Groningen, Leiden, Haarlem, and Enschede. The company was eventually to take its name from the initials of the Brenninkmeijer brothers' first names, opening the first official C&A store in 1861. Many of Clemens and August Brenninkmeijer's descendants were active in the company throughout its history. Indeed, for a time, male members of the family, upon reaching the age of 14, were given the choice of entering the family business or joining the Catholic priesthood. Even then, family members entering the business were subjected to the family's codes of conduct and secrecy.

Expansionism Before World War II

The second Clemens Brenninkmeijer became the driving force behind the family's expansion into Germany. In 1911 he opened C&A, the family's first large German department store, in Berlin. In the next year he opened another Berlin clothing store. In 1913 new branches were opened in Hamburg and Cologne and in 1914 another store was established in Essen. World War I presented the family with few international problems, because Holland remained neutral throughout the conflict.

Company Perspectives:

We put the customer first, always, by offering the best quality fashion clothing at the most competitive prices across a wide range of merchandise—high fashion items or just basics—to meet the many different needs and tastes of customers. In doing this, we are committed to a simple ethic: to contribute to the well-being of our customers, our staff, our suppliers and our partners, by observing standards of behaviour that respect the individual and the collective interest.

We call this approach "the C&A formula" and it has served the individual C&A companies well, since we started over 150 years ago.

After World War I, Germany became the major focus of expansion, despite its inflation and other economic problems. By hard work and constant travel between branches, Clemens Brenninkmeijer made a success of the German operation. By 1928, C&A had eight stores, and at the outbreak of World War II, there were 17.

Clemens Brenninkmeijer's efforts at further international expansion were only partially successful. The first British store was opened in London's Oxford Street in 1922. Later in the decade, other British stores were opened in Birmingham and Liverpool.

In contrast, C&A's most successful field of operations, Germany, was coming under the control of the strongly nationalist and anti-Semitic Nazi regime. The Dutch Catholic family had to come to terms with this new German government. C&A's Dutch background put its German expansion plans at risk. Nazi laws required the firm to gain government permission to open new branches. Some Nazis were also suspicious of the firm's church connections.

The firm emphasized its pre-Nazi, anti-Jewish hiring policies and the family's distant German origins. In a 1937 application to open a store in Leipzig, the board asked for assistance from Hermann Göring, the author of the state economic plan, and successfully argued that it had struggled against Jewish-owned business and prohibited the employment of Jews in the past, writing that the family had "penetrated the power held by the Jewish textile industry."

Against further 1938 allegations by influential Nazi party members that C&A was Dutch, the firm's Berlin representatives stressed the Brenninkmeijer family's German roots in Mettingen. They claimed the family had been forced to take Dutch citizenship by a 1787 law.

World War II brought hardship as the officially neutral firm was cut off from its stores in England by the German invasion of Holland in 1940, and merchandise supplies became harder to obtain because of rationing. As the tide of the war began to turn in favor of the Allies, the Brenninkmeijers began to return to the Netherlands. By the end of the war, only two of the firm's 17 German locations remained relatively unscathed by bombing and fighting. In liberated Holland, however, the company faced government scrutiny, when the Dutch government insisted on

inspecting the company's financial records from during the war. At that time, the Brenninkmeijers changed the company's status from a limited company to a wholly private concern. The company was to take a similar tactic later in Germany. In the meantime, secrecy remained a family policy. The company's growing international interests were presented as independent, country-specific organizations with no connection to the German company—soon to be the largest part of C&A's organization—and the original Dutch branch.

Postwar International Growth

As the West German Wirtschaftswunder—economic miracle—proved to be a powerhouse in the rebuilding of the wider European economy, the Brenninkmeijers returned to make Germany the focal point of their business empire again. The 1950s and 1960s were boom years for C&A in Germany. From 1952 to 1971, the number of C&A clothing and textile stores rose from 17 to 72. By 1982 there were 116 branches worldwide. Düsseldorf became the company's center of operations in the early 1950s.

The booming economic climate of the 1960s stores encouraged C&A to spread its name beyond Holland, England, and Germany. The company opened its first Belgian store in 1963, later building a network of 37 stores in that country by century's end. As the Brenninkmeijers came under pressure from German authorities to publish their company's financial information, Belgium was to become still more important to the company as the city of Vilvoorde was chosen for the site of its headquarters. C&A was also looking to expand into the U.S. market. In 1963 the company fulfilled that long-cherished dream with the acquisition of seven Nathan Ohrbach retail stores.

Throughout the postwar period, secrecy remained a pillar of C&A corporate policy. Important members of the Brenninkmeijer family on the governing board were hardly known outside of Europe's financial circles. When any of C&A's management were quoted in the press, statements tended to remain limited to company sales policy, such as "No store sells cheaper" or—the most famous statement—"We let our merchandise speak for us."

The desire for secrecy was so important that it led the firm to change its legal status again. After the German Bundestag passed new disclosure rules for the GmbH (Gesellschaften mit beschränkter Haftung), C&A Brenninkmeijer became a KG (Kommanditgesellschaft), or limited partnership, in September 1969. The move allowed the family to withhold much of the company's financial information from the public.

Secrecy seemed to insulate the company from change and criticism of other policies that appeared anachronistic. The company's paternalism and preference for hiring Catholics attracted particular criticism from the media. Recruits were required to be devout Catholics and attend mass. The rest of the week was devoted to work training and study for compulsory examinations. If managers became engaged, they were required to give the company details on the betrothed's parents and religion. Non-Catholic affianced partners were expected to convert or, in accordance with the Catholic Church's teachings, to at least agree to a Catholic ceremony and Catholic religious

Key Dates:

1841: Brothers Clemens and August Brenninkmeijer open their first store in Sneek, Netherlands.
1861: Company adopts C&A store name, after the initials of the founders.
1911: C&A expands into Germany.
1922: Company opens first U.K. stores.
1945: C&A converts to a private company.
1950: C&A transfers headquarters to Dusseldorf.
1963: Company moves into Belgium.
1972: Company opens stores in France.
1977: C&A enters markets in Switzerland and Brazil.
1982: Company launches operations in Luxembourg.
1983: C&A begins operations in Spain.
1984: Company enters Austria.
1991: Company opens its first store in Portugal.
1995: C&A opens Denmark store.
1996: Company enters Argentina.
1998: Company enters Ireland.
1999: C&A enters Czech Republic and Mexico.
2001: C&A closes entire U.K. operations.

education for the couple's children. The company's governing board and top management positions remained dominated by members of the Brenninkmeijer family and those related to them through marriage.

Meanwhile, the company's success in Belgium encouraged it to extend its stores and fashions to other European countries. In 1972, the company opened its first C&A stores in France. These were followed by Switzerland in 1977, Luxembourg in 1982, Spain in 1983, and Austria in 1984. The company also brought its stores to Brazil, where it quickly built a leading market position. Despite its international expansion, C&A maintained centralized buying policies, helping it to reduce its costs and offer fashionable clothing at low prices. Yet, while the company was finding success in its new markets—in France, the company's retail chain was to reach more than 50 stores by century's end, while Switzerland was to boast 30 retail stores of its own—in the United Kingdom, C&A was entering a long, slow decline. A chief cause of its problems in that market was the company's slow reaction to the growing fashion awareness of the U.K. consumer—a situation brought on in part by the family's centralized buying operations. In the 1970s and 1980s, C&A began to play catchup in the U.K. market, attempting to reinvent itself as a seller of trendy fashions. Nonetheless, the company, which extended its chain to 110 stores throughout the United Kingdom, enjoyed a position as that market's leading retailer.

C&A proved equally slow to react to the collapse of the East German regime in November 1989 and to subsequent German unification. This initial reluctance was partly its usual caution, but was also due to the need to settle property questions over prewar store sites in Leipzig and elsewhere. After C&A's inexpensive fashions proved popular with East Germans living near the border, making a strong contribution to 1990 profits, the company required no more convincing to expand into the former East Germany.

By autumn 1991, new C&A stores had opened in Guntherstadt, Chemnitz, formerly Karl Marx Stadt, and Magdeburg. There were plans to reopen a C&A on a prewar site in Leipzig. West German expansion continued, however, with new stores planned in Lunen, Ingolstadt, Ravensburg, and Regensburg. Some expenditures and expansion plans elsewhere were reduced in order to concentrate on investment in a unified Germany.

Growing Toward 21st-Century Openness

In the 1990s, C&A continued to identify new national markets in which to establish its store. The company targeted Portugal in 1991, opening five more stores through the decade. C&A also attempted to enter Denmark in 1995, with more limited success when faced with Scandinavian rival H&M. In 1996, C&A moved to South America, opening the first of five stores in Argentina, where the company pledged to invest $2000 million. C&A also entered the Irish market in 1998. Meanwhile the company's U.K. operations were coming under increasing pressure. A wave of new competition, such as the expanding Marks & Spencer chain, New Look, Next, and many other, more fashionable clothing retailers, had knocked the steam out of the company's U.K. sales. The dominant influence of Germany on C&A's clothing fashions proved disastrous for its U.K. branch, as the two country's fashion senses appeared wholly different. By 1995, the company's U.K. operation was losing money.

C&A attempted to revive its U.K. branch in 1998, announcing a £200 million investment program in upgrading its stores, coupled with the closing of a number of its poorest performers. The company also suggested that it intended to move toward a greater openness, shedding at least part of its historical secrecy. In 1997, the company had already taken a first step toward opening up to the financial world when it appointed two non-family members to its board of directors for the first time. The company, which had been juggling a portfolio of more than 20 different fashion brands, also streamlined its brands to just ten, including Clockhouse, for which the company began developing its own retail store concept. By 2001, the company had six Clockhouse stores in operation

C&A's hopes to restore its U.K. operations proved to be in vain. In 2000 the company suddenly announced its intention to exit the U.K. market entirely, closing its remaining 109 stores and placing nearly 5,000 employees out of work. The last C&A store closed its doors in January 2001, ending nearly 80 years of C&A operations in the United Kingdom.

Instead, C&A turned its attention to building its name in new markets. The company began investing in Mexico, opening two stores by 1999 and announcing its intention to open as many as 30 stores in that country by 2009. C&A was also becoming interested in the growing economies of the East European countries. In 1999, the company opened its first store in the Czech Republic.

Despite its growing openness, C&A remained wholly controlled by its founding Brenninkmeijer family, which ranked among the world's wealthiest families with a fortune estimated to be worth more than $5 billion. Entering the 21st century, the internationally operating company exhibited little interest in changing its private status.

Principal Subsidiaries

C&A Unterstutzugskasse GmbH; C&A Nederland CV; C&A Mode AG (Switzerland).

Principal Competitors

Benetton Group S.p.A.; Esprit Holdings Limited; Etam Développement; H&M Hennes & Mauritz AB; New Look Group plc; Next plc; Metro AG; Pinault-Printemps-Redoute SA.

Further Reading

"C&A Opens Second Store in Mexico, Plans 30 by 2009," *Infolatina*, February 9, 1999.

Cope, Nigel, "C&A Ends Secret Counter-Culture," *Sunday Telegraph*, September 4, 1998.

Hardcastle, Elaine, and Arindam Nag, "Retailer C&A Shocks with British Shutdown," *Reuters* June 15, 2000.

"Our Story," April 2001, http://www.c-and-a.com.

"The Rise and Fall of an Institution," *Sunday Mail*, January 28, 2001, p. 20.

Stuart, Jim, "Tears and a Last-Minute Rush at the End of an Acrylic Era," *Independent*, January 27, 2001, p. 10.

—Clark Siewert
—update: M.L. Cohen

C.H. Robinson Worldwide, Inc.

8100 Mitchell Road
Eden Prairie, Minnesota 55344-2248
U.S.A.
Telephone: (952) 937-8500
Fax: (952) 937-6714
Web site: http://www.chrobinson.com

Public Company
Incorporated: 1905 as C.H. Robinson Company
Employees: 3,677
Sales: $2.88 billion (2000)
Stock Exchanges: NASDAQ
Ticker Symbol: CHRW
NAIC: 488510 Freight Transportation Arrangement;
    422480 Fresh Fruit and Vegetable Wholesalers;
    541614 Process, Physical Distribution, and Logistics
    Consulting Services

As one of the leading third-party logistics firms in North America, C.H. Robinson Worldwide, Inc. manages the transportation and distribution of materials, parts, supplies, and finished goods for its customers. From a network of 137 offices in the United States, Canada, Mexico, Europe, and South America, the company during 2000 handled more than 2.3 million shipments for a wide range of customers, numbering more than 14,000. As a third-party logistics company, C.H. Robinson does not itself own transportation equipment but rather contracts with transportation carriers to coordinate the movement of its customers' freight. Just in the area of North American motor transport, the company has contracts with more than 20,000 carriers. About 85 percent of the company's revenues are derived from these transportation activities. Generating about 10 percent of sales are C.H. Robinson's sourcing operations (the founding business), which comprise one of the largest fresh fruits and vegetables distribution networks in North America. Among the produce distributed by C.H. Robinson is its own line, marketed under the brand The Fresh 1, as well as national brand names. The remaining 5 percent of revenues derive from the company's transportation-related information services, which include payroll, fuel management, and payment services. C.H. Robinson began as a small brokerage business, functioning as intermediary between buyer and seller. With the development of the interstate highway system in the 1950s, however, the Minnesota company steadily evolved into a full-service transportation management supplier.

Produce Shipping Roots

The company traces its origin to the early 1900s, when Charles H. Robinson established a small brokerage firm in Grand Forks, North Dakota, to ship produce to customers throughout the Red River Valley region of northeastern North Dakota and northwestern Minnesota. In May 1905, Robinson formed a partnership with Grand Forks-based Nash Brothers, the forerunner of the Nash Finch Company and the leading wholesaler in North Dakota. The partnership was incorporated as C.H. Robinson Company, and Robinson was named the company's first president. According to popular legend, related by Lee Egerstrom in the *St. Paul Pioneer Press,* Robinson "sold out a couple of years later and ran off with Annie Oakley, the showgirl shootist of Buffalo Bill Cody's Wild West Show fame," dying shortly thereafter in 1909. Historical evidence has shown, however, that if such a relationship existed, it would have concluded before 1905. Moreover, Robinson did not die in 1909, nor were his shares in the company acquired by the Nash brothers and Harry Finch at that time. Nevertheless, by 1913 the partnership had ended, and the principals of Nash Finch Company were the sole owners of C.H. Robinson Co.

The Robinson subsidiary served primarily as a produce procurement vehicle for Nash Finch and expanded rapidly by establishing branch offices in Minnesota, Iowa, Wisconsin, Illinois, and Texas—virtually everywhere that Nash had established its own warehouses. In 1919, Minneapolis became Robinson's headquarters, from which the company continued to expand until World War II intervened some two decades later.

During the early 1940s, Robinson also faced action by the Federal Trade Commission (FTC), which concluded that the subsidiary and Nash Finch were in violation of the Robinson-Patman Act because of the price advantage Nash received over that of other wholesalers. As later explained in the *Chronicle*

Company Perspectives:

C.H. Robinson Worldwide is a non-asset-based company. We invest in bright, dedicated people. In early 2001, we had approximately 3,700 employees to serve our customers. New employees, hired for their high creativity, flexibility, and customer service skills, receive training on the job and during internal workshops. Our employees work in 138 offices worldwide, and have the expertise and technology to move products from origin to destination, anywhere in the world, door to door.

Last year, more than 14,000 customers entrusted us with more than 2.3 million shipments worldwide. Every day, CHRW develops and executes solutions to shipping challenges. Our service begins with multimodal transportation, extends to global logistics management of supply chains, and covers every point in between. We are experts in many industries and through our extensive carrier network we have the flexibility to meet nearly any logistics need.

There are many transportation companies. But only CHRW can execute a full range of transportation, logistics and sourcing services with a single call.

(Fall 1988): "Rather than taking the case to court, C.H. Robinson Co. was split into two separate companies. The first company, C.H. Robinson Co., was formed by all offices selling produce to Nash-Finch warehouses, and the ownership of this company was sold to all Robinson employees. The other company, C.H. Robinson, Inc., was comprised of the remainder of the offices and was still owned by Nash-Finch Co."

1960s and 1970s: Moving into Trucking and Becoming Employee Owned

Up until this time, Robinson, like its competitors, was limited to rail transport for the majority of its shipments. Massive funding of the interstate highway system was about to alter that. The Federal Highway Act of 1956 catapulted Robinson into the trucking business. Initially working through its Omaha branch office, C.H. Robinson began capitalizing on opportunities for truck brokerage, launching what may have been the first such brokerage operation in the country. This involvement in managing the transport of "exempt" commodities (perishables that were exempt from government regulation) spread to ten branches by the 1960s. Around mid-decade C.H. Robinson Co. and C.H. Robinson, Inc. consolidated their operations under the name C.H. Robinson Co. Wholesaler Nash Finch still held a minority stake of approximately 25 percent in the brokerage company, with Robinson employees owning the remainder.

This structural arrangement led to a natural conflict of interests, with Nash requesting more Robinson dividends to invest in its own operations and Robinson wishing to retain more earnings in order to accelerate the company's growth. Finally, in 1976, both companies were satisfied when all remaining Nash shares were bought out and Robinson Co. became an entirely employee-owned business. A year later, D.R. "Sid" Verdoorn was installed as company president and CEO, and Looe Baker was named chairman of the board. "With this new leadership in place," recorded the *Chronicle,* "Robinson remained on its successful path—with a new commitment to data processing, and a continued dedication to the expansion of transportation and produce branch offices."

1980s and Early 1990s: Emphasizing Logistics

In 1980, the federal government deregulated the transportation industry through the Motor Carrier Act, which effectively broadened competition in the field. Robinson responded by establishing a contract carrier program and promoting itself not only as a purveyor of food products but also as a freight contractor, or middleman sourcing operation, for virtually all shippable goods. In just five years, the company's average annual growth, measured by truckloads, doubled. The company was now posting more than $700 million in sales, with roughly 40 percent generated by truck brokerage and most of the remainder through produce sales. Commenting on Robinson's evident edge in the truck contracting industry, John J. Oslund, of the *Minneapolis Star Tribune,* wrote, "Unlike most of its competitors, who are relative newcomers, Robinson has developed its expertise over more than 50 years in the dicey and competitive world of produce delivery."

In January 1988, in a concentrated effort to become a full-service, multiple carrier provider, the company launched its Intermodal Division (intermodal denotes shipping that involves more than one mode, such as both truck and rail). As explained in the *Chronicle* (Winter 1994), "By combining its truck strengths with the recently improved service of rail carriers, Robinson saves customers significant dollars on long-distance shipments." In a number of subsequent moves, Robinson increasingly solidified its reputation as a well-rounded, globally positioned transportation and logistics company. For example, in addition to systematically opening a number of new branch offices each year, in 1990 the company expanded its international service through the formation of C.H. Robinson de Mexico. Two years later, international freight forwarding and air freight operations were added through the acquisition of the oldest and largest freight forwarder, C.S. Greene International Inc.

During 1993, a particularly dynamic year for the company, C.H. Robinson made its first foray into the general food and beverage business with the acquisition of New York-based Daystar International Inc., a $40 million distributor of fruit juice concentrates. As Vice-President Looe Baker III told Tony Kennedy, in an interview for the *Star Tribune:* "It's a big deal for us, and you'll see us make more moves. . . . [We're] searching for ways to expand into diversified segments of the food market."

During this time, C.H. Robinson continued to rely primarily on a vast network of independent truck operators, who together offered some 730,000 pieces of equipment, from containers on flatcars to refrigerated vans. Nevertheless, the company began to relax its policy of operating as a non-asset-based service firm by acquiring trucking fleets of its own. In early 1993, Robinson bought a trucking operation based in Sioux Falls, South Dakota, in order to service Carlisle Plastics, whose Western Division was also based there. Other fleet purchases, designed "to provide customer-specific service to large, heavy-volume accounts like Frito Lay" and to create greater flexibility for the company, included 100 48-foot refrigerated containers and 90 48-foot

Key Dates:

1905: Charles H. Robinson joins with Nash Brothers to form a partnership, C.H. Robinson Company, to ship produce to customers in the Red River Valley.

1913: With end of partnership, Nash Finch Company (successor of Nash Brothers) gains sole ownership of C.H. Robinson Co.

Early 1940s: Company is divided in two, with one company owned by its employees and the other owned by Nash Finch.

Mid-1960s: The two successor firms are consolidated under the name C.H. Robinson Co., with Nash Finch owning about 25 percent and employees the remainder.

1976: Nash Finch's shares are bought out and the firm becomes entirely employee owned.

1980: U.S. government deregulates the transportation industry; C.H. Robinson responds by promoting itself as a contract carrier for virtually any shippable product.

1988: Company enters the intermodal business.

1992: Freight forwarder C.S. Greene International is acquired.

1997: Company goes public and changes its name to C.H. Robinson Worldwide, Inc.

1998: Preferred Translocation Systems and Comexter Group are acquired.

1999: Three acquisitions are completed: Norminter S.A., Vertex Transportation Inc., and American Backhaulers, Inc.

2000: Trans-Consolidated Inc. is acquired, marking C.H. Robinson's entry into a new segment, refrigerated partial truckload shipments for perishable food manufacturers.

insulated containers. During this time, Robinson worked with over 14,000 shippers and moved more than 500,000 separate shipments annually.

Before the end of 1993, the company enhanced its European presence by acquiring a 30 percent stake in Transeco, a French motor carrier; Robinson later acquired the remaining shares for full ownership of Transeco. Other international activity included the opening of offices in Mexico City; Santiago, Chile; and Valencia, Venezuela. In 1994, on the verge of celebrating its 90th anniversary, Robinson expanded its intermodal strategy with two purchases, Atlanta-based Commercial Transportation Services Inc. and Boston-based Bay State Shippers Inc., both for undisclosed amounts. The company also had plans to broaden it's the Fresh 1 line to include more value-added items. Annual volume for the 28-item line numbered between six and eight million packages. Careful not to underestimate the potential of the brand, Robinson believed it could yet become ''as recognizable to the trade and consumers as the likes of Dole, Del Monte and Chiquita.''

Late 1990s and Beyond: Going Public and Expanding Through Acquisitions

C.H. Robinson continued to expand its logistics capabilities in the late 1990s. In 1995 the company entered the full-service logistics market through the formation of C.H. Robinson Logistics. This new division focused on developing and managing the logistics operations of customers throughout the entire supply chain. Two years later, the company entered the burgeoning market for expedited freight transportation, focusing on full trailerload shipments, through another new division, CHR-Ex.

At this time, the company remained entirely owned by current and former employees. With a number of the shareholders wishing to cash in at least part of their stakes, the company went public in October 1997. An initial public offering that month of about 25 percent of the company, or 10.6 million common shares, sold for $18 per share (which exceeded the expected price of $15 to $17) and generated about $190 million for the 101 people who sold shares. The initial market value of the company, which was at this time renamed C.H. Robinson Worldwide Inc. to reflect its increased international profile, totaled $743 million. Shares began trading on the NASDAQ under the symbol CHRW. Gross revenues for 1997 reached $1.79 billion, while net revenues amounted to $206 million, a 15.1 percent increase over the previous year. (Net revenues were considered by the company to be a more accurate gauge of performance than gross revenues, as they deducted from gross revenues the cost of the transportation contracted for by the company and the purchase price of the products sourced by the company.) Overseas markets accounted for 16 percent of revenues in 1997.

Sid Verdoorn, CEO of the firm since 1977, was named to the additional post of chairman in 1998. John P. Wiehoff, who was named senior vice-president and CFO in July 1998, was promoted to president of the company in December 1999. The leaders initiated a string of acquisitions in 1998, as C.H. Robinson continued to seek opportunities for growth and as the transportation industry entered a period of heightened consolidation. During 1998 two acquisitions were completed: Preferred Translocation Systems, a non-asset-based third-party logistics firm specializing in partial truckloads; and Comexter Group, an Argentinean firm specializing in South American transportation, freight forwarding, trading, and customs brokering. Another overseas acquisition, that of Norminter S.A., was consummated the following year. Based in Caen, France, Norminter was a non-asset-based third-party logistics company with offices in France, Germany, Spain, and the United Kingdom. Also in 1999, C.H. Robinson acquired Vertex Transportation Inc., which was based in East Rochester, New York, and provided third-party logistics services throughout North America. The largest of this string of acquisitions came in December 1999 when C.H. Robinson paid about $136 million in cash and stock for American Backhaulers, Inc., a privately held logistics firm based in Chicago. American Backhaulers specialized in over-the-road transportation services and had annual gross revenues of about $285 million. In August 2000 C.H. Robinson entered a new segment of the market through the purchase of Brooklyn Center, Minnesota-based Trans-Consolidated Inc., which was a third-party logistics firm specializing in refrigerated partial truckload shipments for perishable food manufacturers.

Results for 2000 highlighted the rapid pace of C.H. Robinson's growth. The gross revenues figure of $2.88 billion represented a 27 percent increase over the previous year, and the net revenues of $419.3 million were a 43 percent gain over the

$293.3 million total of 1999. Looking to the new century, the company was aiming to continue to increase its net revenues by at least 15 percent each year. Strategies to achieve this growth included the development of customer-specific logistics solutions, rapid growth in the partial truckload and short-haul sectors, the addition of more domestic branches and the expansion of intracontinental distribution networks, and an increased use of technology to aid in communication with customers and to improve efficiency. With no debt, strong cash flow, and a motivated workforce that continued to own the bulk of the company stock, C.H. Robinson appeared likely to maintain and solidify its position in the rapidly growing third-party logistics industry.

Principal Subsidiaries

C.H. Robinson International, Inc.; C.H. Robinson Venezuela, C.A.; C.H. Robinson de Mexico, S.A. de C.V.; C.H. Robinson Company (Canada) Ltd.; C.H. Robinson Company; C.H. Robinson Company, Inc.; CHR Aviation, LLC; Daystar-Robinson, Inc.; Fresh 1 Marketing, Inc.; C.H. Robinson Worldwide-LTL, Inc.; Robinson Holding Company; C.H. Robinson Company LP (99%); Wagonmaster Transportation Co.; Robinson Europe, S.A. (France); Robinson Italia S.r.L (Italy; 95%); C.H. Robinson Poland Sp. Zo.o; Comexter Robinson S.A. (Argentina); Comexter Trading Company; Comexter Cargo, Inc.; Robinson Europe (France); C.H. Robinson (UK) Limited; Robinson France SARL; Norminter Iberica (Spain; 98%); E.G.C. SARL (France); T.E.A. 100% Payment & Logistics Services, Inc.; T-Chek Systems, Inc.; Robinson Logistica Do Brasil Ltda. (Brazil).

Principal Competitors

Ryder System, Inc.; GeoLogistics Corporation; Exel plc; BAX Global Inc.; EGL, Inc.; Schneider National, Inc.; CNF Inc.; GATX Corporation; CSX Corporation; FedEx Corporation; Fritz Corporation.

Further Reading

Barshay, Jill J., "C.H. Robinson Plans to Go Public," *Minneapolis Star Tribune,* August 16, 1997, p. 1D.

Beal, Dave, "Robinson Celebrates a Big Year," *St. Paul Pioneer Press,* September 12, 1992.

C.H. Robinson Company: Multimodal Capabilities, Minneapolis: C.H. Robinson Company, 1993.

"C.H. Robinson Sells Robco Name, Assets to Atlanta Transport Firm," *Minneapolis Star Tribune,* September 3, 1986, p. 1M.

Chronicle (Minneapolis), Fall 1988; Winter 1994.

"Company News," *Minneapolis Star Tribune,* March 27, 1990, p. 8D.

Dukart, James R., "Local Autonomy: C.H. Robinson Lets Employees Work Like They Own the Place," *Corporate Report-Minnesota,* August 1999, pp. 34+.

Egerstrom, Lee, "Annie Oakley Key Figure in Company Legend," *St. Paul Pioneer Press,* October 6, 1986.

"Food, Transport Broker Enjoys Life in the Middle," *St. Paul Pioneer Press,* October 6, 1986.

Hickey, Kathleen, "Joining the Competition," *Traffic World,* July 27, 1998, p. 43.

Kennedy, Tony, "Robinson Co. Acquires N.Y. Juice Firm," *Minneapolis Star Tribune,* May 18, 1993, p. 3D.

Levy, Melissa, "C.H. Robinson Worldwide to Acquire American Backhaulers for $136 Million," *Minneapolis Star Tribune,* November 19, 1999, p. 3D.

"Marketplace Pulse," *Minneapolis Star Tribune,* September 3, 1986, p. 1M.

Oslund, John J., "Trucking Broker Rolls over Stereotypes," *Minneapolis Star Tribune,* December 16, 1985, pp. 1M, 7M.

"Roadway, Robinson Enter Critical-Shipments Market," *Logistics Management,* May 1997, pp. 29–31.

3 on C.H. Robinson, Eden Prairie, Minn.: C.H. Robinson Company, 1994.

Youngblood, Dick, "Mover and Shaker," *Minneapolis Star Tribune,* March 23, 1998, p. 11D.

—Jay P. Pederson
—update: David E. Salamie

The Carbide/Graphite Group, Inc.

The Carbide/Graphite Group, Inc.

One Gateway Center, 19th Floor
Pittsburgh, Pennsylvania 15222
U.S.A.
Telephone: (412) 562-3700
Fax: (412) 562-3739
Web site: http://www.cggi.com

Public Company
Incorporated: 1988 as Carbon/Graphite Group, Inc.
Employees: 907
Sales: $207.36 million (2000)
Stock Exchanges: NASDAQ
Ticker Symbol: CGGI
NAIC: 335991 Carbon and Graphite Product
    Manufacturing; 324199 All Other Petroleum and Coal
    Products Manufacturing; 32512 Industrial Gas
    Manufacturing; 325188 All Other Basic Inorganic
    Chemical Manufacturing

The Carbide/Graphite Group, Inc. produces massive graphite electrodes for use in steel manufacturing; needle coke, a raw ingredient used to form these electrodes; and calcium carbide and related products for use as fuel, in chemical manufacturing, and for other specialized applications. The company's sales are primarily to U.S. customers, with approximately a quarter of its revenues derived from sales to European, Asian, and Central and South American countries. A downturn in demand for electrodes, and the costs associated with antitrust charges levied against the company, have forced a recent restructuring and cuts in both staff and operations.

Roots

The origins of the present-day Carbide/Graphite Group extend back to 1899, when the Speer Carbon Company was founded in St. Mary's, Pennsylvania, by chemist John Speer and financier Andrew Kaul. Speer Carbon began operations as a producer of carbon brushes for electric motors and generators.

In 1920 a plant was added in Niagara Falls, New York, to graphitize carbon electrodes that were being made at the Pennsylvania facility. These electrodes were used as consumable tools in the electric manufacturing of steel, which was then a relatively new process. Twelve years later another unit, Speer Resistor Corporation, was established to manufacture carbon resistors for radios.

In 1961 Speer Carbon was purchased by Airco, a producer of gases for industrial and healthcare use, and renamed Airco Speer. Speer and Airco both sold their products to the same types of industrial customers. The following year Airco began a $47 million modernization and expansion of Speer's carbon and graphite operations, and Airco Speer soon became the second largest company in its field. In 1966 Airco acquired National Carbide, which had been formed before World War II to produce calcium carbide at a plant in Louisville, Kentucky, and had later acquired a government-built acetylene plant. Calcium carbide, made from lime and coke, became acetylene gas when mixed with water, which was used for a variety of industrial purposes such as chemical manufacturing and welding.

In 1978 Airco was acquired by British industrial gas giant BOC Group, and four years later BOC launched a new $250 million upgrade program. An electrode manufacturing plant in Ridgeville, South Carolina, and a petroleum needle coke plant in Seadrift, Texas, were built, with the latter producing the raw material used to make carbon electrodes.

A decline in steel production led to a drop in electrode prices during the early 1980s, and in 1988 BOC sold its calcium carbide and graphite producing operations to management and an outside investment group in a $150 million leveraged buyout. As part of the arrangement the electrode plant in South Carolina was sold to Showa Denko of Japan. The newly created company was named the Carbon/Graphite Group, Inc., which was changed slightly to the Carbide/Graphite Group, Inc. in 1992. By this time the company had become the leading U.S.-based maker of graphite and calcium carbide products for industrial use, and the only one producing its own needle coke, which it also sold to outside companies. Graphite products, primarily electrodes, accounted for more than two-thirds of revenues.

Company Perspectives:

The Carbide/Graphite Group is a major U.S. manufacturer of graphite electrode products and calcium carbide products. Graphite electrodes are used as conductors of electricity, and are consumed, in the electric arc furnace (EAF) steelmaking process common to all minimill steel producers. Calcium carbide and derivative products, primarily acetylene, are used in the manufacture of specialty chemicals, as a fuel in metal cutting and welding and for iron and steel desulfurization. Carbide/Graphite Group is the only manufacturer of graphite electrodes that produces its own requirements of needle coke, the principal raw material used in the manufacture of graphite electrodes. The Carbide/Graphite Group also sells needle coke to other manufacturers of graphite products.

A Delayed IPO in the 1990s

In 1992 Carbide/Graphite announced plans to issue three million shares of common stock, but later postponed the offering, citing unfavorable market conditions. In 1995 the company sold its specialty graphite producing operations to competitor SGL Carbon AG of Germany for $62 million, a third of which would be plowed back into plant upgrades. Manufacturing facilities in St. Mary's, Pennsylvania; Dallas, Texas; Kitchener, Ontario; and Montreal, Quebec, were given up in the deal.

The initial public offering (IPO) was revived soon afterward, following a successful stock offering from Carbide/Graphite's top competitor, UCAR International. At this time the company's largest stockholder, Centre Capital Investors, sold its 58 percent stake in the company. Former CEO James Baldwin and several others also sold their shares, with a total of 5.4 million put on the market. Carbide/Graphite's revenues at the time of the IPO stood at $240 million, with half derived from foreign sales. The resurgence of the steel market in the early 1990s had seen the cost of electrodes reach $1.33 a pound, up more than a third from the 1990 price. The company was doing well enough to repurchase substantial chunks of its debt.

The main products manufactured by Carbide/Graphite, massive graphite electrode rods, were now in high demand in the steel industry for use in "minimill" steel mills. Unlike the traditional steelmaking process in which oxygen was blown through iron that had been separated from ore in a blast furnace, minimills used scrap metal that was melted down by a huge infusion of electricity conducted by graphite electrodes. These electrodes, as large as nine feet long and two tons in weight, were themselves consumed in the process of steelmaking, lasting only about eight hours before they were burned up. The electrodes were manufactured in a time-consuming process in which coal tar pitch and needle coke, a petroleum byproduct, were mixed and formed into rods. They were then baked, with more pitch added, and cooked again in a 5,000 degree oven. This step converted them to graphite, a heat resistant electrical conductor. The entire process took as long as three months to complete.

In 1997 the company named Walter B. Fowler, Jr., president and CEO, replacing Nicholas Kaiser, who had served as CEO since 1994 and president since 1991. Fowler previously had headed Carbide/Graphite's electrode operations. The company was continuing to thrive at this time, reporting annual sales of $259 million and profits of $12.1 million. Its stock price had been climbing steadily as well, topping $29 in early 1997, up from the offering figure of $15 less than two years before. A $28 million efficiency-improvement program was now in the works.

Charges of Price Fixing in 1997

In the spring of 1997 the U.S. Justice Department launched an investigation of the major graphite electrode makers for evidence of price fixing, with subpoenas issued to UCAR International, SGL Carbon, Carbide/Graphite Group, and two others. Executives of Carbide/Graphite were offered immunity from prosecution in exchange for their testimony before a grand jury in Philadelphia. The company also participated in the Department of Justice's Corporate Leniency Program with its promise of full cooperation in the ongoing investigation. Electrode prices had been escalating at a rate greater than inflation, and the U.S. Justice Department alleged that meetings had been held in which the companies agreed to raise prices, restrict manufacturing capacity, withhold technology from other competitors, and split up the world market among themselves.

On the heels of this probe, a group of U.S. steel manufacturers joined a class-action lawsuit against the top electrode companies, seeking damages for the alleged price fixing. In early 1998 Showa Denko Carbon of Japan agreed to pay a $29 million fine to the United States in an admission of guilt in the case, quickly followed by UCAR, which paid a record $110 million. UCAR also later settled a lawsuit brought by 27 steelmakers for $80 million.

Despite the investigation, Carbide/Graphite continued paying down its debt and arranged for $120 million in revolving credit, while initiating a $10 million stock repurchase program. The company also set aside $38 million for potential fine and lawsuit payments. In the aftermath of the antitrust investigation, sales of the company's electrodes began to taper off, mainly because of an influx of lower-cost imported steel, and Carbide/Graphite announced that it was expecting lower earnings figures for the foreseeable future. The company subsequently laid off 100 workers at its St. Mary's, Pennsylvania plant, closed its graphitizing and baking operations there, and postponed plans to spend $40 million to upgrade its Niagara Falls plant.

More bad news came in November 1998 when Dow Chemical Co. closed a magnesium production plant in Texas that used Carbide/Graphite-manufactured graphite anodes, thus canceling contracts worth $11 million to the company. A total of 230 additional layoffs, representing 20 percent of Carbide/Graphite's workforce, was announced in February 1999. Shortly after this, SGL Carbon AG agreed to pay a $145 million fine, eclipsing UCAR's as the largest in U.S. antitrust history. The amount included $10 million paid by SGL CEO Robert J. Koehler. By some accounts SGL had been the driving force in the price fixing conspiracy, and several SGL executives were given

Key Dates:

1899: Speer Carbon is founded in St. Mary's, Pennsylvania.

1920: Speer begins manufacturing graphite electrodes for steel production.

1961: Airco purchases Speer Carbon and renames it Airco Speer.

1966: Airco Speer purchases National Carbide, a maker of calcium carbide.

1978: British BOC Group acquires Airco Speer, which becomes its Carbon/Graphite Division.

1982: BOC launches $250 million expansion of Carbon/Graphite operations.

1988: Management of BOC's Carbon/Graphite Division lead a leveraged buyout.

1992: Company becomes known as the Carbide/Graphite Group, Inc.

1995: Stock is offered on the NASDAQ exchange; specialty graphite business is sold.

1997: U.S. Justice Department investigates major electrode makers for price fixing.

1998: Carbide/Graphite sets aside $38 million to settle potential claims from lawsuits, taking an additional charge of $7 million the following year for the same purpose.

1999: Company restructures, lays off more than 20 percent of its workforce.

2000: Joint ventures with Austrian and Pittsburgh-based companies are launched.

prison terms. SGL's U.S. operating unit had filed for bankruptcy protection the previous December.

Carbide/Graphite continued to soldier on, reducing inventory levels and further improving the efficiency of its operations. A total of 180 employees were temporarily laid off while this took place, but they were called back ahead of schedule. In the spring of 1999 a reorganization of the company's graphite electrode operations was begun in which several top executives were replaced, operations were consolidated, and 35 additional jobs were eliminated through an early retirement and severance program. Business conditions remained difficult, however, with electrode prices hitting a low of $1.13 a pound. Fiscal 2000 figures showed a loss of $9.7 million for the year, mainly attributed to costs associated with plant closings and an additional amount of money set aside for legal costs. A $30 million hydrosulfurization complex planned for the Seadrift coke plant was put on hold. By this time the company had paid out much of the money it had earmarked for lawsuit settlement costs, for an estimated 96 percent of its total liability. Other cases were still pending in Canada and Europe, and the company was cooperating with European investigations into the antitrust situation.

A joint venture was launched by Carbide/Graphite in 2000 with MetallpulverGesellschaft mbH & Co. KG of Austria. The

50/50 venture involved international magnesium production and utilized Carbide/Graphite's calcium carbide production capacity. Initial plans for the venture's purchase of Reactive Metals and Alloys Corp. were canceled, however. A second joint venture was formed with Pittsburgh-based Power Quality Systems, Inc. to jointly market electric-arc furnace efficiency optimization systems made by the two companies.

Although it was still recovering from the legal troubles of the late 1990s, Carbide/Graphite Group, Inc. was looking to the future with several new joint ventures and a more efficient, slimmed-down organization. The company's fortunes continued to rise and fall on the somewhat mercurial steel market, however, and the graphite electrode business, upon which Carbide/Graphite was still in large part dependent, appeared likely to remain erratic.

Principal Subsidiaries

C/G Specialty Products Management Corp.; Carbide/Graphite Management Corp.; Carbon/Graphite International.

Principal Competitors

Conoco, Inc.; Nippon Carbon Co., Ltd.; SGL Carbon AG; Showa Denko K.K.; Superior Graphite Co.; Tokai Carbon Co., Ltd.; UCAR International, Inc.

Further Reading

Boselovic, Len, "Asia's Woes Dog Carbide/Graphite," *Pittsburgh Post-Gazette,* July 25, 1999, p. F4.

——, "Carbide/Graphite Lays Off 100 in Elk County," *Pittsburgh Post-Gazette,* November 7, 1998, p. D1.

——, "The Carbide/Graphite Group Stirs Up Steel Refining with Electrodes," *Pittsburgh Post-Gazette,* June 1, 1997, p. C4.

Burgert, Philip, and John E. Sacco, "Investigators Probe Electrode Sales," *American Metal Market,* June 9, 1997, p. 1.

"Electrode Suppliers Investigated for Price-Fixing," *New Steel,* August 1, 1997, p. 14.

Fox, Lauren, "Graphite Electrode Makers Face Price-Fixing Probe," *Dow Jones News Service,* June 5, 1997.

Houser, Mark, "Steelmakers Going Wild for Electric Furnaces," *Tribune Review,* October 8, 1995, p. 1.

"IPO Spotlight Recommendation: Carbide/Graphite Group Buy," *Emerging & Special Situations,* August 14, 1992, p. 8.

"Minimills Look to Recoup Overcharges for Electrodes," *Iron Age New Steel,* October 1, 1998, p. 60.

"New Issues—Carbide/Graphite Group Avoid," *Emerging & Special Situations,* September 18, 1995, p. 17.

"Price Fixing Fallout Tars Graphite Firms," *Pittsburgh-Post Gazette,* February 24, 1998, p. E1.

Sacco, John E., "Carbide/Graphite Will Throttle Back Output," *American Metal Market,* October 27, 1999, p. 1.

——, "Exec Shake-Up Under Way at Carbide/Graphite Group," *American Metal Market,* April 12, 2000, p. 3.

Ward, Joe, "Management Officials Buy Out BOC's Airco Carbide Division," *Courier-Journal,* March 8, 1988, p. 8.

—Frank Uhle

Cargill, Incorporated

Post Office Box 9300
Minneapolis, Minnesota 55440-9300
U.S.A.
Telephone: (612) 742-7575
Fax: (612) 742-7393
Web site: http://www.cargill.com

Private Company
Incorporated: 1936
Employees: 84,000
Sales: $47.6 billion (2000)
NAIC: 112112 Cattle Feedlots; 112310 Chicken Egg
Production; 212392 Phosphate Rock Mining;
212393 Other Chemical and Fertilizer Mineral
Mining; 311111 Dog and Cat Food Mfg.; 311119
Other Animal Food Mfg.; 311211 Flour Milling;
311212 Rice Milling; 311213 Malt Mfg.; 311221
Wet Corn Milling; 311222 Soybean Processing;
311223 Other Oilseed Processing; 311330
Confectionery Mfg. from Purchased Chocolate;
311611 Animal (Except Poultry) Slaughtering; 311612
Meat Processed from Carcasses; 311615 Poultry
Processing; 311911 Roasted Nuts and Peanut Butter
Mfg.; 311942 Spice and Extract Mfg.; 325193 Ethyl
Alcohol Mfg.; 325310 Fertilizer Mfg.; 331111 Iron
and Steel Mills; 422470 Meat and Meat Product
Wholesalers; 422510 Grain and Field Bean
Wholesalers; 422590 Other Farm Product Raw
Material Wholesalers; 422720 Petroleum and
Petroleum Products Wholesalers (Except Bulk
Stations and Terminals); 422910 Farm Supplies
Wholesalers; 422990 Other Miscellaneous Nondurable
Goods Wholesalers; 483111 Deep Sea Freight
Transportation; 483113 Coastal and Great Lakes
Freight Transportation; 483211 Inland Water Freight
Transportation; 522293 International Trade Financing;
523140 Commodity Contracts Brokerage

Cargill, Incorporated is the largest private corporation in the United States. Long known as a commodities merchant, Cargill in the early 21st century stood as one of the largest diversified services companies in the country, involved in nearly four dozen individual lines of business. In addition to merchandising grains, oilseeds, and other commodities, Cargill is a processor of beef, pork, and poultry (through the number three U.S. meat processor, subsidiary Excel Corporation), and several other products, including animal feed, cocoa, eggs, fertilizer, flour, and rice; a transporter of commodities; a manufacturer of steel (through subsidiary North Star Steel Co.); and a financial and technical services provider.

Cargill's corporate philosophy, shaped by its participation in the grain trade, emphasizes secrecy and an intricate worldwide intelligence network. Robert Bergland, former secretary of agriculture, told the *Minneapolis Star and Tribune* that "they probably have the best crop-marketing intelligence available anywhere, and that includes the CIA." While secrecy provides an enormous operational advantage to Cargill, it creates problems as well. For example, during difficult times, Cargill's low profile left no reservoir of favorable public opinion. After becoming president of Cargill in 1957, an exasperated Cargill MacMillan complained that the company received public attention only when it was involved in a court case. This situation remained largely unchanged until late in the 20th century when the company launched an unprecedented advertising campaign designed to bolster its public image.

Grain Trading Roots

William Wallace Cargill began his career in the grain business in 1865 in Conover, Iowa. The business grew as it followed the expansion of the railroad into northern Iowa after the Civil War. In 1875 William Cargill moved the headquarters of his company to La Crosse, Wisconsin. He formed several different partnerships with his brothers, Samuel and James. With Samuel he formed W.W. Cargill and Brother in 1867, which became the W.W. Cargill Company in 1892. James Cargill operated in the Red River Valley in North Dakota and Minnesota with a partner, John D. McMillan. In 1882 the partners sold their Red River Valley grain elevators to William Cargill in order to raise more capital. Then in 1888, James, William, and Sam Cargill formed Cargill Brothers. In 1890 this firm became the Cargill Elevator Company, headquartered in Minneapolis, Minnesota.

In 1895 William W. Cargill's daughter married John Hugh MacMillan, and later his son William S. Cargill also married a MacMillan. When the elder Cargill died in 1909, John Hugh MacMillan forced out William S. Cargill and took control of the company. An ensuing feud simmered for decades, but control of the company now rests firmly in the hands of the MacMillan family, although some Cargills still hold stock (along with a number of employees).

John MacMillan ran the company until 1936, leading it through a difficult period after the struggle for power. Mac-Millan was a cautious manager who established the rule that the company would not speculate in commodities, a careful policy that helped establish the company's reputation in banking circles—an important consideration since the large deals that became Cargill's mainstay required huge lines of credit.

After World War I, MacMillan took two steps that helped lay the foundation for the future growth of the company. Since its beginnings in 1865, Cargill had been based entirely in the Midwest, selling to eastern brokers. When brokers from Albany, New York, began to open offices in the Midwest, by-passing Cargill as a middleman, Cargill opened an office in New York in 1922. In 1929 Cargill opened a permanent office in Argentina to secure immediate information on Latin American wheat prices. In 1936 the Cargill Elevator Company merged with other Cargill firms to become Cargill, Incorporated.

John MacMillan, Jr., became president of Cargill in 1936. While maintaining many of his father's cautious policies, he also brought an imaginative and visionary quality to the company. During the Great Depression, Cargill invested heavily in the storage and transportation of grain, secure in the knowledge that a recovering economy would find Cargill prepared to reap maximum benefit. He also left his mark on grain transportation. Unsatisfied with the standard barge design, he and some associates designed a new type of articulated barge and submitted the design to shipyards. When no company would build the barges, Cargill established its own unit to construct them. Soon Cargill built barges at half the typical cost and with twice the capacity of standard barges.

At the same time, the aggressive nature of MacMillan's management style also created problems for the company, most notably in the September Corn Case of 1937. The 1936 corn crop had been poor, and the 1937 crop would not be available until October. The Chicago Board of Trade and the U.S. Com-modity Exchange Authority accused Cargill of trying to corner the corn market. After Cargill refused a Board of Trade order to sell some of its corn, the board suspended Cargill Grain Company, the subsidiary that conducted trading, from membership. When the board eventually lifted its suspension, Cargill refused to rejoin. For decades, Cargill carried on its trading through independent traders and proclaimed its satisfaction with the greater security this method afforded. Nevertheless, it did rejoin in 1962.

Diversifying from the 1940s to the 1970s

By 1940, 60 percent of Cargill's business involved foreign markets, and World War II had a crippling effect on business. While Cargill did build ships for the U.S. Navy, this enterprise could not replace its lost international business, so the company began a major diversification program, entering into vegetable oil and animal feed. The two activities are closely related: pressing oil leaves high-protein meal, which is then used in animal feed. In 1943 Cargill entered the soybean processing business through the purchase of plants in Cedar Rapids and Fort Dodge, Iowa, and Springfield, Illinois. In 1945 Cargill purchased Nutrena Feeds, an animal-feed producer, thereby doubling its capacity in poultry and animal feeds. Corn and soybean processing were two of the most rapidly expanding agricultural areas in the 20 years after World War II, however, and oil processing soon outstripped the value of animal feeds. By 1949, Cargill had made a major entry into soybean processing, and its researchers were already exploring the value of safflower and sunflower oil.

John MacMillan, Jr., and his brother Cargill MacMillan were determined to expand the company after the war, but in a cautious manner that minimized risk. Cargill took the lead among the major grain companies in efforts to combine a network of inland grain elevators with the ability to export large quantities of grain. Two developments in the 1950s helped to establish Cargill in world trade. In 1953 Cargill opened a Swiss subsidiary, Tradax, to sell grain in Europe. Eventually, Tradax grew into one of the largest grain companies in the world. In 1960, Cargill opened a 13-million-bushel grain elevator in Baie Comeau, Quebec. This facility allowed Cargill to store grain for shipment during the months that winter weather closed the Great Lakes to traffic. The grain elevator also cut the cost of midwestern grain bound for Europe by 15 cents a bushel. In order to maximize profit, the barges that took grain to Baie Comeau hauled back iron ore. Similarly, in 1954 barges that carried grain to New Orleans began to backhaul salt up the Mississippi. Both practices would lead to profitable new enterprises for Cargill. Before the end of the decade, Cargill's sales topped the $1 billion mark.

Cargill became involved in grain sales to communist countries at an early date. In the early 1960s, Cargill began to sell grain to Hungary and the Soviet Union, while its Canadian subsidiary also played a significant role in trade with the Soviets. After a lapse in trade of several years during the late 1960s, Soviet leader Leonid Brezhnev resumed grain deals as part of his effort to improve the Soviet standard of living. At the same time, the United States, anxious to improve relations with the Soviet Union, eased trade restrictions. These developments set the stage for the famous grain purchase of 1972. The

Key Dates:

1865: William Wallace Cargill enters the grain business in Conover, Iowa.

1875: Cargill relocates his business to La Crosse, Wisconsin.

1888: William, James, and Sam Cargill form Cargill Brothers.

1890: Cargill Brothers becomes Cargill Elevator Company, headquartered in Minneapolis.

1909: John Hugh MacMillan, son-in-law of William Cargill, takes control of the company.

1922: Cargill opens an office in New York City.

1936: Cargill Elevator and other Cargill firms are merged to form Cargill, Incorporated.

1943: Company enters the soybean processing business.

1945: Nutrena Feeds is acquired, doubling the company's capacity in poultry and animal feeds.

1953: Tradax, a Swiss subsidiary, is formed to sell grain in Europe.

1954: Company begins backhauling salt up the Mississippi River.

1967: Company expands into wet corn milling through purchase of a mill in Cedar Rapids, Iowa.

1972: Cargill enters the flour milling business.

1974: Company purchases Ralston Purina's turkey processing and marketing division; Caprock Industries, a cattle feedlot operator; and North Star Steel Company.

1975: Hohenberg Bros. Company, a cotton merchandiser, is acquired.

1979: Cargill acquires MBPXL Corporation, a beef processor.

1981: U.K.-based Ralli Bros. and Coney, a major international commodity trader, is acquired.

1982: MBPXL changes its name to Excel Corporation.

1990: Major reorganization of North American operations is undertaken.

1992: Implementation of employee stock ownership plan enables some family members to cash in their ownership shares.

1997: The North American salt business of Akzo Nobel NV is acquired.

1999: Cargill acquires the worldwide grain storage, transportation, export, and trading operations of Continental Grain Company.

2000: Cargill announces plans to acquire Agribrands International, a major animal feed maker.

U.S.S.R. purchased 20 million tons of wheat—roughly one-fourth of the American harvest—of which Cargill sold one million tons.

While Cargill actually lost money on the sale, the ensuing change in the market was more important. The massive sale of wheat, combined with a worldwide drought, drove up agricultural prices and increased Cargill's profits in all areas of operations. Sales increased from $2.2 billion in 1971 to $28.5 billion in 1981. Together with Cargill's success in high-fructose corn syrup (it had entered the wet corn milling market in 1967 through the purchase of a mill in Cedar Rapids, Iowa) and animal feed, this boom financed a significant expansion: during that decade Cargill purchased 137 grain elevators, companies in the coal, steel (North Star Steel Company, bought in 1974), and cattle feedlot (Caprock Industries Inc., in 1974) industries; and Ralston Purina's turkey processing and marketing division (1974). The company also entered the flour milling industry through the purchase of Burrus Mills, which was based in Saginaw, Texas, in 1972; and began merchandising cotton in 1975 with the acquisition of Memphis, Tennessee-based Hohenberg Bros. Company. In 1979 beef processing was added to Cargill's growing array of operations with the purchase of MBPXL Corporation of Wichita, Kansas, which was renamed Excel Corporation in 1982. Also in 1979 came the purchase of the Laurent malt plant in France, which initiated Cargill's involvement in the malting business. Finally, in 1981, Cargill beefed up its trading operations with the acquisition of Ralli Bros. and Coney, a U.K.-based international trader of cotton, rubber, wool, and fiber.

Suffering from Slower Growth in the 1980s

The 1980s brought economic problems that slowed Cargill's growth. A 1980 U.S. government embargo on grain sales to the Soviet Union left Cargill long on grain. While the government provided support for companies that were damaged by the embargo, a rise in the value of the dollar and a debt crisis in developing countries further burdened American agriculture firms. Cargill continued to search for opportunities in the depressed business cycle. Typical of its approach was the purchase of Ralston Purina's soybean-crushing plants in 1985. Overcapacity in the soybean industry did not dissuade Cargill. Whitney MacMillan pointed out that when a business is not doing well there is more room for improvement, and Cargill remained confident that investment during hard times would reap major rewards during the next rise in the business cycle.

Despite periodic downturns, Cargill had exhibited an impressive compound annual growth rate of 15.8 percent sustained over a 25-year period, based on net worth (from $95 million in 1966 to $3.7 billion in 1991). Part of this success was credited to its consistently strong management. Early in the 1930s, Cargill began one of the first management-trainee programs in the country. Cargill did not rely on business-school graduates but took trainees from a wide range of backgrounds and introduced them to the company's system. Cargill placed young executives in responsible positions quickly and groomed those who succeeded. This system proved its worth in 1960 when John MacMillan, Jr., died. For 16 years nonfamily employees ran the company under the leadership of Erwin Kelm. When Kelm retired in 1976, Whitney MacMillan, great-grandson of founder W.W. Cargill, became chairman. Most upper-level administrators at the company were graduates of Cargill's training program, and these officers, like family members, took the long view in planning for the welfare of the company.

As Cargill increasingly depended upon nonfamily members for leadership, the company faced several challenges starting in the mid-1980s that would force it to undergo its most dramatic transformation to date. From the mid-1980s through the early 1990s, Cargill consistently failed to meet its company-wide sales targets primarily because of continued difficulties in grain merchandising, a sector that had never recovered from the 1980 embargo. Cargill's successes had also led to a bloated operation in which ConAgra Inc., its biggest customer, had to purchase products from 18 different Cargill divisions. Chairman Whitney MacMillan and most of the other senior leaders were nearing retirement age with no clear successor from the younger ranks in sight. Finally, some of the family members were lobbying for the opportunity to cash in on Cargill's success through more than the relatively modest annual dividends they received from their stock.

Reorganizing in the Early 1990s

With the help of consultants McKinsey & Company, MacMillan initiated a major reorganization of Cargill's North American operations in 1990. The previous organization along product lines was replaced with a ''soft matrix'' type of structure, which intermixed product line and geographical area management. In order to bring fresh ideas into the organization, Cargill's board of directors was overhauled to include five members from management, five family shareholders, and five outside directors (the first outsiders in 40 years). The structure was also intended to allow the board to mediate between family members and Cargill management.

Such mediation would become more and more critical since Cargill faced the prospect of its first nonfamily CEO since the Erwin Kelm era of 1960–76. Only two fifth-generation family members worked for the firm, and neither had enough experience to take over when MacMillan retired. Eventually MacMillan selected Ernest S. Micek, former president of Cargill's food sector, as his successor. Micek was named president and chief operating officer in 1994 before taking over as CEO and chairman in August 1995. Still, at age 59, Micek was anticipating a short tenure (especially by Cargill standards), since company rules mandated retirement at age 65. MacMillan had retired after more than 44 years at the company.

Meanwhile, and amid false rumors that Cargill would finally go public, the issue of company ownership was at least temporarily settled through the implementation of an employee stock ownership plan in 1992. Family members were given the opportunity to cash in as much as 30 percent of their ownership stake in Cargill. It turned out that only 17 percent was sold, for a total of $730 million, funded through borrowing. About 20,000 Cargill employees in the United States were eligible to receive the resulting stock, ending a long history of ownership exclusively by Cargills and MacMillans.

To reduce Cargill's dependence on the perpetually fickle grain business, the company committed to a program of radical diversification. One aspect of this program was to no longer simply be a commodity merchandiser, but to process the commodities as well—what many called ''moving up the food chain.'' Already an established meatpacker in the United States through its Excel subsidiary, Cargill opened a new plant in Alberta, Canada, in 1989 in the midst of a downturn in meat sales and became the top meatpacker in Canada by 1992. The company also began producing brand-name products for sale to consumers, such as its Sun Valley Poultry chickens and turkeys in England and its Honeysuckle White and Riverside turkeys in

the United States. Through these efforts, Cargill was attempting to gain ground on competitors such as ConAgra, which had moved heavily into branded products throughout the 1980s. By 1993 Cargill was the third largest U.S. food company, behind only Philip Morris and ConAgra, and its annual food sales had reached as high as $22 billion.

A second area of diversification was the development of Cargill's Financial Markets Division. Based on knowledge gained through decades of trading in the world markets, this operation supported the efforts of the parent company and its subsidiaries through a full spectrum of financial services. Started in the mid-1980s and expanded rapidly in the early 1990s, the division generated almost $100 million in earnings for the 1992–93 fiscal year out of the company total of $358 million.

By the mid-1990s, Cargill had surprised many observers by its diversity in both operations and the locations of those operations. In addition to being the top grain company in the world and the number three food company in the United States, the company also boasted the eighth largest U.S. steel producer in its North Star Steel subsidiary, the top position in European cocoa processing, and the number one ranking among pet food processors in Argentina. For the fiscal year ending in May 1995, Cargill reported that its revenues exceeded the $50 billion mark for the first time, totaling about $51 billion, with net income standing at $671 million.

Early in the next fiscal year, Cargill exited from the U.S. chicken processing market when it sold five plants in Georgia and Florida to Tyson Foods Inc. The deal also involved the transfer of ownership of a pork processing facility in Marshall, Missouri, from Tyson to Excel, bolstering that subsidiary's position among the top five U.S. pork producers. Cargill retained its non-U.S. chicken operations as well as its turkey business. For fiscal 1996, Cargill reported record net income of $902 million on record sales of $55.98 billion. In 1997 the company became one of the largest producers and marketers of salt in the world with the purchase of the North American salt business of Akzo Nobel NV, an operation with annual revenues of about $450 million.

Economic Volatility and Major Transactions at the Turn of the Millennium

The economic turmoil that erupted in mid-1997 in Asia and then spread to Latin America and Russia sent global commodity markets into a deep slump, depressing both sales and earnings at Cargill. The company's financial services arm also suffered setbacks as it was involved in trading Russian financial instruments when that country's economy turned sour in the summer of 1998; the unit also lost millions through bad loans to buyers of mobile homes. Cargill earned only $468 million on revenues of $51.42 billion in fiscal 1998 and $597 million on $45.7 billion in sales the following year.

In the midst of these travails, in early 1998, Warren R. Staley was promoted from executive vice-president to president and COO. Staley became president and CEO in April 1999, then was named chairman as well in August 2000, following the retirement of Micek. This period was noteworthy for a number of major deals that Cargill was involved in. In early 1998 Cargill and Monsanto Company formed a biotechnology joint venture whereby Cargill would contract with farmers to grow crops containing Monsanto genes and would then process the resulting harvests into food and livestock feed ingredients. Then in October 1998 Cargill sold its foreign seed operations to Monsanto for about $1.4 billion. In September 1998 Cargill agreed to sell its North American seed operations, which controlled about 4 percent of the U.S. corn seed market, to AgrEvo GmbH, a joint venture of Hoechst AG and Schering AG, for $650 million. Soon thereafter, however, Pioneer Hi-Bred International Inc. sued Cargill, Monsanto, and one other firm alleging that they had wrongfully obtained and used genetic material developed by Pioneer. Following an internal investigation, Cargill admitted that an employee had in fact improperly used Pioneer genetic material in his work at Cargill. Almost immediately, AgrEvo pulled out of the Cargill deal. Cargill was also forced to destroy some of its seed lines, which reduced the value of the business it sold to Monsanto, leading Cargill to return more than $200 million to Monsanto. In May 2000 Cargill agreed to pay $100 million to Pioneer to settle the lawsuit. Cargill then sold its North American seed operation in late 2000 to Dow Chemical Company for an undisclosed sum.

Meantime, in November 1998, Cargill agreed to acquire the worldwide grain storage, transportation, export, and trading operations of its chief rival, Continental Grain Company for an undisclosed sum that industry observers estimated at several hundred million dollars. The deal quickly aroused bitter opposition from farm groups and legislators across the Farm Belt concerned that Cargill would gain too much control of grain exports in a market already suffering from depressed commodity prices. The U.S. Justice Department filed a lawsuit to block the deal. An agreement was reached in July 1999 whereby the government approved the deal contingent upon Cargill divesting nine grain-handling and transport facilities in eight states. This constituted a significant divestiture as it represented about 25 percent of Continental Grain's business.

In the midst of the Pioneer seed debacle and the contentious purchase of the Continental Grain assets, the normally secretive Cargill launched a surprising corporate image campaign. In January 1999 the company launched a three-year, $30 million ad campaign with a Super Bowl television spot and a full-page ad in the *Wall Street Journal*. The timing of the launch was purely coincidental as it had been planned the previous summer. The ads were aimed at farmers and food manufacturers and highlighted long-term relationships between the company and its customers. According to Micek, the company's executives hoped to "put more of a human face on Cargill" through the campaign.

In January 2000 Cargill and Dow Chemical announced that a 50–50 joint venture called Cargill Dow Polymer would begin construction of a manufacturing plant in Blair, Nebraska, where a new kind of plastic made from plants rather than petroleum would be produced. In December 2000 Cargill announced that it had reached an agreement to acquire Agribrands International, Inc. for $580 million, a deal that foiled a planned merger between Agribrands and Ralcorp Holdings Inc. Agribrands would be folded into Cargill Animal Nutrition, maker of feeds under such brands as Nutrena and Acco Feeds. Cargill would

gain a much larger international presence through Agribrands' 70 plants in 17 countries, producing feeds under the brand names Purina, Chow, and Checkerboard. Agribrands had fiscal 2000 earnings of $45 million on revenues of $1.2 billion. Through this acquisition, Cargill would continue its steady expansion beyond its grain trading roots. At the dawn of the new millennium, the increasingly diversified Cargill seemed destined to remain one of the most powerful companies in the world.

Principal Subsidiaries

Caprock Industries Inc.; Cargill Citro-America, Inc.; Cargill Energy Corporation; Cargill Ferrous International; Cargill Fertilizer Inc.; Cargill Investor Services Inc.; Cargill Marine and Terminal, Inc.; Cargill Technical Services; Excel Corporation; Hohenberg Bros. Company; Illinois Cereal Mills Inc.; North Star Steel Co.; Wilbur Chocolate Company Inc.; Cargill Limited (Canada); Ralli Bros. and Coney (U.K.); Seaforth Corn Mills (U.K.).

Principal Competitors

Archer Daniels Midland Company; ConAgra Foods, Inc.; IBP, inc.; Smithfield Foods, Inc.; Hormel Foods Corporation; Sara Lee Corporation; Corn Products International, Inc.; Ag Processing Inc.; Agribrands International, Inc.; Cenex Harvest States Cooperative; ContiGroup Companies, Inc.; Saskatchewan Wheat Pool; Ajinomoto Co., Inc.; Eridania Béghin-Say; Farmland Industries, Inc.; Perdue Farms Incorporated; Tate & Lyle PLC; The Dow Chemical Company; E.I. du Pont de Nemours and Company.

Further Reading

Ahlberg, B., "Cargill: The Invisible Giant," *Multinational Monitor,* July/August 1988, pp. 36–39.

Barshay, Jill J., "Cargill Inc. Shuts Book on Bad Year," *Minneapolis Star Tribune,* August 11, 1999, p. 1D.

——, "Cargill's Quiet Man," *Minneapolis Star Tribune,* June 7, 1999, p. 1D.

——, "Government Approves Cargill-Continental Deal," *Minneapolis Star Tribune,* July 9, 1999, p. 1A.

——, " 'Invisible Giant' Cargill Speaks Up in New Ads," *Minneapolis Star Tribune,* March 5, 1999, p. 1D.

Berss, Marcia, "End of an Era," *Forbes,* April 29, 1991, pp. 41–42.

Brissett, Liz, "Still the One," *Corporate Report-Minnesota,* May 1999, pp. 32+.

Broehl, Wayne G., Jr., *Cargill: Going Global,* Hanover, N.H.: University Press of New England, 1998, 419 p.

——, *Cargill: Trading the World's Grain,* Hanover, N.H.: University Press of New England, 1992, 1,007 p.

"Cargill Inc. Names Ernest Micek to Post of Chief Executive," *Wall Street Journal,* March 29, 1995, p. B12.

"Cargill: Not Just Grain Any More," *Business Asia,* December 18, 1995, p. 12.

"Cargill Still to Contest Charges," *Minneapolis Star Tribune,* June 15, 1996, p. 1D.

Davies, Michael, "Reaping the Harvest?," *Corporate Location,* November/December 1994, pp. 26–29.

Deogun, Nikhil, and Scott Kilman, "Cargill Has Deal to Acquire Agribrands After Cutting in on Ralcorp's Offer," *Wall Street Journal,* December 4, 2000, p. A4.

Greising, David, William C. Symonds, and Karen Lowry Miller, "At Cargill, the Ties That Bind Aren't Binding Anymore," *Business Week,* November 18, 1991, pp. 92–93, 96.

Henkoff, Ronald, "Cargill's Heir-Raising Future," *Fortune,* July 1, 1991, p. 70.

——, "Inside America's Biggest Private Company," *Fortune,* July 13, 1992, pp. 83–90.

The History of Cargill, Incorporated, 1865–1945, Minneapolis: Cargill, 1945.

"How to Feed a Growing Family," *Economist,* March 9, 1996, p. 63.

Kennedy, Tony, "Cargill Chickens Out: It Plans to Sell U.S. Broiler Operation to No. 1 Tyson," *Minneapolis Star Tribune,* July 15, 1995, p. 1D.

Kilman, Scott, "Cargill Agreement to Sell Seed Business to Germans for $650 Million Collapses," *Wall Street Journal,* February 5, 1999, p. A4.

——, "Cargill Hires Minneapolis Agency to Create a Corporate Identity," *Wall Street Journal,* July 23, 1998, p. B11.

——, "Cargill's Staley to Succeed CEO Micek, Who Is Stepping Down Early from Post," *Wall Street Journal,* April 15, 1999, p. B15.

——, "Monsanto Co. Agrees to Pay Cargill $1.4 Billion for Foreign Seed Business," *Wall Street Journal,* June 30, 1998, p. A4.

Kilman, Scott, and Joseph B. Cahill, "Cargill to Buy Continental Grain Assets in Deal to Expand Control of Supplies," *Wall Street Journal,* November 11, 1998, p. A10.

Kilman, Scott, and Susan Warren, "Monsanto, Cargill Team Up for Crop Processing," *Wall Street Journal,* May 15, 1998, p. A3.

Kneen, Brewster, *Invisible Giant: Cargill and Its Transnational Strategies,* East Haven, Conn.: Pluto Press, 1995, 232 p.

——, "The Invisible Giant: Cargill and Its Transnational Strategies," *Ecologist,* September/October 1995, pp. 195–99.

——, *Trading Up: How Cargill, the World's Largest Grain Trading Company, Is Changing Canadian Agriculture,* Toronto: NC Press, 1990, 136 p.

Looker, Dan, "Will the Giant Be Tied Down?," *Successful Farming,* January 1999.

MacMillan, W. Duncan, *MacMillan: The American Grain Family,* Afton, Minn.: Afton Historical Society Press, 1998, 336 p.

Miller, James P., "Cargill Agrees to $100 Million Settlement with Pioneer over Genetic-Seed Traits," *Wall Street Journal,* May 17, 2000, p. A3.

Morgan, Dan, *Merchants of Grain,* New York: Viking Press, 1979, 387 p.

Murphy, Dan, "Taking the High Road: Excel Beef," *National Provisioner,* April 1994, pp. 24–39.

Oslund, John J., "A Career to Remember: Whitney MacMillan Kept Cargill Successful, Private," *Minneapolis Star Tribune,* August 14, 1995, p. 1D.

Pehanich, Mike, "The Quiet Giant Climbs the Value Chain," *Prepared Foods,* October 1993, p. 22.

Schafer, Lee, "Cargill and the Ultimate Commodity," *Corporate Report-Minnesota,* April 1994, pp. 52+.

——, "Executive of the Year," *Corporate Report-Minnesota,* January 1993, pp. 46+.

——, "A New Era: Ernest Micek Will Build on Cargill's Past As He Prepares It for the 21st Century," *Corporate Report-Minnesota,* July 1996, pp. 28–37.

Schmitz, Andrew, *Grain Export Cartels,* Cambridge, Mass.: Ballinger Publishing, 1981, 298 p.

Warren, Susan, "Cargill, Dow Chemical to Make 'Natural Plastic,'" *Wall Street Journal,* January 11, 2000, p. A3.

Westervelt, Robert, "Cargill, Dow Bet $300 Million on Corn-Based Polymers," *Chemical Week,* January 19, 2000, p. 9.

Wilke, John R., "U.S. Demanding Sales by Cargill for Continental Buyout Approval," *Wall Street Journal,* July 9, 1999, p. A4.

Work, John L., *Cargill Beginnings: An Account of Early Years,* Minnetonka, Minn.: Cargill, 1965, 154 p.

—Joseph Bator
—update: David E. Salamie

CASIO Computer Co., Ltd.

6-2, Hon-machi, 1-chome
Shibuya-ku
Tokyo 151-8543
Japan
Telephone: (03) 5334-4111
Fax: (03) 5334-4921
Web site: http://www.casio.co.jp

Public Company
Incorporated: 1957
Employees: 19,325
Sales: ¥410.34 billion ($3.87 billion) (2000)
Stock Exchanges: Tokyo Osaka Amsterdam Frankfurt
Ticker Symbol: 6952
NAIC: 333313 Office Machinery Manufacturing; 334111
   Electronic Computer Manufacturing; 334119 Other
   Computer Peripheral Equipment Manufacturing;
   334220 Radio and Television Broadcasting and
   Wireless Communications Equipment Manufacturing;
   334310 Audio and Video Equipment Manufacturing;
   334518 Watch, Clock, and Part Manufacturing;
   339992 Musical Instrument Manufacturing

CASIO Computer Co., Ltd. (Casio) manufactures desktop electronic calculators, digital and analog timepieces, pocket and office computers, digital diaries, electronic musical instruments, audiovisual products, computers, LCD televisions, digital cameras, and other consumer and industrial electronic products. The company also manufactures telecommunications products, including pagers, mobile phones, and wireless telephone handsets. In 1969 Casio was among the first Japanese manufacturers to fully automate an assembly plant, and this sort of innovation has allowed the firm to remain cost-competitive with other larger electronic manufacturers. Much of Casio's success has been based not only on its technological and assembly innovations but also on its aggressive marketing and sales strategies. As a result of its assertive marketing, the company sells its diverse products in more than 140 countries.

Early History

The company was founded in Tokyo in 1946 by the Kashio family under the name Kashio Manufacturing. Four Kashio brothers—Toshio, Kazuo, Tadao, and Yukio—and their father envisioned a business that was to be managed under a "spirit of creation"; ever since, the company philosophy has remained that of "creativity and contribution." Three of the Kashio brothers still own about 10 percent of all outstanding Casio stock, and the Kashio family has retained effective financial control of the company. The Kashio brothers remain active in the management and operation of the company as well: Toshio Kashio serves as chairman, and Kazuo Kashio is president.

The company was incorporated in 1957 as Casio Computer Co., Ltd. The name Casio is an anglicized version of Kashio, demonstrating that early on the company was acutely aware of the economic significance of international marketing. The Kashios believed that in the post-World War II environment a Westernized name would render the company's consumer and business products more marketable, both domestically and internationally. The incorporation occurred around the same time as Toshio Kashio's invention of the first purely electric—as opposed to electromechanical—small calculator. The company capitalized on this invention and became the only Japanese manufacturer to specialize in electric calculators. After the introduction of semiconductors in the mid-1960s, electromechanical technology was replaced with electronic technology, and in 1965 Casio introduced the world's first desktop electronic calculator with a memory. Over the succeeding decades, Casio consistently sought to expand its product line while relying upon calculators as its primary base of operations.

Prior to 1965 electromechanical calculators were large and expensive. Electromechanical calculators were literally desktop size, ranged in price from $400 to $1,000, and could complete only four functions—addition, subtraction, division, and multiplication. These earlier devices, limited in function and speed, were also prone to mechanical failure. The development of semiconductor and integrated-circuit technologies during the 1960s began to reduce the size and cost of electronic calculators dramatically and simultaneously enhanced their reliability. Electronic calculators were also easier to read, despite their

---

Company Perspectives:

"Starting out initially as a computer manufacturer, CASIO Computer Co., Ltd. has developed calculators, digital watches, electronic musical instruments, liquid crystal televisions, and other products that serve to put information into the hands of people everywhere. Today it is becoming much easier to exchange multimedia data, including images and sound, which will usher in an era where more people around the world start to share more common values. This has generated demand for world-standard data processing devices that are easy to use. At CASIO, the emphasis has always been on the individual consumer, which is why we are working towards our goal of 'personal multimedia' through such products as pagers, PHS telephones, and other communication products, as well as our LCD digital camera and other image data products.

We firmly believe that our products must make the lives of people more enjoyable and comfortable. They must be easy to operate, versatile, and affordable, while offering the highest level of quality possible. To accomplish all of this, we make research and development of totally new products a central theme of our business philosophy. We also place a great deal of emphasis on system equipment, software, electronic devices, and other fundamental areas in our quest to produce products that make the dreams of people everywhere come true.''
                                                    —Kazuo Kashio, president

---

smaller size, because of technical breakthroughs in light-emitting diodes (LED) and liquid crystal displays (LCD), and these new technologies required significantly less power to operate. Casio helped to develop LED and LCD technologies, and by the 1980s these technologies played an increasingly important role in the development of Casio's digital-timepiece and LCD-television markets.

In 1964 the first transistorized, programmable, desktop calculators were introduced, and Japanese manufacturers, including Casio, began to assemble electronic calculators. The entire output from all Japanese electronic manufacturers in 1965 was only about 5,000 units. In 1969 Casio's Kofu factory became the first Japanese plant to mass produce electronic calculators. Very few of these early Japanese electronic calculators were destined for the U.S. market. In 1965 the United States imported just 69 electronic calculators from Japan, and in 1966 Japanese calculators accounted for less than 1 percent of the U.S. market. Casio did not begin to market its own products in the United States until 1970.

In the 1970s Japanese electronic products, particularly consumer electronics, began to capture a larger share of the expanding U.S. market. By the mid-1970s Japanese electronic manufacturers came to dominate the U.S. electronic-calculator market. Japanese companies competed fiercely for market share, and eventually only Sharp and Casio were left. Casio aimed for the bottom of the market, selling small, low-cost calculators with a variety of novel functions. The Casio Mini, which debuted in 1972, was in fact the world's first calculator aimed at the mass market.

The calculator division grew steadily, manufacturing standard electronic calculators, high-performance scientific calculators, pocket computers, and digital diary systems. Electronic notepads and digital diaries greatly expanded Casio's markets, particularly its domestic sales. The electronic-timepiece division also prospered, making a variety of digital and analog watches, many with built-in memory and storage features. The company had entered the digital watch sector in 1974 with the introduction of the Casiotron, which displayed the year, month, date, hour, minute, and second.

By the 1980s Japan had become the world's leading electronics exporter while the United States was the largest consumer of electronic products. As U.S. firms concentrated on military, industrial, and commercial products, Japanese firms instead emphasized consumer products.

Expanding Product Lines in the 1980s

After years of market expansion during the 1970s and 1980s, however, Casio found that market demand in timepieces became stagnant. As a result of market saturation, Casio introduced a number of new timepieces to maintain market demand during the late 1980s, including such products as watches that measured altitude, depth, and barometric pressure; phone-dialing watches; and watches that could record caloric consumption or serve as a pedometer.

Casio moved into a new product area in 1980 with the launch of the Casiotone 201, an electronic keyboard. It was marketed to amateur players who could not afford to buy or were not willing to shell out the money required to buy a traditional piano. In addition to keyboards, the electronic musical instrument division was eventually involved in manufacturing such products as digital synthesizers, guitar synthesizers, digital horns, and other sound generators. One of the Kashio brothers, Toshio, was responsible for the company's move into electronic instruments. He had been interested in mass-marketing musical instruments for a while, but manufacturing costs were too steep. New chip technology that was developed in the late 1970s, however, made cheaper electronic instruments possible.

U.S. sales of electronic keyboards began to take off in the mid-1980s. In 1983 the total number sold in the United States numbered less than 300,000. By 1987, American consumers bought close to five million. Most of these were low-end instruments, retailing for less than $300. By the end of the decade, Casio had captured roughly 55 percent of the electronic instrument market. Its pianos were principally low-cost products, but they provided lots of effects. With digital sampling and memory, keyboards could store dozens of sounds, songs, and patterns. Musical products suffered from potential market saturation, however, and the company lavished millions on advertising in order to keep its products fresh in consumers' minds. After an initial surge in sales, the company began to market enhanced or new lines of products to maintain market demand. During the late 1980s Casio began working to expand its musical markets by appealing to professional musicians and by developing sound products for use in live performances.

Other new products introduced during the 1980s included pocket-sized LCD televisions (1983), a Japanese-language

Key Dates:

1946: Kashio family founds Kashio Manufacturing in Tokyo.

1957: Company introduces the first purely electric small calculator; incorporates as CASIO Computer Co., Ltd.

1965: Casio introduces the first desktop electronic calculator with a memory.

1972: Casio Mini, the first calculator for the mass market, debuts.

1974: Company enters the digital watch field with the launch of the Casiotron.

1980: With introduction of the Casiotone 201, Casio begins producing electronic musical instruments.

Late 1980s: Company begins moving much of its manufacturing outside of Japan.

1991: Casio acquires a stake in Asahi Corporation.

1995: Casio's PHS telephone begins commercial service in Japan; company introduces the first mass-market digital camera.

1996: The Cassiopeia handheld PC featuring Windows CE debuts.

1999: Company posts the first full-year loss in its history.

word processor (1985), and portable TV/VCR combination units (1987). In 1988 Casio introduced a new automated data-processing product line. An integrated business system designed to be used without costly programming, Casio referred to the product as an Active Data Processing System (ADPS). It included a processing unit which Casio hoped would create a universal business data format and a data management system. Casio launched full-scale marketing of this new computer in early 1991 and strengthened its sales network.

Since research and development plays a crucial role in the long-term viability of electronic manufacturers, Casio has consistently devoted about 4 percent of its annual sales revenues to research and development. Among the innovations pursued by Casio was COF (chip-on-film) technology, a method of mounting information on a computer chip that allows increased functional capabilities in lighter and thinner settings. The company adapted COF technology for use in electronic calculators, digital diaries, and printers. The company also began to incorporate this technology into smaller and lighter watches, LCD televisions, computers, and memory cards. In 1990 the company set up a subsidiary, Casio Electronic Devices, to promote the sale of its chip-on-film and LCD components.

Continued Innovation in the 1990s and into the 21st Century

Casio attempted to expand its markets not only through technical enhancements and new product lines, but it also moved aggressively to increase the scope of its operations by expanding internationally. The company began to move some of its manufacturing facilities outside of Japan, to combat the expense of the strong Japanese yen. Casio first opened plants in nearby Taiwan

and Hong Kong. Then in 1990, the company opened plants in California and in Mexico. Both Casio Manufacturing Corporation in San Diego and Casio Electromex in Tijuana were devoted to producing electronic musical instruments.

In 1991 Casio acquired an interest in the Asahi Corporation, a manufacturer of electronic appliances, calculators, and telephone answering machines, and began to diversify into new and promising product areas. It developed a "personal digital assistant" (PDA) with the Tandy Corporation, a small computer that could interface with traditional personal computers, as well as recognize handwriting and send e-mail. Casio's digital diaries became extremely popular with children in the mid-1990s. These handheld devices combined traditional datebook function—calendar, alarm clock, phone directory, memo pad—with functions of immense appeal to school-age consumers, including fortune-telling, secret passwords, a matchmaking adviser, and the "virtual pet." When the user pressed the "pet" button, a puppy would appear on the screen and do tricks. Casio's diaries were such a hit that production had to expand 20 percent in 1994 to keep up with demand. Later models had built-in infrared beam technology that allowed users to send messages to friends' diaries.

Sales of the diaries helped Casio increase its revenues in Japan in 1994, but the strong yen continued to cut into the profitability of the company's exports. Casio increased the amount of its manufacturing that was done overseas in order to combat this trend. While only 30 percent of Casio's production was overseas in 1993, two years later 80 percent of the company's products were made in foreign plants. By 1996 Casio had plants in Singapore, Malaysia, Thailand, and Korea, in addition to its Hong Kong, Taiwan, and North American plants.

Casio began to expand into mainland China as well. In 1993, the company set up two joint ventures in China to manufacture pagers and other electronic devices, and in 1995 two more manufacturing and marketing joint ventures were established in China. Casio Electronics Co. in Zhongshan made electronic diaries and scientific calculators, and another company in Zhuhai produced electronic keyboards. This gave Casio another lower-cost Asian base for manufacturing and also gave the company a foothold in the Chinese consumer market, which was expected to grow markedly. Casio also began marketing pagers in India, under a joint agreement with Mitsui and the Indian company Bharti Telecom, beginning in 1995.

Casio found a promising new market in the mid-1990s as a result of deregulation of telecommunications in Japan. Pagers had not been allowed for sale directly to consumers until March 1995. This changed as part of a liberalization of Japan's telecommunications industry, and Casio experienced record growth in its pager sales. In what seemed a typical move for Casio, which had enjoyed great success with kids' electronics in other areas, the company introduced a pager aimed at schoolchildren. Its "Bell-Me" pager translated telephone signals into text messages coupled with various happy or sad faces. Casio also developed a small mobile telephone it called the "personal handy-phone system" (PHS), which began commercial service in July 1995. This was similar to the digital mobile phones already in use in the United States. The PHS was tailored to the Japanese urban environment. It required an antenna within 100 to 300 meters, but it functioned ideally in Japan's densely populated cities.

Other telecommunications devices Casio marketed in the mid-1990s included the videophone. Previous videophones had been unsuitable for general consumers because of high cost and poor quality. Only large businesses with complex digital networks in place had been able to use videophones with success. Casio began marketing a home-use videophone in 1995 that was reasonably priced and worked well on regular analog telephone circuits. Consumers did not have to change their phone lines in order to use the new phones.

Casio also introduced a low-cost digital camera in 1995. Like the videophone, the digital camera had been used in the corporate world but was previously not convenient for the general public. Casio introduced a moderately priced, pocket-sized model that could be used by consumers with a personal computer. Although the quality of the pictures was not nearly the equal of standard film-based photographs, the Casio camera offered its users an instant view of the picture just taken via an LCD screen on the back of the camera. An unwanted shot could be immediately deleted. Priced around $500, Casio's digital camera was an instant hit, and by mid-1997 the company was churning out more than 80,000 units per month. Even with the quick entrance of numerous competitors, Casio still held 47 percent of the Japanese market at that time.

Another hot product for Casio in the mid-1990s was its G-Shock line of shock-resistant watches. First introduced in 1983, the watches became a craze in the mid-1990s both in Japan and in other developed countries, particularly among younger people. By early 1998, some 500 different models had been introduced and more than 19 million units had been sold.

Casio teamed up with Microsoft Corporation to develop the Cassiopeia handheld PC, which was launched in North America in November 1996. The device featured an operating system called Windows CE, a scaled-down version of Microsoft's Windows. In June 1998 the Cassiopeia E-10 was introduced into North America. This was a palm-sized model, again running on Windows CE, and featuring pen-based operations and a variety of software applications, including personal calendars and contact databases. The Cassiopeia and other handhelds using Windows CE proved to be no match for the sleeker, more lightweight, and simpler-to-use personal digital assistants introduced by Palm Inc., which held almost 80 percent of the handheld market in the late 1990s. Various Windows CE handhelds as a group garnered only a 10 percent share.

Meanwhile, Casio continued to develop high-tech wristwatches and increasingly emphasized wireless capabilities in new products. The PC Cross watch debuted in June 1998, featuring the ability to transmit data to and from PCs using infrared technology. One year later, Casio introduced the world's first wristwatch with a built-in global positioning system (GPS) function, a product aimed particularly at hikers wanting to know their exact location at all times. Unfortunately, a sharp decline in sales for the once-hot G-Shock series of watches helped contribute to the company's dismal results for the fiscal year ending in March 1999. Casio posted the first loss in its entire history, a net loss of ¥8.53 billion ($70.5 million) on net sales of ¥451.14 billion ($3.73 billion). Other factors in the decline included a falloff in sales of pagers and PHS handsets due to the rapid growth of cellular telephone services and a sharp rise in the value of the yen, which made Japanese exports more expensive in the United States, leading to sales declines there. Casio initiated restructuring efforts and inventory writedowns during that fiscal year, taking charges of ¥14.64 billion ($121 million).

Casio returned to the black in fiscal 2000, posting net income of ¥6.17 billion ($58.2 million) on revenues of ¥410.34 billion ($3.87 billion). Among the initiatives taken that year were the formation of a number of alliances in the areas of mobile and wireless technologies. Continuing its collaboration with Microsoft, Casio unveiled the Cassiopeia EM-500, which featured Microsoft's retooled operating system, dubbed Pocket PC, as well as software for the wireless streaming of video. In December 1999 Casio entered into an alliance with a unit of Siemens AG of Germany for the development of a next-generation Pocket PC that would include multimedia, wireless Internet, and mobile telephone capabilities. Casio next agreed to jointly develop what it called a "mobile e-mail terminal" with Vodafone AirTouch Plc of the United Kingdom. New products released by Casio around the turn of the millennium included the Wrist Audio Player, a wristwatch that could also play MP3 audio files downloaded from the Internet; and the Wrist Camera, a wristwatch that doubled as a digital camera, taking postage-stamp-sized black-and-white pictures, which could be transferred to a PC via an infrared adapter. During fiscal 2000, Casio also entered the highly competitive market for digital cellular handsets, attempting to differentiate its model by touting its water and shock resistance.

Throughout the 1990s and into the 21st century, Casio had shown its strength in translating new technology into desirable consumer items. Casio's genius was for making high-tech electronics into small, light, cheap, and intriguing gadgets. It had done this with calculators, watches, keyboards, digital diaries, digital cameras, and handheld computers. The company believed it was positioned for long-term growth using this strategy coupled with an emphasis on mobile and wireless technologies.

Principal Subsidiaries

DOMESTIC: Yamagata Casio Co., Ltd.; Casio Micronics Co., Ltd. (93.2%); Aichi Casio Co., Ltd.; Casio Electronic Manufacturing Co., Ltd.; Kochi Casio Co., Ltd.; Kofu Casio Co., Ltd.; Casio Techno Co., Ltd.; Casio Information Systems Co., Ltd. (99.4%); The Casio Lease Co., Ltd.; Casio Electronic Devices Co., Ltd.; Asahi Corporation (89.4%). EUROPE: Casio Electronics Co., Ltd. (U.K.); Casio Computer Co., GmbH Deutschland (Germany; 60%). ASIA: Casio Computer (Hong Kong) Ltd.; Casio Korea Co., Ltd.; Casio Taiwan Ltd.; Casio (Malaysia) Sdn. Bhd.; Casio Asia Pte., Ltd. (Singapore); Casio India Co., Ltd. (91%); Casio Electronics (Zhuhai) Co., Ltd. (China; 66%); Casio Electronics (Zhondshan) Co., Ltd. (China; 70%); Casio Electronics (Shenzhen) Co., Ltd. (China); Casio Electronics (Guangzhou) Co., Ltd. (China; 53%); Asahi Electronics (Singapore) Pte., Ltd.; Asahi Electronics (Thailand) Co., Ltd.; Asahi Industries (Malaysia) Sdn. Bhd. NORTH AMERICA: Casio Holdings, Inc. (U.S.A.); Casio, Inc. (U.S.A.; 80%); Casio Soft, Inc. (U.S.A.; 72.8%); Casio Canada Ltd.; Casio Manufacturing Corporation (U.S.A.); Casio Electromex S.A. de C.V. (Mexico).

Principal Competitors

Hitachi, Ltd.; Fujitsu Limited; Mitsubishi Electric Corporation; NEC Corporation; Matsushita Electric Corporation; Mitsubishi Electric Corporation; Sharp Corporation; Sony Corporation; The Swatch Group Ltd.; Citizen Watch Co., Ltd.; Seiko Corporation; Timex Corporation; Apple Computer, Inc.; Compaq Computer Corporation; Dell Computer Corporation; Hewlett-Packard Company; Koninklijke Philips Electronics N.V.; Canon Inc.; Eastman Kodak Company; Fuji Photo Film Co., Ltd.; Minolta Co., Ltd.; Nikon Corporation; Olympus Optical Co., Ltd.; Palm, Inc.; Motorola, Inc.; Oki Electric Industry Company Limited; Ricoh Company, Ltd.; SANYO Electric Co., Ltd.; Yamaha Corporation.

Further Reading

Alpert, Bill, "Hand-to-Hand Combat," *Barron's,* November 13, 2000, pp. V8, V10.

"Casio: A Halt in Its Fast Growth Prompts a Move into New Fields," *Business Week,* July 27, 1981, pp. 50 l .

Cignarella, Patricia, "Casio's Quest to Become the Pied Piper," *Adweek's Marketing Week,* January 16, 1989, p. 24.

Cottrell, Robert, "Casio Spearheads Printer Revolution," *Financial Times,* October 11, 1984, p. 26.

"Digital Snap," *Economist,* August 30, 1997, pp. 49–50.

Holyoke, Larry, William Spindle, and Neil Gross, "Doing the Unthinkable," *Business Week,* January 10, 1994, pp. 52–53.

Tanikawa, Miki, "The Clock Is Ticking at Casio," *Business Week,* April 20, 1998, p. 25.

—Timothy E. Sullivan
—updates: A. Woodward, David E. Salamie

Christian Dalloz SA

147, rue de Paris
94227 Charenton-le-Pont Cedex
France
Telephone: (+33) 1-49-77-42-54
Fax: (+33) 1-49-77-44-26
Web site: http://www.cdalloz.com

Public Company
Incorporated: 1958
Employees: 1,500
Sales: EUR 256.3 million (FFr 1.68 billion) ($240
   million) (2000)
Stock Exchanges: Euronext Paris
Ticker Symbol: DAL
NAIC: 339113 Hard Hats Manufacturing; 339115
   Ophthalmic Goods Manufacturing; 327215 Glass
   Product Manufacturing Made of Purchased Glass

Christian Dalloz SA is one of the world's leading manufacturers of protective equipment for the work environment. The company and its subsidiaries produce safety and protection products ranging from eyewear to fall protection equipment; through its Sunoptics subsidiary, the company also produces lenses for sunglasses. Based in France's Jura region, Dalloz has built up a diversified, international portfolio of subsidiaries and products, including: WGM Safety Corp., based in the United States; Bilsom, based in Sweden; the company's founding Christian Dalloz Sunoptics operations in France; and such late 1990s and early 2000s acquisitions as Germany's Söll, the European leader in high-access equipment; and Fendall Company, based in the United States, the world's leading manufacturer of portable emergency ocular wash equipment, acquired in August 2000. More than 95 percent of the company's annual sales, which topped EUR 250 million in 2000, come from the United States and Europe. The United States accounts for the largest share of sales, at 64 percent. Fall protection products represent the largest single product category, at 40 percent of the company's sales, while head protection—including hearing protection, protective filters, eye protection, and hard hats and other head protection—combines to contribute 57 percent of sales. The company's Sunoptics sunglass lenses add just 3 percent to Christian Dalloz's revenues. Listed on the Euronext Paris stock exchange, the company remains majority controlled by holding company Financière Christian Dalloz, itself held by Ginette Dalloz, widow of the company's founder, and French optical products manufacturer Essilor.

Plastics to Polycarbonates in the 1960s

Christian Dalloz established the company that was to bear his name in 1958 as a small manufacturer of injection-molded plastic products. During the 1960s, however, the company began to specialize in eyewear, particularly sun protection lenses. Developing its own lenses, Christian Dalloz launched its first organic lenses in 1970. In the early 1970s, however, the company's development interests turned toward new, stronger polycarbonate materials. The company's research and development efforts enabled it to trademark its own Cridalon polycarbonate. Dalloz's lenses were quickly adopted by many of the leading sunglass manufacturers. The company continued to develop new features and specifications to maintain its position as a high-end provider of sunglass lenses. In 1982, Christian Dalloz introduced a new anti-scratch protective coating.

The company remained modest-sized into the mid-1980s. In 1985, however, the company laid out a new growth strategy based on the diversification of its product lines and the internationalization of its activity. The company's polycarbonate lenses and its background in sun protection led it to look for growth in the work safety equipment market. Christian Dalloz also made its first foreign moves, setting up a new subsidiary, Société Tunisienne de Lunetterie, giving it a foothold in French-speaking North Africa.

To fund its expansion moves, Christian Dalloz went public in 1986, listing on the secondary market of the Lyons stock exchange. That listing was later transferred to the Paris stock exchanges, after France's regional stock exchanges were merged into the Paris Bourse, which itself became part of the Euronext stock exchange partnership at the end of the century. Joining the company was another fast-growing, and closely

Company Perspectives:

Christian Dalloz is a serious business partner in a serious business, protecting the quality of life. Personal safety is a global issue and it calls for a company with a global perspective and a large pool of resources to meet all the challenges.

related, French company, Essilor International. The two companies entered a strategic agreement, giving Essilor a minority stake in Christian Dalloz, with an option to take over the company after founder Dalloz, who had no children, retired. Meanwhile, Christian Dalloz, which sought to expand deeper into the occupational safety sector, began preparing to make an acquisition that was to transform the company into an important player in a soon-to-be consolidated global industry.

That acquisition came in 1989, when Christian Dalloz made a successful bid to acquire 100 percent of WGM Safety Corp. in the United States. The acquisition of the far larger, and more diversified, company gave Christian Dalloz immediate access to the vast North American market, the largest market for occupational safety equipment. The WGM Safety acquisition gave the company a line of products including fall protection equipment, such as harnesses and straps; protective gloves and shoes; hard hats and other protective headgear; breathing filters and equipment; and ear protection, under the well-known Miller and Willson brands.

Not only did the WGM purchase greatly expand Dalloz's arena of operations, it also shifted the company's geographical focus—by 1990, more than 90 percent of the company's revenues came from North America. The company also had taken a prime place in the worldwide safety equipment market, with revenues boosted to past FFr 350 million. The WGM purchase had other repercussions for Christian Dalloz, particularly in the creation of a new holding company, Financière Christian Dalloz, in which Essilor took a one-third minority stake.

Expansion: 1990s–2001

The far larger company almost immediately stubbed its toe. The beginning of a recession in the United States, further exacerbated by the outbreak of war in the Persian Gulf, saw the company extremely exposed to the collapse of its U.S. market. With its revenues slipping some 40 percent, and profits plunging as well, the company also faced a huge debt burden—much of which was subject to an 11 percent interest rate. At the same time, Dalloz attempted to enter a new market, turning its expertise in manufacturing lenses to making intra-ocular implants in 1991. This move required the company to invest heavily in new manufacturing equipment, as well as in marketing and distributing its new line of products. Yet the company's entry proved ill-timed, as competition and other factors sent prices for ocular implants into a downward spiral. Dalloz was forced to exit that market by 1992.

By then, Dalloz also marred by tragedy, after founder Christian Dalloz was killed in an automobile accident in May 1991. The company fell into the hands of Dalloz's widow, Ginette,

who took up a temporary position as company president. Soon after, the company named a new president, Philippe Alfroid, to continue its late founder's drive for expansion. Despite the company's troubles at the start of the decade, its long-term prospects remained solid. The company was able to count on its strong shareholding—Mme. Dalloz maintained the family's majority control of the company, while ally Essilor International's 39 percent in Financière Christian Dalloz, and 10 percent of voting rights, gave the company protection from any threat of a hostile takeover.

Dalloz also sought to shore up its slipping sales in its now crucial U.S. market by rolling out new products, particularly by broadening its product line. Where WGM Safety had long held the leading position in the U.S. market for high-end protective gear, the company now began to introduce products to give it a rising share of the larger market for mid-range equipment.

Dalloz also was helped by a growing trend toward tighter legislation governing safety in the workplace in the United States, a trend that was shortly to spread overseas with the European Community preparing for the coming economic union. As the U.S. economy returned to the growth track, by 1994, Dalloz saw its revenues on the rise again. Toward the end of 1994, however, Christian Dalloz looked to a new acquisition to boost its scale.

The company's vulnerability to cycles in the U.S. economy—where it continued to register more than 80 percent of its profits—encouraged it to seek greater geographical balance. In October 1994, the company found a promising counterweight to its North American operations when it reached an agreement to acquire hearing protection specialist Bilsom, based in Sweden and held through a subsidiary of the Wallenberg group, for FFr 107 million. The purchase more than doubled Christian Dalloz's revenues—nearly FFr 800 million in the first full year after Bilsom's consolidation—and raised its European operations to nearly 30 percent of its total sales. Bilsom also helped balance Dalloz's product line, giving it a fourth major category of protective equipment operations.

The company benefited from new legislation passed in the United States controlling fall protection standards in the workplace, which saw Dalloz's fall protection sales jump in 1995. The company also saw new growth in its sunglass lens division, after it acquired a small Italian company specializing in lenses for the mid- and high-end sunglasses market. The acquisition helped Dalloz reorient its sunglass lenses sales and attract new interest among the world's major sunglasses manufacturers. By 1995, the company's lenses sales had expanded by more than 50 percent.

In 1996, the company restructured its operations around its three principal activities: head protection, fall protection, and lenses for sunglasses. These were placed under the new divisions Dalloz Safety, Dalloz Fall Protection, and Dalloz Sunoptics, respectively. The company then returned to the acquisition table, buying up two British companies, Pulsafe Safety Products and Troll. Although these acquisitions were less spectacular than the WGM and Bilsom acquisitions, they nevertheless boosted the company's product range for eye protection and extended into safety rescue and sports equipment.

Key Dates:

1958: Christian Dalloz founds plastics company.
1970: Company begins production of lenses for sunglasses.
1974: Company switches lenses production to polycarbonates.
1982: Company launches scratch-resistant protective coating.
1985: Company develops expansion strategy; creates Société Tunisienne de Lunetterie.
1986: Company is listed on Lyons Bourse secondary market; shareholder agreement is made with Essilor International.
1989: WGM Safety Corp. (U.S.A.) is acquired.
1991: Company enters market for intra-ocular implants; Christian Dalloz dies in automobile accident.
1993: Bilsom (Sweden) is acquired.
1996: Core businesses undergo reorganization; Pulsafe Safety Products and Troll (U.K.) are acquired.
1997: Komet (France) is acquired.
1998: Moxham (Australia) is acquired; restructuring of industrial park begins.
1999: Söll (Germany) is acquired.
2000: Fendall Company (U.S.A.) is acquired.

Christian Dalloz continued to add new acquisitions to its portfolio. In 1997, the company paid £2.4 million to U.K.-based Blagden Industries for its French operations, Komet. The move enabled Blagden to concentrate on and expand its core chemicals operations, while transferring the Komet protective equipment operations and brand to Dalloz. In that year, Essilor increased its holding in the company beyond the 33 percent mark, which normally was required by French law to trigger a full-scale takeover offer. Essilor and Ginette Dalloz reached a shareholder's agreement, however, in which each was given the right to acquire any of Dalloz's shares the other might put up for sale, allowing Dalloz to remain independent.

Dalloz then continued its expansion, buying up Australia's Moxham in 1998, boosting the company's fall protection assets and giving it new access to the Australian and New Zealand markets. In that year, also, the company prepared to resolve lawsuits brought against its subsidiaries in Texas, which threatened to approach FFr 40 million in settlement costs, while depressing Dalloz's stock price.

As the worldwide market began to move toward consolidation, Dalloz determined to be among the industry's major players. Increasing its European position, the company acquired Germany's Söll, the leading manufacturer of high-access safety equipment. That acquisition strengthened the share of European sales, adding nearly FFr 200 million. The following year, Dalloz returned to the buying trail, when it purchased Fendall Company, based in Illinois, one of the industry leaders in the manufacture of portable emergency eyewash equipment. The Fendall acquisition, which cost the company $17 million, fitted neatly into Dalloz's extensive range of protective eye equipment.

Entering 2001, Dalloz engaged on a restructuring of its industrial base, a process begun in 1998, which included the shutting of several facilities to concentrate its production and the installation of a computerized system across its worldwide activities—the company's products were now present in more than 75 countries. While continuing to seek new acquisitions, Dalloz also started the new century focused on three main priorities, continued restructuring of its production facilities; launch of new product innovations; growing dominance in the consolidating protective equipment industry.

Principal Subsidiaries

WGM Safety Corp.; Willson Fall; Christian Dalloz Sunoptics; Financière Dalloz Christian; Miller-Dalloz Fall Protection.

Principal Competitors

Abatix Corp.; Bacou USA, Inc.; Lakeland Industries, Inc.; Mine Safety Appliances Company; Vallen Corporation; Worksafe Industries Inc.

Further Reading

"Blagden to Expand with Komet Cash," *Independent,* May 2, 1997, p. 26.
"Christian Dalloz change de dimension," *Les Echos,* August 3, 1994 p. 6.
"Christian Dalloz joue la carte de la croissance externe," *Les Echos,* June 26, 1995 p. 15.
Le Masson, Thomas, "Christian Dalloz optimiste pour l'exercice 2000," *Les Echos,* June 9, 2000 p. 18.
——, "Christian Dalloz souffre d'un manque de visibilité," *Les Echos,* June 25, 1999 p. 12.
Texier, Michel, "Des perspectives positives pour Christian Dalloz," *La Tribune,* May 2, 1995.

—M. L. Cohen

Christofle

Christofle SA

9 rue Royale
75008 Paris
France
Telephone: (+33) 1 49 22 40 00
Fax: (+33) 1 48 09 33 65
Web site: http://www.christofle.com

Private Company
Incorporated: 1930
Sales: EUR 113.8 million ($105 million) (2000 est.)
NAIC: 3322 Cutlery and Handtool Manufacturing;
   332211 Cutlery and Flatware (Except Precious)
   Manufacturing; 339912 Silverware and Hollowware
   Manufacturing; 327112 Vitreous China, Fine
   Earthenware, and Other Pottery Product
   Manufacturing

Christofle SA commands respect worldwide for its luxury table service products, including the company's traditional silverware lines and extending to include nearly all items found on and around the well-to-do dining table, including porcelain dishes and linen napkins and tablecloths. Founded in 1830, Christofle remains under the guidance—and ownership—of the founding family, now represented by Maurizio Borletti. Christofle operates manufacturing facilities in France and Brazil, as well as its own retail distribution network, including 75 Pavillon Christofle retail stores and 400 Christofle in-store boutiques placed in larger department stores and home decoration and related specialty shops. Christofle has always been known for its innovative designs and its willingness to commission new designs from noted artists and designers. After producing a line of table service designed by Christian Lacroix in the late 1990s, Christofle has turned to Christian Dior for a new series of designs beginning in 2001. Christofle, formerly listed on the Paris stock exchange, was taken private in 1998 as Borletti and the company's other major shareholders agreed to assume 100 percent ownership of Christofle into a new holding company, Luxury Brand Development, created in Luxembourg and intended to allow the group to invest in other luxury goods companies without compromising the Christofle name. Borletti, seconded by CEO Thierry Fritsch, hopes to build the company, which posted an estimated EUR 113.8 million in sales in 2000, into a strong rival for such larger competitors as Tiffany and Waterford.

Luxury Pioneer in the 19th Century

The Christofle family began their manufacturing career as makers of sequins and jewelry components at the end of the 18th century. The family soon extended their production to include such diverse products as mother-of-pearl and gold buttons, silver-threaded cloth, epaulettes for French army officers' uniforms, as well as jewelry. The Christofle name was already associated with a certain degree of innovation, as the family was awarded a number of patents during the early years of the 19th century. Among the family's businesses was a jewelry workshop located in Paris's Marais quarter. Sales by the end of the 1820s reached FFr 300,000.

The start of Christofle's worldwide fame came in 1830, when Charles Christofle, then 25, took over as head of the Marais enterprise. Charles Christofle was backed by his elder sister Rosine, who had married Joseph Bouilhet, a wealthy French notable. With the far older Bouilhet's wealth, Christofle began to expand his company. From the start, Christofle looked toward the international arena. Among the company's commissions were the crown for Queen Ranavallo of Madagascar and a series of ceremonial swords produced for customers throughout Latin America. By the end of his first decade as head of the family firm, Christofle had driven sales to more than FFr 2 million.

The company continued to manufacture its traditional range of products. The death of Joseph Bouilhet in 1837 left his widow Rosine Christofle-Bouilhet in charge of the family's fortunes. Charles Christofle himself became part of that fortune when his older sister persuaded her daughter to marry her much older uncle. Rosine Bouilhet's other child, Henri, just seven years old at the time of his father's death, was to play a still more central role in the development of the family empire.

In the 1840s Charles Christofle led the family business into a new direction that was to establish the company's name worldwide. In 1842, Christofle acquired the exclusive rights to exploit a series of patents held by Count Henri de Ruolz and British goldsmiths Georges and Richard Elkington. The patents detailed a method of silver- and gold-plating using electrolysis—a radical departure from traditional silver- and gold-plating methods, which used mercury and were both time-consuming and highly toxic.

By 1845, Christofle had opened a manufacturing facility dedicated to the new plating techniques, placing the whole of the family business's future on the success or failure of this new endeavor. Christofle's factory marked one of the first uses of electricity as a production tool. Christofle's technique enabled the plating of a wider variety of objects than ever before, and permitted the application of plating to more common—and less expensive—metals. At the beginning, however, Christofle preferred to establish a reputation for high-quality, limiting his activities to plating works created by other gold and silversmiths.

Yet Christofle found few customers for his plating techniques. Indeed, the company was quickly confronted by a growing number of counterfeit products. Backed by the Bouilhet fortune, Christofle successfully defended his exclusive patent rights before the French tribunals. Christofle also began adding a trademark to his products, a guarantee to his customers of the quality of the silver used for his plated objects. Christofle had already established the company's silver plating to a far higher percentage—92.5 percent—of silver than his competitors. Meanwhile, unable to find commissions for his plating technique, Christofle decided to launch the family into the production of its own line of products.

In 1846, Christofle extended his factory's production to include a variety of objects, especially related to table service. In this, Christofle seemed to have captured the spirit of the times, as a rising class of French bourgeoisie began to aspire to similar luxuries as the country's fading nobility. The so-called "arts de la table" suddenly became part of the required dining room furnishings. Christofle offered the new middle-class silverware and table service with the same commitment to quality but far less expensive than traditionally crafted silver items. Before long, the Christofle name became something of a generic name for silver-plate.

The company received a strong boost when Christofle became the official provider of table service for King Louis-Philippe and the entire House of Orléans. In 1850, the company received a new and important benefactor when Louis-Napoléon Bonaparte commissioned Christofle to produce a table service for the Palais de l'Elysée. Christofle's relationship with Bona-

parte continued after the later became known as Emperor Napoleon III. Christofle's official titles of "Goldsmith to the King" and the "Emperor's Provider" provided the company with the foundation with which to achieve a new international expansion. Founding a factory in Karlruhe, Germany, the company began providing such foreign dignitaries as the Kaiser of Germany and the royal households of the Austro-Hungarian Empire, the Ottoman Empire, and the Tsar of Russia.

Christofle also proved to have a strong commercial sense. Hiring a dedicated sales staff, Christofle arranged a number of contracts with retailers worldwide. In exchange for giving a merchant the exclusive right to sell Christofle's products in a particular town, Christofle claimed space in the merchant's street-side shop windows—while the retailer agreed to carry only Christofle's line of table service in his shop. At this time, Christofle also established the Pavillon Christofle retail store in Paris.

Charles Christofle was joined by nephew/brother-in-law Henri Bouilhet in 1852. The new generation—Henri Bouilhet took over the business when Christofle died in 1863—expanded the company's business and firmly established the business's industrial approach to luxury goods, a departure from the traditional artisan-based industry of the time. Bouilhet was not only a shrewd businessman, but an astute engineer; working with Hermann von Jacobi, of Saint Petersburg, he invented a new method of plating not only silver and gold, but bronze, copper, and other metals as well. The new method, called galvanizing, permitted Christofle to begin producing more monumental works. Among the company's most notable productions were the gold-plated bronze winged statues at the Opéra Garnier in Paris, the railroad car for Pope Pius IX, and a ten-meter tall statue for the Notre Dame de la Garde church of Marseilles.

Changing Fortunes in the 20th Century

The period leading up to World War I represented something of a peak for the Christofle name. The collapse of a great deal of Europe's royalty after the war and the Soviet revolution saw the company lose a large portion of its business. Seeking capital, the company listed on the Paris stock exchange in 1926. Yet the company was soon after hit hard by the Depression, which helped to wipe out much of its remaining customer base. Regrouped under Tony Bouilhet, Henri Bouilhet's grandson, the company shut down its German factory and other foreign operations and transferred all of its manufacturing operations to its Saint Denis, Paris factory.

One of the more fortuitous decisions made by Tony Bouilhet was his marriage to Carla Borletti, a member of a wealthy Milan-based family. In 1930, Christofle was reincorporated as a public limited company, becoming Christofle SA and taking on the Borletti family as major shareholders and important financial backers into the next century. Carla Borletti was not merely a source of new capital for the company, she also proved inspirational in building a new generation of Christofle renown.

Borletti brought in a whole new breed of designers, calling upon many of the Art Deco period's great names to recreate the Christofle image. At the same time, Borletti helped establish a new retail concept for the brand, using the Pavillon Christofle name established by Charles Christofle in the mid-1800s. The company began opening its first foreign branches of the Pavillon Christofle retail chain. The Borletti family's sponsorship enabled Christofle to convince its banks to provide new investment capital. By the dawn of World War II, the company had put its financial problems behind it.

If the war years presented a new interruption to Christofle's growth, the great economic expansion of the postwar period helped the company achieve a new scale of international expansion. Now led by Albert Bouilhet and his brothers Henri and Marc, Christofle once again began expanding its manufacturing capacity, opening manufacturing and distribution subsidiaries, including production and distribution subsidiary Sadoga, launched in Buenos Aires, Argentina, in 1950. Other subsidiaries followed, in the United States, Italy, Belgium, and Germany, culminating in the creation of a new Brazilian manufacturing and distribution subsidiary, Pataria Universal SA Brasil, in 1974. The company once again succeeded in establishing an international reputation for its high quality, luxury products. At the same time, Christofle maintained its market leadership in France, where the company represented more than 50 percent of the market.

Sixth Generation for the 21st Century

Christofle remained a profitable company through the high-flying 1980s. Yet the company's attempt to diversify during the decade nearly brought it disaster. Christofle attempted to join the rising brand label awareness of the period by attaching its name to a variety of products, including a line of wristwatches and jewelry. At the same time, the company continued to produce its core product line of highly priced dining table products, such as a $30,000 tea service and similarly priced place settings. The collapse of the world economy at the end of the 1980s caught the company short. By the beginning of the 1990s, Christofle saw its sales shrink and its profits slip into the red. The company attempted to restructure, cutting out more than 150 jobs, adding to its burdens with some FFr 50 million in restructuring costs. By 1992, the company's losses had topped

FFr 39.5 million for the year and its level of short-term debt had topped FFr 200 million—a heavy load for a company with just FFr 620 million in sales.

Christofle once again looked to its Italian benefactors. In 1993, Albert Bouilhet tapped first cousin Maurizio Borletti to take over leadership of the flagging family-controlled company. Borletti, then only 26 years old, had already proved himself in business. At the age of 18, Borletti had borrowed $20,000 from his father, who ran a company manufacturing clocks for automobile dashboards, and started his own construction business. After his father's death four years later, Borletti took over his family's business, while also managing the Borletti family's investment portfolio.

Borletti agreed to step over to Christofle, paying $10 million to acquire a 55 percent stake in the company. Borletti then set to work restructuring the company, including imposing new cutbacks on its staff. The most important change Borletti made to the company was a refocus on the company's core tableware production, shedding attempts to diversify into other product categories.

Christofle instead diversified within its core business, adding new lines of products to expand the company's production to include the wider range of table service items, such as porcelain serving dishes, china, and table linens. Rather than simply attaching its label to products produced by licensed manufacturers, Christofle now brought control of its diversified range in-house, guaranteeing the same commitment to quality the company brought to its table service.

Borletti boosted the company's advertising budget, adopting modern-style publicity campaigns for a company that had long relied primarily on its world-renowned name. The company also launched new designs, once again turning to outside artists. Such was the case with a line of table service designed by Christian Lacroix, launched in 1997.

On the retail side, Christofle began stepping up the opening of new Pavillon Christofle stores, entering new markets around the world. By the end of the century, the company operated 75 retail stores and had placed Christofle boutiques in another 400 stores, giving it retail representation in 120 countries. The company's retail customers also were more likely to find something to buy—no matter the budget. Taking a page from far-larger rival Tiffany, Christofle launched new lines of more democratically priced products—such as $40 chopsticks—to accompany its continued production of high-end silver- and gold-plated products.

Christofle's return to profits and sales growth was aided by new financial trends in the 1990s. The booming economies in a number of Asian markets had created new classes of luxury goods shoppers. At the same time, Christofle benefitted from the strong economic recovery in the United States—as well as from the sudden explosion of so-called "Internet millionaires." The new ranks of nouveaux riches quickly turned to Christofle for their silverware needs.

By the end of 2000, Maurizio Borletti had given Christofle a new future. The company's sales had seen steady growth in the late 1990s, topping FFr 750 million (EUR 113 million) in 2000.

Borletti's control of the company had also become more solid. In 1998, Borletti led the company's other major investors— primarily other family members—in the creation of a holding company registered in Luxembourg, Luxury Brand Development (LBD), which took 100 percent control of Christofle, removing it from the stock market. LBD represented a new vehicle with which to achieve Christofle's continued interest in diversifying into the wider luxury goods arena; this time, however, the Christofle name was placed in safekeeping as the group explored acquisitions of other brand names.

Christofle entered the new century in good economic health and with strong growth prospects. In 2001, the company commissioned a new line of designs from famed Parisian fashion leader Christian Dior, a move certain to increase Christofle's position in the world tableware market. Meanwhile, Maurizio Borletti continued to expand his vision of the company's future. As he told *Forbes*, "We want to be the Gucci . . . the Hermes of our business." After 170 years and a place in world history, Christofle seemed to have recaptured its youth.

Principal Subsidiaries

Argenteria Christofle spa (Italy); Pavillon Christofle.

Principal Competitors

Brown-Forman Corporation; Corning Incorporated; Guy Degrenne SA; International Cutlery, Ltd.; Lifetime Hoan Corporation; Mikasa, Inc.; Noritake Co., Limited; Oneida Ltd.; Royal Doulton plc; Swiss Army Brands, Inc.; Taittinger S.A.; Waterford Wedgwood plc; WKI Holding Company, Inc.

Further Reading

Berman, Phyliss, "Polishing the Family Silver," *Forbes*, July 6, 1998.
Callahan, Michael, "Turning the Tables," *Success*, December 1998, p. 34.
"Christofle gravit la 'route du luxe,'" *Les Echos*, April 27, 1999, p. 49.
"Christofle, l'ancêtre du luxe français," *Les Echos*, December 10, 1996 p. 60.
de Ferrière. Marc, *Christofle, deux siècles d'aventure industrielle,* Paris: Le Monde Editions, 1994.
——, "Entre tradition et modernisme, une aventure exemplaire," *L'Expansion*, December 20, 1993.
"Le Saga Christofle, orfèvre à Paris depuis 1830," Paris: Christofle SA, 2001.

—M. L. Cohen

Chrysalis Group plc

The Chrysalis Building
Bramley Road
London, W10 6SP
United Kingdom
Telephone: 020-7221-2213
Fax: 020-7221-6455
Web site: http://www.chrysalis.com

Public Company
Incorporated: 1968 as Chrysalis Records
Employees: 758
Sales: £168.2 million (2000)
Stock Exchanges: London
Ticker Symbol: CHS
NAIC: 51223 Music Publishers; 513112 Radio Stations;
   51211 Motion Picture and Video Production; 51113
   Book Publishers; 51221 Record Production

Chrysalis Group plc is a U.K.-based media and entertainment company that owns radio stations, produces television programs, sells books, releases music recordings, and controls a large catalog of music copyrights. Originally formed as a record company to issue recordings by such rock groups as Jethro Tull and Procol Harum, Chrysalis sold that operation in the late 1980s to focus on other media endeavors. During the 1990s the company reentered the record business with the newly formed Echo and Pavilion labels. Cofounder Chris Wright still owns more than 25 percent of the publicly traded company.

Beginnings

The Chrysalis Group's origins date to the late 1960s and the rock music business of that era. Chris Wright, 22, and Terry Ellis, 23, were young managers and bookers of music groups who decided to found a talent agency in 1967, which they called Ellis Wright. The pair found success booking bands to play at British colleges, and soon moved their growing business into an office in the West End of London. Two of the bands represented by Ellis Wright were blues-rockers Ten Years After, who would later gain renown for their appearance at the Woodstock rock festival, and the more eccentric Jethro Tull, led by flautist and composer Ian Anderson. Seeking recording opportunities for the groups, Ellis and Wright hit on the idea of forming their own label. They arranged to license the initial discs by the bands to leading independent Island Records, which agreed to give Wright and Ellis their own label if the early releases were hits.

The idea worked, and Chrysalis Records was formed within a year. The company's name was derived from a phonetic amalgam of its founders' names. Other acts, including Procol Harum and Blodwyn Pig, were soon signed, and the label began to take off. The 1970s were a fertile period for Chrysalis, with major success in both Britain and the United States for Tull, and other hits by new artists including Scottish rocker Frankie Miller, electrified folk group Steeleye Span, former Procol Harum guitarist Robin Trower, Leo Sayer, and UFO.

The late 1970s saw the musical landscape change dramatically as a new generation of rockers sporting spiky hair and short, poppy songs emerged to steal the spotlight from the established stars of the day. Chrysalis signed several key members of the so-called punk and new wave movements including Ultravox, Generation X (featuring Billy Idol), and Blondie, and had hits with each. In England, where Jamaican ska and reggae music had been popular for years, homegrown ska bands such as the Specials and Madness were also now gaining fame, and Chrysalis launched a sub-label called 2-Tone to release these acts.

English musical trends came and went swiftly, and punk and new wave were soon followed by the more mannered New Romantic movement. Chrysalis duly signed one of its leading exponents, Spandau Ballet, to the new Reformation imprint. The company also purchased another label, Ensign, which brought in new artists including Sinead O'Connor. By now Chrysalis's U.S. operations were being run in Los Angeles by Terry Ellis, and hits were achieved by Pat Benatar, Huey Lewis & the News, and Billy Idol, among others. It was getting progressively more difficult for independent labels to make an impact, however, and the music industry soon found itself in a period of consolidation. To stay in the game, the label made a deal to distribute its recordings in the United States through Columbia Records, one of the industry's leaders.

In early 1985 Terry Ellis sold his stake in the company to partner Wright, and later that same year Chrysalis went public following a reverse takeover of Management Agency and Music plc (MAM), which was a joint venture of singers Tom Jones and Englebert Humperdinck. An acquisition was also made of music goods wholesaler Lasgo Exports, which became Chrysalis's Media Products division.

The company had also launched a Visual Programming division, and in 1986 this unit landed in the spotlight for its creation of Max Headroom, a computer-animated hipster who briefly had a TV show in America after appearing in a $25 million Coca-Cola ad campaign. Chrysalis's record business was in a slump, however, and the injury of Billy Idol in a motorcycle accident and the controversial, unpopular behavior of Sinead O'Connor further hurt the label's revenues. Diversification was on the horizon, and in 1988 the FIRST Information Group, a producer of software, was acquired. The following year the company got its feet wet in radio, purchasing a 20 percent stake in station chain Metro Radio.

Sale of Record Label, Corporate Rebirth: 1989–94

In 1989 Chris Wright sold 50 percent of the Chrysalis Records label to industry giant Thorn EMI for $73 million plus the assumption of a portion of the company's debt. Thorn EMI received an option to buy the rest at a later date, and did so in 1991, this time paying only $30 million plus $25 million in debt. The last year of joint operation had seen the label's mounting losses cost the Chrysalis Group $8.7 million. The company as a whole was $14.3 million in the red on revenues of $170 million. Chrysalis had lost other money on a television equipment rental company it was operating, which it later shut down. The one bright spot was the music publishing arm, which reported profits of nearly $2 million.

The Chrysalis Group now consisted of only the music publishing business and a coin-operated amusement and vending operation left over from the MAM merger. Wright, who retained ties with Chrysalis Records by serving as non-executive chairman, was required to avoid reentering the record business for two years after the sale, and he now focused on pursuing new business ventures. These included the construction of a London recording studio in partnership with Pioneer Group of Japan, and offering news and entertainment on airliners, including showing the Olympic games aboard planes.

Looking for additional video production and television opportunities, Wright sought a franchise from cable company ITV, though he failed to win one. A music division was created, which would encompass music publishing, recording, and interests in the Hit record label, The Speaking Book Company, and Air/Edel Associates. The company also formed a new branch, Chrysalis Sport, to produce Italian Football games for television.

In August 1993 the company launched a new record label, Echo. Music division head Steve Lewis declared that the new imprint would seek to position itself as a major independent company, much like the original Chrysalis had done. An investment of $17.5 million was made by Pony Canyon, Japan's third largest record company, giving it a 25 percent stake. The year 1993 also saw the sale of FIRST Information Group to that firm's management.

On other fronts, Chrysalis purchased Red Rooster Film and Television Entertainment, bought a stake in the Sheffield Sharks basketball team, and formed a Radio division, run by Richard Huntingford. After winning a license bid, the first station was launched in Birmingham in September 1994 with the company's new adult-oriented rock and pop Heart format. That same year Chrysalis sold its struggling jukebox and vending business MAM Holdings, and released the first records on the Echo label, which had signed a number of performers including Julian Cope and Shaquille O'Neal. Half of a Dutch television production company, IDTV, was also purchased, as was a 49 percent stake in Scala, an independent British film company. The costs of these activities were affecting the bottom line, however, with losses of more than $25 million reported for the year.

Building the Radio Business: 1995–99

Seeking to expand its radio operations in 1995, the company sold its stake in Metro Radio to facilitate bidding on a license to broadcast in Yorkshire, England, and launched a Heart format station in London. Chrysalis also purchased a Welsh company, Bristol Channel Broadcasting, which ran a station that employed the Galaxy format, a dance music mix that was targeted at a younger audience. Chrysalis's television arm grew during the year with 50 percent investments in television production companies Watchmaker, Bentley, Cactus, and Lucky Dog.

The company was still operating in the red, and in 1996 Wright decided to abandon two money-losing operations. The move to close Chrysalis's film production and international film sales divisions was so sudden that two company directors quit in protest. Despite added losses from the record label and radio stations, the company remained committed to seeing them through. During the year Chrysalis also traded its 49.9 percent stake in the Dutch IDTV concern for 50.1 percent of CVI Media, a new television production company formed in conjunction with VNU of the Netherlands.

In 1997 Chrysalis acquired two more radio licenses in Yorkshire and Manchester, England, from Faze FM for approximately £20 million. The Yorkshire station was the same one it had unsuccessfully bid on several years prior. The two stations would be relaunched with the Galaxy music mix. The next year Choice FM in Birmingham was acquired, and was rebranded as a Galaxy station as well. One third of a New Zealand television venture, South Pacific Pictures Investments, Ltd., and a stake in a joint digital radio venture with Border Television were also bought in 1998.

At the end of the 1990s Chrysalis undertook the assessment and evaluation of its full music catalog, a process that took 18 months. A master list of some 50,000 works was generated, and each was checked for the validity of copyright and ownership.

A value of some £150 million was placed on the holdings. Following the lead of rocker David Bowie, who had sold stock in his music copyright company, Chrysalis used part of the catalog as collateral in obtaining a £60 million loan. This was used to pay off existing debt and to finance new ventures in the Internet and other new media categories. During the decade Chrysalis Music had continued to acquire copyrights, including some from its own staff writers, and had opened offices in Paris, Stockholm, Los Angeles, and Nashville. Further copyrights were obtained with the winter 1999 purchase of Global Music of Germany for $8 million. Global owned some 15,000 titles, and controlled the publishing rights for numerous blues and rock classics in Germany, Switzerland, and Austria.

Book Publishing, Recording, and Other Activities: 1999–2001

At the same time, Chrysalis's Media Products division was undergoing a transformation, investing in numerous book publishers including "remainder" distributor Ramboro Books, Brasseys, B.T. Batsford, Salamander, Greenwich Editions, Conway, Putnam, Zig-Zag, and C&B Publishing. Division anchor Lasgo Exports, still run by founder Peter Lassman, was now one of the top three music and video exporters in the United Kingdom.

Despite having occasional hits, the company's record business continued to struggle financially. Wright was determined to persevere, however, and in the summer of 1999 he announced the formation of a new imprint, Papillon, which would handle older artists that were being ignored by mainstream labels. The first signing brought one of the company's earliest successes

back into the fold. Rejoining Wright after nearly a decade away was Jethro Tull, who had been hitless for some time but continued to tour and record. Papillon also signed Sir Cliff Richard, the perennial British pop singer whose career stretched back to the late 1950s.

Chrysalis also began exploring the possibility of using the Internet as a method of transmitting music content, forming a New Media Division and buying 65 percent of Internet radio startup Ride The Tiger and 30 percent of web site host Citipages, among others. The company also helped form the MXR consortium with a host of other companies, and this group won digital radio licenses for large portions of the United Kingdom. A Latin music publishing joint venture, ChrysalisClip Music S.L., was launched in Spain with Ediciones Musicales Clipper's to acquire new material and license Chrysalis works in Spanish-speaking markets. Chrysalis was also operating a Retail Entertainment division, which distributed music videos and set up listening kiosks in stores, among other endeavors.

In the fall of 2000, Richard Huntingford was named Chrysalis Group CEO, reflecting Chris Wright's less direct involvement with the company he had founded. Though he still maintained a strong presence, he was also increasingly involved in his own ventures, which included several athletic teams. At this time Chrysalis was enjoying a 35 percent growth in radio advertising revenues, compared with the 15 percent industry average. The radio group's market capitalization had also doubled during 1999 and 2000. On top of this good news, Chrysalis had an advantage over its three chief competitors in seeking additional radio licenses. Government rules limited acquisitions based on a chain's total audience share, and all but Chrysalis had reached the limit of 15 percent. A new classic rock format, The Arrow, was being prepared as well. On other fronts the stake in the Sheffield Sharks was sold, while the company's television production arm continued to prosper, churning out popular programs such as Midsomer Murders and Formula One for ITV, The Clarkson Show for the BBC, and Channel 4's music series Top Ten. Results for fiscal 2000 were the best ever, with pretax profits of £1 million on revenues of £168.2 million.

After years of building up steam, the Chrysalis Group was finally reaching cruising altitude. With its radio broadcasting, music publishing, and television production divisions leading the way, and new ventures in book publishing and digital radio broadcasting in the works, the company's future appeared bright.

Principal Subsidiaries

The Chrysalis Group has more than 75 subsidiaries and joint ventures in the United Kingdom and abroad, including: Chrysalis Holdings Ltd.; Chrysalis Books Ltd.; Chrysalis Music Ltd.; Global Chrysalis Music Group GmbH (Germany); Chrysalis Copyrights Ltd.; The Echo Label Ltd. (75%); The Hit Label Ltd.; Lasgo Exports Ltd.; Ramboro Books plc; Salamander Books Ltd.; BT Batsford Ltd.; Quadrillion Publishing Ltd.; Assembly Film and Television Ltd.; Bentley Productions Ltd.; Cactus TV Ltd.; Chrysalis Television Ltd.; CVI Media Group BV (Netherlands; 50.1%); ID&D Film and Video Productions BV (Netherlands; 50.1%); Red Rooster Television Ltd.; Tandem Television Ltd.; Watchmaker Productions Ltd.; Chrysalis Radio Ltd.; Galaxy Radio Northeast Ltd.; Puremix Ltd. (65%); Chrysalis Retail Entertainment Ltd.

Principal Divisions

Radio; Music; Visual Entertainment; Media Products; New Media.

Principal Competitors

AOL Time Warner, Inc.; British Broadcasting Corporation; Bertelsmann AG; Capital Radio plc; Carlton Communications plc; Emap plc; EMI Group plc; Forever Broadcasting plc; Granada plc; GWR Group plc; The McGraw-Hill Companies, Inc.; Pearson plc; Random House; Scottish Radio Holdings plc; SMG plc; Sony Music Entertainment, Inc.

Further Reading

Ayres, Chris, "Tuned in to the Sound of the Suburbs," *Times of London*, January 9, 1999, p. 24.

Bateman, Louise, "Chrysalis Shuts Film Production, Sales Divisions," *Hollywood Reporter*, September 10, 1996, p. I4.

"Chrysalis Sees FY OPG 'Broadly' in Line with Market Expectations," *AFX*, September 3, 1999.

Clark-Meads, Jeff, "Chrysalis' Wright Regroups: Chair Shows Flair for Publishing," *Billboard*, January 11, 1992, p. 29.

"Company Vitae: Chrysalis Group," *Guardian*, January 4, 1997, p. 17.

Frean, Andrea, "Chrysalis Focuses on Media As Losses Top Pounds 14M," *Times of London*, December 18, 1993.

Grover, Ronald, Scott Ticer, and Jonathan Birchall, "Max Headroom Is Half-Human, Rude—And a Huge Hit," *Business Week*, October 13, 1986, p. 47.

Lindsay, Robert, "Chrysalis Grows and Then Flies into Profit," *Birmingham Post*, May 12, 2000, p. 21.

Mason, Tania, "Radio Gaga: Richard Huntingford, Group Chief Executive, Chrysalis Group," *Marketing*, December 14, 2000, p. 20.

Masson, Gordon, and Matt Benz, "Chrysalis Uses Catalog As Collateral for Loan," *Billboard*, March 17, 2001, p. 8.

McClure, Steve, and Dominic Pride, "Pony Canyon Moves West with Echo," *Billboard*, September 18, 1993, p. 57.

Pride, Dominic, "Chrysalis Group Bounces Back into A&R with Echo Releases," *Billboard*, August 13, 1994, p. 8.

——, "Wright Seeing That Indie Label Gets Off on Right Foot," *Billboard*, January 16, 1993, p. 8.

Sexton, Paul, "The Music Group," *Billboard*, October 31, 1998.

Shepherd, John, "Media Transformation Costs Chrysalis Dear," *Independent-London*, June 9, 1995, p. 34.

Stark, David, "Chrysalis Music Publishing," *Billboard*, October 31, 1998.

"Twenty Questions: Richard Huntingford," *Independent-London*, March 21, 2001, p. 4.

White, Adam, "Chrysalis Acquires Publisher Global Music," *Billboard*, February 6, 1999.

—Frank Uhle

Ciments Français

Tour Ariane
La Défense Cedex
92800 Paris
France
Telephone: +33 1 42 91 75 00
Fax: +33 1 47 76 11 35
Web site: http://www.cimfra.fr

Public Company (72% Owned by Italcimenti Group)
Incorporated: 1881 as Société des Ciments Français et
  des Portland
Employees: 13,000
Sales: EUR 2.64 billion (FFr 17.34 billion) ($2.5 billion)
  (2000)
Stock Exchanges: Euronext Paris
Ticker Symbol: CMFAY
NAIC: 3273 Cement and Concrete Product
  Manufacturing; 327310 Cement Manufacturing

One of Europe's leading manufacturers of cement and concrete products, Ciments Français also provides the foundation for the international operations of parent and 72 percent shareholder Italcimenti of Italy. With manufacturing operations in 12 countries spanning more than 30 cement plants, 300 ready-mixed concrete production facilities, and 98 aggregates quarries, Ciments Français is among the top three cement and concrete providers in most of its market areas, including the number two position in France, number three in Belgium, Greece, and the United States, and number one in Basque Spain and Bulgaria. Ciments Français is also active in Thailand, where the company's acquisition of Asia Cement in 1999 has given it the number four position. Ciments Français continues to target the Asian market for growth; in January 2001, the company reached an agreement to acquire 50 percent of Zuari Cement, part of India's Zuari Industries—Ciments Français's first entry into the Indian market. Ciment Français posted EUR 2.6 billion in sales in 2000, two-thirds of which was provided by its cement products. At nearly half of total sales, France remains the company's largest market; combined with the other Euro-pean countries, some two-thirds of sales remain within Europe. Since Italcimenti first acquired a shareholding in Ciments Français in 1992, the Italian cement leader has steadily increased its shareholding in its French counterpart. In an effort to reduce costs, the two companies now share most of their top management positions, with Italcimenti's Rodolfo Danielli taking the position of director general for both companies, while Ciments Français Yves-René Nanot is the group's CEO. Nonetheless, and despite Italcimenti's majority position, the two companies expect to remain separate, publicly listed entities for the near future, preferring to invest instead in developing the group's international operations.

Cementing France in the 20th Century

Ciments Français was formed as the Société des Ciments Français et des Portland in Boulogne-sur-Mer in 1881. Joined by Compagnie des Portland, in Desvres, the two companies combined to form the Société des Ciments Français in 1941. The company profited from France's postwar construction boom, as the country rebuilt from the damage caused by World War II, and entered into an extended period of economic growth that came to a peak during the 1960s. It was during this time, too, that Ciments Français—the company would not, in fact, simplify its name until 1989—began to impose itself on the national market.

An important development in Ciments Français's history was French banking powerhouse Paribas's investment in the company, which placed Ciments Français as part of Paribas's growing portfolio of industrial investments and gave Ciments Français the capital to begin its national and international expansion. Ciments Français's first major acquisition came in 1967, when it purchased Société des Matériaux de Construction de la Loisne.

That acquisition was the first of several that extended through the 1970s and established the company as one of France's leading construction materials firms. Another major step in this development came in 1970, when Ciments Français acquired the industrial and commercial operations of Ciments Portland de Rombas et d'Hagondange. It was the acquisition the following year of the cement operations of Poliet et Chausson, another Paribas holding, however, that placed Ciments Français among the leaders in the French cement market.

Like Ciments Français, Poliet et Chausson had been founded at the turn of the century; initially focused on lime production, Poliet et Chausson had quickly added the production of concrete, cement, and other construction materials. By the 1930s, the company had captured the leadership position in cement production in France. Following World War II, Poliet et Chausson turned its focus to building up a distribution network for its construction materials, and by the 1960s was the French leader in this activity as well. The investments needed to build its position, however, brought Poliet et Chausson under control of Paribas by 1969. Paribas replaced Poliet et Chausson's management with its own team in 1970 and restructured the company, now focusing its future on its distribution wing. The transfer of Poliet et Chausson's cement production operations to Ciments Français was accomplished for the price of FFr 70 million and a 25 percent share of the enlarged cement production empire.

Expansion and Diversification into the 1990s

The Poliet et Chausson acquisition had cemented Ciments Français's position in its French home market. During the 1970s the company turned to international expansion. Moving into new markets was expected to protect the company from the traditionally cyclical nature of its business—as construction activity slowed during the winter seasons—as well as from economic downturns in its single-market focus. The effects of just such a downturn, as France weathered the recession brought on by the Arab Oil Embargo in the early 1970s, encouraged Ciments Français to make its first international move at mid-decade. In 1976, the company acquired Coplay Cement Manufacturing Company, which became Ciments Français's spearhead into the large U.S. and North American market.

At the end of the 1970s, the company also shored up its French operations, purchasing Sablières Modernes, boosting its supply of sand and other raw materials. This move marked the beginning of a diversification drive, bringing Ciments Français into the granulates and ready-mix concrete markets. Toward the middle of the 1980s, the company stepped up its expansion moves. In 1985, the company acquired Louisville Cement, boosting its U.S. activity. Ciments Français extended deeper into the North American market with the purchase of Lake Ontario Cement, in Canada, in 1986. Mexico was to follow two years later when the company acquired a shareholding in Grupo Lacosa.

Meanwhile, after adding Ciments de Champagnole to its French operations in 1986, Ciments Français entered the Spanish market, acquiring an interest in Cementos Molinos in 1987.

The following year marked an intensification of the company's expansion, with the acquisition of France's Entreprises Leon Chagnaud and the establishment of two new foreign subsidiaries, Promsa, in Spain, and Terrazul in Portugal. At the same time, the company restructured its growing U.S. operations into a new subsidiary, Essroc Corporation.

The company adopted the simplified name of Ciments Français in 1989. Its activities, however, were increasingly international. Spain became one of its most important foreign markets beginning that year with the acquisition of Cementos Rezola et de Financiera y Minera. The company then entered an entirely new market, with the purchase of Anadolu Cimento, in Turkey. Overseas, Essroc grew with the purchase of Virginia Precast. Up in Canada, the company also acquired Gormley.

New Owners for the 21st Century

At the start of the 1990s, Ciments Français continued to invest massively in its expansion. In 1990, the company made a number of major acquisitions, including those of Compagnie de Ciments Belges, Moreau, and CBF, giving it a leading share in the Belgian market. Ciments Français then turned to Germany, acquiring Stuna GmbH and Unitbeton GmbH. Other new markets included Greece, with the acquisition of Halyps, and the establishment of its Ciments du Maroc operations in Morocco. In the United States, the company acquired San Juan Cement, topping a year that saw the company mark a new period as a major cement, concrete, aggregates, and granulates group.

Yet the company's aggressive expansion quickly made it highly vulnerable. The collapse of the worldwide construction market and the lapse into an extended recession now placed the debt-heavy company under new pressures. By 1992, the company had come under the control of Italian cement leader Italcimenti, which had acquired a majority of Ciments Français's shares from Paribas. Until then, Italcimenti had been entirely concentrated on its domestic market; the takeover of the majority of Ciments Français gave it the international scope it had been missing as well as the leading position among European cement and concrete manufacturers. Yet the purchase quickly led to scandal, as Ciments Français's losses—which neared FFr 700 million in 1993—exposed a series of alleged insider trading and other illegal practices by Paribas management, leading to a refund of a significant portion of the Ciments Français purchase price to Italcimenti.

A new management, led by Yves-René Nanot, who had previously helped rescue a number of struggling Total subsidiaries, coupled with a revised strategy, helped reduce the company's losses to FFr 171 million by 1994 and restore Ciments Français to profitability by 1995. The company's strategy emphasized four main points: a refocus on the company's core cement operations; a streamlining of the company's international activities; a cost reduction drive; and the shedding of the company's high debt burden. Among the concrete steps taken at this time was the elimination of the company's North American industrial concrete operations and the exit from the Portuguese, Czech Republic, and German markets. Coupled with the prevailing economic downturn, the company's sales dropped by more than FFr 1 billion into the mid-1990s, from a high of FFr 13.5 billion in 1993 to FFr 12.2 billion in 1996.

The two companies also began moving closer together during the late 1990s, combining a number of key operations. Italcimenti continued to build up its shareholding position, which rose to 72 percent of Ciment Français's voting rights by the end of the decade, culminating in the adoption of a common group identity and logo in 1997. Meanwhile, Ciments Français had returned to profitability, posting profits of FFr 318 million in 1996 and then, with revenues once again rising to FFr 13 billion in 1997, reaching profits of FFr 615 million for the year.

Ciments Français returned to developing new markets in 1998, when it acquired Bulgaria's Devnya Cement. The company also bought up cement operations in Kazakhstan, then made its first entry into the Asian market, buying a 49 percent share in Thailand's Jalaprathan cement company. The next year the company bought up 70 percent of that country's Vulkan, placing Ciments Français as the leader in the Bulgarian market. The company's Ciments du Maroc at the same time captured the second place in Morocco's market with the acquisition of that country's Asmar. The company then turned to the Asian market, buying a share of Asia Cement Public, Thailand's fourth largest such company. These moves helped to counter criticism that Ciments Français's absence from the Asian and South American market hampered its competitiveness against the larger players in the global cement market.

Ciments Français continued to post strong revenue increases as the century drew to an end, with sales rising to FFr 13.68 billion (EUR 2.09 billion) in 1998 and profits nearing FFr 900 million (EUR 136.9). One year later, the company's revenues had soared to FFr 13.68 billion (EUR 2.37 billion), and its profits topped FFr 1.16 billion (EUR 177 million). Yet the company's relatively small size and its less developed international structure left it vulnerable to a number of market fluctuations. Chief among these was the price of fuel oil, particularly as the company found its production facilities unable to meet demand in some of its core markets, including the United States. As a result, Ciments Français was forced to import from its other operations, with the added transport and fuel costs cutting directly into the company's margins. The rise in the company's sales to EUR 2.64 billion (FFr 17.34 billion) in 2000 was barely reflected in the company's profits for the year, which reached just EUR 178 million.

Together with Italcimenti, Ciments Français went on a cost-cutting drive in 2001, switching some of its facilities to other fuel sources, such as coal in Bulgaria. The companies also moved to reduce a number of redundancies in its top management slots. Italcimenti's director general took over the same position at Ciments Français, while a number of positions were similarly streamlined to just one executive for both companies. Despite the apparently de facto merger of the two companies' operations, Italcimenti announced that it had no intention to complete its control of Ciments Français—the company's other major shareholder, Italian bank Mediabanco, held 9 percent of voting rights, while the remaining 19 percent was held by private shareholders. Instead, both companies stated a preference to direct their investment interest toward building Ciments Français's position on the international market. The company took a new step toward boosting its global presence in February 2001, when it reached an agreement to acquire 50 percent of India's Zuari Cement.

Principal Subsidiaries

Asia Cement Public Co Ltd. (Thailand; 50%); Asment de Temara (Morocco); Axim; Afyon Cimento Sanayi (Turkey); Ciments Calcia; Ciments de l'Adour; Ciments de Maroc; Ciments Français Europe (Netherlands); Ciments Français International (Luxembourg); Essroc Corporation (U.S.A.); Financiera y Minera (Spain); Socli; Calixa; Cimalit; Compagnie des Ciments Belges; Compagnie Financière des Ciments (Belgium); CTG Spa (Italy); Halyps (Greece); Italmed (Cyprus); Jalaprathan Cement Public (Thailand); Procimar (Morocco); Set Group (Turkey); Vulkan (Bulgaria).

Principal Competitors

Blue Circle Industries PLC; Cemex, S.A. de C.V.; "Holderbank" Financière Glaris Ltd.; Holnam Inc.; Lafarge SA.

Further Reading

Barjonet, Claude, "Ciments Français bien parti pour boucler une très bonne année," *Les Echos*, September 10, 1999, p. 10.

——, "Ciments Français veut reduire ses couts," *Les Echos*, February 20, 2001, p. 14.

——, "Italcimenti et Ciments Français lancent un plan d'economies tous azimuts," *Les Echos,* September 7, 2000, p. 21.

Betts, Paul, and Andrew Jack, "Italcimenti in French Move," *Financial Times,* March 2, 1998.

"Ciments Français poursuite son développement dans les pays emergents," *Les Echos,* July 26, 1999, p. 12.

"Ciments Français Says Cost Cuts Will Offset Possible Slowdown," *AFX Europe,* February 15, 2001.

Jacquin, Jean-Baptiste, "Nanot blanchit les Ciments Français," *L'Expansion,* January 23, 1995, p. 19.

—M. L. Cohen

Cinar Corporation

1055 Rene Levesque Boulevard East
Montreal, Quebec H2L 4S5
Canada
Telephone: (514) 843-7070
Fax: (514) 843-7080
Web site: http://www.cinar.com

Public Company
Incorporated: 1976 as Cinar Films
Employees: 876
Sales: C$172.64 million (1999)
Stock Exchanges: Toronto
Ticker Symbol: CIF.A
NAIC: 51211 Motion Picture and Video Production

Cinar Corporation produces children's television shows and markets supplemental educational materials through two divisions: Cinar Entertainment and Cinar Education. Cinar's most popular television series is *Arthur*, a two-time Emmy award winner. Other programs include *Wimzie's House*, *The Busy World of Richard Scarry*, *The Adventures of Paddington Bear*, *Caillou*, and *Zoboomafoo*. Through a handful of subsidiaries, Cinar Education markets teaching aids and curriculum products such as vocabulary cards, classroom decorations, and software.

Origins

Ronald Weinberg and Micheline Charest first met in 1976, marking the beginning of a courtship that led to marriage and the beginning of a business relationship that led to the formation of Cinar. For the couple, Cinar came before marriage. The business was conceived in New Orleans and born in New York City. Charest, a film graduate, traveled to New Orleans in 1976 to attend a film festival. There, she met the festival's organizer, Weinberg, and the pair immediately began making long-term plans for their future together. They moved to New York and, before the end of 1976, started a business named Cinar Films to distribute foreign-language films to art cinemas.

From its start, Cinar was directed by circumstance rather than strategy. Weinberg and Charest struggled to make a living by distributing foreign films. "New York was very hungry," Charest recalled in a May 14, 1999 interview with *Canadian Business*. "We had absolutely no money," she added. To supplement what little income they generated by peddling foreign films, the couple was forced by necessity into the field of animation. They purchased foreign cartoons, dubbed the cartoons in English, and sold the short animated features to customers in the United States. Neither Weinberg nor Charest had any experience in animation—and presumably little interest in the field—but the combination of the two businesses enabled them to pay their bills. Subsistence was the primary objective during this first era of Cinar's history, a period that endured for approximately seven years. The fortunes of the company and the expectations of Weinberg and Charest improved dramatically once the couple left New York. It was a move forced by necessity.

In 1984, Weinberg and Charest became parents. The birth of their first son caused the couple to reevaluate their approach to Cinar and choose a less expensive setting in which to raise a child. The years of eking out a living in New York were over. The family moved to Montreal, back to Charest's native province, where the cost of living was much lower and, as it would happen, where the business climate was primed for Cinar's growth. Weinberg and Charest were greeted by a federal government receptive to the dreams of aspiring filmmakers, a mood, most importantly, that was expressed financially. The Canadian government was subsidizing the country's film industry, which existed in the shadow of the much larger film industry across the border. Through tax reductions and the dispensation of funds, the government hoped to promote the growth of Canadian film companies, which provided the financial means required to make a small company like Cinar a profit-making success.

More good news awaited them after they settled in Montreal. At the time, newly founded cable networks in the United States were beginning to capture the attention of viewers, but they were in dire need of programming to fill their daily broadcast schedules. It was the emergence of the burgeoning U.S. cable industry coupled with the financial support from federal coffers that gave Weinberg and Charest an opportunity to succeed. The move to Montreal gave them the means and the market to develop Cinar into a legitimate production house, but at first the couple operated Cinar as a distribution company. Once the transformation was complete, Cinar emerged as a major player in the entertainment industry, both in Canada and in the United States.

Faced with far greater prospects in Montreal than in New York, Weinberg and Charest began talking with several cable stations. They entered into agreements with a number of cable broadcasters, including Nickelodeon, to air Cinar productions. The couple began distributing European and Japanese cartoons to its new customers before branching out into production. Working with Japanese and American partners, Cinar created its first original animated production in 1987, *The Wizard of Oz,* narrated by Margot Kidder. The program was followed by a series of Cinar productions, as the company focused on the new cable and specialty channel market to lay its foundation as a production house. Toward this end, the company's first original production established characteristics that would define its success in later years. Cinar became known as a producer of nonviolent children's programming, creating ''pro-social'' content hailed by critics during the 1990s. The company also enjoyed a solid reputation for converting children's books into animated programs, a niche in the entertainment industry that Cinar would exploit to its advantage. In Cinar's *The Wizard of Oz,* both of the company's defining talents were demonstrated, establishing important precedents for future Cinar programming. Although symbolically significant, the company's inaugural production did not make the Cinar name widely known throughout the North American entertainment industry.

At approximately the same time Weinberg and Charest first met in New Orleans, Marc Brown created what would become a hugely successful character named Arthur. Half-aardvark, half-eight-year-old boy, Arthur was created by Brown as the central character in bedtime stories he read to his daughter. Eventually, Brown wrote a series of books featuring Arthur, but the author refused numerous requests to turn Arthur into a television series. ''I just knew what would happen to Arthur,'' Brown said in the May 14, 1999 issue of *Canadian Business.* ''In no time, they'd have him carry a weapon in his backpack.''

Brown rejected all proposals to make Arthur a television character until 1994, when he met Carol Greenwald. Greenwald represented the Public Broadcasting Service's station in Boston, WGBH. In contrast to commercial networks, the Public Broad-

casting Service (PBS) received its programming from its member stations, and WGBH ranked as the network's largest producer of programming. Greenwald prevailed where others had failed by convincing Brown that an Arthur television series could be used to encourage children to read. Once Brown agreed to the project, Greenwald had won only half the battle, however. WGBH did not own its own animation studio, so a producer had to be found, one who could support the project financially and one whom Brown could trust to preserve the sanctity of Arthur. A worldwide search was begun, as Greenwald and Brown spent months visiting production houses around the globe. After a lengthy vetting process, Cinar emerged as the winner, giving Weinberg and Charest the project that would cement their reputation as industry leaders.

Cinar's production of *Arthur* was an unmitigated success. By the end of the decade, after garnering Daytime Emmy awards in 1998 and 1999, the show ranked as the most popular preschool series in the United States. Weinberg and Charest reached celebrity status within the industry, earning praise for their ability to transform children's books into popular, nonviolent television programs. A handful of other Cinar-produced programs added further confirmation of the couple's talents. Programs such as *The Busy World of Richard Scarry, The Adventures of Paddington Bear,* and *Are You Afraid of the Dark?* turned Cinar into a leading production house not only in North America but overseas as well. By the end of the 1990s, the company supplied programming in 40 languages to roughly 150 countries, boasting more programming on television in France, for instance, than any other producer in the world. Revenues inched past the $100 million mark in 1998, and Weinberg and Charest, who had formed international alliances with Viacom, Sony, Time Warner, and Polygram, benefited enormously from the financial success of their company. In 1999, the couple's stake in Cinar was worth an estimated $151 million.

Late 1990s Diversification

Cinar's achievements in the entertainment industry during the latter half of the 1990s were complemented by diversification into other markets. Weinberg and Charest set their sights on the U.S. market for supplementary education products, an estimated $10 billion business. To spearhead their expansion efforts, the couple relied on Hasanain Panju, who served as the company's chief financial officer and its third-in-command. Panju oversaw Cinar's foray into educational supplies, figuring as the chief strategist in acquiring businesses complementary to the company's widely popular animated characters. Industry observers hailed the diversification as a ''mini-Disney'' in the making, as an effort to capitalize on the popularity of the company's characters by absorbing subsidiary businesses that could generate ancillary sources of profits.

Panju fulfilled his strategic plan through acquisitions. In 1997, he spent $56.1 million to acquire Carson-Dellosa Publishing Co. Inc., a Greensboro, North Carolina, company that made teaching aids. Carson-Dellosa's educational materials included classroom decorations, supplemental books, and curriculum material such as vocabulary cards. These products, which were intended for ages preschool through eighth grade, were marketed through annual catalogues sent to every teacher in the United States. A year after the Carson-Dellosa acquisition, Panju acquired

Key Dates:

1976: Cinar is formed in New York City to distribute foreign language films.
1984: Founders Ronald Weinberg and Micheline Charest move to Montreal.
1987: Animated version of *The Wizard of Oz*, Cinar's first original production, is completed.
1994: WGBH and Cinar agree to produce *Arthur*.
1997: Cinar acquires Carson-Dellosa Publishing.
1999: Cinar acquires Edusoft Ltd.
2000: Rocked by financial scandal, Cinar's board fires Weinberg and Charest.

HighReach Learning Inc. for approximately C$40 million. With customers throughout the United States and in Mexico and Japan, HighReach operated as a direct supplier and creator of early childhood educational materials, designing its products for children ranging in age from three months to seven years.

After Panju had begun to create another dimension to Cinar's business, the company's corporate structure was changed. In December 1998, Cinar Films was renamed Cinar Corporation, which was divided in two divisions, Cinar Entertainment and Cinar Education. Cinar Education, headed by Steve Carson, one of Carson-Dellosa's founders, gained another valuable asset in March 1999 when Cinar acquired Edusoft Ltd. A multimedia company based in Israel, Edusoft developed educational software for English-as-a-Second-Language (ESL) instruction. With the addition of Edusoft, Cinar gained the ability to publish multimedia software that incorporated its television characters, exemplifying the synergy between the company's two divisions. Industry pundits applauded Cinar's diversification strategy, pointing to the high profit margins recorded in the educational materials market, but their words of praise soon took on a different tone. As Cinar prepared to exit the 1990s, it became embroiled in controversy and scandal. The first hint of trouble surfaced in October 1999.

1999: Management Ripped Apart by Scandal

Cinar's troubles began with a letter. A group of 71 Canadian writers published a letter claiming that Cinar was using U.S. writers instead of Canadian writers, an accusation that had profound implications. At stake was the financial support Cinar received from the Canadian government, support that was contingent upon Cinar's status as a Canadian producer. In 1999, Cinar relied on tax credits for 20 percent of its production budget. Analysts estimated that the company also received $2 million annually from federally chartered Telefilm Canada. Cinar risked losing both of these sources of financial aid if U.S. writers were responsible for the content of the company's television programs. In October 1999, the Royal Canadian Mounted Police began investigating Cinar. Luc Dionne, president of the Montreal-based Societés des Auteurs & Compositeurs Dramatiques, which represented Canadian writers, offered his version of what had transpired. Cinar, he charged, had received tax breaks because the company's written work was credited to Charest's sister, Helene, who was listed as a Cana-

dian writer using the pseudonym Erika Alexandre. Dionne and others claimed Helene Charest was not a writer and, therefore, Cinar was not eligible for the financial support it had received. Cinar responded by launching an internal audit that exacerbated its problems.

The audit revealed that $122 million in investments had been made in high-yield, short-term bonds through Norshield International Ltd., a Bahamas-based company. Cinar's directors were stunned. The funds had been set aside for acquisition purposes, not for investment, which left the company's board of directors searching for an explanation. On March 6, 2000, Panju was fired. At the same time, Weinberg and Charest resigned as co-chief executive officers, but both retained their seats on the company's board. One day after the announcement, Cinar's share price plummeted 70 percent, falling to $5.56 per share. Before the allegation surfaced that the company had used U.S. writers instead of Canadian writers, Cinar's stock value reached a peak of $30.25 per share.

As the search began to locate the lost funds, a new chief executive officer was hired. Barrie Usher, a former chief executive officer of New York Life Insurance Co. of Canada, assumed control over the beleaguered company in the spring of 2000. Under new management, the company stated that Weinberg and Charest were unaware of the investments made without the board's approval. Instead, the company blamed Panju. In the April 10, 2000 issue of *Business Week*, Panju stated that he had made the investments "for the sole benefit" of Cinar and "with its knowledge." Weinberg and Charest did not escape the wrath of Cinar's board for long, however. In August, the founders were told to vacate their seats on the board, as the extensive investigation into the company's finances deepened. Company officials announced they were revising financial statements for 1997, 1998, and 1999.

By November 2000, Cinar had reached an agreement to recover all of the misappropriated funds, but the turmoil was far from over. Consequently, the company entered the 21st century facing an uncertain future. In early 2001, Cinar filed a $19 million lawsuit against Weinberg, Charest, and Panju. According to the February 14, 2001 issue of *Electronic Education Report*, Weinberg, Charest, and Panju had revealed plans to sue Cinar. While the battle ensued, industry observers reported that the company was considering putting itself up for sale, with rival Nelvana Ltd., a Toronto-based animation company, mentioned as an interested buyer.

Principal Subsidiaries

Edusoft, Ltd.; Carson-Dellosa Publishing Co. Inc.; HighReach Learning Inc.; The Wild Goose Company.

Principal Divisions

Cinar Entertainment; Cinar Education.

Principal Competitors

The Walt Disney Company; Fox Entertainment Group, Inc.; Scholastic Corporation; Nelvana Ltd.

Further Reading

Austen, Ian, "Move Over Mickey Mouse," *Canadian Business,* May 14, 1999, p. 30.

"Cinar Files Legal Proceedings to Recover Remaining Funds," *Educational Marketer,* April 3, 2000, p. 36.

"Cinar Recoups All of $122 Million Investment in Settlement with Globe-X," *Electronic Education Report,* November 8, 2000, p. 3.

Clark, Andrew, "No More Laughter: Scandals Pummel Kids' TV Heavyweight Cinar and Its Once-Golden Husband-and-Wife Team," *Maclean's,* March 20, 2000, p. 36.

Gray, John, "Behind Closed Doors," *Canadian Business,* November 27, 2000, p, 36.

Kelly, Brendan, "Cinar Scandal Spells Trouble for Biz," *Variety,* March 13, 2000, p. 41.

——, "Cinar Sights Missing Cash," *Variety,* March 27, 2000, p. 63.

——, "Cinar Sues Ex-Exex for $19 Million," *Variety,* February 5, 2001, p. 32.

"Toontown Confidential," *Business Week,* April 10, 2000, p. 98.

"Youthful Vision: Two Parents Concerned About Their Kids and TV Tell How They Created a Programming Giant," *Time International,* August 9, 1999, p. 64.

—Jeffrey L. Covell

Comerica Incorporated

Comerica Tower at Detroit Center
500 Woodward Avenue, M/C 3391
Detroit, Michigan 48226
U.S.A.
Telephone: (248) 371-5000
Toll Free: (800) 521-1190
Fax: (313) 965-4648
Web site: http://www.comerica.com

Public Company
Incorporated: 1871 as The Detroit Savings Bank
Employees: 11,000
Total Assets: $41.98 billion (2001)
Stock Exchanges: New York
Ticker Symbol: CMA
NAIC: 52211 Commercial Banking; 52222 Sales
   Financing; 524113 Direct Life Insurance Carriers;
   52392 Portfolio Management; 52393 Investment
   Advice; 523999 Miscellaneous Financial Investment
   Activities

Comerica Incorporated is a multi-state financial services company based in Detroit. In 2001, Comerica had $42 billion in total assets, making it the 23rd largest bank in the United States. It operated 335 branch and supermarket offices and 700 ATMs. Except in Michigan, where its retail offerings are strong, Comerica tailors its products to small and medium-sized companies.

Born in Crisis

The Detroit of the mid-19th century was quite different from the modern Motown. The population of only 19,000 traveled on dirt roads; lumber and shipbuilding were the main industries. Similarly, the institution that preceded Comerica gave little hints of its future scale.

The Detroit Savings Fund Institute was created on March 5, 1849. Michigan governor Epaphroditus Ransom had decreed its founding to provide a safe place for wage-earners to invest their savings after a wave of bank failures. Detroit had three other banks at that time, but they were focused on business clients.

The Institute opened for business on August 17, 1849. At the end of its first day, the Institute had $41 in deposits and six customers. By year's end, this increased to $3,000 and 56 customers. Receipts reached $25,000 within two years and the number of customers increased to 300.

Elon Farnsworth, formerly Michigan's attorney general, served as the first president. The Institute was not a real bank, since it had no shareholders or capital stock. Its managers were unpaid. The Institute hired its first full-time cashier in 1855.

By 1870, the Institute had assets of $1 million. It changed its name to The Detroit Savings Bank in 1871 and reorganized as a corporation.

By 1900, Detroit Savings was a $6 million bank. The new automobile industry was beginning to fuel explosive growth in the area. Detroit's 1906 population of 290,000 would more than triple in the next quarter century.

Detroit suffered with the rest of the country after the stock market crash of October 1929. Detroit Savings was the only bank allowed to remain open during a statewide bank holiday in 1933. Soon, however, President Roosevelt's national bank holiday forced it to close. Detroit Savings changed its name to The Detroit Bank in 1936.

Creation of Future Partner: 1933

Another bank was formed in 1933 whose history would one day be linked to that of Detroit Savings. The Manufacturers National Bank of Detroit was created in 1933 by Edsel B. Ford, Henry Ford's son, and continued to hold strong ties to the Ford Motor Company.

Beginning with $3 million of Ford money, the bank's assets reached $11 million by the end of its first day in business, August 10, 1933. Unlike Detroit Savings, Manufacturers National focused on mid-sized and large corporations. It soon bought several other banks in varying degrees of solvency.

Manufacturers was originally headquartered in Detroit's historical Penobscot Building, then the tallest skyscraper in town, but moved to a renovated office building in 1944.

Detroit's factories attracted thousands of workers during World War II. More women began to take teller positions, previously a job mostly held by men. Detroit Bank's president, Joseph M. Dodge, negotiated contracts for the U.S. military and worked on economic restoration programs for the defeated Axis powers.

Manufacturers bought United States Savings Bank in 1952. It merged with Industrial National Bank in 1955. That same year Detroit Bank acquired the Detroit Trust Company, forming Detroit Bank & Trust, which itself merged with The Birmingham National Bank, Ferndale National Bank, and Detroit Wabeek Bank and Trust Company in 1956. Detroit Bank's assets were more than $1 billion by the 1960s, at which time the company purchased its first computer.

Detroit Bank built a new headquarters building, completed in 1964, next to the former Detroit Trust Company building. Manufacturers moved its headquarters to the Renaissance Center in 1977.

Industry Changes in the 1970s and 1980s

The American banking industry changed substantially in the 1970s. Detroit Bank installed its first ATM (automated teller machine) in 1971. A Master Charge credit card program was adopted soon after.

The holding company DETROITBANK Corporation was formed in 1973 to exploit new industry regulations. As a holding company, DETROITBANK could offer more varied types of financial services than its bank subsidiary. It could also offer them in other states, as well as create new out-of-state banks.

A period of bank deregulation in the United States began in 1980. DETROITBANK changed its name to Comerica Incorporated in 1982. The company followed its retiring snowbird clients south, forming Comerica Trust Company of Florida, N.A. the same year.

The company and its future merger partner Manufacturers National were both moving to increase their presence beyond Michigan. Comerica bought its hometown rival Bank of the Commonwealth in 1983. Manufacturers National acquired Illinois-based Affiliated Banc Group, Inc. in 1987. The same year, Comerica opened a lending office in Texas.

Comerica acquired a Texas bank, Grand Bancshares, Inc., in 1988. Twenty other acquisitions of Texas banks followed. By 2000, this bank division had $3.8 billion in assets and 49 locations.

In 1991, Comerica expanded its California operations with the acquisition of Plaza Commerce Bancorp in Silicon Valley and InBancshares. The company had started an auto financing business there in 1983, which by 1988 was serving other types of businesses. By 2000, Comerica Bank-California had become the state's tenth largest bank, with 30 branch offices.

In the Sun Belt states, wrote *USBanker,* "[Comerica's] focus is on lending to small and middle market companies, using products like a state-of-the-art management system to take share from local competitors. Retail customers are basically 'an accommodation.' " Comerica preferred to operate in growing cities with plenty of smaller businesses, particularly industrial ones.

Needing more space, Comerica abandoned the Detroit Bank & Trust Building for offices at the corner of Woodward and Larned, which became known as the Comerica Tower at Detroit Center.

A "Merger of Equals" in 1992

Comerica and Manufacturers National merged in 1992. Both banks were approximately the same size in assets ($14.3 billion and $12.5 billion, respectively) and employees (7,000 and 6,000).

The banks' CEOs promoted the merger to avoid either company being taken over by an out-of-state bank. Manufacturer's CEO Gerald V. MacDonald was picked to head the combined company, which retained the Comerica name as well as the Manufacturers blue trapezoid logo. MacDonald was succeeded in 1993 by Eugene Miller, a Comerica veteran since 1955.

Miller restructured the company, eliminating unprofitable enterprises, and led it into Canada and Mexico. About 60 out of 348 branches were closed, and 1,800 jobs were cut, mostly through attrition. This reengineering project was dubbed "Direction 2000," and lasted through 1998. Besides hiring a consulting firm, Comerica enlisted the help of its employees, receiving 2,000 suggestions on improving the bottom line.

One new area of growth was in life insurance sales, a business that states were gradually opening to banks. Comerica acquired an existing agency, Access Insurance Services, which it renamed. In 1995, the new Comerica Insurance Services began selling life, disability, and long-term care insurance at 274 branch offices in Michigan.

In early 1995, Comerica was also expanding its investment business via a merger with Munder Capital Management, based in Birmingham, Michigan. This was combined with Comerica's existing Woodbridge Capital Management and World Asset Management units, which together had $22 billion in assets to Munder's $8 billion. Comerica took a minority interest in the venture. Also in 1995, Comerica bought W.Y. Campbell, a Detroit-based investment banking operation, which became the basis for its capital markets group.

In 1996, Comerica sold off two subsidiaries, Comerica Bank-Illinois (formerly Affiliated Banc Group) and John V. Carr & Son, Inc. ABN-AMRO Holdings bought the bank,

Key Dates:

1849: Detroit Savings Fund Institute is chartered after wave of banking failures.

1871: The Institute becomes a corporation called The Detroit Savings Bank.

1900: Detroit Savings has $6 million in assets.

1933: Edsel B. Ford creates Manufacturers National Bank of Detroit.

1936: Detroit Savings becomes The Detroit Bank.

1952: Manufacturers buys the United States Savings Bank.

1955: Manufacturers merges with Industrial National Bank; Detroit Bank acquires Detroit Trust Company.

1956: Detroit Bank & Trust merges with three other banks.

1964: Detroit Bank & Trust builds a new headquarters.

1973: DETROITBANK Corporation is formed as a holding company for Detroit Bank.

1982: DETROITBANK becomes Comerica Incorporated.

1983: Comerica buys Bank of the Commonwealth, expands into Florida and California.

1987: Comerica expands into Texas; Manufacturers buys Illinois-based Affiliated Banc Group.

1992: Comerica and Manufacturers merge.

1993: Eugene Miller succeeds former Manufacturers head Gerald MacDonald as CEO.

1995: Comerica begins selling life insurance, acquires Munder Capital.

1997: Comerica enters Mexico.

1998: Comerica enters Canada.

which Comerica abandoned after determining it could not grow in Illinois.

The Direction 2000 restructuring induced a short-term loss in 1996; however, the bank was again posting winning numbers in 1997. Comerica began operating in Canada in 1998 to benefit from its increasing trade with the states in which Comerica already operated. A Mexican subsidiary had been created in 1997.

Continuing Consolidation: 2000

The wave of giant banking mergers accelerated in 1998, with BankAmerica Corp. joining NationsBank Corp., Norwest Corp. joining Wells Fargo & Co., and Banc One Corp. joining First Chicago/NBD Corp., which brought Banc One, a strong retail bank, into Comerica's Detroit home. These new superbanks dwarfed Comerica in terms of assets, geographic reach, and range of products. Comerica's keys to survival were a focus on its core markets, innovation, and credit quality.

Miller took over the duties of president Michael Monahan upon his retirement in June 1999. Miller was required by company bylaws to retire at age 65 in 2003; he would most likely be succeeded by one of three vice-chairmen: John Lewis, Joseph Buttigieg, or Ralph Babb, Jr. Monahan went on to head the Munder Capital Management unit after its president quit in the fall of 1999. Comerica had been planning to reduce its majority stake in the company.

In 2000 Comerica had 11,000 employees, 1,000 of whom worked at its Detroit headquarters; it also had operations in Michigan, Florida, Texas, California, Colorado, Illinois, Indiana, Ohio, Nevada, New York, and Tennessee, as well as Mexico, Canada, and Hong Kong. Seeing a challenging future in spite of his success, CEO Eugene Miller told a meeting of the Newcomen Society in October 2000, ''Japan has one bank for 1.5 million people. . . . In the U.S. we have one bank for every 25,000 people, and if you factor in credit unions, it's one for every 10,000. There simply are not enough customers to keep all, or even most, U.S. banks in business.''

Principal Subsidiaries

Comerica Bank; Comerica Bank-California; Comerica Bank-Canada; Comerica Bank Mexico, S.A.; Comerica Bank, N.A.; Comerica Bank-Texas; Comerica Insurance Services, Inc.; Comerica Leasing Corporation; Comerica Securities, Inc.; Comerica Trust Company of Bermuda, Ltd.; Comerica West Incorporated; Munder Capital Management (94.7%); Professional Life Underwriters Services, Inc.; Wilson, Kemp & Associates; W.Y. Campbell & Company.

Principal Operating Units

Business Bank; Individual Bank; Investment Bank.

Principal Competitors

Banc One Corp.; Bank of America Corporation; Citigroup Inc.

Further Reading

Duclaux, Denise, ''The $5 Trillion Enigma,'' *ABA Banking Journal,* October 1995, pp. 107+.

Hunter, George, ''Comerica Picks Triumvirate to Groom for the Top Post,'' *The Detroit News,* March 24, 1999.

Klinkerman, Steve, ''The Road Less Taken,'' *Banking Strategies,* July/August 1998, pp. 14–18.

Marshall, Jeffery, ''Buying Munder's Thunder,'' *USBanker,* June 1997, pp. 51–54.

——, ''Sticking to Business,'' *USBanker,* May 1998, pp. 55–56.

Miller, Eugene A., ''Comerica Incorporated: Promises Kept, Promises Renewed,'' New York: Newcomen Society, 2000.

''One for All,'' *Executive Excellence,* December 1996, pp. 15–16.

—Frederick C. Ingram

COMFORCE Corporation

415 Crossways Park Drive
Woodbury, New York 11797
U.S.A.
Telephone: (516) 437-3300
Toll Free: (888) 275-4273
Fax: (516) 396-9528
Web site: http://www.comforce.com

Public Company
Incorporated: 1939 as American Photocopy Equipment
    Co.
Employees: 650
Sales: $480.33 million (2000)
Stock Exchanges: American
Ticker Symbol: CFS
NAIC: 56131 Employment Placement Agencies; 56132
    Temporary Help Agencies

COMFORCE Corporation is a leading provider of specialty staffing, consulting, and outsourcing solutions focused on the needs of the largest companies in the growing information technology, telecommunications, professional, technical, and financial market sectors. By maintaining a large global database of permanent, contracting, and consulting employees, COMFORCE brings clients together with qualified people around the world. Its labor force consists mainly of computer programmers, systems consultants, telecommunications engineers, analysts, engineers, technicians, scientists, researchers, and skilled office support personnel. The company's predecessors had eventful histories in a variety of business endeavors.

Apeco: 1939–85

American Photocopy Equipment Co. was founded in Chicago in 1939. The small duplicating concern was on the verge of bankruptcy in 1944, when Samuel G. Rautbord, its part-time legal counsel, scraped up $85,000—mostly from relatives and friends—to buy out one of the partners. He bought out the remaining partner in 1945 for $120,000—also mostly borrowed—and put the company, whose name was commonly contracted to Apeco, back on track by cutting costs. Annual revenue rose to $2 million, even though Apeco's wet photocopying process was awkward to use. In 1953 the company introduced an improved model based on a principle similar to the one used by the Polaroid Land camera. It was immediately successful. Apeco, which made its initial public offering in 1957, became a glamour technology stock of its time. The price of the shares soared tenfold before a 1960 stock split. Revenues reached $35 million and net income amounted to $4.9 million in fiscal 1961. Born into poverty, Rautbord now had a nine-room apartment overlooking Lake Michigan, a chauffeur-driven Rolls Royce convertible, and a Florida-based 80-foot yacht with a crew of four.

Ironically, Apeco's glory days began to fade around the same time, when Xerox Corporation revolutionized the photocopy industry with its dry-process, plain-paper 914 model. Apeco introduced its own dry-process machine, but the complex model suffered from technical problems, and coated-paper copiers were losing ground to plain-paper ones. Apeco fell into the red in fiscal 1966 and began to diversify, first by purchasing a manufacturer of graphic arts supplies, then by acquiring companies in totally different fields. During 1968–69 it acquired a recreational vehicle division that included firms building boats, travel trailers, and truck campers, and a mobile home division that grew to encompass four factories. Net income reached a record $6.1 million in fiscal 1971 and net sales were a record $133.7 million in fiscal 1972. That year the company also purchased Cascade Data, Inc., a manufacturer of data processing systems and computer software.

Apeco lost nearly $6 million in fiscal 1973 and got out of the computer business. The Arab oil embargo and consequent sharp rise in gasoline prices devastated the recreational vehicle industry, while higher interest rates damaged the mobile home industry. As Apeco's losses mounted, the company sold its marine division (1975) and graphic arts division (1977). After losing nearly $22 million in fiscal 1976, the company filed for chapter 11 bankruptcy protection, shed six European subsidiaries, and phased out production of photocopiers. (An Italian subsidiary continued making them until 1981.) Apeco emerged from bank-

Company Perspectives:

At COMFORCE, our mission is to improve our clients' profits while providing our people with unique and rewarding employment opportunities.

ruptcy in 1980 but continued to lose money every year except fiscal 1982. It liquidated its photocopy sales and distribution activities in 1983.

Lori and COMFORCE: 1985–97

In 1982 Peter and John Harvey, Chicago-based brothers, purchased a controlling interest in Apeco through a subsidiary of Artra Group Inc., a Harvey-controlled enterprise that specialized in buying troubled companies for their tax losses and then merging them with profitable ventures. Two years later Apeco purchased R.N. Koch, Inc., a company based in Providence, Rhode Island, that designed, distributed, and sold low-cost costume jewelry, for about $29 million. The following year Apeco sold its mobile home business and renamed itself Lori Corp. The company acquired three more costume jewelry businesses during 1985–86 at a combined cost of $20 million. Sales reached a peak of $128 million in 1987, but the company lost almost $2 million. The following year it lost more than $7 million on only $92 million in sales. Losses continued to mount, while sales volume dropped. R.N. Koch—renamed New Dimensions Accessories Ltd.—fell into chapter 11 bankruptcy in 1992. It emerged from bankruptcy the following year but ceased operations in 1994, when Lori eliminated most of its $22.7 million bank debt by issuing quantities of its own stock and that of Artra to its creditors.

In 1995 Lori exited the costume jewelry field and entered a new line of business by purchasing an employment agency, Spectrum Global Services, Inc., a subsidiary of Spectrum Information Technologies, Inc., for about $6.4 million in cash and stock. Founded in 1987 and acquired by Spectrum Information in 1993 as YIELD TechniGlobal, this firm was providing telecommunications and computer specialists and expertise to *Fortune* 1000 international companies on a temporary, contractual basis. Annual revenue was about $9 million, and the company was operating slightly in the red. Now controlled by the acquired firm's cofounders, who purchased a 26 percent stake from Artra for about $10 million, and based in Lake Success, Long Island, Lori changed its name to COMFORCE and renamed Spectrum Global COMFORCE Global. COMFORCE Global continued providing technical staffing services to the telecommunications sector as COMFORCE Telecom Inc.

COMFORCE acquired a number of firms in 1996, including Williams Communication Services, Inc.; Project Staffing Support Team, Inc.; RRA, Inc.; Datatech Technical Services, Inc.; Force Five; AZATAR Computer Systems, Inc.; and Continental Field Services Corp., plus its affiliate, Progressive Telecom, Inc. That year it had 33 offices, $55.9 million in sales, and a profit of $1.4 million. In early 1997 COMFORCE purchased RHO Co. Inc. Later in the year it acquired Uniforce Services

Inc.—a company more than twice as big as its purchaser—for $106 million, also assuming Uniforce's debt of $35 million.

Uniforce: 1966–97

Reared in Manhattan's tough Hell's Kitchen area, John Fanning opened his first employment agency in 1954 with $6,000 saved, in part from a newspaper delivery route. He sold this company to his employees in 1967 but also had, with two others, formed a temporary agency in 1961 that later became Uniforce Temporary Personnel Services, Inc. Fanning began franchising local Uniforce offices in 1974 or 1975 and had his first dozen franchisees about two years later. Uniforce had net income of only $18,000 on sales of $16.39 million in 1982 (compared with $10.5 million in 1979), but in 1984, the year the company made its initial public offering, it had 30 offices and earned $1.09 million on revenues of $43.45 million. Armed with $4 million collected by selling stock, Fanning promptly acquired ten companies. The next year the number of offices reached 55, mostly in California, Florida, and Texas. By 1990 there were 110 franchised offices nationwide—mostly in towns and small cities of 10,000 to 50,000 people. Revenues reached $110.44 million, on which Uniforce earned $3.88 million. Headquarters were in New Hyde Park, Long Island.

Uniforce collected gross revenues and took a 45 percent royalty—the industry standard—before forwarding the remainder to its franchisees. In return it managed all of the licensee's internal operations, including payroll, personnel training, accounting, and insurance, paid for advertising, and often invested capital as well. By paying the salaries of the temporary personnel directly, Uniforce eliminated the cash-flow problem franchisees faced by having to wait four to six weeks to receive payment from clients.

Uniforce's stock was selling for about five times the initial offering price in 1989, but business slumped during the 1990–91 recession, so much so that the company had to take back some of its own franchises and was waiving its $15,000 initial franchise fee for prospective licensees. Although Uniforce remained modestly profitable, revenues slumped to $82.93 million in 1992. By early 1993 only 64 offices remained, and Fanning adopted a strategy of converting the remaining franchised operations to company-owned ones. By the end of 1994 Uniforce's company-owned units outnumbered the franchised ones. A number of the Uniforce units were specialized ones operated by subsidiaries such as LabForce of America, PrO Unlimited, and Uniforce Information Services. "Temporary" was dropped from the parent company's name in 1995. The change in strategy was successful and, after several years of increased earnings, Uniforce's net income, in 1996, surpassed the 1989 peak.

COMFORCE Plus Uniforce: 1998–2000

Uniforce Services Inc.'s sales came to $142 million and profit amounted to $3.7 million in 1996. After its purchase by COMFORCE, it became a subsidiary, with Fanning—who said the sale was for him mostly a matter of estate planning—still in charge as chief executive. Acquisitions enabled COMFORCE to raise its revenues to $216.52 million in 1997, but it incurred a net loss of $3.7 million. In September 1998—less than a year

---

Key Dates:

1939: American Photocopy Equipment Co. (Apeco), COMFORCE's predecessor, is founded.
1957: Company goes public.
1976: Apeco files for Chapter 11 bankruptcy protection.
1985: Apeco is renamed Lori Corp. after entering the costume jewelry business.
1995: Lori enters the employment agency business and renames itself COMFORCE.
1997: COMFORCE acquires Uniforce Services Inc., a larger employment agency firm.
1998: Uniforce's founder, John Fanning, purchases COMFORCE.

---

after the sale—Fanning bought out COMFORCE's founders and took the titles of chairman and chief executive of the firm. COMFORCE subsequently moved its headquarters to Woodbury, Long Island.

In 1998 COMFORCE acquired Camelot Consulting Group Inc., Camelot Communications Group Inc., Camelot Control Group Inc., and Camelot Group Inc. With these and the Uniforce acquisition, COMFORCE more than doubled its revenues, to $459.02 million, that year. Despite sharply higher interest expenses of $21.49 million, it earned a small net profit of $825,000. Revenues fell to $436.22 million in 1999, and the company incurred a net loss of $2.04 million. In 2000 COMFORCE made one more acquisition, Gerri C. Inc., a New York City-based provider of staffing, permanent placement, and training services. Revenues grew significantly, to $480.33 million. The company lost $397,000 before taking an extraordinary gain of $2.78 million because of early debt extinguishment. The total debt at the end of the year was $197.42 million.

COMFORCE had 62 offices—48 company-owned and 14 licensed branch offices in 19 states—at the end of 2000. The Staff Augmentation segment was providing information technology, telecom, and other staffing services. The Human Capital Management Services segment was providing contingent workforce management services through the PrO Unlimited subsidiary. The Financial Services segment was providing payroll, funding, and back-office support services to approximately 130 independent consulting and staffing companies. In 1999, the first two segments provided 74 percent of revenues and 67 percent of operating profits, while the latter accounted for the remainder.

The Staff Augmentation segment was providing highly skilled programmers, help-desk personnel, systems consultants and analysts, software engineers, and project managers for a wide range of technical assignments in information technology. It also was providing skilled telecom personnel to plan, design, engineer, install, and maintain wireless and wireline telecommunication systems. In addition, it was providing a broad range of other staffing services, including laboratory support (through the Labforce division), medical office support, and professional,

scientific, clerical, and call-center staffing. Human Capital Management Services was a market leader in providing end-to-end web-enabled solutions for the effective procurement, tracking, and engagement of contingent or non-employee labor, primarily to *Fortune* 500 customers.

Fanning family members owned 31 percent of Comforce's stock in 2000; Artra retained a 9 percent stake. The company's clients included Sun Microsystems, Bellsouth Telecommunications, Boeing, and Microsoft. COMFORCE's four largest customers accounted for about 28 percent of company revenues in 2000.

Principal Subsidiaries

COMFORCE Information Technologies, Inc.; COMFORCE Operating, Inc.; COMFORCE Technical Administrative Services, Inc.; COMFORCE Technical Services, Inc.; COMFORCE Telecom, Inc.; Labforce of America, Inc.; PrO Unlimited, Inc.; Uniforce Payrolling Services, Inc.; Uniforce Services, Inc.; Uniforce Staffing Services, Inc.; UTS of Delaware, Inc.

Principal Divisions

Financial Services; Human Capital Management; Staff Augmentation.

Principal Competitors

Butler International; CDI Corporation; Modis Professional Services.

Further Reading

"Apeco Is Back in the Picture," *Business Week*, August 17, 1968, pp. 88–90.

"Apeco Moves to Halt Its Losing Streak," *Business Week*, September 14, 1974, pp. 30–31.

Clabby, William R., "Lawyer Routbord Buys Tiny Photocopy Firm, Prospers As It Grows," *Wall Street Journal*, July 1, 1960, pp. 1, 16.

"'Driven' to Command Comforce," *Newsday*, September 10, 1998, pp. 53–54.

Garrett, Echo Montgomery, "Big Profits, Small Towns," *Success*, March 1989, pp. 68, 70, 72.

Koselka, Rita, "A Long Way from Hell's Kitchen," *Fortune*, July 9, 1990, pp. 59–60.

"Lori Corp. Restructures $22.7 Million Bank Debt," *WWD/Women's Wear Daily*, August 29, 1994, p. 10.

Marlow, Hal, "Apeco Corp.," *Wall Street Transcript*, February 14, 1972, pp. 27, 153–27, 156.

Mason-Draffen, Carrie, "Staffing Companies to Merge," *Newsday*, August 15, 1997, p. A65.

Mulqueen, John, "Liberating the Workforce," *OTC Review*, April 1985, pp. 14, 16.

Tracy, Eleanor Johnson, "Heading for the Big Time in the Part-Time Game," *Fortune*, April 29, 1985, p. 12.

Welling, Kathryn M., "Fatal Attraction?," *Barron's*, September 25, 1989, p. 58.

—Robert Halasz

CODELCO

Corporacion Nacional del Cobre de Chile

Huerfanos 1270
Casila Postal 150-D
Santiago
Chile
Telephone: (562) 690-3000
Fax: (562) 690-3059
Web site: http://www.codelcochile.com

Government-Owned Company
Incorporated: 1976
Employees: 17,313
Sales: $2.89 billion (1999)
NAIC: 212234 Copper Ore & Nickel Ore Mining;
   331411 Primary Smelting & Refining of Copper Ore

The state-owned Corporacion Nacional del Cobre de Chile (Codelco) is the world's largest producer of copper, accounting for more than 18 percent of Chile's exports and more than 3 percent of its gross domestic product in the mid- and late 1990s. Codelco controls one-fifth of the world's known reserves of copper and was producing over 1.6 million metric tons of copper a year at the end of the 20th century. Its largest two mines, Chuquicamata and El Teniente, are the world's largest open-pit and underground copper mines, respectively. Codelco is also the world's second largest producer of molybdenum, a byproduct of copper mining. In addition to mining, the company further processes copper ore through its smelting, leaching, electrowinning, refining, and metalworking facilities.

Under U.S. Control: 1904–71

El Teniente, a large deposit of copper ore rimming a dormant volcano on the western slope of the Andes Mountains about 50 miles north of Santiago, the capital of Chile, had been mined on a small scale for centuries before William Braden, an American mining engineer, took an option on the property in 1904. He began work on a mine, complete with tunnels, plus a rope tramway, mill, and 40-mile railway, but the project proved too expensive to complete on his own, and he sold a controlling share of his Braden Copper Co. to the Guggenheim Exploration

Co. (Guggenex), in 1909. The facility, including a smelter and refinery, was completed at a cost of $25 million. By 1915 it was turning out 50 million pounds of copper a year at a production cost of less than eight cents a pound. When Guggenex was disbanded that year, 95 percent of the Braden Copper Co. passed to the newly founded Kennecott Copper Corp., which was also controlled by the Guggenheims.

El Teniente, at an average elevation of 7,000 feet above sea level, was to become the largest copper mine in the world. At mid-century the property encompassed 300 square miles. Miles of tunneling extended into ore deposits that ran deep around the edges of the volcano. The complex also included 43 miles of railroad, an aerial tramway, extensive mining, milling, smelting, and refining facilities, and housing and community facilities to meet the needs of 16,000 people living on a barren mountainside. By 1955 it had yielded 238 million tons of ore and 8.68 billion pounds of copper.

Chuquicamata, the world's largest copper deposit, in northern Chile's Atacama Desert, was mined by the Incas as early as 1536 and was brought to the attention of M. Guggenheim's Sons in 1900 by an employee who reported that it could be purchased for less than $250,000. The Guggenheims passed on the opportunity. Albert C. Burrage, a Boston mining engineer, bought the property himself but lacked the resources to develop it. In 1910 he sold it to the Guggenheims for stock valued at $25 million in the Chile Exploration Co., the operating arm of the Chile Copper Co., the company they had founded to exploit the ore at this desolate site. To do so, they built a modern port and electric-power plant at Tocopilla, 90 miles to the west, with cables to bring power to the mine, and a 55-mile aqueduct over the mountains to bring in water. The mine opened in 1915 and employed the porphyry-reduction processes perfected by Guggenheim engineers in Utah.

Chuquicamata became the world's most productive and profitable copper mine; in 1923, it produced refined copper for less than six cents a pound–the lowest price in the world. Even so, in the commodities slump that followed World War I, it was losing money. Anaconda Copper Co. bought 51 percent of Chile Copper in 1923 for $70 million and the remaining 49 percent in 1929. Chuquicamata was developed into the world's largest open-pit copper mine. By the end of 1955 it had yielded 413 million metric tons of copper ore and 11.54 billion pounds of copper.

Braden also took out an option in 1913 on Potrerilleros, a copper-yielding property about 100 miles south of Chuquicamata that had been mined casually since 1875. He sold it in 1916 to Anaconda, which established a subsidiary to exploit it. Work began in 1920 and was completed in 1928 at a cost of $35 million. By the time the open-pit deposits were exhausted in 1955, some 181 million metric tons of ore had been mined and 1.58 million metric tons of copper produced. Work then began on the El Salvador mine, below the surface of Potrerilleros. It came into full production in 1959. Not long after, the Cerro de Pasco Corp. began developing the Andina open-pit mine at another location. It opened in 1970, and an underground addition went into production in 1984.

The Chilean copper operations of Anaconda and Kennecott were highly lucrative for many years. An income tax was not introduced until 1922, when a mild 12 percent rate went into effect. By 1952 the total tax burden was over 70 percent of income, but both companies continued to do well; Kennecott's pretax income between 1955 and 1965 per dollar of sales was 59 cents, and Anaconda's was 47 cents. Nevertheless, production did not rise significantly during the 1950s, as copper began losing ground in world commodity markets to aluminum, lighter and cheaper. Moreover, the percentage of Chilean copper ore refined in Chile dropped from 89 percent to 45 percent.

Kennecott considered a substantial increase in production at El Teniente, but only if the tax rate was reduced and it received what it considered an effective 20-year guarantee of inviolability from nationalization. Instead, in 1966 Kennecott sold 51 percent of the operation to the Chilean government. Kennecott received a ten-year contract to continue managing the joint venture after making a commitment to a huge increase in production. Anaconda kept ownership of its mines and agreed, in return for a tax-rate cut, to raise production markedly, but in 1969 it sold 51 percent to the Chilean government. After President Salvador Allende's left-wing government came into power, the private shares of these enterprises were nationalized, with the government agreeing to pay compensation over 30 years. The government also nationalized Cerro's Andina mine, agreeing to pay a sum corresponding to book value.

Nationalization Under Codelco: 1976–94

Following the overthrow of Allende in 1973, the military junta headed by General Augusto Pinochet cracked down on labor unrest in the mining sector. The four mines of Andina, Chuquicamata, El Salvador, and El Teniente produced 682,300 metric tons of Chile's total output of 828,300 metric tons in 1975. Codelco was established in 1976 to operate these mines. Full production resumed in mid-1976, and the following year

Codelco's mines turned out about 890,000 metric tons of copper, of which Chuquicamata alone accounted for about 579,000—a world record—and El Teniente for about 276,000. In that year the Pinochet government increased the military's share of Chile's copper income–by law 10 percent of net profits–to 10 percent of Codelco's gross export revenues.

Codelco's production was up to 1.1 million metric tons by 1983, when its sales reached $1.8 billion. Its production costs–the world's lowest–of 44 cents a pound enabled its net income to reach $220.6 million. Codelco paid $678.5 million in taxes in 1983 and provided Chile with 46 percent of its foreign exchange. For most of the 1980s, however, world copper prices slumped because of the development of fiber optics and superconductors, the more limited use of raw materials in manufactured products, and the substitution in many cases of aluminum and plastics. Codelco's administration was marked by frequent changes in management, contradictory policies, inadequate investment, and stagnating production, although its mines significantly reduced their production costs. During 1988–89 the price of copper rose appreciably again, enabling Codelco's revenues on 1.24 million metric tons of copper to reach $3.4 billion in 1989. Taxes and dividends transferred to the state comprised 30 percent of Chile's revenues.

In 1990 Codelco's four copper mines produced only 1.14 million metric tons of copper because of production problems at Chuquicamata. The company's debt had reached about $1.5 billion. A new chief executive reduced payroll, persuaded unions to tie pay raises to productivity gains, and secured the passage of a law allowing Codelco, for the first time, to form partnerships with private firms. Net sales reached $3.02 billion in 1992, and net income was $304.72 million. The long-term debt was $1.43 billion.

Codelco suffered a grievous blow when it was discovered that an employee had cost the company at least $175 million between 1989 and 1994 by making bad commodities trades in the futures market. The employee, Juan Pablo Dávila, blamed his wild speculative binge on an effort to make up for the disastrous effects of a data-entry error. Codelco, however, charged him with receiving millions of dollars in a scandal involving major brokerage firms and metals dealers. The scandal led to the resignation of Codelco's chief executive and seven other senior executives and a net loss for 1993. Dávila was convicted of fraud and tax evasion and sent to jail. In 1997 Merrill Lynch & Co. agreed to pay Codelco $25 million to settle a lawsuit in connection with his trading activity. The following year Codelco sued Winchester Commodities Group Ltd. as part of its effort to recover losses.

Two More Mines, Higher Production: 1994–99

Codelco, in 1994, sold 51 percent of the El Abra property, about 30 miles north of Chuquicamata, to Cyprus Amax Minerals Co., the second largest U.S. copper-producing firm (later acquired by Phelps Dodge Corporation, the largest), for $330 million. El Abra was expected to become the third-largest copper-producing mine in Chile, yielding 225,000 metric tons a year of refined copper. Codelco earned a profit in 1994 and enjoyed a banner year in 1995, with net earnings of $636.72 million on sales of $3.93 billion, as world copper prices soared

Key Dates:

1909: U.S. mining engineer William Braden sells controlling share of his Braden Copper Co. to the Guggenheim Exploration Co. (Guggenex); the site of the operation is El Teniente in the Andes Mountains north of Santiago.

1910: Another Guggenheim-owned company purchases rights to the Chuquicamata site, in northern Chile's Atacama Desert.

1915: The Chuquicamata and El Teniente copper mines are in operation.

1966: Guggenheim-controlled Kennecott sells 51 percent of its mining operations in Chile to the Chilean government.

1971: Four mines, including the aforementioned two, have been fully nationalized under the rule of Salvador Allende.

1976: Corporacion Nacional del Cobre de Chile (Codelco) is established to operate the four mines for the Chilean government.

1996: El Abra mine, 49 percent owned by Codelco, opens.

1998: Codelco opens its newest copper mine, Radomiro Tomic.

---

to an average of $1.30 a pound. That year the company produced 1.16 million metric tons of copper and 16,717 metric tons of molybdenum.

The El Abra open-pit mine opened in 1996. That year Codelco sold 51 percent of Inversiones Tocopilla Ltd., its thermoelectric power company, to a three-firm consortium, receiving a payment of $178 million. In 1998 Codelco opened its newest mine, Radomiro Tomic, near Chuquicamata. The company also formed a number of joint ventures, including, in 1999, taking 49 percent of a partnership with the Mexican firm Mineras Peñoles, S.A. to seek copper deposits in the Mexican state of Sonora. None of these years was as profitable as 1995, however, as world copper prices fell to an average low of 70 cents a pound in 1999, the lowest in 12 years and the lowest, in real terms, in 60 years. Sales came to $2.89 billion for the year and net income to $143.32 million. The company's long-term debt was $1.43 billion at the end of the year, not including notes payable and deferred taxes, which totaled another $830.34 million.

Of Codelco's record copper production of 1.69 million metric tons in 1999, Chuquicamata accounted for 39 percent; El Teniente, 21 percent; Andina, 15 percent; Radomiro Tomic, 12 percent; Codelco's share of El Abra's production, 7 percent; and El Salvador, 6 percent. In 2000 Codelco approved a $422 million expansion of El Teniente expected to boost production from the current 350,000 metric tons a year to 480,000 by 2003. Of Codelco's copper sales in 1999, Asia accounted for 40 percent; Europe, 35 percent; North America, 16 percent; and South America, 9 percent. By country, South Korea, Germany, China, and the United States were the largest customers, in that order. Molybdenum production was 23,079 metric tons.

Speaking to industrial analysts in New York in 1999, Codelco president and chief executive officer Marcos Lima Aravena said his company's productivity had increased 80 percent and its direct cash costs had dropped more than 30 percent—to 40 cents per pound—since 1993. This was achieved as part of an emergency plan involving job cuts, pay freezes, and productivity agreements with the workers. Because Codelco's profits had increased in 1999 despite the fall in copper prices, Lima Aravena became the first Latin American to be named "Man of the Year" by the Copper Club in New York. He was succeeded as CEO in 2000 by Juan Villarzu.

Principal Subsidiaries

Chile Copper Ltd. (U.K.); Codelco France (France); Codelco Group Inc. (U.S.A.); Codelco Kupferhandel GmbH (Germany).

Principal Divisions

Andina; Chuquicamata; El Teniente; Radomiro Tomic; Salvador; Talleres.

Principal Competitors

Grupo Mexico, S.A. de C.V.; Phelps Dodge Corp.; Rio Tinto plc.

Further Reading

Bande, Jorge, and Ricardo Ffrench-Davis, *Copper Policies and the Chilean Economy, 1973–88.* Santiago: Corporación de Investigaciones Económicas para Latinoamerica, 1989.

Calian, Sara, Jonathan Friedland, and Suzanne McGee, "Metal Dealers Shudder As Chilean Firm Seeks Culprits in Big '94 Loss," *Wall Street Journal,* February 16, 1996, pp. A1, A4.

"Codelco Keeps the Copper Coming," *Euromoney,* September 1987, special supplement, pp. 24–25.

"Codelco Sues Winchester to Recover Trading Losses," *Wall Street Journal,* January 7, 1998, p. A17.

"Copper Pays Its Way," *Euromoney,* September 1990, special supplement, p. 30.

Jackson, Susan, "Codelco Enters a New Era," *Business Latin America,* June 27, 1994, p. 6.

Moran, Theodore H., *Copper in Chile,* Princeton, N.J.: Princeton University Press, 1974.

Parsons, A.B., *The Porphyry Coppers,* New York: American Institute of Mining and Metallurgical Engineers, 1933.

——. *The Porphyry Coppers in 1956,* New York: American Institute of Mining and Metallurgical Engineers, 1957.

Phelps, Richard W., "Radomiro Tomic," *E/MJ/Engineering and Mining Journal,* March 1998, pp. 28–31.

Sisselman, Robert, "Chile's Chuquicamata: Looking to Stay No. 1 in Copper Output," *E/MJ/Engineering and Mining Journal,* August 1978, pp. 59–71.

——, "Chile's El Teniente Mine: Meeting the Challenge of Declining Ore Grades," *E/MJ/Engineering and Mining Journal,* June 1978, pp. 141–50.

Wernick, David, "Losing Mettle?" *LatinFinance,* November 1999, pp. 21, 22, 29.

"Why Chile Is King of Copper," *Business Week,* December 17, 1984, p. 67.

Yafie, Roberta C., "Exec Says Codelco-Chile Is Still the One to Beat," *American Metal Market,* December 7, 1999, p. 7.

—Robert Halasz

Covington & Burling

1201 Pennsylvania Avenue, NW
Washington, D.C. 20004-2401
U.S.A.
Telephone: (202) 662-6000
Fax: (202) 662-6291
Web site: http://www.cov.com

Partnership
Founded: 1919
Employees: 900
Sales: $165 million (1999 est.)
NAIC: 54111 Offices of Lawyers

One of the United States' preeminent law firms, Covington & Burling, with its more than 450 lawyers, provides expertise in virtually all legal specialties. It is probably best known, however, for helping clients deal with the maze of federal laws and regulations. For example, it represented Microsoft Corporation as the federal government accused it of antitrust violations. For about 30 years it has served state governments in their disputes with the federal government. The firm represents not only many large companies but also more than 100 trade associations with legislative or regulatory concerns. For several decades it has helped write major laws. Covington & Burling has a strong sports practice with clients such as the National Basketball Association, National Hockey League, and the National Football League. It serves foreign governments and businesses in a wide range of concerns, from taxation issues and disputes over mineral rights to intellectual property lawsuits and mergers and acquisitions. Covington & Burling also sets a good example for other law firms by being a leader in providing pro bono services to clients with limited resources. One of the firm's prominent lawyers was Dean Acheson, secretary of state under President Truman, who played a key role in the early years of the Cold War.

Origins and Early History: 1919–45

Covington & Burling began with the distinguished political and legal career of J. Harry Covington. After graduating from the University of Pennsylvania Law School in 1894, he prac-

ticed law in his home town of Easton, Maryland. He was elected to the U.S. House of Representatives in 1908, 1910, and 1912. From 1914 to 1918 he served as the chief justice of the Supreme Court of the District of Columbia. During World War I, Covington served the Wilson administration but also realized new opportunities abounded because of the expanded power of the federal government. War contracts, the recently passed federal income tax, and increased government regulations influenced Covington to start a private law practice.

On January 1, 1919 Covington and Edward B. Burling formed the law partnership of Covington & Burling. A native of Eldora, Iowa, Burling graduated from Harvard Law School in 1894 and had practiced law in Chicago before moving to Washington, D.C., to start the new partnership.

The biggest case for the young partnership resulted from a dispute during World War I. The Christiana Group of Norwegian Shipowners claimed that the U.S. government owed them about $18 million in compensation for deciding to build its own ships. The Christiania Group persuaded the Kingdom of Norway to join them in pursuing the claim. With the help of Covington & Burling, Norway and the shipowners prevailed in arbitration at The Hague, the headquarters of the League of Nations, winning an award of almost $12 million in 1922.

The law firm kept busy after World War I by serving other clients, including the National Canners Association, du Pont de Nemours, W.R. Grace, Price Waterhouse, United Fruit, Bethlehem Steel, Goodyear, the American Institute of Accountants, and the State of Arizona. It added new partners, the most notable being Dean Acheson, who had graduated from Harvard Law School in 1918 before joining the partnership during the Norwegian shipping case. By the end of 1933 the firm consisted of 18 lawyers, including seven partners.

From the beginning, Covington & Burling intended to represent local, national, and international clients. For example, it helped New York investment banker Eugene Meyer move the Madeira School from Washington, D.C., to rural Virginia, which resulted in the firm representing Meyer and the *Washington Post* (which Meyer purchased in 1933) for many years. In the early 1930s the firm advised the president of Columbia in

Company Perspectives:

For more than 80 years, Covington & Burling has enjoyed a broad reputation for two paramount qualities— representation of clients according to the highest professional standards and dedication to public service.

helping that nation solve oil disputes and end an undeclared war against Peru. This range of legal services made the young law firm a challenging business to work for, even if it was not as big or as profitable as the Wall Street law firms.

During World War II, the law firm hired female lawyers for the first time. This was a rather typical development at many law firms that needed to replace male lawyers who had left for military or government service. After the war, however, most firms returned to the earlier trend of hiring almost all men. It was not until the 1970s that women joined large law firms in significant numbers.

Postwar Practice and Challenges

In the aftermath of World War II, the firm assisted Iran as it worked with the United Nations to get the Soviet Union to remove its troops. Once that was accomplished, Iran used the firm for other matters.

After World War II, the law firm experienced considerable growth. In 1948 it had 57 lawyers and 69 staff workers. In 1963 it reached 102 lawyers and 162 staff employees.

In 1969 Covington & Burling began representing states, an important part of its practice in the years to come. Most of the original 13 states hired the firm when the federal government filed a claim in the U.S. Supreme Court that it owned the continental shelf, the relatively shallow area along the Atlantic coast. The court accepted the federal government's claim in *United States v. Maine* in 1975.

Meanwhile, in 1971 the firm began representing New Jersey, and later other states, in a conflict over whether or not the federal government should provide states with funds for social services under the Social Security Act. In *State of Florida v. Mathews* (1976), the states, helped by Covington & Burling, won their case in district court. During the appeal, the parties settled out of court. The federal government agreed to pay $543 million to the states, and in 1978 Congress finally appropriated that amount. Since that time, the law firm has served various state governments on different issues.

Covington & Burling assisted General Dynamics in the early 1980s when the defense firm and the Navy argued over massive cost overruns from building nuclear submarines. Each side blamed the other. The Navy accused General Dynamics of fraud, mismanagement, and poor training, while General Dynamics claimed that the Navy made thousands of new design modifications after the initial contracts had been signed. This dispute lasted several years and was the subject of intense media scrutiny.

In the 1980s the law firm also represented Puerto Rico when the Reagan administration wanted to eliminate a section of the

tax code that gave U.S. companies tax breaks for money earned in Puerto Rico. Meanwhile, Covington & Burling served the Tobacco Institute of America as the controversy over health risks from smoking heated up, and the Bank of Boston when it was charged with money laundering for alleged mobsters.

Covington & Burling opened its first office outside of Washington, D.C. in 1989 by setting up a London branch that focused on international arbitration and assisting clients with investments in the United States and Europe. The *Wall Street Journal* pointed out on March 27, 1989: "Competition is intense among law firms in the international arena, and Washington firms appear to be playing a game of catch-up. Most large New York firms have had European branch offices for years."

In 1989 Covington & Burling lawyer Paul Tagliabue left to become the commissioner of the National Football League (NFL). Since he had joined the firm in 1969, his practice had focused on various NFL issues, and the law firm continued to represent the NFL in the years to come.

The Partnership in the 1990s and Beyond

In 1990 Covington & Burling joined the growing number of American law firms in Brussels, the European Community (EC) headquarters. They came to help prepare their corporate clients for the EC's effort to create uniform business rules and regulations in its 12 member nations by 1992. In 1988 only eight American firms were in Brussels, but the number had grown to 25 by 1990. Most either merged with Belgian law firms or hired local lawyers.

Covington & Burling lawyers assisted leaders of both the Republican and Democratic parties. For example, Charles F.C. Ruff during a four-year absence from the firm served as President Bill Clinton's counsel during the impeachment crisis. During the 2000 electoral disputes in Florida, George W. Bush used lawyers from many leading law firms. Covington & Burling's Bobby Burchfield, an expert on evaluating ballot chads, assisted Bush in the recount controversy. Covington & Burling assisted the District of Columbia when it tried to gain representation in the Congress. The D.C. government and 57 residents used the law firm when they filed the lawsuit *Alexander v. Daly* to gain full voting privileges. In 2000, however, the U.S. Supreme Court ruled against the District of Columbia after a two-year struggle. This was a good example of Covington & Burling's pro bono cases.

As part of Texaco's 1996 settlement of a racial discrimination lawsuit, the company established a Task Force on Equality and Fairness. In June 1997 Covington & Burling's Thomas Williamson, Jr., became the chair of the Texaco Task Force, a model used later for Coca-Cola's task force.

Covington & Burling assisted Microsoft Corporation in the late 1990s when the federal government investigated it for antitrust violations. Firm attorney Charles Ruff testified on Microsoft's behalf in 1997 hearings of the Senate Judiciary Committee.

In 1999 Exxon Corporation chose Covington & Burling for advice on antitrust issues when it merged with Mobil Corpora-

Key Dates:

1919: The partnership of Covington & Burling is founded in Washington, D.C., on January 1.
1921: The firm is renamed Covington, Burling & Rublee.
1949: The firm becomes known as Covington, Burling, Rublee, O'Brian & Shorb.
1951: The firm returns to its original name of Covington & Burling.
1989: The London office is opened.
1990: Covington & Burling opens its Brussels office.
1997: The firm enters an exclusive cooperation agreement with France's August & Debouzy.
1999: The firm establishes an office in San Francisco in March; the firm merges with Howard, Smith & Levin of New York City in October.

tion. Both sides hired several major law firms to help in various aspects of this $79 billion merger that created Exxon Mobil.

Covington & Burling's tax attorneys assisted Computer Associates in its 2000 acquisition of Sterling Software. According to *International Tax Review* in April 2000, this $4 billion acquisition made it "the largest software deal ever." The firm also represented Computer Associates in its acquisitions of Platinum Technologies, Legent, and Computer Management Sciences.

Continuing its tradition as a key player in legislative and regulatory matters, in the 1990s Covington & Burling's lawyers helped write important laws, including the 1992 Energy Policy Act, the Sports Blackout Legislation of 1993, the 1994 Dietary Supplement Health Education Act, the 1996 Telecommunications Act, and the 1997 Food and Drug Modernization Act.

Covington & Burling for many years represented numerous trade associations. In the late 1990s the Association of Publicly Traded Companies hired the firm to lobby Congress for laws limiting liability from possible computer failures in 2000 due to the so-called Y2K problem. Other association clients were the Council for Marketing & Opinion Research, the Grocery Manufacturers Association, the Association of American Medical Colleges, and the National Food Processors Association. Covington & Burling's clients in the 1990s or in the new millennium also included Bacardi, Monsanto, Union Pacific, Merck, Warner-Lambert, Eli Lilly, Turner Broadcasting, the Smithsonian Institute, Procter & Gamble, Public Broadcast System, IBM, General Motors, ASARCO, Warburg Dillon Read, Granaria Holdings, the National Treasury Employees Union, the government of Vietnam, BankBoston Corporation, and the Motion Picture Association of America.

While recognizing corporations' need for lawyers, consumer activist and lawyer Ralph Nader often criticized corporate lawyers who destroyed documents, harassed citizens groups, overcharged clients, or in other ways were unethical. But Nader and Wesley Smith, in their book *No Contest: Corporate Lawyers and the Perversion of Justice in America,* praised Covington & Burling attorney Charles Horsky for his 1952 book *The Washington Lawyer,* which outlined the principles of an ethical corporate law practice.

Covington & Burling was criticized in the 1990s, however, for its role in the tobacco industry. A lobbying firm named State Affairs Company organized Contributions Watch to be a nonpartisan group that examined political campaign contributions. In 1996 Contributions Watch released a study on trial lawyers' contributions. The *Washington Post,* however, found documents indicating that Philip Morris, State Affairs Company, and Covington & Burling influenced the work of supposedly independent Contributions Watch. The *Washington Post* also reported that the law firm allowed Philip Morris to give more than $1 million to fund a company that often testified that only minimal health damages came from secondhand smoke indoors, but the law firm denied any illegal actions.

As part of a law firm consolidation trend, in October 1999 Covington & Burling's 340 lawyers merged with the New York City firm of Howard, Smith & Levin. The 60-lawyer firm represented General Electric's GE Capital section and the Bank of New York Company and had a significant capability in litigation and mergers and acquisitions.

The merger with Howard, Smith & Levin was not counted in the *American Lawyer*'s annual ranking of the United States' largest law firms. Thus based on its 1999 gross revenue of $165 million, Covington & Burling was ranked number 79. Gross revenues of $152 million in 1998 resulted in a number 70 ranking. In 1997, Covington & Burling had $143 million in gross revenue, making it number 61 in the annual ranking.

Although it had declined in the rankings by the *American Lawyer,* Covington & Burling seemed well prepared for the challenges of the new millennium. With a heritage of major contributions to the legal profession, the firm's more than 450 lawyers continued to provide its clients with legal counsel in many areas of American and international law.

Principal Competitors

Arnold & Porter; Hogan & Hartson; Skadden, Arps, Slate, Meagher & Flom; Akin, Gump, Strauss, Hauer & Feld.

Further Reading

Abramson, Jill, "Two Law Firms in U.S. Opening Offices Abroad," *Wall Street Journal,* March 27, 1989, p. 1.

Abramson, Jill, and Timothy Noah, "In GOP-Controlled Congress, Lobbyists Remain As Powerful As Ever—And Perhaps More Visible," *Wall Street Journal,* April 20, 1995, p. A14.

Albiniak, Paige, and Chris McConnell, "Cohen Named MPAA [Motion Picture Association of America] Counsel," *Broadcasting & Cable,* September 21, 1998, p. 34.

Bowers, Diane K., "CMOR [Council for Marketing and Opinion Research]: A Look Back and a Look Ahead," *Marketing Research,* Spring 1995, p. 45.

Brinkley, Douglas, "Architect of a New World," *Washington Post,* August 9, 1998, p. X01.

"Campaign Watchdog Group Has Ties to Philip Morris," *Los Angeles Times,* October 1, 1996, p. 8.

Chace, James, *Acheson: The Secretary of State Who Created the American World,* New York: Simon & Schuster, 1998.

"Covington & Burling Coordinates Software Merger," *International Tax Review,* April 2000, p. 9.

"Covington & Burling Moves into French Market," *International Financial Law Review,* December 1997, p. 5.

"Covington & Burling Plan Continues Merger Trend," *Wall Street Journal,* September 21, 1999, p. A14.

Goodwin, Jacob, *Brotherhood of Arms: General Dynamics and the Business of Defending America,* New York: Times Books, 1985.

Grimaldi, James V., "Having a Ball While Thanking All the President's Lawyers for a Job Well Done," *Washington Post,* January 22, 2001, p. E8.

Havemann, Joel, "Doing Business U.S. Law Firms Chasing New Clients in Brussels . . . ," *Los Angeles Times,* December 4, 1990, p. 4.

Howard, Theresa, "Coke Settles Bias Lawsuit for $192.5M: Company Will Pay More Than 2,000 Black Employees, Set Up Diversity Programs," *USA Today,* November 17, 2000, p. B1.

Ingersoll, Bruce, "SEC Begins Inquiry of General Dynamics' Disclosure of Cost Overruns on Submarines," *Wall Street Journal,* October 3, 1984, p. 1.

Lachica, Eduardo, "Puerto Ricans Fear Tax Overhaul Would Force Island's Retreat to 'Rum-and Textile' Economy," *Wall Street Journal,* February 13, 1985, p. 1.

Lasseter, Earle F., "Power Play Incorporated," *American Bar Association Journal,* May 1997, p. 112.

Lieber, Jill, "NFL's Driving Force/Father's Work Ethic Set Tone Early," *USA Today,* January 25, 1996, p. 1C.

McAllister, Bill, "2000 Reasons to Lobby," *Washington Post,* October 29, 1998, p. A25.

Miller, Bill, "D.C. Loses Bid for Vote in Congress," *Washington Post,* October 17, 2000, p. A1.

Parker, Merrick, *History of the Firm's First Fifty Years,* Washington, D.C.: Covington & Burling, 1969.

"$79 Billion Exxon/Mobil Merger," *International Financial Law Review,* January 1999, p. 6.

Shiver, Jube, Jr., "Bans, Red Ink Smoking: A Burning Work Issue," *Los Angeles Times,* November 21, 1985, p. 1.

Spiess, Gary, "Expanding in Latin America," *International Financial Law Review,* September 1998, p. 72.

"Success Stories: The Fortune 25," *International Commercial Litigation,* March 1997, pp. 12–13.

"Texaco Inc.," *Wall Street Journal,* January 14, 1999.

"Unusual Lawyer Mourned by Unique Client; Clinton Praises Charles Ruff, White House Counsel During Impeachment," *Washington Post,* December 17, 2000, p. A13.

Wain, Barry, "Law Firm Says Vietnam Is Entitled to Oil, Gas Deposits," *Wall Street Journal,* June 16, 1995, p. A11.

Wessel, Davis, and Bob Davis, "Under a Cloud: Bank of Boston Faces Image Problem Likely to Linger for Years . . . ," *Wall Street Journal,* March 7, 1985, p. 1.

Westwood, Howard C., *Covington & Burling: 1919–1984,* Washington, D.C.: Covington & Burling, 1986.

—David M. Walden

Cranswick plc

Driffield, East Yorkshire YO25 9PF
United Kingdom
Telephone: (+44) 1377 270649
Fax: (+44) 1377 275001
Web site: http://www.cranswick.co.uk

Public Company
Incorporated: 1974
Employees: 972
Sales: £157.35 million ($250.5 million) (2000)
Stock Exchanges: London
Ticker Symbol: CWK
NAIC: 311119 Other Animal Food Manufacturing;
112210 Hog and Pig Farming; 311611 Animal
(Except Poultry) Slaughtering; 311612 Meat
Processed from Carcasses; 311613 Rendering and
Meat Byproduct Processing; 311612 Meat Processed
from Carcasses

England's Cranswick plc has transformed itself from a regional pork and pig feed producer into a diversified company operating in three core yet related markets: agribusiness, food products, and pet and pet food products. The company's agribusiness company is grouped around its historical pig marketing and pig feed operations, under the Cranswick Mill subsidiary. The company manufactures pig feed at its original Driffield site in East Yorkshire, and at its Wellingore plant, in Lincolnshire, acquired in March 2000. The acquisition has helped boost the company's production to 250,000 tons per year, while extending its range into the important pig rearing region of Lincolnshire. Wellingore also has enabled the company to extend its feed production to poultry feed. Cranswick Mill oversees Cranswick's pig marketing operations, buying pigs from pork farmers—many of whom are customers for the company's feed products—in and beyond its home regions for sale to pork products producers, including Cranswick itself. The company manufactures pork products, including sausages, hams, and other meats, under its Cranswick Country Foods subsidiary. Cranswick Country Foods oversees the vertical integration of Cranswick's pork, feed, and food operations. The company's food products, manufactured in five production plants, include a 15 percent share of the U.K. market for premium quality sausages, under the Cranswick, Cranswick Gourmet, George Lazenby (which is also the exclusive licensee for the brand Duchy Original Sausages, produced from the Prince of Wales pig herd), and other company-owned and private-label brands. The company's food division has overtaken its pig feed division in turnover, accounting for two-thirds of the company's sales. Cranswick's third area of operations is linked to its core activities: the company's Tropical Marine Centre is Europe's largest importer, breeder, and distributor of tropical fish and invertebrates, as well as a leading manufacturer of fish foods. The Pet division's other subsidiaries, George Buckton and Magnet, produce bird seed. Cranswick is led by chairman and cofounder Jim Bloom, and by CEO Martin Davey, who has helped lead the company's diversification since the late 1980s.

Pig Feed to Pig Farmer in the 1970s

Cranswick was founded in 1974 by East Yorkshire farmers Jim Bloom, Mike Field, and others to manufacture pig feed from their farms' production. Into the late 1970s, the company began to rear and market pigs as well. In 1980, Cranswick extended its operations again, now entering the grain trading market. An outbreak of the highly contagious foot-and-mouth disease in the early 1980s devastated the United Kingdom's livestock population, as animals were forced to be destroyed. The resulting chaos in Cranswick's industry, and the industry's cyclical nature even in the best of times, encouraged the company to seek to diversify its operations by the late 1980s.

Martin Davey, who had joined the company in 1985, was named the company's CEO in 1988 and was instrumental in transforming Cranswick into a small but growing—and profitable—diversified company. In 1988, Cranswick took its first step beyond its agribusiness core, which operated under the Cranswick Mill name, when it bought a small pork butchery. The purchase enabled the company to extend its operations from pig rearing and pig feed production into the processing of pork cuts for the United Kingdom's wholesale and retail markets.

In the early 1990s, Cranswick, which went public with a listing on the London Stock Exchange, extended its growth strategy to boost its food production activities. The company remained closed to its core pork-based operations, however. In 1992, Cranswick added new food processing activities with the acquisition of FT Sutton & Son (Rossendale) Limited, a ham and other processed pork products manufacturer that was to form the basis of the company's Cranswick Country Foods subsidiary. Other acquisitions made in the 1990s allowed the company to extend into packaged retail and branded name products, while remaining close to its focus on fresh and processed pork products. The company also launched its own development team to invent new products, to be sold under the Cranswick name, but also under private labels for such grocery chains as Sainsbury.

Diversified Group for the 21st Century

Yet Cranswick's feed interests led it to diversify into new areas of operation. In 1993, the company acquired George Buckton & Sons Limited. That company, which had been founded in the early 19th century, originally had operated as a drysaltery business until the mid-20th century. Acquired by Harry Henderson, who had seen his Hull, Yorkshire-based shipping business destroyed in World War I, Buckton became one of the United Kingdom's leading producers of bird seed, particularly well known for its corn-based feed created especially for the pigeon racing circuit. The Buckton acquisition seemed a natural extension of Cranswick's existing feed production business. It also led the company into exploring other areas of the market for pets and pet foods.

The company's new interest in the pet market led it to acquire Tropical Marine Centre, the leading supplier of live tropical fish and invertebrates to the European market. Founded in 1970 by Richard Sankey, Tropical Marine Centre also had developed a manufacturing arm for the production of aquarium-related equipment, such as UV cleansing and sterilizing equipment. The company also produced fish foods and, in the mid-1990s, began to develop the first successful tropical fish hatcheries. The Tropical Marine Centre acquisition was completed in 1995. A few months later, at the beginning of 1996, Cranswick boosted its pet division with the purchase of Magnet, adding that company's production of bird food and foods for small animals. Magnet was subsequently placed under the company's George Buckton subsidiary. These acquisitions helped boost the company's revenues to £79 million by the end of 1995. They also encouraged the company to dispose of its grain trading business in 1996.

In the late 1990s, Cranswick turned to boosting its pork products activities. The company found new markets for a number of pork products that were less popular in its core U.K. markets. As such, in 1998, the company began seeing growing sales to the Chinese market for pigs' feet, as well as sales of pork bellies to South Korea and pig tails to the West Indies. In its home market, meanwhile, Cranswick had been building a successful range of gourmet sausages and ham under the Cranswick Country Foods and other brands. These were proving so successful, not only in the United Kingdom, but also in Germany, where the company established its first foreign subsidiary, that its specialty food products now represented its fastest growing segment of operations. The company was expanding its production capacity, adding a new production line in its main pig feed facility.

At the end of 1998, Cranswick boosted its gourmet sausage operations with the acquisition of Cambury Plc, which traded under the retail brand name of Mr. Lazenby. Founded by Richard Lazenby in 1982, the Teeside-based company also held the exclusive license to manufacture the Duchy Original Sausages brand produced from the pig stock of the Prince of Wales. At a cost of £3.5 million, the Mr. Lazenby brand helped fill out Cranswick's strong position in the high-end market.

Cranswick remained relatively unharmed by the outbreak of mad cow disease in the United Kingdom, which had come to full steam by the end of the 1990s, but remained confined to the country's beef industry. Indeed, Cranswick was even to profit somewhat by the growing consumer demand for the type of high-end meat products niches the company had carefully chosen, including the development of its own organic meats and meat products. The company continued to add to its specialty operations in 1999, buying a 33 percent share of Gourmet Sausage Co. Founded only in 1995, the young company was renamed Cranswick Gourmet Sausage Co. after Cranswick boosted its shareholding in 2000 to 67 percent.

Another important acquisition for the company came in September 1999 when Cranswick paid nearly £15 million to acquire Pethick & Co. Founded by meat industry veteran David Pethick and a number of friends in 1989, Pethick & Co., which produced delicatessen meats, particularly hams, for such large-scale customers as the ASDA supermarket chain, helped round out Cranswick's range of processed meat production. By then, the company's food division had outpaced its original feed production, representing some two-thirds of Cranswick's annual sales.

Cranswick's successful transformation into a diversified, yet unified feed-food-pet group made it a favorite among stock market analysts. The company's consistent gains in turnover were matched by strong profits. While still modestly sized, Cranswick's diversified interests helped it ride out the Europe-wide slump in pork prices that caused a number of its closest competitors to go out of business at the end of the decade. Meanwhile, its pet division was seeing strong gains, more than doubling its revenues in the second half of the 1990s. Tropical Marine Centre also was making history with its industry-leading hatchery program—the company had recorded a number of notable successes, including the first successful breeding of fire shrimps (Lysmata debelius) in 1997, then pipefishes (Doryrhamphus multi-annulatus) in 1998, and cleaner shrimps (Lysmata amboinensis) in 1999.

Key Dates:

1970: Richard Sankey founds Tropical Marine Centre.
1974: Jim Bloom, Mike Field, and other farmers form pig feed manufacturing company Cranswick; Cranswick eventually extends operations to include pig rearing and marketing.
1980: Company begins grain trading business.
1982: Richard Lazenby founds Cambury Plc.
1988: Company adopts diversification strategy to counteract market cycles; acquires pork butchery.
1989: Pethick & Co. is founded.
1992: Company acquires FT Sutton & Son (Rossendale) Ltd.
1993: Company acquires George Buckton & Sons Ltd.
1995: Company acquires Tropical Marine Centre; Gourmet Sausage Co. begins operations.
1996: Company exits grain trading business.
1998: Company acquires Cambury/Mr. Lazenby's.
1999: Company acquires Pethick & Co. Ltd; acquires one-third of Gourmet Sausage Co.
2000: Company purchases Wellingore (Lincolnshire) feed manufacturing plant; increases share of Gourmet Sausage Co. (renamed Cranswick Gourmet Sausage Co.) to 67 percent.
2001: Company plans to acquire full control of Cranswick Gourmet Sausage Co.

Cranswick continued to grow into the new century. In 2000, the company acquired a second feed production facility, Wellingore, in nearby Lincolnshire, which not only extended the company's pig marketing and feed production capacity into that important pig farming region, but also added Wellingore's poultry feed production to Cranswick's growing operations. At the beginning of 2001, Cranswick prepared to continue its growth, announcing its intention to become sole owner of Cranswick Gourmet Sausage Co. during the year. Yet the company faced new troubles at the beginning of 2001 as the country was once again devastated by a new outbreak of foot-and-mouth disease. Measures imposed in an effort to contain the spread of the disease effectively shut down major portions of the industry, as well as saw a new destruction of the company's livestock. Nevertheless, Cranswick's strong diversification throughout the previous decade helped to buffer the company's losses, particularly as its U.K. consumer base turned more and more toward the high-end organic and gourmet specialties that had become core Cranswick niches.

Principal Subsidiaries

Cambury Limited; Cranswick Mill Limited; Cranswick Country Foods Plc; Cranswick Deutschland; Cranswick Gourmet Sausage Company Limited (67%); George Buckton & Sons Limited; Magnet; Mr. Lazenby's; Pethick & Co. Ltd.; Tropical Marine Centre Limited.

Principal Competitors

Hazlewood Foods Plc; I£Inc.; Moksel AG; Northern Foods Plc; Smithfield Foods Inc.; Uniq Plc.

Further Reading

Arends, Berndt, "China's Taste for Trotters Helps Cranswick Fill Out," *Daily Telegraph,* May 21, 1998.
"Cranswick Is the Market Pet," *Independent on Sunday,* March 15, 1998, p. 6.
Denny, Charlotte, and John Vidal, "Crippled Industry May Cost Economy £1 Billion Loss," *Guardian,* March 1, 2001.
"Foot and Mouth Crisis: Lay-Off Pay Plight of Industry's Workers," *Birmingham Post,* March 1, 2001, p. 8.
Gray, Joan, "Diversification Helps Cranswick," *Financial Times,* May 25, 2000.
"Large Company Tips: Cranswick," *Investors Chronicle,* December 15, 2000.
Urry, Maggie, "Cranswick Beats Pig Turmoil," *Financial Times,* November 17, 2000.

—M. L. Cohen

Cummins Engine Company, Inc.

500 Jackson Street
Columbus, Indiana 47202-3005
U.S.A.
Telephone: (812) 377-5000
Toll Free: (800) DIESELS; (800) 343-7357
Fax: (812) 377-3334
Web site: http://www.cummins.com

Public Company
Incorporated: 1919
Employees: 28,000
Sales: $6.60 billion (2000)
Stock Exchanges: New York Pacific
Ticker Symbol: CUM
NAIC: 336399 All Other Motor Vehicle Parts
   Manufacturing; 333618 Other Engine Equipment
   Manufacturing; 335312 Motor and Generator
   Manufacturing; 336322 Other Motor Vehicle
   Electrical and Electronic Equipment Manufacturing;
   336399 All Other Motor Vehicle Parts Manufacturing

No one makes more large diesel engines than Cummins Engine Company, Inc. The company's other products— filtration and exhaust systems, natural gas engines, engine components, and electronic systems—have come to provide most of the company's profits, however, as the truck engine market has shrunk. In addition to trucks, Cummins diesel engines are used for drilling rigs, boats, industrial locomotives, compressors, pumps, logging equipment, construction equipment, agricultural equipment, municipal and school buses, and a variety of other applications.

Origins

The company's founder and the man who adapted Rudolf Diesel's engine design for mobile use was Clessie L. Cummins, the chauffeur of a 1909 Packard touring car owned by Will G. Irwin, a wealthy industrialist and philanthropist in Columbus, Indiana. Cummins was regarded by Irwin as indispensable, since he was the only man who could keep the Packard in running condition. When shortly before World War I, Cummins demanded a pay hike to $85 a month, Irwin threatened to fire him. The two men reached a compromise, however. Cummins would accept a salary reduction if the family garage were equipped with tools so that he could do engine repair work. In 1917, Cummins began making wagon hubcaps for the U.S. Army, while reading news about Germany's diesel-powered U-boats. Most diesel engines at that time were large and smoky, and entirely impractical for any kind of transportation.

Cummins started working full-time on diesels in 1919 when he heard that Sears, Roebuck & Co., would buy three-horsepower farm diesels made on a European patent. He persuaded Irwin to negotiate a contract with Sears and established Cummins Engine Company, Inc. The beginning was inauspicious; Sears said the engines were defective, and Irwin had to financially rescue his chauffeur. Neither Irwin nor Cummins was quitting, however. Irwin gave Cummins $10,000 to correct the initial defect and, eventually, poured more than $2.5 million into the company.

The problem with diesel engines at that time was that engineers kept adding devices to them to give them more power. Cummins accepted only one common premise, that of "combustion ignition," or fuel oil in the cylinder bursting into flames to provide power, and systematically disposed of any other "add on" parts. He initially reduced engine horsepower, but ultimately got his diesel to run faster than other models. For ten years his experimental engines ripped the bottoms out of fishing boats or tore themselves to remnants, but Cummins still would not quit. His breakthrough was what he called "the Sneezer," a device that discharged every last particle of fuel oil into the cylinder to ensure that no oil was released as smoke. He also created a fuel injector experts described as "simpler than a fountain pen."

With his diesel at last perfected, he installed it in a Packard and drove the 792 miles from Columbus to New York City on $1.88 worth of heating oil without refueling. He then exhibited the car in the 1930 New York Automobile Show. When skeptics suggested that he had used more fuel than he admitted, Cummins proved them wrong by driving across the country on $9.36 worth of fuel. He also entered a Duesenberg race car at the Indianapolis Motor Speedway and finished 13th while establishing a record speed for a diesel-powered car of 80.389 mph.

Company Perspectives:

At Cummins, we provide the technologies that power the world and support its economies. We conduct our business with the consent of society and we strive to improve the quality of life of all people.

Cummins's fuel pump and injector were now regarded as the best in the industry, but truck manufacturers refused to use them and continued to manufacture gasoline engines, while trying to design their own diesel engines. Irwin came to Cummins's rescue by having the engines of delivery trucks used by his grocery chain of Purity Stores in California replaced by Cummins diesel engines. The truckers liked these new engines, which were powerful, fuel-efficient, and reliable. As these truckers recommended the engine to their colleagues, the business began to flourish.

First Profit in 1937

Irwin's grandnephew, J. Irwin Miller, a young man with a pronounced taste for Greek and Latin but no business training, was appointed as head of the company. Miller was an unlikely manager: he had stuttered as a child, was something of an outcast at school, and knew nothing about engines. He had been expecting to inherit some facet of the family business, however, and applied himself rigorously.

Miller replaced the chauffeur's hand tools with production equipment and constructed a full-scale plant. He then helped employees organize the Diesel Workers Union, and he solicited business during the Great Depression by pointing out to cash-starved truckers that they would save money if they bought only those trucks that offered Cummins engines as options. Miller referred to this strategy—going to the users and not the suppliers—as a "back-door approach." Fortunately for the young company, the trucking business prospered in the 1930s because of improved roads and demand for point-to-point deliveries. Diesel engines for large trucks that needed maximum fuel efficiency were increasingly in demand. In 1937 the young company turned its first profit. Selling engines to competitors was an uncertain way of doing business, but it worked and remained, however unorthodox, the Cummins approach. Miller, who was admired as a scholar and philanthropist, and who served as the first lay president of the National Council of Churches, later acknowledged, "We're in the business of selling engines to engine makers, which is surely not the smartest way to make a living."

The company was not just unorthodox in its marketing approach. It contributed 5 percent of its pretax profits each year to a number of charitable and social service projects. Years later, Cummins became one of the first companies in its industry to hire blacks for other than janitorial jobs. Miller helped beautify the company's hometown, Columbus, Indiana, with the creation of a unique endowment that paid the architect's fees for many public buildings. The fund helped draw some of the country's finest architects to the Midwest town. In 1992, the Business Enterprise Trust recognized Miller's magnanimity and philan-

thropy when it awarded him its Lifetime Achievement Award. Miller's sense of justice and scholarly background helped him at times decide against prevailing business trends as well. For example, when asked why Cummins was resisting pressure to diversify, Miller told *Forbes,* "This may be counter to trends, but we believe that by diversifying you are liable to lose confidence in the value of a good product."

The company doubled its sales in five years and continued to double sales every five years into the 1960s. Sales in 1946 hit $20 million; a decade later they reached more than $100 million. Cummins's best-selling engine was a 2,590-pound diesel for trucks of 13 tons or more. To maintain the high demand for Cummins engines, the company had to stay ahead of the competition, which soon included Mack Trucks, Caterpillar, and GM's Detroit Diesel. In 1952 the company unveiled a turbo-diesel, which used exhaust gases to turn a gas turbine supercharger. The device increased the horsepower of each Cummins engine by 50 percent without raising fuel consumption. That year Cummins demonstrated the engine at the Indianapolis Motor Speedway, where it malfunctioned. Miller was nonplussed. "We have progressed from failure to failure," he said, confidently predicting that the turbo-diesel would soon be perfected and marketed, which it was.

Cummins stayed way ahead of its competition in the 1950s by securing up to 60 percent of the heavy-duty truck market in North America. Its in-line six-cylinder engines were renowned for their power and longevity. Cummins distributors, who handled nothing but Cummins engines and parts, were regarded as highly reputable because of their expertise with the single product line. Although it faced competition from Caterpillar and Euclid, Cummins also began selling engines for off-road construction. "We'll build the roads and then we'll run on them," said Miller.

Downhill in the 1960s

The heavy truck market appeared to be saturated by 1960, however. To expand into alternative markets Cummins crafted a new line of V-6 and V-8 engines, based on an "oversquare" gasoline engine design. Since the diameter of the cylinder in oversquare engines is greater than the piston stroke, the engines produce more power at high speeds. Diesel engines had been long-stroke, but Cummins's engineers found the right combination of fuel and air to inject into the combustion chamber and make their engines workable.

The new engines, the Vim (a V-6 model with 200 horsepower), the Vine (a V-8 with 265 horsepower), and the Val (a V-6 with 120 horsepower), represented Cummins's first attempt at penetrating the lighter truck market. At that time, 44 percent of trucks 13 tons and over had diesel engines, but fewer than 1 percent of the trucks from eight to 13 tons were diesel-powered. With heavier trucks representing just 6 percent of the market, and the lighter trucks 22 percent, management concluded that manufacturing smaller engines would raise revenues. Nevertheless, the lighter truck market proved difficult to enter. Gas was cheap and diesel engines, which at that time cost $1,000 to $4,000 more than gasoline engines, were seen as economical only if the vehicles were driven approximately 4,000 hours per year.

In the early 1960s Cummins began a slow decline. Sales and profits fluctuated. A new line of engines with more than 300 horsepower, introduced by the company in 1962, failed to gain a dominant market share for more than two years. Management was criticized for being behind in both product development and market share.

Part of the problem was Cummins's policy of diversification. Beginning in the late 1950s Cummins started acquiring an interest in companies that produced diesel-related products. By the late 1960s it had become genuinely diversified, purchasing a ski manufacturer, a bank, and even an Irish cattle-feeding outfit. Management had decided to make these acquisitions due to the slow growth of the diesel market. Whereas Cummins's sales averaged 15 percent annual growth, the diesel market was projected to expand at half that rate. A number of new diesel competitors, such as GMC Division and Perkins, compounded the problem.

By 1967 Cummins's share of the crucial heavy-truck market had slipped to less than 45 percent. Earnings were off 78 percent. A strong truck market helped sales rebound in 1968, reaching a record of $365 million. Vigorous sales continued over the next few years, but earnings were erratic. Miller's hand-picked young successor, Henry Schacht, who joined the company after graduating from Harvard Business School and assumed the presidency just two years later, blamed surprisingly strong demand for the thin margins. Instead of preparing for an increased truck demand, Cummins had diverted resources to its nondiesel holdings. To catch up to the competition, Cummins operated its factories 24 hours a day, seven days a week, and paid a large amount in overtime wages. A two-month-long strike only exacerbated the company's difficulties.

"We clearly left the door open to competitors," Schacht told *Forbes*. Demand exceeded supply, and customers went elsewhere. There was criticism that Cummins met the demands of only its biggest customers and that smaller consumers were forced to buy from the competition. Cummins's share of the large truck market reached a low point of less than 40 percent in the early 1970s. The company elected to sell its other holdings and concentrate on meeting the unexpectedly high diesel demand.

The main challenge was to devise a marketing strategy for engines that remained about 5 percent more expensive than that of the competition. The company refused to downgrade its product line. Management believed that the most significant problem for truckers who drove their vehicles 240,000 miles and more a year was downtime. Consequently, the company's response to its slipping market share was to make its engines more powerful, which in turn made them more reliable. In this way Cummins held on to its largest customers. Furthermore, the company expanded its overseas operations. It had a worldwide network of 3,000 service outlets and a computerized analysis of 50,000 miles of major highways, allowing it to match the best engine to the customer's requirements. Its reputation helped it gain access to new markets. By the mid-1970s, 25 percent of the company's revenues came from overseas, and additional profits were being made in the agriculture, construction, and marine enterprises for which Cummins was designing extra-large engines of 1,200 horsepower.

Then Cummins made an apparent mistake and introduced a line of 450-horsepower engines. This was 50 percent more power than a truck needed to haul a loaded rig at 65 mph on a level highway. Cummins was marketing power in its engines, but the problem was the new 55 mph speed limit. The company confronted this issue with an advertising campaign that stressed "reserve power." According to the ads, the new engines could easily maintain 55 mph even on uphill grades, so truckers could travel at the maximum allowable speed. Furthermore, constant speed and less shifting would actually increase fuel efficiency.

The new engines did not sell very well at first, as the truck market in 1975 slumped 40 percent. The following year, however, the market rebounded, and Cummins took the lion's share. Sales reached $1 billion and earnings were $59 million. Cummins benefited from the erratic enforcement of the 55 mph speed limit. Furthermore, the company outperformed its competitors by introducing a turbo-charged, slower-running version of its large-block engine, offering 5 percent better economy.

Nonetheless, management was increasingly concerned about the volatile truck market. While automating company plants in order to stay competitive within the truck engine industry, Cummins increased its profit from nonhighway engines until they accounted for nearly 25 percent of revenues. This stabilized the company, for the demand for agricultural and construction equipment ran in cycles that were unrelated to the demand for truck engines. Cummins also established plants in Scotland and England to penetrate the European market while avoiding European tariffs. It faced new rivals, such as Renault in France and Iveco in Italy, which placed only their own engines in trucks they were manufacturing. But Cummins, which had faced a similar obstacle in the 1930s, was undeterred. New laws allowing trucks of up to 38,000 pounds on European highways, in addition to the escalating costs of fuel, convinced Cummins management that Europe was the new market for Cummins's diesel engines. For Cummins, the European market grew slowly but steadily.

Leaner in the 1980s

In the meantime, Cummins faced a Japanese incursion on the domestic market. These new competitors sought to establish a foothold in the United States by offering their diesel engines at 10 percent to 40 percent below Cummins's prices. Cummins met the challenge with its own price cuts, a strategy that helped prevent the new rivals from capturing a significant share of the market. To maintain profitability, Cummins's CEO, Schacht, instituted a program of austerity and restructuring. From 1979 to 1986, the company cut employment by 22 percent, set up flexible production methods that reduced inventory, increased productivity, and launched outsourcing programs. In addition, although the company lost millions in the early 1980s, Schacht committed about $200 million annually to capital investments and improvements, maintaining Cummins's dividend.

In 1986 the company entered a period of continuous, comprehensive restructuring that embraced every aspect of the business. The adoption of an employee training and empowerment program known as JDIT-Kaizen helped transform the corporate culture. The acronym JDIT stood for the well-known catch phrase "just do it." Kaizen was one of a number of Japanese management techniques that were in vogue at the time. It encouraged creativity at all levels, with the ultimate goal of continuous, gradual improvement. This management strategy may have helped ease labor relations at Cummins, which earlier had moved production to nonunion factories in the southern United States to avoid labor disputes. (In 1993, in fact, the independent Diesel Workers Union—representing workers at four Indiana plants—gave Cummins an overwhelming vote of confidence when it ratified an extraordinary 11-year contract.) Furthermore, a consolidation trimmed operations in the United Kingdom and shuttered two U.S. plants, reducing floor space for worldwide engine manufacturing and distribution by 19 percent.

Notwithstanding these efforts, Schacht and Cummins also made some significant missteps during the last half of the 1980s. Some industry observers criticized the company's downsizing efforts when a resurgence in demand compelled the company to pay overtime rates to keep up. In response to ever more stringent emission control regulations, the company hurried to beat its competitors in bringing a compliant engine to market. Although the new model met U.S. EPA standards, tests conducted after the engine's launch revealed significant shortcomings. At the same time, rival Detroit Diesel Inc. introduced an electronic engine that drew customers away in droves. Cummins's share declined steadily throughout the late 1980s and early 1990s, from more than 60 percent in 1984, to 55 percent in 1988, 50.3 percent in 1989, and 40 percent in 1991, its lowest level in two decades. During this same period, the company lost more than $300 million and recorded only one year of meager profitability.

In 1990, Schacht convinced Ford Motor Co., Tenneco Inc., and Kubota Ltd. to invest a combined total of $250 million in a 27 percent stake in Cummins. The CEO used the infusion of capital to pay down debt and expand European operations. When sales of long-haul trucks bounced back in the early 1990s, Cummins's long years of preparation paid off. In 1993, the company enjoyed its first annual profit since 1987. In 1994, after seeing the company through one of its most difficult periods, Schacht announced that he was stepping down as CEO.

That year—Cummins's 75th in business—the company achieved record sales of $4.74 billion and, perhaps more important, record profits of $252.9 million. James A. Henderson succeeded Schacht as CEO, and Theodore M. Solso became president and chief operating officer. They inherited a company well-positioned to capture significant shares of the vital Japanese and European markets. Henderson became chairman and Solso became president in 1995.

Retooling in 1995

About a decade after Japanese diesels began pouring into the United States, Cummins announced a number of joint ventures with foreign manufacturers in Japan, Finland, and India. Increasing construction abroad was expected to create more demand for the company's engines and generators.

The company's plant at home, in Columbus, Indiana, was making 160 engines a day. Less than 0.5 of these per hundred were found in need of repair; workers were progressing toward a goal of measuring quality in repairs per million.

Cummins invested heavily in research during good times and bad. Its R&D budget of 5 percent of annual sales was twice that of competitors. A $20 million, 50,000-square-foot engine testing facility was completed in 1996.

The company developed SmartPower in 1995. This used a computer embedded in the engine to capture 160 types of performance data, with another 100 customized performance features. The first Interact System engines using SmartPower were released in April 1997. Cummins was committed to extending this program to all of its electronic engine models by 2000. By 1999, the company had invested $1 billion in the program. At the same time, it was participating in a collaborative effort to develop a standard for the transmission of engine data over the Internet.

Unfortunately, the first of these engines manufactured suffered reliability problems, costing the manufacturer millions in warranty costs. The Asian financial crisis also hit Cummins hard, causing orders in that region to drop 50 percent between 1997 and 1998. A downturn in the domestic farm machinery market added to the damage.

In October 1998, the seven largest makers of heavy diesel engines, including Cummins, agreed to pay the Environmental Protection Agency (EPA) $1 billion to settle a suit claiming the group used computerized timing devices to evade emissions tests. Cummins's share price fell as its troubles compounded, leading to takeover rumors.

Forbes reported that 1998 was the truck industry's best year to date. Even so, Cummins lost $21 million on sales of $6.3 billion. The magazine found that the massive Interact System investment was necessary, however, and many of the company's troubles were unavoidable. To combat the losses, CEO James Henderson aimed to raise the company's gross margin to 25 percent and reduce engineering and overhead slightly to 16 percent of sales to achieve an operating margin of 9 percent by 2001.

A growing market was a requisite for these targets. Unfortunately, truck engine sales declined precipitously after peaking at 305,000 in 1999. Cummins's engine shipments for the heavy-duty truck market fell by more than 50 percent in 2000. By this time, the company had closed three plants and cut 1,100 jobs. Henderson retired at the end of 1999 at the age of 65. His chief operating officer and president, Theodore "Tim" Solso, succeeded him as CEO.

In the summer of 2000, *Barron's* noted, Cummins shares were worth what they had been in 1972. The North American diesel engine market was in a slump, and the company's market share had fallen from 60 percent in the 1980s to less than 30 percent, thanks in part to Caterpillar, Inc. Nevertheless, Cummins was considerably more diversified than it had been, with power generation and filtration divisions supplying most of its profits. In 1996, Cummins had restructured its business units according to its primary markets: auto, industrial, power generation, and filtration. At the end of 2000, Cummins announced plans to cut 350 jobs from its diesel engine unit while "fundamentally rethinking" its role in the market. Another loss of 100 jobs soon followed, bringing the total number to 900 for the year.

In early 2001, Cummins signed a more exclusive agreement with Paccar Inc., the Bellevue, Washington-based manufacturer of Peterbilt and Kenworth trucks. Solso told the *Wall Street Journal* that the company would exit the North American truck engine business if that type of relationship did not work. Once the company's sole *raison d'etre*, this sector accounted for only 16 percent of revenues in 2000.

Principal Subsidiaries

Cummins Brasil Ltda.; Cummins Engine Company PTY (Australia); Cummins India Ltd.; Cummins Korea, Ltd.; Cummins Mexicana, S.A. de C.V. (Mexico); Cummins Natural Gas Engines, Inc.; Cummins Power Generation, Inc.; Cummins Power Generation Limited (U.K.); Fleetguard, Inc.; Holset Engineering Company Limited (U.K.); Kuss Corporation; Newage International Limited (U.K.); Onan Corporation; Power Systems India Ltd.; Separation Technologies; Swagman International PTY Ltd. (Australia); Universal Silencer.

Principal Operating Units

Engine; Power Generation; Filtration and Other.

Principal Competitors

Caterpillar Inc.; Detroit Diesel Corporation; Mack Trucks, Inc.

Further Reading

Bary, Andrew, "In Low Gear," *Barron's*, July 17, 2000, p. 24.

Basralian, Joseph, "Cummins Engine: Upshift," *Financial World*, March 14, 1995, pp. 18.

Benway, Susan Duffy, "Geared Up for a Turn: Cummins Comes Through a Rough Patch," *Barron's*, September 22, 1986, pp. 13, 41.

Bergstrom, Robin Yale, "Old Measures, New Rules," *Production*, June 1994, pp. 62–64.

——, "Quick Comments on Quality Solutions at Cummins," *Automotive Manufacturing & Production*, February 1997, p. 64.

Caldwell, Bruce, "Cummins Keeps Pace," *Informationweek*, July 21, 1997, pp. 87–88.

Cimini, Michael H., and Susan L. Behrmann, "Developments in Industrial Relations," *Monthly Labor Review*, July 1993, pp. 56–58.

"Cummins Engine Puts Customers in the Driver's Seat," *Mechanical Engineering*, December 1993, p. 75.

Faltermeyer, Edmund, "Cummins Engine: A Long Term Bet Pays Off at Last," *Fortune*, August 23, 1993, pp. 79–80.

Fialka, John J., and Carl Quintanilla, "Diesel-Engine Makers Agree to Penalty Over $1 Billion in EPA Pollution Case," *Wall Street Journal*, October 23, 1998, p. A6.

Gold, Jacqueline S., "The Twelve Labors: To Hell and Back with Henry Schacht of Cummins Engine," *Financial World*, June 9, 1992, pp. 60–61.

Hallinan, Joseph T., "Cummins Agrees to Supply Truck Engines to Paccar—Risky Strategy Is a Bold Attempt to Revive Dwindling Market Share," *Wall Street Journal*, February 12, 2001, p. B4.

——, "Cummins to Cut 350 Salaried Jobs from Engine Unit," *Wall Street Journal*, November 7, 2000, p. B5.

Henkoff, Ronald, "The Engine That Couldn't," *Fortune*, December 18, 1989, p. 124.

Kelly, Kevin, "A CEO Who Kept His Eyes on the Horizon," *Business Week*, August 1, 1994, p. 32.

——, "Does Cummins Have the Oomph to Climb This Hill?," *Business Week*, November 4, 1991, pp. 66, 68.

"Latest Entry to Cummins $1 Billion Investment in New Product Line Now Moves into Production," *Fleet Equipment*, October 1999, pp. 45–46.

Marcial, Gene G., "Will a Euro Buyer Rev Up Cummins?," *Business Week*, November 30, 1998, p. 128.

Marsh, Harry L., and J. Branch Walton, "An Ironclad Case for Professionalism," *Security Management*, February 1992, pp. 70 + .

McManamy, Rob, "Market Focus: Columbus, Inc., the Town That Builds First Class," *ENR*, April 6, 1992, pp. 36C7–36C12.

Merrick, Amy, "Cummins Expects Loss in Fourth Quarter amid Restructure Charge, More Job Cuts," *Wall Street Journal*, December 2000, p. C22.

Miller, J. Irwin, "The Service Ethic," *Executive Excellence*, October 1992, p. 17.

Mohan, Suruchi, "Engine Manufacturer Cuts Costs Worldwide," *Info-World*, April 6, 1998, p. 66.

Morris, John, "Cummins Comes Back," *CFO*, April 1993, p. 20.

Parker, Jocelyn, "Cummins Engine's Layoffs May Grow As Sector Declines," *Wall Street Journal*, November 20, 2000, p. B13.

Pratt, Tom, "Warburg Leads Biggest US Stock Deal Yet for Cummins Engine," *Investment Dealers' Digest*, December 13, 1993, p. 10.

Quintanilla, Carl, "Cummins CEO Henderson to Retire, and Solso Is Successor," *Wall Street Journal*, September 30, 1999, p. B4.

——, "Cummins Engine Says Weak Asia Sales and Warranty Costs Will Hurt Results," *Wall Street Journal*, March 23, 1998, p. A8.

Rose, Robert L., "In the Lab: Truck-Engine Research Has Its Mr. Clean," *Wall Street Journal*, December 15, 1992, p. B5.

Ross, Chuck, "A Research Facility Driven to Succeed," *Consulting-Specifying Engineer*, December 1996, pp. 38–41.

Schultz, Ellen E., "Pension Protestor: Fired for Complaining?," *Wall Street Journal*, February 11, 1999, p. C27.

Smith, Geoffrey N., "The Yankee Samurai," *Forbes*, July 14, 1986, pp. 82–83.

Taylor, David L., and Ruth Karin Ramsey, "Empowering Employees to 'Just Do It,'" *Training & Development*, May 1993, pp. 71–76.

Townsend, Blaine, "The Corporate Responsibility Hall of Fame," *Business & Society Review*, Spring 1992, pp. 47–50.

Upbin, Bruce, "This Time Is Different—Maybe," *Forbes*, May 31, 1999, pp. 52–53.

—updates: April Dougal Gasbarre,
Frederick C. Ingram

DANZAS

Danzas Group

Peter Merian-Strasse 88
CH-4002 Basel
Switzerland
Telephone: (+41) 61-274-74-74
Fax: (+41) 61-274-74-75
Web site: http://www.danzas.com

Wholly Owned Subsidiary of Deutsche Post AG
Incorporated: 1840 as Maison de Commission et
   d'Expedition Danzas & l'Eveque
Employees: 38,000
Sales: SFr 11.7 billion ($7.5 billion) (2000)
NAIC: 541614 Process, Physical Distribution, and
   Logistics Consulting Services; 488510 Freight
   Transportation Arrangement; 481212 Nonscheduled
   Chartered Freight Air Transportation

Danzas Group is one of Europe's leading logistics groups, the European leader in overland freight-forwarding and logistics, and the world's leading air cargo forwarder. The company is also a subsidiary of Germany's Deutsche Post, overseeing that growing and soon-to-be privatized company's logistics operations. Danzas continues to operate from its Basle, Switzerland-headquarters. Yet, through Deutsche Post, Danzas has been on a buying spree that has tripled its sales in a little less than two years. Danzas's acquisitions at the turn of the millennium include Air Express International, ASG AB, and Nedlloyd ETD, bringing total sales to nearly SFr 12 billion and expanding the company's worldwide workforce to nearly 40,000. Danzas has also been expanding throughout Eastern Europe, notably in Hungary, with its takeover of that country's Danubiasped, and in South America, with the integration of Chile's Deca Express SA. The company's operations are structured into three primary divisions: Intercontinental, Eurocargo, and Solutions. Danzas is led by Peter Wagner, whose official title is chairman and CEO of Deutsche Post's Logistics Corporate Division. That company has been preparing its initial public offering in advance of the ban on postal monopolies among European Community member countries, to be implemented in 2003.

Rising from Defeat at Waterloo

Danzas's history traces back to the European conflict that culminated in the battle of Waterloo in 1815. For much of the company's history, Danzas, first French, then Swiss, struggled to maintain its communication and transportation links against a background of European wars and political troubles.

After the resounding defeat of Napoleon's Grande Armée at Waterloo, a demobilized young French lieutenant named Marie Matthias Nicholas Louis Danzas, or Louis Danzas for short, joined a small freight forwarding company, Michel l'Evêque, Etablissement de Commission et d'Expédition, in St. Louis, France, just across the border from Basel, Switzerland. Within a very short time he was appointed the company's procureur général et spécial. Louis Danzas was an Alsatian, but his family traced their origins to Gascony and Spain; the name was originally spelled D'Anzas.

In 1840 Danzas and his brother-in-law Edouard l'Evêque formed the Maison de Commission et d'Expédition Danzas & l'Evêque a St. Louis. Seven years later Danzas and l'Evêque took their first step toward expansion by opening a branch in the nearby city of Mulhouse, France.

The company was well placed to take advantage of the new technology and the rapidly expanding rail and steamship routes in this part of Europe. Danzas began to build up a worldwide network of agents. In order to handle the regular groupage—the organization of combined freight units for joint transportation—traffic between Zürich and Basel, they merged with the transport companies Favier-Gervais Vonier and Ouzelet & Cie to form a new general partnership, Danzas, Ouzelet & Cie, in 1855. The firm then had Ouzelet's former offices in Basel as a Swiss branch. The new service accéléré may have been the world's first rail groupage service. In 1859, the firm was renamed Danzas, l'Evêque & Minet—the latter was a partner in the former Ouzelet firm—but the company remained French, headquartered in St. Louis, and Louis Danzas remained the undisputed senior partner of the rapidly expanding company until he died in 1862.

His son, Emile Jules Danzas, succeeded him. Initially he had favored a military career, but his father wanted to found a Danzas

Company Perspectives:

Among international logistics firms, Danzas now occupies a leading position in all business sectors. The transformation process is by no means finished, however. In view of the changing needs in today's market, every logistics company has to remain flexible and innovative. Services have to be continually optimized and extended if the group is to be capable of meeting tomorrow's requirements. That's why unwavering orientation to market demands and thus to the needs of individual customers takes center stage in Danzas's philosophy.

business dynasty and sent Emile to work and train in the ports of Hamburg and Le Havre. When Emile received draft papers from the French army during the Crimean War in 1855, Louis Danzas found a young bricklayer to take his son's place in the military for FFr 900 and used his influence to persuade the local authorities to accept the substitution. Edouard l'Evêque retired in 1865, and the company's name was changed to Danzas & Minet, Commissionaires, Expéditeurs, Correspondence avec les Chemins de fer, Agence en Douane, à Bâle & St. Louis.

Alsace became German at the end of the Franco-Prussian War in 1871. As a consequence, the Danzas company would eventually become Swiss. Jules Danzas was a French patriot and could not live under the new German Empire. He moved his family and business, first across the new border to Belfort, France, and then to a more geographically advantageous base at Basel, where he signed a declaration of French citizenship before the French consul. He began to expand his branch network in Switzerland.

Rising Swiss prosperity, new mountain tunnels, and rail links enhanced Basel's role as a trade center on the Rhine River at the point where Germany, France, and Switzerland meet. The Danzas company took advantage of this geographic position to forward freight between these countries and to the larger continent beyond. In 1884 Danzas obtained a subcontract from the Swiss post office for international post deliveries. Even at this time, the company was able to guarantee 24-hour Switzerland-to-London postal service.

In 1878 Jules Danzas had converted Danzas & Minet into a sole proprietorship, but he had no son. By 1884 he had made his colleague Laurent Werzinger a partner; by 1886 Danzas sold most of his interest to Werzinger and retired to Paris, where he died in 1917. Alsace reverted to France a year later after the German defeat in World War I, but by that time the company had established firm roots in the major Swiss commercial city of Basel.

Growth in the 20th Century

Under Laurent Werzinger the company expanded its branch network and acquired an interest in a Rhine steamship company, Basel Rheinschiffahrt AG. High priority was given to the development of branch offices and international groupage services. Because Danzas had become a national household name and was also known internationally, Werzinger decided to retain the name when he incorporated the company as Danzas

& Co. AG on January 1, 1903, with a share capital of SFr 2 million, divided into 400 registered shares with a nominal value of SFr 5,000 each. He also diversified into the travel agency business, opening offices in all regions of Switzerland and also in France. The firm retained a family character when Albert Werzinger, who had joined Danzas in 1883, succeeded his father as chairman in 1911. He remained chairman for 37 years and saw the company through the difficult political problems posed by Switzerland's neutrality in World War I and World War II. At the end of World War I, the company's international operations were threatened by French government reprisals for supposed disloyalty by the legally neutral Danzas company. Werzinger's negotiating skills and tact in putting French notables on the Danzas board contributed to ending the crisis and restoring normal Danzas business in France, the company's most lucrative market. By 1908 the Paris office had a staff of 80, engaged in—among other things—the import of Swiss fabrics for Paris fashion houses, but Danzas also was able to incorporate a separate German subsidiary, Danzas GmbH, in 1919. The company became increasingly involved in seagoing traffic out of the northern European ports.

Danzas incurred substantial losses in the aftermath of the stock market crash of 1929 and found the going rough in the generally depressed world trade scene of the 1930s. A brief upswing in its fortunes was brought to an abrupt end with the outbreak of World War II. Branches in France and Germany were largely shut down in 1939 and those in Italy were closed in 1940. Danzas concentrated its efforts on Switzerland's supply line via neutral Portugal. Hans Hatt, a future Danzas chairman, spent the war years in Lisbon helping maintain this traffic.

Danzas suffered great material and personnel losses during World War II, but its base in neutral Switzerland remained intact, allowing the company to make a speedy postwar recovery. In 1948 Hans Hatt's 73-year-old father, Fritz, succeeded Albert Werzinger as chairman. Under his leadership the network of branches was expanded in Switzerland, France, Germany, and Italy. The company's name was changed to Danzas AG in 1960.

After Hans Hatt became chairman in 1963, the company began to expand outside, as well as within, Europe. New branches were established in Greece, Spain, and Portugal. Representative offices were set up in Latin America and New York and other commercial centers. Many of these were to become the basis for future subsidiary companies. Danzas Travel, concentrating on business and custom-tailored trips, continued to grow.

In 1979 David Linder, a lawyer and member of the Swiss Parliament, was appointed to the dual position of chairman and president. Danzas's registered shares began to be traded on the Basel Stock Exchange in 1985, after shareholders' approval of increased capitalization to SFr 10 million at an annual general meeting. Two years later, at another annual general meeting, the creation of participation certificate capital shares to be traded on the Basel, Zurich, and Geneva exchanges was approved.

International Expansion in the 1980s

International expansion continued throughout the 1980s with the takeover of the British Gentransco Group and the founding of new subsidiaries in Belgium and the Netherlands. By 1984, the Danzas office in Australia became a full-fledged subsidiary. In the following year, Danzas took over several important distribution companies including SATEM S.A. in France and S.A.D. S.A. in Spain, and to cover the United States founded Danzas Tuya S.A.—a Panamanian-registered company—in Miami, Florida.

In 1987, Danzas took over SBT NV in Belgium. New affiliate companies were established in Japan, Taiwan, and Hungary. With the purchase of Northern Air Freight of Bellevue, Washington, in 1989, Danzas had established representative offices in 36 countries and 41 U.S states. By 1991 the company was entering a period of restructuring and consolidation to absorb these new acquisitions.

Capital assets also increased as Danzas developed a policy of providing its own in-house facilities and resources. Investment in real estate, vehicles, and telecommunications assets grew throughout the 1980s. Danzas also promoted its organizational expertise in storage and transportation. In a notable agreement, Jacobs Suchard, the chocolate maker, hired Danzas to set up an automated warehouse system.

On April 1, 1989, David Linder was appointed president of the board of directors. He was succeeded as delegate of the board and chairman of the executive committee by Bernd Menzinger.

The European Community (EC) made a significant step toward deregulation of transportation on July 1, 1990, when it ended national restrictions that had prohibited trucks based in one country from carrying goods within the borders of another member state. The move, along with the opening of East European borders and markets, was widely seen as starting a process that would transform the goods transportation industry.

Some observers predicted an industry shakeout with the removal of protectionist measures. Small- and medium-sized trucking firms were faced with selling out to larger rivals or allying themselves to the majors as subcontractors. In addition, new overseas competitors appeared on the scene, including

Mitsui from Japan, TNT from Australia, and Federal Express from the United States.

Danzas and other big freight transport companies were meeting this challenge not just with acquisitions but by diversification and by expanding their European networks with new routes and methods. For example, the company's new, computer-controlled Cargovia system organized large, full-load shipments for industrial firms across Europe. Its Danznet information system allowed the company to coordinate warehousing and distribution.

Danzas GmbH, the German subsidiary that contributed 20 percent of the company's turnover, spearheaded a move into eastern Germany. A new terminal in Halle would enable the firm to offer exporters and importers regular groupage services to East Germany. An Eastern Europe coordination department was set up to maintain contacts, evaluate opportunities, and set priorities. Danzas was negotiating with many Eastern European countries on possible new companies and joint ventures. Elsewhere in Europe, Danzas created a "flexible pipeline" to allow Bosch, a German electronics manufacturer, to supply the British car-manufacturing industry through the Danzas terminal in Colehill, West Midlands.

Global Logistics Powerhouse for the 21st Century

The *Wall Street Journal* of July 23, 1990, predicted that only ten to 15 European companies would survive deregulation of the freight transportation industry. Danzas was expected to be one of these firms. Along with two other major Swiss contenders, Kühne & Nagel and Panalpina, it suffered the disadvantage of not having headquarters in a European Community member state, but emphasis on an international identity and the importance of its subsidiaries, particularly its powerful French company, with a staff of more than 5,000, minimalized the problems. More troubling for Danzas, however, was its unwieldy empire of hundreds of small companies, lacking for the most part any form of central direction.

Peter Gross took over the company's top spot in 1992, in time to lead Danzas through a new crisis. The end of customs barriers throughout the European Community resulted in a sales drop of 35 percent in 1993. By 1995, the company's sales of SFr 6 billion had managed to return a profit of just SFr 5 billion. In response, Gross led Danzas through a complete reorganization, restructuring itself as a modern holding company with a more streamlined and efficient management structure. Danzas began looking for a partner to help boost it snugly into the big leagues of global logistics providers. Meanwhile, Peter Wagner was appointed as CEO to help turn around the troubled company.

Danzas's restructuring helped restore the company to strong profit growth by 1997. Under Wagner, the company was now refocused on four core areas of operations—Intercontinental, Eurocargo, Consumer Solutions, and Industry Solutions—while Danzas began looking to make a number of strategic acquisitions and partnerships to broaden its international scope. Among the company's possibilities was an alliance with its two big Swiss rivals, Kuhne & Nagel and Panalpina, to form a single giant Swiss corporation. Wagner, however, chose a different route, explaining to *Bilanz:* "There would have been quite a bit of overlapping. The strategic course would have been affected and then there was the cultural aspect. Danzas and Panalpina, for example, are simply incompatible.''

Instead, at the end of 1998, Danzas surprised the logistics community when it allowed itself to be acquired. In December of that year, the company reached an agreement with the German postal monopoly—and Europe's largest postal service—to be acquired as part of Deutsche Post's plans to emerge sometime later as the publicly traded World Net. The acquisition gave Wagner the war-chest to pursue Danzas's ambitious acquisition program. Even as its acquisition was still being finalized in early 1999, Wagner had already begun to shop for new additions to the company.

The first two came in April 1999, when Danzas acquired Sweden's ASG AB for EUR 374 million. The company immediately followed that purchase with the acquisition of the Netherland's Nedlloyd's ETD unit. Wagner prepared his biggest surprise for the end of 1999, when the company announced its intention to acquire Air Express International, the leading freight forwarder in the United States, for $1.4 billion. These three purchases helped to triple the company's sales, and by the end of 2000, Danzas had become an international giant with sales of nearly SFr 12 billion and leading positions in much of its primary markets, including the European leadership in overland cargo and worldwide leadership in air cargo transport. Each of the company's new operations were now united under the Danzas name—as Danzas AEI, Danzas ASG, etc.—as the company began preparations to merge its acquisitions into its existing structure.

After spending all of 2000 absorbing these acquisitions, Danzas set out to boost its positions in selected geographic markets in 2001. Such was the case with its integration of Chile's Deca Express, formally the exclusive agent of Air Express International in that country, as Danzas AEI Chile SA. The company also moved to take full control of a former AEI joint-venture in Lebanon. The Danzas AEI Lebanon unit was then poised to function as the company's operational center for Syria, Lebanon, Jordan, Iraq, and Iran. Back home, Danzas prepared to take part in Deutsche Post's forthcoming initial public offering, expected to be valued at DM 9 billion. With its domestic postal monopoly to be ended in 2003—yet with ambitious plans to extend its position across the European Community—Deutsche Post looked on its Danzas Group operations as a central piece in an empire that could one day make even Napoleon proud.

Principal Subsidiaries

Danzas AIE; Danzas ASG; Danmar Lines AG; Danzas Reisen AG; Imadel AG (95%); Danzas Pty Ltd. (Australia); Danzas AG (Austria); Danzas NV (Belgium); SBT NV (Belgium); Danzas GmbH (Germany); Danzas & Dittes GmbH (Germany; 50%); Danzas HP (France); O.G.T. SA (France), Transvet SA (France; 50%); Danzas AE (Greece); Danzas (UK) Ltd.; Overall Transport (UK) Ltd.; C.A.T. Nationwide Carriers Ltd (U.K.); Baker Britt & Co Ltd (U.K.); Chemoldanzas KFT (Hungary; 50%); Delta Transport S.p.A. (Italy); Italdanzas S.p.A. (Italy); Samec S.p.A. (Italy); Danzas K.K. (Japan); Danzas BV (Netherlands); Danzas (Singapore) Pte Ltd.; Danzas (Southern Africa) Transport (Pty) Ltd.; Danzas SAE (Spain); Danzas Corporation (U.S.A.).

Principal Competitors

Aéroports de Paris; Grupo Aeroportuario del Sureste, S.A. de C.V; BAA plc; Chicago Airport System; Dallas & Mavis Specialized Carrier Co; DSC Logistics; GeoLogistics Corporation; ICTS International N.V.; Kühne & Nagel International AG; M.A.C. Freight Services, Incorporated; Panalpina World Transport (Holding) Ltd; Phoenix International Freight Services Ltd.; Pilot Air Freight; Royal Vopak NV; Stinnes AG; Tibbett & Britten Group plc; Transport Development Group PLC.

Further Reading

Ambuhl, Iso, "Wagner Shows the Way with Danzas," *Cash*, January 26, 2001.
Danzas from 1815–1990, Basel: Danzas AG, 1990.
Ewing, Jack, "Pushing the Envelope," *Business Week International,* September 11, 2000, p. 22.
The History of Danzas: From Waterloo to the New Millennium, Basel: Danzas Group, 2001.
Parker, John, "Danzas Expands," *Traffic World,* February 12, 2001.
Simpson, Ian, "Deutsche Post Buys Air Express," *Reuters,* November 15, 1999.
Wild, Karl, "Badly Underestimated," *Bilanz,* January 2000.

—Clark Siewert
—update: M.L. Cohen

Dentsu Inc.

11-1, Tsukiji
Chuo-ku, Tokyo 104-8426
Japan
Telephone: (81) 3-5551-5111
Fax: (81) 3-5551-2013
Web site: http://www.dentsu.co.jp

Private Company
Incorporated: 1907 as Nihon Denpo-Tsushin Sha
Employees: 10,841
Sales: $2.46 billion (2000)
NAIC: 54181 Advertising Agencies

Dentsu Inc. is the largest advertising agency in Japan, with a domestic market share of over 20 percent and an extensive network of overseas subsidiaries. The company also has strong ties to Japanese media, with shares in a number of newspapers and television networks. It is also the leading advertising company in Asia, with offices in 11 countries. For over 20 years Dentsu has maintained seven subsidiaries in the United States through a joint venture with Young & Rubicam. The company further strengthened its international position in 2000, when it assumed a 20 percent stake in Bcom3 Group, Inc.–the result of a merger between advertising firms The Leo Group and The MacManus Group—the fourth largest advertising holding company in the world.

Early History

Dentsu traces its origins to 1901, when Hoshiro Mitsunaga, a journalist from Osaka, founded two closely related companies: Telegraphic Service Company, an international news wire service; and Japan Advertising Ltd., a broker of advertising space. Mitsunaga often took payment for his wire service in the form of ad space in newspapers, then resold the ad space to his clients. The two companies merged in 1907, under the name Japan Telegraphic Communication Company (Nihon Denpo-Tsushin Sha). This compound name became shortened to Dentsu. Dentsu secured monopoly rights to distribute the United Press wire service in Japan, giving the company unique

leverage over the newspapers it serviced. Dentsu was able to use its influence to get favorable rates for advertising space and, as early as 1908, the company was the acknowledged leader in Japan's communications industry. Dentsu began collecting and publishing statistics on advertising volume in 1909, the first to do so in Japan. By 1912, the company had headquarters in Tokyo's fashionable Ginza district.

Dentsu was the largest broker of advertising space in Japan almost from its inception. However, the agency was practically dismantled in the prewar years. In 1936, the Japanese government formed its own news service, Domei, and Dentsu had to surrender its wire service. Then in 1943, the government consolidated all existing advertising agencies into 12 entities. Dentsu controlled four of the 12 agencies, but because of the war, business dwindled. Founder Mitsunaga died in 1945. There were two intervening presidents, and then the company began to rebuild under the leadership of the remarkable Hideo Yoshida. Yoshida had worked for Dentsu through the war, and he took over the presidency in 1947.

Postwar Ascendance

Yoshida was known as "the big demon," and Dentsu's ad men were "little demons" for their frantic hard work. Yoshida expected Dentsu's executives to report to work one hour earlier than the rest of the staff, and required daily written reports from department heads for his personal perusal. The staff yearly tested its strength with an overnight trip to climb Mount Fuji, but Yoshida showed his management skill as much in whom he hired as in what he had them do. Immediately after the war, Dentsu hired dozens of former government and military officials. Dentsu also made it a practice to recruit sons of officials and prominent businessmen, so that the company soon had a wealth of personal contacts with its corporate and government clients. Beyond this, Yoshida's most prescient step was to invest in Japanese radio and television.

Dentsu is credited with founding commercial radio in Japan. The agency submitted the first application for a commercial radio station in the country just months after the war ended, and Yoshida spoke before the Japanese Diet in 1950 on the impor-

Company Perspectives:

For almost 100 years we have pursued a single mission: to offer our clients the most innovative, distinctive, and diversified communications solutions. The Total Communications system, which Dentsu pioneered, is the key to creating integrated platforms that address each client's specific needs. We are fully committed to creating new solutions that effectively capture the public's imagination through a wide range of communications tactics and activities.

Dentsu's communications solutions are built upon insights into our global marketplace, and upon in-depth knowledge of consumer behavior. These insights give rise to creative ideas that have the power to influence people and, at times, to even impact the structure of the market. Our top priority is to tap this creativity to ensure that even more great ideas see the light of day.

The ideas and the creativity are made possible by the people of Dentsu, the company's greatest asset, and the best assurance that Dentsu clients everywhere will continue to succeed and prosper. Worldwide, the people of Dentsu give the company its special presence, the unique combination of intellect, sensitivity, imagination, compassion and vitality. It is the people of Dentsu that have made the company what it is today, and will continue to do so in years to come.

tance of commercial broadcasting. The company invested in what later became Tokyo Broadcasting System, one of five major commercial radio networks in Japan. Dentsu invested heavily in television as well. Dentsu loaned start-up funds to local stations, found them crucial advertising sponsors, and even provided personnel to manage them. Dentsu's patronage basically made television possible in the postwar years. As a result, as radio and television grew into a modern industry, Dentsu grew too. Because of the company's complex personal and financial ties, Dentsu was given the lion's share of advertising time. Dentsu was able to set aside huge blocks of prime time television for itself—as much as 60 percent of lucrative prime time advertising slots. Thus the company was virtually guaranteed clients. Companies had to come to Dentsu if they wanted the best advertising exposure. Dentsu also had a similar ''block buying'' arrangement with major newspapers, buying from 30 percent to 50 percent of space in national dailies. Dentsu was an investor in the major daily *Mainichi Shimbun*, as well as in a dozen other newspapers. Overall, its position with the media was unparalleled. No other agency had anything like the access that Dentsu had to all Japan's major advertising venues. By 1957, there were close to 800 advertising agencies in Japan, and Dentsu's billings alone made up more than a quarter of the industry total.

The Japanese economy grew in double digits in the 1960s and 1970s, carrying Dentsu with it. By 1968, Dentsu's billings were just behind the leading American firms J. Walter Thompson, Young & Rubicam, and Interpublic. The company had 5,000 accounts, including the biggest Japanese firms and the Japanese business of some American companies. Dentsu had made it standard practice to accept the accounts of competitive companies, for example doing advertising for both carmakers Honda and Nissan, and for rival electronics firms Matsushita

and Toshiba. Dentsu handled competing accounts in separate buildings, or, if that was not possible, at least on separate floors. This arrangement seemed to work well, and it was one more way that Dentsu dominated Japanese advertising. With its enormous media clout, and its willingness to serve everyone, Dentsu surpassed every other agency in the country by a wide margin. In 1974, Dentsu overtook J. Walter Thompson and became the largest advertising agency in the world.

At least 95 percent of Dentsu's billings came from within Japan. Dentsu had opened offices in New York, Bangkok, Chicago, Los Angeles, Paris, Melbourne, Taiwan, Singapore, and Hong Kong in the 1960s, but only three of these actually offered advertising services. The company was cautious about expanding abroad, even though by the late 1970s this was clearly the agency's next step. Differences between Japanese and American or European advertising style made it difficult for Dentsu to go abroad, and the company was built on Japanese-style personnel management, which included at that time lifetime guarantees of employment in exchange for corporate loyalty. In an interview with *Advertising Age* in 1977, Dentsu's then president Hideharu Tamaru noted that these factors would constitute a difficulty if Dentsu were to acquire a foreign agency. Tamaru suggested that Dentsu would initiate a joint venture with an international agency in order to expand overseas.

Expansion in the 1980s

However, the international link was slow in coming. Dentsu found new ways to extend its market in Japan, designing huge events like the celebration of America's bicentennial in Japan, an International Ocean Exposition, and completing a government commission for a new museum of telecommunications. Dentsu worked on the design of shopping centers, specializing in such aspects as people movement patterns. It worked with the government, compiling information on leisure time, doing public opinion surveys, and working for such government agencies as the National Railways. The domestic market still was not big enough for Dentsu, however, and by the end of the 1970s advertising spending began to dip in Japan. The proportion of Dentsu's billings from television advertising began to decline, while the company increased its billings from sports and other large promotions. Without the high earnings from television, Dentsu's overall profitability began to sink.

It was clear that Dentsu had to move beyond Japan to tap more lucrative markets. One result of Dentsu's effective lock on domestic advertising was that its competitors had already established international partnerships. Japan's number two agency, Hakuhodo, had been involved in a joint venture with the American firm McCann-Erickson since 1960, and a dozen other Japanese ad agencies had similar partnerships by 1980. In 1981, Dentsu finally made its move and announced a joint venture with Young & Rubicam. The arrangement, called DYR, gave Young & Rubicam entry into Japan and let Dentsu access Young & Rubicam's expertise in the American and European markets. Initial billings were $70 million, but this grew to $246 million within four years. Dentsu also opened a Shanghai office in 1981. China was not seen as a particularly promising market at that time, but Dentsu saw growth potential. The company worked patiently to make itself known in China. It planned and promoted a huge ''popular concert for youth,'' televised in both

---

Key Dates:

1901: Hoshiro Mitsunaga founds Telegraphic Service Company and Japan Advertising Ltd.
1907: Telegraphic Service Company and Japan Advertising Ltd. merge to form Nihon Denpo-Tsushin Sha (later shortened to Denstu).
1936: Domei news service is formed.
1945: Hoshiro Mitsunaga dies.
1947: Hideo Yoshida becomes president.
1981: Dentsu enters into joint venture with Young & Rubicam.
1987: HDM Worldwide is formed.
1994: Beijing Dentsu is formed.
1998: Dentsu acquires minority stake in Leo Burnett.
2000: Bcom3 Group, Inc. is formed.

China and Japan, with 300 Japanese musicians performing for a crowd of 30,000 young Chinese in Beijing.

Dentsu used its contacts with Young & Rubicam to enter the American and European markets. It established Young & Rubicam-Dentsu offices in New York and Los Angeles in 1983, and in 1984 formed DYR S.A., a joint management company to administer the company's international sales network. Dentsu opened its own subsidiaries in France and Great Britain in the next few years. In spite of this, the company's profits fell in the mid-1980s. Though Dentsu still led the world in billings, by 1984 its profits had fallen behind those of Young & Rubicam. Despite all its efforts, still less than 5 percent of Dentsu's billing was from export advertising. Japanese companies were spending billions of yen on advertising abroad, but it was mostly placed through foreign agencies. Dentsu got a new president in 1985, Gohei Kogure, and he reaffirmed the agency's commitment to international expansion. He resolved to cut costs at home by reducing staff, and he engineered a new image for Dentsu, with the slogan "Communications Excellence Dentsu."

In 1987, Dentsu and Young & Rubicam retooled their earlier link, teaming up also with Eurocom France, Europe's leading ad agency. The new, three-way partnership was called HDM Worldwide. The new company linked 39 cities in Asia, Europe, and the United States. Dentsu hoped to win new clients, and to increase its percentage of overseas billings to 20 percent. Dentsu also opened another subsidiary in the United States in 1987, DCA Advertising, and established offices in Germany and the Netherlands.

While Dentsu looked abroad for new, profitable markets, the company also changed the way it did business in Japan. In 1987, Dentsu premiered the first comparison ad on Japanese television. Advertising in which one product is directly compared to a rival had not been done in Japan, since it was considered in poor taste. A Japanese Fair Trade Commission issued guidelines in 1986 stating that comparative advertising was allowable, and Dentsu was the first to try it. In a $1 million campaign for All Nippon Airways, Dentsu's ads claimed that All Nippon's seating was more comfortable than that of unnamed "others." Mild by American standards, the ad nevertheless demonstrated that

Dentsu was willing to explore new techniques. The agency did well in the late 1980s, riding a consumption boom in Japan.

The 1990s

Eurocom left the three-way joint venture HDM in 1990. The venture was renamed Dentsu, Young & Rubicam Partnerships, concentrating on Asia, America, and Australia and New Zealand. To make up for the loss of its European partner, Dentsu invested in another European advertising network, the London-based Collett Dickinson Pearce International Group. Dentsu then began a streak of acquisitions and investment partnerships, buying part or all of nine agencies in Europe between March 1990 and September 1992. Only a week apart in September 1992, Dentsu acquired 100 percent of BLD Europe, a Brussels firm, and a minority stake in another firm called Publi-Graphics. Publi-Graphics was based in Paris but handled advertising primarily in the Middle East, with such large clients as Johnson & Johnson, Seiko, Nintendo, Eastman Kodak, and Nestlé.

Two years later, Dentsu's international expansion plans changed direction. Many multinational companies had initially expanded to Asia because of low-cost manufacturing, but by the mid-1990s, the consumer markets in Asian countries were also attracting interest. Dentsu began investing in Asian advertising agencies and expanding its own offices to Asian cities in order to capitalize on this trend. In 1994, Dentsu formed a joint-venture in China with two advertising firms there. The joint-venture was named Beijing Dentsu, with offices in Beijing and Shanghai. The company began with only one client, a personal products company called Kao Corp., but Beijing Dentsu expected to bill $10 million in its first year, and grow by 15 percent to 20 percent annually. Dentsu also invested in ventures in Singapore and Malaysia.

Besides looking to Asia for new growth, Dentsu turned to new technologies as a source of future income. In 1996 Dentsu launched a new subsidiary in Japan, called Dentsu Tec Inc., with the Tec standing for "*Te*chnology for *E*xciting *C*ommunication." This company aimed to develop new promotional opportunities using digital and networking technologies. Dentsu also founded Japan's first firm specializing in Internet advertising. The joint venture with Tokyo's Softbank Corporation was called Cyber Communications Inc., or CCI. CCI planned to buy and resell advertising space on the Internet and to help develop and deploy Internet technology in Japan.

New Business Models for the 21st Century

By the late 1990s Dentsu was still looking for ways to establish a strong international presence. The company's revenues outside of Japan totaled $315 million in 1996, a small sum compared to $1.93 billion in domestic earnings. Furthermore, the prolonged slump of the Japanese economy was starting to change the nature of advertising in Japan, in a way that threatened Dentsu's dominance at home and made overseas expansion even more critical to the company's future growth. Traditionally, while Japanese agencies might devote a certain amount of energy to promoting the reputations of their clients, the bulk of their efforts went to securing advertising space and time slots. In this regard, Dentsu's extensive media ties had always given it an enormous advantage over the competition. However, a significant drop in consumer spending in the mid-1990s forced agencies to look toward the American advertising model, based on building customer loyalty through the development of brand-name recognition, for ways to gain larger market share. This increased attention to the creative aspect of the business exposed Dentsu's weaknesses; in 1997, only 12 percent of the company's employees were in creative development.

Nor was the rising demand for distinctive advertising the only development that threatened Dentsu's supremacy. The proliferation of new media including cable TV and the Internet, while not yet nearly as popular in Japan as in the United States, promised a wider range of options for companies seeking new advertising avenues. While the growth of these technologies also promised new opportunities for Dentsu, the broadening of the overall availability of ad space posed a definite threat to the company's 22 percent market share. At the same time, advertising conglomerates from Europe and the United States. were beginning to gain a foothold in Japan, driving home the point that global reach was becoming a key factor in uncovering new opportunities.

Dentsu adopted two basic strategies to help it confront these changes in the industry. In January 1998 the company announced plans to go public, with listings on both the Tokyo and New York Exchanges, by 2001. Dentsu hoped that the increased investment capital would bolster its relatively weak overseas subsidiaries, enabling them not only to compete for new accounts, but also to provide a higher level of service for established Japanese clients with extensive international operations, including Sony and Toyota. By offering on the New York Stock Exchange, the company would not only make its shares available to investors from around the world, but would also make great strides toward developing its reputation as an international company.

In reaction to the growing threat from multinational advertising conglomerates, Dentsu became more aggressive in its pursuit of a powerful international alliance of its own. The company finally found a good match in December 1998, when it acquired a minority stake in Leo Burnett (later reorganized as The Leo Group), an American firm with an established international network and a number of high-profile clients, including Coca-Cola and McDonald's. This partnership took on a whole new dimension when The Leo Group merged with The MacManus Group in November 1999; the three firms formed a new holding company with a potential market value of $2 billion, with Dentsu becoming the majority shareholder with a 20 percent interest. The companies formalized the agreement the following March, and officially became known as Bcom3 Group; in April Dentsu announced its decision to consolidate its U.S. agencies under the Bcom3 name. With a potentially powerful international alliance in place, a conceivable initial public offering (IPO) in 2001, and plans (albeit postponed until 2002) for an IPO of Bcom3 stock as well, Dentsu appeared poised to take a commanding position in the new century as an advertising giant of global proportions.

Principal Subsidiaries

Dentsu East Japan Inc.; Dentsu West Japan Inc.; Dentsu Kyushu Inc.; Dentsu Hokkaido Inc.; Dentsu Tohoku Inc.; Dentsu Okinawa Inc.; Ad Dentsu Tokyo Inc.; Ad Dentsu Osaka Inc.; Ad Dentsu Inc. (Nagoya); Ad Dentsu Inc. (Hokkaido); Dentsu Eye Inc.; Dentsu Tec Inc.; Dentsu, Young & Rubicam Inc.; Dentsu Public Relations Inc.; impiric dentsu Inc.; Dentsu Research Inc.; Dentsu Casting and Entertainment Inc.; Information Services International Dentsu, Ltd.; Dentsu Music Publishing Inc.; cyber communications inc.; Creative Associates Ltd.; Dentsu.Com, Inc.; Music Gali Inc.; B2i inc.; K.K. DENTSUmarchFIRST; iWeb Technologies Japan KK; Dentsu Kosan Service Inc.; Dentsu Management Services Inc.; Dentsu Holdings USA, Inc.; Dentsu Business Development Holdings, Inc. (U.S.A.); Dentsu Business Development Group, LLC (U.S.A.); DCA Advertising (U.S.A.); Dentsu Communications Inc. (U.S.A.); Renegade Marketing Group, LLC (U.S.A.); Sports Culture Excellence Inc. (U.S.A.); DCC Communications Inc. (Canada); Dentsu Holdings Europe Ltd. (U.K.); Collett, Dickenson, Pearce UK Advertising Ltd.; Sharp Image Creative Services Ltd. (U.K.); Travis Sully Harari Ltd. (U.K.); Cayenne Werbeagentur GmbH (Germany); indigo Werbeagentur GmbH (Germany); BlueChip Agentur für Public Relations & Strategie GmbH (Germany); Dentsu Business Development Europe SA (Netherlands, Germany); BLD Europe S.A. (Belgium); Production Concepts S.A. (France); CCP Positioning srl (Italy); Rose Abascal, S.A. (Spain); Phoenix Communications Inc. (South Korea); PDS Media Inc. (South Korea); Beijing Dentsu Advertising Co., Ltd. (China); Beijing Dentsu Shanghai Branch (Dentsu Shanghai, China); Beijing Dentsu Guangzhou Branch (China); Shanghai Oriental Rihai Advertising Co., Ltd. (China); Beijing Oriental Rihai Advertising Co., Ltd. (China); Dentsu (Taiwan) Inc.; Media Palette (Taiwan) Inc.; Dentsu Commex, Inc. (Taiwan); Kuohua Inc. (Taiwan); Dentsu Singapore Pte. Ltd.; Dentsu (Thailand) Ltd.; Pro Q Ltd. (Thailand); Taiwan Advertising Co., Ltd.; Kuohua Inc. (Taiwan); Beijing Dentsu Advertising Co., Ltd.; Dentsu (Malaysia) Sdn. Bhd.; Pt. Inter Admark (Indonesia); NAP-TV Kft. (Hungary); ISL Marketing AG (Switzerland); Dentsu Oceania Pty. Ltd. (Australia); Dentsu Pacific Pty Ltd. (Australia); SSB Advertising Pty. Ltd. (Australia); Advertising Investment Services Pty Ltd. (AIS) (Australia); AIS Media (South) (Australia); AIS Media (Queensland) (Australia); AIS Media (Adelaide) (Australia); Mediactive Pty Ltd. (Australia); Great White Light Pty Ltd. (Australia).

Principal Competitors

Hakuhodo Incorporated; Omnicom Group Inc.; WPP Group plc.

Further Reading

Bechtos, Ramona, "Dentsu Gives Itself a Broader Label: Consultants on Life Styles and Society," *Advertising Age,* August 23, 1976, pp. 22–25.

"Big Demon Adman," *Fortune,* October 1958, p. 92.

Burton, Jack, " 'Dark Horse' Will Keep Dentsu on Global Path," *Advertising Age,* June 10, 1985, pp. 3, 100.

——, "Media Clout Is Source of Dentsu Power," *Advertising Age,* October 24, 1983, pp. M11, M14.

Chase, Dennis, "Y&R, Dentsu Eyeing Worldwide Linkup," *Advertising Age,* May 25, 1981, pp. 1, 78.

"The Demons of Dentsu," *Newsweek,* March 24, 1969, p. 75.

"Diverse Dentsu Nudges Aside JWT for Global No. 1 Status," *Advertising Age,* January 21, 1974, pp. 3, 60.

Harney, Alexandra, "Dentsu Search Over for International Partner," *Financial Times* (London), December 10, 1998.

Holden, Ted, and Amy Dunkin, "Japan Is Getting Too Small for Dentsu," *Business Week,* October 26, 1987, pp. 62–66.

Kilburn, David, "Comparison Ads Make First Flight in Japan," *Advertising Age,* June 8, 1987, p. 61.

——, "Dentsu Concentrates on Growing in Asia," *Advertising Age,* May 23, 1994, p. 54.

——, "Dentsu Expanding to Mideast, Europe," *Advertising Age,* September 7, 1992, p. 4.

——, "Dentsu Looks Inward," *Advertising Age,* April 20, 1987, p. 63.

——, "Dentsu Opening U.S. Promo Shop," *Advertising Age,* July 8, 1991, pp. 3, 34.

——, "How Dentsu's New President Fights Recession," *Advertising Age,* June 21, 1993, pp. 4, 48.

Link, Luther, "Dentsu Critic Calls It 'Public Menace'," *Advertising Age,* January 21, 1974, pp. 69–70.

Madden, Normandy, "Dentsu Signals New Western Ambitions," *Ad Age Global,* January, 2001.

Matsuda, Mat, "Dentsu Eases Through Open Door," *Advertising Age,* December 14, 1981, p. S9.

——, "Dentsu's Tamaru: 'Bridging the 21st Century'," *Advertising Age,* November 9, 1981, pp. 74–78.

Phalon, Richard, "A Japanese Setback," *Forbes,* October 7, 1985, pp. 110–14.

"Promoting Brands. The Perils of Maturity," *Economist* (U.S. Edition), August 2, 1997.

Thompson, John R., "International Growth a Main Priority for No. 1 Dentsu Shop," *Advertising Age,* October 10, 1977, pp. 26–27.

Toga, Mitsuo, "Waves of Globalization Are Hitting the Ad Industry; Dentsu President Sees Public Offering As Step to Compete," *Nikkei Weekly,* January 19, 1998.

—A. Woodward
—update: Stephen Meyer

Deutsche Bank ◪

Deutsche Bank AG

Taunusanlage 12
60262 Frankfurt am Main
Germany
Telephone: (69) 910-91000
Fax: (69) 910-34227
Web site: http://www.deutsche-bank.de

Public Company
Incorporated: 1870
Employees: 98,311
Total Assets: EUR 940.03 billion (2000)
Stock Exchanges: Berlin Bremen Düsseldorf Frankfurt
   Hamburg Hanover Munich Stuttgart Vienna Antwerp
   Brussels Paris Tokyo Luxembourg Amsterdam Swiss
   London
Ticker Symbol: DBK
NAIC: 522110 Commercial Banking; 522210 Credit Card
   Issuing; 522291 Consumer Lending; 522293
   International Trade Financing; 523110 Investment
   Banking and Securities Dealing; 523120 Securities
   Brokerage; 523920 Portfolio Management; 523991
   Trust, Fiduciary, and Custody Activities; 525910
   Open-End Investment Funds; 551111 Offices of Bank
   Holding Companies

Deutsche Bank AG has weathered two world wars, three depressions, and a divided Germany to become one of the world's leading financial institutions, entering the 21st century as the second largest bank in the world. Its operations are divided into two customer-oriented business groups. The Corporate and Investment Bank Group serves corporate and institutional clients, offering investment banking and corporate financing services on a worldwide basis. The Private Clients and Asset Management Group focuses on retail banking, mostly in Germany, and the worldwide provision of asset management services for both individuals and institutions.

19th-Century Origins

Deutsche Bank was founded in Berlin on March 10, 1870, with the approval of the king of Prussia. The company opened its doors for business a month later under the directorship of Georg von Siemens, with five million thalers in capital.

The company's creation coincided with the unification of Germany. After Germany's victory in the Franco-German War, France was required to pay an indemnity of FFr 5 billion, which greatly stimulated German industry, trade, and consumption. Deutsche Bank naturally assumed a position of leadership in the country's expanding economy. The founding of the Second German Reich in 1871 led to another important development: the thaler was replaced by the mark, a new currency based on gold.

Within two years, the bank had established domestic branches in Bremen and Hamburg and expanded into eastern Asia with offices in Shanghai and Yokohama. In 1873 it opened a London branch, and capital stood at 15 million thalers.

Many joint-stock banks, including Deutsche Bank, had been created in the wake of the liberalization of requirements for starting new companies, but many failed within a few years. During the financial crisis of 1873–75 it appeared that the entire economic system was on the verge of collapse; small shareholders as well as wealthy businesspeople were ruined, and in Berlin alone nearly 50 banks filed for bankruptcy.

But Deutsche Bank, because of its concentration on foreign operations, was largely unscathed by the financial panic. With its assets intact, the young bank began to make significant acquisitions, including Deutsche Union-Bank and the Berliner Bankverein, both completed in 1876. These purchases transformed Deutsche Bank into one of Germany's largest and most prestigious banks.

In 1877 Deutsche Bank joined a syndicate of leading private banks popularly known as the "Prussian consortium." The bank was also employed by the government for the issue of state loans, and it grew rapidly in both influence and assets. By 1899 it was able to offer to float, without help from other financial institutions, a 125 million mark loan for Prussia and, at the same time, a 75 million mark loan for the German Reich.

Throughout the 1880s and 1890s Deutsche Bank was a leader in electrical development. It helped to form finance and holding companies and issued bonded loans and shares for the construction of dynamos, power plants, electric railways, tramways, and municipal lighting systems. By 1897, there were 750 power plants located across Germany. The bank also invested in the Edison General Electric Company in the United States and began to build a power plant in Argentina.

During the same period, the bank was a driving force behind railway development. In 1888, Deutsche Bank obtained a concession to build an east-west railway to open up Asiatic Turkey. A decade later, 642 miles of the Anatolian railway were in operation in Turkey. At the same time, in the United States the bank participated in the financial reorganization of Northern Pacific Railroad. All of this, of course, was done in addition to contributing significantly to the development of Germany's own extensive network of surface and underground railways.

Consolidation and Growth in Early 20th Century

The continuity of bank operations was uninterrupted when von Siemens died in October 1901. At Deutsche Bank, like most other German banks, all decisions are made by the board of directors, and the board customarily takes credit for the company's successes. The firm has no official chairman, but selects one board member to act as "spokesman." Thus the absence of von Siemens had little effect on the bank, since management by consensus was the bank's guiding principle.

By the early years of the 20th century, the company had acquired interests in the Hannoversche Bank, the Oberrheinische Bank, and the Rheinische Creditbank, and in Italy, had participated in the 1894 founding of Banca Commerciale Italiana. In 1914 the acquisition of Elberfeld-based Bergische-Märkische Bank and its branches in the Rhineland-Westphalia region increased Deutsche Bank's branch network from eight outlets to 46. The bank's capital was now more than six times the amount it was founded with.

The bank then entered a period of consolidation and growth: it built up its subbranches; improved and extended customer services; paid particular attention to the deposit business; and promoted checks for personal use. In association with numerous regional banks, Deutsche Bank also became involved in a wide range of business activities, including transportation, coal, steel, and oil, as well as railways and electrification. Shortly before World War I, with 200 million marks in capital backed by a 112.5 million mark reserve and deposits and borrowed funds of

1.58 billion marks, the *Frankfurter Zeitung* called it the world's leading bank. Growth continued during the war with the 1917 purchase of the Schlesischer Bankverein, which was based in Breslau (which became Wrocław, Poland, following World War II).

Deutsche Bank weathered the many economic problems during World War I; at the end of the conflict, the bank had offices at 182 locations throughout Germany, and a staff of nearly 14,000. But with the war lost, the German empire gone, and the transition from monarchy to democracy threatened by revolution, Allied demands for reparations totaling 132 billion gold marks pushed the German banking system to the brink of ruin. By 1923, one gold mark was worth 1 trillion paper marks.

The Depression and Nazi Eras

In 1929, as financial chaos loomed, Deutsche Bank merged with its 20-year rival, the Disconto-Gesellschaft. The new entity was called Deutsche Bank und Disconto-Gesellschaft, a name that was used until 1937 when it was changed back to simply Deutsche Bank. At the time of their merger the banks were the two largest in Germany; combined, their capital, reserves, and deposits were each at least twice as large as that of any competitor. The merger, designed to cut administrative costs by closing competing operations, was very successful, and the resulting bank had enough capital and reserves to withstand the economic crisis. Before the collapse, Deutsche Bank and Disconto-Gesellschaft had handled about 50 percent of all business conducted by Berlin banks. By 1931, the bank was relying heavily on its undisclosed reserves and had twice reduced capital, but it remained solvent and required no government aid.

Under orders from the National Socialist government that came to power in 1933, unemployed workers were put to work under a "reemployment" plan. At first, the government concentrated only on projects that were meant to counteract the high unemployment rate; the autobahns were the chief showpiece of this strategy. But by 1936, a significant percentage of industrial production had been switched to the manufacture of weapons and munitions and "reemployment" had become "rearmament." Deutsche Bank supported the program through the purchase of government securities. Also, in 1933 and 1934, three Jewish members of the board of managing directors—Oscar Wassermann, Theodor Frank, and Georg Solmssen—were forced to resign.

During World War II, the government financed its budget deficit by printing new money, a misguided practice that quickly led to spiraling inflation. The problem was artificially suppressed by questionable banking measures; more treasury paper began to appear among the bank's assets. Deutsche Bank's enormous losses were made known only when Germany surrendered to the Allies in April 1945.

After the war, Allied occupation authorities investigating possible war crimes committed by German banks found that Deutsche Bank and its rival Dresdner Bank bore substantial responsibility for the war through their lending to the Nazi government, their purchase of government securities, and the influence that they exerted over large industrial concerns through their shareholdings and corporate directorships. Both

Key Dates:

1870: Deutsche Bank AG is founded in Berlin.
1873: A London branch is opened.
1876: Deutsche Union-Bank and Berliner Bankverein are acquired.
1914: Acquisition of Bergische-Märkische Bank increases the branch network from eight outlets to 46.
1929: Deutsche Bank merges with Disconto-Gesellschaft to form Deutsche Bank und Disconto-Gesellschaft.
1933: The Nazis come to power in Germany, beginning the period of collaboration between Deutsche Bank and the Hitler regime; Jewish board members are ousted.
1937: The bank's name is changed back to Deutsche Bank.
1945: With eastern Germany occupied by the Soviets, Deutsche Bank is run out of Hamburg; the bank has been forced to give up all of its international holdings.
1947/48: In western Germany, Deutsche Bank is divided into ten separate institutions.
1952: The ten West German successor banks are combined into three joint-stock banks.
1957: The three joint-stock banks are merged to form a single Deutsche Bank AG, based in Frankfurt.
1960s: Reestablishment of international operations begins.
1968: Deutsche Bank helps found the European-American Bank & Trust Company in New York.

1972: The bank helps found the European Asian Bank (Eurasbank).
1979: First U.S. branch office opens in New York.
1986: Banca d'America e d'Italia S.p.A. is acquired.
1989: U.K. investment bank Morgan Grenfell is acquired.
1990: German reunification leads Deutsche Bank to quickly reestablish itself in Eastern Germany.
1993: Banco de Madrid, a Spanish bank, is acquired.
1994: Deutsche Bank posts losses from the collapses of Jurgen Schneider's property group and Balsam and the near-collapse of Metallgesellschaft.
1995: Global investment banking operations are consolidated under a new London-based unit, Deutsche Morgan Grenfell; Bank 24, a full-service telephone bank, is launched in Germany.
1998: Investment banking operations are restructured and the Morgan Grenfell name is deemphasized.
1999: U.S. investment bank Bankers Trust Corp. is acquired; the retail banking network is merged with Bank 24 to form Deutsche Bank 24.
2000: Deutsche Bank announces merger with archrival Dresdner Bank but the deal collapses.
2001: Operations are reorganized into two units: the Corporate and Investment Bank Group and the Private Clients and Asset Management Group.

banks also had close ties to SS chief Heinrich Himmler and other Nazi officials, had exploited conquered nations by seizing the assets of their financial institutions, and had helped disenfranchise Jews in Germany. Four directors (including one Nazi Party member) and two executives of Deutsche Bank were arrested by the Allied authorities, but were never tried. Further investigations into Deutsche Bank's collaboration with the Nazis began to be conducted in the 1990s and shed additional light on this dark chapter in the bank's history.

Postwar Reorganization, Expansion into Retail Banking, and International Growth

With the division of Germany into zones of occupation, and with Berlin in the Soviet zone, Deutsche Bank closed its head office there in 1945. The bank was run out of Hamburg. It lost all of its branches in what eventually became East Germany (in 1949 they became the basis for the newly formed Berliner Disconto Bank AG). In 1947–48, the western operations of Deutsche Bank were divided into ten separate regional institutions. After lengthy negotiations with the occupying forces, these ten institutions were formed into three banks: Norddeutsche Bank AG, Rheinisch-Westfälische Bank AG, and Süddeutsche Bank AG served the northern, central, and southern areas of West Germany, respectively. In 1957, these three banks were again reorganized, this time to form a single Deutsche Bank AG with corporate headquarters in Frankfurt. At the time of its reunification, the bank employed more than 16,000 people and its assets totaled 8.4 billion marks. Hermann J. Abs, the strategist behind the reorganization of the bank and one of the key figures in West Germany's financial recovery, became its spokesman.

In the 1960s Deutsche Bank concentrated on improving services for its smaller depositors. The bank launched programs for personal loans of up to DM 2,000 and medium-sized loans up to DM 6,000 for specific purchases, as well as an overdraft facility of up to DM 1,000 for consumers. Other services included personal mortgage loans, improvements in savings facilities, and the establishment of a eurocheque system. By the end of the decade, the bank had become the largest provider of consumer credit in West Germany.

Under the direction of Abs, Deutsche Bank began to reestablish its international operations (it had lost all of its worldwide holdings after the war). It first reopened offices in Buenos Aires, Sao Paulo, and Rosario, Argentina, and then in Tokyo, Istanbul, Cairo, Beirut, and Teheran. In 1968, Deutsche Bank joined the Netherlands' Amsterdam-Rotterdam Bank, Britain's Midland Bank, and Belgium's Societé Generale de Banque in founding the European-American Bank & Trust Company in New York. In 1972 Deutsche Bank founded Eurasbank (European Asian Bank) with members of the same consortium.

When Hermann Abs retired in 1967, Karl Klusen and Franz Heinrich Ulrich took his place, becoming cospokesmen. Abs had wielded such a great concentration of economic and financial power that a special law limiting such influence was named after him—"Lex Abs" reduced the number of supervisory-board seats a single person could hold simultaneously in West Germany.

During the 1970s Deutsche Bank became the dominant financial institution in West Germany. Under the guidelines of the "universal banking" system in place in Germany for more than a century, commercial banks were allowed to hold unlimited interests in industrial companies, underwrite and trade securities on their own, and play the foreign currency markets, in addition to providing credit and accepting deposits. Deutsche Bank took advantage of this rule during the 1960s and 1970s by investing in a wide range of industrial companies. In 1979, the bank held seats on the supervisory boards of about 140 companies, among them Daimler-Benz, Volkswagen, Siemens, AEG, Thyssen, Bayer, Nixdorf, Allianz, and Philipp Holzmann.

But the bank's extraordinary influence in West Germany aroused concern about the extent of the bank's instruments in other companies. As a result of these concerns, Deutsche Bank began to reduce its industrial holdings in the 1970s. This trend, however, was briefly interrupted in 1975 when Middle Eastern concerns flush with petrodollars supplanted the big banks as a source of capital investment. At the request of Chancellor Helmut Schmidt, Deutsche Bank purchased a 29 percent interest in Daimler-Benz from industrialist Friederich Flick to ensure that it would stay in German hands, with the understanding that the bank would resell the shares once the crisis had passed. Deutsche Bank already owned 25 percent of the famed automaker. In December of that year, it resold the shares to a consortium that included Commerzbank, Dresdner Bank, and Bayerische Landesbank.

Becoming a Global Power in the Late 20th Century

During the 1980s, Deutsche Bank made major expansions in its foreign operations, both in commercial banking and investment banking. It opened its first U.S. branch office in New York in 1979, and by 1987 had bought out all its partners in the Eurasbank consortium and renamed it Deutsche Bank (Asia), providing 14 more branches in 12 Asian countries. At nearly the same time, the company's capital-markets branch began operating and trading in Japanese, British, and American securities. By the end of 1988, the bank had approximately 7.2 million customers at 1,530 offices, more than 200 of them outside of West Germany.

In 1980 Deutsche Bank was the only one of the West German Big Three banks to turn a healthy profit. Unlike Commerzbank and Dresdner Bank, the other two of the Big Three, Deutsche Bank did not overexpand, but remained cautious in the face of high interest rates and continued recession. In 1984 it acquired a 4.9 percent stake in Morgan Grenfell, the British securities firm; in 1985 it bought scandal-plagued industrial giant Flick Industrieverwaltung from Friederich Flick, with the intention of taking it public; and in 1988 it acquired a 2.5 percent interest in the automaker Fiat. Another sign of Deutsche Bank's aggressive pursuit of foreign markets was the fact that in the wake of the stock market crash in October 1987, at a time when massive layoffs were taking place in the securities industry, its American securities affiliate, Deutsche Bank Capital Corporation, expanded its workforce. In 1988 Deutsche Bank entered the treasury securities market at a time when many foreign firms were leaving. Two years later, the U.S. Federal Reserve recognized Deutsche Bank Government Securities Inc. as a primary dealer of government securities.

At home, Deutsche Bank took a large and controversial step toward becoming a one-stop financial service center in 1989

when it created its own insurance subsidiary to complement its commercial and investment banking businesses. Immediately, it was considered a strong rival for the Allianz Group, the West German-based company that was Europe's largest insurer.

Wilhelm Christians and Alfred Herrhausen became Deutsche Bank's new cospokesmen in 1985. When Christians retired in early 1988, Herrhausen was appointed sole spokesman for the bank. Following Herrhausen's assassination by terrorists on November 30, 1989, Hilmar Kopper became spokesman.

In the late 1980s and early 1990s, Deutsche Bank bolstered its investment banking arm through additional acquisitions, aiming to become a global investment bank. After acquiring the Toronto-based investment bank McLean McCarthy Ltd. in 1988, it purchased the remainder of Morgan Grenfell in 1989 for $1.5 billion. It also took a more aggressive approach to the North American market. In 1992 Deutsche Bank North America was formed—with John A. Rolls as chief executive officer—to coordinate and manage all of Deutsche Bank's North American operations, including those in investment banking which included McLean McCarthy and C.J. Lawrence Inc., the latter a U.S. investment bank acquired in 1986. The following year Deutsche Bank Securities Corporation was formed to specifically manage such areas as investment banking, securities transactions, and asset management services.

At the same time it aimed to become a global investment bank, Deutsche Bank also pursued a strategy of extending its position as a universal bank beyond Germany. Initially, it focused on Western Europe. But with the fall of communism throughout Eastern Europe in 1989 and 1990, Deutsche Bank sought to become a Europe-wide universal bank. To that end, in 1986 it had acquired Banca d'America e d'Italia S.p.A. from the Bank of America for $603 million (in 1994 this bank was renamed Deutsche Bank S.p.A.). In 1993 Deutsche Bank increased its presence in Italy when it purchased a majority interest in Banca Popolare di Lecco. That same year, the bank purchased Banco de Madrid in Spain, later integrated into Deutsche Bank, S.A.E. By 1994 Deutsche Bank operated 260 branches in Italy and 318 branches in Spain, and in both countries it was the largest foreign bank.

Following German reunification, Deutsche Bank quickly capitalized on the opportunity by entering into a joint venture with Deutsche Kreditbank to begin to restake its claim to eastern German territory. By 1994, Deutsche Bank had more than 300 branches in eastern Germany. It also opened offices elsewhere in Eastern Europe: Bulgaria, the Czech Republic, Hungary, Poland, and Russia.

The early 1990s were a time of rising fortunes for Deutsche Bank as net income more than doubled from 1990 to 1993. This trend was reversed in 1994 when a series of problems hit within a short period. First the bank suffered huge losses from loans of DM 1.2 billion it had made to a property group run by Jurgen Schneider, which collapsed in early 1994. Then two firms in which Deutsche Bank had invested heavily ran into trouble—Balsam filed for bankruptcy and Metallgesellschaft (MG), an engineering conglomerate, nearly collapsed after losing $1.33 billion on speculative oil trades. Kopper provoked additional controversy and public resentment when he called bills amounting to $33 million that the Schneider property group owed to construction workers "peanuts." Early in 1995 the former head of MG sued Deutsche Bank over who was responsible for MG's downfall. Also in early 1995, Deutsche Bank's ties to the Nazi government of Hitler were dredged up when East German files were made public for the first time.

The losses it suffered in 1994 forced Deutsche Bank to increase its loss reserves, which contributed to a reduction in net income to DM 1,360 billion. In 1995 Deutsche Bank made significant moves to further establish itself as a global investment bank. Deutsche Bank North America acquired ITT Commercial Finance Corporation for $868 million to strengthen its presence in asset-based lending. The acquisition was immediately renamed Deutsche Financial Services Corporation. Later in 1995 Deutsche Bank consolidated all of its investment banking operations into Morgan Grenfell under a new unit, Deutsche Morgan Grenfell (DMG), based in London and headed by Ronaldo Schmitz. The move shifted more than half of Deutsche Bank's business to London control rather than that of Frankfurt, a shift that the *European* called a "corporate revolution." The short-term consequence of this revolution was the creation of much bad blood between the bank's staffs in Frankfurt and London. To build up its investment banking operations, DMG poached some of the top names in investment banking from rival firms in New York and London, infuriating these companies.

In September 1995 Deutsche Bank unveiled Bank 24, the first full-service telephone bank in Germany. At the same time, the company was in the midst of a four-year effort, ending in 1996, to reduce the domestic staff by 20 percent, with much of these cuts coming from the traditional branch-based retail network. Further innovation came to the domestic operations in 1996 when Deutsche Bank opened its first supermarket banks. That same year, a scandal rocked DMG when a fund manager assigned bogus values to some securities in his portfolio. Reacting quickly, Deutsche Bank management fired four managers and spent $280 million to cover potential losses at two funds. In late 1996 Kooper announced his resignation from his position as spokesman (but remained chairman of the supervisory board), and Rolf-Ernst Breuer, who had headed up the investment banking operations, became the new spokesman in early 1997.

During 1997 Deutsche Bank sold its 48-branch operation in Argentina to BankBoston Corporation for about $255 million. That year the bank set up an independent historical commission to research its role during the Nazi era. Such investigations were becoming increasingly common in the wake of the Cold War's end and the opening up of archives in the former Communist states of Eastern Europe. In 1998 the bank admitted that it had profited from gold looted from Holocaust victims and that bank officials at the time likely knew the source of the gold. An $18 billion lawsuit was soon filed against Deutsche Bank and other German lenders in relation to such looted gold. Deutsche Bank revealed in 1999 that it had helped finance the construction of Auschwitz, the infamous Nazi death camp in Poland.

With problems continuing at DMG, Deutsche Bank in early 1998 transferred most of the management control of the investment banking operations back to Frankfurt. The Morgan Grenfell name itself began to be deemphasized. Having failed to make much headway in the important U.S. investment banking market through DMG—primarily because of a clash of cultures between DMG's American investment bankers and those hailing from Germany and England—Deutsche Bank turned to the acquisition route for another U.S. invasion. In November 1998 the company announced that it would acquire Bankers Trust Corp., a New York firm that specialized in underwriting securities for smaller companies and emerging markets. Bankers Trust was the seventh largest bank holding company in the United States. It had purchased Baltimore-based investment banking house Alex. Brown & Sons in 1997 and had subsequently renamed the unit BT Alex. Brown Inc. (under Deutsche Bank, it was rechristened Deutsche Banc Alex. Brown). Also in 1998 Deutsche Bank transferred several of its major industrial holdings, a total of DM 40 billion ($24 billion) in stock, to a separate subsidiary in an effort to increase the transparency of its holdings. Among the transferred holdings were stakes in Allianz AG (7 percent), DaimlerChrysler AG (12 percent), and Metallgesellschaft AG (9.3 percent). This move was also seen as a prelude to the eventual unloading of some of these stakes.

The EUR 9.7 billion ($10 billion) takeover of Bankers Trust was completed in June 1999 but not before Deutsche Bank had received a great deal of negative publicity about its activities during the Nazi era. Under pressure from Holocaust survivors and others, Deutsche Bank finally agreed to contribute to a fund set up to settle Holocaust-era claims. The bank refused, however, to be held liable for its holdings in industrial companies that used forced laborers during that period. With the purchase of Bankers Trust, Deutsche Bank became the largest bank in the world with assets of about $750 billion. This position of preeminence proved short-lived, however, as the company was soon surpassed by Mizuho Holdings, which was formed in 2000 from the merger of three Japanese banks.

With the integration of Bankers Trust, investment banking was becoming an increasingly important part of the Deutsche Bank operations, accounting for 56 percent of pretax operating earnings for 1999, a huge jump from the 22 percent figure of 1998. On the other hand, the company was being bogged down by its inefficient retail banking operations, which accounted for only 5 percent of operating earnings in 1999. That year, the retail network was merged with the electronic banking unit Bank 24 to form Deutsche Bank 24 (DB24), which could then offer customers an array of online, telephone, and traditional branch services.

In March 2000 Deutsche Bank appeared to have a solution to its retail banking woes, namely offloading them, through a EUR 31 billion ($30 billion) merger with its longtime archrival Dresdner Bank. The deal would have included the combination of the retail networks of the two banks under the Deutsche Bank 24 unit, which would then have been spun off within three years, with Allianz, the number two insurer in Europe, taking a majority stake. The merger unraveled within weeks of its announcement, however, over the fate of Dresdner's investment banking unit, Dresdner Kleinwort Benson (DKB). Initially, Breuer agreed to merge DKB into Deutsche Bank's investment banking operations. The bank's investment bankers, however, felt that DKB's operations overlapped too much with their own, forcing Breuer to renege on his promise to absorb DKB and to insist that the unit be divested as a precondition to the merger.

The Dresdner's board refused to go along with this and pulled out of the deal.

The failed merger was a huge blow to Deutsche Bank's aspirations to become an even bigger player in global investment banking. In the immediate aftermath, the company invested heavily in its e-commerce operations and announced that it would expand DB24 throughout Europe with a combined "clicks-and-bricks" retail structure. DB24 gained control of the bank's retail operations in Belgium, France, Italy, Poland, Portugal, and Spain, a network that included more than 2,000 branches and 21,000 employees. Another significant development was a February 2001 reorganization that divided the bank's operations into two business units: the Corporate and Investment Bank Group and the Private Clients and Asset Management Group. The former encompassed the investment banking and corporate banking units, while the latter subsumed the retail banking (including DB24), private banking, and asset management units. Through the reorganization, Deutsche Bank hoped to facilitate cross-selling among the units, such as the selling of asset-management products through DB24.

Deutsche Bank's prospects in the early 21st century were clouded somewhat by the aftereffects of the collapse of the Dresdner deal. Deutsche Bank attempted to negotiate a cooperation agreement with Allianz whereby the latter would distribute insurance products through DB24. But in March 2001 Allianz announced that it would acquire Dresdner. Deutsche Bank continued to seek partners, including negotiating with AXA, the French insurance firm, about a distribution deal. Despite the setbacks that Deutsche Bank had suffered in the late 20th century, the bank remained one of the most powerful financial institutions in the world.

Principal Subsidiaries

DB Industrial Holdings AG; DEBEKO Immobilien GmbH & Co Grundbesitz Berlin OHG; DEBEKO Immobilien GmbH & Co Grundbesitz OHG; DEUBA Verwaltungsgesellschaft mbH; Deutsche Asset Management Europe GmbH (93%); Deutsche Asset Management International GmbH; Deutsche Bank 24 Aktiengesellschaft; Deutsche Bank Bauspar-Aktiengesellschaft; Deutsche Bank Lübeck Aktiengesellschaft (94.04%); Deutsche Bank Saar Aktiengesellschaft (96.6%); Deutsche Bank Trust Aktiengesellschaft Private Banking; Deutsche Gesellschaft für Mittelstandsberatung mbH (96%); Deutsche Grundbesitz Management GmbH; Deutsche Immobilien Leasing GmbH; DWS Investment GmbH; EUROHYPO Aktiengesellschaft Europäische Hypothekenbank der Deutschen Bank (96.02%); GEFA Gesellschaft für Absatzfinanzierung mbH; Nordwestdeutscher Wohnungsbauträger GmbH; Versicherungsholding der Deutschen Bank Aktiengesellschaft (75.86%); Deutsche Bank S.A. (Argentina); Deutsche Australia Ltd.; DB (Belgium) Finance S.A./N.V.; Deutsche Bank S.A. - Banco Alemao (Brazil); Deutsche Bank (Canada); db Services SARL unipersonnelle (France); Deutsche Bank S.A. (France); Deutsche-Equities S.A. (France); Deutsche Securities Ltd. (Hong Kong); Deutsche Bank Rt. (Hungary); Deutsche Bank Società per Azioni (Italy; 93.53%); Finanza & Futuro S.p.A. (Italy; 99.99%); DMG Trust Bank Ltd. (Japan; 95%); DB Finance (Luxembourg) S.A. (99.92%); DB Re S.A. (Luxembourg); Deutsche Bank Luxembourg S.A.; Deutsche Bank (Ma-

laysia) Berhad; Deutsche Bank de Bary N.V. (Netherlands); Deutsche New Zealand Ltd. (99.99%); Deutsche Bank Polska Spólka Akcyjna (Poland); Deutsche Bank (Portugal), S.A.; Deutsche Bank OOO (Russia); DB (Asia Pacific) Training Centre Pte. Ltd. (Singapore); Deutsche Bank Asia Pacific Holdings Pte. Ltd. (Singapore); Deutsche Capital Singapore Ltd.; Deutsche Bank, Sociedad Anónima Española (Spain; 99.63%); Deutsche Bank (Suisse) S.A. (Switzerland); DB Equity Ltd. (U.K.); DB Investments (GB) Ltd. (U.K.); Deutsche Morgan Grenfall Group plc (U.K.); Morgan Grenfell & Co. Ltd. (U.K.); Deutsche Sharps Pixley Metals Ltd. (U.K.); Deutsche Bank Financial Inc. (U.S.A.); Deutsche Sharps Pixley Metals Inc. (U.S.A.); Taunus Corp. (U.S.A.); Bankers Trust Corp. (U.S.A.); Deutsche Banc Alex. Brown LLC (U.S.A.).

Principal Operating Units

Corporate and Investment Bank; Private Clients and Asset Management.

Principal Competitors

Dresdner Bank AG; Bayerische Hypo- und Vereinsbank Aktiegesellschaft; Commerzbank AG; Goldman Sachs Group Inc.; Merrill Lynch & Co., Inc.; J.P. Morgan Chase & Co.; Credit Suisse First Boston; Morgan Stanley Dean Witter & Co.; HSBC Holdings plc; UBS AG; Westdeutsche Landesbank Girozentrale; Landesbank Baden-Württemberg; Bankgesellschaft Berlin AG; DG BANK Deutsche Genossenschaftsbank AG; Kreditanstalt für Wiederaubau; Bayerische Landesbank Girozentrale.

Further Reading

"Allianz and Deutsche: And They Lived Unhappily Ever After," *Economist*, April 1989, p. 90.

Ball, Robert, "A Two-Headed Bank Nibbles at the United States," *Fortune*, August 24, 1981, pp. 102+.

Beckett, Paul, "Deal Is Likely to Take Deutsche Bank on Bumpy Ride: Integrating Bankers Trust into Fold Could Be Most Difficult Challenge," *Wall Street Journal*, November 27, 1998, p. B4.

Brady, Simon, "Deutsche Makes Its Mark," *Euromoney*, June 1992, pp. 24–28.

Brierley, David, "Corporate Revolution in the Air As Deutsche Moves to London," *European*, July 21, 1995, p. 17.

Carey, David, "Under Siege," *Financial World*, March 7, 1989, pp. 64+.

Coleman, Brian, and Dagmar Aalund, "Deutsche Bank to Cash Out of Industrial Stakes," *Wall Street Journal*, December 16, 1998, p. A17.

"The Competitive Spirit of Deutsche Bank," *Euromoney*, July 1983, pp. 22+.

Delamaide, Darrell, "The Deutsche Bank Juggernaut Will Keep on Rolling," *Euromoney*, January 1990, p. 32.

"Deutsche Makes Its Pan-European Move," *European Banker*, September 22, 2000.

"Deutsche's Wayward Wunderkind," *Economist*, September 14, 1996, pp. 76–78.

Duyn, Aline van, "A Truly Universal Bank," *Euromoney*, September 1994, p. C30.

Fairlamb, David, "Vorstandsdammerung?," *Institutional Investor*, December 1995, pp. 50+.

Fairlamb, David, and Stanley Reed, "Damage Control at Deutsche: The Failed Dresdner Deal Leaves German Banking in Turmoil," *Business Week,* April 17, 2000, pp. 150–51.

Fallon, Padraic, "The Battle Plans of Hilmar Kopper," *Euromoney,* January 1994, p. 28.

Fisher, Andrew, "Tough Guy at the Bank," *Financial Times,* November 21, 1994, p. FTS4.

Fuhrman, Peter, "A Faster Ship in a Richer Sea," *Forbes,* November 26, 1990, pp. 40–41.

Gall, Lothar, "Hermann Josef Abs and the Third Reich: 'A Man for All Seasons,'?" *Financial History Review* 6, 1999, part 2, pp. 147–200.

Gall, Lothar, et al., *Die Deutsche Bank, 1870–1995,* Munich: Beck, 1995, 1,014 p.

"The German Example: Three Rich, Powerful Banks Dominate the Economy," *Business Week,* April 19, 1976, p. 89.

Grant, Charles, "Sturm und Drang at Deutsche Bank," *Euromoney,* October 1985, pp. 126+.

Greenhouse, Steven, "Deutsche Bank's Bigger Reach," *New York Times,* July 30, 1989.

Grigsby, Jefferson, "Deutsche Bank uber Alles," *Financial World,* May 15, 1990, pp. 42–43.

Gumbel, Peter, "Humbled Giant: Long Highly Praised, Deutsche Bank Finds Itself in Some Trouble," *Wall Street Journal,* November 16, 1995, pp. A1+.

Guyon, Janet, "The Emperor and the Investment Bankers: How Deutsche Lost Dresdner," *Fortune,* May 1, 2000, pp. 134–36, 138, 140.

——, "Why Deutsche Is Banking on Debt," *Fortune,* January 11, 1999, p. 90.

"Herr Dobson's Fishing Trip," *Economist,* May 11, 1996, pp. 67–68.

"Herrhausen's Last Deal," *Economist,* December 2, 1989, pp. 87+.

James, Harold, *The Deutsche Bank and the Nazi Economic War Against the Jews,* New York: Cambridge University Press, 2001, 254 p.

Kantrow, Yvette, "John Rolls' Grand Plan," *Investment Dealers' Digest,* August 29, 1994.

Kopper, Christopher, *Zwischen Marktwirtschaft und Dirigismus: Bankenpolitik im "Dritten Reich," 1933–1939,* Bonn: Bouvier, 1995, 400 p.

Kopper, Christopher, Manfred Pohl, and Angelika Raab-Rebentisch, *Stationen,* Frankfurt: W. Kramer, 1995, 111 p.

Kraus, James R., "Changing to Make Its Mark," *American Banker,* September 20, 1994.

Miller, Karen Lowry, "Fixing Deutsche Bank," *Business Week,* July 19, 1999, pp. 56–58.

Muehring, Kevin, "The Kopper Era at Deutsche Bank," *Institutional Investor,* December 1990, pp. 136–39.

"New Dreams at Deutsche Bank: Germany's Grandest Bank Has a New Vision of Its Future—A Rather More Modest One Than in the Past," *Economist,* June 22, 1991, pp. 79–81.

Norman, Peter, "Deutsche Bank Looking Abroad As West German Market Shrinks," *Wall Street Journal,* September 3, 1985.

Pluenneke, John E., John Templeman, and William Glasgall, "Deutsche Bank Makes a Bid to Become All Europe's Banker," *Business Week,* December 22, 1986, p. 34.

Quint, Michael, "German Giant's Big U.S. Plans," *New York Times,* May 22, 1989, p. D1.

Reich, Cary, "Wilfried Guth, Chairman, Deutsche Bank," *Institutional Investor,* June 1987, pp. 398+.

Rescigno, Richard, "The View from Deutsche Bank," *Barron's,* November 18, 1991, pp. 8–12.

Rhoads, Christopher, "Behind the Books: Holzmann's Woes Can't All Be Tagged on Former Managers," *Wall Street Journal Europe,* December 21, 1999.

——, "Deutsche Bank Discloses Involvement in the Financing of Nazi Death Camp," *Wall Street Journal,* February 5, 1999, p. A13.

——, "Deutsche Bank Probably Knew Nazi Gold's Source, Report Says," *Wall Street Journal,* August 3, 1998, p. A11.

——, "Deutsche Bank to Give BT 'No Autonomy,'" *Wall Street Journal,* December 1, 1998, p. A3.

——, "Making It Work: Deutsche Bank Does What They Said Couldn't Be Done—Purchase of Bankers Trust Starting to Pay Off for World's Biggest Bank," *Wall Street Journal Europe,* November 18, 1999.

Roth, Terence, and Michael R. Sesit, "Leading Lender: As East Bloc Changes, Deutsche Bank Is Set to Play a Bigger Role," *Wall Street Journal,* November 24, 1989.

Seidenzahl, Fritz, *100 Jahre Deutsche Bank, 1870–1970,* Frankfurt: J. Weisbecker, 1970, 457 p.

Shirreff, David, "Deutsche's Anglo-Saxon Gamble," *Euromoney,* January 1995, pp. 24+.

Steinberg, Jonathan, *The Deutsche Bank and Its Gold Transactions During the Second World War,* Munich: Beck, 1999, 176 p.

Steinmetz, Greg, "Fiscal Accounting: A German Historian Probes Nazi-Era Deeds of His Father's Bank," *Wall Street Journal,* October 16, 1997, pp. A1+.

Steinmetz, Greg, and Silvia Ascarelli, "Deutsche Bank Chairman Kopper Resigns," *Wall Street Journal,* October 31, 1996, p. A18.

Templeman, John, "Deutsche Bank Makes a Bid for Global Power," *Business Week,* March 28, 1988, pp. 78+.

Templeman, John, et al., "Deutsche Bank's Big Gamble," *Business Week,* October 14, 1996, pp. 122, 124.

Walker, Marcus, "Deutsche Bank Shuffles Its Management," *Wall Street Journal,* January 26, 2001, p. A10.

——, "Deutsche Bank to Reorganize, Cutting Number of Divisions to Two," *Wall Street Journal,* December 5, 2000, p. A21.

Zweig, Phillip L., "Deutsche Bank Goes on the Attack," *Business Week,* July 17, 1995, pp. 83–84.

—update: David E. Salamie

Diedrich Coffee, Inc.

2144 Michelson Drive
Irvine, California 92612
U.S.A.
Telephone: (949) 260-1600
Toll Free: (800) 354-5282
Fax: (949) 260-1610
Web site: http://www.diedrich.com

Public Company
Founded: 1972
Employees: 1,336
Sales: $74.5 million (2000)
Stock Exchanges: NASDAQ
Ticker Symbol: DDRX
NAIC: 445299 All Other Specialty Food Stores

Diedrich Coffee, Inc. is the second largest specialty coffee company (behind Starbucks) in the United States. The company operates more than 380 coffeehouses in 38 states and six foreign countries. Diedrich coffeehouses sell gourmet coffee, cappuccino, latte, gourmet coffee beans, and other beverages along with some food items. Diedrich coffeehouses are modeled after traditional European coffeehouses with overstuffed sofas and chairs and high-end baked goods. Diedrich coffeehouses serve as friendly town meeting places where neighbors gather and socialize. Each Diedrich coffeehouse is uniquely designed to reflect the atmosphere and people in its neighborhood. Many have outdoor patios and live entertainment on weekends. Diedrich also operates a mail-order coffee business and a wholesale coffee division that sells coffee-brewing equipment to the hospitality foodservice industry. In 1999 the company acquired Coffee People, Inc., a leading chain of mall-based coffee stores.

An Inheritance in 1916

The first Diedrich coffeehouse opened in 1972, but the company actually began in 1916 when German-born Charlotte Diedrich inherited a coffee plantation in Costa Rica. Charlotte left Germany occasionally to visit the plantation and learned a great deal about growing and roasting coffee beans. Her hard work paid off and she began shipping her rich coffee beans to people around the world. Charlotte maintained the plantation through the 1930s, but lost it during the upheaval of World War II.

However, losing her plantation did not weaken Charlotte's passion for growing coffee beans. She perfected her skills and passed her ambitions onto her son, Carl. Before joining his mother in the coffee business, Carl Diedrich served as a conscripted infantry soldier in the German army and was a successful mechanical engineer. In 1964, Diedrich traveled the world to learn more about the coffee business. He studied coffee roasting in Naples, Italy, and toured traditional coffeehouses in the Middle East. He even studied coffee's origins in Yemen, where the people are believed to have grown coffee beans since the sixth century. Diedrich lived for a while with the people of Yemen, so he could learn as much as possible about growing coffee beans and making coffee.

A New Plantation in Guatemala in 1966

Diedrich returned to Germany in the early 1950s and married Inga Zeitz, whose family had been coffee merchants since the mid-1800s. In 1966 the Diedrichs, along with several partners, purchased a 45-acre coffee plantation in Antigua, Guatemala, and harvested about 400 sacks of coffee beans each year. The rich Guatemalan soil and 5,500-foot elevations helped the Diedrichs grow dense, rich Arabic coffee beans. During his six years in Antigua, Carl Diedrich did business with many of the Central American coffee traders who once worked with his mother. He even built a special device—the first coffee roaster for the company—on his family's back porch.

Diedrich was dedicated to his business and he passed his knowledge on to his sons, but he also encouraged them to pursue their own dreams.

A New Venture in 1972

In 1972 political turmoil in Guatemala made living and working difficult, so Diedrich sold the plantation and decided to import his gourmet coffee into the United States. He and his family filled up their 1962 Volkswagen bus with beans from their plantation and headed north from Guatemala to Newport Beach, California. Diedrich set up a wholesaling operation in a garage and sold his coffee beans to dealers. Word of his rich coffee spread. Within three years, he moved to a larger location. Although Diedrich was successful, his work was often grueling and his income modest. Every two months, he had to embark on a two-week journey to Guatemala in his Volkswagen bus to get more beans.

Carl Diedrich's sons showed little interest in their father's business at first. Michael, his oldest, sold body-care products and cosmetics in Germany. Bernhard opted for a career with the United Parcel Service in Washington. Sons Stephen and Carl, Jr., also steered away from Diedrich Coffee. Son Martin did join the business, but he was unhappy at first and did not like living in California. "I didn't feel like I belonged in Orange County (California)," Martin Diedrich recounted in an article in the *Los Angeles Times Magazine.* "I grew up in Latin America, where there is a strong sense of community. I felt displaced here and had constant longings to leave and go somewhere else."

The First Coffeehouse in 1985

It was the younger Diedrich's feelings of displacement that led the company to open its first coffeehouse. In 1985, he persuaded his father to let him open a coffeehouse to help bring people in the neighborhood together. The first Diedrich coffeehouse was very popular, and the following year the company opened a second. "I realized later I was building the kind of places that I found missing in Orange County. They were the fulfillment of my desire to make a home for myself here. At the same time, the community embraced what I was doing. The two came together like a hand in glove," Diedrich said in a *Los Angeles Times Magazine* article.

In time Carl, Jr., joined the business and persuaded his brother Stephen to leave his career in aviation to manage the coffee bean roasting division of the company. With Stephen's help, Carl began building coffee roasters unlike anything the industry had ever seen.

Some industry experts predicted that Diedrich coffeehouses would have trouble competing with the giant Starbucks, a national chain of gourmet coffeehouses. The *Los Angeles Times Magazine* reported that analysts believed that "smaller vendors

would be crushed beneath the Starbucks steamroller." Martin Diedrich believed, however, that Starbucks converted a lot of institutional coffee drinkers to specialty coffees, which helped smaller coffeehouse chains, including Diedrich.

Going Public in 1996

Diedrich Coffee launched an initial public offering (IPO) in 1996, which put Diedrich in direct national competition with Starbucks. Adams Harkness analyst Kim Galle summarized the situation when she said, "There is no Pepsi to their (Starbucks) Coke." Starbucks was much too powerful to compete with directly.

Diedrich expanded rapidly, but its stock slumped. According to the *Los Angeles Times Magazine,* Diedrich stock peaked at $11 and then plunged to less than $2.50. The company lost more than $1 million in 1996.

Restructuring in the Late 1990s

Martin Diedrich attributed the company's financial woes to inexperienced management and restructured the company. He named John Martin as chairman. Martin had worked for Taco Bell for 13 years and was credited with much of the company's success. Martin helped Taco Bell grow from $600 million in sales and 1,500 outlets to more than $4.5 billion in sales and more than 25,000 outlets.

Martin Diedrich also hired Tim Ryan as president and chief executive of the company. Ryan had pulled Sizzler USA out of bankruptcy and had worked with Martin for seven years at Taco Bell. Martin invested $1 million in Diedrich, making him one of the company's largest shareholders. Martin managed the "overall strategy, vision, and support" of the company while Ryan managed the day-to-day operations. According to an article in the *Orange County Register,* the duo planned to transform Diedrich "from a struggling regional player into an international chain with a globally recognized name." Martin and Ryan closed unprofitable stores and solidified agreements with franchises to give Diedrich a stronger national presence, especially on the East Coast. Said Martin in the *Orange County Register:* "We have a lot of dough and we want to grow."

Ryan saw the specialty coffee market as three different segments: mall-based coffee shops, dominated by Coffee People's Gloria Jean's; espresso bars, dominated by Starbucks; and coffeehouses, the niche in which Diedrich hoped to take the lead. Diedrich elaborated on the company's plans in *Nation's Restaurant News* by explaining that Diedrich Coffee planned to further differentiate itself from Starbucks on a national level by providing a more inviting atmosphere tailored to individual neighborhoods and by using custom-roasting procedures. "Coffee is like wine," he said. "If you were to roast all coffee identically as our number one competitor does, it would be like aging all wines identically."

In 1997 Martin Diedrich announced that he was stepping down from his role as chairman to take the new position of vice-chairman and chief coffee officer. Diedrich planned to concentrate on buying the highest quality coffee beans.

Key Dates:

1916: Charlotte Diedrich inherits a coffee plantation in Costa Rica.
1964: Charlotte's son, Carl, travels the world to learn about the coffee business.
1966: Carl and wife Inga purchase a plantation in Antigua, Guatemala.
1972: Diedrichs sell their plantation and move to the United States.
1985: Martin Diedrich opens the first Diedrich coffeehouse.
1996: Diedrich Coffee goes public.
1998: Diedrich signs deals with Taco Bell and other franchises.

Coffee People in 1999

In 1998 Diedrich signed deals to offer Diedrich Coffee in national food franchises, including Taco Bell. The deals allowed Diedrich to sell its coffee in carts and kiosks to franchise customers. The Taco Bell alliance covered 44 units in North Carolina and gave Diedrich its first presence in the eastern United States. "It would take us 10 years to build out what we can do in less than half that time using franchises," Ryan said in *Nation's Business News*. He also claimed that franchises could tailor the concept to local markets better than the company could.

The following year Diedrich acquired the Coffee People, Inc. chain, whose Gloria Jean's and Coffee People and Coffee Plantation outlets totaled 315 stores in 36 states and six countries. The $14.25 million deal ranked Diedrich as the number two specialty coffee retailer in the United States, second only to Starbucks. Coffee People's 280 Gloria Jean's stores held a dominant position in mall-based coffee locations, which gave Diedrich an edge in both the coffeehouse segment of the market and the mall-based store segment.

A Bright Outlook for the Future

In 2001 analysts believed Diedrich Coffee was doing well in rebounding from its earlier losses. The company's profits at the end of 2000 were about $1 million higher than in 1999. John Martin believed the company was now in a position to move ahead with expansion plans and open many new stores. As of 2000 he hoped to open 1,200 to 1,500 new units over the next five years. In 1999 and 2000 the company signed two agreements with M & P Coffee, Ltd., a national franchise operator, to develop 50 coffeehouses in southern California and 17 coffeehouses and an undetermined number of kiosks in Nevada. In 2000 former Boston Chicken executive J. Michael Jenkins replaced Tim Ryan as president and CEO when Ryan retired.

Principal Subsidiaries

Coffee Plantation; Gloria Jean's Gourmet Coffee; Coffee People, Inc.

Principal Competitors

Starbucks Corporation; Tully's Coffee Corporation; Kraft Foods North America; Einstein/Noah Bagel Corporation.

Further Reading

Banoo, Sreerema, "Coffee House Wafting in Aroma of Success," *Business Times* (Malaysia), December 10, 1999.
"Diedrich Coffee to Acquire Six-Unit Café Chain," *Nation's Restaurant News,* 1997, p. 24.
"Diedrich Expands Further in Colorado," *Denver Business Journal,* July 14, 2000, p. 13A.
Hamstra, Mark, "Diedrich Coffee Inks Franchise Deal with Taco Bell," *Nation's Business News,* September 28, 1998.
Hardesty, Greg, "Chairman Plans Big Growth at Diedrich Coffee Inc. of California," *Knight-Ridder/Tribune Business News,* November 19, 1997.
Hirch, Jerry, "Diedrich Coffee Inc. Lost Half Its Market Value Over the Week," *Knight-Ridder/Tribune Business News,* March 14, 1997.
Martin, Richard, "Martin Debuts Start-Up, Bites into BBQ As Diedrich Regroups," *Nation's Restaurant News,* April 27, 1998, p. 1.
Mouchard, Andre, "Despite Booming Sales at New Locations, Coffee Company Must Sell Stores," *Knight-Ridder/Tribune Business News,* April 30, 1997.
Smith, Martin J., "Of Human Beings & Coffee Beans," *Los Angeles Times Magazine,* July 26, 1998, pp. 14+.
Spector, Amy, "Diedrich Coffee Taps Ex-Boston Chicken Chief Jenkins As CEO," *Nation's Restaurant News,* October 9, 2000, p. 4.
——, "Diedrich to Gulp Coffee People, Brew Up No. 2 Segment Ranking," *Nation's Restaurant News,* February 22, 1999, pp. 6, 108.
——, "Quarterly Return Brews Profit, But Diedrich Has to Perk Up Unit Growth," *Nation's Restaurant News,* February 21, 2000, p. 11.

—Tracey Vasil Biscontini

Diesel SpA

Via dell' Industria 7
36060 Molvena, Vicenza
Italy
Telephone: (+39) 424-477-555
Fax: (+39) 424-411-955
Web site: http://www.diesel.com

Private Company
Incorporated: 1978 as Genius Group
Employees: 1,000
Sales: L 640 billion ($350 million) (2000 est.)
NAIC: 315 Apparel Manufacturing; 3159 Apparel
 Accessories and Other Apparel Manufacturing; 448
 Clothing and Clothing Accessories Stores

Based in the small village of Molvena in the north of Italy, Diesel SpA is one of Europe's top manufacturers of designer jeans and other apparel, including the upscale DieselStyleLab brand, the extreme sports-inspired 55-DSL sportswear line, and Diesel Kids children's clothing. Diesel also licenses its brand for a number of accessory products, including eyewear, manufactured by Italy's Safilo; shoes and other footwear by Global Brand Marketing USA; luggage and other leather goods by Principe, in Italy; and perfumes and cosmetics, under the Diesel Plus Plus and Zero Plus labels, manufactured by Germany's Marbert. Diesel's irreverent advertising campaigns have driven its strong implantation in more than 10,000 chain and department stores in more than 80 countries worldwide—the company insists on maintaining essentially identical marketing and branding activities across its global market. Diesel also has been building up a network of company-owned and franchised Diesel retail stores, which feature its jeans and the DieselStyleLab labels. By 2001, the company operated nearly 150 retail stores. The expansion of its retail operations indicated the long-private Diesel might go public early in the new century. Diesel, led by founder Renzo Rosso, posted L 640 billion in revenues in 2000.

Designer Crop of the 1970s

Renzo Rosso was born in 1955 in Brugine, in northeastern Italy, where his family operated a small farm. Rosso's talent for business was evident early on, however. At the age of ten, Rosso began breeding rabbits—starting with a single rabbit given to him as a gift. Rosso's rabbit farm quickly counted more than 100 rabbits, giving him his first taste for fast-growing profits. Rosso's distaste for schoolwork, however, left him with modest plans for his future, as he told *Interview:* "My dream as a kid was just to be a little more than a simple workman."

At the age of 15, however, Rosso heard of the opening of a new textile manufacturing school. "I didn't like to study," Rosso told *Interview,* "and the rumor was that at this new school that had just opened—the first fashion school in Italy—it would be very easy to graduate." Rosso did graduate and at the same time discovered a flair for fashion design. At the age of 20, Rosso began designing his own clothes; then, in 1975, he joined a local textiles company, Moltex, led by Adriano Goldschmied, that specialized in producing trousers. Rosso's position as production manager was quickly placed in doubt when Goldschmied sought to dismiss Rosso. Instead, Rosso convinced Goldschmied to keep him on, reducing his salary and placing him on a commission. "This gave me an incredible incentive," Rosso told *Interview,* "The company completely turned around, and not long after I said to him, 'Thank you very much, now it's time for me to move on.'"

Rosso proposed that he and Goldschmied form a partnership based around the promotion of new designer labels. Goldschmied agreed, selling Rosso 40 percent of the new company, called the Genius Group, which was launched in 1978. The Genius Group was responsible for creating a number of successful brand names, including Goldie, Ten Big Boys, Martin Guy, and Katherine Hamnett, and, of course, Rosso's own Diesel jeans brand.

Rosso had chosen the Diesel brand name especially for its international appeal. Pronounced more or less the same all over the world, the Diesel name fitted in with Rosso's concept of a single global market segmented not along national borders but

Company Perspectives:

Beginning as a company focused on making quality clothing, Diesel has become part of youth culture worldwide. It can legitimately claim to be the first brand to believe truly in the global village and to embrace it with open arms.

along age and lifestyle lines. Rosso also was eager to test his own ideas of style. By 1979, he had created his first full menswear collection around the Diesel name; the company's first international sales came in 1981. The following year, the group opened a factory outlet store for its designs.

Rosso's involvement with the Diesel brand remained entirely hands-on. In 1984, he debuted a new line, Diesel Kids, extending the company's jean-based fashions to cover the entire range of youth markets. Sensing the potential of the Diesel brand, Rosso bought out Goldschmied and the other Genius Group partners in 1985. By then, sales of Diesel-branded clothing amounted to about $5 million per year.

Campaigning for Global Recognition in the 1990s

With 100 percent control of his company and brand, Rosso set out to develop a new way of creating fashion. Diesel began hiring a new generation of design staff—all hand-chosen by Rosso himself—bringing in young design school graduates from across the world and giving them the mandate to ignore what the rest of the world's fashion community was doing and instead create clothing to reflect their own, and Rosso's, personalities. Designers were encouraged to allow free reign to their creativity—and ultimately to design the clothing they themselves would want to wear. In addition, Rosso instituted a new sort of "research trip." Designers were required to travel at least two times a year, were given complete freedom and an unlimited budget to choose their destinations, and in turn were invested with the mission to return to the company's headquarters with the inspiration to create the next season's line of Diesel clothing.

Such unorthodox design methods quickly helped the company develop a reputation for offbeat, even avant-garde design, and proved immensely appealing to the company's core European youth market. The debut of the company's Diesel Female collection in 1989 further expanded the company's target markets. Until then, the company's sales had remained for the most part within Italy; Rosso now determined to spread the company internationally, boosting its presence to some 40 countries, with sales topping $130 million, by the start of the decade. The company also attempted to enter the U.S. market, turning to a U.S.-based manufacturer, Russ Togs, to handle its distribution.

The year 1991 represented a hallmark in the company's history. In that year, Diesel hired Stockholm, Sweden-based advertising firm DDB Paradiset to help it fashion a new, global advertising campaign. Developed in conjunction with Diesel's own in-house creative team, the Paradiset campaign had as its objective to roll out a single advertising image to all of the Italian firm's international markets. The resulting advertising campaign, a mix of social and political commentary with a heavy sauce of black humor, catapulted Diesel to the world's

attention. In an era that had seen such controversial advertising campaigns as those of Benetton and Calvin Klein, the new Diesel ads took "in-your-face" to new extremes. An example of the Diesel campaign was a print ad featuring a teenager with a gun and the tagline: "If they never learn to blast the brains out of their neighbors what kind of damn FUTURE has this COUNTRY of ours got?"

As one industry observer remarked: "With one ad, Diesel got a whole new presence in the market. They went for the jugular, and any time an advertiser does that, it's bound to upset some people." The more upset their parents became, the more eagerly the company's target youth market bought the Diesel line. Just as the world market for jeans began to see dozens of new competitors, Diesel had managed to make itself one of the most well-known jeans makers, and this despite prices that started at $99 per pair and ranged up to $200 per pair.

If the company managed to impose itself on the European market, where it became one of the top-selling jeans labels during the 1990s, it was less successful in the United States. The financial collapse of Russ Togs at the start of the decade cut severely into the company's growth in that market. Despite the advertising campaign's success at attracting attention to the company's products, finding Diesel jeans and clothing remained difficult for many customers until the middle of the decade. Nonetheless, the company succeeded in placing its line in such prestigious locations as Bloomingdale's and Barney's New York and quickly built up a cult image.

After discovering the pleasures of snowboarding, Rosso was inspired to launch the company into a new category of clothing. The company debuted its new brand, 55-DSL, in 1994. Although initially meant to develop clothing for the extreme sports market, the label quickly encompassed a wide range of sportswear bearing the Diesel name and style. The company also began a licensing program to place its name and logo on a variety of items. The company's first license was granted to Italy's Safilo, which launched its Diesel Shades line in 1994. Safilo managed to capture Diesel's flair for irony, with such model names as Porn Star, Nose Job, and Atomic Sun. The sunglasses became a quick success, prompting the company to develop other licensed products, such as a line of Diesel perfumes and fragrances manufactured by Germany's Marbett, and then extending to footwear, luggage, and, in a license granted in 1999, watches made by Fossil.

Retail Empire in the 21st Century

After relying on chain stores and department stores for its sales, Diesel turned toward building its own retail empire. The company opened its first 14,000-square-foot flagship store in New York City in 1996. The following year saw a second store, opened in London's Covent Garden. The company quickly built up its retail operations, topping 25 stores by 1998. By the end of 2000, the company operated more than 120 company-owned or franchised Diesel stores in 80 countries. The company's strong growth—as it topped the L 500 billion mark by mid-decade—increasingly brought Diesel and Rosso to the attention of the world's business community. In 1997, Renzo Rosso's success was crowned with Ernst & Young's Entrepreneur of the Year award.

Key Dates:

1975: Renzo Rosso joins textile firm Moltex.
1978: Rosso helps found Genius Group.
1979: Diesel brand is launched.
1981: International sales begins.
1982: Factory outlet store is opened.
1984: Diesel Kids line is launched.
1985: Rosso acquires full control of Diesel.
1989: Diesel Female is launched.
1991: International advertising campaign begins.
1994: 55-DSL brand is launched; license for Diesel eyewear is acquired.
1996: First retail store is opened.
1998: DieselStyleLab label is launched.
2000: Staff International is acquired.
2001: Company expands to Spain and Portugal.

Declines in the jeans market toward the end of the 1990s led Diesel to begin looking for ways to expand its range of clothing. The company debuted a new line of upscale, more fashion-conscious clothing under the label DieselStyleLab. The company took care to separate its new line, which was nonetheless sold in its retail stores and in-store boutiques, from its youth-market Diesel line—seen as a necessary move to preserve the company's trendsetter status among its core youth market.

Diesel confirmed its ambitions to move deeper into the upscale category when it acquired Staff International in April 2000. That company, which had been manufacturing Diesel's DieselStyleLab, also owned several luxury-class brands, as well as the licenses for such upscale labels as Red Label, by British designer Vivienne Westwood, and Martin Margiela. Although Staff International had been near bankruptcy before the Diesel purchase, it represented a step toward Rosso's avowed goal of becoming a key player in the luxury goods market, while nonetheless sticking to the company's core casual wear segment.

The company continued to boost its name recognition and sales through its irreverent advertising. In 2000, the company prepared to launch the career of a "fake" celebrity, building a global advertising campaign around its sponsorship of an unknown Polish singer—complete with CD release, tabloid hype, and fan club. Diesel nevertheless remained down-to-earth in its business growth, mapping out a new expansion program, with the possibility of the company making a public listing to finance an aggressive expansion drive. In February 2001, the company targeted the Spanish and Portuguese markets for further growth, replacing its third-party distributor with its own domestic subsidiaries, with plans to expand its retail operations in both countries. Successfully steering the twists and turns of trendiness, Diesel expected to continue to clothe and inspire its customers through the 21st century.

Principal Subsidiaries

Staff International.

Principal Competitors

Giorgio Armani S.p.A.; Benetton Group S.p.A.; Bill Blass Ltd.; Calvin Klein, Inc.; Donna Karan International Inc.; Esprit Europe AG; Gianni Versace SpA; Guess, Inc.; Hugo Boss AG; Levi Strauss & Co.; Naf Naf S.A.; OshKosh B'Gosh, Inc.; Polo Ralph Lauren Corporation; Tommy Hilfiger Corporation; Groupe Zannier.

Further Reading

Blanchard, Tamsin, "Jeans Genius," *Independent,* April 23, 1996, p. 14.

Campbell, Lisa, "Diesel Fights to Keep Cult Image," *Marketing,* September 10, 1998.

"Diesel May Go Public to Finance Expansion," *Financial Times,* July 28, 1998.

Goldfarb, Brad, "We Take You to the Leader," *Interview,* November 1, 1998.

Horovitz, Bruce, "Fuming over Diesel's Shocking Ads," *Newsday,* May 24, 1993, p. 31.

Rickey, Melanie, "Diesel's Driving Force," *Independent,* July 29, 1998, p. 8.

—M. L. Cohen

EBSCO Industries, Inc.

P.O. Box 1943
Birmingham, Alabama 35201-1943
U.S.A.
Telephone: (205) 991-6600
Fax: (205) 991-1479
Web site: http://www.ebsco.com

Private Company
Incorporated: 1943 as Military Service Company
Employees: 4,000
Sales: $1.25 billion (2000 est.)
NAIC: 23311 Land Subdivision and Land Development;
314999 All Other Miscellaneous Textile Product
Mills; 332994 Small Arms Manufacturing; 42191
Sporting and Recreational Goods and Supplies; 51114
Database and Directory Publishers; 514199 All Other
Information Services; 51421 Data Processing
Services; 54186 Direct Mail Advertising; 54189 Other
Services Related to Advertising

EBSCO Industries, Inc. is a diverse and international conglomerate that built itself on magazine subscription services. As technology has advanced, the company has become a leader in supplying information to libraries through its CD-ROM products and online services. EBSCO also manufactures such diverse items as fishing lures, hunting rifles, and promotional products.

Selling Magazines, Then Anything: 1930s–70s

When Elton B. Stephens graduated from the University of Alabama School of Law in 1936, he figured he could earn ten times the salary of a lawyer by selling magazines. Selling was not new to Stephens. Growing up in a poor family of eight children in rural Clio, Alabama, Stephens told *Forbes* he spent his youth selling "everything I could get my hands on." He had paid for college selling magazines door-to-door and selling socks and shirts in a dry goods shop. Though he was an enthusiastic salesman, Stephens told *Forbes* he hated selling magazines door-to-door. "You'd get the door slammed in your face. You'd get cussed at by husbands. You had to bounce back." Nevertheless, he went on selling and eventually hired others to sell for him. By 1937 Stephens purchased a Keystone Readers' Service franchise.

During World War II, Stephens realized the great potential for success in selling to military bases, and in 1943 he and his wife, Alys Robinson Stephens, had invested $5,000 into their own partnership, the Military Service Company, which sold magazines, personalized binders, and racks. When Keystone fired Elton Stephens for spending too much time with his own company, Stephens offered the publishers who had supplied Keystone better terms and took their business. Stephens' treatment of Keystone became typical of his management style. If a supplier impeded the progress of a division, EBSCO would start its own venture or acquire another to replace it.

Stephens's desire to make his business as effective as possible and his youthful drive to "sell anything he could get his hands on" set the stage for EBSCO's growth. In an interview with *Forbes,* Stephens estimated that he launched between 60 to 80 companies over his 60 years in business, noting that 30 percent of them had failed. He recalled telling someone once "that I'd like to have five companies. That way, if one or two of them don't make it, I'll still have something to hang my hat on." By the 1990s, EBSCO would be active in 28 industries.

Stephens started his company with the idea that he would work on an all-cash basis, and for 20 years he managed his company without a long-term loan. With cash on hand, Stephens formed Metal Fabricators and Finishers to manufacture display stands, Vulcan Binder and Cover to make binders, and Vulcan Enterprises to provide community-related messages for binder covers; he purchased Hartsfield Printing Company to supply personalized stationary to the military, and acquired Hanson-Bennett Magazine Agency of Chicago and National Magazine Company of San Francisco. By 1964, Stephens had learned that loans help businesses to grow and thus took on EBSCO's first long-term debt. Remembering a lost opportunity because of his reluctance to take on debt, Stephens told *Forbes* "Had I done that, I would probably be worth another three or four million dollars. But I'm not."

Company Perspectives:

*We guide ourselves with seven values: Customer First—
Our jobs and our company's future come from the customer.
Sales—We communicate, educate and persuade to offer our
products and services as far and wide as the market opportunity exists. Growth—We are committed to finding and
growing revenues and business activities. Profitability—
Profits provide the resources to maintain operations, to
invest to improve them, to develop new opportunities and to
ensure a financially secure organization. Engineering—We
must constantly seek to identify and to develop ways to
realize opportunities and to change shortcomings. Thrift—
The need for economy stands as an eternal verity. People—
People make the difference when they work together as a
knowledgeable, productive and motivated team with mutual
respect for one another. We are thankful for our historical
progress. We are inspired by our opportunities. We will
continue to seek improvement and growth.*

Nevertheless, since the 1960s, EBSCO—so-called after the
initials of its founder's name along with the abbreviation for
"company"—continued to grow, as did Stephens's fortune. In
1971, Stephens turned over EBSCO's presidential duties to his
son, J.T. Stephens. Under the leadership of J.T. Stephens,
EBSCO flourished. One year after taking the presidential position, J.T. Stephens saw EBSCO's sales volume double with the
purchase of Franklin Square Agency, Ziff-Davis's international
subscription service. Like his father, J.T. Stephens seemed to be
comfortable selling just about anything.

While the company remained focused on maintaining the
prominence and leadership of its magazine subscription division, it broadened its base of operations to include unrelated
industries such as National Billiard, Fine Craft Carpets, and
PRADCO, the country's largest manufacturer of fishing lures.
Elton B. Stephens remained as chairman of EBSCO, overseeing
the company's charitable contributions and profit sharing investment trust. In 1981, he started his second career as a banker,
launching Alabama Bancorp.

Information Leaders in the 1980s

To maintain its leadership in the magazine subscription services industry, EBSCO was sensitive in its role as an information handler. EBSCO researched the needs of each of the different types of libraries it serviced: academic/research, law,
biomedical, school, public, and special/corporate. Staff members organized seminars and forums to create a mutually beneficial working relationship with customers, seek electronic connections between EBSCO and automated library systems, and
develop special reports that aided libraries in analyzing their
journal collections. EBSCO employees also helped develop
library communication standards and supported the library profession through membership and active participation in the
American Library Association, Medical Library Association,
Special Libraries Association, National Information Standards
Organization, Serial Industry Systems Advisory Committee,
and the International Committee on Electronic Data Interchange

for Serials. EBSCO strove to make subscription management as
easy and efficient as possible. To that end it developed the
world's first online data communications network for serial
management. Developed in the late 1970s to connect all
EBSCO Subscription Services regional offices with the central
computer in Birmingham, in the 1990s EBSCONET acted as a
link between EBSCO and customers worldwide. Customers
could place orders and claims, order missing issues, search
EBSCO's title database, send e-mail to EBSCO or other
EBSCONET users, review their list of subscriptions ordered
through EBSCO, access the Internet, and search for and order
individual articles through the CASIAS (Current Awareness
Service/Individual Article Service) option.

EBSCO's understanding of the importance of accessing information quickly and easily helped it become one of America's
leading producers of CD-ROM reference products. In the
1980s, EBSCO Publishing was formed to combine two acquisitions, *Popular Magazine Review*—a publisher with abstracting
and indexing capabilities which EBSCO renamed Magazine
Article Summaries in 1987, and Horizon Information Systems,
a producer of CD-ROM search and retrieval software. EBSCO
Publishing's first product was *The Serial Directory: An International Reference Book*. The archives of Magazine Articles Summaries were converted to electronic format and published on
CD-ROM in 1989.

EBSCO Publishing was the first to provide abstracts and
keyword searching to full text or general magazines in electronic format. In 1993, Carol Tenopir and Péter Jacsó noted in a
study for *Online* that given a choice between indexes with or
without abstracts they thought most users would choose those
with abstracts "every time." The leading CD-ROM indexes for
the layperson in 1993 were H.W. Wilson Company's Readers'
Guide Abstracts, UMI's Periodical Abstracts Ondisc (and its
subfile, Resource-One), and EBSCO's Magazine Article Summaries. Tenopir and Jacsó attempted to differentiate between
these competitors based on the quality of their abstracts. The
authors looked at the consistency of style and readability in the
abstracts, the extent to which the ANSI standard (The American
National Standards Institute's standards for abstracts developed
in 1979) was observed, and the informativeness of the abstracts.
Readers' Guide Abstracts best met the test for informativeness
and were two-and-a-half times longer than the others. The Magazine Article Summaries abstracts were very brief, but described the information in the article. The authors noted that
EBSCO did not claim to offer full abstracts but rather summaries of articles.

Such a test might not indicate the desires of those who use
indexes, however, and that was the market EBSCO desired
most to please. Tenopir and Jacsó wrote that some instructors
and librarians preferred "an index with shorter, less informative
abstracts because they didn't want students to rely on abstracts
without having to go to the original article." Indeed, EBSCO's
customers were the center of product development. Joseph Tra-
gert, EBSCO Publishing's manager of product development,
remarked in *Information Today* that "our objectives for 1996
are a direct result of focus groups, surveys, communication with
industry professionals, and feedback from our customers and
our sales team regarding the needs of libraries." In describing
the product development cycle at EBSCO Melissa Kummerer

noted in *CD-ROM Professional,* "We can never consider a product to be finished. We can always make it better: by adding features, adding editorial content, or reducing memory requirements. We believe that quality is not a static term." In 1996 EBSCO planned to increase the number of titles abstracted and indexed to over 3,800 and full-text titles covered to over 1,500.

In keeping with EBSCO's interest in developing new products, it began offering an online search and retrieval system called EBSCOhost in 1996. EBSCOhost featured the same searching capabilities made popular by CD-ROM but could be accessed on the Internet. Jacsó hailed the emergence of EBSCO online because, he said, "for many magazines, EBSCO is the only abstracting/indexing and/or full-text source."

EBSCO's growth has strengthened the company and its surrounding community. Elton B. Stephens founded the Alabama "%" Club, whose member companies donate 2, 5, or 10 percent of their pretax income to foundations or other charitable projects. EBSCO was a member at the 5 percent level. In addition, EBSCO funded the nation's largest endowment for a chair of library science at the University of Alabama. Of the company's success, Elton B. Stephens told *Forbes,* "I never dreamed that we would accomplish anything like what we have."

New Developments Near the Millennium

EBSCO continued to update its offerings. By the end of 1997, all the company's CD-ROMs carried a Windows interface and EBSCOhost became available for Macintosh users. EBSCOhost was integrated with the EBSCOdoc document delivery service by this time.

The EBSCOdoc division reverted to its original name, EBSCO Document Services, in December 1997. The unit had begun in 1979 as an independent information brokerage called Dynamic Information. It was acquired by EBSCO in 1994.

By 1998, EBSCO's Collectanea service was providing corporate users with access to more than 1,600 periodicals dating back to 1990. However, it lacked the content of market leaders Dow Jones, Lexis-Nexis, and Dialog. Other specialized products targeted the medical market.

In developing new products, wrote Mike O'Leary in *Information Today,* EBSCO followed a "second-wave" strategy—benchmarking and improving upon the existing offerings of competitors such as Information Access Company (a unit of Gale Group), OCLC, and UMI. The company incorporated "relevance searching" into the 2.0 version of its EBSCOhost periodicals database for libraries, which allowed users to find the most relevant documents to their queries more efficiently—only the largely home consumer-based Electric Library service offered a similar interface at the time. EBSCOhost 2.0 also featured redesigned graphics.

By the end of 1998, EBSCO Document Services had folded, a casualty of competition, restrictive publisher licensing, and changing technology, according to J.T. Stephens. EBSCO continued to offer access to the same material via its electronic services, and planned to add the ability to order documents from third-party suppliers. Other recent casualties in the document delivery business included UMI's Information Store and Knight-Ridder Information's SourceOne. Nevertheless, during the year EBSCO had acquired Network Support Inc., maker of the Relais line of document supply systems.

EBSCO developed a new service in late 1998, EBSCO Online, which allowed libraries to access and manage its Internet journals from one source. It promised to become the online equivalent of EBSCO Subscription Services—linking publishers with libraries. Even as it was released, EBSCO Online was being integrated with the EBSCOhost databases.

EBSCO replaced the Collectanea service with Corporate ResourceNet (CRN) in 1999. CRN integrated periodical databases with Internet and third-party sources. The heavy use of Internet sources allowed EBSCO to price CRN below Dow Jones Interactive, Lexis-Nexis, and Dialog, which dominated the corporate market.

EBSCO bought NoveList, a reader's advisory in fiction, from CARL Corporation in June 1999. At the turn of the millennium, EBSCO was sealing partnerships with Dun & Bradstreet, ABC-CLIO, and Salem Press, to enlarge its databases. In late 2000, EBSCO Book Services extended its online book ordering to end users, chiefly libraries.

In late 1999, EBSCO and its partner, the Open Society Institute (OSI), announced plans for the "largest information consortium in the world," called Electronic Information for Libraries Direct (EIFL Direct). Participants included academic, research, medical, national, and public libraries in 39 countries, mostly in the third world or Eastern Europe. EBSCO provided access to several of its databases, available either on CD-ROMs or over the Internet, depending on the technological sophistication of the user.

While EBSCO's information products developed at a rapid pace, the company was also growing its sporting goods businesses. By 1998, EBSCO had acquired eight lines of fishing lures to add to its original Rebel brand. It also launched a new brand of its own, Excalibur. The company had become one of the world leaders in fishing lures, manufacturing at seven locations in the southern United States and Latin America.

Beginning with the 1997 purchase of Knight & Hale Game Calls, based in Cadiz, Kentucky, EBSCO widened its outdoor lines to include hunting products. The next year, it bought Knight Rifles of Centerville, Iowa. Knight manufactured muzzleloader rifles used to hunt deer. The Knight Rifles acquisition was EBSCO's largest yet. Knight's Green Mountain Barrel Company subsidiary in New Hampshire produced 70,000 rifle barrels a year.

EBSCO soon bought a hunting scent business called Code Blue and combined it with Knight & Hale. Other late 1990s acquisitions included Canton, Alabama-based Wayne Industries, a manufacturer of lighted signs, and Tinker Business Forms, a small operation in Pelham, Alabama.

EBSCO also sold personalized promotional items to 7,000 distributors through its Vitronic and Four Seasons product lines. By 1999, EBSCO Development Company had begun developing a residential subdivision in an 8,000 acre property along Double Oak Mountain in Shelby County, Alabama.

Principal Divisions

Carry-Lite Decoys & Accessories; Code Blue; Directional Advertising Services; EBSCO Book Services; EBSCO CardMember Services; EBSCO Consumer Magazine Services; EBSCO Curriculum Materials; EBSCO Development Company; EBSCO Magazine Express; EBSCO Media; EBSCO Promotional Products; EBSCO Publishing; EBSCO Realty; EBSCO Reception Room Subscription Services; EBSCO Subscription Services; EBSCO Teleservices; Four Seasons & Vitronic; Green Mountain Rifle Barrel Co.; Kinescope Interactive; Knight & Hale Game Calls; Knight Rifles; Luxor; Military Service Company; Mt. Laurel; NSC International; PRADCO Outdoor Brands; Publisher Promotion & Fulfillment; Publishers' Warehouse; Tinker Business Forms; Wayne Industries; H. Wilson Company; Valley Joist; Vulcan Industries; Vulcan Information Packaging; Vulcan Service.

Principal Operating Units

Information Services; Sales; Manufacturing.

Principal Competitors

DAS; Dialog; Dow Jones & Company, Inc.; Electric Library; Information Access Company; Lexis-Nexis Group; OCLC; UMI.

Further Reading

Beiser, Karl, "From Print to Electronic Form: The Sum Greater Than the Parts," *Database,* October 1993, pp. 97–99.

Bell, Suzanne S., "The Serials Directory/EBSCO CD-ROM," *Information Today,* October 1993, pp. 24–25, 27.

Duberman, Josh, "Collectanea Desk Top Library: The Future of Corporate End-User Searching?" *Online,* March/April 1998, pp. 88–90.

Duval, Beverly K., and Linda Main, "Microcomputer Applications in the Library—Part 1B: EBSCOhost's New Face," *Library Software Review,* June 1998, pp. 120–128.

"EBSCO Document Delivery Division Announces Name Change," *Information Today,* December 1997, p. 19.

"EBSCO Offers New Search and Retrieval System for Libraries," *Information Today,* September 1995, p. 43.

Jacsó, Péter, "CD-ROM Publishers Come Online," *Information Today,* September 1995, pp. 32–33.

Kummerer, Melissa, "Perpetual Product Development: EBSCO's CD-ROM Development Strategy," *CD-ROM Professional,* November 1993, pp. 104–08.

McMenamin, Brigid, "The Afterlife of a Salesman," *Forbes,* May 24, 1993, pp. 206–08.

Milazzo, Don, "EBSCO Is a Category Killer," *Birmingham Business Journal,* November 6, 1995, p. 1.

Miller, Kathy, "EBSCO Integrates Services," *Information World Review,* June 1999, p. 5.

——, "EBSCO: Subscriptions to Online Realm," *Information World Review,* December 1998, pp. 41–42.

"News from EBSCO Publishing," *Information Today,* March 1996, p. 4.

"OCLC and EBSCO to Offer Full-Text Images of Articles from 1,000 General Reference Journals," *Information Today,* April 1995, p. 18.

O'Leary, Mick, "EBSCO Carves a Niche for EBSCOhost," *Information Today,* June 1996, pp. 27ff.

——, "EBSCOhost 2.0 Enriches Search Power," *Information Today,* June 1998, pp. 19, 22ff.

——, "EBSCO Joins Business Info Fray," *Information Today,* May 1999, pp. 12–13.

"Online Data Communications Network Provides Speedy Customer Service," *Data Management,* December 1985, pp. 46–48.

Pollard, Jonathan, and Anne Marie Downing, "Ziff Boosts Computer Library Availability with Major Distribution Agreements," *Business Wire,* November 2, 1988.

Quint, Barbara, "EBSCO Industries Folds EBSCO Document Services," *Information Today,* October 1998, pp. 4, 6.

Rifkind, Eugene, "EBSCO Primary Search," *Information Today,* January 1995, pp. 20–21.

Rogers, Michael, "EBSCO Acquires CARL's NoveList," *Library Journal,* June 1, 1999, pp. 33–34.

——, "EBSCO Adds Book Search Services for Libraries and Users," *Library Journal,* November 15, 2000, p. 23.

——, "EBSCO and OSI Creating Global Library Consortium," *Library Journal,* November 1, 1999, p. 27.

——, "EBSCO Debuts New Products," *Library Journal,* May 1, 1997, p. 23.

——, "EBSCO Partners with ABC-CLIO," *Library Journal,* August 2000, pp. 30–32.

Rosen, Linda, "EBSCO Magazine Article Summaries Full Text Elite CD-ROM," *Information Today,* June 1993, pp. 26–27.

Stephens, James T., "EBSCO Industries, Inc.," New York: Newcomen Society, 1999.

"Subscription Service Credits Its Swiftness to On-line Net," *Computerworld,* March 19, 1984, p. 38, 40.

Tenopir, Carol, and Péter Jacsó, "Quality of Abstracts," *Online,* May 1993, pp. 44–55.

Tenopir, Carol, and Timothy Ray Smith, "General Periodical Indexes on CD-ROM," *CD-ROM Professional,* July 1990, pp. 70–81.

—Sara Pendergast
—update: Frederick C. Ingram

ELEMENTIS

Elementis plc

One Great Tower Street
London EC3R 5AH
United Kingdom
Telephone: (020) 7398-1400
Fax: (020) 7398-1401
Web site: http://www.elementis.com

Public Company
Incorporated: 1908 as Harrisons & Crosfield Ltd.
Employees: 2,971
Sales: £573.8 million ($928 million) (2000)
Stock Exchanges: London
Ticker Symbol: ELM
NAIC: 325131 Inorganic Dye and Pigment
    Manufacturing; 325188 All Other Basic Inorganic
    Chemical Manufacturing; 325998 All Other
    Miscellaneous Chemical Product and Preparation
    Manufacturing; 326291 Rubber Product
    Manufacturing for Mechanical Use; 326299 All Other
    Rubber Product Manufacturing; 422690 Other
    Chemical and Allied Products Wholesalers

Specialty chemicals producer Elementis plc holds world-leading positions in three areas: chromium chemicals, which are used in such areas as leather tanning, timber treatment, metal alloys and finishing, and ceramics; synthetic iron oxide pigments, the applications for which include pigmented concrete used in construction, decorative paints and other coatings, and cosmetics; and rheological additives, which are key ingredients in such products as paints, inks, hand lotions, and grease. Among the company's other operations, Elementis owns Linatex, a leading brand of abrasion-resistant rubber. The firm adopted the Elementis name only in 1998, but the company history actually begins in 1844 with the formation of Harrisons & Crosfield (H&C), which eventually developed into a large conglomerate. The fortunes of H&C were closely linked to Britain's position in the international marketplace, and its history was molded by a succession of strong personalities.

19th-Century Origins in the Tea Trade

The partnership between Daniel Harrison, Smith Harrison, and Joseph Crosfield was formed in Liverpool on January 1, 1844. The Harrison brothers, the eldest and youngest sons in a family of 17 children, already were working as tea merchants in Liverpool. Joseph Crosfield was too young to have established himself in business, but at only 23 he was already recognized as an ambitious man and was reluctant to lose his independence by committing himself to a formal partnership.

Nevertheless, Joseph Crosfield's parents persuaded their son to accept the favorable agreement offered by the Harrison brothers. In return for contributing one-quarter of the initial capital of £8,000, Joseph Crosfield was to receive three-tenths of the partnership's profits. With Daniel Harrison as chairman, Smith Harrison as the firm's representative at tea sales, and Joseph Crosfield in charge of the office, the partnership began its long history of trading.

For over 200 years the trade in tea had been controlled by the East India Company, which had obtained a monopoly when granted a royal charter in 1600. The Charter Act of 1813 canceled the East India Company's monopoly and opened both India and China to wider enterprise. The removal of tariffs and shipping restrictions, increasing demand for tea in Britain, and the building of canals and roads in India further encouraged new trading ventures, but, because of the prohibitive expense of setting up plantations, the new firms that entered the market had to begin as agency houses rather than as primary producers.

In its first year of trading H&C made a modest profit of £3,000 on a turnover mostly derived from tea but with a small element of coffee trading. It expanded rapidly and in 1854 moved from Liverpool to Great Tower Street in London, where it was based until 1989. The partners' benevolent attitude toward their staff was shown in their provision of free accommodation for unmarried employees and of free lunches for all workers. The firm now concentrated solely on the tea trade and benefited from its proximity to the tea markets of Mincing Lane. In just ten years the small provincial firm had become an established national organization with international aspirations.

During the middle of the 19th century, Britain's trade with its colonies exceeded that of France, Germany, Italy, and the United States combined. The year 1869 marked a crucial point in the history of the tea trade. The opening of the Suez Canal made transportation quicker and cheaper while the building of all-steel ships made wooden-composite ships such as the *Cutty Sark*—launched in 1869—something of an anachronism. Furthermore, a plague of coffee leaf disease devastated the 1869 coffee crop, forcing planters to focus their attention on producing tea, an obvious substitute that could be grown successfully on the old coffee plantations. H&C benefited from all of these changes and in 1882 its annual sales of tea exceeded 100,000 crates for the first time.

Daniel Harrison's son Joseph was admitted to the partnership in 1855, where he was to remain until his death in 1915. His father retired in 1863 to be replaced by Smith Harrison, who served as chairman of the firm for the next 20 years. By 1883, however, all of the original partners were dead, and despite the continued involvement of members from both families, the future of the firm was beginning to look less secure than during the first decades of rapid growth. Change came in 1894 when two salaried partners joined, representing the new management that was to initiate another period of expansion.

Turn of the 20th Century: Becoming Plantation Owners and Expanding into Rubber

Charles Heath Clark was an expert tea-blender who quickly grasped the commercial possibilities of expanding the range of products offered by the main office in London. H&C began to package tea for provincial merchants and it was a short step for the firm to produce its own brand for retail sale. The demand and supply of tea were both good and H&C benefited from a high margin on sales of Nectar, its proprietary brand. Heath Clark initially launched the brand in South Africa as he was unwilling to antagonize H&C's customers in Britain by appearing to establish a competing brand. Indeed, when Nectar was launched in the United Kingdom in 1904, the cost of advertising the product was greater than any increase in income, and the loss of customer goodwill led H&C to sell the brand to Twinings.

The dynamic Arthur Lampard, a risk-taking entrepreneur, was to lead H&C into the 20th century. His strategy was to turn H&C into a firm with truly international interests, not only as tea agents but also as plantation owners. Lampard visited Russia in 1895 to set up a trade route from Ceylon to Moscow via Odessa in order to cut handling costs for H&C's increasing number of Russian customers. In the same year Lampard visited Colombo, Ceylon, and set up Crosfield, Lampard & Co. to buy tea directly from plantation owners in Ceylon. Despite an unexpected fall in the market price of tea in 1901, Lampard continued his policy of overseas expansion, and by 1907 branch offices had been opened in New York, Montreal, and Kuala Lumpur.

H&C's reliance on the tea market was soon to be reduced by its entry into the rubber market. In 1900 over two-thirds of the world's annual supply of 40,000 tons of rubber was produced in Brazil, with the remainder coming from equatorial Africa. In 1903 Herbert Brett and W.S. Bennett, two names synonymous with the British rubber trade, enlisted Lampard's help to issue a prospectus for the Pataling Rubber Estates Syndicate, a venture based on an old coffee plantation in Malaysia which had been converted to rubber growing.

H&C was appointed as agent and secretary to the company and Lampard persuaded his more cautious board members to make an investment of £1,000. Lampard was prepared to go without profit for the plantation's first years, for he had forecast that a recent invention, the motor car, was likely to survive as rather more than a fashionable plaything for the rich, and that rubber for tires would eventually be in great demand.

In 1905 Lampard and Brett, the latter by now an employee of H&C, purchased several small estates in Malaysia for £50,000 and amalgamated them into the Golden Hope Rubber Estate. Whereas the Pataling Syndicate had been undersubscribed, shares in Golden Hope were sold at a substantial premium. The following year Lampard visited the east coast of Sumatra and set up a plantation with a Swiss planter, Victor Ris, who shared Lampard's vision of large plantations organized in the same efficient manner as Sumatra's huge tobacco plantations.

These ventures in Malaysia and Sumatra carried more risk than those in Ceylon, which was perceived as a maturing economy run by professional and experienced planters. By supporting Malaysian and Sumatran plantation owners—for example, by underwriting new crops, providing fertilizers and harvesting equipment, and acting as sales agents—H&C ensured the success of the plantation and, as an obvious consequence, its investment. The company took responsibility for bookkeeping and the raising of finance and sent powerful visiting agents to inspect the plantations. In this way the fledgling plantations benefited from high-quality advice on both the financial and agricultural aspects of the business.

Lampard had forecast astutely that his plantation rubber would be of a superior quality to that harvested in wild conditions in Brazil and Africa and his move into rubber growing was followed swiftly by Michelin, Dunlop, and Firestone. Britain's previously unenthusiastic financial sector, which had curtailed investment overseas because of the Boer War of 1899 to 1902, was now impressed by the prominent Lampard who worked ceaselessly to establish the industry worldwide. When the price of rubber rose from around four shillings per pound in 1902 to 12 shillings in 1905, Lampard's willingness to take risks was justified totally.

Key Dates:

1844: Daniel Harrison, Smith Harrison, and Joseph Crosfield form a partnership in Liverpool to trade tea and coffee.

1854: The firm's headquarters are moved to London.

1894: New managers—Charles Heath Clark and Arthur Lampard—join firm and initiate expansion into plantation ownership.

1903: Business enters the rubber market.

1908: Partnership is turned into a limited-liability company under the name Harrisons & Crosfield Ltd.

1920: Company expands into timber through the purchase of the China Borneo Company.

1923: Company begins production of Linatex, an abrasion-resistant form of rubber.

1935: The Harcros chain of builders' merchants is launched.

1947: Chemical manufacturing begins through joint venture with Durham Chemicals.

1973: British Chrome & Chemicals is acquired.

1979: American Chrome & Chemicals is acquired.

1982: Three large plantation groups are sold to Malaysian concerns; company goes public as Harrisons & Crosfield plc.

1985: Pauls Plc, maker of malt and animal feed, is acquired.

1988: The firm's chemical interests are amalgamated as Harcros Chemical Group.

1989: Edward Baker, a specialist pet-food company, is purchased.

1990: Most of the company's general trading unit is divested; Crossley chain of builders' merchants is acquired.

1994: The Indonesian plantations are divested.

1996: Company makes final exit from the plantation business.

1997: The Harcros builders' merchant business is sold, beginning the divestment of all nonchemical units.

1998: Company changes its name to Elementis plc; Rheox, maker of rheological additives, is bought from NL Industries; remaining nonchemical units are divested.

2001: Company effectively puts itself up for sale.

The next important step taken by the partners of H&C was to turn the firm into a limited-liability company. For several years it had been felt that a partnership, with its reliance on capital that could be withdrawn on the death or retirement of a partner, was too restrictive for an organization with ambitious expansion plans. Obtaining limited liability would make extensive capital expenditure possible—and most importantly for a business that was still run largely by the scions of two families—the shareholders of the company could vote against nepotistic elections to positions of responsibility.

A prospectus was issued by the brokers Foster and Braithwaite in May 1908 and the issue was fully subscribed. Existing partners exchanged their partnership capital for £150,000 of ordinary share capital and the first new directors took up 150,000 management shares of one shilling each. Friends, employees, and customers took up large blocks of shares and only £50,000 out of a total issued share capital of £307,500 was bought by private and institutional investors who had no direct link with the company. Years of steady profits and a stated aim of building up reserves rather than recklessly distributing profits ensured the success of the issue.

The worldwide increase in rubber planting was bound to lead to oversupply when crops were harvested four or five years after the first seeds were sown. The price dropped to between three or four shillings per pound in 1906, and reached a low of less than three shillings following the U.S. bank crisis of 1907. H&C weathered several difficult years until 1910, when the internal combustion engine became available, making the mass-production of cars economically viable. The demand for tires led to an annual demand for rubber of 100,000 tons in 1911, and H&C made excellent profits as rubber soared to 12 shillings per pound. The rubber boom forced H&C into building new accommodations to deal with increased paperwork flowing through the London office.

1910s Through 1930s: Rocky Times and Further Diversification

Charles Heath Clark became chairman of H&C in 1911, replacing James Crosfield, who had served the company for 46 years. He took over during a period of rapidly falling rubber prices and slow growth in tea sales. The seaman's strike of 1911 led to riots at Liverpool Docks and a one-month embargo on unloading ships. The London Dock Dispute of the following year further damaged H&C when 100,000 men were called out over a very minor dispute. Nevertheless, an issue in 1912 of £150,000 worth of £1 ordinary shares at a premium of ten shillings was oversubscribed.

The outbreak of World War I hit H&C badly. Britain diverted its resources to the manufacture of heavy engineering goods to support the war effort and communication with the plantations became increasingly difficult. Shipping restrictions and a low level of demand for tea caused a decline in international trade and many of the staff were called up to serve in the army. To compound the company's misfortune Arthur Lampard died in 1916, and no adequate successor could be found to take over the leadership of the plantation companies until the war was over.

Henry Welch was an important addition to the board in 1917. A solicitor who had built up an extensive practice in the City of London, Welch had experience as a director of several public companies and was responsible for the founding of the National Institute of Industrial Psychology in 1921. His main task was the reorganization of the company's balance sheet as soon as the war was over, when he restructured the share capital of the company to reflect the massive changes that H&C had experienced in the ten years since its incorporation.

Despite the war the directors of H&C did not ignore the possibility of new ventures abroad. Chinese green-leaf tea remained popular in Russia, the United States, and north Africa and H&C set up a joint venture with an established Chinese company to form Harrisons, King and Irwin in 1917. Based in Shanghai, with branch offices in Hankow and Foochow, the office was to be one of the casualties of the Japanese invasion during World War II.

Heath Clark, exhausted by his efforts in leading H&C through the war years, resigned from his position as chairman at the end of 1918. George Croll, who had worked for H&C in the Far East, was elected as his successor, but the young man whose energy had made a great impact on the company's plantations was to be dogged continually by ill health. Two successful issues of £150,000 in ordinary shares were made in January and July 1919, and the board was strengthened to include a complement of nine full-time members.

An issue of £400,000 ordinary shares made in December of the same year, however, was undersubscribed, and for the first time in the company's history a substantial portion of the issue had to be taken up by the underwriters. It was a time of national and international economic gloom and prices for tea and—in particular—rubber plummeted. Plantations were operating at a loss; and Heath Clark became a prime mover in the Rubber Growers' Association, which voluntarily agreed to cut production in India, Ceylon, and the Dutch East Indies. Immediate profits were sacrificed, but future production in a more stable market was guaranteed by withdrawing 25 percent of possible output in 1921. Heath Clark formally reassumed his old position of chairman on the death of George Croll in 1922.

A significant new venture was begun in 1920 when H&C and the Chartered Company of British New Guinea acquired the assets and goodwill of the China Borneo Company. H&C was given exclusive rights to cut and develop timber and received Borneo government backing to develop the timber industry in Borneo. Production rose from 1.1 million cubic feet in 1919 to six million cubic feet in 1940. The timber-supplies division of H&C grew to include ventures in Australia and the United States and gained a particularly strong brand image in its Harcros chain of builders' merchants which was started in 1935.

In 1921 H&C's relatively minor interests in tobacco plantations were sold to Dutch companies. H&C felt that it lacked the experience necessary to turn the growing of tobacco, always a delicate crop to harvest, into a regular source of profits. Profits from tea enjoyed a renaissance in the late 1920s but the boom contained the seeds of its own destruction as increased plantings were to lead to an excess of supply in the early 1930s. Expenditure on research and development gave a boost to the company, however, when Linatex was invented by Bernard Wilkinson, an assistant on a Malaysian rubber plantation. The Linatex process, which treated rubber to allow its use as an abrasion-resistant lining, had the twin advantages over mild steel of increased strength and lower cost and continued to be a valuable source of income for the firm.

H&C also diversified into growing coconut palms in the Philippines, Ceylon, and on the Malabar Coast. Once the kernel of the coconut is dried it turns into copra, which is then crushed to produce coconut oil. H&C initially sold this as a raw material for the production of soap and candles but the postwar shortage of butter led to demand for substitute products. Margarine, which is composed largely of coconut oil, became increasingly

popular, and production of copra reached one million tons annually during the 1930s. The depression suffered by the company's rubber interests was partially offset by this boom.

Eric Miller, a director of H&C since 1911, had been largely responsible for the Stevenson Report, which attempted to control the build-up of rubber stocks after the end of World War I. Miller had many close links with the heads of banks and rubber-growing companies and was a born diplomat. He convinced Winston Churchill that sales of British rubber at a good price to the United States would do much to pay off Britain's war debt to that country. As with previous similar agreements, the plan was to restrict production in India, Ceylon, and the Dutch East Indies as a method of stabilizing world prices.

The Wall Street crash of 1929 precipitated the Depression. This was to be a severe test for Eric Miller, who was now chairman of H&C. The company's profits for 1932 fell to £183,000, less than half the amount recorded in 1929. The world withdrew from international trade, putting up tariffs and imposing quotas on imports. Exchange rates fluctuated wildly and companies were reluctant to grant any form of credit as insolvencies became commonplace. H&C was forced again into a voluntary reduction of one of its commodities as the Tea Regulation Scheme limited exports from India, Ceylon, and the Dutch East Indies. Despite these measures, the company was forced to close several of its plantations.

The situation for rubber was even worse. The International Rubber Regulation Committee, to which Eric Miller was appointed by the government of British Malaya, signed an agreement in May 1934 that allocated each rubber trading company a strict production quota. With only a very few exceptions, new plantings of rubber were prohibited.

The outbreak of World War II was a further immense blow to the company as shipping lines closed and trade slumped. The entry of the Japanese into the war in October 1941 led to the invasion and subsequent loss of many of the Far Eastern plantations.

Postwar Era: Commodity Travails, Rising Interest in Chemicals

The end of the war saw more years of difficult trading for H&C. Demand for commodities was dampened by economic recession in the United Kingdom and transportation was difficult because of disruption to shipping lines. As in World War I, H&C lost many employees to the armed forces, and the Nazi bombardment of the City and the docks of east London further hampered international traders. Many plantations in the East had been destroyed by the invading Japanese, and when H&C attempted to reestablish operations abroad it was dismayed to see the effects of years of neglect.

The early 1950s saw a deterioration in the relationship between countries in the Far East and those countries that had controlled the majority of their trade. It was a time when war-damaged Britain was losing its old empire and the former colonies were no longer content to accept their traditional role of primary producer to foreign profit-takers. Governments imposed stringent restrictions on the transference of profits from their country to foreign agents and began to seek control over commodity prices. When H&C sought to renew its plantation leases in Indonesia it was forced to surrender one-third of its land to the Indonesian government. The outbreak of civil war in 1958 and increasing unrest in Malaysia and Sumatra left H&C unable to meet the commodity requirements of many of its customers.

H&C reacted to these problems by becoming increasingly involved in new technologies. A process to manufacture cyclized rubber was developed at the Rubber Research Institute of Malaysia and in the mid-1950s H&C began large-scale production. This rubber, which is used in printing inks and paints, was distributed by Durham Raw Materials Ltd., a joint-venture company half owned by H&C. The development of crumb rubber, and the introduction of standard grades for Malaysian rubber from 1965 onwards, did much to stabilize the rubber industry and, as a consequence, to make H&C's profits from this sector more consistent.

H&C also decided to take over the full ownership of the British Borneo Timber Company as part of a strategy to increase the importance of this sector. Throughout the 1970s the company, through its Harcros subsidiary, began to buy up small timber yards throughout the United Kingdom. The acquisition of larger timber merchants, such as the Sabah Timber Company, gave H&C a powerful distribution network from which to pursue further expansion. It was a logical step to use these existing sites to establish a chain of builders' merchants, still under the Harcros name, that supplied a full range of materials to the construction industry.

Eric Miller was knighted in 1958 after being replaced as chairman by Sir Leonard Paton in 1957. Although Paton served as chairman for only five years, he can be considered responsible for beginning the transformation of H&C, arguing long and hard to guarantee an adequate supply of timber from the Borneo plantations. Paton was replaced in 1962 by Finlay Gilchrist, who devised a complex system of defensive crossholdings between the H&C holding company, its subsidiaries, and its associates. By deliberately forging an intricate structure, Gilchrist was able to protect all of the group's interests from predators looking to take over a small, but nonetheless valuable, subsidiary.

Tom Prentice became chairman in 1973 during a turbulent time for the company and needed to rely on all of the skills he had learned in the timber industry in the East. The nationalization of plantations in Sri Lanka—formerly Ceylon—was soon followed by changes in Malaysia which required foreign companies to relinquish 70 percent of their interests by 1990. The group, supported by Baring Brothers merchant bank, undertook a further complicated restructuring designed to unite the group's interests in order to protect the value of shareholders' investments. Throughout the 1970s this complicated structure withstood the efforts of corporate raiders—most noticeably the Rothschild Investment Trust—and Prentice was able to lead H&C away from its dependence on plantations to encompass fully the opportunities offered by chemicals, building supplies, and agriculture.

Transformation via Series of Purchases and Disposals: 1980s Through Mid-1990s

The 1980s showed the effects of this diversification away from a reliance on commodities that proved too cyclical to guarantee consistent profits. In 1982 three large plantation groups—Golden Hope, Pataling, and London Asiatic—were sold to Malaysian concerns for £146 million. In 1984 H&C sold a large portion of its Malaysian investments to Permodalan, the state-controlled investment company. The remaining 30 percent was sold in 1989 for £145 million, but the plantations in Sumatra still remained in H&C's ownership. H&C was floated on the London Stock Exchange in 1982—as Harrisons & Crosfield plc—and began reshaping its activities with a series of purchases and disposals.

In 1985 H&C made a significant acquisition with the purchase of Pauls Plc, a manufacturer of malt and animal feeds, for £116 million. Profits from this company formed the backbone of H&C's food and agriculture division, which was strengthened by the acquisition of Edward Baker, a specialist pet-food company, in 1989. George Paul, the chief executive officer of Pauls, was elected to the board of H&C and, along with Thomas Prentice, became joint chief executive officer of the company.

By 1986 H&C intensified its aim of moving away from tropical soft commodities. Palm oil prices had dropped by nearly 50 percent during the year, and profits from the rubber market were depressed by expenditure on research into disease control. George Paul identified the company's problems as overdiversification, a reliance on primary agricultural products, and weak management in certain sectors. Paul instigated a rationalization plan and hinted that noncore companies would be sold off even if they were of historical importance to the company. As an example, Durham Chemicals Distributors Ltd. was sold in 1987, leaving H&C to concentrate on chemical manufacture rather than distribution.

Paul also took steps to improve H&C's image in the City. Perceived as a steady but rather dull holding company, the board took on the former head of M and G Fund Management, David Hopkinson, to convince the City of the group's intrinsic worth. After frequent allegations of insider dealing, fund managers began to see well-established conglomerates such as H&C as perfect vehicles for regular, long-term growth. Dependence on the plantations was reduced rapidly and by 1986 they accounted for less than one-quarter of the group's profits. The City, which had always preferred to deal directly with the commodity market rather than through holding companies with interests in commodities, was becoming increasingly enamored with H&C.

In November 1988 H&C announced the reorganization of its chemical interests under the new name of the Harcros Chemical Group. Its component parts included British Chrome & Chemicals (acquired in 1973) and American Chrome & Chemicals (acquired in 1979), world leaders in manufacturing chromium chemicals, and Troyfel Ltd. and Hardman Inc., which specialized in iron oxide technology and adhesives. At the time of the reorganization George Paul stated that the company's intention was to double the size of this group, through organic growth and selective acquisitions, within five years.

The deal making continued in the 1990s, further altering the composition of H&C. In 1990 the company sold off the bulk of its general trading unit in a further deemphasis of the founding business. The Crossley chain of builders' merchants was bought from Bowater Industries for £113 million in May 1990 and then amalgamated into Harcros, the flagship of the group's timber and building supplies division. That same year, H&C bolstered the pigments side of its chemicals unit through the purchase of Pfizer Pigments from the U.S. drug firm Pfizer Inc. for about £40 million ($65 million). This deal moved H&C into the number two position worldwide in the production of synthetic iron oxide pigments, used in construction, coatings, and cosmetics. Profits suffered in the early 1990s from the effects of recession and the resulting slump in the building industry, a slump that affected both the building supplies and chemical operations of H&C.

In 1992 H&C beefed up its animal feeds unit, known as Pauls Agriculture, with the £67 million purchase of several agricultural units of Unilever, including BOCM-Silcock, a maker of animal feed through its 22 U.K. feed mills; Unitrition, an oil miller; and Fulmar, a maker of fish feed based in Scotland. By 1994, Bill Turcan had taken over as chief executive. The new leader effectively ended a chapter in the long history of Harrisons & Crosfield that year by selling off the firm's Indonesian plantations to a group of four Indonesian businessmen for £176 million ($273 million) in cash. Also in 1994 came the divestment of two consumer food units that specialized in private-label cereals. H&C, by and large, now consisted of the building supplies, chemicals, and animal feeds operation, although it would be 1996 before the company's final plantation interest, one located in Papua New Guinea, was sold off.

Late 1990s and Beyond: Emerging As Elementis

The company's conglomerate holdings continued to result in poor profits and a weak share price, leading to a decision in 1997 to focus full attention on specialty chemicals, the sector in which management felt that, based on growth prospects, H&C could best enhance shareholder value. Late that year, the Harcros builders' merchant business was sold to Meyer International for £318 million. Over the next year, the remaining nonchemical units—in timber, food, agriculture, and pet food—were sold off, and at the start of 1998 H&C changed its name to Elementis plc.

Part of the proceeds from the divestments were returned to shareholders in the form of a special distribution totaling £402 million ($643 million). Much of the remainder was used for the purchase of Rheox from NL Industries Inc., a £280 million ($450 million) deal completed in early 1998. Rheox was a maker of rheological additives used to control the flow characteristics of such products as paints and cosmetics. Elementis thus ended its first full year of operation with several main units: chromium chemicals, where it was the world leader; pigments; specialties, which included Rheox and other businesses, such as performance polymers and zinc products; Linatex, maker of abrasion-resistant rubber; and Harcros Chemicals, a U.S. chemical distributor. Late in 1998 Turcan, having shepherded H&C through its transformation into Elementis but not having a chemicals background, was replaced as chief executive by Lyndon Cole, who had been an executive at GE Plastics, a division of the U.S. giant General Electric Company. Sales from continuing operations for 1998 totaled £534.2 million ($850 million).

Market difficulties led to a restructuring in 1999 that eliminated more than 300 jobs from the workforce and aimed for annual cost savings of more than £10 million. Competitive pressures, particularly in the company's core area of chromium chemicals, contributed to the sinking of the company's share price to an all-time low early in 2000. Rumors of a takeover of Elementis began to circulate and continued throughout 2000. In December of that year, the company's shares rose sharply after an approach was made by a private equity capital firm regarding a possible takeover. Meantime, restructuring efforts had resulted in better financial results for 2000, including a 12 percent increase in operating profit and a 14 percent gain in profits before taxes. Sales increased 7 percent to £573.8 million ($928 million). The future of the company remained in doubt in early 2001, however, as the firm essentially put itself up for sale in March of that year, seeking acquisition offers that might be "in the best interests of shareholders."

Principal Subsidiaries

Elementis UK Limited; Linatex Limited; Elementis Chromium LP (U.S.A.); Elementis Pigments Inc. (U.S.A.); Elementis Specialties Inc. (U.S.A.); Harcros Chemicals Inc. (U.S.A.); Linatex Corporation of America Inc. (U.S.A.).

Principal Divisions

Elementis Chromium; Elementis Pigments; Elementis Specialties; Harcros Chemicals; Linatex.

Principal Competitors

Imperial Chemical Industries PLC; Clariant Ltd.; Laporte plc; Akzo Nobel N.V.; E.ON AG; BASF Aktiegesellschaft; Bayer AG; OM Group, Inc.; Air Products and Chemicals, Inc.; E.I. du Pont de Nemours and Company; The Dow Chemical Company; Rohm and Haas Company.

Further Reading

Batchelor, Charles, "Bid Approach Boosts Shares in Elementis," *Financial Times,* December 7, 2000, p. 30.

Blackwell, David, and Richard Tomkins, "H&C Acquires Rheox for £280m," *Financial Times,* December 31, 1997, p. 15.

Coates, Austin, *The Commerce in Rubber: The First 250 Years,* Oxford: Oxford University Press, 1987, 380 p.

Donnithorne, Audrey, *British Rubber Manufacturing,* London: Jill Duckworth & Co., 1958, 159 p.

Drabble, J.H., *Rubber in Malaya, 1876–1922,* London: Oxford University Press, 1973, 256 p.

Edgecliffe-Johnson, Andrew, "Meyer to Buy Harcros Builders' Merchants for £300m," *Financial Times,* October 13, 1997, p. 27.

"Elementis Puts Itself Up for Sale," *Chemical Market Reporter,* March 5, 2001, p. 6.

"Elementis Supplement," *Chemical Market Reporter,* September 28, 1998, pp. E4+.

Ensor, Sir Robert, *England, 1870–1914,* Oxford: Oxford University Press, 1936.

Frin, David, "Elementis Revamp Paying Off," *Financial Times,* August 3, 2000, p. 22.

Gain, Bruce, "Harrisons & Crosfield Launches Chemicals Business As Elementis," *Chemical Week,* October 29, 1997, p. 20.

Hume, Claudia, "Cole: Rallying the Troops at Elementis," *Chemical Week,* April 28, 1999, p. 42.

Malkani, Gautam, "Elementis to Shed 300 Jobs This Year," *Financial Times,* August 6, 1999, p. 18.

One Hundred Years As East India Merchants, London: Harrisons & Crosfield, 1943.

Peel, Michael, "Farewell to a Conglomerate," *Financial Times,* October 25, 1997, p. 5.

——, "Harrisons' Taste Changes to Special Blend," *Financial Times,* October 22, 1997, p. 26.

Pugh, Peter, *Great Enterprise: A History of Harrisons & Crosfield,* London: Harrisons & Crosfield, 1990, 271 p.

Tieman, Ross, "Harrisons & Crosfield Ponders Its Direction," *Financial Times,* March 12, 1997, p. 21.

Warren, Susan, "NL Agrees to Sell Rheox Business to British Firm," *Wall Street Journal,* December 31, 1997, p. C20.

Young, Ian, "Buyer Approaches Elementis," *Chemical Week,* December 13, 2000, p. 7.

——, "Elementis Emerges from the Shadows," *Chemical Week,* August 19, 1998, pp. 72–73.

——, "Elementis's Dramatic Entrance," *Chemical Week,* January 14, 1998, p. 6.

—Andreas Loizou
—update: David E. Salamie

Elizabeth Arden, Inc.

14100 NW 60th Avenue
Miami Lakes, Florida 33014
U.S.A.
Telephone: (305) 818-8000
Toll Free: (800) 277-2445
Fax: (305) 818-8010
Web site: http://www.frenchfragrances.com

Public Company
Incorporated: 1911
Employees: 1,300
Sales: $382.3 million (2001)
Stock Exchanges: NASDAQ
Ticker Symbol: RDEN
NAIC: 32562 Toilet Preparations Manufacturing

Elizabeth Arden, Inc. is one of the world's leading makers of prestige perfumes and cosmetics. Key brands include Elizabeth Taylor's White Diamonds, White Shoulders, Red Door, 5th Avenue, Green Tea, and Sunflowers. The company also sells a line of Elizabeth Arden brand color cosmetics, and skin care products under the names Ceramides, Visible Difference, and Millennium. Elizabeth Arden goods are sold in over 90 countries worldwide, with major markets in the United States and Europe. A world leader in the cosmetics industry since the 1920s, Elizabeth Arden was acquired by Unilever PLC, a conglomerate of consumer product companies, in 1990. It became an independent, publicly owned company in 2001, when it was purchased by FFI Fragrances. That company took the Elizabeth Arden name.

Erratic Beginnings

Elizabeth Arden, who founded the company in 1911, can be credited with singlehandedly laying the foundations of the modern American cosmetics industry. Elizabeth Arden was born Florence Nightingale Graham in Canada during the late 1870s. Named for the renowned nurse who served during the Crimean War, Graham grew up in a large, poverty-stricken family. When she was unable to finish high school because her family lacked the finances, she persuaded herself that nursing was her true vocation and began training for that profession. Graham quickly realized her mistake. It was sales, not suffering humanity, that finally lured her and tapped her real talents.

While a student nurse, Graham had met a chemist experimenting with a facial cream that could help acne sufferers. The concept intrigued her, leading to her conviction that most women would give anything for beauty. An unsuccessful early attempt to start a mail-order business marketing her own version of face cream failed largely because of her father's impatience with his madcap daughter's strange concoctions. Instead Graham toiled at a series of jobs in Toronto that afforded her a chance to display her salesmanship. At one point employed as a dental assistant, she doubled the dentist's revenues in a short time when she hit upon the idea of persuasively writing each patient to explain the necessity of regular dental check-ups.

Nearly 30 years old and unwilling to marry for fear of losing her independence, Graham set off for New York City in 1908. Landing a job as a bookkeeper for the prominent Squibb Pharmaceutical Company, she was impressed by the state-of-the-art laboratories and the constant attention to research and development. This inspired her to fashion a small lab of her own, where she might "scientifically" test out her own ideas for beauty products. Before venturing into this unknown arena, however, Graham quit her job at Squibb to become an assistant in a newly established beauty culture salon. Catering to a wealthy clientele, these early beauty parlors came to be the nucleus of the future cosmetics industry. They emphasized skin care rather than hair care, and the methods for achieving glowing skin did not rest with makeup as much as with skin massage and the applications of creams and lotions.

Unfamiliar with the concept of beauty salons before coming to New York, what she learned there helped Graham lay the foundations for the cosmetics industry she was to eventually build. Graham was hired as a "treatment girl" to deliver facial massages, mix the facial concoctions of the owner, Mrs. Eleanor Adair, and give manicures. Graham displayed unusual talent and sales ability, and quickly learned all the aspects of the beauty culture field.

Until then, Florence Nightingale Graham had never worn cosmetics. Even in the early 20th century, a proper woman simply hoped for a healthy complexion—facial "paint," usually applied without skill or finesse, was considered disreputable. However, higher levels of female education coupled with the women's suffrage movement provided the stimuli for change. By the time Graham arrived in New York, shorter hair and cosmetics were becoming increasingly associated with emancipation.

Soon Graham felt confident enough to go into business for herself. Without funds to finance the endeavor on her own, however, she formed a partnership with Elizabeth Hubbard in 1910. While the nameplate bore the partner's name—Florence Nightingale was rejected as suggestive of a hospital ward—the cosmetic mixtures and other ideas were clearly Graham's. She dubbed her pricey lotions and powders "Grecian," endowing them with a romantic allure and prestige that would become her trademark.

Instead of a parlor, the establishment was referred to as a salon, since Graham thought it would appeal to higher class society women. Although the partners could barely afford the rent, Graham had insisted on lavish quarters in a brownstone on New York's Fifth Avenue, which was rapidly turning into a major business district. The partners quarreled soon after their salon opened its doors, however, and Elizabeth Hubbard abruptly departed, leaving Graham to pay the huge rent. Borrowing $6,000 from her brother to keep her salon open, Graham worked as a manicurist after hours to supplement her income.

In addition to the problems of trying to pay the rent, it was necessary for Graham to decide on a name for her salon. While the suffragettes were taking steps towards women's rights, their emancipation had not reached the point where "Miss" connoted respectability, and Graham decided to use "Mrs." Her former partner's name, Elizabeth, appealed to her, although a new last name was harder to come by. She finally chose Arden after reading the name in a poem by Alfred, Lord Tennyson. The new name seemed to evoke the prestige and understated glamour that Graham not only craved for her business, but for herself as well. Thus Florence Nightingale Graham became Elizabeth Arden.

After hours, when she was not manicuring nails for extra income, Arden experimented with cosmetics. One of her distinctive contributions was the addition of fragrance to the lotions and powders of the day, which had been lacking scent. The

facial creams sold at the time were greasy and heavy, but Arden hired a chemist to formulate a light, fluffy cream that became an instant success. It was at this point that she developed her "total beauty" idea. The concept initially involved sharing her salon quarters with a "prestige" hairdresser and a milliner; later a clothing shop was included. Eventually the idea was further expanded to include beauty spas.

Elizabeth Arden's hard work and imagination paid off, making her salons enormously profitable. Without serious competitors for the first several years after establishing her business, her success was also aided by changing attitudes toward equality of the sexes. Emancipation had progressed so far as to soften the prejudices against women who wore short hair and cosmetics. Times were changing so rapidly that by 1914, Elizabeth Arden removed the "Mrs." from her nameplate and substituted "Miss." It was good for business.

A steady stream of products was marketed in the initial years of Elizabeth Arden's business, including rouges and fragrant, tinted powders that she taught her "girls" to apply with subtlety and finesse. In 1914, on the eve of the outbreak of World War I, Arden traveled to Paris, her first trip abroad. During her summer-long sojourn, Arden became acquainted with the more sophisticated Parisian techniques of beauty culture and makeup application. She brought these techniques back with her, in addition to the cosmetic products, including the eye makeup worn by wealthy dames of Paris society. Though chemists improved on the products, Arden found it difficult to convince her clients to apply it—eye makeup for many was going too far. It was America's entry into World War I, however, that provided the necessary catalyst. While the men were away at war, women found themselves employed in many lines of work formerly closed to them, and as they gained even greater independence, many of the restrictive taboos became outdated. Women began experimenting with Elizabeth Arden's eye makeup, the first to be introduced in the United States.

Elizabeth Arden's Venetian line of cosmetics along with her velvety Cream Amoretta—in her signature chic bottling—were being sold in department stores all over the East Coast, and her salon with the famous red door was duplicated in Washington, D.C., in 1914, proving an instant success. A year later Arden perfumes were introduced, further expanding the line of products offered in the salons. However, her reign as undisputed queen of cosmetics was not due to last. After the war, competition came to the fore, marking the beginning of the lifelong personal animosity between Elizabeth Arden and her chief rival, Helena Rubenstein. The cosmetics industry began growing at a rapid pace and became steadily more lucrative, especially to women, for whom it was one of the few lines of business in which they could rise to the top and be leaders.

Increasing Success: 1920s–30s

However, Elizabeth Arden was, more often than not, the industry standard bearer. By the start of World War II in Europe, there were dozens of Elizabeth Arden salons all over the world, and hundreds of products being marketed, including soaps, bath salts, even toothpaste, as well as perfumes to go with either morning, afternoon, or evening dress. No one advertised cosmetics as frequently nor as lavishly as Elizabeth Arden. This was in accord with her philosophy, held throughout her life, that in order to make money, one had to spend it. Meanwhile, American women were in fact spending $6 million annually on cosmetics by 1925, barely 15 years after Elizabeth Arden had hung up her shingle. That year her company reaped over $2 million in sales, a figure that doubled only four years later.

During the Depression, Elizabeth Arden predicted—and advertised accordingly—that the American woman would not stint on beauty. Unlike most American businesses, Elizabeth Arden's company earned handsome profits during those years, even making strides with innovative lipsticks which, until 1932, had come in only a few basic shades. Elizabeth Arden believed that just as perfume should go with the costume, so too should lipstick. Her "lipstick kit" containing several different shades was a big hit at the height of the Depression, creating a sensation in the industry as competitors scrambled to imitate the concept. Then in 1934 she established her extremely successful "beauty spa" in Maine—another was opened in Arizona in 1946—where women shed excess pounds and immersed themselves in Elizabeth Arden bath salts and afterbath lotions for $500 per week. By the mid-1930s there were 29 Elizabeth Arden salons around the world, while her company manufactured and marketed 108 different products.

The outbreak of World War II, which spelled a loss of overseas markets and raw materials, did not catch Elizabeth Arden by surprise. Just as she had done before World War I, Elizabeth Arden stocked up on raw materials early, and offset the loss of income from her overseas salons by concentrating on expanding her domestic market. Her products were not only carried in department stores coast to coast, but the war years saw Arden expanding into all of the major drugstore chains of the day. Consequently in 1944, at the height of the war, business at Elizabeth Arden's was booming, and the company remained a pacesetter. A line of clothing was added in the 1950s, and Elizabeth Arden became the first in the industry to target male customers by marketing men's fragrances and opening a "men's boutique."

Changing Hands After Arden's Death

Elizabeth Arden continued her reign as grande dame of the cosmetics industry until her death in 1966. By then the cosmetics industry in the United States had grown into a multibillion-dollar business, and large corporations were mass producing personal care products that, while lacking in prestige, could be sold at much lower prices. Friends and relatives had urged Arden to sell her profitable business as early as 1929, when a $15 million offer was made. She refused, and no further mention of selling or merging occurred. However, negotiations for the sale of the company began shortly after her death. Elizabeth Arden Co. was finally acquired in late 1970 by the pharmaceutical company, Eli Lilly & Co., which cut costs and instituted streamlined procedures before putting it up for sale again in 1987. The company changed hands twice more until 1990 when it was purchased by the Anglo-Dutch conglomerate Unilever PLC. Two years later Unilever established the Prestige Personal Products Group, which included Elizabeth Arden Co. and Calvin Klein.

A constant during these changeovers was Elizabeth Arden's president and CEO, Joseph F. Ronchetti, who had joined the company after Arden's death. In 1986, when the company was still a subsidiary of Eli Lilly, Ronchetti devised a five-year plan to revitalize Elizabeth Arden Co. and make it more competitive. While the budget for advertising—especially targeted at baby boomers—was doubled, more modern packaging and innovative bottling was instituted. Ronchetti stuck with the plan throughout the changes in ownership. By the end of the five years, advertising was conducting an average of 200–300 promotions a month, and research and development had created many pace-setting products, including a line of ultraviolet (UV) sun protection creams and lotions that was distinguished by awards from the Skin Cancer Foundation. In addition, Elizabeth Taylor's White Diamonds became the number one selling fragrance in 1991 after the famous actress personally introduced the scent in ten U.S. cities. Elizabeth Arden had also become more responsive to its social environment—animal-testing of its cosmetics was virtually never done, and considerable donations were made to such causes as AIDS research and child welfare.

Revolving Door at the Top in the 1990s

Unilever's purchase of Elizabeth Arden, coupled with that of Fabergé, Inc. in 1990, made the conglomerate the second largest cosmetics company in the world. With a distribution network in virtually every country on earth, in addition to state-of-the-art research facilities, Elizabeth Arden Co. stood to benefit from its acquisition by the corporation. Yet under Unilever's umbrella, Elizabeth Arden suffered years of poor direction and disappointing earnings. In what was billed as a "surprise resignation," Joseph Ronchetti stepped down from the presidency of Elizabeth Arden in 1992. In two years with Unilever, Elizabeth Arden had seen substantial sales growth despite a general slowdown in the prestige cosmetics market, and it had introduced the highly successful White Diamonds and then Red Door perfumes. According to a June 1992 *New York Times* article, Ronchetti had transformed the Arden brand from "a line for grandmothers into a brand that younger career women wanted to wear." Ronchetti claimed he wanted to leave Elizabeth Arden while everything was going well. But filling his job was difficult for the company. The presidency of Arden was taken by Robert M. Phillips, who had been chairman of Unilever's Chesebrough-Ponds, Calvin Klein, and Arden units.

Phillips left after two years, to become worldwide director for Unilever's personal products businesses. Kim Delsing then became president and CEO of Elizabeth Arden. Delsing, who had previously run Unilever's Calvin Klein unit, came in during a restructuring of Arden's global business. The company consolidated management for its Western Hemisphere business, and its two U.S. divisions were combined. Elizabeth Arden was estimated to have sales of around $1 billion worldwide in the early 1990s, but by 1994 one of the reasons given for the management changes was to boost profitability. Kim Delsing was replaced in 1995, having lasted just a year. At that point, the financial rockiness of Elizabeth Arden was exposed. Though the company had seemed to be doing well just a few years earlier, Delsing's job was described as pushing Arden through a difficult turnaround. Gross margins were said to have eroded, and inventories were obsolete. The other half of Unilever's prestige products division, Calvin Klein, was said to have a profit margin of around 20 percent. Industry estimates put Arden's profits at just 4 percent in

1994. Sales volume was also estimated to have slid, from $1 billion in 1993 to only $850 million two years later. To add to its problems, it was not clear what direction the company was moving in. Delsing had run into difficulties with the launch of a new perfume, Elizabeth Taylor's Black Pearls. A dispute with several major department stores led Arden to introduce Black Pearls at mass market stores such as J.C. Penney and Sears. The deemphasis on high-end stores chipped away at Arden's prestige image. Peter England took over the shaky Arden from Delsing, and worked to assure the industry that his company was not turning into a mass market business. But Arden's sales fell, hurting profits at Unilever's personal products division. Unilever's chairman Michael Perry told *WWD* (February 21, 1996) that the 1995 losses at Arden were "a hiccup," not a disaster, and estimated that the unit would be profitable again in 18 months. Poor financial results for the personal products division in 1997 were again blamed on Elizabeth Arden. At that time, Unilever had announced plans to sell off underperforming units. Unilever's chairman claimed that Arden was not yet in the sell-off group. Sales and profits at Arden improved in 1999, especially after the introduction of a new fragrance, Splendor.

Despite Arden's recovery, Unilever sold the unit in 2001 to FFI Fragrances. FFI, formerly French Fragrances, Inc., was a perfume marketer that dealt in prestige as well as mass market products. FFI paid roughly $190 million in cash for Elizabeth Arden, plus an exchange of stock which gave Unilever an approximately 18 percent stake in the publicly owned company. FFI changed its name to Elizabeth Arden, Inc. At the time of the transaction, annual sales at Arden were estimated at $890 million. This was still below the company's peak in the early 1990s. The company's new leadership hoped to improve Arden's international business, and to streamline order fulfillment and materials management.

Principal Competitors

The Estée Lauder Companies Inc.; Coty, Inc.; Inter Parfums, Inc.

Further Reading

"Arden's Colorbox Blockbuster to Assist Children's Charity," *Women's Wear Daily,* September 25, 1992, p. 6.

Born, Pete, "Arden-Delsing Split: Trying for Too Much with Too Little Clout," *WWD,* August 18, 1995, p. 1.

——, "Arden Regroups; Masturzo, Janney Out," *WWD,* August 12, 1994, p. 7.

——, "England's Mission at Elizabeth Arden: Picking Up the Pieces," *WWD,* November 10, 1995, p. 1.

"Elizabeth Arden Company Creates In-House Media Department," *New York Times,* February 4, 1991, p. C9(N), D9(L).

Elizabeth Arden: The Woman, the Company, the Legacy, New York: Elizabeth Arden Co., 1993.

Fallon, James, "Unilever Personal Unit Hurt by Arden in 1995," *WWD,* February 21, 1996, p. 2.

——, "Unilever Reports Elizabeth Arden Back in Black, Met Targets for '98," *WWD,* February 24, 1999, p. 23.

Lewis, Alfred Allan, and Constance Woodworth, *Miss Elizabeth Arden,* New York: Coward, McCann & Geoghegan, 1972.

Naughton, Julie, "Beattie: Welcome to the New Elizabeth Arden," *WWD,* January 26, 2001, p. 4.

Raj, D.D., "Global Cosmetics & Household Product Industry—Industry Report," *Merrill Lynch Capital Markets,* December 1, 1992.

Rice, Faye, "Elizabeth Arden: Profiting by Perseverance," *Fortune,* January 27, 1992, p. 84.

Stern, Aimee L., "How Elizabeth Arden Gave Itself a Makeover," *AdWeek's Marketing Week,* September 9, 1991, pp. 18–19.

Strom, Stephanie, "Elizabeth Arden Chief in Surprise Resignation," *New York Times,* June 13, 1992, p. 37.

Unilever United States, Inc. 1991 Report to Employees, New York: Unilever United States, Inc., 1991.

Zinn, Laura, "Beauty and the Beastliness," *Business Week,* June 29, 1992, p. 39.

—Sina Dubovoj
—update: A. Woodward

English China Clays Ltd.

John Keay House
St. Austell, Cornwall PL25 4DJ
United Kingdom
Telephone: 44(0)172-67-4411
Web site: http://www.imerys.com

Wholly Owned Subsidiary of Imerys
Incorporated: 1919 as English China Clays Ltd.
NAIC: 212324 Kaolin and Ball Clay Mining; 325192
    Cyclic Crude and Intermediate Manufacturing; 325998
    All Other Miscellaneous Chemical Product and
    Preparation Manufacturing (pt)

English China Clays Ltd. is perhaps best known as the world's largest producer of kaolin, a fine white clay used primarily for finishing glossy paper. This product as well as other specialty mineral pigments and chemicals produced by the company are used in the manufacture of high-quality printing and writing paper as well as in the manufacture of ceramics, paints, and polymers. Sales outside the United Kingdom accounted for 87 percent of the company's revenue in 1995. In April 1999 English China Clays became a wholly owned subsidiary of the French company Imetal S.A., which later changed its name to Imerys.

Historic Origins of China Clay

Kaolin (literally "white hill") takes its name from the mountain in China from which European manufacturers of ceramics originally obtained their supplies of the raw material. The increasing demand for ceramics in Europe stimulated a search for raw materials nearer home and, by the early 18th century, china clay deposits had been located in Bohemia, Thuringia, Saxony, and near Limoges in France. In the United Kingdom china clay deposits that were found to be of a finer quality than elsewhere in Europe were discovered in Cornwall in the middle of the 18th century; their exploitation created the United Kingdom's china clay industry. Its development in the 19th century was economically most important to Cornwall, since its growth took place at a time when the industry upon which Cornwall had previously depended for employment and wealth creation, tin mining, was being forced into decline by foreign competition. Changes in the papermaking industry and its expansion in the second half of the 19th century created a new and growing market for china clay.

Twentieth-century processes of extracting, refining, and drying china clay remained in essence the same as they were in the 19th century, although the application of technology transferred to machines much of the work done by manual labor in the early days, improved the purity of the final product, and made it possible to extract other minerals that formerly went to waste. Even so, waste remained a formidable problem for the English china clays; despite the use of sand and the application of much research, the production of one ton of clay still created seven tons of waste. The first process, the pit operation, involved exposing china clay deposits by removing the overburden. Some deposits may be as close to the surface as three feet while others may be hundreds of feet below ground. Hydraulic mining, by firing water jets from a cannon at the clay deposits, freed the deposits and created a slurry that also contained sand and mica. The slurry was then pumped out and the coarser sand removed before the refining process proceeded. This process took out unwanted minerals such as quartz, mica, and feldspar.

Geologically, china clay is formed in granite rocks by the decomposition of feldspar. At this stage chemical bleaching to remove the stains in the clay caused by mineral salts, particularly iron oxide, can add value to the final product, a technological advance not available until after World War II. ECC operated six refining plants in Devon and Cornwall that took clay from a number of pits and mixed it in the quantities required for finished products of varying characteristics. The final drying process, which usually took place in natural gas-fired driers, was originally done in coal-fired kilns and even, at some pits, by wind and sun.

1919: The Formation of English China Clays Ltd.

In the first half of the 19th century, production of china clay was in the hands of many small proprietors, some of whom owned the land on which the mine lay and some of whom leased it. Although some consolidation took place later in the century, in 1914 there were still some 70 individual producers. At that time the industry was characterized by low wages, overproduction, and price-cutting. These problems were exacerbated by the outbreak of World War I, particularly for an industry that depended on exporting for some 70 percent of its output. During the war, shipping capacity for goods such as china clay, which had little or no military purpose, was severely limited. By 1917 many china clay producers were making losses and few, if any, were making profits. A trade association, Associated China Clays, was established in that year, and in its seven-year existence—it terminated in 1924—had some success in stabilizing the industry by setting prices and sales quotas. In 1919, the three largest producers in Cornwall—Martin Brothers Ltd., established 1837; the West of England and Great Beam Company, established 1849; and the North Cornwall China Clay Company, established 1908—merged to form English China Clays Ltd. (ECC).

Reginald Martin of Martin Brothers was chairman of the new company but the most influential figure, until his premature death in 1931, was T. Medland Stocker of the West of England Company. Stocker was a qualified mining engineer, anxious to see technical improvements and investment in an industry whose development was inhibited by fragmentation and a lack of capital; his company had before 1919 absorbed a number of smaller china clay companies. Stocker was very much the architect of the 1919 merger. Two more acquisitions, the Melbur China Clay Company and John Nicholls & Company, made shortly after the incorporation of English China Clays, gave English China Clays 21 pits to operate. With an annual output three times the tonnage of its nearest competitor, Lovering China Clays, ECC was the largest company in the industry. It was not, however, the only company involved in restructuring in the industry; in 1919 H.D. Pochin & Company acquired one of Cornwall's oldest china clay companies, J.W. Higman & Company, and their combined output made Pochin the third largest producer.

Overcapacity and Acquisitions: 1920s–30s

Through the 1920s ECC faced the difficulties caused by the slump that followed the immediate postwar boom. Excess capacity in the china clay industry internationally, as world demand remained below prewar levels, engendered fierce price-cutting competition, which became even worse after the failure of the

trade association in 1924. The success of a new association, formed in 1927, was short-lived—it lasted only until 1929—although it was reflected in ECC's improved profits in 1929. Over the decade ECC increased its dominance of the industry by further acquisitions. Four companies were acquired in 1927, the North Goonbarrow, the Great Halviggan, the Imperial Goonbarrow, and the Rosevear, and in 1928 the Hallivet China Clay Company was purchased. There were four more smaller acquisitions in 1929, Burthy China Clays, New Halwyn China Clays, the Carbis China Clay & Brick Company, and the Trethowal China Clay Company, and, more important, because of its consistent refusal to join any trade association, William Varcoe & Sons was acquired in two stages by ECC in 1929 and 1930.

During the Great Depression, the china clay industry was severely affected. Production fell in the United Kingdom by 34 percent between 1929 and 1931, and remained below the 1929 level throughout the 1930s. Although the effect of the Great Depression was not as severe in the United Kingdom as it was in the United States, it was enough to provide a powerful stimulus to consolidation and amalgamation among the china clay producers, as in many other industries. In the interwar years rationalization, in large part taken to mean the merger of small-scale manufacturing units in order to gain the benefit of economies of scale, became as widely practiced as diversification was to become in the 1950s and 1960s.

In these circumstances the merger of English China Clays with its two major, though smaller, competitors, Lovering China Clays and H.D. Pochin & Company, in 1932 was the next logical step toward rationalizing the industry. ECC became a holding company, owning 63 percent of its new operating subsidiary, English Clays Lovering Pochin & Company (ECLP). The remaining shares were held by members of the Pochin and Lovering families. The first chairman of ECLP was the Honorable Henry D. McLaren, who in 1935 succeeded his father as Lord Aberconway. Reginald Martin, who remained chairman of ECC until 1948, when he was older than 70, was managing director of ECLP from 1932 to 1937. Martin's assistant managing director in 1932, who was to succeed him in 1937 and to exercise a major influence over the company until 1963, was John Keay—Sir John Keay from 1950, when he was knighted. An accountant by profession, Keay had joined ECC in 1929 and was responsible, with Reginald Martin, for the success of the negotiations leading to the 1932 merger.

The integration of so many diverse companies—another 12 china clay producers were acquired during the 1930s—would not have been easy at the best of times. In the 1930s when falling demand, surplus capacity, and low prices meant there was little spare cash for investment, it was even more difficult. Some progress was made, however, in modernizing, mechanizing, and making the industry more efficient. The engineering facilities at the company's 42 pits were reorganized and with the acquisition in 1935 of the Charlestown Foundry, despite its poor condition, the company had a nucleus for engineering. Electrification was extended to more of the company's pits and processes, and in 1936 a new central power station was commissioned at Drinnick, to supply all the company's operations. The company developed brickmaking using the high-temperature-resistant substance malachite and looked for other uses for this material. A research department was established, initially to work on fractionating clay particles to produce the more highly refined selected particle size (SPS) clay required by paper manufacturers, especially in the United States.

Diversification and the Postwar Boom

World War II offered ECLP little hope of improving trading conditions. With home demand expected to fall and no hope of maintaining the export trade that, through the 1930s, had taken up nearly 65 percent of output, a 50 percent reduction of capacity was enforced by the Board of Trade under its wartime powers. For ECLP, the only bright spot was the Charlestown Foundry, which was able to undertake armaments contracts and, re-equipped with machinery and tools that were to prove of immense benefit to the company in the immediate postwar years, worked to full capacity throughout the war.

When the war ended, it soon became clear that the demand for china clay would expand rapidly. Although ECLP had formulated plans for postwar development, shortages of men, building materials, and fuel precluded any immediate expansion, nor was it an easy task to reopen pits that had been closed for the duration of the war. After representations had been made to the government, a Board of Trade working committee was appointed to look for ways of increasing production. Its report, published in March 1946, recommended short-term measures to alleviate the labor, materials, and fuel problems and suggested a wider ranging inquiry. A Board of Trade committee was appointed, therefore, with John Keay from ECLP as its vice-chairman. Its report, delivered two years later, condemned the industry, but not ECLP, for among other things, its failure to innovate, poor research, and lack of welfare facilities for its workers. In 1950 an advisory council, on which sat representatives of all parts of the industry, was established. For ECLP, the immediate postwar years meant steady growth and recovery. One innovation for which it was responsible in those years made a major alleviation in the United Kingdom's postwar housing shortage. Cornish Unit houses, jointly designed and developed by ECC's subsidiaries Selleck Nicholls and John Williams, were bungalows built from concrete using china clay sand. In the ten years immediately after the war, 40,000 were built. ECC's building subsidiaries went on to extend the range of prefabricated building components for both housing and industrial use.

In the early 1950s, restructuring and reorganization paved the way for the emergence of what would be known as the ECC group. In 1951 and 1954 ECC was able to buy the shares in ECLP previously held by the Lovering and Pochin families and, with a financial reorganization in 1956, ECLP became a wholly owned subsidiary. The activities of the group's subsidiaries were then reorganized into four trading divisions, each one covering one of ECC's main operations: china clay, building, quarrying, and transport. The changing nature of the business since 1956 later resulted in transport being moved to the ECCI division, and the new IDF division being created.

ECC International (ECCI) was the operation concerned predominantly with the production and sale of china clay, a raw material used by a number of industries. In the late 1980s, some 80 percent of china clay output was used by the paper industry, 12 percent by the ceramic industry, and 8 percent by miscellaneous industries, mainly in the manufacture of paint, rubber, and plastics. ECCI also produced and sold calcium carbonate and other industrial minerals. In 1989 the division's sales of industrial minerals exceeded six million tons for the first time. It also had transport operations and a small waste-disposal business. Production facilities were located in the United Kingdom in Devon and Cornwall, as well as in the United States, Brazil, and Australia. In 1994, this business was split; ECCI Europe's sales contributed nearly half of the group's operating business turnover of £877.6 million; ECCI Americas/Pacific accounted for 29 percent.

The operations of the ECC Construction Materials (ECCCM) division included the production and sale of quarry material, macadam, concrete products, and industrial sand in the United Kingdom and the United States, and a U.K. waste-disposal business. ECCCM contributed 34 percent of group turnover in 1989.

Two smaller divisions also operated under the ECC Group. ECC Construction (ECCC) was concerned with the construction, development, and refurbishment of private housing, and, trading as SNW Homes and Bradley Homes, was responsible for building houses in the United Kingdom. This division accounted for approximately 4 percent of group turnover in 1989, and by the mid-1990s, English China Clays was preparing to discontinue these operations entirely. The other division, IDF International, supplied drilling fluids to the oil and gas exploration industry and accounted for 6 percent of group turnover in 1989.

Further Acquisitions in the 1980s

The 1950s and 1960s saw considerable growth and profitability for ECC. Large amounts of capital were invested during this time in modernizing all parts of the china clay production process, and as research and technological developments offered scope for further improvements, the process continued in the 1970s and 1980s. Oil-fired driers replaced the coal-fired kilns in the 1960s; these, in turn, were replaced with natural gas-fired driers in the 1980s. From the 1960s onward increasing quantities of china clay were transported as slurry.

ECC continued to steadily acquire the remaining independent china clay producers as well as allied quarrying, stone, building and building materials, and concrete companies, and extended its transport interests. It expanded its activities overseas. A sales presence in the United States that dated back to 1920 became, with the addition of clay manufacturing facilities in Georgia acquired in 1942, the Anglo-American Clays Corporation in 1956. The plant at Sandersville, Georgia, was expanded in the 1980s and specialized in the production of high-brightness hydrous clays and calcined clays. Southern Clay Products in Texas produced ball clay products, and in 1986 ECC acquired the Sylacauga Calcium Products Division of Moretti-Harrah Marble Company, which produced high-quality ground marble. In 1987 the U.S. construction aggregate producer J.L. Shiely was acquired.

In the 1980s ECC, like other U.K. companies, started to look at the Pacific region and the Far East as possible areas for development. In 1986, Fuji Kaolin Company, in which ECC already had a 50 percent interest, became a wholly owned subsidiary of the group, as did the Kaolin Australia Pty Ltd. in the same year. It entered a technology transfer agreement with the People's Republic of China in 1987. International expansion would remain a priority into the 1990s, as ECC opened offices in Singapore and a calcium carbonate plant in South Korea.

Divestitures in the 1990s

Under the leadership of Andrew Teare, who was appointed chief executive in 1990, ECC entered a new era. It redefined itself as a specialty chemicals manufacturer as well as a supplier of industrial pigments and minerals. English China Clays relocated its headquarters to Reading, England, in 1991, after occupying the John Keay House, at St. Austell, Cornwall, for more than 25 years. Wary of remaining, in Teare's words, "almost a conglomerate," the company divested itself of a dozen businesses, including the company's construction materials division, which was sold in June 1994 and began trading under the name CAMAS.

The company also made acquisitions to strengthen its core product line. After selling a number of smaller companies worth together around $160 million, ECC bought Pittsburgh-based Calgon Water Management in 1993 from Merck and Co. for $307.5 million. The entry into the specialty chemicals market permanently changed ECC's outlook. Teare pointed out numerous ways Calgon would strengthen ECC, for example, in research and development and global marketing, particularly to the paper industry. The results were immediately apparent; sales of paper chemicals increased 35 percent in 1994, when turnover for Calgon was £158.5 million.

Kaolin remained vitally important to English China Clays during the 1990s, although by 1995 specialty chemicals already accounted for 21 percent of the company's sales. Kaolin, worth 43 percent of sales ($620 million) in 1992, was predicted to account for 57 percent ($901 million) in 1996, in part on the strength of a recovery in the international paper industry. Calcium carbonate was also important, worth 15 percent ($217 million) of the company's sales in 1992. In 1995, ECC sought to strengthen these businesses by negotiating with Redland Plc for the fine-ground calcium carbonate operations of Genstar Stone Products Co. of Hunt Valley, Maryland. The company also had plans to invest £34 million on these types of operations in Sweden and the United States.

With the restructuring project finally at an end, ECC by mid-decade was in a position both to dramatically increase its market share of the paper-whitening pigment industry and to become a major player in the specialty chemicals business. In 1995 the company made a pair of strategic acquisitions designed to boost its calcium carbonate holdings: In March it invested SKr 200 million in a Swedish carbonate plant, which would provide an annual yield of 100,000 tons, while in October it acquired the calcium carbonate products division of Genstar for $35 million. In January 1996 ECC combined its Calgon paper operations with subsidiary ECCI AmPac to form the ECCI AmPac Paper Group. By early 1996, ECC's paper operations accounted for 60 percent of the company's total business.

Unfortunately, the company did not anticipate the drastic drop-off in the demand for kaolin and calcium carbonate that soon followed. By early 1996 the paper industry was in the midst of a significant destocking trend; this downturn in the market, combined with a sudden wave of inexpensive imports from Brazil, caused ECC's paper-whitening business to decline 15 percent. At around the same time it became apparent that the company's specialty chemicals line was not doing as well as originally hoped, showing only a £10 million profit on more than £200 million invested for the year 1995. In June SBC Warburg issued a profit downgrading for the company, which hit the stock value hard: shares dropped to 243 pence by July and continued to plummet until the end of the year, reaching a five-year low of 167½ in early December. Meanwhile, production levels in the paper industry also remained low.

The financial hit taken by the company was extreme. The year 1996 saw a loss of £42.9 million, compared with net earnings of £95.1 million in 1995. In an attempt to halt this downward spiral, in January 1997 the company initiated a comprehensive cost-cutting plan, reducing its workforce by 10 percent and consolidating some of its North American operations. The changes brought some relief, and additional reductions in September helped boost ECC's share price back to 264½ pence. The company also could boast a first half profit of £41.6 million, a significant improvement over a near disastrous 1996.

This streamlining effort had no effect on the dismal state of the paper industry, however, as paper sales continued to flounder. By September 1998 ECC stock had dropped to 145 pence per share. To help increase its sinking value, the company implemented a share buy-in plan in late 1998, purchasing several million shares of its own stock throughout the months of November and December, all at prices hovering between 160–175 pence. These maneuverings allowed the company to claim a profit of £84.4 million for the year, only a slight drop from 1997.

A remedy arrived in January 1999, when French metals processing firm Imetal S.A., the world's third largest producer of paper-whitening pigments, made a hostile offer of £680 million for English China Clays. The news of Imetal's offer caused the company's stock to leap more than 50 percent to 242½. In light of this sudden increase, ECC rejected the deal, claiming that it failed to reflect the company's value. In February Imetal proposed a second offer of £756 million, which ECC accepted. In April the European Union approved the deal and Imetal, which was now engaged solely in the minerals processing industry—having divested its metal interests—became Imerys. English China Clays Ltd. continued to operate as a wholly owned subsidiary of the new company, dedicated, as always, to the production of kaolin and calcium carbonates.

Principal Competitors

Engelhard Corporation; Kerr-McGee Corporation; NL Industries, Inc.

Further Reading

Bruce, Robert, "The Down to Earth Approach to People," *CA Magazine,* November 1994, p. 6.

Byrne, Harlan S., "English China Clays, Renamed, Geared for 'Nineties Expansion," *Barron's,* February 19, 1990, pp. 39–40.

German, Clifford, "French Bid for China Clays," *Independent* (London), January 12, 1999.

Harrington, Maura J., "ECC Returns to Start for System Building," *Computerworld,* June 18, 1990, p. 36.

Hudson, Kenneth, *The History of English China Clays,* Cornwall: ECC Ltd., 1969.

Kay, Helen, "Dividing the Spoils," *Director,* April 1995, pp. 26–32.

Kiesche, Elizabeth S., "English China Clays Dives into Specialty Chemicals with Calgon Buy," *Chemical Week,* June 23, 1993, p. 9.

Kindel, Stephen, "English China Clays: Old Product, New Markets," *FW,* May 11, 1993, p. 21.

Layman, Patricia L., "Specialty Chemicals Signal New Era for English China Clays," *Chemical & Engineering News,* July 31, 1995, pp. 12–15.

Mortished, Carl, "Paper Slowdown Hits English China Clays," *Times* (London), March 14, 1996.

Oates, David, "English China's World Ambitions," *Director,* September 1987, pp. 56–60.

Stevenson, Tom, "China Clay Rejig Bears Some Fruit," *Independent* (London), September 14, 1995.

There Is More to ECC Than China Clay, Cornwall: ECC Group, 1989.

—Judy Slinn
—updates: Frederick C. Ingram, Stephen Meyer

Exabyte Corporation

1685 38th Street
Boulder, Colorado 80301
U.S.A.
Telephone: (303) 442-4333
Toll Free: (800) EXABYTE; 392-2983
Fax: (303) 417-7170
Web site: http://www.exabyte.com

Public Company
Incorporated: 1985
Employees: 1,053
Sales: $222.2 million (2000)
Stock Exchanges: NASDAQ
Ticker Symbol: EXBT
NAIC: 334112 Computer Storage Device Manufacturing

Exabyte Corporation designs, develops, produces, and sells tape subsystems for data storage applications. The company primarily makes a full range of eight-millimeter, four-millimeter, and quarter-inch minicartridge tape drives and tape libraries, as well as data cartridges and media supplies. Exabyte also provides worldwide service and support for its full line of products. These products provide reliable compact data storage for discrete but fast growing segments of the computer industry, including mid-range systems, networks, workstations, and personal computers. Exabyte's products offer a range of storage applications for data acquisition and interchange, data and software distribution, automated storage management, and archiving.

The Drive for Faster Storage Systems in the 1980s

Exabyte was founded in 1985 by Kelly Beavers, Juan Rodriguez, and camera buff Harry Hinz, who saw the possibilities of turning camcorder technology into an ultrafast, high-capacity data storage medium. Rodriguez had 20 years of computer experience at IBM and then as cofounder of Storage Technology, a producer of disk drives. Hinz and Beavers were fellow Storage Technology employees. The founders initially sought to produce and sell high-capacity, self-operating, eight-millimeter tape

drives for use as data backups for mid-range computers. Before the creation of Exabyte, producing backup data was a laborious process, requiring the use of conventional tape technology and the presence of operators tediously changing reels or cartridges as they slowly filled with data. This process could take hours, sometimes days. With Exabyte's innovation, backup operations could be performed quickly and without the presence of manual operators. The company's success relied primarily on the quickly changing computer industry and the increasing need to manage, store, and retrieve vast amounts of essential data.

The innovation of high speed backup systems was a relatively recent phenomenon. Early computers were designed for calculating rather than for storing and managing data, which was largely done on punch cards. Rapid advancements in computers rendered these machines obsolete, giving way to workstations, minicomputers, networks of personal computers, and supercomputers used for a host of academic, commercial, and scientific purposes. Central to these advancements were rapid innovations in the microprocessor, governing the speed and power of computer systems. Equally important were advancements in the ability of computers to collect, store, and retrieve huge quantities of data. The phenomenal growth in storage capacity, usually in the form of nonremovable disks, created a parallel need for efficient backup systems in case of data loss. While computer manufacturers had considerably increased disk drive capacities, innovations in tape backup systems lagged far behind. Exabyte was originally conceived for this purpose.

Exabyte's beginnings were not without difficulty. Rodriguez's reported run-ins with venture capitalists over product marketing, after only six months of testing the technology, almost torpedoed the company's chances. When the venture capitalists withdrew their backing, Exabyte had to fire all 11 of its employees. Enough local investors came forward, however, for the company to rehire them. After overcoming these obstacles, Exabyte's early success relied mostly on forging strategic partnerships to gain additional capital and manufacturing expertise. In 1986, the Japanese giant Sony Corporation agreed to produce mechanisms for the tape drives. Other agreements with Japan's Kubota to make tape drives and Solectron of Silicon Valley to produce circuit boards permitted Exabyte to limit its manufactur-

Company Perspectives:

Founded in 1985, Exabyte Corporation is known around the world for innovative tape storage solutions and premium quality media. Exabyte designs, manufactures and markets data storage products for midrange, high availability networks. Available through OEMs, distributors and resellers around the world, Exabyte tape products include the award-winning M2 drive: fast, high capacity and self-cleaning.

ing role to final assembly, testing, and customization. The 1987 partnership with Kubota also brought in a large cash infusion, which considerably boosted Exabyte's cash flow.

With the backing of these partnerships, Exabyte introduced in 1987 the EXB-8200 eight-millimeter tape drive to support minicomputers and networks of personal computers. The tape backup system packed 2.3 gigabytes of data onto a videocassette and sold for $2,055. As anticipated, the tape drive was self-operating and represented a breakthrough in adapting consumer video recording technology to the storage of computer data. Applying helical scan recording technology, which had been used in video products for 30 years, Exabyte produced a compact, relatively inexpensive eight-millimeter tape cartridge drive which could hold unprecedented amounts of data. Unlike other backup systems at the time, the tapes could also be conveniently removed and stored in a vault. The EXB-8200 was the world's first "eight-millimeter helical scan computer storage subsystem," reducing considerably both the labor and media cost for saving backup data. The product was also designed for other conventional data processing uses, including data acquisition, software distribution, archiving, and data interchange. In the realm of data acquisition, the EXB-8200 could record and archive seismic, satellite, telemetry, and other scientific information. It also proved useful for medical and other imaging systems. In contrast to conventional tape drive technology, Exabyte's helical scan device employed relatively slow-moving tape using heads mounted on a rapidly rotating drum. This method offered several advantages contributing to high recording density. The need for "tight tolerance" was considerably reduced as the tape drive used only one or two short tracks at a time, rather than multiple, lengthier tracks found in conventional parallel track recording. This method meant that recording tracks could be run closer together. In addition, the helical scan technology permitted the tape to run at a slower rate producing far less stress on the tape. In turn, less stress meant that thinner metal particle tape could be used to record at high densities.

Rapid Growth in the Early 1990s

In 1987, Peter Behrendt joined Exabyte as president, after more than 26 years at IBM, where, along with other positions, he directed its worldwide electric typewriter business and international marketing strategy for storage products. When Behrendt arrived at Exabyte, the company employed just 50 people and had sold only 69 tape drives worth $170,000. With Behrendt, sales tripled to $89 million in 1989 and then increased to $287 million in 1992, making Exabyte one of *Fortune* magazine's 100 fastest growing companies in the United States. In 1991, Behrendt became CEO. He then succeeded

cofounder Juan Rodriguez as chairman, after Rodriguez left in January 1992.

Several months later, in September 1992, eight complaints were filed against Exabyte in the U.S. District Court for Colorado, alleging that top officials hyped Exabyte's earnings potential in order to sell off large blocks of personal stockholdings before having to release bad news. The complaints came immediately after a 38 percent one-day drop in Exabyte's stock price following news that its 1992 third-quarter earnings would fall far below analysts' predictions. On January 21, 1993, the plaintiffs filed a consolidated amended complaint alleging primarily the same action. The District Court dismissed the consolidated complaint, however, after the plaintiffs failed to establish an actionable claim.

In 1990, Exabyte introduced the EXB-8500, the first in a series of second generation eight-millimeter tape subsystems, which included improved data recording capabilities, storage capacity, and retrieval and transfer speed. Exabyte produced its family of eight-millimeter drive subsystems with capacities ranging from 2.5 to ten gigabytes largely for the high end of the market. The products accounted for approximately 80 percent of total revenue from 1991 through 1993. In 1994, the company also introduced the Mammoth eight-millimeter cartridge tape subsystem, the industry's fastest, highest capacity tape drive. When shipped, the product would offer a major technological leap forward with a storage capacity of 20 gigabytes.

In addition, starting in 1992, Exabyte began a series of strategic acquisitions to move from focusing exclusively on eight-millimeter data storage products to providing a full range of eight-millimeter, four-millimeter, and quarter-inch tape solutions. In 1992, it entered the low- to mid-range tape system market with the acquisition of R-Byte, a producer of four-millimeter cartridge subsystem tape products. In 1993, Exabyte purchased the Mass Storage Division of Everex Systems, Inc., which designed and produced quarter-inch minicartridge subsystems for the low-end and mid-range network and high-end personal computer market. The company then bolstered its position in the eight-millimeter market through the 1994 acquisition of German-based Grundig Data Scanner GmbH, adding helical-scan tape component research and manufacturing capabilities. The production and distribution of automated tape libraries made Exabyte the leading supplier of this product in the world.

These strategic acquisitions considerably enhanced Exabyte's share of the tape drive market. In 1993 alone, the company announced nine new products spanning three tape drive technologies, as well as automated tape libraries. Between 1987 and 1993, the company's workforce went from just 50 to more than 1,000. Moreover, Exabyte had also installed approximately 650,000 eight-millimeter tape drives throughout the world worth more than $1 billion. From a product line of one eight-millimeter tape drive subsystem with 2.5 gigabytes, Exabyte by 1994 was producing more than 30 distinct products in the eight- and four-millimeter, and quarter-inch formats, as well as library products that automatically stored between 50 gigabytes and 3.2 terabytes of data, a huge jump in storage capacity.

Exabyte's full range of products proved remarkably efficient and gained wide use among operators of personal computer networks, workstations, and mini- and personal computers. Even before the advent of its second generation of products, Exabyte counted among its customers IBM, Sun Microsystems, Motorola, NCR, Nixdorf, and Northern Telecom, to name a few. Since then, Exabyte added other customers including AT&T, Data General, Hewlett-Packard, Unisys, and many others. By 1990, the company had installed more than 100,000 tape subsystems to backup computers.

Exabyte produced its eight-millimeter and quarter-inch tape drives at its facility in Boulder, Colorado. The California firm, Solectron, manufactured Exabyte's four-millimeter products at its plant in Penang, Malaysia. The company's production strategy relied on "just-in-time" manufacturing techniques, which emphasized flexibility and continuous flow. Exabyte also customized its subsystems for selected customers. In 1993, the company acquired Tallgrass, a marketer of storage products, to sell and support Exabyte's full range of subsystems and tape libraries to distributors in North and South America. Exabyte also established a wholly owned subsidiary in the Netherlands and sales and technical support offices in Amsterdam, Frankfurt, Manchester, Paris, Singapore, and Tokyo to sell its products throughout Europe and Asia. In 1990, Exabyte established another subsidiary in Cumbernauld, Scotland, to provide repair services to European customers. The company later relocated these services in 1994 to a large facility in nearby Falkirk. In 1995, the company announced the opening of its Shanghai, China, office to meet the needs of the burgeoning Chinese market.

Since Exabyte went public in 1989, the storage market became highly competitive and subject to rapid technological innovation. A number of manufacturers with alternative technologies entered the market and competed for a limited number of customers. Many companies, some considerably larger than Exabyte, were also engaged in producing and commercializing data storage systems, including IBM, DEC, and Hewlett-Packard, which sought to incorporate their own storage systems in their computer products. The industry had also undergone consolidation. In 1992 and 1993, the industry experienced ten mergers and acquisitions, resulting in fewer but much larger multibillion-dollar competitors. This trend was attributed to the move toward single suppliers providing multiple products. In addition, these companies moved to restructure themselves and to form strategic alliances to adapt to changing market conditions and growing competition. While Exabyte appeared to have a lock on the

market for eight-millimeter tape subsystems for data storage in the mid-1990s, some speculated that other companies would soon enter the lucrative market. At that time, Exabyte's competition came primarily from companies manufacturing and distributing four-millimeter products, which because of their lower cost and smaller size rivaled the eight-millimeter products at the low-end computer workstation market. Exabyte's four-millimeter products also competed directly with these offerings. In 1994, the company stated that "more than ever before, Exabyte is running a tough race for market leadership. While the company's expansion into new technology areas is designed to enhance its future growth prospects, it also means there are more fronts on which to fight the competition."

Heading into the 21st Century: New Competitors, New Challenges

A number of setbacks in the mid-1990s served to cloud Exabyte's future. Many of the difficulties were beyond the company's control. One major challenge facing the company was the continually evolving nature of technology, coupled with the constant demand for new products. While its talent for innovation was what originally enabled Exabyte to rise above the competition, by 1995 the company found itself selling off large portions of its inventory at cost, or sometimes even at a loss, as demand for faster, more efficient tape drives rendered a number of its products obsolete. Sales actually rose 7.6 percent in the first six months of 1995, compared to the same period in 1994, but earnings dropped 36.6 percent, from $14.5 million to $9.2 million. The dramatic increase in value of the yen, and subsequent rise in the price of parts manufactured in Japan, also took a bite out of Exabyte's earnings, since the company depended on Sony for a third of its components.

These difficulties, part of the nature of the business, were largely unavoidable. However, the delayed release of Exabyte's long-awaited Mammoth eight-millimeter tape drive proved to be near fatal to the company. Mammoth was launched in March 1996, to great fanfare; unfortunately, it also arrived two years behind schedule. The quality of the product, like Exabyte's other offerings, was never in question: Mammoth was capable of storing 40 gigabytes of data at a rate of 21 gigabytes per hour, a substantial improvement upon Exabyte's previous storage technology. It was, in many respects, worth the wait. However, the company's failure to provide a mid-range product during the interim allowed the competition—most notably Quantum, maker of the Digital Linear Tape (DLT 7000) tape drive—to make inroads into the market. Exabyte executives insisted on the superiority of their technology to Quantum's, claiming that the "helical scan" method resulted in less wear and tear than the linear method; however, in terms of sales they had already missed the boat. While Mammoth did enable Exabyte to strike important deals with Apple and Siemens, these contracts could not make up for the lost customer base.

During this period, Exabyte attempted a number of new sales and product development initiatives in an effort to resuscitate its sagging profits. In August 1996 the company's Eagle retail division—formed in 1995 with the aim of developing storage products for PC users and small businesses—released the Eagle TR-3 minicartridge tape drive. Hoping to make an immediate impact on the $750 million—and growing—desktop tape storage business, the company offered the new product for half of what rivals were asking for similar devices. In an effort to create a faster, more efficient means of meeting demand for its products, the company launched its Strategex Partner Program in early 1997, giving computer resellers more direct access to its marketing, inventory, and technical support systems.

Unfortunately, these efforts did little to reverse the company's losses, and in late 1997 Exabyte was forced to restructure. The company reduced its job force by 15 percent, cut funding for research and development, and discontinued a number of its less profitable products. CEO William Marriner pledged to renew the company's focus on the high-capacity storage devices that formed its core business, placing great hopes in the release of the Mammoth-2 (M2) eight-millimeter tape drive, slated for late 1999. The company also entered the expanding storage area networking market in May 1999 with the launch of NetStorM ("Networking, Storage, Management"), an integrated storage solution for a range of businesses.

In spite of a tremendous sales push and rave reviews, the M2 did not restore Exabyte to profitability. The company suffered another loss of $14 million in the first quarter of 2000, and was forced to lay off another 250 employees in March 2001. However, there were still a few bright spots on the horizon. By August 2000 demand for Exabyte's products was still exceeding capacity, and the company was on schedule to release its latest eight-millimeter tape drive, the Mammoth-3 (M3), in mid-2001. The company also had high hopes for both NetStorM—with the network storage product market expected to reach $15 billion by 2002—and CreekPath Systems, a former

subsidiary specializing in data storage for Internet firms, which was spun off in July 2000, with Exabyte retaining a minority interest. Still, at the dawn of the new century it remained to be seen whether these new developments would help lift the company to the level of profitability it enjoyed in the early 1990s.

Principal Divisions

Drives & Storage Media Division; Storage Automation & Solutions Division.

Principal Competitors

Quantum Corporation; Seagate Technology, Inc.; Sony Corporation.

Further Reading

Backover, Andrew, "Mammoth-2 Tape Drive May Be Big Lift for Boulder, Colo.-Based Exabyte," *Denver Post*, November 13, 1999.

Deutschman, Alan, "America's Fastest Growing Companies," *Fortune*, October 5, 1992, pp. 59–82. Graham, Sandy, "Exabyte Has Problem Everyone Wants," *Denver Rocky Mountain News*, August 20, 2000, p. G3.

Kokmen, Leyla, "Exabyte Bets Future on Going Back to Basics," *Denver Post*, February 2, 1998, p. C1.

Wiegner, Kathleen K., "Attention Packrats!" *Forbes*, May 14, 1990, p. 126.

Zeiger, Dinah, "Storage Firms Have to Run Just to Keep Up," *Denver Post*, October 16, 1995, p. C1.

—Bruce Montgomery
—update: Stephen Meyer

Famous Dave's of America, Inc.

7657 Anagram Dr.
Eden Prairie, Minnesota 55344
U.S.A.
Telephone: (952) 294-1300
Fax: (952) 294-1301
Web site: http://www.famousdaves.com

Public Company
Incorporated: 1994
Employees: 1,800
Sales: $70.2 million (2000)
Stock Exchanges: NASDAQ
Ticker Symbol: DAVE
NAIC: 72211 Full Service Restaurants

Famous Dave's of America, Inc. is a growing restaurant business that was founded in 1994. Forty-five Famous Dave's barbeque restaurants operate in seven states in three different types of theme styles: roadhouse barbeque shack, hunting lodge, or blues club. The Minnesota-based company has an aggressive expansion and franchisee plan to create more restaurants each year and is well known, not only for its unique atmospheres but its barbecue fare, which is also marketed outside its establishments to other retail outlets.

Beginning of Famous Dave's: 1994–95

Dave Anderson opened his first restaurant in 1994 and named it "Famous Dave's BBQ Shack." Anderson's background included sales for a major *Fortune* 500 company, and an instrumental position in Grand Casinos, Inc. A Chicago native and fan of barbeque, Anderson claims to have searched for the perfect barbeque sauce for twenty years before opening his first restaurant. Located in a Hayward, Minnesota resort he had purchased, the restaurant was a quick success and soon Anderson was serving huge crowds of up to 1,000 daily. The restaurant began as a hobby for Anderson but soon grew to an investment as he spent $2 million into building the restaurant. The restaurant featured his "famous" sauces—Rich & Sassy, Hot Stuff, Texas Pit, Georgia Mustard, and Devil's Spit.

In 1995 a second location was added in Minneapolis with seating for 75 when the screened-in porch was in use. The "shack" concept with Americana antiques was featured in the restaurant. That same year, Famous Dave's earned a blue ribbon in the "Best BBQ Sauce in America" contest at the American Royal International Barbeque Contest.

Going Public in 1996

By 1996, Anderson was thinking about growth. His restaurants were generating over $1 million in annual revenues and he was ready to set his sights on a new theme and the national expansion of his dream.

As a Chicago native, Anderson knew that a combination of barbeque and blues music was hard to resist, so in September 1996 he opened a new concept restaurant, featuring both ribs and blues music, in Minneapolis with 9,000 square feet and at a cost of $1.4 million.

In October 1996, the business announced its initial public offering. Traded on the NASDAQ market under the ticker DAVE, the restaurant's shares saw opening day prices rise from $6.25 to $11.25 on 2.3 million units.

In an article in *Nation's Restaurant News,* Chairman Dave Anderson said, "We've learned a lot coming out this year. We're looking to triple our current store base in 1997 with anywhere from six to eight units. We've begun to identify sites for 1998 that will take us to out-of-state locations such as Madison, Wisconsin, Chicago and possibly Indianapolis."

Despite the strong showing in the stock market, the business itself was not producing a profit. At the end of 1996, Famous Dave's reported a loss of $706,598, compared to a loss of $306,190 for 1995.

New Leadership in 1997

In 1997, Douglas Lanham was named chief executive officer of Famous Dave's with Anderson still serving as chairman of the board. Mark Payne became president of the company to oversee the finance, real estate, and construction areas.

Company Perspectives:

Our mission. "Be Famous." Famous Dave's of America is committed to creating environments that transcend current restaurant offerings by serving the highest quality, flavor intense foods in surroundings that are stimulating, interesting, and fun. We will be guided by our values and beliefs, creating a culture of productive and empowered associates that provide a service atmosphere certain to delight our guests beyond their expectations. This will result in maximized value to our shareholders and partners. Our passion: "Be Famous." Famous Dave's is a flavor intense eating experience that smells great, musically makes you feel good, and visually creates an overwhelming impression that our guests will never forget. We provide exceptional service that wows our guests beyond their expectations, full portions that are value priced, and great flavorful food that creates a craving so strong that our guests are excited to return again with friends. Our purpose: "Be Famous." We are committed to becoming the best providers of barbeque in the nation. We create the best concept, prepare the best food, develop the best brand, and execute the best sensory experience for our guests. We are single-minded in being "Famous."

Regarding the management changes, Dave Anderson said, "I have been on a 20-year quest to bring the best barbeque to America. As part of that mission, I made a commitment at the end of 1996 to assemble the very best team of professionals to execute my vision and take this concept into the future. That team is now in place and ready to implement our expansion plans."

The company announced plans to open ten locations in 1997, and another 24 in 1998, with a goal to be the first national chain of barbeque restaurants. *Nation's Restaurant News,* a Chicago-based trade journal, named Famous Dave's one of the "Hot Concepts" in 1997. In June 1997, Dave Anderson received the emerging entrepreneur award from Ernst & Young.

In December, a new concept for the restaurant was launched in addition to the barbeque shack and the blues club themes. This new concept, the Lodge, was based on the northwoods lodges of the 1930s and 40s. Other new restaurants were opened in Stillwater and Highland Park, Minnesota.

At the end of 1997, the news from NASDAQ was as disappointing as the business' expected losses. The stock fell 44 percent in December based on reports that the company would not be meeting earnings expectations. At the end of the year, the loss was $4.6 million.

Readjusting in 1998 and 1999

At the beginning of 1998, Famous Dave's was facing two major challenges: falling stock prices and lagging sales. Just a year earlier, its executive team had called for an aggressive expansion, but in 1998, the company revised its plans in favor of more "controlled expansion."

Corporate layoffs also resulted from the unexpected loss and change of expansion plans. President Mark Payne, Chief Finan-

cial Officer Steven Odpahl, Marketing Vice-President Stan Herman, and Franchising Vice-President Tom Ragan all left the company.

Careful evaluation of locations for profitability caused the closing of one of the restaurants in Madison, Wisconsin with the second location remaining open. At the end of 1998, the company reported a loss of $4.4 million, including $2.7 million in charges for closings and corporate restructuring. Overall sales, however, continued to rise by over 124 percent.

Famous Dave's opened its 24th location in May 1999. The new location, a second "Famous Dave's Ribs n' Blues," was opened in downtown Chicago and could seat 500. Also in 1999, Anderson published a new cookbook, *Famous Dave's Backroads & Sidestreets.*

In August 1999, President and CEO Doug Lanham left the company and was replaced by Martin O'Dowd, former president of Rainforest Café, Inc. Again, management changes came after falling stock prices. The stock price had fallen from a high of $8.50 in 1998 to a low of $2.56 in 1999. The company also reported a loss of $310,000 for the second quarter of 1999. The net loss for 1999 was $6.61 million.

Turning the Company Around in 2000 and Beyond

The purchase of a D.C.-based Red River barbeque chain created an expansion into the nation's capital in 2000. Four of the five Red River restaurants were converted to Famous Dave's joints. The entire acquisition was less expensive than building just one Famous Dave's location from the ground up.

President and CEO Martin Dowd focused on improving the company and its growth. "To grow this company appropriately, we'll do it in three ways. We'll grow our own stores, through acquisition and through franchising," he said. With two franchises at the beginning of the year, the company focused on marketing its franchise opportunity—even giving one franchise away in a lottery as a promotional effort.

The company also planned to distribute sauces and other food to retail outlets as well as offering stands and stores everywhere from sporting events to airports. Famous Dave's already had a stand at the Metrodome Plaza and a location at the Minneapolis-St. Paul airport.

In January 2001, the company announced three new contracts that would increase the franchised locations to 27 restaurants in Illinois, Iowa, Georgia, Tennessee, Kentucky, Ohio, Florida, and West Virginia.

For fiscal 2000, the company earned its first profit since going public in 1996. Famous Dave's reported an income of $2.1 million for 2000 compared to a $6.61 million loss in 1999. Contributing to the positive numbers was a 47 percent increase in revenue to $70.1 million.

"Fiscal 2000 was the first full year of implementation of our three-pronged growth strategy. Even though we have yet to realize the potential of this program, we have had very favorable results in the early stages," said Martin O'Dowd, president and CEO.

Key Dates:

1994: Dave Anderson opens first Famous Dave's restaurant.
1996: New blues-theme restaurant opens; Famous Dave's is listed on the NASDAQ.
1997: New management is selected; lodge theme restaurant opens.
1998: Martin O'Dowd is named CEO.
2000: Famous Dave's posts first profits since going public.

The first quarter of 2001 exceeded expected revenues with an increase of over 3 percent in revenues. As of April 2001, the company operated 35 restaurants with ten franchises.

As Famous Dave's refocused on the future, a combination of new stores and franchises were planned to add to growth, a strategy perhaps not as aggressive as in the past but one which promised to preserve the now profitable company. The focus remained on the food and the recipes of the company's founder, Dave Anderson, whose guiding motto was, "May you always be surrounded by good friends and great barbeque."

Principal Competitors

Applebee's International Inc.; Hooters of America, Inc.; Timber Lodge Steakhouse, Inc.

Further Reading

Bertagnoli, Lisa, "Making CONVERTS," *Restaurants & Institutions,* February 15, 2000, p. 55.

Carlino, Bill, "Famous Dave's Sizzles with Three Units and a $15 M IPO," *Nation's Restaurant News,* December 2, 1996, p. 13.

Franklin, Jennifer, "Famous Dave's Spreads Barbecue Concept," *Minneapolis-St. Paul CityBusiness,* February 25, 2000, p. 3.

Hoogesteger, John, "Famous Dave's Seeking Farther-Reaching Fame," *Minneapolis-St. Paul CityBusiness,* January 12, 2001, p. 10.

Johnson, Tim, "Famous Dave's to Scale Back Expansion," *Minneapolis-St. Paul CityBusiness,* March 27, 1998.

Kahn, Aron, "Three Executives Leave Famous Dave's Barbecue Restaurant Chain," *Saint Paul Pioneer Press,* April 1, 1998.

Levy, Melissa, "Famous Dave's Goes for Growth," *Star Tribune* (Minneapolis), June 16, 2000, p. 1D.

McCartney, Jim, "Award-Winning Minneapolis Restaurant Names New CEO," *Saint Paul Pioneer Press,* August 3, 1999.

——, "Minnesota's Famous Dave Hopes Investors Will Help Make Ribs Famous, Too," *Saint Paul Pioneer Press,* August 19, 1996, p. 8.

Merrill, Ann, "Famous Dave's Stock Really Cooks During First Day of Trading; Barbecue Chain Plans to Use Proceeds to Open More Roadhouse-Style Eateries," *Star Tribune* (Minneapolis), October 22, 1996, p. 1D.

——, "The Ribs Race; Anderson Is Ready to Smoke out Rivals on Barbecue Sauce," *Star Tribune* (Minneapolis), May 19, 1997, p. 1D.

Phelps, David, "Famous Dave's Stock Gets off to a Famous Start; Hype, Changing Demographics, Rainforest Success Help Fuel Rise," *Star Tribune* (Minneapolis), October 28, 1996, p. 1D.

Reilly, Mark, "Famous Dave's Feeds Franchising Efforts," *Minneapolis-St. Paul CityBusiness,* March 31, 2000, p. 11.

Walkup, Carolyn, "Famous Dave's BBQ Shack Eyeing the Big Picture," *Nation's Restaurant News,* July 22, 1996, p.8.

——, "Famous Dave's Eyes Improvement As Newer Ribs n' Blues Concept Expands," *Nation's Restaurant News,* May 31, 1999, p. 8.

Youngblood, Dick, "Dave Is Famous for Good Reasons; From Casinos to Barbecue Joints, He Does Things in a Big Way," *Star Tribune* (Minneapolis), April 22, 1996, p. 1D.

Zuber, Amy, "Famous Dave's: Boning up on the Competition," *Nation's Restaurant News,* May 12, 1997, p. 116.

—Melissa Rigney Baxter

First Choice Holidays PLC

First Choice House
London Rd.
Crawley, West Sussex RH10 2GX
United Kingdom
Telephone: (+44) 129 356-0777
Fax: (+44) 129 358-8680
Web site: http://www.firstchoiceholidaysplc.com

Public Company
Incorporated: 1973 as Owners Abroad (Wholesale) Ltd.
Employees: 11,178
Sales: £1.88 billion ($2.73 billion) (2000)
Stock Exchanges: London
Ticker Symbol: FCD
NAIC: 561510 Travel Agencies; 561520 Tour Operators

Having escaped a hostile takeover attempt by larger rival Airtour Plc, and at the same time seeing the collapse of a proposed merger with Switzerland's Kuoni Travel that would have propelled it into the European big leagues, U.K. tour and travel operator First Choice Holidays PLC has changed direction for the new century. The fourth largest travel agent and tour operator in the United Kingdom, First Choice has made a successful move into the booming specialist travel segment, building up a steady portfolio of acquisitions that have extended its operations across Europe. First Choice operates in four principal areas: Air Inclusive Holidays; Charter Airline Operations; Travel Retailing; and Yachting and Watersports Holidays. These activities are supported through an extensive network of subsidiaries organized into four divisions: UK & Ireland Tour Operations, including mainstream and specialist businesses; International Tour Operations; Canadian Tour Operations; and Airline & Aviation, including the company's own Air 2000 charter airline. Among the company's brand names are the Bakers Dolphin, Travel Choice, and Holiday Hypermarkets retail chains, long-haul operators Hayes & Jarvis and Unijet; and premium niche companies such as Meon Villas, Longshot Golf Holidays, Sunsail, and Flexigroup. First Choice has been actively expanding its European continental holdings, boosted by the acquisitions in 2000 of the European tour operating business of Ten Tour Group and the travel division of Spain's Barcelo. These acquisitions extended First Choice's operations into the French, Spanish, Belgium, Austria, German, Swiss, and Irish markets. Fueling these acquisitions is the £200 million investment agreement with Caribbean Cruise Lines, which gave the U.S. company a 20 percent stake in First Choice—and coincidentally formed a poison pill defense against possible future hostile takeover attempts. First Choice, a money-loser in the mid-1990s, is led by CEO Peter Long and non-executive chairman Ian Clubb, who orchestrated the company's turnaround strategy. After consolidating acquisitions, First Choice's turnover neared £2 billion in 2000, with industry-leading operating margins of 5.4 percent.

Start and Restart in the 1970s

First Choice Holidays started life in the early 1970s, when Continental Air Brokers and Economy World Travel merged to form Owners Abroad (Wholesale) Ltd. in 1973. The company's initial focus was on discounted airfares. As the *Guardian* described the company's beginnings, Owners Abroad was a "bucket shop selling surplus airline tickets at knock-down prices." The transformation of the British holiday landscape during the 1970s—which saw the country shift from traditional British shore-based holidays to increasing numbers of vacationers booking airplane flights—encouraged Owners Abroad to increase its position as a tour operator and travel agent. The company began to build up its portfolio by acquiring other established businesses.

One of Owners Abroad's first acquisitions was that of Falcon Leisure, based in Ireland, which had been set up by John Boyle during the 1970s. Boyle was among the first to recognize the growing demand for flight-only travel; left with empty seats during a Falcon-organized charter flight, Boyle placed an ad selling the seats alone. The company quickly found buyers. British legislation at the time, however, restricted tour operators from selling only airplane seats; to circumvent that law, Boyle added cheap hostel beds to the flights. Falcon's early position in this market gave it a long head-start when the legislation was finally changed. With the acquisition of Falcon Leisure, made in 1983 for £2 million, Owners Abroad placed itself in position to grow quickly through the 1980s.

Company Perspectives:

First Choice is a leading European leisure travel company comprising mainstream and specialist tour operations, travel retail and aviation businesses.

By then, Owners Abroad had sold part of the company in a public listing on the London secondary market, raising the capital not only to acquire Falcon Leisure but to begin a steady diet of acquisitions, including that of the youth-oriented tour operator 2twentys, added in 1984. By the middle of the decade, Owners Abroad had transformed itself into a full-fledged tour operator. Supporting its growing travel package sales, the company decided to begin its own charter airline operations. In 1986, the company purchased two Boeing 757s; by 1987, the company was ready to launch its airline, dubbed Air 2000. The new airline enabled the company to offer some 35 weekly flights from the Manchester airport to destinations throughout the Mediterranean. Backing the launch of Air 2000 and the company's impending expansion was a full-listing on the London primary market, in 1987. In that year, the company took on Howard Klein as chairman.

Air 2000 enjoyed rapid success, enabling the company to build up a fleet of nine airplanes by the end of the decade. The company was also enjoying a reputation for quality, with Air 2000 winning a number of awards for being among the United Kingdom's best charter airlines. By the beginning of the 1990s, Owners Abroad had built up a position as one of the top five travel companies in the United Kingdom.

Meanwhile, Owners Abroad continued branching out, in 1988 acquiring 25 percent of Canada's International Travel Holidays (ITH), which had been founded in 1972 as Adventure Tours Canada. The share purchase by Owners Abroad encouraged ITH to begin its own expansion drive, as the company moved to establish nationwide operations, principally through the acquisition of a number of strong regional players. ITH also began cruise operations, forming Encore Cruises in 1991. In 1994, Owners Abroad acquired 100 percent of ITH, which by then had become Canada's leading travel and tour operator. The acquisition helped balance Owners Abroad's traditionally summer-based business in the United Kingdom with Canada's winter-based travel season. Owners Abroad then changed ITH's name to Signature Vacations in 1995.

Resistance in the 1990s

By then, Owners Abroad had changed its own name and weathered a crisis that nearly saw its end as an independent company. Chairman Klein had begun informal talks with rival Airtours, another fast-growing tour and travel operator, about the possibility of merging the two companies in the early 1990s. Talks broke off, however; instead, Owners Abroad sold a 10 percent stake to Westdeutsche Landesbank, through its Thomas Cook travel subsidiary, based in the United Kingdom, in 1992. The following year, however, Airtours, which had managed to avoid a monopoly inquiry, launched an all-out hostile takeover bid for Owners Abroad. The company fought to defend itself, at

a cost of £5 million, and finally succeeded when its German investor increased its stake to 20 percent.

At the same time, the combination of a shrinking, recession-era travel market and the company's own market missteps—the company missed the renewed interest in Spanish holidays in the early 1990s—wiped out the company's profits. The resulting scandal among shareholders forced the resignation of Klein and other members of the company's management. Owners Abroad then hired Francis Baron as chairman.

Baron immediately took the company on a rebranding and restructuring exercise. After market tests revealed that many of the company's half dozen or more brand names enjoyed virtually no brand recognition among British consumers (compared with more than 50 percent recognition for rival Thomson); meanwhile, the company's name itself had led to a great deal of confusion among consumers, who were convinced that Owners Abroad was little more than a time-share operator. In 1994, therefore, the company scaled back its number of brand names to just three, and changed its corporate name to First Choice Holidays. The company's smaller range of brand names were also restructured around three main business categories, those of family vacations, single holidays, and luxury travel.

Baron did not last long with First Choice. Although credited with successfully bringing First Choice through its rebranding, Baron quickly alienated others in First Choice's management with what was described as an "authoritarian" management style; Baron's management also led to strains between First Choice and Westdeutsche Landesbank, which began reducing its shareholding in the company. Meanwhile, First Choice, which was by then the United Kingdom's number three travel company, was seeing its market share gradually being eroded. Operating margins were also dismal, posting at just 1 percent, compared with as much as 5 percent elsewhere in the industry. At last, in 1996, after other members of First Choice's management threatened to quit, Baron was packed off with a £650,000 severance check.

Baron was replaced by Peter Long as CEO, while Deputy Chairman Ian Clubb took the company's chairmanship. The new heads quickly inaugurated a turnaround strategy, promising to restore operating margins to 4 percent by 1999. Not only were Long and Clubb successful—the company's operating margins topped 5.4 percent in 2000—they also successfully steered First Choice through a new expansion that gave the company a position as one of the U.K.'s strongest specialty operators—the industry's highest-margin sector—and also expanded it as a European-wide operator. At the same time, First Choice moved to become a vertically integrated operator, adding a long-absent retail division, boosted by the acquisitions of Bakers Dolphin—which traced its history back to the late 1800s—and Intatravel. The company also began opening retail stores under the Travel Choice and Travel Choice Express brands, and joined in on the formation of the Holiday Hypermarkets joint venture. The company took full control of Holiday Hypermarkets in 2000.

By 1998, First Choice was ready to begin an extended acquisition drive. In that year, the company bought up two of the U.K.'s leading long-haul specialists, Unijet—the country's

Key Dates:

1973: Owners Abroad (Wholesale) Ltd. is formed.
1982: Company changes name to Owners Abroad Group Plc and lists on London secondary market.
1983: Company acquires Falcon Leisure (Ireland).
1987: Company is listed on London primary market.
1988: Owners Abroad acquires stake in International Travel Holidays (ITH; Canada).
1992: Thomas Cook assumes 10 percent stake in company.
1993: Airtours attempts hostile takeover; Thomas Cook raises stake to 20 percent.
1994: Owners Abroad acquires full control of ITH; changes name to First Choice Holidays.
1995: Company changes ITH brand name to Signature Holidays.
1996: Peter Long becomes CEO, announces three-year restructuring plan.
1999: First Choice attempts merger with Kuoni Travel (Switzerland); Airtours launches new hostile takeover attempt; company begins Holiday Hypermarket joint venture; acquires Bakers Dolphin and Intatravel to launch retail division.
2000: First Choice acquires Meon Travel, Sunsail International, and FlexiGroup; launches Travel Choice Direct; acquires full control of Holiday Hypermarkets; acquires Ten Tour Group's European tour operating business; acquires Barcelo (Spain) travel division.
2001: Company acquires 75 percent of CIT Holidays.

fifth largest tour operator—and upscale vacation packager Hayes & Jarvis. The two deals, for £134 million, helped to spark a century's end industry consolidation frenzy.

First Choice itself was caught up in the consolidation whirl, announcing its agreement in 1999 to merge its operations with those of Switzerland's Kuoni Travel and thereby create one of Europe's leading travel operators. That deal unraveled after Airtours returned with a new hostile bid for First Choice—quickly rallying First Choice's shareholders to its cause. Kuoni dropped out of the proposed merger and First Choice's hopes rested on the European Community's Mergers and Monopoly review board, which rejected the takeover attempt.

By the time the dust settled on the hostile takeover, the consolidation of Europe's travel industry was in full swing, with U.K. market leader Thomson Holidays being snatched up by German travel giant Preussag, among other deals. First Choice, however, was now content to remain on the sidelines of the consolidation drive and instead quietly build up its portfolio in what was to become widely viewed as the key travel growth market in the 21st century, that of specialist travel. Between 1999 and early 2001 First Choice had completed more than half a dozen acquisitions and had solidly positioned itself as a leader in the high-margin specialty market. The company also made significant strides overseas, acquiring the European tour operating business of Ten Tour Group and the travel division of

Spain's Barcelo, giving it a foothold in most of the primary European markets.

Fueling this new acquisition drive—and providing a significant war chest for future acquisition moves—was the May 2000 agreement with Caribbean Cruise Lines that gave the latter a 20 percent stake in First Choice for its £200 million investment. The two companies also agreed to begin preparations for a launch of a new joint-venture cruise company to begin operations possibly by 2002. The deal was well greeted by industry analysts, who pointed out the investment gave First Choice a large-scale investor capable of thwarting any future hostile takeover attempts. First Choice quickly showed its continued interest in international expansion: in March 2001, the company announced its acquisition of 75 percent of CIT Holidays, a U.K.-based company with extensive operations in Spain and Italy.

Principal Subsidiaries

First Choice Holidays & Flights Limited; Unijet Travel Limited; Air 2000 Limited; Ski Bound Limited; Viking Aviation Limited; Hayes & Jarvis (Travel) Limited; Bakers World Travel Limited; First Choice Retail Limited; Sunsail International Limited; Meon Travel Limited; Holiday Hypermarkets (1998) Limited; Sunquest Holidays (UK) Limited; Crown Holidays Limited; Falcon Leisure Group (Overseas) Limited (Ireland); Taurus Reiserveranstalter GesmbH (Austria); Bosphorous SA (Belgium); Groupe Marmara SA (France); Stardust Yacht Charters SA (France); Nazar Holiday Reiserveranstaltung GmbH (Germany); Taurus Tours AG (Switzerland); Royal Vacaciones S.A. (Spain); Viajes Barceló, S.L. (Spain); Signature Vacations Inc. (Canada).

Principal Divisions

UK & Ireland Tour Operations; International Tour Operations; Canadian Tour Operations; Airline & Aviation.

Principal Competitors

Airtours Plc; American Express Company; Carlson Wagonlit Travel; Kuoni Travel Holding Ltd.; Preussag AG; Thomas Cook Holdings Ltd.

Further Reading

Aliosi, Silvia, and Keith Weir, "First Choice Aims to Fly Solo," *Reuters*, July 9, 1999.
Cope, Nigel, "Travel Giants Tighten Their Grip," *Independent*, June 19, 1998, p. 19.
"First Choice Holidays," *Investors Chronicle*, December 22, 2000.
"Flying Clubb Class to Holiday Success," *Observer*, March 21, 1999.
Jones, David, "First Choice Picks Europe for Growth," *Reuters*, December 14, 1999.
Pain, Steve, "First Choice Has Holiday in Profit Sun," *Birmingham Post*, December 13, 2000, p. 27.
Pandya, Nick, "Company Vitae: First Choice," *Guardian*, June 10, 2000.
Phelps, John, "First Choice Cruising After Holiday Alliance," *Scotsman*, May 19, 2000.

—M. L. Cohen

The Gambrinus Company

14800 San Pedro Avenue
San Antonio, Texas 78232-3733
U.S.A.
Telephone: (210) 490-9128
Fax: (210) 490-9984

Private Company
Incorporated: 1986
Employees: 300
Sales: $425 million (1999 est.)
NAIC: 42281 Beer and Ale Wholesalers; 31212
   Breweries

Based in San Antonio, Texas, The Gambrinus Company imports, brews, and distributes beers on a regional and national basis. The company is owned by its chief executive officer, Carlos Alvarez, who was instrumental in introducing the Mexican beer Corona Extra to the United States. It is now America's top imported beer, after surpassing Heineken in 1997. Gambrinus is licensed to distribute Corona in Texas and the states east of the Mississippi River. Canada's Moosehead beer became the company's first nationally distributed import. Gambrinus expanded beyond the distribution side of the business in 1989 when it began to purchase small specialty breweries. The company owns America's number two craft brewer, Pete's Brewing Company, maker of Pete's Wicked Ale.

Beginning of Gambrinus Company: 1986

The founder and owner of The Gambrinus Company, Carlos Alvarez, grew up in Acapulco, Mexico. He went to work for the Modelo brewery, located in Mexico City, starting out in the sales department. By the late-1970s he had risen to become the company's export director. He convinced Modelo to sell its Corona Extra beer outside of Mexico. First imported to the United States in 1981, Corona caught on mostly with a younger demographic and soon enjoyed explosive growth. By 1985 sales reached five million cases. A year later 13 million cases of Corona were sold in the United States.

It was in 1986 that Alvarez left Modelo to distribute Corona on his own, creating The Gambrinus Company, named after the mythic Flemish king known for his love of beer. Alvarez was granted Corona distribution rights in Texas and 24 eastern states. Barton Brands Ltd. of Chicago controlled the rest of the country. Corona continued its extraordinary growth during 1987, reaching 20 million cases sold, with Barton distributing the beer throughout its 25-state territory and Gambrinus only selling in Texas and five eastern states. The beer was so popular that in many instances it had to be rationed to bars, restaurants, and stores. Corona eclipsed Canada's Molson as America's number two imported beer and appeared poised to pass the Netherlands' Heineken, which according to the beverage industry publication *Impact* had been the top selling import since the repeal of Prohibition in 1933.

Corona, however, would become a victim of its own success. Lacking market data, Gambrinus and Barton did not really know who was buying Corona and why. Its growth was a flash explosion, rather than something sustainable. Drinking Corona had become a fad, as a number of consumers simply tried the beer then returned to their usual domestic brand. To make matters worse, Corona became the subject of unfounded rumors. In the eastern distribution territories, the word was that Corona was heavy on calories, a charge that Gambrinus answered with full-page ads to set the record straight. The problem in Barton's territory was more troubling and difficult to address: the story churning through the rumor mill was that either ABC's *20/20* or CBS's *60 Minutes* reported that Corona beer was contaminated by urine. Sales dropped in markets as the rumor spread. Despite the danger of simply spreading the rumor further by fighting it, Barton aggressively went after rival distributors that it accused of starting the rumor, demanding letters of retraction and threatening to sue any other distributors that could be linked to the rumor. It also publicized the results of a beer-testing company, which found Corona free of contaminants.

Although the rumors were dispelled, Corona sales plummeted in 1989. The importers stayed the course with the beer's "vacation in a bottle" message and simply waited for the fad drinkers to leave the market and allow the brand to build on it base of loyal customers in a sensible manner. Gambrinus had an additional problem in its eastern states by charging the same price as Heineken. Market research indicated that consumers believed a Mexican beer should be priced cheaper than a beer imported from Europe. When in late 1990 and early 1991, a federal excise tax was increased, Gambrinus recognized a chance to make a price adjustment. The distributor convinced Modelo, as well as wholesalers and retailers, to absorb the tax increase, which amounted roughly to 50 cents per six-pack. Barton did not follow suit, but later in the year it decided to absorb a California statewide tax hike. Aided by an increased marketing budget, Corona was then able to renew its pattern of growth, which many in the beverage industry had thought to be highly unlikely.

Acquisition of Spoetzl Brewery: 1989

In addition to Corona, Gambrinus distributed several other Modelo beers and in 1989 entered the brewery business itself with the purchase of the Spoetzl Brewery, maker of Shiner Beer, located in the small town of Shiner, Texas. Alvarez became aware of Spoetzl's signature beer, Shiner Bock, when using Austin as a test market for Corona. Shiner had something of a cult following among the city's young adults and was making inroads in Houston and Dallas. Alvarez began negotiations to buy the brewery from the Great Texas Brewing Company, created by a group of Houston investors who had purchased Spoetzl in 1984 and were now looking to sell. One of the partners, who was devoted to the brewery almost to the point of obsession, however, refused to sell and went to court to block the Gambrinus deal. Eventually Alvarez would have to pay $3.5 million for an operation that, based on its annual revenues, was worth around $1 million. In the end, he paid the price because he liked the beer.

The town of Shiner, Texas, was established in 1888 when Henry B. Shiner donated land for a railroad right of way and a town site in Lavaca County. The rich farming area attracted German and Czech immigrants. A group of local investors created the Shiner Brewing Association in 1909 in order to satisfy the immigrants' taste for Old World beer, but the brewery failed to produce a suitable product. In 1914 the Association brought in Kosmos Spoetzl, a Bavarian brewmaster with his own family recipe, and leased the facilities to him. A year later he purchased the brewery that would then bear his name.

Spoetzl was hardly aggressive in marketing Shiner beer, mostly driving around in his truck, accompanied by his dog, giving away samples to farmers as they worked, or at community gathering places. Selling in a 75-mile range of Shiner,

Spoetzl was starting to succeed with his beer when Prohibition went into effect. Until repeal the brewery managed to survive by making ice and producing "near beer," which contained an allowable 0.5 percent of alcohol. Local legend maintained that Spoetzl would occasionally forget to boil off the alcohol in select batches. When regular beer production resumed in 1933, Spoetzl became prosperous enough to replace the original wood and tin building with a stone structure. With her father's death in 1950, Spoetzl's daughter Cecelie ran the brewery until 1966 when the business passed out of family hands and a succession of owners then struggled to keep the operation profitable.

Although Alvarez had no intention of tampering with the brewing process, he made other changes as soon as Gambrinus took over the Spoetzl Brewery. He canceled all of the contracts to brew other companies' brands, even though the work amounted to one-quarter of the brewery's annual revenues. Alvarez anticipated that he would need all of his production capacity to support the projected demand in Shiner beers. He also canceled all out-of-state agreements for Shiner beers, which had been sold to anyone willing to buy a shipment, even as far away as Arizona and Ohio. Alvarez wanted to make sure that the product was handled properly, and so for the sake of quality control and long-term growth he contracted the sales territory. Finally, and to some observers the most surprising move, he immediately raised the price of Shiner beer, which under the previous owners had cost less than Budweiser and now cost 75 percent more. Alvarez wanted to position the product in the premium category, and although Shiner beer had a loyal following that might be disenfranchised, it was small, and Gambrinus stood to gain considerably by establishing the higher price with customers unfamiliar with the brand.

Gambrinus also invested millions to upgrade the facilities. It added new fermentation tanks, created the brewery's first testing laboratory for quality control, and built a new warehouse. The changes made by new ownership soon began to show results. The brewery produced 35,000 barrels in 1990, but by 1995 the number had increased to 138,000, as Shiner Bock became America's best-selling bock beer. Spoetzl was now the largest specialty brewery in the Southwest and the seventh largest in the country.

Addition of BridgePort Brewery: 1995

With the rising popularity of specialty beers, the three major industry giants—Anheuser-Busch, Miller, and Coors—looked to create their own internal specialty product lines or to simply buy up the microbreweries. Gambrinus, with its Spoetzl operation in sound shape, became involved in this consolidation of the craft brewer segment by purchasing the BridgePort Brewing Company in 1995. BridgePort was the oldest operating microbrewery in Oregon, an area which had become a hotbed for craft brewing.

BridgePort was established in Portland, Oregon, in 1984 as the Columbia River Brewery by wine-makers Dick and Nancy Ponzi. They hired Karl Ockert, a University of California, Davis Brewing graduate, to build and run the brewery. His recipe for BridgePort Ale proved popular and fueled the brewery's growth. In 1986 the company changed its name to BridgePort Brewing Company and opened the BridgePort BrewPub to the public. It introduced a number of craft beers, which it began to bottle in 1989 and distribute to retail stores in Oregon and Washington. Other area microbreweries, however, expanded more rapidly through public offerings of their stock. They surpassed privately funded BridgePort, which never devoted money to promotions or marketing. The Ponzis knew they either had to curtail expansion plans, step up their commitment, or sell out to a company with deeper pockets and better sales and marketing capabilities. In the end, they chose to sell the business to Gambrinus.

Gambrinus, as it had done with Spoetzl, instituted a number of immediate changes. It brought back Ockert, who had left BridgePort in 1990, to run the brewery; it invested $3.8 million in equipment, including a new bottling line and a quality control laboratory; it pulled BridgePort from weaker markets, then redesigned the packaging and paid to create a new proprietary bottle; and it instituted the first-ever advertising campaign for BridgePort beers.

In 1997 Gambrinus gained its first national distribution deal for an imported beer when it acquired the distribution and marketing rights for Canada's Moosehead beer from the Guinness Import Corporation. Despite industry insiders who discounted the possibility of reversing the trend of declining sales with Moosehead, Gambrinus looked to apply some of the lessons it had learned with Corona beer.

In the meantime, Corona sales were so strong that Modelo decided to renew import rights with Barton and Gambrinus for an additional ten years, despite the fact that Anheuser-Busch now owned a major stake in the Mexican brewer and was itself interested in acquiring the distribution rights to Corona. Modelo had good reason to be pleased with its American partners. In 1997 Corona passed Heineken to become the largest-selling imported beer in the United States. Building on its U.S. success, Corona was now sold in more than 140 countries and had become the top-selling Mexican beer in the world and the fifth largest overall.

Gambrinus added to its brewery businesses in 1998, purchasing Pete's Brewing Company for $69 million. Although a strong second to microbrewer Boston Beer, makers of the Sam Adams line of beers, Pete's struggled in an environment in which the craft segment of the beer industry suffered a sharp drop in growth. Sales declined in late 1997 and early 1998, forcing Pete's to look for a buyer.

Pete's Brewing Company was founded in 1986 by a former engineer named Pete Slosberg and a group of investors. With its Pete's Wicked Ale and savvy advertising strategy, the company was an early success story in the rising microbrewery business. Sales jumped from $130,000 in 1988 to $5.5 million in 1992. The company made an initial public offering of stock in 1995, debuting at $18 a share and reaching a high of $26.50. Then the bubble for the microbrewers burst. As Gambrinus had discovered in the early days of distributing Corona, growth resulting from the white-hot enthusiasm of a fad was impossible to sustain. Faced with a dizzying array of specialty beers in the

cooler that included seasonal and commemorative brews in addition to year-round offerings, many consumers opted for old standbys like Corona. Even venerable Guinness enjoyed a new-found popularity with younger beer drinkers. Pete's lost $6 million in 1997 and its stock plummeted. Under terms of the acquisition, Gambrinus paid $6.375 per share.

As Gambrinus worked to grow Pete's and its other specialty breweries and to revitalize Moosehead sales, its future continued to be very much tied to the success of Corona. Because it was deliberate about expanding distribution in its eastern territory, Gambrinus had more of an upside than Barton in generating greater sales. The major brewers were also aggressively promoting competing products, such as Anheuser-Busch's Tequiza, making the future less certain for Gambrinus. While sticking to their basic marketing program, Modelo, Gambrinus, and Barton also took measured steps to maintain Corona's position as the top imported beer. Although the beer was known for its distinctive bottle, the partners decided in June 2000, after years of development, to introduce Corona in cans. The new package was intended to fill a gap, providing customers with Corona in places that prohibited bottles, such as airplanes, stadiums, and golf courses. To accommodate a lime wedge, so often associated with the beer, the can was designed with a wide mouth opening. The Corona partners also looked to sell more to the Latin community, targeting individual Hispanic groups, rather than lumping them together. As a privately held company, Gambrinus was less susceptible to shareholder pressure and was thus able to follow a conservative and steady game plan that had served it well since its creation.

Principal Subsidiaries

Spoetzl Brewery; BridgePort Brewing Company; Pete's Brewing Company.

Principal Competitors

Anheuser-Busch Companies, Inc.; Boston Beer Company; Heineken N.V.; Miller Brewing Company.

Further Reading

Antosh, Nelson, "San Antonio Company to Buy Shiner Brewery," *Houston Chronicle*, August 12, 1989, p. 1.

Cox, James, "Corona Importer Puts a Cap on Rumor," *USA Today*, July 20, 1987, p. 6B.

Earvolino, Patrick, "Beer Necessities," *Texas Monthly*, November 1996, pp. 12, 108.

Hassell, Greg, "Brewer Takes Shot at Growth," *Houston Chronicle*, February 2, 1992, p. 1.

"Importer Gambrinus to Buy Struggling Pete's Brewing Co.," *Houston Chronicle*, May 23, 1998, p. 2.

Jacobson, Louis, "A Good Head for Beer," *Wall Street Journal*, April 19, 1999, p. 12.

Kermouch, Gerry, "Gambrinus' Gamble," *Brandweek*, February 24, 1997, p. 32.

Slosberg, Pete, *Beer for Pete's Sake: The Wicked Adventures of a Brewing Maverick*, Boulder, Colo: Siris Books, 1998, 258 p.

—Ed Dinger

Gaz de France

23 rue Philibert-Delorme
75840 Paris, Cedex 17
France
Telephone: (+33) 1-47-54-20-20
Fax: (+33) 1-47-54-38-58
Web site: http://www.gazdefrance.com

Government-Owned Company
Incorporated: 1946
Employees: 32,000
Sales: EUR 11.2 billion ($10.5 billion) (2000)
NAIC: 221210 Natural Gas Distribution; 211112 Natural
  Gas Liquid Extraction; 234910 Water, Sewer, and
  Pipeline Construction; 213112 Support Activities for
  Oil and Gas Operations

Not content to be Europe's third largest provider of natural gas, Gaz de France (GDF) is gunning for that market's top spot. The state-owned company has stepped up its acquisitions at the turn of the century, boosting its natural gas reserves to more than 30 billion cubic meters while expanding its operations worldwide to transform itself into a vertically integrated company capable of supplying customers "from wellhead to burner tip." The company has already achieved production levels of two billion cubic meters, with plans to raise production to 15 percent by the year 2003. GDF's ambitions have been spurred by the liberalization of the utilities markets in European Community member states, which has—on paper, at least—ended the traditionally monopolistic nature of these markets since August 2000. Faced with increased competition in its domestic market, which accounts for some 75 percent of the company sales (and in which GDF has already reportedly some 5 percent of its top corporate clients), GDF has been busy establishing positions in other markets—including the United Kingdom, the Eastern European countries, and Mexico and other Latin American markets. The company intends to boost its 10 percent of the European market to 20 percent by 2003. GDF remains wholly owned by the French government. However, the government is unable to provide the massive levels of investment capital needed for GDF to achieve its ambitious growth plans. An opening of its capital—most likely to fellow French-government controlled companies such as TotalFinaElf and EDF (Electricité de France)—is therefore seen as a likelihood for the early years of the century, possibly as early as 2002. Nonetheless, company chairman and CEO Pierre Gadonneix, appointed by the government in 1996, has steadfastly ruled out a privatization of the company.

Founding a French Utility Monopoly in the 1940s

GDF was first established in order to concentrate the production and distribution of gas in France. Before 1946 gas was mainly manufactured from coal, in more than 500 gas works, located throughout the country, which were owned by companies of various sizes: large companies supplied the areas around major cities, whereas subsidiaries of coal companies, such as Les Houillères Nationales, now Charbonnages de France (CDF), delivered gas to mining areas. For economical, political, and social reasons, the energy industries were nationalized soon after World War II by the Gouvernement provisoire, a tripartite government consisting of Mouvement Republicain Populaire, Socialist, and Communist parties.

Nationalization took place on the recommendation of Général Charles de Gaulle, the former head of government, and Marcel Paul, the communist minister of industry. On April 8, 1946, the Nationalization Act was effected, nationalizing the production, transport, distribution, import, and export of electricity and combustible gas; and establishing two new public corporations—Gaz de France and Electricité de France (EDF). Several gas producers remained exempt from nationalization, particularly those whose main activity was not gas production, transmission, or distribution including the producers of natural gas and gas manufacturing companies with an annual production of less than six million cubic meters. Gas distributors supplying less than this quantity were also exempt from nationalization. These included local authorities and in 1991, 21 municipal utilities remained as independent companies.

Eventually the mixed enterprises, those companies providing both gas and electricity, were absorbed by EDF, includ-

Company Perspectives:

Gaz de France is determined to pursue its ambitious strategy of development along the entire gas chain, from the wellhead to the burner tip, by combining internal and external growth to strengthen its position among leading gas operators in Europe. In 2001, we intend to strengthen our role as a public service addressing local needs while accelerating our European development.

ing the gas activity which was later to be allocated to GDF. Under the Nationalization Act, these companies were financially autonomous and consequently commercially and technically independent. Initially, to simplify and unify the organization, EDF was in charge of the management of GDF whose first chairman, George Reclus, was under the authority of EDF's chief executive officer, Roger Gaspard. On January 4, 1949, however, GDF was partially separated from EDF when a law came into force giving it financial autonomy, with a credit of FFr 6 billion and the order to separate its management from EDF within 6 months.

On February 23, 1949, Jean Le Guellec, former General Inspector of Industry and Commerce, was elected first chairman of Gaz de France, with George Combet, former chairman of Société de Gas et d'Electricité de Nice, as chief executive officer. Their first task was to modernize and concentrate gas manufacturing facilities and to develop the local transmission networks. The first long-distance pipeline was established in 1953, from the Nancy area to Paris, to open up a new market for the Lorraine coal gas. In southwest France, meanwhile, several small natural gas fields remained unexploited. A new law, the Loi Armengaud, came into force on August 2, 1949, excluding natural gas transmission from GDF's monopoly. This was in opposition to the Nationalization Act, which excluded only natural gas production from GDF's monopoly.

In 1951, the Lacq gas field in southwest France, then one of the largest in the world, was discovered by Elf Aquitaine and launched in 1957. The first transmission system, 4,000 kilometers long, was built to supply gas to southwest France, Brittany, and the Paris area. As a result, sales of natural gas increased threefold over the following five years from 1957 to 1962. Cities connected to the mains switched progressively to natural gas and by 1965 approximately half of France was supplied with natural gas. This was known as the natural gas revolution. The period was marked by the birth of the Fifth Republic and the arrival in 1959 of Général de Gaulle as head of state. It was also the period of the Algerian War and the loss of this colony was to be significant for French energy resources. In 1958, a special regime was established for the transmission and sale of natural gas in France. The Société Nationale des Gaz du Sud Ouest (SGNSO), owned by GDF, retained a monopoly within its area and the Compagnie Française du Méthane (CFM), owned 50 percent by GDF, 40 percent by TOTAL Compagnie Française des Pétroles and 10 percent by Elf, was established to carry out all operations relating to transmission and sale outside southwest France. With these subsidiaries GDF had a virtual monopoly of gas transport and distribution in France.

Choice of Natural Gas in the 1960s

By the end of the 1960s, 70 percent of gas supplied to customers by gas utilities was natural gas, as opposed to 99.5 percent in 1991. Supplies from Lacq were insufficient and it was necessary to import gas. The French tradition of strong government intervention and involvement in the energy sector influenced negotiations for contracts. The purchase of gas was a useful diplomatic ploy, as confirmed by the first contract with Algeria, which procured gas from the Hassi R'Mel gas field. Signed in 1965 with the Algerian company Sonatrach, this initiated GDF's international involvement. The second gas import contract was signed with the Netherlands in 1967, linking GDF with the Dutch company Gasunie until 2005. Gas from the Groningen field was carried by pipeline via Belgium to northern and eastern France, leading to the extension of the transport network in Europe as well as in France, where the network reached a length of 13,000 kilometers in 1970.

Aware of its important role in the national program and in international energy markets, GDF extended its research and development, particularly in the field of high-pressure pipelines and gas liquefaction, to improve transmission and storage facilities. GDF participated in the construction of the first natural gas liquefaction plant, GL4Z, in Algeria; designed and built the LNG (liquefied natural gas) receiving terminal at Le Havre; and ordered its first LNG carrier, the Jules Verne. Later, the Fos-sur Mer, Provence, and Montoir de Bretagne, Brittany, terminals were designed and built, the latter being larger and more efficient. Underground storage facilities had been in operation since 1956 and GDF had pioneered the development of storage engineering. From a strategic and load-matching viewpoint, these needed to be developed to allow GDF to cope with winter's peak demand. The largest unit, 2,760 million cubic meters, was put into service in 1968 at Chémery in central France and in 1991 was still the world's largest underground storage facility.

In 1969 Robert Hirsh, a former state representative at Commissariat à l'Energie Atomique (CEA) and a member of the board of Electricité de France, replaced Jean Le Guellec as chairman of Gaz de France. Hirsch's nomination was particularly significant for the French energy policy. The period leading to the 1973 oil shock was characterized by cheap oil which boosted France's industrial development and more than doubled energy consumption. The use of oil greatly increased, demand for gas and electricity grew substantially, and the French nuclear power program was started. The period of the two main oil price rises, 1973 to 1979, boosted natural gas consumption in France and throughout the world.

In response to the first oil price shocks, French government policy was to adopt a far-reaching nuclear power strategy, enabling France to rely more on nuclear power for energy production. This resulted in significant diversification of primary energy suppliers. The idea was to avoid a situation where one supplier accounted for more than 5 percent of France's total energy supply and this remained the case in 1991. To follow this policy, GDF looked for alternative suppliers of natural gas, resulting in the purchase of Soviet and Norwegian North Sea gas in addition to the former Algerian and Dutch contracts. With the most important natural gas reserves in the world, Russia became its largest producer. Three contracts were signed between GDF and

Soyouzgazexport, one from 1976 to 2000 for 2.5 billion cubic meters per year, one from 1980 to 2000, and the third, from 1984 to 2009, for eight billion cubic meters per year. The Norwegian contracts were signed with four separate producers—Ekofisk in 1977, Statfjord in 1985, Heimdal in 1986, and Gullfaks in 1987. In 2003 other deliveries were planned to come from Norway—Troll and Sleipner—after contracts agreed with Norway's Statoil. Two more contracts were signed with Algeria, one in 1973 for 3.5 billion cubic meters per year, and one in 1982 for five billion cubic meters. Both were long-term contracts, 25 years and 20 years long, respectively, and have been renegotiated.

In 1976 Robert Hirsch left Gaz de France and Jean Blancard became chairman after a long career in the energy sector. In 1979 Blancard was in turn replaced by Pierre Alby, former chief executive manager of GDF. The nomination of such distinguished representatives of the energy industry demonstrated the government's concern with the gas industry. Furthermore, by 1979 Paris was relying solely upon natural gas. Production of manufactured gas had ceased and GDF was importing huge quantities of natural gas to meet increasing French consumption. GDF had been induced to align with other gas companies in managing the transmission of purchased gases and in supplying security clauses. The 1970s, marked by the energy crisis, saw the total transformation of Gaz de France into an active member of the international energy market and network.

Natural gas consumption's share of primary energy, which was 7.9 percent in 1973, increased to 12.7 percent in 1979, while the electricity share increased from 9.2 percent to a mere 11.7 percent. The competition between the two sources was strong, and GDF, aware of changing times ahead for the enterprises, whether private or public, developed a new attitude toward its friendly rival Electricité de France (EDF). GDF was divided into a number of operating divisions which dealt only with GDF. At a local distribution level, GDF and EDF shared a joint role. Distribution regions were divided into a number of distribution areas. Each distribution area had a budget for each type of energy, but for the general public EDF and GDF were closely connected with private consumers of both gas and electricity generally invoiced on the same bill.

To differentiate between gas and electricity as energy sources was a daunting task for GDF. GDF programs and rates were regulated by the Minister of Industry and the Minister of Economy and Finance. Despite this close link with the government, GDF was ostensibly run as a commercial enterprise, financially independent and taxed in the same way as a private firm. In the early 1900s GDF recorded severe losses which it was necessary to restrict.

Historically, GDF had a difficult position in the national economy compared to EDF. France traditionally exported electrical energy and EDF had to face overcapacity of electricity, whereas huge quantities of gas were imported. In 1985 Pierre Alby, then chairman of GDF, summed up the problem in a speech on the competition between natural gas and nuclear power during the 15th World Conference of the International Gas Union when he said that in France, a country lacking major national gas resources, "the gas industry is a factor which cannot be neglected by a policy striving to establish a balance between imports and exports." He added, however, that the gas industry could not isolate itself from balance of trade concerns. His analysis of the position of gas as opposed to nuclear energy revealed the new policy GDF decided to adopt. After major technical achievements at national and international levels, GDF needed, he said, to accept the laws of competition on the energy market and, above all, nuclear competition.

Independent Utility in the 1980s

Once again GDF was ready to accept a new commercial challenge. GDF could not compete with lower prices as the government controlled these closely. Initially GDF continued to implement its strategy of promoting the export of French gas expertise by becoming involved in several trans-European pipeline companies and obtaining part ownership of two tankers used to transport LNG from Algeria. In this respect, GDF developed its industrial activity and thereby reduced the import bill.

The next stage was to promote a modern image of the gas industry to the general public as well as domestic, commercial, and industrial users, in order to compete with electricity. To this end natural gas was promoted as a plentiful, flexible, powerful, and clean source of energy. The environmental safety of the product, particularly important in the industrial sector, helped GDF to increase its market share significantly. The promotion of clean energy was also welcomed by the increasingly vocal ecology movement, which was strongly against nuclear energy. Fondation du Gaz de France was established to promote protection of the environment.

To tackle the domestic and commercial market was, however, more difficult. GDF was in fierce competition with EDF for the domestic market, the new housing sector being one of the main targets. EDF had an advantage with the public authorities who were concerned about the excess of electric energy and tended to favor electrical installations. GDF therefore had to develop efficient marketing methods as well as new communication skills and the company structure was modified to cope equally with government control and with the competitive energy market. The new logo, a single flame designed in 1987, was a sign of this change.

During the mid-1980s, the European gas market had become considerably more international in character, including significant developments regulating competition, the establishment of a European Economic Community internal market program, and environmental issues. Jacques Fournier, who, before his appointment as GDF chairman in 1986, was secretary general of the former Socialist government, was at the same time chairman of the CEEP, European Center of Public Enterprises, and was thus aware of the importance of an internal European market. During a meeting organized by the Fondation Europe et Société early in 1988, he said that GDF would have to adapt itself to the changing situation in Europe concerning standardization, markets, and the fiscal system, at the same time declaring that public services and the spirit of enterprise were not in opposition. State control, he said, was necessary in order to preserve GDF's autonomy. Francis Gutmann, former French ambassador in Madrid, appointed GDF chairman in August 1988, continued the battle for the autonomy of his company while the monopoly of imports and distribution began to be contested at national and European levels.

GDF showed a loss of FFr 96 million in 1990 on a turnover of FFr 41.8 billion—more than twice the loss of 1989. Despite these losses, the company had by 1991 proven an ability to cope with technological changes and marketing adaptations. With its industrial assets, research facilities, and expertise, GDF's active part in worldwide gas development made the company a major factor in French economic growth. The need to make a profit was recognized.

EC Market Liberalization for the 21st Century

A contract signed with the government in February 1991 enabled GDF to make a profit. Based on discussions underway since the fall of 1989, the contract covered objectives and management during the period 1991 to 1993. At the press conference held soon after its signing, Francis Gutmann declared: "At a time when natural gas is recognized as a major source of energy and when GDF continues to increase its strategic weight in France and abroad, the new contract provides the responsibility and the autonomy necessary to accomplish a continually improved public service." The tariff policy was also covered in the contract allowing GDF, among other things, to follow the fluctuations of supply costs. This enabled GDF to stand up to international competition and protect its distribution monopoly from challenges by the French parliament and the European commission.

In France, as Elf Aquitaine and Total threatened GDF's gas market shares, a parliamentary amendment was signed which changed the statute of 1946. The new amendment gave communes, the basic units of French local government, freedom in organizing their own gas distribution. This amendment, known as the Desrosiers amendment, was later revoked. At the same time, the European commission continued efforts to break up national energy policies.

Those efforts bore fruit toward the end of the 1990s when a schedule was put into place ending domestic utilities monopolies in all European Community countries by August 2000. GDF responded to this imminent revolution—which was to open up utilities markets to competition for the first time in more than 50 years—by transforming itself into an internationally operating utilities giant. By the end of the decade, GDF had

nearly doubled its sales, and established strong positions in a number of its European neighbor markets.

One of GDF's first international expansion moves came in 1994, when the company bought control of EEG (Erdol-Erdgas Gommern) of Germany. The company also joined the GASAG joint venture to win the gas distribution contract for the Berlin market in 1997.

By then, the appointment of Pierre Gadonneix as company chairman and CEO in 1996 had marked the beginning of a new and ambitious growth strategy. By the end of the decade, GDF expected to boost its number of French customers to more than ten million—a target the company had reached by 2000. GDF also sought to add production capacity, with plans to build its own production to account for 15 percent of its total reserves by 2003. GDF also began developing ancillary operations, products, and services, such as cogeneration operations.

GDF moved into Italy, acquiring that country's Agip Servizi in 1997, which, coupled with the extension of its Cofethec Servizi subsidiary, gave the leading position in Italy's heating, ventilation, and air-conditioning (HVAC) services markets. The following year, GDF introduced itself to the Mexican market, through its MaxiGas Natural subsidiary, which began supplying the state of Tamaulipas in the northeast of the country. By 2000, GDF had begun to assert itself as a major utility company in the Mexican market, particularly with its acquisition of 67 percent of Energia Mayakan and 100 percent of Transcanada del Bajio, both gas transmission pipeline operators. GDF also won new gas distribution permits in Mexico, in Mexico City in 1998 and in the Puebla Tlaxcala region in 2000. During the same period, GDF was building its interests in the United Kingdom, which had already liberalized its market, acquiring that country's Volunteer Energy Ltd.

The year 2000 also saw GDF restructure its operations as it prepared for the August 2000 liberalization of its home market. In April of that year, the company reorganized its business into five major business units: Services; Distribution; Infrastructures; Trading; and Exploration-Production. The new organization represented the company's drive to become, as Pierre Gadonneix stated, a provider of natural gas services "along the entire gas chain, from the wellhead to the burner tip."

In August 2000, GDF acquired the "exploration-production" component of its new organization when it paid EUR 371 million for Transcanada International Netherlands (TCIN), as well as a 38.5 percent share of Noordgastransport BV, giving GDF offshore drilling and production capacity for the first time in the company's history. Soon after, in October 2000, GDF added the oil and gas reserves held by Statoil, of Norway, giving it a 20 percent share of the Njord oilfield in the Norwegian Sea, and a 12 percent share of Snohvit oilfield in the Barents Sea. Together these new assets helped boost the company's projected 2001 production to more than 2.5 billion cubic meters. The company ended that year with rising sales, which topped EUR 11.2 billion. Despite higher oil prices and a high dollar, the company's net income remained strong at EUR 431 million.

The European Community's utilities industries were technically liberalized in August 2000. Pressure from France's unions, however, helped reinforce the French government's reluctance to implement the full scale of liberalization policies. Meanwhile, GDF, faced with the massive investment cost of its ambitious growth plan, was forced to consider opening its capital to outside investors. While remaining steadfast in its intention of maintaining government control of the company, the French government and GDF leadership indicated their willingness to allow a limited number of outside investors, such as fellow French government-controlled bodies TotalFinaElf and EDF to acquire shares in GDF. That decision, however, was postponed by the Socialist-led government for at least until after the 2002 elections.

In the meantime, GDF was able to secure government agreement to help finance the continuation of its growth strategy into 2001. The company began the new century by forging an agreement with Sonatrach of Algeria and Petronas of Malaysia to take a share of gas production in Algeria's Ahnet basin. In February 2001, GDF began anticipating further expansion, acknowledging its interest in acquiring part of Lithuania's state-owned Lietuvos Dujos gas utility, up to 51 percent of which was scheduled to be put up for sale. GDF's international expansion—which had enabled it to build up a client base of more than two million customers outside of its domestic market—placed it in a strong position to contend for the top spots in the world's gas utility market.

Principal Subsidiaries

CFM (16%); Cofathec Servizi (Italy); Coriance (86%); Degaz (Hungary; 55%); EEG (Germany; 40%); EMB (Germany; 64%); Estag (Austria; 68%); Gazocean Armement (55%); Gaz de Bordeaux (43%); Gazinox; Gaz Metropolitain (Canada; 81%); Gaztransport & Technigaz (93%); GDF (U.K.; 49%);

GES; Gensel; Messigas (50%); Methane Transport (75%); Portgas (Portugal); Pozagas (Slovakia); SPBVergaz (Russia); Societe Girondine de Cogeneration (86%); Termoraggi (Italy; 85%); Volunteer (U.K.; 50%).

Principal Competitors

BG Group plc; Centrica plc; Eni S.p.A.; Gas Natural SDG, S.A.; N.V. Nederlandse Gasunie; OAO Gazprom; Italgas - Societa Italiana per il Gas p.A.; Westcoast Energy Inc.

Further Reading

Environmental Pressures and the Response of the European Gas Industry, Report of the Institution of Gas Engineers of the 10th W.H. Bennett Traveling Fellowship, 1988.
"Gaz de France Keeps Mum on Opening Its Capital," *Reuters,* March 21, 2001.
"Gaz de France Open to Alliances," *Europe Energy,* December 23, 1999.
"Gaz de France's Development May Be Slowed by Lack of Funds," *Europe Energy,* May 26, 2000.
"Gaz de France Subsidiary Expands into Northern Mexico," *Infolatina,* March 22, 2001.
Lyle, C.D., and R.O. Marshall, *Gas Regulation in Western Europe,* London: Financial Times Business Information, 1990.
Magada, Dominique, "GDF Prepares for European Gas Spot Market," *Reuters,* February 14, 2001.
Mémoire Ecrite de L'Electricité et du Gaz, Paris: EDF-GDF, 1990.
Mougin, Pierre, *Mémoires,* Paris: Imprimerie Barneoud, 1966.
Picard, Bertrand, *Bungener, Histoire de l'EDF,* Paris: Dunod, 1985.

—Florence Protat
—update: M.L. Cohen

GEICO Corporation

One Geico Plaza
Washington, D.C. 20076
U.S.A.
Telephone: (301) 986-3000
Toll Free: (800) 841-3000
Fax: (301) 986-2851
Web site: http://www.geico.com

Wholly Owned Subsidiary of Berkshire Hathaway Inc.
Incorporated: 1936 as Government Employees Insurance
Company
Total Assets: $9.4 billion (1999)
NAIC: 524126 Direct Property and Casualty Insurance
Carriers (pt)

GEICO Corporation writes auto insurance for good drivers. The company, which is the seventh largest American auto insurer, got its start during the Depression in Texas. Drawing from a pool of government employees, the company grew rapidly after World War II and gradually expanded its customer base beyond its original franchise. After near failure in the mid-1970s, GEICO returned to financial health in the 1980s and 1990s. The company became a wholly owned subsidiary of Berkshire Hathaway Inc. in 1995.

Insurance for Good Drivers: The 1930s and 1940s

GEICO was founded in 1936 in San Antonio, Texas, by Leo Goodwin. Goodwin was a 50-year-old employee of U.S.A.A., an insurance company that served the needs of officers in the U.S. military. It was here that Goodwin got the idea of setting up his own insurance company, which would select good drivers as customers. With a pool of better-than-average drivers, and no insurance agents or salesmen as middlemen, he calculated that it would be possible to sell a policy that ordinarily cost $36 or $37 for only $30 and still make money. At the time that Goodwin formulated these plans, this discrepancy represented a huge savings, since many people's weekly salary was less than $30.

Goodwin sought out Fort Worth banker Cleaves Rhea, who agreed to invest $75,000 in his company if Goodwin could put up $25,000. After raising the money, Goodwin chartered the Government Employees Insurance Company (abbreviated GEICO) on September 1, 1936, at the height of the Great Depression. He held one-fourth of the company's stock, and Rhea took possession of the other three-fourths, in keeping with the proportion of his contribution.

In seeking out a pool of good drivers, Goodwin targeted government employees as people who were likely to be responsible and to have a steady income. Since the largest pool of government employees in one place was, logically enough, in Washington, D.C., Goodwin and his wife, Lillian, moved to the city in 1937 and rechartered their company on November 30, 1937. GEICO set up offices in the Investment Building, at 15th and K Streets in the northwest quadrant of the city. Once in Washington, Goodwin and his wife worked tirelessly to make their fledgling enterprise a success. They labored 12 hours a day, 365 days a year, establishing principles to select good drivers and sending out direct mail solicitations to government employees and military personnel. GEICO's direct mail operations took the place of a sales force of insurance agents and helped to keep the company's rates low. On weekends, Goodwin went out to local military bases and personally solicited customers, or hand-wrote responses to customer inquiries and complaints. At the end of the company's first year in business, GEICO had written $104,000 worth of premiums.

Each year Goodwin's underwriting losses declined, until 1940, when the company showed a $5,000 underwriting gain and a $15,000 profit. In an effort to strengthen these financial gains, Goodwin stressed customer service. In 1941, for instance, a large hailstorm severely damaged thousands of cars in the Washington area. Goodwin arranged with repair shops to work 24 hours a day on the company's customer's cars, and he also had automotive glass specially shipped to Washington to fill the sudden demand. As a result of these efforts, his policyholders had their cars repaired far sooner than many others.

The entry of the United States into World War II at the end of 1941 brought significant strain to GEICO, as its pool of military and federally employed policyholders moved about the country frequently and were shipped overseas. As the American economy was converted to wartime production, rationing, price freezes, and shortages of essential goods resulted. Goodwin relied on family members and a group of young female employees to keep GEICO afloat during the war years.

GIs Coming Home: Expansion in the Postwar Years

In the wake of the war, GEICO's business expanded dramatically as millions of soldiers returned home and purchased cars and houses, which GEICO was able to insure. In 1946 the company's net income quadrupled, and premiums reached $2.5 million, 50 percent more than the previous year. To handle this new business, GEICO augmented its staff with a group of young returning veterans who would form the backbone of the company's management in the postwar years.

By 1948, GEICO's value had reached approximately $3 million. At this time, Goodwin's original co-investor, the Rhea family, sold its stake in the company to the Graham-Newman Corporation of New York, E.R. Jones and Company of Baltimore, and David Lloyd Kreeger, a private investor who lived in Washington, D.C. Later that year, Graham-Newman distributed its portion of the company's 175,000 shares to its stockholders, and GEICO became a publicly traded company. In the following year, GEICO bought a building to house its rapidly expanding operations, at 14th and L Streets Northwest, in Washington. The six-story structure cost $725,000 to buy and renovate, offered 48,000 square feet of space, and was ready for occupation within a year.

Also in 1949 GEICO began to branch out, offering services beyond basic property insurance for the first time. The company incorporated the Government Employees Corporation (GECO), a Delaware finance company that made loans for the purchase of cars and boats. After GEICO customers began to ask if they could buy life insurance from the company, GEICO set up the Government Employees Life Insurance Company (GELICO) in Washington with $300,000 in capital raised from GEICO shareholders. In setting up these two spinoff companies, GEICO separated them from the parent company to avoid jeopardizing the financial health of GEICO by taking risks in unfamiliar fields. When each new company was formed, GEICO shareholders were offered the opportunity to buy stock in the new enterprises, so the three companies had many owners in common. Although their shares were traded separately on the stock exchange, they also shared services and office space, as well as key management with GEICO. By the end of 1949 the parent

company of these new offspring had passed the $1 million mark in profits for the first time.

In 1950 GEICO expanded its geographical reach, winning a license to sell insurance in the key New York market as well as in nine other states. The company further expanded its potential market of policyholders in 1952 when it made all state, county, and municipal workers eligible for coverage. As a result of this change, more than 41,000 new policyholders joined the company in that year. Written premiums jumped by more than 50 percent, to $15.2 million. To handle some of the influx of new customers, GEICO opened an information office in New York City, at 125 Broadway. This facility was so heavily used that an underwriting staff was added later in 1952 and a claims staff was installed the following year.

Also in 1953, GEICO purchased the old Federal Housing Administration Building at Vermont Avenue and K Street Northwest in Washington, D.C.; in 1955, it was renamed the GEICO Operations Building. That same year GEICO expanded the types of insurance coverage it offered when it began writing fire insurance for dwellings and personal belongings in Washington, D.C., Maryland, and Virginia.

In 1956 GEICO took its first step toward automating its operations when it installed an IBM Type 500 Magnetic Drum Data Processing Machine at its operations facility. By the following year, premiums had increased to $36.2 million. In 1958 GEICO expanded its customer pool further when it added civilian professional, technical, and managerial occupation groups to those who were eligible for insurance coverage. With this enlargement, the company's number of policies rose to 485,443. Its customers were spread throughout the nation. The following year, GEICO moved again to a bigger facility; its 1,100 employees were transferred to a newly built Operations Center in Chevy Chase, Maryland, a suburb of Washington.

The company continued its technological innovation the following year when a new telephone system was installed in Chevy Chase that could handle up to 50 incoming calls at once. Also in 1960, GEICO extended the services it offered when it began to market a homeowners insurance package to its policyholders. By the following year, this package was being offered in 36 states and the District of Columbia. In 1961 GEICO also organized the Criterion Insurance Company to provide automobile insurance for enlisted military personnel who did not meet GEICO's good driver standards. Along with this expansion in the types of coverage it offered, GEICO continued its geographical expansion in 1961 when it opened the company's first West Coast office, in San Francisco. Employees in this office handled sales, policy service, and claims settlement. A year later the company opened a second western office, in Denver. This facility was the headquarters of the Government Employees Finance Company (GEFCO), which was set up to make personal and educational loans. Nine years after its inception, this company was merged with the Government Employees Corporation (GECO), another loan outfit.

In 1964 GEICO passed the one million policyholders mark, and the following year, the company opened its first drive-in auto claim center in Chevy Chase, Maryland, to serve Washington-area policyholders. GEICO and its various subsidiaries continued to expand throughout the 1960s. By 1968, the company

Key Dates:

1936: Leo Goodwin founds the Government Employees Insurance Company (GEICO) in San Antonio, Texas.
1937: GEICO is moved to Washington, D.C.
1949: GEICO begins offering life insurance, loan products.
1952: GEICO makes products available to all state, county, and municipal workers.
1960: GEICO begins marketing a homeowners insurance package to policyholders.
1964: GEICO signs its one millionth policyholder.
1979: GEICO Corporation is formed.
1995: Berkshire Hathaway Inc. acquires GEICO Corporation; company phases out its homeowners insurance plan.
1998: GEICO launches $100 million marketing campaign.

had offices in 24 states and three foreign countries: England, West Germany, and Japan. GEICO's foreign offices were located near large concentrations of U.S. servicemen.

By 1971, GEICO had become the fifth largest publicly held auto insurance company in the United States. In the following year, the company passed the two million policy mark. Its number of policies written had doubled in just eight years. After this remarkable postwar growth streak, however, GEICO began to lose its way as the structure of the insurance industry started to change.

Redrawing the Line: The 1970s

In 1973 GEICO abolished the last of its occupational restrictions on eligibility for insurance. This step was taken only after a seven-month period of study, during which company executives decided that new computerized data bases, which provided information on an individual's driving record, provided sufficient means for determining who was a good driver. In place of reliable driver record information, the company previously had generalized on the basis of occupation about a driver's probability of mishap, but with access to new data, GEICO felt that it could safely expand its pool of potential clients. With this step, the company made its services available to the entire population. By the end of the year, this move had helped the company to become the fourth largest publicly held auto insurer, with more than $479 million in annual premium income.

To solicit further growth in the population at large, GEICO ran advertisements, sent out 25 million pieces of direct mail a year, and relied on word of mouth from its policyholders. In addition, the company had 123 field offices where salaried agents sold insurance policies. A network of regional offices with switchboards and operators also was being built, and the first center, a $13.1 million facility in Woodbury, New York, was dedicated in October 1973. With a greater emphasis on regional operations, the company hoped to entice more customers west of the Mississippi, where only 20 percent of its policyholders lived.

Despite this push for new customers, GEICO continued to insist that it insured good drivers only. By this time, however, the company's reliance on good drivers to keep its claims down was becoming less and less feasible as no-fault insurance laws swept the nation. Under the old system, the insurer of the driver at fault in an accident paid for everything. Since GEICO drivers were rarely at fault, the company paid out little in fees, which enabled it to keep its premiums down. Under the new system, however, claims were determined by how much damage was done, not by who was at fault. In addition, GEICO found itself squeezed by regulatory restrictions on its rates, as public outrage about rising insurance costs caused states to pass laws limiting the amounts that companies could charge. These new laws, along with GEICO's headlong expansion, brought the company to the brink of disaster in the mid-1970s. The company had overestimated its own financial strength and discovered that it had underestimated its losses by $100 million. In 1975 GEICO reported a loss of $126.5 million, as high claims for hospital and auto repair fees battered its bottom line.

In May 1976 GEICO appointed a new chairman, and the company undertook an aggressive program to stay afloat. With the assistance of the District of Columbia's Insurance Superintendent and the rest of the insurance industry, a rescue plan was devised for the company. A consortium of 27 insurance firms took over one quarter of the company's policies, on a commission basis, so that the company would not fail and thus shake public confidence in the insurance industry. A stock offering of $76 million, to be used to pay off claims, was successfully completed, and GEICO also instituted a stringent cost-containment program, called Operation Bootstrap, in which policyholders in certain states were dropped and other high-risk drivers were eliminated, among other measures.

Although losses for 1976 equaled $26.3 million, by 1977 GEICO was proclaiming that it had returned to financial solvency, and the company entered a period of retrenching and reorganizing. In 1978 GEICO began to acquire the stock of its three sister companies in an effort to diversify the company's lines of business. In January 1979, a holding company for all of the GEICO properties was formed and named the GEICO Corporation. By the start of the 1980s, GEICO was a much smaller company than it had been at its height in the 1970s, and it began to move cautiously into new areas. In 1981 the company formed Resolute Group, a reinsurance subsidiary set up to insure other insurers. Also in that year, the company formed the GEICO Investment Services Company.

After selling off its 66 percent interest in GELICO, GEICO made a series of acquisitions. In 1982 the company bought a property casualty insurance company, which wrote standard insurance, and named it GEICO General. The company also bought the Garden State Life Insurance Company and renamed it the GEICO Annuity and Insurance Company. The Criterion Casualty Company also was formed to write policies for young male drivers who could not obtain insurance elsewhere.

In 1984 GEICO increased its level of automation, and this investment was rewarded with lower costs and higher profits. Throughout the 1980s GEICO stuck to its core business of writing insurance policies for good drivers, and the company's financial position steadily improved. By 1991, its profits had reached $193.8 million, and the company had become the country's seventh largest automobile insurer. In an effort to expand its market, GEICO formed an automobile club to compete with the American Automobile Association (AAA) and also tried to increase its market share in the homeowner's insurance field. In addition, the company continued its policy of buying up its own shares, further strengthening its financial position. As GEICO moved into the mid-1990s, the firm appeared to be well suited for continued financial stability. After its close brush with oblivion in the mid-1970s, the company had returned to its original franchise of low-cost insurance for good drivers, using no middlemen, and demonstrated that it could thrive in this niche.

Strength in Numbers: A Merger for the 21st Century

In April 1995, as part of its push to strengthen its position as a premier auto insurer, GEICO made the controversial decision to phase out its homeowners insurance plan. To ease the transition for the more than 438,000 policyholders affected by the change, the company entered into an agreement with Aetna, whereby Aetna would automatically assume responsibility for GEICO's homeowner policies once they expired. Although GEICO went to great lengths to reassure its policyholders that Aetna's rates would be comparable to its own, the change still caused a number of problems, particularly for GEICO policyholders in Alaska, Hawaii, and Mississippi, where Aetna did not offer coverage. Meanwhile, the company's earnings remained strong in the early part of 1995, with first quarter profits up more than 75 percent from the year before.

GEICO's financial profile changed dramatically in August, however, when majority stockholder Warren Buffett, founder and CEO of Berkshire Hathaway Inc., announced his intention to acquire the remaining shares in the company for $2.3 billion. Buffett's involvement with GEICO spanned more than 40 years, starting in 1951 when, as a 20-year-old business student at Columbia, he invested 70 percent of his net worth in the auto insurer. By 1976 Buffett was able to purchase an additional $45.7 million worth of shares, giving him a 15 percent stake in the company. Over the next 20 years this investment grew to be worth more than $2 billion.

Buffett attributed much of Berkshire Hathaway's profit increases during the following two years to the GEICO acquisition. The parent company's second quarter profits in 1997 surpassed $275 million, an increase of more than $85 million from 1996, and in January 1998 Berkshire Hathaway's Class A stock surpassed the $50,000 mark per share for the first time.

Buffett also had big ambitions for his new company. Intent on increasing its market share from 3 to 10 percent, GEICO began relaxing its formerly strict standards regarding driving records. In March 1998 GEICO launched a $100 million marketing campaign that targeted a wider range of drivers, including college students. The company also sought to expand its presence geographically, launching a renewed effort to expand its client base west of the Mississippi. GEICO's direct sales strategy paid off; by mid-year the company was adding 10,000 new drivers a week. During this growth spurt the company was able to expand its regional operations, adding 2,500 new jobs to its Macon, Georgia offices and renovating its Virginia Beach facilities. The company also was able to lower its rates in a number of states, including Maryland, Texas, and California.

The year 1999 brought hard times for the company, however. It began in the early part of the year, when allegations of customer fraud surfaced in Scottsdale, Arizona. According to complaints, a number of auto insurers, including GEICO, had been demanding that repair shops use aftermarket parts when repairing vehicles for which they were liable. Although GEICO's auto insurance policy clearly stated that repairs would be made with parts of "like kind and quality," these "imitation" parts were arguably inferior, and potentially dangerous. The scandal eventually led to litigation, and in September 1999 the city of Scottsdale, Arizona, filed suit against the company.

During this same period, an increase in the number of underwriting losses resulted in weaker profits for the company, and in the first quarter of 2000 GEICO suffered a total underwriting loss of more than $86 million. Although the company had increased its market share at least 40 percent under Berkshire's ownership, the sudden downturn made rate hikes inevitable. By 2001 it remained to be seen if GEICO's more liberal driver policy would pay off.

Principal Subsidiaries

Government Employees Insurance Company; GEICO General Insurance Company; GEICO Indemnity Insurance Company; GEICO Casualty Insurance Company.

Principal Competitors

The Allstate Corporation; State Farm Insurance Companies; Travelers Property Casualty Corp.

Further Reading

Barboza, David, "Following the Buffett Formula; Geico Chief May Be Heir to a Legend," *New York Times,* April 29, 1997.

Bremner, Brian, "GEICO's Acceleration Is No Accident," *Business Week,* March 30, 1992.

Dickson, Martin, "Lessons from History: Martin Dickson on Berkshire Hathaway's Plans to Buy the Rest of Geico," *Financial Times* (London), August 28, 1995.

Everly, Steve, "Insurer's Phaseout Draws Fire; GEICO Tells Customers It Intends to Drop Homeowner Coverage," *Kansas City Star,* April 15, 1995.

"Geico Builds on New Confidence," *New York Times,* August 16, 1979.

"GEICO's Financial Position Strong," *Journal of Commerce,* November 10, 1977.

"Is the Party Over?," *Forbes,* November 15, 1973.

Lowe, Janet, "Buffett's GEICO Saga Called a Lesson in Investing," *Omaha World Herald,* September 5, 1995.

Meyer, Gene, "Auto Parts Verdict Has a Lot of Experts Guessing," *Kansas City Star,* October 10, 1999.

"Why GEICO Is Acquiring More of Itself," *Business Week,* September 12, 1983.

Zonana, Victor F., "Geico Says '77 Net May Top $32 Million, A Sharp Turnaround from Recent Losses," *Wall Street Journal,* March 31, 1977.

—Elizabeth Rourke
—update: Stephen Meyer

General Cable

General Cable Corporation

4 Tesseneer Drive
Highland Heights, Kentucky 41076-9753
U.S.A.
Telephone: (859) 572-8000
Fax: (859) 572-8458
Web site: http://www.generalcable.com

Public Company
Incorporated: 1927
Employees: 8,600
Sales: $2.69 billion (2000)
Stock Exchanges: New York
Ticker Symbol: BGC
NAIC: 335929 Other Communication and Energy Wire Manufacturing

General Cable Corporation, with its headquarters located in Highland Heights, Kentucky, is the third largest wire and cable manufacturer in the world, and the largest in the United States, with sales approaching $3 billion a year. General Cable designs, manufactures, and distributes products for the communications, energy, and electrical markets. Its communications' wire and cable, including fiber optics, is used in a variety of voice, data, and video applications. Its energy cables are used for power transmission either suspended in the air, or laid underground or underwater. General Cable's electrical wire and cable products are used in the wiring of buildings as well as in common consumer goods. Its more recognizable brand names include Romex, Carol, Aniconda, BICC, and Brand Rex. The company operates a total of 38 manufacturing facilities in nine different countries.

Formation of General Cable: 1920s

General Cable has undergone a number of name changes and ownership arrangements over the years. The original corporation dates back to the 1920s when a dozen cable and wire manufacturers were combined, many of which could boast rich histories of their own. The oldest was the Standard Underground Cable Company, founded by the prolific American inventor George Westinghouse in 1882. In that year, Thomas Edison ushered in the age of electricity when he built the Pearl Street generating station to distribute power to the Wall Street district of Manhattan. Edison relied on direct current, which could travel only short distances, thus requiring a large number of power generating plants. Westinghouse, on the other hand, focused on alternating current, which could be transmitted long distances, required fewer power plants, and could be located in less populated areas. As he did with most of his inventions, Westinghouse formed companies to supply the necessary support products, such as cables in the case of his power generating enterprise. Westinghouse would lose control over most of his companies during the financial panic of 1907.

General Cable came together in two phases. First in 1925 Safety Insulated Wire & Cable Co. of Bayonne, New Jersey, acquired two smaller companies to create Safety Cable Co. After further acquiring two Chicago companies, Safety Cable in 1927 was then combined with Standard Underground Cable and several other companies in a deal executed by the banking firm of Kissel, Kinnicutt & Co. to form the General Cable Corporation. One of the acquisitions was a copper sheet mill that would be unloaded the following year, when the new corporation would also bring yet another cable company into its fold. In essence, this merger of a dozen companies was a banker's attempt at vertical integration, a move reminiscent of J.P. Morgan's creation of United Steel. This was a different era, however, and the benefits of combining so many assets in the cable and wire industry were not as apparent.

The many transactions left General Cable saddled with a great deal of debt. Many of its 22 manufacturing plants, spread across 14 different locations, were out of date and virtually worthless, serving only to falsely inflate the corporation's worth. The integration of a number of operations held some promise for General Cable, which had become one of only six companies with the capability of producing wire from start to finish; but whatever benefits it might derive were offset by a top-heavy management structure, which included 37 corporate officers. Each of the company's five main divisions operated separately and boasted its own set of highly paid executives. At one point, General Cable devoted a large open room in its New

York headquarters to serve as a visiting vice-president's lounge. Not surprisingly, General Cable's many executives scrambled for position in the corporate hierarchy.

The flush economic times of the late 1920s covered over a number of potential problems. General Cable posted an impressive profit of $5 million in 1929. With the crash of the stock market and the onset of the Great Depression, however, General Cable was forced to face some hard realities. Because its business was so dependent on copper, the company had focused a good deal of its attention, and hope for profit, on speculation of the raw commodity. Unfortunately, when the music stopped in 1929 General Cable was left holding a huge inventory of copper that it had bought at 24 cents a pound. The price would drop all the way to five cents a pound in 1932, a major factor in the five straight years of losses that the company would suffer.

Dwight Palmer: Steering Company Through the Depression

An executive named Dwight R.G. Palmer, who came to the company through the smallest of the 1925 acquisitions, would change the fortunes of General Cable. With the company on the verge of collapse in 1932 it was Palmer who found a new source of business in the Hoover Dam. The city of Los Angeles had already drawn up plans to build a power line from the dam but lacked the funds to implement it. Palmer helped Los Angeles to get funding from Washington, then won the bid to provide the cable. That work would lead to other major power line contracts at the Bonneville and Grand Coulee dams. As a result of his efforts, Palmer was named president of General Cable in 1933. At odds with the chairman of the board over the company's speculation on copper and the need to trim fat, particularly in the management structure, Palmer eventually won out. In 1936 the General Cable board named him the chief executive officer of the company.

General Cable enjoyed its best year since 1929 when it posted a $1.65 million profit in 1936, but the rest of the 1930s proved less successful. Like most of American industry, General Cable would have to wait until World War II before it completely overcame the effects of the Depression. As early as 1938 Palmer recognized that war was inevitable, and despite being called a warmonger, he made a public appeal for a defense program. In the meantime, while other companies shied away from military contracts, General Cable became France's sole supplier of wire until the country fell in 1940; likewise, it became Britain's first and most important source of wire. When the United States did become involved in the war, General Cable was prepared to ratchet up production to unprecedented levels. Virtually overnight, the company expanded from operating six plants with 2,000 employees to operating ten plants with 12,000 employees, who worked around the clock, seven days a week.

General Cable was recognized for its wartime production. It supplied 80 percent of all communication wire used by the Army Signal Corps and allied armies, a third of all Navy wire and cable needs, and 56 percent of the wire and cable used by the Maritime Commission. In all, General Cable produced ten times more wire and cable during the war than its nearest competitor. When Palmer was told by the Pentagon to cut back on production in 1944 in anticipation of the end of the war, Palmer actually stepped up production and the military bought every inch that General Cable could turn out. Then in May 1945, with the military advising against it, Palmer began to cut back. Projecting that the war would end by September 1, he had but a two-week supply of goods on hand when the Japanese finally surrendered in August, bringing World War II to a close. Thus, when some $66 million in orders were subsequently canceled, General Cable was not left holding excess inventory.

General Cable did not make huge profits, but it came out of the war with a much more solid business going forward. It cut back to operating just six manufacturing plants, finally liquidated facilities that it had closed in the 1930s, and for the next few years worked to eliminate the debt that had hindered its growth in the past. It was not until the 1950s that General Cable initiated an expansion plan. It built new plants in Illinois, California, Florida, and Texas. General Cable also began to acquire other companies. In 1955 it purchased the outstanding stock of General Insulated Wire Works. A year later it added the Clifton Conduit Company, Alphaduct Wire & Cable, and General Insulated Wire Works. In 1957 General Cable acquired the Metal Textile Corporation, and in 1959 the Cornish Wire Company.

In addition to manufacturing its traditional wire and cable products, General Cable now produced galvanized steel wire and strand, terminal housings, and equipment for cable installation and maintenance. It also moved into the communications field. Profits that stood at $3.4 million in 1950 reached $8.7 million by the end of the decade. At its peak in 1956, General Cable posted a $12 million profit.

General Cable underwent both expansion and contraction in the 1960s. The number of plants, which stood at just six in 1950, would reach a peak of 41 in 1967. By 1970 the number would be reduced to 35. General Cable closed some plants while building new ones, as well as forming joint ventures to expand its business overseas. The best year of the 1960s was 1966 when General Cable realized a profit of $31.2 million.

Business was generally sluggish during the lean economic years of the early 1970s. In 1973 General Cable moved its executive offices from Manhattan to Greenwich, Connecticut. The company made a major acquisition in 1976 with the $67 million purchase of Sprague Electric Company, makers of electronic and electrical circuit components, and the largest U.S. manufacturer of fixed capacitors. In that same year, General Cable completed pioneering work with fiber optics cable for the U.S. Air Force.

In 1978 General Cable made a number of moves that would further diversify its business and launch the company onto a new path. It sold its Power & Control operation to Pirelli Cable

---

Key Dates:

1882: Oldest of General Cable companies, Standard Underground Cable, is established by George Westinghouse.

1927: Twelve companies are merged to create General Cable.

1933: Dwight Palmer is named president and CEO.

1973: Corporate headquarters are moved from Manhattan to Greenwich, Connecticut.

1979: Name is changed to GK Technologies.

1981: Company is acquired by Penn Central Corporation.

1992: Penn Central spins off wire and cable assets to reform General Cable with corporate headquarters in Kentucky.

1994: Wassall PLC acquires company.

1997: General Cable becomes independent via public stock offering.

1999: General Cable acquires energy cable business of BICC Plc for $440 million.

Corporation for $58 million in March 1978, then in May acquired Automation Industries for $106 million to gain a presence in engineering and technical services as well as environmental products. In September General Cable raised $53 million on a new issue of stock, which it then used to purchase 2.8 million shares of stock in the British company BICC Limited.

Changing Name to GK Technologies: 1979

To better reflect its new mix in business, the company changed its name in 1979 to GK Technologies (although it legally preserved the General Cable Corporation name). A year later it would see sales reach $1.2 billion and realize a profit of more than $70 million. It also began discussions to sell the company to the Penn Central Corporation, controlled by Cincinnati financier Carl H. Linder, whose company held varied interests in electronics, defense, telecommunications, and energy. In May 1981, Penn Central acquired all of the stock of GK Technologies and merged it with other assets to form a separate unit within the corporation. Penn Central added to its cable and wire businesses during the 1980s, although Linder was experiencing some troubles with his finances. By 1987 one of the businesses he controlled, Los Angeles-based Mission Insurance, was operating under Chapter 11 of the U.S. Bankruptcy Code. In that same year, Penn Central talked about spinning off the Sprague Electrical Company that General Cable had acquired in 1976. Sprague was part of Penn Central's electronics division, which lost almost $155 million in 1986.

When a downturn in the construction industry in the early 1990s left Penn Central holding an excess in wire inventories, it was the wire and cable assets that were spun off in 1992. Reclaiming the name General Cable Corporation, this new entity was still owned by Linder. After some sparring between Ohio and Kentucky, General Cable was induced by tax breaks to locate its corporate headquarters in Highland Heights, Kentucky. The company, however, did not fare well. It lost more than $69 million in 1992 and another $57.8 million in 1993.

General Cable was purchased for $270 million in cash and assumed debt in June 1994 by Wassall PLC, a British manufacturing holding company.

Wassall hired Stephen Rabinowitz, a former General Electric executive, to take over General Cable. He faced a situation similar to that of Palmer 60 years earlier: too many executives operating their own enclaves within the corporation. Rabinowitz quickly cut down the size of the senior staff, as well as inventory and overhead costs. He returned annual sales above the $1 billion mark and, after a net loss in 1994, began to post increasing profits. Rabinowitz developed a "Power of One" strategy, which essentially concentrated on the company's large customers. General Cable sought to provide one-stop shopping for all wire and cable needs, forming joint ventures and relying on sourcing contracts to fill in the gaps. The most surprising line of business for the new General Cable was the old product of copper-based cable. While many competitors left the field in favor of fiber optics, General Cable found that the need for copper-based products was never higher. Fiber optics was little more than a product that General Cable produced because its customers wanted to buy it and the Power of One concept required it.

In order to concentrate on other areas, Wassall sold off 80 percent of its interest in General Cable through a public stock offering in May 1997. It sold the remaining interest a few months later. Rabinowitz remained in charge of General Cable, which now traded on the New York Stock Exchange under the symbol BGC. The company continued to enjoy healthy growth in sales and profits in both 1997 and 1998. Then in 1999 General Cable made a major acquisition when it purchased the energy cable business of BICC Plc for $440 million. BICC was reportedly troubled by takeover rumors and was selling off interests in order to focus on its core construction business. The BICC deal instantly made General Cable one of the largest wire and cable companies in the world. While retaining the General Cable corporate name, the company began operating as BICC General.

The assimilation of the BICC assets, however, did not proceed as smoothly as Rabinowitz had hoped. Although sales almost doubled, topping $2 billion, profits in 1999 fell from $71.2 million the year before to just $34.3 million. In order to pay down debt, General Cable sold off its under-performing BICC-acquired businesses in Europe, Africa, and Asia to a subsidiary of the Italian company Pirelli S.p.A. for $216 million. At the time of the divestiture, the company once again began using General Cable as its go-to-market name. General Cable then moved to expand its business into Mexico, the Caribbean, and Central and South America, using the $23 million purchase of Mexican cable maker Telmag to gain a presence in the region.

Although it lost $26 million in 2000, General Cable posted record sales of $2.7 billion. With a solid management structure in place, and the BICC deal fully digested, General Cable appeared ready to take its place as a global leader in the wire and cable industry.

Principal Subsidiaries

BICC General Cable Company; Carol Cable; GK Technologies; Marathon Manufacturing Holdings, Inc.; MLTC Company.

Principal Competitors

Alcatel S.A.; Cable Design Technologies; Corning; Pirell S.p.A.; Sumitomo Electric Industries; Tyco International Ltd.

Further Reading

Deutsch, Claudia H., "Rising Stock Price and Profits Reflect a Tough Three Years of Revamping at General Cable," *New York Times,* November 28, 1997, p. D2.

Frazier, Mya, "General Cable Returning to Profitable Outlook," *Cincinnati Business Courier,* December 8, 2000, p. 24.

"General Cable," *Fortune,* October 1947, pp. 99–104, 184–90.

"General Cable to Buy BICC Cable Business for About $440 Million," *Wall Street Journal,* April 8, 1999.

Rishtmyer, Richard, "General Cable Is on a Roll," *Electronic Buyers' News,* November 9, 1998, p. 33.

Yafie, Roberta C., "General Cable, BICC Linkup Is Synergistic," *American Metal Market,* April 9, 1999, p. 4.

—Ed Dinger

General Dynamics Corporation

3190 Fairview Park Drive
Falls Church, Virginia 22042-4253
U.S.A.
Telephone: (703) 876-3000
Fax: (703) 876-3125
Web site: http://www.gendyn.com

Public Company
Incorporated: 1925 as Electric Boat Company
Employees: 43,400
Sales: $10.36 billion (2000)
Stock Exchanges: New York Chicago Pacific
Ticker Symbol: GD
NAIC: 334419 Other Electronic Component Manufacturing; 334511 Search, Detection, Navigation, Guidance, Aeronautical, and Nautical System and Instrument Manufacturing; 335312 Motor and Generator Manufacturing; 336411 Aircraft Manufacturing; 336413 Other Aircraft Parts and Auxiliary Equipment Manufacturing; 336414 Guided Missile and Space Vehicle Manufacturing; 336611 Ship Building and Repairing; 336992 Military Armored Vehicle, Tank, and Tank Component Manufacturing

General Dynamics Corporation is a leading defense contractor, with nearly 60 percent of the company's net sales coming from contracts with the U.S. government. The company's largest operating unit is Marine Systems, which accounts for about one-third of sales, is the leading supplier of combat vessels to the U.S. Navy, and includes Electric Boat Corporation (the founding company), maker of the Seawolf and Virginia-class submarines; and Bath Iron Works (acquired in 1995), maker of destroyers and amphibious assault ships. The Combat Systems unit, which generates about 12 percent of net sales, produces the M1 tank for the U.S. Army (a business purchased from Chrysler Corporation in 1982) as well as other land and amphibious assault vehicles; it also makes gun and ammunition handling systems, reactive armor, and ordnance. Accounting for nearly one-quarter of sales is the Information Systems and Technology unit, which offers to both defense and commercial customers a wide range of technologies, including communication, computer, defense, electronic, information, and telecommunications systems. The Information Systems unit was created out of a series of acquisitions that began in 1997. Generating the bulk of General Dynamics' revenues from commercial customers is its Aerospace unit, which consists of Gulfstream Aerospace (acquired in 1999), one of the world's leading makers of business aircraft. Approximately 30 percent of overall revenues are derived from the operations of Gulfstream.

The Early Decades As Electric Boat

General Dynamics has a long history in weapons production, originating in the late 19th century with an Irish-American inventor named John Holland. Associated with the Fenians, a secret New York City organization sympathetic to the struggles of the Irish nationalists, Holland was commissioned to construct a submarine capable of destroying British naval vessels. While previous submarine designs had been attempted by other inventors, none were effective warships, and, in fact, several of Holland's first submarines sank. Moreover, his ill-conceived attempts at secrecy soon drew the attention of American law enforcement authorities, who prevented Holland from achieving his mission for the Fenians. Nevertheless, Holland remained interested in building a viable submarine, and, toward that end, he founded the Electric Boat Company in 1899, with financial backing from investors that later would include various members of Congress.

Once he developed a prototype, Holland had difficulty finding a market for his submarine, as the U.S. Navy was not initially interested in the project. Then, lawyer, financier, and battery and electronics magnate Isaac Leopold Rice offered to finance the development of subsequent Holland submarines in return for an interest in Electric Boat. Holland was persuaded to relinquish his patent rights and management authority to Rice, who successfully made sales to the U.S. Navy and several other foreign naval services. Holland effectively lost control of the company and found himself earning a salary of $90 per week as chief engineer, while the company he founded was selling submarines for $300,000 each.

Electric Boat gained a reputation for unscrupulous arms dealing in 1904–05, when it sold submarines to Japan and Russia, who were then at war. Holland submarines were also sold to the British Royal Navy through the English armaments company Vickers. Submarines, which had once been denounced in Britain as "damned un-English"—considered too sly and cowardly for use in a proper gentleman's war—were now legitimized as genuine naval weapons by the world's most powerful navy.

During this time, Holland lost patience with Rice and resigned in protest at being excluded from his company's affairs. A frail man plagued by a respiratory condition since birth, Holland died shortly thereafter in 1914. He was replaced as chief engineer by Lawrence Spear who, in close association with Vickers, redesigned the Holland submarine. Speed was improved, a conning tower and periscope replaced the Holland observation dome, and torpedo tubes were incorporated for the first time. The full potential of the submarine, however, was not fully recognized until World War I, when German U-boats caused serious disruptions in British shipping.

Isaac Rice died in 1915 and was replaced by his associate Henry Carse. Under Carse, Spear was given greater control over the company's operations. Electric Boat had a substantial backlog of profitable orders and was financially strong enough to purchase several companies, including Electro Dynamics (involved in ship propulsion), Elco Motor Yacht (builders of pleasure boats), and New London Ship & Engine of Groton, Connecticut (manufacturers of diesel engines and civilian ships). The company's name was changed to the Submarine Boat Corporation in 1917.

When the United States became involved in World War I, Carse made the crucial decision to devote the company's resources to the construction of disposable cargo vessels rather than submarines. Eventually realizing his mistake, Carse began to retool for submarine production; before the process could be completed, however, the war had ended, and the company had lost a great deal of money. Moreover, the U.S. Navy then decided to devote most of its reduced postwar budget to surface ships. Faced with bankruptcy, Carse reorganized the company, emphasized production of surface ships, and brought back the Electric Boat Company name in 1925.

On the eve of World War II, the business practices of Electric Boat came under investigation by the U.S. government and several independent groups; the company was accused of being a "financial beneficiary" of foreign wars. Electric Boat was also found to have inadvertently given design secrets to officials of the increasingly hostile government of Japan. In an investigation led by Senator Gerald Nye, Electric Boat was accused of profiteering, graft, and unethical business practices.

Carse responded that, because the U.S. Navy had suspended all major contracts for ten years, Electric Boat had been forced to deal with foreign governments—many of which were corrupt—in order to remain financially solvent.

During this time, the German remilitarization and hostile Japanese activities forced the Roosevelt Administration to reassess its position on military preparedness. Consequently, the government placed orders for submarines and PT (patrol/torpedo) boats from Electric Boat facilities at Groton and the Elco plant in New Jersey. The new orders led to the revitalization of Electric Boat, now led by John Jay Hopkins, appointed in 1937 by the retiring Lawrence Spear, who himself had taken over when Henry Carse retired. While Spear continued to offer advice from his retirement, Hopkins was thoroughly in charge and fully responsible for the company's strong reemergence.

Following the American declarations of war against the Axis powers, Electric Boat and its Elco Yacht and Electro Dynamic subsidiaries mobilized for production at full capacity. This sudden expansion in output caused a serious labor shortage, which was filled by women, who took jobs as welders and riveters. During the war, the Electric Boat companies produced hundreds of submarines, surface ships, and PT boats, contributing greatly to the success of island fighting in the Pacific. When the war ended in 1945, the Navy reduced its orders for new vessels. Only 4,000 of the company's 13,000 wartime employees were retained after the war, and Electric Boat stock fell in value from $30 per share to $10.

Diversifying in the Postwar Era As General Dynamics

As a result, Hopkins initiated another reorganization of Electric Boat, which included a diversification into related commercial and defense industries. In 1947 Electric Boat purchased Canadair Limited from the Canadian government for $22 million. Canadair produced flying boats and modified DC-4s during the war, but had greatly diminished sales during peacetime. A series of events, including the Berlin Blockade, Soviet detonation of an atomic bomb, and the war in Korea, stimulated demand for new aircraft, including the T-33 trainers, F-86 Sabres, and DC-6s built under contract by Canadair. By the early 1950s, Canadair's success began overshadowing that of Electric Boat; some business advisers even suggested that Canadair purchase Electric Boat and operate it as a subsidiary. Instead, on February 21, 1952, a new parent company called General Dynamics Corporation was established to manage the operations of Canadair and Electric Boat.

With substantial profits from its Canadair subsidiary, General Dynamics purchased Consolidated Vultee Aircraft from the Atlas Corporation in 1954. Consolidated, which became General Dynamics' Convair Division, manufactured a variety of civilian and military aircraft, including the 440 passenger liner, F-102 and F-106 fighters, Atlas and Centaur rockets, and the B-24, B-36, and B-58 Hustler bombers.

Convair led the development of the American nuclear aircraft program, enthusiastically supported by the Pentagon. CEO Hopkins was a strong advocate of nuclear power and its numerous applications, but the nuclear airplane, or "N-bomber," was

Key Dates:

1899: Electric Boat Company is founded to build submarines.

1917: Company's name is changed to Submarine Boat Corporation.

1925: Company is reorganized and reincorporated as Electric Boat Company; expansion into surface ships begins.

1937: John Jay Hopkins joins company and is instrumental in its revival through the production of hundreds of submarines, surface ships, and PT boats during World War II.

1947: Canadair Limited is acquired.

1952: General Dynamics Corporation is established as a successor to Electric Boat and as a parent company for Electric Boat and Canadair.

1954: General Dynamics acquires Consolidated Vultee Aircraft, which becomes the Convair Division; Electric Boat launches the first nuclear submarine, the *Nautilus.*

1959: General Dynamics and Material Services Corporation merge.

1971: Company relocates its headquarters to St. Louis.

1976: Canadair is sold back to the Canadian government.

1978: Fort Worth Division begins production of the F-16 combat fighter.

1982: General Dynamics purchases Chrysler's battle tank division, which becomes the Land Systems Division.

1985: Cessna Aircraft Co. is acquired.

1991: With end of Cold War, new CEO William A. Anders begins divestment program that reduces the company to two businesses by 1994: submarines and armored vehicles.

1992: Cessna is sold to Textron Inc.; company headquarters is moved to Falls Church, Virginia.

1993: The Fort Worth Division is sold to Lockheed Corporation.

1994: The Space Systems Division is sold to Martin-Marietta.

1995: Bath Iron Works, a major shipbuilder, is acquired.

1997: The company's Information Systems and Technology unit begins to be built through a series of acquisitions.

1998: National Steel and Shipbuilding Company, owner of a San Diego naval shipyard, is acquired.

1999: General Dynamics completes two major acquisitions: Gulfstream Aerospace Corporation, maker of business jets, and three information systems units of GTE Corporation.

later found to be impractical, and the project was abandoned. Electric Boat enjoyed greater success with nuclear power; in 1954 it launched the first nuclear submarine, the *Nautilus.*

The company's development of commercial jetliners came near the end of Hopkins' tenure. While Douglas and Boeing were developing their DC-8 and 707 passenger jets, Convair was unable to introduce its jetliner because the company was

delayed by contractual obligations to TWA and its eccentric and intrusive majority shareholder Howard Hughes. Specifically, Convair was bound to incorporate numerous design changes suggested by Hughes. As the result of a financial crisis that postponed TWA's purchase of jetliners and eventually forced Hughes out of TWA, Convair was unable to recover from the delayed entry of its 680 and 880 models into the jetliner market. General Dynamics was forced to write off the entire passenger liner program with a $425 million loss.

The financial position of General Dynamics was so seriously weakened by the Convair jetliner program that the company was targeted for a takeover by Henry Crown, a Chicago construction materials magnate. Crown offered to merge his profitable Material Services Corporation with General Dynamics in exchange for a 20 percent share of the new company's stock, and the proposal was accepted in 1959. Two years later, Crown appointed Roger Lewis as chairperson of General Dynamics. Under Lewis, General Dynamics purchased the Quincy shipbuilding works from Bethlehem Steel in 1963 for $5 million. Quincy, then an outdated facility requiring costly improvements, held promise as a builder of surface ships.

In the early 1960s, the U.S. Defense Department invited American defense contractors to bid for the production of a new aircraft, the F-111, slated to replace the Department's aging fleet of B-52 bombers. General Dynamics entered the competition in partnership with the Grumman Corporation, against a design submitted by Boeing. Even though many regarded the Boeing F-111 as the better built and the more capable plane, the General Dynamics/Grumman version was consistently declared superior by Pentagon officials and industry experts. An investigation of impropriety in the selection process was interrupted when President Kennedy was assassinated in November 1963 and was not concluded until 1972.

General Dynamics continued to develop its version of the F-111 at its Convair facility in Fort Worth, Texas. The Air Force and Navy amended their design specifications and requested the addition of so many devices that the prototype could barely fly. With its utility as a replacement for the B-52 greatly diminished, the aircraft's role was reassessed, and the project was eventually identified by congressional critics as an example of gross mismanagement, organizational incompetence, and financial irresponsibility. The F-111 project consumed an inordinate amount of the defense budget and delayed by six years the introduction of Grumman's similar—and in many ways superior—F-14 Tomcat.

In 1966, Lewis removed Crown from the company by repossessing his 18 percent share of nonvoting company stock. Crown was paid $120 million for his shares, but lost control of both General Dynamics and Material Services Corporation. Over the next few years, Crown continued to purchase substantial numbers of shares of voting stock, expanding his interest until he emerged in 1970 with control over the board of directors. Lewis was summarily fired and replaced by David Lewis (of no relation). Crown subsequently moved the company from New York to St. Louis in February 1971.

That year, the Electric Boat division of General Dynamics and its chief competitor, Newport News Shipbuilding, were awarded contracts to manufacture a new submarine, the 688, or *Los Angeles* class. Two years later, General Dynamics hired Takis Veliotis to take charge of the Quincy shipbuilding yard. Once in charge at Quincy, Veliotis concluded an agreement to build liquefied natural gas tankers in conjunction with a cold storage engineering firm called Frigitemp.

During this period, the Defense Department announced a $200 million competition for the production of a new jet fighter. Careful to avoid the problems that plagued the F-111, General Dynamics initiated its development of the F-16. The F-16 program closely followed its development and budget schedules, and the first prototype exceeded specifications.

Although it was apparently chosen over the Northrop F-17 Cobra, the F-16 faced an unexpected challenge from McDonnell Douglas's independently developed F-15 Eagle. The lower-priced F-15 took a significant portion of the fighter market away from General Dynamics, whose Fort Worth Division began producing the F-16 in 1978. The U.S. government, however, compensated General Dynamics by promoting sales of the F-16 to NATO countries and other American allies. Canadair, which manufactured aircraft for Commonwealth countries, was sold back to the Canadian government in 1976 for $38 million.

The following year, Admiral Rickover publicly berated Electric Boat for poor workmanship and cost overruns on 18 *Los Angeles* class submarines. Rickover was particularly upset about the U.S. Navy's contractual obligation to absorb a large portion of the overruns, which were running as high as $89 million per vessel. A dispute then arose between the Defense Department and Electric Boat, wherein Electric Boat threatened to halt production of the submarines unless its share of the losses were covered as well. General Dynamics sought the protection of Public Law 85-804, which was originally intended to protect ''strategic assets,'' such as Lockheed and Grumman, from bankruptcy due to cost overruns.

General Dynamics won a settlement from the Pentagon but soon realized that its problems at Groton were not merely financial. Productivity was seriously compromised by absenteeism and an employee turnover rate of 35 percent. Management lost control over inventories, and poor workmanship resulted in costly reconstruction. In October 1977, David Lewis transferred Takis Veliotis from Quincy to Groton, with instructions to reform the operation. Within months Veliotis had restored discipline, efficiency, and financial responsibility at Electric Boat.

Addition of Tanks/Land Systems: 1980s

Veliotis left Electric Boat in 1981 to take a seat on the General Dynamics board of directors and to serve as international sales-person and ''company ambassador.'' Later that year, however, Veliotis resigned in protest over a dispute with David Lewis, whom Veliotis claimed had promised him the position of chief executive officer. Soon thereafter, Veliotis was indicted by government prosecutors for illegal business practices. He fled to Greece, maintaining that he had possession of damaging evidence of fraudulent overcharges made by General Dynamics.

In 1982, General Dynamics purchased the Chrysler Corporation battle tank division, with plants located in Warren, Michigan, and Lima, Ohio. The division, renamed Land Systems,

had already secured a government contract to build the Army's next main battle tank, the M-1. Developed in response to newer Soviet tanks such as the T-72, the M-1 was to be powered by a jet turbine and capable of speeds of up to 50 miles per hour. The M-1 also included a computer-guided gun-aiming mechanism designed to assure a high degree of accuracy while the tank was traveling over rough terrain at high speeds.

When the first M-1 prototypes were delivered from Land Systems, several basic design flaws were noticed by Pentagon officials. First, exhaust from the engine was so hot that infantry could not come near the tank for cover under fire. Moreover, the M-1 was fast but prone to breakdown, and it required so much fuel that logistical support became questionable. Finally, the M-1's ammunition bay was too small to carry more than 40 shells. Critics recommended that the M-1 project be canceled in favor of its predecessor, the durable, battle-tested M-60. During this same period, General Dynamics won a government contract to service and maintain TAKX supply ships for the American Rapid Deployment Force.

Also at this time, Lewis and other company officials were called to testify before a congressional subcommittee, which suggested that the company had overcharged the government for supplies and personal expenses. The proceedings initiated separate investigations by the Justice Department and the Internal Revenue Service. Soon after Admiral Rickover was involuntarily retired by Navy Secretary John Lehman, General Dynamics was awarded a government contract to manufacture a number of new boats, including the $500 million Ohio class Trident submarine. The contract eliminated many of the company's disputed charges to the Pentagon and, as a result, led to the cessation of the congressional investigation. Wisconsin Senator William Proxmire criticized these developments by remarking that ''defense contractors like General Dynamics have so much leverage against the government they can flout the laws that govern smaller companies and individuals.''

David Lewis retired in 1985 and was replaced by Stanley C. Pace, formerly head of TRW. Oliver Boileau, president of General Dynamics, was passed over for the position at the insistence of the board of directors and the Crown family, all of whom wished to see an end to the policies of Lewis and his protégés. Pace made several changes at General Dynamics, even before Lewis had left the company. He sold the Quincy shipyard and founded a new division called Valley Systems, established to win contracts for the Reagan Administration's Strategic Defense Initiative. In 1985 he purchased Cessna Aircraft Co. Pace also helped clean up General Dynamics' image by instituting an ethics program, which resulted in the firing of 27 employees.

Post–Cold War Transformation

Several external forces helped shape the conduct of business at General Dynamics in the late 1980s and early 1990s. The U.S.S.R.'s collapse revealed it a much weaker military foe than had previously been believed. The subsequent end of the Cold War soon brought Congressional and public pressure to cut domestic defense budgets. These factors compelled General Dynamics to transform itself into a smaller, more focused company with a higher concentration of international sales. The

Persian Gulf conflict helped boost General Dynamics' tank and F-16 fighter sales to Turkey, Egypt, and Saudi Arabia and opened Middle East markets to the military manufacturer.

In January 1991, William A. Anders was assigned to reorganize General Dynamics according to the new market realities. He assumed the chief executive office, while Stanley Pace took a seat on the company's board of directors. Anders's strategy in the face of industry changes was to cut employees, trim research and development, divest peripheral businesses, and reduce capital spending. By June 1992, Anders had cut 25 percent of the workforce (24,800 employees) and put $1.7 billion in assets up for sale. Gains from divestments were rolled back to shareholders, and, by 1993, almost $600 million in debt was paid, which helped boost the company's share price. General Dynamics, which had suffered a $578 million loss in 1990, recovered to realize a $305 million profit the following year.

Despite the improving financial picture, General Dynamics came under criticism from the Pentagon and Department of Defense for a lucrative executive Gain-Sharing plan that was tied to increases in the company's share price. In 1991 alone, as General Dynamics whittled away at its employee roster, *Business Week* reported that 25 top managers received $18 million in incentive bonuses. The company, meanwhile, relocated its headquarters from St. Louis to Falls Church, Virginia, in 1992.

Anders pronounced the transformation of General Dynamics complete in 1993's annual report. After selling its Missile Division to Hughes Aircraft Company for $450 million and Cessna Aircraft to Textron Inc. for $600 million, both deals coming in 1992, and its Fort Worth Division to Lockheed for $1.5 billion in 1993, as well as reaching an agreement to sell its Space Systems Division (which had been created out of Convair in 1985) to Martin-Marietta (a $209 million deal that was completed in 1994), the company emerged with two primary business segments: nuclear submarines and armored vehicles. The corporate workforce had shrunk from about 86,000 in 1991 to 30,500 in 1993, and debt decreased 94 percent during this period. Government contracts still comprised 94 percent of the company's annual sales, which remained essentially flat over the reorganization period. Operating earnings, however, increased by $98 million, from $211 million in 1991 to $309 million in 1993. That year, Anders relinquished the chief executive office to former president James Mellor and assumed General Dynamics' chair as a transitional measure through April 1994.

Even after the special distributions to shareholders, the company still had more than $1 billion in cash and virtually no debt by late 1994. From this position of strength, Mellor began pursuing acquisitions of related niche businesses to build on General Dynamics' two remaining units. In September 1995 the company acquired Bath Iron Works for $300 million from an investor group led by Prudential Insurance Co. As a result of the deal, General Dynamics owned two of the six major private naval shipyards in the United States: Electric Boat's submarine facility in Groton, Connecticut, and Bath's shipyard in Bath, Maine. Bath, which traced its origins back to the founding of Bath Iron Foundry in 1833, was under contract with the U.S. Navy to build 11 guided-missile AEGIS destroyers. Around the time of the acquisition, the Seawolf submarine program was nearly killed by Congress, an event that might have shut down

Electric Boat's shipyards. Despite objections that the Navy did not need a third Seawolf submarine, Electric Boat was awarded a $1.5 billion contract to build the final such sub, to be called the USS *Jimmy Carter*.

In 1996 the company's Land Systems Division was awarded a $217 million contract to build a new amphibious assault vehicle for the U.S. Marines. Eventual production of more than 1,000 of these vehicles was projected to be worth more than $4 billion through 2014. That same year, Bath was part of an alliance that won a contract to build 12, $800 million amphibious assault ships, the LDP-17, for the Navy. In January 1997 General Dynamics continued its acquisition program with the purchase of two businesses from Lockheed Martin Corporation for $450 million: Armament Systems, a maker of advanced gun and fire-control systems, and Defense Systems, producer of turrets and transmissions for combat vehicles. The bulk of these operations were combined within a new Armament Systems Division, which became part of General Dynamics' Combat Systems unit alongside the Land Systems Division.

In mid-1997 Nicholas D. Chabraja took over as CEO from the retiring Mellor, having previously served as an executive vice-president and general counsel and having played a prominent role in the company's post–Cold War transformation. He almost immediately faced a setback when the company, seeking to expand its position in the area of Army vehicles, was blocked from acquiring United Defense L.P., a maker of military vehicles, because of potential antitrust concerns. Undeterred, Chabraja shifted his immediate acquisition focus to a new niche area: electronics and systems integration, a growth area in which he felt General Dynamics had some expertise. Thus came the formation of a third company operating unit: the Information Systems and Technology unit (Marine Systems and Combat Systems being the other two). The new unit was built through a series of acquisitions that began in 1997. In October of that year Advanced Technology Systems was acquired from Lucent Technologies Inc. for $267 million. Advanced Technology produced undersea surveillance systems, signal processing, and vibration control systems. In December 1997 General Dynamics acquired Computing Devices International, a division of Ceridian Corporation, for $500 million. From this deal came three more pieces of the Information Systems puzzle: General Dynamics Information Systems, Inc.; Computing Devices Canada Ltd.; and the U.K.-based Computing Devices Company Limited. In June 1998 the company acquired another systems integration business called Computer Systems & Communications Corporation.

Chabraja continued to look for acquisition targets in shipbuilding as well. In November 1998 General Dynamics spent $415 million to acquire NASSCO Holdings Incorporated, parent company of National Steel and Shipbuilding Company (NASSCO), which owned a Naval shipyard in San Diego. The addition of NASSCO helped diversify the line of ships built by the Marine Systems unit as the newly acquired company produced hospital ships and combat support ships for the U.S. Navy as well as commercial ships such as oil tankers. General Dynamics now owned half of the six private yards that made Navy ships but when the company made an unsolicited $1.4 billion bid for Newport News Shipbuilding Inc. in early 1999, touting the potential cost savings of the combination, the Pentagon blocked the takeover attempt, citing the dominate position in shipbuilding that General Dynamics would thereby gain.

Once again hardly skipping a beat, General Dynamics concluded two large deals later in 1999. In July 1999 the company returned to the aviation market and also greatly increased the percent of revenues it generated from the commercial market with the acquisition of Gulfstream Aerospace Corporation, a leading maker of business jets, in a stock swap valued at about $5 billion. In September 1999 General Dynamics further bolstered its Information Systems and Technology unit through the $1.01 billion purchase of three business units from GTE Corporation. The units, reorganized within a new entity called General Dynamics Government Systems Corporation, specialized in command, control, communications, and intelligence systems; electronic defense systems; and information systems for defense, government, and industry. The acquisition spree helped propel revenues from the $4.97 billion mark of 1998 to $8.96 billion in 1999. Net income more than doubled, from $364 million to $888 million.

During 2000 NASSCO won a $650 million contract to build three double-hull oil tankers for BP Amoco plc. Also that year a joint venture between the Land Systems Division and General Motors Corporation was selected by the U.S. Army to build an eight-wheeled armored vehicle, the LAV III. The program had a total cost of $4 billion for about 2,100 units. General Dynamics reported net income of $901 million on sales of $10.36 billion for 2000. Early in 2001 the company acquired Primex Technologies Inc., maker of munitions, propellants, satellite propulsion systems, and electronics products, for $520 million. Primex was renamed General Dynamics Ordnance and Tactical Systems and was integrated into the Combat Systems unit.

Principal Subsidiaries

American Overseas Marine Corporation; Bath Iron Works Corporation; CD Plus S.A.R.L. (France); Computer Systems & Communications Corporation; Concord I Maritime Corporation; Concord II Maritime Corporation; Concord III Maritime Corporation; Concord IV Maritime Corporation; Concord V Maritime Corporation; Convair Aircraft Corporation; The Elco Company; Electric Boat Corporation; Electrocom, Inc.; GDIC Corp.; General Dynamics Advanced Technology Systems, Inc.; General Dynamics Armament Systems, Inc.; General Dynamics (C.I.) Limited (Cayman Islands); General Dynamics Defense Systems, Inc.; General Dynamics Foreign Sales Corporation (Virgin Islands); General Dynamics Government Systems Corporation; General Dynamics Information Systems, Inc.; General Dynamics International Corporation; General Dynamics Land Systems Inc.; General Dynamics Limited (U.K.); General Dynamics Manufacturing Limited (Canada); General Dynamics Marine Services, Inc.; General Dynamics Properties, Inc.; General Dynamics Shared Resources, Inc.; Gulfstream Aerospace Corporation; Material Service Resources Company; NASSCO Holdings Incorporated; Patriot I Shipping Corp.; Patriot II Shipping Corp.; Patriot IV Shipping Corp.; S-C 1969 Credit Corporation.

Principal Operating Units

Aerospace; Information Systems and Technology; Marine Systems; Combat Systems.

Principal Competitors

Lockheed Martin Corporation; Raytheon Company; The Boeing Company, Textron Inc., Newport News Shipbuilding Inc.; Airbus Industrie; Bombardier Inc.; Dassault Aviation SA; Electronic Data Systems Corporation; Harris Corporation; L-3 Communications Holdings, Inc.; Litton Industries, Inc.; Racal Electronics Plc; United Defense Industries, Inc.

Further Reading

"Air, Land, and Sea: Big Defense Backlog Suggests Better Days for General Dynamics," *Barron's,* August 30, 1982, pp. 37+.

Berss, Marcia, " 'Are We in the Wrong Business? No,' " *Forbes,* December 25, 1989, pp. 38+.

Bremner, Brian, "General Dynamics Takes a Tomahawk to Itself," *Business Week,* June 22, 1992, p. 36.

Byrne, Harlan S., "Bloody but Unbowed: Despite the Flak, General Dynamics Is Stronger Than Ever," *Barron's,* November 4, 1985, pp. 6+.

Chakravarty, Subrata N., " 'We've Got a Lot of Depth,' " *Forbes,* May 11, 1981, pp. 199+.

Coulam, Robert F., *The Illusion of Choice: The F-111 and the Problem of Weapons Acquisition Reform,* Princeton, N.J.: Princeton University Press, 1977.

Crock, Stan, "General Dynamics Sounds the Charge," *Business Week,* May 19, 1997, pp. 136+.

Curley, John, "General Dynamics Is Facing the Issue of How to Grow As Defense Outlays Slow," *Wall Street Journal,* April 8, 1985.

——, "On the Defensive: Business Is Just Fine at General Dynamics, Yet Troubles Abound," *Wall Street Journal,* May 18, 1984.

Dobrzynski, Judith H., et al., "General Dynamics Under Fire: Inside the Dynasty That Controls General Dynamics," *Business Week,* March 25, 1985, pp. 70+.

Ellis, James E., "General Dynamics: All Cleanup Up with No Place to Grow," *Business Week,* August 22, 1988, pp. 70+.

——, "Layoffs on the Line, Bonuses in the Executive Suite," *Business Week,* October 21, 1991, p. 34.

Frank, Allan Dodds, "The One That Got Away," *Forbes,* January 16, 1984, pp. 31+.

Franklin, Roger, *The Defender: The Story of General Dynamics,* New York: Harper & Row, 1986, 385 p.

"General Dynamics: Striking It Rich on Defense," *Business Week,* May 3, 1982, pp. 102+.

"General Dynamics: The Tangled Tale of Takis Veliotis," *Business Week,* June 25, 1984, pp. 114+.

"General Dynamics: Winning in the Aerospace Game," *Business Week,* May 3, 1976, p. 86.

Goodwin, Jacob, *Brotherhood of Arms: General Dynamics and the Business of Defending America,* New York: Random House, 1985, 419 p.

Greenberger, Robert S., "General Dynamics Temporarily Barred from New U.S. Work After Indictment," *Wall Street Journal,* December 4, 1985.

Miller, William H., "Defense Conversion: The Fourth Time Around," *Industry Week,* April 4, 1994, pp. 20–22+.

Mintz, John, "Attempting to Get Back on Course: Failure of Rocket Launch Shakes General Dynamics," *Washington Post,* April 6, 1993, p. D1.

——, "General Dynamics Flies a Little Lighter," *Washington Post,* March 2, 1993, p. D1.

——, "General Dynamics to Buy Shipyard for $300 Million," *Washington Post,* August 18, 1995, p. D1.

——, "Muscular or Moribund?: It's a Matter of Opinion When It Comes to the Fate of General Dynamics," *Washington Post,* December 26, 1994, p. F1.

Pasztor, Andy, "General Dynamics May Have to Rethink Game Plan," *Wall Street Journal,* August 28, 1997, p. B4.

——, "General Dynamics to Build Through Acquisitions," *Wall Street Journal,* May 18, 1999, p. A4.

——, "General Dynamics to Press Ahead on Acquisition Trail," *Wall Street Journal,* April 15, 1999, p. B12.

Perry, Nancy J., "General Dynamics' Selling Strategy," *Fortune,* January 11, 1993, p. 56.

Rosenberg, Hilary, "Throwing Away the Textbook," *Financial World,* October 1, 1982, pp. 12+.

Smart, Tim, "General Dynamics to Acquire Gulfstream," *Washington Post,* May 18, 1999, p. E1.

——, "Run Silent, Run Profits: Low-Key General Dynamics Is a Top Gun Again," *Washington Post,* November 16, 1998, p. F12.

——, "Virginia Shipbuilder's Sale Scuttled," *Washington Post,* April 15, 1999, p. E1.

Squeo, Anne Marie, "General Dynamics Looks Beyond Tanks to Technology," *Wall Street Journal,* July 25, 2000, p. B4.

Taylor, Robert E., "Defense Firm, NASA Chief Are Indicted: General Dynamics and Aides Said to Have Charged Cost Overrun Improperly," *Wall Street Journal,* December 3, 1985.

Tyler, Patrick, *Running Critical: The Silent War, Rickover and General Dynamics,* New York: Harper & Row, 1987, 374 p.

Worthy, Ford S., "Mr. Clean Charts a New Course at General Dynamics," *Fortune,* April 28, 1986, pp. 70+.

Yenne, Bill, *Into the Sunset: The Convair Story,* Lyme, Conn.: Greenwich Publishing Group, 1995, 112 p.

—April Dougal Gasbarre
—update: David E. Salamie

Gonnella Baking Company

2006 W. Erie St.
Chicago, Illinois 60612
U.S.A.
Telephone: (312) 733-2020
Toll Free: (800) 262-3442
Fax: (312) 733-7670
Web site: http://www.gonnella.com

Private Company
Incorporated: 1886
Employees: 500
Sales: $69 million (2000 est.)
NAIC: 311812 Commercial Bakeries

Gonnella Baking Company is a baker of Italian and French style bread operating primarily in the Chicago area. From fresh bread to frozen dough, Gonnella sells to retailers and restaurants alike through both regional and national distribution. A privately owned family company, Gonnella has built a loyal following in its over 110-year history. It has been ranked as one of the nation's top 100 bakeries and produces nearly 1.5 million pounds of bread products per week. Besides Italian bread, the company also makes frozen dough, fresh frozen baked bread, buns, rolls, breadsticks, and bread crumbs.

A Rising Business in the 1880s and 1890s

In a small storefront on south side Chicago's DeKoven Street, Alessandro Gonnella, an immigrant from Barga, Italy, opened his version of the American dream—a bakery. Alessandro was a hands-on manager because as the store's only employee he was baker, delivery service, salesperson, and accountant. The business, fed with the yeast of Alessandro's dedication, grew and soon allowed his wife, Marianna Marcucci, to join him in the United States from Italy.

In 1896, the business had become so successful that a new location—on Sangamon Street near Ohio Street—was necessary. Soon, the business required more employees as well and help arrived when more family emigrated from Italy to work in

the bakery, namely Alessandro's brothers-in-law—Lawrence, Nicholas, and Luigi Marcucci.

Building for the Future: 1910s–60s

By 1915, Gonnella Bakery was in need of more space once again and a new plant was built on Erie Street in Chicago. As the company had grown delivery methods had also progressed. Now, delivery wagons drawn by horses were required to make over 200 stops each per day.

Several distribution changes throughout the decades changed the customer base that Gonnella served. While once fresh baked bread delivered to homes constituted the biggest percentage of the business, the climate soon changed. An evolution away from home-delivered sales led to higher volume sales to restaurants and grocery stores.

Delivery was no longer reliant on wagons either; the advent of the automobile gave Gonnella a new distribution method—the truck. Soon, Gonnella trucks became a symbol for fresh baked goodness delivered throughout Chicago.

New Products and Challenges in the 1970s

In the early part of the 1970s, a federal investigation looked into antitrust and monopoly complaints regarding Chicago's Italian bakers. Part of the Sherman Act established by Congress on July 2, 1890, antitrust laws were written "to protect trade and commerce against unlawful restraints and monopolies." The complaint against Gonnella was initially filed in October 1972 and settled out of court in August 1974. The final judgment decreed that Gonnella Baking, as well as codefendant Turano Baking Co., were not to "fix, determine, maintain or stabilize prices, discounts or other terms or conditions for the sale of bread to any third person" or "divide, allocate or apportion markets, territories or customers, or refrain from soliciting or accepting bread business from customers doing business with any other person engaged in the baking or sale of bread."

With the threat of antitrust legislation behind it, the company moved into the future with new products. Gonnella introduced frozen bread dough in the mid-1970s. These ready-to-bake

---

Company Perspectives:

Our mission, which springs from our family tradition, is to provide our customers with bakery products of the highest quality combined with a special standard of service. At Gonnella, outstanding breads are only part of our story. Ask any of our clients why they choose Gonnella and you'll understand that the Gonnella name is a name built on service. We were founded on the credo that offering superior service by focusing on the customer's needs is what sets one company apart from another. Today, over a century later, we still remain true in every sense of the word to our founding mission. Every one of our employees from our president to our receptionist will go out of their way to deliver on our promise of customer satisfaction. Whether it's making sure that the special order called in is delivered fresh and on-time, helping you iron out a difficult technical issue, choosing the right mix of products for your operation, or a friendly greeting when you call, we always put our customers first. Put simply, when you deal with Gonnella you're guaranteed to have the best service possible.

---

products allowed the company to sell to grocery stores and restaurants in a larger geographical area. The frozen dough, when shipped to restaurants and groceries, was thawed and baked on location to give more consumers access to fresh-baked bread. The Gonnella trucks were no longer confined to Chicago but were dispatched throughout Illinois and in surrounding states.

Building in the 1980s

In 1980, Gonnella Bakery purchased a plant in Schaumburg, Illinois, to produce frozen dough. The increased manufacturing space and capabilities extended the reach of the bakery into supermarkets, delis, and restaurants in 35 states.

As the company prepared for its 100-year anniversary in 1986, it also began plans to market its fresh frozen bread products nationally. Part of that decision was based on demand from consumers for Gonnella bread in a larger geographic area. "We get calls for bread from Arizona, Florida, places like that," said Louis Marcucci, Gonnella president in *Crain's Chicago Business.* "But we don't ship fresh bread any farther than Indiana." In 1986, the company's revenues were $26 million with profits estimated at $700,000.

Frozen Products Bringing Growth in Early 1990s

The names of some of the employees at Gonnella in the late 20th century were remarkably similar to those who worked in the business over 100 years earlier. In fact, 33 members of the Gonnella and Marcucci families, descendants of the first owners of the business, worked for the company throughout the 1990s.

In 1990, Gonnella's rivalry with Turano Baking hit a new level when both bakeries introduced new products aimed at serving a larger market area. While Turano introduced dry pasta and frozen cannoli, Gonnella introduced a new line of frozen garlic bread.

Sales were estimated at $32 million in a November 12, 1990 article in *Crain's Chicago Business* with rival Turano ringing up sales of $26 million. Frozen bread accounted for one third of Gonnella's sales, which allowed the company to sell to an area of more than 35 states.

In 1994 Gonnella made the decision to outsource its delivery. President Robert A. Gonnella said, "We serve over 4,000 restaurants a day and another 500 institutional customers and retailers."

The decision was a difficult one, as the Gonnella trucks were not only part of the Chicago landscape but a part of Gonnella heritage as well. "One of the ways my grandfather used to measure the success of his business was by the number of trucks we owned," said Gonnella. "One of the most emotional decisions that I ever had to make in business was outsourcing our trucks."

The change, however, was the right thing for the business, noted Gonnella. "We were trying to be experts in everything. We're not in the transportation business, we're in the business of baking."

The following year, *Crain's Chicago Business* reported that half of Gonnella's estimated $41 million in revenues were from frozen dough sold to grocery stores. "No matter how fast or good you are, you can't bake (bread) and get it on the shelf within an hour. In-store bakeries can," said President Robert Gonnella, explaining the popularity of the frozen dough being sold to grocery store chains.

As the demand for fresh food rose, Gonnella found more customers for its frozen dough in the grocery business—such as Jewel Food Stores and Dominick's Finer Foods, Inc. Varieties of frozen dough included Italian, wheat, white, and French.

Creating Opportunity: 2000 and Beyond

In 1999 Gonnella Baking was listed as one of the largest privately held companies in Chicago, according to *Crain's Chicago Business. Crain's* estimated revenues at $84.4 million, and the company had 330 employees. For 2000, sales dropped to $69 million but the number of employees increased to 500. Lou Gonnella was president and CEO of the company; George Marcucci served as CFO.

In 2000, Gonnella was selected as the "official hot dog bun supplier at Wrigley Field." Wrigley Field was renowned as the home ballpark of Major League Baseball's Chicago Cubs. "We view this as a great opportunity to put a greater focus on our hot dog bun business at the retail level. Gonnella has been in business for 114 years and is as much a part of Chicago as the Cubs. Given the appeal of Wrigley Field and its audience demographics, we think we have a winning program for the 2000 baseball season," said Tom Marcucci, vice-president of sales and marketing, in a company press release.

The company found additional promotional opportunities in the form of signage with the Wrigley Field contract and agreed to sponsor "This Week in Cubs History" on the marquee. Paul Gonnella, director of sales said, "the Gonnella name is well recognized in the Chicago area and we believe this arrangement

Key Dates:

1886: Alessandro Gonnella opens the Gonnella Bakery.
1896: The bakery moves to a larger location.
1915: The plant which would later become the corporate headquarters is built.
1970s: Gonnella enters the frozen dough market.
1974: Gonnella reaches out-of-court settlement in federal antitrust case.
1980: Gonnella purchases plant in Schaumburg, Illinois.
1986: The company begins distributing fresh frozen bread products nationally.
1994: Gonnella outsources bread delivery after more than a century of maintaining its own distribution vehicles.
2000: Company is selected as the official hot dog bun supplier to Wrigley Field, home of the Chicago Cubs.

will help our business regionally. We are prepared to increase our market share by dedicating our South Side facility exclusively for the increased production of pan breads, including hot dog buns.''

Also, in 2000 the company launched a web site at www.gonnella.com. The web site offered everything from product lists and distributor information to recipes from the Gonnella cookbook.

What started as a storefront bakery producing a few hundred loaves of bread a week had grown into a thriving manufacturing company with three plants producing more than 1.5 million pounds of bread products each week. Two plants in Chicago and one in Illinois as well as two additional sales/distribution offices in Indianapolis and Wisconsin employed a total of 500 people. Gonnella distributed to an area of 35 states, stretching from coast to coast. The company enjoyed the distinction of being listed several times on *Bakery Production and Marketing Magazine*'s list of the nation's top 100 bakeries.

Principal Competitors

The Earthgrains Company; Heinemann's Bakeries; Interstate Bakeries Corporation.

Further Reading

Anderson, Veronica, ''Consumers Fresh Demand Stirs the Pot for Food Firms; As Some Frozen Sales Cool, Processors Scramble,'' *Crain's Chicago Business*, September 11, 1995.

''Baker Decides to Leave the Driving to the Pros,'' *Food Logistics*, January/February 1998.

Cleaver, Joanne, ''Gonnella Reaches for Slice of Fresh-Frozen Bread Market,'' *Crain's Chicago Business*, March 24, 1986, p. 49.

Crown, Judith, ''Breaking with Bread; Rival Italian Bakers Seek Dough in Pasta, Frozen Foods,'' *Crain's Chicago Business*, November 12, 1990, p. 19.

Mikus, Kim, ''Gonnella Hits Home Run with Cubs;'' *Chicago Daily Herald,* April 13, 2000, p. 1.

—Melissa Rigney Baxter

Groupe Guillin SA

Zone Industrielle
25290 Ornans
France
Telephone: (+33) 481-40-23-23
Fax: (+33) 481-62-15-92
Web site: http://www.groupeguillin.com

Public Company
Incorporated: 1972 as Guillin Emballages
Employees: 740
Sales: EUR 144.83 million ($126.5 million) (2000)
Stock Exchanges: Euronext Paris
Ticker Symbol: GIL
NAIC: 326112 Unsupported Plastics Packaging Film and
Sheet Manufacturing; 541420 Industrial Design Services

Groupe Guillin SA is one of Europe's leading manufacturers of plastics packaging products for the food and related industries. The company holds a leading 65 percent share in its home French market and up to 30 percent of the total European market. Operating through four primary subsidiaries—Guillin Emballages, Alphaform, Dynaplast, and Nespak—Groupe Guillin transforms some 45,000 tons of PET, polypropylene, and polystyrene plastics into more than two billion products per year. The company, which has long played a leading role in the development of new plastics-based packaging products, produces containers and packaging products for supermarket, catering, and general food industries, as well as packaging and products for the fruit and vegetable industry. Led by founder, Chairman, and CEO François Guillin, the company is looking forward to expanding rapidly in the early years of the new century, with plans to double its annual revenues by 2005. The company expects this growth to come as much from acquisitions as from internal expansion. A possible acquisition target is that of Socamel-Rescaset, a French manufacturer of disposable dishes, cookware, and packaging products for the restaurant industry. Since 1999, Guillin has bought up nearly 20 percent of Socamel's shares. In the meantime, Guillin continues to invest in its existing businesses, spending upward of FFr 100 million per year on capital investments to increase and modernize its production capacity. The company has been traded on the public stock market since 1989, beginning with the Lyons stock market before moving to the Paris secondary market. The Guillin family continues to hold 55 percent of the company's stock.

Garage-Based Growth in the 1970s

Groupe Guillin had its start in a garage in the tiny village of Mouthier-HautePierre, in the Loue valley, in 1972. François Guillin, then 24 years old, had installed a machine for pressing plastic trays and found customers for his products among the region's university cafeterias. The company early on concentrated on so-called "short-life" packaging products for fresh foods.

During the 1970s, Guillin turned toward the booming supermarket sector, which was quickly transforming the French retail landscape. The rise of the hypermarket—a particularly French style of department store and supermarket combined in a single, massive sales space—created a new breed of retail empire, which quickly grew to dominate the country's retail scene. It had opened a new market for Guillin, who developed a range of containers especially for the bakery departments of the country's supermarkets and hypermarkets. Among Guillin's earliest customers was the Carrefour chain, credited with inventing the hypermarket concept.

Carrefour's interest in Guillin's products helped put the company on the map. As Guillin commented to *L'Expansion:* "After that, it was fireworks!" Guillin quickly expanded production to include a variety of packaging designs for the various pastries, breads, cakes, and other products found in Carrefour's bakery departments. Other supermarket chains rapidly caught on, turning to the growing Guillin company.

One of the features that marked the company from the beginning was its willingness to innovate, placing a large percentage of its resources into research and development to create new products. In the 1980s, the company extended its range of supermarket containers to the deli department, creating a range of packaging and products specifically designed for the department's meats and prepared foods. Meanwhile, Guillin was finding success beyond the supermarket sector; the company's

Company Perspectives:

Based on its experience and innovation ability, the Guillin Group intends to pursue its development in the service of its customers in order to continually strengthen its rank in Europe and to offer its colleagues and shareholders an environment which meets their expectations.

Key Dates:

1972: François Guillin establishes Guillin Emballages; during its first decade, the company develops a line of pastry containers.

1980: Company develops line of containers for catering and deli counters.

1989: Company is listed publicly on Paris secondary market.

1990: Alphaform and Dynaplast are acquired.

1993: Nespak (Italy) and Gattini are acquired.

1997: Gattini, a money-losing operation, is sold off.

1999: Shares in Socamel-Rescaset are acquired.

2000: Holding in Socamel-Rescaset is increased to 19 percent.

packaging products soon became sought after across much of France's retail catering industry.

By the end of the 1980s, Guillin had moved its headquarters to nearby Ornans and had become a growing company of 120 employees posting sales of FFr 120 million per year. In that year, Guillin, seeking to expand the company, brought it onto the Lyons stock exchange, with a listing on the secondary market. The Lyons stock exchange later was merged with France's other regional exchanges into the single Paris Bourse. Guillin's listing was then transferred to the Paris Bourse's secondary exchange. While the listing helped the company to raise capital for a new period of growth, the Guillin family remained, nonetheless, in majority control of the company's shares.

External Growth in the 1990s

The public listing enabled Guillin to go on a bit of a shopping spree in the early years of the next decade. In 1990, Guillin acquired two companies, Alphaform and Dynaplast. The first of the two, Alphaform, based in the Drôme region, expanded the company's range of plastic trays and containers, while also extending it into the disposable dish and tableware segments. Dynaplast, based in the Yonne region, was to prove a significant addition to Guillin, adding not only its own range of products but especially PET production capacity, bringing Guillin into this fast-rising packaging segment. Dynaplast also manufactured PET sheets for use by other plastics products manufacturers and featured its own strong research and development capacity. Dynaplast was, indeed, to become one of the driving forces of Guillin's continued product innovation.

Instead of integrating its new acquisitions under the existing company, Guillin reformed itself as the Groupe Guillin holding company, placing Dynaplast, Alphaform, and Guillin Emballages as subsidiaries under the new parent. They soon were joined by two new acquisitions. In 1993, Guillin acquired Nespak, based in Italy and Gattini, based in France's Vaucluse region. Nespak expanded Guillin into a new category, that of fruits and vegetables, which quickly became one of the company's fastest growing segments. Gattini, too, added a new product range, that of protective plastic films; yet the Gattini acquisition quickly turned sour and began posting losses through the mid-1990s. After losing some FFr 10 million per year through Gattini, Guillin put the Vaucluse operations up for sale in 1997.

In the meantime, Guillin had come through another crisis. A dramatic rise in raw plastics prices placed Guillin, along with the rest of the packaging industry, under extreme pressure. Faced with customer resistance to any changes in the

company's own prices, Guillin was forced to take a loss in 1994, its first ever year in the red, posting FFr 10.5 million in losses on sales of FFr 650 million. The crisis, which saw prices for the different types of plastics between 25 and 85 percent, also signaled a coming consolidation of the packaging industry, which remained highly fragmented among both large- and small-scale companies. As one analyst described the market to *L'Usine Nouvelle:* "There isn't enough room for everyone anymore. Tomorrow, it will be necessary to be a certain size in order to follow one's clients into all the markets."

Market pressures helped place Guillin's Dynoplast subsidiary under bankruptcy protection by 1996, while the group as a whole recovered its profitability. Meanwhile, after attempting to restructure its Gattini subsidiary, Guillin announced its intention to sell those operations in 1997. The company also had redeveloped its strategy, targeting two core markets for its future growth, those of catering and fruits and vegetables. Through Nespak, Guillin already was able to claim a position as one of Europe's leaders in the fruits and vegetables category. Meanwhile, Guillin began a newly aggressive investment program, construction of a 3,500-square-meter extension of its Guillin Emballages production facility, as well as investing FFr 15 million in a new extrusion line for the Dynoplast operations, while Alphaform was given a FFr 12 million extension into PET plastic sheeting production. Nespak, too, was slated to receive a FFr 20 million investment to increase its production capacity, helping to counteract the loss of FFr 45 million in annual sales as a result of the sell-off of Gattini.

The return to profitability of Dynoplast also helped it stake out new growth prospects, particularly with the company's continued introduction of innovative packaging materials and products. The company's heavy investment program continued into 1998, when it spent FFr 100 million to add thermoforming and extrusion capacity across its part of production facilities.

Guillin promised to grow bigger at the turn of the century. Envisaging new acquisitions, François Guillin told *La Tribune:* "The experience with Gattini permitted us to clarify our strategy and to fix a minimum revenue level of 150 million francs for companies in the group."

At the end of the decade, Guillin appeared to have identified its next acquisition target. In 1999, the company began buying up shares in fellow French packager Socamel-Rescaset. By the middle of 2000, as Guillin's share of Socamel climbed toward 20 percent, Guillin acknowledged its interest in acquiring Socamel, while Socamel's primary shareholder announced its interest in a possible sale. The addition of Socamel not only would add some FFr 450 million in annual sales to Guillin's books, but also would permit Guillin to extend its operations into the restaurant sector. Such moves fitted in well with Guillin's determination to double its annual sales by 2005. At the same time, Guillin expected to expand its international sales—which already accounted for 42 percent of its sales in 2000—positioning itself not only as France's leader in its market segment, but among the top European leaders as well.

Principal Subsidiaries

Alphaform; Dynaplast; Guillin Emballages; Nespak SpA.

Principal Competitors

Amcor Ltd.; Ball Corporation; Bunzl plc; CarnaudMetalbox SA; Crown Cork & Seal Company, Inc.; Huhtamaki Van Leer; Italmobiliare S.p.A.; Pactiv Corporation; Rexam PLC; Sealed Air Corporation; Sonoco Products Company; UNITIKA LTD.

Further Reading

Meyer, Jean-Michel, "L'emballage sous pression," *L'Usine Nouvelle,* October 12, 1995.

Nezzar, Samira, "L'emballeur Guillin cible l'agroalimentaire européen," *La Tribune,* March 5, 1998.

Robert, Martine, "François Guillin: Une mutation industrielle extraordinaire," *Les Echos,* September 23, 1996, p. 51.

——, "Guillin paré pour l'Europe," *Emballages Magazine,* May 29, 2000.

——, "Guillin révolutionne la barquette plastique," *Les Echos,* September 23, 1996, p. 53.

——, "Guillin vise toujours l'international," *Emballages Magazine,* January 29, 2001.

—M. L. Cohen

Grupo Ferrovial, S.A.

Principe de Vergara, 135
28002 Madrid
Spain
Telephone: (+34) 91-586-25-00
Fax: (+340 91-586-26-77
Web site: http://www.ferrovial.es

Public Company
Incorporated: 1952
Employees: 12,488
Sales: EUR 3.6 billion ($3.25 billion) (2000)
Stock Exchanges: Madrid
Ticker Symbol: FER
NAIC: 541330 Engineering Services; 234120 Bridge and
   Tunnel Construction; 234110 Highway and Street
   Construction; 234930 Industrial Nonbuilding Structure
   Construction; 233220 Multifamily Housing
   Construction; 234990 All Other Heavy Construction;
   488119 Other Airport Operations

Grupo Ferrovial, S.A. is the second largest construction group in terms of market capitalization in Spain, behind Fomento de Construcciones y Contratas (FCC). Ferrovial is active in nearly every branch of the construction business, from civil and public works projects, engineering to residential construction, with a strong background in large-scale works—such as the construction of Chile's tallest office tower and the construction of the new Guggenheim Museum in Bilbao, Spain—and highway, bridge, and road construction. Construction continues to account for more than 80 percent of Ferrovial's annual revenues; the company has embarked, however, on a diversification program intended to increase the contribution of diversified operations to at least 50 percent by 2004. The company's diversification remains nonetheless closely linked to its core construction business, with operations in toll road, parking, and airport management concessions; real estate; and services, such as waste disposal. Real estate is handled chiefly by Ferrovial Inmobiliaria, which accounted for 9 percent of company revenues in 2000 and in that year became Spain's leading real estate construction and management com-

pany. Concessions fall under subsidiary Cintra (Concesiones de Infraestructuras de Transportes, S.A.), created in 1998 to take advantage of synergies with Ferrovial's toll road construction activities. Cintra has rapidly built up a strong portfolio of toll road concessions, in Spain, Portugal (including the Scut highway concession awarded in 2000), Latin America, and North America, with a stake in the H-407 toll road concession in Toronto, Canada. Cintra is also a fast-growing airport management company, owning nine airports in Mexico, the Bristol Airport outside of London, England, and the 99-year concession for Niagara Airport in Niagara Falls. Concessions accounted for just 7 percent of Ferrovial's total revenues in 2000, but is expected to be among the company's fastest-growing revenue sources. The company's Ferroser services subsidiary is active in public services, such as street cleaning and waste management, and maintenance and facilities management service. That division added another 3 percent to the company's sales in 2000. The company also has taken an interest in constructing the information superhighway, acquiring minority shareholdings in Spanish telecommunications and internet services companies Cableuropa/ONO and Uni2. Based in Madrid, and still majority owned by the founding del Pino family, Ferrovial posted sales of EUR 3.6 billion in 2000. Spain continues to account for more than 80 percent of the company's total sales. Nonetheless, the company has been involved in international activities almost from its start, and foreign sales represent an increasingly strong source of revenue growth for the company.

Working on the Spanish Railroad in the 1950s

Born in 1920, Rafael del Pino y Morena became one of Spain's leading industrialists. At the conclusion of the Spanish Civil War, del Pino entered the country's prestigious Universitaria de Ingenieria de Caminos, Canales y Puertos (Road, Canal, and Port Engineering), receiving a doctorate in 1947. Del Pino's university career was also to help him establish important political contacts that became essential for the company he was to found. Upon completing his doctorate, Del Pino joined Vias y Construcciones S.A., where, within a short time, he rose to a director's position.

Del Pino left Vias y Construcciones in 1952 to spend the summer traveling across Europe and plotting out his next career

Company Perspectives:

Ferrovial feels a connection with its clients. Obtaining their satisfaction and contributing to society's development are the basis of Ferrovial's activities. Its management is defined by principles of profitability and growth.

move. Returning to Spain, del Pino launched his own construction company. Called Ferrovial—literally, "railroad"—del Pino's company initially specialized in construction of railroad ties but quickly extended itself to the construction of railroads themselves. Del Pino's initial holding in his company was just 50 percent, with the remainder held by members of his family. Through the 1950s, however, del Pino steadily bought out the other family members' shares, gaining 100 percent control by the beginning of the 1960s.

Del Pino's political connections helped his company secure a number of important railroad construction contracts. The company also branched out in the early 1960s into other public works projects, notably with the construction of the Salto 2 hydroelectric plant on the Sil River. International operations were also an early feature of Ferrovial, such as the award for the contract for Libya's Hedjaz railroad in the early 1960s.

Government contracts remained the most important source of revenues for the fast growing Ferrovial. The beginning of massive infrastructure investments by the Spanish government under Francisco Franco marked a period of strong growth for Ferrovial as the company extended its operations to include highway and roadway construction. The inauguration of the National Toll Highway Program in the mid-1960s gave Ferrovial a number of important contracts to build the country's toll road system. The company also joined with Europistas to win the concession to operate Bilbao-Behobia toll road in 1968.

Into the 1970s, Ferrovial began to branch out, creating a number of new subsidiaries to operate its diversifying interests. By 1975, the company had created its Ibervial S.A. real estate subsidiary, which later was to become Ferrovial Immobiliaria. The company also established Cadagua S.A. as it entered public services operations, such as waste management and street cleaning services. Ferrovial's expanding interests in concessions led it to form Eurovias, which was granted the concession to operate the highway between Burgos and Arminon. Del Pino himself was gaining prominence among Spain's industrial community. In 1972, he was named president of the management committee overseeing the Empresa Nacional del Gas (National Gas Company), charged with creating the new Enagas company. Del Pino subsequently was named president of Enagas, a position he held until 1974. The Enagas position helped del Pino win new friends among Spain's energy industry, such as Claudius Boada, who later was to become president of the American Hispanic Bank.

In 1976, Ferrovial began construction of its first large-scale housing development, the Covibar development in Madrid. That development, which was to reach more than 4,400 homes, gave the company an important boost toward becoming a leader in the Spanish residential development sector. Meanwhile, as the Spanish construction market entered a slump following the death of Franco, Ferrovial found increasing heavy construction clients in such countries as Libya, Mexico, Paraguay, and Kuwait. As the Spanish construction crisis deepened, international contracts came to represent a larger proportion of the company's revenues. At the height of the slump, which lasted from 1979 to 1984, more than a third of Ferrovial's construction revenues came from its foreign operations.

Construction Boom in the 1980s

Joining del Pino in 1981 was eldest son Rafael del Pino y Calvo-Sotelo, a fellow graduate of the Ingenieria de Caminos, Canales y Puertos university, who also received an M.B.A. from the Massachusetts Institute of Technology. The younger del Pino started his career at the company's Libyan operations, learning the business from the ground up, before taking on increasingly central positions in the company in the late 1980s.

The Spanish construction industry entered a new boom phase in the middle of the 1980s and Ferrovial's Spanish construction operations once again generated the largest share of its growing business. By then, the company had begun to formulate its strategy for becoming one of Spain's leading construction companies. After winning the concession for the Sant-Cugat-Terrassa-Manresa highway, Ferrovial captured a strong share of the building boom sparked by the approach of Barcelona's hosting of the 1992 Olympic Games.

Diversified Construction and Concessions Leader for the 21st Century

If Spain had long been Western Europe's poor cousin, the beginning of the 1990s marked a period of new economic growth for that country. Ferrovial was by then in primary place to capture a strong share of the booming construction market. The privatization of much of Spain's industrial base also presented a variety of opportunities for the company in the early 1990s. During this first half of the decade, Ferrovial established several new subsidiaries as it again began to diversify its operations. Ferrovial Conservacion S.A. was established to spearhead the company's entry into infrastructure and facility maintenance and conservation services. The company coupled the creation of Ferrovial Immobiliaria with the launch of its first foreign real estate developments, notably in neighboring Portugal. Ferrovial also played a major role in the construction of Spain's high-speed train railroad network.

In 1995, Ferrovial took a giant step forward in its quest to become Spain's leading construction firm when it acquired a majority shareholding in struggling, publicly traded rival Agromán S.A. While Ferrovial itself had long resisted a public offering, preferring to maintain its family-owned status, the Agromán acquisition was to lead to a public offering by Ferrovial in 1999 as the company moved to acquire the remaining shares of Agromán. The Agromán acquisition helped Ferrovial's sales jump to nearly EUR 1.6 billion in 1996. The company's strong growth through the second half of the decade was to enable it to nearly double its revenues in less than five years.

After merging its own construction operations with those of Agromán's to form the new subsidiary Ferrovial Agromán

Key Dates:

1952: Rafael del Pino y Moreno founds Grupo Ferrovial, S.A.
1955: Hydroelectric plant construction begins.
1966: Company enters road construction.
1968: Company wins Bilbao-Behobia highway concession.
1981: Rafael del Pino y Calvo-Sotelo, eldest son of the founder, joins company.
1986: Company begins Olympics construction projects.
1991: Construction of high-speed train projects begins.
1995: Company acquires Agromán S.A.; launches Ferrovial Servicios.
1996: Ferrovial Agromán Internacional S.A. is formed.
1997: Guggenheim Museum in Bilbao is completed; company acquires Ferogasa.
1998: Company launches Cintra concessions subsidiary.
1999: Public offering is made.
2000: Company acquires majority stake in Budimex (Poland); wins Scut highway (Portugal) concession.

Internacional S.A., Ferrovial continued to boost its other operations. In 1996, the company turned to the South America market, where it was awarded highway concessions in Chile. That year, the company also completed construction of the headquarters building for Compania de Telecomunicaciones de Chile (CT), the country's tallest building and one of the tallest on the South American continent.

Another high-prestige Ferrovial project was completed the following year, when the Guggenheim Museum in Bilbao became one of the decade's architectural highlights. Meanwhile, Ferrovial continued to build up its concessions operations, acquiring urban services group Ferogasa in 1997. By 1998, Ferrovial tagged its concessions operations for further growth, creating a new subsidiary, Cintra, to hold its operations in that sector. Cintra immediately began its own expansion, launching into airports facilities ownership and management with the acquisition of nine airports in Mexico. Cintra also stepped into the car park market with a number of key acquisitions, including those of Dornier, Reinrod, Femet, and ESSA. By the end of 1999, the company's parking concessions topped 110,000 spaces.

Ferrovial went public in 1999, selling nearly 35 percent of its shares in what was Spain's largest public offering to date. The del Pino family nonetheless retained their majority control of the company, with more than 57 percent of outstanding shares. The public offering enabled the company to make a number of new moves, notably in the concessions market. By 2000, it had increased its number of airport concessions to 12, including the purchases of the Bristol Airport in England, and the winning of concessions contracts for the Cerromoreno Airport in Antofagasta, Chile, and a 99-year contract to operate the Niagara Falls airport. The company also achieved a number of

new highway concessions contracts, including the H-407 toll road in Canada.

Rafael del Pino y Moreno retired from the company he had founded, giving up his chairman's position to son Rafael del Pino y Calvo-Sotelo. The younger del Pino had been one of the driving forces behind the company's diversification, leading the company into such areas as telecommunications—with the mid-1990s purchases of stakes in Cableuropa/ONO and Uni2. Ferrovial, which had nearly achieved its goal of becoming Spain's leading construction company (only rival FCC had a larger market capitalization), now adopted a new goal of boosting its diversified operations to account for at least 50 percent of total sales by 2004. Yet the company was far from neglecting its core construction business. Those operations took on a new international vigor when the company announced its acquisition of 58.5 percent of Budimex, Poland's leading construction company, opening new markets for the company in Eastern Europe and Germany.

Principal Subsidiaries

Agromán Gibraltar, Limitada; Agro-Rutas, S.A.; Aplicacion Recursos Naturales, S.A.; Cintra, Concesiones de Infraestructuras de Transportes, S.A. (68%); Compañía de Obras Castillejos, S.A.; Constructora Agromán-Ferrovial Limitada; Ditecpesa, S.A.; Ferroconservación, S.A.; Ferrovial Construç, Gestao y Manutençao, S.A.; Ferrovial Agromán, S.A.; Ferrovial Agromán Chile, S.A. (78%); Ferrovial Agromán Colombia, S.A.; Ferrovial Agromán Internacional, S.A.; Ferrovial Agromán Puerto Rico, S.A.; Ferrovial Agromán Uruguay, S.A.; Ferrovial Bélgica, B.V.; Ferrovial Inmobiliaria, S.A.; Ferrovial Inmobiliaria Chile, S.A.; Ferrovial Servicios, S.A.; Ferrovial Telecomunicaciones, S.A.; Gijonesa de Cementerios, S.A. (90%); Lar 2.000, S.A.; Sitkol, S.A.; Tecpresa, S.A.; Urbaoeste, S.A.

Principal Competitors

Acciona, S.A.; ACS, Actividades de Construcción y Servicios, S.A.; Balfour Beatty Plc.; Bechtel Group Inc.; Grupo Dragados SA; Fomento de Construcciones y Contratas, S.A.; Hyundai Engineering & Construction Co., Ltd.; Kvaerner ASA; Odebrecht S.A.; VINCI SA.

Further Reading

"Construction Lifts Ferrovial Profits," *Financial Times,* November 3, 2000.
"Ferrovial Buys Canadian Highway Concession," *Reuters,* May 11, 1999.
"Grupo Ferrovial Does Not Rule Out Growth Through Acquisitions," *AFX Europe,* April 19, 1999.
Kozlowski, Pawel, "Ferrovial Wants Budimext to Diversify into Telecoms," *Reuters,* May 31, 2000.
Parsons, Claudia, "Ferrovial Rises After Spain's Biggest Private IPO," *Reuters,* May 5, 1999.

—M. L. Cohen

Grupo Mexico, S.A. de C.V.

Baja California 200
Mexico City 06760
Mexico
Telephone: (525) 564-7066
Fax: (525) 564-7677
Web site: http://www.grupomexico.com

Public Company
Incorporated: 1965 as Asarco Mexicana, S.A.
Employees: 30,407
Sales: 17.32 billion pesos ($1.81 billion) (1999)
Stock Exchanges: Mexico City
Ticker Symbol: GMEXICO
NAIC: 212112 Bituminous Coal Underground Mining;
212221 Gold Ore Mining; 212222 Silver Mining;
212231 Lead Ore & Zinc Ore Mining; 212234 Copper
Ore & Nickel Ore Mining; 212299 All Other Metal
Ore Mining; 331411 Primary Smelting & Refining of
Copper Ore; 331419 Primary Smelting & Refining of
Nonferrous Metal; 482111 Line-Haul Railroads

Grupo Mexico, S.A. de C.V. is Mexico's largest mining company and the world's third largest producer of copper, fourth largest of silver, and fifth largest of zinc. It also engages in the mining and processing of other minerals, principally gold, lead, and molybdenum. In addition to its holdings in Mexico, Grupo Mexico owns ASARCO, Inc., a company with many mining facilities in the United States and a majority stake in Southern Peru Copper Corporation Grupo Mexico also holds the majority share in Mexico's longest railway.

Under U.S. Ownership: 1892–1965

Grupo Mexico originated not with a Mexican company but with the activities of the Guggenheim family of the United States, through their M. Guggenheim's Sons partnership, which had been investing in U.S. mining and smelting operations since 1880. In 1889 Simon Guggenheim persuaded some Mexican mine owners to send their silver ores to the Guggenheim smelter in Pueblo, Colorado. After Congress imposed a heavy duty on imported ores the following year, the Guggenheims established smelters in Monterrey (1892) and Aguascalientes (1895) and first leased, then bought, mines in Mexico yielding lead, iron, silver, and copper. By 1901 Guggenheim-owned smelters were processing 40 percent of the lead and 20 percent of the silver mined in Mexico. Meanwhile, industrialists in the United States were forming a cartel-like trust of large smelting operations, founded in 1899 as the American Smelting and Refining Co. (ASARCO). The Guggenheims declined to join and, when the trust ran into difficulty, purchased a controlling stake in ASARCO in 1901 for $45.2 million.

The Guggenheim Exploration Co. bought for $5 million, in 1902 or 1903, a copper, lead, and zinc mine at Velardena, Durango, which was turned over to ASARCO. This company also very early acquired a lead and zinc mine at Santa Eulalia, Chihuahua. A smelter completed in 1907 near Chihuahua became, in the 1920s, the largest lead smelter in the world. The Tiro General mine at Charcas, San Luis Potosi, was acquired by ASARCO in 1911, and a smelter and refinery were built nearby.

Mexico was now entering the decade of civil war following the fall of President Porfirio Diaz. By supporting the ambitions of Pancho Villa in the north of Mexico, ASARCO was able to keep five of its plants open, while all the others farther south had to close. Also during this period, the company acquired a vein system in the mineral-rich (lead, zinc, and copper) Santa Barbara, Chihuahua district. In 1919 ASARCO acquired the Rosita coalfields near Sabinas, Coahuila. Coal from this property would be the fuel to generate the electricity needed for the company's mining and smelting operations. The facility cost $8.5 million to develop, including coke ovens, Mexico's only zinc smelter, and a showpiece model town. ASARCO gained control of the San Potosi smelter in 1923. The Monterrey and Aguascalientes smelters were abandoned as antiquated in the 1920s, but ASARCO opened a Monterrey lead refinery in 1929.

Profits from its Mexican properties helped ASARCO sustain itself during the Great Depression. In 1947 11 ASARCO plants in Mexico were treating 6,100 metric tons of ore a day and producing 29,700 tons of lead, zinc, copper, and iron concentrates a month. The Rosita coal mine was producing 600,000

Key Dates:

1892: M. Guggenheim's Sons opens its first Mexican facility, a smelter in Monterrey.

1911: Guggenheim-controlled ASARCO now owns many mines and smelters in Mexico.

1947: ASARCO has 11 Mexican facilities and is the nation's largest private employer.

1965: ASARCO sells 51 percent of its Mexican subsidiary to Mexican investors.

1978: As Grupo Industrial Minera Mexico, the now independent company begins selling stock to the public.

1979: Company opens La Caridad, Mexico's second largest copper mine.

1990: Company acquires a majority stake in Cananea, Mexico's largest copper mine.

1994: Grupo Industrial Minera Mexico is reorganized as Grupo Mexico, S.A. de C.V.

1997: Grupo Mexico purchases a 74 percent share of Mexico's longest railway.

1999: Grupo Mexico purchases ASARCO, its former owner, for $2.2 billion.

tons a year. ASARCO was the largest private employer in Mexico at this time.

ASARCO's Mexican revenues came to perhaps $80 million in 1962, but its earnings were estimated at only $2 million. The company's executives complained that its profit margins were almost being eliminated by taxes and export duties, especially the latter, which was raised to 28 percent for refined products in 1954. The Mexican government allowed a reduction of the export duty when foreign properties came under majority Mexican ownership, and ASARCO expressed its willingness to make such an arrangement but said it was having trouble finding Mexican partners. Low metal prices apparently were making it impossible for wealthy Mexicans to achieve a rate of return on equity high enough to make ASARCO a worthwhile investment.

Thriving on Copper: 1965–90

Prodded to comply with the law requiring certain enterprises, such as mining concerns, to be Mexican-controlled, ASARCO sold a 51 percent share of its Mexican subsidiary in 1965 for between $30 and $40 million to a group headed by industrialist Bruno Pagliai. The ensuing company, Asarco Mexicana, S.A., became Industrial Minera Mexico, S.A. (IMM) in 1974, when another 15 percent was sold to Mexican investors, reducing ASARCO's stake to 34 percent. In 1978 this company was placed under Grupo Industrial Minera Mexico, S.A. de C.V., a holding company with all-Mexican equity that began selling stock on the Mexico City stock exchange. A subsidiary, Mexico Desarrollo Industrial Minero, S.A. de C.V. (Medisma) remained 34 percent owned by ASARCO.

The group's richest holding was the La Caridad copper mine in the state of Sonora. In 1968 Asarco Mexicana signed agreements with two government agencies to explore intensively a site within a national mining reserves area. Important copper

production in the area—the Nacozari district—had begun around 1900 but had ended in 1949 because of low copper prices. The company's efforts culminated in the 1979 opening of Mexico's second largest copper mine, an open-pit operation with reserves of 680 million tons of ore, plus a smelter to produce blister (rough) copper and a refinery to purify it further. IMM was acting as the sales agent for Mexicana de Cobre, S.A., which was 44 percent owned by the Mexican government. In 1985 Mexicana de Cobre was constructing a new smelter to handle the ore, which was being extracted at the rate of 72,000 metric tons a day, and to meet the demands of the refinery.

Grupo Industrial Minero acquired 92 percent of the government's share of Mexicana de Cobre in a 1988 public auction and increased its share in 1997 to 98.5 percent. The company was producing 57 percent of Mexico's copper in 1990, when it bought 77 percent of the Cananea mine for $475 million. Located in the state of Sonora not far south of the Arizona border, Cananea was Mexico's largest copper mine, an open-pit operation worked on a small scale in the late 19th century by General Ignacio Pesqueira. An Arizona prospector, William C. Greene, took out an option in 1898 from his widow for $47,000 and began large-scale exploitation. A miner's strike was bloodily repressed in 1906, and in 1911 the mine was producing six million pounds of copper a month. Anaconda Copper Mining Co. purchased Greene Cananea Copper Co. in 1928. The Mexican government and private companies acquired 51 percent of the shares in 1971, but Anaconda remained the largest single stockholder until 1982 of what became Mexicana de Cananea.

Grupo Mexico in the 1990s

Grupo Industrial Minera Mexico's net sales came to 3.41 billion new pesos ($1.13 billion) and net income amounted to 729.44 million new pesos ($241.86 million) in 1991. The following year was almost as good, but in 1993 sales dropped and the company incurred a net loss. In 1994 Grupo Mexico, S.A. de C.V. was established as a holding company with the objective of replacing Grupo Industrial Minera Mexico and consolidating all of the company's subsidiaries. This was accomplished through the acquisition of all of the shares representing the foreign investment in Medisma, which now included Mexicana de Cananea as well as Mexicana de Cobre. ASARCO announced later in the year that it expected to sell most of its 24 percent stake in Grupo Mexico within the next two years. The purchase was completed in 1997 for $323 million.

Grupo Mexico's mineral production in 1994 included 289,882 metric tons of coal and 186,361 metric tons of zinc. Copper production in 1995 totaled 303,685 metric tons. The company was operating ten mines and seven plants. Jorge Larrea Ortega, Grupo Mexico's chairman and chief executive officer and known as Mexico's "King of Copper," yielded his posts in 1994 to his son German Larrea Mota-Velasco. After this difficult year, marked by capital flight and a peso devaluation, Grupo Mexico made a comeback—aided by higher copper prices—in 1995, earning 3.83 billion pesos (about $563 million) on sales of 10.07 billion pesos (about $1.48 billion). This proved to be Grupo Mexico's best result in the 1990s.

In 1997 a consortium of three companies that included Grupo Mexico and the U.S. company Union Pacific Corp. purchased a 50-year operating concession of government-owned Ferrocarril Pacifico del Norte, S.A. de C.V., for $527 million, with Grupo Mexico taking 74 percent. The rail network of roughly 4,000 miles connected Mexico City with such cities on the U.S. border as Ciudad Juarez and Mexicali and included a passenger run for tourists through the Copper Canyon. Grupo Ferroviario Mexicano was established by the partners to run the railway. "We combine a cyclical company with a cash cow and the end result is the stabilization of cash flows," was the reason for the acquisition that the chief financial officer of Grupo Mexico gave to Alex Mathias of *Euromoney.* "Copper prices are low right now but the rail business subsidiary is good." A government official later credited Larrea with acting shrewdly. "When Grupo Mexico bought the Pacific Northern line he paid cash," the official told Joel Millman of the *Wall Street Journal.* "Then he went to Wall Street and asked for better financing than even the government gets."

Grupo Mexico made a bigger acquisition and brought its relationship with ASARCO full circle in 1999, when it bought this company for $1.18 billion in cash and the assumption of $1.02 billion in debt. The purchase of ASARCO, which held a number of U.S. mines, smelters, and refineries and a majority stake in Southern Peru Copper Corporation, made Grupo Mexico the world's third largest copper producer. It was hotly contested by Phelps Dodge Corporation, the largest U.S. copper producer, which had earlier made a bid for ASARCO in order to keep it from merging with Cyprus Amax Minerals Co. Grupo Mexico won the bidding war not by offering to pay more but to pay all in cash. To help finance the acquisition, Grupo Mexico quickly sold Enthrone-OMI, Inc., ASARCO's specialty chemicals division, to Cookson Group plc for slightly more than $500 million. In 2000 it sold American Limestone Co., another ASARCO business, to CSR America, a unit of Australian-based CSR Ltd., for more than $211 million.

In 2000 Grupo Mexico's mining subsidiary, Grupo Minero Mexico, consisted of three principal operating units: Mexicana de Cobre, Mexicana de Cananea, and Industrial Minera Mexico. The former two were operating the La Caridad and Cananea mines, respectively. IMM consisted of eight underground mines producing zinc, gold, silver, copper, lead, and coal in central and northern Mexico. Among them was Charcas, the nation's largest zinc producer, and San Martin, the nation's largest underground mine, in the state of Zacatecas. Grupo Minero Mexico's processing facilities consisted of two copper smelters; three refineries—for copper, zinc, and precious metal; and leaching and solvent extraction/electrowinning (SX/EW) facilities at La Caridad and Cananea. Grupo Mexico's rail operations were under the Grupo Ferroviario Mexicano subsidiary.

Aside from the La Caridad (copper, molybdenum, gold, and silver), Cananea (copper, gold, and silver), Charcas (silver, copper, lead, and zinc), and San Martin (silver, lead, zinc, and copper) mines, Grupo Mexico was still operating mines at Santa Eulalia, Chihuahua (silver, lead, and zinc), and Nueva Rosita, Coahuila (coal). The mines at Velardena, Durango (silver, copper, lead, and zinc), and Santa Barbara, Chihuahua (gold, silver, copper, lead, and zinc) also had long been exploited by the company's predecessors. Another mine, at Taxco, Guerrero (gold, silver, lead, and zinc), was near one of Mexico's most popular tourist cities and the historic home of silver treasures.

Grupo Mexico also was operating a mine at Rosario, Sinaloa (lead, zinc, silver, and gold). La Caridad was the site of a copper smelter and refinery, silver and gold refinery, SX/EW and sulfuric-acid plants, and a rod mill. Cananea had a copper smelter and SX/EW plant. San Luis Potosi was home to a copper smelter, a sulfuric-acid plant, and zinc and arsenic refineries. A silver and gold refinery was in Monterrey and a lime plant in Agua Prieta Sonora. The company was pursuing exploration and development projects at El Arco, Baja California Norte; Bolanos, Jalisco; Buenavista, Sonora; and Angangueo, Michoacan.

ASARCO included four zinc mines in Tennessee and three copper and silver mines in Arizona. The other two U.S. mines were in Colorado and Montana. There were three smelters—in Arizona, Montana, and Texas; two refineries in Amarillo, Texas; and two SX/EW facilities in Arizona. Southern Peru Copper was producing copper, silver, molybdenum, and gold in Cuajone and Toquepala, which also had an SX/EW plant. Ilo had two refineries, a smelter, and a sulfuric-acid plant.

Of Grupo Mexico's revenues of 17.32 billion pesos (about $1.81 billion) in 1999, copper accounted for 48 percent, transport services for 28 percent, and zinc for 10 percent. Mexico accounted for 52 percent of company sales, and the United States for 44 percent. Grupo Minero Mexico accounted for more than 80 percent of the parent company's 497,057 metric tons of copper sold. It also accounted for more than 95 percent of the 152,984 metric tons of zinc sold. Grupo Ferroviario Mexicano (Ferromex) transported 32.6 million metric tons of cargo an average distance of 728 kilometers (452 miles). Some $238 million was spent as part of a five-year program of modernization, including the rehabilitation of 202 kilometers (126 miles) of road and the laying of 23,835 metric tons of new rail. A total of 50 locomotives were acquired, and work began on a yard in Guadalajara. Grupo Mexico's net income was 1.88 billion pesos (about $195 million).

Principal Subsidiaries

ASARCO, Inc. (U.S.A.); Grupo Ferroviario Mexicano, S.A. de C.V. (74%); Grupo Minero Mexico, S.A. de C.V.; Southern Peru Copper Corporation (U.S.A.; 54%).

Principal Operating Units

Ferrocarril Chihuahua-Pacifico; Ferrocarril Mexicana; Industrial Minera Mexico; Mexicana de Cananea (98.5%); Mexicana de Cobre (96.4%).

Principal Competitors

Corporacion Nacional del Cobre de Chile; Phelps Dodge Corporation.

Further Reading

"All Aboard," *LatinFinance,* August 1998, pp. 49, 52.
Anderson, Jenny, "Copper-Topped Battering," *Institutional Investor,* January 2000, p. 93.
"Asarco Plans to Sell Most of Its 24% Stake in Grupo Mexico SA," *Wall Street Journal,* November 25, 1994, p. C13.

Baldwin, Letitia, "Mexican Copper Producers Eye Rebound," *American Metal Market,* April 3, 1985, pp. 3, 18.

Bernstein, Marvin D., *The Mexican Mining Industry, 1890–1950,* Albany, State University of New York, 1964.

Chase, Martyn, "Mexico to Become Sixth in World Copper Output," *American Metal Market,* June 13, 1979, pp. 1, 12.

Contreras, Oscar, *Cananea,* Mexico City: Miguel Angel Porrea, 1998.

Macdonald, John, "The Big New Kicker at Asarco," *Fortune,* January 1963, pp. 82–83.

Marcasson, Isacc F., *Metal Magic: The Story of the American Smelting & Refining Company,* New York: Farrar, Straus and Co., 1949.

Mathias, Alex, "Grupo Mexico: King Copper with Railway," *Euromoney,* December 1998, p. 68.

Millman, Joel, "Grupo Mexico Sets Bold Plan to Go Global in Copper," *Wall Street Journal,* September 28, 1999, p. A18.

Sisselman, Robert, "La Caridad Copper," *Engineering and Mining Journal,* October 1979, pp. 72–84, 87–89.

—Robert Halasz

Guilford Mills Inc.

4925 W. Market St.
Greensboro, North Carolina 27407
U.S.A.
Telephone: (336) 316-4000
Fax: (336) 316-4056
Web site: http://www.guilfordmills.com

Public Company
Incorporated: 1946
Employees: 6,200
Sales: $814.2 million (2000)
Stock Exchanges: New York
Ticker Symbol: GFD
NAIC: 313210 Broadwoven Fabric Mills; 314121 Curtain and Drapery Mills; 314129 Other Household Textile Product Mills; 313249 Other Knit Fabric and Lace Mills

Guilford Mills Inc. is the leading producer in the United States of warp, or flat, knit fabric. The company knits, dyes, and finishes nylon, acetate, and polyester yarn and sells finished fabrics to the apparel, automotive, and home furnishings industries. Guilford fabrics are used in lingerie, sportswear, loungewear, swimwear, bedsheets, mattress ticking, bedspreads, upholstery, and draperies. In the automotive industry, Guilford fabrics are used for automobile roof interiors and seat covers. Guilford has substantial international sales, and operates mills in Mexico, Brazil, Portugal, and the United Kingdom.

Postwar Founding

Guilford Mills was founded in 1946 in Greensboro, North Carolina. James Hornaday set up shop in a garage with half a dozen employees and six warp-knit machines to produce synthetic fabrics for ladies' lingerie. The company's first permanent knitting plant was built four years later in Greensboro, and in 1961, Guilford started its first dyeing and finishing plant, which Hornaday hoped would enable Guilford to charge more for its material. Charles (Chuck) Hayes, who later became

Guilford's chairman and CEO, was hired that same year to oversee the new operation. At that point, Guilford had 60 machines and was a medium-sized operation.

Guilford quickly introduced innovative dyeing and finishing techniques that included laminating, napping, embossing, and coating. From its beginnings in lingerie, Guilford branched out and supplied warp knit fabric to manufacturers of sleepwear, dresses, swimsuits, and other apparel. The company also supplied fabric for window treatments, automotive interiors, shoes, and luggage.

Twenty-one years after its founding, Guilford launched a second dyeing and finishing plant. By 1968, Hayes, at 33, was president of the company, which had turned increasingly to the production of warp knit fabrics. Warp knit is a specialized fabric made by a machine knit process. The nylon, acetate, and polyester yarns run in a lengthwise direction in the fabric, forming interlocking loops. With progressive production strategies, the company quickly grew to $3 million in sales.

Hayes is credited with building the company from a small knitter of synthetics into one of the world's largest and most efficient producers of warp knit fabric. Under Hayes's direction, the company won business away from larger competitors and made shrewd acquisitions and partnerships. Guilford became adept at producing low-priced synthetic knockoffs of more expensive, natural-fiber fabrics.

Acquisitions in the 1970s and 1980s

The company went public in 1971. Hayes became the chairman and CEO one year later, and the company listed its stock on the American Stock Exchange. In the early 1970s, Guilford acquired Astrotex, Ltd., of New York and launched the Guilford-National joint venture in Kenansville, North Carolina. When velour, a velvety cotton fabric priced at a steep $8 a yard, became popular in the 1970s, Hayes and his team of fellow executives decided to develop a cheaper, synthetic substitute. Although the company had to invent a new way to dye the velour-like material, Guilford perfected a synthetic velour in 1978 that generated six to eight years of profitability. During the late 1970s, Guilford acquired the Chadalon Nylon Extruding

Plant in Georgia and started a major bonding and laminating division at the Greensboro, North Carolina site.

In 1981 Guilford organized a joint venture in the United Kingdom with Carrington-Viyella plc. The new company was called Guilford-Kapwood Ltd., and Bryan Lodder, a Briton, was appointed to oversee it. Two years later, Guilford bought out the British company, which was renamed Guilford Europe. Lodder was in charge of European operations.

Guilford's executives refer to 1984 as the company's "golden year." Stock was listed on the New York Stock Exchange. During the previous five years, Guilford's sales had increased 70 percent. In 1984 the company earned $24.3 million on sales of $456.9 million—a 5 percent margin that was the envy of the industry. Giants such as Burlington and J.P. Stevens had margins of two and 1.1 percent, respectively. "Commodity, the volume, our low cost, our low overhead—everything was just in place, and we were it," Guilford CEO Hayes was quoted as saying in the May 1992 issue of *Business—North Carolina*. "It all came together because at that time we had the most advanced line of warp-knit products in the world and had replaced a lot of woven fabrics at lower selling prices, but at better margins to us. It all clicked at the same time."

Guilford took advantage of the "click" and used profits to embark on an aggressive acquisitions campaign. The market in synthetics was beginning to fade by the mid-1980s and, to survive, Guilford realized it needed to increase market share. The company acquired two competitors in 1985—TRT Corp., of Augusta, Georgia (a fabric printing operation), and Lumberton Dyeing & Finishing Co. of North Carolina. The following year, 1986, Guilford bought up Gold Mills Inc. of Pennsylvania and FEF Industries of North Carolina. The company bought into Grupo Ambar, S.A. de CV, a warp knitter in Mexico City in 1987. These acquisitions doubled sales between 1984 and 1988 and gave Guilford a 60 percent share in warp knitting, its primary business.

In addition to acquisitions in the warp knit business, Hayes pushed Guilford to learn new technologies. The company branched into the circular-knit business. Circular knits are twice the size of the standard 60-inch fabric width and are produced on special knitting machines. Wide-width circular knit fabric is popular with apparel makers because more garments can be cut from less fabric.

Guilford began producing circular knit fabric in 1989, using prototype equipment. Because the fabric was double the standard width, Guilford needed new machinery to dye it. The company converted its Augusta, Georgia, printing plant into a state-of-the-art, circular-knit finishing facility. The conversion eventually cost Guilford more than $30 million in equipment and resulted in millions of dollars in losses.

By the mid-1980s, Guilford was one of Greensboro's major employers. In 1987 the company had sales of $539.1 million, and in 1988, Guilford was number 461 on the *Fortune* 500 list. In 1988 the company combined Guilford/U.K. and Guilford/U.S. manufacturing facilities to form the International Marketing Division. The company also set up a partnership with Suminoe Textile Co. of Japan, a leading supplier of textiles to the automotive industry. The two companies planned to share marketing resources and technical knowledge and supply American and Japanese car manufacturers with fabric for head and door liners. Guilford had pioneered the automobile headliner market in 1986 and was eager to expand into car upholstery and other auto interior fabrics.

In 1988 industrial fabrics, including automotive, made up 24 percent of Guilford's business. Apparel fabrics constituted 62 percent of the company's sales, and home furnishings were 14 percent. The company's headliner fabrics could be found in more than half of all American cars, and its seat cover business was booming. Also in 1988, Guilford acquired Krislex Knits, Inc., which had been one of Guilford's major suppliers of circular knit fabric.

By the end of the 1980s, Guilford had more than 4,500 employees working at 14 plants. But the company was having trouble making the transition from warp knits to the realm of circular knits, which required a fashion- and consumer-oriented approach and involved higher raw material costs and stricter quality control. In making warp knits, running 100,000 yards of seconds was of little consequence—it was prohibitively expensive with circular knits.

According to CEO Hayes, speaking in the May 1992 *Business—North Carolina* article, Guilford was ill-prepared for the transition. "The mentality was warp knit," he said. "There was a tremendous difference in culture that did not mesh together."

On top of the circular knit problems, Guilford suffered growing pains in the latter half of the decade and had difficulty integrating the six companies it had acquired since 1984. Growth slowed in 1989, the same year that a Miami Beach financier began building a stake in Guilford. Industry analysts wondered if the financier Victor Posner, owner of the Graniteville Co. corduroy plant, planned a takeover.

Hayes appointed Bryan Lodder as president of the company. Hayes retained the titles of chairman and CEO, but assured Lodder that he would have total autonomy. Lodder was president until 1991, when Hayes assumed that position.

Changes in the 1990s

By the end of the decade, a number of factors had converged to cut into Guilford's profits. A slump in clothing sales and a growing flood of cheap imports, along with a decrease in automotive production, slowed growth considerably. By 1990, Guilford stock had fallen to $21 from its high of $39.50 in 1987. That year, the company lost $22.6 million when it closed the Augusta, Georgia, circular-knit dyeing and finishing plant. The operation was moved to facilities in Lumberton and Greensboro. Sales for 1990 were $544.1 million.

Guilford marked 1990 with innovation, becoming the first U.S. mill to introduce microdenier specialty fabrics, which have a high-filament count that gives a silk-like feel to stretchy fabrics. The company also began a market launch into sports and fashionwear made with cotton Lycra spandex. In 1991, Guilford launched the Feminine Mystique Foundations Lines and the Infiknits wide-width circular knits line of natural fibers and Lycra blends. The production of fine denier specialty yarns allowed Guilford to create unique, exclusive fabrics. That year, Guilford's sales were $528.8 million and net income was $15.9 million; the company had slipped to the last slot on the *Fortune* 500 list. Guilford was not alone in its struggles—the *Wall Street Journal* of April 2, 1992, reported that profits for the *Fortune* 500 companies were "an unparalleled disaster" in 1991. Profits for the group fell 41 percent that year.

Guilford continued its program of restructuring and redirecting itself in 1992. CEO Hayes took on the additional roles of president and chief operating officer. The company planned to invest $100 million in new machinery and equipment and set a goal to become a global contender in the automotive market, building on its sales to Toyota, Nissan, and Honda in addition to General Motors and Ford Motor Co.

The year 1992 also saw Guilford's continued development of its wide-width circular knits business. The company showed strong growth for Infiknits, its naturally finished, 100 percent cotton and cotton/Lycra spandex fabric line. Against the backdrop of a slow rebound in the textile industry, Guilford's share of the women's domestic swimwear market continued to rise, driven by innovations in fabrication. Guilford formed a partnership with Hunter-Douglas, a major player in the home fashions industry, to produce the Silhouette line of vertical blinds and pleated shades.

Guilford's automotive business unit also showed recovery, with worldwide growth in automotive and van interiors and residential upholstery. The unit emerged as a technological and design innovator, selling its bodycloth and headliner fabrics to automakers in the United States, Europe, and Japan.

Always driven to research and innovation, Guilford began developing a technical center in Greensboro to combine its engineering, technology, research, and product divisions under one roof. The company focused in 1992 on the further development of microdenier fabrics. Improvements in process technology and modifications of equipment were also high priorities. As the 1990s progressed, Guilford revved up, exploring new markets geographically and in interesting niches. CEO Hayes was dedicated to making Guilford a truly global player. The company had major customers who were already worldwide companies, and Guilford decided to follow their lead. The company opened a sales, marketing, and distribution office in Guatemala City, Guatemala, in 1995, in order to focus its business in South America. Its automotive fabrics division planned to enter new markets in Brazil and Argentina, as well as in India and China. In apparel, the company aimed to get out of some of its mature U.S. markets, such as sleepwear, and explore specialty products, possibly using Guilford's patented high-tech products. The company spent $100 million in 1993 to upgrade its machinery and to investigate new technology. Interest in technology continued through the 1990s. In 1998 a Guilford executive told industry journal *Sporting Goods Business* that the company was "buying one of every new, interesting, state of the art machine technologies applicable to the business."

Guilford made a major acquisition in 1996, buying up Hoffmann Laces, a Cobleskill, New York-based manufacturer of lace fabrics. Hoffmann had annual sales of around $100 million at the time of the acquisition, and it sold its lace to apparel makers, intimate apparel makers, and the home furnishings market. Hoffmann's biggest customer was J.C. Penney, and it also did business with Kmart and Wal-Mart. Guilford was interested in latching onto niche markets using specialty fabrics. Its new subsidiary filled a large order for Penney in 1997, making the fabric for a new kind of popular sheet made of a cotton/lycra blend. Guilford continued to lavish money on research and development, outspending almost all its competitors in order to find new niche products. By 1997, apparel industry sales made up close to 40 percent of Guilford's total revenue. It had such major customers as Victoria's Secret for its lace and lycra-blend fabrics, and it was one of the premier manufacturers of swimwear fabric. But Guilford also found itself filling unusual market slots, such as making so-called air compression spacers for leading shoe manufacturer Nike and its Air System sneaker line. Guilford also made fasteners used in disposable diapers, and sold specialty "dazzle" fabrics and high-tech active wear fabrics to global marketers such as Fila and Adidas. It manufactured fabric with special attributes such as wind resistance and moisture wicking, and even introduced a fabric for the hunting and outdoor industry that could adjust temperature.

By the late 1990s, Guilford was about evenly split between the apparel business and its automotive line, with each making up approximately 40 percent of sales. Sales of home furnishings fabrics grew, so that this business accounted for close to 15 percent of sales by 1998. The company continued its trend toward international markets. It had growing sales to Japanese automakers, and in 1998 Guilford announced plans for a major expansion of its Mexican textile plant. Goods from the Mexican plant were earmarked for South American markets as well as customers in the United States, with plans to sell later to Europe and directly to Mexico.

Chuck Hayes, who had worked for Guilford since 1961 and overseen its rise to a global corporation, stepped down as CEO in December 1999. In 2000 the firm attempted to consolidate some of its domestic manufacturing plants, and then moved some jobs to Mexico as it suffered a disastrous third quarter. Apparel fabric sales fell off precipitously, forcing the company into the red for that quarter. Some of its apparel business was affected by cheaper imports, and in 2000 Guilford announced it would no longer make any fabric for sleepwear and robes since this market was too competitive. Apparently the company was vulnerable to even relatively small decreases in its apparel markets. Its equipment was state of the art and very expensive. The plants that used this high-tech machinery were not profitable unless they were running at or near full capacity. An overall sales drop of just a few percentage points hurt Guilford's bottom line quickly. Overall in 2000, its four U.S. mills ran at only 60 percent capacity. Guilford reported a loss for the next quarter of 2000, and then for the first quarter of 2001 as well. Sales at both the apparel and automotive divisions slid as 2001 opened. In early 1998 Guilford had predicted it would soon break the $1 billion mark in sales, but the next few years were disappointing. By 2001 the company had to reevaluate its options, as it entered what looked like a worsening retail environment.

Principal Subsidiaries

Hoffman Laces, Ltd.; American Textil, S.A. de C.V. (Mexico); Guilford Europe, Ltd. (U.K.); Guilford Kapwood GmbH (Germany); Guilford Texla N.V. (Belgium); Tybor, S.A. (Spain).

Principal Divisions

Apparel, Home & Industrial Fabrics; Automotive & Upholstery Fabrics.

Principal Competitors

Burlington Industries, Inc.; Milliken & Company Inc; Unifi, Inc.

Further Reading

Avery, Sarah, "Salesman Orients Textile Firm to Japan," *Greensboro News & Record,* February 13, 1989, p. C4.

Bailey, David, "Look Back in Anger: For Guilford Mills to Face the Future, Chuck Hayes Had to Come to Grips with Where He'd Been," *Business-North Carolina,* May 1992, p. 28.

Clune, Ray, "Guilford Mills Sees Best Growth in Automotive Area," *Daily News Record,* February 18, 1998, p. 14.

——, "Guilford to Spend $100M to Expand Mexican Operations," *Daily News Record,* March 18, 1998, p. 13.

"Fiber Selection: Wet Processing Implications," *Textile Industries,* August, 1970, pp. 144–69.

"For Guilford Mills, Added Value Multiplies Profits," *Textile World,* December 1983.

"*Fortune* 500 Group Had 41 Percent Plunge in '91 Profits," *Wall Street Journal,* April 2, 1992, p. C21.

Geremski, Terence E., "Guilford Mills Reports Record Second Quarter Earnings," *PR Newswire,* January 18, 1993.

Gridley, Clark, "Guilford Expectant of Record Year," *Daily News Record,* February 8, 1996, p. 9.

——, "Guilford's Hoffman Takeover Allows Firm to Sell to Stores Directly" *Daily News Record,* February 17, 1997, p. 64.

Grish, Kristina, "Warp Speed," *Sporting Goods Business,* February 4, 1998, p. 128.

Heerwagen, Peter, "North Valley Home to Fortune 500," *North Valley Business Journal,* June 1992, p. 1.

Hopper, Kathyrn, "First Quarter Loss Pressures Guilford Mills," *Greensboro News & Record,* February 19, 1990, p. C1.

——, "Guilford Mills Eyes Deal with Financier," *Greensboro News & Record,* May 22, 1990, p. A6.

Kunz, Mary, "What Makes a Survivor?" *Forbes,* January 26, 1987.

Luber, Diane, "Guilford Mills: Digesting New Ventures," *Greensboro News & Record,* January 23, 1989, p. C8.

——, "Guilford Mills to Sell One Plant in Lumberton, Expand Another," *Greensboro News & Record,* September 29, 1988, p. C5.

Malone, Scott, "Guilford in Red, Cuts Jobs," *WWD,* July 28, 2000, p. 2.

Maycumber, S. Gray, "Guilford Restructures Fabric Units," *Daily News Record,* January 10, 2000, p. 2.

McCurry, John, "Guilford Speeds Apparel Realignment," *Textile World,* December 2000, p. 19.

McNamara, Michael, "Hayes Maps Global Goal for Guilford Mills," *WWD,* November 14, 1995, p. 9.

Mildenberg, David, "Posner Raises Guilford Mills Stake: Company to Phase out Georgia Plant," *Greensboro News & Record,* January 27, 1990, p. A7.

O'Hanlon, James, "Knitting Up a Storm," *Forbes,* January 21, 1980, p. 81.

Patterson, Ramona, "Guilford's Krislex Purchase Creates Room to Grow," *Business Journal—Charlotte,* January 11, 1988, p. 11.

Robinson, Russ, "Textiles, Tobacco, Furniture Continue to Reign in Triad," *Business—North Carolina,* May 1986, p. 31.

Seidel, Leon, "Everything's Coming Up Tricot," *Textile Industries,* January, 1970, pp. 94–95, 154.

Smith, William C., "Industrial Textiles Mood: Upbeat Despite Economy," *Textile World,* December 1992, pp. 70–72.

Snow, Katherine, "Textiles' Recovery Needs Consumers to Catch Up," *Business Journal—Charlotte,* December 30, 1991, p. 12.

Waxler, Caroline, and Dolly Setton, "Panty Line," *Forbes,* October 6, 1997, p. 141.

Young, Vicki M., "Guilford Posts Quarter Loss," *WWD,* February 6, 2001, p. 20.

—Marinell Landa
—update: A. Woodward

Hallmark Cards, Inc.

2501 McGee Street
Post Office Box 419580
Kansas City, Missouri 64141-6580
U.S.A.
Telephone: (816) 274-5111
Fax: (816) 274-5061
Web site: http://www.hallmark.com

Private Company
Incorporated: 1923 as Hall Brothers, Inc.
Employees: 25,000
Sales: $4.3 billion (2000)
NAIC: 511191 Greeting Card Publishers; 322233
Stationery, Tablet, and Related Product
Manufacturing; 322299 All Other Converted Paper
Product Manufacturing; 339942 Lead Pencil and Art
Good Manufacturing; 512110 Motion Picture and
Video Production; 512120 Motion Picture and Video
Distribution; 513210 Cable Networks; 531120 Lessors
of Nonresidential Buildings (Except Miniwarehouses);
541921 Photography Studios, Portrait

Hallmark Cards, Inc. is the world's largest greeting card company, creating 30,000 different designs and related products each year in more than 30 languages, and distributing them in more than 100 countries. In addition to the Hallmark flagship, the company also markets cards under the Ambassador and Expressions from Hallmark brand names. The company's products are sold in Hallmark retail outlets, through mass merchandise stores, and via the hallmark.com web site. Over the years, Hallmark has branched out into other products and services that use creativity and emotion to help people connect, including stationery, party goods, gift wrap, photo albums, cut flower arrangements, home decor, collectibles, books, and Christmas ornaments. In the late 1990s, the company acquired several specialized greeting card companies that operate as wholly owned subsidiaries, including DaySpring Cards, Inc., the leader in Christian personal expression products; InterArt Holding Corporation, maker of high-quality greeting cards and related products including the Mary Engelbreit and Holly Pond Hill

lines; and William Arthur, Inc., which offers customized holiday cards, wedding invitations, fine stationery, and other high-end products. Hallmark's Binney & Smith Inc. subsidiary specializes in personal skill development products, including Crayola crayons, Magic Markers, modeling material, creativity software, model kits, and art supplies for professionals and students. Hallmark also creates family-oriented television programming through its Hallmark Entertainment, Inc. subsidiary. Hallmark Entertainment holds a controlling majority stake in Crown Media Holdings, Inc., operator and distributor of two cable television channels: the Hallmark Channel and the Kermit Channel. Yet another wholly owned subsidiary is The Picture People, operator of more than 250 mall-based portrait studios in 26 states. Even with the firm's diversification, the greeting card remains Hallmark's mainstay—so much so that Hallmark has often been mistakenly credited with inventing it.

Early History

Hallmark was founded by Joyce C. Hall, a native of Norfolk, Nebraska, who as a teenager ran a postcard company with his older brothers. In 1910 Hall, still only 18, left the family business he had founded after a traveling salesman convinced him that Kansas City, Missouri, would serve him better as a wholesaling and distribution center. Almost immediately after arriving in Kansas City, Hall set up a mail-order postcard company in a small room at the Young Men's Christian Association, where he remained until his landlord complained about the volume of mail Hall was receiving. The new company was named Hall Brothers, a name justified the following year when Rollie Hall came to Kansas City to join his brother in the business.

At that time, picture postcards were all the rage in the United States, with the best ones imported from Europe. Very early on, however, Joyce Hall came to believe that the postcard's appeal was quite limited. They were novelty items rather than a means of communication; with the leisure time required to write long letters diminishing, and the long-distance telephone call still a rare phenomenon, people would need a shorthand way of reaching each other by mail. Greeting cards suggested themselves as a viable alternative, so in 1912 Hall Brothers added them to its product line.

Company Perspectives:

This Is Hallmark: We believe: *That our* products and *services must enrich people's lives and enhance their relationships. That creativity and quality—in our concepts, products and services—are essential to our success. That the people of Hallmark are our company's most valuable resource. That distinguished* financial performance *is a must, not as an end in itself, but as a means to accomplish our broader mission. That our* private ownership *must be preserved.*

The values that guide us are: Excellence *in all we do.* Ethical and moral conduct *at all times and in all our relationships.* Innovation *in all areas of our business as a means of attaining and sustaining leadership.* Corporate social responsibility *to Kansas City and to each community in which we operate.* These beliefs and values guide our business strategies, our corporate behavior, and our relationships with suppliers, customers, communities and each other.

The outbreak of World War I bore out Hall's contention. The supply of postcards from Europe dried up, but domestic products were of inferior quality and their popularity waned. Greeting cards stepped into the breach. In 1914 Hall Brothers bought a small press and began publishing its own line of Christmas cards. In 1915 a fire destroyed the company's entire inventory, putting it $17,000 in debt, but Joyce and Rollie Hall rebuilt the business. In 1921 they were joined by their brother William Hall. By 1922 Hall Brothers had recovered to the point where it was employing 120 people, including salespeople in all 48 states. Also that year, it diversified for the first time and started selling decorative gift wrap.

In 1923 the company formally incorporated under the name Hall Brothers, Inc., and two years later the Hallmark brand name appeared on the company's products for the first time. Over the next two decades, the company would attack its market aggressively through advertising. In 1928 Hall Brothers became the first greeting card company to advertise nationally when it took out an ad in *Ladies Home Journal.* In 1936, with the national economy emerging from the worst of the Great Depression, Hall Brothers went on the attack again, introducing an open display fixture for greeting cards that Joyce Hall had developed with the help of an architect. Previously, cards had always been kept under store counters, out of customers' sight and usually in a disorganized state. In 1938 Hall Brothers advertised in the broadcast medium for the first time when it began sponsoring "Tony Won's Radio Scrapbook" on WMAQ radio in Chicago. Meantime, the company's first licensing deal was concluded in 1932, when it gained the right to use Walt Disney characters on its products.

When the United States entered World War II, the company pitched an appeal to friends and loved ones of military personnel with the slogan "Keep 'em happy with mail." Hall Brothers would find its most famous and enduring slogan in 1944, however, when it started using the tagline "When you care enough to send the very best," which had been suggested a few years earlier by Sales and Advertising Manager Ed Goodman. After the war, a staff artist created the company's logo, consisting of a five-pointed crown and the Hallmark name in script letters. Hall Brothers trademarked the logo in 1950.

1950s and 1960s: Hallmark Hall of Fame, Retail Shops, Ambassador Cards

The company established another landmark in advertising on Christmas Eve 1951, when it sponsored a television production of Gian Carlo Menotti's opera *Amahl and the Night Visitors.* This was the first of the famous Hallmark Hall of Fame series, which two years later presented a production of *Hamlet* starring the noted British Shakespearean actor Maurice Evans. That broadcast marked the first time the entire play had ever been seen on U.S. television. As Joyce Hall himself once said, "Good taste is good business."

Also in the early 1950s, Hall Brothers began opening the first of thousands of retail shops specializing in Hallmark cards. In 1954 the company changed its name to Hallmark Cards, Inc., having already used Hallmark as a brand name for 31 years. In 1959 the company introduced its Ambassador Cards line to tap into the lucrative market presented by shoppers at mass merchandisers such as supermarkets, discount stores, and drugstores. The next year Hallmark introduced its own line of party decorations and began featuring characters from Charles M. Schulz's "Peanuts" comic strip on its products.

In 1966 Joyce Hall retired as president and CEO of the company he had founded. Handing the reins to his son, Donald Hall, Joyce Hall nevertheless remained active in company affairs as chairman until his death in 1982. Joyce Hall was not only a wealthy and successful businessman when he died, but also a member of the French Legion of Honor and a commander of the British Empire. He had been friends with British Prime Minister Winston Churchill and with U.S. Presidents Harry Truman and Dwight Eisenhower. For the latter Hall Brothers custom-designed an official presidential Christmas card in 1953.

Among Donald Hall's first important moves as CEO of Hallmark were the 1966 establishment of Hallmark International to further expand the company abroad and the 1967 acquisition of Springbok Editions, maker of jigsaw puzzles. The next year, the company broke ground on the Crown Center, a $500 million retail, commercial, and residential complex intended to revitalize an area near downtown Kansas City and financed entirely with company funds. Hallmark created a new subsidiary, Crown Center Redevelopment Corporation, to oversee it.

1980s Acquisitions

In 1979 Hallmark acquired Georgia-based lithographer Litho-Krome Corporation. In 1981 the company formed a division, Hallmark Properties, to create and administer licensing projects. This division went on to create Hallmark's Rainbow Brite, Purr-Tenders, and Timeless Tales character merchandise, and also oversaw the company's licenses for Peanuts and Garfield cartoon characters. Later still, this division would be renamed Hallmark Licensing (in 1992) and its licensed properties would include Harry Potter, Dr. Suess, Barbie, Winnie the Pooh, Looney Tunes, Blue's Clues, and Batman.

The Crown Center development suffered a disaster in 1981 when two suspended walkways at the center's Hyatt Regency hotel collapsed, killing 114 people and injuring 225. After his father's death in 1982, Donald Hall added the chairmanship to his duties as CEO. In 1984 Hallmark acquired Binney & Smith, the Pennsylvania-based maker of Crayola crayons and Liquitex

Key Dates:

1910: Joyce C. Hall sets up a mail-order postcard company in Kansas City, Missouri.

1911: Hall's company begins operating under the name Hall Brothers.

1912: Greeting cards are added to the product line.

1923: Company is incorporated as Hall Brothers, Inc.

1925: The Hallmark brand name is used for the first time.

1928: Hall Brothers becomes first greeting card company to advertise nationally with an ad in *Ladies Home Journal.*

1938: First radio advertising through sponsorship of "Tony Won's Radio Scrapbook" on Chicago's WMAQ.

1944: First use of the slogan "When you care enough to send the very best."

1950: Company trademarks its famous logo, consisting of a five-pointed crown and the Hallmark name in script letters.

1951: Hallmark Hall of Fame series is launched with the company's sponsorship of a television production of the opera *Amahl and the Night Visitors.*

Early 1950s: First retail shop specializing in Hallmark cards opens.

1954: Company changes its name to Hallmark Cards, Inc.

1959: The Ambassador Cards line is launched to serve shoppers at mass merchandisers.

1967: Springbok Editions, maker of jigsaw puzzles, is acquired.

1984: Binney & Smith, maker of Crayola crayons and other art products, is acquired.

1986: Shoebox Greetings line of nontraditional cards is launched.

1994: RHI Entertainment, Inc. is acquired and is later renamed Hallmark Entertainment, Inc.; the Hallmark Gold Crown Card, a frequent-buyer reward program for customers of selected Hallmark retail stores, is introduced.

1997: Expressions from Hallmark is launched, marking the debut of the Hallmark brand in the mass merchandising market; William Arthur, Inc., maker of customized and prepackaged stationery products, is acquired; company web site adds e-commerce features.

1998: Hallmark completes several acquisitions: U.K.-based Creative Publishing, Editions DALIX of France, and InterArt Holding and Tapper Candies, both U.S.-based; a significant stake in the Odyssey channel is acquired.

1999: A line of 99-cent greeting cards is introduced under the Warm Wishes brand; DaySpring Cards and The Picture People are acquired; company launches a ten-year strategic plan, aiming to triple revenues by 2010, to $12 billion.

2000: A partial offering of stock in Crown Media Holdings Inc. is completed.

2001: The Odyssey channel is relaunched as the Hallmark Channel.

art materials. In 1986 Donald Hall retired as CEO and handed the post to the company president, Irvine O. Hockaday, Jr.

In 1987 Hallmark, after being a prominent advertiser in the broadcast media for many years, became an owner as well when it acquired a group of Spanish-language television stations from Spanish International Communication. The next year, it added another station purchased from Bahia de San Francisco Television. Also in 1988, Hallmark acquired a Spanish-language network, Univision, and amalgamated all of its holdings in a subsidiary, Univision Holdings. Based in New York, the subsidiary ran the nine full-power stations under the name Univision Station Group.

During the mid-1980s small greeting card companies began competing for Hallmark's market position with a diverse array of cards that became favorites. In the mid-1980s Hallmark fought back with its Personal Touch and Shoebox Greetings series (the latter debuting in 1986). Many of these cards, however, bore a resemblance to rival designs that some found too striking. In 1986 Blue Mountain Arts, Inc., which produced non-occasion cards featuring poetry and pastel illustrations to produce a concentrated emotional effect, sued Hallmark for copyright and trade infringement and unfair competition. The initial decision went against Hallmark, which appealed ultimately to the Supreme Court. When the Supreme Court refused to hear the case in 1988, Hallmark agreed to discontinue its Personal Touch line. Financial terms of the settlement were not disclosed.

1990s into the 21st Century: Diversifying in the Face of Increasing Competition

Hallmark's biggest challenge during the early 1990s was confronting its continuing loss of market share to the number two and three companies in the greeting card industry, American Greetings Corporation and Gibson Greetings, Inc., respectively. From 1990 to 1995, it was estimated that Hallmark's market share fell from 50 to 45 percent. In the mid-1990s, some industry experts were even suggesting that American Greetings would overtake Hallmark sometime between 1999 and 2004.

The reason for Hallmark's decline rested in the very backbone of its empire—the specialty card and gift shops that sold the Hallmark brand, which by the early 1990s numbered more than 10,000. Over a long period, these shops had fallen victim to changing buying patterns in particular among women, who still bought 90 percent of all cards sold. Pressed for time, more and more consumers were opting to purchase cards at one-stop shopping outlets—supermarkets, drugstore chains, and large discounters—such as Wal-Mart. In the early 1970s more than half of all cards were sold in specialty shops; by the early 1990s only about 30 percent were. American Greetings and Gibson, which did not have such extensive ties to the card shops, were able to recognize the trend and shift to accommodate it. Hallmark, however, was in a bind. Continuing to rely so heavily on specialty shops would do nothing to halt its market share decline, but it could not simply abandon the shops, for doing so would bankrupt many of them, not something a company as paternalistic as Hallmark could seriously consider.

One strategy was to diversify away from greeting cards even further. In 1990 Hallmark acquired Willitts Designs, a maker of collectibles, but then sold the company only three years later. Likewise, Hallmark's venture into Spanish-language television was abandoned in 1992 at a loss of $10 million when Univision was sold to Grupo Televisa. Cable television was Hallmark's next foray with the 1991 formation of a Crown Media Inc. subsidiary to which was added Cenom Cable in St. Louis, through the purchase of a controlling interest for $1 billion. In 1994 this venture too was cast aside when Hallmark sold Crown Media to Charter Communications Inc. for $900 million.

During this period Hallmark also updated its product line, offering a more high-tech approach to card purchasing. In 1991 the "Personalize it!" in-store kiosk was introduced (later called Touch-Screen Greetings), through which customers were able to create computer-generated personalized greeting cards. The following year Hallmark filed suit for infringement of its kiosk patent against American Greetings and its Creata-Card kiosk. The suit was settled in 1995 with each company receiving a worldwide, nonexclusive license to use the technology; no other details on the settlement were provided at that time.

Moreover, in 1994, Hallmark developed recordable greeting cards in partnership with Information Storage Devices. Initially retailing for $7.95 each, these cards allowed the sender to record his personal message, which would then play back each time the card was opened. Also in 1994 came the debut of the Hallmark Gold Crown Card, a frequent-buyer reward program for customers at selected Hallmark retail stores. Two years later, the Hallmark stores participating in the reward program were rebranded under the Hallmark Gold Crown name through a $100 million remodeling program in which the stores were also provided with a fresh look. In addition to the frequent-buyer program, the Gold Crown stores differed from regular Hallmark stores in several respects; they had their own lines of cards and exclusive merchandise, and they were all owned by individuals and were not franchises.

In the face of declining profits brought on by declining market share, Hallmark went through a series of reengineering and restructuring efforts in the early 1990s in an attempt to hold costs down. U.S. and Canadian operations were consolidated, and a 1995 restructuring brought together for each Hallmark card brand its administrative, marketing, and product development functions.

Additional diversification moves in the area of entertainment were made in the mid-1990s. In 1994 Hallmark acquired RHI Entertainment Inc. for $365 million. RHI was the television production company responsible for Hallmark's Hall of Fame productions. Hallmark thus acquired the world's leading producer of family-oriented entertainment, which it promptly renamed Hallmark Entertainment, Inc. and set up as a subsidiary of Hallmark Cards. Then in 1995, Hallmark purchased a 9.9 percent stake in European broadcaster Flextech for $80 million. Flextech and Hallmark created a family-oriented international cable television network, the Hallmark Entertainment Network, which commenced operations in Ireland and the United Kingdom in 1996.

Next, Hallmark Entertainment, Inc. teamed up with the Jim Henson Company in 1998 to launch the Kermit Channel, a pay television channel featuring general family entertainment fare. Also in 1998, Hallmark purchased a significant stake in the Odyssey channel, a cable network that had been launched in 1988 as a religious channel and that was in the process of being transformed into a family-oriented entertainment channel.

Given the uneven success of Hallmark's other ventures, greeting cards remained the company's most important endeavor. New promotions of Hallmark cards in the mid-1990s included a "sneak-a-peek" advertising campaign, comprising a series of commercials in which people were caught looking at the backs of the cards they had received, just to make sure they were Hallmarks. Continuing to seek ways to reverse the decline in its share of the greeting card market, the Hallmark brand was introduced into the mass merchandiser market for the first time with the 1997 launch of Expressions from Hallmark. The cards featured the Hallmark logo on the back and were initially marketed though more than 5,000 discounters, supermarkets, and drugstores. This move angered many owners of Hallmark retail stores, who feared that their sales would suffer. In 1999 came the debut of yet another new line called Warm Wishes, which featured cards priced at 99 cents and aimed at increasingly value-conscious consumers. The Warm Wishes line debuted in more than 17,000 retail outlets across the United States. The new initiatives appeared to be working, as Hallmark reported that its share of greeting card sales in the U.S. retail market increased from 47 percent in 1997 to 51 percent in 1998 to 52 percent in 1999.

Although the company had been involved in the online world in various ways since the mid-1980s, Hallmark's first serious move into the Internet came in 1996 with the launch of its corporate web site, hallmark.com. Primarily offering corporate news and product information, the site did offer some early versions of free electronic greeting cards (or e-cards). In November 1997 an overhauled hallmark.com went live with a much more extensive selection of free e-cards, some e-cards that sold for $1.50, and new e-commerce features, such as the online retailing of gift products, including jewelry, flowers, and stuffed animals. In late 1999 Hallmark began offering all of its e-cards free of charge.

The pace of acquisitions quickened in the late 1990s as Hallmark continued to diversify. In 1997 the company purchased William Arthur, Inc., a West Kennebunk, Maine-based maker of customized and prepackaged stationery products. Overseas growth was pursued as well in response to U.S. greeting card sales being flat for several years. Hallmark in 1998 acquired Creative Publishing plc, a leading U.K. maker of boxed and seasonal cards, for about $310 million. Creative was merged into the company's existing U.K. business, which was renamed Hallmark Cards (Holdings) UK. The purchase of Creative increased Hallmark's share of the U.K. greeting card market to nearly 30 percent, making it the number one player there. Hallmark similarly expanded in France in 1998 through the purchase of Editions DALIX. Two more acquisitions were completed in the United States in 1998: Bloomington, Indiana-based InterArt Holding Corporation, maker of high-quality greeting cards and related products whose product line included items designed by artist Mary Engelbreit; and Tapper Candies, a maker of candy, toys, and party favors based in Cleveland. During 1999 Hallmark acquired DaySpring Cards, Inc., the leading creator of Christian personal expression products. Adding the Siloam Springs, Arkansas-based DaySpring provided Hallmark with increased access to the fast-growing Christian card market. A second acquisition in 1999 brought The Picture People into the Hallmark fold. Based in Foster City, California, The Picture People operated a national chain of mall-based portrait studios.

In mid-1999 Hallmark launched an ambitious ten-year strategic plan, aiming to triple revenues by 2010, to $12 billion. The company planned to remain centered around its core greeting card business, but would also pursue growth and expansion in five additional business platforms: "caring gift solutions, memories, life celebrations, personal development, and family entertainment." Subsequent developments in greeting cards included the launch of Hallmark en Español, a line of more than 1,000 Spanish-language greeting cards; the introduction of Hallmark Fresh Ink, a line of hipper, sometimes risque cards aimed at women between the ages of 18 and 39; and the signing of Maya Angelou to a licensing deal to develop cards and specialty gifts featuring newly written poetry and sentiments from the poet laureate. As the 21st century began, Hallmark had to contend with an enlarged competitor in the form of American Greetings, which purchased the number three card company, Gibson Greetings, in 2000. According to Ashlea Ebeling writing in *Forbes,* the market share battle had now grown even tighter, with Hallmark holding 45 percent of the U.S. card market and American controlling 40 percent.

In the area of family entertainment, meantime, Hallmark in May 2000 made a partial offering of stock in Crown Media Holdings Inc., a subsidiary of Hallmark Entertainment that operated and distributed the Hallmark Entertainment Network, the Kermit Channel, and the Odyssey channel. Hallmark retained a 49.1 percent stake in Crown Media and 90 percent of its voting rights. In 2001 Odyssey's name was changed to the Hallmark Channel, and the network began stepping up its showings of Hallmark Hall of Fame productions. Crown Media also began rebranding its Hallmark Entertainment Network outlets located outside the United States under the Hallmark Channel name.

Principal Subsidiaries

Binney & Smith Inc.; Crown Center Redevelopment Corporation; DaySpring Cards, Inc.; Gift Certificate Center; Hallmark Entertainment, Inc.; Hallmark International; Halls Merchandising, Inc.; InterArt Holding Corporation; Irresistible Ink; Litho-Krome Company; The Picture People; Tapper Candies; William Arthur, Inc.; Hallmark Cards Australia Ltd.; Binney & Smith Ltd. (Canada); Hallmark Cards Canada; Hallmark Group France, S.A.; Hallmark Mexicana, S. de R.I. de C.V. (Mexico); Hallmark Cards Nederland B.V. (Netherlands); Uitgeverij Spanjersberg B.V. (Netherlands); Verkerke Reprodukties, N.V. (Netherlands); Hallmark Cards New Zealand Ltd.; Hallmark Cards Iberica, S.A. (Spain); Hallmark Cards (Holdings) UK.

Principal Competitors

American Greetings Corporation; CSS Industries, Inc.; Amscan Holdings, Inc.; Factory Card Outlet Corp.; Thomas Nelson, Inc.; Blue Mountain Arts, Inc.

Further Reading

Beatty, Sally, "Hallmark, Media Firms Pool Interests to Build Network," *Wall Street Journal,* July 5, 2000, p. B4.

Chandler, Susan, "Can Hallmark Get Well Soon?," *Business Week,* June 19, 1995, pp. 62–63.

Coleman, Calmetta Y., "Hallmark to Buy U.K. Card Firm for $310 Million," *Wall Street Journal,* July 10, 1998, p. B4.

Ebeling, Ashlea, "Wild Card," *Forbes,* November 13, 2000, pp. 250–51.

Fitzgerald, Kate, "Hallmark Alters Focus As Lifestyles Change," *Advertising Age,* October 25, 1994, p. 4.

Flint, Joe, "Odyssey Cable Network to Change Its Name to Hallmark Channel," *Wall Street Journal,* March 29, 2001, p. B15.

Frazier, Mya, "Battle for Retail Real Estate: American Greetings, Hallmark Duke It Out in $7 Billion Industry," *Cleveland Plain Dealer,* November 8, 2000, p. 1C.

"From Someone Who Loves You," *Economist,* August 10, 1991, p. 63.

Fuller, Jennifer Mann, "Going for the Gold: Hallmark Cards Makes Strong Investment to Ensure Success of Its 4,800-Store Network," *Kansas City Star,* December 17, 1997, p. B1.

Hall, Joyce C., with Curtiss Anderson, *When You Care Enough,* Kansas City, Mo.: Hallmark, 1979, 269 p.

Hamilton, Martha M., "Floral Retailers Bunch Up in a Crowded Field: Is There Room to Bloom for New Competitors?," *Washington Post,* February 12, 2000, p. E1.

Hayes, David, "Cyber Greetings: Sending Instant Holiday Cards Is Just a Click Away," *Kansas City Star,* December 21, 1996, p. B1.

Helliker, Kevin, "Hallmark Finds Another Market Niche: The Sorrowful," *Wall Street Journal,* December 24, 1998, p. B1.

Hirshey, Gerri, "Happy Day to You," *New York Times Magazine,* July 2, 1995, pp. 20+.

Howard, Elizabeth G., "Hallmark's $4 Billion Formula," *Kansas City Business Journal,* June 16, 1995, p. 17.

Kinni, Theodore B., "The Reengineering Rage," *Industry Week,* February 7, 1994, p. 11.

Mann, Jennifer, "Angelou, Hallmark Team Up," *Kansas City Star,* November 14, 2000, p. D4.

——, "Greeting Card Firms in Patent Dispute: Suits Come and Go Between Hallmark, American Greetings," *Kansas City Star,* February 1, 2001, p. C1.

——, "Hallmark Attacking Competitor over Technology: Web Site for American Greetings Corp. Is Focus of Lawsuit," *Kansas City Star,* June 3, 2000, p. C1.

——, "Hallmark Plans Buyout in U.K.," *Kansas City Star,* July 10, 1998, p. A1.

——, "Hallmark to Start a Site for Retailers: Ebizmix.com Has Already Lined Up 70 Suppliers," *Kansas City Star,* June 7, 2000, p. C1.

——, "Progress Is Slow for Hallmark.com: Web Site Has Plenty of Visitors So Far, but Few Purchases," *Kansas City Star,* June 13, 2000, p. E9.

Nelson, Emily, "Dearest Mom, Greetings from My CD-ROM," *Wall Street Journal,* September 4, 1996, p. B1.

Orenstein, Susan, "Roses Are Red, Violets Are Blue, Hallmark's Online, but What Can It Do?," *Industry Standard,* November 20, 2000.

Schiller, Zachary, and Ron Grover, "And Now, a Show from Your Sponsor," *Business Week,* May 22, 1995, pp. 100–02.

Stern, William M., "Loyal to a Fault: Its Brand Name Is August, Its Profits a Wow! But Hallmark Cards Had Better Get with It—Now!," *Forbes,* March 14, 1994, pp. 58–59.

Weiner, Steve, "Do They Speak Spanish in Kansas City?," *Forbes,* January 25, 1988, p. 46.

Young, Gordon, "Card Sharks," *Utne Reader,* May/June 1993, p. 132.

—Joan Harpham
—updates: Douglas Sun and David E. Salamie

Hammerson

Hammerson plc

100 Park Lane
London W1Y 4AR
United Kingdom
Telephone: (+44) 20-7887-1000
Fax: (+44) 20-7887-1010
Web site: http://www.hammerson.co.uk

Public Company
Incorporated: 1953 as Hammerson Property and
    Investment Trust
Employees: 171
Sales: £141.1 million ($235.67 million) (2000)
Stock Exchanges: London
Ticker Symbol: HMSO
NAIC: 531311 Residential Property Managers; 531312
    Nonresidential Property Managers

Hammerson plc's more than £3.3 billion in property assets in the United Kingdom, France, and Germany make it one of Europe's heavyweight real estate companies. Hammerson's portfolio is tilted toward the retail sector, with nearly 60 percent of its assets represented by shopping centers. The remainder of the company's real estate holdings is in the office building sector. Hammerson owns or holds long-term leases on a number of prime U.K. properties, including the 16 Old Bailey office complex, the 26-floor 99 Bishopsgate complex, the Brent Cross shopping center, a 50 percent share in the 800,000-square-foot West Quay shopping center in Southampton, and a share in the Bull Ring development in Birmingham, expected to be completed early in the new century. In France, Hammerson owns the Italie 2 shopping center, 54 Boulevard Haussmann, 56 percent of the Bercy 2 shopping center, and a 36 percent share of the Les 3 Fontaines shopping complex in Parisian suburb Cergy Pontoise. In Germany, Hammerson has concentrated on the Berlin market, where it owns a majority share of Forum Steglitz, and a 98 percent interest in Markisches Zentrum. In addition to the Bull Ring development, Hammerson has a number of other prominent developments under construction, including the 13-story One London Wall office complex expected to be completed by summer 2003, and two neighboring buildings in Paris's seventh

arrondissement, the former headquarters of Seita on the Quai d'Orsay and a nearly 12,000-square-meter building on the Rue d'Université, both offering frontage on the River Seine. Once present in a dozen international markets, including the United States and Canada, Hammerson has concentrated its portfolio on its three core markets since the late 1990s.

Building a Building Business in the 1950s

The Hammerson family, who had been operating a business in the garment industry, entered the real estate market during the years of World War II. Led by Lewis Hammerson, the family sold off its garment business and used that capital to begin buying up London-area properties. The company renovated the properties (often single-family houses), transforming them into apartment buildings and then reselling them. Incorporated as L.W. Hammerson & Co., the company's steadily increasing profits enabled it to enter the market for retail and commercial properties by the end of the 1940s.

In the early 1950s, the company performed a reverse takeover of older company Associated Investment Trust, that not only boosted the company's size but gave it a listing on the London stock exchange. Taking on the name of Hammerson Property and Investment Trust, the company slowly began to assert itself on the London market, building up one of the United Kingdom's largest real estate portfolios.

Leading the company's major growth was Sydney Mason, who took over after Lewis Hammerson's death in 1958. Mason turned the company's interest to a relatively new type of building development, that of the shopping center. As rising numbers of automobiles and better highways enabled more of the population to move outside of the city centers, the shopping center offered an alternative to the typical High Street urban shopping district. Hammerson began developing its own shopping centers. Its first center was built at the end of the 1950s in Bradford, in the Yorkshire region.

Hammerson had begun, meanwhile, to develop another interest: international growth. With financial backing from such institutional investors as Standard Life Assurance and Royal London Mutual Insurance, Hammerson started to acquire properties in other parts of the English-speaking world. During the 1960s, Hammerson expanded into Australia, New Zealand, and

---

Company Perspectives:

Hammerson offers shareholders an exposure to key European real estate markets. Its strategy is to focus on major shopping centres and office buildings. The group is performance oriented, balancing the allocation of capital between income producing properties and developments and recycling its resources to maximise returns. Hammerson operates well managed properties which provide attractive and efficient environments both for occupiers and their customers.

---

the United States. The company's international growth was spurred on by the passage of legislation in the early 1960s. The so-called Brown Ban of 1964 had placed severe limits on the rate of new developments in the United Kingdom and especially Hammerson's core London market. Hammerson's overseas presence helped it to continue its growth.

Global Growth in the 1960s

By the end of that decade, the company had extended into Canada, a market that was to become one of the company's most important foreign markets. Back at home, Hammerson also found a new headquarters building, at 100 Park Lane, in London. Formerly known as Dudley House, the building originally had been built in 1827 by the first Earl of Dudley. Damaged during the air raids of World War II, the building was only partially restored with funds provided by the War Damage Act. A full restoration of the property was not begun until 1969, when Hammerson, then seeking a new headquarters, agreed to carry out the needed repairs.

At the same time, Hammerson looked closer to home, across the North Sea, entering Dutch and Belgian property markets in the late 1970s. Back at home, the effects of the Brown Ban had cut deeply into the company's new development efforts. Instead, Hammerson concentrated on renovating and improving its existing portfolio of properties. Hammerson's revenues were by then generated by its net rental income rather than by its earlier practice of ''flipping'' its renovated buildings. If these factors meant that the company's growth in the early 1970s had been more modest than in the decade before, they also helped protect the company during the long slump in the property market that began in 1974. Coupled with a long-lasting recession, itself brought on by the Arab Oil Embargo of 1973, the bottoming out of the property market spelled the ruin of many of Hammerson's more speculative competitors. Hammerson's own low vacancy levels helped to protect it from the worst of the downturn in the real estate market.

Not all of the company's holdings were performing equally, however. The company's Australian and New Zealand holdings left it particularly vulnerable to the struggling markets in those countries. The return to health of the European and United Kingdom markets encouraged Hammerson to turn its focus to those markets, which, toward the middle of the decade, had entered into a new boom period.

This time, Hammerson joined its competitors in the buoyant market for new property developments that was helping to transform the skylines of many of the world's major cities.

Hammerson built up a large portfolio of speculative developments, and its holdings boosted it to the rank of number five in the United Kingdom's real estate investment sector by the end of the decade. The company averted one disaster—a hostile takeover attempt from Dutch property investment giant Rodamco in 1989—to rush headlong into a new building market crash. This time, Hammerson's portfolio left it highly vulnerable to the sudden slump in rents and the soaring vacancy rates that marked the beginning of the 1990s.

Described by the *Independent* as ''a hopelessly over-extended, unfocused world-wide property investor,'' Hammerson was hit hard by the crash in the worldwide property market that hit bottom in 1992. The company's angry shareholders, which had seen their investments cut in half, agreed to help the company raise new capital in a rights issue with the condition that Hammerson shed its management, including longtime leader Sydney Mason. Taking Mason's place in 1993 was industry veteran Ron Spinney, who previously had held the top position at rival property developer Greycoat.

Refocusing for the 21st Century

Spinney placed Hammerson on an immediate diet, leading a vast sell-off of the company's holdings, including its entire Australian portfolio AMP Limited in 1994. Proceeds from that sale and from the sale of other properties in now noncore markets were placed in expanding Hammerson's U.K. portfolio and developing its positions in just two carefully chosen foreign markets, those of Paris and Berlin. The company's choices were to prove the right ones as those two markets began a return to health by the middle of the decade. Meanwhile, the refocus on a smaller number of markets helped the company cut its costs, improving its profit margins.

Hammerson coupled its property sales with the acquisition of new properties, enhancing its commercial and office building portfolio. In 1994, the company made a number of purchases, including 99 Bishopsgate, which had been heavily damaged in an IRA bombing in 1993, and the £140 million cash and share purchase of six buildings from the PosTel post office pension fund. The following year, Hammerson began boosting its French holdings, focusing on Paris, with the acquisitions of 54, Boulevard Haussmann, giving the company more than 10,000 square meters on one of the city's busiest shopping streets. Just outside of Paris, Hammerson bought a share in the Espace St. Quentin shopping center, as well as a holding in the 3 Fontaines shopping center in Cergy Pontoise. The company added another Parisian site, 40–46, rue de Courcelles, in 1996, paying £67 million.

In 1996, Hammerson boosted its small portfolio of German properties with the acquisition of a controlling interest in Berlin's Markisches Zentrum shopping complex, for the purchase price of £81.5 million. Hammerson extended its new growth strategy not only to the acquisition of existing buildings but to the development of new office and commercial complexes. One such development was the new London landmark building Globe House, a 20-story structure with a view of the Thames River. The company also joined in with partners for the development of the ambitious Bull Ring development designed to revitalize the Birmingham city center. That development was slated to be completed by 2001.

Key Dates:

1942: Lewis Hammerson sells garment business and begins real estate activity
1948: L.W. Hammerson & Co. is incorporated; company begins commercial property purchases.
1953: Reverse takeover of Associated Investment Trust is accomplished; company is listed on the London Stock Exchange; name changes to Hammerson Property and Investment Trust.
1958: Lewis Hammerson dies; Sydney Mason takes over company direction; shopping center development begins.
1960s: Company undertakes foreign expansion into Australian, New Zealand, and U.S. markets.
1968: Company expands into Canada.
1969: Headquarters moves to 100 Park Lane, London.
1970: Company expands into Europe.
1989: Rodamco attempts hostile takeover.
1993: Ron Spinney takes over as CEO.
1994: Company sells Australian and New Zealand assets.
1995: Company buys 54, Boulevard Haussmann (Paris).
1996: Company acquires share in Espace St. Quentin and 3 Fontaines shopping centers (Paris region), Rue de Courcelle (Paris), and Markisches Zentrum (Berlin).
1998: Company sells off Canadian holdings.
1999: Company buys Euston Square (London).
2000: Company acquires Forum Steglitz (Berlin), Les Trois Quartiers (Paris); begins development of One London Wall.
2001: Company sells Rue de Courcelle.

Unlike the company's property developments during the speculative 1980s, most of its new properties were pre-let before completion. Such was the case with Globe House, for example, which had already found BAT as its major tenant.

Hammerson attempted to gain weight in 1997 when it began merger talks with U.K. rival MEPC, which held extensive holdings in the North American market. Although analysts greeted the idea of such a merger warmly, the merger fell through by the end of the year.

Hammerson's realignment was more or less completed in 1998 when the company agreed to sell its Canadian assets, which accounted for some 17 percent of its total portfolio, to OMERS Realty Corp. for C$600 million. The company turned the proceeds of that sale toward boosting its presence in the Paris market, buying up two Parisian shopping centers and their management, including the Italie 2 shopping complex. Back in the United Kingdom, Hammerson reached an agreement with Land Securities, then developing the Martineaux Galleries in Birmingham, to combine that structure with the Bull Ring development, creating a single shopping complex worth some £800 million. Soon after, Hammerson paid £83 million to buy Euston Square, in London, from Japanese company Kajima.

Ron Spinney announced his intention to step down from day-to-day management of the company he had resurrected in May 1999. Taking instead a part-time position as company chairman, Spinney explained to the *Financial Times:* "I am 58 years old and the business is just about in the shape that I want it to be. It is the first time I have been able to say to myself that there are no buildings in our portfolio which I wouldn't want to own." Spinney was replaced by John Richards, who had already been serving to coordinate the company's U.K. and European expansion efforts.

Richards continued to guide Hammerson along the strategy developed by his predecessor. At the beginning of 2000, the company acquired a new Berlin site, the 28,000-square-meter Forum Steglitz shopping center. In Paris, the company acquired the office and retail property of Les Trois Quartiers, in Paris, for £127 million, and then a majority interest in the Bercy 2 shopping complex, for £44 million. The company's West Quay, Southampton shopping complex opened in September 2000. At the end of that year, Hammerson announced the start of construction of the One London Wall complex, a 19,300-square-meter office complex expected to be completed in 2003. Helping to finance these and future developments was the sale, in March 2001, of the company's refurbished rue de Courcelles building, to Munich Re in a deal worth £101 million.

Principal Subsidiaries

Hammerson Cergy Pontoise SAS (France); Hammerson Europe BV (Netherlands); Hammerson GmbH (Germany); Hammerson Group Management Ltd; Hammerson Haussmann 54 SAS (France); Hammerson International Holdings Ltd; Hammerson Italie SAS (France); Hammerson Madeleine SAS (France); Hammerson Oracle Investments Ltd; Hammerson SA (France); Hammerson Saint Quentin Ville SAS (France); Hammerson UK Properties Ltd; MV Geschaftshaus Verwaltung GmbH & Co.; Markisches Zentrum KG (Germany; 98%); SCI SDPH (France; 64.5%).

Principal Competitors

Assurances Générales de France; American International Group, Inc.; Bail Investissement S.A; British Land Plc; Capital Shopping Centres Plc; CB Richard Ellis Services, Inc.; Credit Suisse First Boston; Foncière Euris S.A.; Gecina SA; Klépierre S.A.; Société Foncière Lyonnaise S.A.; Peel Holdings Plc; Société Immobilière de Location pour l'Industrie et le Commerce (SILIC); Simco SA; Wates City of London Properties.

Further Reading

Branson, Clive, "Spinney Refocuses Hammerson," *European,* February 24, 1995, p. 25.
Pain, Steve, "High Street Hammering for Hammerson," *Birmingham Post,* March 6, 2001, p. 17.
Roberts, Dan, "City: Hammerson Vows to Keep European Holdings," *Daily Telegraph,* September 1, 1999.
"Ron Spinney to Step Down As Hammerson Chief," *Financial Times,* May 14, 1999.
Stevenson, Tom, "Hammerson Gets into Shape," *Independent,* March 19, 1996, p. 18.
Yates, Andrew, ed., "Hammerson Backs the Boom," *Independent,* March 17, 1998, p. 24.

—M. L. Cohen

Headway Corporate Resources, Inc.

850 Third Avenue
11th Floor
New York, New York 10022
U.S.A.
Telephone: (212) 508-3560
Fax: (212) 508-3589
Web site: http://www.headway.com

Public Company
Incorporated: 1986 as Phoenix Capital Corporation
Employees: 10,500
Sales: $360.7 million (1999)
Stock Exchanges: American
Ticker Symbol: HEA
NAIC: 541612 Human Resources and Executive Search
Consulting Services

New York–based Headway Corporate Resources, Inc., provides resource and staffing services primarily to the financial services industry, which includes banks, insurance companies, and associated businesses such as accounting and law firms. Headway offers executive search services through its subsidiary, the Whitney Group, which has an international presence in Hong Kong, Japan, Singapore, and the United Kingdom. Employing a hub-and-spoke organization, Headway's temporary staffing business operates out of regional offices. In addition to providing clerical support staff through its Office Temps Division, Headway also places production and design specialists through its Graphics Staffing Division; computer programmers and an array of information technology specialists through its Technical Staffing Division (Headway Technology Resources); and food-service workers, light industrial workers, and medical support staff through its Support Services Division. In some cases Headway acts as a "vendor-on-premises" to provide administrative functions for temporary staff, in effect acting as an outsourced Human Resources Department. In recent years Headway has been extremely aggressive in acquiring smaller staffing companies in order to diversify the mix of industries and regions it serves, as well as to expand beyond the financial sector

to media/entertainment, Information Technology, telecommunications, consumer goods, and e-commerce. Headway also has taken steps to incorporate the Internet into its recruiting efforts.

Emergence of Temporary Staffing Industry After World War II

The two largest temporary employment services companies, Kelly Services and Manpower, were both founded shortly after World War II. Following a stint in the Army's Quartermaster Market Center, where he became familiar with office procedures and equipment, William Russell Kelly opened a general office services company in Detroit, Michigan, in 1946. Working out of his home initially, Kelly and his employees performed typing, copying, and accounting work for local companies. Kelly then began to send personnel and equipment to his clients' offices. Before long he simply sent the personnel, his "girls." By 1957 Russell Kelly Office Services would change its name to Kelly Girl Service.

In the meantime, Manpower was created in Milwaukee, Wisconsin, in 1948 when law partners Elmer L. Winter and Aaron Scheinfeld recognized that the booming U.S. economy following World War II had created the need for agencies that could provide temporary employees. At first the emphasis at Manpower was on industrial workers, but eventually shifted to office workers. In the 1970s the temporary services industry began to expand rapidly as companies radically changed their approach to temporary employees. Rather than simply viewed as fill-ins for permanent employees, temps became part of a plan to reduce costs, at a time when the expense of hiring and maintaining employees reached as much as 150 percent of wages. Only when work flow demanded would companies bolster staffs through temporary employment agencies. During periods of downsizing, especially in the early 1990s, companies' reliance on temporary employees became even heavier. A trend to hire employees on a project basis also fueled growth in the temporary staffing industry, which generated $28.9 billion in revenues in 1993 and grew to $62 billion by 1998. Moreover, it was estimated that 90 percent of all U.S. companies used temporary workers, provided by some 8,000 staffing companies in what can only be described as a highly fragmented industry.

Company Perspectives:

Headway offers a complete range of outsourcing solutions through Permanent, Temporary and Vendor on Premise staffing. We supply the full spectrum of Today's most demanded job titles in Information Technology and internet Development, Graphic Design, Financial Services, as well as core support Administrative, Clerical, or Light Industrial Staffing.

Creation of Headway Corporate Resources in 1996

Headway Corporate Resources arose out of a 1991 merger between an executive search firm, the Whitney Group, and an advertising and public relations agency, AlbertFrank-Guenther Law. The new company, AFGL International, would be headed by Gary Goldstein, chairman of Whitney Partners, the corporate parent of the Whitney Group. The corporation's initial purpose was to serve as a holding company for a number of consulting firms, including prominent financial consultant Furash & Co., acquired in 1995. In 1996, however, AFGL began to narrow its focus to the human resources business. While retaining Whitney's executive search business, it sold off its advertising and public relations interests, and through a newly formed subsidiary, Headway Corporate Staffing Services, Inc., acquired Irene Cohen Temps (as well as other assets of Irene Cohen Personnel, Inc.), Corporate Staffing Alternatives, Inc., Certified Technical Staffing, and Vogue Personnel Services—at a total cost of approximately $12 million for the New York–area agencies. AFGL International in November of 1996 reincorporated in the state of Delaware, changing its name to Headway Corporate Resources, Inc. Goldstein's stated intention was to increase the company's revenues from $70 million to more than $250 million within two years. In addition to clerical temps, he anticipated placing highly skilled financial professionals in a banking industry that was increasingly opting to hire on an assignment basis. Goldstein also wanted Headway to manage human resources departments, as well as to provide strategic planning for the hiring of temporary staff.

Headway's 1996 acquisition of temporary staffing agencies gave the company an immediate presence in the important Manhattan market. It developed a decentralized hub-and-spoke strategy as a way to expand its business beyond New York. Its large hub offices were intended to cut down on overhead costs, providing a competitive edge in pricing, a model that also granted Headway national stature while allowing for local differences. In 1997 Headway opened a Western hub in Montebello, California, with just three staff and five temporary employees, working out of a 500-square-foot office. Within a few years the hub would have 44 staff members overseeing some 2,500 temporary employees, becoming one of the top five staffing companies in southern California. Headway's philosophy of decentralized control gave local management the leeway to take advantage of a large pool of unemployed actors in a way that would not be appropriate in other regions.

Headway continued to make acquisitions in 1997, as it looked to expand its reach geographically while making the company less reliant on the financial services sector. In addition

to New York–based Administrative Sales Associates Temporaries, Inc. and Administrative Sales Associates, Inc., Headway bought Advanced Staffing Solutions, Inc., based in Raleigh-Durham, North Carolina, and E.D.R. Associates, Inc. and Electronic Data Resources, L.L.C., both located in Windsor, Connecticut. Furthermore, Headway refined its focus by selling off Furash & Co., which according to Goldstein no longer fit in with the long-term thinking of the company.

In 1998 Headway turned to one of its clients, NationsBank Corporation, for $110 million in financing not only to fuel its program of strategic acquisitions but to refinance debt. Through the course of the year, Headway would make seven more acquisitions and expand into four new regions. It acquired Cheney Associates and Cheney Consulting Group, located in Hamden, Connecticut; Shore Resources, Incorporated, located in Los Angeles, California; substantially all of the assets of the Southern Virginia offices of Select Staffing Services, Inc.; Staffing Solutions, Inc. and Intelligent Staffing, Inc., located in Miami Lakes, Florida; Phoenix Communication Group, Inc., located in Woodbridge, New Jersey; and Staffing Alternatives International, Inc. and VSG Consulting, Inc., located in Dallas, Texas. Headway also would supplement its executive search business with the acquisition of Chicago-based Carlyle Group Ltd.

By the end of 1998, Headway would have regional hubs in California, Connecticut, Florida, New Jersey, North Carolina, and Virginia. Recent acquisitions, especially in North Carolina's Research Triangle, would increase substantially the company's expansion into Information Technology staffing, boosting the IT share of its 1998 revenues to 20 percent. Overall, revenues would be more than double those of the previous year, rising from $142.8 million in 1997 to $291.3 million in 1998. Goldstein's two-year goal to reach $250 million in revenues was, as a result, easily surpassed.

Due to a robust economy in the late 1990s that resulted in an extremely low unemployment rate, the number of potential temporary employees available to Headway and other staffing agencies was reduced significantly. Heavy emphasis was placed on recruiting, evaluating, and training, and on keeping employees. By the end of 1999 Headway employed almost 10,000 temporary staffers in a typical week. To maintain its roster Headway recruited through newspaper advertisements, referrals from employees and clients, and outreach to job fairs, educational institutions, and community groups. While it did not think that the Internet was a complete answer, Headway did use Internet sourcing as one of a number of recruiting tools. (Moreover, in 1999 the company formed a strategic alliance with JobDirect.com to help fill entry-level positions in the lucrative college recruiting market.) To make sure candidates for temporary employment were able to fulfill the needs of its clients, Headway employed a thorough screening process, which included a careful check of references and what it termed a "total person interview," the purpose of which was to determine a candidate's aptitude in terms of handling responsibility, as well as motivation and enthusiasm. Headway also evaluated skill levels to be certain that candidates would be able to perform the tasks required by clients. In addition, Headway provided computer tutorials for employees wishing to upgrade basic office skills. Although such training helped in retaining its base of temporary employees, more important was the fact that

---

Key Dates:

1986: Phoenix Capital Corporation is organized in Nevada.
1991: Company merges with the Whitney Group.
1996: Company sells off public relations interests to focus on Human Resources; business is reincorporated in Delaware as Headway Corporate Resources.
1999: Company acquires U.K. executive search firm Tyzack and Partners Ltd.
2000: Company agrees to serve as the exclusive U.S. agent representing information technology specialists from the People's Republic of China.

Headway paid competitive rates and offered benefits to qualified employees, including insurance, vacations, holidays, and 401(k) programs.

In 1999 Headway continued to pursue its plan of strategic acquisitions that could easily be folded into its operation. In June of that year it purchased the information technology staffing division of Nine Rivers Technology Corporation, which included 85 employees in offices located in Raleigh, North Carolina; Dallas, Texas; and Boca Raton, Florida. Not only did Headway bolster its presence in North Carolina's important Research Triangle, it added market share in two other fast-growing high-tech areas of the country. Headway expanded its executive search business and its overseas business with the acquisition of England's oldest executive search firm, Tyzack and Partners, Ltd. Consolidated with Whitney's London office, which focused on the financial sector, Tyzack brought much needed experience working in media/entertainment, telecommunications, consumer goods, IT, venture capital, and e-commerce. Overall, Whitney showed strong growth in 1999 and was ranked as the top recruiter in the financial services industry in a survey of more than 2,000 HR professionals and line managers. The fact that almost 40 percent of the placements made by Headway's executive search division were nonfinancial proved that the company was making great strides in diversification.

Headway Stock Languishing Despite Success in the Late 1990s

Results for 1999 showed continued growth for Headway. Revenues climbed 24 percent, reaching $361 million. Net income increased by 18 percent, rising from $6 million to $7.1 million. Nevertheless, Goldstein was frustrated that the price of Headway stock did not reflect the company's strong numbers, efforts to diversify, and potential growth. The company seemed to be lumped in with other staffing companies with less than stellar performances. After reaching a high of $11.75 in 1998, Headway stock fell to a low of $3.19, a level at which it floundered. With a market capitalization in the range of $38 million, Headway with its $361 million in revenues was valued by investors at barely more than a tenth of sales. Goldstein

began to seriously consider turning to private equity investors in order to take the company private. Not only would such a move increase Headway's value, it also would forestall the tempting possibility of a hostile takeover that could be accomplished with a lowball bid.

In 2000 Headway initiated a major deal that could have a significant impact on its future growth. The company signed a letter of intent with the Shanghai Foreign Service Company (FSCO) to serve as the exclusive agent representing information technology specialists from the People's Republic of China to work in the United States. Tied closely to the Chinese government, FSCO was the largest provider of human resources services to multinational companies doing business in China. Due to a severe shortage of IT professionals in the United States, Headway looked to prosper with access to the world's largest untapped resource of trained workers.

Whether Headway went private or remained a publicly traded company, it appeared poised to continue its pattern of growth and diversification. Because of tight labor conditions, many companies opted for the security of permanent workers over temporaries, causing many staffing companies to languish, and putting a further drag on the price of Headway stock. Underperformers also made themselves inviting acquisition prospects. With thousands of staffing companies in the industry, and the need for their services likely to rebound, Headway was expected to continue making selective acquisitions and blend the new resources into its highly successful hub-and-spoke organization. Although it was far from ready to rival giants Kelly and Manpower in size, by the beginning of the 21st century Headway was fashioning a solid national and international reputation.

Principal Subsidiaries

Headway Corporate Staffing Services; Whitney Partners, L.L.C.; Tyzack Holdings Limited; Carlyle Group.

Principal Divisions

Office Temps; Graphics Staffing; Technical Staffing; Support Services.

Principal Competitors

Adecco; Kelly Services Inc.; Manpower, Inc.

Further Reading

Gandel, Stephen, "Forgotten Firms Seek to Exit Market; Nontech Firms Go Private; Not Your Father's LBO," *Crain's New York Business,* April 3, 2000, p. 1.
"NationsBank to Lend $110M in Funding for Headhunter," *American Banker,* February 4, 1998, p. 5.
Rosenblatt, Robert A., and Stephen Gregory, "Worker-Starved Companies Go Hire and Hire," *Los Angeles Times,* May 9, 1998, p. 1.
"Temporary Jobs Claim More Downsized Professionals," *American Banker,* July 1, 1996, p. 3A.

—Ed Dinger

━H▇IDELBERG━

Heidelberger Druckmaschinen AG

Kurfürsten-Anlage 52-60
69115 Heidelberg
Germany
Telephone: (+49) 622-1920
Fax: (+49) 6221926999
Web site: http://www.heidelberg.com

Public Company
Incorporated:
Employees: 24,177
Sales: EUR 5.0 billion ($4.39 billion) (2000)
Stock Exchanges: Frankfurt
Ticker Symbol: HDD
NAIC: 333293 Printing Machinery and Equipment
   Manufacturing

Heidelberger Druckmaschinen AG (Heidelberg) is the world's largest maker of printing equipment, ahead of second place Xerox Corporation. The Heidelberg, Germany-based company holds a 30 percent share of the world market for offset printing presses, its core market. Yet Heidelberg has been extending its range of products to include pre-press, post-press and digital printing technologies to reinvent itself as an all-in-one systems provider for the 21st century. In all, the company's more than EUR 5 billion in annual sales give it some 20 percent of the total world printing equipment market. Some 85 percent of the company's sales are made internationally. Europe generates about half of Heidelberg's sales, while the United States adds another 30 percent of total sales. Heidelberg is well-positioned in the Asian market as well, which is expected to match the market potential of the United States and Europe in the early decades of the 21st century. Heidelberg, which celebrated its 150th anniversary in 2000, has been listed on the Frankfurt exchange only since 1997. Most of its shares are held by institutional investors, with German utility concern RWE alone holding 56 percent of Heidelberg's shares. However, Heidelberg announced plans to increase its free-float shares to more than 30 percent and up to as much as 80 percent by 2002.

Ringing in the 19th-Century Printing Industry

While Gutenberg's invention of the printing press revolutionized society, the printing industry remained largely unchanged into the 19th century. The advent of the industrial revolution was to bring large-scale transformations to the printing industry, as the use of new production techniques and the advent of new power sources enabled the engineering of larger and faster printing presses. The source of much of this innovation remained in southern Germany, where Gutenberg had first invented his press. An important step forward was the invention of the high-speed press, known as the "schnellpresse" in 1810; soon after, the first steam-driven presses were placed in service.

Georg Hamm went into business in 1844, opening a machine factory and bell foundry in Frankenthal. Hamm's 26-year-old younger brother Andreas took over his brother's company. Joining with partners, Hamm renamed the business Hemmer, Hamm und Compagnie in 1850, marking the official start of Heidelberg's history. Andreas Hamm left the company the following year in order to found his own business, combining his two interests, bell-making and printing presses. In 1863 Hamm joined up with another printing machine maker, Andreas Albert, who had completed an apprenticeship with printing press manufacturer Koenig und Bauer (the future KBA). The new company, Maschinenfabrik Albert & Hamm, continued founding bells, but also began production of a series of printing presses that were to give the company quick renown. By the middle of the decade, the company had produced 14 presses, finding customers as far away as Odessa.

The partnership lasted until 1873—Hamm wanted to continue bell-making, competing for and winning the command to cast the 27-ton emperor bell for the Cologne Cathedral. The partners became competitors, with A Hamm OHG Schnellpressenfabrik und Eisengiesserei gaining the upper hand with the 1875 debut of Hamm's "high-speed cylinder letterpress." This press quickly won international acclaim. Hamm continued to innovate up until his death in 1894, introducing another successful press, the Pro Patria, which was to sell more than 500 units, and gain the company an international clientele of more than 400 customers.

Company Perspectives:

Heidelberg develops solutions for the entire Printing and Publishing Industry. Our commitment is to be the best partner to the graphic arts industry, offering forward-looking solutions. Worldwide.

After Hamm's death, the company was taken over by his son Carl, who sold off the printing machinery division two years later to Wilhelm Muller, a Heidelberg-based industrialist. Muller transferred the assets and equipment of Hamm's company to a Heidelberg factory in 1896. Three years later, the printing press company was opened up to private shareholders in order to increase its capital. The company was now named Schnellpressenfabrik A Hamm AG Heidelberg. Hamm's name was soon dropped, and the company was renamed Schnellpressenfabrik AG Heidelberg. The company's Pro Patria line was meanwhile enjoying steady increases in sales both in Germany and internationally.

World War I interrupted the company's expansion, cutting off its international sales. By 1916, the company had converted its production to support the German war effort, manufacturing armaments, including grenade blanks. The company also received a new shareholder, Mannheim industrialist Richard Kahn, who, by 1919, had taken over the Heidelberg printing press operation entirely. Kahn was to stimulate the development of the company's first platen ("tiegel" in German) printing machines, and particularly the introduction of automated sheet-feeding. Early models were capable of processing more than 1,000 sheets per hour, and speeds were doubled by the 1920s. The process helped to revolutionize the printing industry during the prewar period, and the Heidelberger Tiegel quickly became one of the top-selling printing presses worldwide.

Postwar World Leader

The company's fortunes were especially helped by the arrival of Hubert H.A. Steinberg to its managing board. Only 29 years old when he started with the company, Steinberg became the driving force for the company's growth over a reign that was to last until the early 1970s. Steinberg proved to be a natural marketer—one of his ideas led the company to install a press on the back of a truck; salesmen could then drive to potential customers to give them a first-hand view of the machine's capabilities. Steinberg also introduced payment plans for its presses. In order to meet the steady rise in demand, Steinberg adapted the production line techniques pioneered by Henry Ford for the company's printing presses. By the end of the 1920s, Heidelberg was able to produce 100 of its Tiegel presses per month. The company merged with two other Kahn-held companies, Maquet AG and Maschinenfabrik Geislingen, in 1929, giving it added production capacity.

The collapse of Kahn's business during the Great Depression led Heidelberg to be acquired by its creditor banks, enabling Schnellpressenfabrik Heidelberg to remain in business. The banks later sold their holding to German utility conglomerate RWE in 1941. Meanwhile, the company had another international top-seller in the 1930s, when it debuted a fully automatic high speed press in 1934.

Yet Heidelberg was quickly falling under the shadow of the Nazi rise to power. Publishing restrictions led to a drastic falloff in the company's domestic orders, and exports were also coming under pressure. Heidelberg opened branches in Los Angeles and New York to help compensate for the drop in European orders, but these were crippled by increasing anti-German import legislation. By 1942, the company was forced to end production of printing presses. Instead, Heidelberg began manufacturing lathes, which saved many of its skilled workers from being sent to the war front. The company had also taken pains to maintain a distance from the Nazi party. This decision was to enable the company to stay in business after the Allies occupied Heidelberg.

The company continued to produce lathes, then began accepting orders for repairs and service of its printing presses, before returning to full-time production of printing presses by 1949. Heidelberg was to become an important part of the German economic miracle. By 1950, as the company celebrated its centenary, its sales had topped DM 21 million. More than 35,000 Heidelberg presses were then in operation around the world. The inauguration the following year of the Drupa international printing and paper trade fair at Dusseldorf was to provide a new showcase not only for Heidelberg but for the German printing press industry as a whole.

The 1950s saw the company expand not only its production capacity, but its entire product range. Heidelberg opened a new state-of-the-art production facility in nearby Wiesloch in 1957; the following year, as the company unveiled a new product line, its Heidelberg facility was expanded as well. After clinging to its letterset printing press technology for its first hundred years, Heidelberg entered the increasingly popular market for offset printing presses as well. The first offset press, the Heidelberg KOR, was introduced in 1962. The expansion of the company's product line led it to take on a new name, Heidelberger Druckmaschinen AG, in 1967.

Industry Heavyweight for Another Century

By the time of his retirement in 1972, Steinberg had led Heidelberg to the top ranks of the world's printing press manufacturers. The company was hard hit during the economic turmoil of the 1970s, yet quickly reasserted itself with the development of a new generation of products, such as the multicolor Speedmaster, introduced in 1974. By the beginning of the 1980s, Heidelberg's sales had topped DM 1 billion. In 1982, Heidelberg further enhanced the scope of its products with the introduction of its first web-offset machines. Three years later the company started production at a new plant, in Amstetten, which had been held up by legal troubles for nearly a decade. The new facility gave the company much needed large founding capacity.

In 1988, Heidelberg made its first large-scale foreign acquisition, buying up Harris Graphics, a U.S.-based maker of web-offset machines, which also had plants in Mexico and France. The loss-making company, which cost Heidelberg $300 million, was returned to profits in the early 1990s, and saw its name

Key Dates:

1850: Andreas Hamm takes over brother's machine shop
1851: Hamm founds own bell foundry and machine factory.
1863: Hamm forms partnership with Andreas Albert.
1873: A Hamm OHG Schnellpressenfabrik und Eisengiesserei is founded.
1875: High-speed cylinder letterpress debuts.
1896: A Hamm OHG is acquired and moved to Heidelberg.
1905: Company changes name to Schnellpressenfabrik AG Heidelberg.
1919: Richard Kahn acquires company.
1920s: Company begins production of platen presses.
1929: Company merges with Maquet AG and Maschinenfabrik Geislingen.
1934: Company launches fully automatic high speed press.
1941: RWE acquires full control of company.
1962: Company begins production of offset presses.
1967: Business changes name to Heidelberger Druckmaschinen.
1974: Speedmaster press debuts.
1982: Company begins web-offset press production.
1997: Company goes public on Frankfurt exchange; forms NexPress joint venture.
1999: Company acquires Kodak's Office Imaging division.

changed to Harris Heidelberg. By then, Heidelberg had developed its new "direct imaging" technology, first incorporated in its machines in 1991. In 1995, Heidelberg launched its first fully direct-imaging press, the Quickmaster DI.

At that time, the company's chairman seat was taken over by Hartmut Mehdorn. The new chairman quickly led the company on the development of a new strategy for the turn of the century. Recognizing the rapidly changing printing industry landscape—customers were increasingly seeking turnkey printing solutions, while the field was rapidly transferring toward fast-developing digital printing technologies—Heidelberg sought to transform itself into a full-service printing solutions provider. In order to meet the goals of its new strategy, Heidelberg needed to extend into pre-press, post-press, and other printing areas. To do this, the company hit the acquisition trail in 1996.

Among the company's acquisitions that year was the purchase of Stork Contiweb, a Netherlands-based maker of reel splicers and dryers. The company followed up that acquisition in July 1996, buying up Eschborn, Germany's Linotype-Hell AG, gaining that company's well-known prepress technology. The two company's operations were merged and centered on Heidelberg's Kiel manufacturing plant in 1997. In the United States, the company completed a 28,000-square-foot extension of its Harris Heidelberg headquarters, boosting its prepress capacity. By then, Heidelberg had expanded its holdings to include post-press operations, with the acquisition of Sheridan Systems, a leader in the United States and United Kingdom markets. Post-press was then expanded in 1998 when Heidelberg acquired Stahl-Gruppe, a worldwide leader in post-press machinery and systems, such as folding, stapling, book threading, and sealing equipment.

Fueling its acquisition drive, which saw its sales rise past EUR 3.5 billion in 1999 and past EUR 5 billion in 2000, Heidelberg went public in 1997, taking a listing on the Frankfurt stock exchange. The company became one of the country's largest companies, in terms of market capital. Yet the limited nature of the offering (only 16 percent of shares were involved in the "free float"; the remainder stayed with Heidelberg's institutional investors) caused its stock to remain consistently undervalued. The company sought to rectify this, announcing its intention to increase the level of its free-float shares in 2000 to at least 30 percent. With the agreement of its institutional investors, including longstanding majority shareholder RWE, the company expected as much as 80 percent of its shares to reach the public market by 2002.

In the meantime, Heidelberg began to take steps to impose itself on the fast-growing digital printing market. The company formed a joint-venture with Kodak, called NexPress, in 1997, with the intention of competing with segment-leader Xerox. Heidelberg was also set to go head-to-head with Xerox when Kodak agreed to sell its Office Imaging division to the German company, further enhancing its digital printing and imaging technology. At the same time, Heidelberg was also taking steps to build up its position in the booming Asian market, acquiring trading company East Asiatic Co., based in Hong Kong, for DM 465 million. The acquisition gave Heidelberg a strong sales network covering most of the Asian markets. These markets, which remained relatively undeveloped, were expected to match those of Europe and the United States in the early decades of the 21st century. From its position as the world's largest seller of printing machinery, 150-year-old Heidelberg looked forward to new printing milestones in the future.

Principal Competitors

Xerox Corporation; Baldwin Technology Company, Inc.; CreoScitex/KBA; Danka Business Systems PLC; Goss Holdings, Inc.; Indigo NV; KBA AG; MAN Roland AG; Presstek, Inc; Quipp, Inc.; Xeikon NV.

Further Reading

"Heidelberg in Focus," *American Printer*, January 1, 2001.
"Heideldruck erhalt 30 Prozent mehr Auffrage," *Frankfurter Allgemeine Zeitung*, February 14, 2001.
Intindola, Brendan, "Kodak Ends Copier Manufacturing with Heidelberger Deal," *Reuters Business Report*, March 17, 1999.
Marsh, Peter, "Heidelberger Looks to Boost 'Free Float,' " *Financial Times*, February 13, 2001.
——, "Leaders of the Global Pack," *Financial Times*, May 18, 2000.
——, "Printing Presses Enter 21st Century," *Financial Times*, April 18, 2000.

—M. L. Cohen

Heilig-Meyers Company

12560 West Creek Parkway
Richmond, Virginia 23238
U.S.A.
Telephone: (804) 784-7300
Fax: (804) 784-7913
Web site: http://www.hmyco.com

Public Company
Founded: 1913
Employees: 7,700
Sales: $2.30 billion (2000)
Stock Exchanges: OTC
Ticker Symbol: HMYRQ
NAIC: 442110 Furniture Stores

Through a rapid expansion in the 1970s and 1980s, Heilig-Meyers Company attained status as the largest publicly traded home-furnishings retailer in the United States by the mid-1980s. By 1998 revenues exceeded $2 billion and the company ran more than 1,250 stores, most of which were in small towns. Difficulty assimilating acquisitions and problems with the company's credit unit pushed Heilig-Meyers into the red in the late 1990s. In August 2000 the company filed for Chapter 11 bankruptcy protection. Then, in April 2001, it announced plans to close all remaining Heilig-Meyers furniture stores in order to focus on its 70 RoomStore units, which sell entire ensembles of furniture designed for particular rooms. Middle and higher income consumers were the target customers for the RoomStore chain, which in 2001 had stores in metropolitan areas of Texas and Maryland as well as in Washington, D.C. Whereas the vast majority of sales at the Heilig-Meyers chain had been made on installment credit plans through the company's own credit unit, the RoomStore's customers had to pay cash, use credit cards, or qualify for a third-party credit program, as Heilig-Meyers had jettisoned its credit unit as part of its restructuring plan.

First 50 Years: From One Store to 14

Heilig-Meyers was founded in 1913, when W.A. Heilig and J.M. Meyers opened a home-furnishings store in Goldsboro,

North Carolina. These two Lithuanian immigrants had entered the retail business in 1911 by peddling piece goods to farmers settled around Goldsboro. The two men drove a horse and wagon over dirt roads to deliver merchandise, or even traveled on foot with the furniture on their backs.

In-house credit, along with effective cost controls, allowed Heilig-Meyers to survive the Great Depression. In 1931, its single year in the red until the late 1990s, the company still lost only $5,000. By 1934 Heilig-Meyers had added stores in Kinston and Wilson, North Carolina. A fourth store opened in Raleigh in 1936 and a fifth in Rocky Mount, North Carolina, in 1939.

The collaboration between Heilig and Meyers ended in 1946 with the Meyers family retaining control of the stores in Goldsboro, Wilson, and Rocky Mount. J.M. Meyers turned over direct management responsibility to his sons Hyman and Sidney. Hyman became president and general manager, and Sidney became director of merchandising. Their father continued, however, to be involved daily with all aspects of the business until his death in 1968. Company headquarters were moved to Richmond, Virginia, in 1951.

By this time Heilig-Meyers had developed its operational philosophy of focusing on small towns and rural areas for its growth. Because newspaper circulation was limited in such locations, management chose to base its advertising on direct mail. The limited customer base meant that the company could not grow if it confined itself to selling furniture. Soon items such as jewelry, electronic goods, small appliances, lawnmowers, and bicycles were being offered as well. In 1965, when Heilig-Meyers had 14 stores, mostly in eastern North Carolina, it opened a central warehousing facility in Rocky Mount.

Rapid Expansion in the 1970s and 1980s

Heilig-Meyers had 19 stores early in 1970, when it merged with the nine-store chain of Thornton Stores of Suffolk, Virginia. George A. Thornton, Jr., founder of Thornton Stores, became chairman of the board of the combined company, a position he held until his death in 1980. Heilig-Meyers had 41 stores when it went public in 1972 to finance further expansion. The officers, besides Thornton, were Hyman Meyers, president,

Key Dates:

1913: Company is founded when W.A. Heilig and J.M. Meyers open a home-furnishings store in Goldsboro, North Carolina.

1951: Headquarters are moved to Richmond, Virginia.

1970: Heilig-Meyers merges with Thornton Stores, a nine-store chain.

1972: Company goes public to fund further expansion.

1986: The 74-unit Sterchi Bros. Co. is purchased for $44 million; Heilig-Meyers now runs 216 stores throughout the South.

1989: Company expands beyond the South, into the Midwest; unit total reaches 277.

1993: Heilig-Meyers spends $65 million for McMahan's Furniture Co., with 92 stores in California, Arizona, New Mexico, Texas, Nevada, and Colorado.

1995: Puerto Rico's largest-volume furniture retailer, Berrios Enterprises, is acquired for $99.3 million.

1996: Rhodes Inc., a 106-store chain based in Atlanta, is acquired for $261.9 million.

1997: Company acquires the RoomStore and Mattress Discounters.

1998: Number of units peaks at more than 1,250; company posts loss for year ending in February.

1999: Rhodes and Mattress Discounters are divested.

2000: Company sells its Puerto Rican division; files for Chapter 11 bankruptcy protection in August; closes more than 300 stores.

2001: Company announces plan to shutter the entire Heilig-Meyers chain and refocus the company on the RoomStore concept.

and Sidney Meyers and Nathan Krumbein (brother-in-law of Hyman and Sidney Meyers), vice-presidents. Heilig-Meyers had revenues of $22.1 million and net income of $1.5 million in 1972. In 1974, when it operated 55 stores in North Carolina, South Carolina, and Virginia, it had net income of $1.7 million on revenues of $34.4 million.

Part of Heilig-Meyers's subsequent growth in the 1970s came by acquisition. The company purchased the assets of Granite Furniture Co. of Mount Airy, North Carolina, in 1975, and Bruce's Furniture Stores of Easley, South Carolina, in 1979. It also bought furniture stores in Richmond, Danville, Virginia, and Kershaw, South Carolina. By 1980 there were 72 stores. Revenues had risen to $81.5 million and net income to $5.1 million. Management considered, but ultimately rejected, a 1979 proposal from an unidentified company to buy Heilig-Meyers for about $36 million in cash and notes. Two years later it turned down a $43.9 million offer from Citicorp Capital Investors Inc. of Chicago and Founders Equity Inc. of Washington.

The Meyers brothers and Krumbein sold much of their stock in 1983 and retired the next year, but remained directors. They turned over the management to two trusted executives still in their 30s, William DeRusha and Troy Peery, Jr. DeRusha, the company president, subsequently became chairman and chief executive officer. Peery advanced from treasurer to senior vice-president and secretary and later became president and chief operating officer.

DeRusha won an award and high praise from the *Wall Street Transcript* in 1984 for his management. A leading industry specialist cited Heilig-Meyers for "the number one management team in the industry." He credited the previous management with having put into place a successful system of how the stores should be run, down to the smallest detail. Another industry analyst said that in 1982, a year of severe economic recession, "Their earnings only flattened when others typically went down 20, 30, 50 percent. They've never closed a store in their 72-year history as a result of nonperformance. . . . What we could say has changed is that they've adopted a more rapid expansion program."

The Heilig-Meyers system of operation called for placing stores in communities of 50,000 or less, where competition from other retailers was limited to local stores. After saturating the market in Virginia, North Carolina, and portions of West Virginia, the company turned in the 1980s to South Carolina, Georgia, Alabama, Mississippi, and Tennessee for expansion. In fiscal 1985 (ending March 31, 1985), when there were 127 stores, net income reached $11.7 million on revenues of $167.9 million. A board of investment analysts told the *Wall Street Transcript* in 1985 that Heilig-Meyers had become "the premier investment play in the retailing side of the [home furnishings] business. . . . They have established a tremendous record—20 percent compounded growth rate in earnings and 15 percent compounded growth rate in sales."

Part of this growth was by acquisition. In 1984 Heilig-Meyers bought a Bristol, Tennessee, furniture company and a West Virginia supply company that it merged into a subsidiary. The purchase of 14 Royal Jackson stores in 1985 for $9.3 million opened up the Mississippi and Alabama markets. In 1986 the company bought the 74-unit Sterchi Bros. Co. for $44 million. These acquisitions brought Heilig-Meyers's total to 216 stores in 175 towns.

Although Heilig-Meyers was selling household goods ranging from VCRs to bicycles and lawnmowers, in addition to furniture, DeRusha told an interviewer for *Dun's Business Month* in 1986 that "We're really in the distribution and credit business." Some 90 percent of the company's 300,000 customers were using its credit plans to make purchases on time, paying annual financing charges of up to 24 percent. Income from credit came to 16 percent of total revenues. In defense of the company's practices, DeRusha pointed out that many of its customers could not pay cash, that there was no minimum monthly payment or penalty for late payment, and that it offered delivery within a week plus a unique repair service.

Heilig-Meyers placed great emphasis on its intensive training program of three to five years for developing its store managers. Once promoted to this level, company personnel were earning $32,000 to $38,000 a year, with an incentive program based on store performance that could double their salaries. As a result, the Heilig-Meyers manager was the highest-paid person in some towns.

In 1987 Heilig-Meyers purchased 22 stores in North Carolina, South Carolina, and Georgia from Reliable Stores Inc. for about $22 million in cash. It was also planning to open 20 to 25 new stores during the year. By early 1988 the company had 258 stores in 11 states, with its reach extending into Florida and Kentucky. Revenue came to $303.5 million in fiscal 1988, and net income to $15.5 million. The following year revenue grew to $351.6 million and earnings rose to $17.1 million. By the fall of 1989 the 277-store chain had entered the Midwest for the first time, in Ohio.

Continuing to Expand Aggressively in the Early 1990s

In February 1990 Heilig-Meyers bought 34 stores and warehouses in Tennessee, Kentucky, West Virginia, and Virginia from Reliable Stores for about $35 million. Over the next year it also acquired six stores from Holthouse Furniture Corp. and nine from The Furniture Center, Inc., for $5.6 million and $10.6 million, respectively. Revenues reached $447.8 million in fiscal 1991, and net earnings $18.3 million. Later in 1991 the company bought five more Furniture Center stores for $2.8 million and 42 stores from WCK, Inc., for $14.4 million.

By 1992 Heilig-Meyers had set a goal of 50 new stores a year. In that year it acquired 13 stores from Gibson McDonald Furniture Co. for $13.7 million, four stores from Reichart Furniture Corp. for $739,000, and 14 stores in Pennsylvania and West Virginia from Wolf Furniture Enterprises for $6.8 million. Of Heilig-Meyers's 401 stores, 60 percent were less than four years old. There were five distribution facilities, each designed to serve between 90 and 125 stores within a 200-mile radius.

Heilig-Meyers purchased Carlsbad, California-based McMahan's Furniture Co. for $65 million in 1993. This acquisition added 92 stores: 65 in California, 12 in Arizona, seven in New Mexico, four in Texas, three in Nevada, and one in Colorado. The company entered the Chicago area by purchasing 11 L. Fish stores. This acquisition of Fish's four downtown and seven suburban stores was a departure from the company's traditional focus on smaller markets, but DeRusha said they were a good geographic fit for Heilig-Meyers, which had been expanding in the Midwest. Also in 1993 the company began sponsoring a NASCAR racing team.

Noting that about 80 percent of its customer sales were being charged to company credit cards, an industry analyst declared in late 1993 that Heilig-Meyers had emerged as the country's most profitable furniture retailer. Its market capitalization of $1.6 billion was said to be the biggest in the business. The only question was whether the chain, with 470 stores, was running out of room to expand at its annual profits growth rate of 30 percent. After Heilig-Meyers reported sales up 31 percent and profits up 45 percent in fiscal 1994, a professor at American University wrote that the company recorded installment purchases in revenues before sales were final and glossed over a negative cash flow of $75 million. Heilig-Meyers's treasurer replied that "The whole report is completely erroneous and full of inaccuracies."

There was no change in the Heilig-Meyers strategy in 1994. It announced plans to open 70 to 90 stores during fiscal 1995, exclusive of acquisitions. Seventy-seven stores were added during 1994, including eight acquired Nelson Bros. units in the Chicago area, bringing the total to 647. For fiscal 1995 (ending February 28, 1995), Heilig-Meyers reported that sales had reached $956 million and total revenues $1.15 billion, an increase of 33 percent over the previous fiscal year. Net earnings were $66.8 million, up 21 percent. The company planned to open at least 50 new stores and to aggressively seek acquisitions that could take it beyond the 700-store mark in 1995. By then a sixth distribution center had opened in Moberly, Missouri, to serve its stores in Illinois, Iowa, and Missouri, and a seventh, in Fontana, California, to serve its California stores. According to company executives, expansion would continue to center primarily on small-town markets in the Southeast and Midwest. The company's long-term debt was $370.4 million at the end of fiscal 1995, up from $248.6 million at the end of fiscal 1994. Dividends had been paid in every year since 1975.

Developing a Variety of Formats in the Late 1990s

In 1995 Heilig-Meyers acquired Puerto Rico's largest-volume furniture retailer, Berrios Enterprises, for $99.3 million. The deal gave Heilig-Meyers 17 more stores and its first presence outside the U.S. mainland. The stores continued to operate under the Berrios name, which had a good reputation in Puerto Rico, breaking with the company tradition of changing the names of its acquired stores to Heilig-Meyers. The company moved into the Pacific Northwest for the first time in 1996 through two acquisitions. The purchase of Santa Monica, California-based McMahan's Furniture Co. included six stores in Washington, 13 in California, and one in Nevada. (This McMahan's, a different corporate entity than the one purchased in 1993, was owned by other members of the McMahan family.) Also acquired was Self Service Furniture Co., a chain based in Spokane, Washington, operating 23 stores in its home state, Oregon, Idaho, California, and Montana.

A larger and more significant acquisition in 1996—the largest acquisition in company history—was that of Rhodes Inc., an Atlanta-based furniture chain with 106 stores mostly located in the Southwest and Midwest. In a deal completed in December 1996, Rhodes was purchased for $69.4 million in stock and the assumption of $192.5 million in debt. Rhodes sold slightly more upscale furnishings than Heilig-Meyers, and its units were located in mid-size markets and large cities rather than the small towns of its new parent. Because of these differences, Heilig-Meyers retained the Rhodes name and its more upscale product line.

During 1997 Heilig-Meyers added three more formats as it quickly and nearly inadvertently developed into a multiformat retailer. It purchased the RoomStore, a ten-unit chain of stores in the Dallas area that sold ensembles of furniture designed for particular rooms. The RoomStore became Heilig-Meyers's format for major metropolitan areas. Heilig-Meyers next purchased a 19-unit North Carolina chain called Star Furniture Co. These units were rebranded under the name ValueHouse Furniture, with ValueHouse becoming the company's format for very small towns, towns even too small for a Heilig-Meyers store. Finally, Heilig-Meyers went in a slightly different direction with its third 1997 acquisition, that of Mattress Discounters Corp., the largest retailer of specialty bedding in the country, with 169 stores located in mid-size and large markets in ten states. By early 1998 the six formats of Heilig-Meyers amounted to a total of more than 1,250 units, and the acquisition spree had led to a 60.9 percent increase in revenues for the fiscal year ending in February 1998, with sales surpassing the $2 billion mark for the first time.

Heilig-Meyers had plans to rapidly expand each of these formats through organic growth and through purchasing other chains and converting the units to the appropriate format. But profits suffered in fiscal 1998 as the company concentrated on assimilating the acquisitions. Also hurting the company was the steady increase in personal bankruptcies from the middle to late years of the decade, which translated into more and more bad loans being carried by the company's credit arm. Furthermore, Heilig-Meyers had attempted to make Rhodes into a more upscale retailer than it had been, which led to the loss of many of that chain's traditional customers.

Heilig-Meyers began restructuring beginning in late 1997, with charges and asset write-downs leading to a net loss of $55.1 million for fiscal 1998. Expansion plans were scaled back, although the company did complete the purchase of 21 stores in the Baltimore-Washington, D.C. area from Reliable Stores Inc. Of these units, 18 were subsequently converted to RoomStores, two to Rhodes, and one to Heilig-Meyers. This restructuring also included the closure during 1998 of about 40 Heilig-Meyers stores in noncore metropolitan areas, such as Atlanta, Cleveland, and Milwaukee. Hundreds of workers lost their jobs. In late 1998, Peery stepped down from his post as president in the midst of another year in the red—a $2 million loss for fiscal 1999.

In March 1999 Donald S. Shaffer, a former executive at Sears, Roebuck and Co. with a reputation as a turnaround specialist, was named president and COO. At the same time, the company decided to reverse some of its recent expansion moves by selling off both Rhodes and Mattress Discounters to focus more on Heilig-Meyers and RoomStore. In July 1999 Rhodes was sold to its management team and certain institutional investors for about $110 million. One month later, Mattress Discounters was sold to an investment group led by Bain Capital for $230 million. Later in 1999, Heilig-Meyers closed down 18 stores located in the Chicago and Milwaukee areas. A loss of $58.6 million was posted for the fiscal year ending in February 2000, by which time the company had been reduced to 906 units. Revenues fell 16.2 percent for the year, to $2.04 billion.

2000s: Declaring Bankruptcy, Focusing on RoomStore

Continuing to shed units acquired only recently, Heilig-Meyers sold its Puerto Rican division in April 2000 for more than $120 million. In July Chairman and CEO DeRusha resigned under pressure after a number of shareholders and analysts began blaming the company's problems on the acquisition spree that he launched in 1995. Shaffer became president and CEO. In need of a financial overhaul, and with its share price dropping below $1, Heilig-Meyers filed for Chapter 11 bankruptcy protection on August 16, 2000. It also announced at that time that it planned to close 302 Heilig-Meyers stores—including all of its stores in California, Idaho, Montana, and other markets in the West—and lay off about 4,400 of its employees. Distribution centers in California and Georgia were

slated for closure. Another key element of this initial restructuring was the elimination of all in-house credit programs in favor of contracting with a third party to handle financing for customers. This last move meant that Heilig-Meyers would no longer face the risk of being exposed to consumer bad debt.

Even these drastic measures quickly proved to be inadequate. Following the store closures in the fall and the elimination of in-house credit, a number of the company's remaining stores turned unprofitable. In January 2001, then, Heilig-Meyers began closing an additional 116 stores, including 97 Heilig-Meyers stores in 20 states, 14 ValueHouse units in North Carolina, and five RoomStore locations in Portland, Oregon. Another 1,000 workers lost their jobs. Despite these additional cutbacks, however, the company was having trouble finding a viable way to escape from bankruptcy in what was a very difficult retailing environment. Heilig-Meyers therefore announced in April 2001 that it would close its remaining 375 Heilig-Meyers stores, shut down three more distribution centers, and concentrate its full attention on its profitable RoomStore chain, which numbered 70 units at that time, all located in metropolitan markets of Texas, Maryland, and Washington, D.C. This would represent a huge slimming down for a company that was once—only a few years previous—the undisputed leader of U.S. furniture retailing, but it perhaps provided a viable way for Heilig-Meyers Company to emerge from Chapter 11.

Principal Subsidiaries

Heilig-Meyers Furniture Company; HMY-RoomStore, Inc.; MacSaver Financial Services, Inc.; MacSaver Funding Corporation, Inc.; MacSaver Insurance Services, Ltd. (Bermuda).

Principal Competitors

Ethan Allen Interiors Inc.; Rooms To Go; HomeLife Furniture Corporation; Havertys Furniture Companies, Inc.; Levitz Furniture Incorporated; IKEA International A/S; Seaman Furniture Company, Inc.; Krause's Furniture, Inc.; Jennifer Convertibles, Inc.; Schottenstein Stores Corporation.

Further Reading

Buchanan, Lee, "Heilig-Meyers Sees 700 Units," *Furniture/Today*, November 14, 1994, pp. 1, 18.

Craft, Leslie, Jr., "What's in Store for Heilig-Meyers?," *Furniture/Today*, October 5, 1992, p. 16.

Engel, Clint, "Heilig-Meyers to Buy 17 Puerto Rican Units," *Furniture/Today*, December 26, 1994, pp. 1, 51.

——, "Heilig-Meyers Hones Strategy," *Furniture/Today*, March 27, 1995, pp. 1, 46.

Epperson, Wallace W., Jr., "Heilig-Meyers Co.," *Wall Street Transcript*, December 3, 1984, p. 76114.

"Furnishings/Residential and Commercial," *Wall Street Transcript*, September 16, 1985, pp. 79200-79202.

Gilligan, Gregory J., "Furnishing Growth: Heilig-Meyers Continues to Increase Sales Despite Difficult Times For Industry," *Richmond Times-Dispatch*, August 26, 1996, p. D14.

——, "Furniture Giant Files Bankruptcy Papers," *Richmond Times-Dispatch*, August 17, 2000, p. A1.

——, "Heilig-Meyers Buys West Coast Chain," *Richmond Times-Dispatch*, August 29, 1996, p. B8.

——, "Heilig-Meyers CEO Oversees Rapid Growth," *Richmond Times-Dispatch,* June 30, 1998, p. C1.

——, "Heilig-Meyers Keeps on Growing: Richmond-Based Furniture Retailer Buying Two Chains," *Richmond Times-Dispatch,* September 18, 1996, p. C1.

——, "Heilig-Meyers Scaling Back to Boost Profitability," *Richmond Times-Dispatch,* December 18, 1997, p. A1.

——, "Heilig-Meyers Sets Sights High," *Richmond Times-Dispatch,* June 16, 1994, p. B8.

——, "Heilig-Meyers to Enter Chicago Area," *Richmond Times-Dispatch,* June 17, 1993, p. B10.

——, "Heilig-Meyers to Rearrange Itself," *Richmond Times-Dispatch,* March 25, 1999, p. B8.

——, "Refurbishing the Home Furnishings Chain," *Richmond Times-Dispatch,* February 7, 1999, p. E1.

——, "The Remaking of Heilig-Meyers," *Richmond Times-Dispatch,* April 17, 2000, p. D16.

——, "Richmond, Va.-Based Furniture Retailer Closes All Remaining Stores," *Richmond Times-Dispatch,* April 12, 2001.

——, "A Room with a View: Heilig-Meyers Strives for High Ground Again with RoomStore Sales Concept," *Richmond Times-Dispatch,* February 18, 2001, p. E1.

——, "Thinking Big: Heilig-Meyers' Purchases Give It a Variety of Approaches," *Richmond Times-Dispatch,* August 25, 1997, p. D16.

Hackney, Holt, "Heilig-Meyers: The Vulture Play in Home Furnishings," *Financial World,* December 8, 1992, pp. 18–19.

Hagerty, James R., "Heilig-Meyers Has a Tough Time Making It in the City: Furniture Firm Struggles to Crack Upscale Urban Market with Rhodes Chain," *Wall Street Journal,* September 30, 1998, p. B4.

Howard, Maria Osborn, "Furniture Firm Here Steps Out: Heilig-Meyers Buys Puerto Rican Chain," *Richmond Times-Dispatch,* December 15, 1994, p. B9.

Levy, Robert, "Heilig-Meyers: Selling Big in Small Towns," *Dun's Business Month,* June 1986, pp. 56–57.

Mollenkamp, Carrick, "Heilig-Meyers Seeks Bankruptcy-Law Protection," *Wall Street Journal,* August 17, 2000, p. A4.

Rorrer, Mollie, "Heilig-Meyers Plans to Buy 34 Stores from Reliable," *Richmond Times-Dispatch,* January 5, 1990, p. A5.

——, "Heilig-Meyers Rings Up Sales Increases amid Home Furnishings Industry Slump," *Richmond Times-Dispatch,* September 9, 1990, p. F1.

Schroeder, Michael, "The Sherlock Holmes of Accounting," *Business Week,* September 5, 1994, p. 48.

—Robert Halasz
—update: David E. Salamie

HELZBERG DIAMONDS

Helzberg Diamonds

1825 Swift
Kansas City, Missouri 64116
U.S.A.
Telephone: (816) 842-7780
Fax: (816) 480-0294
Web site: http://www.helzberg.com

Wholly Owned Subsidiary of Berkshire Hathaway
Incorporated: 1915
Employees: 3,000
Sales: $400 million (2000 est.)
NAIC: 44831 Jewelry Stores

Helzberg Diamonds is one of the country's largest jewelry retailers, with a chain of some 200 stores nationwide. The firm began in Kansas City, and gradually expanded to become the largest jewelry chain in the Midwest. Helzberg now has a presence in most of the 50 states, with locations primarily in enclosed shopping malls and strip malls. Its stores are Helzberg Diamond Shops and a sister chain of larger format stores called Jewelry3. The retail chain was operated by the descendants of founder Morris Helzberg until 1995, when it was sold to Berkshire Hathaway, the holding company of investor Warren Buffett.

From Father to Son: 1910s–20s

The nationwide chain that became Helzberg Diamond Shops Inc. began as a small jewelry store in Kansas City, opened in 1915 by a Russian immigrant, Morris Helzberg. Helzberg had five children, two girls and three boys. The children helped out in the shop, and the whole family was involved in making decisions regarding the business. Within a few years of starting the store, Morris Helzberg suffered a disabling stroke. His oldest son, Morton, was away at college studying dentistry, and the next oldest son, Gilbert, was soon to be shipped out to fight in World War I. The responsibility for running the family business fell to the youngest of the five children, Barnett, who was all of 14 years old. An uncle ran the store during the day, and Barnett took over when he got out of school at three o'clock. This seemed like it should have been a temporary

arrangement until Gilbert returned from overseas. But when the older brother came back to Kansas City, he found that Barnett relished working in the store, and was full of plans for expansion. The rent on the original store was something around $30 a month. Barnett wanted to lease a bigger place, for $150 a month. This was a quite a jump in rent, but the teenage Barnett eventually prevailed. In 1920 he opened his own shop, called Shaw Diamond Shop, in the more expensive space, while Gilbert ran the original store. Within only a few months, Shaw Diamond was doing as much business as the old shop. Brother Gilbert decided to shut the old store and join Barnett in the new place, renamed Helzberg Diamonds.

Barnett was ambitious, and a big fan of advertising. He spent thousands of dollars on newspaper ads, some of which featured the two brothers' serious faces, with the slogan "Meet the Helzberg Boys, Wear Diamonds." Gilbert was seemingly content to keep the business as it was, but Barnett was full of bold advertising campaigns and such gimmicks as free car and airplane rides for customers who made significant purchases. Barnett began offering customers payment plans by the mid-1920s, so they could buy on credit. This allowed the store to sell to people who might not otherwise be able to afford Helzberg jewelry. By the mid-1920s, the Helzberg brothers had grown into a small chain of stores. Gilbert opened a shop in Wichita, and Barnett moved the Kansas City store to a new location and opened another store in Topeka, Kansas. In 1928 Barnett opened another bigger store in Kansas City.

Expansion in the Midwest in the 1930s and 1940s

The prosperity of the 1920s gave way to the Great Depression after the stock market crashed in 1929. Barnett Helzberg continued to run his stores undeterred. He married the daughter of another prominent Kansas City jeweler in 1930, and in 1932, despite the poor economic conditions, he began a major overhaul of the flagship Helzberg store. Helzberg's doubling of the size of its 11th and Walnut Street store was the single major business expansion in Kansas City for that year. The scope of the job was so extraordinary in view of the overall business climate that Helzberg's cabinet maker hung a huge placard in front of the jewelry store announcing how many men were at

Company Perspectives:

Our mission: to serve each and every customer in a very special way, always reflecting our 86-year heritage of excellence and value.

work and boasting that the cabinet plant was running at full capacity. Barnett Helzberg continued to run the small jewelry chain with panache, dreaming up more eye-catching promotions such as offering special deals on children's bicycles. He also advertised on the radio, sponsoring a popular weekly music show. Gilbert Helzberg died in 1934, in an automobile accident. Barnett Helzberg then purchased Gilbert's Wichita store, and a few years later opened a new location in Des Moines, Iowa. The firm lost money one year during the Depression, but otherwise weathered the downturn well. By 1940, the chain of five stores was deemed the largest jewelry business in the Midwest.

During World War II, Helzberg churned out advertisements with patriotic themes. The stores advertised special "Certified Perfect" diamonds, a scheme Helzberg evolved that tagged certain items as having been declared "perfect" under ten-power magnification. This scheme apparently had great resonance with Helzberg customers, and set the chain's products apart from its competitors.

By the late 1940s, Helzberg Diamonds had grown to include 11 shops in the Midwest. In 1948 Helzberg opened a grandiose shop called House of Treasures in Kansas City's Country Club Plaza. The swank, three-story jewelry, china, and silver store was a step up from the other Helzberg shops, which sold on credit to middle-income customers. The House of Treasures was meant for Kansas City's elite. Also in 1948 Helzberg relocated the old Wichita shop and transformed it, too, into a large and luxurious emporium. However, these two stores apparently made a disproportionate strain on the rest of the Helzberg chain. Other new stores that opened later were not on as grand a scale.

Retrenching to the Suburbs in the 1960s and 1970s

Barnett Helzberg, Jr., joined the diamond firm in 1956, after getting a degree in business from the University of Michigan. The chain continued to open new stores in the Midwest throughout the 1950s. By 1963, when Barnett, Jr., became president of the company, Helzberg Diamonds had 39 shops, almost all in downtown shopping districts. But the rise of the suburban shopping mall in the 1960s began to pull customers away from traditional business districts, and Helzberg Diamonds suffered. When Barnett, Jr., took over the top job, he began closing the chain's downtown locations. By 1970, Helzberg Diamonds had shrunk to only 15 stores. These were all new stores opened in suburbs and shopping centers, except for the luxurious Country Club Plaza store opened in 1948.

With the move to the suburbs, Helzberg Diamonds began to court a more youthful image. The signal representation of the company in this era was the "I Am Loved" campaign from 1967. Helzberg manufactured lapel buttons bearing the words "I Am Loved" as a store giveaway, and the slogan became a

huge success. "I Am Loved" was the inspiration of Barnett Helzberg, Jr., who according to lore thought of the button gimmick after proposing marriage to his girlfriend Shirley Bush. The initial ad copy suggested that, if you could not give your love a diamond, you could at least speak your feelings with the "I Am Loved" pin. Helzberg made up 50,000 of the buttons for the 1967 debut of the campaign. These sold out very quickly, and the "I Am Loved" slogan was soon carried on everything from drinking glasses to golf balls. The company gave away an estimated 18 million "I Am Loved" buttons before it was through. Hospitals passed out Helzberg "I Am Loved" buttons to homesick young patients, and the buttons made their way to soldiers serving in Vietnam. It was a marketing campaign that far surpassed the company's expectations.

In the 1970s, Helzberg began opening more stores, aiming for three a year through the decade. The company exited some of its ancillary lines of business. Helzberg had had a mail-order business since the early 1950s, serving mainly rural customers who were exposed to Helzberg's advertising but could not drive in to the stores. Barnett, Jr., sold off the mail-order business in the early 1970s, and also sold the company division that had run licensed jewelry departments in stores including Kmart and Woolco. Helzberg also eventually stopped selling watches, long a jewelry store tradition, and focused on diamonds and gems. Its mall stores took on a new format, meant to be more enticing to customers. This was an open floor plan, with the jewelry counter located right inside the open border to the mall. Instead of peering in the windows, customers who were "just looking" might come right in.

The chain increased its pace in the 1980s, opening many more stores. By the end of the decade, Helzberg Diamonds had essentially doubled its size, ending 1989 with 81 stores. Barnett Helzberg, Jr., had made essential changes while he was president of the company. The old downtown stores were gone, and Helzberg Diamond Shops had been reinvented as sleek suburban mall stores. The firm's territory covered 19 states by the end of the 1980s. Financially, the chain seemed to prosper, and even expanded when many other jewelry chains were showing little or no growth. Annual sales for the company were estimated at around $70 million for 1986, and some Helzberg stores were bringing in $2 million each in the late 1980s. By the end of the decade, the Helzberg chain was accounted the 12th largest jewelry retailer in the United States. Only a few jewelry chains nationwide had more than 100 stores at the end of the 1980s, and Helzberg was on its way to catching up to these leaders, such as the Texas-based Zale, and California's Barry's Jewelers (later Samuels Jewelers).

Outside Management from the Late 1980s Onward

In 1988 the firm hired a new president, Jeffrey Comment. Formerly an executive with a Philadelphia department store, Comment was the first to hold that top managerial spot outside the Helzberg family. Other outside executives also joined Helzberg around this time, and the chain again worked on refocusing its mission so it could expand further. Customer service had always been extremely important to Helzberg stores. Company advertising sometimes featured thank yous from satisfied customers, and the firm thrived on bringing in repeat business. When Comment took over, he re-stressed

Key Dates:

1915: Morris Helzberg opens first jewelry store.
1932. Barnett Helzberg expands Kansas City store despite Depression.
1967: Helzberg's "I Am Loved" ad campaign provokes nationwide attention.
1988: First company president from outside Helzberg family is hired.
1995: Helzberg chain is bought by Berkshire Hathaway.

customer service, which was backed up by sophisticated database management. Customers were asked for information when they made purchases, including dates of birthdays and anniversaries. Helzberg used this to generate mailings, hitting prime customers dozens of times a year. Mailings included catalogs, announcements of special sales, and personal notes such as birthday cards.

Comment also revamped the store format. Stores opened after 1988 were larger than their predecessors, averaging 1,500 to 1,600 square feet. Comment also introduced an even larger "superstore" format. The superstore was named Jewelry3, because it offered three times the selection of most jewelry stores. The first superstores opened in strip malls, with a 4,000-square-foot floor plan. New stores, both the regular format and the Jewelry3 design, blanketed the Midwest and moved into the Southeast as well. Sales for 1993 were estimated at over $250 million. Comparable store sales rose markedly, from about $700,000 each annually in 1983 to around $1.7 million a decade later.

In 1995, the *Kansas City Business Journal* reported that Barnett Helzberg, Jr., was thinking of taking the family firm public. Helzberg was 61 that year, and he was apparently concerned about preserving the value of his business when it passed to his heirs. Helzberg Diamonds had reportedly already held preliminary talks about a public offering with investment banker Morgan Stanley when the story came out in January, 1995. Two months later, talk of the public offering was canned when the firm was sold to Berkshire Hathaway, the holding company of renowned investor Warren Buffett. A Helzberg company publication claimed that the sale to Berkshire Hathaway had come about through a chance meeting on the street in New York between Buffett and Barnett, Jr. For an undisclosed sum, Buffett's holding company took over Helzberg, which had grown to be the third-largest jewelry retailer, with 148 retail outlets and annual sales around $300 million. Berkshire Hatha-

way owned an array of companies in many sectors, including financial services, beverages, consumer products, and retailing. It also owned Borsheim's Inc., another regional jewelry chain based in Omaha, Nebraska. Barnett Helzberg, Jr., gave up his post as chairman and was no longer associated with the firm after the buyout. Jeffrey Comment continued as president.

After it became a subsidiary of Berkshire Hathaway, Helzberg Diamonds continued uninterrupted on the growth plan Comment and his team had mapped out in the late 1980s. Store openings were increased from 20 to 30 a year, with more of the Jewelry3 large-format stores in the mix. The company also worked to continue to raise comparable store earnings. In early 1996 the sales average per store was over $2 million, already up from $1.7 million three years earlier. The company aimed to bring the sales average up to $3 million over the next few years. Helzberg shops also began entering markets in a splashy way, saturating particular areas with large numbers of stores. When Helzberg planned to begin retailing in Philadelphia in 1996, it anticipated not one or two store openings, but eight, all in the superstore concept. The Chicago region already had ten Helzberg stores by 1996, but the firm planned to add 11 more by the end of the year.

Helzberg continued its expansion through the late 1990s and into the 2000s. By 2001 it had over 200 stores, and was one of the largest jewelry retailers in the nation. Stores had been opened in most of the 50 states.

Principal Competitors

Zale Corporation; Signet Group Plc; Samuels Jewelers Inc.

Further Reading

"Berkshire Hathaway Reaches Pact to Buy Jewelry Store Chain," *Wall Street Journal*, March 13, 1995, p. C6.

Butcher, Lola, "Helzberg Deftly Mixes Continuity, Change, with Love, Growth," *Kansas City Business Journal*, April 17, 1989, p. 1.

Flynn, Michael Kephart, and Linda Kephart Flynn, "The Diamond of Databases," *Ingram's*, July 1994, p. 61.

Hazel, Debra, "Keeping the Sparkle in Retail," *Chain Store Age Executive*, November 1993, p. 28.

"Helzberg's Purchased by Berkshire," *WWD*, March 13, 1995, p. 12.

Henderson, Barry, "Helzberg May Make Initial Public Offering," *Kansas City Business Journal*, January 20, 1995, p. 1.

Schulte, Ann E., *So Far: The Story of Helzberg Diamonds*, Kansas City: Helzberg Diamond Shops, Inc., 1990.

Schuster, William George, "Helzberg, Barry's Aim for Growth," *Jewelers' Circular Keystone*, April 1996, pp. 140–41.

—A. Woodward

HIT Entertainment PLC

Maple House
149 Tottenham Court Road
London W1T 7NF
United Kingdom
Telephone: (+44) 20-7554 2500
Fax: (+44) 20 7388 9321
Web site: http://www.hitentertainment.com

Public Company
Incorporated: 1989
Employees: 92
Sales: £20.3 million ($30 million) (2000)
Stock Exchanges: London
Ticker Symbol: HTE
NAIC: 512110 Motion Picture and Video Production

Up and comer HIT Entertainment PLC (the HIT originally stood for Henson International Television) wants to be the world's leading independent developer of television characters for the preschool set. With a strong stable of existing media properties—including U.K. mega-hit *Bob the Builder,* recently imported to the United States, the dancing mouse *Angelina the Ballerina,* and *Kipper* the dog—the London-based company has taken a giant leap into the U.S. market. In February 2001, HIT Entertainment reached an agreement to take over Texas-based Lyrick Corp., the developer of smash success *Barney the Dinosaur.* The deal, worth more than $275 million in cash and stock, has catapulted HIT's market capitalization to more than £600 million (the company posted just £20.3 million in revenues in 2000), and will result in a company with total sales worth the equivalent of some $200 million. Production of the *Barney* operations, which include a new 40-show deal with PBS to extend the dinosaur's run to at least 2007, as well as a new licensing deal with Fisher Price Toys to begin in 2002, will remain in Texas, even as HIT uses its international connections to make a fresh attempt to take *Barney* worldwide. Meanwhile, Lyrick's strong distribution network in the United States provides HIT with instant access to the U.S. retail market, where the company will promote its *Bob the Builder* and other series. *Bob the Builder,* which began broadcasting on Nickelodeon's

Nick Jr. cable television channel in January 2001, has already proved one of the fastest-growing preschool programs in the United States. Through its HIT Wildlife division, the company is also a leading producer of wildlife and nature programming. HIT is led by CEO and founder Peter Orton, who formerly worked for the Children's Television Workshop and The Jim Henson Company. Following the Lyrick acquisition, HIT became tipped as a possible purchaser for Orton's former employer, after Germany's GM.TV, which acquired The Jim Henson Company in 2000 and then ran into financial problems, was seeking a buyer for its new acquisition.

Distributing Success in the 1990s

HIT Entertainment already boasted a prominent pedigree when Peter Orton founded the company in 1989. Having formerly worked for the Children's Television Workshop, and then following *Muppets* creator Jim Henson into the formation of The Jim Henson Company, Orton became head of Henson International Television, the company's international distribution arm. When Disney began talks to acquire The Jim Henson Company in the late 1980s, Orton and other employees at Henson International Television convinced Jim Henson to allow them to spin off the distribution arm as an independent distribution company. Henson agreed, and Orton persuaded his coworkers in Henson International Television ''to hold hands and jump off the cliff,'' as Orton told the *Independent.* Taking the initials from the division's former name, Orton established HIT Entertainment, based in London.

HIT's business initially remained limited to distributing character properties. Among the company's early products were popular British series *Postman Pat* and the long-running *Alvin & the Chipmunks* series. Other popular programs financed and distributed by HIT Entertainment included animated features based on classic children's books such as *Wind in the Willows* and the *Peter Rabbit* books. Helping to fund the company was an investment by British satellite and cable TV operator Flextech made in 1990, which bought 23 percent of HIT for approximately £600,000.

In the early 1990s, HIT began to branch out into programming production, notably with the formation of a new division,

Key Dates:

1989: Peter Orton founds HIT Entertainment, which formerly operated as the distribution arm of The Jim Henson Company; worldwide distribution deals are signed for *Postman Pat* and *Alvin & the Chipmunks*.

1990: Flextech invests in HIT.

1993: Company launches production of wildlife programming under HIT Wildlife.

1995: HIT opens office in Los Angeles.

1996: Company goes public on British AIM market; acquires *Bob the Builder* license.

1997: HIT joins London Stock Exchange primary market; launches HIT Video division; begins inhouse properties development: launches *Brambly Hedge, Kipper,* and *Percy the Park Keeper*.

1998: Company starts HIT HOT animation studios; forms HIT Consumer Products division.

1999: HIT launches *Bob the Builder* television series (U.K.); forms HIT Consumer Products USA division.

2000: Company announces five-for-one stock split; reaches agreement with Nickelodeon for *Bob the Builder* series in the United States; agrees to licensing contract with Hasbro for *Bob the Builder* products.

2001: HIT announces acquisition of U.S.-based Lyrick Corp. and *Barney the Dinosaur* rights; signs worldwide licensing contract with Fisher Price Toys for Barney products.

HIT Wildlife, in 1993. The new division began producing wildlife and nature-oriented programming. HIT Wildlife rose to become one of the company's chief revenue generators, claiming as much as 35 percent of the company's sales by the mid-1990s. As Orton pointed out to *Kids TV*, "With wildlife [series], you can dub them and they carry no cultural baggage. Usually, if a drama is sold to 15 or 20 markets, that's a lot, but these series can go to many more."

HIT's foray into nature-oriented programming quickly gave it a taste for production in its other core area, that of children's programs, and particularly programs for the preschool market. That market had been undergoing dramatic changes since the days when Orton's former employer's *Muppets,* and especially their initial vehicle, *Sesame Street,* ruled the toddler set. The appearance of a new character—a purple dinosaur named Barney—in the late 1980s had opened an entire new category of children's programming.

Created by Sheryl Leach, reportedly in order to entertain her hyperactive child, the Barney character was to sweep the preschool set off its feet, and became one of the most popular and highest-selling characters of all time. By the early 1990s, Barney and ancillary products were bringing in some $250 million per year for Lyrick Corp., the Texas-based company set up by Leach's father-in-law Dick Leach to develop the Barney character. HIT was able to become part of the Barney phenomenon by handling international distribution activities for the character.

The success of Barney and the growing popularity of other preschool directed characters, which were later to include such unusual stars as the Teletubbies, encouraged HIT to begin production of its own stable of characters. Instead of simply distributing characters and their series, HIT now sought to become involved in their development—not only producing television programs, videos, and films, but also in controlling lucrative licensing activities. In order to fund this transition, the company went public, listing its shares on London's AIM market in 1996. The listing gave the company a market capitalization of just £18 million, but enabled it to launch its new HIT Video division, which began production of video programming targeting the company's core preschool audience.

A new character came to the company's attention in 1996, when advertising executive and would-be cartoonist Keith Chapman pitched his idea to HIT Entertainment. Chapman's character was a little builder named Bob the Builder, with such friends as Scoop the Digger, Muck the Bulldozer, and Roley the Steamroller. While a number of other producers had turned down the idea, HIT recognized its potential and bought the rights to developing the Bob the Builder character into a television series. The following year, HIT joined the London Stock Exchange's primary market, boosting its market capitalization to £50 million and raising an additional £8 million through a rights issue. The new funds went toward the production of the company's first three programs: *Brambly Hedge, Percy the Park Keeper,* and *Kipper,* a series about a dog that became the company's first hit series.

Building a Preschool Empire for the 21st Century

HIT opened its own animation studies in 1998, dubbed HOT Animation. The company also launched its Consumer Products Division in order to generate revenues through character licensing. By then, the company's *Kipper* series had proven a hit across the United Kingdom. Initially broadcast on Britain's ITV network, *Kipper* was brought across the Atlantic, when HIT signed a broadcasting deal for the series with the Nickelodeon television network. That deal was just the first for HIT, as it quickly lined up buyers for a number of its other series in the United States. By the end of 1998, HIT had an impressive customer list, including Starz/Encore, which bought the *Brambly Hedge* and *Percy the Park Keeper* series; and HBO Family, which bought HIT's *Anthony Ant* cartoon series. The company's wildlife programming was also finding success in the United States, with the Animal Planet channel buying the rights to air *Wyland's Ocean World*.

By then, HIT had also found an eager buyer in the BBC for the *Bob the Builder* program as development of the initial installment of the series, created in the company's HOT Animation studios, neared completion. At the same time, HIT's *Kipper* series went on to win the BAFTA award for Best Children's Animation, as HIT built on its reputation for quality animation—in an era that was witnessing an increasing number of cheaply animated Japanese series flooding the world's children's programming markets. A new offering of shares, raising an additional £14 million in development funding, helped boost the company's market capitalization to £82 million by the end of that year.

At the beginning of 1999, HIT, which by then boasted ten first-run series on American television, launched a new Consumer Products USA subsidiary to exploit the growing success of its characters on that market. The company took a leap into television history, however, when Bob the Builder finally made his television debut on the BBC in April 1999. The series proved an instant hit among the United Kingdom's preschool market. Surprisingly, the show quickly gained popularity in other markets as well, and by the end of 1999, Bob the Builder was recognized as the United Kingdom's fastest-growing preschool series character.

After a new stock placement in July 1999, which raised HIT's market capitalization to £170 million, the company performed a five-for-one stock split in January 2000. HIT began preparing to bring *Bob the Builder*—which achieved quick success in Germany as well—to the vast U.S. market, inking a deal with Nickelodeon in December 1999 that called for 78 *Bob the Builder* episodes and broadcasting rights for five years. HIT had also built up a strong merchandising business for Bob-related products, which sold for more than £60 million through 2000. HIT was also continuing development on a number of new character projects, including production of a TV film called *Faeries,* which HIT hoped to develop into a full-scale series franchise. The company was also rolling out a new character series based on a dancing mouse, called *Angelina the Ballerina.* That series, which the company expected to bring to the United States, was backed by a five-year licensing agreement signed with Mattel at the end of 1999.

HIT, which had long been suggesting that it intended to expand its character stable through acquisitions, nearly found a partner in early 2000, when the company held talks with Britt Allcroft, the British company that held the licenses to such popular characters as Thomas the Tank Engine, Captain Pugwash, and Sooty. The two sides were unable to agree on a price, however, and the merger fell through. HIT continued to search for a new acquisition, while concentrating on the growing fortunes of *Bob the Builder.* The series' enormous popularity in the United Kingdom continued to build throughout 2000, culminating with the release of the first *Bob the Builder* song and CD. The song, released during the all-important Christmas season, quickly grabbed the number one spot.

Soon after, *Bob the Builder* debuted in the United States. The series began airing five times per week on Nickelodeon's Nick Jr. station in January 2001. By the end of February, the show already boasted an audience of more than 12 million—and had taken the top spot among the most popular preschool children's characters. The success of the *Bob the Builder* series was also set to blossom into a wide variety of licensed products, with strong revenues more or less guaranteed. The launch of the *Bob the Builder* video was scheduled for May 2001, with an initial run of 500,000 copies. At the same time, the company reached an agreement with Sears to set up 850 "Bob Shops" across the retailer's countrywide network. Even before HIT's *Bob the Builder* merchandising effort got underway, demand was already building. As Peter Orton told the *Guardian* in March 2001, "We're already getting reports from Florida of British children on holiday being rugby tackled by American kids looking to snaffle their Bob branded towels and clothes."

HIT Entertainment had by then done a bit of "snaffling" of its own when it announced in February 2001, its acquisition of Lyrick Corp. and its Barney the Dinosaur and other characters.

The deal, which included a cash payment of $110 million and newly issued HIT shares collectively worth $160 million, helped boost HIT Entertainment's market capitalization to more than £600 million. It also gave the British company Lyrick's powerful Barney-based retail distribution network. As Orton told the *Toronto Star,* "What it does immediately for us is create a relationship that would take us 10 years to achieve if we were doing it on our own, which would be to get into Wal-Mart, get into Target, get into these major retail outlets." Meanwhile, if Barney no longer quite inspired the success of its early 1990s heyday, it remained one of the most popular preschool children's characters in the United States. The character's limited penetration overseas also presented HIT with the opportunity of developing new international markets. Meanwhile, the Lyrick acquisition was immediately backed up by three important agreements, the first, an extension of *Barney's* PBS contract, with an agreement to purchase 40 new programs and extend *Barney's* run until 2007; the second, a new deal with Fisher Price Toys to develop and market a new range of Barney toys and games, beginning in 2002; and the third, the transfer of Lyrick's money-losing publishing operations to a third-party publisher, which guaranteed at least seven-figure sales.

The Lyrick acquisition put HIT Entertainment on the world map. If the company remained tiny compared to such industry heavyweights as Disney, HIT's ambitions called for the company to build up a leading position in its core preschool market. The company was also interested in pursuing new acquisitions. One possible target was seen in Orton's former employer, The Jim Henson Company. That company had been acquired by Germany's GM.TV in 2000. Yet, when GM.TV, which had also acquired a 50 percent share in Formula One racing rights, began facing financial problems, Henson Company was widely tipped to be sold off again. Fast-growing HIT Entertainment, which continued to be led by Henson alumnus Orton, seemed like a natural to build the next home for the now classic Muppets.

Principal Subsidiaries

HIT Entertainment USA Inc.; Ludgate 151 Ltd.; HOT Animation Ltd; Entermode Ltd.;

Principal Competitors

Walt Disney Company; Cinar Corporation; Fox Family Worldwide, Inc.; Scholastic Corporation.

Further Reading

Bulkely, Kate, "Bob Builds a Future with Barney," *Independent,* February 28, 2001, p. 3.
Cassy, John, "Bob Builds Ratings Empire in the US," *Guardian,* March 13, 2001.
"Hit Posts Record Result and Goes After Rights," *Kids TV,* October 26, 1998.
MacIsaac, Mary, "Animated Way of Building up Solid Financial Returns," *Scotland on Sunday,* February 18, 2001.
O'Connor, Ashling, "HIT Plans to Develop 'Bob Shops' in US," *Financial Times,* March 13, 2001.
Reddall, Braden, "Barney's Happy Family Grows," *Toronto Star,* February 10, 2001.

—M. L. Cohen

HITACHI

Hitachi, Ltd.

6, Kanda-Surugadai 4-chome
Chiyoda-ku
Tokyo 101-8010
Japan
Telephone: (03) 3258-1111
Fax: (03) 3258-5480
Web site: http://www.hitachi.co.jp

Public Company
Incorporated: 1920
Employees: 337,911
Sales: ¥8.0 trillion ($75.48 billion) (2000)
Stock Exchanges: Tokyo Osaka Nagoya Fukuoka Kyoto Sapporo Amsterdam Frankfurt Luxembourg New York Paris
Ticker Symbol: HIT
NAIC: 234930 Industrial Nonbuilding Structure Construction; 234990 All Other Heavy Construction; 326220 Rubber & Plastic Hoses & Belting Mfg.; 331200 Steel Product Mfg. from Purchased Steel; 331319 Other Aluminum Rolling & Drawing; 331421 Copper Rolling, Drawing, & Extruding; 333120 Construction Equip. Mfg.; 333295 Semiconductor Machinery Mfg.; 333298 All Other Industrial Machinery Mfg.; 333314 Photographic & Photocopying Equip. Mfg.; 333415 Air-Conditioning & Warm Air Heating Equip. & Commercial & Industrial Refrigeration Equip. Mfg.; 333516 Rolling Mill Machinery & Equip. Mfg.; 333611 Turbine & Turbine Generator Set Unit Mfg.; 333613 Mechanical Power Transmission Equip. Mfg.; 333911 Pump & Pumping Equip. Mfg.; 333912 Air & Gas Compressor Mfg.; 333921 Elevator & Moving Stairway Mfg.; 333991 Power-Driven Handtool Mfg.; 333999 All Other Misc. General Purpose Machinery Mfg.; 334111 Electronic Computer Mfg.; 334112 Computer Storage Device Mfg.; 334113 Computer Terminal Mfg.; 334119 Other Computer Peripheral Equip. Mfg.; 334210 Telephone Apparatus Mfg.; 334220 Radio & TV Broadcasting & Wireless Communications Equip. Mfg.; 334290 Other Communications Equip. Mfg.; 334310 Audio & Video Equip. Mfg.; 334411 Electron Tube Mfg.; 334412 Bare Printed Circuit Board Mfg.; 334413 Semiconductor & Related Device Mfg.; 334419 Other Electronic Component Mfg.; 334510 Electromedical & Electrotherapeutic Apparatus Mfg.; 334512 Automatic Envir. Control Mfg. for Residential, Commercial, & Appliance Use; 334515 Instrument Mfg. for Measuring & Testing Electricity & Electrical Signals; 334516 Analytical Laboratory Instrument Mfg.; 334613 Magnetic & Optical Recording Media Mfg.; 335110 Electric Lamp Bulb & Part Mfg.; 335121 Residential Electric Lighting Fixture Mfg.; 335211 Electric Housewares & Household Fan Mfg.; 335212 Household Vacuum Cleaner Mfg.; 335222 Household Refrigerator & Home Freezer Mfg.; 335224 Household Laundry Equip. Mfg.; 335311 Power, Distribution, & Specialty Transformer Mfg.; 335312 Motor & Generator Mfg.; 335314 Relay & Industrial Control Mfg.; 335911 Storage Battery Mfg.; 335921 Fiber Optic Cable Mfg.; 335929 Other Communication & Energy Wire Mfg.; 335999 All Other Misc. Electrical Equip. & Component Mfg.; 336510 Railroad Rolling Stock Mfg.; 511210 Software Publishers

Hitachi, Ltd. is both Japan's largest electronics manufacturer and one of the largest conglomerates in the world. Fittingly, Hitachi is often called the General Electric of Japan, and is in fact considered to be one of the "Big Five" *sogo denki,* or general electric companies, a group that is typically said to also include Fujitsu Limited, Toshiba Corporation, Mitsubishi Electric Corporation, and NEC Corporation. Hitachi's full range of electronics products includes semiconductors, personal computers, computer peripherals, consumer audio and video equipment, telecommunications equipment, and medical electronics equipment. Beyond electronics, the company is involved in power and industrial systems, including nuclear and hydroelectric power plants, control equipment, elevators and escalators, trains, automotive equipment, and construction machinery; home appliances such as air conditioners, refrigerators, washing machines, microwave ovens, and vacuum cleaners; and materials manufacturing, including pipes, wires, and cables, and prod-

---

Company Perspectives:

Hitachi, Ltd. celebrated its 90th anniversary in 2000, and with the motto "reliability and speed," we are determined to enter the 21st century with enthusiasm and confidence. We have recently announced a new strategy for growth called "i.e. Hitachi," a medium-term consolidated business plan. With our wealth of knowledge and strength in information technology, we will make effective use of the Internet to offer customers higher value and become their "Best Solutions Partner." Further, in order to achieve our goal of becoming "Hitachi, the brand of choice," we have created a new corporate slogan: Inspire the Next. It is a statement of our intention to invigorate the next era, as we focus our corporate activities in directions aimed at making Hitachi the most trusted company in the world.

ucts made from iron, steel, copper, and rubber. Approximately 30 percent of the company's sales are derived outside of Japan. Hitachi is part of the Fuyo *keiretsu,* a loose grouping of affiliated companies linked through history and tradition, as well as cross-shareholdings.

Roots in Motors

Hitachi's historical foundations can be traced back to 1910, when Namihei Odaira took his first engineering job with Kuhara Mining. The recent graduate of the Tokyo Institute of Science soon became frustrated with his company's reliance on technology imported from Europe and the United States. Odaira used his engineering skills to build small five-horsepower electric motors that rivaled the imports in quality and durability. His employer soon became his first, and—for a few years—only customer.

While Odaira's motors worked efficiently for the copper mine, he had trouble selling them to other Japanese firms. It was not until the outbreak of World War I that he was able to gain some large customers. A major power company found that, because of the war, it could not obtain the three large turbines it had ordered from Germany and was forced to turn to Hitachi in the absence of a better alternative. Odaira made the most of his opportunity, delivering the 10,000-horsepower generators in five months. Impressed with his work, the power company soon ordered more equipment. Soon other corporations came to Odaira for help in improving their industrial capabilities.

Odaira incorporated his company in 1920 and named it for the town of Hitachi, where he had made his first sale. True to the company name, which means "rising sun," Odaira's success increased rapidly in the interwar era. In the 1920s Hitachi expanded its operations to meet the growing demand of Japan's burgeoning industrial economy. Through the acquisition of other companies, Hitachi evolved into the nation's largest manufacturer of pumps, blowers, and other mechanical equipment. The company also became involved in metal working and began manufacturing copper cable and rolling stock. These developments served to consolidate Hitachi's ability to build

and supply a major manufacturer without outside help. In 1924 it also built Japan's first electric locomotive.

The ascendancy of the Japanese military government in the 1930s forced some changes at Hitachi. Although Odaira struggled to maintain corporate independence, his company was nonetheless pressured into manufacturing war material, including radar and sonar equipment for the Imperial Navy. Odaira, however, was successful in preventing Hitachi from manufacturing actual weapons.

World War II and its aftermath devastated the company. Many of its factories were destroyed by Allied bombing raids, and after the war, American occupational forces tried to disband Hitachi altogether. Founder Odaira was removed from the company. Nevertheless, as a result of three years of negotiations, Hitachi was permitted to maintain all but 19 of its manufacturing plants. The cost of such a production shutdown, though, compounded by a three-month labor strike in 1950, severely hindered Hitachi's reconstruction efforts. Only the Korean War saved the company from complete collapse. Hitachi and many other struggling Japanese industrial firms benefited from defense contracts offered by the American military. Meanwhile, Hitachi went public in 1949.

Postwar Moves into Electronics and Household Appliances

During the 1950s Chikara Kurata, who had succeeded Odaira as president of Hitachi, directed the company into an era of market expansion. Anticipating the future of electronic engineering, he established technology exchanges with General Electric and RCA. He also initiated a number of licensing agreements which allowed Hitachi to compete, through affiliates, in the worldwide market. In the 1960s the firm also began marketing consumer goods, introducing its own brand of household appliances and entertainment equipment.

Perhaps Hitachi's most important decision, however, was investing in computer research. In 1957 Hitachi built its first computer and entered into the high-tech age. During the 1960s Hitachi developed Japan's first online computer system, and emerged as the world's largest producer of analog computers, which were used in scientific research to compile complex statistical data.

Despite its technical advances, Hitachi and most other Japanese electronics companies still lagged behind U.S.-based International Business Machines Corporation (IBM). The Japanese Ministry of International Trade and Industry took direct action to narrow the gap and make Japan competitive. It funded a cooperative research and development effort which involved most of Japan's major technical firms. Hitachi benefited greatly from this program, and ended its overseas policy of non-confrontation. From that point forward, the high-tech competition between America and Japan, and between IBM and Hitachi in particular, was underway. In 1974 Hitachi developed and launched what were then known as "plug compatible mainframes." These "clones" cost less than but were compatible with IBM's machines, which set the industry standard.

Hitachi has long been recognized for its ability to adapt to changing economic conditions. Its flexibility was especially

Key Dates:

1910: Namihei Odaira begins making small five-horse-power electric motors.
1915: Company manufactures a large 10,000 horsepower generator.
1920: Odaira incorporates his company as Hitachi, Ltd.
1924: Company builds Japan's first electric locomotive.
1939–45: Company is forced to make war material, and many of its factories are destroyed by Allied bombing raids.
1949: Hitachi goes public.
1957: Hitachi builds its first computer, marking the beginning of electronics production.
1960s: Production of household appliances begins.
1964: Hitachi builds the first cars for Japan's bullet train.
1974: Company produces its first IBM-compatible computer.
1982: Hitachi and 11 of its employees are indicted on charges of stealing confidential design secrets from IBM.
1988: Company forms joint venture with Texas Instruments to develop a 16-megabyte DRAM chip.
1989: Hitachi acquires controlling interest in National Advanced Systems, a U.S. distributor of mainframe computers; National is renamed Hitachi Data Systems.
1991: Through an alliance with IBM, Hitachi begins reselling IBM notebook computers in Japan under the Hitachi name.
1999: Company announces a ¥336.92 billion ($3 billion) net loss for the fiscal year ending in March; major restructuring efforts ensue.

evident during the 1974 OPEC oil crisis that devastated Japan (which imported nearly 95 percent of its energy) and its industrial sector. Drastic cost-cutting measures were taken to keep the firm financially solvent, and company executives voluntarily took 15 percent pay cuts. Following 1975, when the company had its first disappointing fiscal year, sales and profits at Hitachi began to increase dramatically.

Scandals and Other Problems in the 1980s

Hitachi worked hard—many said too hard—to transform itself into the IBM of Asia in the 1980s. In July 1982, Hitachi and 11 of its employees were indicted on charges of commercial bribery and theft. Apparently some employees at Hitachi had been stealing confidential design secrets from IBM so as not to lose ground in the intense race for technological superiority. The FBI and the U.S. Justice Department arranged an operation that caught Hitachi employees paying for IBM documents.

Penalties for the offense were, on the surface, quite light. Hitachi was fined $24,000 and only two employees were given jail sentences. The negative publicity caused by the scandal damaged Hitachi considerably, however. News of the trial appeared just as the company was beginning a full-scale marketing campaign for its products in the United States. Many

American companies canceled their orders or refused to receive shipments. A civil suit brought by IBM won the American company at least $24 million in annual royalty payments over the ensuing eight years and the right to examine Hitachi's new software releases for five of those years.

Hitachi recovered from this unfortunate set of circumstances, but soon faced other problems. Marketing had always been the company's weakest department, seriously hampering its competitiveness abroad. For many years, Hitachi's products were sold under competitors' names, thereby undermining the company's brand recognition. In 1986, profits dropped for the first time in a decade, down 29 percent from 1985 to $884 million. Part of the decline could be attributed to external market factors: the strong yen made Hitachi's products comparatively more expensive; a global decline in semiconductor sales hamstrung that industry; and competition from low-cost manufacturers in Korea and Taiwan put a squeeze on profit margins. But Hitachi's sliding profits were also attributable to its concentration in mature and slow-growth markets. Its two largest sectors, industrial equipment and consumer products, were not all that promising: the conglomerate's large industrial customers had cut back on orders, and lackluster marketing efforts made Hitachi virtually indiscernible from the plethora of consumer electronics brands. The company was simply not positioned to enter into fast-growing markets.

To deal with these problems, Hitachi president Katsushige Mita sought to change the company's approach to its business. "We cannot live with tradition alone," he said. "I have to make Hitachi a more modern company." To this end, Mita reorganized Hitachi's operations and instituted new business strategies in the mid-1980s. Cost-cutting measures such as increased automation helped reduce labor expenses and helped the corporation compete more effectively with its rivals in Southeast Asia. The transfer of production to other countries helped diffuse fluctuations in the exchange rate. The 1989 purchase of a controlling interest in National Advanced Systems (NAS), an American distributor of mainframe computers, helped shore up Hitachi's sales efforts in that important market. The subsidiary, renamed Hitachi Data Systems, hoped to challenge segment leaders IBM and Amdahl Corporation with machines that ran 20 percent faster than their competitors.

Increased investments in research and development helped the company stay in the technological vanguard, especially in semiconductors, consumer electronics, and computers. With the support of the Japanese government, Hitachi and its domestic competitors formed a research and development alliance known as the Very Large Scale Integration (VLSI) Project. The joint effort proved very fruitful, enabling Hitachi to stay one technological step ahead of its overseas competitors, continuously developing semiconductors with ever-higher memory capacity. By the early 1990s, Hitachi's R&D expenditures amounted to 6 percent of all corporate R&D spending in Japan. It also ranked as that country's top patent holder, and was even a contender for that standing in the United States.

Technical superiority, however, proved insufficient for the company; it also sought market share dominance. A 1985 memo leaked to the public revealed what American competitors had suspected: Hitachi was "dumping" its semiconductors on overseas markets. Dumping, or selling goods in foreign markets at significantly lower prices than those set in domestic markets, is an anticompetitive practice. Once again, the company faced the wrath of the U.S. government.

Restructuring: 1990s and Beyond

An apparently contrite Hitachi charted a new, more cooperative course in the late 1980s and early 1990s. In 1988 it formed a trendsetting venture with Texas Instruments Incorporated to jointly develop a 16-megabyte dynamic random access memory (DRAM) chip. In the early 1990s, Hitachi formed alliances with Hewlett-Packard Company, TRW Inc., and even longtime rival IBM. The latter partnership, which began in 1991, involved Hitachi reselling IBM notebooks in Japan under the Hitachi name.

Still, Hitachi was unable to parlay its technological leadership into earnings growth: while the conglomerate's sales were essentially flat at around ¥7 trillion from 1991 to 1994, its profits dropped more than 71 percent, from ¥230 billion to ¥65 billion. In 1990, President Mita announced a reorganization that focused, in part, on transforming the conservative corporate culture that some observers blamed for Hitachi's declining earnings. The leader shifted the company's primary emphasis from heavy industrial equipment to information systems. Organizational changes focused on the dismantling of a "plant profit center" scheme. Sometimes known as just "pc," this system integrated production, quality, and cost control as well as product design and planning within each factory. The new plan reorganized some divisions into autonomous operations in an effort to emphasize consumer demands over production requirements. Pay freezes and cuts of up to 15 percent for white-collar workers were also instituted.

Mita became chairman in 1991 as Tsutomu Kanai took the reins as president. As Hitachi struggled to improve its profitability, it continued to gain renown in Japan for the bullet trains that it built. Having built the first cars for the bullet train in 1964, Hitachi introduced a new model in 1993 that boasted maximum speeds of 270 kilometers (167 miles) per hour. This achievement was a prime example of why Hitachi suffered from such low profit margins throughout the 1990s. Although best known as an electronics manufacturer, the company was saddled with numerous slow-growth, low-margin product lines that were holdovers from earlier decades in the company's history. At mid-decade Hitachi's workforce totaled more than 330,000 workers, comprising the largest private labor force in Japan, and the company had more than 860 subsidiaries. Many U.S. observers believed that Hitachi and the other Japanese conglomerates needed massive restructurings involving huge workforce reductions and the selling off or closing down of large numbers of noncore operations. Although often compared to General Electric, Hitachi had nothing like the strategy of GE chief Jack Welch, who professed to abandon any business in which his company could not attain the number one or number two position. Such ruthless business practices, particularly any action involving mass layoffs or firings, remained taboo in Japan. Hitachi was seen by many as a lumbering giant, unable to move quickly enough to improve profitability or develop new products in a timely manner.

Compounding Hitachi's travails was the prolonged economic stagnation that afflicted Japan in the wake of the bursting of the bubble economy of the late 1980s. Then the Asian economic crisis erupted in mid-1997, sending demand for, and the prices of, semiconductors and other electronics products tumbling. Hitachi barely eked out a profit for the fiscal year ending in March 1998, before plunging into the red the following year, posting a net loss of ¥336.92 billion ($3.33 billion). This was the company's first loss since it began using consolidated accounting in 1963 and one of the largest on record in corporate Japan.

Kanai in 1998 announced a restructuring involving a workforce reduction of 4,000. Then in April 1999 Kanai was named chairman, and Etsuhiko Shoyama was promoted from executive vice-president to president. Shoyama began implementing other restructuring efforts, including the reorganization of the company into ten divisions (which Hitachi called "companies"), each of which had its own president with broad autonomy whose pay was linked to performance. The size of the company's board of directors was cut to help speed up decision-making. A semiconductor plant in Irving, Texas, was shut down and 650 people were laid off. Certain product lines, such as mainframe computers, were abandoned. To counter the company's engineering-driven culture, which tended to create products without regard to market needs, product developers were forced to get feedback from the marketing staff.

In another break with tradition, Hitachi abandoned its insistence on developing major products internally and turned to alliances and joint ventures with its competitors. In November 1999 Hitachi and NEC formed a joint venture, Elpida Memory Inc., to make DRAM memory chips. One month later, Hitachi joined with Taiwan-based United Microelectronics Corporation to form Trecenti Technologies, Inc., a venture focusing on the fabrication of semiconductor wafers. By early 2001 Hitachi had similarly entered into several other alliances, including ventures with: Fujitsu to develop, make, and sell large-screen plasma display panels for the widescreen television market; Computer Sciences Corporation of El Segundo, California, to offer information technology systems and services in Japan; Clarity Group to develop optical components for telecommunications through a U.S. venture called OpNext, Inc.; NEC on the joint development of next-generation optical transport systems; Omron Corporation of Japan in the area of factory automation control systems; Fuji Electric Co., Ltd. and Meidensha Corporation on the development, design, and production of equipment and components for facilities devoted to the transmission and distribution of electric power; and Kawasaki Heavy Industries to pursue contracts for overseas railway systems.

Hitachi also began pursuing acquisitions as a means of gaining positions in burgeoning high-tech companies in the United States and Japan. One of the company's main strengths was its huge hoard of cash, which totaled $15 billion at the end of the 1990s. Leveraging this asset, Hitachi planned to spend about $3 billion on acquisitions from 2000 through 2003. One of the first purchases was a $175 million deal for U.S.-based e-Business Consulting Group, which was renamed Experio Solutions Corporation. In another streamlining move, Hitachi announced in February 2001 that its instruments group and its semiconductor manufacturing equipment group would be merged into Nissei Sangyo Co., Ltd., a publicly traded firm controlled by Hitachi through a majority ownership. Nissei Sangyo had already been handling sales for the two groups, and this move was aimed at improving efficiency. Other mergers of subsidiaries and affiliates were accomplished as well.

Although relatively tame by U.S. standards, the restructuring efforts undertaken were certainly significant for a Japanese giant such as Hitachi. Less certain was the program's chances for success, although the emphasis on profitability was never more prominent at Hitachi as Shoyama made delivering a return on equity of 8 percent by March 2003 the main goal of the restructuring.

Principal Subsidiaries

Babcock-Hitachi K.K.; Chuo Shoji, Ltd.; Hitachi Air Conditioning Systems Co., Ltd.; Hitachi Building Systems Co., Ltd.; Hitachi Cable, Ltd. (53%); Hitachi Capital Corporation; Hitachi Chemical Co., Ltd. (56%); Hitachi Construction Machinery Co., Ltd. (55%); Hitachi Denshi, Ltd. (64%); Hitachi Electronics Engineering Co., Ltd. (61%); Hitachi Electronics Services Co., Ltd.; Hitachi Engineering & Services Co., Ltd.; Hitachi Engineering Co., Ltd.; Hitachi Hokkai Semiconductor, Ltd.; Hitachi Hometec, Ltd.; Hitachi Information Systems, Ltd. (51%); Hitachi Keisho, Ltd.; Hitachi Kiden Kogyo, Ltd. (57%); Hitachi Life Corporation; Hitachi Maxell, Ltd. (53%); Hitachi Media Electronics Co., Ltd.; Hitachi Medical Corporation (65%); Hitachi Metals, Ltd. (55%); Hitachi Mobile Co., Ltd.; Hitachi Plant Engineering & Construction Co., Ltd. (56%); Hitachi Printing Co., Ltd. (98%); Hitachi Semiconductor and Devices Sales Co., Ltd.; Hitachi Service & Engineering (East), Ltd.; Hitachi Service & Engineering (West), Ltd.; Hitachi Software Engineering Co., Ltd. (53%); Hitachi Techno Engineering Co., Ltd.; Hitachi Telecom Technologies, Ltd.; Hitachi Tohbu Semiconductor, Ltd.; Hitachi Tokyo Electronics Co., Ltd.; Hitachi Transport System, Ltd. (61%); Hitachi Via Mechanics, Ltd.; Japan Servo Co., Ltd. (53%); Nissei Sangyo Co., Ltd. (58%); Hitachi (China), Ltd.; Shanghai Hitachi Household Appliances Co., Ltd. (China; 60%); Hitachi Computer Products (Europe) S.A. (France); Hitachi Semiconductor (Europe) GmbH (Germany); Hitachi Semiconductor (Malaysia) Sdn. Bhd. (90%); Hitachi Consumer Products (Asia) Corp. (Philippines); Hitachi Asia Ltd. (Singapore); Hitachi Consumer Products (S) Pte. Ltd. (Singapore); Hitachi Electronic Devices (Singapore) Pte. Ltd. (85%); Hitachi Nippon Steel Semiconductor Singapore Pte. Ltd. (54%); Taiwan Hitachi Co., Ltd. (62%); Hitachi Europe Ltd. (U.K.); Hitachi Home Electronics (Europe) Ltd. (U.K.); Hitachi America Ltd. (U.S.A.); Hitachi Automotive Products (USA), Inc.; Hitachi Consumer Products (America), Inc. (U.S.A.); Hitachi Data Systems Holding Corp. (U.S.A.); Hitachi Electronic Devices (USA), Inc.; Hitachi Home Electronics (America), Inc. (U.S.A.); Hitachi Semiconductor (America), Inc.

Principal Competitors

Fujitsu Limited; Toshiba Corporation; Mitsubishi Electric Corporation; NEC Corporation; Sony Corporation; Hewlett-Packard Company; International Business Machines Corporation; Compaq Computer Corporation; Matsushita Electric Industrial Co., Ltd.; Samsung Group; Intel Corporation; Texas Instruments Incorporated; Bull; Telefonaktiebolaget LM Ericsson; Motorola, Inc.

Further Reading

Anchordoguy, Marie, *Computers, Inc.: Japan's Challenge to IBM,* Cambridge, Mass.: Harvard University Press, 1989.

Beauchamp, Marc, " 'We Have to Change,' " *Forbes,* September 22, 1986, pp. 84–92.

Fulford, Benjamin, "Jack Welch Lite," *Forbes,* June 14, 1999, pp. 64–68.

Gross, Neil, "Inside Hitachi," *Business Week,* September 28, 1992, pp. 92–98, 100.

Hamilton, David P., "Harder Drive: Decade After Failing, Japan Firms Try Anew to Sell PCs in U.S.," *Wall Street Journal,* June 5, 1996, pp. A1+.

——, "Japan's PC Firms Boot Up to Invade U.S.: Hitachi and Fujitsu Are Leading Latest Foray," *Wall Street Journal,* November 3, 1995, p. A10.

Hara, Eijiro, "Hitachi: The Shackles of Past Glory, and Faith in Technology," *Tokyo Business Today,* March 1991, pp. 34–37.

"Hitachi's Snail-Like Progress," *Economist,* October 3, 1998, pp. 69–70.

Hof, Robert D., " 'The Japanese Threat in Mainframes Has Finally Arrived,' " *Business Week,* April 9, 1990, p. 24.

Imori, Takeo, "Hitachi: Too Little Too Late?," *Tokyo Business Today,* December 1992, pp. 12–13.

Keenan, Faith, and Peter Landers, "Staggering Giants," *Far Eastern Economic Review,* April 1, 1999, pp. 10–13.

Kunii, Irene M., "High-Tech Giants on the Ropes," *Business Week,* November 30, 1998, p. 74.

Landers, Peter, "Broken Up: Japan's Biggest Players Get Serious About Restructuring," *Far Eastern Economic Review,* February 11, 1999, p. 50.

Landers, Peter, and Robert A. Guth, "Japan's Hitachi Plans High-Tech Shopping Spree: Domestic and U.S. Stakes Are Sought As a Giant Changes," *Wall Street Journal,* January 5, 2000, p. A19.

Mattera, Philip, *World Class Business: A Guide to the 100 Most Powerful Global Corporations,* New York: Holt, 1992.

Port, Otis, "What's Behind the Texas Instruments-Hitachi Deal," *Business Week,* January 16, 1989, pp. 93, 96.

Tsurumi, Yoshi, *Multinational Management: Business Strategy and Government Policy,* Cambridge, Mass.: Ballinger, 1977.

Smith, Lee, "Hitachi: Gliding Nowhere?," *Fortune,* August 5, 1996, pp. 81–84.

Sobel, Robert, *IBM vs. Japan: The Struggle for the Future,* Briarcliff Manor, N.Y.: Stein & Day, 1985.

—April Dougal Gasbarre
—update: David E. Salamie

The Hoover Company

101 East Maple Street
Canton, Ohio 44720
U.S.A.
Telephone: (330) 499-9200
Fax: (330) 497-5808
Web site: http://www.hoover.com

Wholly Owned Division of Maytag Corporation
Incorporated: 1910 as Hoover Suction Sweeper Co.
Employees: 5,000
NAIC: 335212 Household Vacuum Cleaner
Manufacturing; 333319 Other Commercial and
Service Industry Machinery Manufacturing

A division of Maytag Corporation since 1989, The Hoover Company is the leading producer of floor care products in the United States. Hoover has a full line of products at both premium and popular price points, including upright, canister, and stick vacuum cleaners; hand-held, wet-dry, and deep cleaners; floor polishers and shampooers; and central vacuum systems. The company also makes commercial vacuum cleaners and extractors. Top selling Hoover products include the WindTunnel family of vacuums, the Hoover Bagless upright vacuum, and the SteamVac deep cleaner. Hoover's manufacturing plants include three in Stark County, Ohio, and one each in Texas and Mexico. Company sales are limited to the North American market.

The Birth of a Legendary Brand

The company's roots date to 1827, when Henry Hoover established a tannery near Canton, Ohio. More than 80 years later, in 1908, W.H. Hoover and his son began selling vacuum cleaners from the family business after purchasing the rights to an electric suction sweeper invented the year before by Murray Spangler, an inventor by profession who was moonlighting as a janitor at a local department store. From a soap box, fan, sateen pillow case, and broom handle, Spangler assembled a crude machine to vacuum the dust that aggravated his asthma when he swept carpets with a broom. On realizing the product's sales

potential, Spangler began a search for investors and found one in his cousin's husband, W.H. "Boss" Hoover. Hoover bought Spangler's patent in 1908, kept Spangler as a partner, and hired six employees to produce the machines in his tannery. Initially called the Electric Suction Sweeper Co., the company was incorporated in Ohio on December 6, 1910, under a new name, The Hoover Suction Sweeper Co.

Soon thereafter, Mr. Hoover began marketing the sweeper in stores throughout the country. His strategy relied on a small magazine ad, which ran in the *Saturday Evening Post,* offering a free ten-day trial period to those who wrote and requested it. Customers would then be directed to a nearby store that had agreed to stock the Hoover sweeper for the duration of the ad. Mr. Hoover's idea was to have selected stores distribute the machines to customers, allow the stores to keep the sales commissions, and then to invite them to become dealers for the company's product. This strategy proved remarkably effective, and the company eventually established a chain of 5,000 reputable dealers from coast to coast. Mr. Hoover's early success relied on door-to-door salesmen who represented each local store; that store, in turn, lent its name for a share of the sale. Hoover also stationed salesmen in dealer showrooms to give free product demonstrations.

Domestic sales aside, Hoover found new markets for the electric sweeper abroad. In 1911, he opened a Hoover plant in Canada and an office in England in 1919. By 1921, Hoover was selling the product worldwide, and by 1923 sales reached $23 million. Also during this time, Hoover began an engineering and development program to design better machines. In 1926, a breakthrough innovation with the "beater bar" utilized the memorable advertising slogan: "It beats as it sweeps as it cleans." The beater bar worked by thumping the carpet to loosen dirt which was then swept up into the bag by a bristle brush aided by strong suction. The company improved on the beater bar with the Quadraflex agitator, which doubled the brushing action and continued as a feature of Hoover vacuum cleaners into the 1990s. Hoover made numerous other innovations, including such convenience features as disposable paper bags, the vacuum cleaner headlight, and the self-mounted attached hose feature, which was patented in 1936.

Adapting to the New Postwar Environment

In 1942, the company turned its manufacturing facilities to the war effort, producing plastic helmet liners and parachutes for fragmentation bombs, as well as four components for the proximity fuse. Owned by the Hoover family since its founding, the company went public in 1943. With the end of the war came new changes for the company. Although Hoover had always prospered with door-to-door selling, changing times made it increasingly difficult to hire these salesmen. As housewives gained employment outside the home, they were no longer the promising sales prospects they had been. Moreover, the advent of the shopping center, greater mobility by automobile, and the explosion in commercial advertising via radio, television, magazines, and newspapers lured the public directly to retailers, undercutting the door-to-door sales system.

Hoover also met with heightened competition. When other companies, including General Electric, began selling through corner appliance stores, Hoover began to feel the pinch. Other companies, such as Electrolux, established Hoover-like sales forces, which also undercut profit margins. By the time Herbert Hoover, Jr. (no relation to the U.S. president) succeeded his father, H.W., as chief executive in 1954, profits represented a mere 3 percent of sales, and the company's market share had fallen. As a result of declining market share, the company jettisoned door-to-door sales marketing, as well as its retail policy. Hoover then expanded its number of U.S. dealers to nearly 30,000. Under Herbert, Jr., the company also set up a subsidiary called Hoover Worldwide in New York to expand the company's management beyond Canton, Ohio.

In 1966, as a result of a proxy battle to oust Herbert Hoover, Jr., Felix N. Mansager became chief executive of the company. Mansager had started with Hoover in 1929 as a door-to-door salesman and rose to become sales manager of Hoover's North and South Dakota sales force. Realizing the obsolescence of door-to-door sales following World War II, he had abandoned the technique in favor of forming a cadre of dealer-supervisors to oversee and train retailers. The plan proved highly effective and was expanded nationwide. This accomplishment won him a position as Hoover's worldwide marketing vice-president in 1959.

While the balance sheet appeared respectable enough, the company suffered from declining market share, lagging domestic sales, and an exceedingly narrow product line. At the time, Hoover essentially produced only two products—vacuum cleaners in the United States and washing machines and vacuum cleaners in England. In the early 1950s, market share precipitously dropped to 9 percent, and for almost a decade domestic sales barely budged from $51.7 million in 1953 to only $54.9 million in 1962. When compared to overseas volume, Hoover's domestic sales were anemic at best. In 1963, a full 55 percent of the company's $242 million in sales came from England, a consumer market considerably smaller than that of the United States. Another 20 percent came from its other overseas operations.

As executive vice-president, Mansager had moved to expand domestic growth through product diversification and acquisitions. With Herbert Hoover, Jr.'s consent, he had added new products, including toasters, irons, and hair dryers, putting the company in direct competition with the likes of Westinghouse and Sunbeam.

Mansager's rise to the top post represented the first time in 58 years that the company's management was dominated by nonfamily members. As the new chief executive, Mansager immediately announced a $20 million expansion of the North Canton plant. He also moved to address the imbalance between domestic and foreign sales through more product diversification and by pushing stronger U.S. sales. As a result, by 1971 Hoover sold more than one-third of all vacuum cleaners in the United States, forcing competitors Westinghouse and General Electric to quit the floor-care market. The company also was selling many products in other markets, ranging from electric fondue pots to washing machines. This product diversification stemmed partly from Mansager's 1969 acquisition of Knapp-Monarch, a producer of small kitchen appliances. In 1971, stronger U.S. sales amounted to 37.8 percent of the total.

1970s and 1980s: Takeover Battles

These promising developments were short-lived, however. In 1974, Hoover's earnings collapsed from $33 million to only $8.7 million, as a result of an overcrowded appliance market. Mansager then retired in 1975, eight months before reaching the mandatory retirement age of 65. His replacement by Merle Rawson heralded a more conservative direction for the company. In 1977, Rawson sold the small appliance unit to focus exclusively on Hoover's core products. He also moved Hoover Worldwide from New York back to North Canton, bringing with him only the remaining key personnel. By 1977, earnings had risen again, albeit not to earlier levels. Although Hoover's one-third share of the domestic vacuum cleaner market had barely moved since 1971, the company remained profitable enough. Its stock had already peaked years ago and now stood at around $11 per share.

In 1979, enticed by Hoover's low stock price, quality products, and its worldwide name, J.B. Fuqua, owner of the Atlanta-based conglomerate Fuqua Industries, targeted the company for a takeover bid. Fuqua's conglomerate specialized in making acquisitions, having purchased about 40 such firms in as many years. In building his conglomerate, with sales totaling $1.6 billion in such diverse areas as trucking, lawn mowers, and photofinishing, he preferred making quiet deals with major stockholders to launching hostile takeovers. What appeared to be an easy and lucrative acquisition, however, turned hostile when the small town family business resisted his overtures. Fuqua's strategy was to get a controlling share of Hoover stock directly from family members by offering $22 a share and then to acquire the rest by offering Fuqua stock and debentures.

Fuqua appeared assured of gaining a significant controlling interest, as Herbert was eager to sell his huge share of stock to

Key Dates:

1907: Murray Spangler invents an electric suction sweeper.

1908: W.H. "Boss" Hoover purchases Spangler's patent and forms the Electric Suction Sweeper Co.

1910: Firm is incorporated under a new name, Hoover Suction Sweeper Co.

1921: Hoover sweepers are being sold worldwide.

1926: The "beater bar," a dirt loosening device, is added to Hoover models.

1943: Company goes public.

1979: Company fends off hostile takeover bid from J.B. Fuqua.

1985: Chicago Pacific Corporation acquires Hoover for $534.7 million.

1989: Maytag Corporation acquires Chicago Pacific for $1 billion, with Hoover becoming a division of Maytag.

1991: Hoover's U.K. and European operations are reorganized as Hoover Europe.

1994: Hoover Australia is sold to Southcorp Holding Ltd.

1995: Hoover Europe is sold to Candy S.p.A., reducing Hoover to its North American operations.

1997: Company introduces its WindTunnel line of upright vacuum cleaners.

Fuqua. On leaving the company, however, he had signed an agreement requiring him first to offer Hoover the option to match any buyout offer. Fuqua bet that the company would not borrow most of the needed $24.2 million and risk the lawsuits that would inevitably follow. He had miscalculated, however, and in the ensuing court battle initiated by Hoover, a federal judge ruled that Fuqua's bid by letter to family members rather than to stockholders constituted an illegal tender offer. Hoover's victory, however, came at a price. At $22 a share, Fuqua's bid was attractive to shareholders. When the deal fell through, angry stockholders filed three suits against management: two class-action complaints charging that management improperly used company funds to block Fuqua's offer through purchase of Herbert's shares, and a third filed by family member Frank Hoover, who first opposed the buyout and now sought to force its acceptance. To appease litigious stockholders, Hoover promised to look for other buyers and to explore financial alternatives.

Nevertheless, just six years later in October 1985, Hoover received another unsolicited $40-a-share acquisition offer from the Chicago Pacific Corporation. Formed in June 1984, Chicago Pacific emerged from the bankruptcy reorganization of the Chicago, Rock Island & Pacific Railroad Company. In 1975, the railroad company (chartered in 1847) entered proceedings for reorganization under section 77 of the Federal Bankruptcy Act. On January 25, 1980, a federal district court ordered that the railroad begin liquidation of its rail assets. With more than $450 million in cash and huge tax credits from the sale, Chicago Pacific began searching for a substantial acquisition. After two failed efforts in 1984 to purchase Textron, Inc. and Scovill Inc., Chicago Pacific focused on Hoover, whose large domestic and overseas markets and famous brand name made it an attractive

target. Given the bid of $40 per share, Hoover's board rejected the offer, directing the company's management to seek other interested buyers to maximize value for shareholders. In October, news of the move sent Hoover's stock up more than $7 in over-the-counter trading to around $43 per share. The tender offer was set to expire on November 1, but in last-minute negotiations, Chicago Pacific signed a definitive agreement to acquire Hoover for $534.6 million. The key to the deal stemmed from Chicago Pacific's willingness to raise the bid to $43 a share, which Hoover's board of directors accepted. The agreement continued a trend on Wall Street that witnessed the takeover of several consumer product companies.

At the time of acquisition, Hoover's net income totaled more than $40 million, up from just $28 million in 1983. Its business consisted of producing and distributing electric vacuum cleaners and accessories, electric floor polishers, and other floor care appliances and supplies, as well as laundry equipment, including washers and dryers. Hoover also had subsidiaries in England, Canada, Mexico, Colombia, Australia, France, South Africa, and Portugal.

1989 Forward: The Maytag Era

In January 1989, Chicago Pacific was acquired for $1 billion in a friendly buyout by Maytag Corporation, a producer of microwave ovens, refrigerators, washers, dryers, and other appliances. The combined sales of the two corporations was expected to exceed $3 billion. Both companies made the deal for similar reasons. Chicago Pacific's efforts to evade a hostile takeover by an investment group prompted it to look for a friendly buyer. Maytag also sought to avoid corporate raiders in the quickly consolidating international appliance market. As the fourth largest producer after General Electric, Whirlpool, and White Consolidated Industries, Maytag seemed an appealing acquisition. The purchase of Chicago Pacific not only would ward off corporate raiders by adding $500 million in debt to its balance sheet, but also would expand its markets overseas with the lucrative Hoover franchise. Maytag had no presence in the international market, while Hoover had 13 plants in eight countries that manufactured vacuum cleaners, washers, dryers, refrigerators, dishwashers, and microwave ovens, distributing them in the United Kingdom and continental Europe as well as in Australia.

The acquisition gave Maytag the foothold in the international market that it needed. In 1991, Hoover reorganized its operations in the United Kingdom and Europe into Hoover Europe, which was responsible for all manufacturing and marketing throughout the region. To increase Hoover Europe's competitive position, $25 million in capital improvements were made to the plant in Wales, which began producing new washers and dishwashers. In 1993, Hoover also consolidated all vacuum cleaner production in Europe at its facility in Scotland, closing its manufacturing facilities in France. This restructuring of the company along pan-European lines produced a minor international row between France and Britain.

The French foreign minister, Roland Dumas, denounced the reorganization resulting in the loss of 600 jobs as a "serious incident." The French government then asked the European Commission (EC) to investigate whether the assistance offered by Britain to transfer the operations constituted a violation of EC rules. Accusations were also made that Britain was engaged in ''social dumping''—attracting foreign investment through eroding workers' rights. In light of Europe's slow economic growth and rising unemployment, the free flow of capital and labor across international borders was a sensitive issue for nations experiencing job losses at home. To remain competitive in the fast emerging global business, Hoover found that it had to concentrate its production facilities in one European plant. The company also reasoned that Scotland would provide a more flexible workforce—an important competitive advantage in many industries—than could be had in France.

In the meantime, Hoover and parent Maytag were suffering from the economic recession gripping much of the world. Hoover's European operations had been squarely in the red since the 1989 takeover, a situation made even worse in 1992 when Hoover Europe, attempting to revive flagging sales, made a serious miscalculation in offering two free transatlantic airline tickets to anyone buying a Hoover product in the United Kingdom for as little as $165. More than 220,000 people responded to this almost-too-good-to-be-true deal, leading not only to financial folly but also to a near public relations disaster when the company delayed getting tickets to people claiming them, as well as to litigation that continued for years to come. The fiasco resulted in the firing of three top executives at Hoover Europe, as well as to Maytag being forced to take $60 million in pretax charges in 1993 to cover the costs of the ill-fated promotion.

The new chairman and CEO of Maytag, Leonard A. Hadley, soon determined that the best course of action would be to retreat back to North America and concentrate on turning around operations there. In late 1994, Hoover Australia was sold to Southcorp Holding Ltd. for $82.1 million in cash. In the second quarter of the following year, Maytag sold Hoover Europe to Italian appliance maker Candy S.p.A. for $164.3 million in cash. Hoover was now reduced to its North America operations, which sold only vacuum cleaners and other floor-care products, including wet/dry utility vacuums, a sector the company had entered in the fall of 1993, and deep cleaners, where Hoover debuted in 1994 with the SteamVac wet-extraction cleaner. Another development in the mid-1990s was the completion in 1994 of a new 255,000-square-foot national distribution center located near one of the company's Stark County plants in Ohio.

In the late 1990s, Hoover, along with all of Maytag, adopted a program called Lean Sigma. This was a combination of so-called lean manufacturing, which focused on cutting waste, and Six Sigma, the improvement initiative that sought to improve quality by reducing defects. Hoover also continued to produce innovative new products. In 1997 the company introduced the WindTunnel line of upright vacuum cleaners, which featured a new head design that was more effective at picking up dirt. This successful line was expanded to include a self-propelled version in 1998. Also debuting in 1997 was the SteamVac Ultra, which added a powered hand tool with two rotating brushes to the popular SteamVac deep cleaner.

Keith G. Minton succeeded the retiring Brian A. Girdlestone as president of Hoover in January 1998. With consumer demand increasing for vacuum cleaners that capture more dust and emit fewer particles into the air, Hoover responded in 1998 with a line dubbed Breathe Easy featuring a filtration bag that captured 100 percent of dust mites and nearly 100 percent of ragweed and pollens; these models also included a washable triple-layer filtration cassette. In 2000 Hoover introduced a bagless upright model that featured two chambers for capturing dirt and other particles and a HEPA filter with a three-year lifespan. This model was followed by the debut of bagless WindTunnel models that incorporated the twin-chamber design. Meantime, Hoover responded to another consumer trend—the increasing popularity of hard-floor surfaces—with the 1999 introduction of the FloorMAX hard-floor cleaner, which could dispense cleaning solution and scrub, polish, and buff floors. Other products introduced in 1999 included the SteamVac WidePath, which featured a nozzle 20 percent wider than that of other SteamVac models, and an upgraded line of lightweight stick cleaners under the Quik-Broom name. In 2001 Hoover added an on-board, powered hard tool to its self-propelled version of the WindTunnel. Through this aggressive approach to developing new and improved products, Hoover was maintaining and solidifying its position as the U.S. leader in floor-care products.

Principal Competitors

BISSELL Inc.; The Black & Decker Corporation; AB Electrolux; Fantom Technologies Inc.; The Kirby Company; Royal Appliance Mfg. Co.

Further Reading

Byrne, Harlan S., ''The Predator or the Prey?,'' *Barron's,* March 3, 1997, pp. 22, 24.

''The Challenger from North Canton,'' *Forbes,* June 15, 1972, p. 60.

Crudele, John, ''Hoover Accepts New Offer,'' *New York Times,* October 30, 1985, p. D1.

David, Gregory E., ''Breaking the Spell: Once the Rodney Dangerfield of White Goods, Maytag Is Finally Getting Respect,'' *Financial World,* May 10, 1994, pp. 34, 36.

''Filling a Power Vacuum at Hoover,'' *Business Week,* October 21, 1967, pp. 84–88.

French, Janet Beighle, ''Sweeping Gains in Rug Cleaning: New Vacuum Cleaners Come with Variety of Options,'' *Cleveland Plain Dealer,* April 7, 1997, p. 7D.

Gerdel, Thomas W., ''Appliance Industry Is Cleaning Up: Favorable Interest Rates and Strong Home Sales Encouraging Purchases of New Appliances,'' *Cleveland Plain Dealer,* September 16, 1998, p. 1C.

——, ''Vacs Compete to Clean Up: Battle Brewing As Area Manufacturers Enter Utility Market,'' *Cleveland Plain Dealer,* March 29, 1994, p. 1C.

Gillman, R.W., ''One Man's Theory Opens a New Door,'' *Nation's Business,* January 1970, pp. 84–85.

Greenhouse, Steven, ''Hoover Rejects Takeover Bid,'' *New York Times,* October 16, 1985, p. D5.

Hill, Andrew, and Michael Cassell, ''Candy Pulls Hoover Away from the Mangle,'' *Financial Times,* May 31, 1995, p. 21.

Holt, Donald, ''Fighting Off Fuqua Was an Unsettling Victory for Hoover,'' *Fortune,* October 22, 1979, pp. 139–140, 144.

Hoover, Frank G., *Fabulous Dustpan: The Story of the Hoover,* Cleveland: World Publishing, [1955], 250 p.

''In the Nick of Time,'' *Forbes,* September 1, 1968, p. 46.

Narbrough, Colin, ''Hoover Sold After Free Flights Fiasco,'' *Times* (London), May 31, 1995.

Salpukas, Agis, ''A Chief Is Elected By Chicago Pacific,'' *New York Times,* April 21, 1984, p. I31.

Semmler, Edward R., "Hoover Introduces Upgraded Models," *Canton (Ohio) Repository,* June 11, 1997, p. A1.

——, "Hoover Plugs in New Line," *Canton (Ohio) Repository,* June 23, 1994, p. 5.

——, "Price War Dictates to Hoover," *Canton (Ohio) Repository,* June 30, 1996, p. A1.

Siler, Julia Flynn, "$1 Billion Merger in Appliances," *New York Times,* October 25, 1988, p. D1.

Upbin, Bruce, "Global, Schmobal," *Forbes,* March 10, 1997, pp. 64, 66.

—Bruce Montgomery
—update: David E. Salamie

IMERYS

Imerys S.A.

Tour Maine-Montparnasse
33, avenue du Maine
75755 Paris Cedex 15
France
Telephone: (+33) (1) 45 38 48 48
Fax: +33 (1) 45 38 74 78
Web site: http://www.imerys.com

Public Company
Incorporated: 1880 as Société Le Nickel
Employees: 14,583
Sales: EUR 2.80 billion ($2.5 billion) (2000)
Stock Exchanges: Euronext Paris
NAIC: 212325 Clay and Ceramic and Refractory
   Minerals Mining; 421320 Brick, Stone, and Related
   Construction Material Wholesalers; 3271 Clay Product
   and Refractory Manufacturing; 212324 Kaolin and
   Ball Clay Mining

Known as Imetal until 1999, Imerys S.A. has transformed itself into one of the world's major minerals and materials processing groups. After exiting its historic metals processing activities at the end of last century, Imerys operates through four primary business groups: Building Materials; Refractories & Abrasives; Ceramics & Specialties; and Pigments & Additives. The company's Building Materials activities, which accounted for 22 percent of the company's sales in 2000, include a leadership position in the French market for clay roof tiles and bricks. Imerys's Refractories & Abrasives division, adding another 21 percent to sales, makes the company the world leader in mining and production of minerals for these product markets. The company is world leader in the market for raw materials and ceramic bodies, including clay and kaolin, and in high-performance graphite production through its Ceramics & Specialties division, which produced 12 percent of sales in 2000. Pigments & Additives, however, boosted by the company's takeover of English China Clays in 1999—which prompted its name change—remains the company's largest sales generator, with 45 percent of Imerys's EUR 2.8 billion in sales in 2000.

Nickel Mining in the 19th Century

Imerys's history dates back to 1863 in the French colony of New Caledonia, when Jules Garnier, an engineer, discovered important nickel deposits. Some ten years later, together with Henri Marbeau, he founded La Société de Traitement des Minerais de Nickel, Cobalt et Autres. Four years later, in 1880, Garnier and Marbeau's company merged with Higginson et Hanckar to form the company's direct predecessor, Société Le Nickel (SLN). Although its headquarters were located in Paris, the SLN built small factories near Marseilles and a blast furnace at Nouméa, New Caledonia. Its early progress was encouraging. However, the first nickel crisis in 1884 slowed down its activities, and after the closing of the main factory at Chaleix, Garnier and Marbeau were forced to relocate production to France, Britain, and Germany.

This was the era of tall sailing ships of 3,000 to 5,000 tons, that were able to cross in 100 days and to transport around 60,000 tons of minerals annually. These transported nickel from New Caledonia to Europe until World War I interrupted the company's expansion. By the end of the war, only the Le Havre factory had escaped damage. The SLN took nearly 15 years to recover from the disaster. In 1931 it entered into partnership with the Société Calédonia and created Calédonickel, a company that managed the large factory of Doniambo, near Nouméa. Six years later, having absorbed Calédonickel, the SLN was the only company exploiting nickel in New Caledonia and was already producing 10 percent of the world's nickel consumption. Calédonickel and, more generally, the SLN were not only responsible for considerable improvements in the Caledonian economy but also played a leading role in the urbanization and social development of the island. They took on workers from abroad, but also trained and employed natives. During World War II, the Doniambo factory's output reached the United States, since a great part of it was sent to help in the construction of U.S. weapons. Although these transactions increased SLN's international status, the war left the company in a precarious state. The need was felt to concentrate and modernize its structure and equipment. This process took SLN about ten years, but in 1950 the company's nickel production (6,900 tons) finally exceeded that of 1939 (6,700 tons). In spite of several other crises, the next 20 years saw the continuation of

Company Perspectives:

Imerys pursues a value-creating growth strategy: using its substantial mineral reserves and sophisticated processing expertise, the Group supplies technically advanced products that are essential to the success of a diversified customer base.

SLN's development from the level of a cottage industry to that of an advanced technology company.

Peñarroya, which was to merge with SLN in 1967, had grown rapidly in parallel with SLN. Although both companies were partly owned by the Rothschild empire, which had been one of the founders of Peñarroya, they had separate identities, management, and operations. Created in 1881 by Charles Leroux in order to exploit the coal and lead mines of the Andalusian village that gave its name to the company, Peñarroya, after a very difficult start, made great progress at the beginning of the 20th century. For his efforts, Charles Leroux received a medal at the Paris Universal Exhibition (Exposition Universelle) of 1900. In 1910, Peñarroya's new chairman, Fréderic Leroux, decided to extend the company's activities beyond Spain. World War I had little effect on Peñarroya, since Spain was not at war with Germany, and the company rapidly turned to the exploitation of nonferrous metals in the Mediterranean basin. It prospected for zinc in North Africa and its French colonies, in Greece, and in Italy. After the shock of World War II, Peñarroya expanded as far as South America and Mauritania, under the influence of the new chairman René Fillon, who used to work for the Banque Rothschild and whose tenure would last until 1961. Peñarroya then became a world leader in zinc but also produced silver, cadmium, germanium, and later—in association with Mokta—uranium and aluminum. In 1961 the company's structure was redefined and Peñarroya found itself in need of a new chairman to replace René Fillon. The Rothschild group proposed Georges Pompidou, who was, however, unable to accept the offer as he was shortly to become prime minister of France. It was therefore Guy de Rothschild himself who became chairman, this being the first time that a Rothschild had personally participated in the management of one of the family's businesses. He also recruited Bernard de Villeméjane, the future chairman of Imetal.

Modernizing in the 1960s

On his arrival at Peñarroya, Guy de Rothschild found that there were numerous problems to solve. To modernize the company's plant, he introduced a new zinc furnace. The commercial problems were more serious, as Peñarroya was not able to sell its own products. Rothschild established and bought small businesses to counterbalance Peñarroya's losses and entered into partnership with several other companies, which included Pechiney, the iron and steel leader. Throughout this period, Rothschild actively sought new sources of financing and revenue. After the metal crisis of 1967, when metal prices plunged, this search gave birth to Imetal.

The year 1967 was important for both SLN and Peñarroya. Through COFIRED, a company owned by the Compagnie du Nord, itself belonging to the Rothschilds, which bought 50 percent of Peñarroya's capital and gave it back to SLN, SLN became the majority shareholder in Peñarroya and therefore controlled it. Yet until 1970, although the two companies were run along the same lines, they retained separate management and headquarters. In 1970, just before the takeover of Mokta, the companies eventually merged and become a single group, SLN-Peñarroya. The nomination of Bernard de Villeméjane as president of the group coincided in 1971 with Mokta's entry into the group, through a public offer of exchange which was accepted by 92 percent of Mokta's shareholders. Created in 1865 to exploit magnetic iron ore deposits in Mokta-el-Hadid, Algeria, Mokta had developed slowly under the control of the Suez Bank. It diversified primarily into manganese and uranium and later became a holding company. With iron interests in Spain, manganese in Gabon and Morocco, and—most importantly—uranium in France, Nigeria, Gabon, and Canada, Mokta was only fully absorbed by Imetal in 1980.

The three Rothschild companies were now faced with the merger of Pechiney and Ugine-Kuhlmann, their direct competitors, in 1971. Three years later, in 1974, the Rothschild group became an industrial holding company. A new name, Imetal, was chosen for its modern connotations although it had no actual meaning. It was a public limited company with headquarters in the 15th arrondissement of Paris and moved in 1977 into the 51st floor of the famous Tour Montparnasse. This concentration and merging was, of course, part of the logical continuation of SLN's growth policy, but was also prompted by the international oil crisis of 1973 that affected the nickel industry more directly in 1975. Although Mokta and its uranium survived the energy crisis quite well, the 30 percent decrease in construction as well as the fall in prices and of the dollar deeply affected the group. Imetal did not recover fully from the crisis until the end of the 1980s.

However, one year after its formation Imetal was to receive international attention through the highly publicized Copperweld case. Imetal was trying to expand into the United States and made a takeover bid for Copperweld, a company created in 1915 that manufactured specialty tubing, bimetallic wire, and alloy steel. Copperweld's employees and management opposed the bid and took the case to court. The court decision in favor of Imetal provoked protests by U.S. workers in the streets of Washington, D.C., and New York. The anti-French movement reached its climax and was fueled by antisemitic slogans directed against Baron Guy de Rothschild. The latter eventually came to Pittsburgh to defend his company and succeeded in turning opinion in his favor. He ended by acquiring 67 percent of Copperweld, and later gained complete ownership.

Rothschild did not stop there, and on his way toward internationalization he bought 25 percent of the Lead Industries Group, formed in 1930 as the result of the amalgamation of a number of U.K. lead manufacturers in the 1920s. Then through Mokta, Imetal managed to take over the largest private uranium-ore company in France, la Compagnie Française des Minerais d'Uranium. The latter is now a major subsidiary of Mokta.

These events were followed in 1976 by the creation of Minemet, which combined in a single entity all of the marketing companies of the Imetal group, together with Minemet

Key Dates:

1863: Jules Garnier discovers nickel deposits in New Caledonia.

1873: With Henri Marbeau, Garnier founds La Société de Traitement des Minerais de Nickel, Cobalt et Autres.

1880: Company merges with Higginson et Hanckar to form Société Le Nickel (SLN).

1881: Charles Leroux founds Penarroya.

1937: SLN merges with Calédonickel.

1967: SLN merges with Penarroya.

1974: Company changes name to Imetal S.A.

1989: Imetal purchases Société Gelis-Poudenx-Sans and Groupe de la Financière d'Angers.

1999: Company takes over English China Clays plc for £756 million; changes name to Imerys S.A.

2001: Imerys acquires Industrial Minerals division of Hecla Mining Company.

Recherche, a subsidiary conducting the major part of its operations at the Trappes Research Center, near Paris, which was opened in 1972. In 1979, Guy de Rothschild, who had passed the retirement age laid down by the company, was obliged to resign, and, Bernard de Villeméjane became chairman of Imetal. In 1980, when SLN celebrated its 100th anniversary, Imetal's consolidated profits totaled FFr 200 million, to which Copperweld had made a major contribution. However, Bernard de Villeméjane had to face another crisis, mainly affecting nickel production and caused by recession in the minerals market. The industry was, if not depressed, certainly in stagnation. Change was urgently needed and the possibility of a change of product line gradually became apparent.

Shifting Focus in the 1980s

At the beginning of the 1980s, Bernard de Villeméjane took a series of measures to reduce the importance of uranium and minerals in Imetal's activities. In his opinion, they were no longer profitable. First, in 1983, he conceded the majority of SLN's shares to Eramet and the latter became Eramet-SLN, of which Imetal now controls only 15 percent. In 1986 the situation had deteriorated still further and Imetal's losses amounted to FFr 586 million. Mokta, which was partly responsible for this, was sold to Cogéma in 1986. In 1987 it was Peñarroya's turn; Imetal's share in the company was reduced from 59 percent to 34.1 percent and later to 15 percent. Peñarroya in the early 1990s was owned by Metaleurop. As Bernard de Villeméjane explained to Le Nouvel Economiste, on August 21, 1987, "Ten years ago, uranium and mining represented 80 percent of our activity. Today, it is less than one fifth."

As it was moving away from its old activities, Imetal was buying new companies and specializing in construction materials. It obtained 100 percent control of Huguenot Fenal, a company constructing roof shingles and with many affiliates. Imetal then bought the Industrie Regionale du Bâtiment (IRB), which included ten companies. Imetal's move into the construction materials sector and its subsequent financial recovery were

spectacular. From losses of FFr 586 million in 1986, the group had moved to profits of FFr 550 million in 1988. After this success, Bernard de Villeméjane decided to diversify into baked clay, tiling, ceramics, and brick. These seem incongruous activities for a mining group but as its chairman stated in Entreprises, December 12, 1988, "it appears to be different from what we used to do, but in reality it does correspond to our company culture." Indeed, the manufacturing technique employed in construction materials is not far removed from that used in nonferrous metals; both rely on the use of kilns. The success of Imetal in this sector can also be explained by the company's considerable experience in energy conservation and the way in which Imetal used this experience to adapt itself to an increasingly competitive sector such as construction.

After the purchase of la Société Gélis-Poudenx-Sans—shingles and bricks—and the Groupe de la Financière d'Angers—slate—in 1989, Imetal became the world leader in shingles and the foremost brick producer in France. Yet Imetal's outlook remained if not regional, at the most national. Naturally, the next step would be internationalization in its new sector. "We are on the threshold of a European development phase" said Imetal's chairman, in La Cote Desfossée, April 4, 1989. Its first two partners were Italy and Germany, through Metaleurop, created in association with Preussag. Then came the United Kingdom, in the form of Steely, a company with which Imetal entered into partnership in September 1990, for the distribution of its products in the United Kingdom. Imetal also maintained good relations with the United States and, having bought all the remaining shares in Copperweld, Imetal acquired CE-Minerals, a subsidiary of Asea Brown Boveri and an important producer of clay.

Materials Group for the 21st Century

"Imetal" was becoming more and more of a misnomer. The company had definitely passed from the nonferrous metal industry to that of construction materials, although its dramatic success in the sector had not kept it from maintaining its former and traditional activities. Although the company tried very hard to justify these changes and to make them seem consistent, there was a paradox in the fact that this company, which once had an enormous network of international branches, was—in 1989—"on the threshold of a European development phase." In spite of its brilliant successes in its new field, Imetal had entered a sector far less prestigious and far more competitive, especially on a European scale, than its former field. As Bernard de Villeméjane stated in l'Usine Nouvelle, on November 11, 1989, "Making money in sectors that one may find less glamorous, is preferable to losing money in other, more prestigious sectors."

Imetal's move away from metals processing took on steam in the 1990s, as the company began adding to its minerals and construction materials operations. In 1992, the company acquired the United States' Dry Branch Kaolin (DBK), based in Georgia, and began building those operations into the world's number three producer of paper-grade kaolin. DBK was only the first of a vast acquisition program carried out during the decade that completely transformed the company. Imetal's acquisitions, ranging from minerals processors in China to its 1995 purchase of Lonza Graphites and Technologies, boosting its graphites production operations, were to double the company's size in just five years. Among the company's acquisitions during the mid-1990s were Georgia Marble, in the United States, adding calcium carbonate production; Timcal, of Switzerland, and Stratmin, of Canada, further boosting the company's graphite operations; C-E Minerals, in the United States, and Plibrico, in Luxembourg, both refractories producers; Ceratera, in France, boosting its clay production; and Refral, in France, and Lombra et Cedonosa, in Spain, enhancing the company's portfolio of technical ceramics production. The company, now led by CEO and Chairman Patrick Kron, continued to seek to gain new scale.

The 1999 takeover of English China Clays—world leader in kaolin production with a 39 percent market share—gave Imetal more than 50 percent of that market and completed the company's transformation. The takeover offer, initially rejected by English China Clays, was finally accepted for a price of £756 million. As a result of its new acquisition, Imetal moved to shed its metals division, selling off its Copperweld subsidiaries in the United States and Canada. The company then changed its name, inventing Imerys to promote its reinvented organization. The company's minerals processing sales had nearly doubled, rising past EUR 2 billion in 1999.

Acquisitions continued to play a major role in Imerys's growth at the turn of the century. In 2000, the company's acquisitions included Honaik, in Malaysia, giving it a foothold in the fast-growing specialty pigments market. That year, the company also acquired the ceramic bodies production operations for Portugal's Vista Alegre, boosting its position in that market in southern Europe. Announcing growing sales, which topped EUR 2.8 billion in 2000, Imerys began the year 2001 with the purchase of the Industrial Minerals division of Hecla Mining Company, based in the United States, giving Imerys the leadership in the sector in both the North American and European markets. Imerys's aggressive growth strategy, if not quite as glamorous as its Imetal past, assured its future position among the world's leading mineral processing companies.

Principal Subsidiaries

Huguenot Fenal; Industrie Régionale du Bâtiment; Gélis-Poudenx-Sans; Financière d'Anger (98%); Mircal; Copperweld (U.S.A.).

Principal Operating Units

Building Materials; Refractories & Abrasives; Ceramics & Specialties; Pigments & Additives.

Principal Competitors

Asahi Glass Company, Limited; CRH plc; ELEMENTIS plc; Engelhard Corporation; Hanson PLC; Hecla Mining Company; Lafarge SA; National Refractories & Minerals Corporation; Owens Corning Corporation; Compagnie de Saint-Gobain; Wienerberger Baustoffindustrie AG; Zemex Corporation.

Further Reading

Baron, Benoit, and Chantal Colomer, "Les Fers au Feu Internationaux d'Imetal," *La Cote Desfossées,* April 6, 1990.

Black, Ralph, "Les Grandes Options de la Stratégie de Peñarroya-Le Nickel," *Les Echos,* January 25, 1971.

Bouvier, Jean, *Les Rothschild,* Paris: Edition Complexe, 1983.

Gout, Didier, "Imetal se Construit un Nouvel Avenir," *l'Usine Nouvelle,* November 16, 1989.

"Imerys Accede Au Premier Rang Mondial Des Abrasifs," *La Tribune,* May 10, 2000

"Imerys se renforce aux Etat-Unis," *La Tribune,* March 1, 2001

"Imetal May Sell Metals Processing Division," *Financial Times,* June 7, 1999.

Le Nickel-SLN, 1880–1980, 100 ans d'une entreprise et d'une industrie, Paris: SLN, 1980.

Peñarroya, 1881–1981, histoire d'une société, Paris: Peñarroya, 1981.

Rothschild, Guy de, *Si j'ai Bonne Mémoire,* Paris: Belfond, 1983.

—Sonia Kronlund
—update: M.L. Cohen

Ispat Inland Inc.

3210 Watling Street
East Chicago, Indiana 46312
U.S.A.
Telephone: (219) 399-1200
Fax: (219) 399-5544
Web site: http://www.inland.com

Wholly Owned Subsidiary of Ispat International N.V.
Incorporated: 1893 as Inland Steel Company
Employees: 10,000
Sales: $2.39 billion (1999)
NAIC: 331111 Iron and Steel Mills; 331221 Rolled Steel Shape Manufacturing

Ispat Inland Inc. is the sixth largest steel producer in the United States. Formerly a unit of Inland Steel Industries, it was acquired by Ispat International N.V. in 1998. Inland has long been one of the most innovative and technologically advanced integrated steel mills. In the early 1980s, when a poor economy coupled with the rising tide of imports and a depressed international steel market took its toll on the whole of the industry, Inland remained a leader in modernization and in utilizing technology. By relying on continued new developments in steel production, Inland was restored to a somewhat tenuous profitability by the early 1990s. Cost-cutting and customer service, as well as some financial juggling, helped the company survive the latter part of the decade.

19th-Century Founding

Inland had its beginnings in the depression of 1893. It was in that year that the Chicago Steel Works, a manufacturer of farm equipment, along with many other companies, went out of business. A group that included a foreman from the defunct company made an attempt to form a new company to begin producing steel on a site that Chicago Steel Works had acquired, in the village of Chicago Heights, Illinois. The necessary capital to finance the venture, however, could not be found, until the group enlisted Joseph Block, a Cincinnati, Ohio, iron merchant, who was in Chicago to visit the World's Fair. He brought his son Phillip D. Block into the venture.

After incorporating as Inland Steel Company in October 1893 and purchasing the idle machinery of Chicago Steel Works, Inland was ready to begin production in early 1894. By the end of the year, another of Joseph Block's sons, L.E. Block, had joined the company. In the next few years, the business grew steadily, with production centered on agricultural implements. Sales were boosted by a new product, side rails for bed frames.

In 1897 sales topped $350,000, and the company, which had been sinking much of its profits into improving machinery at the mill, purchased the East Chicago Iron and Forge Company and renamed it Inland Iron and Forge. The new addition was operated by L.E. Block and produced equipment for the railroad industry. The plant was sold in 1901 for ten times its original purchase price of $50,000.

By the end of the 19th century Inland was doing well, and sales were growing steadily. In 1901 it found itself in a position to accept an offer by a real estate developer promising 50 acres of land to any firm that would spend at least $1 million to build a steel plant on the site. The patch of land was beside Lake Michigan, which could provide water needed for operating a mill and a waterway for transporting material. The land was also near several major railroad lines. In 1902, when the first phase of construction of the new Indiana Harbor, Indiana, plant was completed, Inland had a steel ingot capacity of 60,000 tons. Due to a general recession, Inland lost $127,000 in 1903–04. For the same reason, from 1901 until 1906 the company did not pay dividends. By 1905, however, the plant got its first big order, for 30,000 tons of steel channels and plates.

In 1906, to meet the growing demand for steel, Inland added its fifth open hearth furnace and constructed the first blast furnace in northern Indiana. By purchasing the lease on an iron mine in Minnesota, Inland ensured itself of a source of iron ore to feed its furnaces that allowed it to reduce costs and significantly increase steel production. Production was increased further as Inland added more open hearth furnaces and sheet mills. In 1911 the Inland Steamship Company was formed to transport ore from Inland's growing mining concerns in Minnesota to the

Indiana Harbor mill. A year later, Inland was manufacturing spikes and rivets for the railroad industry.

Innovations and Expansion in the Early 20th Century

By 1914, when Joseph Block died, Inland had a steel ingot capacity of 600,000 tons. Capacity reached one million tons by 1917, and to accommodate the world market's growing demand for steel, Inland completed construction of a second plant at Indiana Harbor that year. Demand for steel increased during World War I, and following the war, between 1923 and 1926, all of the mills and machinery at the new plant were completely electrified, which provided the most efficient production. When the war ended, the railroad industry became Inland's top customer, replacing agriculture. When Phillip D. Block became president of Inland in 1919, Inland started to improve working conditions and to provide benefits for its employees. It was one of the first companies in the steel industry to introduce an eight-hour workday. The measure was soon abandoned, however, when the rest of the industry did not follow suit. In 1920 Inland was the first steel company to adopt a pension plan for its employees.

In the early 1920s Inland began to make steel rails in its 32-inch roughing and 28-inch finishing mills that previously had been used only for rolling structural shapes. This was an innovation in the steel industry, and within a short time rolling and finishing rails was Inland's most successful operation in terms of both sales and earnings. At the same time, the company spent $1 million to build a structural steel finishing mill. During this period, Inland continued to modernize and expand. Millions of dollars were spent to improve quality and efficiency as demand for steel rose and sales skyrocketed.

The early 1920s were not only a time of great prosperity for the steel industry, they were also a period of upheaval. The second great wave of mergers and attempted mergers in the steel industry since the beginning of the century commenced in 1921. As it had been in the early 1900s, Inland was again the object of schemes designed to merge smaller independent companies into one huge corporation. A plan initiated in 1921 envisioned the consolidation of seven large steel companies—Inland, Republic Steel Corporation, Brier Hill, Lackawanna, Midvale Steel and Ordnance, Youngstown, and Steel and Tube Company of America. Rumors of the proposed plan circulated

in the press in late 1921 and early 1922, but in May 1922 Lackawanna withdrew from the plan. Negotiations continued between Republic, Inland, and Midvale. After the Federal Trade Commission (FTC) issued a complaint in August 1922, however, executives of the three companies announced that financing would be difficult while the legal issues raised by the FTC complaint were being resolved. The plan was dropped.

Sales at Inland increased, and while the company continued to spend on expansion, it became the number one U.S. steel company in rate of return on fixed assets in the period from 1926 to 1930. In 1928 Inland was able to acquire a limestone quarry on the upper peninsula of Michigan, and formed Inland Lime and Stone Company. Inland acquired another source of raw materials by purchasing 15 acres of land in Kentucky holding high-grade coking coal.

Inland's expansion continued through the late 1920s and did not stop even when the Great Depression hit in 1929. Between 1929 and 1932 Inland spent $30 million on expansion. In 1932, the only Depression year in which Inland was not in the black, the company unveiled the widest continuous hot-strip mill in the United States. At a cost of $15 million, the mill was 76 inches wide and would later be used to roll sheet for the auto industry and for the U.S. Navy during World War II. While 1932 was a financially dismal year for Inland, which was operating at only 25 percent of capacity, that figure was one-third higher than that for the balance of the industry. During the period from 1931 to 1935, Inland's operating profit in terms of fixed assets was 6.1 percent, the highest in the industry.

At the time that Inland built the new mill, competition in the steel industry was intense, and Inland was forced to compete with companies like United States Steel, among others, that had their own warehouse operations through which to market their products. To remain competitive with its rivals, Inland chose to go into the steel warehouse business and in 1935 acquired Joseph T. Ryerson & Son Inc., a steel warehousing and fabricating chain. Ryerson provided an outlet through which Inland's customers could buy steel and have it custom processed. In 1936 Inland acquired Milcor Steel Company of Milwaukee, Wisconsin, which made a wide variety of steel products and had plants and warehouses in seven cities. Milcor provided Inland with a market for the products of its sheet-rolling mills.

War and Labor Unrest in the 1940s

When World War II began, Inland, still under the direction of Chairman Phillip D. Block, immediately began a program of expansion to provide added capacity by building new blast furnaces and coke ovens to provide steel for bombs, shells, tanks, ships, and planes. By 1944 Inland had become completely integrated. The company controlled its own sources of raw materials including coal, ore, and limestone. With Inland's total ingot capacity of 3.4 million tons by 1944, sales in the years between 1940 and 1950 ranged from $200 million to $400 million per year.

In the 1940s prosperity was tempered somewhat by a series of labor disputes in which the United Steel Workers of America (USWA) sought higher wages and certain benefits for its members. Although labor and industry had agreed to a no-strike, no-

Key Dates:

1893: Inland Steel starts with surplus Chicago Steel equipment.

1901: Inland begins building a plant next to Lake Michigan.

1906: Minnesota iron mine is leased.

1911: Inland Steamship Company is formed to transport ore.

1928: Sources of limestone and coking coal are acquired.

1935: Joseph T. Ryerson & Son is acquired.

1936: Milcor Steel is acquired.

1966: Expansion program is completed.

1978: After recession, Inland has a banner year.

1986: Inland buys J.M. Tull; company reorganizes as Inland Steel Industries, Inc., a holding company for Inland Steel Company and Inland Steel Services.

1989: High-tech joint venture with Nippon Steel is launched.

1994: Inland sees first profit in five years, expands globally.

1998: Ispat International N.V. buys Inland Steel Company; the remaining U.S. holding company, Inland Steel Industries, renames itself after subsidiary Ryerson Tull, Inc.

lockout pledge during the early 1940s, steel workers across the country went on strike to demand a $1 a day wage increase in March 1942. The effects of the strike on war production were not significant, and Inland and the USWA signed a contract covering working conditions for the company's 14,000 employees at both Indiana Harbor and Chicago Heights.

A much more serious strike, involving 750,000 steel workers, took place in 1946 and virtually crippled the steel industry as production fell to its lowest level in half a century. The strike lasted 26 days and affected 11,000 employees at Inland's Indiana Harbor and Chicago Heights plants. Only after Inland and the other companies involved agreed to a wage raise of 18.5 cents per hour did the strike end. Inland was then able to continue to produce the steel required by the huge postwar demand for consumer products. The steel Inland produced then went primarily to the automobile and home-appliance industries. After the war, Inland continued to expand its facilities for sheet and strip and also acquired more property from which to mine raw materials, in Minnesota, Michigan, and Kentucky. In 1945 Phillip D. Block resigned as chairman after serving for more than 22 years. He was replaced by his brother, L.E. Block, who served until 1951.

The Postwar Period

During the early 1950s expansion slowed at Inland. From 1952 to 1955 steel production capacity increased by 700,000 tons. This was half the amount needed to close the gap between Chicago area demand and capacity. In the years between 1947 and 1958 Inland's capital expenditures of $121 million were the most modest among the major steel companies. Expansion, however, picked up during the steel boom of 1956, when Inland began a new program

in which the company spent $360 million to modernize its plants, to acquire new mining properties, and to build a steel building to serve as its new headquarters in downtown Chicago. The stainless steel for the curtain walls of the 19-story building had to be purchased from another steel company because Inland was still producing carbon steel almost exclusively.

Although the early 1950s were relatively unremarkable for Inland in terms of production and growth, they marked the beginning of a decade that was to include two bitter and costly disputes between the steel workers and the industry. The first conflict began in November 1951 when the USWA notified the industry that it wanted to bargain for a wage increase. In December, after no agreement was reached, union president Phillip Murray called for a strike. Almost immediately, President Harry S. Truman referred the case to the Wage Stabilization Board. The board held hearings and made a recommendation accepted by the union but rejected by the industry. In April 1952 the board tried unsuccessfully to avert a strike. A few days later, on the eve of a strike, President Truman issued an order for the nation's steel mills to be seized by the government to keep them open and avert a strike. The industry was outraged by the president's order and Inland's president, Clarence B. Randall, was chosen to give the industry's viewpoint in an address that was broadcast on nationwide radio and television. Randall called the president's order an "evil deed" that he had no legal right to issue. The U.S. Supreme Court agreed that the move was not legal and in June 1952 ordered that the mills be returned to their owners. Within a few hours, 600,000 workers walked off their jobs to begin a strike that would affect 95 percent of the nation's steel mills and would last for 55 days.

Randall became chairman of Inland in 1953. After a few years of calm, the industry and the USWA became involved in another dispute that was to prove the longest and most costly in the industry's history. The dispute began in May 1959 when the industry called for a wage freeze. When negotiations stalled in July, 500,000 steel workers went on strike. In October, President Dwight D. Eisenhower applied for an 80-day injunction under the Taft-Hartley Act, ordering the workers back to the plants while negotiations continued. The Supreme Court upheld the injunction, and the plants reopened in November. In January 1960, the USWA won an agreement that gave it a substantial wage increase. The agreement brought to an end the 116-day strike that had shut down the steel industry and forced the closing of automobile plants because of a shortage of steel.

The 1960s: New Facilities and Processes

As the 1960s began, the steel industry planned record production to fill consumer orders and replenish inventories left depleted by the strike. Inland's steel shipments in the years 1961 to 1965 averaged 4.1 million tons per year, compared to 3.6 million tons per year in the previous five years. To keep up with new production demands, Inland embarked on a new expansion program in 1962. The plan included a new 80-inch continuous hot strip mill as well as Inland's first oxygen steelmaking shop. The new shop meant a shift away from the open hearth steelmaking process. It had a capacity to produce more than two million tons per year and enabled Inland to close down its oldest open hearth furnace plant, which had been operating for 60 years, since 1902.

The expansion plan was completed in 1966 and helped Inland to lower costs, improve product quality, and increase capacity. An important milestone for Inland was the completion in 1967 of its new research facilities in East Chicago, Indiana, where company scientists could investigate new processes in steel metallurgy and production. The large amount of capital that Inland invested in expansion in the mid-1960s, along with stronger competition, had the effect of lowering earnings by 25 percent in the period from 1964 to 1967. Joseph L. Block, who succeeded Randall as chairman in 1959, believed that the expansion was important for the future, as Inland faced stiff competition for its midwestern market.

When Joseph L. Block retired in 1967, he had earned a reputation as a maverick in the steel industry. In 1962, when the steel industry had clashed with President John F. Kennedy over a proposed rise in steel prices, Block broke with industry ranks and insisted that the time was not right for a steel price hike. In 1966, however, Block took the lead in raising prices with the largest increase since 1963. Block was well known, as reported in *Time* magazine, for strengthening "Inland's reputation as a civic-minded company" by among other things supporting a fair-employment law in Illinois as well as a redevelopment project for East Chicago.

New Leadership for the 1970s

Block was replaced as chairman by his cousin Phillip D. Block, Jr. Under the new chairman, Inland maintained its share of the midwestern market and also achieved the highest profit-to-sales ratio among the big-eight steel makers. In the late 1960s, as competition increased from foreign imports and markets eroded, Inland began a diversification program. The first step was into the housing market with the acquisition of Scholz Homes Inc. and later the formation of Inland Steel Urban Development Corporation. By 1974 diversification had led Inland into areas such as steel building products, powdered metals, and reinforced plastics.

The steel business started off slowly in the 1970s for the whole industry. Profits were down, and Inland's net profit declined from $81.7 million in 1968 to $46.7 million in 1970. By 1974, however, things had turned around, and the steel industry experienced one of the biggest booms in its history. After a tight period in the previous two years, demand for steel increased dramatically in 1974, and Inland's sales climbed to $2.5 billion. With demand showing no evidence of slowing, Inland, under Chairman Frederick G. Jaicks, who had replaced Phillip D. Block, Jr., in 1971, made plans for a $2 billion expansion, which it planned to finance from strong earnings and outside financing. Inland, however, along with the rest of the industry was hurt by the recession of 1975, and by 1977 the industry, plagued by overcapacity, faced another downturn, as imports flooded the market at prices domestic companies were unable to match. Inland's earnings slumped as costs went up and demand dropped, forcing the company to hold up the first phase of its expansion plan.

Business turned around for Inland in 1978, a record year for the company, in which it was able to capture 6.5 percent of the domestic steel market. The company produced 8.6 million tons of steel and generated profits of $158.3 million on $3.25 billion in sales. By the early 1980s, however, the steel industry was in trouble again. A combination of factors, including the high level of imports, decreased demand, and an oversupply of steel drove down prices at the same time that costs such as labor and energy were on their way up. These factors, combined with high investment expenses as well as depressed Midwestern industries—autos, farming, construction, and appliances—caused Inland's profits to drop 64 percent from their 1978 peak to $57.3 million in 1981.

Inland suffered four straight years of losses totaling $456 million in 1982 through 1985. The company was forced to shut down some of its steel mills and to lay off some workers. Yet Inland continued to develop new products and improve production efficiency. The company had success with lightweight, high-strength, and corrosion-resistant steel for the auto, farm, and construction industries; in 1981 it was able to push its market share to a record 6.7 percent.

Recovering from Industry Downturns

In order to survive in a depressed industry, Inland—under Chairman Frank Luerssen, who took over in 1983—cut costs by shutting down unprofitable operations and divesting itself of certain assets. Inland began to sell various subsidiaries, including companies that had supplied it with raw materials. In addition, seven major operations at the Indiana Harbor works were shut down. Steel making capacity was reduced by 30 percent. While producing less steel, Inland began to shift its efforts into more profitable areas such as its highly successful steel distribution operations which it sought to expand by acquiring J.M. Tull Metals Company, a large metal-products maker, processor, and distributor, in 1986.

In May 1986 Inland made a move to separate its waning steel manufacturing operations from its profitable steel distribution sector by reorganizing as Inland Steel Industries, Inc., a holding company for Inland Steel Company, and Inland Steel Services, Inland's service center operations. Inland executives hoped that the reorganization would facilitate diversification and joint ventures.

Shortly thereafter, Inland formed a partnership with a Japanese firm, Nippon Steel Corporation. The partnership, known as I/N Tek, was created to construct a continuous cold rolling facility near New Carlisle, Indiana. The I/N Tek facility was the only U.S. continuous cold rolling mill. By combining five basic operations that were usually done separately, the facility was able to complete in less than an hour a process that had taken as many as 12 days. The cold rolled steel produced by the plant was used for, among other applications, autos and appliances. Another joint venture with Nippon Steel, I/N Kote, was started in 1989 to construct and operate two steel-galvanizing lines adjacent to the I/N Tek facility. The project was to be used in combination with I/N Tek to galvanize the cold rolled steel.

With profits having declined 54 percent in 1989, and losses of $21 million for 1990, Inland expected its continued expansion and modernization through projects such an I/N Tek and I/N Kote to result eventually in profits nearly double the then record $262 million earned in 1988. Such a turnaround would ensure that Inland would remain an industry leader in growth and technology, while once again becoming a top industry performer.

The 1990s and Beyond

By 1994, the steel industry began to recover. The overall economy had picked up and there was an increased demand for cars—good news for Inland, which was a leading supplier of steel to such automakers as Honda, Toyota, Ford, General Motors, and Chrysler. In addition, the dollar remained inexpensive so that foreign competitors did not have the advantage of asking lower prices, and difficulties with labor unions were resolved.

As a result of these combined factors, in 1994 Inland enjoyed its first profit since 1989. Other moves by the company also ensured greater revenues and profits. Inland closed some units that were unprofitable; sold off businesses that were outside its core steel business; and began the search for emerging markets overseas to compensate for slower growth in the domestic market. A separate operating unit, the company's third, was created. Called Inland International, the unit sold and distributed products to industrial customers all over the world.

One market was Mexico, where the company formed a joint venture in 1994 with Altos Hornos de Mexico S.A., to be called Ryerson de Mexico. In 1995, a joint venture was created with China's Baoshan Iron and Steel, called Ryerson de China; and another to deal with exports was formed in Hong Kong with two partners: South African Macsteel and Canada's Federal Industries. In 1996, a partnership was formed in India between Inland Steel Industries and Tata Iron and Steel Co. of Numbai, called Tata-Ryerson, which provided industrial materials management services to Indian customers.

Inland had focused on serving high-end customers with high quality steel bars and other products. However, some quality problems resulted in the loss of some customers and the company returned to the commodity steel markets.

New Steel noted that both Old Steel and New Steel paradigms existed within Inland Steel. Yet the future seemed to belong to more progressive modes of doing business. After a precedent-setting contract with the United Steelworkers of America in 1993, ISI's workers took on more responsibility in exchange for improved job security and working conditions.

The company had to buy coke since shutting down its coke batteries in the early 1990s; this resulted in cost penalties of around $25 million a year. Inland's empowered workers continued to look for ways to improve yields. At the same time, automotive customers, led by the transplants (factories established by such foreign makers as Toyota, Honda, BMW, and Mercedes-Benz in the United States), were growing ever more demanding in terms of quality.

Inland exited the unprofitable steel plate business in 1995. Ninety percent of Inland's steel output ended up in consumer goods, a third of it in automobiles. Unfortunately, Inland suffered disproportionately when auto sales fell. At the same time, a weaker dollar was helping the American steel industry increase its exports, and sales at Inland's Mexican unit doubled in 1995 to $150 million. All told, Inland had one of its most

profitable years ever in 1995, although the next year's results were much less impressive.

Inland Steel Industries CEO Robert Darnall told *New Steel* that the company needed to help its customers exploit its technical expertise in order for it to survive the next economic downturn. As late as the fall of 1995, Darnall was dismissing the idea that the company spin off its profitable Materials Distribution Group, which included Joseph T. Ryerson and J.M. Tull Metals. "Maybe it gives a little pop for current shareholders," he told *Financial Times,* "but it . . . really doesn't create long-term shareholder value."

Nevertheless, a fraction of Ryerson Tull was spun off in 1996, helping to reduce Inland's considerable debt load. (An initial public offering sold 13 percent of Ryerson's shares, netting $60 million.) Frustrated by persistent production problems, Darnall replaced several executives early in 1996.

In July 1998, Ispat International N.V. bought Inland Steel Company—the steelmaking operations of Inland Steel Industries—for about $1 billion. Inland Steel Industries, the holding company, then renamed itself after its prime remaining subsidiary, Ryerson Tull, Inc. Inland Steel Company became known as Ispat Inland, Inc.

Ispat was a $2 billion a year global player that had grown to an immense size by buying troubled government-owned mills. Its acquisition of Inland Steel Company gave Ispat a major presence in the competitive U.S. market. The deal also suggested a new period of consolidation for an industry troubled by excess capacity worldwide, according to *Industry Week.* As it had with its other acquisitions, Ispat immediately went to work cutting costs at Inland. In its first year and a half as an Ispat subsidiary, Inland realized $275 million in annualized cost savings.

Information technology (IT) had become a key competitive tool by 2000. Automotive customers in particular demanded just-in-time delivery of products; Inland also used integrated databases to coordinate multichannel service.

At the turn of the millennium, Ispat Inland was the sixth largest integrated steel producer in the United States, accounting for 5 percent of national steel production. Its largest division, Flat Products, made carbon and high-strength, low-alloy flat rolled steel, primarily for automakers and appliance and furniture manufacturers. This division accounted for 85 percent of revenues. Bar Products supplied a variety of markets with special quality carbon, alloy, and free machining bar products. The company operated a steelmaking plant in East Chicago and two state-of-the-art finishing plants near New Carlisle, Indiana (both joint ventures with Nippon Steel), as well as a Minnesota iron mine.

Principal Divisions

Ispat Inland Flat Products; Ispat Inland Bar Products.

Principal Competitors

Commercial Metals Company; Earle M. Jorgensen; Worthington Industries, Inc.

Further Reading

Berry, Bryan, "Inland Steel Redefines Itself," *Iron Age/New Steel,* August 1995, p. 18.

Byrne, Harlan S., "Inland Steel: Plotting a Return to Consistent Top Earnings," *Barron's,* March 15, 1993, pp. 45–46.

——, "Revival, Part II," *Barron's,* July 22, 1996, p. 22.

Cimini, Michael H., and Susan L. Berhmann, "Win-Win Contract at Inland Steel," *Monthly Labor Review,* October 1993, p. 74.

Colkin, Eileen, "Traditional Values in a High-Tech World," *Informationweek,* September 27, 1999, pp. 233–38.

Evans, Richard, "Man of Steel," *Barron's,* March 23, 1998, p. 13.

Geer, John F., Jr., "Steel Wallflower," *Financial World,* November 21, 1995, p. 40.

Gilbert, R., and W. Korda, *The Story of Inland Steel,* Chicago: Inland Steel Company, 1974.

"Help Thy Customer, Help Thyself," *Forbes,* December 18, 1995, pp. 196–97.

"Ispat Inland Settles Louisiana Fraud Case with U.S. for $30 Million," *IBJ Daily,* January 18, 2001.

Kafka, Peter, "Steel Steal," *Forbes,* April 20, 1998, p. 486.

Mehta, Manik, "Steel's Still-Growing Giant," *Industry Week,* January 18, 1999, pp. 120–23.

"Nelson Retires As President of Inland Steel Co.," *Metal Center News,* May 1996, p. 118.

"New Lease on Life," *Forbes,* May 9, 1994, pp. 82–87.

"Picking Nickels Off the Floor," *Forbes,* October 26, 1992, pp. 106–08.

Samuels, Gary, "Help Thy Customer, Help Thyself," *Forbes,* December 18, 1995, p. 196.

Sheridan, John H., "A Global Future?," *Industry Week,* January 18, 1999, pp. 124–28.

—Patricia Leichenko
—updates: Dorothy Kroll, Frederick C. Ingram

Jillian's Entertainment Holdings, Inc.

1387 S. Fourth Street
Louisville, Kentucky 40208
U.S.A.
Telephone: (502) 638-9008
Fax: (502) 638-0984
Web site: http://www.jillians.com

Private Company
Incorporated: 1988 as Jillian's Billiards Club
Employees: 5,500
Sales: $110 million (2000 est.)
NAIC: 71395 Bowling Centers; 71312 Amusement
Arcades; 71399 All Other Amusement and Recreation
Industries; 72241 Drinking Places (Alcoholic
Beverages); 72211 Full-Service Restaurants

Jillian's Entertainment Holdings, Inc. operates a chain of 40 restaurant and entertainment complexes in the United States and Canada. The company's sites typically combine several drinking and dining options with billiards, bowling, high-tech video games, and a dance club. The privately held firm has put IPO plans on hold but is continuing to expand using funding from investors.

1988 Founding in Boston

The first Jillian's was opened in Boston, Massachusetts, by Stephen Foster. Foster, a 1978 graduate of Boston University Law School, had been working in New York as a corporate lawyer when he noticed people roller skating to pop music in Central Park. Inspired to create a club where people could do this indoors, he quit his job and sought help from his father, a Newton, Massachusetts judge. The elder Foster mortgaged his home to provide funds for the venture, which would be located in Boston on the top floor of an old brick stable building. In August 1979, after installing 10,000 square feet of maple flooring, the skating club was opened. Called Spinoff, it did well for a few years until the roller disco craze faded; the venture folded in 1987. In the meantime Foster had founded another new business, an oil brokerage firm called United Fuels International.

When the club closed its doors, Foster and Spinoff manager Kevin Troy sought a subtenant so they could take advantage of their long-term lease at the locked-in rate of $4 a square foot, heat included. A laser-tag franchise was lined up, but the deal fell through when its parent company went out of business. While still seeking a tenant, Foster read a magazine article about billiards on a trip to New York, and he decided to investigate the subject. He found that the dingy pool hall he visited contained not just the expected hustlers and "low-lifes," but also a smattering of yuppies and models. Sparked to research the topic further, Foster discovered that billiards' somewhat seedy reputation was mostly a recent phenomenon, and that it had earlier been considered a refined, even royal, diversion. He also took note of the fact that the game was one that could be enjoyed by both novices and experts and seemed to work well as a social "icebreaker." Figuring that they had little to lose, Foster and Troy decided to take a chance and purchased 41 pool tables to install in their still vacant space. In the summer of 1988 they opened Jillian's, named after Foster's wife Gillian (but spelled with a more "feminine" first letter).

Although business was slow at first, word of the elegantly appointed pool hall soon got around. By the following winter, with a newly installed bar in place, Jillian's was doing turn-away business. Sensing a trend in the making, Foster decided to form a new company to market the concept around the country. A second club was opened in Miami, and locations soon were being scouted in other cities. To obtain more financing, a merger was effected with the publicly traded MetalBanc Corp., which recently had sold its main business, a precious metals trading operation (MetalBanc also owned a building and development subsidiary in south Florida). After the merger MetalBanc's name was changed to Carom Capital Corporation, with Foster named president and CEO. In April 1990 another club was opened in Seattle, with one in Cleveland following in July; both were located in revitalized waterfront areas. Renamed Jillian's Entertainment Corp. in late 1991, the company began preparing to open more clubs during 1992 and was looking for buyers for the real estate business acquired in the MetalBanc merger.

In November 1991 Jillian's found itself in the unenviable position of denying allegations of drug distribution and money

Company Perspectives:

Jillian's Management believes that it is on the cutting edge of the "Eat! Drink! Play!" industry. With its tightly managed and fully conceived program, consistently profitable unit economics, the visionary leadership of its founder, and the recent partnership with the J.W. Childs Group of Boston, Jillian's is uniquely positioned to dominate its target markets. Its aggressive expansion strategy, powered both by new builds and by acquisitions, should enable Jillian's to secure its position as market leader and to establish its brand further in the national consciousness.

laundering that related to activities of the previous regime at MetalBanc, with no current employees or administrators named in court documents. The company quickly formed a separate subsidiary to encapsulate the remaining assets from this earlier period, which might be subject to forfeiture if the case was lost. MetalBanc's former leadership and Orexana, the company that had taken over the precious metals trading operation, also were named in the case. Several months later the government dropped its charges against the justifiably relieved Jillian's, which resumed its focus on developing new locations.

In the spring of 1992 Jillian's began looking at ways to franchise the billiards concept, retaining International Franchise Development, Inc. for this purpose. The company's newest club, its second in the Cleveland area, opened late in the year after the city of Cleveland Heights granted a variance on laws requiring pool halls to close by midnight. The club, which featured 23 billiard tables, a bar, and kitchen, was seeking major pool tournaments and stars such as Minnesota Fats to give exhibitions, according to the company.

Focus on Expansion in the 1990s

During 1993 Jillian's announced that it had leased sites for new clubs to be located in Champaign, Illinois; Annapolis, Maryland; and Worcester, Massachusetts. A billiards club in Pasadena, California, also was purchased. Each new outlet was set up as a separate subsidiary of the company. The year 1993 was Jillian's first profitable one, with earnings of $162,000 on revenues of $3.6 million. By the end of 1994 the company had a total of eight locations, and its growth continued at a measured pace over the next several years.

In 1997 a restructuring took place whereby a company called Jillian's Entertainment Holdings, Inc. took ownership of Jillian's Entertainment Corp., thus taking the company private. The new firm was owned by J.W. Childs Equity Partners LP and seven other shareholders, including Stephen Foster. J.W. Childs had reportedly invested $25 million. In the winter Jillian's headquarters was moved to Louisville, Kentucky, to be closer to the center of the widening chain.

With the new infusion of capital, Foster was able to step up the pace of expansion, adding four new locations by the end of the year and six more in 1998. In addition to billiards, some clubs were now also offering "high tech" games such as virtual

horse racing and skiing, plus sports cafes that featured large-screen televisions showing live games.

To accommodate the widening range of activities, Jillian's was looking for larger spaces to lease, with a minimum of 20,000 square feet required. Development costs could run as much as $5 million per site, depending on the location. A company spokesman emphasized the fact that, despite the sports-associated atmosphere, Jillian's was intended to appeal to a broad cross-section of the public, and the company was planning to feature even more diverse activities, including ten to 16 bowling lanes and a dance club, at future locations.

In early 1999 Jillian's opened its first New York location, in Albany, and additional clubs were soon under construction in the towns of Rochester and Farmingdale. The company was now operating more than 25 sites around the country. It also had taken over two "America Live" operations in Phoenix and Minneapolis, the latter located at the Mall of America. This 50,000-square-foot entertainment complex was the company's largest to date.

Putting IPO on Hold in 1999 and Moving into the 21st Century

In September the company announced plans for an initial public stock offering, citing the need for capital to fuel its continuing expansion. The offering was expected to bring in $46 million. In the face of the increasingly rocky IPO market the offering was shelved, however, with the company obtaining funding from private investors instead. Jillian's reported revenues of $59.7 million for 1999 with a loss of $2.5 million, which it attributed to the cost of its ongoing expansion.

The company partnered with Sony in early 2000 to offer HyperBowl, a Sony-developed virtual bowling game, at its locations around the country. HyperBowl utilized a full-sized bowling ball that was rolled in a way that interacted with a computer. A video projection system displayed the "lane," which could be depicted as the heaving deck of a sailing ship, a curving street in San Francisco, or the ruins of Rome. Sony had introduced the game at its own Metreon Entertainment Center in San Francisco the previous summer.

Jillian's locations now offered a unique blend of entertainment options that appealed to upscale 20- and 30-somethings, and even a few baby boomers. In the Hibachi Grill, groups of diners were seated around a Japanese-style grill run by an entertainer/chef wearing a distinctive hat. The chef would flip balls of rice or popcorn shrimp into the mouths of diners while cooking as many as seven courses of food at the table. In the Amazing Game Room, Hyperbowl was joined by a NASCAR racing simulator (the full-sized car's windshield was a video screen displaying a simulated race), an F-16 flight simulator patterned after actual military training models, a basketball game that required players to shoot at a moving hoop, and many more. Games did not require money or tokens, but used credit card-sized swipe cards that could be reloaded with value as the evening progressed. An onsite ATM was available if needed. In the retro-styled Hi-Life Lanes neon-colored bowling balls were rolled down one of a dozen or so black light-illuminated lanes in a room that was ringed with video screens and pulsated with of the Jillian's experience all contributed to the company's success.

Key Dates:

1988: Stephen Foster founds the first Jillian's Billiards Club in Boston.
1990: Jillian's merges with MetalBanc Corp.; name is changed to Carom Corp.
1991: Name is changed to Jillian's Entertainment Corp.
1997: Jillian's goes private; $2.? million is invested by J.W. Childs Equity Partners.
1998: Headquarters is moved to Louisville, Kentucky.
1999: IPO is announced, but later withdrawn.
2000: Jillian's teams with Sony Corporation to distribute HyperBowl virtual reality game.
2001: First Canadian site opens; chain grows to 40 locations.

Principal Subsidiaries

Jillian's Entertainment Corp.

Principal Competitors

AMF Bowling, Inc.; Champps Entertainment, Inc.; Dave & Buster's, Inc.; dick clark productions, inc.; Fashion Cafe; Hard Rock Cafe International, Inc.; HOB Entertainment, Inc.; Hooters of America, Inc.; Johnny Rockets Group, Inc.; Planet Hollywood International, Inc.; Total Entertainment Restaurant Corp.

Further Reading

Bergendorf, Dennis, "It's Hardly Traditional," *Bowlers Journal International,* April 2000.
"CEO Interview: Jillian's Entertainment Corporation," *Wall Street Transcript,* May 16, 1994.
Drexler, Michael, "Jillian's Hustles to Open Hall," *Plain Dealer Cleveland Ohio,* September 19, 1992.
Fischler, Marcelle S., "Like a Disneyland for Evenings on the Town," *New York Times,* March 26, 2000.
Flynn, Sara, "Clubs: Pinball Wizards," *Boston,* February 1997.
Gray, Andy, "Play with Your Food—Game Rooms Add Flavor to Jillian's," *Tribune Chronicle,* July 15, 1999.
Karman, John R., "Strong Growth Is Still Jillian's Game Plan Despite Pulling IPO," *Business First of Louisville,* January 28, 2000, p. 4.
Milliken, Peter H., "Entertainment Complex Has a Variety of Diversions," *Vindicator,* June 11, 1999.
O'Connor, Bill, "Night Moves," *Sunday Beacon Magazine,* June 21, 1998.
Redding, Rick, "Jillian's to Put IPO on the Table," *Business First of Louisville,* September 10, 1999, p. 1.
Schooley, Tim, "Jillian's Scouts Sites," *Pittsburgh Business Times & Journal,* November 5, 1999, p. 1.
Von Bergen, Jane M., "A Retro, Transcendental Spin on Dining, Playing," *Philadelphia Inquirer,* June 25, 1999.
Werbock, Sunshine, "Jillian's: It's All Just Fun and Games," *Northeast Times,* July 1, 1999.

—Frank Uhle

amplified music and crashing pin-strike sounds, while a nearby bar served drinks. Other areas of the facility included the Groove Shack video dance club and bar, the billiards club/bar combo, and the Video Cafe & Bar sports lounge. The newest locations also featured the Blue Kat Live club, which featured a mix of rock, blues, and "acid jazz" performers.

Although Jillian's targeted, for the most part, single adults and corporate groups, the company's offerings were easily adaptable to families, and its sites were popular destinations for teens on weekend afternoons. Noting the broad appeal of the concept, and the number of markets with no similar "eatertainment" establishment, the company projected that it could open as many as 150 or more additional clubs in North America. Its first location outside the United States, in Montreal, Canada, was scheduled for completion in the summer of 2001, bringing the number of sites in the chain to 40.

After more than ten years in business, Jillian's had distilled its concept into one that was bigger and bolder than ever. With many potential markets left to tap, its expansion was not likely to slow down any time soon. The broad audience base, the wide range of entertainment offerings, and the energy and excitement

Kasper A.S.L., Ltd.

77 Metro Way
Secaucus, New Jersey 07094
U.S.A.
Telephone: (201) 864-0328
Toll Free: (800) 223-7698; (877) 435-7537
Fax: (201) 864-7768
Web site: http://www.kasper.com

Public Company
Incorporated: 1975 as Sassco Fashions, Ltd.
Employees: 1,600
Sales: $400.8 million (2000)
Stock Exchanges: OTC
Ticker Symbol: KASP
NAIC: 315234 Women's & Girls' Cut & Sew Suit, Coat,
     Tailored Jacket & Skirt Manufacturing; 42233
     Women's, Children's & Infants' & Accessories
     Wholesalers; 44812 Women's Clothing Stores

Kasper A.S.L., Ltd., the world's largest women's suit manufacturer, designs, markets, sources, manufactures, and distributes women's career and special occasion suits, sportswear, and dresses under Kasper A.S.L., Anne Klein, Albert Nipon, and Le Suit trademarks. The company also grants licenses for the manufacture and distribution of certain other products under the Anne Klein, Kasper, and Nipon names, including women's watches, jewelry, footwear, coats, eyewear, and swimwear, and men's apparel. In addition, the company operates retail outlet stores throughout the United States under the Kasper A.S.L. and Anne Klein names. Fabrics are selected primarily from Europe and Asia. The clothing is manufactured in the Far East.

Sassco Fashions: 1975–97

Arthur S. Levine, president of the Kelly Arden dress and suit lines of Bobbie Brooks, bought this division in 1972 and made it an independent company. In 1975 he secured a license for suits and dresses under the Sasson label and named his company Sassco Fashions, Ltd. Levine sold Sassco Fashions to Leslie Fay Inc. in 1980. It continued as a division of Leslie Fay, with Levine as its head. In addition to the Sasson label, Leslie Fay was, in 1980, marketing jeans designed by Herbert Kasper and women's apparel under the name "Kasper for Joan Leslie," although it is not clear whether these items were under the Sassco division at this time.

After a period as a private company following a leveraged buyout, Leslie Fay reemerged in 1986 as a public company under the name The Leslie Fay Companies, Inc. The Sassco division line now consisted of moderate- and better-priced dresses and suits under a number of labels, including Kasper for A.S.L., Sasson, and Suits by Dallas. The Kasper for A.S.L. designs and colors were intended to appeal to young career women. Moderate-priced suits in classic designs with specialty fabrics were offered under the Suits by Dallas name. By 1988 Sassco was the largest suit manufacturer based in Manhattan's Seventh Avenue garment district. Sassco added Nolan Miller special occasion suits—aimed at older consumers—in 1987 and recorded sales of almost $130 million that year. Sassco acquired Albert Nipon designer- and bridge-collection dresses and suits in 1988. The division had seven units of its own that year: the Kasper suit and dress lines, the Sasson and Dallas suit collections, Nolan Miller, Albert Nipon, and a private-label suit business.

By 1992 the division was doing about $300 million in annual sales volume, of which branded suits and dresses accounted for $250 million and private-label merchandise for the remainder. These sales were all wholesale, but for late 1992 the division added a retail Kasper coat collection and a line of 200 or so in-store shops in major department stores. The target, in August 1992, was to be in 40 Federated Department Stores units, including units in the company's Abraham & Straus, Bloomingdale's, Bon Marche, Burdine's, Jordan Marsh, Lazarus, and Rich's stores, and in 40 May Department Stores, including the Filene's, Kaufman's, and Lord & Taylor divisions. Where the division—commonly but not officially known as Kasper for A.S.L.—did not have in-store shops, retailers were urged to move its offerings out of the suit department and into prime sportswear areas, as it responded to the more casual workplace by introducing seasonless fabrics, less structured tailoring, pantsuits, three-piece items, and suits sold with sweaters.

Leslie Fay, it was discovered soon after, had submitted false numbers for its 1992 results, and the following year the company fell into Chapter 11 bankruptcy. The Sassco Fashions division continued to offer moderate- to designer-priced suits under a number of different labels, including Kasper for A.S.L., Kasper II for A.S.L., Le Suit, Albert Nipon, and Nolan Miller. It also offered moderate- and better-priced dresses under the Kasper for A.S.L. label and better-priced sportswear under the Kasper and Company for A.S.L. label.

At a bankruptcy court hearing in 1994, Leslie Fay's president testified that Levine wanted to purchase Sassco Fashions back from the company. Sassco was the company's strongest and most profitable division, with its fiscal 1993 sales of $300–$350 million accounting for roughly half of Leslie Fay's $661 million in sales that year. Seemingly for that very reason, however, Leslie Fay was unwilling to sell the division to Levine, who reportedly offered $225 million but was unable to secure financing. In early 1996 an investor group offered to buy Sassco for about $240 million in cash and stock, but Leslie Fay rejected this offer as well. Because Levine and Gregg Marks, Sassco's president, were considered essential to the business, the proposal reportedly called for them and other division executives to receive 25 percent of the stock for remaining at the helm.

Independent Company: 1997–99

Leslie Fay finally conceded defeat in 1997 in its effort to retain Sassco. As part of the reorganization plan under which it emerged from bankruptcy, the company spun off Sassco Fashions, Ltd., which issued notes and distributed 6.8 million shares, collectively valued at $110 million, to Leslie Fay's creditors. Members of management received stock options for about 20 percent of the shares. The new company traded initially over the counter and was renamed Kasper A.S.L., Ltd. later in the year. The company was at this time making and marketing suits and dresses under the labels Kasper for A.S.L., LeSuit, b. bennett, and Albert Nipon, as well as Kasper & Co. sportswear and Nina Charles knitwear (which was dropped in 1999). During 1997 the number of company outlet stores grew from 36 to 47. Net sales, at $311.71 million, were flat.

Sales remained about the same in 1998. Net income of $3.17 million reflected interest and financing costs of $17.79 million, mostly on Kasper's long-term debt of $110 million that it inherited from the Leslie Fay breakup. That year the company launched its first major advertising campaign in several years, displaying its name on buses and billboards around the country. In 1999 the campaign was taken to print advertising in magazines.

Kasper purchased Anne Klein Co. in early 1999 for an estimated $75 million. It was founded by the eponymous designer in 1968, with her work continued after her death in 1974 by Louis Dell'Olio and Donna Karan. Karan left in 1985 to found her own company. With business on the decline, Dell'Olio was replaced in 1993, first by Richard Tyler and then by Patrick Robinson. Neither was successful commercially, and in 1996 Anne Klein dropped its designer collection line, concentrating on its bridge collection of jackets, pants, and skirts that could be worn in numerous combinations (''bridge'' being the name for the share of the marketplace between couture and ready-to-wear). Isaac Franco and Ken Kaufman, designers from rival Emanuel/Emanuel Ungaro, were hired to design this line, which was renamed Anne Klein 2.

Anne Klein registered $94.5 million in sales in 1998 and was the third most recognized designer name, according to a consumer survey by the publisher of *WWD* (*Women's Wear Daily*), but the company lost money in both 1997 and 1998 as the volume of its mainstay bridge sportswear business declined. Whereas Kasper dominated the women's suit market at prices of $200 and under, Anne Klein clothing was more expensive and sold at better-class department stores such as Neiman Marcus and Saks Fifth Avenue. Its core customer was seen by Kasper management as an upper-level executive, while Kasper's own customer was likely to be a junior executive or secretary. Anne Klein had its headquarters in Manhattan and its warehouse in Secaucus, New Jersey; Kasper maintained a showroom and offices in Manhattan but had its warehouse and headquarters in Secaucus.

In Financial Difficulty in 2000

Franco and Kaufman were re-signed to direct the design of the new Anne Klein division of Kasper and to oversee creative direction of all Anne Klein licenses. They continued to produce the Anne Klein bridge collection and its casual counterpart, A Line Anne Klein. There were plans to expand distribution to Europe and Asia. In 2000 the division introduced Anne Klein Suits, a bridge line priced to retail around $400 to $500, and in competition with—among others—Albert Nipon. Kasper was hoping the new label would inherit Nipon's reputation among merchants for suits that consistently fit well and could be supplied and resupplied to stores quickly. The new Anne Klein suits included 45 styles in an array of colors. Many of them incorporated key fabrics from the sportswear collection, and detailing included Anne Klein's signature pick stitching, dolman sleeves, double-faced fabrics, snap buttons, leather details, and detachable fur collars. Among those well received by observers was a two-tone beaded gray flannel pantsuit, a one-button textured winter white wool skirt suit, and a rust-colored mohair jacket worn over an espresso turtleneck and wool trousers. Also unveiled for the fall of 2000 was a revival of the dormant Anne Klein 2 label for better-priced sportswear.

The Anne Klein acquisition also included licensed watches under the Anne Klein 2 and Anne Klein Swiss names and footwear under the Anne Klein 2 name, but the latter (and perhaps the former as well) were inactive by this time. By 2001 the Anne Klein licensing division had 17 licensing agreements in place and was offering a wide range of products bearing its trademarks, including watches, jewelry, footwear, coats, eyewear, sleepwear, swimwear, handbags, small leather goods, scarves, socks and hosiery, sewing patterns, and umbrellas. Kasper had licensing agreements covering women's coats and blouses; men's woven sports shirts; sweaters and casual pants; and handbags, portfolios, and wallets. (A Kasper footwear license in the mid-1990s had not proven successful.) Nipon had licensing arrangements including men's tailored clothing, neckwear, and small leather goods, and women's and girls' coats and outerwear.

Kasper invested $1 million in a comprehensive web site that made its debut in 1999. In partnership with Planet Direct and ZineZone, the company introduced a "Kareer Center" page as a comprehensive resource to organize their workday and personal agenda, and a "Kasper Klothing" page to display the company's ready-to-wear and sportswear lines. Planet Direct's custom portal enabled Kasper to offer features including e-mail, an online calendar, real-time stock quotes and portfolio management, news, and local weather. ZineZone offered access to career, industry, investing/personal finance, and business news libraries. Online shoppers could view photos and descriptions of current clothing offerings, with zoom software allowing them to view textures, colors, and features of selected apparel, and a sizing chart for misses', petite, and women's sizes.

Kasper's net sales dropped $1 million, to $311.21 million, in 1999. Operational expenses rose by almost $15 million—chiefly to revive Anne Klein—and interest and financing costs increased by almost $3 million. The company incurred a net loss of $4.77 million. For the first half of 2000, the company reported a loss of $3 million on $191.3 million in revenue. On September 30, Kasper announced that it would not make its semiannual interest payment of about $7.2 million to the holders of its senior notes, who were receiving an annual interest rate of 12.75 percent. The company said it was in the midst of a liquidity crisis because of costs tied to the launch of the new Anne Klein 2 line and a difficult spring for Kasper and Anne Klein goods.

Chase Manhattan Bank and eight other creditors of Kasper agreed in November 2000 to waive the company's compliance with certain financial covenants and all existing defaults so that the company could restructure its financial obligations and improve its ability to meet long- and short-term strategic plans. The nine creditors had extended Kasper a revolving-credit and letter-of-credit line of $160 million in 1999, and this remained valid, according to a company spokesperson. As of the end of that year, Kasper had borrowed $53.44 million directly from the credit line and about $22.74 million in letters of credit. Kasper closed 2000 with sharply higher net sales of $400.8 million. Royalty income came to an additional $14.91 million. Costs were also up, however, including $25.58 million for interest and financing and $2.34 million in restructuring charges. The company's net loss for the year was $25.19 million.

Kasper was placing its hopes for the fall 2000 season on a revival of the suit business, which had been sagging for the past five years because of the rise of casual dress in the workplace. Retailing data from the spring and summer indicated that shoppers were finally ready to update their sweater sets with jackets, but the trend was not yet well established enough to afford any degree of certainty. Kasper ranked ninth among women's suitmakers in a biannual survey of consumer brand awareness and preferences taken in late 1999.

In early 2001 the company was selling its products in about 2,000 department and specialty stores in the United States, Canada, and Europe. These included Federated (Bloomingdale's, Macy's East, Macy's West, Rich's/Lazarus, Bon Marche), May Company (Lord & Taylor, Hecht's, Robinsons-May, Foley's, Kaufman Famous-Barr, Filene's, Meier & Frank), Saks, Inc. (Parisian, Proffitt's, Carson Pirie Scott), Marshall Field's, Dillard's, and Belk. In all, department stores accounted for about 66 percent of gross sales in 2000. The company also was selling its products in 66 company-operated retail outlets under the Kasper A.S.L. name and in 29 company-operated retail outlets under the Anne Klein and Anne Klein 2 names. These stores were selling licensed as well as company-produced items. They accounted for about 19 percent of the company's net sales in 2000.

The Kasper collections in 2001 were Kasper A.S.L., Kasper Dress, Kasper & Company Sportswear, Kasper & Company Woman, Kasper Woman, Le Suit, and Le Suit Woman. Kasper A.S.L. held about 70 percent of the "upper moderate" women's suit market in the United States in 2000 and remained the company's core business, responsible for about 36 percent of net domestic wholesale sales in that year. The Le Suit line was a less expensive alternative and accounted for about 16 percent of net domestic wholesale sales. Kasper also was manufacturing suits under the Albert Nipon label and was designing and manufacturing suits under private labels for various department stores. Kasper and Company A.S.L. sportswear accounted for about 11 percent of net domestic wholesale sales in 2000. Anne Klein and A Line Anne Klein sportswear accounted for about 14 percent of net domestic wholesale sales. Anne Klein 2 accounted for another 8 percent.

Each of the company's product lines had its own design team. A manufacturing facility in China went into production in 1998 and accounted for about 5 percent of finished goods in 2000. The rest of its goods were being turned out by more than 30 contractors located primarily in China, Hong Kong, the Philippines, and Taiwan.

Kasper's principal shareholders in March 2001 were Whippoorwill Associates, Inc., 18.1 percent; Bay Harbor Management, L.C., 15.9 percent; and ING Equity Partners, L.P. I, 9.5 percent. Trading of Kasper stock moved from the NASDAQ to the OTC (Over-The-Counter) bulletin board in February 2001 because the company was no longer meeting certain NASDAQ listing requirements. As of March 20, 2001, a share of stock was trading for less than ten cents.

Principal Subsidiaries

Asia Export Limited (Hong Kong); Kasper A.S.L. Europe, Ltd. (U.K.); Kasper Holdings Inc.

Principal Competitors

Jones Apparel Group; Leslie Fay Companies, Inc.; Liz Claiborne, Inc.; McNaughton Apparel Group Inc.

Further Reading

Agins, Teri, "Leslie Fay's Levine Seeks to Buy Back Sassco Fashions Unit from Company," *Wall Street Journal,* July 5, 1994, p. A5.

Curan, Catherine, "Apparel Firms Pressing Their Suit with Women," *Crain's New York Business,* September 11, 2000, pp. 4, 52.

——, "New Owner Plans to Spur Comeback for Anne Klein," *Crain's New York Business,* April 12, 1999, pp. 4, 39.

Friedman, Arthur, "Anne Klein's New Era: Kasper to Buy Name, Aims for Megabrand," *WWD/Women's Wear Daily,* March 17, 1999, pp. 1, 10–11.

——, "Kasper Maps In-Store Shop Plan," *Women's Wear Daily,* August 4, 1992, pp. 2, 19.

——, "Kasper's Klein Franchise Gets Kaufman, Franco," *WWD/Women's Wear Daily,* August 3, 1999, pp. 2, 19.

——, "Kasper Starts Up Kasper.com with $1 Million," *WWD/Women's Wear Daily,* August 12, 1999, p. 5.

Karr, Arnold J., "Kasper Structures New Terms," *WWD/Women's Wear Daily,* November 21, 2000, p. 12.

"Kasper Returns to Footwear Business with Takeover of Anne Klein Brand," *FN/Footwear News,* March 22, 1999, p. 9.

"Leslie Fay Emerges from Reorganization in Bankruptcy Court," *Wall Street Journal,* June 5, 1997, p. B12.

Michals, Debra, "Sassco: Moving Beyond Suits," *Women's Wear Daily,* August 9, 1988, p. 8.

Strom, Stephanie, "$240 Million Is Offered for Leslie Fay Unit," *New York Times,* January 10, 1996, p. D2.

Wilson, Eric, "Anne Klein Suits Kasper Just Fine," *WWD/Women's Wear Daily,* March 14, 2000, p. 10.

——, "Old Names with New Games," *WWD/Women's Wear Daily,* January 24, 2000 supplement, pp. 38, 96.

—Robert Halasz

Kelley Drye & Warren LLP

101 Park Avenue
New York, New York 10178-0002
U.S.A.
Telephone: (212) 808-7800
Fax: (212) 808-7897
Web site: http://www.kelleydrye.com

Partnership
Founded: 1836 as Mulligan & Barney
Employees: 800
Sales: $127.5 million (1999)
NAIC: 54111 Offices of Lawyers

Kelley Drye & Warren LLP is one of the oldest and largest law firms in the United States. Started in 1836 as a two-man partnership in New York City, the firm has over 300 lawyers in New York; Washington, D.C.; Los Angeles; Chicago; Stamford, Connecticut; Parsippany, New Jersey; Brussels; and Hong Kong, as well as affiliated overseas offices in Tokyo, Bangkok, Jakarta, Manila, and Mumbai, India. Kelley Drye & Warren provides legal counsel in virtually all legal specialties, including traditional areas such as real estate and banking to newer fields such as environmental law and the Internet-based economy. For decades Kelley Drye & Warren has represented major corporations or their predecessors, including Union Carbide Corporation, Chrysler Corporation, and The Chase Manhattan Bank.

Origins and Practice in the 1800s

Hiram Barney began in 1836 a partnership that evolved into Kelley Drye & Warren LLP. He became the junior partner in the New York firm of Mulligan & Barney. In 1838 it became Waterman & Barney after Mulligan died and William Dwight Waterman teamed up with Barney. From 1841 to 1849 the partnership was called Barney & Mitchell with the addition of William Minott Mitchell.

Barney's first client was George Catlin, the famous painter of Indian and Western scenes. The lawyer also represented the estate of Francis Scott Key, author of "The Star Spangled Banner."

Barney's notable legal career included trips to the Iowa Territory in 1840 and 1841 to help resolve land claims and title questions concerning the so-called Half Breed Tract located between the Mississippi and Des Moines rivers near Keokuk, Iowa. The Sac and Fox tribes had ceded the tract to the federal government in 1836 after their defeat in the Black Hawk War.

Originally an anti-slavery Democrat, Barney joined the new Republican Party and became a friend of Abraham Lincoln, who in 1861 appointed him the Collector of the Customs of the Port of New York. As the collector, Barney was responsible for overseeing 1,100 individuals, the largest federal agency at the time.

After the Civil War, widespread corruption led some in the legal profession to seek reforms. Thus the firm's early lawyers in 1870 helped organize The Association of the Bar of the City of New York that fought against Tammany Hall and its leader "Boss" Tweed.

In 1875 name partner William Allen Butler helped establish the Central Trust Company of New York, which became a long-term client. He also was a prominent litigator, especially in maritime law. According to the Kelley Drye firm history, Butler wrote that he had "the opportunity of aiding in establishing the jurisdiction of the Admiralty courts under the Constitution of the United States upon the basis of the ancient maritime law of continental Europe as distinguished from the circumscribed statutory law of England. . . ."

The Firm from 1900 to 1945

In 1905 Butler, Notman, Joline & Mynderse split into two partnerships. Butler, Notman & Mynderse retained the predecessor firm's admiralty practice. The other new partnership of Joline, Larkin & Rathbone kept most of the previous firm's corporate practice, including Central Trust Company of New York. In 1907 the Joline firm helped the Metropolitan Street Railway and the New York City Railway successfully reorganize after they declared bankruptcy. Others reorganized by the Joline firm included Westinghouse Electric & Manufacturing Company in 1908, St. Louis & San Francisco Railroad in 1913, Maxwell Motor Company, Inc. in 1913 and 1921, American Writing Paper Company in 1926 and 1927, Detroit United

Company Perspectives:

The time is now. The next century is approaching. New revolutions and industries are unfolding, from genetic engineering to virtual reality. The shape of the world is changing and Kelley Drye is bringing its industry knowledge and cross-disciplinary skills to bear for a diversified group of clients. We're not only helping the well-established corporations of today, but also advising the Chase Manhattans, Union Carbides, and GTEs of tomorrow, the potential success stories of the next 160 years.

Railway in 1928 and 1929, International Mercantile Marine Company in 1929, and the Oklahoma Natural Gas Corporation in 1933. The firm's attorneys in the early 20th century also represented Lanston Monotype Machine Company, Sloss-Sheffield Steel & Iron Company, Pressed Steel Car Company, The Virginian Railway, United States Industrial Alcohol Company, and Lever Brothers.

In 1917 the firm organized the Surdna Foundation for banker John E. Andrus. That foundation, which always kept a member of the Joline or successor firms on its board of directors, started with little money but by 1985 had $225 million in assets. The law firm also drew up the will of Augustus D. Juilliard and set up the Juilliard Musical Foundation and its Juilliard School of Music.

In 1921 the law firm hired Nicholas Kelley as a new partner. Kelley had graduated from Harvard University and then the Harvard Law School in 1909, worked for New York's Cravath law firm, and served as Wilson's and Harding's assistant secretary of the Treasury Department before he joined the firm.

In 1921 the firm represented The Guaranty Trust Company when it negotiated with the government of Peru for a $50 million loan, but that country was not financially sound enough to warrant such a large loan.

The firm also helped the Maxwell Motor Company gain a loan from Chase Securities Corporation so that it could build the first Chrysler automobile, and then it incorporated Chrysler Corporation under Delaware law in 1925. With the law firm's help, Chrysler Corporation in 1928 acquired Dodge Brothers and thus became the nation's third largest auto maker. Chrysler remained one of the firm's major long-term clients in the decades to come.

The Post-World II Practice

During World War II, Chrysler Corporation had converted its factories from auto production to making tanks, B-29 engines, guns, and other war-related items. The law firm played an important role helping return Chrysler to the peacetime production of civilian vehicles. In the 1950s the firm assisted Chrysler in its acquisitions of the Briggs Manufacturing Company and three foreign companies.

Other clients soon after the war included the Board of Governors of The Society of The New York Hospital, Lake

Tankers Corporation, National Oil Transport Corporation, The Virginian Railway, and Norfolk & Western Railroad Company.

With the 1935 passage of the National Labor Relations Act, often called the Wagner Act, some law firms began labor practices since unions representing unskilled workers grew rapidly. The firm's lawyers after the war helped draft the 1947 Taft-Hartley Act, a major piece of union legislation. The law firm continued in the decades ahead to represent many companies involved in labor issues, a specialty that Robert M. Lunny said in his history was "unique for a large 'Wall Street' or 'Park Avenue' law firm."

The firm of Rathbone, Perry, Kelley & Drye in 1951 included 20 partners, 23 associates, and 64 staff and clerical workers. In 1965 the law firm began representing the New York Giants, which led to work for other NFL teams, the National Football League itself, and the NFL Management Council that represented the players in collective bargaining. In the 1960s the firm also represented The Holmes Protection Group in an antitrust case that went to the U.S. Supreme Court.

In the 1970s the firm's real estate practice expanded, so that by the mid-1980s it managed real-property investments for Connecticut General Life Insurance Company, Equitable Life Assurance Society of the United States, Metropolitan Life Insurance Company, Rouse Company, the Society of the New York Hospital, and the New York Province of the Society of Jesus (Jesuits).

In October 1974 the law firm included 84 lawyers, eight accountants, and 115 staff members. The passage of many new federal laws and regulations in the 1960s and 1970s stimulated the growth of the legal profession.

Two other events in the 1970s brought major changes to the nation's large law firms. First, advertising and public relations significantly increased after the U.S. Supreme Court ruled that professional associations' restrictions on advertising violated the First Amendment's guarantee of free speech. Second, the *National Law Review* and the *American Lawyer* were started to publish information on internal law firm management practices and their financial performance. Such legal journalism led to firms becoming more business-oriented as salaries skyrocketed in order to prevent lateral hiring by competing firms.

Like other elite corporate law firms, Kelley Drye & Warren grew rapidly in the 1980s. From 93 lawyers in New York in January 1979, the firm exploded in size to 210 lawyers in January 1984 in offices in New York; Miami; Los Angeles; San Francisco; Tokyo; Washington, D.C.; Morristown, New Jersey; and Stamford and Danbury, Connecticut.

Chrysler Corporation, one of Kelley Drye's historic clients, almost collapsed due to excessive debt and its poor performance compared to Japanese and German companies that made more fuel efficient cars during the 1970s energy crisis. To meet the strict requirements of a huge federal loan guarantee, Chrysler used Kelley Drye but mainly relied on New York's Debevoise, Plimpton, Lyons & Gates as its lead counsel in what Stewart called the "largest corporate rescue mission ever attempted."

Kelley Drye, since shortly after World War I ended, had been representing Union Carbide and Carbon Corporation,

Key Dates:

1836: Mulligan & Barney is founded.

1838: Partnership is renamed Waterman & Barney.

1841: Barney & Mitchell becomes the new name.

1849: Firm is renamed Barney & Butler.

1851: Barney, Humphrey & Butler becomes the new name.

1859: Partnership is renamed Barney, Butler & Parsons.

1874: Partnership adopts the new name of Butler, Stillman & Hubbard.

1896: Partnership's new name is Butler, Notman, Joline & Mynderse.

1905: New name of Joline, Larkin & Rathbone is chosen.

1918: Larkin & Perry is formed.

1920: Larkin, Rathbone & Perry becomes the firm's new name.

1943: Rathbone, Perry, Kelley & Drye is established.

1952: Kelley, Drye, Newhall & Maginnes is the partnership's new name.

1961: In its first merger, the firm acquires Barr, Robbins & Palmer.

1962: Kelley, Drye, Newhall, Maginnes & Warren is formed.

1965: Firm starts an affiliated office called Roberts & Hayden in Jersey City, New Jersey.

1969: Firm is renamed Kelley, Drye, Warren, Clark, Carr & Ellis after a merger.

1975: Kelley Drye & Warren LLP is chosen as the firm's permanent name.

1979: Merger with Cross, Brodrick & Chipman results in new offices in Stamford and Danbury, Connecticut.

1981: Firm starts a Washington, D.C. office.

1982: Miami office is opened; New York headquarters are moved to 101 Park Avenue.

1983: Firm merges with New York's Miller, Montgomery, Sogi & Brady, P.C.

1984: Firm opens offices in San Francisco, Los Angeles, and Morristown, New Jersey.

1997: Kelley Drye becomes affiliated with a law firm in Jakarta, Indonesia.

2001: Firm opens its new office in Tysons Corner, Virginia.

which became Union Carbide Corporation in 1957. The firm helped Union Carbide from 1957 to 1963 when the federal government charged it with antitrust violations. After using Kelley Drye for many purposes, Union Carbide again relied on its longtime outside counsel when it faced a major crisis that threatened its very existence. On December 3, 1984, a plant owned by a Union Carbide subsidiary in Bhopal, India, released toxic pollutants into the air that killed about 8,000 persons and injured about 300,000. Multiple lawsuits were filed that sought many billions of dollars in damages. Some thought Union Carbide would turn to a larger law firm, as Chrysler had done just a few years earlier. However, Kelley Drye had gained expertise in mass tort litigation when it helped Hercules Inc. successfully settle Agent Orange litigation filed by lawyers representing thousands of Vietnam War veterans. According to Kelley Drye's web site, "we had [Bhopal] suits on behalf of the more than 500,000 claimants consolidated and dismissed from U.S. courts, and were instrumental in designing a favorable settlement with the Indian government."

Developments in the 1990s and Beyond

Some of the firm's corporate clients in the 1990s included GTE, a leading telecommunications company; ADT Security Systems; venture capital company Sevin Rosen; Mission Energy Company; and Qwest Communications. By the beginning of the new millennium the firm's Project Finance and Infrastructure Group had provided legal advice to various sponsors, investment banks, and others involved in 100 projects in 40 nations.

To strengthen its Asian practice, Kelley Drye in 1997 affiliated with the law firm of Soebagjo, Roosdiono, Jatim & Djarot in Jakarta, Indonesia. Kelley Drye for 20 years had represented both Indonesian and non-Indonesian clients in transactions involving power, telecommunications, and other areas.

In the late 1990s Kelley Drye represented several foreign telephone companies that opposed proposed Federal Communications Commission changes. The FCC wanted U.S. long-distance companies to change their payment to international carriers for overseas calls. Fearing such changes would hurt their businesses and were indeed treaty violations, Hong Kong Telecom, Guyana Telephone & Telegraph, the Caribbean Association of National Communications Organizations, and several other entities engaged Kelley Drye to fight the FCC's changes.

To assist mainly its telecommunications and Internet-based clients, Kelley Drye in 2001 established an office in Tysons Corner, Virginia. The firm shared the 12th floor of the Tycon Tower with other companies, such as Nokia Venture Partners, LP, that together offered a wide range of legal, investment, financial consulting, public relations, and other business services. Without formal corporate mergers, this joint effort provided one-stop business assistance.

Responding to an increasingly globalized economy, Kelley Drye in the late 1990s made lateral hires to establish an International Trade and Investment Group and strengthen its Financial Institutions Group. The firm intended to bolster its Asian/Pacific practice in particular. Oracle Corporation in 2001 recognized Kelley Drye's expertise in that region when it chose the law firm to participate in its VentureNetwork web site that would give Asian companies more opportunities to learn about the New York law firm's services and how they could use online business methods.

Kelley Drye lawyer Robert L. Haig made a major contribution to his profession when he served as editor-in-chief of a 1998 six-volume work called *Business and Commercial Litigation in Federal Courts*. Michael A. Pope said this extensively documented book "rates a very special place in the library of today's litigator."

In 2000 Kelley Drye & Warren represented Amedeo Hotels Ltd. owned by Prince Jefri Bolkiah of oil-rich Brunei. The government sued the prince to recover billions that he allegedly embezzled. The law firm's international practice also included helping the American subsidiary of Germany's Daimler-Chrysler to set up its first American plant to build Mercedes-Benz automobiles. Similar globalization developments assisted by large law firms such as Kelley Drye occurred in many industries.

Although Kelley Drye & Warren did not rank among the world's 50 largest law firms, the *American Lawyer* included it in its annual listing of the 100 largest U.S. firms. Based on its 1997 gross revenue of $110.5 million, the firm ranked number 85. In 1998 it was number 89 with $120.5 million gross revenue, and in 1999 it declined to number 96 based on its gross revenue of $127.5 million. Its competitors in the new millennium included many larger American law firms and also foreign law firms such as London's Clifford Chance with its approximately 3,000 lawyers worldwide.

Principal Operating Units

Litigation; Corporate and Banking; Labor and Employment Law; Employee Benefits; Bankruptcy; Tax; Real Estate; Personal Services.

Principal Competitors

Baker & McKenzie; Jones, Day, Reavis & Pogue; and Skadden, Arps, Slate, Meagher & Flom.

Further Reading

Friedman, Robert, "Carbide Should Make Interim Payments to Bhopal Disaster Victims, Judge Says," *Wall Street Journal,* April 17, 1985, p. 1
"Kelley Drye & Warren Poaches Top Partners for Expanding Practices," *International Financial Law Review,* January 1999, p. 5.
"Kelley Drye Links with Jakarta Firm," *International Financial Law Review,* November 1997, p. 7.
"KPN and Qwest to Form Europe's Biggest Internet Traffic Network," *International Financial Law Review,* January 1999, p. 7.
Kurzman, Dan, *A Killing Wind: Inside Union Carbide and the Bhopal Catastrophe,* New York: McGraw-Hill Book Company, 1987.
Lunny, Robert M., *Kelley Drye & Warren: An Informal History, 1836–1984,* New York: Kelley Drye & Warren, 1985.
Luxner, Larry, "Back and Forth on Foreign Billing," *Telephony,* October 5, 1998, pp. 62–64.
Pope, Michael A., "Business and Commercial Litigation in Federal Courts," *Defense Counsel Journal,* July 1999, pp. 411–12.
Shari, Michael, et al, "Brunei's Battle Royal," *Business Week,* April 3, 2000, p. 24.
Stewart, James B., "Bud Holman of Kelley Drye Is in Spotlight As He Assembles Union Carbide's Defense," *Wall Street Journal,* December 20, 1984, p. 1.
——, "Chrysler: Debevoise, Plimpton, Lyons & Gates," in *The Partners: Inside America's Most Powerful Law Firms,* New York: Simon and Schuster, 1983, pp. 201–44.
——, "Suits Against Union Carbide Raise Issues for Lawyers, Multinationals," *Wall Street Journal,* December 17, 1984, p. 1.
Wilcox, Fred A., *Waiting for an Army to Die: The Tragedy of Agent Orange,* Cabin John, Md.: Seven Locks Press, 1989.

—David M. Walden

A World of Difference

Kuoni Travel Holding Ltd.

Neue Hard 7
CH-8010 Zurich
Switzerland
Telephone: (+41) 1-277-44-44
Fax: (+41) 1-271-52-82
Web site: http://www.kuoni.com

Public Company
Incorporated: 1906 as Travel Bureau
Employees: 6,552
Sales: SFr 4.11 billion (2000)
Stock Exchanges: Swiss
Ticker Symbol: KUNN
NAIC: 561510 Travel Agencies; 561520 Tour Operators

Kuoni Travel Holding Ltd. oversees one of Europe's top five travel and tour groups. Based in Zurich, Switzerland, the company is particularly strong in both its domestic and U.K. markets, but is also present throughout Europe, especially in Scandinavia, with a rising presence in the United States and Asian markets. Kuoni Travel operates in three primary areas of business: Leisure Travel, which accounts for more than 85 percent of the company's sales; Business Travel, through its BTI unit, which handles travel coordination activities for the small and mid-sized and large-scale corporation markets; and Incoming Services, which provides travel destination services, such as touring and sightseeing packages. The company markets it high-end tours and travel packages under the Kuoni name. Discount travel packages are offered under the Helvetica brand name. Switzerland remains the company's single largest market, representing slightly less than one-third of its total sales. The U.K. and North American markets together provide less than one-third of sales. The European continent, including Scandinavia, added another roughly 30 percent to Kuoni's total sales, which topped SFr 4 billion in 2000. Kuoni has been stepping up the pace of its acquisitions at the turn of the century. After being thwarted in its attempt to merge with the United Kingdom's First Choice Holidays Plc, which would have helped the company create a counterweight to Europe's market-

leading Preussag-Thomson alliance announced in early 2000, Kuoni has changed direction, targeting the Scandinavian, Indian, and North American markets for its future growth. Listed on the Swiss stock exchange, Kuoni is led by Chairman Daniel Affolter and President and CEO Hans Lerch.

Early Twentieth-Century Travel Pioneer

A native of Chur, Switzerland, Alfred Kuoni moved to Zurich to open a travel agency in 1906. If the company's name—Travel Bureau—was not all that original, Kuoni quickly established itself as a pioneer in exotic travel destinations. One of the company's first organized tour packages took Swiss citizens on a guided tour to far-off Egypt. In 1925, Kuoni reincorporated as a joint-stock company, with shares remaining within the Kuoni family. Through the years leading up to World War II, Kuoni expanded from its original location to include a number of sales offices throughout Switzerland. Despite its success in its home market, the company recognized early on that Switzerland was too small for its growing ambitions. The company also opened its first international office, in Nice, in the south of France. Further international moves were thwarted by the buildup to and outbreak of World War II.

Kuoni's international expansion began almost immediately after the end of the war. In 1948, the company opened its first international subsidiaries, in Italy and France. Kuoni also continued to pioneer new and exotic travel destinations, such as the organization of the first charter flights to Africa. In 1957, the Kuoni family established the Kuoni and Hugentobler Foundation under which to group their holding; much later, with Kuoni's public listing, the foundation would became the company's primary shareholder.

Kuoni began looking farther afield in the 1960s. In 1963, the company made its first entry into the Asian markets with the opening of a branch office in Japan. Two years later, Kuoni entered what was later to become one of its most important single markets when it acquired the United Kingdom's Challis & Benson Ltd. The importance of the U.K. market to Kuoni was seen at the beginning of the 1970s when the company changed its name—and its U.K. operations' name—to Kuoni Travel Ltd.

Company Perspectives:

We are committed to creating best value for people: our customers, employees, shareholders and business partners. We strive to be successful in our core business activities: Leisure Travel, Business Travel and Incoming. We motivate our staff by encouraging entrepreneurship and innovation at all levels. We think and act internationally. We strive to enhance shareholder value. We support environmentally friendly solutions. Kuoni stands for reliability, best value for money, quality and fairness in business.

The company's listing on the Swiss stock exchange provided fuel for new growth, while opening up the company's shares to new partners, including SwissAir, which built up a 30 percent share in Kuoni. The public listing enabled the company to step up its international growth. After opening a subsidiary in Austria at the beginning of the decade, Kuoni now launched subsidiaries in Germany and Spain, both in 1973, and a subsidiary in Greece the following year. The year 1974 also saw Kuoni step up its position in the U.K. market, when it acquired Houlders World Holidays, based in England.

While building up its international network, Kuoni also was launching new products. In 1977, the company began marketing its first around-the-world tour. In the 1980s, Kuoni began to acquire properties in many of its most popular destinations, adding a number of hotels, including the Hawksbill Beach Hotel in Antigua in 1981 and the Discovery Bay Beach Hotel in Barbados, bought in 1984. In 1986, Kuoni became the first tour operator to offer around-the-world charter flights on the Concorde supersonic jet. Although this latter product catered to the company's strong high-end and high-margin clientele, Kuoni also launched a new brand name, Helvetica, to encompass its discount tour and travel operations.

Takeover Target in the 1990s

The worldwide travel industry remained highly fragmented in the 1990s, with numerous small-scale operators competing against a smaller number of quickly growing industry heavyweights. Kuoni, which had already captured the lead in the Swiss market, was determined to maintain a leadership position as the travel industry headed into a drawn-out consolidation drive leading up to the turn of the century. The company acquired Reiseburo NUR Neckermann in 1987, boosting its position in the Austrian market. Three years later, the company regrouped its Austrian activities, launching the NUR Neckermann Reisen AG joint venture with Germany's Neckermann Touristic. Kuoni's part of the joint venture remained at 49 percent.

Back home, the company continued to consolidate its dominance of the Swiss market, acquiring Privat Safaris, the country's leading operator of tours to eastern Africa, and Reiseburo Popularis, which combined retail offices with direct sales operations marketing discount tour and travel packages. Yet Kuoni's strong position in the Swiss market and its growing share internationally soon led it to become the target of a takeover attempt. The sale of SwissAir's 30 percent holding

created the opening for Germany's Krauthof AG department store group to acquire a 50.1 percent majority of Kuoni in 1992.

Kuoni, through the Kuoni and Hugentobler Foundation, nonetheless retained majority control of the company's voting rights—which provided the leverage to the resolution of the takeover attempt. In 1995, the Kuoni and Hugentobler Foundation bought out Krauthof's stake in the company. The company then changed its name to Kuoni Travel Holding, a move that also reflected a new diversification drive: in 1995 the company acquired Danzas Reisen AG, a Switzerland-based specialist in business travel services. The Danzas acquisition led Kuoni to create a dedicated business travel unit. The company also acquired retailer Kewi Reisen, while integrating its majority share of Railtour Suiss SA, acquired the year before.

Industry Consolidator for the 21st Century

With its independence assured, Kuoni launched its own acquisition drive in the late 1990s. In 1996, Kuoni added France's Voice SA, and Scanditours, focused on the Nordic region. The company moved into The Netherlands with the acquisition of Special Traffic that same year. Kuoni also looked to the potentially huge market of India for the first time, acquiring SOTC Holiday Tours, which provided the basis for its Kuoni India Ltd. subsidiary. Two other acquisitions completed the company's busy years, those of Rotunda Tours, expanding Kuoni into South Africa, and CIS Intersport, a Swiss company catering to the growing demand for sports-oriented holiday packages. In 1996, also, the company's Edelweiss Air launched its charter flight operations.

Kuoni's expansion campaign continued strongly through the end of the century, including the launch of the P&O Travel Ltd. joint venture with Peninsular and Oriental Steam Navigation Company, based in Hong Kong, with offices in Bangkok and Singapore. The 1997 joint venture strengthened Kuoni's position in the Asian market, which, despite the austere economic climate in the region at the end of the decade, promised to become one of the world's stronger holiday markets. Closer to home, Kuoni continued lining up acquisitions, especially Voyages Jules Verne, a U.K. upscale tour operator, and Switzerland's Manta Reisen, which specialized in scuba and other deep-sea holidays. The company also acquired German business travel specialist Euro Lloyd Reisenburo, which it combined with its other German operations into the new subsidiary BTI Euro Lloyd, one of that market's top five business travel companies. Also in 1998, Kuoni launched a joint venture with Italy's Gastaldi Tours.

The next year saw Kuoni face a major setback. At the beginning of 1999, the company announced its agreement to merge with the United Kingdom's number three travel operator, First Choice Holidays. The merger, agreed to by both sides, was thwarted by a surprise takeover attempt from rival U.K. operator Airtours Plc, which offered a higher per-share price. When the majority of First Choice's shareholders chose to back the Airtours offer—which itself was blocked by the European monopolies commission—Kuoni pulled out of the merger talks.

The First Choice merger might have allowed Kuoni to become not only a major player in the U.K. travel market but to

Key Dates:

1906: Alfred Kuoni opens Travel Bureau in Zurich.
1907: Kuoni organizes first guided tour to Egypt.
1925: Company is incorporated as a joint-stock company.
1948: Subsidiaries in France and Italy are opened.
1951: First charter flights to Africa are launched.
1957: Kuoni and Hugentobler Foundation is established.
1963: Japanese branch office is opened.
1965: Challis & Benson Ltd (U.K.) is acquired.
1970: Austria office is opened; name is changed to Kuoni Travel Ltd.
1972: Company is publicly listed on Swiss stock exchange.
1973: German and Spanish subsidiaries are established.
1974: Houlders World Holidays (U.K.) is acquired; Greece subsidiary is opened.
1981: Hawksbill Beach Hotel (Antigua) is acquired.
1984: Discovery Bay Beach Hotel (Barbados) is purchased.
1987: Reisburo NUR Neckermann (Austria) is acquired.
1990: Privat Safaris and Resieburo Popularis are acquired.
1992: Krauthof AG makes takeover attempt.
1994: Kuoni acquires Railtour Suisse SA.
1995: Name is changed to Kuoni Travel Holding Ltd.; Danzas Reisen and Rewi Reisen are acquired; Edelweiss Air AG is founded.
1996: Kuoni acquires Voice SA (France), Special Traffic (Netherlands), SOTC Holiday Tours (India), Rotunda Tours (South Africa), and CIS Club Intersport.
1997: P&O Travel Ltd. joint venture is launched.
1998: Voyages Jules Verne (U.K.), Manta Reisen (Switzerland), and Euro Lloyd Reiseburo (Germany) are acquired; Kuoni Gastaldi Tours joint venture is formed.
1999: Merger is attempted with First Choice Holidays (U.K.); Intrav (U.S.A.) is acquired.
2000: Kuoni acquires T Pro (U.S.A.), Sita Travel (India), Apollo Resor (Sweden), and Dane Tours (Denmark).
2001: Scandinavian holdings are restructured.

boost its position to the top ranks in all of Europe. After the collapse of the merger, however, Kuoni redirected its strategy to other markets. Three markets in particular were to receive its attention: the United States, Scandinavia, and India. In 1999, Kuoni acquired upscale travel company Intrav, based in St. Louis, Missouri; the Intrav acquisition, which cost Kuoni $115 million, gave it a strong opening into the booming U.S. market for luxury vacations. The following year, the company acquired T Pro, an incoming services specialist based in New York and the number three incoming services provider to the U.S. market.

The year 2000 saw Kuoni not only strengthen its hold on the Swiss travel market—taking a 49 percent share in ITV, Switzerland's third largest tour group and subsidiary of Germany's Preussag—but also expand its presence in its new target markets of Scandinavia and India. The first was served by the acquisition of 49 percent of Apollo Resor, based in Stockholm, Sweden, and then boosted by the acquisition of Denmark's Dane Tours. In March 2001, the company announced its decision to restructure most of its Scandinavian holdings into a single subsidiary.

On the Indian subcontinent, which represented one of the world's single largest potential markets, the company formed a cooperation agreement with that country's Tata conglomerate at the beginning of 2000. That year the company also acquired India's travel leader, Sita Travel, which was then merged into the company's Kuoni Travel subsidiary. Kuoni was now the leading travel group in India. As the company entered the new century, it promised to continue its acquisition drive to reinforce its new geographic objectives. To fuel its continued expansion, Kuoni performed a ten-for-one stock split, raising another SFr 144 million.

Principal Subsidiaries

Alletiders Rejser A/S (Denmark; 95%); Cosmos Internationales Reise- und Touristenburo GmbH (Austria); Edelweiss Air AG (73%); Euro Lloyd Reiseburo GmbH (Germany); Hellenic Tours SA (Greece); Jet Tours AG; Kuoni Gastaldi SpA (Italy; 55%); Kuoni India Ltd.; Kuoni Japan KK; Kuoni Reisen AG; Kuoni Travel Inc. (U.S.A.); Kuoni Travel Ltd (U.K.); Kuoni Travel Nederland BV; Kuoni Travel (Scandinavia) A/S (Denmark); Kuoni Utazasi Iroda Kft (Hungary); Manta Reisen AG (90%); P&O Travel Ltd. (Hong Kong); Railtour Suisse SA; Voyages Jules Verne Ltd (U.K.); Voyages Kuoni SA (France).

Principal Competitors

Airtours Plc; American Express Company; Carlson Wagonlit Travel; First Choice Holidays Plc; Preussag AG; Thomas Cook Holdings Ltd.

Further Reading

Carey, Christopher, "Intrav Accepts $115 Million Buyout from Swiss Travel Firm," *St. Louis Post-Dispatch,* July 20, 1999, p. C12.
Court, Mark, "We'll Fight Them on the Beaches," *Sunday Telegraph,* May 2, 1999, p. 6.
Drees, Caroline, "Kuoni Slips on Capital Increase News," *Reuters,* March 28, 2000.
Gelnar, Martin, "Kuoni's First Choice Merger Seen Falling Through," *Reuters,* June 2, 1999.
"Kuoni Maps Out European Expansion Strategy," *Financial Times,* March 29, 1999.
"Kuoni on Hunt for Takeovers," *Financial Times,* March 29, 2000.
Pitcher, George, "Patient Players Triumph in Travel Industry Takeovers," *Marketing Week,* May 18, 2000.

—M. L. Cohen

Lego A/S

Astvej 1
Billund DK-7190
Denmark
Telephone: 75 33 11 88
Fax: 75 35 83 77
Web site: http://www.lego.com

Private Company
Incorporated: 1944 as Legetojsfabrikken LEGO Billund
    A/S
Employees: 7,821
Sales: $1.1 billion (1999 est.)
NAIC: 339932 Games, Toys, and Children's Vehicles;
    71311 Amusement and Theme Parks

Lego A/S is the holding company for a global toy manufacturer that is the largest toy maker in Europe and the fifth largest in the world. Lego's core product is a line of plastic, interconnecting building bricks. Children can use Lego bricks in a variety of ways, making them into structures of their own imagining, or following the manufacturer's plans to assemble specific toys. Legos are aimed for children from birth through roughly age 14, though in some countries a significant proportion of sales are made to adults. The Duplo line of Lego bricks is aimed for preschoolers, and more sophisticated lines, such as Technics and Mindstorms, are geared towards older children. Lego Dacta is the company's educational products division, while the Lego Lifestyles division handles licensed lines of children's clothing, watches, and backpacks. The company also operates three theme parks, with a fourth set to open in Germany in 2002. Lego is one of the most recognized brand names in Europe, where it ranks with such other global sellers as Coke and Levis. Lego operates 24 subsidiary companies to cover different national markets, and runs ten manufacturing plants. The company is privately held by the family of founder Ole Kirk Christiansen.

Rough Beginnings

The Lego brand of toys was created in 1932 when Ole Kirk Christiansen, a Danish carpenter, decided to extend his carpentry business by manufacturing a line of simple, hand-carved, wooden toys. (The spelling of the family name was later changed to Kristiansen.) He called his new toy business "Lego" as a contraction of two Danish words, "leg godt," meaning "play well." Years later when Lego construction toys became immensely popular in Europe, people pointed out that Lego also means "I assemble" in Latin, but Christiansen always claimed that this double meaning was purely serendipitous. During the bleak years of the 1930s, Christiansen sold his simple wooden toys door to door in the tiny farming community of Billund, Denmark, where he lived. After facing near bankruptcy in 1932, Ole Kirk managed to survive by combining the production of his wooden toys with more mundane household implements such as ladders and milking stools. In one memorable year, the small woodworking firm became involved with the international yo-yo craze. Lego began large scale production of the toy only to discover that, like most toy fads, the yo-yo boom died as suddenly as it had begun. His storerooms crammed with thousands of the unwanted wooden discs, Christiansen converted yo-yo halves into wheels for a new toy truck that became very popular with Danish children.

After the turmoil of World War II and a disastrous fire that destroyed the toy factory in 1942, Ole Kirk Christiansen decided to rebuild his enterprise. A larger and more modern factory was constructed near the site of the old warehouse in Billund and the company was converted from a sole proprietorship to a private limited toy manufacturing company named Legetojsfabrikken LEGO Billund A/S (The LEGO Billund Toy Factory Ltd.). Ole Kirk took the title of senior manager and appointed his son Godtfred as junior manager. By 1947, the Lego company had matured into a prosperous family enterprise which manufactured almost 150 different kinds of carved wooden toys and employed about 40 people.

In the postwar period, good quality plastic became widely available for the first time, prompting Lego to add plastic toys to its line of merchandise. Initially, these plastic toys were coolly received by Danish consumers, with one journalist pointing out that "plastics will never take the place of good, solid wooden toys." Despite this early setback, Lego continued to experiment with plastic toys; in 1949, Lego made its first tentative step into toy history when the company introduced Automatic Binding Bricks, a plastic building toy in which the blocks could grip

Company Perspectives:

Children are our role models because they are curious, creative and imaginative. They embrace discovery and wonder. They are natural learners. These are precious qualities that should be nurtured and stimulated throughout our lives.

The LEGO brand is an integrated universe of experiences contributing to more fun and play. But the LEGO brand represents much more than just play. "Play" in the LEGO sense is learning. By helping children to learn, we build confident, curious and resourceful adults. For their future. And ours.

together to prevent block towers from toppling on little children. These blocks had studs on top, like today's Lego bricks, but their undersides were hollow, allowing the blocks to grip only when they were placed directly on top of one another. These bricks were not well received by toy consumers and many were returned from retailers unsold.

Birth of Modern Lego Toys: 1950s

The concept for the Lego System was born in 1954 when Ole Kirk's son Godtfred visited a local toy fair. One of the buyers at the fair complained to Godtfred that all of the toys being offered at the exposition were alike and that no toy company offered a comprehensive toy system that would encourage creativity in children. Godtfred felt challenged by this complaint and returned to the Lego toy factory determined to come up with an original toy system. He drew up a list of ten requirements that he felt were essential for a quality line of toys. Among the more obvious criteria, like high quality and good play value, were some particular qualities that would distinguish the future Lego brick system. These criteria included the requirement that the toy line be enjoyable for either sex, that it cover a wide age group, that the system include a large number of components, and that compatible pieces be available for adding on to the parts already purchased. Upon reviewing more than 200 toys already being produced by the Lego company, Godtfred decided that the Automatic Binding Bricks, which at this time accounted for only about five percent of sales, held the most promise as the basis for an integrated toy system.

In 1955, the building bricks, manufactured in bright red, yellow, white, and blue, were renamed the "Lego System of Play" and marketed not just as building blocks but as an integrated toy system. Packaged with model street signs, cars, and trucks, the construction set encouraged children to create whole city blocks instead of just one building. The great virtue of the Lego System was that it was infinitely expandable; a parent could purchase a set with bricks and accessories and then be encouraged to buy limitless numbers of add-on sets. In succeeding years, the small Billund toy factory was deluged with orders for the Lego System of Play, due in large measure to Godtfred's insistence on extensive advertising and personal sales meetings with the major Danish toy retailers.

Although sales of the new toy system exceeded expectations, the company continued to experiment with the design of

the product. A major breakthrough came in 1957 when, after testing a variety of models with local children, the company introduced the now famous Lego brick with studs on top and tubes underneath. This new design not only held the bricks together more firmly, but it allowed a child to place the bricks together in any configuration. Three eight-studded bricks could now be combined in 1,060 ways. A child could build tall structures of practically any shape or size, limited only by the number of Lego bricks at his or her disposal.

With the new and improved bricks, soaring Danish sales, and a newly renovated and expanded factory, Lego executives felt that it was time to make a serious effort at marketing their toy system internationally. Initially, Lego had exported their products on only a limited basis by means of wholesale agents in other European countries; however, by the late 1950s they began to set up their own foreign sales subsidiaries. In 1956, the first foreign sales office was opened in Germany, to be followed quickly by offices in Switzerland, Belgium, France, Sweden, and Great Britain. Through these subsidiaries, the Lego company began to consider the whole of Europe as their home market for the Lego product and to use this base to extend sales overseas. By the early 1960s, licenses for the North American production and distribution of the plastic toy had been sold to the Samsonite Corporation; further, the Lego Overseas division recruited sales agents to sell the plastic bricks in Africa, Asia, Australia, and South America.

From the start of this international expansion, Lego executives had decided that only the Lego construction system would be marketed internationally. This decision would mark the first step in Lego's move to become a one product company as the small plastic bricks began to account for larger and larger shares of sales. The fate of the wooden toys that had been the mainstay of the business for more than 20 years was finally sealed in 1960 when a fire destroyed the portion of the factory in which they were produced. Lego managers decided not to rebuild the wooden toy division, but instead to concentrate all production facilities on the Lego construction toy system.

American distribution of Lego products began in 1961 when the giant Samsonite Corporation acquired the American and Canadian license to manufacture and distribute the popular Danish construction toy. Samsonite was looking to diversify its growing company and felt that its experience in plastics and retailing corresponded well with the plastic toy industry. Samsonite opened plants in Stratford, Ontario, and Loveland, Colorado, to manufacture Lego bricks and established a separate sales force to market the product. Although Samsonite managed to sell a respectable $5 million in Lego products annually in North America, the sales figures never matched the huge success that Lego was having in the European market. As a result, Samsonite relinquished its Lego System license in 1973. "Our managerial expertise was better suited to consumer durables than to toys, so we eased out of the toy business," a Samsonite executive stated in a 1976 article in *Business Week*. The Lego Group moved in immediately, establishing an American sales company, Lego Systems, Inc., in Brookfield, Connecticut. In only two years, through heavy investment in advertising and promotion, the subsidiary was able to raise sales levels by more than ten times; to meet this enormous increase in demand, the Lego Group set up a huge 143-acre site in Enfield, Connecticut, in 1975 for the manufacture and sale of

Lego products. By 1976, annual retail sales in the United States had reached $100 million, accounting for almost one third of Lego sales worldwide.

Multinational Growth in the 1970s and After

By the early 1970s, the Lego company employed 1,000 workers at its Billund headquarters, was earning $50 million annually, and was responsible for nearly one percent of Denmark's industrial exports, according to toy historian Marvin Kaye. As the sales of the Lego construction toy system grew and new foreign sales subsidiaries were opened, it became imperative for Lego A/S to reorganize its administrative structure. Under the directorship of Godtfred Kristiansen, who had assumed control of the company after his father's retirement in 1956, Lego began to transform itself from a small family business into a multinational corporation. Although this evolution was begun in the 1960s, with the creation of separate divisions to handle product development, technological development, and sales and promotion, the pace and scale of these changes increased dramatically in the mid-1970s. In 1976, partly at the urging of Godtfred's son Kjeld Kirk Kristiansen, the Lego company was split into five sister companies.

International management and coordination was transferred to a new company called Interlego A/S (later to be renamed Lego A/S) and for the first time an outsider, Vagn Holck Andersen, was appointed to head overall operations. Lego System A/S would retain responsibility for the manufacture and direct supervision of European sales companies, Lego Systems Inc. would oversee North American sales and production, Lego Overseas A/S would coordinate sales in those countries without their own sales companies, and Lego Futura ApS would be responsible for product development. According to a 1974 article in *International Management,* Godtfred was reluctant to give up direct control over the day to day management of Lego, but he eventually agreed to create a more efficient management system. However, Godtfred was firm in his determination to keep the company private in spite of suggestions that going public would provide the capital for a more rapid expansion. In 1979, the Kristiansen family regained direct administrative control of the company with the appointment of Godtfred's son Kjeld Kristiansen as president of Interlego A/S.

The basic Lego brick remained virtually unchanged since its introduction in 1958. The mechanical properties and raw material of the bricks were improved so that they fit together more easily, but a brick made in 1958 would still join with one made

in the mid-1990s. However, many new components were added to the Lego system with the basic requirement that all new products be compatible with all other elements of the system. In the 1960s, the Lego System sets began to be organized around specific themes, including trains, spaceships, and airplanes. By the 1990s, these theme-related sets had evolved into ten product lines: Freestyle, Belville, Town, Space, Castle, Pirates, Ships, Trains, Aquazone, and Model Team. Each product line included many different sets with components geared to each specific theme, but nonetheless compatible with the components of all the other product lines.

One of Godtfred Kristiansen's original principles for his toy system was that it be attractive to both boys and girls. Although girls had always formed a share of the Lego market, market research revealed that the majority of Lego sets were being bought for boys. Over the years, Lego had attempted to broaden its appeal to girls. In 1979, the company introduced a Lego block based jewelry set, but it failed to capture the imagination of the five- to seven-year-old girls for which it was designed; the line was discontinued after a couple of years of mediocre sales. Undaunted, Lego introduced a new segment of its Basic product line oriented specifically toward girls. Called Paradisa, the principal feature of the new line was its color. Pale pink, pastel, purple, and turquoise blocks were considered more attractive to girls than the traditional primary colors of the Lego System products. According to David Lafrennie, Lego's American PR director, the Paradisa line was very successful, and Belville, a girl-oriented set with a "role-playing" theme, was launched in 1994.

Another of Godtfred Kristiansen's principles was that the toy system be fun for all ages. From its introduction, Lego System was designed for a fairly broad age range of three to 16 years, but the Kristiansens felt that they could strengthen either extreme of this range by adding lines specifically developed for pre-schoolers and the older child. In 1969, Duplo Toys were introduced. Using the same principle of the interlocking brick as the Lego System, Duplo bricks were larger and easier to manipulate with small hands; further, they could also be combined with the smaller Lego bricks as the child grew. Lego Technic, introduced in 1977, was designed to bolster the other end of the age range and bring Lego play into the teen years. With Lego Technic the older child could build technically realistic models using the gears, pulleys, beams, and other special pieces found in Lego Technic sets.

By the early 1980s, Lego had amassed an enormous share of the worldwide construction toy segment. Sales grew at an average rate of about ten percent a year through the 1980s and early 1990s in spite of overall slow growth in the toy industry. In the late 1980s, total sales had soared to about $600 million, much of the increase due to the huge gains made in the United States and Canada. This steady growth was capped by an astounding 18 percent increase in 1991, at a time when overall toy industry sales rose by only four percent. In 1992, Lego controlled about 80 percent of the construction toy market, according to *Advertising Age.* By the mid-1990s, the small Billund carpentry business had grown into a group of 45 companies on six continents employing almost 9,000 people.

The largest threat to Lego's dominance of the construction toy market in the 1980s and 1990s did not come from competing construction toys but from Lego imitators. One of the great virtues of the Lego System was the simplicity of its basic building blocks, but this simplicity also proved to be a liability, since other companies could easily reproduce the basic design. Compounding this problem was the fact that the patent on the design for the Lego brick expired in 1981, forcing Lego to enter lawsuits with other companies involving trademark infringement on packaging, logos, and accessories but not on the brick design itself. Although a number of small companies produced cheap imitations of Lego using names like Rego, Dalu, or even Leggo, these small-scale unpromoted brands proved to be little more than an irritant to the giant Lego Group. A much greater threat came from the established toy company Tyco Toys, Inc., which in 1984 launched its Super Blocks series featuring plastic building blocks that were interchangeable with Lego bricks. Lego Systems sued Tyco in both the United States and Hong Kong courts but, after four years of litigation, they were unsuccessful in stopping sales of Super Blocks. Tyco's copycat product, while never approaching Lego sales volumes in the United States, nonetheless managed to capture some ten percent of U.S. sales of construction toys in the late 1980s. Even more importantly, the lower price of Super Blocks put pressure on Lego to keep prices at a competitive level.

Although Lego had essentially been a single brand company since the early 1960s, the 1990s witnessed growth in the non-toy segment of the Lego Group. This new market included the extension of Lego licenses to a variety of children's items including clothing, children's room decor, and books. Since 1968, an invaluable part of the Lego marketing campaign in Europe had been the Legoland Park in Billund, Denmark. Built from some 42 million Lego bricks, the theme park attracted more than 20 million visitors, all of whom went home with a new vision of the potential of Lego toys. A new Lego theme park opened outside London in 1996, followed by an American park in Carlsbad, California, in 1999. A fourth park, in Gunzburg, Germany, was scheduled to open in 2002.

Lego marketers attributed the tremendous success of their construction system to an integrated marketing approach and an emphasis on brand building. "We put all our eggs in one basket, and we market that basket," Dick Garvey, vice-president of marketing, stated in a 1992 article in *Advertising Age*. However, a toy analyst with Kidder, Peabody & Co. told *Advertising Age*'s Kate Fitzgerald in 1991 that Lego's phenomenal growth could not last: "Lego's been allowed to grow by leaps and bounds for the past decade mainly because they had a lot of catching up to do. The construction-toy market in the U.S. was wide open. . . . Lego is only now reaching the saturation point in the U.S. and they're going to have a hard time keeping up their momentum."

New Product Lines in the Late 1990s

Lego seemed to take Fitzgerald's words to heart, and it worked particularly hard in the 1990s to build its brand image so that it could catapult into new market areas. Lego spent heavily on advertising, increasing its ad budget by 25 percent annually in the early 1990s. Marketing dollars went not only to plug new product introductions, but to touting the Lego brand in general. In the early 1990s, Lego's U.S. subsidiary flouted industry logic by refusing to hire executives with a background

in toys. Its marketing vice-president came to Lego from Quaker Oats, and the company insisted that the Lego brand, not the toys, was its main interest. Yet 30 to 40 percent of the Lego line was new each year, with a range of products including girls' Lego sets, licensed home furnishings, and even at one point a test line of Legos for senior citizens. By the mid-1990s it was clear that the company would have to do more to retain its market share. Lego's largest national market had long been Germany, but sales dropped 2 percent there in 1994, even though Lego expected growth of more than 10 percent. Sales in the United States also fell around 8 percent, the first dip in 17 years. Lego hoped to expand sales into Asia and India, where rising incomes meant growing opportunity for toy makers. To facilitate movement into these markets, the company streamlined its management in the mid-1990s, breaking into 24 wholly owned subsidiary companies, each of which covered one national market.

By the late 1990s, the company had come up with a new goal. A company spokesperson quoted in *Marketing* for July 2, 1998 revealed the new mission: "In the year 2005, we want the Lego brand to be the most powerful in the world among families and children." What this seemed to mean was that Lego was willing to use its brand equity to bring out new sorts of Lego toys, entering areas it had previously shied away from. A U.S. Lego executive told the *Wall Street Journal* (December 27, 1994) that "You'll never see us doing Pink Pony or E.T. . . . they're fads that pass." But the company began latching onto popular movies such as *Star Wars* in the late 1990s, marketing tie-in toys. Lego also began putting out building sets with electronic components, vying for a share of the electronic game market. Electronic games had held a growing piece of the overall toy market since the 1980s. By 1998, video games accounted for over 26 percent of the U.S. toy market, and more than that in France and the United Kingdom, other leading Lego markets. In 1998 Lego introduced Mindstorms, a Lego set aimed for older children, that had computer controls embedded in the plastic bricks. Kids could make remote-control robots from the Mindstorms set. Mindstorms was apparently also popular with adults. The core 700-piece kit retailed for under $300 in the United States, and included an infrared transmitter, motors, and light and touch sensors. A similar line extension in 2000 was a Lego video camera kit that could be connected to a home computer and programmed to react to sound, light, or motion. Lego pushed farther into the electronic realm in the early 2000s, entering a venture with computer giant Microsoft to help create content for some of Microsoft's computer games, and enlisting Hollywood film director Steven Spielberg to help market a Lego movie camera kit. Lego launched Lego Technic Bionicle in 2001, a line of toys and CD-ROMs accompanied by a mythic story available on a web site. Other new products for 2001 capitalized on the Harry Potter book series and the third of the *Jurassic Park* movies.

With its fourth Legoland theme park due to open in Germany in 2002, its clothing line a leading children's brand in Europe, and a slew of new electronic Lego kits and movie and book tie-in kits, Lego seemed to have moved beyond the "classic toy" category it had held for so long. While the private company did not release full financials to the public, Lego seemed to be struggling in the late 1990s. It lost money in 1998, and in 2000 Lego again announced that it had run a deficit and had an extremely disappointing year. Even with these recent stumbles, in 2001 Lego reiterated that its overall goal was to make itself the world's leading brand for children by 2005.

Principal Subsidiaries

Lego Overseas A/S; Lego AG (Switzerland); Lego S.P.A. (Italy); Lego Systems, Inc. (U.S.A.).

Principal Divisions

Lego Dacta; Lego Lifestyles; Lego Software.

Principal Competitors

Hasbro, Inc; Walt Disney Company.

Further Reading

"A Danish Toymaker Puts It Together in the U.S.," *Business Week,* September 6, 1976, pp. 80, 83.

Derwent, Charles, "Lego's Billion-Dollar Brickworks," *Management Today*, September 1995, p. 64.

Eidson, Christy, "If You Build It, Will They Come?" *Across the Board*, July-August 1999, p. 64.

50 Years of Play, Billund, Denmark: The Lego Group, 1982.

Fitzgerald, Kate, "Lego: Dick Garvey (The Marketing 100)," *Advertising Age,* July 8, 1992, p. S20.

——, "Toyland's Elusive Goal—Win Over Both Sexes," *Advertising Age,* February 8, 1993, pp. S2, S18.

Hirsch, Jerry, "Danish Family Business Builds on Bricks," *Knight-Ridder/Tribune Business News*, March 25, 1999, p. OKRB99084101.

Kaye, Marvin, *The Story of Monopoly, Silly Putty, Bingo, Twister, Scrabble, Frisbee et cetera,* New York: Stein and Day, 1973, pp. 155–59.

Kostin, Ileah, "Nothing Like a Dane," *Forbes,* November 3, 1986, pp. 145, 148.

"Lego and Tyco Blocks," *New York Times,* November 15, 1988, p. D13.

"Lego Builds on Its Manufacturing Image," *International Journal of Retail & Distribution Management*, Winter 1995, p. 5.

"Lego: Fighting the Video Monsters," *Economist*, January 30, 1999, p. 57.

"Lego Taps New Markets, but Keeps an Eye on Its Image," *Brandweek,* February 8, 1993, p.28.

"Lego to Launch Toy with CD-Rom Package," *Marketing Week*, February 1, 2001, p. 6.

Meeks, Fleming, "So Sue Me," *Forbes,* November 28, 1988, pp. 72, 74.

Morais, Richard C., "Babes in Toyland?," *Forbes,* January 3, 1994, pp. 70–71.

Oates, David, "The King of the Lego Castle," *International Management,* January 1974, pp. 32–36.

Rogers, Danny, "Lego to Be Danish Disney," *Marketing*, July 2, 1998, p. 19.

Rohwedder, Cacilie, "Lego Interlocks Toy Bricks, Theme Parks," *Wall Street Journal*, December 27, 1994, p. B2.

—Hilary Gopnik
—update: A. Woodward

The Loewen Group Inc.

4126 Norland Avenue
Burnaby, British Columbia V5G 3S8
Canada
Telephone: (604) 299-9321
Fax: (604) 473-7330
Web site: http://www.loewengroup.com

Public Company
Incorporated: 1985
Employees: 10,800
Sales: $896.1 million (2000)
Stock Exchanges: OTC Toronto
Ticker Symbols: LOWGQ; LWN
NAIC: 81222 Cemeteries and Crematories (pt); 81221
  Funeral Homes; 524113 Direct Life Insurance
  Carriers; 53121 Offices of Real Estate Agents and
  Brokers

The Loewen Group Inc. is a funeral service corporation located in British Columbia, Canada. The largest funeral service corporation in Canada and the second largest such firm in North America, The Loewen Group owns and operates 847 funeral homes, 23 cemeteries, 12 crematoria, and three ambulance companies in Canada, the United States, and Puerto Rico. With more than 10,000 employees, the company provides a full range of funeral services, including prearrangement, family consultation, the sale of caskets and related funeral items, the preparation of the body and removal of the remains, the use of a funeral home for both visitation and worship, various transportation services, and, in addition to the traditional burial items, a cremation service.

Early History

The roots of The Loewen Group can be traced to A.T. Loewen, the director of a small funeral home in Steinbach, Manitoba. Opening his business in 1961, Loewen operated a highly successful, but small-volume, operation in a rural area in one of the great western provinces of Canada. When A.T.

Loewen fell sick and was unable to continue as director of the funeral home, his son Ray assumed control of the entire business. Ray Loewen had just completed his degree in theology from Briercrest Theological College in Saskatchewan. He had not intended to follow in his father's footsteps; given the circumstances, however, Ray dutifully continued what his father had begun.

Not satisfied with the state of funeral care and services in Manitoba, Ray Loewen came up with an idea to create a chain of funeral homes that would arrange to share resources such as hearses and services such as body preparation. Unfortunately, not many people were won over by his idea. The young entrepreneur could not find many funeral homes that were willing to become part of a national chain, and the idea of economies of scale was alien to him. Part of Loewen's initial difficulties in establishing a funeral home chain was the result of unusually high barriers to entering the funeral home business. Because of the longstanding reputations and recognition of family-run funeral homes within individual communities, it was almost unheard of for an outsider to arrive in a small town and suddenly open a funeral home. Therefore, the resistance to the idea of establishing a funeral home chain was disappointing to Loewen, but not altogether surprising.

Unable to fulfill his dream, in 1969 Loewen decided to move his family to British Columbia, where he operated a funeral home and also delved into real estate and transportation businesses. Although he was able to acquire a number of funeral homes during this time, Loewen became increasingly disillusioned with the funeral home industry. In 1975, Loewen abruptly turned over all responsibility and management of his business holdings to one of his most trusted managers and campaigned successfully as a member of the Conservative Party for a seat in the provincial legislature of British Columbia. Loewen served as a member of the legislature for a period of four years and was much admired by his fellow Conservative Party colleagues for his trustworthiness and knowledge of the political issues of the day. In 1979, Loewen left the political arena as abruptly as he had entered it and set up a major real estate development and management company. When the real estate market began to suffer during the early 1980s, Loewen

Company Perspectives:

*The Loewen Group is committed to surpassing the expecta-
tions of the families we serve. Our dedicated men and
women strive daily to provide extraordinary service and
compassionate care to families during their time of great
need.*

*By focusing on how we manage all aspects of the com-
pany and by investing in our employee teams through better
training and new systems of accountability, we will provide
families with even better service and care.*

thought he would take another chance at fulfilling his dream of
building a chain of funeral homes.

Creating a Company During the Mid-1980s

Loewen had more luck the second time around. In the
United States, Houston-based Service Corporation International
was in the process of an aggressive acquisitions campaign,
buying up funeral homes at a rapid pace across the country.
When Service Corporation International entered the Canadian
market, funeral home owners in Manitoba, British Columbia,
and other provinces began to think about selling their businesses. Suddenly, Loewen found himself flooded with acquisition opportunities primarily consisting of ''mom and pop''
family-run funeral homes in small communities that preferred
to sell their businesses to a large Canadian consolidator.

Incorporated as The Loewen Group, Inc. in October 1985,
and encompassing funeral services, real estate, and insurance,
the company was operating 45 funeral homes throughout the
western provinces of Canada within two years. Loewen had also
learned the meaning of economies of scale, and he had centralized the firm's purchase of such items as embalming fluid,
coffins, advertising, and other essential ingredients to the funeral service industry. During the late 1980s, Loewen's wide
range of funeral service offerings, his ability to create economies of scale, and his successful advertising resulted in a phenomenal 65 percent increase in revenue for each funeral service
conducted under the auspices of his growing company.

In 1987, The Loewen Group reported earnings of $786,000
on revenues of approximately $14 million. Yet this was not
enough capital to expand the company as rapidly as Loewen
wished. Consequently, the founder decided to sell 10 percent of
the company to the public and, as a result, raised $4.6 million to
fund his ever-growing list of acquisitions. As it happened, however, the year reflected a very mediocre performance for the
worldwide stock exchanges, diminishing the inflow of capital
that Loewen initially had expected. His ability to make acquisitions was curtailed, and, as he experienced unexpected difficulties turning around the acquisitions he had recently made,
Loewen arranged a management conference in Vancouver to
discuss the direction of the company. At the conference,
Loewen asked how many of the former funeral home owners
who were now within The Loewen Group had previous experience managing their business within the framework of a budget.
Out of a total of 160 former owners, only four people had such

experience. Loewen immediately initiated a comprehensive
plan to teach each funeral home director the intricate details of
balancing a budget. Loewen's commonsense strategy was that it
was much easier to teach a funeral home director how to do
accounting than it was to teach an accountant how to treat
grieving relatives of the deceased.

Acquisition and Expansion During the Late 1980s

At the beginning of fiscal 1988, The Loewen Group owned
and operated 98 funeral homes and five cemeteries. One year
later, that number had risen to more than 120 funeral homes and
ten cemeteries. The focus of Ray Loewen's acquisition strategy
during these years, a strategy that has remained relatively unchanged, was his concentration on small, family-operated funeral homes and cemeteries. Loewen's modus operandi was to
acquire a funeral home or cemetery, keep the existing management in place, retain the name of the acquired funeral home, and
provide funeral directors with generous stock options in the
company.

Loewen's unique strategy of ''regional partners'' also
proved highly successful. Regional partners were the leading
operators of acquired businesses who were allowed to strike a
formal affiliation with The Loewen Group and were permitted
to retain an interest of approximately 10 percent in the future
appreciation of the company's entire regional operation. This
arrangement gave the regional partner the ability to benefit from
The Loewen Group's financial support, while the parent company benefited from the regional partner's involvement in the
local community and ability to identify potential candidates for
acquisition. Loewen's ''regional partner'' strategy worked so
well that within two years nearly 30 percent of all company
acquisitions of family-run funeral homes had been identified by
regional partners.

The Loewen Group was also able to take advantage of the
stability of what had come to be called the ''death care provider'' industry. From 1983 onward, demographic statistics
showed that not less than two million people in North America
would die each year. As baby boom survivors reached the age of
65, it was projected that the annual death rate would surpass
three million. Thus, regardless of economic conditions, the
death rate assured the industry of a regular customer base. By
continuing its strategic acquisition policy of ''mom and pop''
family funeral homes and capitalizing on the gradual rise in
death rates across North America, by the beginning of 1990 the
company had acquired almost 300 funeral homes and approximately 25 cemeteries.

Growth During the 1990s

In April 1991, to accommodate the growth of the company
and the expansion of its administrative offices, The Loewen
Group moved its headquarters to a large, three-story building in
Burnaby, British Columbia. Always cognizant of the welfare of
its employees, during this period the company established an
employee share ownership program for both full-time and eligible part-time employees. By the end of fiscal 1993, The Loewen
Group had acquired an additional 83 funeral homes and 33
cemeteries; by the end of fiscal 1994, the company had acquired
another 108 funeral homes and 46 cemeteries. The total number

```
┌─────────────────────────────────────────────┐
│              Key Dates:                      │
│                                              │
│ 1961:  A.T. Loewen opens funeral home in     │
│        Steinbach, Manitoba.                  │
│ 1985:  Ray Loewen forms Loewen Group, Inc.   │
│ 1991:  Loewen Group moves headquarters to    │
│        Burnaby, British Columbia.            │
│ 1996:  Loewen Group settles lawsuit with     │
│        Jerry O'Keefe, a Mississippi funeral  │
│        home operator; Loewen ac-             │
│        quires Prime Succession Inc., the     │
│        largest private funeral home business │
│        in North America, for $295            │
│        million.                              │
│ 1999:  Loewen Group files for Chapter 11     │
│        bankruptcy protection in June.        │
│ 2000:  Company announces plans to shift its  │
│        headquarters to Toronto.              │
└─────────────────────────────────────────────┘
```

of funeral homes and cemeteries owned by The Loewen Group on September 18, 1995 was 764 and 172, respectively, an astounding sixfold increase since 1989.

Along with this phenomenal period of acquisition and expansion, however, came an event that threatened the very existence of the company. The Loewen Group, in the course of its expansion strategy, acquired several local funeral homes in the immediate area of Biloxi, Mississippi. Valued at a cost of $8.5 million, two of the funeral homes belonged to Jerry O'Keefe, a former mayor of the city of Biloxi. The purchase ended O'Keefe's exclusive arrangement to sell his own insurance in the funeral homes that The Loewen Group had purchased. Therefore, O'Keefe decided to sue The Loewen Group for the right to sell his own insurance. Rather than litigate over what management at The Loewen Group regarded as a minor issue, the company agreed to combine funeral-insurance operations in the funeral homes purchased from O'Keefe.

When The Loewen Group backed out of the agreement, O'Keefe returned to court and sued the company for fraud and antitrust violations. O'Keefe had hired an extremely enterprising lawyer who convinced the local jury to award his client between $100 million and $400 million in compensatory and punitive damages. These amounts would have wiped out the net worth of The Loewen Group, and the company decided to appeal the verdict. To make matters worse, however, the Mississippi judge ruled that The Loewen Group would have to post 125 percent of the award within one week, a total of $625 million, if the company wished to continue with the appeal. Company management was understandably stunned. They considered a range of alternatives, from borrowing the money for the bond to declaring bankruptcy under Chapter 11. At the 11th hour, after endless meetings and sleepless nights, management at the company's headquarters in Burnaby, British Columbia, finally agreed to settle out of court for $240 million.

Although the company's stock fell from a high of $41 per share to an all-time low of $8 during the litigation, Ray Loewen was determined not to let this episode prevent him from forging ahead. In early 1995, Loewen acquired the Osiris Holding Company for $103.8 million. Located in Philadelphia, Pennsyl-

vania, Osiris owned and operated 22 cemeteries and four combination funeral home/cemetery facilities, all within the United States. In August 1995, the company purchased MHI Group, Inc., an operator of 13 funeral homes, four cemeteries, and three crematories in the state of Florida, and five additional properties in Colorado. One of the most significant properties involved in this transaction was the Star of David funeral home/cemetery facility that served a large Jewish community in Fort Lauderdale, Florida. During late 1995 and early 1996, the company concluded two more major acquisitions, including the Shipper Group and Ourso Investment Corporation. Shipper Group owned and operated a total of seven cemeteries in the New York/New Jersey area, including Beth Israel Cemetery in Woodbridge, New Jersey. Beth Israel Cemetery was the largest cemetery serving the Jewish community in the state of New Jersey. Ourso Investment Corporation, located in Louisiana, was the owner of 15 funeral homes, two cemeteries, and a growing life insurance business. The Loewen Group expected high returns from Ourso, which had annual revenues of more than $70 million, within a very short time.

In addition to aggressive expansion of its network of funeral homes and cemeteries in North America, in the early 1990s the company established The Loewen Children's Foundation, a nonprofit organization formed to promote and support hospice care for terminally ill children in both Canada and the United States. The company was also a founding sponsor of Canuck Place, the first freestanding hospice facility to care for terminally ill children and the needs of their families in North America.

The Loewen Group became the second largest provider of death care services in North America, ranked along with the leader in the industry, Service Corporation International, and third place Stewart Enterprises. These three companies, however, represented less than 8 percent of the industry's total properties and less than 15 percent of its total revenues. With more than 85 percent of the funeral homes within the United States still family-owned or under private ownership in the mid-1990s, The Loewen Group felt confident that there would be ample opportunity to continue its growth through acquisition strategy.

Assessing the Damage: The Late 1990s

With the potentially disastrous O'Keefe lawsuit behind it, the Loewen Group was determined to pursue an aggressive acquisition strategy in order to boost profitability. The two most substantial deals were done in conjunction with the New-York-based Blackstone Group. The first acquisition was for Prime Succession Inc. of Chicago, the largest private funeral home operator in North America, for $295 million. Under the terms of the agreement, Loewen would own a 20 percent stake in Prime Succession until the year 2000, when it would have the option to purchase the remaining 80 percent from Blackstone. Ultimately, the merger would give Loewen an additional 146 funeral homes and 16 cemeteries in the United States. Loewen entered into a similar agreement with Blackstone in the buyout of the Rose Hills Memorial Park Association of Los Angeles for $240 million. While such partnerships were unusual for the Loewen Group, the two agreements pushed the total value of the company's acquisitions for 1996 over the $1.4 billion mark, a clear indication that Ray Loewen was intent on expansion.

In the midst of this buying spree came an unexpected—and uninvited—buyout bid from Loewen's much larger American rival, Service Corporation International. The terms of the offer were very generous: $2.1 billion, in addition to the assumption of $1.1 billion of Loewen's debt. However, Ray Loewen, who owned a 15 percent stake in the company, valued Loewen's independence above all else, and he urged board members and shareholders to reject the deal. Service Corporation subsequently raised its bid to $3.24 billion. This second offer amounted to $59 a share, significantly higher than Loewen's stock value of approximately $40 per share. Ray Loewen, however, managed to persuade the shareholders that his ambitious acquisition plan would, in the long-term, provide a much higher return on their investment, and once again Service Corp. was rebuffed. In January 1997 Service Corp. officially withdrew its bid, and Loewen was free once again to pursue its independent vision.

Unfortunately, the decision to decline Service Corp.'s offer almost precipitated the untimely death of the Loewen Group. Although profits for 1996 were a respectable $63.6 million, investor confidence in the company was still shaken by the O'Keefe settlement, and the shareholders were beginning to become impatient with the company's sagging share value. Loewen attempted a major restructuring in September 1997, cutting 540 jobs and closing a number of its less lucrative units, in an effort to reduce operating expenses by $25 million a year.

However, a series of quarterly losses forced stock prices to fall steadily over the course of 1997 and 1998, and by January 1999 shares had dropped to $5.65, a steep decline from their $40 value only a year earlier.

This downward spiral proved too much for the founder and CEO, and in October 1998 Ray Loewen stepped down as head of the company. While a merger now seemed like a good idea, interest in the company was no longer as strong as it had been, and by March 1999 the company's creditors were pounding on the doors. After suffering a 77 percent drop in profits for the first quarter of 1999, the company was forced to file for protection in U.S. Bankruptcy Court in June, in an effort to restructure its debt and try to stay afloat. This it did, and losses for 2000 were reduced to $72.5 million, compared to $465.2 million in 1999. After relocating to Toronto and selling off over 300 holdings, the company submitted an updated filing in March 2001, and seemed to have some chance of survival.

Principal Subsidiaries

Loewen Group International, Inc.; TLGI Management Corporation.

Principal Competitors

Carriage Services, Inc.; Service Corporation International; Stewart Enterprises, Inc.

Further Reading

Bailey, Ian, "Loewen Bullish on Expansion: Funeral Chain Earnings Hit $63.9 million," *Toronto Star*, March 6, 1997.

Bohner, Kate, "Tasteless," *Forbes*, July 3, 1995, p. 18.

Carlisle, Tamsin, "Loewen to Settle Provident Lawsuit for $30 Million," *Wall Street Journal*, February 13, 1996, p. A8(E).

Constantineau, Bruce, "Loewen's Gamble Proves Deadly: Funeral-Chain CEO's Rapid-Growth Strategy Following Lawsuits Leads to His Resignation," *Gazette* (Montreal), October 13, 1998.

"Crisis for a Funeral Giant," *MacLean's*, February 5, 1996, p. 40.

Day, Eileen, "Beyond Breaking Records," *Vision, The Loewen Group, Inc.*, November 1995, p. 5.

Hassell, Greg, "SCI Wants to Buy Its Biggest Rival; $2 Billion Bid for Loewen," *Houston Chronicle*, September 18, 1996, p. 1.

Hyndman, Peter, "Closure in Mississippi," *Vision, The Loewen Group, Inc.*, March/April 1996, p. 8.

Joyce, Greg, "Loewen Shares Rocket After Deal; Out-of-Court Settlement in Thorny U.S. Case," *Gazette* (Montreal), January 30, 1996, p. C1.

"Loewen Group," *Wall Street Journal*, November 7, 1995, p. B4(E).

"Loewen Group Buys U.S. Firm," *Wall Street Journal*, March 20, 1995, p. B4(E).

McMurdy, Deirdre, "Mississippi Blues," *MacLean's*, February 12, 1996, p. 50.

Olsen, Walter, "A Small Canadian Firm Meets the American Tort Monster," *Wall Street Journal*, February 14, 1996, p. A15(E).

Osterman, Cynthia, "Funeral-Home Mogul Loewen Fights Back; Scrambles to Regain Investors' Confidence," *Toronto Star*, January 27, 1997, p. B4.

Stuart, Scott, "Loewen's Search Could Hit Dead End; Death Care Giant Is Likely Too Late in Its Efforts to Find a Mate," *Mergers & Acquisitions Report*, August 10, 1998, p. 1.

——, "Vultures Pick Over Loewen: Erstwhile Deathcare Giant May Soon Be Digging Its Own Grave, *Mergers & Acquisitions Report*, March 15, 1999.

"Undertaker Lives On," *MacLean's*, February 12, 1996, p. 68.

—Thomas Derdak
—update: Stephen Meyer

LUMINAR
plc

Luminar Plc

41 King Street
Luton
Bedfordshire LU1 2DW
United Kingdom
Telephone: (+44) 1582-589-400
Fax: (+44) 1582-589-401
Web site: http://www.luminar.co.uk

Public Company
Incorporated: 1987 as Leadwise Leisure
Employees: 3,000
Sales: £74.1 million ($117 million) (2000)
Stock Exchanges: London
Ticker Symbol: LMR
NAIC: 722110 Full Service Restaurants; 72221 Limited-
Service Eating Places; 722410 Drinking Places
(Alcoholic Beverages)

Luminar Plc is the United Kingdom's leading nightclub owner and operator, with more than 250 nightclubs, bars, and restaurants throughout England and Scotland, including the famed Hippodrome in central London. Luminar Plc has long backed its growth on a number of core club concepts, particularly its Chicago Rock Café theme restaurant-nightclub chain. The company also has been rolling out an increasing number of club themes, including the minimalist Liquid nightclub, which uses DVD, MPEG, and oil filter lighting technology to "decorate" the dance hall; the Latin-inspired Rhythm Room; Jumpin' Jaks, featuring live entertainment; and the family restaurant chain Tucker's Smokehouse. Other brands include Life café and "the" bars. Luminar has been expanding aggressively since the late 1990s, leading an industry consolidation in the United Kingdom. In 1999, the company bought 27 nightclubs— including the Hippodrome—from rival Allied Leisure. The £392 million acquisition of larger rival Northern Leisure in mid-2000 catapulted Luminar to the first rank of U.K. nightclub operators, adding some 200 nightclubs and restaurants, including the Jumpin' Jaks brand, and doubling the company's revenues. Luminar is led by founder and CEO Stephen Thomas. The

company's shares trade on the London Stock Exchange. Mercury Asset Management, which funded Luminar's growth in the early 1990s, maintains a 52 percent share of the company.

Disco Fever in the 1980s

Stephen Thomas began his career in the entertainment field in the early 1970s, when he joined the Rank Organisation, at the time one of the United Kingdom's top pub and nightclub companies, as a trainee assistant in 1972. Thomas remained with the Rank Organisation through the end of the decade. The buoyant disco music trend of the era laid the groundwork for a growing market for nightclubs in traditionally pub-oriented England. Thomas began developing his own ideas on how to run a nightclub business. "I would love to have run the Rank Organisation and turned it around," Thomas told the *Independent,* adding: "I really fancied being CEO but they never asked me because I was so far down the organisation. I was second spear-thrower on the left."

Thomas's ambitions led him to look elsewhere. At the beginning of the decade he left the Rank Organisation to join pub and brewery group Whitbread, which had begun developing its own nightclub division. Thomas became director of Whitbread's Aureon Entertainment subsidiary, overseeing the operations of 35 discotheques and theme bars.

In 1987, Thomas determined to launch his own nightclub operations and test out his management ideas. Leadwise Leisure, Thomas's new company, began operations in 1988, with just £24,000 in capital. Thomas initially began buying struggling nightclubs—which, for the most part in the United Kingdom, were held by single owners, rather than by large corporations—and redeveloping them into profitable businesses. Yet Thomas quickly saw the advantages of developing a growing new niche in nighttime entertainment.

Strict closing laws limited pubs from remaining open after 11 p.m.; people in most of England and the rest of the United Kingdom, at least outside of the major cities, thus had few opportunities for late-night entertainment. Thomas saw an opportunity to serve these markets by exploiting a loophole that allowed later opening times for restaurants. Changing his com-

---

pany's name to Luminar Leisure, Thomas began developing a new theme restaurant format. Dubbed the "Chicago Rock Café," Thomas's new formula combined restaurant, bar, and nightclub features under a single roof, inspired by what the company described as, according to the *Independent,* "the sort of bars you would find if you got lost in Chicago and ended up in the blue-collar working class areas off the tourist track." The company added to the café's American-style theme by maintaining a "classic" music policy, playing songs that were at least ten years old. "The idea," Thomas told the *Daily Telegraph,* "is that people don't ask 'Have you heard this?' but say 'Do you remember this' and sing along."

Although other companies had begun developing theme restaurant formats in the 1990s, taking the cues from such fast-growing chains as Hard Rock Café and Planet Hollywood, Luminar could boast that the Chicago Rock Café was the only venue to boast dancing, dining, and drinking in a single place. The company opened the first Chicago Rock Café in King's Lynn in 1990. Luminar quickly began scouting for new locations, sticking to the small- and medium-sized town markets where it could gain more or less a monopoly on the town's night time entertainment market.

To finance the expansion of the Chicago Rock Café chain, Luminar sold a majority of its shares to Mercury Asset Management in the early 1990s. Meanwhile, Luminar continued to expand its interest in discotheques, building up a portfolio of mostly provincial discos. This category also was undergoing strong growth as the booming rave culture—propelled by the popularity of the house and techno music styles developed in the late 1980s—began to attract increasing numbers of the youth market to the United Kingdom's discotheques and nightclubs. Over the course of the 1990s, the nightclub scene slowly began to lose its negative aura—nightclubs were often associated with violence, a hangover from the punk scene of the late 1970s. The newer, disc jockey oriented nightclub scene was to gain its own negative image, notably with the rise of hallucinogenic drug use that accompanied the techno scene. Yet nightclubs began to take a larger share of the night time entertainment scene in the United Kingdom.

The vast majority of the company's nightclubs remained small, single-owner venues. Yet a number of corporations, like Luminar, began building strong portfolios of discotheques. Luminar's rivals were to include the JD Wetherspoon restaurant chain, Northern Leisure, Allied Leisure, and Thomas's former employer, the Rank Organisation. The industry remained far from consolidation in the mid-1990s, however. Less than 15 percent of the country's nightclub scene—venues with capacity of more than 400—was held by the six largest players.

Luminar was fast on its way to joining the top ranks of nightclub operators. By the end of 1995, Luminar Leisure had grown to revenues of £21 million. At the beginning of 1996, the company's operations included 14 Chicago Rock Cafés and a growing portfolio of 18 discotheques and nightclubs. In that year, Luminar shortened its name to Luminar Plc and took a listing on the London Stock Exchange. The relatively modest offering, which raised just £5 million and left Mercury Asset Management in majority control of the company's shares, enabled it to pay down debt and begin a more aggressive expansion program.

"Lifestyle Interpretation Company" for the 21st Century

In the mid-1990s Thomas and Luminar began rolling out a number of new theme bars and nightclubs, expanding its offering to capture an increasingly segmented night-going public. As Thomas told the *Sunday Telegraph,* "There is a dissection of age and a dissection of the market. Younger people 18 and 24 prefer nightclubs, older consumers prefer the bar experience. You have to understand how each market works. You have to have a clear strategy for getting people into both. You have to run them differently, otherwise people get confused."

Thomas was quick to show his own understanding of the night-going market. At the end of 1996, Luminar rolled out its Cuba-inspired Rhythm Room bar-restaurant-disco concept for the somewhat older customer; the chain was to become one of the company's key brands. Luminar also prepared to debut its venture into family-style restaurants, opening the first Tucker's Smokehouse in 1997. Meanwhile, the company's Chicago Rock Café underwent a strong expansion, opening ten new locations in 1997 alone.

Luminar's expansion continued strongly into 1998, when the company opened nearly 15 new Chicago Rock Cafés. By the end of that year, Luminar's portfolio included 60 venues, and Thomas was asserting that his company could one day grow to more than 600 locations. Luminar also was debuting a new discotheque concept, the minimalist Liquid clubs. With little more decoration than its bare white walls and empty space, Liquid represented a new type of "virtual" disco, using DVD and MPEG technology, coupled with oil-based filters and related "liquid" graphics to create constantly changing decors.

Luminar's growth had brought it to the number four position in the United Kingdom's nightclub industry by the beginning of 1999. Yet the coming year was to mark the beginning of a transformation of the country's nightclub scene. As the industry's leading corporate players began a consolidation process, others sought to exit the nightclub market in favor of other entertainment areas. Such was the case, for example, of then market leader First Leisure, which spun off its nightclubs division in a management buyout. In 1999, several major deals were transforming the country's nightclub market. Rank Organisation sold its 37 nightclubs to fast-growing Northern Leisure, while Allied Domecq acquired European Leisure, which, among other venues, owned the famed Hippodrome in London.

Luminar had no plans to remain on the sidelines of the growing industry consolidation. After expressing an interest in acquiring First Leisure's nightclub operations, Luminar turned to another dance partner. Allied Leisure's acquisition of European Leisure had been merely a prelude to its exit of the nightclub circuit, concentrating its operations instead on its newly enlarged bowling alley, pool and snooker, and related holdings. Luminar now showed its interest in leading the consolidation dance, announcing its agreement to acquire Allied's 27 clubs, including the Hippodrome, in a cash deal of £34.5 million. The Allied acquisition not only strengthened Luminar's position in a number of English markets, it also brought the company's operations into Scotland for the first time. Most of the Allied venues were rebranded under one of Luminar's formats; the company disposed of seven of the former Allied properties.

The Allied acquisition proved, however, merely an appetizer for a larger meal to come: in May 2000, Luminar and Northern Leisure announced their intention to merge operations. The all-share transaction, worth more than £390 million, folded Northern Leisure's more than 150 nightclubs—including those acquired from Rank Organisation some months earlier—into the undisputed industry leader, with nearly 250 nightclubs and more than 10 percent of the United Kingdom's nightclub market, and total sales expected to top £600 million by the end of the 2001 fiscal year. The two companies, which had first held talks in mid-1999, were also highly complementary, both having long targeted the small- and medium-sized town circuits.

Absorbing its new holdings, Luminar also added Northern Leisure's own lineup of brands to its stable, including the Jumpin' Jaks live entertainment format. Unlike Luminar, however, Northern Leisure had preferred to develop its properties as unbranded venues, giving Luminar an opportunity to convert its new locations to one of its existing brand names. Meanwhile, Luminar continued to boost its Chicago Rock Café format, opening its 45th site in early 2000. By the end of March 2001, the company was operating some 60 Chicago Rock Cafés.

As it moved into the first year of the new century, Luminar gave no sign of resting in its expansion drive. While the company pursued continued expansion of the Chicago Rock format, it also was developing its other existing brands, such as the Liquid disco concept, which now boasted eight nightclubs. Luminar also was developing other brands, including the "the" chain of bars, Life nightclubs, and a new chain of jazz and blues clubs, Jamhouse, which was to see its first openings in such cities as Birmingham, London, Edinburgh, Cardiff, and Dublin in 2001. As many in the world had come to view England as one of the world's most vibrant nightclub scenes, Luminar's moves were certain to keep it a major player on that country's dance floor.

Principal Subsidiaries

Luminar Leisure Ltd; The Chelsea Brewery Company Ltd; Tucker's Smokehouse Ltd; Chicago Rock Café Ltd; Savoy Leisure Ltd; Rhythm Room Ltd; Fitness Ltd; Luminar Properties Ltd; Intercede 1485 Ltd.

Principal Competitors

Carlson Restaurants Worldwide Inc.; Enterprise Inns Plc; Granada Plc; Greene King Plc; JD Wetherspoon Plc; Planet Hollywood International, Inc.; Punch Taverns Group Ltd.; Rainforest Café, Inc.; The Rank Group Plc; Scottish & Newcastle plc; Whitbread Plc; The Wolverhampton & Dudley Breweries, Plc.

Further Reading

Blackwell, David, "Buys Help Luminar," *Financial Times,* November 2, 2000.
——, "Wetherspoon and Luminar Celebrate," *Financial Times,* January 10, 2001.
Lafferty, Fiona, "Twenty Questions: Stephen Thomas, Founder and CEO of Luminar Plc," *Independent,* August 30, 2000.
"Luminar Dances the Night Away," *Investors Chronicle,* November 1, 2000.
"Luminar Has Found a Niche," *Independent,* October 24, 1997, p. 26.
"Luminar Is Looking for a Minimum Growth Development of 20% Year on Year," *Wall Street Transcript,* October 23, 2000.
"Luminar Takes Northern Leisure in All-Share Deal," *Financial Times,* May 11, 2000.
Reece, Damian, "The Big Remix," *Sunday Telegraph,* October 24, 1999, p. 12.

—M. L. Cohen

Lund International Holdings, Inc.

911 Lund Boulevard
Anoka, Minnesota 55303
U.S.A.
Telephone: (612) 576-4200
Fax: (612) 576-4297
Web site: http://www.lundinternational.com

Public Company
Incorporated: 1965
Employees: 3,100
Sales: $194.4 million (1999)
Stock Exchanges: NASDAQ
Ticker Symbol: LUND
NAIC: 336399 All Other Motor Vehicle Parts
   Manufacturing; 326199 All Other Plastics Product
   Manufacturing (pt); 332510 Hardware Manufacturing

Lund International Holdings, Inc. (Lund) is the nation's largest maker of light truck accessories. Through its subsidiaries, Lund Industries, Incorporated, Deflecta-Shield Corporation, Ventshade Company, and Smittybilt, Incorporated, the company designs, manufactures, and distributes aftermarket automotive accessories and other products for light trucks, sport utility vehicles, vans, passenger cars, and heavy trucks. The company sells 70 product lines through dealers, distributors, catalogs, and chain stores. Products include side window ventvisors, windshield visors, hood shields, bug deflectors, running boards, tonneau covers, aluminum storage boxes, tubular products, and suspension lift systems. Through acquisitions of leading brands in all of the major product categories, Lund items are clear market leaders or are in a strong secondary position. Lund's hood shields, window vents, cab visors, molded boards, and grille covers are considered the number one brands on the market. Customers include Ford, Toyota, Navistar, and Freightliner.

Company Beginnings in 1965

Lund International was founded in 1965 by Allan W. Lund, an entrepreneur highly skilled in the design of fiberglass prod-

ucts. Prior to producing accessories for the truck market, Allan Lund was a teacher and insurance salesman. He began producing prototype work for snowmobile, boat, and other recreational vehicle makers, and started making sun visors in a Coon Rapids, Minnesota chicken barn in 1974. The Lund SunVisor attached to the cab of a truck or van. By the late 1970s, as light truck sales increased, Lund began producing appearance accessories for light trucks. He developed several new product lines in the 1980s and by 1990, the visors, available for 940 different makes, models, and years of vehicles, were producing revenues of an estimated $15 million per year.

Lund's second product was a cab spoiler. An authorized dealer program was established to sell products through auto parts stores, auto body and trim stores, and car washes. Dealer-expediters, who customize new trucks before they leave the lot, significantly boosted product sales. The company soon expanded to offer 20 additional product lines, including bug shields, fender extensions, and grill inserts. One of the company's fastest growing lines from this period was running boards, mainly because women, who were driving trucks in greater numbers, found them helpful for getting in and out.

Accelerated Expansion in 1994

Lund consolidated operations and doubled its production capacity as a means of keeping up with demand for its products, which soared 41 percent in the first nine months of fiscal 1994, compared with results of a year earlier. In 1993, sales had increased 58 percent over 1992 results. The company reported at the time that its consolidation meant vacating two leased buildings in Coon Rapids totaling 97,000 square feet, and two additional leased areas in nearby Mounds View and Blaine. Plans were under way to construct a new 200,000-square-foot office, manufacturing, and warehouse building in Anoka, Minnesota.

The fast-growing firm also organized the sale of 800,000 shares of stock in an effort to allow large-scale investors a chance to buy into the company. According to the SEC filings, all proceeds from the sale would go to CEO Allan Lund, who owned 52 percent of the company and would retain 33.5 percent after the sale. Allan Lund received approximately $17 million for his stock and the company benefited from having more of its

Company Perspectives:

We set out to become a one-stop shop for accessories: to sell everything but the truck. Today we offer the market's broadest line of accessory products. We consciously instituted world-class quality standards. Our mission is, and always has been, to be the leader in satisfying customer needs for automotive accessories. Today we have the sales momentum to prove our leadership in service, engineering and innovation. And like the vehicles themselves, Lund International is powerful, responsive and aggressive in seeking new opportunities. We continue to drive ahead of the competition in automotive accessories.

shares available for public trading. "Most institutions have shied away from the company because relatively few shares have been available for purchase," according to Piper Jaffray analyst Blair Frantzin in *City Business.* He said that five or six institutions already owned significant portions, but the company expected to double the number through the offering. Lund maintained very low debt and was well positioned for growth. The company reported a profit margin in excess of 40 percent, but because of rapid growth, the company was forced to subcontract some of its manufacturing, depressing profit margins for 1994 and 1995. In 1994, Lund won approval to sell its products in Europe. William McMahan, who had led the company from 1988 through 1991, left to take a position with Anagram International, but he returned in 1994.

A surge in truck sales accounted for much of the company's success. Offering a broad line of branded products, the company kept its name highly visible by sponsoring NASCAR races. Lund unveiled three new products in late 1995. The company introduced a running board that came in four variations and fit 22 different sport utility vehicles, a market that was just beginning to develop. The second product introduced that year was a rounded exterior sun visor that did not require screws to attach to the vehicle. Representing a new product area for Lund, the third introduction was a tonneau cover, a flat seal over a pickup's cargo hold. The cover featured an easy-to-use seal that saved customers the cost of installation. Lund experienced very favorable orders for both the tonneau covers and sun visors. Company officials reported that the new headquarters and new automated manufacturing plant allowed the company to fill orders more efficiently and rapidly.

A Major Acquisition in 1997

In the winter of 1997, Lund signed a merger agreement to acquire a much larger competitor, Deflecta-Shield Corporation of Indianola, Iowa. Deflecta-Shield was founded in 1961 and successfully sold hood shields. The company developed product lines to include running boards, side window deflectors and covers, visors, tonneau covers, and other styling accessories. In 1994, Deflecta-Shield acquired a leading aluminum products manufacturer, which enabled the company to extend product offerings to a more diverse market. Products included aluminum running boards, storage boxes, bed protection, and other accessories.

Lund primarily sold to wholesale distributors, who in turn sold to retailers. The majority of Deflecta-Shield sales were to auto manufacturers like Ford, General Motors, and Chrysler. Lund offered to pay $16 per share for the publicly traded company, which had been selling at about $15.75. Lund CEO William McMahon said at the time that the acquisition would form a new company with more breadth of products and sales clout than its competitors. "The industry is very fragmented and young, and we expect to be market leaders and the low-cost providers by sharing our resources," McMahon said. Most competing companies in the market had sales of less than $40 million, while Deflecta Shield reported sales of $72.3 million in 1996. The two companies represented the leading players in the plastic and fiberglass truck accessories market. Together, the merged companies were expected to generate close to $130 million in sales for 1998, according to a *Plastic News* report.

A key catalyst for the acquisition was New York-based investment banker Harvest Partners, Inc., which had acquired 38.4 percent of Lund in September 1997 by buying out company founder Allan Lund, who retired as chairman. According to *Plastic News,* as part of the Deflecta-Shield deal, Harvest committed debt financing of $87 million and increased its economic stake in Lund to 60 percent and its voting share to 49 percent. Harvest Managing General Partner Harvey Wertheim said at the time, "When we made our first investment in Lund, we knew we were entering an industry with a good growth cycle but with a lot of little players. What we plan to do is change the position of the market by growing quickly and keeping our eyes open for new acquisitions to bring into the fold. We're looking for companies that overlap and fit into what we acquired." In addition to making plastic parts through injection molding, thermoforming and drape molding, which involves placing preheated resin over an open mold, Deflecta-Shield also made aluminum accessories and suspension products.

For five years in a row, *Forbes* and *Fortune* listed Lund among the top 100 growth companies in the United States, but the company had experienced problems getting newly developed products to market, resulting in net declines of 3.6 percent. A downturn in the automotive accessories market led to a dip in sales the next year. Margins improved by the last quarter of 1997. Company officials remained optimistic and estimated that by 2000, more than half the vehicles sold in the United States would be light trucks. The add-on accessories market was a $2 billion industry made up of approximately 2,000 small companies. McMahon reasoned that the fragmented industry was ideal for consolidation.

Lund acquired 100 percent of the outstanding common stock of Ventshade for $67 million and of Smittybilt for $18 million, in 1998 and 1999, respectively. Ventshade had been established since 1935 in Jacksonville, Florida. The company was founded by the current president's father, who built the business with the Ventshade, a device mounted above car windows to keep out rain. The company made window shades, hood shields, light covers, and other accessories. Smittybilt, a Corona, California company, was also a long established business that engineered and manufactured accessories for cars, sport utility vehicles, pickup trucks, and heavy over-the-road vehicles on a national level. Smittybilt specialized in offering a broad line of tubular products, including the Outland and SureStep brands. Harvest

Key Dates:

1965: Business is founded by Minnesota entrepreneur Allan W. Lund.
1994: Company begins selling its products in Europe.
1997: Company signs merger agreement to acquire Deflecta-Shield Corporation.
1998: Lund International acquires Ventshade Company.
1999: Company acquires Smittybilt, Incorporated.

Partners committed to investing additional equity in Lund and structured the financing for the transactions. Belmor, a company established in 1921, was a nationally recognized manufacturer of class 8 truck accessories located in Chicago, Illinois. Belmor became a subsidiary of Lund at the time of the Deflecta-Shield merger.

Acquisition-related expenses caused a revenue loss in 1998. That year, Dennis Vollmershausen, who headed a construction equipment company, Champion Road Machinery, replaced CEO McMahan, who retired. Vollmershausen said in an *Atlanta Business Chronicle* article, "In order to lead in the industry, our strategy is to build a broader product offering. Clearly, part of the attraction of [acquiring] Auto Ventshade is its manufacturing proficiency and capacity." Board directors Ira Kleinman and Harvey Wertheim became owners of nearly 50 percent of the company. Also in 1999, the company sold the assets of its Fibernetics specialty and plastics division in Compton, California, for approximately $1 million. Fibernetics President Jim Covone reported in *Plastic News,* "We really didn't fit in [Lund's] long-term plans because Lund is primarily proprietary." The company processed plastic, fiberglass, carbon fiber, and urethane materials.

According to Vollmershausen, Lund enjoyed more than 10 percent of a $1.6 billion market for accessories and suspension products by the end of 2000. The expansion program resulted in sales growth from $42 million in 1997 to $194 million in 1999. The company introduced five new products for the year, including Eclipse hood scoops, X-Terminator wrap bug shields, Stainless Interceptor wrap bug shield, Ultima storage boxes, and the Smittybilt Sure-Step box step.

Outlook for 2001 and Beyond

Early on, Lund sold its products principally through warehouse distributors. With increased sales of light trucks in later years, competition from mass merchandisers, national automotive retailers, and original equipment manufacturers significantly shifted a portion of sales away from warehouse distributors and created pricing pressures, especially in the plastic and fiberglass product lines. In addition, the automotive accessory market began undergoing consolidation in both the manufacturing and distribution areas. In response to changing market conditions, the company reported that it had reorganized its sales and marketing functions to better accommodate each of its market channels. Lund also had restructured and consolidated its manufacturing and warehouse operations. The company continued to develop new cost-competitive products in response to weaker than anticipated sales in fiscal 2000, and anticipated strong longer-term demand for light truck and heavy truck accessories. The company announced in 2000 that it would begin outsourcing its production of fiberglass products.

Principal Subsidiaries

Lund Industries, Incorporated; Deflecta-Shield Corporation; Ventshade Company; Smittybilt, Incorporated.

Principal Divisions

Light Truck; Heavy Truck; Suspension and Ventshade; Product Supply Companies.

Principal Competitors

DaimlerChrysler AG; Discount Auto Parts, Inc.; Donnelly Corporation; Durakon; Eagle-Picher Industries, Inc.; General Motors Corporation; Lancaster Colony Corporation; Textron Inc.; Toyota Motor Corporation; Williams Controls.

Further Reading

Fredrickson, Tom, "Lund Intl. to Swell in Size," *Minneapolis-St. Paul City Business,* May 6, 1994, p. 1.
——, "Minnesota Growth 40," *Minneapolis-St. Paul City Business,* February 9, 1996, p. 7.
Koelln, Georgann, "Lund International of Minnesota Buys Deflecta-Shield for $90 Million," *Knight-Ridder/Tribune Business News,* Nov. 27, 1997, p. 1127BO948.
"Lund Sells Fibernetics Unit to Investors," *Plastic News,* February 15, 1999, p. 3.
"Lund Unveils Five New Light Truck Accessories," *Aftermarket News,* December 2000, p. 22.
Martin, Justin, "Companies to Watch," *Fortune,* October 3, 1994, p. 148.
——, "Lund International Holdings," *Fortune,* October 3, 1994, p. 148.
Moriarty, George, "Lund Nets $30 Million Via Private Placement," *Private Equity Week,* February 8, 1999.
Paire, Jennifer Rampey, "Lawrenceville Auto Accessories-Maker Acquired," *Atlanta Business Chronicle,* November 20, 1999, p. 18A.
Pryweller, Joseph Lund, "Deflecta-Shield to Unite," *Plastic News,* December 8, 1997, p. 3.
Schafer, Lee, "Lund Intl. Holdings, Inc.," *Corporate Report-Minnesota,* June 1990, p. 73.

—Terri Mozzone

Mars, Incorporated

6885 Elm Street
McLean, Virginia 22101
U.S.A.
Telephone: (703) 821-4900
Fax: (703) 448-9678
Web site: http://www.mars.com

Private Company
Incorporated: 1911 as Mar-O-Bar Co.
Employees: 30,000
Sales: $14 billion (2000 est.)
NAIC: 31132 Chocolate and Confectionery
    Manufacturing from Cacao Beans; 31134
    Nonchocolate Confectionery Manufacturing; 31152
    Ice Cream and Frozen Dessert Manufacturing; 311111
    Dog and Cat Food Manufacturing; 311212 Rice
    Milling; 311919 Other Snack Food Manufacturing;
    311991 Perishable Prepared Food Manufacturing;
    311999 All Other Miscellaneous Food Manufacturing;
    333311 Automatic Vending Machine Manufacturing

From its origins in candy and confectionary products, Mars, Incorporated has diversified to become a world leader in several other markets, including snack foods, pet care products, main meal foods, electronic automated payment systems, and soft drink vending. In spite of its large size and geographic reach, the company remains privately owned. It has fostered an ostensibly egalitarian corporate culture since the 1960s. The company is notoriously secretive despite the millions it spends to promote its products. Although lagging behind rival chocolatier Hershey domestically, Mars has stronger global operations and controls 15 percent of the world candy business.

Origins in 1911

Mars began in 1911 as the Mar-O-Bar Co., a snack food business founded by Frank C. Mars of Tacoma, Washington, who made a variety of buttercream candy in his home. Quality and value were the foundations of his first candy factory, which employed 125 people. In 1920 Frank Mars relocated to larger quarters in Minneapolis, where Snickers (without the chocolate coating) and Milky Way bars were created. The company posted a loss of $6,000 in 1922, but by 1924, sales exceeded $700,000. Mars changed his company's name to Mars Candies in 1926. With the rapid growth of the company, Mars sought larger quarters and built a new plant in suburban Chicago in 1928. Sales actually quadrupled during the lean years of the Depression and new products were introduced, including the Mars Almond Bar, Snickers Bar (now sporting a chocolate covering), and 3 Musketeers.

Frank Mars hired his son Forrest E. Mars to work in the candy operation after his graduation from Yale, but the two reportedly had a stormy relationship. In the early 1930s, Frank, giving Forrest some money and the foreign rights to manufacture Milky Way, ordered his son to start his own business abroad. Moving to England, Forrest established a confectionery and a canned pet food company, which met with great success.

In 1940 Forrest Mars returned to the United States and founded M&M Limited in Newark, New Jersey, to manufacture chocolate candies in a sugar shell. At that time, stores reduced their stock of chocolate in the summer because of the lack of air conditioning, and Forrest hoped to capitalize on the unique construction of M&M's to sell the candy year round. The name of the candy was derived from the initials of Mars and an associate, Bruce Murrie. M&M's Peanut Chocolate Candies were introduced in 1954, the same year the famous slogan "the milk chocolate melts in your mouth—not in your hand" was first used.

Frank Mars's business was also experiencing great success. In 1943 Mars ventured into the main meal business, which included a wide selection of rice products, including whole grain, savory, boil-in-bag, fast cook, instant, and frozen rice as well as other products. Uncle Ben's rice utilized a rice processing technology called parboiling, which was developed in England and was first used in the United States by a Texas food broker with whom Forrest E. Mars, Sr., formed a partnership. Several months after their first production facility was completed, they began selling rice to the U.S. Army, which they continued to supply throughout World War II.

After the war, the company introduced converted rice to the
American public, and by 1952 it sold the country's number one
brand of rice. Around this time, the company adopted the name
"Uncle Ben" for a locally famous rice grower known for
producing high quality rice crops. Uncle Ben's eventually be-
came the leading brand of rice worldwide, sold in more than 100
countries, with manufacturing facilities in the United States,
Australia, Belgium, German, the Netherlands, and the United
Kingdom. Other popular brands included Country Inn rice,
Dolmio spaghetti sauces, pasta, and oriental dishes named Suzi
Wan, primarily sold in Europe and Australia.

United in 1967

Because of increased production, Mars constructed a new
plant in Hackettstown, New Jersey, in 1958. In the early 1960s,
facilities were extended to Europe with a factory at Veghel in
the Netherlands. In 1967 Forrest merged his business with the
Mars Company owned by his father and took over operation of
the new company. He established a radically egalitarian system
at the company in which workers were called associates and
everyone—from the president down—punched a time clock.
Offices were eliminated and desks were arranged in a wagon-
wheel fashion, with the higher-ranking executives in the center,
to facilitate communication between individuals and functional
areas. Notoriously demanding, Forrest rewarded his associates
with salaries that were substantially higher than those in other
comparably sized companies.

In 1968 Mars—already the largest dog food packer in the
world, with subsidiaries in Europe, South America, and Australia—acquired Kal Kan Foods, Inc., a dog food company
founded in 1937 that later supplied food for dogs in the U.S.
military during World War II. With assistance from Mars, Kal
Kan expanded by adding a second canned pet food plant in
Columbus, Ohio, and a dry pet food plant in Mattoon, Illinois,
while expanding into midwestern and eastern markets. New
product development of Mars pet-care products was aided by
the creation of the Waltham Centre for Pet Nutrition in the
United Kingdom, which was formed to study the nutritional
preferences and needs of pet animals. Nutritional studies were
published regularly in scientific and veterinary journals, and
Waltham became a world authority on pet care and nutrition.

Mars Electronics International (MEI) began operating in
Britain in 1969 and expanded to the United States in 1972. MEI
was responsible for the introduction of electronics to the
vending machine industry. In 1985 MEI expanded its product
line to include advanced bill technology and cashless payment
systems. In addition to serving the vending industry, MEI also
provided products for use in pay phones and amusement parks.
MEI's electronics technology had also been applied to data

acquisition and laser scanning devices. In 1987 the company's
British and American operations were merged to form the largest international manufacturer of electronic coin machines. In
addition to its two manufacturing facilities, MEI had marketing
and sales offices throughout the United States, Europe, Australia, and the Far East.

Forrest, Sr., retired from Mars in 1973. His elder sons,
Forrest E. Mars, Jr., and John Mars, took over Mars as
co-presidents—joined in 1983 in the office of the president by
their sister Jackie, who took a lesser role in running the company. In his retirement, Forrest, Sr., started a candy business
named Ethel M. Chocolates (after his late mother) to produce
premium boxed chocolates. Around 1988 Ethel M. Chocolates
was purchased by Mars.

Sweet Battle in the 1970s and 1980s

Despite its unorthodox corporate culture, the Mars company
thrived. Hershey Foods and Mars historically fought a battle to
hold the number one spot in the U.S. candy market, an honor
which passed between them. Mars took over the top spot in the
early 1970s and by late in the decade had pushed its market
share 14 percentage points ahead of Hershey. According to an
industry executive quoted in *Fortune,* "it took the Hershey
people seven or eight years to realize that Mars was not going to
go away.... Then it took them another five years to get their act
together." Hershey responded with a flurry of new product
introductions, heavy advertising, and innovative marketing efforts. In the mid-1980s Mars tried to combat this by creating a
new image for candy as a sweet snack, not just junk food. Mars
paid $5 million to have M&M's and Snickers named "the
official snack foods of the 1984 Olympic Games." Commercials featured athletes getting quick energy from sugary snacks.
By 1985 industry analysts noted that the two companies were
neck and neck, with Mars's recent brand introductions including Bounty Bars, Combos, Holidays M&M's, Kudos, Starburst,
Skittles, and Twix Cookie Bar.

Mars added frozen snacks to its repertoire when it acquired
Dove International in 1986. The Dove Bar, a hand-dipped ice
cream bar with a thick chocolate coating, was created in 1956
by Leo Stefanos, the proprietor of a Chicago candy shop. For
many years, the bar was only available in the Chicago area; it
appeared in selected U.S. markets during the early 1980s.
Doveurope was established in 1988. Other Mars frozen treats
included Dove miniatures and ice-cream versions of 3 Musketeers, Milky Way, and Snickers bars.

In 1988 Hershey Foods Corporation surpassed Mars as the
largest U.S. candy maker when it acquired Cadbury
Schweppes's U.S. division, boasting the Mounds and Almond
Joy brands. In 1989 Mars suffered another setback when it tried
to launch Sussande chocolate bars, a high priced European-style
bar, which, according to a report in *Forbes,* was a costly failure.

More Brands for the 1990s

The company rivalry between Mars and Hershey reversed
itself in 1991, when Mars increased its percentage of the total
candy market from 16.7 percent to 17.9 percent while Hershey's
market share remained flat at 17 percent, according to the *Wall*

Key Dates:

1911: Frank C. Mars starts a candy factory in Tacoma, Washington.
1920: Mars relocates to Minneapolis; company begins selling Snickers and Milky Way bars.
1926: Business is renamed Mars Candies.
1928: A new plant in Chicago is built.
1940: After starting operations in Europe, son Forrest brings M&M's to United States.
1943: Mars begins making parboiled (instant) rice for the U.S. Army.
1954: Peanut M&M's debuts.
1958: Mars builds a new plant in New Jersey; facilities soon extend to the Netherlands.
1967: Frank and Forrest Mars merge their respective businesses.
1968: Mars, already a leading dog food maker, buys and expands Kal Kan.
1969: Mars Electronics International begins developing high-tech vending machines.
1973: Forrest Mars retires; elder Mars children become co-presidents.
1986: Mars enters frozen snack business with purchase of Dove International.
1991: Numerous new candy and pet food brands are added.
1999: Founder Frank Mars dies.
2000: Cocoapro.com web site celebrates the magic of chocolate.

Street Journal. Mars was very successful with its 1990 introduction of peanut butter M&M's, which took a toll on Hershey's number two-ranked Reese's peanut butter cups. Mars launched 12 new products in 1991, including a dark chocolate candy bar under the Dove name, mint and almond M&M's, Milky Way Dark, and Peanut Butter Snickers.

Also in 1991 Mars introduced Expert, a super-premium dog and cat food line meant as an alternative to Hill's Science Diet and Iams, which was sold only in pet stores and feed shops. An industry analyst noted in the *New York Times* that "people are feeding their pets like they feed their children. The nutrition kick has moved over to our pets." To meet customer demand, Mars quickly moved into the specialty pet food area, but made the product accessible by selling it in supermarkets. Mars's other pet-care lines continued to do well. According to company literature, Kal Kan was the fifth largest pet food manufacturer in the United States. Other top sellers in Australia, Europe, and the United States included Pedigree and Partners dog foods; Whiskas, Sheeba, and Brekkies cat food; and Winergy Horsesnacks.

Mars also explored healthier alternatives for its traditional snack products when, in 1992, the company became the first customer of Procter & Gamble Co.'s caprenin, a low-calorie cocoa butter substitute. Mars used caprenin in Milky Way II bars, launched on the West Coast in April 1992. Made of fatty acids naturally found in other fats such as peanut oil, cheese, and milk, caprenin was not subject to Food and Drug Adminis-

tration approval as were fat substitutes. Some of the sugar in Milky Way II was replaced with polydextrose, a low-calorie carbohydrate. The resulting candy bar was 25 percent lower in total calories and had 50 percent fewer calories from fat than the original Milky Way. By introducing Milky Way II, Mars became the first candy manufacturer to try to gain or retain calorie- and fat-conscious customers.

The company did not ignore its strengths, however. In late 1992, Mars began testing Mahogany, a line of premium chocolates, in Germany. These candies included truffles, bars, and boxed chocolates in reddish-brown and gold packaging with such South American motifs as palm trees and colonial style houses. The candy was relatively expensive, with a small box of eight truffles costing almost $4 and a 50-gram chocolate bar selling for more than $1.

Analysts questioned Mars's future stability, particularly in light of the Mars brothers' reputed inability to share power with top managers who did not carry the family name, and it remained unclear who would assume control of the company when they retired. In the early 1990s, though, the company rested near the top of the confectionery products, dog and cat food, and rice milling industries. With numerous internationally recognized brands, including the perennially top-ranked Snickers, Kal Kan, and Uncle Ben's, Mars enjoyed a unique recipe for success.

John and Forrest Mars, Jr., had trouble through three presidents in the first four years in the early 1990s. Demanding taskmasters, they often paid double the going rate for management talent. In the middle of 1993, as its competitors downsized, the company offered voluntary separation agreements to its U.S. employees.

"Waking Up" in the Mid-1990s

Market share in several categories slipped in the early 1990s; the overall European market was shrinking. Mars suffered a conspicuous lack of successful new products, an area in which archrival Hershey excelled. However, reported *Fortune,* the Mars brothers seemed unfazed, likely more focused on long-term concerns than momentary fluctuations in sales. *Fortune* questioned the effectiveness of the company's "one world, one brand" policy, maintaining regional differences were still an important factor in marketing. Mars, however, still beat Hershey's overseas; it was estimated to have shipped 100,000 tons of chocolate to Russia alone in 1993.

Mars dumped its ad agency, Bates Worldwide, in favor of BBDO in 1995. Mars wanted a more image-building approach such as had been successful for Visa and Pepsi. The company did hire former Bates executives to head its European marketing.

Mars tried several new tricks in the late 1990s. It acquired a small organic foods marketer, Seeds of Change, in late 1997. The reportedly foul-tasting VO2 Max Energy Bar, Mars's shot at a $300 million a year market, was launched but quickly pulled due to poor sales. A version of M&M's with crisped rice added to the chocolate center was much more successful; it began shipping in late 1998.

Forrest Mars, Sr., died in Miami in July 1999 at the age of 95. His children had been legally barred from selling the company without his consent until his death, leading to speculation that the company would go public or change hands within a few years. After its founder's death, the company began to consolidate several divisions and agencies. It planned to merge its candy, pet care, and food businesses in continental Europe into a single unit.

Forbes believed Mars, Incorporated had already become sluggish and, being private, inattentive to the quarterly profit demands of Wall Street. Its chocolates trailed ten points behind those of its rival from Pennsylvania. The Uncle Ben's division, once the leading rice producer in the United States, let market share fall to Quaker Oats' Rice-A-Roni and Carolina and Mahatma rice from Riviana Foods until it actually lost money in 1998. In 1999, after terminating 100 of its 540 "associates," the division found a hit in frozen dinners—microwaveable bowls of rice topped with meat, vegetables, and sauce.

In early 2000, Mars launched a web site, Cocoapro.com, dedicated to celebrating recent research claiming health benefits for certain of chocolate's plant-derived components. The company's extensive process for manufacturing chocolate was also presented.

In spite of its market share setbacks, Mars, Incorporated was still a serious marketing force around the world. At the beginning of the millennium, the company had facilities in more than 60 countries and sold products in more than 150. It was spending $850 million a year advertising brands such as M&M's candies, Snickers candy bars, Uncle Ben's rice, and Pedigree dog food.

Principal Subsidiaries

Ceipa France; Dolma Italy; Kal Kan Foods.

Principal Divisions

Snack Foods; Pet Care; Main Meals; Electronics; Drinks.

Principal Competitors

Cadbury Schweppes; Hershey Foods Corporation; Nestlé S.A.; Ralston Purina Company.

Further Reading

Beirne, Mike, "Mars Extends M&M's Crisp-Ward; Toy Candy Surges Past Fad Status," *Brandweek*, June 29, 1998, p. 8.

Benady, David, "Mars Acts to Halt European Decline," *Marketing Week*, September 6, 1996, pp. 24ff.

Brabbs, Cordelia, "Unwrapping the Changing Future of Mars," *Marketing*, January 13, 2000, p. 13.

Branch, Shelly, "Chocolate Lovers, Relax! Mars Points to Web Site Touting Cocoa's Benefits," *The Wall Street Journal*, January 28, 2000, p. B2.

Brenner, J.G., *The Emperors of Chocolate*, New York: Random House, 1999.

——, "Planet of the M&M's," *Washington Post Magazine*, April 12, 1992.

Cantoni, Craig J., "Quality Control from Mars," *Wall Street Journal*, January 27, 1992.

Dixon, Mark, "Bar Wars," *Accountancy*, June 1998, pp. 32–34.

Fairclough, Gordon, "Mars Inc.'s Future Is Unclear After Death of Patriarch," *Wall Street Journal*, July 6, 1999, p. A22.

Fisher, Christy, "Milky Way Cuts Calories," *Advertising Age*, January 20, 1992.

Fucini, Joseph J., and Suzy Fucini, *Entrepreneurs: The Men and Women Behind Famous Brand Names and How They Made It*, Boston: G.K Hall & Co., 1985.

Hwang, Suein L., "Peanuts and Caramel Combine to Create Sticky Competition," *Wall Street Journal*, April 14, 1992.

Johnson, Bradley, "Kal Kan Goes Upscale," *Advertising Age*, September 24, 1990.

Katayama, Frederick H., "Snickers Ice Cream Bar," *Fortune*, August 13, 1990.

Kitt, Janette, "Securing a Foothold for Confectionery," *Candy Industry*, July 1992.

Koselka, Rita, "Candy Wars," *Forbes*, August 17, 1992.

Lawrence, Steve, "Bar Wars: Hershey Bites Mars," *Fortune*, July 8, 1985.

Leonhardt, David, "It's Not All Kisses in Candyland" (review of *The Emperors of Chocolate*), *Business Week*, February 22, 1999, p.18.

Levitt, Craig, "Sweet Success," *Discount Merchandiser*, October 1997, pp. 35–38.

"A Little Illustrated Encyclopedia of M&M/Mars," Hackettstown, N.J.: M&M/Mars, 1992.

"Mars Acquires the Dove Bar," *New York Times*, August 12, 1986.

"Mars Merger Talks Denied by Nestlé," *New York Times*, September 20, 1991.

McNatt, Robert, and Roy Furchgott, "It's the Taste, Stupid," *Business Week*, June 1, 1998, p. 6.

Mehegan, Sean, "Mars Attacks," *Brandweek*, May 13, 1996, p. 1.

Mistry, Bhavna, "On a Global Mission," *Marketing*, October 9, 1997, pp. 39–42.

Mussey, Dagmar, and Laurel Wentz, "Mars Tries Premium Chocolate in Europe," *Advertising Age*, December 14, 1992.

Noble, Barbara Presley, "Will the American Pet Go for Haute Cuisine?," *New York Times*, December 16, 1990.

O'Leary, Noreen, "New Life on Mars," *Brandweek*, May 6, 1996, p. 44.

"On the Wings of a Dove," *Washington Post*, May 13, 1991.

"Our Most Important Ingredient Is Quality," McLean, Va.: Mars, Incorporated, 1980.

"P&G Sells Caprenin to Mars, Achieving Product's First Sale," *Wall Street Journal*, January 20, 1992.

Palmeri, Christopher, "Wake Up, Mars!," *Forbes*, December 13, 1999.

Rutherford, Andrea C., "Candy Firms Roll Out "Healthy' Sweets, But Snackers May Sour on the Products," *Wall Street Journal*, August 10, 1992.

Saporito, Bill, "The Eclipse of Mars," *Fortune*, November 28, 1994, p. 82ff.

——, "Uncovering Mars' Unknown Empire," *Fortune*, September 26, 1988.

Sprout, Alison L., "Milky Way Light," *Fortune*, February 24, 1992.

Steinhauer, Jennifer, "America's Chocoholics: A Built-In Market for Confectioners," *New York Times*, July 14, 1991.

—Janet Reinhart Hall
—update: Frederick C. Ingram

MBC Holding Company

882 West Seventh Street
St. Paul, Minnesota 55102
U.S.A.
Telephone: (651) 228-9173
Fax: (651) 290-8211
Web site: http://www.grainbelt.com

Public Company
Incorporated: 1991 as Minnesota Brewing Company
Employees: 150
Sales: $19.2 Million (1999)
Stock Exchanges: NASDAQ small cap
Ticker Symbol: MBRW
NAIC: 42281 Beer and Ale Wholesalers

MBC Holding Company is a corporation whose subsidiaries include Minnesota Brewing Company, Gopher State Ethanol, and MG-CO2. The companies are involved in the production of beer and ale, ethanol, and carbon dioxide gas for industrial uses. Chairman Bruce Hendry owns 52 percent of MBC Holding Company. MBC's flagship operation, Minnesota Brewing Company, produces beer and beer related products under the Premium and Grainbelt, Pig's Eye, Brewer's Cave, and Yellow Belly logos. The Brewing Company is currently the 12th largest brewer in the nation and, in addition to producing its proprietary brands, MBC performs contract production for third parties, bottling and packaging both beer and sparkling water.

A Minnesota Tradition: 1855–1991

The state of Minnesota had long been associated with the production of beer. German immigrants settled in Minnesota and began brewing beer as early as the mid-1800s. By the late 19th century Minnesota had 112 breweries operating within its borders. MBC Holding Company resulted from the joining of the old Seventh Street brewery site in St. Paul, and the Grainbelt product line of Minneapolis Brewing.

The brewing facility on Seventh Street, now known as the Minnesota Brewing Company, began its history in 1855 as the Cave Brewery. The Cave Brewery established itself early as one of the principle brewing operations in the state. Throughout its years the brewery changed ownership and produced beer and other related products under many labels. Despite its frequent change of ownership the brewery remained in the same location for its 146 years. The location was chosen for its underground caverns along the banks of the Mississippi River in St. Paul.

Caverns or underground vaults were essential elements to the brewing and winemaking process in an age that predated modern refrigeration. Brewers relied on cold storage to provide a constant temperature range for their beer making, particularly the fine German lagers and ales that were in demand in Minnesota at the time. A Bavarian immigrant and brewery by trade, brewer Christopher Stahlmann went in search of caves and clean springfed water along the Mississippi until finding the brewery's ideal location in St. Paul.

Soon the brewery became Minnesota's largest beer producer and the caves were further excavated. The expanded facility allowed for brewing operations on three separate levels, and extended the production space well over a mile. A natural spring provided the water to the brewery throughout its history and has been measured to be over 1,100 feet deep. The Brewing Company claimed the water to be "diamond clear and regarded as some of the best water in the world."

Minnesota's early brewing operations were also aided by climate and topography. Abundant farmland allowed the breweries to purchase local barley and the Mississippi River trade brought quality hops and malt, essential ingredients for beer production.

Many of the settlers in the Midwest, particularly the Germans and the Irish, had rich brewing traditions in their native countries and created a demand for the local product. Despite the Cave Brewery's success, shortly after its founding the Stahlmann family sold the operation to the St. Paul Brewing Company. In 1900 the business was sold again and renamed The Jacob Schmidt Brewery.

Meanwhile in Minneapolis, another brewery was thriving. Minneapolis Brewing Company had produced a very successful

Company Perspectives:

MBC Holding Company operates a full-scale brewery in St. Paul, Minnesota. Today the brewery employs over 150 people and produces various proprietary brands of beer as well as a number of private label and contract brands of beer and water. The product line includes regular beer, light, non-alcoholic, malt liquor, and micro-style-brews.

product in its Golden Grain Belt beer. First introduced in 1893, the beer was enjoying wide success regionally. Minneapolis Brewing also produced beers under the brand names Zumwalt, Gilt, and Minnehaha Ale and gained attention for its technological advances. The brewery was one of the first partially automated facilities in the city, relying on labor saving devices for much of its production process.

The political and social climate regarding alcohol took a dramatic turn in the 1920s. The prohibition of the manufacture and distribution of alcoholic beverages in January 1920 threatened to destroy the brewing operations in the state. Fortunately, the two breweries, Jacob Schmidt in St. Paul and what was now referred to as Grain Belt Brewery in Minneapolis, were able to stay in business by producing legal beverages such as soft drinks and non-alcoholic beers.

When the 18th amendment was repealed by the 21st constitutional amendment in 1933, and the distribution of alcohol was once again legalized, Grain Belt and Schmidt beer products were reintroduced.

The Grain Belt label was promoted through an innovative marketing plan as the company pushed to gain back its market share after the industry upheaval of Prohibition. Grain Belt was dubbed ''The Friendly Beer'' in an advertising campaign that lasted through the 1930s.

In the 1940s, the company set out to distinguish itself as a producer of a high-quality product. Grain Belt Premium, bottled in 1947, was the result. A large neon billboard erected on Nicollet Island in downtown Minneapolis helped to link clear name recognition with the association of a quality premium beer. The outcome was a winning combination for Grain Belt. The brewery worked on presenting its Premium beer in packaging that was unique. The company used a distinctive clear glass, long-necked bottle. Grain Belt Premium captured the notion of superiority in its packaging with the slogan, ''The beer of exceptional quality.''

Throughout the 1950s and 1960s both breweries continued to produce beer and ale, though the St. Paul brewery changed owners several times. Despite its place among the top 20 breweries in the country, in the early 1970s Grain Belt was suffering from financial difficulties. In 1972 G. Heileman Brewing Company of La Crosse, Wisconsin, purchased the struggling plant. Heileman at the time also owned and operated the Jacob Schmidt Brewery in St. Paul. The combination of a big brewing facility in St. Paul and a strong brand name product from Grain Belt made Heileman a potentially formidable regional contender in the beer market.

The 1970s were an era when national brands were impacting the formerly regional beer market. National brands would undercut costs and had significant advertising budgets that eventually overturned local customer loyalty. In 1976 Heileman moved Grain Belt production out of Minneapolis to the St. Paul plant. Grain Belt sales were on a decline, though Grain Belt Premium still had a sound reputation in the industry and a small but committed following. Production in St. Paul continued through the 1980s.

In 1989 Heileman was bought by an Australian firm and it decided to consolidate all of the company's operations. Heileman's plans to close the St. Paul facility and move all operations to La Crosse met with a lot of opposition from the people of St. Paul. A campaign was mounted to get Heileman to reconsider the pullout or at least to sell the business to other investors, but the campaign met with little success and the brewery remained closed for two years.

Rising from the Ash Heap— Minnesota Brewing Company: 1991–96

In 1991 Heileman relented and signed an agreement with newly formed Minnesota Brewing Company to take control of the St. Paul Brewery. As part of the negotiation, Minnesota Brewing secured the Grain Belt and Premium brand names and logos.

In the early 1990s, the contract brewing market for beer and sparkling water was increasing. At the same time, original domestic beers sales were down, though exports had increased.

Beer production in the 1990s was a changing field; microbreweries were on the rise and there was an international interest in beers of regional character. The Minnesota Brewing Company took Grain Belt Premium and returned to its original recipe in an attempt to recapture the success it had in its early days.

The Pig's Eye Pilsner line of beer was also introduced in the spring of 1992. Pig's Eye paid homage to the first white settler of St. Paul, Pig's Eye Parrant. The Pig's Eye brand included: Pig's Eye Pilsner, Pig's Eye Lean, Pig's Eye Ice, Pig's Eye Red Amber, and Pig's Eye N.A. Pig's Eye Ice won a silver medal at the Great American Beer Festival for Minnesota Brewing in 1994 and Pig's Eye Red Amber won a bronze the following year at the same event. Pig's Eye N.A., Minnesota Brewing's non-alcoholic beer, won numerous awards since its introduction, including a gold medal in the non-alcoholic beer category. With the success of Premium, and the introduction of the Pig's Eye line of beers, Minnesota Brewing saw sales increase 28 percent in 1992 and another 27 percent in 1993.

Minnesota Brewing Company made the decision to go public in October 1993. The company did a lot of marketing to promote its proprietary brands in the wake of its IPO. Minnesota Brewing reported increasing its advertising budget some $300,000 in an effort to expand its market share. By 1994 Grain Belt Premium was entered in the Great American Beer Festival in Denver. Premium took top honors in the American Lager Division. The 1994 gold medal combined with the marketing campaign of 1993 led to a significant increase in domestic sales in 1995.

Key Dates:

1855: Cave Brewery is founded in St. Paul by Christopher Stahlmann.
1893: Minneapolis Brewing Company begins selling Grain Belt.
1897: Stahlmann family sells Cave Brewery to St. Paul Brewing Company.
1900: Business is again sold and renamed Jacob Schmidt Brewing.
1920s: Companies produce non-alcoholic beer during Prohibition.
1950s: Both the Minneapolis and St. Paul breweries remain active, though the latter changes hands several times.
1972: G. Heileman purchases the Grain Belt operations; Heileman also now owns and operates the Schmidt brewery.
1987: Acquisition of Heileman by Australian company leads to closing of St. Paul brewery location.
1991: Brewery is sold to Minnesota Brewing Company; business reopens for Octoberfest.
1992: Pig's Eye brands debut; Pig's Eye Ice wins silver medal at beer festival.
1993: Company completes initial public offering; Pig's Eye Red Amber wins bronze medal at beer festival.
2000: Minnesota Brewing changes its name to MBC Holding Company and Minnesota Brewing Company becomes a wholly owned subsidiary.

Unfortunately for Minnesota Brewing, earnings did not stay strong for long. In 1995 Pete's Brewing Company, a contract partner with the Minnesota Brewing Company for beer production, packaging and distribution, decided to move its production to another facility. In the wake of this decision Minnesota Brewing quickly took action to find other parties to replace its lost contractual work.

Later that year, Minnesota Brewing negotiated agreements with two other parties. It signed a contract to produce powdered malt liquids for home brewing (an emerging interest among beer enthusiasts), and another party contracted with Minnesota Brewing to create a base product that could be used in wine coolers.

Minnesota Brewing Company was faced with another set of problems when Winterbrook Inc., owner of LaCroix water, declared bankruptcy. Minnesota Brewing had been a contract packer for Winterbrook, providing bottling, packaging, and distribution. The two companies worked out an agreement to keep the business with Minnesota Brewing while Winterbrook remained under bankruptcy protection.

Having lost much of its contract work, Minnesota Brewing was eager to branch out into new enterprises. In 1996 the company signed a licensing agreement to distribute Yellow Belly, a new lemon flavored malt beverage. The brewery was optimistic that a contract with Southern Wine and Spirits of Cerritos, California, to be its wholesaler would lead to promising sales. The company now ranked 5th in regional beer sales

and had won six medals for its products at the annual beer festival, but it was still struggling to increase profits.

New Ventures: 1997–2001

Minnesota Brewing brought Jack Lee on board as president and CEO in 1997. The brewery continued to pursue new products, trying to recapture some of the contract sales figures it had lost with the conclusion of the Pete's Brewing business. Minnesota Brewing signed an agreement with Basix Foods of Hollywood, Florida, to begin producing and bottling a ''new age'' energy drink by the name of Blue Jeans Power Drink. The drink had seen remarkable success in European markets and the company had hoped it would find a share of the U.S. sports drink market as well. Later that year Minnesota Brewing also signed a contract to produce and distribute Rhino Chasers beer and ales.

The company had been given a $2.5 million line of credit from Minnesota Brewing Limited Partnership and when the line expired in early 1999 the company found itself in default. In the end, Minnesota Brewing Limited Partnership agreed to accept preferred stock holdings in lieu of the outstanding debt.

Perhaps the brewery's most controversial move began in January 1998 when Minnesota Brewing filed an application with the Minnesota Pollution Control Agency to begin exploring the commercial production of ethanol at the downtown brewery. Minnesota Brewing converted and retooled a portion of the downtown brewery to produce and market ethanol. The company wanted to diversify its interests and ethanol production seemed a good fit for the brewery. Minnesota Brewing also signed an agreement to partner with MG Industries of Malvern, Pennsylvania, to produce commercial grade carbon dioxide. Carbon dioxide was a natural byproduct of ethanol production.

In 2000, Minnesota Brewing Company changed its name to MBC Holding Company. With interests in beer production, ethanol, and commercial carbon dioxide, the new company name reflected its broader industrial base. In a press release the company explained the change by saying, ''The company had proposed the name change because it felt the name Minnesota Brewing no longer accurately reflected all of the company's operations and interests. The board believes the new name will benefit the company in its efforts to diversify its operations through the formation of subsidiaries and participation in joint ventures while preserving the name Minnesota Brewing for its brewing operations.''

The year 2000 saw sales for the company rising, and the diversification into other industries seemed to be working. Soon, however, another byproduct of MBC's ethanol production had neighbors of the plant protesting. Odor and noise related to the conversion of thousands of tons of corn into ethanol was causing a backlash in the community around the St. Paul plant. Eventually the matter was taken from protests in the streets and letters to the editor to the St. Paul City Council chambers. The City Council agreed to file a nuisance action against the ethanol plant, earmarking $100,000 to investigate the possible health impact to the neighborhood. Lee, president of both Minnesota Brewing and Gopher State Ethanol, promised to try to work with the city to remedy the problems.

At the dawn of a new century, the company began producing several specialty beers to celebrate the heritage of the brewery. Known as Brewer's Cave beers, they included Amber Wheat Ale, Golden Caramel Lager, and Roasted Black Barley Ale. The company also promoted tours at the St. Paul plant and operated an historic Rathskellar for visiting groups.

MBC Holding Company and its wholly owned subsidiaries, Minnesota Brewing Company, Gopher State Ethanol, and MG-C02, were attempting to build and grow a business by diversifying and utilizing connected industries. The brewing facility, while historic, had struggled throughout its years. The Minnesota Brewing Company's products, while doing well in competitions, had yet to reach remarkable sales levels. Whether the company could establish itself as a premiere brewing operation remained to be seen. MBC Holding Company, in its attempt to use the plant and its resources to its fullest potential, had made controversial choices that could possibly affect how the public perceived the company for years to come.

Principal Subsidiaries

Minnesota Brewing Company; Gopher State Ethanol LLC; MG-CO2.

Principal Competitors

Miller Brewing Company; Anheuser-Busch Companies, Inc.; Gluek Brewing Company.

Further Reading

"Calling All Bellies," *Beer Scope,* May 1997, p. 26.
"Minnesota Brewer Revives Grain Belt Golden Label," *St. Paul Pioneer Press,* April 3, 1998.

—Susan B. Culligan

Merrill Lynch

Merrill Lynch & Co., Inc.

4 World Financial Center
New York, New York 10080
U.S.A.
Telephone: (212) 449-1000
Fax: (212) 236-4384
Web site: http://www.ml.com

Public Company
Incorporated: 1959 as Merrill Lynch, Pierce, Fenner &
   Smith
Employees: 72,000
Total Assets: $407.2 billion (2000)
Stock Exchanges: New York Chicago Pacific Paris
   London Tokyo
Ticker Symbol: MER
NAIC: 523110 Investment Banking and Securities
   Dealing; 523120 Securities Brokerage; 523130
   Commodity Contracts Dealing; 523140 Commodity
   Contracts Brokerage; 523920 Portfolio Management;
   523991 Trust, Fiduciary, and Custody Activities;
   524113 Direct Life Insurance Carriers; 551112 Offices
   of Other Holding Companies

Merrill Lynch & Co., Inc. is one of the largest financial institutions in the world, with total corporate assets in excess of $400 billion and client assets of nearly $1.7 trillion, as of year-end 2000. The firm stands as the largest retail brokerage house in the United States, as well as one of the leading U.S. investment banks, and is among the global leaders in debt and equity underwriting, bond underwriting, and merchant banking. Long committed to the needs of the small investor, Merrill has continually diversified its offerings from the late 1960s into the 21st century. Now a global giant in the industry, increasingly active in a variety of investment fields outside the retail business, Merrill has evolved far from its original concentration on what its founder called ''people's capitalism.''

1885–1959: From Burrill & Housman to Merrill Lynch, Pierce, Fenner & Smith

Merrill Lynch's oldest direct predecessor was the partnership of Burrill & Housman, founded in 1885. In 1890 William

Burrill left the firm he had created, and the next year Arthur Housman's brother Clarence joined what was then A.A. Housman & Company. When Arthur Housman died in 1907, he left behind one of Wall Street's leading brokerage houses.

That same year, Charles Merrill and Edmund Lynch arrived in New York, where they met and became friends. The two 22-year-old entrepreneurs had both recently finished college and gravitated to Wall Street to seek their fortune. At that time, the stock market was chiefly the domain of a small number of eastern businessmen, but Merrill quickly realized the vast potential of financial markets funded by a broad spectrum of middle-class Americans. He received his initial training in the bond department of Burr & Company, and then set up his own firm in 1914. The following year he persuaded Edmund Lynch to join him, and Merrill, Lynch & Company was born.

The company prospered and grew quickly, earning a strong reputation in financial circles for financing the newly emerging chain-store industry. Merrill himself was a founder of Safeway Stores, and the company underwrote the initial public offering for McCrory Stores. By the late 1920s, Merrill, Lynch was reaping the benefits of that decade's prolonged economic boom, but Charles Merrill gradually became uneasy about the frantic pace of investment. He predicted that bad times were ahead as early as 1928, warning his clients and his own firm to get ready for an economic downturn. When the crash came in 1929, Merrill, Lynch had already streamlined its operations and invested in low-risk concerns. Despite this foresight, in 1930 Merrill and Lynch decided to sell the firm's retail business to E.A. Pierce & Company and concentrate on investment banking.

E.A. Pierce & Company was the direct descendant of A.A. Housman & Company. The company was named for Edward Allen Pierce, who had joined Housman in 1901, become a partner in 1915, and the managing partner in 1921. After World War I, Pierce concentrated on building the firm into a nationwide network of branches connected by telegraph, in order to reach more customers. After a 1926 merger with Gwathmey & Company, the firm was renamed E.A. Pierce & Company the following year.

Like most brokers, Pierce struggled through the Depression years, and in 1939 he persuaded Charles Merrill to rejoin him in

Company Perspectives:

Our Vision is to be the preeminent financial management and advisory company in the world. It is a drive firmly rooted in the things we value most: our intelligence, our principles and our optimism. Achieving preeminence is more than a goal. It is a means to an end. Preeminence affords us a leadership position in our chosen markets, a reputation as the best place to work, and the two most important benefits that accrue to the best-managed companies—client and shareholder value second to none.

the retail business. In 1940 Merrill Lynch, E.A. Pierce & Cassatt opened its doors, dropping the comma between Merrill and Lynch for the first time and adding Cassatt & Co., a Philadelphia firm that had sold part of its business to Pierce and part to Merrill, Lynch in 1935.

The new firm was devoted to the radical concept of offering to its investors a "department store of finance." Clients were urged to research their financial options, and Merrill Lynch saw itself as a partner in that process, even providing educational materials. In 1941 the firm merged again; this time it became Merrill Lynch, Pierce, Fenner & Beane when it absorbed Fenner & Beane, a New Orleans company that was the nation's largest commodities house and the second largest "wire house" (an investment firm that, like E.A. Pierce, depended on its private telegraph wires for a broad-based business).

During World War II the company benefited greatly from the economic turnaround brought by increasing military spending. Throughout the bull market of the postwar period and the 1950s, Merrill Lynch continued to be an innovator and a popularizer of financial information. The firm erected a permanent Investment Information Center in Grand Central Station, distributed educational brochures, ran ads with such titles as "What Everybody Ought to Know About This Stock and Bond Business," and even sponsored investment seminars for women. These new ideas made Merrill Lynch the best-known investment firm of the day. Charles Merrill's reputation soared to such heights that shortly before his death in 1956 one Wall Street historian referred to him as "the first authentically great man produced by the financial markets in 50 years."

In 1958 the firm juggled names again. Alpheus Beane, Jr., dropped out of the firm, and since Winthrop Smith had taken over as directing partner two years earlier, the firm was renamed Merrill Lynch, Pierce, Fenner & Smith. The next year it became the first large Wall Street firm to incorporate, and earnings reached a record high of $13 million.

1960s Through Mid-1980s: Diversification and International Expansion

During the 1960s the company began to diversify and expand internationally. In 1964 Merrill Lynch entered the government-securities business when it acquired C.J. Devine, the nation's largest and most prestigious specialist in that market. Over the course of the decade the firm also entered the fields of real estate financing, asset management, and economic consulting, and added 20 new overseas offices. The company paid

special attention to establishing a European presence, which allowed participation in the developing Eurobond market, and by 1964 had succeeded in becoming the first U.S. securities firm in Japan. In that same year Merrill Lynch was named lead underwriter for the $100 million public offering of Comsat, builder of the world's first telecommunications satellite, thus solidifying its position as one of the country's major investment banking firms. The company underwrote the sale of Howard Hughes's TWA stock in 1965, and in the next ten years added significant new business with firms such as Commonwealth Edison, Fruehauf, and Arco. By the end of the decade Merrill was managing about $2 billion annually in such offerings.

One of these projects, a 1966 debenture issue for Douglas Aircraft, led to an investigation by the Securities and Exchange Commission (SEC) and a substantial rewriting of the regulations governing full-service investment firms such as Merrill Lynch. The SEC charged that Merrill had passed on to some of its institutional clients confidential information about Douglas gathered while serving as the latter's investment banker. The company neither admitted nor denied the allegations but did agree to pay some fines, and the SEC took the opportunity to tighten its rules regarding insider trading and the prevention of unwarranted intraoffice disclosures.

Net income in 1967 was a handsome $55 million, representing an increase of 300 percent during the previous eight years. In the following year, Donald T. Regan was named president of Merrill Lynch, and two years later he became chairman and CEO. Regan guided Merrill Lynch in an ambitious program of diversification aimed at making the company a "one-stop investment and estate-planning institution." This included Merrill Lynch's first determined entry into the real estate field with the 1968 acquisition of Hubbard, Westervelt & Motteley, enabling it to offer to customers a range of mortgages, leasebacks, and other options; a major move into the mutual fund markets; and the purchase of Royal Securities Corporation of Canada, significantly strengthening Merrill Lynch's position in that country.

The firm also absorbed the New York Stock Exchange's fifth largest brokerage house, Goodbody & Company, in 1970 when that company fell victim to Wall Street's so-called "paper crunch disaster." Overextended trading houses were generating more transaction records than their accounting departments could keep up with, resulting, in the case of Goodbody and many others, in massive confusion and eventual collapse. The exchange asked Merrill Lynch to step in and help Goodbody, and Merrill Lynch ended up acquiring the firm at the end of 1970. The bailout cost little and brought Merrill Lynch new expertise in the area of unit trusts and options trading.

In 1971 Merrill Lynch became the second member of the New York Stock Exchange to invite public ownership of its shares, and in July of that year became the first to have its own shares traded there. During the telecast of the World Series that year, Merrill Lynch introduced its famous slogan, "Merrill Lynch is bullish on America." The company adopted its present name in 1973, forming a holding company called Merrill Lynch & Co., Inc., with Merrill Lynch, Pierce, Fenner & Smith as its principal subsidiary.

Regan's diversification program continued with a 1972 move into international banking. London-based Brown-Shipley Ltd.

Key Dates:

1885: Burrill & Housman is founded as a partnership.

1891: Following the departure of one of the founders, the company is renamed A.A. Housman & Company, which soon becomes one of Wall Street's leading brokerage houses.

1901: Edward Allen Pierce joins A.A. Housman, becoming a partner in 1915.

1915: Merrill, Lynch & Company is formed by Charles Merrill and Edmund Lynch.

1927: A.A. Housman is renamed E.A. Pierce & Company.

1930: Merrill and Lynch, aiming to concentrate on investment banking, sell their retail business to E.A. Pierce.

1935: Philadelphia-based Cassatt & Co. sells part of its business to Merrill, Lynch and part to E.A. Pierce.

1939: Merrill, Lynch merges with E.A. Pierce.

1940: Firm emerges as Merrill Lynch, E.A. Pierce & Cassatt.

1941: Firm is renamed Merrill Lynch, Pierce, Fenner & Beane following the acquisition of New Orleans-based Fenner & Beane.

1958: With the departure of Alpheus Beane, Jr., and the naming of Winthrop Smith as a directing partner, the firm changes its name to Merrill Lynch, Pierce, Fenner & Smith.

1959: Company becomes the first large Wall Street firm to incorporate.

1964: Firm enters the government-securities business through purchase of C.J. Devine.

1971: Firm goes public with listing on the New York Stock Exchange.

1972: Company expands into international banking through acquisition of Brown-Shipley Ltd., which is soon renamed Merrill Lynch International Bank.

1973: A new holding company is formed called Merrill Lynch & Co., Inc., with Merrill Lynch, Pierce, Fenner & Smith becoming its principal subsidiary.

1977: Merrill Lynch introduces the Cash Management Account, an innovative integrated-investment vehicle aimed at individuals.

1987: Wall Street crash sends profits reeling.

1995: The leading independent securities firm in England, Smith New Court PLC, is acquired.

1997: Mercury Asset Management PLC, the leading U.K. money management firm, is acquired.

1999: Merrill Lynch Direct, a web site offering online trading of securities, debuts.

---

soon became Merrill Lynch International Bank, and in 1974 Merrill Lynch acquired the Family Life Insurance Company of Seattle, Washington. In 1976 Merrill Lynch formulated a strategy to meet the challenge of the increasingly complex international financial marketplace by offering "a diversified array of securities, insurance, banking, tax, money management, financing, and financial counseling." Formerly clear demarcations between the various money professions were rapidly blurring, as Merrill Lynch demonstrated in 1977 when it announced the creation of the Cash Management Account (CMA). This unique account allowed individual investors to write checks and make Visa charges against their money market funds. Banks did not appreciate this incursion into their territory and mounted a number of legal campaigns to stop it, to no avail. By 1989, fully half of Merrill Lynch's $304 billion in customer accounts were placed in CMAs, and most of the other leading brokerage houses had developed similar integrated-investment vehicles.

Despite its sustained attempt to achieve a steady level of profit through diversification, Merrill Lynch's earnings reflected the volatile nature of its core securities business. For example, 1971 profit reached a new high of $70 million, but was followed by the difficult oil embargo years of 1972–74; and while 1975's record $100 million was not equaled for several years afterward, 1980 saw record highs of $218 million in profit and $3 billion in revenues. That year also marked the end of the Regan era at Merrill Lynch, as new U.S. President Ronald Reagan named Donald T. Regan secretary of the treasury and later made him White House chief of staff.

Roger Birk became the company's new chairman and CEO, followed in 1984 by William A. Schreyer. Schreyer, unhappy with Merrill Lynch's failure to match the earnings of some of its more flamboyant competitors, made increased profitability his chief goal. To that end, Schreyer reorganized the vast company, strengthened its trading, underwriting, and merger and acquisition departments, and made a $1 billion move into new offices in the World Financial Center. The firm also cut spiraling operating costs and trimmed 2,500 employees from its ranks.

In 1985 Merrill Lynch met a longstanding goal when it became one of the first six foreign companies to join the Tokyo Stock Exchange. The following year, when the firm became a member of the London Exchange, Merrill Lynch was able to offer round-the-clock trading. Later in 1986 Merrill Lynch sold its real estate brokerage unit as part of Schreyer's plan to unload low-profit concerns so that the company could focus more on using its powerful retail divisions to sell the securities its investment banking department brought in. The strategy worked; profits increased to a record $453 million during that year.

Also in 1986, scandal hit when Leslie Roberts, a 23-year-old Merrill Lynch broker, was arrested by the FBI for mail fraud. Roberts's complex fraud scheme involved huge sums—as much as $10 million from a single investor's account. The Roberts case typified for many the money fever of pre-crash Wall Street, and the incident attracted international attention.

Focusing on Profits Following 1987 Crash

Then in April 1987, the company was caught speculating in hugely unsuccessful fashion when it lost $377 million trading mortgage-backed securities—the largest one-day, one-company trading loss in Wall Street history. Coupled with the crash of October 1987, profits were sent reeling and Merrill Lynch was forced to freeze salaries, cut bonuses, dismiss employees, and slash commission payouts to its sales force. But profits increased dramatically the next year, reaching a record high of $463 million. During 1988 Merrill Lynch also achieved a long-held goal when it edged out Salomon Brothers to become the largest underwriter in the United States. The following year Merrill Lynch realized another long-term goal: the firm became the world leader in debt and equity securities, this time besting First Boston Corporation in the race for the top spot. Merrill Lynch remained in the thick of the hot merger-and-acquisition business as well, earning, for example, a tidy $90 million for helping put together the $25 billion leveraged buyout of RJR Nabisco Inc. that year.

Although Merrill Lynch's revenue and assets under management grew steadily from 1988 to 1990, its return on equity continued to lag behind other firms in the industry. Observers particularly cited the company's traditional inability to control costs—according to *Business Week,* it was "powerful but awkward and overweight . . . hobbled by a costly, bloated bureaucracy." Schreyer embarked on an ambitious reorganization that created 18 operating divisions, the managers of which were accountable for all costs therein. Merrill Lynch also downsized, reducing its head count from 48,000 in 1989 to 37,000 in 1991 and eliminating unprofitable subsidiaries such as Merrill Lynch Realty, Inc. and its clearing service Broadcort Capital Corp. It made additional cuts in its non-U.S. operations. Schreyer's overall cost-containment program paid off by reducing costs $400 million from 1989 to 1991.

Perhaps most important, however, Schreyer changed the mindset of the company from an obsession with generating revenue to a focus on earning profits. Compensation programs tied to the production of revenue were scrapped to make room for new schemes based on return on equity (ROE). Schreyer set an overall company goal of 15 percent ROE, but also held Merrill Lynch divisions to this standard as well. As a result, Merrill Lynch's ROE figures improved dramatically in the early 1990s—5.8 percent in 1990, 20.8 percent in 1991, 22 percent in 1992, and 27.3 percent in 1993. This achievement did not, however, come at the expense of growth. From 1990 to 1993, gross revenues increased from $11.15 billion to $16.59 billion, while assets under management increased from $110 billion to $161 billion. In the midst of this success, Schreyer retired in 1993 and was replaced as chairman and CEO by Daniel P. Tully, who had been president and COO.

By 1994 Merrill Lynch had achieved an average ROE of at least 15 percent across business cycles. Other firms in the industry struggled in 1994 as a series of U.S. Federal Reserve interest rate hikes battered the bond market and reduced underwriting dramatically. Merrill Lynch—though its profits were down significantly in the second, third, and fourth quarters—still managed an ROE of 18.6 percent for the year on record gross revenues of $18.23 billion. Since the company had the ability to offer its customers a full range of financial services and investment opportunities, it could generate revenues—and profits—in all types of market environments. Merrill Lynch's continuing growth in the global market—highlighted in 1994 by its first-time leadership in Eurobond and global bond underwriting—also promised to help the firm overcome downturns in the economies of individual countries or regions. Another international milestone reached in 1994 was the opening of an office

in Beijing, making Merrill Lynch the first U.S. securities firm to open an office in the People's Republic of China.

The year 1994 did leave a cloud hanging over the otherwise sunny forecast for Merrill Lynch's future. Orange County, California, was forced to file for bankruptcy late in 1994 after losing nearly $2 billion in a $7.6 billion county investment fund. Throughout the 1990s, the Orange County treasurer had leveraged the fund in order to purchase securities that would increase sharply if interest rates fell. The scheme worked very well until the 1994 Federal Reserve rate hikes sent the fund's securities into a tailspin. The county subsequently sued Merrill Lynch for $2 billion, claiming that the firm had advised the treasurer to make investments that exceeded state-mandated limits on risk. Merrill Lynch denied that it had done anything wrong, and claimed that it had not been the treasurer's financial adviser. In 1998, however, Merrill Lynch paid fines in excess of $400 million in connection with its business activities involving Orange County; Merrill Lynch settled related lawsuits over the next few years, paying additional sums to the parties involved.

In mid-1995 Merrill Lynch became the largest investment bank in the world in terms of equity sales, trading, and research through its acquisition of England's biggest independent securities firm, Smith New Court PLC. With the $803 million purchase, Merrill Lynch not only increased its presence in England but also gained businesses in several countries where it had none, such as South Africa, Malaysia, and Thailand. The acquisition thus brought further geographic diversification to Merrill Lynch's operations, at the same time that it significantly enhanced the firm's position in the mergers and acquisitions side of investment banking in Europe. Further international deals and branch openings meant that by 1996, 30 percent of revenues was generated outside the United States. Among the deals were the acquisitions of brokerages in Spain (FG Inversiones) and Australia (McIntosh Securities Limited) and the purchases of stakes in brokerages in Italy, India, Thailand, Indonesia, and South Africa.

In April 1997, 28-year company veteran David H. Komansky succeeded Tully as CEO. Komansky made an immediate impression with the year-end 1997 acquisition of Mercury Asset Management for $5.3 billion in cash. Mercury was the leading money management firm in the United Kingdom with about $170 billion in funds under management. Almost instantly, Merrill Lynch now had an international asset-management business, with overseas strengths in Europe and Asia, and ranked as the third largest retail and institutional money manager in the world with more than $610 billion in assets under management. On a broader basis, Merrill Lynch also became at the end of 1997 the first brokerage firm to have more than $1 trillion in customer assets.

Further expansion in Asia came in 1998 with the purchase of 33 branches and the hiring of 2,100 employees from the failed Japanese firm Yamaichi Securities. Merrill Lynch now had 200 offices located outside the United States, far more than most of its U.S.-based competitors. The firm also acquired Midland Walwyn Inc., a Canadian broker-dealer, in 1998 for $850 million. Net earnings for 1998 suffered, however, from a variety of factors, including the aftereffects of the Asian financial crisis and the meltdown in the Russian economy. Merrill Lynch suffered its first quarter in the red since 1989 when it posted a $900 million bond trading loss in the third quarter of 1998. The firm also had loaned money to the Long-Term Capital Management hedge fund, which nearly collapsed; as part of a bailout led by the Federal Reserve, Merrill Lynch chipped in $300 million. Finally, there was the $400 million in fines from the Orange County debacle. In the midst of these travails, the company announced that it would fire 5 percent of its 64,800-employee workforce.

Meantime, Merrill Lynch cautiously joined in the late 1990s online investing revolution with the 1997 introduction of Merrill Lynch Online, which initially provided only account balances, news, and research reports. Online trading soon followed, but on a limited basis only, as the company had to tread cautiously because of its 18,000 commissioned brokers. Under increasing pressure from Internet-savvy competitors, such as Charles Schwab Corporation, Merrill Lynch belatedly took the plunge into online trading in December 1999 with the launch of Merrill Lynch Direct. This web site offered brokerless trading at $29.95 for stocks, mutual funds, and bonds; access to initial public offerings being underwritten by Merrill Lynch; more research offerings; and other enhancements to its predecessor.

With the repeal in the fall of 1999 of the Glass-Steagall Act, the last barriers between banks, brokerage firms, and insurance companies had been torn down. Early the following year, Merrill Lynch moved into banking with the rollout of a federally insured, interest-bearing account that was tied to customers' investment accounts. Any cash in such accounts not invested in securities would be swept into the new bank accounts. In December 2000 Merrill Lynch and London-based HSBC Holdings plc launched a joint venture aiming to offer online banking and investment services to people in Europe and Asia having more than $100,000 to invest and wanting to make their own financial decisions. Other developments in 2000 included the acquisition of Herzog Heine Geduld Inc., a leading NASDAQ market maker, and the promotion of E. Stanley O'Neal to head of Merrill Lynch's brokerage operations, making him the first African American in that position, which was generally considered a stepping stone to the CEO office at Merrill Lynch.

As the markets soured in the latter months of 2000 and into 2001—highlighted of course by the spectacular bursting of the Internet stock bubble—Merrill Lynch began trimming expenses. Noncore units were placed on the block and the company sold its mortgage-servicing and origination unit and its energy-trading business. Some job cutting took place as well, including the elimination of nearly 2,000 jobs in the brokerage unit. In the volatile financial times of the early 21st century, Merrill Lynch, despite its cost-cutting initiatives, appeared to be better positioned to thrive than many of its rivals thanks to its stability, size, and highly diversified operations—diversified both by product and by geography. Proof of this was found in the results for 2000, which were highlighted by record earnings of $3.8 billion, a 41 percent increase over the $2.7 billion figure of the previous year.

Principal Subsidiaries

Merrill Lynch, Pierce, Fenner & Smith Incorporated; Merrill Lynch International (U.K.); Merrill Lynch Government Securities, Inc.; Merrill Lynch Capital Services, Inc.; Merrill Lynch Investment Managers, L.P.; Merrill Lynch Investment Managers Limited (U.K.); Merrill Lynch Bank USA; Merrill Lynch Bank & Trust Co.; Merrill Lynch International Bank Limited (U.K.); Merrill Lynch Capital Markets Bank Limited (Ireland).

Principal Operating Units

Corporate and Institutional Client Group; Private Client Group; Merrill Lynch Investment Managers.

Principal Competitors

Goldman Sachs Group Inc.; Morgan Stanley Dean Witter & Co.; J.P. Morgan Chase & Co.; Citigroup Inc.; Credit Suisse First Boston; The Bear Stearns Companies Inc.; Lehman Brothers Holdings Inc.; Paine Webber Group Inc.; Quick & Reilly/ Fleet Securities, Inc.; The Charles Schwab Corporation; Mellon Financial Corporation; Deutsche Bank AG; AXA Financial, Inc.; Nomura Securities International, Inc.; FMR Corp.

Further Reading

"American Municipalities: Merrill Lynched," *Economist,* December 17, 1994, pp. 76–78.

Byrnes, Nanette, and Leah Nathans Spiro, "Will Merrill Take a Hit in Orange County?," *Business Week,* February 13, 1995, p. 86.

Clifford, Mark L., and Leah Nathans Spiro, "How Merrill Lynch Is Winning the East," *Business Week,* September 1, 1997, pp. 79–80.

"The Culprits of Orange County," *Fortune,* March 20, 1995, pp. 58–59.

Doherty, Jacqueline, "Ride 'em, Dave: Can Komansky Get the Merrill Lynch Bull to Dance to a Different Tune?," *Barron's,* November 30, 1998, pp. 27–31.

Friedman, Jon, "The Remaking of Merrill Lynch," *Business Week,* July 17, 1989, pp. 122–25.

Hecht, Henry, ed., *A Legacy of Leadership: Merrill Lynch, 1885–1985,* New York: Merrill Lynch, 1985.

Holson, Laura M., "Merrill's Bull in China's Shop," *New York Times,* March 26, 2000, p. 1.

LaPlante, Alice, "Merrill's Wired Stampede," *Forbes,* June 6, 1994, pp. 76–80.

Lenzer, Robert, "Merrill at the Half-Trillion Mark," *Forbes,* April 26, 1993, pp. 42–43.

McGeehan, Patrick, "Poised to Take Merrill by the Horns," *New York Times,* October 29, 2000, p. 1.

Michels, Antony J., "Get Lean When the Times Are Fat," *Fortune,* May 17, 1993, pp. 97–100.

Nash, Jeff, "Merrill Flexes Its Muscle," *Money,* March 2001, pp. 52–53.

Norton, Leslie P., "Merrill's Big Bet: Is Mercury Asset Management Worth What the U.S. Giant Is Paying?," *Barron's,* November 24, 1997, p. 39.

Perkins, Edwin J., *Wall Street to Main Street: Charles Merrill and Middle-Class Investors,* Cambridge: Cambridge University Press, 1999.

Reed, Stanley, and Leah Nathans Spiro, "A Jolly Good Deal for Merrill Lynch," *Business Week,* December 1, 1997, p. 154.

Regan, Donald T., *The Merrill Lynch Story,* New York: Newcomen Society in North America, 1981.

Savitz, Eric J., "Bull in a China Shop?: Merrill Lynch May Be Getting a Bum Rap from Investors," *Barron's,* September 17, 1990, pp. 10–11, 20.

Schifrin, Matthew, "Merrillizing the World," *Business Week,* February 10, 1997, pp. 146–51.

Schifrin, Matthew, and Erika Brown, "The Bull Has an Identity Crisis," *Forbes,* May 5, 1999, pp. 108–14.

Spiro, Leah Nathans, "Merrill May Be a Merger Mogul at Last," *Business Week,* May 27, 1996, p. 134.

——, "Merrill's E-Battle," *Business Week,* November 15, 1999, pp. 256–60+.

——, "Raging Bull: The Trimmer New Look of Merrill Lynch," *Business Week,* November 25, 1991, pp. 218–21.

Strom, Stephanie, "Japan's Investors Become Bullish on Merrill Lynch," *New York Times,* January 6, 2000, p. C1.

Thornton, Emily, and Stanley Reed, "A Scrambler at Merrill," *Business Week,* June 19, 2000, pp. 234–38.

Tully, Shawn, "Merrill Lynch Bulls Ahead," *Fortune,* February 19, 1996, pp. 76–79, 82–84.

——, "Merrill Lynch Takes Over," *Fortune,* April 27, 1998, pp. 138–40+.

Wozencraft, Ann, "Bias at the Bull: Merrill Lynch's Class-Action Settlement Draws a Crowd," *New York Times,* February 27, 1999, p. C1.

—Wallace Ross
—update: David E. Salamie

A *Responsible Care*® Company

Methanex Corporation

1800 Waterfront Centre
200 Burrard Street
Vancouver, British Columbia V6C 3M1
Canada
Telephone: (604) 661-2600
Fax: (604) 661-2676
Web site: http://www.methanex.com

Public Company
Incorporated: 1991
Employees: 846
Sales: $1.06 billion (2000)
Stock Exchanges: NASDAQ Toronto
Ticker Symbols: MEOH; MX
NAIC: 325191 Gum and Wood Chemical Manufacturing

Based in Vancouver, Canada, Methanex Corporation is the world leader in the production and marketing of methanol. Produced from natural gas, methanol is used in the production of formaldehyde, MTBE (methyl teniary butyl ether), acetic acid, and in wood adhesives, plastics, paints, building products, foams, explosives, herbicides, pesticides, and poultry feed additives. End uses of methanol include acting as a substitute for chlorofluorocarbons in aerosol products and as a deicer and windshield washer fluid. MTBE's use as a gasoline additive to reduce carbon monoxide emissions has not only spurred industry growth, but has created a degree of controversy, leading to Methanex filing a claim under the North America Free Trade Agreement (NAFTA) against the government of the United States.

Roots of Methanex: 1968

Much of the assets of Methanex were originally part of Ocelot Industries, an oil and natural gas company that was formed in 1968 to exploit resources in Canada's Alberta Province. The company enjoyed some success, but by 1985 it was saddled with high debt and crippled by weak oil prices, resulting in a $40.4 million loss for the year. After a write-down of assets, the company reported a further loss of $167.2 million in

1986. As foreign firms began to take over poor-performing Canadian energy companies in 1987, Ocelot, with its own losses continuing to mount, worked with bankers and institutional investors to create a refinancing pact. It also promoted a 33-year-old executive, Brooke Wade, to the post of president in a management reorganization. In 1988 Ocelot began to sell off some of its major oil and gas producing properties to help reduce its debt of $770 million, but by the following year the company retained a Toronto securities dealer to help it consider acquisition, merger, or other investment proposals in order to maximize shareholder value in the company.

Ocelot's chemical division took advantage of the company's natural gas holdings by producing methanol in its Kitimat, British Columbia, plant. In the late 1980s methanol emerged as a possible alternative to gasoline as an automotive fuel, prompting oil companies to develop cleaner, reformulated gasolines. Nevertheless, methanol was a primary raw material in methyl teniary butyl ether (MTBE), an additive that made up approximately 15 percent of reformulated gasoline. With passage in the United States of the 1990 Clean Air Act amendments (as well as separate regulations in California) mandating the use of reformulated gasoline in much of the country by 1996, the manufacture of methanol appeared to have a tremendous upside. The chemical was considered a mature commodity, enjoying a steady but generally modest increase in demand each year. Only once in the 1980s did methanol see a sharp rise in price, and that was caused by the unexpected outage of a major plant. Because of the future need for MTBE in reformulated gasoline, however, the potential for the methanol industry was greatly enhanced. Plants that had been shut down were now being brought back into production and new facilities were being built.

In 1991 Ocelot spun off its Kitimat methanol plant, as well as its ammonia business, to create a separate, publicly traded company called Methanex, with Wade serving as president and chief executive officer. As part of the spinoff, the German conglomerate Metallgesellschaft AG (MG) merged its North American and Caribbean methanol assets with the Ocelot interests in exchange for a 28 percent equity stake in Methanex. The Methanex board would later be expanded from six to eight to accommodate MG, whose chairman and CEO, Heinz Schimmelbusch, would also serve as chairman for Methanex.

With the clear intent of becoming the world's leading producer of methanol, Methanex was quick to make deals to bolster its production capacity. It acquired MG's interest in a joint venture with American Cyanamid Co. for $11.7 million in cash and 2.9 million shares of Methanex stock, thereby increasing MG's interest in the company to 35 percent. The Cyanamid venture would convert an idle ammonia plant near New Orleans into a methanol facility. Methanex also entered into a joint venture with Dallas-based Hoechst Celanese Chemical to restart methanol production in a Clear Lake, Texas, plant. With both new plants expected to be operational by the end of 1992, Methanex expected to double its annual production of methanol.

Majority Shareholders, Changing Twice: 1993

Impressive as these transactions may have been at the moment, they were soon overshadowed early in 1993 when Methanex agreed to acquire the assets of the world's leading methanol producer, New Zealand's Fletcher Challenge Ltd., a diversified forestry company with interests in energy, construction, and agricultural-services. After acquiring a wide range of businesses in the mid-1980s, Fletcher was now looking to sell off assets to pay down debt. For Fletcher's methanol interests Methanex paid $250 million in cash and nearly 74 million common shares of stock for a total consideration in excess of $700 million. Fletcher, with a 43 percent equity stake, now became the largest shareholder of Methanex, as MG's position dropped to 10 percent. As part of the deal, the head of Fletcher's methanol unit, Dr. Brian Hannan, became Methanex's chief executive officer, with Wade now serving in a secondary position. From Fletcher, Methanex acquired two methanol plants in New Zealand as well as a plant in Chile. With additional production capacity in hand, Methanex then canceled the deal it had earlier negotiated with Hoechst Celanese.

Fletcher, however, would be the controlling shareholder of Methanex for just a brief interlude. By the end of 1993, Canada's Nova Corp., a chemical and pipeline concern, would agree to merge its methanol interests with Methanex in exchange for common shares worth $145.9 million and the right to purchase additional shares for $139.8 million in cash. Because it would have to spend $166.5 million to retain a controlling interest and was uninterested in holding a minority stake, Fletcher opted to sell 15.5 million of its Methanex shares to Nova, with the remainder offered for resale to the public. MG further agreed to sell stock to Nova, thus reducing its Methanex holdings from 10 percent to 6 percent. Hannan continued to serve as president and CEO, but less than a year later he would return to his native New Zealand to run Methanex's Southern Hemisphere and Asian operations. He was replaced by Pierre Choquette, the president and chief operating officer of the parent corporation's Novacorp International unit. Wade left

Methanex to start up an investment firm, but he would continue to serve on the company's board as a strategic adviser.

Although the use of reformulated gasoline did not increase as much as anticipated, a shortage in methanol in 1994 led to an unprecedented spike in the commodity's price and, in turn, resulted in massive profits for Methanex. Priced around 30 cents a gallon in 1993, methanol reached $1.55 per gallon on contract sales and as high as $1.80 on the spot market. For the year, Methanex posted a net income of $442.7 million on sales of $1.5 billion, compared to $10.7 million in net income on sales of $533 million the year before. A number of chemical companies now began making plans to reopen shuttered methanol plants or to build new facilities, prompting fears that the market would eventually become glutted as these new sources of the commodity became available.

Taking advantage of its leading position in the industry, Methanex was able to build a war chest in excess of $400 million in order to ride out the inevitable downturn in methanol pricing. Aside from the cyclical nature of the business, methanol faced more serious political and marketing challenges from a rival alternative fuel: ethanol, which was derived from corn and backed by powerful agribusinesses. In the midst of methanol's price run-up in 1994, the safety of MTBE was called into question by U.S. ethanol lobbying groups, who alleged that MTBE could cause headaches and dizziness when drivers filled up at the pump in cold weather. The price of Methanex stock suffered a downturn but quickly recovered.

Methanol prices in early 1995 fell as quickly as they had risen the year before. The increase in the cost to manufacture MTBE due to high methanol prices had put a damper on the sale of reformulated gasoline, and states successfully petitioned the Environmental Protection Agency for leeway on meeting the goals of the reformulated gasoline program. Furthermore, foreign countries were not converting to reformulated gasoline as much as had been expected. Decrease in demand coupled with new production capacity led to a fall in the price of methanol as well as Methanex stock. The formaldehyde business remained strong, however, and the government mandate for cleaner fuels appeared to insure a continuing need for MTBE, making the drop in price more a correction than a crisis for a company like Methanex. Nevertheless, it agreed to sell off a jointly owned ammonia plant for $84 million to Mitsui & Co. in order to focus on its core business. Although not as successful as it had been in 1995, Methanex still realized a net income of $191.7 million on revenues of $1.25 billion.

Methanol Prices Recover in 1996

After bottoming out in 1995, the price of methanol began to rise again in 1996. Methanex began implementing a strategy to build on its competitive edge in the industry. It reduced its cost structure, primarily by replacing high-cost facilities, such as those located in New Zealand and North America, in favor of new low-cost plants in Chile. Furthermore, Methanex improved operating efficiencies and lowered shipping costs. It also signed long-term charter agreements on a fleet of dedicated methanol tankers as well as invested in terminal facilities. In all, Methanex was positioning itself to be able to prosper in any part of the methanol price cycle. In 1996 the company saw its sales

Key Dates:

1968: Ocelot Industries is incorporated.
1991: Ocelot spins off Methanex Corporation, with Met-allgesellschaft as major shareholder.
1993: Merger leads to Fletcher Challenge becoming company's major shareholder; Nova Corp. gains control by the end of the year.
1994: A sharp increase in methanol prices leads to record profits.
1999: Company files NAFTA claim in response to California ban on MTBE, a gasoline additive.

drop to $945.7 million. After taking a write-down of $93 million in order to close high-cost facilities, it reported a net loss of $7.9 million.

The methanol industry was consolidating in 1997, divided up among three primary players: Methanex, producers in Saudi Arabia, and producers in Trinidad and Tobago. Methanex tried to strengthen its position by acquiring the Trinidad Tobago Methanol Company, but was thwarted by the German petrochemical company, Helm AG, which had first-refusal rights to the 69 percent stake controlled by the government of Trinidad and Tobago. Methanex made other plans to expand low-cost production capacity by building a new plant in Asia that would begin operations in 2002. The company also formed a joint venture with Qatar General Petroleum Corp. to build a methanol plant in Umm Said, giving Methanex a presence in the Middle East. With its size and liquidity, Methanex was also able to buy methanol on the spot market in order to prop up the price in 1997. The company would produce what it designated as the second best year in its history. Net earnings of $202 million were realized on sales of almost $1.3 billion.

The following year, however, would see Methanex and the industry as a whole suffer through one of its worst years. The price of methanol plunged to its lowest level in a decade, caused in part by weak demand for MTBE and a financial crisis in Asia, but mostly attributed to an overabundance of supply. New production capacity far outstripped the world's need for methanol. Methanex reported a net loss of $68 million on sales of just $721 million. With a new low-cost plant in Chile ready to come onstream in 1999, Methanex decided to shut down high-cost facilities in North America, but with two other large plants of competitors scheduled to begin production the oversupply of methanol would continue to hurt the industry.

Demand for methanol derivatives was actually quite strong in both the United States and worldwide. The robust U.S. economy was expanding rapidly and the demand for both acetic acid and formaldehyde used in building supplies and consumer goods had a positive effect on methanol sales. Methanex, as it lowered its production costs, was in a better position than its competitors to take advantage of the increasing need for methanol when the oversupply of methanol invariably corrected itself. More and more the sore spot was MTBE. Its potential to spur methanol sales had been a major factor in the creation of Methanex and had caused chemical companies to add produc-

tion capacity that had resulted in a glutted market. Increasingly MTBE came under fire from environmentalists and the producers of ethanol.

The methanol industry suffered a blow with potentially devastating effects when in March 1999 California Governor Gray Davis signed an order to phase out the use of MTBE by 2002 because of concerns that the additive was contaminating groundwater. Because California alone accounted for 6 percent of the company's sales, Methanex replied aggressively. It argued that the real environmental problem was leaking underground gasoline storage tanks that the state had failed to properly monitor, pointing out that MTBE was just one of a number of chemicals in reformulated gasoline that was leaking into the groundwater. The company further argued that stronger emission standards on boat engines would also protect drinking water, and that by banning MTBE the state, in addition to raising the price of gasoline, was more likely to add to air pollution than it was to alleviating water pollution.

Methanex then turned to the investor rights provisions of NAFTA to file a claim against the U.S. government for $970 million in damages for business lost due to California's MTBE ban. In the ten days following the governor's decision, Methanex stock lost $150 million in value, and the company contended that its stock had also declined in the two years since the MTBE safety issue was first raised in California. The company was more likely interested in reaching a compromise with California on environmental issues than actually receiving monetary damages. As the State Department determined who would negotiate on behalf of California, as provided by NAFTA, Methanex filed another NAFTA-based complaint. It charged that California violated U.S. treaty obligations by not enforcing state and federal environmental laws, namely California's failure to make property owners meet a December 1998 deadline to upgrade some 16,000 underground gasoline tanks. The spokesperson for California's Environmental Protection Agency dismissed the claim, saying that "the allegation has nothing to do with the enforcement of environmental laws and everything to do with Methanex desperately trying to hold on to the California market for MTBE."

As its claims against California slowly proceeded through the legal system, Methanex announced results in 1999 that were even poorer than the previous year. On sales of $695 million the company posted a net loss of $150 million. Demand for methanol, including MTBE, was high, but oversupply remained a source of trouble. With its cash reserves Methanex remained healthy and began efforts to consolidate industry-wide production in order to stabilize the price of methanol. As part of this effort, Methanex acquired Houston-based Saturn Methanol for $28 million in April 2000. The company also looked to develop new uses for methanol by joining automakers and other companies in developing cars that run on fuel cells using methanol.

Methanex rebounded in 2000, posting net earnings of $145 million on sales of $1.06 billion. Because of high natural gas prices in North America, methanol production essentially shut down in the continent, allowing Methanex with worldwide facilities to take advantage of the resulting rise in the price of methanol. Going forward in 2001, the company's fight with California over MTBE continued to linger. It heated up in

March 2001 when Methanex charged, in an amendment to its NAFTA claim, that Governor Davis was improperly influenced by political contributions from Archer-Daniels-Midland Co., a maker of ethanol. Although Governor Davis acknowledged that his campaign received about $200,000 from Archer-Daniels, he denied that his decision to ban MTBE was influenced by the contributions.

Whatever the outcome of the company's claims against California, Methanex with its cash reserves was well positioned for the future. Aside from MTBE, methanol would continue to be needed by a variety of industries. Furthermore, if Methanex's efforts at diversification were successful, the company could expect continued growth.

Principal Subsidiaries

Methanex Fortier Inc; Methanex Methanol Company; Waterfront Shipping Company Limited (Barbados); Methanex New Zealand Limited; Methanex Chile Limited; Methanex Europe NV (Belgium).

Principal Competitors

Borden Chemicals; Celanese Corp.; Millennium Chemicals Inc.

Further Reading

"Canadian Energy Industry Expects Takeovers by Foreigners to Go On," *Houston Chronicle,* January 19, 1988, p. 6.

Carlton, Jim, "Canada's Methanex Alleges Contributions Swayed California MTBE Gasoline Ban," *Wall Street Journal,* March 8, 2001, p. B13.

Cavanaugh, Tim, "Methanol Prices Hit All-Time High," *Chemical Marketing Reporter,* June 20, 1994, p. 3.

Collier, Robert, and Glen Martin, "Canadian Firm Sues California Over MTBE," *San Francisco Chronicle,* June 18, 1999, p. A1.

Lifsher, Marc, "State's Stand on Additive Is Challenged," *Wall Street Journal,* November 3, 1999, p. CA1.

"Methanex Guns for Pole Position in the Methanol Market," *Chemical Week,* August 26/September 2, 1992, p. 9.

"Methanex, Nova Blossom on Methanol Price Runup," *Chemical Marketing Reporter,* February 6, 1995, p. 8.

"Methanex Sticks to Its Knitting," *Chemical Week,* April 30, 1997, p. 57.

"Methanex Streamlining and Adding New Capacity," *Chemical Marketing Reporter,* December 9, 1996, p. 11.

"Methanex Wants Lead in Methanol," *Chemical Marketing Reporter,* August 24, 1992, p. 3.

Palmeri, Christopher, "Methanol Blues," *Forbes,* October 11, 1993, p. 44.

Parkinson, David E., "Methanex Plans 2 Ventures to Boost Methanol Output," *Wall Street Journal,* August 19, 1992, p. B5.

—Ed Dinger

Metropolitan Opera Association, Inc.

Lincoln Center
New York, New York 10023
U.S.A.
Telephone: (212) 799-3100
Fax: (212) 870-4508
Web site: http://www.metopera.org

Nonprofit Company
Incorporated: 1932
NAIC: 711110 Theater Companies and Dinner Theaters

Since 1932 the Metropolitan Opera Association, Inc. has run New York City's internationally acclaimed Metropolitan Opera. With an annual operating budget of approximately $200 million, the Metropolitan Opera stages more than 200 performances during the course of a season that runs 30 to 32 weeks. In addition to the more than 800,000 people who attend performances at the Opera's home in the Lincoln Center for the Performing Arts, millions more across the world partake through weekly radio broadcasts and occasional television productions, as well as through touring shows and recordings. A separate organization, the Metropolitan Opera Guild, helps raise a significant portion of the approximately $70 million in contributions made to the Metropolitan Opera each year. The Guild also handles the Opera's merchandising. Because ticket sales only cover 40 percent of the Met's operating budget and government grants only account for less than 2 percent, fundraising and ancillary income are of paramount importance. After enduring many periods of financial struggle during its 120 years of existence, the Metropolitan Opera has never been healthier than it is today.

Creation of the Metropolitan Opera: 1880

In the 1840s in New York as many as four theaters presented opera, creating what was deemed New York's first golden age of opera. With its opening in 1854, the Academy of Music, located near fashionable Union Square, became the leading opera house, the place where high society gathered to admire itself. As post–Civil War industry produced a generation of nouveau riche, however, the Academy's 18 boxes were unable to accommodate the newcomers who, in any case, were less than enthusiastically received by the old-line Knickerbocker aristocracy. The Academy's begrudging offer to build 26 additional boxes was considered inadequate, and in April 1880 the Metropolitan Opera was incorporated by several wealthy benefactors. In all, 70 shareholders were enlisted to provide the $1.7 million required to buy the land and build an opera house at 39th and Broadway. The mansions of the wealthy and the entertainment district, which had been marching uptown for many years, would soon leave the Academy in the backwaters of Manhattan. By 1886 it abandoned the field to the Met, as New York's reconstituted high society and new opera house reigned virtually unopposed for the next 20 years.

From the outset, the Metropolitan Opera house, which opened in 1883, was considered inadequate, despite its fine acoustics. The configuration of the building's property lines resulted in cramped dressing rooms, and limited rehearsal and storage space. In fact, scenery stored under the stage contributed greatly to a fire that in 1892 destroyed the interior of the theater. The expense of rebuilding also led to a new organization, the Metropolitan Opera and Real Estate Company, which would in effect act as landlord to the independent producers who actually ran the opera season, presumably at a profit. The shareholders of the Metropolitan Opera and Real Estate Company, who paid for taxes, maintenance, and repairs of the theater through a yearly assessment, received use of a box for every performance of the opera season in lieu of rent. It was this subsidy that would permit the producers to return a profit, or at least keep losses to a minimum. The Metropolitan Opera Company became the official producing entity in 1908.

For three seasons in the early 1900s the Metropolitan Opera faced stiff competition from a maverick impresario named Oscar Hammerstein and his Manhattan Opera House. Although Hammerstein did not curry favor with high society, his opera house, which featured exciting new French opera and fresh talent, began to draw fashionable patrons. In what was nothing less than an opera war, both Hammerstein and the Metropolitan Opera spread their operations to other cities. In the end, Hammerstein was choked by debt and on the verge of ruin, yet the Metropolitan Opera generously paid him $1.2 million to quit the business.

Company Perspectives:

From its opening in 1883, the Metropolitan Opera has been one of the world's leading opera companies. Today, the Met's preeminent position rests on the elements that established its reputation: high quality performances with many of the world's most renowned artists, a superior company of orchestral and choral musicians, a large repertory of works, and the resources to make performances available to the public.

Although grand designs of controlling opera in other major cities, including Chicago and Philadelphia, were never realized, the Metropolitan Opera firmly established itself as America's major producer of opera and a true international venue.

For 20 years, until the stock market crash of 1929, the Metropolitan Opera would enjoy a period of artistic achievement and financial stability. Until 1920 the major attraction was tenor Enrico Caruso. Gustav Mahler and Arturo Toscanini became principal conductors at the Met, which presented the American premiere, and in some cases the world premiere, of many notable operas. Along with the U.S. economy, the Metropolitan Opera thrived in the 1920s, so much so that it could decline the offer of funding from the Juilliard Foundation, created by textile mogul and longtime Met boxholder A.D. Juilliard. The Met's lack of interest in meeting Juilliard requirements would free up the funding that would be used to establish the Juilliard School of Music. Rising production costs during this period were offset by increased ticket prices and new sources of secondary income: The Victor Talking Machine Company paid an annual fee to sign Met singers for recordings, and NBC paid for the exclusive right to bring Met singers to the radio. In addition, the Metropolitan Opera rented out its house, sold the rights to its concessions and programs (plus a share of advertising revenues), and earned $15,000 a year from a piano endorsement. Times were so flush that building a new opera house seemed almost a certainty. The collapse of Wall Street in 1929, however, would delay that dream for many years.

The high water mark during this affluent period for the Metropolitan Opera was the 1927–28 season, when the company realized a profit of $141,000, with subscription revenues that totaled $55,000 per week. The 1929–30 season would see the Met lose money for the first time in 20 years, despite record receipts. With the economy in shambles the Metropolitan Opera saw subscriptions drop and tours canceled. Otto Kahn, longtime president and chairman of the Metropolitan Opera Company, was replaced by his attorney Paul D. Cravath, who also represented Westinghouse and RCA. He quickly signed a generous radio contract for the Met, which received $5,000 for each of 24 live broadcasts of operas.

The first radio broadcast of a Met opera, *Hansel und Gretel,* occurred on Christmas Day 1931, and was carried by the largest network of stations ever assembled at the time. The entire Red and Blue Networks of NBC were augmented by shortwave transmission over the BBC as well as Canadian and Australian networks. By the 1933–34 season the Saturday afternoon broadcasts had found a sponsor, Lucky Strike Cigarettes. A year later Listerine would back the show. Aside from the much needed revenue that radio brought the Metropolitan Opera, it also lent the company national stature. No one was sure about the number of listeners until the Met appealed for contributions over the radio. The enthusiastic and widespread support of the broadcasts could now be measured in the tangible form of money.

Establishment of Metropolitan Opera Association: 1932

As the losses mounted in the 1930s, the Metropolitan Opera had no choice but to change its approach to business. The concept that opera could be made profitable was abandoned; to produce a season was now a matter of funding, not investment. In 1932 Cravath reorganized the producing entity by creating the Metropolitan Opera Association, a nonprofit corporation that would be free of federal entertainment taxes. Because it was now deemed an educational enterprise, the Met was also able to apply for funding from the Juilliard Foundation. The 50th season of the Metropolitan Opera was only saved by a fundraising campaign that scraped together $300,000 from various sources, including $100,000 from the radio audience and $50,000 from the Juilliard Foundation.

In 1935 Mrs. August Belmont founded the Metropolitan Opera Guild to raise money for the Metropolitan Opera, as well as to develop an audience for opera through education. By 1937 regular matinee performances for students were held, and soon the Guild would bring opera to the schools. By the end of the century the Guild would contribute more than $75 million to the Metropolitan Opera. With an annual budget of approximately $17 million, the Guild would boast 100,000 members, becoming the largest organization of its kind.

Although it was far from healthy, the Metropolitan Opera saw its income steadily increase in the late 1930s, enough to ward off the very real danger of collapse as it waited for the U.S. economy to recover. Then in the summer of 1939 the Opera Association was informed that a number of boxholders that comprised the Metropolitan Opera and Real Estate Company refused to pay the annual assessment levied on their shares. Therefore, the lease on the opera house would not be renewed when it expired on May 31, 1940, and the property would be put up for sale. Cravath's successor, Cornelius Bliss, is credited with saving the Metropolitan Opera by negotiating a selling price of $1.97 million for a property that was assessed for tax purposes at $5.4 million, and spearheading an effort to convince shareholders to accept the deal. He also initiated a million-dollar fundraising campaign to provide the financing. Thus, on May 31, 1940, the Metropolitan Opera Association assumed the title of the opera house itself.

Also in 1940 the Metropolitan Opera radio broadcasts finally landed a long-term sponsor in the Texas Company (Texaco), which had recently suffered bad press over its dealings, however legal, with Axis countries in the period before the United States entered World War II. Because a prominent display of philanthropy was deemed an appropriate public relations response, the oil company decided to back the Met. The goodwill that would accrue to Texaco over the next 60-plus years for sponsoring the weekly opera broadcasts cannot be estimated. Furthermore in

---

Key Dates:

1880: Metropolitan Opera is founded.
1883: Metropolitan Opera house opens.
1892: Fire destroys interior of house and leads to reorganized Metropolitan Opera and Real Estate Company.
1908: Metropolitan Opera Company becomes official producing entity.
1932: Nonprofit Metropolitan Opera Association assumes control.
1940: Metropolitan Opera Association buys the Metropolitan Opera house from the Metropolitan Opera and Real Estate Company.
1966: Metropolitan Opera moves to new home in Lincoln Center.
1977: First PBS telecast of a Metropolitan Opera production is aired.

1940, the Metropolitan Opera would first turn to television, another medium in which Texaco would eventually serve as sponsor. An initial concert of selected material was telecast from the NBC studios. The first telecast from the stage of the Metropolitan Opera would be November 29, 1948, when ABC would present the season's opening night production of *Otello.*

World War II hurt attendance and, until New York State tax laws were modified, the Metropolitan Opera was burdened with heavy real estate taxes. Another public appeal for money was made in 1943–44, but with the end of the war and the resumption of touring and increased ticket sales, the Metropolitan Opera was able to post a modest $6,000 profit. The 1946–47 season would produce $3 million in income for the first time since the 1920s, yet the Metropolitan Opera lost more than $200,000. Even though scenery and costumes were becoming threadbare as operas that had been mounted 20 and 30 years earlier were recycled, rising production costs had clearly outstripped the amount of revenue that could be generated through ticket sales and ancillary income. Periodic fundraising appeals to the radio audience in order to avert pending disaster became a way of life at the Met.

Plans for a New Opera House: 1950s

The tonic that would restore the Metropolitan Opera to financial health, in the opinion of many, was a new opera house, offering not only increased seating capacity but storage facilities and updated technology. The idea had been advanced a number of times over the decades, but it finally took shape in the 1950s. Federal urban renewal legislation gave the government broad powers of eminent domain to seize property. Robert Moses, New York's legendary and autocratic builder of parks and roadways, was in charge of the "Title I" program in the city. He identified a slum that was in the vicinity of Columbus Circle that he offered to make available to the Met. In the meantime it appeared that Carnegie Hall might be torn down and that the New York Philharmonic might be in need of a new home. The Met and the Philharmonic joined forces and turned to the Rockefeller family, whose foundation had already de-

cided to fund the performing arts. The result would be Lincoln Center, Inc. and the building of a complex that not only included a 3,750-seat Metropolitan Opera and Philharmonic Hall (later named Avery Fisher Hall), but also a multipurpose theater (the State theater), a library, and an educational facility that would eventually become the Juilliard School of Music.

Plans for a new opera house had always assumed that the project would be funded by selling the old facility. Because of Lincoln Center, the Metropolitan Opera Association would be able to raze the old building and lease its valuable mid-town property. It was not surprising that efforts to "Save the Met" were not welcomed by the Association's management as it prepared to move into its new theater. In the end, the old opera house began to crumble on its own accord, and the Metropolitan Opera Association was able to sign a long-term lease for the property that would create an endowment fund the organization had never been able to accumulate. Rather than a contingency fund to meet deficits, the endowment was intended to expand the opera company's repertory and allow the production of new operas as well as the revival of older works that had limited box office appeal.

Although Philharmonic Hall was completed in 1962, the new Metropolitan Opera did not open until 1966. The finances of the Metropolitan Opera Association, however, were still not in sound shape. Banker George S. Moore became president of the organization in 1967 and began to put the Metropolitan Opera on a sound financial footing. Production budgets were adhered to and ticket prices raised. Moore cut costs, going so far as to postpone the opening of the opera season and canceling a production of *Don Giovanni.* When longtime general manager Rudolph Bing left in 1972, the Metropolitan Opera entered another crisis state. It lost star performers and attendance fell, as did contributions. To many observers in the late 1970s it seemed that only a massive government subsidy, as much as 30 percent of the Met's fundraising budget, would be able to keep the Met, and American opera, alive.

It was in 1977 that the Metropolitan Opera began regular telecasts on PBS, with Texaco serving as the sole corporate sponsor. The initial show, a production of *La Bohème,* was seen by some four million viewers. Not only were more people now exposed to opera through television, the Metropolitan Opera was exposed to more people. Aggressive marketing and fundraising, and tighter management would pay off in the early 1980s as the Metropolitan Opera achieved its best fiscal health since the 1920s. It was now in a position to begin work on a new $100 million endowment fund.

Unlike other prosperous times in its history, the Metropolitan Opera did not slip backwards; rather, it continued to thrive on its success. By 1989 merchandising sales alone would exceed $6 million, allowing the Metropolitan Opera Guild to contribute a record $4.1 million. In 1990 the Texaco-Metropolitan Opera International Radio Network began to deliver live broadcasts to 22 countries in Europe, thus solidifying the Met's international presence. Also in 1990 the Metropolitan Opera Association was solvent enough to complete 82 capital projects at a cost of $15 million.

Named general manager in 1990, Joe Volpe, who began work at the Met in 1964 as an apprentice carpenter, led the

Metropolitan Opera into a new century. Under his watch the Met strengthened its position, financially and artistically, at a time when other major opera companies around the world were struggling. Thus, Volpe became the most powerful man in opera, and his job the most coveted. When Lincoln Center began to make plans for a $1.5 billion renovation, Volpe and the Metropolitan Opera Association were in a position in January 2001 to withdraw from the project and begin their own renovation plans, which would include expanding the Met's lobby. Despite being the largest and richest occupant, contributing 30 percent of Lincoln Center's shared operating costs (and receiving 30 percent of common revenues), the Metropolitan Opera had no more say in the renovations than the smallest of the Center's 12 constituent groups. Volpe's surprise notice of resignation to Lincoln Center came just a week after the city committed $240 million to the project. Although the relationship between the Met and Lincoln Center had been occasionally contentious over the years, a 99-year lease would likely insure that the two parties would work out the details over the renovations. In any case, the Metropolitan Opera Association had reached a mature enough state to fund whatever work that needed to be done. Its financial outlook, at least in the near term, appeared quite solid.

Further Reading

Blumenthal, Ralph, "Midlife Hits Lincoln Center with Call for Rich Face Lift," *New York Times,* June 1, 1999, p. 1.

Blumenthal, Ralph, and Robin Pogrebin, "Lincoln Center Renovation Plan Has Opera Houses at Odds," *New York Times,* January 25, 2001, p. B1.

Briggs, John, *Requiem for a Yellow Brick Brewery: A History of the Metropolitan Opera,* Boston: Little, Brown, 1969, 359 p.

Eaton, Quaintance, *The Miracle of the Met: An Informal History of the Metropolitan Opera, 1883–1967,* Westport, Conn.: Greenwood Press, 1976, 490 p.

Kolodin, Irving, *The Metropolitan Opera, 1883–1966: A Candid History,* New York: A.A. Knopf, 1966, 762 p.

Mayer, Martin, *The Met: One Hundred Years of Grand Opera,* New York : Simon and Schuster : Metropolitan Opera Guild, 1983, 368 p.

Merkling, Frank, *The Golden Horseshoe, the Life and Times of the Metropolitan Opera House,* New York: Viking Press, 1965, 319 p.

"Mighty Joe Opera," *Forbes,* June 15, 1998, p. 302.

Pogrebin, Robin, "Making Waves Is Nothing New for Met's Maverick," *New York Times,* January 25, 2001, p. B6.

——, "Paying for Billion-Dollar Cultural Dreams," *New York Times,* January 30, 2001, p. E1.

—Ed Dinger

Mitsubishi Heavy Industries, Ltd.

5-1, Marunouchi 2-chome
Chiyoda-ku, Tokyo 100
Japan
Telephone: +81-3-3212-311
Fax: +81-3-3212-9800
Web site: http://www.mhi.co.jp

Public Company
Incorporated: 1964
Employees: 39,366
Sales: ¥2.45 trillion ($27.25 billion) (2000)
Stock Exchanges: Tokyo Osaka Nagoya Kyoto Hiroshima
Fukuoka Niigata Sapporo
NAIC: 336611 Ship Building and Repairing; 336411
Aircraft Manufacturing (pt); 23595 Bridge and Tunnel
Construction (pt); 221113 Nuclear Electric Power
Generation; 33312 Construction Machinery
Manufacturing; 3332 Industrial Machinery
Manufacturing; 333291 Paper Industry Machinery
Manufacturing; 3334 Ventilation, Heating, Air-
Conditioning, and Commercial Refrigeration
Equipment Manufacturing; 333611 Turbine and
Turbine Generator Set Units Manufacturing

Mitsubishi Heavy Industries, Ltd., Japan's largest shipbuild-
ing and machinery maker, is a mammoth company involved in
an array of industrial concerns. With nearly 150 subsidiaries,
Mitsubishi Heavy Industries (MHI) operates in 11 key
sectors—Shipbuilding, Nuclear Energy Systems, General
Machinery and Components, Paper and Printing Machinery,
Steel Structures and Construction, Machinery and Plants, Air-
Conditioning and Refrigeration Systems, Machine Tools,
Power Systems, Aerospace Systems, and Industrial Machinery—and produces everything from cruise ships and oil
tankers, to construction machinery, newsprint machines, turbines, airplanes, gasoline engines, and gear cutting machines.
The company also builds nuclear power plants, bridges, and
sports stadiums. MHI traces its history back to the latter part of
the 19th century, and has demonstrated its ability to withstand
periodic downturns in the Japanese economy. These economic
vagaries have prodded the company to shift its focus among
various sectors over the years. Shipbuilding, for example, was
once the heart of MHI, but the company has concentrated more
recently on aerospace and power systems as demand for its
large ships has waned. MHI's adaptive skills were looking to be
tested again at the dawn of the 21st century, as the company
addressed various management problems and redundancies.

MHI's Origins: The 19th Century

Since the 1880s the diversified collection of industrial manufacturers now known as MHI has constituted the heart of the
vast Mitsubishi group. Essentially all of Mitsubishi's many
industrial offspring were developed as adjuncts to its shipbuilding business, begun in 1884. The Mitsubishi interest in shipping
and shipbuilding extends back to the group's founding in 19th-
century Japan. Yataro Iwasaki, born in 1834 to a rural samurai
family, early in his life became an official with the Kaiseken,
the agency responsible for regulating trade in his native Tosa
domain, on the island of Shikoku. By adroitly straddling the
roles of public official and private entrepreneur, Iwasaki was
able to start a small shipping company in the late 1860s. In 1875
the Japanese government gave Iwasaki the 13 steamships that
he had operated on its behalf during a brief military engagement
with Formosa, making his newly named Mitsubishi Shokai—or
Three-Diamond Company, the source of the firm's logo—the
dominant shipping agent in Japan.

With extensive mining interests and a talent for currency
speculation, Iwasaki became so successful that the government
created a rival shipping firm, the KUK, to foster competitive
pricing. After a short fare war that threatened the ruin of both
firms, Mitsubishi's shipping assets were merged with those of
the KUK in 1885 to form a single, state-sponsored company.
Mitsubishi retained a small amount of stock and exercised some
control in the new firm, but its interest shifted to land-based
industries, in particular mining and shipbuilding. In 1884, unable to make a go of shipbuilding, the Japanese government had
loaned and then transferred outright its two leading shipyards to
the private sector. Mitsubishi took control of the best of these,
located in Nagasaki, and became Japan's premier builder of

Company Perspectives:

Today, we are expanding our businesses through technological innovations stemming from a global perspective and the development of enterprises aimed at achieving harmony in the international community. Starting with the construction of various facilities which provide comfort and adhere to local culture and customs, we have in recent years been grappling with issues of common concern to all of mankind like the development of new sources of energy and environmental protection. Marching toward the 21st century, MHI will continue to challenge issues that will be confronting us in the future such as ocean development and space programs. Our determination to conduct business on a global scale is supported by, and reflected in, a fundamental philosophy: utilization of technological expertise accumulated over more than a century to assess changes that occur with the passage of time while continuously developing previously unexplored areas. Together with the trust we have earned today, our untiring effort has become the driving force for building a new tomorrow.

Insuring harmony between mankind, technology and nature. Seeking a more prosperous future, MHI is moving steadily ahead.

ships and the only one capable of competing in the international marketplace.

Japan's shipbuilding industry was still relatively primitive, however, and remained so until the 1896 Shipbuilding Promotion Law combined with the Sino-Japanese War to spur domestic demand. Mitsubishi, by this time known as Mitsubishi Goshi Kaisha, became the favorite supplier of large oceangoing vessels to the state shipping company NYK, building 43 percent of all ships ordered between 1896 and World War I. Despite the close ties between the two companies, it appears that Mitsubishi did not receive preferential treatment. Indeed, although Mitsubishi gained fame in 1898 as the supplier of Japan's first oceangoing steamship—the 6,000-ton Hitachi Maru—its delivery was so tardy that the NYK awarded a second, similar contract to a British firm.

From 1896 through 1904, the eight years between Japan's wars with China and Russia, Mitsubishi's shipbuilding business increased by nearly 300 percent. In 1905 it acquired a second dockyard, in Kobe, and by 1911 employed some 11,000 workers at Nagasaki alone. Mitsubishi's shipbuilding division was not yet especially profitable—a disproportionate amount of the parent company's profits still came from mining and stock dividends—but it soon gave rise to a panoply of subordinate industries that supplied the yards with raw materials and parts. For example, in 1905 the Kobe yard spawned what would eventually become Mitsubishi Electric Corporation, a leading manufacturer of generators and electric appliances. Other shipbuilding divisions grew into power plants and independent producers of airplanes, automobiles, and heavy equipment. Bolstered by its highly profitable mining interests, Mitsubishi was able to afford the vast sums of money and years of work required to transform its subsidiaries into world leaders.

The Early 20th Century and World War I

When World War I began in 1914, Japanese shipping lines were unable to procure a sufficient number of foreign ships to maintain their booming business, and so turned to local manufacturers such as Mitsubishi. Japanese production increased more than tenfold between 1914 and 1919, with Mitsubishi leading the field. So great was the surge in business that the Iwasaki family, still in control of Mitsubishi Goshi Kaisha—the group's holding company—decided to spin off a number of its leading divisions into separate, publicly held companies, thereby gaining access to outside capital without substantially weakening the company's dominant position. In 1917 the Mitsubishi Shipbuilding Company (MSC) was created, along with Mitsubishi Bank, Ltd., Mitsubishi Iron Works, and a trading company for the entire group, now called Mitsubishi Corporation. The major components of the Mitsubishi *zaibatsu*, or conglomerate, were thus in place by 1920, although the ensuing years would bring many modifications to its structure.

As is generally the case, the wartime buildup in ship orders was followed by a severe depression. As business declined below prewar levels many shipbuilders were bankrupted and all were forced to impose drastic layoffs. The slump continued throughout the 1920s, merging into the Great Depression. Mitsubishi's lack of shipbuilding contracts continued until the beginning of World War II. In the meantime, however, MSC was actively pursuing a number of other technological developments, most notably the airplane and the automobile. Having made its first airplane in 1916 and first automobile in the following year, MSC grouped these products under the name Mitsubishi Internal Combustion Engine Manufacturing Company in 1920. This offshoot went through several changes before taking the name of Mitsubishi Aircraft Company in 1928, at which time it was already one of Japan's leading manufacturers of military aircraft. After six years of independence, however, the aircraft and automobile facilities were once again united with MSC to form Mitsubishi Heavy Industries in 1934. It is not clear why this strategy was adopted, but the imminent prospect of war with China may have suggested the need for a more unified industrial force.

World War II

To stimulate the moribund shipping industry, the Japanese government instituted the Scrap and Build Scheme in 1932. This policy called for shipowners, aided by government subsidies, to replace their older vessels with a smaller number of new, more efficient ships. In this way Japan's excess capacity could be reduced while simultaneously modernizing its fleet and promoting new shipbuilding technology. As the leading Japanese builder, Mitsubishi Heavy Industries (MHI) greatly benefited from this program, and even more so from the program's successor, the 1937 Superior Shipbuilding Promotion Scheme. This campaign was clearly prompted by Japan's preparations for war, as it subsidized the construction of large cargo ships with an eye to their eventual use for the transportation of troops and supplies. In the years following, government intervention in shipbuilding escalated to outright control, as the Imperial Navy placed all dockyard facilities under its direct command in 1942. The MHI yards at Nagasaki and Kobe produced a wide range of government warships, including the world's largest battleship, the *Musashi*. In addition, MHI used its aircraft experience to build 4,000 bombers and some 14,000 of the famous Zero fighters, widely recognized as the finest flying machine in the Pacific during the war's early years. The Zero provided an early example of the cost efficiency and quality that marked Japanese industrial design. A lightweight machine, the Zero could be produced quickly and economically, yet it boasted superior aerobatic abilities and heavy firing power. The Zero made Mitsubishi infamous in the West, discouraging postwar marketers of other Mitsubishi products from highlighting the company name in advertising.

At the end of the war in 1945, an estimated 80 percent of Japan's shipyards were still in usable condition. Mitsubishi's main yard at Nagasaki, however, did not escape the effects of the world's second atomic explosion. At war's end the occupying Allied forces halted all shipbuilding activity, restricting the heart of Japan's industrial economy. During the two years in which this ban remained in effect, MHI kept busy by repairing damaged vessels and even using its massive plants for the manufacture of furniture and kitchen utensils.

Challenges After World War II

With the growing realization that Japan could be a strategic asset in the postwar battle against Asian communism, the Allies relaxed the more stringent limitations, and many Japanese companies resumed production. For MHI, occupation forces waited until 1950 to chop its mighty assets into three distinct and geographically separated firms: West Japan Heavy Industries, Central Japan Heavy Industries, and East Japan Heavy Industries. Part of an effort to destroy the Mitsubishi *zaibatsu* as a recognizable entity, the division of MHI was intended to force the three companies to compete against each other for contracts, thus hindering their growth.

The rest of the Mitsubishi group was similarly fragmented, and although it gradually reassumed its former shape, the Iwasaki family no longer controlled the various subsidiaries by means of a single holding company. Instead, each of the major Mitsubishi companies acquired stock in its fellow companies, and a triumvirate composed of the former MHI companies, Mitsubishi Bank, and the group's trading company became the unofficial head of what remained a voluntary economic entity. It is remarkable that this loosely connected portfolio of war-ravaged corporations

should then have proceeded to outperform its global competitors over the next few decades. The three heavy-industry companies, in particular, faced an almost impossible situation. Forced to compete with one another, forbidden from pursuing the military contracts that had formerly provided a huge portion of its business, and confronted by international competitors whose technological progress had not been interrupted by the war, the new MHI trio appeared destined for failure.

Several factors combined to help MHI get past this critical period. The 1947 Programmed Shipbuilding Scheme provided low-interest government loans to the shipping companies that needed but could not afford new vessels. In effect, the government decided which ships should be built and helped pay for them, injecting the capital needed to restart a business cycle that had nearly ground to a halt. Secondly, the three companies were able to use some of their idle aircraft facilities in the manufacture of motor scooters and automobiles. Under the direction of the head designer of the Zero, Kubo Tomyo, the rejuvenated auto division sold about 500,000 scooters before the government asked it to resume making small autos in 1959. Thirdly, Japan's shipbuilders realized that the Japanese economy depended on ships and their manufacture, and that if Japanese ship producers could not compete in the postwar international market the entire nation would suffer.

Driven by such a threat to its existence, the former MHI companies hired an increasing number of highly competent engineering graduates from Japan's leading universities and set them to work emulating the advanced technology of the United States and Western European countries. Able to rely on trade unions that were loyal and flexible in the extreme, they were soon producing oceangoing vessels equal in quality to but less expensive than anything made in the West. The Korean War of 1951–53 triggered a huge increase in orders and, after surviving the short depression following the war, the companies were able to exploit the rapidly developing worldwide demand for oil tankers. The tanker market was in turn given a tremendous jolt by the Suez Canal crisis of 1956, since the canal closing sparked a surge of orders for larger, more efficient ships able to complete the long journey around Africa. Between 1954 and 1956 total orders at Japanese builders more than tripled to 2.9 million gross tons, of which at least two-thirds were placed by foreign shipping companies.

Growth in the 1960s and 1970s

The post-Suez depression in shipbuilding was severe enough to prompt fresh diversification at MHI. Increased research financing was devoted to civil engineering, plant construction, and automobiles, all of which MHI's years of experience in heavy industry had well prepared it to undertake. In 1958, in cooperation with 23 other Mitsubishi Group corporations, Mitsubishi Heavy Industries created Mitsubishi Atomic Power Industries. Since then, MHI continued to dominate contemporary Japanese production of atomic power. Automobile production rose steadily, if not as quickly as at rivals Toyota and Nissan, and by 1964 the Nagoya plants were manufacturing 4,000 cars per month. Even aircraft production had been resumed by the early 1960s.

With the world increasingly dependent on imported oil and Japan's construction skills honed to perfection, Mitsubishi was hit by an avalanche of orders for tankers during the 1960s and early 1970s. To accommodate this extraordinary boom, the three parts of MHI were once again united, resulting in the 1964 rebirth of Mitsubishi Heavy Industries. This giant's 77,000 employees and $700 million in sales were spread among a handful of the most important heavy industries, but shipbuilding commanded the bulk of MHI's resources. A new dock with 300,000-gross-ton capacity was built at Nagasaki in 1965, followed by the 1972 completion of a mammoth 1-million-gross-ton supertanker facility at the same yard. This ultra-efficient dock enjoyed only a short life, however—the oil crisis of 1973 and 1974 soon brought tanker orders to a near standstill, permanently crippling the entire Japanese shipbuilding industry.

Economic Downturn: 1975–85

The economic downturn was devastating. By 1975, the last of the peak tanker years, 40 percent of MHI sales and one-third of its workers were involved in shipbuilding. By 1985 those numbers had plummeted to 15 percent and 17 percent, respectively. But MHI managed to shift its assets quickly enough to survive. Having already spun off its automobile division to form Mitsubishi Motors Corporation in 1970, MHI aggressively pursued clients in the power-plant and factory-design fields. It also reclaimed its position as the top supplier of military hardware to Japan's growing defense force. At the same time, MHI streamlined its production facilities by shifting employees from older industries such as shipbuilding to newer ones such as machinery and power-plant production, and simultaneously allowed natural attrition to shrink its overall labor bill. Thanks in no small part to this diversification, MHI emerged successfully from the disastrous downturn of the shipbuilding industry, and became an industrial leader in other areas as well.

The 1990s

The early 1990s brought a fresh set of challenges to MHI. A weakening of the global economy and the post-Gulf War oil shock caused a downturn in the company's sales. Moreover, the strength of the Japanese Yen made it difficult for MHI's ships and heavy equipment to compete in the global market against equipment produced in countries—especially South Korea—with weaker currencies. To compensate, MHI's shipbuilding division embarked on a program of heavy cost-cutting in 1992. But the situation took a toll, and the company's other division continued to account for greater percentages of MHI's total sales.

By the mid-1990s it looked as though MHI had weathered the storm to become an even stronger force. Its construction and power sectors flourished as the company won a number of lucrative contracts. In February 1996, for example, MHI was selected to build six gas turbine thermal power plants for Dubai Electricity and Water Authority in the United Arab Emirates. Two months later, MHI received an order to construct a fertilizer plant for R.P. G. Industries of India, and also teamed up with two Chinese companies (Baoshan Iron & Steel Corp. and Changzhou Metallurgical Equipment Corp.) to produce steel-making parts and equipment in China.

The resurgence of Japan's shipbuilding industry in the mid-1990s seemed to complete MHI's revival. The yen had at last begun to weaken, making it easier for Japanese companies

such as MHI to compete effectively against their Korean rivals. In addition, global demand for tankers and ships boomed, since the world's commercial fleets had aged. By 1996, in fact, roughly 41 percent of all tankers were more than 20 years old and approaching the end of their useful life span. In this new environment, MHI's shipbuilding division benefited from the company's cost-cutting measures of the early 1990s, as well as from more recent advances in computer-aided design that maximized efficiency.

Prudently, MHI did not abandon its efforts to emphasize its other divisions despite the renaissance in the shipbuilding sector. In fact, MHI not only looked to new sectors in Japan to drive its recovery, it also sought out new markets abroad for its equipment and services. Southeast Asia and the Middle East sorely needed new power sources, and as the global economy boomed, the private and public sector undertook major construction projects—which drove demand for MHI's equipment. Late in 1996, MHI won a $1.1 billion contract to install a 2,400 megawatt power plant for the Saudi Consolidated Electric Co., as well as a contract worth about $127.8 million to supply generators for Taiwan Power Co.'s new nuclear power plant. MHI continued to boom in 1997. After winning a contract to build a fertilizer ammonia plant for Indonesia's PT Kaltim Pasifik Amoniak, MHI was selected by Saudi Yanbu Petrochemical Co. to build polyethylene and ethylene glycol plants.

The year 1998, however, saw a dramatic reversal of this positive trend. Dragged down by the repercussions of the currency crisis that rocked Thailand and other developing countries, Japan's economy slumped along with the rest of Asia. MHI's sales slowed as its key customers cut back on construction and infrastructure projects in response to the growing "Asian economic crisis." By October 1998, though, it was clear that MHI could not blame its problems entirely on outside economic forces. MHI had counted on foreign markets to make up for sluggish sales at home through the first part of the 1990s. In an effort to boost its profits even more, MHI had outsourced much of its foreign production to subcontractors—without ensuring appropriate supervision. The result was that some of the massive construction and power projects MHI had undertaken in Southeast Asia and the Middle East were hindered by poor quality. As the *Asian Wall Street Journal* reported, these quality control issues severely undercut the profitability of MHI's foreign operations. In fact, the company eventually had to redo some of the work itself—hurting its earnings.

The company's sales and profits dropped further in 1999, as Japan remained mired in the Asian economic crisis. Nobuyuki Masuda stepped down as MHI's president to become chairman of the board. In his place Takashi Nishioka was appointed president. Nishioka had won the admiration of shareholders during his tenure as head of MHI's aerospace operations, playing an essential role in moving that division away from its longstanding reliance on defense contracts. Instead, Nishioka had looked to the private sector for business, focusing particularly on bolstering MHI's business ties with Boeing.

Upon taking the helm, Nishioka announced a massive restructuring program, involving 7,000 job cuts, a reorganization of the company's engine and motor operations, and an expansion of its aerospace division. Perhaps more importantly,

Nishioka promised to end MHI's policy of "matrix management," in which the company's branch offices competed among themselves and with the division headquarters. In place of this inefficient system, Nishioka pledged to unify management functions.

These changes would take time to implement, though. In 2000, with Japan's domestic economy still in the doldrums, MHI reported its first net loss since the company had been reunified in 1964. Despite this significant setback, Nishioka remained optimistic that MHI would recover from its latest problems. He predicted that the company would return to profitability by 2003.

Principal Subsidiaries

Mitsubishi Heavy Industries America, Inc. (U.S.A.); MHI Corrugating Machinery Company (U.S.A.); Mitsubishi Engine North America, Inc. (U.S.A.); MHI Forklift America, Inc. (U.S.A.); Bocar-MHI S.A. de C.V. (Mexico); Mitsubishi Brasileira de Industria Pesada Ltda. (Brazil); CBC Indústrias Pesadas S.A. (Brazil); ATA Combustao Tecnica S.A. (Brazil); Mitsubishi Heavy Industries Europe, Ltd. (U.K.); MHI Equipment Europe B.V. (Netherlands); Saudi Factory for Electrical Appliances Company, Ltd. (Saudi Arabia); Bohai & MHI Platform Engineering Co., Ltd. (China); Mitsubishi Heavy Industries (Hong Kong) Ltd.; MHI-Mahajak Air-Conditioners Co., Ltd. (Thailand); Thai Compressor Manufacturing Co., Ltd. (Thailand); Highway Toll Systems Sdn. Bhd. (Malaysia); MHI South East Asia Pte. Ltd. (Singapore).

Principal Competitors

Ishikawajima-Harima Heavy Industries Co., Ltd.; Kawasaki Heavy Industries, Ltd.; Mitsui Group; NKK Corporation.

Further Reading

"Airbus and the Japanese," *New York Times,* November 21, 1991.

Bates, Daniel, "Systems Modeling in Distribution Pact with Tokyo Goliath," *Pittsburgh Business Times & Journal,* March 9, 1991.

Blustein, Paul, "High-Tech's Global Links: Industry's Huge Costs Unite Former Rivals," *Washington Post,* July 16, 1992.

Chida, Tomohei, and Peter N. Davies, *The Japanese Shipping and Shipbuilding Industries: A History of Their Modern Growth,* London: Athlone Press, 1990.

Kanabayashi, Masayoshi, "Ship Firms That Diversify Win Favor of Analysts," *Asian Wall Street Journal,* June 6, 1995.

Lamke, Kenneth, "Miller Park Is Just One of Mitsubishi's Problems," *Milwaukee Journal Sentinel,* October 30, 1999.

Lubar, Robert, "The Japanese Giant That Wouldn't Stay Dead," *Fortune,* November 1964.

"Mitsubishi: A Japanese Giant's Plans for Growth in the U.S.," *Business Week,* July 20, 1981.

"Mitsubishi Heavy Industries Ltd.," *Oil and Gas Journal,* November 23, 1992.

"Mitsubishi Heavy Industries Pact," *Wall Street Journal,* November 2, 1992.

"Mitsubishi Heavy Now Expects Deeper FY Group Net Loss," *Dow Jones International News,* March 28, 2001.

"Mitsubishi: The Diamonds Lose Their Sparkle," *Economist,* May 9, 1998.

"Nishioka Named President of Mitsubishi Heavy Industries," *Japan Weekly Monitor,* April 5, 1999.

Smith, Maurice, "A Touch of the Mitsubishis (Mitsubishi Heavy Industries),"

Accountant's Magazine, January, 1991.

Tindall, Robert E., "Mitsubishi Group: World's Largest Multinational Enterprise?," *MSU Business Topics,* Spring 1974.

"Westinghouse Electric Corp.," *Wall Street Journal,* March 24, 1992.

Wray, William D., *Mitsubishi and the N.Y.K., 1870–1914: Business Strategy in the Japanese Shipping Industry,* Cambridge: Harvard University Press, 1984.

—Jonathan Martin
—updates: Sina Dubovoj, Rebecca Stanfel

The Motley Fool, Inc.

123 North Pitt Street
Alexandria, Virginia
U.S.A.
Telephone: (703) 838-3665
Fax: (703) 684-3603
Web site: http://www.fool.com

Private Company
Incorporated: 1994
Employees: 375
NAIC: 51331 Wired Telecommunications Carriers (pt)

The Motley Fool, Inc. offers personal financial advice and investing strategies to readers through a variety of media. The company maintains a presence online through America Online and through its own web site, www.fool.com, which attracts more than two million visitors per month. Its founders, brothers David and Tom Gardner, reach millions of readers through books, nationally syndicated newspaper columns, and weekly radio shows. The company also operates a web site for investors in the United Kingdom, located at www.fool.co.uk.

Origins

The multimedia blitzkrieg of personal finance information launched by brothers David and Tom Gardner began modestly, receiving only tepid response from the public. In July 1993, the Gardners, along with a college friend, Erik Rydholm, created a 16-page print newsletter that combined investing information and humor written for the individual investor. The unusual slant of irreverent stock advice was published under the banner "The Motley Fool," an investment guide geared for the layperson and produced by unabashed novices in the arena of investment analysis.

The title of the newsletter was drawn from a line in Shakespeare's *As You Like It:* "A fool, fool! I met a fool i' the forest, a motley fool." It was a fitting reference considering the background of the newsletter's writers. David and Tom Gardner were English majors at college, neither with any formal training in finance, but both were convinced that their approach to personal investment would attract a broad audience of aspiring investors. In Elizabethan literature, the fool was the one person at court who could speak truthfully to the king without fear of losing his life. David and Tom Gardner, iconoclasts wearing jester caps, perceived themselves as the fools of Wall Street. They would teach and amuse, and along with their audience, learn the secrets of investing.

The elder of the two Gardner brothers, David, graduated as a Morehead scholar from the University of North Carolina in 1988. At Chapel Hill, David majored in English, while his brother studied English and creative writing at Brown University, graduating with honors. Rydholm attended Brown University as well, earning a degree in political science in 1989. David Gardner eventually began writing for a financial newsletter, *Louis Rukeyser's Wall Street*, before he teamed with his brother and Rydholm to create the first issue of *The Motley Fool*. Initially, the trio developed a list of potential subscribers by using wedding lists gathered from their friends and relatives. A mailing list was created and sample issues of the newsletter were sent to those on the list, along with an invitation to subscribe. Few chose to do so, but the young entrepreneurs persisted. Working out of David Gardner's house, the partners published 12 monthly newsletters before they abandoned the project, never gaining more than 300 subscribers.

Debut of America Online Forum: 1994

Their first attempt failed, but the Gardner brothers soon found another medium to explore. In November 1993, Tom Gardner posted a note in the personal finance area maintained by Internet service provider America Online (AOL). He provided his telephone number and offered free copies of *The Motley Fool* newsletter. By the following day, three messages were on his answering machine, one from Texas, one from Maine, and one from Minnesota. Sensing an opportunity to reach a large audience with their offbeat approach to investing, the Gardners set up a message board on AOL to serve as a forum for exchanging investment information. They explained they were novices, but offered to answer any questions anyone might have, and encouraged others to offer any advice of their own. By February 1994, the Gardners' bulletin board had become the most popular personal finance site on AOL.

Officials at AOL noticed the popularity of the Gardners' site and invited the brothers to establish an official presence on what ranked as the country's leading online service. The invitation came with a modest sum of start-up money—less than $10,000—enabling the Gardners to move their operation into the ground floor of a townhouse in Alexandria, Virginia. More computers were purchased and employees were hired, as The Motley Fool took on the trappings of a legitimate business. The forum, in its new, official guise, debuted in August 1994 and quickly became a haven for those pursuing financial independence. The electronic conversations and the writings of the site's editors centered on the demystification of investing, on tearing down the barriers that distanced the ordinary investor from Wall Street. In a July 1997 interview with *Entrepreneur* magazine, David Gardner explained The Motley Fool perspective. "When we began," he said, "we looked at Wall Street, and what we perceived was a huge world that had gotten rich managing other people's money because people didn't know what to do with their money. There was no incentive for the institutions to teach them. If they taught them, people would stop paying fees. Wall Street has many such conflicts of interest, where its interests are not fully aligned with the customers it is serving. That's why it's both easy and powerful to teach people about investing."

Starting with 60 readers its first day, the forum on AOL quickly flourished, spawning the establishment of the Gardners' own site, www.motleyfool.com (later shortened to www.fool.com). Aside from offering advice and managing the flow of questions and answers on the forum, the Gardners established the "Fool Portfolio," a collection of stocks funded with $50,000 of their own money. Later renamed the "Rule Breaker Portfolio," the assortment of stocks served as the testing ground for the techniques, theories, and strategies explored by the Gardners and the online investment community that was gathering around them. Users—the fellow "Fools" who participated in the forums and frequented the web sites—were invited to watch and learn from the company's own mistakes and successes, an opportunity that an increasing number of investors chose to take.

For their first year as system operators running a forum, the Gardners anticipated annual revenues of $25,000. Their projection was based on their percentage of the $2.95 hourly rate AOL charged visitors to the forum, but the brothers soon found their popularity fueling grander expectations. AOL itself was recording mushrooming growth, its subscriber rolls swelling month by month, and the financial markets were beginning to demonstrate unprecedented vitality, attracting more and more individual investors. Allied to both of these powerfully growing phenomena, The Motley Fool was swept up into the frenzy, feeding the insatiable appetite for up-to-the-minute financial information and stock tips. By mid-1995, the Gardners had added three new forums on AOL, which increased revenue estimates to $1.5

million. The success of the Rule Breaker Portfolio, whose eight stocks were up 22.5 percent by May 1995, led the company to establish additional portfolios that served as case studies for a variety of investing strategies. A half-dozen teach-by-example portfolios were created, bearing titles such as the "Boring Portfolio," which was created in January 1996 to illustrate a more conservative approach to investing.

As the depth of The Motley Fool's online presence increased, so too did the breadth of the Gardners' burgeoning business empire. Through the Internet, the brothers had gained the attention of a large audience of individual investors, which led them to introduce their signature blend of humor and investing advice through a variety of media formats. Beginning in 1996, the brothers began writing books through a partnership with publisher Simon & Schuster. The first book, *The Motley Fool Investment Guide*, became an unmitigated success, ranking as a *New York Times* bestseller. During the next three years, two more books were published, *You Have More Than You Think* and *Rule Breakers, Rule Makers*, both of which were also *New York Times* bestsellers. The Gardners' publishing success spawned the creation of a line of self-published titles released under the Fool Publishing label, representing one facet of the Gardners' smorgasbord of personal finance information.

After the public's embrace of *The Motley Fool Investment Guide*, the Gardners' unique perspective was fed into other media channels. Nationally syndicated weekly newspaper features debuted in 1997, giving The Motley Fool a ubiquitous presence in many of the country's newspapers. Three years after the Gardners began writing weekly columns, more than 170 newspapers across the nation featured the instructive writings of The Motley Fool's editors and analysts. One year later, in 1998, a joint venture with Cox Radio led the way for a nationally syndicated radio show, "The Motley Fool Radio Show," which over the course of the ensuing two years was broadcast every weekend on more than 120 radio stations nationwide. In 1999, the company added yet another tributary to its broadening flow of information and advice, launching *The Motley Fool Monthly* magazine.

The Motley Fool's online activities intensified during the late 1990s as well. The company reached overseas for the first time in 1998, when Motley Fool UK was established. Designed specifically to meet the investment and personal finance needs of the United Kingdom, the site, www.fool.co.uk, was established on AOL UK and found a receptive audience. Visitors to the site reached into the millions within a matter of months, prompting the company to hatch plans for a German site, which was expected to launch in 2000. The Motley Fool also began diversifying as it expanded, including a foray into mortgage services. In 1998, the company announced an agreement with E-Loan, the leading online mortgage marketplace, to provide online mortgage services through a co-branded Mortgage Center. The exclusive two-year agreement provided Fools with access to services such as customized loan recommendations, mortgage quotes, online applications, and rate comparisons, enabling users to electronically shop for the best price among local and national lenders.

A New CEO for the Future

As The Motley Fool prepared for the end of the 1990s and its future in the new century, it did so with a new chief executive

Key Dates:

1994: The Motley Fool forum debuts on America Online.
1996: *The Motley Fool Investment Guide,* the first of a series of books, is published.
1997: Nationally syndicated newspaper columns first appear.
1998: A web site for U.K.-based investors is established.
1999: C. Patrick Garner is hired as chief executive officer.

officer. The company began looking for a new strategic leader in July 1999, hoping to find someone able to steward the company in its new, multifaceted form. The search lasted ten months, ending with the arrival of C. Patrick Garner, a former senior executive with the Coca-Cola Company. Garner boasted three decades of experience at Coca-Cola, figuring as one of the company's leading business and marketing strategists. His arrival at The Motley Fool occurred at a critical juncture in the company's history, taking place just as the country's financial markets were beginning to show less robust signs of growth. The frenetic growth of the 1990s had fueled The Motley Fool's remarkable rise to prominence, but many observers wondered whether the company could continue to proliferate as a brand during a market downturn. Such was the challenge facing Garner as he assumed control over the company in mid-2000, and the early evidence showed that the challenge was daunting.

At roughly the same time Garner began his tenure at The Motley Fool, the company announced the launch of Soapbox.com. Debuting in August 2000, Soapbox.com was an online venue that allowed anyone to post investment research reports for sale. After a promising start, the forum quickly sputtered, failing to realize expectations because, critics contended, the quality of the investment reports was poor. Soapbox.com was shut down in February 2001, its failure just one of the casualties suffered by The Motley Fool that month. The company's attempt to establish a Germany-based operation also was scuttled, ending a year after it began because the company was unable to find a local partner. The most distressing news of the month affected the entire organization, providing a clear signal that the rampant confidence of the 1990s

had begun to wane. The Motley Fool announced it was reducing its staff by one-third because advertising revenue was declining. At the company's Alexandria headquarters, 109 jobs were eliminated as well as another six positions in London. "We're adopting an old economy approach to profitability," a company spokesperson told the *Financial Times* on February 9, 2001.

As The Motley Fool prepared for the future, the events of early 2001 signaled the beginning of a new era for the company. Continued success depended on its ability to thrive amid declining market conditions and ebbing investor enthusiasm, which threatened to drain the company of its remarkable vitality. With Garner plotting the company's next strategic moves, however, The Motley Fool stood well positioned to progress positively through the transition and to remain a prominent fixture in the media.

Principal Subsidiaries

FoolMart.

Principal Competitors

Raging Bull, Inc.; TheStreet.com, Inc.; Yahoo! Inc.

Further Reading

"Brothers Find Fool's Gold Mine," *Tennesseean,* March 2, 1998, p. 1E.

Cohen, Adam, "A Chorus of True Believers," *Time,* June 17, 1996, p. 48.

Graves, Jacqueline M., "All Systems Going Green for Sys-Ops," *Fortune,* May 15, 1995, p. 28.

Harper, Philipp, "A Fool's Paradise," *Forbes ASAP,* February 19, 2001, p. 75.

Jenkins, Patrick, "Motley Fool Sheds a Third of Its Staff," *Financial Times,* February 9, 2001 p. 29.

Keating, Peter, "When Fools Are Bored, Wise Men Should Worry," *Money,* April 1998, p. 31.

McGarvey, Robert, "Only Fools Cash In," *Entrepreneur,* July 1997, p. 110.

"Motley Fool to Launch Soapbox.com," *Financial Net News,* May 8, 2000, p. 7.

—Jeffrey L. Covell

NEWCOR

Newcor, Inc.

1825 S. Woodward Avenue, Suite 240
Bloomfield Hills, Michigan 48302
U.S.A.
Telephone: (248) 253-2400
Fax: (248) 253-2413
Web site: http://www.newcor.com

Public Company
Incorporated: 1933 as National Electric Welding
    Machines Company
Employees: 1,583
Sales: $238.1 million (2000)
Stock Exchanges: AMEX
Ticker Symbol: NER
NAIC: 333298 All Other Motor Vehicle Parts
    Manufacturing; 33518 All Other Industrial Machinery
    Manufacturing

Newcor, Inc., with corporate headquarters located in Bloomfield Hills, Michigan, is a manufacturing company that is organized into three operating groups. Precision Machined Products accounts for 70 percent of Newcor sales, producing shafts, axles, and other large iron and steel castings for the automotive, medium, and heavy-duty truck, and agricultural vehicle industries. The Rubber and Plastic group makes parts, both cosmetic and functional, primarily for automakers. The Special Machines group designs and builds machines for the automotive, appliance, and other industries to perform such manufacturing functions as welding, assembly, forming, heat treating, and testing. After rapid expansion in the mid-1990s, Newcor has incurred heavy debt, which became a burden on the company as it experienced a series of poor financial results. Losses have not only crippled the price of Newcor stock, but have made the company an inviting takeover target.

Newcor's Origins Dating Back to 1933

The making of specialty machines was at the heart of Newcor's heritage. Its direct ancestor was the National Electric Welding Machines Company, incorporated in Michigan in 1933 with a manufacturing facility in Bay City. The company was a welding machine maker for more than 30 years, listed on the American Stock Exchange, and created growth internally, with the exception of the 1946 acquisition of the Smalley-General Company. In 1967 National Electric Welding purchased a Canadian firm, Volta Welders, Ltd. A year later a Delaware corporation was formed to merge with National Electric Welding. On February 14, 1969, the reorganized corporation was named Newcor. Volta Welders would form the basis of Newcor Canada.

The reconstituted Newcor slowly added to its business. In 1972 it ventured overseas, establishing Newcor, N.V., in Belgium. The following year it made an acquisition, paying $1.5 million for the Wilson Automation Company. In 1975 Newcor created Machine Tool Company. Newcor made yet another acquisition in 1977, buying Eonic, Inc., makers of cams and camshafts, at the cost of more than $4 million in cash, plus notes and stock. In 1978 the company founded Newcor Ohio, but closed the unit after just two years. Newcor made a public offering of its stock in 1980 and began trading on the NASDAQ. A year later it bought a controlling interest in Indocomp, followed in 1982 with the $7.1 million acquisition of Dearborn Tool & Machine Corp. In 1985 Newcor continued its strategy of growth through acquisitions by acquiring a 51 percent interest in Arbotech Systems, followed by an 81 percent stake in Rochester Gear, Inc., for which it paid $2 million. Several months later Newcor would purchase the remaining 19 percent of Rochester Gear.

For all its attempts at diversification, which extended the company into seven lines of business, Newcor still relied on the making of specialty machines to provide the lion's share of its revenues, an area that was subject to downturns. With a sputtering economy in the late 1980s, Newcor was forced to retrench. The Belgium operation was liquidated in 1986. Indocomp was liquidated in 1987. The company's stake in Arbotech was sold in 1988. By 1989 Newcor retained the firm of Kidder, Peabody to help it explore the possibility of selling all or part of the company's assets. Late in that year, Newcor entered into discussions with an unnamed suitor about selling off its machine manufacturing group and did not dismiss the possibility of selling the entire company. Early in 1990, however, management announced that it had ended all talks and that it now planned to focus on what it called internal strategies to strengthen the company. Little more than two weeks later, Newcor closed its Canadian operations, citing poor sales of the subsidiary's custom welding and assembly equipment business. The company's other facilities were expected to provide enough capacity to support customer demand.

The 1990 Clean Air Act Amendments Spurring Growth

Far more important to the fortunes of Newcor than any belt-tightening measures were the 1990 Clean Air Act amendments passed in the United States, which created tougher emission and fuel-efficiency standards for vehicles. Newcor was positioned to capitalize on the auto industry's need to increase spending on engines and transmissions. The company began a run of strong growth. Sales jumped from $79.9 million in 1990 to $98.7 million in 1991, with profits increasing from $1.2 million to $5 million. In 1992 Newcor moved to achieve a better balance between its special machine and precision parts businesses by acquiring the Midwest Rubber Co. unit from Sudbury Inc. for approximately $3.2 million. Midwest Rubber manufactured transmission shift boots and seals, as well as healthcare equipment parts.

Prospects in the auto industry continued to look promising for Newcor in 1993. Car manufacturers began ordering new machine-tool equipment in an effort to increase productivity, cut costs, and roll out new products more quickly. Newcor, in turn, was catching the eye of many investors. By 1994, however, the company was suffering another downturn, which management attributed, for the most part, to cost overruns. Almost 60 percent of its business still came from the manufacture of specialty machines and only 40 percent from precision parts. In February 1995, after several consecutive quarters posting poor results, Newcor named W. John Weinhardt as its new president and chief executive officer.

To help move the company from what he called slow- to no-growth businesses to more stable businesses, Weinhardt added to Newcor's Rubber and Plastics group, augmenting Midwest Rubber with the purchase of three separate companies: Boramco, Production Rubber Products, and Rubright Industries. The total cost of these acquisitions was approximately $11.6 million. The deals were finalized by early 1996. Shortly thereafter, Newcor sold the Wilson Automation division to ABB Flexible Automation. To further narrow the focus of Newcor, Weinhardt then announced that he was looking to sell

off the company's Machine Tool and Eonic divisions, which he characterized as stand-alone businesses that provided little synergy with Newcor's other interests. In October 1996, he sold the Machine Tool operation, and several months later divested Newcor of its Eonic division. In the meantime, Weinhardt added to the Rubber Plastics business by purchasing for approximately $8 million Plastronics, Inc., a Wisconsin company with $16 million in annual sales. In essence, Newcor sold off half its sales base, which it replaced through acquisitions. Now 80 percent of Newcor sales came from components, and Weinhardt was predicting that the company could top $300 million in annual sales by the end of the century. He also was talking about even further acquisitions, an ambitious plan given that the company had lost money in 1994 and 1996 and posted a meager profit of $900,000 in 1995. The company would realize record sales of $130.8 million in 1997 and net income of $3.9 million, but Newcor had not shown strong results for a long enough period of time to justify Weinhardt's optimism.

Nevertheless, late in 1997 Newcor closed on a deal to acquire Machine Tool & Gear Inc., makers of pinion and side gears, output shafts, and rear-axle shafts for auto manufacturers. It also signed an agreement to purchase the Deco Group, which made precision components for cars and trucks. Then early in 1998 Newcor signed an agreement to purchase Turn-Matic Inc., maker of such automotive parts and components as oil-filter adapters, main-bearing caps, and intake and exhaust manifolds. For the quarter ending on January 31, Newcor announced that it would lose more than $1 million, but Weinhardt maintained that a poor first quarter would not have a long-term impact on the results for the year, once all the recent acquisitions had been digested.

Wall Street investors, however, were not as enthusiastic about Newcor as was Weinhardt. The company had incurred heavy debt in acquiring its new acquisitions. As a result, the price of Newcor stock was soft. Its average price in 1994, the year before Weinhardt shifted the company away from specialty machines, was $9.20. During the first six months of 1998 Newcor stock averaged $9.06, and on July 13 dipped to $7.81. Weinhardt insisted that the stock was undervalued and predicted that the company would still post record sales of $250 million by the end of the year, despite a strike at General Motors, one of Newcor's major customers.

Naming Keith Hale President and CEO in 1998

Newcor failed to meet Weinhardt's expectations. Losses mounted over the final two quarters of 1998 and the price of Newcor stock fell accordingly. It dropped to the $4 range by October and reached a low of $3.38 on December 2. But by that time Weinhardt was out. According to a company press release, he left "to pursue other interests." Named to replace him as president and CEO was Keith Hale, who had served as general manager at Deco International before it had been acquired by Newcor. The 58-year-old Hale had originally planned to retire from business, but opted to take the Newcor position after he was approached by the company's board.

Hale quickly set about establishing credibility for Newcor. He admitted in an interview, "Our stock has not performed well for investors. We have not delivered to our bottom line the last several months, and we have no choice but to turn that around.

Key Dates:

1933: National Electric Welding Machines Company is incorporated in Michigan.
1969: Company is renamed Newcor, Inc.
1990: U.S. Clean Air amendments trigger company growth.
1995: W. John Weinhardt is named president and CEO.
1998: Keith Hale replaces Weinhardt.
2000: Poor health forces Hale to step down.

. . . It is not, however, anything that isn't fixable.'' Some of the changes Hale instituted were minor, such as moving the end of the company's fiscal year from October 31 to the calendar year ending on December 31. More significantly, he closed a rubber and plastics plant located in Auburn Hills and replaced the head of the Machine Tool & Gear group. Furthermore, he looked to expand sales to Europe and to investigate ways to consolidate and cut costs.

By March 1999 Hale was initiating additional efforts to revitalize Newcor. He announced that the company would invest $7 million to expand production capabilities in the Metals group to support new business that had been captured in the first six weeks of the year. He further announced a stock repurchase plan that would not only acquire shares for a stock option program but also demonstrate that the company had confidence in itself. After Newcor lost $1.15 million in 1998, Hale struck an optimistic note about prospects for 1999, projecting $275 million in sales and a net profit. He also hoped to see Newcor stock trading in the $8 range. In June, as part of an effort to consolidate operations, Hale decided to close the Livonia plant that Newcor had acquired just two years earlier in the Production Rubber Products transaction. The company also elected to trade its stock on the American Stock Exchange instead of the more volatile NASDAQ. Financial analysts, however, remained skeptical about Hale's moves. Wall Street at the time preferred the stock of automakers over auto suppliers, and money managers favored much larger companies than Newcor. By midyear, Newcor stock still traded below $5. Unfortunately for Hale, he also suffered health problems that led to surgery in 1999. His recovery hindered his effectiveness during a crucial period for Newcor.

In late September 1999, Hale was forced to admit that the company would not be able to meet expectations for the year. Investor response was swift and harsh. The price of Newcor stock reached its lowest point since the company went public in 1980, plunging on October 19 to a low of $1.44 a share. For the year, Newcor would lose $11.6 million, despite posting record sales of $258.5 million. Although the bottom line was weak, the company clearly was generating business, leading many to speculate that with its depressed stock price Newcor might make an attractive acquisition target.

Exx Inc., a Las Vegas-based holding company, began to acquire shares of Newcor stock. On October 18 it bought 50,000 shares at $1.50 each, and another 250,000 the next day when Newcor stock reached its nadir of $1.44. Exx bought 272,000 shares on October 20. Then flying under the radar, Exx acquired stock in much smaller blocks, ranging from 900 to 2,000. By January 2000 it had accumulated 13.25 percent, or 652,200 shares, of Newcor, with Exx's chairman and CEO, David Segal, owning an additional 24,000 shares. Exx described itself as a company that specialized in turning around depressed businesses. Among its varied interests were an electronics division that made wiring for the telecommunications business and motors for vending machine and floor cleaners; toy manufacturers Handi Pac and Harry Gordy International, holders of the license to make products based on the children's television show the *Power Rangers*; and Hi-Flier Manufacturing Co., a kite maker.

Newcor responded to a potential takeover by instituting what it called a "shareholders rights plan" and Exx deemed a "poison pill." A further deterrent was contained in a bond indenture agreement that would require the immediate repayment of $125 million in debt if any party amassed 35 percent of Newcor's outstanding stock—a provision that would add substantially to the purchase price. Moreover, once a party obtained as little as 10 percent of Newcor's stock, the company's board could trigger its unspecified shareholders rights plan if it judged that the investor was "seeking short-term financial gain which would not serve the long-term interests of the company." Although Segal and Exx controlled more than the necessary level of stock, Newcor's board held off, awaiting developments.

In April 2000, Hale resigned because of continuing health problems. He was replaced on an interim basis by James J. Connor, who Hale had brought in to serve as the company's chief financial officer and who had served earlier as acting president for six months following Hale's surgery. By the end of the month Exx finally formally declared its intentions by making a proposal that would essentially purchase Newcor at a price of $4 per share. Exx maintained that it had sought to negotiate a mutually acceptable transaction with Newcor's board of directors but never received a meaningful response. While urging shareholders to take no action until the unsolicited offer was reviewed, Newcor management was clearly under the gun. Exx increased its stake to 15 percent, publicly urged the board not to activate its poison pill provision, and pleaded its case for representation on the board, pointing out that Exx now held more stock in Newcor than all of its officers and directors combined. In August, Exx proposed that it purchase newly issued shares of Newcor stock, which would increase its stake to almost 35 percent, and then acquire effective control of Newcor, by having Segal become chairman and CEO and by gaining control of three board seats. The offer was rejected. A few days later, Exx withdrew its original $4 per share offer, citing the board's refusal to negotiate or withdraw its poison pill measure. Segal did not dismiss the possibility, however, that Exx might continue to purchase additional shares of Newcor stock in the open market.

As the Newcor board removed the interim title to make Connor its president and CEO in August 2000, the company continued to struggle. It announced that it would shut down the Turn-Matic plant, laying off its 75 workers. Year-end results were also disappointing, with another net loss anticipated. By February 2001 the Newcor board finally compromised with Segal and Exx, which now owned 17.5 percent of the company's stock. Segal, plus a director to be nominated by Exx, would be added to the board, which would increase in size from seven to nine. Newcor also would amend its shareholders rights plan to allow Exx to increase its ownership stake to 23.5 percent by December 31, 2001; 25.5 percent by December 31, 2003; 27.5 percent by December 31, 2004; and 30 percent thereafter. In turn, Exx agreed to forgo any proxy contest through December 31, 2004. With so many variables in its operations and management, the prospects for Newcor would remain uncertain for the foreseeable future.

Principal Subsidiaries

Rochester Gear, Inc.; Plastronics Plus, Inc.; Deco Technologies; Deco International, Inc.; Turn-Matic, Inc.

Principal Operating Units

Rubber and Plastic; Special Machines; Precision Machined Products.

Principal Competitors

Allied Devices; BFGoodrich Company; Dana Corporation; Delphi Automotive Systems; Eaton Corporation; GKN Sinter Metals; Twin Disc, Inc.

Further Reading

Lauzon, Michael, "Newcor Buys Auto Parts Molder," *Plastic News,* January 20, 1997, p. 3.

McCracken, Jeffrey, "Bumpy Ride for Newcor," *Crain's Detroit Business,* October 18, 1999, p. 2.

——, "In Line for a Takeover? Las Vegas Company Buying Stock in Newcor," *Crain's Detroit Business,* January 3, 2000, p. 2.

——, "Newcor Doubling Size, Shifting Gears," *Crain's Detroit Business,* January 26, 1998, p. 3.

——, "New Core of Newcor: CEO Plans Plant Closing and Other Changes," *Crain's Detroit Business,* December 21, 1998, p. 2.

——, "New Newcor Stock Lags," *Crain's Detroit Business,* July 20, 1998, p. 2.

Serwach, Joseph, "Newcor Sheds 3rd Unit, Buys 4th Firm, Sees Revised Growth," *Crain's Detroit Business,* March 17, 1997, p. 22.

——, "Newcor to Sell 2 Divisions, Acquire 2 Firms," *Crain's Detroit Business,* June 24, 1996, p. 3.

—Ed Dinger

Nordea AB

Hamngatan 10
SE-10571 Stockholm
Sweden
Telephone: (+46) 8-614-7000
Fax: (+46) 8-105-069
Web site: http://www.meritanordbanken.com

Public Company
Incorporated: 1997 as Nordic Baltic Holding
Employees: 19,300
Sales: EUR 5.89 billion ($5.6 billion) (2000)
Stock Exchanges: Stockholm Helsinki Oslo
Ticker Symbol: NBH
NAIC: 522320 Financial Transactions Processing,
    Reserve, and Clearinghouse Activities; 551111 Offices
    of Bank Holding Companies; 523110 Investment
    Banking and Securities Dealing; 522110 Commercial
    Banking; 522120 Savings Institutions

First off the starting block among pan-European banking mergers—a trend expected to boom in the early years of the 21st century—Nordea AB has created Scandinavia's largest bank, with primary operations in Sweden, Denmark, and Finland, as well as subsidiaries in Estonia, Latvia, Lithuania, and Poland. Nordea's main subsidiaries are MeritaNordbanken in Sweden and Finland, Unibank in Denmark, and Christiana Bank og Kredietklasse in Norway. One of Nordea's fastest-growing brands, however, has bypassed the national route altogether and has hitched the parent holding company to the Internet. Solo, Nordea's Internet-banking business, is the world's leading Internet banking service, with more than two million active customers consulting the company's range of Internet-based services, which include its Solo Market, a network of some 1,000 online stores allowing secure online payment directly from the Solo web site. Nordea's total customer base of nine million private customers and 700,000 corporate clients, including such global heavyweights as Nokia and Eriksson, combine to give the company 40 percent of the Finnish banking market, 25 percent of the Danish banking market,

20 percent of Sweden's banking sector, and 15 percent of the market in Norway. The company holds similarly strong positions in the Scandinavian life insurance markets. The company claims more than EUR 230 billion in assets in 2001. Formed through a long series of mergers, the immediate predecessor to Nordea was the 1997 Nordic Baltic Holding merger between Merita and Nordbanken. The additions of Christiana Bank and Unibank in 1999 extended the bank across most of Scandinavia. At the beginning of 2001, the bank adopted the new Nordea name—standing for "Nordic Ideas"—while keeping its existing bank brands. Nordea is traded on the Stockholm, Helsinki, and Oslo stock exchanges.

A Trail of Bank Mergers into the 20th Century

The formation of Nordea at the beginning of the 21st century was the result of a long series of mergers through more than 150 years of Scandinavian banking history. Each of the major banks that made up the first pan-Scandinavian—and one of the first pan-European banks—traced their histories to the 19th century and the beginnings of the modern Scandinavian banking industry. Many of the components that created the future Nordea group had also been operated as government-owned banking institutions.

Sweden's Nordbanken alone represented more than 170 years of banking history and the product of the mergers of some 80 separate banks. The oldest of the Nordbanken banks was Wermlandsbanken, founded in 1832. Another early Swedish bank was Smålands Bank, founded in 1837. In 1848, a group of merchants in Gothenburg founded their own bank, Göteborgs Privat Bank. Like Wermlandsbanken and Smålands Bank, this youngest bank operated primarily on local and regional levels.

The mid-19th century saw the formation of a number of other banks. In 1864, the Sundsvallsbanken was created and quickly became the primary financial institution for Sweden's forestry industry. Skaragborgsbanken, founded in 1865, captured that local market; the same year saw the formation of Uplandsbanken.

The first mergers among Sweden's banking industries began to appear toward the end of that century. Among these were the

Company Perspectives:

Vision: We shall be valued as the leading financial services group in the Nordic and Baltic financial markets with a substantial growth potential. Ambition: We shall be number one or number two or show superior and profitable growth in every market and product area in which we choose to compete. We shall have the leading multichannel distribution with a top world ranking in e-based financial solutions. Mission: We help customers fulfil their aspirations. By creating value for our customers we create value for shareholders. We offer opportunities that enable us to keep, develop and attract employees with the highest competence and talents.

mergers of Göteborgs Privat Bank with Stockholm's Enskilda Bank, which in 1898 merged with another Stockholm-based bank, Diskontobank. This step also marked an increasing tendency of the country's largely locally and regionally based banks to begin consolidating towards a more nationally focused market.

Another piece of the puzzle that was to become Nordbanken was the creation of Lantmannabanken in 1917. This bank was formed specifically to focus on Sweden's agricultural market. After a financial collapse in 1923, Lantmannabanken was restructured as Jordbrukarbanken and placed under the Swedish government's control—becoming the country's first state-owned bank. This bank was subsequently renamed Sveriges Kreditbank, underlying its national character.

The formation of the predecessor to Sveriges Kreditbank was accompanied in the private sphere by a series of mergers that transformed Uplandsbanken into a major nationally operating bank. That bank merged with Sundsvall Handelsbank in 1917, then with both Gefleborgs Folkbank and Hudiksvalls Kredibank in 1920. The newly enlarged bank became known as Uplandsbanken. Meanwhile, the Göteborgs bank was also growing, acquiring Kopparsbergs Enskilda Bank in 1922.

This same period had seen similar activity in Finland, leading toward the creation of Merita Bank in the mid-1990s. Finland's first commercial bank was formed in 1862 operating under the name of Suomen Yhdyspankki. Where Sweden's banks remained largely local and regional, however, the new Finnish bank established national operations from the outset. The bank gained new competition in 1889, when Kansallis-Osake-Pankki was founded. The two banks remained limited to commercial and corporate banking until after World War II, when both banks established private customer services. In the meantime, the Suomen Yhdyspankki bank, renamed Pihjoismaiden Yhdyspankki after a merger in 1919, had become one of the country's leading commercial banks.

In Norway, meanwhile, Christiania Bank had followed a steadier course than its Scandinavian neighbors. Formed in 1848 in what was then known as Christiania—before the Norwegian capital city's name was changed to Oslo—the bank was originally known as Christiania Kredietklasses, before changing its name to Christiania Bank og Kredietklasse in 1851.

Lastly, in Denmark, Privatbanken had been founded in 1857 and grew to become that country's largest bank. Led by Danish financial baron CF Tietgen, who had been behind such large-scale Danish companies as Tuborg, DFDS, the Great Northern Telegraph Company, and De Danske Spritfabrikker, Privatbanken faced competition from other nationally operating rivals. These included Andelsbanken, founded in 1925 and which had its origins among the country's agricultural community before investing in Denmark's manufacturing industry. Another large-scale Danish bank was SDS Bank, which represented the grouping of many of the country's local and regional banks.

National Mergers in the 1970s

The formation of the European Community led to increasing consolidation among Scandinavia's banking communities in the 1970s. Each national market saw the mergers of many of their major players to create more powerful nationally operating banks with more capacity to compete on an international level, and to compete against other international banks which were by then making strong inroads in their domestic markets. The process of consolidation created a small number of dominant players in each of the Scandinavian markets, including Nordbanken, Unidanmark, Merita, and Christiania Bank og Kredietklasse—the major components of the future Nordea.

Consolidation in Sweden began in earnest in 1972 with the merger of Göteborgs Bank with Smalandsbanken, forming Götabanken. Two years later, Sveriges Kreditbank merged with another state-owned bank, Postbanken, operated by the country's postal system. That merger created Post-och Kredietbanken, or PKBanken, then the largest bank in Sweden. That bank was to sink to third place, behind SE Banken and Svenska Handelsbanken, after the recession of the early 1980s. Teaming up with Oslo's Christiania Bank og Kredietklasse, however, PKBanken began its first international operations, opening joint-venture locations in Asia, the United States, the United Kingdom, and Brazil. After the Swedish government placed PKBanken on the Stockholm stock exchange, the bank ended its association with Christiania Bank to focus again on the national market. PKBanken made two major acquisitions at the end of the 1980s, those of Sveriges Investeringsbank, founded by the Swedish government in 1967, and another state-owned body, the Carnegie Fondkommision brokerage house, acquired in 1988.

The Nordbanken name first appeared in the mid-1980s, with the merger of Sundsvallsbanken and Uplandsbanken in 1986. When PKBanken acquired regionally focused Nordbanken in 1990, the latter name was maintained for the whole of the newly merged bank. That same year saw the creation of Göta Bank, formed through the combination of Götabanken, Wermlandsbanken, and Skaraborgsbanken. Nordbanken then acquired Göta Bank in 1993. By then, however, Nordbanken had once again come under full control of the Swedish government, which had been forced to rescue the bank from its financial collapse in 1992. Crippled by the global recession and the bottoming out of the country's real estate market, Nordbanken underwent replacement of its management, the sale of its bad debt portfolio to the Swedish government, and a reduction of its staff by some 20 percent.

By 1995, Nordbanken once again took a public listing on the Stockholm exchange as the government reduced its ownership

Key Dates:

1972: Merger of Göteborgs Bank with Smalandsbanken forms Götabanken.
1974: Sveriges Kreditbank merges with Postbanken to form PKBanken.
1975: Phjoismaiden Yhydspankki changes name to Union Bank of Finland.
1984: PKBanken is listed on Stockholm stock exchange.
1986: Union Bank of Finland merges with Bank of Helsinki; Sundsvallsbanken and Uplandsbanken merger forms Nordbanken.
1988: PKBanken acquires Carnegie Fondkommision.
1989: PKBanken acquires Sveriges Investeringsbank.
1990: Unibank is formed; PKBanken acquires Nordbanken, adopts Nordbanken name; Gota Bank is created.
1993: Nordbanken acquires Gota Bank
1995: Union Bank of Finland merges with Kansallis-Osake-Pankki to form Merita Bank
1997: Nordbanken and Merita merge to form Nordic Baltic Holding.
2000: Unibank and Christiania Bank og Kredietklasse join Nordic Baltic Holding; company changes name to Nordea AB.

position. Meanwhile, its Finnish neighbors were also undergoing a consolidation process. Phjoismaiden Yhydspankki, which had begun expanding internationally, anglicized its name to Union Bank of Finland in 1975. The bank had also begun to pioneer the use of electronic banking systems during that decade. In 1986, Union Bank of Finland was boosted by the merger with Bank of Helsinki, then the country's third largest bank. The recession of the early 1990s forced the breakup of another leading Finnish bank, Suomen Säästöpannki (Savings Bank of Finland), in 1993, with Union Bank and Kansallis-Osake-Pankki each taking a share of that bank's operations. By then, Kansallis-Osake-Pankki had grown through the 1992 merger with Suomen Työväen Säästöpannki, the savings bank operated by the Finnish labor movement. Three years later, Union Bank of Finland, through its holding company Unitas Ltd., was merged with Kansallis-Osake-Pankki, creating Merita Bank.

In Norway, Christiania Bank had grown through mergers with Andresens Bank in 1980 and Fiskernes Bank in 1983. Hit hard by the recession of the early 1990s, Christiania was rescued by the Norwegian government, which became the bank's sole shareholder. By the late 1990s, however, the Norwegian government had placed the bank back on the public market, reducing its holdings to just 35 percent by the end of the decade.

The recession had also brought losses to Denmark's Unibank. That bank had only been formed in 1990, merging the operations of Andelbanken, SDS Bank, and Privatbanken. Recovering from the crisis, Unibank strengthened its investment banking wing in 1996, when it established Aros Securities in a merger between its own equity business and the international investment operations of the ABB Group. That company be-

came Fleming Aros in 1998 in another joint venture, which was ended after Unibank's entry into Nordea.

Unidanmark, parent company of Unibank, merged with the largest Danish insurance company, Tryg-Baltica, to create an enlarged financial services company. Unibank next looked toward Sweden, where it bought up a controlling share of Trevise AB, an asset management business. Unibank then converted Trevise into a full-fledged private bank operation with offices in Sweden and Finland. Unibank also moved into Norway, acquiring that country's Vesta, making Unibank one of Scandinavia's leading insurance companies.

Cross-Border Mergers for the 21st Century

Unibank's moves across Scandinavia represented the first of several sudden consolidations within the Scandinavian banking industry. Sharing similar and often intertwined histories, the Scandinavian countries were seen as good matches for partnerships. The coming of the single European currency spelled the dawn of a new era for the European banking industry as a whole, which had remained largely centered on domestic markets. While the banking industries in most of the European Community countries concentrated on consolidating their domestic markets—a process that remained largely unfinished at the turn of the century, the Scandinavian markets, which had already undergone national consolidation efforts, were able to look beyond their borders for future growth.

Nordbanken and Merita were also among the first and largest to surf the new wave of cross-border mergers. The two banks merged in 1997, forming MeritaNordbanken. An important product brought to the new bank was its Solo Internet-based banking operation, which was fast on its way toward becoming one of the world's leading online banking services. That name soon proved too tight a fit as the newly enlarged banking group looked across Scandinavia for other potential partners. The next member joined in March 2000, when Unidanmark agreed to merge with MeritaNordbanken in a deal valued at $4 billion.

The new company, which took on the larger name of Nordic Baltic Holding in order to contain its continuing Nordbanken, Merita, and Unibank banking and financial services brands, soon added to its scope. At the end of December 2000, Christiania Bank og Kredietklasse became part of the leading financial services company in Scandinavia, a process begun in September 1999. By the time Christiania was added, Nordic Baltic Holding had chosen a new name for itself. The bank was now to be known as Nordea, a name built from the words ''Nordic'' and ''Idea,'' suggesting the bank's willingness to extend its success beyond its Scandinavian base to the global scale.

While Nordea pledged to continue operating under its national brands, the company nonetheless moved to the integration of its operations to create a single, pan-Scandinavian brand. One such move toward this end was the renaming of the former Unibank's Aros investment banking unit as Nordea Securities in April 2001. As analysts forecast a coming wave of cross-border banking mergers in a rapidly consolidating European industry, Nordea appeared in a prime position to take a leading place in the world banking market in the new century.

Principal Subsidiaries

Nordea Companies (Finland) (NCF); Nordea Companies (Denmark) (NCD); Christiania Bank og Kredietklasse (Norway); Merita Bank (Finland), Nordbanken, Unibank (Denmark); Bank Komunalny (Poland); NB Industrikredit; Merita Finance (Finland); Nordea Finance (Latvia); (Latvia); Nordea Finance Lit (Lithuania); Nordbanken Finans; Norgeskreditt (Norway); K-Finans (Norway); Unifactoring (Denmark); Unifinans (Denmark); Unikredit Realkreditaktieselskab (Denmark); Unileasing (Denmark); Christiania Forsikring (Norway); Fondforsikring (Norway); Livsförsäkring AB Livia; Livia II; Merita Life Assurance (Finland); Norske Liv (Norway); Tryg-Baltica (Denmark); Vesta Forsikring (Norway); K-Fondene (Norway); K-Kapitalförvaltning (Norway); Merita Asset Management (Finland); Merita Fund Management (Finland); Nordbanken Kapitalförvaltning; Nordea Securitiesz.

Principal Competitors

Den Danska Bank; SE Banken; Svenska Handelsbanken; Swedbank.

Further Reading

Brown-Humes, "Nordea Plans Online Boost," *Financial Times*, February 22, 2001.

"E*Europe: Bank Leads by a Click over Mortar," *Time International*, May 1, 2000, p. 54.

"Merita, Nordbanken Merge, Want Others to Join," *Reuters Business Report*, October 13, 1997.

"Scandinavian Models," *Economist*, May 20, 2000.

Wallace, Charles P., "Admire Our Busy Signal," *Time*, June 19, 2000, p. B22.

—M. L. Cohen

NPC International, Inc.

720 West 20th Street
Pittsburg, Kansas 66762
U.S.A.
Telephone: (316) 231-3390
Fax: (316) 231-5115
Web site: http://www.npcinternational.com

Public Company
Incorporated: 1974 as Southeast Pizza Huts, Inc.
Employees: 15,200
Sales: $455.62 million (2000)
Stock Exchanges: NASDAQ
Ticker Symbol: NPCI
NAIC: 72211 Full-Service Restaurants

NPC International, Inc. is the largest franchisee of Pizza Hut restaurants, operating roughly 12 percent of all of the Pizza Hut restaurants in existence. NPC International controls approximately 850 Pizza Hut restaurants in 27 states, but the company has reached an agreement with its franchisor, Pizza Hut, Inc., to operate as many as 1,300 Pizza Hut units. Formerly the owner of the Skipper's seafood chain and the Tony Roma's barbecue rib chain, NPC International is focused exclusively on maintaining and expanding its network of Pizza Hut restaurants.

Origins

When two brothers from Wichita, Kansas, opened a pizza parlor in 1958, the concept that drove NPC International's growth was born. Frank and Dan Carney borrowed $600 from their mother to open their first restaurant, a small, brick pizza parlor they named Pizza Hut. A year later, the first Pizza Hut franchise opened in Topeka, Kansas, marking the birth of a franchise system that 12 years later would help make Pizza Hut the largest pizza restaurant chain in the world. Not long after this period of frenetic growth began, O. Gene Bicknell joined the Pizza Hut franchise network, opening his first Pizza Hut in Pittsburg, Kansas, in 1962. Bicknell's restaurant, for which he paid $75 per month in rent, represented the first unit of what would become the largest Pizza Hut franchise in the system, Bicknell's NPC International, Inc.

The Carneys' Pizza Hut, Inc. (PHI) expanded at a dizzying pace during the 1960s. Bicknell shared in the chain's success by aggressively expanding his own fiefdom of Pizza Hut franchises, which primarily included rural areas in the southeastern United States. Bicknell succeeded by keeping close attention to costs and maximizing the profit margins recorded by his string of restaurants. In 1974, he incorporated his Pizza Hut operations as Southeast Pizza Huts, Inc. and continued to expand. Bicknell acquired Pizza Hut franchises that were performing poorly and applied his cost-cutting measures to transform the underperforming units into profit-generating outlets. In 1977, the year the 3,000th Pizza Hut unit opened, PHI was acquired by soft drink conglomerate PepsiCo, Inc., whose vast financial resources fueled the expansion of the Pizza Hut chain. Bicknell, who paid a franchising fee to his new franchisor, PepsiCo, expanded his portfolio of Pizza Hut properties as well, but to fulfill his ambitious growth plans he needed capital. In 1984, he took his company public, renaming it National Pizza Company, the direct predecessor to NPC International.

By the time of National's debut as a publicly traded company, Bicknell had 94 Pizza Huts in operation and was collecting more than $35 million in annual sales. His territory of operation covered nine states, but as the name of his new company suggested, Bicknell aimed for a broader geographic presence. National's initial public offering (IPO) of stock provided the capital to finance a greatly accelerated expansion program. By the end of the decade, less than six years after its IPO, National ranked as the largest Pizza Hut franchisee, presiding over more than 320 units and collecting more than $113 million in sales. The enormous growth had been achieved through the development of franchise territories and the acquisition of units from other franchisees, a mode of expansion that Bicknell wanted to continue to employ. His policy of targeting underperforming Pizza Hut franchises and reversing their fortunes was fueling rapid growth, but during the late 1980s his growth strategy collided against a formidable obstacle. Bicknell found himself butting heads against the power and might of PepsiCo.

As Bicknell rapidly expanded the size of National, PepsiCo, through PHI, pursued a similar plan of attack. Both PHI and National were pushing forward with growth-through-acquisition strategies, but in their respective races to capture a larger portion of the country's pizza market, PHI enjoyed considerable advantages over National. Pizza Hut franchisees were bound by their licensing agreements to offer their businesses to PHI before selling to another party. Bicknell was intent on maintaining his rapid expansion pace into the 1990s, but PHI possessed the right of first refusal. Bicknell could only obtain a Pizza Hut franchise after PHI had decided against acquiring the property for itself, leaving Bicknell to pick over the least desirable acquisition candidates. With increasing frequency during the late 1980s, PHI was exercising its right of first refusal, which forced Bicknell to look outside the Pizza Hut system for the vehicle to satisfy his desire for growth. "National wasn't going to sit back and let Pepsi steal all their deals," a restaurant analyst was quoted as saying in the February 13, 1989 issue of *Nation's Restaurant News*.

1989 Acquisition of Skipper's

Forced to look elsewhere, Bicknell set his sights on Skipper's, a quick-service, fish-and-chips chain based in Bellevue, Washington. The process of acquiring Skipper's proved difficult. Initially, PepsiCo disapproved of Bicknell's foray outside the Pizza Hut system, citing another right of the franchisor to preclude a franchisee from owning any businesses other than Pizza Hut franchises. After nearly a year, officials at PepsiCo relented to the arguments presented on behalf of National, but the struggle to acquire Skipper's did not end there. In 1988, Bicknell offered Skipper's management $24.5 million in cash for the 214-unit chain, but Skipper's officials said the price was too low. Eventually, in November 1989, Bicknell prevailed, paying $31.2 million for the $120-million-in-sales company.

At the time, Skipper's was losing money, but National's management had its growth vehicle in its possession. Officials stated that it would likely require a 12- to 18-month period before Skipper's could achieve profitability, but after that hurdle was cleared, the company's plans were bold. Bicknell was aiming to take the 214-unit regional chain concentrated in the Pacific Northwest and turn it into a 700-unit national fast-food chain. Not long after Skipper's became part of the National fold, the euphoria pervading the company's headquarters evaporated. Disappointment set in, and the dark mood would endure for years.

By mid-1991, National had reached the point at which Skipper's was projected to begin delivering profits. The profits had not materialized. Expectations for profitability had been quashed by a 40 percent increase in the price of pollock, the primary fish used by Skipper's, which severely eroded the chain's profit margins. Frustrated National managers announced it would be another 18 months before Skipper's could begin delivering its expected results. Meanwhile, the company's chain of Pizza Huts continued to expand, albeit at a slower pace than Bicknell and his colleagues desired. National

controlled 366 Pizza Hut restaurants by mid-1991, but their performance was being diluted by the lackluster Skipper's chain. Considerable attention was devoted to injecting Skipper's with the vitality that would enable Bicknell to actualize his expansion plans. By the end of 1991, company executives believed they had found an answer.

In January 1992, a new breed of Skipper's restaurants made its debut. Instead of trying to resurrect the fish-and-chips chain as a volume producer, the company created a more upscale version called Skipper's Seafood Broiler. Offering a new menu that eschewed Skipper's traditional fried food items, the new restaurants featured higher-priced, broiled seafood items. Nearly twice the size of traditional Skipper's units, the Seafood Broiler restaurants replaced the chain's nautical-themed interior design with a more modern design, and included drive-through service and banquet rooms. Concurrently, as preparations were made to establish 30 Seafood Broilers by April 1992, National began shuttering unprofitable stores, hoping the elimination of poorly performing units coupled with a new higher-priced, higher-profit-margin approach to its seafood business would at last cure the chain's ills. Another year passed, and, to Bicknell's chagrin, there were no great signs of improvement.

The move toward a more upscale concept failed to deliver expected results. Customers balked at the high prices of a Seafood Broiler meal, and the company was forced to spend mid-1992 trying to recapture lost customers by offering discounts and coupons. By 1993, three years after acquiring Skipper's, National had fallen far short of greatly expanding the Skipper's chain. The size of the chain was essentially the same as three years earlier, while meaningful profitability remained elusive. The company began experimenting with an English recipe in 1993, taking a back-to-basics approach to stimulating growth, but few outside observers expressed any belief that a return to lower-priced, fried fish would lead to a dramatic turnaround. One restaurant analyst, as quoted in the May 21, 1993 issue of the *Puget Sound Business Journal*, offered his perspective. "They have been trying to find a formula that will work and so far they haven't produced the profit results. Should they go for the value price with volume or go for the high-quality food and service and get margins? They've been flip-flopping back and forth on that. They don't really know what package is going to work best."

1993 Acquisition of Tony Roma's

As the search for a solution dragged on, National executives pinned their hopes on a new expansion vehicle. In May 1993, the company announced its intention to acquire Tony Roma's, A Place for Ribs Inc. Unlike the Skipper's acquisition, PepsiCo officials offered little resistance to National's desire to purchase Tony Roma's, approving the transaction within 24 hours of learning of Bicknell's intentions. Based in Dallas, Tony Roma's was a privately owned rib and barbecue chain with 27 company-owned restaurants and 114 franchises. National paid $20 million for the chain, completing the acquisition in June 1993. The addition of Tony Roma's marked National's entry into the casual-theme restaurant business and, perhaps more importantly, imbued National's headquarters with a renewed spirit of optimism. In the coming years, the expansion of Tony Roma's was expected to fuel National's growth, while plans for Skipper's development were put on hold until profitability was achieved.

Key Dates:

1962: Bicknell opens his first Pizza Hut franchise.
1974: Southeast Pizza Huts, Inc. is incorporated.
1984: The firm, renamed National Pizza Company, debuts as a publicly traded corporation.
1989: National Pizza acquires the Skipper's seafood chain.
1993: Tony Roma's is acquired.
1994: National Pizza is renamed NPC International.
1996: Skipper's is sold.
1998: NPC International reorganizes, assuming only a minority interest in Tony Roma's.

A new corporate title was adopted by National roughly a year after the Tony Roma's acquisition. In acknowledgment of its diversified composition, the company changed its name to NPC International, Inc. in July 1994, but it would lose some of its diversity in the coming years. Skipper's continued to chip away at NPC International's earnings in the wake of the Tony Roma's acquisition. In the company's fourth fiscal quarter ending March 1995, officials announced that the company was incurring a $35 million charge to cover the cost of the closing of as many as 95 Skipper's outlets. By the end of the company's next fiscal year, it had decided to abandon the business altogether. After more than five years of frustration, NPC International divested its problematic quick-service seafood chain in March 1996, enabling it to focus more of its resources on the development of the Tony Roma's chain.

During its first three years of NPC International ownership, Tony Roma's expanded and launched a new prototype, as NPC International experimented with the casual-theme concept. In 1995, a $1.9 million prototype was opened in Grapevine, Texas, as part of NPC International's attempt to attract younger customers and to strike more of a balance between male and female customers. The prototype featured multilevel dining rooms, a visible kitchen, and a menu with 19 new items. Instead of focusing primarily on barbecue ribs, the menu offered salads, seafood, and steaks. Tony Roma's vice-president of marketing explained the reasoning behind the changes in an April 8, 1996 interview with *Nation's Restaurant News.* "We certainly want to increase the frequency and give the customers a chance to make this a regular stop rather than one time a year for Uncle Harry's birthday."

Late 1990s: A Company Strictly Focused on Pizza

As NPC International entered the late 1990s, it again altered its strategic course. The company expanded Tony Roma's to more than 190 restaurants and increased its annual revenue volume to more than $350 million before deciding to assume a far less active role in its development. In June 1998, NPC International teamed with a private equity firm named Sentinel Capital Partners to execute a recapitalization of Tony Roma's. The move left NPC International with only a minority stake in the restaurant chain, leaving it free to devote all of its human and financial resources toward the growth of its chain of Pizza Huts.

As part of a massive restructuring program, PepsiCo spun off its restaurant holdings in 1997, including PHI. TRICON

Global Restaurants, Inc., formerly a subsidiary of PepsiCo, became the new parent company of PHI and, as a consequence of the spinoff, inherited a considerable amount of debt from PepsiCo. To reduce its debt, TRICON began selling operations to its franchisees, adopting a strategy that dovetailed with Bicknell's desire to expand his Pizza Hut system.

Held in check for years, NPC International began acquiring Pizza Hut units in earnest during the late 1990s. Not all of the units acquired by NPC International came from PHI: In mid-1997, for example, NPC International acquired 100 units from fellow franchisee Jamie B. Coulter, who in 1965 opened the first Pizza Hut franchise east of the Mississippi. TRICON's strategic goal of paring down its operations, however, undoubtedly helped accelerate Bicknell's expansion plans. During the last four years of the decade, NPC International acquired a staggering 482 Pizza Hut units, giving the company a total of 837 restaurants as it entered the 21st century. An agreement between NPC International and TRICON set the stage for further strident expansion in the future. According to filings with the Security and Exchange Commission, NPC International had the option to acquire additional Pizza Hut units up to a total of 1,300 restaurants. Based on this agreement and Bicknell's penchant for expansion, NPC International promised to figure as the most powerful Pizza Hut franchisee for years to come.

Principal Subsidiaries

NP Acquisition Corp.; National Catering Co. Inc.; NPC Management Inc.; NPC Restaurant Holdings Inc.; Seattle Restaurant Store; NPC INTL Inc.

Principal Competitors

Little Caesar Enterprises, Inc.; Papa John's International, Inc.; Domino's Pizza, Inc.

Further Reading

Baker, M. Sharon, "Battered By Low Margins, Skipper's Baits New Hooks," *Puget Sound Business Journal,* May 21, 1993, p. 14.
Boulton, Guy, "Pizza Hut, Major Franchisee to Swap Restaurants in 12 States," *Knight-Ridder/Tribune Business News,* June 8, 1994, p. 06080118.
Hamstra, Mark, "NPC International Plans to Acquire 100 Pizza Huts," *Nation's Restaurant News,* May 5, 1997, p. 5.
Howard, Theresa, "Skipper's Debuts Seafood Broiler, Shutters 8 Restaurants," *Nation's Restaurant News,* March 2, 1992, p. 3.
Papiernik, Richard L., "NPC Fishes for Pizza, Beef Sales As Skipper's Put to Sea," *Nation's Restaurant News,* June 10, 1996, p. 11.
Prewitt, Milford, "National Pizza Nabs Tony Roma," *Nation's Restaurant News,* May 31, 1993, p. 1.
——, "NPC Intl. Eyes $35M 4-Q Charge to Cover Skipper's Closing Costs," *Nation's Restaurant News,* February 6, 1995, p. 2.
——, "Pizza Hut Inks Pact As PepsiCo Earnings Slip," *Nation's Restaurant News,* June 20, 1994, p. 3.
Prinzing, Debra, "Rising Fish Prices Take Their Toll on Skipper's Bottom Line," *Puget Sound Business Journal,* May 13, 1991, p. 4.
Romeo, Peter, "National Pizza Alters Course with Bid for Skipper's Chain," *Nation's Restaurant News,* February 13, 1989, p. 1.
Ruggless, Ron, "Tony Roma's Unveils New Prototype, Menu Items," *Nation's Restaurant News,* April 8, 1996, p. 3.

—Jeffrey L. Covell

OAO LUKOIL

11 Stretenski Boulevard
101000 Moscow
Russia
Telephone: +7-095-927-4444
Fax: +7-095-928-9841
Web site: http://www.lukoil.com

Public Company
Incorporated: 1991
Employees: 120,000
Sales: $9.75 billion (1999)
Stock Exchanges: OTC
Ticker Symbol: LUKOY
NAIC: 324110 Petroleum Refineries; 211111 Crude
   Petroleum and Natural Gas Extraction

OAO LUKOIL is one of Russia's most successful efforts at capitalism following the breakup of the Soviet Union in 1991. An integrated oil company, involved from the exploration stage to the gas pump, LUKOIL was created when the oil and gas industry was chosen to be Russia's first attempt at privatization. The state-run, western Siberian companies of Langepasneftegaz, Uraineftegaz, and Kogalymneftegaz were merged together to form LUKOIL, with the initials of the three combined to coin the name for the new giant company. LUKOIL, although not the largest of Russia's new private oil companies, is unquestionably the most advanced, attracting foreign investors and partnerships, and trading on the New York Stock Exchange. Russia's oil and gas reserves are sizeable, with eastern Siberia seen as the world's last great unexplored territory that could add greatly to the country's wealth. LUKOIL, which produces about 24 percent of Russia's crude, also operates in 25 other countries. It has a presence in the United States through its purchase of Getty gas stations.

Breakup of Soviet Union and Creation of LUKOIL: 1991

For many years the Soviet Union produced more oil than any other country in the world, even more than Saudi Arabia or the United States. Its great wealth, however, was essentially squandered, used to prop up an inefficient, militarized economy and to enrich Soviet government ministers. With the collapse of Communism and the breakup of the Soviet Union, the control of oil fields, pipelines, and refineries became a matter of vital importance to both Russia and the Soviet republics that quickly broke free and sought to exploit their own natural resources. Russian production of crude oil fell steadily as the Soviet Union declined, due in large part to a lack of government investment, which resulted in rotting surface equipment, and the overall failure of the Soviet planned economy. Under Soviet rule, Russia's oil industry was divided among 33 ''associations,'' many of which were huge enterprises but essentially operated as fiefdoms. Based on 1991 data, 16 of the Russian associations would have been ranked among the world's top 30 oil companies.

Efforts to privatize the oil and gas industry began soon after the fall of Communist rule. By the end of 1991, four large holding companies had been formed out of the old oil associations, the most strategically positioned being LUKOIL, led by Vagit Alekperov. The son of an oil worker, Alekperov grew up in the oil town of Baku (now part of independent Azerbaijan), where many Westerners made their fortunes—including the Nobel brothers, better known today for Alfred Nobel's endowment of the annual prizes for peace, science, and literature that bear his name; and Marcus Samuel, who established Shell Oil. After studying engineering at a petrochemical institute, Alekperov went to work in the emerging oil industry in western Siberia, where oil was first discovered in 1964. In 1983 he became director of oil production in the town of Kogalym (its oil association, Kogalymneftegaz, would one day become a linchpin of LUKOIL), which was located in one of Russia's richest oilfields yet only pumped a few million barrels of crude annually. By 1990 the association under Alekperov's leadership would be producing 240 million barrels a year. In that year, at the age of 40, Alekperov would be summoned to Moscow and appointed deputy minister of oil production, at a time when not only the Soviet oil industry was falling apart, but the entire Soviet system of government was on the edge of collapse.

Alekperov was quick to recognize what the future held. He began meeting with Western oil executives to pick their brains about creating an integrated oil company, and in the process learned a great deal about the workings of private enterprise.

Company Perspectives:

LUKOIL is the first Russian integrated oil company operating according to the principle "from oil well to filling station."

Alekperov asked British Petroleum (BP) to form a strategic partnership, but was turned down by executives who could not fathom the possibility of valuable Soviet oil assets becoming privatized.

In Moscow, Alekperov's foresight was seen as a threat by Communist hardliners, who were anything but receptive to his proposal that the oil industry be divided among a dozen integrated companies. On the verge of being fired, he was the beneficiary of a failed coup attempt by hardliners that included his boss, the head of the oil ministry. When the plotters were thwarted and Soviet President Mikhail Gorbachev remained in charge, Alekperov became acting oil minister. As the Soviet structure continued to disintegrate, he was able to set the future direction of the oil industry. Following a decree by Russian President Boris Yeltsin, Alekperov established LUKOIL for his own control, acquiring some of Russia's best properties and most talented engineers, while placing loyal ministry subordinates at the head of other oil companies.

The transition to capitalism in Russia, however, was not without complications. Oil facilities that had for years essentially run themselves now resisted being merged into the new integrated companies. The Samara Refinery, for instance, had struck its own exporting deal with a Belgian company that had connections to a Russian gangster. Somehow, export earnings never seemed to return to Russia. When one of the integrated oil companies, Yukos, tried to exert control over the refinery, its appointed general manager was murdered outside his home. Three months later the head of the Belgian company was critically wounded when his Mercedes was ambushed on the streets of Moscow, and another executive of the company was subsequently killed. With that, Yukos was able to proceed with incorporating the Samara Refinery into its operations.

First Russian Company to Offer Stock: 1994

Overall, ten large integrated Russian oil companies were formed. In 1994 LUKOIL was the first to begin offering shares of stock on the new Russian Trading System, with the Russian government temporarily controlling a third of the company and retaining a long-term 5 percent stake. Because Russian law did not require disclosure, it was uncertain how much of the company Alekperov owned, but there was no doubt that he held voting control and ran the affairs of LUKOIL with a firm hand.

Alekperov began to address the problems LUKOIL faced as it transformed itself into a Western-style corporation. First, production had to be increased. Because of decaying Soviet-era equipment, output had dropped by 15 percent in 1993 and was expected to drop another 5 percent in 1994. In order to finance the purchase of equipment to put wells back into production, LUKOIL signed an agreement to sell 70,000 barrels of oil a day to Chevron, then pledged the revenues to guarantee a $700

million loan from the Japanese trading house of Mitsui. To further increase output LUKOIL also began to buy up smaller Russian oil companies.

LUKOIL also had to improve efficiency and maintain cash flow. Too many of LUKOIL's customers, such as Russia's collective farms, were state mandated and simply did not pay their bills. The Lukoil Financial Company was formed to deal with the non-payment crisis that was forcing the company to cut output and place workers on compulsory leave. The new company would assume control over the flow of goods and cash within LUKOIL. It also began conversations with the government about the mutual cancellation of debt.

LUKOIL's relationship to the Russian government, due to its sheer size as well as close ties to the oil ministry, gave it a distinct advantage over its rival Russian oil companies. In some cases LUKOIL was seen as acting as proconsul for the government, or the government as the agent for the oil company. After a BP-led consortium of oil companies pursued a deal for three years with Azerbaijan to develop oil fields in the Caspian Sea, despite civil war and a coup d'état, Russia began pressuring Azerbaijan to include LUKOIL in the deal. First the Russian Minister of Energy proposed that LUKOIL should be granted a 20 percent stake in the consortium, then a few months later the Russian government sent a formal note to the British embassy to lay a claim to the oil reserves. Finally, Alekperov flew in to close the deal, demanding a 10 percent, equity-free slice of the project, which the Azerbaijan government, in the interests of improving relations with Moscow, eventually agreed to. For many observers it was more a matter of extracting oil tribute from a former vassal than negotiating a business deal.

LUKOIL received further bad press during the early days of its existence when it was sued for $660 million in U.S. federal court by a Texas unit of Frankenburg, a Liechtenstein company. Lukoil was accused of conspiracy, fraud, and money laundering. In 1991 Frankenburg had been hired by Kogalymneftegaz to repair abandoned wells, but quit work a year later when it was not paid. The suit alleged that non-payment was simply a way to drive Frankenburg out so that work could then be diverted to a new oil services company set up in the British Virgin Islands by Alekperov and other LUKOIL executives, and aided by former Frankenburg employees. The fact that one of the alleged conspirators was American was used as entree to the U.S. courts. LUKOIL heatedly denied the charges, and Frankenburg eventually elected to drop the suit, but at the very least the affair introduced the oil company to further complexities of the free enterprise system. Such embarrassment was not helpful at a time when LUKOIL was trying to distance itself from the image of Russian corruption in order to attract foreign investors.

In 1995 LUKOIL made an offering of bonds that would convert to stock in the company and lead to trading in Western financial markets, but was met with less than anticipated enthusiasm. Nevertheless, the Atlantic Richfield Co. (ARCO) eagerly purchased $250 million of the bonds, which would give it a 5.7 percent stake in the company and represent the largest single foreign investment in Russia. It was also the first time that a foreign oil company had acquired equity in a major Russian oil company. The relationship made sense for both parties. LUKOIL would receive cash to upgrade facilities, as well as access to much

Key Dates:

1991: LUKOIL is formed in aftermath of the dissolution of the Soviet Union, through consolidation of the western Siberian companies Langepasneftegaz, Uralneftegaz, and Kogalymneftegaz.

1994: LUKOIL becomes first Russian company to offer stock.

1995: Offering of convertible bonds leads to listing on New York Stock Exchange.

1998: LUKOIL enters into agreement with Conoco to drill in the northern territories of Russia.

2000: LUKOIL acquires U.S. Getty gas stations.

needed technical and management expertise. ARCO, heavily dependent on the shrinking reserves of Alaska, would gain access to new reserves and was already skilled in operating under conditions similar to Siberia. Several months later ARCO upped its stake in LUKOIL and signed an 18-year agreement to commit $5 billion to jointly develop projects in Russia.

Attempting to Enter U.S. Gasoline Market: 1997

By 1997, with privatization of the oil industry far from complete, LUKOIL was generally considered an unparalleled Russian success. With a market capitalization of $9 billion, it planned to issue ten million new preferred shares of the company. The Russian government, in need of cash, also decided to sell off 15 percent of its ownership. Although the company announced strong financial results for 1996, LUKOIL still needed to bring its accounting up to international standards in order to attract further foreign investment. In the meantime, it continued to pursue its ambitious goals. LUKOIL gas stations not only spread across Russia, replacing the tanker parked on the side of the road where motorists traditionally filled up, they began cropping up in former Soviet republics and other Eastern European countries. In July 1997 LUKOIL made an attempt to enter the U.S. gasoline market when it teamed with Nexus Fuels of Irving, California, to establish 5,000 fueling centers next to the outlets of several supermarket chains, which saw the move as a way to recapture some of the revenue lost to the oil companies that had expanded their onsite convenience stores. The deal fell apart, however, when, according to Nexus, LUKOIL failed to provide the necessary cash.

The Russian oil industry experienced its first taste of merger mania in 1998 when AO Yukoa and AO Sibneft combined to create AO Yuksi, instantly becoming the third largest private oil producer in the world. Rumors then spread that Lukoil would combine with AO Sidanco, a possible move that investors questioned by bidding down LUKOIL stock by more than 10 percent. Despite a Russian obsession with size, Yuksi had little to offer. In effect, two cash-strapped, poorly run companies were thrown together. In the end, LUKOIL would remain the choice of investors even if it remained somewhat smaller than Yuksi.

With a 1998 drop in oil prices, Russia's oil industry was hurt and the country's economy thrown into crisis, eclipsing further talks of mega-mergers. A number of foreign oil companies, also

adversely affected by low oil prices, pulled out of Russia, electing instead to invest in West Africa and the Middle East, where it cost less to operate. Companies also feared that Russia and its unstable government might create a state oil company and possibly reverse course on privatization of the industry. Moreover, Russian taxes were onerous, based on revenues rather than profits.

Nevertheless, LUKOIL was strong enough to press on. In 1998 it teamed with Conoco to develop oil and natural gas reserves in the northern territories of Russia. It also joined a consortium of oil companies, including Texaco and Exxon, to drill in the Timan Pechora region, an oil shelf that was projected to contain several billion barrels of oil. Lukoil purchased a Russian exploration company which held licenses to drill in some of the best sites in Timan Pechora, and also purchased Komitek, another company in the region with proven reserves of 1.36 billion barrels.

After annual revenues fell from $9 billion in 1997 to below $4 billion in 1998, oil prices began to rise again, so that in 1999 LUKOIL generated a record $9.75 billion. It continued its outward expansion, upgrading domestic facilities and establishing foreign refinery capacity. LUKOIL looked once more to entering the U.S. gasoline market in 2000 when it agreed to purchase a chain of 1,300 gas stations from Petty Petroleum for $71 million. The company also faced charges at home that it and the other major Russian oil companies were using offshore firms and trading schemes to avoid paying taxes, which were estimated to total some $9 billion a year. LUKOIL maintained that all its taxes were paid, but also warned Moscow that any tightening of regulations would prevent the company from continuing to upgrade its aging production equipment and soon lead to a drop in oil production that would have a dire effect on the economy. With world oil prices soaring, however, such predictions of doom for LUKOIL carried little weight.

The economic climate for Russia was also improving. In 2000 the country's economy grew for the first time since the fall of the Soviet Union. With oil reserves that could possibly top 100 billion barrels, Russian territory was looking even more promising than the five billion to 16 billion barrels that could be realized in Alaska's Arctic National Wildlife Refuge that President George W. Bush indicated he would allow to be tapped. Russian officials went on a road show to urge U.S. oil companies to drill in Russia, which they maintained would be faster and provide far more oil than the Refuge. With forecasts indicating that over the next 20 years the world would continue to increase its oil consumption, any supply of crude not controlled by OPEC (the Organization of Petroleum Exporting Countries) would have to be viewed as an inviting prize.

LUKOIL, with the vast potential of Russian oil reserves backing it up, appeared poised in 2001 to join the ranks of the world's major oil companies, the so-called seven sisters. In order to be less dependent on the fluctuation of crude oil prices, LUKOIL invested widely in downstream businesses in Europe and the United States. Aside from expanding European refining capacity, LUKOIL looked to buy a gas retailer, such as Austrian Avanti. In the United States it looked to acquire an East Coast refinery to supply its chain of Getty gas stations. As long as the Russian government and economy remained relatively stable, there was no reason to believe that LUKOIL would be unable to find enough Western partners to help it continue to grow.

Principal Divisions

Refining; Supplies; Marketing; Transportation.

Principal Competitors

Exxon Mobil Corporation; Royal Dutch/Shell Group; BP Amoco p.l.c.; Total Fina Elf S.A.; Texaco Inc.; Chevron Corporation; Conoco Inc.; Repsol YPF, S.A.; Petróleos de Venezuela S.A.; Petróleo Brasileiro S.A. - Petrobras; Petróleos Mexicanos; Norsk Hydro ASA; CITGO Petroleum Corporation; Ultramar Diamond Shamrock Corporation; Occidental Petroleum Corporation; Sunoco, Inc.; Amerada Hess Corporation; 7-Eleven, Inc.; Koch Industries, Inc.; Kerr-McGee Corporation; Tatneft; Yukos.

Further Reading

Brzezinski, Matthew, "Russian Oil Mergers Run a Big Risk of Creating Inefficiency on Larger Scale," *Wall Street Journal,* January 26, 1998, p. A15.

Friesen, George, "The Foreign Game Revisited," *Oil & Gas Investor,* November 1994, p. 36.

Ivanovich, David, "Houston Oil Firm Accuses Russian Client of Fraud," *Houston Chronicle,* February 8, 1994, p. 3.

Khartukov, Eugene M., "Incomplete Privatization Mixes Ownership of Russia's Oil Industry," *Oil & Gas Journal,* August 18, 1997, pp. 36–40.

Klebnikov, Paul, "The Seven Sisters Have a Baby Brother," *Forbes,* January 22, 1996, p. 70.

Knott, David, "Big Challenge: Reform Russia's Oil Industry," *Oil & Gas Journal,* August 8, 1994, p. 32.

——, "A Closer Look at Lukoil," *Oil & Gas Journal,* June 20, 1994, p. 24.

"Lukoil: Vagit Rockefeller," *Economist,* July 16, 1994, p. 57.

"Russian Oil: A Gusher Under Ice," *The Economist,* December 10, 1994, p. 64.

"Russia Prepares Sales of Oil Companies," January 1994, *Project & Trade Finance,* p. 22.

"Russia's Emerging Energy Giants," *Euromoney,* April 1998, pp. 86–92.

Stevenson, Richard W., "Russia's Lukoil Sets Sights on Joining Ranks of the Majors," *Houston Chronicle,* October 30, 1994, p. 11.

Stoughton, Sheldon, "Decree to Change Shape of Russian Oil Industry," *Oil & Gas Journal,* December 14, 1992, p. 20.

Rubinfien, Elisabeth, "Russian Oil Man and Firm He Formed, Lukoil, Are Making Mark on Industry," *Wall Street Journal,* April 25, 1994, p. A8.

Tavernise, Sabrina, "Russian Oil Company Buys U.S. Gas Station Chain," *New York Times,* November 4, 2000, p. C2.

—Ed Dinger

"Adhering to Excellence"™

Pacer Technology

9420 Santa Anita Ave.
Rancho Cucamonga, California 91730
U.S.A.
Telephone: (909) 987-0550
Fax: (909) 987-0490
Web site: http://www.pacertechnology.com

Public Company
Incorporated: 1984
Employees: 148
Sales: $47.7 million (2000)
Stock Exchanges: NASDAQ
Ticker Symbol: PTCH
NAIC: 32552 Adhesive and Sealant Manufacturing

Pacer Technology is a leading manufacturer and supplier of high-performance glues, adhesives, and epoxies sold to consumer, hobby, automotive, and industrial customers. The company is best known as the maker of Super Glue, a classic adhesive brand acquired in 1994. The 1998 acquisition of Cook Bates Inc. nearly doubled Pacer's size. Cook Bates is a leading manufacturer of nail care products such as pumice stones, emery boards, tweezers, scissors, and nail clippers, which are sold under brand names such as Gem, Kurlash/Diamon Deb, Oleg Cassini, and Brut. Pacer covers five key areas of retailing: discounting chains, drug chains, supermarket chains, hardware and home centers, and hobby and craft outlets. Pacer also maintains licensing agreements to produce products "behind the scenes" for other brand names. Pacer's products are sold in 75,000 U.S. retail outlets including Wal-Mart, Kmart, Target, The Home Depot, Walgreens, and Eckerd. While the company's sales have risen sharply in the late 1990s and early 2000s, its profits have declined, due in part to costs associated with the integration of its Cook Bates facilities.

Model Airplanes in the 1970s

Pacer was founded in the early 1970s as a maker of model airplane kits. The company soon realized, however, that the secret to its success was in the adhesives used to assemble the kits rather than in the kits themselves. Within a few years, Pacer reincorporated as an adhesive manufacturer and supplier and relocated from Wyoming to California.

The company put much thought into the packaging of its adhesives. It acquired plastic injection and blow-molding machinery and began to manufacture plastic packaging for its products. Producing its own packaging saved the company money, which allowed it to invest more in the development of its adhesives.

New Divisions in the 1980s

The company divided its new adhesive products into several distinct categories and marketed these products under different brand names. Its popular hobby adhesives, used to assemble crafts and models, were marketed under the Zap brand name. Pacer marketed a wide range of adhesives and sealants to industrial customers, such as manufacturers of automobile and heavy-duty equipment, subassemblies and components, medical devices, and electronic components for maintenance and repair operations. These products were sold under the Pacer Tech brand name.

Pacer also manufactured a line of automotive adhesives designed to withstand the high temperatures and heavy wear-and-tear associated with the operation of automobiles. These products included high-performance sealants and instant gaskets and were marketed mainly under the Pacer's ProSeal brand name.

Super Glue in 1994

To diversify its product line, Pacer acquired several companies in the 1990s, including the Super Glue Corporation. President and CEO James Munn arranged the 1994 takeover of Mexlonic, formerly the Super Glue Corporation of Ridgewood, New York. Super Glue products include a high-performance line of adhesives and plastic molded clips used in homes, schools, and offices. The move was considered risky at the time. "They were doing about $12 million in sales, and we were doing close to the same," said W. Thomas Nightingale III, a Pacer marketing executive at the time of the takeover. The acquisition caused Pacer to post a net loss that year and "it took

347

Company Perspectives:

Pacer is a world-class manufacturer and distributor of items we all know, use, and see in stores throughout 70 countries in the world. The quality of our products' packaging and deployment have achieved a world-class caliber reputation with our customer base. Branded products include Super Glue, Zap hobby products, Oleg Cassini, GEM, Kurlash/Diamon Deb, Elvira, and Brut personal health and beauty items. Pacer is also the "behind the scenes" manufacturer for many major household adhesives and nail care items. Pacer's mix of products is varied. There are two components that "tie it all together." First, we are in total control of the basic manufacturing process. We know how to maintain quality and meet production deadlines within tight budgets. Second, we enjoy excellent relations with the top retailers in the nation and around the world.

some time to discover which Super Glue products were going to be the most profitable for Pacer," according to the *Inland Empire Business Journal.*

Pacer also acquired other companies around the time of the Super Glue takeover. It purchased Novest, Inc. in 1993, a private corporation that manufactured adhesives, sealants, and lubricants for engine and body parts, and California Specialty Chemicals, Inc., in 1997, a producer of proprietary sculptured acrylic nail liquids and powders.

Pacer soon realized that Super Glue would be its ticket to success in the future. In 1995 it redesigned Super Glue containers to make them more convenient for users. Its new tubes had smaller-but-deeper diaphragms to minimize leakage and better conserve the unused portion of the product. The new design was the first alteration to the product since its introduction in 1977.

Pacer introduced a new line of Super Glue in 1995 called Future Glue. Unlike most adhesives, Future Glue was designed to be applied to dirty surfaces and was stronger than Super Glue.

In 1997 Pacer signed exclusive agreements with Home Depot and Target that would generate millions in Super Glue sales. According to the *Tribune Business News,* the Home Depot agreement stipulated that Super Glue would be the only general-purpose cardboard mounted glue product on display in its 115 existing stores and in the 500 new stores it expected to open by 2000. Target agreed to put Pacer's Handi-Tak reusable putty adhesives near its 6,000 checkout counters in its 750 stores.

Cook Bates in 1998

In March 1998 Pacer acquired the massive Cook Bates, which nearly doubled Pacer's size. Headquartered in Venice, Florida, Cook Bates was a division of London International Group, Inc. The 102-year-old company had been operating since 1896 and was a leading manufacturer of nail care products such as pumice stones, emery boards, nail clippers, scissors, and tweezers. Analysts believed the Cook Bates purchase was a good move for Pacer. Cook Bates had a longstanding reputation

for high-quality, innovative products sold in about 70 countries. Cook Bates had particularly high seasonal sales and marketed special holiday products such as new leopard-skin manicure sets and hot colors manicure sets.

Since Pacer already had a strong presence in retail outlets throughout the United States, the company was in a unique position; it could market Cook Bates products along its already existing channels. "This acquisition will open up key shelf space for Pacer's existing products and offer us the opportunity to leverage our global distribution and marketing capabilities by cross-selling Cook Bates' products with ours," said Munn. Vice-President Jim Gallagher said in an article in *Chain Drug Review:* "There were tremendous synergies with Pacer's marketing, manufacturing, and distribution capabilities. Because of that we were able to combine both operations relatively quickly."

As more women entered the workforce, Pacer saw tremendous growth for its Cook Bates products in Western Europe. "The size, demographic mix and limited amount of competition make overseas markets particularly attractive. Demand for our nail-care products is very strong in Europe, a market that is estimated to be growing at 20 percent annually," Munn explained.

Although the Cook Bates acquisition helped Pacer boost its sales, Pacer suffered a drop in profits. Some of Cook Bates's operations overlapped with Pacer's and forced the company to pay too much for its operations. Pacer also paid more than $3 million in charges relating to the integration of Cook Bates.

Restructuring in Early 2000

Pacer's top priority in early 2000 was to increase profits. The company was nearly delisted on the NASDAQ when its stock dropped to less than $1 per share. Pacer's board of directors terminated President and CEO James Munn and assembled a new management team to turn the company around. It appointed Nightingale president and CEO. Robert R. Vanderlaan, a former Sherwin Williams executive, was named chief operating officer (COO). In 2000 Pacer successfully rebuffed a proxy takeover attempt by Munn and some disgruntled board members.

To boost its income, Pacer concentrated on increasing its presence in Home Depot and Kmart "by expanding its shelf space and placement in multiple sections of stores." It closed a Memphis, Tennessee distribution center and consolidated operations in Rancho Cucamonga, the location of the company's headquarters. "We will be focusing on reducing the number of products we make," said Nightingale. "We are looking at profitability and margins for each product."

The company also obtained the exclusive rights from Pen-Tel Products to sell Bondini adhesive products, including Bondini 2 and Bondini Everything Gel. Because it bonds with nearly all surfaces, Bondini became known as "Bondini the Magic Glue." In 2000 Bondini was sold at Wal-Mart, Kmart, Sears, and other retail outlets. Nightingale stated in a company press release that the Bondini acquisition broadened Pacer's retail presence and that Pacer planned to increase the number of items in the Bondini product line.

Key Dates:

1975: Pacer is founded as a maker of model airplanes.
1978: Company goes public.
1980: Pacer enters the industrial market
1984: Company reincorporates and relocates from Wyoming to California.
1993: Pacer acquires Novest, Inc.
1994: Pacer acquires Super Glue Corporation.
1997: Pacer acquires Cook Bates Inc.
2000: Company restructures to increase profits.
2001: Company obtains exclusive rights to sell Bondini adhesive products.

Pacer also continued to develop new products. In 2001 the company was performing trials on a cyanoacrylate formulation topical skin-closure device to be sold to the medical field. The company expected to begin selling the product in 2002. It also was seeking government approvals on its Rectite adhesives. Rectite was a poultry adhesive designed to reduce the bacterial contamination of food.

As of 2001, industry experts believed that Pacer would soon be back on track and highly profitable. Although there was a trend in retailing toward consolidating operations and using fewer vendors, analysts believed the immensely popular Super Glue was probably here to stay.

During the next few years Pacer planned to further expand into overseas markets and sell its products in lesser-developed countries. In 2000 nearly 20 percent of Pacer's revenues stemmed from sales in more than 70 countries in Europe, South America, the Pacific Rim, Mexico, and Eastern Europe. Pacer's revenues rose from $46 million in 1999 to $47.7 million in 2000, but its net income dropped from $1.3 million in 1999 to $0.3 million in 2000.

Principal Competitors

Minnesota Mining & Manufacturing Company; Dow Chemical Co.; Borden, Inc.; Henkel Manco Inc.; Devcon; 3-Bond; Alteco.

Further Reading

Benson, Don, ''Turnaround Ace to Head Ailing California Gluemaker Pacer Technology,'' *Knight-Ridder/Tribune Business News,* April 7, 2000, p. 0009902A.

''Maximizing Super Glue Tube Convenience,'' *Packaging Digest,* August 1995, p. 77.

''Pacer Big Presence in a Range of Categories,'' *Chain Drug Review,* June 19, 2000, p. 246.

''Pacer Technology Acquires Leading Manufacturer of Nail Clippers, Emery Boards, and Related Manicure Products; Acquisition of Assets of Cook Bates to Add $20 Million in Revenues,'' *Business Wire,* March 4, 1998, p. 3041032.

Padilla, Mathew, ''Fly Boy Leads Pacer Technology to New Heights,'' *Inland Empire Business Journal,* November 1997.

''Rapid Growth Continues at Pacer Technology,'' *Chain Drug Review,* June 7, 1999, p. 256.

Scott, Gray, ''Pacer Technology Says Major Contracts Will Add Millions in Sales,'' *Knight-Ridder/Tribune Business News,* June 14, 1997, p. 714B1098.

—Tracey Vasil Biscontini

The Pepsi Bottling Group, Inc.

One Pepsi Way
Somers, New York 10589
U.S.A.
Telephone: (914) 767-6000
Fax: (914) 767-7761
Web site: http://www.pbg.com

Public Company
Incorporated: 1999
Employees: 38,700
Sales: $7.98 billion (2000)
Stock Exchanges: New York
Ticker Symbol: PBG
NAIC: 312111 Soft Drink Manufacturing; 312112 Bottled
Water Manufacturing

The Pepsi Bottling Group, Inc. (PBG) is the world's largest manufacturer, seller, and distributor of Pepsi-Cola beverages. Separated from parent PepsiCo, Inc. in 1999, it accounted that year for 55 percent of Pepsi-Cola beverages sold in the United States and 32 percent worldwide. Pepsi Bottling Group's strongest presence is in the United States and Canada, but it also holds exclusive Pepsi franchises in Greece, Russia, and Spain as well as in most U.S. states and Canadian provinces. The company delivers its products directly to stores without using wholesalers or other middlemen. In addition to its extensive production and distribution facilities, PBG leases and operates about 20,000 vehicles and owns more than 1.1 million soft drink dispensing and vending machines. PepsiCo holds a controlling interest in the firm.

Pepsi-Cola Bottling and Distribution to 1975

Caleb D. Bradham founded the original Pepsi-Cola Co. in 1902, shortly after devising, and before patenting, the syrup in his New Bern, North Carolina drugstore. He established a syrup and bottling factory in New Bern in 1904. Bradham began franchising the product to other bottling companies almost immediately; by the end of 1909 there were 250 in at least 24 states.

Pepsi-Cola suffered losses in 1919 because of the high sugar prices that followed the end of World War I price controls. Bradham bought the sugar he needed at high prices as a hedge against even higher prices. When the sugar bubble burst in 1920, prices fell from 26 cents a pound to below two cents a pound within months, and he was ruined, declaring bankruptcy in 1923. A few bottlers remained, and Roy Megurgel purchased the company's trademark, business, and goodwill for $35,000, moving the enterprise to Richmond, Virginia. However, in 1931 his National Pepsi-Cola Corp. also went bankrupt.

Charles G. Guth's Loft, Inc. was operating candy stores with soda fountains when a grievance against the Coca-Cola Co. drove him to found a new Pepsi-Cola Co. Megurgel purchased the prior company's trademark, business, and goodwill for $10,500 before coming to terms with Guth. By 1934 the company was profitable, due to Guth's fortuitous decision the previous year to offer the soft drink in 12-ounce bottles instead of the usual six, but for the same five cents. Guth established bottling plants in Baltimore, New Orleans, Philadelphia, and Pittsburgh to supplement the original one in Long Island City, an industrial area in New York City's borough of Queens. He also acquired a Montreal plant in 1934 and formed a Canadian subsidiary. Coca-Cola challenged the Canadian Pepsi trademark, taking its case all the way to the British empire's highest court, which in 1942 ruled in favor of Pepsi-Cola.

Like Bradham, Guth generally relied on franchisees to grow the Pepsi-Cola business, establishing four U.S. regional territories to sign up bottlers. They brought in 167 licensees during 1935–36, and by the end of 1939 the number had nearly doubled. Loft, Inc. shareholders won a proxy fight against Guth in 1936, and three years later he withdrew from Pepsi-Cola by terms of a settlement. Loft was merged into Pepsi-Cola in 1941. During World War II sugar supplies were rationed, so the company bought the sweetener in Mexico and processed it into a syrup there before shipping it to bottlers. The federal government halted this practice in 1944. Pepsi-Cola began packaging its product in cans as well as bottles in 1948.

Alfred N. Steele, a former Coca-Cola manager, was chief executive of Pepsi-Cola during the 1950s. Steele revived the flagging company through a variety of measures, including a shakeup of management, a new advertising campaign, and a change in the formula of the drink to make it less sweet. On taking charge he also concentrated on reviving the morale of Pepsi-Cola's often-fractious 500-odd independent bottlers. Usually local businessmen, the bottlers had been prone to selling out because of dissatisfaction with stagnating sales in the late 1940s. As business improved in the 1950s, Steele still regarded the bottlers as a problem, because, in his opinion, they were inclined to become complacent and lazy in good times. Accordingly, Steele bought the franchises of several bottlers who were not getting good results in major markets and assumed operation of these territories directly. By 1959 Pepsi-Cola was its own bottler in 22 major U.S. markets, including metropolitan New York City, Houston, Philadelphia, Pittsburgh, and St. Louis.

Pepsi-Cola began expanding overseas in the 1950s. One territory that remained unserved, however, was the Soviet Union, although a trademark was registered in Moscow in 1938. The company scored a public relations coup in 1959, when, as the representative of the U.S. soft drink industry at the Moscow Trade Fair, its kiosk was visited on a hot summer day by Soviet Premier Nikita Khrushchev and U.S. Vice-President Richard Nixon. While the cameras whirled, the Soviet leader quaffed a cup of Pepsi and proclaimed it "very refreshing." In 42 days, visitors there drank Pepsi at the rate of 10,000 cups an hour. The nation remained out of bounds commercially until 1973, however, when Moscow made Pepsi-Cola the sole soft drink company allowed to bottle in the Soviet Union. Parent PepsiCo, Inc. (the company had changed its name following its 1965 merger with Frito-Lay) sold the concentrate to the Soviet government, which provided the bottling and distributing facilities. Some two billion bottles were being sold annually in 1978.

A Growing Company-Owned Network: 1975–99

Although there were still hundreds of Pepsi-Cola licensees in the United States alone—some of them grouped into sizable chains—the company, in 1975, was reserving for itself bottling and distribution facilities in ten choice metropolitan territories. This network was administered by a Metro unit that was renamed Pepsi-Cola Bottling Group in 1977. In 1978 subsidiaries of PepsiCo operated 19 plants, in Dallas, Houston, Los Angeles, Milwaukee, the New York City metropolitan area, Orlando, Philadelphia, Phoenix, and Pittsburgh, the entire state of Rhode Island, and all of Michigan except the Upper Peninsula. Pepsi-Cola Bottling Group was manufacturing, selling, and distributing carbonated soft drinks and syrups bearing trademarks owned by PepsiCo, including Pepsi-Cola, Diet Pepsi-Cola, Pepsi-Cola Light, Mountain Dew, Teem, Patio, and Aspen. The 34 company-owned units abroad run by Pepsi-Cola International went under the name United Beverages International.

A vexing issue for PepsiCo at this time was perennial overdog Coca-Cola's huge lead in fountain sales and vending machine locations. Pepsi's franchise agreements—unlike Coke's—gave its licensees and not the company the right to sell to soda fountains in their territories. Pepsi-Cola Bottling Group executives complained that the bottlers were hurting the company by neglecting this area. Craig Weatherup, the PBG executive who later became first CEO of independent Pepsi Bottling Group, later recalled to *Beverage World* that "the continual loss of fountain accounts hit this organization like a series of bombs." PBG attempted to solve the problem by establishing a unit that called directly on fast-food operations and other large users of soft drinks without regard to franchise territorial lines. If the salesman won an account, PBG contracted with the local bottler to co-pack the beverages and to service the fountain machinery.

Acquisitions in the late 1970s and early 1980s increased Pepsi-Cola Bottling Group's share of Pepsi-Cola USA's overall soft drink system to 21 percent by 1985. The unit's revenues increased from $1 billion in 1984 to more than $2.5 billion in 1986—in part because of further acquisitions, such as Allegheny Beverage Corp. and MEI Corp.—raising its share to 32 percent. Weatherup, who became president of Pepsi-Cola Bottling Group in 1986 and graced the cover of *Beverage World* in August 1987, later described this era to the magazine as "a stretch of six to eight years in which it seemed we could do little wrong." The system now consisted of 45 plants grouped in 25 business units reporting to four business regions—eastern, central, southern, and western. Headquarters were in Somers, New York, just down the road from PepsiCo headquarters in Purchase.

Interviewed by Tim Davis of *Beverage Group* at this time, Weatherup denied that Pepsi-Cola Bottling Group had a plan for further physical growth. "We are prepared to be larger—we don't see ourselves getting smaller," he conceded, but added, "Every acquisition we've made has been triggered by some circumstance, the most common being change in family ownership. That has keyed the vast majority of acquisitions over the last 10 years. We have not solicited anyone's franchise, ever, that I know of, or forced anyone to sell. . . . We absolutely are not looking to take a floundering bottler under our wing. That has not been a criterion for 10 years." The following year—1988, however, PepsiCo agreed to buy its third largest independent U.S. bottling operation from Grand Metropolitan plc for $705 million. In outbidding two groups led by existing Pepsi franchisees, PepsiCo indicated that the territories were desirable because they were adjacent to existing PBG bottlers.

By this time Pepsi-Cola Bottling Group had been dissolved, a company reorganization having folded PBG, Pepsi-Cola USA, and the USA Fountain Beverage Division into four U.S. regional divisions of Pepsi. Under whatever name, however, the operation continued to grow. In 1990 PepsiCo was operating on a company-owned basis about 55 of the 190-odd soft drink plants in the United States, accounting for about 47 percent of the Pepsi-Cola beverages sold in the United States. The company also had a minority interest in about 25 more plants. In 1995 the number of company-owned plants in the United States and Canada was about 70 (of about 200 total), accounting for 56 percent of Pepsi beverages sold in North America.

In Spain, PepsiCo held only a 14 percent market share of the cola market in 1988 and trailed Coca-Cola by five to one. Pepsi-Cola International's poor performance was attributed mainly to

---

Key Dates:

1902: Caleb D. Bradham founds the original Pepsi-Cola Co.

1936: Pepsi bottling plants have been established in five U.S. cities and Montreal.

1948: Company begins packaging its product in cans as well as bottles.

1959: Pepsi-Cola is its own bottler in 22 major U.S. markets.

1965: Company is renamed PepsiCo, Inc. following its merger with Frito-Lay.

1978: Pepsi Bottling Group is founded for company-owned bottling and distribution.

1988: PepsiCo purchases its third largest independent bottling operation, from Grand Metropolitan plc, for $705 million.

1999: Pepsi Bottling Group becomes an independent company.

---

a distribution problem, which was addressed by refranchising several key markets, including Madrid. By 1991, however, joint ventures in which Pepsi-Cola International took a part were operating Spanish plants, and in 1993 these became completely company-owned. With the fall of the Soviet Union, PepsiCo lost its soft drink monopoly there. Pepsi-Cola International restructured its Russian operations, sharing bottling and distribution with local partners, but during the next five years Coca-Cola outspent PepsiCo by six to one and drew even in market share. The company, in 1996, said it would work with Whitman Corp.'s General Bottlers unit—Pepsi's second largest bottler—and insurer Leucadia National Corp. to add 11 plants over the next five years. In 1999 Pepsi Bottling Group purchased operations in St. Petersburg from Whitman.

Independent Company: 1999–2000

In March 1999, PepsiCo spun off its soft drink bottling and distribution operations—what was known within the organization as Pepsi COBO (company-owned bottling operations)—as The Pepsi Bottling Group Inc. In the fifth largest initial public offering in U.S. stock market history, PepsiCo sold 100 million shares at $23 a share. Retaining a 40 percent interest in the newly public company, PepsiCo placed two senior officials on its board of directors. In addition, PBG was required to submit its annual operating plan to PepsiCo for its approval and was using only PepsiCo-approved vendors. In return, PBG was expecting a high level of funded marketing support from PepsiCo.

Pepsi Bottling Group was focusing on enhancing the one-third of its business defined as "cold drink" or single serve. This profitable area had been growing rapidly as consumers increased their snacking. PBG doubled its spending on new coolers and vending machines between 1997 and 1999, adding about 175,000 new pieces of equipment. The company also was acquiring more bottlers in areas primarily contiguous to its existing operations, in order to realize cost savings in raw materials, manufacturing, warehousing, logistics, and general administration. Weatherup, who had been president and chief

executive officer of Pepsi-Cola North America (1990–96) and chairman and CEO of its parent, Pepsi-Cola Co. (1996–99), and who then became the first chairman and CEO of Pepsi Bottling Group, said the company intended to grow 1 to 2 percent a year by acquisitions, averaging six to ten deals a year.

One pressing problem was to increase Pepsi Bottling Group's operations outside North America, which were accounting for only 8 percent of total revenues. Russian operations suffered a heavy blow in 1998, when the value of the ruble collapsed, leading to a $212 million restructuring asset writedown. But in its first year as an independent company, PBG registered $7.51 billion in revenues—a 13 percent gain over the previous year. Net income was $118 million. These figures improved to $7.98 billion and $229 million, respectively, in 2000.

Pepsi-Cola Bottling Group had 67 production facilities (60 owned) and 320 distribution facilities (258 owned) at the end of 2000 in parts of 41 states, the District of Columbia, eight Canadian provinces, Spain, Greece, and Russia. PBG's brands included Pepsi Cola, Diet Pepsi, Mountain Dew, Lipton Brisk, Lipton's Iced Tea, Pepsi One, Slice, Mug, Aquafina (bottled water), Starbucks Frappaccino, Fruitworks, and, outside the United States, 7UP, Pepsi Max, Mirinda, and Kas. PBG also had the right to manufacture, sell, and distribute soft drink products of other companies in some territories. About 80 percent of PBG's volume in 2000 was sold in the United States. In 1999 Pepsi-Cola brands held about 29 percent of the carbonated soft drink market in the United States, compared with 40 percent for Coca-Cola Co. brands. The long-term debt was $3.27 billion at the end of 1999. PepsiCo owned 37.9 percent of PBG's outstanding common stock in February 2001. It also held all of the outstanding Class B stock.

By the terms of Pepsi Bottling Group's master syrup agreement with PepsiCo, PBG had the exclusive right to manufacture, sell, and distribute fountain syrup to local customers in its territories and to act as a manufacturing and delivery agent for national accounts within its territories that specifically requested direct delivery without using a middleman. Also under this agreement, PBG had the exclusive right to service fountain equipment for all of the national account customers within its territories. PBG was purchasing the concentrates to manufacture PepsiCo's soft drink products. Other raw materials were generally being purchased from multiple suppliers, but with PepsiCo acting as the agent.

By the terms of Pepsi Bottling Group's master bottling agreement with PepsiCo authorizing PBG to manufacture, package, sell, and distribute the cola beverages bearing the Pepsi-Cola and Pepsi trademarks, PBG was required to pay the concentrate prices determined by PepsiCo and to deploy the types of containers authorized by PepsiCo. PepsiCo also had the right to approve PBG's annually presented three-year financial plan but did not have the right to withhold approval unreasonably. Failure to carry out the approved plan in all material respects could result in a termination of the agreement. PBG had the right to determine the prices at which it sold its products. Although PBG had an extensive distribution system in the United States and Canada, in Russia, Spain, and Greece, it was using a combination of direct store distribution and distribution through wholesalers.

Principal Subsidiaries

Bottling Group, LLC.

Principal Competitors

Coca-Cola Enterprises Inc.

Further Reading

Banerjee, Neela, "Pepsi Pledges $550 Million for Russia, Aiming to Regain Footing Against Coke," *Wall Street Journal,* April 26, 1996, p. A7C.

Davis, Tim, "What Drives PBG?," *Beverage World,* August 1987, pp. 32, 34, 36, 38, 81–83.

"Driving Blue Highways," *Beverage World,* August 15, 1999, pp. 40–46.

Helyar, John, "PepsiCo to Buy Big U.S. Bottler for $705 Million," *Wall Street Journal,* June 23, 1988, p. 10.

Martin, Milward, *Twelve Full Ounces,* New York: Holt, Rinehart and Winston, 1962.

"Pepsi Takes on the Champ," *Business Week,* June 12, 1978, pp. 90–92.

"Resurgent Pepsi Gets a New Boss," *Business Week,* May 30, 1959, pp. 106, 108, 110.

Specht, Marina, "Pepsi Challenges Coke in Spain," *Advertising Age,* March 14, 1988, p. 63.

Springmann, Christopher, "Weatherup Takes on the Pepsi Challenge," *Chief Executive,* November 2000, pp. 20–21.

Steinriede, Kent, "Formally Separated from Its Pepsi Concentrate Siblings . . . PBG Charts Its Own Course," *Beverage Industry,* May 1999, pp. 26–30.

—Robert Halasz

Phillips Petroleum Company

Phillips Building
Bartlesville, Oklahoma 74004
U.S.A.
Telephone: (918) 661-6600
Fax: (918) 661-6279
Web site: http://www.phillips66.com

Public Company
Incorporated: 1917
Employees: 12,400
Sales: $21.22 billion (2000)
Stock Exchanges: New York Pacific Toronto
Ticker Symbol: P
NAIC: 211111 Crude Petroleum and Natural Gas
　　Extraction; 211112 Natural Gas Liquid Extraction;
　　213111 Drilling Oil and Gas Wells; 324110
　　Petroleum Refineries; 325110 Petrochemical
　　Manufacturing; 325211 Plastics Material and Resin
　　Manufacturing; 326122 Plastic Pipe and Pipe Fitting
　　Manufacturing; 422710 Petroleum Bulk Stations and
　　Terminals; 447110 Gasoline Stations with
　　Convenience Store; 447190 Other Gasoline Stations;
　　486110 Pipeline Transportation of Crude Oil; 486210
　　Pipeline Transportation of Natural Gas; 486910
　　Pipeline Transportation of Refined Petroleum Products

Phillips Petroleum Company is one of the largest oil companies in the United States. Its main emphasis in the early 21st century is exploration and production of crude oil and natural gas, with exploration activities in 19 countries and production in nine. Key regions for these operations include the North Slope of Alaska; Venezuela; the North Sea (including the U.K., Norwegian, and Danish sectors); Nigeria; Kazakhstan; China; and the Timor Sea (located between East Timor and Australia). The company has three other main segments: the refining, marketing, and transportation of crude oil and petroleum products, including the marketing of the famous Phillips 66 brand of gasoline; the gathering, processing, and marketing of natural gas, an activity conducted through Duke Energy Field Services, LLC, in which Phillips holds a 30.3 percent stake (with the remainder held by Duke Energy Corporation); and the manufacturing and marketing of petrochemicals and plastics, which is conducted through Chevron Phillips Chemical Company LLC, a 50–50 joint venture between Phillips and Chevron Corporation.

Early History

Phillips is named after brothers Frank and L.E. Phillips and was organized in 1917 to acquire their original venture in the oil business, Anchor Oil and Gas Company. Raised on an Iowa farm, the Phillips brothers left Iowa after Frank heard rumors of vast oil deposits in Oklahoma, then part of the Indian Territory. Along with others Frank Phillips founded Anchor Oil and Gas in 1903. After a struggle, Frank Phillips, joined by L.E., finally began to make money from oil in 1905. They reinvested their profits, founding a bank. Eventually, the brothers decided to leave the uncertain oil business for good and concentrate on banking. They were forestalled, however, when World War I broke out and the price of crude jumped from 40 cents to more than $1 a barrel. The brothers founded Phillips Petroleum Company in 1917, headquartered in Bartlesville, Oklahoma.

From the very beginning, the Phillips brothers found much natural gas while drilling for oil. Most drillers considered the gas useless and burned it off at the wellhead, but the Phillips brothers sought to turn it into a cash crop. In 1917 Phillips opened a plant near Bartlesville for extracting liquid byproducts from natural gas. The byproducts could be used in motor fuels. The company's research into the uses of natural gas received further impetus in 1926, when it won a patent infringement suit brought against it by Union Carbide over Phillips's process for separating hydrocarbon compounds.

Phillips prospered throughout its first decade. By 1927, it was pumping 55,000 barrels of oil a day from more than 2,000 wells in Oklahoma and Texas. Its assets stood at $266 million, compared with the $3 million it had when it was founded. The company also decided to enter the refining and marketing businesses in 1927, in response to automobile sales and as an outlet for its growing production. In 1927, it began operating a refinery near the Texas town of Borger. It also opened its first gas station, in Wichita, Kansas.

Phillips's entry into retailing presented it with the problem of finding a brand name under which to sell its gasoline. According to company lore, the solution presented itself as a Phillips official was returning to Bartlesville in a car that was road-testing the company's new gasoline. He commented that the car was going "like 60." The driver looked at the speedometer and replied, "Sixty nothing . . . we're doing 66!" The fact that the incident took place on Highway 66 near Tulsa only strengthened the story's appeal to Phillips's executives. The company chose Phillips 66 as its new brand name, one which has endured and achieved classic status.

In 1930 Phillips added to its refining and retailing capacities when it acquired Independent Oil & Gas Company, which was owned by Waite Phillips, another Phillips brother. The Great Depression hit the company early and hard. In 1931 Phillips posted a $5.7 million deficit in its first ever loss-making year. As a consequence, it cut salaries and laid off hundreds of employees. Phillips stock plunged to $3 a share, down from $32. The company quickly regained its profitability, however, posting a modest surplus the next year.

Before the decade was out, Phillips also would make two personnel changes to help secure its future for the longer term. In 1932 a promising young executive named K.S. (Boots) Adams was promoted to assistant to the president, Frank Phillips. Six years later, he succeeded Phillips as president when the company's founder assumed the post of chairman. Boots Adams—a boyhood nickname, inspired by his affection for a pair of red-topped boots—was 38 years old when he became president, and he and Phillips made rather an odd couple at the top of the chain of command. They often disagreed as to how the company should be run, but Phillips seems to have known that the future ultimately belonged to his protégé. "Mr. Phillips liked me, but not my ideas," Adams later recalled. "He said to me: 'I'm going to object to everything you do, but you go ahead and do it anyway.'"

Phillips's strength in research and development paid off during World War II. In the late 1930s, the company developed new processes for producing butadiene and carbon black, two key ingredients in synthetic rubber, which became all the more crucial to the United States after Japanese conquests in Indonesia and Indochina cut off the supply of natural rubber in 1941. Phillips also developed high-octane aviation fuels, an early

version of which powered British fighters in the Battle of Britain. The fuels were widely used by the Allied air forces.

Postwar Growth and International Expansion

In the years immediately following the war, Phillips began to reap in earnest the harvest of its research and commitment to natural gas. It generated substantial income by licensing its petrochemical patents to foreign companies. At home, the company was eminently positioned to take advantage of the sudden growth of cross-country pipelines in the 1940s and the consequent surge in natural gas prices. By the middle of the next decade, its reserves would total 13.3 trillion cubic feet, worth an estimated $931 million. Phillips also invested heavily in oil exploration, refining, natural gas drilling, and petrochemical plants. In 1948 it formed a new subsidiary, Phillips Chemical Company, and entered the fertilizer business when it began producing anhydrous ammonia.

Although Phillips had the advantage over its competitors in natural gas and chemicals, it fell behind in the postwar foreign oil rush because of Frank Phillips's opposition to overseas ventures. Even though his company had begun drilling in Venezuela in 1944, Phillips was determined to keep the company a mainly domestic enterprise and turned down the exclusive rights to the lucrative concession in the neutral zone between Saudi Arabia and Kuwait in 1947. The company eventually acquired a one-third stake in American Independent Oil, which took the Middle East concession, but it required all of Boots Adams's persuasive powers to get his boss to agree to it.

Frank Phillips died in 1950 and Adams, long his heir-apparent, succeeded him as chairman and CEO. Under Adams, Phillips continued to focus on its interest in natural gas and was the nation's largest producer in the 1950s. Its program of capital expansion was ambitious, with expenditure reaching a peak of $257 million in 1956. Phillips also began to break out of the constricting mold that its late founder had built for it. In 1952 the company started expanding its marketing network beyond the Midwest, opening Phillips 66 stations in Texas and Louisiana. Phillips continued to march through the deep South, then up the Atlantic seaboard, as far as it could extend its supply lines from its refineries. It also was becoming apparent that Frank Phillips had erred in refusing to develop overseas sources of oil, as the cost of finding and pumping crude in the United States increased. Finally, as the decade neared its end, Adams went on an around-the-world fact-finding trip. When he returned, he set a five-year timetable for expanding Phillips's international operations.

Phillips's practice of licensing its patents overseas without acquiring an interest in the new ventures had yielded royalties but no growth; so in 1960 the company took a 50 percent interest in a French carbon black plant using Phillips technology. Petrochemical joint ventures in Asia, Afric, Europe, and Latin America followed. Phillips also acquired drilling concessions in North Africa, the North Sea, New Guinea, Australia, and Iran. These foreign ventures were still not profitable when Boots Adams retired in 1964 and handed the reins to President Stanley Learned, but the company had begun to make up for lost time.

Under Learned, Phillips continued to diversify and expand. In 1964 it acquired packaging manufacturer Sealright Inc. as part of its move into plastics. Two years later, Learned himself broke ground on a petrochemical complex in Puerto Rico that would produce chemical raw materials and motor fuels. Phillips also expanded its domestic oil operations. In 1960, it had tried to break into the California market by acquiring 15 percent of Union Oil Company of California, but litigation by Union Oil and the Justice Department prevented Phillips from pursuing a takeover; in 1963 Phillips sold its stake to shipping magnate Daniel K. Ludwig. Instead, Phillips acquired the West Coast properties of Tidewater Oil Company in 1966 for $309 million. The deal took four months to complete and required great secrecy. When the purchase was announced, the Justice Department filed an antitrust suit to dissolve it, but a U.S. District Court allowed the acquisition to stand, pending an appeal to the Supreme Court. By 1967 there were Phillips 66 stations in all 50 U.S. states.

Learned retired in 1967 and was succeeded as CEO by William Keeler. In addition to his career with Phillips, Keeler, who was half Cherokee, was named chief of the Cherokee nation by President Harry S. Truman in 1949. Keeler used this position to campaign on behalf of Native American causes. Now he assumed responsibility for the eighth largest oil company in the United States, and one in which some serious problems were beginning to manifest themselves. Foremost among these prob-

lems was dependence on outside sources of crude oil. For years, Phillips had not pumped enough to supply its refineries, so it had to buy crude from other producers. In 1969 Phillips made an unsuccessful offer to acquire Amerada Petroleum Corporation, a major crude producer with no marketing operations. Phillips was more successful with its new exploration strategy, under which it considerably slowed exploration in the continental United States, the most thoroughly prospected area in the world, and concentrated on Alaskan and overseas locations. This paid off in 1969, when Phillips discovered the massive Greater Ekofisk field under the Norwegian North Sea. Phillips joined with several European partners to develop the field. The discovery of a major field in Nigeria soon followed. In the early 1970s, Phillips joined with Standard Oil Company of New Jersey (later Exxon Corporation), Atlantic Richfield Company, Standard Oil Company of Ohio, Mobil Oil Corporation, Union Oil Company of California, and Amerada Hess Corporation to form Alyeska Pipeline Service Company. Alyeska would build the trans-Alaska pipeline, which allowed the exploitation of the massive deposits in Prudhoe Bay, Alaska.

Turbulent 1970s

During this time Phillips suffered from overexpansion and ailing chemical ventures. Some petrochemical projects fared badly because of falling propane and fertilizer prices. In plastics, Phillips found that it could not compete with smaller companies that had lower capital costs. Keeler addressed these problems by installing tighter controls on corporate planning. Phillips executives also found that having gas stations in all 50 states was no advantage when the company's presence in many markets was too small to ensure a profit. In 1973 Phillips divested most of its stations in the Northeast. A price war in California had drained the 3,000 stations acquired from Tidewater from the start, and it never made money; in 1973 the Supreme Court finally ordered Phillips to divest the Tidewater assets, and two years later the company sold most of its Pacific Coast properties to Oil Shale Corporation.

Keeler retired in 1973 and was succeeded as CEO by President William Martin. The remainder of the 1970s would be turbulent years for Phillips. In 1973 Phillips was one of the first and most prominent U.S. corporations to be accused of making an illegal contribution to President Richard Nixon's reelection campaign. Phillips pleaded guilty and admitted donating $100,000 illegally. Over the course of the next two years, Phillips would admit that the company had made illegal contributions to 65 congressional candidates in 1970 and 1972, as well as to Lyndon B. Johnson's 1964 presidential campaign and Nixon's 1968 campaign. The money came from a secret $1.35 million fund set up by Phillips executives for that purpose and channeled through a Swiss bank account. The company paid $30,000 in fines.

In 1975 the Los Angeles-based Center for Law in the Public Interest filed a class action suit against Phillips on behalf of several small shareholders. In settling the lawsuit, the company agreed to give up the strong majority that its executives had always held on its board of directors. The board was reconstituted, with nine of the 17 directors coming from outside the company.

In turn, these legal difficulties were followed by even greater disasters. In 1977, Phillips's Bravo platform in the Ekofisk field blew out during routine maintenance and spewed oil into the North Sea for eight days. Two years later, 123 people were killed when a floating hotel for Ekofisk workers capsized in a storm. Also in 1979, an explosion at Phillips's Borger, Texas refinery injured 41 people. Meanwhile, William Keeler's strategy of exploring in foreign lands began to backfire as it produced more dry holes than reserves, while other oil companies were discovering new fields in the Rocky Mountains and in Louisiana.

Fending Off Takeovers in the 1980s

William Martin retired in 1980 and was succeeded by William Douce. In 1982 Phillips's fortunes revived somewhat when a joint exploration venture with Chevron found substantial reserves under the Santa Maria Basin, off the coast of California. The company added even further to its crude supplies in the following year, when it acquired General American Oil Company, for $1.1 billion, stepping in as a white knight to thwart a takeover bid from Mesa LP. It would not be Phillips's last encounter with Mesa and its chairman, T. Boone Pickens, Jr. In 1984 Phillips acquired Aminoil, Inc. and Geysers Geothermal Company from R.J. Reynolds Industries for about $1.7 billion. Observers noted that the deal made Phillips, now the subject of takeover rumors, a less attractive buyout candidate because of the debt it would have to assume.

The takeover rumors became reality early in December 1984, when Pickens announced that his company had acquired 5.7 percent of Phillips's stock and intended to try for a majority stake. Douce, though scheduled to retire shortly, had prepared for such an event and was determined to fight. "Boone Busters" T-shirts appeared in Bartlesville, which feared for its life should Phillips ever be taken from it, and the company launched a barrage of lawsuits. One suit charged that Mesa was violating a pact it had signed before withdrawing its bid for General American Oil, in which it promised never again to attempt to take that company over. When the dust cleared a month later, Phillips had driven Pickens away and preserved its independence, but Phillips agreed to buy out Mesa's holdings as part of a restructuring that would ultimately cost $4.5 billion, loading itself with debt and requiring the disposal of $2 billion in assets. For his part, Pickens conducted an orderly retreat laden with spoils—$75 million in pretax profits plus an additional $25 million to cover his expenses.

No sooner had Pickens left the field, however, than other attacks began. In January and February 1985, financiers Irwin Jacobs, Ivan Boesky, and Carl Icahn all bought up large blocks of Phillips stock. Then, on February 12, Icahn struck, launching a $4.2 billion offer to buy 45 percent of the company. Combined with the 5 percent he already owned, this would give Icahn a controlling stake. In early March, faced with shareholders willing to sell to Icahn owing to dissatisfaction with the Pickens deal, Phillips executives came up with a plan to exchange debt securities for half of its outstanding stock, including Icahn's 5 percent, at $62 per share, compared with the $53 per share it had paid Pickens. Icahn accepted and he, too, left with his spoils.

The task of rebuilding the battered company—now saddled with $8.9 billion in debt—was left to C.J. (Pete) Silas, who succeeded William Douce as chairman in May 1985. Under Silas, Phillips sold off the necessary $2 billion in assets within 18 months of Icahn's repulse. Among those to go were Aminoil and Geyser Geothermal. The company also cut 9,000 jobs by 1989. As a result of its forced restructuring, Phillips gave up becoming an integrated, worldwide energy company, and refocused on its core oil and gas businesses. In the late 1980s, unexpectedly strong earnings from its petrochemical businesses more than offset the effect of lower oil prices and raised hopes for Phillips's long-term recovery.

These hopes received a setback in October 1989, however, when an explosion occurred at Phillips's plastics plant in Pasadena, Texas, killing 23 people and causing $500 million in damage. The disaster temporarily eliminated Phillips's U.S. capacity to manufacture polyethylene, which is used to make blow-molded containers and other products.

Transforming Operations for a New Millennium

Phillips entered the 1990s still saddled with nearly $4 billion in debt from its battles with corporate raiders. Its debt-to-equity ratio stood at nearly 60 percent. The early 1990s were difficult years for the company as the economic downturn hit the oil and gas industry particularly hard. The company completed additional workforce reductions and asset sales. In 1992 Phillips reorganized its operations into strategic business units, which were given greater autonomy and more profit and loss responsibility. That year also saw Phillips create GPM Gas Corporation, a subsidiary that assumed control of the natural gas gathering, processing, and marketing activities. Phillips planned to sell 51 percent of GPM through an initial public offering to raise funds to further reduce the debt load, but the poor energy market of early 1992 forced Phillips to cancel the IPO.

Wayne Allen was promoted from president and COO to chairman and CEO in 1994. Under Allen's leadership, Phillips increased its exploration and production operations. The company had already, in 1993, proven the viability of drilling for oil and gas beneath the immense sheets of salt that cover more than half of the Gulf of Mexico. The salt layers had stymied previous attempts to seismically map the deeper layers, but Phillips developed a 3-D seismic technology that enabled it to see clearly beneath the salt. So-called subsalt production in the Gulf began in late 1996. Meantime, international exploration efforts led to the company's first production of oil in China in 1994 and a major gas discovery in the Timor Sea located between East Timor and Australia. Also in 1994 Norway's parliament approved Ekofisk II, a $2.5 billion improvement project involving the replacement of five aging platforms with two new ones, along with the extension of the production license to 2028. Phillips expected that by that year, Ekofisk II will have produced one billion barrels of oil. The construction of Ekofisk II was completed in 1998.

On the marketing side of its operations, Phillips's profits were weaker than those in exploration and production. The company worked to expand its network of gas stations and convenience stores in the mid-1990s. As part of an industry trend toward consolidation and the sharing of costs through joint operations, Phillips and Conoco Inc. in 1996 discussed merging their refining and marketing businesses but failed to reach an agreement. That year Phillips posted net income of $1.3 billion on sales of $15.73

billion, enabling it to reduce its debt load to $3.1 billion and its debt-to-equity ratio to 39 percent.

Pressure to consolidate continued to build in the late 1990s as two megamergers rocked the industry: British Petroleum plc's merger with Amoco Corporation to create BP Amoco p.l.c. and Exxon Corporation's merger with Mobil Corporation to form Exxon Mobil Corporation. The new giants dwarfed Phillips with their revenues in excess of $100 billion. In late 1998 Phillips and Ultramar Diamond Shamrock Corporation reached a preliminary agreement to combine their refineries and gas stations in a joint venture, but the deal fell apart early the following year. Meantime, Phillips in 1998 made its largest discovery since Ekofisk in a field in Bohai Bay, off the northeastern coast of China. At the time, this was the largest find off the shore of China.

During the second half of 1999 James J. Mulva took over as chairman and CEO from the retiring Allen. Mulva would oversee some of the most dramatic events in the company's history soon after taking over, as Phillips decided to focus even further on exploration and production by either selling or placing into joint ventures its other three units. The company at first planned to sell its GPM Gas unit, but instead in March 2000 Phillips combined GPM with the gas gathering, processing, and marketing operations of Duke Energy Corporation to form a joint venture called Duke Energy Field Services, LLC, with Duke initially holding 69.7 percent of the new entity and Phillips holding the remaining 30.3 percent. In April 2000 Phillips substantially bolstered its exploration and production operations through the acquisition of the Alaskan assets of Atlantic Richfield Company for about $7 billion, the largest acquisition in company history. This deal enabled BP Amoco to complete its $28 billion acquisition of Atlantic Richfield. For Phillips, the addition of the Alaskan assets increased its daily production by 70 percent and doubled its oil and gas reserves. Phillips completed a third major deal in July 2000 when it combined its worldwide chemicals businesses with those of Chevron to form a 50–50 joint venture called Chevron Phillips Chemical Company LLC. Through the new entity, whose annual revenues would be nearly $6 billion, the two companies hoped to reap annual cost savings of $150 million.

Plans to shift the company's refining and marketing operations into another joint venture were apparently abandoned with the announcement in February 2001 that Phillips would acquire Tosco Corporation for $7.49 billion in stock and debt. The deal, if completed, would make Phillips the number two refiner in the United States, trailing only Exxon Mobil, and the number three gasoline retailer, with more than 12,000 outlets in 46 states (Tosco's main brands included 76 and Circle K). Mulva called this deal, through which the company would have strong positions in both the upstream and downstream sides of the oil industry, the "final step" in the company's plan to become one of the major integrated oil companies. It would cap a whirlwind transformation for a company that many had written off in the wake of the takeover battles of the 1980s.

Principal Subsidiaries

66 Pipe Line Company; Phillips Alaska Holdings, Inc.; Phillips Alaska, Inc.; Phillips Alaska Natural Gas Corporation; Phillips China Inc. (Liberia); Phillips Coal Company; Phillips Gas Company; Phillips Gas Company Shareholder, Inc.; Phillips International Investments, Inc.; Phillips Investment Company; Phillips Kazakhstan Ventures, Ltd. (Liberia); Phillips Oil Company (Nigeria) Limited; Phillips Petroleum Canada Ltd.; Phillips Petroleum Company Norway; Phillips Petroleum Company United Kingdom Limited; Phillips Petroleum Company Western Hemisphere; Phillips Petroleum International Corporation; Phillips Petroleum International Investment Company; Phillips Petroleum Kazakhstan, Ltd. (Liberia); Phillips Petroleum Resources, Ltd.; Phillips Petroleum Timor Sea Inc.; Phillips Petroleum Timor Sea Pty Ltd (Australia); Phillips Petroleum UK Investment Corporation; Phillips Petroleum (91–12) Pty Ltd (Australia); Phillips Pipe Line Company; Phillips Receivables Company, LLC; Phillips Texas Pipeline Company, Ltd.; Phillips Transportation Alaska, Inc.; Phillips-San Juan Partners, L.P.; Phillips 66 Capital I; Phillips 66 Capital II; Polar Tankers, Inc.; Sooner Insurance Company; WesTTex 66 Pipeline Company.

Principal Competitors

Exxon Mobil Corporation; Royal Dutch/Shell Group; BP Amoco p.l.c.; Total Fina Elf S.A.; Texaco Inc.; Chevron Corporation; Conoco Inc.; Repsol YPF, S.A.; Petróleos de Venezuela S.A.; Petróleo Brasileiro S.A. - Petrobras; Petróleos Mexicanos; Norsk Hydro ASA; CITGO Petroleum Corporation; Ultramar Diamond Shamrock Corporation; Occidental Petroleum Corporation; Sunoco, Inc.; Amerada Hess Corporation; 7-Eleven, Inc.; Koch Industries, Inc.; Kerr-McGee Corporation; The Dow Chemical Company; E.I. du Pont de Nemours and Company.

Further Reading

Barrionuevo, Alexei, "Chevron and Phillips to Form Venture with $5.7 Billion in Revenue," *Wall Street Journal,* February 8, 2000, p. A4.

——, "Phillips Petroleum to Delay Finding Partner for Venture," *Wall Street Journal,* November 16, 2000, p. A6.

——, "Suit Over BP Amoco-Arco Pact Halted: Move Follows Disclosure of Phillips Plan to Buy Arco's Alaskan Assets," *Wall Street Journal,* March 16, 2000, p. A3.

Barrionuevo, Alexei, and Steve Liesman, "Phillips Petroleum, in Strategy Shift, Seeks Sales or Ventures for Some Units," *Wall Street Journal,* September 24, 1999, p. B6.

Biesada, Alexandra, "The Levitation," *Financial World,* June 23, 1992, p. 36.

Blalock, Dawn, "Phillips Petroleum, Long Buried in Debt, Frees Itself," *Wall Street Journal,* April 15, 1996, p. B3.

Blumenthal, Karen, and Christopher Cooper, "Phillips and Ultramar Call Off Plans to Join Refining, Marketing Operations," *Wall Street Journal,* March 22, 1999, p. B8.

Borrego, Anne Marie, "Phillips Petroleum to Cut Staff by 8 Percent, Capital Spending," *Wall Street Journal,* January 7, 1999, p. A4.

——, "Ultramar Diamond Shamrock, Phillips to Combine Refineries and Gas Stations," *Wall Street Journal,* October 9, 1998, p. A3.

Brown, Wesley, and John Stancavage, "Phillips Called Ripe for Merger," *Tulsa World,* August 19, 1998.

"Chevron, Phillips to Form Giant Chemical JV," *Oil and Gas Journal,* February 14, 2000, pp. 24–25.

Deogun, Nikhil, and Alexei Barrioneuvo, "Phillips to Buy Tosco in $7.49 Billion Deal: Move Reflects Strategy Shift for Firm That Set Focus on Output, Exploration," *Wall Street Journal,* February 5, 2001, p. A3.

Gill, Douglas, "Fillip for Phillips: An Exciting New Find Brightens Its Future," *Barron's,* November 1, 1982, pp. 13+.

Gold, Jackey, "Phillips Petroleum: Take a Trip on Route 66," *Financial World,* October 15, 1991, pp. 16+.

"How They Won the West—and More," *Business Week,* January 28, 1967.

Jones, Billy M., *L.E. Phillips: Banker, Oil Man, Civic Leader,* Oklahoma City: Oklahoma Heritage Association, 1981.

Kvendseth, Stig S., *Giant Discovery: A History of Ekofisk Through the First 20 Years,* Tananger, Norway: Phillips Petroleum Company Norway, 1988.

Liesman, Steve, "Phillips Petroleum Again Is Hunting for Partner, with Chevron a Possibility," *Wall Street Journal,* September 20, 1999, p. A4.

——, "Phillips Petroleum CEO Says Discovery in China Is Stronger Than Expected," *Wall Street Journal,* February 9, 2000, p. A10.

Meyer, Richard, "The Final Straw," *Financial World,* January 26, 1988, pp. 39+.

Norman, James R., "The Sharks Keep Circling Phillips," *Business Week,* February 11, 1985, pp. 24+.

——, "What the Raiders Did to Phillips Petroleum," *Business Week,* March 17, 1986, pp. 102+.

"Phillips Aims at 'Built-in Value,'" *Business Week,* June 27, 1959.

"Phillips, Duke Enter Agreement to Combine Certain Businesses," *Oklahoma City Journal Record,* December 17, 1999.

"Phillips Petroleum: Laying the Groundwork," *Forbes,* February 1, 1965.

Phillips: The First 66 Years, Bartlesville, Okla.: Phillips Petroleum Company, 1983.

"Phillips to Acquire Tosco in Multibillion-Dollar Deal," *Oil and Gas Journal,* February 12, 2001, pp. 33–35.

Ray, Russell, "Phillips' 'Final Stop,'" *Tulsa World,* February 6, 2001.

Rublin, Lauren R., "Phillips Pays the Price and T. Boone Pickens Makes Another Big Score," *Barron's,* December 31, 1984, pp. 13+.

Ryan, Christopher, "Phillips Plans Cutbacks," *Tulsa Tribune,* November 21, 1991, p. 1A.

Schein, Chris, "Phillips Has Plans for More Layoffs," *Tulsa World,* November 13, 1991, p. B1.

Smith, Rebecca, "Duke Energy and Phillips Petroleum Form Gas-Gathering, Processing Firm," *Wall Street Journal,* December 17, 1999, p. A4.

Tuttle, Ray, "Deep Drilling: Phillips Believes Mahogany Field May Contain 100 Million Barrels of Oil," *Tulsa World,* September 1, 1996, p. E1.

Vogel, Todd, "Phillips Climbs Up from the Bottom of the Barrel," *Business Week,* January 16, 1989.

Wallis, Michael, *Oil Man: The Story of Frank Phillips and the Birth of Phillips Petroleum,* New York: Doubleday, 1988.

—Douglas Sun
—update: David E. Salamie

Powell's Books, Inc.

7 NW 9th Avenue
Portland, Oregon 97202
U.S.A.
Telephone: (503) 228-0540
Fax: (503) 228-1142
Web site: http://www.powells.com

Private Company
Founded: 1971
Employees: 450
Sales: $41.8 million (2000)
NAIC: 451211 Book Stores; 453310 Used Merchandise
Stores

Powell's Books, Inc. sells new, used, out-of-print, and rare books at its four full-service stores and three specialty stores in the Portland metro area (Powell's Technical Books, Powell's Travel Store, and Powell's Books for Cooks & Gardeners) and online at powells.com. Its world famous flagship store, Powell's City of Books, covers a city block and contains roughly 1.5 million volumes, new, used, and rare. The company's online outlet provides access to each of the seven stores and its Hoyt Warehouse.

A Start in Used Books: 1970

Powell's history begins in Chicago, where Michael Powell opened his first bookstore in 1970. Powell was a University of Chicago graduate student with an undergraduate degree in political science, who loved to read medieval histories. He hailed from Oregon, where he had worked summers as a commercial fisherman and his great-grandfather had homesteaded in the 1890s. Encouraged by friends and professors, including novelist Saul Bellow, Powell borrowed $3,000 from sociologist Morris Janowitz to assume a lease on a bookstore where he bought and sold used books. Within two months, he had paid off the loan and was on his way to building a profitable business. "The book business was much more exciting [than graduate school], "according to Powell in a 1987 article in the *Business Journal*. "I'd go to flea markets on Sunday in Chicago and buy books, then sell them on campus for food money."

In the summer of 1971, Powell's father, Walter, managed his son's store for a month, while the younger Powell went on vacation. He, too, caught the bookselling bug, and after returning to Portland, Oregon, opened his own used bookstore there with 100 boxes of books purchased at a local rummage sale. The older Powell, a retired painting and wallpapering contractor of 25 years, had also worked as a newspaper reporter and publicity director, sold advertising specialties, and taught industrial arts. Unencumbered by bookseller traditions, he followed an unorthodox formula: He shelved used and new, hardcover and paperback books side by side in his store at Southwest 12th Avenue and Burnside. Even Michael Powell was uncertain what to make of his father's practice. "In the used book world," he was later quoted in company literature as saying, "mixing paperbacks and hardbacks was not so much of a stretch, but when my dad had the idea of bringing in new books too, I had no sympathy." Yet Powell's Books, open 365 days a year and staffed by knowledgeable and dedicated book lovers, "had synergy beyond what we expected."

Michael Powell later offered the opinion in the August 28, 1983 edition of the *Oregonian* that his father's unorthodox formula worked because it benefited both bookseller and book buyer. Booksellers make more on used books than new ones. The profit margin on a new book ran about 40 percent in the late 1970s and early 1980s, while on used volumes, it ran to 50 or 60 percent. With new and used books shelved together, "[e]veryone profits." The customer was likely to buy the used copy and "bless you for the bargain," according to the younger Powell. As business grew, Walter Powell moved his store to a larger site across the street and, finally, to its present location, in an old car dealership, which he expanded from its original 24,000 square feet to 30,000 square feet in 1983.

By 1979, the older Powell appealed to the younger Powell to return to Portland to take over management of Powell's Books, which by then employed eight people, each of whom was expert in a number of fields and responsible for buying books in his or her areas. Michael Powell joined his father in running Powell's Books, which was on its way to becoming one of the three largest bookstores in the country. The other two largest stores were Strand's Books in New York and the Tattered Cover in

Company Perspectives:

We are innovative Booksellers challenged by readers, the community, the industry, and ourselves. We value books, new, used, and rare. We support the personal and professional development of all members of the company. We recognize the value of each person's contribution to the company. We are committed to open and harmonious relations in our workplace. We are committed to ethical business practices with customers, vendors, and each other. We recognize the uniqueness of each store and will work to heighten cooperation among all stores. We accept the responsibility to do quality work. We value our customers and expect each of us to be knowledgeable, courteous, and helpful. We encourage the development and implementation of new ideas. We recognize that profitability is essential to our continued business and professional development. We serve as an important resource to our community through our books, ourselves, and by actively bringing people together for the exchange of ideas and information. We have a social responsibility to the community and our industry to fight censorship, promote literacy awareness, and encourage authors and their works. We are committed to reflecting the cultural, ethnic and experiential diversity of the larger community through our hiring practices and by making books and information available to people with special needs or interests.

Denver. In 1982, Walter Powell sold Powell's Books to his son, although he remained involved in its everyday management until his death at 72 in 1985.

Years of Impressive Growth: The Early 1980s

The late 1970s and early 1980s were years of impressive growth for Powell's Books. While independent booksellers nationwide were closing their doors due to economic recession and the spread of bookstore chains and discounters, Powell's increased its sales by 38 percent annually from 1979 to 1983. Its sales total reached $2 million in fiscal 1983; by 1987, that number was $5 million. In 1983, Powell's purchased the entire stock of the Midwest's former largest bookstore, located in Cleveland, Ohio—700,000 books for $300,000—which it began shipping by truck to Portland. The store still did not advertise except for in the local yellow pages and occasionally in the *Oregonian*, although it gained in national renown when an article by a travel writer in a 1983 issue of *Newsday* listed it among Portland's tourist destinations. Powell's was known for the no-hassle policy of its management, who viewed a bookstore as a place to come read as well as buy. To help the uninitiated find their way through Powell's stacks and yet maintain a self-service set-up, maps of the premises were available in the front lobby, and the entire stock was labeled and cross-referenced.

In fact, Powell's was at the time gaining something of an international reputation as well. In 1985, a delegation of Chinese educators visited the store on its tour of American educational institutions. The educators wanted technical books, including English language aids, such as dictionaries, for which they wanted to barter fruit; however, Powell's insisted upon monetary payment. The store made its first sale of used books to the Pacific Rim in late 1986 with a large shipment of paperback novels and magazines to the Philippines. To assist in overseas sales, Powell's began a project that entailed cataloging about 10,000 titles, mostly used and out-of-print publications, ranging from neuroscience to nuclear physics; it offered these lists of titles to overseas university libraries and other potentially interested entities. By 1987, it was the moving force behind an exchange shipment with the provincial library in Fujian Province, China. In 1992, it organized the first major shipment of goods—books—to Vietnam from the United States.

Powell's also was interested in expanding its local market in the 1980s. In late 1984, it opened a second 8,500-square-foot store (four times the size of the average chain bookstore) in a shopping mall in the Portland suburb of Beaverton. In late 1985, the Anne Hughes Coffee Room opened at Powell's main store, followed shortly by Powell's Travel Store, in the lower level of downtown Portland's Pioneer Courthouse Square. At 3,000 square feet and close to 10,000 volumes, Powell's first specialty store was small by Powell's own standards, but large for a bookstore with a specific focus. According to Michael Powell, who was quoted in an *Oregonian* article in November 1985, the distinguishing feature of Powell's Travel Store was its "integration of guidebooks, maps and periodicals with literature and social studies about a region." Alongside books for tourists were mood-setting works of fiction and books about the arts of places and regions. There were also newspapers and periodicals, and free information about Portland. A section of the store offered travel products, such as small binoculars, electric converters, hair dryers, shaving kits, passport holders, and money belts. In addition, a coffee shop with seating for 18 sold espresso coffee and cookies. By 1987, with 12,000 to 15,000 books in stock, Powell's Travel Store was meeting initial sales projections of $1,000 a day.

In late 1986, Powell's also opened a technical publications annex and, in the summer of 1987, a specialty cookbook and gardening store. Powell's 2,500-square-foot Books for Cooks & Gardeners was located on one of Portland's more popular shopping streets with a stock of about 10,000 volumes, tapes and videotapes, including new, used, and rare cookbooks, books on wine, and literary essays or narratives dealing with food and drink. By this time, sales for its main Portland store, Powell's City of Books, had reached between $4 million and $5 million a year, and sales at its Beaverton bookstore had risen more than 28 percent every year since its opening in 1984.

Michael Powell was by then a well-known Portland figure. He lived in southeast Portland with his wife, Alice, a social worker who, due to the success of Powell's Books, was able to do a portion of her work on a pro bono basis. The couple had a young daughter, Emily. Powell sat on six local boards devoted to causes ranging from chamber music to mental health and was an outspoken advocate of the rights of Portland's gay and homeless populations. In addition, he was in line to become the next president of the American Booksellers Association. He had a reputation for being decisive, somewhat taciturn, and witty, a man well-respected by his community with a commitment to giving something back. Books, Powell believed, were a vital

Key Dates:

1970: Michael Powell opens his first bookstore in Chicago.
1971: Walter Powell opens Powell's Books in Portland, Oregon.
1979: Michael Powell joins Walter Powell in running Powell's Books.
1982: Walter Powell sells Powell's Books to Michael Powell.
1983: Powell's Books expands from 24,000 to 30,000 square feet.
1984: Powell's opens a second store in a shopping mall in the Portland suburb of Beaverton.
1985: Walter Powell dies; the Anne Hughes Coffee Room opens at Powell's main store, followed by Powell's Travel Store in Portland's Pioneer Courthouse Square.
1990: Powell's enlarges its main store to 43,000 square feet.
1992: Powell's organizes the first major shipment of goods to Vietnam from the United States.
1993: Powells.com begins selling books online.
1996: Powells.com becomes the web site for all store inventories.
1999: Powell's increases its retail space to 68,000 square feet.
2000: Unionized Powell's employees and management sign their first three-year contract.

tool in fighting ignorance and ensuring democracy. He often wandered the bookstore and worked the counter from time to time, and his office was off the store's front room, a cluttered room that he shared with a handful of other employees.

Expansion on Two Fronts: The Internet and at Home

By 1990, Powell's was growing at a rate of 25 percent annually and totaling $10 million in sales per year. The main store shelved about 750,000 volumes, covering almost 500,000 titles. A typical weekday brought in 3,000 to 5,000 shoppers. Portland's Design Review Commission approved a $1.1 million, 20,000-square-foot, two-story expansion to Powell's, which, when completed in late 1990, added capacity for another 250,000 books and a total of 43,000 square feet. This addition made the bookstore potentially the largest in the nation. However, despite the expansion, Powell's remained, according to the *San Diego Union-Tribune*, a "low-tech" wonder, "a warren of warehouse-type shelves, makeshift signs, and concrete floors" in color-coded rooms. Powell's still stuck to its manual system of inventory cards, maintained by the 75 people who ran the store's sections. Section heads met regularly with 30 used book buyers, who scoured the Northwest for books, and bought books locally from a steady stream of clients. The buyers put on something of a show for shoppers by sifting through books at a table just inside the store's entrance during business hours.

Powell's had come to exemplify what many publishing professionals believed was the resurgence of the independent bookstore, which in the early 1990s enjoyed 32 percent of book sales nationally after a decade of sales dominance by bookseller chains: catering to local interests and stocking a large number of titles. These independents showed signs of vigor while the chains, emphasizing bestsellers, suffered from a recession-related decline in shopping mall traffic. Powell's was unique and vital even among independents, a social hangout with more than 20 readings or literary events a month, doing business in excess of $10 million and selling about two million books a year.

However, by the mid-1990s, the success of the independents was on the wane; by the late 1990s, their market share had dropped to 17 percent as the chain stores and book discounters, once again, prevailed. Beginning in the mid-1990s, Powell's sales increases tapered off to the single digits, and in 1997 and 1998, sales were flat. In response to this turn of events, the store availed itself of online marketing. In 1993, Powell's had begun selling technical titles online; in early 1996, Powells.com became the web site for all of the business's inventories.

Sales through the company's web site doubled each subsequent year, amounting to a little less than 10 percent of total revenue, or $3.3 million for the year ended June 1999. Yet despite the size of its Internet revenues, Powell's Books' focus remained on used and hard-to-find titles in 2001. Seventy percent of its stock was still used, out-of-print, and rare books. According to Michael Powell, while the Internet expanded the bookselling market, it did not simply substitute one venue of sales for another. On the Internet, "interest and need are higher. . . . You can sell a more obscure book, but you don't have to sell it cheaply." Books that were too narrow in appeal to warrant display at a Powell's store would be stored in its Hoyt Warehouse, a space large enough to hold 40,000 volumes, until that day someone, or some other store, came looking for them. Powell's thus could continue to expand its already stupendous inventory, better serving customers directly while also supplying the growing network of competing virtual bookstores. Powell's made its inventories available through Half.com in 2001. It was also a regular supplier of books to Amazon.com beginning in the late 1990s and, in 2000, it began offering electronic books for sale online.

To house its ever increasing stock of books, Powell's completed construction in 1999 of a $3.5 million, four-story tower on its main store, Powell's City of Books, increasing its total retail space to 68,000 square feet. Anchoring the store's new entrance was its Pillar of Books, a carving in Tenino sandstone of eight of the world's great books stacked one on top of the other, on a base inscribed in Latin: Buy the book, read the book, enjoy the book, sell the book.

With expansion and renovation came reorganization. Powell's began computerizing operations in the mid-1990s and, in 1998, against many employees' wishes, it abandoned its former system of narrow employee specialization in particular subject areas in favor of team leaders responsible for broad categories, such as performing arts and genre fiction. Powell's also eliminated merit raises and cut back on annual cost-of-living increases in the fall of 1998. Responding to these changes, a majority of the store's 350 employees narrowly voted in April 1999 in favor of being represented by the International Longshore & Warehouse Union. During the ensuing ten months of contract negotiations, there was much friction between labor and management. Finally in August 2000, the two groups signed a three-year contract.

While the contract did not significantly affect Powell's bottom line, its attendant increases in employee wages and benefits translated into delays in some computer upgrades and store maintenance. Powell's was still going strong, however, with more than 1.5 million titles and sales of $41.8 million for the year ended June 2000. Some 3,000 to 5,000 people walked through Powell's Books' doors daily, and the store purchased about 3,500 used books each day. In addition, 44,000 book lovers browsed Powell's virtual shelves via the Internet on a daily basis.

Principal Competitors

Amazon.com, Inc.; Barnes & Noble, Inc.; Borders Group, Inc.

Further Reading

Balzar, John, ''A Novel Method to Sell Books,'' *Los Angeles Times*, August 7, 1998, p. 1.

Gauntt, Tom, ''Michael Powell: Retailer Turns a Page in Bookselling Trade, Makes a Mark As an Activist,'' *Business Journal*, June 8, 1987, p. 12.

Hamilton, Don, ''Michael Powell: Leaving His Imprint on Portland,'' *Oregonian*, July 5, 1987, p. 1.

Hill, Gail Kinsey, ''Bookseller Finds Niche in Used, Rare Books,'' *Oregonian*, August 17, 1999.

—— ''Powell's Employees Say Changes in Pay, Operations Forced Union Push,'' *Oregonian*, March 12, 1999, p. B1.

Hill, Gail Kinsey, and Jeffrey Kossoff, ''Rules Change As Powell's Contract Signed,'' *Oregonian*, August 15, 2000, p. E1.

Miller, Matt, ''Be They Browsers or Bibliophiles . . . Powell's Is One for the Books,'' *San Diego Union-Tribune*, July 31, 1990, p. D1.

Pintarich, Paul, ''Powell's Sets Aside Space for the Rare,'' *Oregonian*, March 15, 1987, p. 18.

Rothenberg, Randall, ''Outside Publishing Centers, A Giant Bookstore Prospers,'' *New York Times*, August 12, 1991, p. D7.

Tripp, Julie, ''Where Books Are Big Business,'' *Oregonian*, August 28, 1983, p. A22.

—Carrie Rothburd

Randall's Food Markets, Inc.

3663 Briarpark Drive
Houston, Texas 77042
U.S.A.
Telephone: (713) 268-3500
Fax: (713) 268-3602
Web site: http://www.randalls.com

Wholly Owned Subsidiary of Safeway Inc.
Incorporated: 1966
Employees: 17,650
Sales: $2.58 billion (1999)
NAIC: 44511 Supermarkets and Other Grocery (Except Convenience) Stores

Randall's Food Markets, Inc. (better known as Randalls, sans apostrophe) operates a chain of 116 supermarkets in Texas, competing in Houston, Dallas, and Austin. The company's stores operate under the names Randalls and Tom Thumb and feature an array of specialty departments. Designed as one-stop-shopping destinations, the supermarkets contain bakeries, florists, coffee shops, pharmacies, banks, delicatessens, gourmet counters, and video rental departments. Randalls has been credited with revolutionizing the grocery business in Houston, where the chain started as a family-owned business.

Origins

The celebrated legacy of the Onstead name in Houston's grocery business began with the family's patriarch, Robert Randall Onstead. Onstead gained his first experience in the grocery business as a teenager, when he delivered groceries for his uncle in Ennis, Texas. The son of a mail carrier, Onstead studied for a premedical degree at the University of North Texas before moving to Houston with his wife in 1954. He arrived in Houston to work for his father-in-law, Blocker Martin, who hired the 23-year-old Onstead to manage a grocery store he owned. Martin served as Onstead's mentor, teaching his son-in-law the value of customer service and innovation. Martin was dynamic and charismatic, while Onstead was described as quiet and conservative, but the pair worked well together.

By 1960, Onstead had become president of the grocery business, which had expanded to include four stores. Although the business existed for only four years after Onstead took charge, the Martin and Onstead pairing made a lasting impression on local shoppers. When the company's second store opened, the two grocery store innovators celebrated the grand opening by wrapping the store in Saran Wrap, a product that recently had made its debut on store shelves in the United States. The television program "Today" broadcast the event live, heralding the marketing flair on display.

The four-store grocery business was sold to Piggly Wiggly in 1964, but Onstead was only beginning what would become a lifelong career as a grocer. For his next foray into the grocery business, Onstead teamed with two industry veterans, Norman Frewin and Randall Barclay, in 1966. The trio started with $85,000 in capital—most of it borrowed—and purchased two Minimax stores in north Houston. The stores were renamed Randalls and tailored into discount supermarkets featuring merchandising innovations that would later become standard characteristics of grocery stores across the country. Special prices were advertised on the stores' large front windows, hot delis were constructed inside, and other specialty departments—trademarks of an Onstead-owned supermarket—were added in a gradual process. The business expanded gradually as well, developing into a small, local chain renowned for catering to the specific needs of its customers. There were four stores by 1970 and eight stores by 1977. Expansion occurred at a measured pace, restricting the company's territory of service primarily to the affluent western suburbs of Houston, but the stores' reputation among customers was growing at a more energetic pace.

"We had a strong following around the sites of our stores," explained Randall Onstead, the son of Robert Onstead and the future leader of the company. "Almost everybody in the area shopped at Randalls," he said, in a May 1987 interview with *Progressive Grocer*. "But there were many neighborhoods in Houston where we had no presence. We needed a plan to expand our operations in the entire market." By the late 1970s, the desire to accelerate expansion intensified. Houston, enjoying a remarkable surge in growth fueled by an oil boom, ranked as one of the fastest growing metropolitan areas in the country. Randalls, tremendously popular in the neighborhoods it occupied, stood poised to share in the growth of the city. At the time, the company controlled 4 percent of the grocery market in the city, the point from which it began pursuing its declared goal of developing into the market leader in Houston. Robert Onstead was ready to expand in earnest and see if his blend of customer service and elaborate supermarkets could attract more Houstonians than all his rivals.

1980: Spurring Expansion with Acquisitions

Onstead spent nearly 15 years forging Randalls' reputation as a high-quality supermarket chain before striking out on the expansion trail with strident steps. The march began in 1980, when Randalls acquired four large retail stores recently vacated by Handy Andy, a supermarket chain that had flirted with the one-stop-shopping concept that would become Randalls' signature trait. Each of the acquired stores was nearly twice as large as Onstead's existing stores, giving him the space to actualize his vision of the premier supermarket. The stores also were situated in affluent Houston neighborhoods with ideal demographics. For future store sites, Onstead chose locations on the periphery of fast-growing Houston, establishing stores near new shopping areas where condominiums and houses would be built once the retail centers were completed.

To capitalize on the opportunity presented by the large, former Handy Andy stores, Randalls developed two supermarket concepts. Both of the concepts would serve as the company's exclusive expansion vehicles for the 1980s. Ranging in size between 50,000 and 56,000 square feet, Randalls' ''super combo'' stores were designed to make the company the market leader in Houston. The stores contained pharmacies, seafood sections, banks, florists, in-store restaurants, and cosmetic departments. The company's other concept, its ''flagship'' format, was roughly the same size as a super combo with all the same specialty departments, but also included a French bakery and 5,000 upscale specialty items scattered throughout the store's shelves.

Onstead's son, Randall, joined the company as an assistant manager at the chain's first flagship store. His arrival at the nine-store chain marked the beginning of an era of unprecedented growth. Between 1977 and 1982, Randalls' market share leaped from 4 percent to 11 percent. By 1987, a year after Randall Onstead was appointed president and chief operating officer, the company had expanded into a 39-store chain with a firm hold on the competitive Houston market. Despite its long-standing policy of refusing to sell beer, wine, or any other alcohol, Randalls controlled 27 percent of the metropolitan

market by 1987, having leveraged its prestigious reputation to create a chain of domineering strength. The national business press took note of the company's strident growth during the 1980s, which lifted annual revenues to $900 million by the decade's end, but success engendered its own problems. To continue its remarkable record of growth into the 1990s, the Onsteads would have to look beyond Houston to satisfy their desire for expansion. By doing so, the father-and-son team was forced to complete a difficult evolutionary process. Randalls, once a local, mom-and-pop business, was transforming into a regional corporation.

Expanding into Dallas: 1992

By 1992, Randalls was a thriving 46-store chain with annual sales in excess of $1 billion. The chain ranked as the fastest growing company in Houston. From this point in its development, Randalls began to greatly accelerate its expansion, eclipsing the robust pace set in the 1980s. In 1992, the company acquired the chain of grocery stores from Cullum Companies. The acquisition doubled the size of Randalls, giving the company a chain of supermarkets that ranked as the market leader in Dallas. Next, in January 1994, Randalls acquired the Austin, Texas-based AppleTree chain, giving the company a presence in three cities and control over 125 supermarkets.

For several years after the acquisitions, Randalls struggled to contend with operational, competitive, and managerial challenges created by absorbing Tom Thumb and AppleTree. Now with stores in Dallas, Houston, and Austin, the Onsteads found themselves presiding over a $2-billion-in-sales regional grocery organization that forced them to change their leadership style. Since the company's inception, Robert Onstead—an active Church of Christ member—had refused to sell alcohol, but the acquisition of the Tom Thumb chain, which sold beer and wine, forced a change in policy. In September 1994, Randalls rescinded its ban on alcohol—just one of several profound changes that occurred during the mid-1990s. In an October 1994 interview with *Progressive Grocer,* Randall Onstead explained: ''The most challenging issue we're dealing with is digesting all of the acquisitions. As similar as our operations were, we couldn't have been more different in our managerial and organizational styles. Randalls had a top-down management style. All decisions were made at the top. Tom Thumb had a consensus-run or bottom-up management style. Well, it didn't take long to figure out that Randalls top-down management style was not going to work in a big company. Very soon after the acquisition of Tom Thumb it became obvious there was friction between the two styles.''

Eventually, the Onsteads realized they needed to relinquish some control over their company. The benign autocracy that had existed for more than a quarter of a century was replaced with a decentralized structure that ceded authority to lower levels of management. Store managers began to exert more influence over the operation of the company, and, for the first time, supermarket employees were asked for their opinions regarding the chain's management. Structurally, Randalls was divided into three management groups to oversee the company's stores in Houston, Dallas, and Austin. Ultimately, the operational problems stemming from the Tom Thumb acquisition were not completely resolved until Robert Onstead moved

Key Dates:

1966: Robert Onstead and two partners open two grocery stores in north Houston.
1980: Four Handy Andy supermarkets are acquired.
1986: Randall Onstead, son of the company's founder, is named president.
1992: supermarket chain is acquired.
1997: Kohlberg Kravis Roberts & Co. acquires controlling interest in Randall's.
1999: Safeway Inc. pays $1.43 billion for Randall's.

to Dallas in 1996 to serve as a liaison between Houston and Dallas. Concurrently, he relinquished his title as chief executive officer to his son, who assumed strategic control over the company as it entered the late 1990s.

Randalls' operational problems began to disappear after 1996, but another aftereffect of the early 1990s acquisition continued to hound the company. The acquisitions had left Randalls strapped for cash and burdened with debt. Although the company continued to expand following the absorption of Tom Thumb and AppleTree, it did so at a lumbering pace, causing its revenue volume to stall at roughly $2.4 billion during the mid-1990s. "We've been under serious capital constraint the last three years, which has made it difficult to grow at the pace we felt we needed to grow," Randall Onstead remarked in the April 7, 1997, issue of *Supermarket News.* "We've opened three or four new stores a year during those three years, and we'd like to grow at a faster pace."

Late 1990s: The End of an Era

To resolve their financial dilemma, the Onsteads chose not to complete an initial public offering of stock, but allied themselves with a financial partner instead. In 1997, the New York investment firm Kohlberg Kravis Roberts & Co. (KKR) purchased a 61 percent stake in Randalls for $225 million. KKR was most widely known for its hostile takeover of RJR Nabisco in 1989, a $25 billion deal that ranked as the largest takeover in business history. Randalls' partnership with KKR gave the Onsteads the capital to reduce their debt and fund the expansion and renovation of their chain. Of the $225 million, the company used $100 million to reduce its debt of $340 million. The balance was earmarked for expansion. Armed with a fresh supply of capital, the Onsteads announced that they were pursuing a goal of $3.5 billion in sales by 2000.

In the wake of the KKR equity investment, Randalls threw itself into an exhaustive renovation and expansion program. Within 18 months, the company had opened ten new stores and had remodeled 39 existing stores. In the spring of 1999, eight new stores were under construction and five major renovations were underway, excluding the $113 million the company planned to spend during the remainder of the year to add 16 new stores and to complete 53 store renovations. Although chainwide sales failed to increase substantially, the sales recorded at individual stores before the KKR investment and after the KKR investment increased an industry leading 8.7 percent as

Randalls headed into the summer of 1999. It was at this point when industry observers heard startling news. The announcement marked the beginning of a new era at Randalls.

In mid-1999, Pleasanton, California-based Safeway Inc. acquired Randalls in a $1.43 billion deal. The $27-billion-in-sales grocery chain operated more than 1,500 supermarkets in the United States and Canada. Safeway had abandoned the Houston and Dallas markets during the late 1980s as part of a restructuring program. Its return to Texas's major markets represented the fulfillment of the company's self-described "fill-in strategy," as it sought to flesh out its North American presence. For Randalls, the acquisition promised to greatly improve the chain's ability to remain competitive. As it had expanded throughout its three-city territory, the company faced stiff competition from rivals Albertson's, Inc. and The Kroger Co., national supermarket chains that enjoyed greater purchasing power than Randalls. By becoming part of the Safeway fold, Randalls gained the ability to negotiate larger discounts when purchasing products, enabling the chain, in turn, to lower its retail prices and more effectively compete against Albertson's, Kroger, and others.

As Randalls entered the 21st century, the company was buoyed by the vast financial support of Safeway. Although the acquisitions of the early 1990s had delivered substantial physical and geographic growth to the chain, the process of absorbing the companies and evolving into a regional chain had proven difficult. Much of the 1990s had been spent resolving operational, managerial, and financial problems stemming from the Onsteads' march into Austin and Dallas, but following its acquisition by Safeway, Randalls' management hoped to conclude the near decade-long struggle. Despite the company's growing pains, its reputation among Texas shoppers remained impressively strong. Randall Onstead stayed on as chief executive officer, and the chain's stores retained their names as well, making the transition into Safeway ownership an imperceptible segue in the eyes of most shoppers.

Principal Subsidiaries

Randall's Food & Drugs, Inc.; Randall's Properties, Inc.; Gooch Packaging Company, Inc.; American Community Stores Corporation; Food Depot, Inc.; Randall's Beverage Company, Inc.; Randall's Management Company, Inc.

Principal Competitors

The Kroger Co.; H.E. Butt Grocery Company; Albertson's, Inc.

Further Reading

Calkins, Laurel Brubaker, "Randalls: Redefining the Way Houstonians Shop for Groceries," *Houston Business Journal,* March 12, 1990, p. 14.
Elder, Laura, "Supermarket Merger Remarkable," *Houston Business Journal,* July 30, 1999, p. 1.
"KKR Takeover Seen As Win-Win Situation for Onstead Family," *Knight-Ridder/Tribune Business News,* March 10, 1998, p. 310B1087.
Kramer, Louise, "Randalls Leaves Its Thumbprint; the First Tom Thumb Store to Open Since Cullum Was Acquired Bears the

Houston Parent's Fresh Foods Stamp,'' *Supermarket News,* March 21, 1994, p. 45.

Mathews, Ryan, ''A Decade of Change,'' *Progressive Grocer,* October 1994, p. 28.

Pybus, Kenneth, ''Grocery Giant Keeps Shelves Stocked with Change,'' *Houston Business Journal,* December 9, 1994, p. 24.

''Randalls Chairman to Add Same Post at Tom Thumb, Give Up CEO Position,'' *Supermarket News,* March 11, 1996, p. 6.

Tanner, Ronald, ''Five Chains That Stand Out,'' *Progressive Grocer,* October 1985, p. 83.

——, ''Randalls: On the Expansion Trail,'' *Progressive Grocer,* May 1987, p. 206.

Turcsik, Richard, ''Deep in the Heart of Texas,'' *Progressive Grocer,* September 1999, p. 11.

Zweibach, Elliot, ''KKR Agrees to Purchase Stake of 61% in Randalls,'' *Supermarket News,* April 7, 1997, p. 1.

——, ''New Role for Randalls,'' *Supermarket News,* September 28, 1998, p. 1.

——, ''Strategies Growth,'' *Supermarket News,* March 8, 1999, p. 29.

—Jeffrey L. Covell

Remington Arms Company, Inc.

870 Remington Drive
P.O. Box 700
Madison, North Carolina 27025-0700
U.S.A.
Telephone: (336) 548-8700
Fax: (336) 548-8629
Web site: http://www.remington.com

Wholly Owned Subsidiary of Clayton, Dubilier & Rice, Inc.
Incorporated: 1816
Employees: 2,500
Sales: $381.2 million (1997)
NAIC: 332994 Small Arms Manufacturing; 332992 Small Arms Ammunition Manufacturing; 339920 Sporting and Athletic Goods Manufacturing; 314991 Rope, Cordage, and Twine Mills

Remington Arms Company, Inc. is one of the oldest manufacturers of firearms in the United States and the largest U.S. producer of rifles. The company also sells the Stren brand of fishing line and other fishing products. A worldwide supplier of small arms, Remington holds a special place in American popular culture, its name having grown synonymous with the taming of the American West in the 19th century. In addition, the company is known for its long history of innovation, and counts the famous breach-loading rifle among its many advancements in technology.

Early 19th-Century Beginnings

Eliphalet Remington, Jr., the progenitor of Remington Arms, was born in 1793 to Eliphalet and Elizabeth Remington. The family moved west—from Connecticut to New York—in 1800 to find land and start a farm. They settled in what is now Ilion, New York. In addition to the farm, Eliphalet set up a forge and blacksmith shop to help him build his farm equipment. Eliphalet, Jr., was drawn to the shop early, and displayed a canny Yankee ingenuity. For example, when the Remington family wanted some silver spoons for Eliphalet, Jr.'s sister, Mary, they sent the young Eliphalet to a silversmith with pieces of rough silver. After watching the silversmith for a day,

Eliphalet, Jr., returned with the silver pieces. He then proceeded to make the spoons himself, to everyone's satisfaction, in the family's blacksmith shop.

Remington acted similarly when he decided to make his own hunting rifle. Unable to afford the purchase price of a new rifle, he fashioned his own from scrap iron. Locals were so impressed with Remington's homemade firearm that they began paying him to make rifles for them. Within a few years Remington's skills were recognized throughout the region and he was deluged with orders for custom-made firearms. Throughout the 1820s Eliphalet, Jr., and his father shipped rifles to customers throughout New England by way of the Erie Canal. In 1828 he expanded the business by purchasing 100 acres of land closer to the canal. With financial backing from friends, he set up a new forge and blacksmith shop. Unfortunately, Eliphalet, Sr., was accidentally killed while transporting equipment to the new location.

Remington's operation continued to blossom during the 1830s as his guns became known for their high-quality craftsmanship. The company received a major boost in 1845 when it landed its first government contract. Also in 1845, Remington crafted the first gun barrel in America to be fashioned from solid steel. Remington's steel rifles quickly garnered a reputation for precision. Orders poured in. Beginning in the 1850s, Remington started designing and manufacturing revolvers. For several years the company sold its popular Beal revolver. It followed that model with the Rider revolver, one of the first self-cocking revolvers. In 1856 Eliphalet and his three sons officially joined forces to form E. Remington and Sons.

Explosive Growth, Diversification, Then Bankruptcy in Later 19th Century

Not surprisingly, E. Remington and Sons experienced explosive growth during the Civil War and contributed to the Union victory. Even before the war started the Remington armory was churning out rifles by the thousands for various government contracts. After the war began, though, production boomed. The company filled one order, for example, for 40,000 rifles priced at $16 each. To keep up with skyrocketing demand, the company built a temporary production facility to make army revolvers and installed a steam generation system to produce power. At times, every man and boy in the town of Ilion worked day and night for periods of weeks to meet contract deadlines. Remington produced nearly $3 million worth of rifles during the war. Importantly, Remington developed its famous breach-loading gun at this time to replace the conventional muzzle-loading rifle.

The demands of wartime production proved to be too much for the 68-year-old Remington. He died during the first few months of the conflict, leaving his three sons to fill his shoes. Philo, the oldest of the three and the best craftsman, became president of the company. Younger brother Samuel, who was known as a savvy businessman, became responsible for finding new contracts. He is credited with extending Remington's reach overseas. In fact, Samuel eventually made his home in Paris and London, and later assumed the title of president of the company in order to enhance his prestige (and ability to get new business) in Europe. Eliphalet, the youngest, was placed in charge of the office and day-to-day operating activities.

Business dropped after the war, but orders surged within a few years as a result of Remington's increasingly popular breach-loading rifles. Besides new orders by the U.S. Army, Remington shipped hundreds of thousands of rifles overseas to countries such as Sweden, France, Egypt, Spain, and Denmark. Samuel eventually secured more than $11 million in contracts with the French government alone, largely as a result of that country's war with Germany. By the 1870s Remington's gun production capacity had surpassed that of the entire nation of England. It employed 1,850 people and, at times, churned out an average of 1,400 rifles and 200 revolvers daily.

International orders slowed during the late 1800s. To keep its workers busy, Remington diversified into a number of unique industries where its penchant for innovation was rewarded. For example, it contracted to build the first 100 Baxter steam cars (streetcars capable of producing 25 horsepower and traveling at speeds of more than 15 miles per hour). Remington was later the first company to manufacture a Baxter steam canal boat. Similarly, the Remington armory manufactured the first 100 velocipedes (vehicles that sported two wooden wheels with attached crank pedals) made in the United States, thus giving birth to the domestic bicycle industry. Remington even shipped a special tandem, or two-seater, model. Other innovations manufactured by Remington beginning in the late 1880s included specialized sewing machines and devices, the typewriter, electric lighting systems, pill- and tablet-making equipment, gaso-

line-powered engines, deep-well pumps, lathes, burglar alarms, and cigar-making machines.

After development by the armory, most of Remington's inventions were contracted out for manufacture or set up as separate operating companies under the constantly unfolding Remington corporate umbrella. Soon, Remington became known as a haven for inventors. At times during the 1870s and 1880s, Remington secured an average of four new patents each week. Inventors were welcomed into Philo Remington's home, where they would present their ideas. If Philo approved, Remington's armory would assist in patenting and producing the device. Meanwhile, the company continued to innovate in the firearms industry. It introduced the James P. Lee military rifle, for example, a type of bolt-action gun that was followed by more advanced Remington models. Remington also developed a rapid-fire naval gun, one of the earliest precursors to the modern machine gun, and a popular double-barreled shotgun. Among other unique novelties was Remington's "gun cane," a gun that looked like a walking stick, and a portable gun designed to project 200 yards of lifeline to the upper floors of burning buildings.

By the mid-1880s Remington had established itself as a pillar of American ingenuity. Unfortunately, the Remington brothers' (Samuel had died in 1882) strategy of diversification had failed to bear fruit and the company was financially troubled. Problems were exacerbated by untimely setbacks, such as the infamous Chicago fire of 1874, which destroyed Remington's sewing machine company. Remington went bankrupt in 1886 and was bought out in 1888 by a partnership led by private investor Marcellus Hartley, who was also a Remington salesman. The town of Ilion was stunned as the Remington family endured its darkest hour. Philo died in 1889, but Eliphalet III lived until 1924. Although he was removed from the company's operations, Eliphalet lived to see the resurgence of E. Remington and Sons as the Remington Arms Company. As the company's performance continued to wane during the 1890s, the new owners shed Remington's non-performing operations, including its long-running farm implements business. Nevertheless, Remington's legacy of innovation continued. It was particularly recognized for its inventions related to the bicycle and the typewriter.

Although Remington experienced financial problems, the company never lost its reputation as the inventor and producer of some of the finest firearms in the world. While Remington became a major player in the northeastern U.S. industrial community, its firearms helped to tame the American West. In fact, many of Remington's rifles and revolvers achieved legendary status. Wild Bill Hickok, for example, was known for carrying a Remington double-barreled Derringer pistol in his vest pocket. Likewise, infamous bank robber Frank James and renowned riverboat gambler Bat Masterson both publicly endorsed Remington firearms in newspaper advertisements. Remington's role in the settling of the country would be recounted endlessly in the Hollywood westerns of the 20th century.

Becoming Affiliate of Du Pont in First Half of 20th Century

Remington's fortunes began to improve following a government order in 1898 for 100,000 guns during the Spanish-

Key Dates:

1816: Eliphalet Remington, Jr., makes his first hunting rifle.
1856: Remington and his three sons form E. Remington and Sons.
1886: Company goes bankrupt.
1888: A partnership led by investor Marcellus Hartley buys out the company and reorganizes it as Remington Arms Company.
1920: Company is incorporated as Remington Arms Company, Inc.
1933: E.I. du Pont de Nemours & Company acquires a 60 percent stake in Remington.
1942: Company sells its two-millionth rifle.
1969: Power tool business is sold to DESA Industries, Inc.
1986: Remington completes a move of its headquarters from Bridgeport, Connecticut, to Wilmington, Delaware.
1992: Company assumes control of the Stren fishing product line from Du Pont.
1993: Du Pont sells Remington to Clayton, Dubilier & Rice, Inc., a private investment group.
1996: Remington moves its headquarters to Madison, North Carolina.

American War. As its firearms business healed, the company bailed out of less successful endeavors, including its large bicycle operation. It kept its typewriter division, the Remington Standard Typewriter Company (renamed Remington Typewriter Company in 1903); in 1927 it folded that company into an affiliated office equipment company called Remington Rand, Inc. Sales were again buoyed with the onset of World War I, first by orders from English and French governments and later by the United States when it finally entered the conflict. During World War I Remington spent about $1 million on new land, buildings, and equipment necessary to meet ballooning demand. After the United States entered the war in 1917, Remington's workforce swelled from about 900 to more than 11,000. That figure eventually climbed as high as 15,000, many of whom were women. Daily output reached a record 3,000 rifles daily.

Remington was better prepared to deal with the postwar sales slide following World War I than it had been after previous conflicts. Specifically, Remington introduced its first cash register in 1918. Sales of the patented device were swift during most of the 1920s. But even that business slumped following the Great Depression. Remington sold the operation to National Cash Register Company in 1931 in an effort to buoy lagging gun sales. By the early 1930s Remington employed only 300 workers at its core Ilion plant. In need of a facelift, Remington sold a 60 percent interest to E.I. du Pont de Nemours & Company in 1933. Under Du Pont's direction, Remington tore down several unneeded buildings and refurbished some of its aging facilities. By the late 1930s Remington was well-positioned for the impending World War II production boom.

Du Pont's interest in Remington was both well-timed and appropriate. Founded in 1802, the company had started as a manufacturer of gunpowder and explosives. By the early 1900s Du Pont controlled the lion's share of the U.S. gunpowder market. Because Remington had augmented its firearms operations with extensive munitions manufacturing, the companies complemented one another. The partnership was particularly beneficial during World War II, when demand for both gunpowder and firearms soared. Remington again shifted into overdrive during that war, hiring more than 9,000 workers to produce its renowned Springfield rifle. The U.S. government accepted delivery from Remington of more than one million rifles during the early 1940s. Remington's factories ran 24 hours each day, seven days per week. The company celebrated the sale of its two-millionth rifle in 1942.

Following the war, Remington again focused on developing and producing firearms for sport. Its payroll was quickly reduced to about 1,500 workers and business was expectedly sluggish. To boost sales from its core firearms and munitions segments, Remington diversified into new arenas. Notable was its entrance into the industrial tool field. Remington developed and began manufacturing a "Cartridge-powered Stud Driver," a device that fired stud fasteners into various structural materials. The model 450, as it was labeled, used cartridges similar to bullet cartridges. The product enjoyed success during the massive postwar housing and construction boom. Remington sold its power tool business to DESA Industries, Inc. in 1969.

Remington continued to glean profits from military contracts and to sell its sporting rifles and shotguns during the mid-1900s. In addition, it branched out into a number of new markets. It continued to produce sewing machines and office equipment through its affiliation with Remington-Rand, for example, although that unit was eventually sold. Remington began producing goods ranging from hunting knives and mens' accessories (such as Remington shavers) to household utensils and tools. As its offerings and sales expanded, Remington's manufacturing infrastructure extended throughout the United States, with both corporate and government-owned plants spreading to Delaware, Connecticut, Arkansas, Ohio, and Oklahoma, among other places.

Wholly Owned by Du Pont: 1980–93

By 1980, Remington was generating approximately $300 million in sales, most of which was attributable to its firearms and munitions divisions. When Du Pont completed its purchase of Remington Arms in 1980 as part of its strategy to diversify out of its core chemical business, which was suffering from a savage petrochemical industry downturn, however, the investment proved a big disappointment. Remington experienced major setbacks during the early and mid-1980s, especially in the face of strong foreign competition. Low-cost gunmakers, particularly in emerging Asian economies, inundated U.S. markets with inexpensive firearms. At the same time, Remington's strongest demographic market segment, midwestern farmers, fell on hard times.

By 1986, Remington's annual revenues had plummeted to a discouraging $200 million. Distressed by the failure of the division, Du Pont initiated a reorganization at Remington that was designed to streamline operations, improve research and development, and ultimately improve profitability. Du Pont closed some of Remington's facilities, among other cost-cutting measures, and made plans to broaden Remington's product line. Items introduced during 1986 included a line of hunting apparel and high-tech deer rifles made with kevlar (a lightweight synthetic material five times stronger than steel). Providing the foundation for those innovations were proven Du Pont performers, including: the Model 700 line of hunting rifles; the XP-100 pistols, which were considered among the most accurate in the world; and popular shotgun models 11-87, 1100, and 870. In 1992 Remington further broadened its product line when Du Pont placed its Stren brand of fishing line and other fishing products within Remington's purview.

During the late 1980s and early 1990s, Remington's financial performance improved significantly, largely as a result of successful product line extensions and new introductions. By 1992, in fact, Remington had nearly doubled its sales over 1986 levels to about $400 million annually. In 1993, Du Pont announced that it had reached an agreement to sell Remington to leveraged-buyout specialist Clayton, Dubilier & Rice, Inc., a private investment group.

The Clayton, Dubilier & Rice Era, 1993 into the 21st Century

Remington enthusiasts were fearful that the company's legacy of quality and innovation might be trammeled by the private investment group. Those concerns were allayed shortly after the new owner announced its long-term plans for Remington. For example, under the direction of Remington's new chief executive, Tommy Millner, Remington announced plans to open a new $5 million research and development center in Elizabethtown, Kentucky. Opened in 1996, it was initially staffed with about 60 employees. Remington also announced its intent to consolidate operations, lower operating costs, and to more actively support legislation related to gun-owner's and hunter's rights. Regarding the latter, Remington joined the American Shooting Sports Council and the Remington Arms Political Action Committee, which were engaged in legal battles with increasing numbers of municipalities, who were suing gunmakers over alleged negligence in the manufacturing, marketing, and distribution of guns. These suits were somewhat similar to the largely successful suits brought against the tobacco industry starting in the mid-1990s. To show its concern about issues of gun safety, Remington spent $1 million on safety-related advertisements and on producing a safety video to be included with most of the company's new firearms. Also, the Remington Shooting School opened in 1995, near the company's plant in Ilion. Under its new ownership, Remington also bolstered its marketing efforts by becoming a major sponsor of NASCAR Winston Cup auto racing.

Other developments in the mid-1990s included Millner's decision to move the company's headquarters to a more rural setting, in keeping with where the bulk of its customers lived. In 1996, therefore, Remington relocated to Madison, North Carolina, a small town about 25 miles north of Greensboro. Further expansion came in 1997 when the company opened a new firearms plant near Mayfield, Kentucky, its first such new plant since 1828.

Remington's financial position was rather precarious in the late 1990s as the company was carrying a fairly heavy load of debt and had to contend with the stagnant sales that were vexing the entire gun industry. The sales slump had a number of causes, including an aging population of gunowners, which was also declining in numbers, and less interest in hunting (coupled with the diminishment of huntable land due to urban sprawl). The potential for additional federal gun-control legislation and the

lawsuits filed against the gun industry placed further clouds over the company's future.

It was against this backdrop that Clayton, Dubilier & Rice began exploring in early 1998 the possible sale of Remington or a public offering of its stock. By mid-2001, however, no deal had been completed to either sell the company or take it public. In the meantime, the gun industry made a bit of a comeback in 1999 when demand for guns surged for the first time in several years, enabling gunmakers to increase their revenues through price increases—Remington boosting its prices from 2.5 to 5.5 percent. The increased demand appeared to stem from a combination of anxiety over potential chaos resulting from the Y2K computer bug and concerns that buying guns might be made more difficult in the future in the wake of the municipal lawsuits and the shooting massacre at a high school in Littleton, Colorado. Of course, the Y2K bug resulted in little chaos, and George W. Bush's ascension to the presidency in 2001 dampened fears about increased federal gun control. It also appeared that the lawsuits might be losing steam as some early court rulings went in favor of the gunmakers.

Principal Competitors

Sturm, Ruger & Company, Inc.; Fabbrica d'Armi Pietro Beretta S.p.A.; Colt's Manufacturing Company, Inc.; Smith & Wesson Corporation; Glock GmbH; SIG Arms Sauer GmbH.

Further Reading

Berger, Loren, ''Remington Faces a Misfiring Squad,'' *Business Week,* May 23, 1994, p. 90.

James, Frank W., ''Remington Answers Shooter's Needs,'' *Shooting Industry,* October 1991, p. 18.

Kerfoot, Kevin, ''The Remington Arms Co. Building New Facility,'' *Kentucky Manufacturer,* June 1996.

Marcot, Roy, *Remington: America's Oldest Gunmaker,* Stevens Point, Wis.: Primedia Special Interest Publications, 1998.

McKee, Kelly, ''Firearms Maker Heads for the Country,'' *Greensboro (N.C.) News & Record,* January 17, 1999, p. R3.

Schulz, Warren E., *Ilion—The Town Remington Made,* Hicksville, N.Y.: Exposition Press, 1977.

Shaw, Donna, ''Legendary Remington Gunmaker Sold to Manhattan Investment Firm,'' *Knight-Ridder/Tribune Business News,* October 21, 1993, p. 102.

Slutsker, Gary, ''The Name Game,'' *Forbes,* December 15, 1986, p. 187.

Stankevich, Debby Garbato, ''Taking Aim,'' *Discount Merchandiser,* July 1998, pp. 41–45.

Sundra, Jon R., ''Following a Year Under New Ownership, Remington Proves to Be in Good Hands,'' *Shooting Industry,* January 1995, p. 20.

——, ''Looking for Hard Facts in the Soft Firearms Market,'' *Shooting Industry,* February 1998, pp. 18+.

Taylor, John M., ''Remington's New Era,'' *American Hunter,* January 1994, p. 12.

——, ''Remington Posts Profits, Still on the Selling Block,'' *Shooting Industry,* August 1998, p. 62.

——, ''Remington Sets the Pace,'' *Shooting Industry,* March 1996, pp. 90+.

Weidner, David, ''Remington Arms Is Moving to North Carolina,'' *Winston-Salem Journal,* September 22, 1995, p. 7.

—Dave Mote
—update: David E. Salamie

Repsol-YPF S.A.

Paseo de la Castellana, 278
28046 Madrid
Spain
Telephone: (+34) 91-348-81-00
Fax: (+34) 91-348-28-21
Web site: http://www.repsol-ypf.com

Public Company
Incorporated: 1987
Employees: 29,262
Sales: $43.08 billion (2000)
Stock Exchanges: Madrid New York
Ticker Symbol: REP
NAIC: 324110 Petroleum Refineries; 324199 All Other
    Petroleum and Coal Products Manufacturing; 486110
    Pipeline Transportation of Crude Oil; 324110
    Petroleum Refineries

Repsol-YPF S.A. is Spain's largest industrial company and is the sixth largest oil company in Europe in terms of sales. Formed in 1987 by the merger of state-controlled oil sector companies, Repsol is now 100 percent privatized and publicly traded on both the Madrid and New York stock exchanges. One of Spain's dominant companies, Repsol-YPF is also Argentina's largest corporation, with the addition of YPF, which Repsol acquired from the Argentinean government in 1999. YPF adds important oil and natural gas exploration and production operations to Repsol's predominantly refining and marketing-based operations. The company now controls about 60 percent of the refining market in Spain and has a 45.5 percent share and controlling management position in Gas Natural, which dominates the Spanish natural gas market. The company also controls nearly 45 percent of Argentina's oil reserves and about 40 percent of its natural gas market. The company exports throughout much of South America. The addition of YPF has catapulted Repsol-YPF into the leading ranks of global oil companies, giving the company the number seven spot.

State Control in the 1920s

In 1539, the Spanish ship *Santa Cruz* transported the first transatlantic oil shipment when it carried a barrel from Venezuela to Spain. It was thought the dark fluid had properties to relieve the gout of King Charles I. History does not record whether he found it to be an effective remedy.

State monopoly and control, a characteristic that persisted in the Spanish industry, was established at the end of the 18th century when King Charles III declared all mining deposits, whether they were of a commercial character or not, to be the property of the crown. Only the crown would have the right to grant exploration or development concessions.

As 19th- and 20th-century Spain fell into a long period of decline and lagged behind the rest of Europe in industrial development, the country failed to develop a strong domestic oil industry. By the mid-1920s only a few unsuccessful attempts at oil exploration had taken place. No refineries were built. The country was heavily dependent on imported foreign oil, supplied by Shell and other major multinationals and distributed through an inadequate and fragmented network.

The corrupt dictatorship of Primo de Rivera, which governed the country between 1923 and 1930, realized that this state of affairs could not continue if Spain were to industrialize. The problem haunted successive Spanish governments and later it became more important as living standards and the number of motor vehicles rose in the period of rapid economic growth that followed World War II. By 1980, 65 percent of Spain's oil was still imported. Rivera's solution was to return to the tradition of state monopoly, a policy that was followed in modified forms by all successive Spanish governments up to 1986. In 1927, the dictator issued a decree expropriating all foreign and domestic oil sector companies and placing them under the control of a state agency. Administration was entrusted to Compañia Arrendataria del Monopolio de Pétroleos Sociedad Anónima (CAMPSA), which had the sole rights to purchase oil from producers at state-controlled prices.

Ironically, the country's first refinery was built in the Canary Islands by Compañia Española de Petróleos S.A. (CEPSA), a private company, in 1930. The islands had been specifically excluded from the decree. CEPSA has remained an important Spanish oil company. Three state-owned refineries were built prior to the disruptions of the 1936–39 Spanish Civil War and the Franco dictatorship's diplomatic isolation and armed neutrality during World War II.

In July 1941, CAMPSA undertook the country's first major exploration, the ''Tudanca'' survey of the northern Burgos region, with negative results. Foreign exchange pressures and CAMPSA's continued failure to discover oil on Spanish territory led the Franco regime to relax rules on foreign participation.

A 1947 law left CAMPSA in control of marketing and distribution, but enabled the government to authorize private and public companies to develop a wide range of activities in trade, industrial handling—especially refining—storage, research, and exploration for production of oil and gas fields.

In practice, the government usually required foreign companies to work under joint participation schemes with CAMPSA or other state-controlled entities. A requirement that both private and public refineries had to sell to CAMPSA continued, and in 1957 it was extended to gasified petroleum products.

The State Monopoly in the 1960s and 1970s

In 1963, the government announced the National Combustibles Plan and it asserted direct control of sales, imports, and production of oil products. The government would determine each refinery's contribution to the national supply. Each refinery had to offer its product to CAMPSA, which then sold to consumers through its monopoly distribution network. To protect the balance of payments, refineries had to purchase a set percentage of their crude requirements from the Spanish government. This was known as the ''Government Quote'' and reached a height of 50 percent in 1980, then declined until it was removed in 1985.

After 169 wildcat failures, an association of Caltex and CAMPSA made the first discovery of oil in the ''la Lora'' concession and produced small amounts of low-grade crude oil in 1964. In 1965 offshore drilling began, and ten years later joint ventures discovered substantial quantities off the Mediterranean coast. By the early 1990s five offshore producing fields were in operation.

The rapid expansion of the Spanish economy created a 15 percent increase in annual oil consumption. In 1965, the government founded Hispanica de Petróleos (Hispanoil) as a state-owned company charged with spearheading exploration and development efforts in Spain and elsewhere.

When the share of imported crude reached 73 percent of the country's total supply in 1973, the government initiated a policy of encouraging more foreign participation to build refineries. It hoped to offset the costs of imported crude with exports of refined products. Shortly afterward, it attempted to cushion the shock of the first Arab oil boycott and OPEC-induced price rises by lowering taxes on products, with the result that only some of the costs were passed on to consumers.

In June 1974, the government announced the merger of the three refineries in which the state had a controlling interest: REPESA, ENCASO, and ENTASA. The state retained 72 percent of the shares. The new company, Empresa Nacional del Petróleo (ENPETROL) was also given the task of coordinating efforts to secure crude supplies through direct bargaining with producing states. An attempt to develop the First National Energy Plan was soon abandoned in 1976 and the country was without a coordinated energy plan until 1979. Authority for the use and production of energy was dispersed among different agencies, departments, and public companies.

Transition to Privatization in the 1980s

Francisco Franco died in 1975 and Spain passed into a new democratic era. In October 1977, the Spanish government and political leaders signed the Pacts of Moncloa, which attempted to establish a consensus for political and economic change. Included were provisions for the reorganization of the energy sector.

The Second National Energy Plan, introduced in July 1979, laid the groundwork for the formation of Repsol. According to the plan, a reorganization of public entities was required because exploration had failed to develop. The structure of the industry was fragmented and lacked vertical integration. CAMPSA, the Spanish banks, and the Department of Finance continued to resist moves toward integration. The second oil crisis and moves toward joining the European Community (EC), however, forced the logic of integration and the creation of Instituto Nacional de Hidrocarboros (INH), Repsol's direct predecessor. On December 18, 1981, all public participations in the oil sector were brought together in one holding company: INH. Minority foreign shareholders in Spanish public oil companies were gradually bought out.

During the 1983–86 negotiations for Spain's entry to the EC, it became increasingly clear that Spain would have to dismantle its formal government monopoly in marketing. CAMPSA shares were split among the refineries, with INH retaining the majority of the shares. Negotiators hoped to avoid a situation in which the EC would require CAMPSA to offer its distribution network and services to every interested foreign company. The refineries agreed to continue to sell products destined for the domestic market to CAMPSA.

In 1985, Hispanoil took over ENIEPSA, a public company formed in 1976 to engage in exploration. Shortly afterward, INH was reorganized into a divisional structure: Hispanoil exploration, Enpetrol refining, Alcudia petrochemicals, Butano liquefied petroleum gas, and Enagas natural gas distribution. In September 1987, all these divisions, except Enagas, were incorporated into the new Repsol S.A., a company then 100 percent

Key Dates:

1963: Spanish government announces National Combustibles Plan.
1965: Hispanoil is created.
1973: Merger of state-controlled refineries occurs.
1979: Second National Energy Plan lays foundation for Repsol.
1981: Instituto Nacional de Hidrocarboros (INH) is formed.
1985: Hispanoil takes over ENIEPSA, an oil exploration firm.
1986: Repsol S.A. is created.
1989: First public share offering takes place; company acquires Naviera Vizcaina, Pemex, (Mexico), and Carless (U.K.).
1991: Compañia Arrendataria del Monopolio de Pétroleos Sociedad Anónima (CAMPSA) is broken up.
1992: Gas Natural is formed.
1996: Company acquires Astra (Argentina).
1997: Repsol is fully privatized.
1998: Company acquires 15 percent of Argentinean government-controlled YPF.
1999: Repsol acquires full control of YPF.
2000: Company gains full management control of Gas Natural.

owned by the Spanish state. The name Repsol, formerly a trademark for lubrication products, was chosen after extensive marketing research because it was short, widely recognized in Spain, and easy to pronounce in other languages. It was envisaged that Enagas would be added to Repsol at some future point. Otherwise, Repsol retained the INH divisional structure but Hispanoil became Repsol Exploración, Enpetrol was renamed Repsol Petróleo, Alcudia became Repsol Química, and Butano became Repsol Butano.

Repsol's Initial Years

In 1986 Spain joined the EC under a phased plan to enable the country's protected industries, including the oil industry, to adapt to EC regulations. With the creation of Repsol, the government hoped to create an integrated national oil company that would be able to compete successfully in the post-1992 single European market. By changing the structure from that of a government agency to a company in which the government retained a majority stake through INH, an arm's-length relationship was established that might satisfy critics of the Spanish government's close involvement with its oil industry. The INH also wanted to have a strong domestic oil company able to develop an overall strategy including exploration, production, refining, and distribution.

The EC Commission was reluctant to accept Repsol's dominant role in CAMPSA because Article 37 of the Treaty of Rome declared that member states should adjust commercial monopolies to the extent that all discrimination in trade between citizens of member states disappeared. Also, Article 48 of Spain's treaty of adhesion to the EC required Spain to open up its frontiers to the importation of oil products originating from the EC. In

December 1987, the EC Commission warned Spain that it would be taken to the European Court if it did not take further steps to liberalize the market.

A decision had already been made to sell 26 percent of Repsol to the public, both in Spain and abroad. Repsol and the government were impressed with similar privatizations in the United Kingdom. It was believed that a partial flotation would not only raise money and make it easier for the company to secure private sector finance, but also introduce a private sector discipline and increase the international stature of the company. INH would continue to hold a two-thirds share to ensure government control.

The May 1989 share issue, on the Madrid and New York stock markets simultaneously, was successful beyond expectations. The initial offering of 40 million shares was heavily oversubscribed and a further issue equivalent to 10 percent of the original had to be made. Overall, the equivalent of more than $1 billion was raised and the company had 400,000 new shareholders (to date this was the largest share offer ever for a Spanish firm and largest of 1989 worldwide). The issues were so attractive that at least three brokerage firms were later successfully prosecuted for irregularities in the flotation by the Comision Nacional de Valores (CNV), the Spanish stock market supervisory body.

At the beginning of 1989, Repsol acquired the Naviera Vizcaina shipping company to increase its own marine fleet and avoid rising charter rates. Later that year, Repsol took over the 34 percent interest of Petróleos Mexicanos (Pemex), the Mexican state oil company, from the Spanish Petronor refinery company in exchange for a 3 percent interest in Repsol. The deal included a five-year supply contract by Pemex and envisaged cooperative ventures in Mexico. It brought Repsol to a holding of 90 percent in Petronor and 70 percent in CAMPSA. In August of that year, Repsol purchased Carless Refining & Marketing and Carless Petroleum from Kelt Energy, the U.K. oil independent. Repsol intended to develop a market for its products in the United Kingdom through the Carless chain of 500 service stations.

International Leader for the New Century

By 1990, Spain still had only 5,000 service stations. The United Kingdom, by comparison, had 20,000. Foreign companies had only opened seven in Spain, and Repsol's Spanish competitors had opened only 180. In November 1989 Leon Brittan, the EC Competition Commissioner, attacked Spain for failure to open markets in heating oils and liquefied petroleum gas (LPG). With 13 million customers, the subsidiary Repsol Butano had 100 percent of Europe's largest market for butane. But prices for liquefied petroleum gas were soon to be liberalized.

Brittan warned that the commission would keep a close watch on Spanish interpretations of regulations, the dominant position of Repsol in CAMPSA, and the slow development of independent outlets. He said the commission would reexamine a possible court action against Spain if the Spanish market were not fully opened up to foreign competitors.

In 1991 Repsol refined more than 60 percent of all the crude processed in Spain, distributed all liquefied petroleum gas, and produced half the petrochemical and oil products. Partially in response to EC criticism, Repsol and the other CAMPSA shareholders decided that CAMPSA's 3,800 service stations and some other retail assets would be divided between Repsol and the CAMPSA minority shareholders—CEPSA, Petromed, and Ertoil. In 1991 the division took place, with Repsol gaining about two-thirds of the stations as well as the use of the service station brand name Campsa (the company continued to also use the Repsol and Repshop brands). CAMPSA continued as a distribution and transportation company, with Repsol in control of the majority of the shares.

Market liberalization continued in Spain into the mid-1990s, resulting in increased competition for Repsol and the loss of some of its clout, such as from the dissolution of CAMPSA. Competitors entering the Spanish market included British Petroleum which took over Petromed, a small refiner, and the French oil powerhouse Elf which bought a stake in CEPSA, the largest private refiner in the country. Altogether about 40 different petroleum companies had been allowed into the Spanish market by the end of 1995.

In response to the growing competition, Repsol pursued an increasingly international strategy of seeking both sources of crude and markets for its products abroad. The company successfully discovered oil in the North Sea, Colombia, Angola, and Egypt and was awarded new exploration areas in Argentina, Angola, Algeria, Dubai, Egypt, and Vietnam. In 1990, it began explorations in Soviet Turkmenistan and agreed to explore in other Soviet areas in cooperation with Total and Petrofina.

Overseeing Repsol since its founding in 1987 was chairman and chief executive officer Oscar Fanjul-Martin. A former economics professor and technocrat, he was instrumental in the negotiations that led to Spain's entry into the European Union. In the early 1990s, Fanjul-Martin succeeded in his efforts to significantly expand Repsol's natural gas operations. In 1992, Repsol and La Caixa, a Spanish bank, merged their natural gas operations to form Gas Natural, with Repsol holding 45.5 percent of the new gas utility. The following year, Repsol gained an even stronger position in natural gas when Gas Natural purchased 91 percent of the Spanish state-owned Enagas, giving Gas Natural a near monopoly on natural gas in Spain. By 1995, Repsol's natural gas and bottled-gas businesses contributed about 25 percent of company earnings, compared to just 9 percent in 1987. The company acquired full management control of Gas Natural in 2000, in exchange for neutrality agreements with Spain's utility companies.

Fanjul-Martin also had the difficult task of guiding Repsol through the oil downturn of 1993, when prices plunged. The company's strengths—including a much stronger downstream operation than such price-sensitive areas as exploration—were clearly in view, however, and by instituting a vigorous cost-cutting program, Repsol was able to increase profits more than 11 percent, outperforming most of its competitors.

The mid-1990s were marked by a significant reduction in the government ownership of Repsol. Share issues in 1993, 1995, and early 1996 reduced INH's stake in the company to 40.5, 21, and about 10 percent, respectively. Each of the issues proved extremely popular in Spain, elsewhere in Europe, and in the United States, testifying to Repsol's strong position. By 1997, Repsol had been completely privatized. The company remained focused primarily on its domestic market, essentially limited to its refining and marketing operations. In 1996, Spanish Prime Minister José María Aznar appointed Alfonso Cortina as Repsol's new CEO. Cortina put into place a new expansion strategy that was to see the company break into the world's top ten by the end of the century.

A chief facet of Repsol's growth was its expansion into the South American market. As many of that continent's oil companies were being privatized, Repsol stepped up as a major bidder. In 1996, the company acquired a 37.7 percent stake in Argentina's Astra, paying $360 million for control of that oil and gas company. Repsol also joined a partnership with another Argentinean company, YPF, and Mobil Oil, to acquire Peru's La Pampilla oil refinery. Also in Argentina, Repsol acquired that country's Pluspetrol service stations. By 1997, Repsol, which made no secret of acquiring a share of Argentinean government-controlled YPF, pledged to invest more than $3 billion to expand its interests across Latin America.

Repsol's moment came in 1998 when the Argentinean government announced its intention to sell a 14.9 percent share of YPF. Repsol won that bid with an offer worth $2 billion. The following year, Repsol—with help from the Spanish government—pressured Argentina to relinquish the rest of its holding in YPF. The government agreed, and Repsol paid another $13 billion to acquire the remaining 85 percent of YPF. The deal not only gave Repsol the strong oil and gas exploration operations it had been lacking, it also propelled the company into the top ten of the world's oil companies, giving it the seventh place spot.

Back home in Spain, Repsol increased its control of Gas Natural in January 2000, reaching an agreement with 25 percent stakeholder LA Caixa that gave Repsol management control of the natural gas company—in time for what many analysts regarded as the beginning of a European industry boom. Meanwhile, Cortina was leading the company along another promising direction, beginning investments in fiber optics. Repsol was also seeking alliances to boost its position. In February 2000 the company began talks with Italy's ENI group about forming an industrial alliance. By the beginning of 2001, both sides were issuing statements denying their intention to go beyond an alliance and into a full-scale merger.

Principal Subsidiaries

Astra C.A.P S.A. (Argentina; 99%); Ajax Petroleum (Uruguay; 34%); Astra Produccion Petrolera, S.A. (Venezuela; 68%); British Solvent Oils (U.K.); Carless Refining & Marketing BV (Netherlands); Compania Logistica de Productos Petroliferos-CLH (60%); Gas Natural SDG, SA (45%); Gaviota Re, S.A. (Luxembourg); Petronor EE. SS., SA (86.58%); Repsol Butano, SA; Repsol Comercial de Productos Petroliferos, SA (96%); Repsol Derivados, SA (99.96%); Repsol Distribucion, SA; Repsol Exploracion, SA; Repsol Intl. Finance BV (Netherlands); Repsol Oil, U.S.A. Repsol Petroleum Ltd. (U.K.); Repsol Petroli S.p.A. (Italy); Repsol S.A. de C.V. Mexico; Repsol YPF Peru (91%); Repsol Petroleo, SA; Repsol Quimica, SA; Repsol (U.K.) Ltd.; YPF (Argentina; 99%).

Principal Competitors

Exxon Mobil Corporation; Royal Dutch/Shell Group; BP Amoco p.l.c.; Total Fina Elf S.A.; Texaco Inc.; Chevron Corporation; Conoco Inc.; Petróleos de Venezuela S.A.; Petróleo Brasileiro S.A. - Petrobras; Petróleos Mexicanos; Norsk Hydro ASA; CITGO Petroleum Corporation; Ultramar Diamond Shamrock Corporation; Occidental Petroleum Corporation; Sunoco, Inc.; Amerada Hess Corporation; 7-Eleven, Inc.; Koch Industries, Inc.; Kerr-McGee Corporation; The Dow Chemical Company; E.I. du Pont de Nemours and Company.

Further Reading

Barghini, Tiziana, "Spain's Repsol Takes Control of Gas Natural," *Reuters,* January 12, 2000.

Calian, Sara, and Carlta Vitzthum, "Demand for Repsol Shares Outstrips Supply in Offering As Investors Expect to Strike Oil," *Wall Street Journal,* January 31, 1996, p. C2.

Correlje, A.F., *The Liberalization of the Spanish Oil Sector: Strategies for a Competitive Future,* Rotterdam: The Centre For Policy Studies, Erasmus University, 1990.

Correlje, Aad, *The Spanish Oil Industry: Structural Change and Modernization,* Amsterdam: Thesis Publishers, 1994, 349 p.

Irvine, Steven, and Elisa Martinuzzi, "Repsol Guarantees Satisfaction," *Euromoney,* September 1995, p. 258.

Kielmas, Maria, "Olé Repsol! The Spanish Oil Company Sets a Swift Pace," *Barron's,* August 7, 1989, p. 15.

"Oscar Fanjul-Martin: Repsol," *Financial World,* July 19, 1994, p. 46.

Parsons, Claudia, "Repsol Clinches Takeover of Argentina's YPF," *Reuters,* June 23, 1999.

"Profits from Adversity," *International Management,* January/February 1994, pp. 36–41.

Santamaria, Javier, *El petroleo en Espana: del monopolio a la libertad,* Madrid: Espasa Calpe, 1988, 210 p.

Wallin, Michelle, "Repsol Clinches $13.1B Bid for YPF," *AP Online,* June 24, 1999.

—Clark Siewert
—updates David E. Salamie, M.L. Cohen

Ropes & Gray

One International Place
Boston, Massachusetts 02110-2624
U.S.A.
Telephone: (617) 951-7000
Fax: (617) 951-7050
Web site: http://www.ropesgray.com

Partnership
Founded: 1865
Employees: 420
Sales: $210.5 million (1999)
NAIC: 54111 Offices of Lawyers

Founded in 1865, Ropes & Gray is one of the oldest and most respected law firms in the nation. A full-service firm, Ropes & Gray provides legal advice to mostly corporate clients, including local Boston companies and large multinational firms in many nations. As Boston's largest law firm, Ropes & Gray represents Harvard University and many other educational institutions, in addition to businesses in a wide variety of other industries. For example, it serves as special or general counsel to more than 100 public companies and assists more than 500 mutual funds or fund boards. Due to their public service, Elliot Richardson and Archibald Cox were two of the better known Ropes & Gray partners.

Origins and Early Practice: 1865–1945

John Codman Ropes and John Chipman Gray, Jr., both grew up in wealthy Salem, Massachusetts families and graduated from Harvard College and Harvard Law School before they formed their partnership in 1865. In the first 13 years they served mainly individuals, plus a few companies, and Harvard, a longtime client.

The two founders made contributions outside their private law practice. Gray taught part-time at Harvard Law School, where he helped begin the use of the case method that became standard procedure in 20th-century law schools. Ropes served as an assistant U.S. attorney and wrote books on the history of the Civil War and Napoleon. The two partners also were the first editors of the *American Law Review.*

In 1878 the firm began changing when it brought in William C. Loring and changed the firm's name to Ropes, Gray & Loring. As counsel to the New York and New England Railroad, Loring shifted the firm's practice from individuals to mainly corporations. That was a general trend of the late 1800s as businesses increased in size and complexity, and many lawyers became business advisors behind the scenes. "These corporate law attorneys became the recognized elite of the profession and the molding force in the profession," wrote Gerald Gawalt, "even though membership in the large law firm was and remains reserved for a very small percentage of American lawyers."

In the 1890s Ropes, Gray & Loring began its public finance practice by helping municipalities sell bonds. In 1890 the firm's net income had increased to $71,108.24 from just $8,331.64 in 1878. In 1899 the firm changed its name to Ropes Gray & Gorham with the departure of Loring to become a justice of the Commonwealth Supreme Judicial Court and the addition of Robert Gorham as the new name partner.

The firm continued to grow in the early 20th century, reaching 11 lawyers and 15 staff personnel in 1910. After Gorham died, in 1914 the partnership became Ropes, Gray, Boyden & Perkins, with Roland Boyden and Thomas Perkins as the two new name partners. By 1920 the firm had grown to 43 lawyers and 53 staff members.

The partnership prospered during the business expansion and bull market of the 1920s, including serving Canadian paper and pulp companies and other foreign interests. A correspondent office operated in New York City from 1920 to 1938. In 1929 the firm opened a Paris office mainly to serve the needs of its client Lee, Higginson & Co., but that operation ended in 1932 because of the Great Depression and a financial scandal.

In 1926 and 1930 the firm gained its first Irish Catholic and Jewish partners, respectively. Most of the firm remained white Protestants, however, typical of most big law firms of that era.

During the Depression, the firm increased its bankruptcy and reorganization practice. For example, all but one firm attorney worked on reorganizing the Brown Company, which owned paper mills and timber properties. Yet overall, the partnership

Company Perspectives:

For over a century Ropes & Gray has been one of the leading law firms in the United States. Through changing times and circumstances, clients of all sizes have consistently sought us out when faced with difficult problems. What brings them here? And what do we bring to them?

We think the answers start from a simple premise about what clients need and how law firms can provide it. Clients need the best lawyers they can find, and the most successful firms are those that combine superior talent with a supportive environment where nothing gets in the way of solving clients' problems. We've done our best to act on this premise. Lawyer by lawyer, client by client, we've built a reputation for first-rate work, a positive outlook, and the highest standards of service and ethics. As a result we've continued to attract excellent clients, challenging assignments—and outstanding lawyers.

suffered as business activity declined. The 1930s was the only decade in the firm's long history when it actually decreased in size, from 58 lawyers and 85 staff employees in 1930 to 49 lawyers and 65 staff in 1940.

In spite of the bad days, some good things happened during the Depression. The firm picked up work on a large International Hydroelectric bond issue. It also gained some work from the flurry of New Deal laws and regulations. Like many other law firms, it developed a labor practice by representing companies that dealt with increased union strength after Congress passed the National Labor Relations Act in 1935. It also helped corporations prepare financial reports for the newly created Securities and Exchange Commission.

In the 1930s the firm also began serving Serge Semenenko, a Russian immigrant who became a lending officer for the First National Bank of Boston. Firm lawyers drew up loan agreements for Semenenko, who introduced the lawyers to the world of Hollywood and entertainment. Thus began a long relationship between the law firm and Boston's preeminent bank.

In 1940 the partnership changed its name to Ropes, Gray, Best, Coolidge & Rugg, making Charles Coolidge, Charles Rugg, and William H. Best the new name partners.

The firm in 1944 began representing Admiral Husband E. Kimmel, who had been the Pacific Fleet commander-in-chief when the Japanese attacked Pearl Harbor on December 7, 1941. The Roberts Commission blamed Kimmel and the Army's top general in Hawaii for not being prepared for the Pearl Harbor attack, but Kimmel, assisted by the law firm's attorneys, spent literally decades trying to clear his name.

Post-World War II Years

Soon after World War II ended, the firm worked on reorganizing the Massachusetts Hospital Life Insurance Company, a complicated matter that some doubted could ever be realized. It also defended the Hood Milk Company in several cases.

The Arnold Arboretum controversy, started in 1946, engaged Ropes & Gray for 20 years. Harvard, the firm's client, wanted the arboretum to be consolidated under control of its Biology Department, while others wanted the arboretum to remain more autonomous. The Massachusetts Supreme Judicial Court finally ruled in Harvard's favor in 1966.

In 1950, 56 lawyers worked at Ropes & Gray. At that time it did considerable work for Paine Webber, located nearby. Other clients included the Eastern Gas and Fuel Associates, the New England Electric System, Sylvania, Brown Company, Gillette, Kendall Company, Jones & Lamson, and several investment companies. For many years the firm also represented Ocean Spray Cranberries, a company it had helped organize.

Ropes & Gray lawyer Charles Coolidge and other leading Boston Protestants began urban renewal projects in the 1960s. Carl Brauer in his firm history said those "efforts helped end the historic division between that group, which largely 'owned' the city, and its Irish Catholic political majority, which largely ran it. . . . That renaissance in turn had more than a little to do with the vitality and growth of Ropes & Gray and other Boston law firms during the 1970s and 1980s."

In 1964 Elliot Richardson, probably the best known Ropes & Gray lawyer, finally left the law firm for good. He had joined the firm back in the 1930s but left frequently for prominent government positions. He held four cabinet posts and other positions in the Eisenhower, Nixon, Ford, Carter, and Bush administrations. Richardson became best known in 1974 when he resigned as U.S. attorney general, rather than comply with President Richard Nixon's demand to dismiss Watergate special prosecutor Archibald Cox, another former Ropes & Gray lawyer.

By the mid-1960s Ropes & Gray's clients included Central Maine Power Company, Maine Yankee Atomic Power Company, Boston Edison, Narragansett Brewing, Cabot Corporation, Copper Range, Boston Filter, American Thread, Morse Shoe, Radio Shack Corporation, John Hancock Mutual Life, Putnam Funds, Investment Trust of Boston, WGBH Educational Foundation, New England Medical Center, Berkshire Hathaway, Massachusetts Port Authority, Hotel Corporation of America, and several others. Most of its corporate clients were based in New England.

After many years of occupying the top floors at 50 Federal Street, in 1965 the firm moved from its old inadequate offices to its new headquarters at the State Street Bank Building at 225 Franklin Street. Two years later Hooks Burr replaced John Quarles as Ropes & Gray's chairman. The firm grew rapidly under Burr's leadership, going from 82 lawyers in 1970 to 137 in 1980. Although it continued to hire many new graduates of Harvard Law School, by the late 1970s it also interviewed graduates from the law schools of Yale, Columbia, Pennsylvania, Michigan, Chicago, Virginia, Boston College, and Boston University. Like other firms, Ropes & Gray hired more minorities and women in the 1970s and also began hiring legal assistants or paralegals.

The firm's litigation department, exceeded in size only by its corporate practice, in 1969 advised the Kennedy family after Senator Edward M. Kennedy was involved in a car accident at Chappaquiddick that resulted in the death of his passenger.

Key Dates:

1865: Partnership of Ropes and Gray is founded in Boston.
1878: Partnership is renamed Ropes, Gray & Loring.
1899: Firm becomes Ropes Gray & Gorham.
1914: Firm is renamed Ropes, Gray, Boyden & Perkins.
1940: Firm becomes known as Ropes, Gray, Best, Coolidge & Rugg.
1942: Partner Albert Boyden publishes a history of the firm.
1961: Firm chooses the permanent name of Ropes & Gray.
1981: Washington, D.C. office is opened on January 1.
1985: Providence, Rhode Island office is opened.
2000: Firm establishes a New York office.

Senator Kennedy was not convicted of any crime in this famous incident. The firm's "major contribution to the affair was in achieving a court decision that set down rules for the conduct of inquests, which had never been articulated before in Massachusetts," wrote Brauer in his firm history.

In the early 1970s Ropes & Gray played a key role in a much publicized crisis. New York City was on the brink of financial collapse, so the Congress authorized a $2 billion loan. Treasury Secretary William Simon chose the Boston law firm to help in this transaction, instead of choosing one of the New York firms. A team of Ropes & Gray lawyers worked long hours to finally make the loan a reality.

Two developments in the late 1970s spurred intense competition among large law firms such as Ropes & Gray. First, the U.S. Supreme Court ruled that professional associations' advertising restrictions violated the First Amendment's guarantee of free speech, which led to more professionals advertising. Second, the *National Law Journal* and the *American Lawyer* began writing articles and evaluating the internal management and financial performance of large law firms. With comparative data available, more experienced lawyers left their firms for greener pastures.

Greater legal specialization also occurred. For example, Ropes & Gray in 1978 recognized its healthcare practice as a distinct specialty, influenced by the growth of hospital corporations and increased Medicare and Medicaid funding, two developments that had begun in the 1960s.

Developments in the 1990s and Beyond

Ropes & Gray played a role in President Clinton's plans to reform healthcare. It served as the legal counsel to The Jackson Hole Group, a well-known group of healthcare providers and insurance leaders that came up with a plan called managed competition. That formed the basis of proposed legislation, but the Congress did not pass Clinton's reforms.

In 1994 Stanford University contracted with Ropes & Gray and two San Francisco law firms to handle about two-thirds of its legal responsibilities, while downsizing its inhouse lawyer

ranks from 21 to eight. Stanford's goal was to reduce its legal fees by paying its outside law firms a monthly fixed fee.

An example of Ropes & Gray's intellectual property practice occurred when it represented State Street in *State Street v. Signature Financial Corporation*. Signature in 1993 had received a patent for its "Hub and Spoke" financial software. State Street tried in vain to license the software, so it sued in the Massachusetts district court, where the judge ruled the software was unpatentable. The Court of Appeals for the Federal Circuit in 1998 found that Signature's software patent was valid, however, and the U.S. Supreme Court in 1999 denied State Street's appeal. "The Court's decision dramatically widens the field of potential patents in the U.S.," according to *Managing Intellectual Property* in June 1999.

In a press release dated March 13, 2001, Managing Partner Douglass N. Ellis said, "Ropes & Gray is in the process of building one of the nation's leading practices in the fields of intellectual property, life sciences, and technology law." At that time, it had more than 50 professionals in that specialty.

In the 1990s the number of product liability lawsuits mushroomed. For example, Johnnie Cochran and other lawyers filed a class action lawsuit against the chemical company that made the fertilizer used to bomb the Oklahoma City Federal Building. The judge dismissed the case, saying the manufacturer was not responsible for how its products were misused.

Then, in a second case, lawyers went after chemical companies that made the explosives used to blow up the World Trade Center. Ropes & Gray defended Norsk Hydro ASA, one of the manufacturers. In these and other cases, the courts dealt with efforts to increase the limits of liability.

Ropes & Gray also represented the chemical industry's Coalition for Effective Environmental Information in dealings with the Environmental Protection Agency, other regulatory bodies, and various private environmental groups. For example, in 1998 the Environmental Defense Fund opened its Chemical Scorecard web site, which proved very popular. The authors of a *Chemical Week* article on June 3, 1998 said the new web site "has begun to achieve something Greenwood [a Ropes & Gray lawyer] has been trying to do for several years: awaken industry—particularly top executives—to the Internet's power to shape public perceptions of environmental issues and companies' environmental performance."

In 1998 Ropes & Gray tax attorneys advised Bain Capital, an investment company, when it spent about $1 billion to purchase 90 percent of Domino's Pizza from founder Thomas Monaghan. The firm's other lawyers provided expertise in most other legal specialties, including real estate, biotechnology, acquisitions and mergers, labor and employment, creditors' rights, and benefits consulting.

Based on Ropes & Gray's 1997 gross revenue of $175 million, the *American Lawyer* in July/August 1998 ranked the firm as the 47th largest in the United States. The following year its gross revenue of $196.5 million ranked it as the 49th largest firm. Its 1999 gross revenue of $210.5 million ranked it as the nation's 53rd largest firm. It had profits per equity partner in 1999 of $750,000, which was better than several higher-ranked firms but also far less than some firms that averaged more than $1 million profits per equity partner.

Operating from offices in Boston, New York, Providence, and Washington, D.C., plus a London conference center, Ropes & Gray in 2001 faced numerous challenges. The firm's competitors included numerous large law firms and also large accounting firms that employed many lawyers. The American Bar Association was considering allowing law firms to include other professionals, such as accountants. Recent trade pacts such as the North American Free Trade Agreement, the introduction of the Euro monetary system in Europe, and technology issues were just a few of the other concerns of Ropes & Gray and their clients at the start of the new century.

Principal Operating Units

Corporate; Creditors' Rights; Employee Benefits & Consulting; Environmental; Health Care; Intellectual Property & Technology; Labor & Employment; Litigation; Real Estate; Tax; Private Client Group.

Principal Competitors

Covington & Burling; Goodwin Procter; Hale and Dorr; Testa, Hurwitz & Thibeault.

Further Reading

"Bain Capital Consults Ropes & Gray," *International Tax Review,* November 1998, p. 7.

Barnes, Bart, "Elliot Richardson Dies at 79; 1973 Resignation As Attorney General Shocked the Nation," *Washington Post,* January 1, 2000, p. B7.

Brauer, Carl M., *Ropes & Gray 1865–1990,* Boston: Ropes & Gray, 1991.

Dietrich, Mark O., "Health Care Reform—The Driving Force Behind Federal Tax Law Change," *Massachusetts CPA Review,* Winter 1994, p. 14.

Fairley, Peter, and Rick Mullin, "Scorecard Hits Home," *Chemical Week,* June 3, 1998, pp. 24–26.

Fisher, Louis, "Public Service As a Calling," *Texas Law Review,* April 1998, pp. 1185–1217.

Gawalt, Gerald W., *The New High Priests: Lawyers in Post-Civil War America,* Westport, Conn.: Greenwood Press, 1984.

Gormley, Ken, *Archibald Cox: Conscience of a Nation,* Reading, Mass.: Addison-Wesley, 1997.

Hairston, Deborah, with Gerald Ondrey, "Liability and the CPI [Chemical Process Industries]," *Chemical Engineering,* September 1996, p. 32.

"Opening the Floodgates," *Managing Intellectual Property,* June 1999, pp. 34, 36.

Stevens, Amy, "Lawyers and Clients," *Wall Street Journal,* November 18, 1994, p. B6.

—David M. Walden

Ryerson Tull, Inc.

2621 W. 15th Place
Chicago, Illinois
U.S.A.
Telephone: (773) 762-2121
Fax: (773) 788-4212
Web site: http://www.ryersontull.com

Public Company
Incorporated: 1842 as Joseph T. Ryerson & Son, Inc.
Employees: 4,500
Sales: $2.86 billion (2000)
Stock Exchanges: New York
Ticker Symbol: RT
NAIC: 331221 Rolled Steel Shape Manufacturing; 42151
   Metals Service Centers and Offices; 42269 Other
   Chemical and Allied Products Wholesalers

Ryerson Tull, Inc. sells three million tons of metal a year, making it North America's leading distributor and processor of metals. Formerly known as Inland Steel Industries, the company merged with and took the name of its main operating unit after selling off the Inland Steel Company business to Ispat International N.V. in 1998. Ryerson now has 70 facilities in the United States and Canada, as well as joint ventures in low-cost steel producing countries such as China and India.

Windy City Origins

Joseph T. Ryerson, the founder of the company, arrived in Chicago in the early 1840s. Working as an agent for a firm of Pennsylvania iron masters, he leased a shop along the Chicago River and advertised for sale such wares as sheet iron, English and German steel, buggy springs, axles, nails, and wrought iron spikes, among other products. With his inventory expanding, Ryerson acquired property and built an iron store in the city's downtown business district. By 1852, Ryerson's operation had again outgrown its space and moved to larger and more convenient facilities alongside the river, where a new dock allowed ships to deliver iron right to the Ryerson store.

In 1871 the company experienced a setback as the Great Chicago Fire devastated Ryerson's warehouse. The founder reopened in temporary quarters, however, and rebuilt his iron store on the same site. In a notice to his customers, Ryerson expressed his determination: ''I shall do everything in my power to serve my customers as usual, in my line of goods. I still live, and intend to do business, not withstanding the awful calamity that has befallen our city, and the citizens generally. I am ready for the fight against misfortune, and I trust my old friends and customers will stand by me.''

Ryerson remained owner and head of the company until 1883, when another family member, Edward L. Ryerson, Sr., took over as owner, president, and chairperson. The founder's son, Joseph T. Ryerson, II, was also an active part of the operation. During this time, the company had pared its offerings to focus on serving boilermakers, which, at the time, were Chicago's primary users of iron and steel. Ryerson also was offering corrugated furnaces for boilers and a variety of boilermaker tools. Indeed, the company would later name its newsletter, established in 1892, the *Boilermaker*. By the end of the decade, as railroads rapidly carved their paths throughout the country, the boiler shops and flue shops that serviced steam locomotives became increasingly important customers to Ryerson. To make room for an increasing demand and inventory, the Ryerson plant expanded several times during this period.

Expanding in the 1900s

In the early 1900s increasing industrialization allowed Ryerson to expand its product lines in serving Chicago's metal users. Specifically, the company supplied rails to a large number of steel consumers in the railroad industry, iron and steel products for farm implement makers, and the steel used in the construction of skyscrapers. In 1908 the entire operation of Ryerson moved to facilities at 16th and Rockwell in Chicago, a plant that would continue in use into the 1990s. In 1909, Ryerson moved for the first time outside of Chicago, opening a plant in New York.

As steel became more popular, so did its derivative ''alloy steel'' materials. The research and applications of alloy had begun in the late 18th century, and as the Industrial Revolution spread throughout the United States, the demand for the stronger, more resilient alloy steels increased. Experiments with chromium and nickel brought the realization that a combination of elements produced a metal superior in many respects to steels alloyed with only one. The toughness and strength of nickel lengthened the service and dependability of gears, crank shafts, and other vital parts of machines used in transportation. Vanadium steel was introduced in 1907 to the U.S. automotive industry by Henry Ford. It was also used for structural steel and high-speed tool steels. Ryerson was a part of this growing trend, and in 1911 made its first offering of alloy stocks, including four grades of nickel, chrome, and vanadium steels, which were well suited for railroad, automotive, and machinery needs.

Another industry development that Ryerson was able to take advantage of was that of stainless steel. In fact, in 1926 Ryerson's stocks of the new stainless steel were among the first available anywhere. The use of stainless steel spread throughout the chemical and drug industries and to other industrial applications because of its ability to stand up against corrosive properties. In 1929 stainless steel trim first appeared on cars and became increasingly popular in the auto industry for its beautiful finish and non-tarnishing quality. Stainless also proved remarkably strong, suggesting structural possibilities and weight-saving economy. In 1934, for instance, the first streamlined train using stainless steel made its appearance in the United States; it was lighter in weight and, thus, capable of greater speeds. Other product introductions by Ryerson at this time included a line of Ryertex thermosetting plastic laminates.

Taken Inland in 1935

The acquisition of Joseph T. Ryerson & Son by Inland Steel began a relationship that would remain in effect into the 1990s. In 1935 it was announced that Inland Steel Company and Ryerson had approved a plan to merge. Inland Steel was a well-established Chicago-based steel producer, engaged in the manufacture of bars, shapes, plates, sheets, strips, rails, track accessories, and tin plate. In fact, the company ranked seventh in size in the steel industry at the time. The acquisition of Ryerson gave Inland an outlet for its products milled at Indiana Harbor and Chicago Heights. Ryerson, with ten plants in midwestern and eastern cities including Detroit, Cleveland, Buffalo, Cincinnati, Boston, New York, and Philadelphia, continued to operate as a wholly owned subsidiary. The combined assets of the two com-

panies at the time of the merger totaled over $116 million. Edward L. Ryerson, Jr., who had taken the reins of the company in 1929, continued to lead Ryerson under the parentage of Inland Steel, until his retirement in 1953.

While wartime was a period of significant expansion for most steel companies, Ryerson, being a distributor, did not initially share such growth during World War II. The War Production Board gave low priority to shipments for service centers, reasoning that channeling steel through middlemen was unnecessary and costly. However, as government contractors began to complain when their materials were not delivered in a timely manner, Ryerson soon proved that its services were essential.

Diversified Product Lines After World War II

The postwar period was marked by expansion, both of the Ryerson product line and of its geographic scope. By 1946 Ryerson had established its first West Coast plant in Los Angeles, bringing the company's total number of service centers to 12. By 1955 the company was offering full stocks of aluminum and polyvinyl chloride (PVC) sheets, pipe, and fittings. The company's new plastics division was further supplemented by the addition of fiberglass structural shapes, pipe, tubing, bars, and sheet in 1963. During the 1970s Ryerson began converting stainless and aluminum coils into flat sheets to service special customer orders. Later, a stainless plate center and new plate processing facility were established in Chicago. Also during this time, Ryerson went through a period of acquisitions to increase its geographic presence, acquiring the Federal Steel Corp. in 1967 and, later, the Vance Iron & Steel Co. in 1975.

However, the country's steel industry began to experience serious problems in the 1960s and 1970s. Factors such as high labor costs, slowing growth in domestic markets, and declining world market share contributed to this downturn. Moreover, foreign competition intensified as did the popularity of such steel substitutes as plastic and aluminum. The decline continued, and between 1982 and 1986, the steel industry suffered a severe depression. Although certainly affected by the adverse conditions, Ryerson seemed to survive these years better than many in the industry. While other service center companies were forced to cut back during this time, Ryerson even experienced some moderate expansion, opening new facilities in Nebraska and Iowa while upgrading its headquarters and plants in Houston, Kansas City, and Milwaukee. According to an April 1984 article in *American Metal Market,* Ryerson reported a 1983 operating profit of $22.5 million, triple that of the previous year, while sales had increased 11.6 percent to $792.5 million. Moreover, in 1984 the company achieved its first billion-dollar sales year.

Restructuring in the 1980s and 1990s

However, to offset the declining U.S. steel market, parent company Inland Steel was forced to restructure. In its service center division, Inland combined subsidiary J.M. Tull Metals with Ryerson's service center networks to create four regional distribution units: Joseph T. Ryerson East, Joseph T. Ryerson West, Joseph T. Ryerson Central, and J.M. Tull Metals. The reorganization called for a 10 percent cut in salaried workforce, but was estimated to save the company about $10 million in 1991. Moreover, according to company officials, the reorgani-

Key Dates:

1842: Joseph Ryerson opens up shop in Chicago as an agent for steelmakers.
1871: Ryerson rebuilds after the Great Fire.
1935: Inland Steel Company (later subsumed under holding company Inland Steel Industries) acquires Joseph T. Ryerson & Son, Inc.
1986: Ryerson subsidiary is combined with J.M. Tull Metals.
1996: Ryerson Tull lists on the New York Stock Exchange in a partial public offering.
1998: Ispat International N.V. buys Inland Steel Company; corporate parent Inland Steel Industries merges with Ryerson, renaming itself Ryerson Tull, Inc.

zation allowed the units to operate closer to their markets, respond better to the needs of their customers, and be more acutely aware of competition.

In the mid-1990s Ryerson went through additional restructuring actions, seeking to consolidate some of its far-flung operations. The company announced in May 1994 that it would close its Boston outlet and move all inventory and processing to its more modern facility in Wallingford, Connecticut. According to company officials, the closing occurred because the Boston facility was inefficient and additional investment in the unit was not justified. In addition, current business volume and projected market growth did not support two Ryerson service centers in the New England market. Further analysis of business volume and projected growth prompted the 1995 closing of Ryerson's Jersey City service center, the operations of which were consolidated in the Philadelphia plant.

Despite necessary closings and the consolidation of operations, Ryerson did witness a growth in demand at its Minneapolis service center. In response the company called for an addition to that plant in 1995, resulting in a 300,000-square-foot facility with new metal processing and distribution equipment. The Minneapolis center received a laser cutting machine and another multi-torch flame-cutting machine, as well as a new overhead crane and an increase in its truck fleet.

The future of the steel industry remained uncertain. In Inland Steel's 1994 annual report, management addressed the issue of whether superior steel and a thriving distribution business would enable the company to remain profitable in a recession. Suggesting that the answer was perhaps "no," management looked toward redefining their business by diversification. As Joseph T. Ryerson & Son also faced such challenges, its reputation for sound leadership and service would no doubt be a valuable asset.

Despite earlier hints of diversification, ultimately Inland's management chose a strategy of consolidation and divestiture, allowing the company to focus on its strongest holding, Ryerson Tull. This unit's global sourcing capacity—a key to survival in the cost competitive industry—was enhanced by joint venture operations in India, China, and Mexico. (The Mexican venture soon boasted 18 locations. Nevertheless, by March 2000

Ryerson was planning to sell its stake to its partner, Altos Hornos de Mexico, S.A. de C.V.) While the U.S. remained the prime market for the steel industry, its higher costs for labor and raw material had many global mill companies setting up operations in Latin America and Asia.

Ryerson Tull had sales of $2.15 billion and net income of $73 million in 1995. It was described as the largest metals service center in the United States, with a market share of 9 percent. It completed an initial public offering of 13 percent of its stock in June 1996. Before this time, the company had been a wholly owned subsidiary of Inland Steel Industries (the holding company for Inland Steel Company), which now owned 87 percent of its shares.

In July 1998, Inland Steel Industries, Inc. sold its Inland Steel Company operating unit to Ispat International N.V. for $1.1 billion. By the end of the year, Ryerson Tull had agreed to merge with Inland Steel Industries. At the same time, Inland Steel Industries changed its name to Ryerson Tull, Inc. (The Inland Steel name continued to be used in those operations earlier acquired by Ispat.) Neil S. Novich became chairman, president, and CEO of the company.

The new Ryerson Tull soon made its first acquisition, buying Washington Specialty Metals from Bethlehem Steel for $70 million in February 1999. Ryerson Tull made the unit the base of its new Specialty Metals Group. The acquisition made stainless steel and aluminum Ryerson Tull's largest product group. By this time, the company was selling almost $3 billion of metals a year from more than 70 facilities in North America.

The *Wall Street Journal* reported that a rise in short-term interest rates in the spring of 2000 hit the steel industry hard. Ryerson Tull's sales volume fell precipitously as demand for construction equipment fell.

To survive in the coming few years, Novich told investors the company was aiming to help customers reduce their total costs through refinements in information and metal processing technologies. It participated in manufacturers' early involvement programs that allowed it a role in designing parts and processes. Ryerson's market of choice was comprised of medium to large original equipment manufacturers (OEMs), which tended to switch suppliers less frequently and to develop deeper relationships with them. They were also most likely to choose Ryerson's value-added services. These strategies helped keep revenues climbing during difficult years, reported *Metal Center News,* but they could do little to prevent falling metal prices from eating away at Ryerson Tull's margins.

In the last six months of 2000, Ryerson restructured, aiming to lower costs. Two regional offices and six service centers were closed. Certain corporate functions were centralized. More than 300 employees were terminated. Total cost savings were estimated to be $30 million a year. Nevertheless, profits continued to slip into the first quarter of 2001.

Principal Subsidiaries

Ryerson Tull Mexico (50%); Tata Ryerson Ltd. (India; 50%); Shanghai Ryerson Ltd. (China; 50%); IMF Steel International Ltd. (Hong Kong; 50%).

Principal Operating Units

Ryerson Tull North; Ryerson Tull South; Ryerson Tull West; Ryerson Tull Coil Processing; Ryerson Tull Procurement Corporation.

Principal Competitors

Reliance Steel and Aluminum Co.; Sumitomo Metal Industries, Ltd.; Worthington Industries, Inc.

Further Reading

Beirne, Mike, "Joseph T. Ryerson Closing Another East Coast Location," *American Metal Market,* July 7, 1995, p. 4.

——, "Ryerson Eyeing New Niche?," *American Metal Market,* July 16, 1991, p. 5.

——, "Ryerson Revamp Seen Clashing with Its Computers," *American Metal Market,* November 13, 1990, p. 4.

——, "Ryerson to Quit Boston," *American Metal Market,* May 9, 1994, p. 2.

Berry, Bryan, "Inland Steel Redefines Itself," *Iron Age New Steel,* August 1995, pp. 18ff.

Bettner, Jill, "Who's Done Better Diversifying?," *Forbes,* June 4, 1984.

Burgert, Philip, "Ryerson to Continue Service Expansion," *American Metal Market,* March 17, 1983, p. 1.

Cochran, Thomas N., "Offerings in the Offing: Ryerson Tull," *Barron's,* June 17, 1996, p. 48.

Fisher, Douglas Alan, *The Epic of Steel,* New York: Harper & Row Publishers, 1963.

Hohl, Paul, "Ryerson and Tull Buoy Inland's Net," *American Metal Market,* January 26, 1988, p. 3.

Kafka, Peter, "Steel Steal," *Forbes,* April 20, 1998, p. 486.

Keefe, Lisa M., "Reassembling Ryerson," *Crain's Chicago Business,* September 3, 1990, p. 1.

Ryerson: Celebrating the First 150 Years, Chicago: Joseph T. Ryerson & Son, Inc., 1992.

Matthews, Robert Guy, "Rate Increases Slow Steel Industry More Than Forecast," *Wall Street Journal,* June 5, 2000, p. B4.

Mehta, Manik, "Steel's Still-Growing Giant," *Industry Week,* January 18, 1999, pp. 120–23.

"Merger Complete; Officers Named," *Metal Center News,* April 1999, pp. 13–14.

"Metal Center CEOs Stress Continued Growth," *Metal Center News,* July 2000, pp. 12–24.

"Metals Distributor Supplies Expertise As Well As Product," *Purchasing,* November 19, 1998, p. 74.

"Ryerson Helps Pole Maker Tower over Competitors," *Metal Center News,* May 2000, p. 14.

"Ryerson Tull Buys Washington Specialty Metals," *Purchasing,* February 11, 1999, p. B31.

Sheridan, John H., "A Global Future?," *Industry Week,* January 18, 1999, pp. 124–28.

"When Honeywell Swapped a Pack of Suppliers for One Close Partnership," *Purchasing,* November 21, 1996, p. 50.

—Beth Watson Highman
—update: Frederick C. Ingram

Sam's Club

608 SW Eighth Street
Bentonville, Arkansas 72712
U.S.A.
Telephone: (501) 277-7000
Fax: (501) 273-4053
Web site: http://www.samsclub.com

Division of Wal-Mart Stores, Inc.
Founded: 1983 as Sam's Wholesale Club
Sales: $24.8 billion (2000)
NAIC: 45291 Warehouse Clubs and Superstores

Sam's Club, a division of discount merchandiser Wal-Mart Stores, is one of the nation's leading operators of members-only warehouse stores. The division runs over 450 stores across the country. Sam's Club sells to some 41 million customers who pay an annual fee to become members. Members can shop at Sam's sprawling stores, which are typically 110,000 to 130,000 square feet, and offer more than 4,000 items, from fresh groceries to auto supplies, clothing, and pharmaceuticals. The clubs also offer additional services such as a mail-order pharmacy, travel club, Internet, and long-distance services, car loans, and discount credit card processing. Mark-up on Sam's Club items is just over wholesale, so goods at these stores are deeply discounted over other vendors. Sam's Club sells to small businesses such as restaurants, daycare centers, and offices, and also markets to individuals. Sam's Club entered the warehouse club market in the mid-1980s, after Wal-Mart founder Sam Walton studied the success of other similar ventures. After some consolidation in the industry, Sam's Club leads the market neck-and-neck with close competitor Costco.

Catching a Trend in the 1980s

Sam's Club was created by Sam Walton, the remarkable retailer who brought the nation Wal-Mart stores. Walton had built a chain of Arkansas five-and-dimes in the 1960s, and increased this to almost 300 stores in the South in the 1970s. Wal-Mart Stores, Inc. incorporated in 1971 and was a billion-dollar operation by 1980. Wal-Mart stores were located in small towns, usually in markets so small that other retailers avoided

them. The stores offered deeply discounted goods, and rural people flocked to them. Wal-Mart continued to expand across the nation in the 1980s, keeping in the main to small towns. Sam's Club debuted in 1983 as something of a corollary to the Wal-Mart small-town strategy. The warehouse stores were designed for an urban market, giving Wal-Mart Stores, Inc. access to customers it did not otherwise reach.

The warehouse club idea did not originate with Sam Walton. The designated father of the warehouse club industry was the aptly named Sol Price, who ran Price Club. Sol Price opened his first Price Club in San Diego in 1976. The chain spread across the West Coast in the 1980s. Price Club stores were huge, on average 108,000 square feet, and ran with no frills and a minimum of employees. Sol Price guided Sam Walton through one of his stores in the early 1980s, and Walton acknowledged that his Sam's Clubs were patterned after the Price chain. The first Sam's opened in Oklahoma City in 1983. It was called Sam's Wholesale Club, the name that stuck with the chain until 1990. By the end of 1983, there were two more stores, one in Kansas City, Missouri, and one in Dallas. Sales the first year were already $40 million. In 1984 the chain added eight stores, and these 11 stores brought in $225 million total that year. Sam's Clubs were located in leased warehouses, usually in rather desolate areas. They were huge, and bare of decoration. Goods were displayed on shipping pallets or on steel shelves which reached almost to the ceiling. "Displayed" might be putting it too strongly, as the items were often simply set out stacked inside torn-open packing boxes. But the goods were brand-name, at prices much lower than elsewhere. Customers usually had to buy large sizes or multiple packs of things.

Sam's Club took advantage of the distribution know-how of the Wal-Mart chain. An analyst for Morgan Stanley quoted in *Discount Store News* for December 9, 1985, described Wal-Mart's distribution network as using "some of the most sophisticated systems currently devised." The chain already knew how to hold down costs, and it amplified this skill at Sam's Clubs. Merchandise was moved mechanically whenever possible, so that few human hands needed to touch it on its journey from factory to customer's car. In addition, Wal-Mart had studied the market carefully before plunging into the warehouse business. The urban market of the warehouse store was a great complement to the small-town market of the Wal-Mart chain. The two chains added to each other without competing. Another analyst quoted in the *Discount Store News* article claimed that Wal-Mart and Sam's together could "serve almost all the potential shoppers in a market." Serving everybody was quite a proposition, but it seemed possible. The Sam's chain grew rapidly, and accounted for a larger portion of Wal-Mart's sales each year through the 1980s.

In 1986 warehouse club sales accounted for less than 1 percent of total U.S. retail sales. But what *Fortune* magazine dubbed a "mini-industry" was nevertheless worth about $4.4 billion annually at that time, and the level of profitability was enticing. The entrenched Price Co. was still the market leader in 1986, with sales of $1.9 billion, and profits of $46 million. One key to the profitability of the warehouse concept was that goods turned over very quickly. Inventory at Sam's Clubs turned over on average 16 to 18 times a year. This high turnover meant that inventory was off the shelves and sold within 30 days, or before the store had to pay for it. Many retailers had jumped on the warehouse trend by the mid-1980s. Besides Sam's Club and Price Club, competitors in the industry included Costco Inc., Pace Membership Warehouse, Warehouse Club Inc., Wholesale Club Inc., BJ's Wholesale Club, and Price Savers. Costco, Pace, Warehouse Club, and Wholesale Club all went public in 1986 to fund further expansion. BJ's also had expansion plans in the mid-1980s, and Price Savers got the backing of the large grocery chain Kroger when it was acquired in August 1985. The industry was getting crowded as chains competed for specific regional markets and then for membership within those markets.

Between its founding in 1983 and 1985, Sam's Clubs opened in urban markets in the South and Southwest. The chain entered the Midwest in 1986. By 1987, Sam's had 84 stores. This included stores it bought in 1987 when Sam's took over the warehouse chain Super Saver Wholesale. Super Saver had gone head-to-head with Sam's in ten southern cities, and had another 11 warehouse stores in the South. But it was not profitable, and in 1987 Sam's took over the chain, closing some stores and reopening others under the Sam's banner. In 1989, Sam's began moving into the Northeast. This region had little exposure to the warehouse store concept, and was not a Wal-Mart stronghold either. Sam's opened its first store in the Northeast in Delran Township, New Jersey, and planned to open other stores in New York, Delaware, Maine, New Hampshire, and Pennsylvania. The other leading warehouse chains also targeted the Northeast at that time. The California-based Price Club chain had started Price Club East, and had 11 stores in the Northeast by 1990. Costco also entered the Northeastern market in 1990, with a revamped store format that included a bakery.

By 1989, the Sam's Club division brought in $4.8 billion in sales, rising more than 25 percent over the previous year. The chain continued to account for a larger portion of Wal-Mart's total sales each year. By 1989, it was providing over 18 percent of Wal-Mart's total sales.

Consolidation and Competition in the 1990s

Sam's changed its name in 1990 from Sam's Wholesale Clubs to simply Sam's Clubs. A judge in North Carolina had ruled that the chain was not entitled to the word "wholesale" in its name, since in that state only from 11 to 15 percent of goods bought at the Sam's stores was actually intended for resale by others. State law required that at least 50 percent of goods sold be intended for resale, to merit the "wholesale" appellation. Though the ruling only applied to North Carolina, the chain thought it would be confusing to have different names in different states. So it adopted the simpler Sam's Club name overall. While the chain was taking "wholesale" out of its name, it coincidentally bought a rival chain called The Wholesale Club. Sam's paid about $175 million for the Indianapolis-based chain of 27 stores. The Wholesale Club was founded in 1982, the year before Sam's. It operated exclusively in the Midwest. The chain had experienced a slow start, then eventually took off, with sales climbing from $165 million in 1987 to approximately $700 million at the time of its acquisition by Sam's in 1990. It was poised to open three stores in the Chicago area when Sam's bought it. Sam's Clubs had been opening stores around Chicago, moving into suburban locations and in smaller towns on the outskirts of the city such as Joliet and Rockford. Sam's acquisition of The Wholesale Club gained it strength in the Midwest just as other chains were also muscling into the area.

By 1990, competition between Sam's and the other leading chains was growing more intense as the big players moved out of their core markets. Where the different warehouse chains met head-on, they tried to differentiate. Some offered a brighter format, or emphasized fresh foods and baked goods. One advantage Sam's had was its relationship with Wal-Mart. Though Sam's had originally been designated for urban markets, where Wal-Marts opened in small towns, increasingly since the late 1980s Sam's opened alongside or nearby Wal-Marts. Because Sam's was for members only, and appealed to small businesses, Wal-Mart's management claimed the two stores did not overlap. Half the new Sam's opened in 1990 were paired with a Wal-Mart. The size of the duo dwarfed other players in the same market.

The booming warehouse store market the various players had struggled to divide since the mid-1980s began to cool in the early 1990s. The expanding warehouse chains could not keep up their momentum. The biggest players were still Sam's Club, Costco, Price, and Pace Membership Warehouse, which was run by the formidable retailer Kmart. A poor retail environment in the early 1990s, combined with the intensity of the competition among the chains as they reached out of their core geographical markets, caused several stumbles. Sam's apparently looked into acquiring Price or Costco, as did Kmart. Eventually Price and Costco merged, forming Price/Costco Inc. in 1993. (Within a few years the name reverted to Costco Companies Inc.) Kmart was unable to keep Pace Membership Warehouse going, and sold 99 of its 113 stores to Sam's in 1993. At this juncture, Sam's was the biggest chain left, with about 400 stores and 1993 sales of $14.7 billion. Sam's also accounted for 22 percent of Wal-Mart's total sales by that year. But Sam's entered a period of doldrums. By the

Key Dates:

1983: First Sam's Wholesale Club opens in Oklahoma City.
1987: Sam's acquires southern competitor Super Saver Wholesale chain.
1990: Chain changes name to Sam's Club.
1993: Company acquires Pace Membership Club, a struggling chain owned by Kmart.
1998: Company undertakes major renovation program.
2000: Sam's, Costco, and BJ's Wholesale rank as the dominant players in the warehouse club industry.

middle of 1994, same-store sales levels had fallen month by month for almost a solid year.

The company decided to refocus on its core of small business customers, targeting specific industries such as nursing homes, restaurants, hotel/motel operators, cleaning companies, and restaurants. It stocked items such as institutional quality sheets, heavy restaurant-grade cutlery, wheel chairs, and wrist splints. In targeting particular businesses, Sam's also moved to carry less of other items, such as housewares, that appealed more to consumers buying for themselves or their families. In 1994 Sam's also began stocking some unusual items, including juke boxes and grand pianos, that were meant to appeal to upscale consumers who enjoyed the thrill of bargain hunting. Sam's got a new president in late 1995, Joseph Hardin, Jr. Hardin resigned in 1997 to take a job at the copy shop chain Kinko's. He was replaced by Mark Hansen. Sales remained slow at the chain, accounting for a shrinking percentage of Wal-Mart's total. Sam's had provided over 20 percent of Wal-Mart's sales in the early 1990s, but by 1997 this figure had dropped to 17.5 percent. In 1998 the company embarked on a major renovation program. It remodeled 70 stores, added bakeries or other new departments to 50 more, and expanded the fresh grocery departments of 120. Some top buying personnel were replaced, and the chain announced it would build a new kind of store, a "Millennium Club," beginning with a model in San Diego. The Millennium Clubs offered more upscale items, such as wine, not found in other Sam's. Sam's Clubs also began offering a host of services, such as Airborne Express shipping service, discounted Internet access, a mail-order pharmacy, software training, and more. It introduced a new private label food line called Members Mark, and assailed its members with direct mail claiming "the secret to living well" could be found at Sam's. All these moves seemed to have paid off, as 1998 was the best year the chain had had in a long time. Sales were close to $23 billion, and operating profits rose 15 percent over 1997.

But there was more turnover at the top, as Sam's Club got a new president, Tom Grimm, in October 1998. Grimm had formerly led the Pace Membership Club, which Sam's acquired from Kmart in 1993. Strong consumer spending in the late 1990s and through 2000 helped Sam's get back on its feet somewhat. Sales and earnings increased in 1999, and the company opened almost 20 new stores. By 2000, the warehouse

club industry had shaken down to only three major players: Sam's, with over 450 stores; Costco, with close to 300; and BJ's Wholesale Club, with just over 100 units. Rivalry between Costco and Sam's continued unabated. Costco had subsumed the Price Club chain that Sam's was originally modeled after, and Sam's continued to take cues from Costco, offering similar goods and services. Sam's and Costco opened stores within the same city, and Sam's increasingly penetrated California, once a Costco stronghold. Also in 2000, Costco announced that it would open a new warehouse store in Arlington, Texas, only blocks from the site Sam's had picked for its new store. Sam's hoped to prevail, enhancing its marketing through ventures such as catalogs geared toward specific groups of members, for example daycare center operators. Sam's also began attaching gas stations to its stores, moving from a pilot of seven in 1999 to a planned hundred or more by the end of the year. Sam's also enhanced its pharmacy operations, and offered other services such as one-hour photo processing and prepared meals. The warehouse store industry had matured and changed markedly between Sam's launch in 1983 and the beginning of the new millennium. From a growing, untapped market with room for many players, it had become a somewhat saturated industry, with head-to-head confrontation for market share within the same geographical area. Though Sam's had recovered from its mid-1990s slump, conditions in the 2000s seemed likely to continue to be colored by the intensive competition between the chain and its closest rivals.

Principal Competitors

Costco Companies, Inc.; BJ's Wholesale Club, Inc.

Further Reading

"Company's Growing Sales Force Seen As Nation's Top Membership Warehouse Chain in a Few Years," *Discount Store News*, December 9, 1985, p. 33.

Halverson, Richard, "Ruling Forces Sam's to Drop 'Wholesale' Name," *Discount Store News*, November 26, 1990, p. 3.

Hisey, Pete, "Membership Merger Mania," *Discount Store News*, November 26, 1990, p. 1.

Liebeck, Laura, "New Leader Hopes to Take Member Club Out of Middle Ground," *Discount Store News*, June 7, 1999, p. 92.

Markowitz, Arthur, "Sam's, Pace Square Off for Midwest Dominance," *Discount Store News*, December 17, 19990, p. 5.

"Sam's Club Out to Prove the Rebound Is for Real," *Discount Store News*, June 8, 1998, p. 118.

"Sam's Expansion Is Key to Wal-Mart's Success," *Discount Store News*, July 16, 1990, p. 85.

Saporito, Bill, "The Mad Rush to Join the Warehouse Club," *Fortune*, January 6, 1986, pp. 59–61.

Thurmond, Shannon, "Sam Speaks Volumes About New Formats," *Advertising Age*, May 9, 1988, p. S26.

"Top Two Raise Bar, Lift Sales," *DSN Retailing Today*, August 7, 2000, p. 43.

Troy, Mike, "Sam's Updates Market Strategies," *Discount Store News*, March 9, 1998, p. 5.

Vance, Sandra, and Roy V. Scott, *Wal-Mart: A History of Sam Walton's Retail Phenomenon,* New York: Twayne Publishers, 1994.

Zellner, Wendy, "Why Sam's Wants Businesses to Join the Club," *Business Week*, June 27, 1994, pp. 48–50.

—A. Woodward

Schmitt Music Company

88 South Tenth Street
Minneapolis, Minnesota 55403-2473
U.S.A.
Telephone: (612) 339-4811
Fax: (612) 339-3574
Web site: http://www.schmittmusic.com

Private Company
Incorporated: 1926
Employees: 525
Sales: $60.2 million (1999)
NAIC: 45122 Prerecorded Tape, Compact Disc and Record
Store; 45114 Musical Instrument and Supplies Store

Schmitt Music Company (also known as Schmitt's) is one of the country's largest full-service music retailers. The company sells pianos, electronic keyboards, church organs, accessories, and printed music. Schmitt operates 11 stores in Minnesota and 13 stores in eight other states. Schmitt Music also teaches more than 170,000 music lessons each year and sells about 20,000 starter band and orchestra instruments. A family owned and operated store for four generations, Schmitt has served the musical needs of the Midwest for over 100 years.

Starting with Sheet Music: 1920s–30s

The company owes its genesis to Paul Schmitt, who in 1890 traveled from New York City to take a job managing the sheet music department for Century Piano in Minneapolis. An unsuccessful salary negotiation led to Schmitt's decision to quit his position and strike out on his own. In 1896, Schmitt founded the company, but did not incorporate until 1926. Initially, Schmitt Music Company concentrated on sheet music sales. The company expanded into publishing its own school choral, band, and orchestra music by the 1930s. Within the decade, Paul's son Robert A. Schmitt joined his father in guiding the business and expanding the company to include record, radio, and phonograph sales. Fostering an appreciation for the enticing power of music, clinics were introduced featuring recitals of new compositions for music educators to offer their students. Creative marketing strategies led

to swelling inventories that demanded larger accommodations. In 1941, Robert A. Schmitt signed the mortgage for a larger location in downtown Minneapolis. He moved the business into the newly purchased building, and made room on the fifth floor for a warehouse and piano-rebuilding shop, which allowed the company to begin selling pianos and organs.

Massive Expansion in the 1950s

Robert P. Schmitt, son of Robert A., became company president in 1958. Almost immediately Robert P. began an aggressive expansion program to acquire other music companies. He purchased Bach Music in Rochester, Minnesota, Day Music Company in Wisconsin, and Hospe Music in Nebraska. In a *Twin Cities Business Monthly* interview, Robert P. said, "once you learn how to play your horn well, there are all sorts of other resources for supplies and music that you might use. Our specialty is education—bringing music to kids at the piano bench." Schmitt developed a plan for locating stores in neighborhoods to accommodate parents in getting their children to and from music lessons. His goal was to make the company indispensable to band and orchestra directors. The company sold and serviced big ticket instruments such as euphoniums, tubas, xylophones, and pianos directly to schools. Sales representatives visited schools to market instruments and purchasing plans to students during band sign-ups.

The company's Minneapolis headquarters became an unofficial landmark when Robert P. Schmitt decided to beautify one of the large exposed exterior brick walls. Like other American cities of the 1970s, citizens and business owners in Minneapolis were concerned about beautifying the older downtown buildings. Schmitt hired the repair of the old bricks and bricked up 32 exterior windows. He asked a company employee to choose notes from a musical score that could be painted as a mural over the enormous facade. The employee searched through the store's sheet music and came up with the most graphically attractive piece of music she could find, Maurice Ravel's "Gaspard de la Nuit." Pianist Van Cliburn posed playing a Steinway concert grand piano in front of the mural for a now famous photograph, which attracted the attention of national newspapers.

Robert's son, Tom Schmitt, took charge of the business in 1985, becoming the fourth generation family president of Schmitt Music. Tom had been accepted to both medical school and law school, but before making a decision, he queried his father about how much the president of Schmitt Music made in a year. He determined that a ten-year apprenticeship with his father would be preferable to graduate school. In 1989, Tom Schmitt bought a four-store Colorado keyboard retailer, Wells Music, adding a musical instrument division to the Schmitt Music Company. Under his direction, one of the company's divisions developed a "Baxstage" section, introduced in 1992. According to Pamela Hill Nettleton in *Twin Cities Business Monthly*, "Baxstage looks like rock-and-roll band heaven, with scores of electric and acoustic guitars hanging on the walls, drums and cymbals set up on the floor and glass counters stocked with microphones and cable." Following the family tradition, Tom convinced his brother Doug to begin learning various areas of the business and to concentrate on the musical instrument stores and printed music.

1990s: Steinways Sold in Suburbs

Schmitt Music became the fourth largest keyboard retailer in the country by the mid-1990s. Predicting that high-end pianos, such as Steinway, Kawai, and Boston, would sell well in the suburbs, Tom Schmitt added separate "Steinway Rooms" to several locations on the outskirts of the Twin Cities. He reasoned that being located outside the typical mall environment would encourage musicians to come in and sample the instruments without the noise and distractions of mall traffic. Piano sales evolved into the major revenue producer for the company, making up over half of Schmitt's total sales in 1994, along with sales of electronic keyboards, digital pianos, and home and chord organs. Total sales for 1994 topped $40 million.

In the Twin Cities metropolitan area, instrument sales competitors included Trestman Music Center, Guitar Center, Groth Music, Knut-Koupee Music Stores, and Roger Dodger Music. In 1999, a music superstore chain called MARS opened in the Twin Cities. When asked what Schmitt's stores offered that MARS did not, Tom Schmitt told a *Star Tribune* reporter that Schmitt's offered great customer service, competitive pricing, community involvement, and knowledgeable employees. The company had became known for hiring well-trained, friendly staff that included professional musicians.

The MARS product line included digital keyboards, guitars, drums, amplifiers, mixing boards, and microphones—catering to rock 'n' roll tastes, although the MARS company also dabbled in the school band market. As the new competition targeted rock bands, Schmitt served the niche market of church and home organ business. Schmitt's was particularly strong on keyboards, sheet music, and band and orchestra instruments and had established strong contacts with regional band directors who appreciated the company's emphasis on customer service. In addition, music lessons had become a lucrative part of the business, evidenced by the fact that the company's Edina store alone was giving approximately 2,000 music lessons per week.

The company offered six free lessons with every instrument purchase, along with affordable purchase plans to allow almost every child the opportunity to engage musically. Under terms of the instrument trial purchase plan, parents could buy an instrument with a low down payment followed by monthly payments. Should a child lose interest, Schmitt permitted a return of the instrument during the contract period without requiring further monthly payments. Unfortunately for the company, 44,000 Minnesota families alleged that Schmitt's Music charged excessive interest on instruments purchased via credit. A class-action lawsuit was filed against the company in February 1993. The suit alleged that the company charged 18 percent interest on instrument sales. Under Minnesota's usury law, 8 percent annual interest was the maximum amount allowed on such transactions. Tom Schmitt told a *St. Paul Pioneer Press* reporter, "We still contend it was a revolving charge account—and it still is." Minnesota law permits up to 18 percent annual interest on revolving charge accounts. "The program has not changed one iota," according to Schmitt, "We did change the contract a little bit, taking a belt-and-suspenders approach so it's even more clear to customers that they're signing a revolving charge application." Schmitt said the company agreed to a settlement because they could not run the risk of losing. "When the stakes are so high, it was literally the whole future of the company," he said. The company agreed to pay about $1.7 million in cash and to provide coupons worth $2 million to customers who said they were overcharged.

Schmitt Music joined the bandwagon of other Twin Cities businesses in promoting community philanthropic deeds. In an effort to provide musical instruments for underprivileged children, Schmitt Music held a drive during the holiday season for used band and orchestra instruments. The Music for Kids Project collected the instruments from families no longer needing them, organized and repaired them, and then donated them to Minneapolis and St. Paul public school music departments. In the program's first year, 300 instruments were collected and donated. According to company records, Schmitt Music also gave 5 percent of its profit to charity each year.

2000: Opening of First California Store

Continuing its westward expansion, in the winter of 2000, Schmitt Music opened a new organ store in Laguna Hills, California. The company also announced that the "landmark" downtown Minneapolis headquarters building was being sold to a group that planned to remodel the retail-and-office space for a business appraisal firm and two tenants. The new owners agreed to maintain the black-on-white mural of "Gaspard de la Nuit"

Key Dates:

1890: Paul A. Schmitt moves to Minneapolis from New York City to manage Century Piano's sheet music department.
1896: Schmitt leaves Century Piano to found a retail music store.
1926: Schmitt Music Company is incorporated.
1932: A record department is added.
1933: Radios and phonographs are added.
1934: Schmitt Music expands and publishes school music.
1937: Company introduces music clinics.
1940: A recording studio is added.
1942: Store is moved to new location on South 10th Street in Minneapolis.
1947: Company enters keyboard business.
1958: Robert P. Schmitt, grandson of the founder, becomes president and adds Martin Guitar line.
1960: Schmitt Music opens stores in St. Paul and Robbinsdale, Minnesota.
1966: Schmitt Music opens store in Edina, Minnesota.
1971: Schmitt buys Rochester, Minnesota-based Bach Music Company.
1973: Schmitt begins rapid expansion.
1985: Tom Schmitt, great-grandson of the founder, becomes president.
1999: Schmitt buys piano store in Independence, Missouri, and an organ store in Antioch, Kansas.

since it had become a favorite local landmark. Tom Schmitt said the company had been considering a move for several years as a means to centralize its administrative, distribution, and warehouse functions. A Brooklyn Center site was chosen because of its proximity to a current store and warehouse. The company had seven stores in the metro area by the end of 2000.

The market for music instruments had grown between 6 and 9 percent over the past decade, according to Brian Majeski, editor of *Music Trades*. That trend was expected to continue, with guitars as the biggest seller, school instruments second, followed by acoustic and digital pianos. The 12- to 24-year-old category of consumers were the largest purchasers of musical instruments and census figures showed that the category was growing. However, Majeski said the industry performed better during times of economic prosperity. Consequently, the slowing economy would likely impact revenues. Tom Schmitt, optimistic about the company's future, said that academic research showed that musical skills boosted children's intelligence and reports of that information created more interest. In regard to the company's long success, Robert P. Schmitt commented, "When I think about the secret of our longevity, I keep thinking that we have good people working for us and that all of us believe that what we do has a benefit. The products and the services we sell are close to our hearts. And," he added, "we all like music."

Principal Divisions

Wells Music; Schmitt's Music.

Principal Competitors

Trestman Music Center; Guitar Center, Inc.; Groth Music; Knut-Koupee Music Stores; Metropolitan; Bodines; MARS.

Further Reading

Carlson, Scott, "Class Action Suit Proceeds Against Minnesota Musical Instrument Firm," *Knight-Ridder/Tribune Business News*, December 13, 1995, p. 12130107.

Hill Nettleton, Pamela, "The Music Men," *Twin Cities Business Monthly*, August 1995, p. 52.

Kalstrom, Jonathan, "Big Firms Spread Holiday Cheer," *City Business*, August 1995, p. 26.

Levy, Melissa, "Schmitt Music Goes Suburban," *Minneapolis Star Tribune*, August 3, 2000, p. 1D.

Meyer, Gene, "Jenkins Music, Kansas City, Mo., Makes Ownership Switch," *Knight-Ridder/Tribune Business News*, November 11, 1997, p. 111B0901.

Moore, Janet, "Selling to a Different Beat," *Minneapolis Star Tribune*, February 21, 1999, p. 1D.

Moylan, Martin J., "Schmitt Settles Lawsuit Over Usury Charges," *St. Paul Pioneer Press*, May 18, 1996, p. 1B.

—Terri Mozzone

SHARP

Sharp Corporation

22-22 Nagaike-cho
Abeno-ku
Osaka 545-8522
Japan
Telephone: +81-6-6621-1221
Fax: +81-6-6627-1759
Web site: http://www.sharp-world.com

Public Company
Incorporated: 1935 as Hayakawa Metal Industrial
   Laboratory
Employees: 60,200
Sales: ¥1.85 trillion ($17.66 billion) 2000
Stock Exchanges: Tokyo Osaka Nagoya Paris
   Luxembourg Zurich Basel Geneva
Ticker Symbol: SHCAY
NAIC: 33431 Audio and Video Equipment Manufactur-
   ing; 33421 Telephone Apparatus Manufacturing;
   333313 Office Machine Manufacturing (pt); 335221
   Household Cooking Appliance Manufacturing

Sharp Corporation develops, produces, and markets advanced consumer electronics, business products, and electronic components. For most of the 1980s Sharp's reputation—and sales—lagged behind those of arch-rival Sony Corporation. In the 1990s, though, Sharp emerged as the leader of the liquid crystal display (LCD) industry. LCD panels are lighter and thinner than the cathode ray tube screens common in televisions, and have revolutionized calculators, computer screens, video recorders, and hand-held devices. However, Sharp is more than an LCD manufacturer. The company also does a brisk business in integrated circuits, digital copiers, fax machines, and household appliances. Although 65 percent of its sales are generated in Japan, Sharp has subsidiaries around the world.

The Hayakawa Metal Industrial Laboratory: 1912–42

The company was founded as a small metal works in Osaka in 1912 by an inventor and tinkerer named Tokuji Hayakawa.

After three years in business, earning a modest income from gadgets and repair jobs, Hayakawa engineered a mechanical pencil he called the "Ever-Sharp." Consisting of a retractable graphite lead in a metal rod, the Ever-Sharp pencil won patents in Japan and the United States. Demand for this simple and durable instrument was immense. To facilitate greater production, Hayakawa first adopted an assembly line and later moved to a larger factory.

Hayakawa's business, as well as his personal life, were dealt a devastating blow on September 1, 1923. On that day, the Great Kanto Earthquake caused a fire which destroyed his factory and took the lives of his wife and children. Hayakawa endured severe depression, and it was a year before he reestablished his factory. The Hayakawa Metal Industrial Laboratory, as the company was called, resumed production of the Ever-Sharp pencil, but Hayakawa became interested in manufacturing a new product: radios.

The first crystal radio sets were imported into Japan from the United States in the early 1920s. Hearing one for the first time, Hayakawa immediately became convinced of its potential. With little understanding of radios, or even electricity, he set out to develop Japan's first domestically produced crystal radio. After only three months of study and experimentation, Hayakawa succeeded in receiving a signal from the broadcasting service which had begun programming—to a very small audience—only a few months before, in 1925.

The radio entered mass production shortly afterward, and sold so well that facilities had to be expanded. Crystal radios, however, are passive receivers whose range is limited. Hayakawa felt that powered radios, capable of amplifying signals, should be the subject of further development. While competitors continued to develop better crystal sets, Hayakawa began work on an AC vacuum tube model. When the company introduced a commercial model, the Sharp Dyne, in 1929, Sharp was firmly established as Japan's leading radio manufacturer. The company expanded greatly in the following years, necessitating its reorganization into a corporation in 1935.

The laboratory, for all its success, was not a leader in a wide range of technologies; it led only in a narrow section of the

391

Company Perspectives:

We do not seek merely to expand our business volume. Rather, we are dedicated to the use of our unique, innovative technology to contribute to the culture, benefits, and welfare of people throughout the world.

It is the intention of our corporation to grow hand-in-hand with our employees, encouraging and aiding them to reach their full potential and improve their standard of living.

Our future prosperity is directly linked to the prosperity of our customers, dealers, and shareholders—indeed, the entire Sharp family.

---

market. In addition, the company did not have the benefit of financial backing from the *zaibatsu* conglomerates or the government. In the realm of the national modernization effort, it was an outsider. This may have been its saving grace, however, as the government had become dominated by a group of right-wing imperialists within the military. Whatever their political opinions, the leaders of Japan's largest corporations were compelled to cooperate with the militarists in their quest to establish Japanese supremacy in Asia. Hayakawa, on the other hand, was for the most part left alone.

World War II and Postwar Challenges

During World War II, though, Hayakawa and his company were forced to produce devices for the military, and even to restructure, as new industrial laws intended to concentrate industrial capacity were passed. Renamed Hayakawa Electrical Industries in 1942, the company emerged from the war damaged but not destroyed. While other industrialists were purged from public life for their support of the militarists, Hayakawa was permitted to remain in business. His biggest concerns were rebuilding his company and surviving Japan's postwar recession.

By 1950 more than 80 of Hayakawa's competitors were bankrupt. But Hayakawa's officials personally guaranteed the company's liabilities when the company suffered a critical drop in sales, and Hayakawa Electric was able to obtain the cooperation of underwriters until the first major expansion in the Japanese economy occurred in 1952.

Hayakawa considered television, a field that had not yet proved commercially successful, a highly promising new area. The company began development of an experimental TV set in 1951, even before plans had been made to begin broadcasting in Japan. Two years later, when television broadcasting started, Hayakawa Electric introduced its first commercial television set under the brand name ''Sharp,'' in honor of the pencil. Hayakawa's good timing was essential in allowing the company to establish and maintain a significant and profitable market share.

Innovation in the 1950s and 1960s

The company started development of a color television in the mid-1950s. In 1960, with the advent of color broadcasting in Japan, Hayakawa introduced a line of color sets. This was followed in 1962 by a commercial microwave oven, and in

1964 by a desktop calculator. The Compet calculator was the first in the world to use transistors. In 1966 the microwave oven received a rotating plate and calculators shrank with the use of integrated circuits.

Hayakawa recognized the great sales potential of the United States; a sales subsidiary was established there in 1962. It served the dual purpose of facilitating sales and observing the market. By the late 1960s, the Sharp brand name had become well-established in North America. Sales in the United States provided the company with a large and increasing portion of its income. In addition, subsidiaries were established in West Germany in 1968 and Britain in 1969.

Hayakawa Electric made two major breakthroughs in 1969. That year the company introduced the Extra Large Scale Integration Calculator, a device now reduced to the size of a paperback book. The other new product was the gallium arsenide light-emitting diode (LED)—in effect, a tiny computer light. Like the radio and television before them, improved versions of both the calculator and LED were subsequently introduced in future years.

New Leadership in the 1970s

Tokuji Hayakawa retired from the day-to-day operations of his company in 1970, assuming the title of chairman. He was replaced as president by Akira Saeki, a former executive director. Saeki oversaw an important reorganization of the company intended to establish a new corporate identity and unify product development efforts. That year, Hayakawa Electric Industries also adopted its new name: Sharp Corporation.

Saeki, who witnessed the Apollo moon landing while in the United States, decided that the company's future efforts should center on the development of semiconductors, the electronic components that had made the lunar mission possible. He initiated construction of a massive research complex called the Advanced Development and Planning Center. The project was a significant investment for Sharp, since its budget was already seriously strained by the construction of an exhibit for Expo '70. Nevertheless construction was begun on a 55-acre research complex in Tenri, Nara Prefecture. When completed, the research complex cost ¥7.5 billion, representing about 70 percent of Sharp's capitalization.

Perhaps the most important product to come out of the Tenri research facility was the Very Large Scale Integration (VLSI) factory automation system. Building upon existing integration technologies, VLSI production lines enabled manufacturers to reduce defects and raise productivity through the use of industrial robots and other mechanical apparatus.

During the 1970s, Sharp consolidated its position in consumer goods by broadening its product line to include refrigerators, washers, portable stereos, copiers, desktop computers, video equipment, and Walkman-type headsets. Perhaps Sharp's most significant development during this period occurred in 1973, when the company introduced the first hand-held calculator using a liquid crystal display (LCD) screen. LCD screens had been discovered in 1963 at RCA Labs, but the American company had been largely uninterested in the discovery. Having just pioneered cathode ray tubes in color, RCA did not see any use for LCD screens. Sharp, on the other hand, incorporated LCD screens into its calculator, making it smaller and lighter. Although Sharp's LCD screen did not seem like a tremendous breakthrough at the time, the technology would later prove central to Sharp's development.

In an effort to head off impending protectionist trade legislation, Sharp built new factories in its largest overseas markets, principally the United States. The company's decision to build a plant in Memphis, Tennessee, was criticized at first. RCA had closed a plant in Memphis in 1966, favoring production in Taiwan. Sharp maintained that RCA had merely suffered from inept management and went ahead with the plant. By pushing its American suppliers for parts with zero defects and incorporating the Japanese concept of full worker involvement, the Memphis plant proved highly successful.

Embracing LCD: 1986–94

President Saeki retired in 1986, continuing to serve the company as an advisor. He was succeeded by Haruo Tsuji, a "numbers man" with an exemplary record in middle and upper management. During Saeki's tenure, Sharp had diversified into a wide range of consumer products. By 1986 Sharp operated 12 research laboratories and 34 plants in 27 countries and its employees were equally divided between Japan and foreign countries. The logistics of running a truly international corporation took a toll on Sharp's earnings, however, particularly as the value of the Japanese yen strengthened against other currencies in the mid-1980s. In 1986, for example, Sharp's earnings plunged 42 percent to ¥20.78 billion ($137.5 million). Nevertheless, Saeki had left his company, with its 18 divisions, poised for a future of vigorous growth.

Eschewing the more glamorous development paths of rivals such as Sony and Matsushita, who expanded by acquiring a number of Hollywood-based entertainment companies during the 1980s, Sharp instead focused on research and development. In consumer electronics and appliances, the company engaged in a measured effort to move upmarket, introducing more expensive, but higher quality, products. By the late 1980s Sharp

had developed a number of innovations in its product line such as a video disc player capable of reproducing three-dimensional images, a cordless telephone with a 100-meter range, and Zarus, a highly successful computerized personal organizer, capable of reading handwritten Japanese text.

But the most significant changes took place in another area of business. New president Tsuji quickly recognized the potential of LCD devices, and unflinchingly focused the company's resources on developing the technology. Tsuji committed 10 percent of Sharp's total sales revenues to research and development. With this push, Sharp soon began to add LCD screens to all its products. By the late 1980s, Sharp succeeded in producing a thin film transistor LCD—a display with impressively sharp definition that opened the door to color laptop computers and portable televisions.

In 1989, Tsuji appointed Kiyoshi Sakashita, a company board member and an expert in industrial design, to lead a team of 50 engineers focused on further exploiting Sharp's LCD technology. Three years and countless brainstorming sessions later, the company unveiled ViewCam, an ingeniously redesigned video camcorder that presented the image on a four-inch LCD screen as it was being recorded. First shown at Japan's prestigious consumer electronics show in Osaka, Sharp's ViewCam "set the industry abuzz," according to the *Far Eastern Economic Review*. The ViewCam represented a direct challenge to Sony's best-selling Handycam. Within two years, over 1.6 million ViewCam units were sold, at an average price of ¥223,000 ($2,275).

Sharp's LCD advances propelled the company forward. Between 1991 and 1994, Sharp's LCD business grew by more than 35 percent each year, and by the close of fiscal 1994, LCD screens accounted for over 30 percent of Sharp's total revenue. While rivals Sony and Matsushita watched their profits drop in 1994, Sharp's earnings rose by 25 percent over the same period.

The company did not rest on its laurels, however, as it remained committed to development. In the early 1990s Sharp completed two new research and development centers: the Makuhari Building in Tokyo, which focused on multimedia, networking, and software for advanced information systems; and Sharp Laboratories of Europe Ltd. in Oxford, United Kingdom, which focused on areas such as pan-European translation technology and opto-electronics. In 1992 alone, the company spent over ¥100 billion ($660 million) on research and development. Sharp also fortified its television manufacturing operations in the United States, Spain, Thailand, and Malaysia, and shifted some of its other production facilities abroad as well. Late in 1994, for example, the company transferred LCD front-end manufacturing facilities to its plant in Camas, Washington. A few months later, Sharp established an LCD production facility in Wuxi, China. During this period, the company also entered into key relationships with Intel Corporation and Apple Computer, Inc. to jointly develop flash memory chips and personal information equipment. In 1994 Tsuji announced that the company would invest $1 billion over three years to build the world's largest LCD plant. By mid-1994, *Far Eastern Economic Review* announced that Sharp was "poised to usurp Sony as the electronics maker to watch in the 1990s—provided it can keep churning out good products."

As its chief competitors struggled to catch up with its advances, Sharp continued to pin its future on LCD technology. In 1995 Sharp announced that it would again increase capital investments in its electronic devices division. In particular, the company planned to pour funds into its LCD and semiconductor manufacturing operations. Sharp's goal was not merely to produce LCD screens. Rather, the company sought to place cutting-edge LCD technology at the core of the emerging multimedia field. Sharp launched a bevy of products to further this agenda, including the Mebius notebook computer, the Super High-Resolution LCD Projector, and the pen-operated infrared transmission LCD Office Station. At the same time, Sharp entered into an alliance with AT&T to jointly develop the next generation of videophone technology. "In the 21st century, I envision the future will be involved with three important things—multimedia, semi-conductors, and LCDs," Tsuji told the *New Jersey Business News* on January 1, 1996.

Overcoming Difficulties: 1996–2001

The economic climate of the late 1990s confronted Sharp with new challenges, however. Starting in 1996, Sharp—like other Japanese electronic companies—saw its sales eroded by the high value of the yen (which made Japanese products more expensive). "The production cost in Japan has become the highest in the world," Tsuji complained to the *Wall Street Journal*. In response, Sharp shifted more of its manufacturing overseas.

As LCD technology continued to go mainstream, the prices the displays commanded began to decline sharply, falling more than 50 percent in 1996 alone. Nevertheless, Sharp continued to boost production. The company also announced that it would produce and sell notebook personal computers in the United States to complement the company's burgeoning sales of copiers to American customers. Thanks to decisions such as these, Sharp appeared to be unscathed by the strong yen and the slumping LCD prices, even as many of its competitors went through painful restructurings. Early in 1997, Tsuji announced that Sharp would increase its production of LCDs by 43.8 percent for the year and would continue to invest heavily in LCD research and development.

But 1997 inaugurated a more difficult period. Sharp's LCD products faced tremendous competition from Matsushita Electric Industrial Co., as well as from manufacturers in Korea and the United States. The competition drove down prices and raised the supply of LCDs. To top if off, Sharp had failed "to develop new high margin products that could guarantee it a steady stream of profits," according to the *Asian Wall Street Journal*. As a result, the company's profits and sales declined for the first time in five years.

Sharp's troubles only grew more intense with the onset of a severe Japanese recession in 1998 (the country's worst since World War II). Sales of Sharp's usually steady "white goods" sector (appliances such as refrigerators, washing machines, and air conditioners) plummeted as Japanese consumers shied away from major purchases. Caught in this crunch, Sharp's profits fell another 43 percent in 1998.

In response to the crisis, Tsuji stepped aside and was replaced by Katsuhiko Machida as president. Describing the situation as "the worst in the history of Sharp," Machida instituted a number of changes to right the foundering company. In August 1998 he announced that Sharp would entirely replace its production of cathode ray tube (CRT) televisions by 2005. In their place, the company would introduce sets using LCD screens—thereby driving demand for the displays in which Sharp specialized. In 1999, Machida also brought sweeping changes to Sharp's production and management systems. According to *Industry Week*, Machida sped up Sharp's decision-making process and allocated more responsibilities to his three deputies. More importantly, he freed the company's numerous subsidiaries, appointing local executives to key positions. In 1999, for instance, he made an American (the first ever) the head of Sharp's U.S. subsidiary. Machida also cut costs—especially in the company's flailing semiconductor segment—and reduced Sharp's product lines.

Sharp recognized that it would have to wait out Japan's economic turmoil for its fortunes to recover completely. But the company also continued to develop new products in the hopes of finding its next "hit." In 2000 Sharp once again boosted capital investments, the bulk of which went to increased production of LCD panels. Sharp also planned to devise a device that combined the functions of television with personal computers. In 2001 Sharp began plans to manufacture next-generation LCDs—low-temperature, liquid continuous-grain silicon display systems that incorporated semiconductor chips. Sharp also looked to strengthen its position in other areas. In 2000, for example, Sharp teamed up with Xerox Corporation to develop next-generation ink jet printers and copiers. With strategies such as these, Sharp appeared well-positioned to confront the challenges and seize the opportunities presented by the new century.

Principal Subsidiaries

Sharp Electronics Corporation (U.S.A.); Sharp Manufacturing Company of America; Sharp Microelectronics Technology Inc. (U.S.A.); Hycom Inc. (U.S.A.); Sharp Electronics of Canada Ltd.; Sharp Electronics (Europe) GmbH (West Germany); Sharp Electronics (Svenska) AB (Sweden); Sharp Electronics (U.K.) Ltd.; Sharp Precision Manufacturing (U.K.) Ltd.; Sharp Electronics GmbH (Austria); Sharp Electronics (Schweiz) AG (Switzerland); Sharp Electronica Espana S.A.; Sharp Corporation of Australia Pty. Ltd.; Sharp Manufacturing France S.A.; Sharp-Roxy Sales (Singapore) Pte. Ltd.; Sharp Electronics (Singapore) Pte. Ltd.; Sharp Electronics (Taiwan) Company Ltd.; Sharp Appliances (Thailand) Ltd.; Sharp-Roxy (Hong Kong), Ltd., Sharp Thebnakorn (Thailand) Co. Ltd. (STLC), Sharp-Roxy Electronics Corporation (M) Sdn. Bhd. (Malaysia), Sharp Laboratories of Europe (England) Ltd.

Principal Competitors

Samsung Electronics Co., Ltd.; Seiko Epson Corporation; Toshiba Corporation; Sony Corporation; Hitachi, Ltd.; Matsushita Electric Industrial Co., Ltd.

Further Reading

Eisenstodt, Gale, "Unidentical Twins," *Forbes*, July 5, 1993, p. 42.

Friedland, Jonathan, "Sharp's Edge: Prowess in LCD Screens Puts It Ahead of Sony," *Far Eastern Economic Review,* July 28, 1994, p. 74.

Gross, Neil, "Sharp's Long-Range Gamble on Its Innovation Machine," *Business Week,* April 29, 1991, pp. 84–85.

Hamilton, David, "Sharp's Edge Dull, Leaving Shares Adrift," *Asian Wall Street Journal,* September 17, 1997.

Morris, Kathleen, "The Town Watcher," *Financial World,* July 19, 1994, pp. 42–45.

Prior, James, "Sharp Pioneers Society's 21st Century Products," *New Jersey Business News,* January 1, 1996.

Teresko, John, "Japan: Reengineering vs. Tradition," *Industry Week,* September 5, 1994, pp. 62–70.

—updates: Maura Troester, Rebecca Stanfel

Shaw Industries, Inc.

616 East Walnut Drive
Dalton, Georgia 30722
U.S.A.
Telephone: (706) 278-3812
Toll Free: (800) 441-7429
Fax: (706) 275-3735
Web site: http://www.shawinc.com

Wholly Owned Subsidiary of Berkshire Hathaway Inc.
Incorporated: 1967 as Philadelphia Holding Co., Inc.
Employees: 30,023
Sales: $4.1 billion (2000)
NAIC: 31411 Carpets and Rug Mills

Shaw Industries, Inc. is the largest carpet manufacturer in the world. The company designs and manufactures more than 3,100 styles of tufted carpet for residential and commercial use, selling its wholesale products to retailers, distributors, and commercial users. Shaw Industries' brand names include: Philadelphia, Cabin Crafts, Shaw Commercial Carpets, Stratton, Networx, Shawmark, Trustmark, Cumberland Evans Black, Salem, Sutton, Tuftex, Queen Carpet, Designweave, Redbook, Minster, and Invicta. A vertically integrated company, Shaw Industries participates in every stage of the manufacturing process, from the production of yarns through the finishing of carpet. The company ranks as the largest producer of polypropylene yarn in the world. Shaw Industries also provides installation services and sells laminate flooring and ceramic tile. The company operates as a subsidiary of Berkshire Hathaway Inc., the publicly traded holding company controlled by famed investor Warren E. Buffett.

Origins

Brothers Robert and J.C. Shaw founded the company that was to be known as Shaw Industries in 1967. According to a profile in the *Atlanta Journal and Constitution,* the brothers were born in Dalton, Georgia, to the owner of Star Dyeing Co., a subcontractor serving the carpeting industry. As young men, they went their separate ways and left Dalton. Upon their fa-

ther's death in 1960, the brothers returned home to decide whether to sell or close the business. They did neither, deciding instead to retool their father's company as a supply firm to the industry, which they called Star Finishing Co. The small company—with ten employees and four machines—dyed and finished carpeting for other companies.

The Shaws first entered carpet manufacturing in December 1967, when they acquired the Philadelphia Carpet Company of Cartersville, Georgia. In order to make the purchase, the company incorporated as Philadelphia Holding Co., Inc., but adopted the name Shaw Industries when it went public in 1971. The company was listed on the American Stock Exchange in March 1972.

The 1970s posed a number of challenges to the young company as it faced the oil embargo and the subsequent energy crisis and inflation. At that time, housing starts slowed and the construction industry suffered. The embargo also affected the availability of petrochemical products used in producing the synthetic carpet yarns. Despite those pressures, the company continued to grow. In June 1972, the company acquired New Found Industries, Inc., a spinner of fine gauge carpet yarns. In the same year, the company started up its own heat-set and twisting operations for processing the continuous filament nylon yarn used in making shag carpeting. Shaw also built a new carpet finishing plant in suburban Los Angeles, California, in order to help supply West Coast markets.

In the 1974 fiscal year, Shaw acquired Elite Processing Co., Inc. of Dalton, Georgia, and Syntex Yarns, Ltd of Calhoun, Georgia. The former purchase allowed the company to increase its capacity for dyeing tufted carpeting, for Elite had newer "beck dyeing" equipment than Shaw then possessed, as well as "TAK" dyeing equipment, which manufacturers use to create designs by sprinkling flecks of dye onto the carpet material. The Syntex acquisition, renamed New Found Yarns, Inc., added approximately 150,000 pounds per week to the company's yarn-producing capacity. That increased capacity added both to Shaw's in-house production and the materials it sold to other producers.

By 1975, however, the energy crisis began to catch up with the company, decreasing orders and backing up inventory. Sales and revenues decreased 11.8 percent, primarily due to downturns in the construction and home furnishing industries. This year was the first and only year when Shaw's revenues declined. In 1976, while inflation continued and housing starts remained sporadic, matters improved for the company, which showed a 16.2 percent increase in sales and revenues, which was offset partially by a decrease in the sales price of the products due to the slow market. At the same time, Shaw Industries was able to spend $5 million to upgrade and expand its production facilities.

The 1977 and 1978 fiscal years marked a significant change of course for the company, as it consolidated all levels of operations. The company had been producing yarn and providing finishing services for its own products and for those of other manufacturers. During this period, however, Shaw determined that the New Found Yarns Division did not have sufficient capacity to meet internal demands as well as those of outside buyers, so it discontinued yarn sales. All of Shaw's other dyeing, printing, and tufting manufacturing facilities were set aside exclusively for the company's own use as well. On the administrative side, the company streamlined management structure in its Dalton offices for greater efficiency. In the course of this restructuring, Bud Shaw, who had been running the Philadelphia Carpet division, assumed a less active role in the corporation's day-to-day operations.

Shaw restructured through acquisitions and sales as well. In 1977, the company acquired the Magee Carpet Company's tufted residential and commercial carpeting operations and sold its own finishing facilities in California. At the end of that fiscal year, it sold its Philadelphia, Pennsylvania carpet-weaving facility to Pennsylvania Carpet Mills, Inc. Neither holding fit into the company's long-range plans, Senior Vice-President for Operations W. Norris Little wrote in a letter to stockholders, and the two sales "allowed us to concentrate our efforts more fully on our Dalton and Cartersville carpet operations," referring to the company's two major centers of production in Georgia.

Over the next few years, the company continued to consolidate as well as grow in the face of fluctuations in the larger economy which affected the price and availability of raw materials as well as the market for new carpeting. In an industry commonly regarded as cyclical, with its dependence on eco-

nomic fluctuations and even less controllable factors such as the effect of bad weather on the construction business, the company continued to stay one step ahead.

1980s: The Rise to Dominance

The next pivotal point in the company's trend toward consolidation came in 1982 at the nadir of the most recent industry cycle. CEO Robert Shaw decided to eliminate the middleman—in the person of outside carpeting distributors—from its sales structure. The company added eight regional warehouses to its original two and expanded its sales force, taking the further gamble of putting the salespeople on salary rather than compensating them through straight commission. In 1982, according to the *Atlanta Journal,* 55 percent of the company's sales were to national or overseas distributors, while 45 percent went directly to retailers. Three years later retailers accounted for 80 percent of sales. In the intervening years, Shaw had become the largest carpet manufacturer in the nation. At the end of 1985, Shaw was the first company ever to sell more than $500 million worth of carpet in the United States in a single year, and that figure was more than double the company's 1982 sales.

In the decade that followed, Shaw's transition to direct sales would be seen as pivotal to its move to world leader. With the benefit of hindsight, analysts could see the change in strategy in more abstract terms. *Fortune* contributor Brian O'Reilly wrote in 1993 that, at that time, "[CEO Robert] Shaw . . . accepted an unpleasant truth about his industry: Carpets are a commodity." That is to say, brand loyalty and brand-name recognition were practically nonexistent in the industry and price had become the major concern of consumers. Apparently this truth, like so many others, came as no surprise to Robert Shaw, who was called "our Iacocca" by one industry observer. Shaw told the *Atlanta Journal:* "we're not really concerned with the normal cycles in the carpet industry because we're in better control of our marketing strategy through the number of customer accounts we have. . . . We're turning over the inventory at the same rate—even though the regional distribution system is larger. The risk factor you face is running your inventory out of control, whether it's in one place or 12."

In the next few years, Shaw Industries continued to grow, expanding its yarn-spinning capacity to meet the increased demand of its own tufting operations. In 1984, it acquired the spinning facilities of Avondale Mills in Stevenson, Alabama. In 1986, the company followed up by acquiring the spinning facilities of the Candlewick division of Dixie Yarns, Inc., also of Dalton.

Shaw Industries' ownership of facilities at all levels of carpet production, or vertical integration, was common within the industry, according to a 1986 article in *Barron's.* "The carpet business . . . is affected significantly by trends in fashion, principally color. Many variations in style of tufted carpet are created by the various ways color is applied through dyeing or printing. Shaw's dyeing facilities rate among the most modern and versatile in the industry," noted *Barron's.* That versatility came in handy in the fall of 1986, according to *Forbes* magazine, when the du Pont and Monsanto companies "turned carpet retailing on its head with the first genuine technological innovation in carpet fibers in five years." That innovation, as most

Key Dates:

1967: Company is incorporated as Philadelphia Holding Co., Inc.

1971: Concurrent with conversion to public ownership, the company changes its name to Shaw Industries, Inc.

1983: New marketing strategy substantially increases sales force and direct sales, igniting growth.

1987: Acquisition of West Point-Pepperell makes Shaw Industries the largest carpet manufacturer in the world.

1992: Salem Carpet Mills, Inc., the fourth largest carpet manufacturer in the world, is acquired.

1998: Shaw Industries' retail division and its U.K. business are sold.

1999: Queen Carpet Corp. is acquired.

2001: Company is acquired, for $2 billion, by Warren Buffett's Berkshire Hathaway Inc.

consumers know by now, was the stain resistant fiber most carpets are sold with today. The breakthrough may have thrown the whole industry for a loop, but Shaw Industries was able to respond quickly, purging its outdated stock and changing over its machinery.

In late 1987, Shaw Industries became the world's largest carpet maker by purchasing the carpet business of West Point-Pepperell of West Point, Georgia, the fourth largest producer in the country. According to the *Atlanta Journal,* West Point's sales and profits had been hurt by its slow transition to stain-resistant technology and its inability to produce sufficient yarn for the company's own needs. Those, of course, were two areas in which Shaw Industries particularly excelled, especially since it acquired an additional yarn-spinning plant in Thompson, Georgia, earlier the same year. West Point then produced Cabin Crafts carpeting, a well-established brand which had been around since 1932.

With the acquisition of West Point, Shaw's revenues topped $1.2 billion, double its nearest competitor, Burlington Industries. The deal, according to *Forbes,* bolstered Shaw in three relatively weak areas of its business: luxury high-pile carpets, durable commercial carpets, and pricier wool carpets. From 1981 to 1988, Shaw's sales had increased fivefold, and income more than tripled. "We just keep adding the zeros," CEO Robert Shaw told *Forbes.*

In December 1989, Shaw acquired the property, plant, equipment, inventories, and businesses of the carpet divisions of Lancaster, Pennsylvania-based Armstrong World Industries, Inc. Armstrong's carpet business was then the fifth largest in the country, and its acquisition increased Shaw's share of the domestic market from approximately 14 to 18 percent. The deal included manufacturing plants in Georgia, North Carolina, Tennessee, and Virginia and was viewed by observers as a coup for Shaw.

The company continued to grow through the end of the decade and into the early 1990s. In 1989, the company held 22

percent of the domestic market, with sales of $1.2 billion and a 41 percent increase in earnings from the year before. In 1990 an industry analyst told the *Atlanta Journal,* "They're in control of their future and I'm not sure if the people they are competing with can say that." That control, the company had shown, came largely from its willingness to put profits back into the company toward the continual updating of equipment. For this reason, *Fortune* estimated, Shaw paid 10 percent less for supplies than its competitors, further increasing its edge.

Miscues and Recovery in the 1990s

In May 1992, the company acquired Salem Carpet Mills, Inc., the fourth largest carpet maker in the world, through a merger agreement. According to the company, that move significantly enhanced the company's position in the residential marketplace by adding the Salem and Sutton labels, both well respected in the industry, to its arsenal. During the same year, the company also expanded its commercial product offerings, and its seven-year-old modular tile business, Networx, continued to grow in a difficult market. In July of the same year, the company acquired the polypropylene carpet fiber manufacturing facilities in Andalusia, Alabama, and Bainbridge, Georgia, from Amoco Fabrics and Fibers Company.

In the early 1990s, the company began to turn more of its attention to international markets. During 1992, the company opened a full-service distribution center in Preston, England, to serve its U.K. and European markets. In March 1993, the company acquired the English company Kosset Carpets, Ltd. of Bradford, England. The largest single-site manufacturer of carpeting in the United Kingdom, it was the producer of the well-known brands Kosset and Crossley . By 1994, Shaw Industries had spent $100 million acquiring three carpet manufacturers in the United Kingdom, as it sought to exploit a highly fragmented market. Company executives believed they could increase productivity at the U.K.-based production sites by introducing Shaw Industries' tufting technology, which was considered to be more efficient and more advanced than the manufacturing processes used in Western Europe.

The push overseas occurred at roughly the same time Shaw Industries made an even bolder move back on the domestic front. Having registered remarkable success in its efforts to vertically integrate its operations, the company decided to take the ultimate step towards absolute control over the carpet market by diversifying into retail sales. As with the U.K. carpet market, company strategists perceived a weakness they believed they could exploit. They considered carpet salespeople in the United States as being inexperienced, guilty of spreading misinformation, and creating a less than desirable atmosphere for carpet shoppers. The first Shaw Carpet Showplace opened in mid-1996 in Pittsburgh, marking the beginning of a $200 million expansion program that eventually gave the company a chain of more than 400 retail outlets.

After several years, it became clear to Shaw Industries executives that the expansion into the United Kingdom and the diversification into retail were mistakes. In Europe, U.K. sales dropped 20 percent within two years, as the company fell victim to a price war waged by local competitors. Belgian carpet manufacturers, benefiting from a weak Belgian franc, proved to be formidable adversaries, in particular. The company's retail operations suffered as well. Shaw Industries' management was undeniably adept at overseeing the production of carpets, but it seemingly possessed little experience in managing the retail side of the business, at least according to one *Forbes* reporter. The company's lack of experience was compounded by the reaction of its largest customers. Customers such as Home Depot, Carpet One, and Abbey greeted Shaw Industries' entry into retail as an attack on their businesses. They stopped buying carpets from Shaw Industries, which had turned from being a supplier to a competitor in their eyes, and handed their business to Shaw Industries' wholesale competitors.

By 1998, Shaw Industries realized it had overreached. Between 1994 and 1998, earnings plunged from $120 million to $20 million. Perhaps equally distressing, the company's market share dropped four percentage points, enabling Shaw Industries' closest rivals to close ground. In April 1998, Shaw Industries sold Carpets International, Plc, its U.K. subsidiary. In August 1998, the company's retail operations were also sold; those stores not included in the sale to The Maxim Group, Inc. were closed.

Refocused on manufacturing and wholesaling, Shaw Industries concluded the 1990s on a more positive note. Not long after the divestiture of the retail operations was completed, Shaw Industries' largest customers renewed their business relationships with the company. In August 1999, the company more than made up for the loss of market share earlier in the decade by completing a massive acquisition. Dalton-based Queen Carpet Corp., an $800 million-in-sales carpet manufacturer, was purchased for $470 million in cash and stock. The acquisition increased Shaw Industries' market share from 27 percent to 35 percent and, for the first time, gave the company a manufacturing presence on the West Coast. The addition of Queen's Los Angeles-based Tuftex division was perceived as a valuable asset for the company's distribution network.

As Shaw Industries entered the 21st century, it embarked on a new era of existence. In late 2000, famed investor and multibillionaire Warren E. Buffett announced his intention to purchase Shaw Industries. In February 2001, the $2 billion deal was concluded, making Shaw Industries a subsidiary of Buffett's holding company and investment vehicle, Berkshire Hathaway Inc. Chairman and CEO Robert Shaw welcomed the acquisition, which left Shaw Industries' management intact. No longer a publicly traded company, Shaw Industries entered a new era as a private subsidiary of a public company, but its prominence as the influential leader of a $10 billion industry promised to keep the company in the public eye.

Principal Subsidiaries

Shaw Financial Services, Inc.; Shaw Transport, Inc.; Shaw Contract Flooring Services, Inc.; Shaw Contract Flooring Installation Services, Inc.; Shaw Retail Properties, Inc.; Shaw Contract Properties, Inc.; SHX Leasing, Inc.; Shaw Funding; Rug Décor by Shaw Corporation; Queen Carpet Corporation; Pro Installation, Inc.; Terza, S.A. de CV (Mexico; 49%).

Principal Competitors

Mohawk Industries, Inc.; Beaulieu Of America, LLC; Interface, Inc.

Further Reading

Brown, Elicia, "Shaw's Red-Carpet Status," *Financial World,* January 8, 1991.
Burritt, Chris, "Bob Shaw Has Quarterbacked His Carpet Company to No. 1," *Atlanta Journal,* December 22, 1986.
——, "Rug Industry Leader Taking a Giant Step," *Atlanta Constitution,* October 13, 1987.
——, "Shaw Industries Acquires Vacant Thompson Factory for a Yarn Plant," *Atlanta Journal,* August 28, 1987.
——, "West Point Deal Hinged on Several Key Issues," *Atlanta Constitution,* November 11, 1987.
Campanella, Frank W., "Clean Sweep: Record Sales, Earnings Year Shapes Up for Shaw Industries," *Barron's,* December 29, 1986.
Flamming, Douglas, *Creating the Modern South: Millhands and Managers in Dalton, Georgia, 1884–1984,* Chapel Hill: University of North Carolina Press, 1992.
Ghosh, Chandrani, "Floored," *Forbes,* November 15, 1999, p. 174.
Hannon, Kerry, "Full Speed Ahead and Damn the Stock Market," *Forbes,* January 25, 1988.
Hawkins, Chuck, "Shaw Industries Is on Top, Thanks to Bold '82 Moves," *Atlanta Journal,* March 17, 1985.
Hendrick, Bill, "Top-Performing Georgia Stock of the Eighties Was Shaw Industries," *Atlanta Journal and Constitution,* January 1, 1990.
Lightsey, Ed, "King of Carpet," *Georgia Trend,* April 1999, p. 10.
Lillo, Andrea, "Buffett Makes Pitch for Struggling Shaw Ind.," *Home Textiles Today,* September 11, 2000, p. 1.
McCurry, John W., "Shaw Industries Nears $3-Billion Sales Plateau," *Textile World,* May 1996, p. 40.
Naughton, Julie, "Shaw Grows As Producer and Retailer," *HFN The Weekly Newspaper for the Home Furnishing Network,* January 8, 1996, p. 20.
O'Reilly, Brian, "Know When to Embrace Change," *Fortune,* February 22, 1993.
Poole, Sheila M., "Carpet Maker Rolling Up Profits," *Atlanta Journal,* May 16, 1990.
——, "Shaw to Buy Armstrong Carpet Units," *Atlanta Journal,* November 11, 1989.
Rouvalis, Cristina, "Carpet Maker Shaw Industries Chooses Butler, Pa. for First Retailer Store," *Knight-Ridder/Tribune Business News,* June 7, 1996, p. 6070016.
"Shaw Approves Sale to Berkshire Investors Group," *Home Textiles Today,* October 23, 2000, p. 2.
"Shaw's Rug Evolution," *HFN The Weekly Newspaper for the Home Furnishing Network,* April 28, 1997, p. 19.
Vermillion, Len, "Floor Covering Retailer Shaw Industries to Close 100 Stores," *Home Improvement Market,* February 1998, p. 19.
Wyman, Lissa, "Shaw Still Eyes Retail, Despite Soured Deal," *HFN The Weekly Newspaper for the Home Network,* January 29, 1996, p. 20.

—Martha Schoolman
—update: Jeffrey L. Covell

Sidley Austin Brown & Wood

Bank One Plaza, 10 South Dearborn
Chicago, Illinois 60603
U.S.A.
Telephone: (312) 853-7000
Fax: (312) 853-7036
Web site: http://www.sidley.com

Partnership
Founded: 1866 as Williams & Thompson
Employees: 2,000
Sales: $446 million (1999)
NAIC: 54111 Offices of Lawyers

One of the world's largest law firms, Chicago-based Sidley Austin Brown & Wood is a legal powerhouse with several branch offices in the United States, Asia, Europe, and the Middle East. The firm has a long history in traditional industries such as electrical utilities, communications, and railroads. After World War II, it began serving clients in new areas such as healthcare, environmental affairs, and high technology. Its specialties cover the full range of a modern law practice, from intellectual property and real estate to mergers and acquisitions and complex financial transactions. As more businesses expand overseas, Sidley Austin Brown & Wood plays a major role in the world's increasingly globalized economy.

Origins

In 1866 Norman Williams and John Leverett Thompson fulfilled an adolescent commitment when they started their law partnership of Williams & Thompson in Chicago. In their first few years their general practice included collecting debts, litigation, real estate work in the booming city, and writing wills. In 1867 Williams was one of the incorporators of Pullman's Palace Car Company, the Chicago company that became famous for making railroad sleeping cars.

The young partnership in 1969 began its long-term representation of Western Union Telegraph Company when it moved its central division headquarters from Cleveland to Chicago. After

Walter L. Newberry died in 1868, the law firm successfully represented Mrs. Newberry in estate litigation. That allowed the Newberry family to use its wealth to build Chicago's Newberry Library, which was officially chartered in 1894.

After the Great Chicago Fire destroyed much of the city in 1871, the firm represented many insurance companies, including the Equitable Life Assurance Society of the United States, which remained a client for over a century. In 1874 the firm gained The Young Men's Christian Association (YMCA) as another long-term client.

The firm played a significant role in the young communications industry. It represented Western Electric Manufacturing Company and its successor Western Electric Company, which made equipment for Western Union and also became the nation's major manufacturer of telephone equipment in the 1880s. When Jay Gould instituted his so-called "telegraph wars," Williams & Thompson served Western Union as it tried to resist but eventually was taken over by Gould in 1881. In 1881 the law firm incorporated the Chicago Telephone Company, one of its major clients well into the 20th century.

The firm's utility practice included incorporating the Western Edison Light Company in 1882, shortly after Thomas Edison developed the first useful light bulb. In 1887 the firm incorporated Chicago Edison Company, which acquired the franchise of the earlier company. The firm also represented the Chicago Arc Light and Power Company in the late 1800s. Building on this experience, the firm continued to have a strong utility practice as it entered the next century.

Meanwhile, the firm helped railroads to expand. It helped the Atchison, Topeka and Santa Fe Railroad lay the legal foundations for its extension from Kansas City to Chicago in the 1880s. For example, it set up land purchases or leases for the railroad, and continued to represent it until 1893.

Shortly after the firm moved to the Tacoma Building in 1889, William P. Sidley joined the firm. He graduated from Williams College, earned his LL.B. from the Union College of Law, and also earned an M.A. from the Harvard Law School. Sidley later became the lead name partner and guided the firm through much of the 20th century.

Key Dates:

1866: Partnership of Williams & Thompson is founded in Chicago.

1889: Partnership changes its name to Williams, Holt & Wheeler.

1900: Firm becomes known as Holt, Wheeler & Sidley.

1913: Holt, Cutting & Sidley is the firm's new name.

1919: Partnership name becomes Cutting, Moore & Sidley.

1937: Sidley, McPherson, Austin & Burgess becomes the partnership's new name.

1944: Firm adopts the name of Sidley, Austin, Burgess & Harper.

1950: Sidley, Austin, Burgess & Smith is the firm's new name.

1967: Firm chooses Sidley & Austin as its name

1969: Firm establishes a branch office in Washington, D.C.

1972: Firm merges with Leibman, Williams, Bennett, Baird & Minow.

1974: Firm opens its London office.

1980: Los Angeles office opens through a merger with the 11-lawyer firm of Shutan & Trost.

1982: Singapore and New York offices are opened.

1990: Partnership opens its Tokyo office.

1996: Dallas office is opened.

1998: Seattle office is started.

2001: Sidley & Austin merges with the 400-lawyer firm of Brown & Wood.

Following the 1893 World's Columbian Exposition, the law firm helped found the Columbian Museum of Chicago as a permanent home for the exposition's numerous mineral, plant, animal, and anthropological items.

In the 1890s the Chicago firm represented the Illinois Steel Company until it was acquired by J. Pierpont Morgan's Federal Steel Company. Morgan in 1901 combined Federal Steel along with Andrew Carnegie's steel company to create U.S. Steel, the nation's first billion-dollar corporation.

The Partnership from 1900 to 1945

The law firm's growing corporate practice included a variety of services. In addition to helping companies become incorporated, buy and sell land, and deal with litigation, it also became involved in large scale financings. For example, in 1908 it represented the Chicago Telephone Company when it increased its capital stock from $20 million to $30 million, mortgaged its property to the First Trust and Savings Bank, and gained approval for $50 million in bonds. In 1910 the law firm represented Western Electric when it issued $15 million in bonds. Those two deals "marked the firm's initial experience in large-scale public financing," according to the firm's history book.

In the early 20th century, the law firm's corporate practice grew with the addition of the American Bicycle Company, American Linseed Company, and American Piano Company as new clients. With the 1890 Sherman Antitrust Act and other antitrust

laws being enforced, the Chicago law firm defended its corporate clients against charges filed by the federal government.

In 1915 the firm gained a new full-time clerk or associate named Edwin C. Austin. Born in 1892, Austin graduated from the University of Wisconsin in 1912 and then in 1915 graduated as the top student from the Northwestern University Law School. Later chosen as a name partner, Austin remained a key figure in the firm for over 60 years.

When the firm then known as Holt, Cutting & Sidley celebrated its 50th anniversary in 1916, it had four partners, four clerks or associates, and ten staff employees. Half of its annual gross income of slightly under $100,000 came from two main clients: Western Electric Company and Chicago Telephone Company. Although still a small firm, its solid reputation was acknowledged by Charles S. Cutting, a former probate judge, serving two terms as the Chicago Bar Association's president.

Under Cutting's leadership, the firm represented numerous prominent Chicago citizens in wills and estate matters. After Richard W. Sears, cofounder of Sears, Roebuck & Company, died in 1914, the firm worked until 1931 to resolve Sears's estate matters. In 1923 the partnership assisted Edith Rockefeller McCormick, the daughter of John D. Rockefeller, when she established the Edith Rockefeller McCormick Trust. After she died in 1931, the firm spent 20 years resolving disputes concerning her estate. In 1932 the law firm handled the estate of William Wrigley, Jr., who had started his chewing gum business back in 1892 in Chicago.

In the 1920s, the law firm prospered as the city grew during America's business expansion. In 1920 it moved to offices in the newly constructed Roanoke Building on LaSalle Street, popularly known as Chicago's "street of lawyers." Chicago grew from 2.7 million to 3.4 million people during the 1920s.

In 1920 the firm assisted its long-term client Chicago Telephone Company to acquire the Central Union Telephone Company and then three weeks later change its name to the Illinois Bell Telephone Company. In the late 1920s it helped the Central Public Service Corporation acquire other companies and thus operate in 24 states and seven foreign countries. However, that client went bankrupt in the early years of the Great Depression.

After graduating from Northwestern University Law School, in 1926 Adlai E. Stevenson became the newest lawyer at the firm. Even as a young lawyer, Stevenson showed a strong interest in government service and foreign affairs. For example, he served in 1933 as the president of the Chicago Council on Foreign Relations, whose national organization often was headed by top partners at elite corporate law firms. In 1933 Stevenson left to work for President Franklin D. Roosevelt. In the years ahead he would work periodically for the law firm and in government service, eventually running unsuccessfully for president, thus becoming one of the law firm's most prominent lawyers.

After reaching its peak income in 1931, the firm's income by 1935 had decreased 40 percent. From the 1930s into the 1950s, it helped several railroads deal with bankruptcy and reorganization, including the Chicago and North Western Railway Company, Denver & Rio Grande Western, and the Wisconsin Central.

New Deal legislation of the 1930s led to more work for corporate law firms. After the government passed the Federal Securities Act of 1933, the law firm represented Halsey, Stuart & Company, its first underwriter under the new securities act.

The firm in the 1940s began its long-term representation of the A.C. Nielsen Company, which became most famous for its Nielsen Television Index Service made possible by using its "Audimeter" device in selected representative homes. In 1941 the law firm included ten partners and 21 associates. During World War II, the firm like many others hired its first female lawyers to compensate for the men who had left to enter military or government service.

The Practice After World War II

The firm grew gradually in the postwar years, from 32 lawyers in 1966 to 48 in 1972. Starting in 1969 with its first branch office in Washington, D.C., the firm added several other offices both in the United States and other nations.

In 1972 Sidley & Austin's 100 lawyers merged with the 53 lawyers of Leibman, Williams, Bennett, Baird & Minow. The smaller firm had originated in 1945 when Robert F. Carney, G. Kenneth Crowell, and Morris I. Leibman formed the partnership of Carney, Crowell and Leibman.

New clients in the 1970s included the American Bar Association and also the American Medical Association as it fought against the Federal Trade Commission having regulatory power over it. In that decade the law firm also represented subsidiaries of the American Natural Resources Company as it developed the Great Plains Coal Gasification Project, the United States' first commercial plant that turned lignite coal into natural gas. Meanwhile, the firm increased its mergers and acquisitions practice when it helped International Minerals & Chemical Corporation acquire coal mines and other resources. One of its long-term nonprofit clients was Chicago's Northwestern University.

For decades law firms seldom let the outside world know about their internal affairs. Outsiders had available a list of partners and associates in the *Martindale-Hubbell* annual reference work, but little was available on their management, finances, and clients. Professional societies discouraged advertising or even cooperating with journalists or historians. For example, when Steven Brill in the late 1970s tried to find out Sidley & Austin's gross annual revenues, it was very difficult. His reporter for the *American Lawyer* had to call most of the Chicago law firm's 175 partners before one finally shared that information.

Brill's magazine and the *National Law Journal* pioneered modern legal journalism by shedding light on what had been more or less secret societies. With more comparative information about large law firms available, lawyers then increased their lateral career moves to firms that offered more financial opportunities. In addition, increased competition for the best lawyers resulted from growing corporations and a multitude of new government laws and regulations. Thus most large law firms grew even faster in the late 1970s and especially the 1980s.

Sidley & Austin's rapid growth paralleled the expansion of the Chicago Bar Association. By 1983 the firm had about 400 lawyers. Meanwhile, the CBA went from about 10,000 members in the mid-1970s to 17,638 in 1983. According to Terence C. Halliday, the CBA in 1983 with "its budget of $4.4 million made it the richest and biggest of all metropolitan associations in the United States. In fact, the CBA budget in 1983 exceeded all but four of the fifty-six state bar associations."

In 1983 former U.S. Solicitor General Rex Lee and Carter Phillips began to build Sidley & Austin's U.S. Supreme Court specialty. In the October 1998 *ABA Journal*, Phillips claimed that only the Chicago firm in 1983 was "consciously and systematically pursuing those cases." That was an important step, for by the late 1990s the Court had reduced the number of cases it reviewed and heard more cases handled by Supreme Court specialists.

When AT&T endured antitrust lawsuits that eventually broke up its monopoly of long-distance phone services, its general counsel was Sidley & Austin's Howard Trienens. Sol Linowitz reported that Trienens remained a Sidley & Austin partner, while preferring not to serve on AT&T's board of directors.

Due to charges of legal malpractice from representing Lincoln Savings, one of the many savings and loan institutions that failed in the 1980s, Sidley & Austin paid $7.5 million to settle those claims made by the federal government. At least five other corporate law firms also paid large amounts to settle other legal liability charges from their work in the S&L crisis, which received extensive media coverage. None of the law firms admitted any wrongdoing, according to Ralph Nader and Wesley J. Smith in their book *No Contest: Corporate Lawyers and the Perversion of Justice in America*.

The Firm in the 1990s and Beyond

When Commonwealth Edison's exclusive energy contract with Chicago was up for renewal in 1990, the utility represented by Sidley & Austin attorneys demanded and received a secrecy agreement that prevented the people of Chicago from seeing any records the utility deemed confidential, although city government officials could look at them. After considerable political criticism, Commonwealth Edison allowed public and media access to most documents it had marked confidential. That led to the city renewing the utility's contract. Ralph Nader and Wesley J. Smith cited Sidley & Austin's behavior in this case as an example of how big law firms help corporations at the expense of average citizens. They argued in their 1996 book that the "imbalances between real people and artificial persons called corporations are growing fast."

In 1994 Sidley & Austin lawyer Scott Bass helped write the Dietary Supplement Health and Education Act. Since that law did not cover foods, later in the decade some companies were adding herbs and other supplements to what were called functional foods. However, Bass said in a 1999 *New York Times* article that, "It's not valid to have a box of cereal that says 'Dietary Supplement.'"

Other clients in the 1990s and after the turn of the century included Health Alliance, Amoco, and Citicorp. It also helped Microsoft's main outside law firm Sullivan & Cromwell when the software giant was accused of antitrust violations.

In November 1998 the *American Lawyer*, assisted by London's *Legal Business*, published its first rankings of the world's major law firms. Based on its 811 lawyers, Sidley & Austin ranked number 12. Only 5 percent of its lawyers were outside the United States, unlike Baker & McKenzie, the most internationalized firm, with 80 percent outside of its home country. Based on 1997 gross revenue of $360 million, Sidley & Austin received a number 11 ranking.

With Baker & McKenzie having over 2,000 lawyers and London's Clifford Chance having about 3,000 lawyers, Sidley & Austin in early 2001 faced challenges from other big law firms competing for the best lawyers and clients. Thus, as part of a consolidating trend, in 2001 Sidley & Austin combined its 900 lawyers with Brown & Wood's 400 lawyers who worked out of offices in New York, Los Angeles, San Francisco, Beijing, Hong Kong, and London.

Principal Competitors

Baker & McKenzie; Mayer, Brown & Platt; Skadden, Arps, Slate, Meagher & Flom.

Further Reading

Carter, Terry, "Another Antitrust Win for the ABA," *ABA Journal*, May 1997, p. 38.
France, Steve, "Takeover Specialists," *ABA Journal*, October 1998, pp. 38–40.
Halliday, Terence C., *Beyond Monopoly: Lawyers, State Crises, and Professional Empowerment*, Chicago: The University of Chicago Press, 1987.
Hays, Constance L., "It's Not Just Food, It's a Supplement," *New York Times*, February 9, 1999, p. 6.
Hofmann, Mark A., "HMO Incentives at Issue," *Business Insurance*, February 28, 2000, pp. 1, 22.
Kogan, Herman, *Traditions and Challenges: The Story of Sidley & Austin*, Chicago: Sidley & Austin, 1983.
Lee, Paul, "The Global Players Revealed," *International Financial Law Review*, November 1998, pp. 23–31.
Linowitz, Sol M., with Martin Mayer, *The Betrayed Profession: Lawyering at the End of the Twentieth Century*, New York: Charles Scribner's Sons, 1994.
"Microsoft Bolsters Legal Team," *InfoWorld*, July 10, 2000, p. 14.
Nader, Ralph, and Wesley J. Smith, *No Contest: Corporate Lawyers and the Perversion of Justice in America*, New York: Random House, 1996.
"Success Stories: The Fortune 25," *International Commercial Litigation*, March 1997, pp. 12–13.

—David M. Walden

SONY

Sony Corporation

7-35 Kitashinagawa 6-chome
Shinagawa-ku
Tokyo 141-0001
Japan
Telephone: (03) 5448-2111
Fax: (03) 5448-2244
Web site: http://www.world.sony.com

Public Company
Incorporated: 1946 as Tokyo Tsushin Kogyo Kabushiki
   Kaisha
Employees: 189,700
Sales: ¥6.69 trillion ($63.08 billion) (2000)
Stock Exchanges: Tokyo Osaka Nagoya Fukuoka
   Sapporo New York Pacific Chicago Toronto London
   Paris Frankfurt Düsseldorf Brussels Vienna Swiss
Ticker Symbol: SNE
NAIC: 334111 Electronic Computer Manufacturing;
   334119 Other Computer Peripheral Equipment
   Manufacturing; 334210 Telephone Apparatus
   Manufacturing; 334220 Radio and Television
   Broadcasting and Wireless Communications
   Equipment Manufacturing; 334290 Other
   Communications Equipment Manufacturing; 334310
   Audio and Video Equipment Manufacturing; 334413
   Semiconductor and Related Device Manufacturing;
   512110 Motion Picture and Video Production; 512120
   Motion Picture and Video Distribution; 512131
   Motion Picture Theaters, Except Drive-In; 512220
   Integrated Record Production/Distribution

Sony Corporation is one of the best-known names in consumer electronics and ranks second worldwide in electronics behind Matsushita Electric Corporation. Since it was established shortly after World War II, Sony has introduced a stream of revolutionary products, including the transistor radio, the Trinitron television, the Betamax VCR, the CD player, the Walkman portable cassette player, and the PlayStation game console. The company's electronics segment—which includes audio and video products, televisions, personal computers, monitors, computer peripherals, telecommunications devices, and electronic components (such as semiconductors)—generates about two-thirds of the overall revenues. Sales of game consoles and software account for about 9 percent of revenues. Another 10 percent of revenues are derived from Sony's music businesses, which include the Columbia and Epic record labels. About 7 percent of revenues come from Sony's motion picture and television business, which includes the Columbia TriStar studio. Sony's other major business segment is insurance, from which about 6 percent of revenues originate.

Early History: From Tape Recorders to Transistor Radios to the Trinitron

Sony was founded by a former naval lieutenant named Akio Morita and a defense contractor named Masaru Ibuka. Morita, a weapons researcher, first met Ibuka during World War II while developing a heat-seeking missile-guidance system and a night-vision gun scope. After the war Ibuka worked as a radio repairman for a bomb-damaged Tokyo department store. Morita found him again when he read in a newspaper that Ibuka had invented a shortwave converter. In May 1946 the two men established a partnership with $500 in borrowed capital, and registered their company as the Tokyo Tsushin Kogyo Kabushiki Kaisha (Tokyo Telecommunications Engineering Corporation, or TTK). Morita and Ibuka moved their company to a crude facility on a hill in southern Tokyo where they developed their first consumer product: a rice cooker, which failed commercially. In its first year TTK registered a profit of $300 on sales of less than $7,000.

But as the Japanese economy grew stronger, demand for consumer goods increased. Morita and Ibuka abandoned the home-appliance market and, with injections of capital from Morita's father, concentrated on developing new electronic goods. Ibuka developed a tape recorder fashioned after an American model he had seen at the Japan Broadcasting Corporation. Demand for the machine, which was introduced in 1950 and was the first Japanese tape recorder, remained low until Ibuka accidentally discovered a U.S. military booklet titled

Company Perspectives:

Recognizing that environmental protection is one of the most pressing issues facing mankind today, Sony incorporates a sound respect for nature in all of its business activities. With this philosophy, Sony has defined environmental conservation as an important part of its management strategy. The Sony Group has created a global action plan and conducts environmental preservation programs. This program has five core components: reducing the environmental impact of business activities and production processes; designing environmentally sensitive products and promoting recycling; developing environmental technologies; promoting the environmental education and full participation of Sony employees; and disclosing environmental information to the public.

Nine Hundred and Ninety-Nine Uses of the Tape Recorder. Translated into Japanese, the booklet became an effective marketing tool. Once acquainted with its many uses, customers such as the Academy of Art in Tokyo purchased so many tape recorders that TTK was soon forced to move to a larger building in Shinagawa.

Norio Ohga, an opera student at the academy, wrote several letters to TTK criticizing the sound quality of its recorder. Impressed by the detail and constructive tone of the criticisms, Morita invited Ohga to participate in the development of a new recorder as a consultant. Ohga accepted, and subsequent models were vastly improved.

Constantly searching for new technological advances, Masaru Ibuka heard of a tiny new capacitor called a transistor in 1952. The transistor, developed by Bell Laboratories, could be used in place of larger, less-durable vacuum tubes. Western Electric purchased the technology in order to manufacture transistorized hearing aids. Ibuka acquired a patent license from Western Electric for $25,000 with the intention of developing a small tubeless radio.

TTK began mass production of transistor radios in 1955, only a few months after they were introduced by a small American firm called Regency Electronics. The TTK radio was named Sony, from *sonus,* Latin for ''sound.'' The Sony radio had tremendous sales potential, not only in the limited Japanese market but also in the United States, where the economy was much stronger.

Traditionally, international sales by Japanese companies were conducted through trading houses such as Mitsui, Mitsubishi, and Sumitomo. Although these trading companies were well represented in the United States, Morita chose not to do business with them because they were unfamiliar with his company's products and did not share his business philosophy. Morita traveled to New York, where he met with representatives from several large retail firms. Morita refused an order from Bulova for 100,000 radios when that company required that each carry the Bulova name. Morita pledged that his company would not manufacture products for other companies and eventually secured a number of more modest orders that assured his company's growth at a measured pace. Another highlight of

The rising popularity of the Sony name led Morita and Ibuka to change the name of their company to Sony Kabushiki Kaisha (Corporation) in January 1958. The following year Sony announced that it had developed a transistorized television, which was introduced in 1960. That same year, after a business dispute with Delmonico International, the company Morita had appointed to handle international sales, Sony established a trade office in New York City and another in Switzerland called Sony Overseas.

A subsidiary called Sony Chemicals was created in 1962 to produce adhesives and plastics to reduce the company's dependence on outside suppliers. In 1965 a joint venture with Tektronix was established to produce oscilloscopes in Japan.

During the early 1960s Sony engineers continued to introduce new, miniaturized products based on the transistor, including an AM/FM radio and a videotape recorder. By 1968 Sony engineers had developed new color-television technology. Using one electron gun, for more accurate beam alignment, and one lens, for better focus, the Sony Trinitron produced a clearer image than conventional three-gun, three-lens sets. In what has been described as its biggest gamble, Sony, confident that technology alone would create new markets, invested a large amount of capital in the Trinitron.

Also in 1968, Sony Overseas established a trading office in England, and entered into a joint venture with CBS Inc. to produce phonograph records. The venture was under the direction of Norio Ohga, the art student who had complained about Sony's early tape recorder, whom Morita had persuaded in 1959 to give up opera and join Sony. The company, called CBS/Sony, later became the largest record manufacturer in Japan. In 1970 Sony Overseas established a subsidiary in West Germany to handle sales in that country.

1970s: Betamax and the Walkman

After a decade of experience in videotape technology, Sony introduced the U-matic three-quarter-inch videocassette recorder (VCR) in 1971. Intended for institutions such as television stations, the U-matic received an Emmy Award for engineering excellence from the National Academy of Television Arts and Sciences. In 1973, the year Sony Overseas created a French subsidiary, the academy honored the Trinitron series with another Emmy.

Sony developed its first VCR for the consumer market, the Betamax, in 1975. The following year the Walt Disney Company and Universal Pictures filed a lawsuit against Sony, complaining that the new machine would enable widespread copyright infringement of television programs. A judgment in favor of Sony in 1979 was reversed two years later. Litigation continued, but by the time the matter reached the U.S. Supreme Court the plaintiffs' original case had been severely undermined by the proliferation of VCRs, making any legal restriction on copying television programs for private use nearly impossible to enforce.

During the mid-1970s, competitors such as U.S.-based RCA and Zenith and Japanese-based Toshiba and Victor Company of

Key Dates:

1946: Akio Morita and Masaru Ibuka found Tokyo Tsushin Kogyo Kabushiki Kaisha (TTK).
1950: TTK introduces the first Japanese tape recorder.
1955: TTK begins selling Japan's first transistor radio; company goes public.
1958: Company's name is changed to Sony Corporation.
1960: Sony introduces the world's first transistor television.
1968: The revolutionary Sony Trinitron color television debuts; Sony enters the record business through a joint venture with CBS Inc.
1975: Company launches the Betamax VCR.
1979: The Sony Walkman is introduced.
1982: Sony introduces the first CD player.
1985: Company introduces its first 8mm video camera.
1987: CBS Records, and its Epic and Columbia labels, is acquired for $2 billion.
1989: Columbia Pictures is acquired for $3.4 billion.
1994: The Sony PlayStation debuts.
1997: The VAIO line of PCs for the home market is launched.
2000: The PlayStation 2, featuring enhanced graphics, processing power, and DVD and broadband capabilities, is released.

Japan (JVC) effectively adopted and improved upon technologies developed by Sony. For the first time, Sony began to lose significant market share, often in lines that it had pioneered. Strong competition, however, was only one factor that caused Sony's sales growth to fall (after growing 166 percent between 1970 and 1974, it grew only 35 percent between 1974 and 1978).

Like many Sony officials, Akio Morita lacked formal management training. Instead, he relied on his personal persuasive skills and his unusual ability to anticipate or create markets for new products. In typical fashion, Sony introduced the Betamax VCR well before its competitors, in effect creating a market in which it would enjoy a short-term monopoly. At this stage, however, Morita failed to establish the Betamax format as the industry standard by inviting the participation of other companies.

Matsushita Electric (which owned half of JVC) developed a separate VCR format called VHS (video home system), which permitted as many as three additional hours of playing time on a tape, but which was incompatible with Sony's Betamax. When the VHS was introduced in 1977, Morita was reported to have felt betrayed that Sony's competitors did not adopt the Betamax format. He appealed to 81-year-old Konosuke Matsushita, in many ways a patriarch of Japanese industry, to discontinue the VHS format in favor of Betamax. When Matsushita refused, many believed it was because he felt insulted by Morita's failure to offer earlier collaboration.

Matsushita launched a vigorous marketing campaign to convince customers and other manufacturers not only that VHS was superior, but that Betamax would soon be obsolete. The marketing war between Matsushita and Sony was neither constructive nor profitable; both companies were forced to lower prices so much that profits were greatly depressed. Although Betamax was generally considered a technically superior product, the VHS format grew in popularity and gradually displaced Betamax as a standard format. Despite its falling market share (from 13 percent in 1982 to 5 percent in 1987), Sony refused to introduce a VHS line until the late 1980s.

In 1979 Morita personally oversaw the development of a compact cassette tape player called the Walkman. Inspired by Norio Ohga's desire to listen to music while walking, Morita ordered the development of a small, high-fidelity tape player, to be paired with small, lightweight headphones that were already under development. The entire program took only five months from start to finish, and the product's success is now legendary—Walkman even became the generic term for similar devices produced by Sony's competitors.

1980s: CD Player, Video Cameras, CBS Records, Columbia Pictures

During the 1970s, Masaru Ibuka, 12 years Morita's senior, gradually relinquished many of his duties to younger managers such as Norio Ohga, who was named president of Sony in 1982. Ohga became president shortly after a corporate reorganization that split Sony into five operating groups (marketing and sales, manufacturing, service, engineering, and diversified operations). While not formally trained in business, Ohga nonetheless understood that Sony was too dependent on an unstable consumer electronics market. In one of his first acts, he inaugurated the 50–50 program to increase sales in institutional markets from 15 to 50 percent by 1990.

During this time, Sony's research and development budget consumed approximately 9 percent of sales (Matsushita budgeted only 4 percent). Another groundbreaking result of Sony's commitment to research and development was a machine that used a laser to reproduce music recorded digitally on a small plastic disk. The compact disk (or CD) player, introduced by Sony in 1982, eliminated much of the noise common to conventional, analog phonograph records. Sony developed the CD in association with the Dutch electronics firm Philips, partly in an effort to ensure broad format standardization. Philips, which had developed the most advanced laser technology, was an ideal partner for Sony, which led in the pulse-code technology that made digital sound reproduction possible. Soon the CD format was adopted by competing manufacturers; by the mid-1990s it had virtually replaced phonograph systems as the recording medium of choice.

Early in the 1980s, Morita began ceding some of his duties to Sony's president, Norio Ohga, the young opera student hired 30 years earlier to improve Sony's tape recorders. Under Ohga, Sony entered into a new acquisitions phase with the intent of protecting itself from the costly mistake it had made with Betamax. One example of the changes Ohga brought about was Sony's video camera, introduced in 1985. Lighter, less expensive, and more portable than VHS cameras, the camera used 8mm videotape, and was incompatible with both Betamax and VHS machines. The key difference between this and earlier Sony products was that Sony developed the new 8mm video format in conjunction with over 100 competitors. While the camera may have been incompatible with the older Betamax and VHS technologies, Sony ensured that it would be compatible with the next generation of video cameras. Within three years of its introduction, the camera captured over 50 percent of the European, 30 percent of the Japanese, and 20 percent of the North American markets.

In May 1984 Sony purchased Apple Computer's hard-disk-technology operations. As a result of this acquisition, Sony was able to control about 20 percent of the Japanese market for workstations, personal computers used in business offices, thus helping to increase the proportion of its sales derived from institutional customers. Ohga also broke a decades-old tradition in 1984 when he established a division to manufacture and market electronics components for other companies. By 1988, fueled by strong sales of semiconductors (once manufactured only for Sony products), the components division had grown to represent about 11 percent of Sony's total sales.

Sony also sought to gain control of the software end of the electronics/entertainment industry. On November 29, 1985 the Sony Corporation of America, which operated several assembly plants in the United States, purchased the Digital Audio Disk Corporation from its affiliate CBS/Sony. Two years later, Sony purchased CBS Records for $2 billion. CBS Records, whose labels included Epic and Columbia, was during this time the largest producer of records and tapes in the world.

Sony had learned through its Betamax experience that a superior product alone would not ensure market dominance; had Sony been able to flood the market with exclusively Beta-formatted movies, the VCR battle might have turned out differently. Looking toward the future development of audio equipment, including digital audio tape (DAT), Sony bought the record manufacturer with an eye toward guaranteeing that the products it manufactured to play music would remain compatible with the medium used to record music. The acquisition marked less of a diversification for Sony than an evolution toward dominance in a specific market.

Sony sought further diversification in U.S. entertainment companies. In 1988, the company considered an acquisition of MGM/UA Communications Company, but decided the price was too high. Then in 1989 Sony made headlines around the world when it bought Columbia Pictures Entertainment, Inc. from Coca-Cola for $3.4 billion. Columbia provided Sony with an extensive film library and a strong U.S. distribution system. It also carried $1 billion in debt, which almost tripled Sony's short-term debt to around ¥8 billion. Industry analysts applauded the move; when a recession hit the film industry shortly after Sony's purchase, however, some began to question Sony's ability to deliver its traditionally strong profits.

1990s and Beyond: PlayStation, VAIO, and the Networked Future

Sony did deliver, however, posting record earnings in 1990 of ¥58.2 billion ($384 million), a 38.5 percent increase over 1989. In 1992, Columbia Pictures and its subsidiary TriStar jointly captured 20 percent of the U.S. market share, far above the shares held by competing studios. By this time the entertainment operation had been renamed Sony Pictures Entertainment, Inc.

The complexities of operating a truly multinational corporation, however, began taking their toll on Sony. Most of the world's largest economies (Europe, Japan, and the United States) were experiencing a slowdown in the early 1990s. This factor created what Sony called "an unprecedentedly challenging operating environment." Although sales in most of Sony's businesses increased in 1992, operating income dropped 44 percent to ¥166 billion ($1.2 billion). Net income increased slightly to ¥120 billion.

The ongoing appreciation of the yen against most major currencies had an even more adverse effect on Sony's bottom line in 1993: net income fell a dramatic 70 percent to ¥36 billion ($313 million) on sales of ¥3.99 trillion ($34.4 billion). Had the yen's value held steady at 1992 figures, Sony's net income would have totaled about ¥190 billion ($1.3 billion).

During that year, Ohga assumed the duties of chief executive in addition to his role as president. He and Morita responded to Sony's tough economic situation by bolstering marketing, reducing inventory levels, streamlining operations, and keeping a watchful control of capital investments. The company also embarked on an extensive reorganization effort with the goal of decentralizing operations and reducing unnecessary management. Despite these measures, Sony was unable to stem the slide. Net income plummeted another 50 percent in 1994 to ¥15 billion, on sales of ¥3.73 trillion.

By this time Morita had relinquished virtually all his duties in the company, having suffered a stroke in late 1993. In Sony's 1994 annual report, his picture and signature were conspicuously absent from the letter to shareholders, implicitly announcing Ohga's new leadership position. Under Morita's leadership, Sony's rise to preeminence in the world consumer electronics market was almost entirely self-achieved; Sony outperformed not only its Japanese rivals, among them associates of the former *zaibatsu* (conglomerate) companies, but also larger American firms, which by 1995 had all but abandoned the consumer electronics market.

In the late 1980s Morita told *Business Week* that he regarded Sony Corporation as a "venture business" for the Morita family, which had produced several generations of mayors and whose primary business remained the 300-year-old Morita & Company. Under the direction of Akio Morita's younger brother Kuzuaki, Morita & Company produced sake, soy sauce, and Ninohimatsu brand rice wine in Nagoya. The company, whose initial $500 investment in TTK was worth $430 million in 1995, owned a 9.4 percent share of Sony.

In April 1995, Ohga ascended to the chairmanship of Sony, and Morita was made an honorary chairman. The company's new president was Nobuyuki Idei, a 34-year veteran of the company, who had founded Sony's French subsidiary in 1970 and had since played a role in many of the company's major accomplishments, including audio CD technology, computer workstations, and the 8mm video camcorder.

Sony's success had been a direct result of the wisdom of its founders, who had the talent to anticipate the demands of consumers and to develop products to meet those demands; Idei's presidency, some suggested, signaled a new era for the company.

Immediate among Idei's concerns were helping Sony become an integral player in the information highway industry. He also hoped to help the company establish an industry standard for DVDs, or digital videodisks, CD-like disks capable of holding full-length films for play on television screens via players. Once again, Sony had teamed up with Philips to develop a DVD format, but the partners quickly discovered they were facing a rival format developed by Toshiba and Time Warner. This rival format quickly gained the support of a number of the world's consumer electronics powerhouses. Rather than face a replay of the bloody battle between the Betamax and VHS formats, Sony and Philips in late 1995 agreed to support the DVD format developed by Toshiba and Time Warner. Sony subsequently introduced its first DVD player in March 1997.

Meanwhile, Sony unexpectedly entered the video game market in the mid-1990s, making an immediate splash. The development of the Sony PlayStation had actually begun in the late 1980s as a joint project with game giant Nintendo Co., Ltd. Nintendo had agreed to help develop a new game console that would combine the graphic capabilities of a computer workstation with Sony's CD-ROM drive, but then pulled out of the project in 1992. Sony decided to develop the new machine solo, introducing the 32-bit PlayStation to the Japanese market in 1994 and the U.S. market one year later. It was an immediate and huge success, in part because of the hundreds of software titles that were quickly available for the console thanks to Sony's ability to entice top Japanese and U.S. developers to create games for the PlayStation. By 1998, the PlayStation had grabbed about 40 percent of the worldwide game market, and Sony's game unit, Sony Computer Entertainment, accounted for 10 percent of the company's worldwide revenue and a whopping 22.5 percent of its operating income.

Unfortunately, the mid-1990s were also marked by continued problems at Sony Pictures Entertainment. Top management at the motion picture arm spent hundreds of millions of dollars on a string of flops, such as *Last Action Hero* and *Geronimo,* in addition to spending lavishly on hiring, studio renovations, and other expenses. Sony ended up taking a $3.2 billion write-off—one of the largest ever by a Japanese company—related to the entertainment unit during the fiscal year ending in March 1995; consequently, the company posted a net loss for the year of $2.8 billion (on sales of $44.76 billion). A major management shakeup occurred as well.

As Sony attempted to turn around its motion picture unit, in electronics the company surprised many observers by entering the crowded and low-margin personal computer business in 1997. That year, through a partnership with Intel, Sony began selling its VAIO line of PCs. Including both desktop and notebook models, the line received plaudits for its quality but got off to a slow start in the United States thanks to its above-average price tags. Sony designed the VAIO computers specifically for the home market, and they sported unique features that made them particularly well-suited to consumers who owned other Sony products. For example, software and ports were included to allow owners of Sony camcorders to transfer their home videos to the VAIO PC and to edit and manipulate the videos in a variety of ways. Sony also continued to stay on the cutting edge in the venerable television field, introducing its first flat-screen TV in 1996 and its first digital, high-definition model two years later. Also in 1998 came the launch of AIBO, a robot dog, which was touted as having the capability of expressing emotions and learning.

During 1999, a year that saw the passing of company co-founder Morita (the other founder, Ibuka, died in 1997), Idei launched a sweeping reorganization to position the company for the future—in Sony's vision, "the network era of the 21st century." In March 1999 Sony announced that it planned to cut its workforce by 10 percent and its manufacturing capacity by one-third before 2003. The cutbacks were slated for areas where growth had been slowing: analog televisions, VCRs, and Walkmans. The company planned to increase the amount of resources committed to such hot areas as digital products and the PlayStation, as well as placing increased emphasis on developing software, hardware, and services for the new networks that were beginning to emerge at the end of the 20th century—home networks, broadband networks, wireless networks. For Idei, the key for Sony was a historic shift in focus: hardware had traditionally driven product development, but Idei instead wanted software development and services to drive hardware design.

Perhaps the first example of such an approach came with the 2000 introduction of the Sony PlayStation 2. Although it was a technical marvel featuring high-end 3-D graphics and more processing power than most desktop PCs, the 128-bit PlayStation 2 was much more than a souped-up version of the original. It was of course designed for game software but it was not just a game console, having been conceived as a home entertainment center. Its DVD drive not only played game software but also audio CDs and DVD movies. It had the capability of connecting to the Internet and as such could be used as a broadband device controlling an Internet-connected home network. Despite manufacturing difficulties that limited production during the first year, the PlayStation 2 had a stellar debut, with about nine million units sold in the first 12 months. The high costs associated with developing and manufacturing the machines, however, depressed profits at Sony for the 2001 fiscal year. Also in the wake of its debut came rival Sega's exit from the game console business in favor of concentrating on developing game titles for other companies' machines, including the PlayStation 2. Sony continued to face competition in the game field from Nintendo, which planned to release a new machine in the fall of 2001, and faced the prospect of a new competitor, Microsoft Corporation, which was also planning a fall 2001 release of its XBox machine.

In June 2000 Idei was named chairman and CEO of Sony, while Kunitake Ando, who had headed the VAIO unit, was named president and COO. Rounding out the new management team was Teruhisa Tokunaka, a former head of the PlayStation unit, who was named deputy president and CFO. The new team faced a myriad of challenges in the rapidly changing high-tech world of the early 21st century. One example was in Sony's music business, which was being rocked by the industry-wide threat of the rampant and unauthorized downloading of digital music files over the Internet. Sony joined other music giants in suing Napster, the most obvious threat to their hegemony. The company also entered into a joint venture with Vivendi Universal S.A. to develop an online subscription service that would allow music downloads through what was called a "virtual jukebox.'' Such a service was part of a new push by Sony into broadband delivery of the audio and video material owned by its content arms. With its aggressive moves in the areas of games, networking, and delivery of digital content, Sony was almost certain to remain a frontrunner in the ever broadening field of consumer electronics and related platforms and services.

Principal Subsidiaries

Aiwa Co. Ltd. (50.6%); Intervision Inc.; Sony Ichinomiya Corporation; Sony Inazawa Corporation; Sony Oita Corporation; Sony Enterprise Co., Ltd.; Sony Kisarazu Corporation; Sony Kita Kanto Corporation; Kibo Industry Corporation; Sony Chemicals Corporation; Sony Kohda Corporation; Sony Kokubu Corporation; Sony Communication Network Corporation; Sony Computer Entertainment Inc.; Sony Components Chiba Corporation; Sony Siroisi Semiconductor Inc.; Sony Life Insurance Co., Ltd.; Sony Senmaya Corporation; Sony Assurance Inc.; Sony/Taiyo Corporation; Sony Digital Products Inc.; Sony Denshi Corporation; Sony Tochigi Corporation; Sony Trading International Corp.; Sony Nagasaki Corporation; Sony Nakaniida Corporation; Sony Neagari Corporation; Sony Hamamatsu Corporation; Sony Pictures Entertainment (Japan) Inc.; Sony Pictures Television Japan Inc.; Sony PCL Inc.; Sony Finance International, Inc.; Sony Plaza Co., Ltd.; Sony Precision Technology Inc.; Sony Broadcast Products Corporation; Sony Broadcast Media Co., Ltd.; Sony Bronson Corporation; Sony Marketing Co., Ltd.; Sony Max Corporation; Sony Mizunami Corporation; Sony Minokamo Corporation; Sony Miyagi Corporation; Sony Music Entertainment (Japan) Inc.; Sony Logistics Corporation; Sony of Canada Ltd.; Sony Computer Entertainment America Inc. (U.S.A.); Sony Corporation of America (U.S.A.); Sony Electronics Inc. (U.S.A.); Sony Latin America Inc. (U.S.A.); Sony Magnetic Products Inc. of America (U.S.A.); Sony Music Entertainment Inc. (U.S.A.); Sony Pictures Entertainment Inc. (U.S.A.); Sony Argentina S.A.; Sony Comercio e Industria Ltda. (Brazil); Sony Componentes Ltda. (Brazil); Sony da Amazonia Ltda. (Brazil); Sony Chile Ltda.; Sony de Mexico S.A. de C.V.; Sony Corporation of Panama, S.A.; Sony Puerto Rico, Inc.; Sony de Venezuela S.A.; Sony Austria GmbH; Sony DADC Austria A.G.; Sony Service Centre (Europe) N.V. (Belgium); Sony Czech, spol. s.r.o.; Sony Nordic A/S (Denmark); Sony France S.A.; Sony Berlin G.m.b.H. (Germany); Sony Deutschland G.m.b.H. (Germany); Sony Europe GmbH (Germany); Sony International (Europe) G.m.b.H. (Germany); Sony Hungaria kft (Hungary); Sony Italia S.p.A. (Italy); Sony Logistics Europe B.V. (Netherlands); Sony Poland Sp.z.o.o.; Sony Portugal Ltda.; Sony C.I.S. A/O (Russia); Sony Slovakia Spol. Sr. O.; Sony España, S.A. (Spain); Sony Overseas S.A. (Switzerland); Sony Eurasia Pazarlama A.S. (Turkey); Sony United Kingdom Limited; Sony Computer Entertainment Europe Limited (U.K.); Sony Entertainment Holdings Europe Ltd. (U.K.); Sony (China) Limited (Beijing); Sony Corporation of Hong Kong Ltd.; Sony International (Hong Kong) Ltd.; Sony India Limited; P.T. Sony Indonesia; P.T. Sony Electronics Indonesia; Sony Electronics of Korea Corp.; Sony Electronics (Malaysia) Sdn. Bhd.; Sony Technology (Malaysia) Sdn. Bhd.; Sony Philippines, Inc.; Sony Electronics (Singapore) Pte. Ltd.; Sony Industries Taiwan Co., Ltd.; Sony Video Taiwan Co., Ltd.; Sony Magnetic Products (Thailand) Co., Ltd.; Sony Mobile Electronics (Thailand) Co., Ltd.; Sony Semiconductor (Thailand) Co., Ltd.; Sony Siam Industries Co., Ltd. (Thailand); Sony Thai Co. Ltd. (Thailand); Sony Vietnam Limited; Sony Australia Ltd.; Sony New Zealand Ltd.; Sony Gulf FZE (United Arab Emirates); Sony South Africa (Pty.) Ltd.

Principal Competitors

Nintendo Co., Ltd.; Matsushita Electric Corporation; Motorola, Inc.; Hitachi, Ltd.; Koninklijke Philips Electronics N.V.; Toshiba Corporation; Yamaha Corporation; Victor Company of Japan, Limited; Sharp Corporation; Bose Corporation; Samsung Group; Pioneer Corporation; SANYO Electric Co., Ltd.; Canon Inc.; AOL Time Warner Inc.; BASF Aktiengesellschaft; Bertelsmann AG; Compaq Computer Corporation; Daewoo Group; Dell Computer Corporation; EMI Group plc; Fuji Photo Film Co., Ltd.; Fujitsu Limited; Harman International Industries, Incorporated; International Business Machines Corporation; Intel Corporation; LG Electronics Inc.; Microsoft Corporation; NEC Corporation; Nokia Corporation; Oki Electric Industry Company Limited; Viacom Inc.; Virgin Group Ltd.; Vivendi Universal S.A.; The Walt Disney Company.

Further Reading

Armstrong, Larry, Christopher Power, and G. David Wallace, "Sony's Challenge," *Business Week,* June 1, 1987, pp. 64+.

Browning, E.S., "Japan's Sony, Famous for Consumer Electronics, Decides That the Future Lies in Sales to Business," *Wall Street Journal,* October 9, 1984.

Brull, Steven V., Neil Gross, and Robert D. Hof, "Sony's New World," *Business Week,* May 27, 1996, pp. 100+.

Carvell, Tim, "How Sony Created a Monster," *Fortune,* June 8, 1998, pp. 162+.

Cieply, Michael, "Sony's Profitless Prosperity," *Forbes,* October 24, 1983, pp. 128+.

Fulford, Benjamin, "Godzilla Needs Batteries: Sony, Japan's Most Famous Company, Is in a Slump," *Forbes,* September 18, 2000, p. 66.

Gross, Neil, and William J. Holstein, "Why Sony Is Plugging into Columbia," *Business Week,* October 16, 1989, pp. 56+.

Kunii, Irene M., and Ron Grover, "Sony Slides into a Slump," *Business Week,* June 5, 2000, p. 68.

Kunii, Irene M., Emily Thornton, and Janet Rae-Dupree, "Sony's Shakeup," *Business Week,* March 22, 1999, pp. 52–53.

Kunii, Irene M., et al., "The Games Sony Plays," *Business Week,* June 15, 1998, pp. 128–30.

Landro, Luar, Yumiko Ono, and Elizabeth Rubinfein, "A Changing Sony Aims to Own the 'Software' That Its Products Need," *Wall Street Journal,* December 30, 1988, p. 1.

Lubove, Seth, and Neil Weinberg, "Creating a Seamless Company," *Forbes,* December 20, 1993, p. 152.

Lyons, Nick, *The Sony Vision,* New York: Crown, 1976.

"Media Colossus: Sony Is Out to Be the World's One-Stop Shop for Entertainment," *Business Week,* March 25, 1991, p. 64.

Morita, Akio, *From a 500-Dollar Company to a Global Corporation: The Growth of Sony,* Pittsburgh: Carnegie-Mellon University Press, 1985, 41 p.

——, *Made in Japan: Akio Morita and Sony,* New York: Dutton, 1986, 309 p.

——, "When Sony Was an Up-and-Comer," *Forbes,* October 6, 1986, pp. 98+.

Morris, Kathleen, "Lonesome Samurai: Under Major Pressure on a Number of Fronts, Sony Goes It Alone As Usual," *Financial World,* May 23, 1995, pp. 26–29.

Nathan, John, *Sony: The Private Life,* Boston: Houghton Mifflin, 1999, 347 p.

Palmer, Jay, "Back in the Game," *Barron's,* April 15, 1996, pp. 31–35.

Schlender, Brent, "Sony on the Brink," *Fortune,* June 12, 1995, pp. 60+.

——, "Sony Plays to Win," *Fortune,* May 1, 2000, pp. 143–46+.

——, "Sony's New President: Here's the Plan," *Fortune,* April 17, 1995, pp. 18–19.

Siklos, Richard, Ronald Grover, and Irene M. Kunii, "Does Sony Really Need a Partner?," *Business Week,* October 11, 1999, pp. 118–19.

Smith, Lee, "Sony Battles Back," *Fortune,* April 15, 1985, pp. 26+.

"Sony: A Diversification Plan Tuned to the People Factor," *Business Week,* February 9, 1981, p. 88.

—Maura Troester
—update: David E. Salamie

Southern Peru Copper Corporation

Avenida Caminos del Inca 171
Chacarilla del Estanque
Santiago de Surco
Lima 33
Peru
Telephone: (511) 372-1414
Fax: (511) 372-0262

Public Company (54% Owned by Grupo Mexico, S.A. de C.V.)
Incorporated: 1952
Employees: 3,682
Sales: $711.09 million (2000)
Stock Exchanges: New York Lima
Ticker Symbols: PCU; PCUC1
NAIC: 212234 Copper Ore & Nickel Ore Mining;
　331411 Primary Smelting & Refining of Copper Ore;
　551112 Offices of Other Holding Companies

Southern Peru Copper Corporation, a holding company, is Peru's largest privately owned concern. It operates the Toquepala and Cuajone mines, some 10,500 to 10,900 feet above sea level in the Andes Mountains, about 610 miles southeast of Lima, Peru. It also operates a smelter and refinery in the Pacific coastal city of Ilo, Peru. Copper is the main mineral produced, but the mines also yield small amounts of molybdenum and silver as byproducts.

Southern Peru Copper Before the 1980s

Originally discovered by a German in the 19th century, Toquepala was a copper deposit in the mountains of extreme southern Peru that attracted relatively little interest because its ore contained only about 1 percent of the metal. Nevertheless, in the late 1930s a Peruvian engineer named Juan Oviedo persuaded the American Smelting and Refining Co. (ASARCO) to take, through its Northern Peru Mining Co. subsidiary, an option on the property and an adjacent one named Quellaveco. In 1945 another U.S.-based mining company, Cerro de Pasco

Corp., purchased Cuajone, a similar property in the area. Cerro also challenged the ASARCO claim but lost in court. In 1955 both companies and two other American ones—Phelps Dodge Corp. and Newmont Mining Corp.—agreed to develop these properties through a new company, Southern Peru Copper Corporation, which had been incorporated in 1952. ASARCO took a 57.75 percent stake, Cerro and Phelps Dodge 16 percent each, and Newmont, 10.25 percent. (Cerro subsequently raised its stake to 22.25 percent, while ASARCO's share dropped to 51.5 percent.)

An article in the 1950 mining code was the basis for the 1954 contract to exploit the Toquepala deposit. It provided for a sharing of 30 percent of Southern Peru Copper's net income with the Peruvian government in place of other taxes. This represented a moderate reduction of the usual Peruvian corporate tax level for the length of time it took Southern Peru Copper to recoup its initial investment in the mine complex. The four companies financing Southern Peru Copper invested $108 million and received a $120 million loan from the Export-Import Bank, a U.S. government agency. The project eventually cost almost $250 million. The Toquepala mine, an open-pit operation, began production in late 1959. Southern Peru Copper also built a smelter in the coastal city of Ilo to producer blister (rough) copper from the ore. A railroad was constructed to link the mine to the smelter. The copper, about 140,000 metric tons a year, was then sent to ASARCO's Baltimore refinery and another in Belgium for final processing.

Contention developed over Southern Peru Copper's interpretation that depreciation and depletion allowances should not be considered profits for the purpose of computing when the company's recovery of its investment had been made. This was poorly received among a population inclined to be hostile to a foreign company engaged in exploiting an extractive, nonrenewable asset, and a congressional commission accused Southern Peru Copper of keeping double or even triple sets of books. The company countered with an advertising campaign pointing out to the public that Southern Peru Copper was the biggest income tax payer in Peru. Moreover, Southern Peru Copper was able to put pressure on the government because it wanted the company to develop the bigger Cuajone copper

---

Key Dates:

1955: Four U.S. companies take stakes in Southern Peru Copper Corporation.

1959: Operations begin at a mine and smelter at Toquepala.

1976: A second, larger mine complex at Cuajone begins operations.

1994: Southern Peru Copper purchases its Ilo copper refinery from the Peruvian government.

1995: Southern Peru Copper sets records for revenues and profits as world copper prices peak; the company makes an initial public offering on the New York Stock Exchange.

1999: Grupo Mexico, Southern Peru Copper's new majority owner, dismisses company managers.

---

deposit, only 12 air miles from Toquepala. In 1968 Southern Peru Copper dropped its interpretation of profit but in exchange received a further period of six years during which only taxes in effect at the time of the 1954 signing would be owed. This settlement was followed almost immediately by the announcement of a projected investment of $355 million in the Cuajone project by the four companies backing Southern Peru Copper, including a connection to the railway line, a system of roads, and an aqueduct.

A Peruvian military coup brought into power a nationalist regime that expropriated a subsidiary of Exxon Corporation in 1968 and also seized other U.S.-owned properties. The new government canceled Southern Peru Copper's Quellaveco concession. It also established a government monopoly to market Peruvian copper and announced plans to build an Ilo copper refinery, which was completed in 1976. As a result of the expropriations, the Cuajone project did not qualify for low-interest Export-Import Bank loans until the United States and Peru reached a settlement in 1974. The government and Southern Peru Copper continued to negotiate, however, and in 1969 settled on a tax rate of 47.5 percent during the recovery period and a maximum rate of 54.5 percent during the six-year postrecovery period. By the time the project got underway, the cost had swelled to $620 million, with financing including $55 million from the Export-Import Bank and $404 million from 54 worldwide lending institutions. Work was completed about late 1976. Cuajone became the largest copper mine in Peru, with annual capacity of ore to produce 170,000 tons a year of blister copper. The eventual cost of the project reached $727 million.

Good Years and Bad: 1980–95

Southern Peru Copper's sales reached $306.71 million in 1983 and $315.57 million in 1984. Its net earnings were slender, however, and the company lost money between 1985 and 1988 because of low world copper prices. The Peruvian government reduced Southern Peru Copper's tax rate to 45 percent in 1986 and 40 percent in 1990. By then the price of copper had risen and Southern Peru Copper was in the black again, earning $7.55 million in net income on $395.03 million of net sales, but the

company lost a small amount in 1991 before recovering in 1992 and 1993. The settlement in 1991 of a four-year-long dispute with the Peruvian government over profits taken out of the country by Southern Peru Copper allowed the company to move ahead with a $445 million expansion and renovation program. This included a secondary recovery operation at each mine using a leaching process to extract copper from rock wasted in traditional mining. Leaching was expected to raise Southern Peru Copper's copper production by 15 percent.

Southern Peru Copper used some of its revenue to invest in Peruvian companies. In the early 1990s, for example, it held 20 percent of Textil Piura S.A., 30 percent of the shares in the textile enterprises of a group directed by Juan Francisco Raffo, and 30 percent of the shares of Cables y Conductores de Cobre S.A., an enterprise producing all types of wire, cables, and electrical and telephonic conductors made of copper. The company's Peruvian critics said it was investing profits that it had first taken out of the country illegally.

Reporting from Peru in 1992, Nathaniel C. Nash of the *New York Times* wrote that Southern Peru Copper's 5,000 workers and their 20,000 dependents received free housing, education, electricity, water, medical care, and food at the mines and Ilo. The company also was subsidizing college education for the children of its workers. "A tour through both Cuajone and Toquepala," he continued, "found them to be more like modern rural United States towns, with manicured lawns, clean buildings and streets. The hospital in Cuajone is considered perhaps the most modern in Peru." Nevertheless, he noted, "Recent surveys have found that 75 percent of the residents do not like the presence of this American corporate giant, dubbed by some as the 'gringo octopus.' " Calvin Sims, another *Times* reporter, in 1995 interviewed Southern Peru Copper workers in Ilo, dozens of whom said that they and their families suffered respiratory problems in reaction to smoke from the smelter. (Southern Peru Copper also purchased the Ilo refinery in 1994, paying $65 million, and installed a sulfuric-acid plant at the smelter in 1995.) The company denied that there was a health problem but said it would spend $151 million on environmental projects in the area. A lawyer representing Ilo residents said Southern Peru Copper had destroyed a 12-mile stretch of coastline by annually dumping 30 million metric tons of untreated mining waste into the Pacific Ocean.

Sustained by high copper prices, Southern Peru Copper was booming in this period. Net sales came to $661 million, of which northern Europe accounted for 34 percent; Asia, 30 percent; Italy, 17 percent; Latin America, 15 percent; and North America, 4 percent. Net income came to $99 million. Copper prices peaked in 1995, and Southern Peru Copper set records for revenue ($928.84 million) and income ($217.75 million). ASARCO's minority partners offered 13 million shares (17.3 percent of the total outstanding) that year on the New York Stock Exchange. Shortly thereafter, ASARCO purchased the Newmont stake in Southern Peru Copper for $116.4 million. In 1995 the company began work on a solvent extraction/electro-winning (SX/EW) facility at Toquepala. Southern Peru Copper was reorganized into a holding company structure, effective at the beginning of 1996. Although now nominally a U.S. corporation, Southern Peru Copper continued to maintain its executive headquarters in Lima.

Further Developments in the Late 1990s

In 1997 Southern Peru Copper secured $800 million in financing for a $1.24 billion, five-year expansion of the Cuajone mine and modernization of the Ilo smelter. Seventeen banks joined in the loan, which represented the largest capital-markets issue ever for Peru and also had the longest final maturity (ten years) and average life (seven years) of any capital-markets issue from Peru. The first phase, a $245 million expansion of the Cuajone open pit and concentrator plant, was completed in 1999, boosting the company's copper output by 19 percent. The upgrading of the smelter would include a new, larger capture-acid plant that would catch 95 percent of all emissions from the smelter's high chimneys and convert them to sulfuric acid, some of it used in the company's own leaching operations. Southern Peru Copper confirmed in 1999 that a two-year drilling program at Toquepala had increased the mine's reserves by more than 160 percent. Although the area would have to be stripped to reach the new reserves, beneath the mine, they would be suitable for leaching. The company also completed expansion of the Toquepala SX/EW facility in 1999 and was exploring many other areas of Peru, including a gold-copper project in the north being conducted as a joint venture.

ASARCO's stake in Southern Peru Copper, now 54.2 percent, passed to Grupo Mexico, S.A. de C.V., when the Mexican mining giant purchased ASARCO in 1999 for $2.2 billion. (The other stockholders at the end of the year were Cerro Trading Co. Inc., a subsidiary of Marmon Group, 14.2 percent; Phelps Dodge Overseas Capital Corp., 14 percent; and public shareholders, 17.6 percent.) The company's top managers, consisting of U.S. executives, were promptly dismissed by German Larrea Mota-Velasco, Grupo Mexico's chairman and chief executive officer, who also assumed these Southern Peru Copper posts himself. "Larrea seemed to be offended by the high level of compensation the ex-pats had, and the fact that they're paid in U.S. dollars," one executive told Robert C. Yafie of *American Metal Market*. Larrea said that Southern Peru Copper would continue with the Toquepala expansion, a planned Cuajone SX/EW facility, and Ilo smelter modernization, but he qualified plans for the latter, the centerpiece of the program. In a statement released to the press, Larrea said that his company was "reviewing time required to execute the investment commitment in the Ilo smelter, taking into consideration what is best economically and financially for Southern Peru Copper as well as the appropriate investment return."

Southern Peru Copper produced 745.61 million pounds of copper in 1999, of which Cuajone accounted for almost 380 million, Toquepala for 256.39 million, and the Toquepala SX/EW facility for 109.23 million. All of these totals appeared to be records. Smelter production came to 638.14 million pounds. The Ilo refinery turned out 552.74 million pounds, for a total refinery output of 661.96 million pounds when adding the SX/EW production. Molybdenum production was (in concentrates) 12.06 million pounds, of which Toquepala accounted for nearly seven million and Cuajone for 5.07 million. Blister silver production came to 3.38 million ounces and refined silver to nearly 2.8 million ounces. Net sales for the year totaled only $584.55 million, a figure below 1997 and 1998 and indicative of a 12-year low for world copper prices. Net earnings were $29.41 million, also down from the figures of the previous two years. Long-term debt was $199.25 million at the end of the year.

Southern Peru Copper's production and income were higher in 2000. Copper production came to 751.04 million pounds, of which Cuajone accounted for 394.55 million, Toquepala 232.89 million, and the Toquepala SX/EW plant, 123.6 million. The Ilo refinery turned out 583.66 million pounds, and the total refined production was 707.2 million pounds. Molybdenum production was (in concentrates) 15.88 million pounds, of which Toquepala accounted for 8.24 million and Cuajone for 7.64 million. Refined silver production came to 3.34 million ounces. Net sales reached $711.06 million, in large part because of higher copper prices and higher sales volume. Net earnings were $92.9 million. The company's long-term debt at the end of 2000 was $322.91 million.

Principal Subsidiaries

Logistics Services Inc.; Los Tolmos S.A. (Peru); Multimines Insurance Company, Ltd. (Bermuda).

Principal Competitors

Corporacion Nacional del Cobre de Chile; Phelps Dodge Corporation.

Further Reading

Bowen, Sally, "Peruvian Copper Group Caught in State of Flux," *Financial Times,* October 15, 1999, p. 36.

Crespo, Mariana, "Southern Peru Copper: Buy on the Restructuring," *Financial World,* June 20, 1995, p. 16.

Goodsell, Charles T., *American Corporations and Peruvian Politics,* Cambridge: Harvard University Press, 1974.

"Huge Peru Copper Mine Slated to Open Late '76," *Journal of Commerce,* March 3, 1975, p. 14A.

Macdonald, John, "The Big New Kicker at Asarco," *Fortune,* January 1963, pp. 81–82.

——, "Why Peru Pulls Dollars," *Fortune,* November 1956, pp. 178, 183.

Malpica Silva Santisteban, Carlos, *El poder economico en el Peru,* Lima: PERU*graph* Editores, 1992, Vol. 3, pp. 1307–08, 1310–12.

Nash, Nathaniel C., "Coup in Peru a Blow to Its Copper," *New York Times,* April 28, 1992, pp. D1, D22.

Sims, Calvin, "In Peru, a Fight for Fresh Air," *New York Times,* December 12, 1995, pp. D1, D4.

Vandell, Jonathan, "Delay in Peruvian Copper Project Underlines Pragmatic Limits of Revolution," *New York Times,* November 28, 1974, pp. 53, 55.

Watkins, Mary, "Introducing Peru," *Project Finance,* February 1998, p. 38.

Yafie, Roberta C., "Grupo Mexico Cuts Cloud SPCC's Return," *American Metal Market,* December 14, 1999, p. 1.

——, "SPCC Execs Appointed: Grupo Mex Sets Tactics," *American Metal Market,* December 21, 1999, p. 2.

—Robert Halasz

Standard Motor Products, Inc.

37-18 Northern Boulevard
Long Island City, New York 11101
U.S.A.
Telephone: (718) 392-0200
Toll Free: (800) 846-7455
Fax: (718) 472-0122
Web site: http://www.smpcorp.com

Public Company
Incorporated: 1926
Employees: 3,400
Sales: $606.45 million (2000)
Stock Exchanges: New York
Ticker Symbol: SMP
NAIC: 336312 Gasoline Engine and Engine Parts
    Manufacturing; 336322 Other Motor Vehicle
    Electrical and Electronic Parts Manufacturing; 336391
    Motor Vehicle Air Conditioning Manufacturing;
    44131 Automotive Parts and Accessories

Standard Motor Products, Inc. is the epitome of stability. Founded in 1919, the company grew up with the automobile age, as a manufacturer and distributor of an ever widening inventory of automotive replacement parts, which it sells primarily to big warehouse distributors and leading auto-parts retail chains. Solidly and consistently profitable, the family-controlled company makes no waves and very little news. Sales have increased in almost every year (but fell in 2000). Standard Motor Products was directed by the same two men for over 40 years.

Standard Motor Products to 1972

Standard Motor Products was founded in 1919 by Elias Fife and Ralph Van Allen. The partnership opened its doors in New York City's borough of Manhattan with ten employees, selling automotive replacement parts to repair shops. Piston rings, ignition parts, and starter and generator brushes were the company's first products, followed soon after by battery cables and clamps. From the beginning, ignition switch keys were its most popular product. Standard Motor Products moved its headquarters in 1921 to Long Island City, an industrial neighborhood in New York's borough of Queens. Van Allen moved to Seattle in 1920 to open a Standard Motor Products branch, and the partnership was dissolved in 1925, with Fife as sole proprietor until the following year, when the firm was incorporated. Van Allen operated a separate company in Los Angeles under the same name and logo until 1936, when he sold it to Fife.

Standard Motor Products introduced its Blue Streak line of premium-quality ignition products in the 1930s. After acquiring Hygrade Products Co. in 1947, it expanded its product line to include carburetor repair parts, fuel pumps, shock-absorber parts, and speedometer cables, and in 1950 it introduced the "Hygrade System" of simplified carburetor kits for tune-ups and light overhauls. In 1959 Fife retired from active management. His son Bernard became president and treasurer, and his son-in-law Nathaniel Sills became vice-president and secretary.

Standard Motor Products made its initial public offering in 1960. The company had warehouses in Chicago, Los Angeles, Montreal, Seattle, and Toronto. Net sales came to $12.93 million that year (about double the 1955 figure) and net income to $769,978. The sale of Class A stock at $15 a share raised nearly $4.5 million. Members of the Sills and Fife families retained 21 percent of this class of stock and all of the Class B, which assured them a voting majority.

Standard Motor Products was, at this time, selling all of its output to the replacement market, through automotive-parts distributors, for use by repair shops, service stations, and related customers. Parts were being manufactured for all domestic models and about 90 percent of imported ones. This output consisted of ignition systems (75 percent); carburetor parts (15 percent); and cables and wires (10 percent), with the majority of items priced under $3. The ignition parts were being sold under the Standard and premium Blue Streak names, carburetor parts under the Hygrade trademark, and cables and wire under the Ektron name. One product in the Hygrade line developed by the company, the "Jiffy Kit," offered repair personnel all the basic items needed to tune up a carburetor. A Canadian subsidiary was responsible for distribution in that country and also performed some manufacturing and assembling of ignition contact sets.

Key Dates:

1919: Standard Motor Products is founded as a partnership in Manhattan.
1926: Partnership is dissolved
1926: Cofounder Elias Fife incorporates the business.
1946–47: Bernard Fife and Nathaniel Sills assume management of the company.
1960: Standard Motor Products offers stock to the public for the first time.
1963: The company begins distributing as well as manufacturing automotive parts.
1978: Standard Motor Products begins manufacturing air-conditioning parts.
1996: The company enters the European auto-parts replacement market.

In 1963 Standard Motor Products established the Marathon Parts division as a wholesale distributor of automotive parts. Management entered this line out of concern that innovations might replace the conventional components of the internal combustion engine that it was manufacturing. By 1970 there were 32 outlets in Connecticut, New York, Ohio, and Pennsylvania. Marathon wholesalers carried parts made by all automotive manufacturers, and less than 5 percent of its sales came from products made by Standard Motor Products. Marathon was contributing about half of Standard's sales and 30 percent of its net income at the end of the 1960s.

Standard Motor Products' sales grew rapidly but profits remained flat until 1967, when net earnings passed the $1 million market for good, reflecting greater manufacturing efficiency and streamlining of the warehouse facilities. Net sales came to $55.05 million and net earnings to $2.95 million in 1971. By then Standard Motor Products had added a subsidiary in Rio Grande, Puerto Rico. The parent company's full-time sales force of more than 130 was one of the largest in the industry. In 1972 the company acquired Universal Automobile Parts Distributors, Inc. of Miami, adding its warehouse to the Marathon Parts division. Also that year, the company purchased Champ Items, Inc., a St. Louis-based manufacturer of a broad line of functional replacements and general-service parts to the wholesale market. This company became a separate division, selling its products under the "Champ" name.

Continuing to Grow in the 1970s and 1980s

Standard Motor Products' sales and earnings grew consistently through the 1970s. Manufacturing was accounting for about 70 percent of sales, and distribution for about 30 percent in 1978. In 1978–79 the company purchased two manufacturers of replacement automotive air-conditioning parts and began selling them under the Four Seasons name. Net sales came to $125.88 million in 1980 and net earnings to $3.29 million (compared to a record $6.15 million in 1978). During this year ignition parts accounted for 56 percent of sales, battery cables and wires for 16 percent, and carburetor parts for 11 percent. In 1981 the manufacture of air-conditioning parts was consolidated in a plant in Grapevine, Texas, and in 1983 this operation became profitable

for the first time on nearly $20 million in revenues. The Champ division moved to Edwardsville, Kansas, in 1981.

Standard Motor Products' net earnings reached $21.07 million in 1983, a mark not exceeded for more than a decade. This prosperity was not reflected in its Long Island City quarters, where the elevator to the executive offices also moved freight, and the top-floor reception room faced one side of the factory, but the company had doubled its market share in its main manufactured-product categories, to 25 percent, since 1977. "Many competitors have become parts of conglomerates and lost their entrepreneurial drive," Fife told a *Business Week* reporter in 1984. "By staying independent, we have gained share from them." During the 1980–82 recession Standard Motor Products kept fully stocked, built a new distribution center, and expanded its sales force to 350. Because many of the 2,000 warehouse distributors to whom the company sold products lacked their own sales forces, Standard Motor Products promoted its wares directly to the auto-supply centers and service stations that were their customers.

In 1986 Standard Motor Products purchased the EIS brake parts division of Parker-Hannifin Corp. and an electronic-ignition assembly plant in Hong Kong from Fairchild Semiconductor Corporation. With carburetors seemingly on the way out, it introduced a line of fuel-injection parts the following year. By this time Standard Motor Products had added plants in Manila, Arkansas; Gardenia, California; Berlin and Middleton, Connecticut; Rural Retreat, Virginia; and West Bend, Wisconsin, plus the Hong Kong facility.

Sills's son Lawrence became president of the company in 1986, but his father and Fife, now described as co-chairmen and chief executive officers, continued in charge. In 1989 *Wall Street Transcript* gave the two its bronze award in the auto parts/replacement industry category for their restructuring program and aggressive marketing effort. The publication quoted an investment advisor, who said, "Frankly, its been a very difficult time for the industry. . . . A manufacturer has to adapt to the changes in the distribution end, because this is not a consumer market. This is a market that is difficult to influence. So I think Standard Motor Products deserves recognition for its aggressive posture in trying to shift operations in low-cost areas, in terms of making acquisitions into a very different product line, in trying to grow its businesses by taking the short-term lumps."

Standard Motor Products introduced a second line of wire and cable products in 1989. This line was steadily expanded to include import coverage and was reintroduced in 1995 under the Tru-Tech brand name. In 1992 the company became the first aftermarket supplier, other than original-equipment manufacturers, to produce mass air flow (MAF) sensors, through a Canadian joint venture.

Further Expansion: 1990–2000

Standard Motor Products' sales passed the half-billion mark in 1990, with about a quarter of its merchandise being sold to retail outlets in the do-it-yourself marketplace. Ignition parts accounted for 33.5 percent; brake parts, 23 percent; temperature control systems, 16.5 percent; wire and cables, 11.2 percent; fuel-system parts, 10.3 percent; and the Champ service line, 5.5

percent. Sales and earnings were stagnant during the ensuing recession, but the company cut its marketing costs, eliminated departments such as maintenance and engineering, and turned over quality control from independent inspectors to its own production workers. After a survey of its Long Island City workers revealed that they thought too much inventory was on hand, the company began establishing "manufacturing cells" in which all of the machines producing a part were grouped together so that unfinished work was not spread around the plant. After the economy improved and sales surged, net earnings reached a new record of $23.67 million in 1994.

Standard Motor Products did not rest on its laurels but continued to expand its manufacturing capacity. In 1995, for example, it acquired two companies—Automotive Dryers, Inc. and Air Parts, Inc.—making and distributing climate control system parts in Cumming, Georgia. Standard Motor Products was now the largest automotive aftermarket producer of air-conditioning replacement parts; climate control systems accounted for 20 percent of its sales.

Also in 1995, Standard Motor Products added an electronic-ignition operation in Herzliya, Israel, and a brake systems plant in Mississauga, Ontario. In addition, it formed part of a joint venture producing brake systems in Ontario, California; added Pik-A-Nut Corp. of Huntington, Indiana, to the Service Line division; and, through its Hong Kong subsidiary, entered into a joint venture in China to produce ignition modules for use in Chinese original-equipment applications. In 1996 the company acquired a firm assembling and distributing ignition wire sets and battery cables in Dallas; purchased a manufacturer of fan clutches and oil coolers; and opened an electric-motor manufacturing and assembly facility in Canada. Standard Motor Products closed its Manila plant in 1995 and no longer retained the one in Gardenia.

Standard Motor Products sold its Service Line division, including the Champ and Pik-A-Nut operations, to P&B Inc., in 1998–99. The company got out of the brake replacement business in 1998, exchanging it for the temperature control business of Moog Automotive, Inc., a subsidiary of Cooper Industries Inc., and converting the Mississauga plant to the manufacture of ignition, wire, and temperature control components. As a result, temperature control accounted for 49.7 percent of Standard Motor sales in 1999. In 2000, however, temperature control sales dropped to 44 percent of the total, which the company attributed to the loss of a major retail customer and cool and wet summer weather in the northeastern and midwestern states.

Between 1996 and 1999 Standard Motors Products acquired majority stakes in three British-based companies supplying ignition and fuel-systems components and rebuilt engine computers to buyers throughout western Europe. The European replacement market was forecast to increase at a rate more than twice that of the United States. A joint venture was begun in 1997 with Valeo, S.A., to remanufacture air-conditioning compressors for this market. Standard Motor Products also acquired, in 1999, Lemark Auto Accessories Ltd., a British-based supplier of wire sets, and a Texas-based unit of Mark IV Industries, Inc. that was manufacturing and distributing fan clutches and oil coolers. In 2000 it completed the purchase of Vehicle Air Condition Parts, a British distributor, and Automotive Heater Exchange SRL, an Italian company.

Of Standard Motor Products' net sales of $606.45 million in 2000, the Engine Management segment accounted for 49.1 percent and the Temperature Control segment for 44 percent. Products of the former included ignition and electrical parts, emission and engine controls, onboard computers, sensors, ignition wires, battery cables, and carburetors and fuel-system parts. Ignition and emission parts accounted for 37.4 percent of the company's net sales, and wires and cables, 10.1 percent. The Temperature Control segment consisted primarily of air-conditioning compressors, clutches, accumulators, filter/driers, blower motors, heater valves and cores, evaporators, condensers, hoses, and fittings. Compressors accounted for 20.1 percent of company sales and other air-conditioning parts for 21.9 percent.

Standard Motors Products' operating profit was $30.66 million in 2000. Engine Management's profit of $37.96 million was more than three times as high as Temperature Control's $11.54 million. All other segments of the company, consisting of items pertaining to corporate headquarters and Canadian and European business units that did not meet the criteria of a reportable operating segment, lost a combined $18.84 million. The United States accounted for 87 percent of company sales; Canada, for 4 percent; and other foreign countries, for 9 percent. Net earnings came to $9.73 million. The company's long-term debt was $150.02 million at the end of 2000.

In 1999 Standard Motor Products relocated two of its wire and cable operations, one in Dallas and the other in Bradenton, Florida, to a new facility in Reynosa, Mexico, which focused on assembly and packaging of the economic wire sets, while the premium line continued to be manufactured in Edwardsville. By this time the company had added plants in Orlando, Florida, and Wilson, North Carolina, for ignition manufacturing, and Corona, California; Fort Worth, Texas; and Elk Grove Village, Illinois, for temperature control. The Puerto Rican manufacturing operation was now in Fajardo, and European manufacturing was in Nottingham, England. The company no longer maintained an Israeli plant. The two Connecticut plants no longer belonged to the company, and the Rural Retreat one had been vacated and subleased.

Fife died in 1997. Three years later, Lawrence Sills succeeded his father as chief executive officer, but Nathaniel Sills, by that time 92, continued as chairman of the board. Members of the Sills and Fife families (by birth or marriage) owned about one-third of the common stock. GAMCO Investors, Inc. held another one-fifth.

Principal Subsidiaries

Four Seasons Europe S.A.R.L. (France); Marathon Auto Parts and Products, Inc.; Motortronics, Inc.; SMP Motor Products Limited (Canada); Standard Motor Products Holdings Limited (England and Wales; 80%); Standard Motor Products (Hong Kong) Limited; Standard Motor Products de Mexico, S. de R.L. de C.V.

Principal Divisions

Engine Management; Temperature Control.

Principal Competitors

Dana Corporation; Federal-Mogul Corporation.

Further Reading

"An Auto Parts Company Running In High Gear," *Business Week*, April 16, 1984, p. 112.

"Corporate Critics Confidential: Auto Parts/Replacement," *Wall Street Transcript,* December 4, 1989, pp. 95,603, 95,619.

Corwin, Philip, "Standard Motor Products Results In High Gear As Demand Warms Up," *Barron's,* Jun 1, 1970, p. 28.

Malanga, Steve, "Productivity Paradox," *Crain's New York Business,* August 2, 1993, p. 23.

Mirabella, Alan, "Standard's Stock Is Out of Neutral," *Crain's New York Business,* May 17, 1993, p. 31.

Robertshaw, Nicky, "Auto-Parts Maker Fine-Tunes Profits," *Crain's New York Business,* March 25, 1991, p. 35.

"Standard Motor Products, Inc.," *Wall Street Transcript,* December 18, 1972, pp. 31,150–31,151.

"Standard Motor Products On Route to Higher Net," *Barron's,* February 22, 1961, pp. 25–26.

Welling, Kathryn M., "He Won't Pay Up," *Barron's,* August 28, 1995, p. 22.

—Robert Halasz

Stroock & Stroock & Lavan LLP

180 Maiden Lane
New York, New York 10038-4982
U.S.A.
Telephone: (212) 806-5400
Fax: (212) 806-6006
Web site: http://www.stroock.com

Partnership
Founded: 1876 as the solo practice of M. Warley Platzek
Employees: 350
Sales: $166 million (1999 est.)
NAIC: 54111 Offices of Lawyers

Stroock & Stroock & Lavan LLP is a prominent New York City-based law firm that provides a full range of legal services such as real estate, litigation, intellectual property, insurance, tax, trusts and estates, finance, and capital markets. Its clients include *Fortune* 500 corporations, small technology firms, investment and commercial banks, overseas businesses, and foreign governments. Originally a Jewish law firm, it served many Jewish clients and helped strengthen Jewish civic and educational nonprofit associations, along with Gentile clients and associations. A small firm of about a dozen lawyers in its early days, the Stroock law firm's rapid expansion finally came in the late 20th century. By 1990 it had started branch offices in Los Angeles, Miami, Washington, D.C., and Budapest, Hungary. Its modern law practice ranges from helping energy companies in the United States and the Middle East to representing more than 250 investment companies, aiding mergers and acquisitions, and assisting clients dealing with the Information Age and the emerging electronic economy. Like other elite law firms, Stroock & Stroock & Lavan is a major player in privatization and other aspects of globalization.

Origins and Early Practice

Stroock & Stroock & Lavan began in 1876 when M. Warley Platzek began an individual law practice in New York City. Platzek studied at the New York University Law School and was trained in two law offices before starting his own practice, which focused on bankruptcy issues.

In 1893 Moses J. Stroock, a graduate of the Columbia College Law School, and Paul M. Herzog, a graduate of the New York Law School, became partners, and the firm became known as Platzek, Stroock & Herzog. With Herzog's departure in 1900, the firm was renamed Platzek and Stroock.

During his career in private law practice, Platzek provided legal counsel to Tammany Hall, the Democratic political machine that ran much of New York City. From 1907 to 1924 he served on the New York Supreme Court.

When Platzek left in 1907, Sol M. Stroock, the younger brother of Moses J. Stroock, became a partner, and the firm was renamed Stroock & Stroock. In the early 20th century the firm's clients included wealthy families that needed help in trusts and estates; Groton, Connecticut's Electric Boat Company, which made the first submarine purchased by the U.S. Navy; Oceanic Cheese & Sausage Company; women's clothing manufacturer Jacob Sperber; and some shipping and railroad companies. After the Prohibition amendment to the Constitution was ratified, the firm began representing the Wholesale Liquor Dealers of New York State. In 1909 the partnership moved to 30 Broad Street close to the New York Stock Exchange, and then in 1918 it relocated to 141 Broadway, its home until 1937.

Platzek and the two Stroock brothers were prominent members of the Jewish community. Firm historian Jethro Lieberman wrote: "It was the 'Our Crowd' German-Jewish clientele for which the firm was mostly, and justly, noted in those days." That included Otto H. Kahn, Felix M. Warburg, Walter N. Rothschild, and Jacob Schiff. The three early Jewish partners contributed to many Jewish organizations, such as the Educational Alliance founded in 1889, the Montefiore Hospital for Chronic Invalids, the Jewish Board of Guardians, the Federation for the Support of Jewish Philanthropic Societies of New York City, and the Jewish Theological Seminary of America. They also served non-Jewish civic and educational institutions.

One major case began soon after World War I ended, when President Wilson signed a law making it illegal to sell alcoholic beverages. The Kentucky Distillers and Warehouse Co. hired the firm to argue that the law was unconstitutional. In 1919, however, the U.S. Supreme Court upheld the federal law.

Until it went bankrupt in the 1930s, United Cigar Stores Company was the small law firm's major client. United Cigar's 409 stores nationwide in 1910 made it a major chain. That client led the firm to other tobacco clients, including George Washington Hill, the head of Lucky Strike cigarettes, and Thomas Fortune Ryan, one of the founders of the American Tobacco Company in the late 1890s. In 1923 the firm represented the French banking firm of De Rothschild Freres in a major bankruptcy case, which the firm lost.

For many decades the firm remained a small operation. In 1924, for example, it included just seven lawyers and about eight staff. The firm's lawyers were not specialists until the 1940s, a general feature of most law firms of those days.

The Depression Years and World War II

In 1936 Sol Stroock served as a member of the Citizens' Anti-Crime Committee appointed by New York Mayor Fiorello LaGuardia to fight organized crime that threatened the city's financial stability. The committee helped Thomas E. Dewey, the city's special prosecutor, gain several convictions, which led to his political career as a prominent Republican.

Peter I.B. Lavan, who had graduated from Columbia Law School in 1918 before joining the firm, in the 1930s brought in considerable work for the firm as it increasingly emphasized its corporate and financial practice. For example, he oversaw the reorganizations of Twentieth Century–Fox and the Tobacco Products Co. He also helped form United Merchants and Manufacturers.

In the 1930s Lavan assisted Henry Rose in his takeover of part of Sears's business and the creation of a new Sears subsidiary. Through that work, Lavan became Sears's outside counsel for New York, and he also helped William Rosenwald, Sears's general counsel, to buy a significant portion of the Empire State Building. Lavan's advice led Rosenwald to organize American

Securities Corporation. Not surprisingly, Rosenwald remained a client of the firm for many years.

Meanwhile, the Stroock law firm and many others in the 1930s gained work from the new laws and regulations approved as part of President Franklin Roosevelt's New Deal. Although many in the legal profession opposed the creation of the Securities and Exchange Commission (SEC), corporations needed more legal assistance to file SEC reports. When the Stroock law firm's Milton Scofield was asked to file an SEC statement for United Merchants and Manufacturers, he admitted in the firm's history book, "No one in the office knew how to do one," so he turned to former law school friends who were part of the SEC.

With just a handful of lawyers, the small Stroock law firm contrasted with several much larger firms also based in New York City. In his 1939 article, Ferdinand Lundberg called the big firms "law factories" that had from 50 to 75 lawyers. Most were based in New York City, and most were "made up predominantly of men of native or Anglo-Scotch stock."

New York City's American Molasses Company, a firm client since 1918, in 1939 won a lawsuit attacking the New York City's sales tax. In 1941 Parev Products Co., Inc. sued I. Rokeach & Sons, Inc., the firm's client, for dropping its kosher oil, for which Parev received royalties, and then selling a new oil product and not paying royalties. The U.S. Court of Appeals for the Second Circuit denied Parev's claims.

When Sol Stroock died in 1941, the firm, then with about $250,000 in gross revenue, faced what Jethro Lieberman described as "its greatest crisis," for Stroock was by far the firm's most experienced and prominent partner. The firm's five partners discussed options such as dissolving the firm, merging, or hiring a prominent lawyer to replace the deceased name partner. They decided to stay together under the new name of Stroock & Stroock & Lavan, formally adopted on January 1, 1943.

During World War II, some firm attorneys left for military or government service. One Stroock lawyer spent most of his time at the Bayonne, New Jersey plant of the Elco and Electro Dynamics Divisions of the Electric Boat Co., a longtime firm client. One of the most important contributions the firm made was a licensing agreement allowing the Elco Division to make PT Boats that helped the U.S. Navy in its war against Japan.

The Post-World War II Practice

The small firm of Stroock & Stroock & Lavan, with no more than 15 lawyers throughout the 1940s, continued in the postwar era to strongly support various Jewish educational and civic organizations, including New York City's Maimonides Hospital and the Jewish Child Care Association of New York. The firm's lawyers also backed non-Jewish causes and groups, such as the National Commission for the Decennial White House Conference on Children and Youth. Meanwhile, according to Jethro Lieberman, clear anti-Semitism continued until the early 1950s in both law schools and many large law firms.

After Haiti's President Jean-Claude Duvalier left the small Caribbean island in 1986, the Haitian government hired the Stroock law firm to recover as much of its assets as possible. The firm tracked money to Duvalier bank accounts in Switzer-

---

Key Dates:

1876: M. Warley Platzek begins his individual practice in New York City.
1893: The firm changes its name to Platzek, Stroock & Herzog.
1900: The partnership becomes Platzek and Stroock.
1907: The name Stroock & Stroock is adopted.
1943: The firm is renamed Stroock & Stroock & Lavan.
1987: The Stroock law firm merges with New York City's Olnick Boxer Blumberg Lane & Troy.
1990: The firm establishes an office in Budapest, Hungary.

---

land and other places as it prepared for legal action in France, where Duvalier and his family lived on the Riviera. This case reminded some of how Iran's shah and Philippines President Ferdinand Marcos took public funds for their own benefit.

In December 1986 the Stroock law firm announced that it would merge with New York's Olnick Boxer Blumberg Lane & Troy as of January 1, 1987. Olnick Boxer specialized in real estate law for major New York City property owners and developers, including Starrett Housing Corporation, American Express, and the Milstein family. In 1986 its 28 lawyers brought in revenue of about $7 million. The Stroock law firm in 1986 had 265 lawyers and about $65 million in revenue. Stroock's real estate clients included Bear, Stearns & Company; Chemical Bank; and E.F. Hutton Inc.

Following the merger, in 1987 Stroock & Stroock & Lavan included more than 285 lawyers and more than 425 secretaries, paralegals, and other staff who worked in New York, Los Angeles, Miami, and Washington, D.C. In 1989 the firm had a total of 339 lawyers, which ranked it as New York City's 19th largest law firm. In 1989 the partnership recorded gross revenue of $120 million, which put it in a three-way tie for the 19th largest New York City law firm.

The Stroock law firm used both inhouse public relations/ marketing professionals and outside experts to promote its practice. For example, the firm's 41-lawyer Los Angeles office in 1988 used the Los Angeles public relations firm of Rogers & Associates. Such efforts occurred as "the staid profession of law becomes the competitive business of law," according to Myrna Oliver in the *Los Angeles Times*.

That was a major change from the law profession's early history, when most law firms were almost like secret societies as they followed the American Bar Association's view that advertising was unprofessional. In 1977 the U.S. Supreme Court ruled that such prohibitions violated the First Amendment's guarantee of free speech, which opened the gates to professionals using various advertising, marketing, or public relations methods.

Thus in the late 20th century the practice of law was transformed in many ways. The dramatic increase in the size of the Stroock law firm and others not surprisingly made lawyer relationships more impersonal as new departments and specialization occurred.

In addition, more women joined the ranks of the nation's elite law firms. In the late 1980s, one-third of the Stroock law firm's associates were women, and it had ten women partners, a typical development that was virtually unknown before the 1970s.

Law Practice in the 1990s and Beyond

With the collapse of communist governments in Eastern Europe and the Soviet Union, many law firms began representing clients in those areas and then opened offices there. Stroock & Stroock & Lavan lawyers based in the United States in 1989 helped Bear, Stearns & Co. and other Western companies either start investment funds or acquire local businesses in Poland, Hungary, East Germany, and the Soviet Union.

In 1990 the Stroock law firm established a branch office in Budapest, Hungary, one of the former Eastern Bloc nations that emphasized rapidly privatizing its government-owned operations following communism's downfall. In 1992 the Hungarian government chose the Stroock law firm as its international counsel to assist in a major ten-year highway privatization effort. The firm also represented AES in its bid to gain energy contracts in Hungary. These were two examples of how Hungary tried to modernize as a prerequisite to applying for membership in the European Union.

The Stroock law firm in the 1990s represented Carl C. Icahn, the largest investor in RJR Nabisco Holding Corporation; DoubleClick, the Internet's major advertising placement firm; and Miami's Premium Sales Corp. In the 1990s most large corporate law firms had some kind of intellectual property (IP) practice as a way of providing a full range of services. The Stroock law firm in 1994 recruited the entire 14-lawyer IP practice of Blum Kaplan to benefit its clients. "Long regarded as gawky technocrats, lacking the polish and the instincts of first-class lawyers, they [IP specialists] now find themselves being courted by New York's elite firms, many of which are anxious to develop IP capabilities," said Philip Sington in the September 1994 *International Corporate Law*. Of course, they competed with some firms that had specialized for years in IP matters such as copyright and patents.

According to the *American Lawyer*'s annual survey of the nation's 100 largest law firms, Stroock & Stroock & Lavan was number 56 based on its 1997 gross revenue of $157.5 million. It declined to number 63 in 1998 with $163 million in gross revenues, and number 78 in 1999 with $166 million in revenues. That was a long way from 1986, when Stroock was one of the nation's 35 largest law firms. The firm's profits per equity partner went from $560,000 in 1997 to $595,000 in 1998 and $630,000 in 1999. Although the firm had grown in the 1990s, its growth was relatively slow compared with some of the nation's other large law firms.

Principal Operating Units

Capital Markets; E-Commerce and Technology; Entertainment; ERISA and Employee Benefits; Health Care; Insolvency and Restructuring; Insurance; Intellectual Property; Labor and Employment; Litigation; Real Estate; Tax; Trusts and Estates.

Principal Competitors

Paul, Weiss, Rifkind, Wharton & Garrison; Skadden, Arps, Slate, Meagher & Flom; Sullivan & Cromwell.

Further Reading

Abramson, Jill, and Arthur S. Hayes, "Law Firms Forge Eastern European Ties," *Wall Street Journal*, November 27, 1989, p. 1.

Cherovsky, Erwin, "Stroock & Stroock & Lavan," in *The Guide to New York Law Firms*, New York: St. Martin's Press, 1991, pp. 193–96.

Forster, Richard, "Hungarian Legal Market Faces Contraction," *International Financial Law Review*, February 1998, pp. 41–43.

Grossman, Laurie M., and Nikhil Deogun, "Premium Sales Corp.'s Investors Lose Big," *Wall Street Journal*, June 14, 1993, p. C1.

Harlan, Christi, "Acquirer of 11 Failed Texas S&Ls Under 'Southwest Plan' Sues U.S.," *Wall Street Journal*, October 14, 1992, p. B9.

Hays, Constance, "Fighting RJR, Icahn Demands That It Spin Off Nabisco Stake," *New York Times*, March 12, 1999, p. 1.

Lieberman, Jethro K., *Stroock & Stroock & Lavan: An Informal History of the Early Years 1876 to 1950*, New York: Stroock & Stroock & Lavan, 1987.

Lipton, Eric, "2 Hired to Calm Fears for Web Privacy," *New York Times*, March 8, 2000, p. B3.

Lowenstein, Roger, "Looking for Loot: Haiti Presses Search World-Wide for Assets Duvalier Appropriated—Former President's Transfer of $103 Million Is Traced, But Recovery Is Difficult   Life and Litigation on Riviera," *Wall Street Journal*, December 2, 1986, p. 1.

Lundberg, Ferdinand, "The Law Factories: Brains of the Status Quo," *Harper's Magazine*, July 1939, pp. 180–92.

Marcus, Amy Dockser, and Wade Lambert, "Suit Claims Eli Lilly Drug Caused Genetic Harm Across Generations," *Wall Street Journal*, March 13, 1990, p. B9.

Oliver, Myrna, "PR Joins the Bar," *Los Angeles Times*, October 17, 1988, p. 1.

Sington, Philip, "New York Turns Intellectual," *International Corporate Law*, September 1994, p. 9.

"Stroock & Stroock Plans a Merger, Bolstering Real Estate Operation," *Wall Street Journal*, December 23, 1986, p. 1.

—David M. Walden

SWAROVSKI

Swarovski International Holding AG

General Wille Strasse 88
CH-8706 Feldmeilen
Switzerland
Telephone: (+41) 1 925 71 11
Fax: (+41) 1 925 73 12
Web site: http://www.swarovski.com

Private Company
Incorporated: 1895 as Daniel Swarovski & Co.
Employees: 12,600
Sales: SFr 1.99 billion (2000)
NAIC: 339911 Jewelry (Except Costume) Manufacturing;
333314 Optical Instrument and Lens Manufacturing;
333515 Cutting Tool and Machine Tool Accessory
Manufacturing

Switzerland-based Swarovski International Holding AG is parent to the Swarovski group of companies based in and around Watten, in the Tyrol region of Austria. Founded in 1895, the Swarovski name has become nearly synonymous with crystal production. The company manufactures crystal jewelry stones, crystal gifts and objects—including its famed collection of miniature animals—and accessories, as well as crystal-based materials for the fashion industry, and components for crystal chandeliers. Swarovski is also well-known for its Swarovski Optik subsidiary's line of high-performance telescopes, gun-sites, and binoculars for hunting and birdwatching enthusiasts. Another company subsidiary, Swareflex, manufactures roadside reflectors and related highway safety products. The company's Tyrolit subsidiary produces a catalog of over 70,000 bonded, grinding, cutting, sawing, and drilling tools and systems. Lastly, the company is part of the Signity joint venture with Swiss gemstone seller Golay Buchel & Cie., created in 1999 to produce genuine and manmade gemstones, cubit zirconia, and similar products. With worldwide operations including factories in the United States, Mexico, Italy, Brazil, Argentina, and elsewhere, Swarovski employs more than 12,000 people. Swarovski remains wholly owned and led by the founding Swarovski family.

Late 19th-Century Crystal

Daniel Swarovski, originally from the Bohemia region of the former Austro-Hungarian empire, came to Wattens, in the Tyrol region of Austria, with a new invention. Originally trained to cut crystal by hand, Swarovski had invented and patented an automatic grinding machine to industrialize the process, and the Tyrolean mountain rivers provided a cheap source of energy to run the machine. Swarovski's invention—and a process that remained a jealously guarded family secret—was to revolutionize the crystal industry and provide the basis for the family company's long-lasting success. Swarovski set up his firm, Daniel Swarovski & Co., in 1895.

Swarovski's invention produced crystal gemstones of outstanding quality—and the patented process enabled the company to become the world's leading producer of crystal gemstones. The company's earliest products were especially valued by the jewelry and fashion industries. By the end of World War I, the company began to target the industrial community as well. In 1917, Swarovski began developing grinding and polishing equipment for its own production uses. By 1919, however, the company saw the opportunity to market these tools as a new product line. In that year, Swarovski launched its first subsidiary and brand name, Tyrolit. Originally designed for cutting and polishing crystal gemstones, the Tyrolit line of products later expanded to include a wide variety of applications.

The 1930s saw several significant developments in Swarovski's history. The first of these was a line of crystal "trimmings," which debuted in 1931. The Swarovski trimmings featured the company's crystal gemstones prepared in a variety of ready-to-use formats for edging, hems, and borders. Also known as rhinestones, Swarovski's gemstones were of such high quality that they were often mistaken for real diamonds.

In the 1930s, also, Wilhelm Swarovski, the son of Daniel Swarovski, began work on a prototype for a pair of field binoculars. The younger Swarovski, who had inherited his father's inventiveness, had joined the family company at the age of 17, and had long been conducting experiments in glass smelting techniques. Wilhelm Swarovski finished his prototype field

Company Perspectives:

SWAROVSKI's corporate culture: Daniel Swarovski, technical genius, humanitarian, and founder of the company, had a crystal clear vision that went far beyond financial or corporate ambitions. One of his primary concerns was to build a democratic company that could offer employees, co-workers and directors a life of dignity and self-respect, of social harmony and cultural experiences. His attitude was shaped by his own early experiences:

"Our fellow workers are our fellow humans. We need to value each individual as a human being, and help him or her to lead a fulfilled life in honour and dignity."

Daniel Swarovski's philosophy was far ahead of its time. At a time when both the term "corporate culture" and acting to implement it were largely unknown, SWAROVSKI already realized the importance of it and valued it as a program for their employees that would provide them with a harmonious social environment. The first step towards his vision, taken as early as 1907, was a housing development scheme, followed by the introduction of sporting activities and cultural events, along with a profit-linked bonus scheme and other fringe benefits. This progressive attitude which continues today at the heart of the company is the key to SWAROVSKI's loyal and fast growing workforce of some 12,600 employees around the world.

glasses in 1935, developing new grinding techniques for the field glasses' hand-ground and polished optical components. The company began production of optical lenses in 1939, on the eve of World War II. The company's field glasses were to remain in the prototype stage, however, until after the war ended.

Swarovski moved into a third area of operations toward the end of the decade when it launched a line of reflective glass that quickly found a number of applications, such as road and rail reflectors, reflector strips for guardrails, and other safety uses. Launched in 1937, these products resulted in the creation of the Swareflex brand in 1950.

Expanding Products in the 1950s

Emerging from World War II, the company built on Wilhelm Swarovski's optical experiments to begin the production of eyeglass lenses in 1945. This was to become an important part of the company's operations and remained a key component of its catalog until the early 1980s. Swarovski not only ground lenses, it also launched an initiative to train opticians for the Austrian market, founding the Industrial and Vocational School for Optics, Glass, Iron, and Metal, which later became the Trade School for Opticians, producing a large share of the country's opticians.

The company's optical glass activities grew quickly. By 1948, production of optical glass had outgrown the company's Wattens glass-cutting headquarters. The company opened a new facility in nearby Absam, forming the operation as the

subsidiary Swarovski Optik KG in 1949. While eyeglass lenses represented the largest share of the new subsidiary's production—up to 300,000 lenses ground per month—Swarovski Optik launched production of its first pair of binoculars, the 7 x 24, which was quickly acclaimed by Europe's hunting enthusiasts.

In the 1950s, Swarovski's reflective glass operations had also begun to grow—the postwar European economic boom and the rapidly growing numbers of automobiles on the continent's highways helped to stimulate demand for the Swareflex range. Meanwhile, Swarovski's Tyrolit operations were also outpacing its Wattens production capacity, and those operations were moved to a new production plant, in Schwaz, Austria, in 1950.

A new generation of Swarovskis had taken a place at the company's leadership, as Daniel Swarovski's grandson Manfred took over the family company's direction in the 1950s. Manfred Swarovski brought the company into a new direction and new acclaim, when, working with designer Christian Dior, the company created its famed multicolored Aurora Borealis crystal stones. The collaboration with Dior marked the beginning of a new era of close cooperation between the crystal company and the world's fashion industry.

The company's other divisions were also producing their share of technical innovations in the 1950s. Through the decade, Swarovski Optik rolled out a number of binocular designs, including the wide-angle Habicht binoculars. The company also began developing a new range of opera glasses, which debuted in 1957. Two years later, Swarovski Optik debuted its first rifle scope, a line that was to become one of its most important. Meanwhile, Tyrolit was enjoying increasing international success, leading the subsidiary to open its first foreign sales office, in Milan, Italy, in 1953. The company's international reputation was equally helped by the launch of a new range of fiberglass-reinforced grinding wheels, launched in 1952.

Light Bulb Moment in the 1970s

Tyrolit was also leading Swarovski's international development. In 1960, the company opened its first manufacturing plant outside of Austria, founding the grinding tool production facility Abrasivos Austromex in Mexico City, Mexico. The company opened a new foreign plant in Buenos Aires, Argentina, in 1968. This expansion coincided with the launch of a new line of resinoid bonded diamond grinding tools the year earlier.

Swarovski's crystal operations were also growing. In 1965, the company began producing crystal chandelier components—dressing up such famed chandeliers as those in the Metropolitan Opera House in New York City and France's Palace of Versailles. Two years later, Swarovski began producing a new range of natural and artificial gemstones, including cubit zirconia. The company developed the first mechanical process for cutting cubit zirconia by the end of the decade.

The 1970s marked the beginning of a new era for Swarovski. Until then, the company had never ventured into the consumer retail market. The worldwide recession of the decade, the result of the Arab Oil Embargo of 1973, had caused a dramatic drop in demand for the company's crystal gemstones. Manfred

Swarovski was searching for a way to prop up the company's sales. As granddaughter, and future company Vice-President Nadja Swarovski told the *Financial Times:* My grandfather was fiddling around in his office with a few little crystals when it occurred to him that the pieces, arranged in a certain fashion, resembled a tiny mouse. That was his light bulb moment.''

That moment led the company to launch the first of what was to become one of the world's most sought-after collector's series, a tiny crystal mouse, in 1976. The mouse and the many other animals in the series, the production of which was placed under a new Tabletop Division, brought the Swarovski name into the consumer world for the first time. The company's consumer products, which at first represented a means to guarantee cash flow during industry down-cycles, nonetheless quickly became an integral part of the company's operations. In 1977 Swarovski followed up the worldwide success of its crystal animals by launching its own line of jewelry. This move led to the creation of a new subsidiary and brand, the Daniel Swarovski line of jewelry and accessories in 1989. By then, the growing international demand for the company's crystal animals also led the company to establish the Swarovski Collectors Society—which quickly boasted a membership of more than 300,000. The company also changed its logo, formerly featuring the Tyrolean edelweiss, to a more elegant swan symbol.

Market Leaders for the New Century

Swarovski continued to build its several businesses through the 1990s. Tyrolit, which had continued to roll out new products, such as laser-welded diamond tools targeted to the stone industry launched in 1984, also continued its international development. After launching a new production plant in San Luis, Argentina, the company moved into North America, buying a

share of Diamond Products, in the United States. In 1997, Tyrolit cemented its North American position with the acquisition of Bay State/Sterling Company, based in Massachusetts, then the number two leading manufacturer of bonded grinding tools in the U.S. market. Tyrolit also built up its European position through the decade, opening a new Stans, Austria plant for high-precision grinding tools in 1992, acquiring the Italian diamond tools producer Vincent in 1993, and capping the decade with the acquisition of HS Veglio S.p.A, a metal bonded diamond tools manufacturer based in Italy.

Swarovski Optik meanwhile had continued to build an international reputation for its high-quality binoculars, telescopes, and gun sites. After discontinuing production of eyeglass lenses in 1983, the company began expanding its range, adding hand-held night-vision binoculars and pocket binoculars during the decade. In 1991, the subsidiary moved into the U.S. market, founding Swarovski Optik North America. Swarovski continued to roll out new products, such as laser range finders, leading to the company's patented LRS product and a rifle scope with integrated range finder, a market first. In the mid-1990s, the company was encouraged to begin designing binoculars for a new market—that of bird-watching enthusiasts. The company rolled out its own line of bird-watching binoculars in 1999.

By then, Swarovski itself was enjoying renewed enthusiasm from the fashion industry. Helping to inspire this trend—which saw Swarovski's crystals glitter from creation of the world's top fashion designers—was Nadja Swarovski, who joined the company's New York branch in 1995. The new generation of Swarovski actively sought partnerships with and sponsorships of such noted designers as Anand Jon, Alexander McQueen, Philip Treacy, and others—helping to raise Swarovski's name from the ''kitsch'' of its crystal animals to the ranks of global haute couture. At the turn of the century, the company also prepared to expand its direction with the formation of a joint-venture with Geneva, Switzerland-based Golay Buchel, to produce precision-cut genuine gemstones and synthetic and imitation stones.

As Swarovski closed out the century, it had built an enviable position as a world leader in nearly all of its product categories. With a new generation of the Swarovski family in position to take over the company's lead, the Swarovski name was poised to provide glitter for a new century.

Principal Subsidiaries

Daniel Swarovski Corporation AG; Daniel Swarovski Paris; Swarovski Selectrion; Swarovski Silver Crystal; Swarovski SCS; Swarovski Crystal Memories; Swarovski Kristallwelten; Swarovski Components (Austria); Signity (50%); SwaroLite; Swareflex; Swarovski Optik AG; Swarovski Optik North America; Tyrolit Schleifmittelwerke Swarovski KG (Austria).

Principal Competitors

Avimo Group Limited; Konica Corporation; Leica Camera AG; Nikon Corporation; Société du Louvre; Tiffany & Co.; Carl-Zeiss-Stiftung.

Further Reading

Adams, Susan, "Hawk Eyes," *Forbes*, November 13, 2000, p. 402.

Becker, Vivienne, *The Magic of Crystal*, New York: Harry N. Abrams, Inc., 1995.

Carpenter, Lea, "A Many Spangled Thing," *Financial Times*, February 10, 2001.

Pongvutitham, Achara, "Crystal Producer Seeks to Relocate to Thailand," *Nation* (Thailand), August 6, 1997.

Rickey, Melanie, "The Glitter Band," *Independent*, December 19, 1998, p. 27.

—M. L. Cohen

Tellabs, Inc.

4951 Indiana Avenue
Lisle, Illinois 60532
U.S.A.
Telephone: (630) 378-8800
Fax: (630) 852-7346
Web site: http://www.tellabs.com

Public Company
Incorporated: 1975
Employees: 6,997
Sales: $3.39 billion (2000)
Stock Exchanges: NASDAQ
Ticker Symbol: TLAB
NAIC: 33421 Telephone Apparatus Manufacturing;
    335313 Switchgear and Switchboard Apparatus
    Manufacturing; 33429 Other Communications
    Equipment Manufacturing

Tellabs, Inc. is a key player in the dynamic and ultra-competitive telecommunications industry. The company designs, manufactures, markets, and services optical networking, next-generation switching, and broadband access solutions. It also provides professional services that support its products. Tellabs' customers include local and long-distance telephone companies, international service providers, wireless networks, businesses and governmental organizations with private voice and data networks, and cable television companies interested in transmitting voice, video, and data communications. These customers use Tellabs' equipment—such as the TITAN digital cross-connect systems, MartisDXX access and transport networks, and FOCUS systems—to handle millions of phone calls and Internet connections. With 14 development centers and six manufacturing facilities, Tellabs is truly a global concern, operating in North America, Europe, Latin America, Asia, Africa, and the Middle East.

Early Years: 1975–84

Tellabs was founded in 1975, when six men, all with various degrees of experience in electrical engineering and sales, got together around a suburban Chicago kitchen table, "drinking coffee and brainstorming." (Of the six, two would stay with the company for over 20 years: Michael Birck, who was Tellabs' CEO and president until 2000, when he became chairman, and Chris Cooney, vice-president of sales.) The group planned to form a telecommunications company that did not fit traditional corporate molds, one that offered customers products and services that met their specific needs.

Between them, the six partners raised start-up capital of $110,000 and incorporated Tellabs in the spring of 1975. The company's research and development department consisted of one man, a handmade wooden workbench, a used soldering machine (purchased for $25), and an outdated oscilloscope. Its sales force consisted of two men and two used Chrysler New Yorkers, chosen for their large trunks. Within months, the company began marketing its first product, an echo suppressor intended for independent telephone companies, such as Continental Telephone and GTE.

During this time, the founding members drew no salaries. Family members supported the new company by going back to work, mortgaging homes, cleaning Tellabs' offices on weekends—even posing as assembly line workers when potential customers were taken through the "plant." By December 1975, Tellabs was enjoying a bit of success. It had 20 permanent employees and sales of $312,000. Soon the company landed an account with Western Union, its first major customer. By 1977, Tellabs was able to move into a permanent facility in Lisle, Illinois, and its sales force had quadrupled to eight. That year, annual sales jumped to $7.8 million.

New Challenges and Opportunities in the 1980s

Tellabs' expansion continued with the opening of its first subsidiary, Tellabs Communications Canada, Ltd., in 1979. The following year, the company expanded its market to the south, with the opening of its Tellabs Texas manufacturing facility, and also became public, trading on the NASDAQ exchange. The company put more money into R&D, developing complex networking systems, as well as a line of digital communications systems for telephone companies and large computer systems. In 1983, with the opening of Tellabs' fourth facility in Puerto Rico, it seemed Tellabs' growth would continue uninterrupted.

In 1989, the company made a significant step towards increasing its European presence with the acquisition of Delta Communications in Shannon, Ireland. Renamed Tellabs Ltd., the subsidiary supplied signaling and conversion systems for Europe's E1 telecommunications markets, a venue previously untapped by Tellabs. By 1992, Tellabs' foreign sales network expanded to cover Belgium, New Zealand, Korea, and Mexico, where government monopolies on telecommunications systems were beginning to dissolve. The following year the company acquired Martis Oy, a Finnish telecommunications supplier, for approximately $70 million. This acquisition further solidified Tellabs' European market presence. With Martis Oy, Tellabs also obtained a product—the DYX multiplexer—that was compatible with synchronous digital hierarchy, which is the digital standard that most of the world (excluding the United States) uses. The DYX multiplexer provided the platform for Tellabs' tremendously successful MartisDXX access and transport networks.

New Products and Soaring Sales: 1991–99

Tellabs' marketing efforts worldwide were boosted by an array of new, state-of-the art technologies. Foremost among these was the TITAN 5500 digital cross-connect system, which Tellabs introduced in 1991. Digital cross-connect systems route telephone calls and Internet transmissions between switching centers in the networks of local and long-distance carriers. Although the TITAN 5500 only generated $13 million in 1991, the equipment quickly became known as the "Cadillac" of the industry, according to Crain's Chicago Business. By 1993, the TITAN accounted for over $80 million of Tellabs' annual revenues.

Although Tellabs focused on its digital cross-connect systems segment in the early 1990s, the company did not overlook its booming business in echo cancelers. In 1991 Tellabs introduced a line of digital echo cancelers designed to work in conjunction with new fiber optics systems. These products provided a huge boost to the company, as sales of echo cancelers alone reached $40 million in 1992 (second only to AT&T in the entire industry). Tellabs' total revenues increased 90 percent between 1992 and 1993, to hit a record high of $320 million. The company's success did not go unnoticed on Wall Street. Tellabs' stock price jumped from $21 per share to just over $69 per share during the same period.

Just as Tellabs had benefited from—and been challenged by—the breakup of the monolithic Bell system in 1984, the company stood to realize significant gains as the telecommunications industry went through a second revolution in the mid-1990s. Traffic on telephone networks grew exponentially as ever increasing numbers of individuals and businesses used the Internet. Telephone companies scrambled to keep up with this surge in demand on their once unchallenged networks. Some turned to fiber optic line, which can carry over ten times as much traffic as conventional copper wire. Others sought new ways to manage the traffic on their existing networks more efficiently.

In 1996 Congress passed the landmark Telecommunications Act, which brought additional changes to the industry. In the wake of this deregulatory legislation, long-distance telephone providers could enter the local calling market, while the seven "Baby Bells" could join the long-distance fray. Competition in the telecommunications industry grew fierce as a result of these tectonic shifts. Local and long-distance telephone companies

Then, in 1984, the monolithic Bell System was dissolved, and several regional "Baby Bell" companies emerged.

Prior to the breakup, the Bell System had designed its own products through its subsidiary Bell Laboratories and produced them through Western Electric, AT&T's manufacturing division. Suddenly, through the divestiture, the previously closed Bell market was wide open. Although analysts had predicted that companies like Tellabs would benefit substantially from the new market, the new arrangement prompted intense competition as a large number of new companies emerged to compete for contracts with the Baby Bells. Regional Bell companies no longer had the financial resources of Ma Bell to rely upon and began looking for the lowest possible bidder when making new purchases. Competition became fierce, and although Tellabs' sales hit $100 million in 1985, gross profit margin dropped from 50 percent in 1984 to 35 percent in 1985.

Company management thus decided to make some internal changes in order to compete more effectively. Tellabs implemented a progressive management system, incorporating the Japanese just-in-time inventory plan, new employee training programs, and replacing traditional manufacturing lines with manufacturing cells, with each employee skilled in a number of interchangeable functions. The company also increased its research and development expenditures by about 40 percent and began developing such products as the $100,000 CROSSNET digital interchange product, CT1 multiplexer, that brought in much higher profit margins than Tellabs' early $200 echo suppressor. As private communications networks sprang up, Tellabs began to customize products to meet their needs. The company's increased efficiency in bringing new products to the market also allowed it to effectively win a bid against Bell Labs and Western Electric for an ongoing contract to supply AT&T with networking multiplexers, an integral component in AT&T's communications operations.

By 1987, Tellabs was back on the road to profitability, with improved sales to regional Bell companies as well as to long-distance service providers. That year, the company signed a $10 million contract with the long-distance carrier Sprint to supply its entire optical fiber network with digital echo cancelers. Sales for 1987 rose 18 percent to $136.1 million; net income rose 27 percent to $10.7 million.

Also that year, Tellabs began boosting efforts to penetrate foreign markets. "We didn't have the staff or the right products to address foreign markets before," CEO Birck told shareholders the following year, noting that "in 1987 we felt we were big enough and had a sufficient array of products to make a real commitment overseas." Birck then predicted that overseas sales, which accounted for 1 percent of revenues in the early 1980s, would rise to 30 percent by 1990. By 1988, Tellabs had opened sales offices in London, Australia, and Hong Kong and had expanded its Canadian operations.

eyed each other's networks hungrily. At the same time, cable television companies recognized that they could do far more than bring cable television into people's homes, as they had already established a network infrastructure that was enviable in its reach.

Tellabs was ideally situated to capitalize on the industry's ongoing fluctuations. More players in the telecommunications industry meant more business for equipment manufacturers like Tellabs. For example, Tellabs teamed up with Advanced Fibre Communications, Inc., and introduced the CABLESPAN 2300 Universal Telephony Distribution System in 1994. This unique equipment allowed a wideband signal—such as those that were common in cable television—to be split, thus enabling companies to offer both voice and video service with the same delivery system that once brought only cable television pictures. The CABLESPAN technology thus gave cable television companies the chance to compete in the burgeoning voice-transmission market without having to build a new system.

At the same time, Tellabs was already in a position to profit from the surge in traffic along established phone networks. The TITAN 5500 helped networks manage digital circuits more efficiently. With the aid of the cross-connect system, carriers could easily reroute circuits, thereby boosting the capacity of their fragile networks. The TITAN became even more essential to carriers as Tellabs periodically released updated hardware and software for the equipment. By 1994, the TITAN could manage 688,000 simultaneous phone calls.

Despite Tellabs' unparalleled success, CEO Birck recognized that his company's future was in no way guaranteed. "You are not going to just grow continuously at the rate we've been growing without getting into new lines," he told *Crain's Chicago Business*. In an effort to expand its reach, Tellabs spent about $76 million in 1996 to acquire Steinbrecher Corp., a manufacturer of extensive wireless technologies. With this purchase, Tellabs entered the potentially lucrative fixed wireless market. Since building traditional wired networks involves monumental commitments of time and money, Tellabs thought that creating wireless local phone systems could be a boon to developing countries.

Instead of laying thousands of miles of wire, these nations could extend local telephone service through wireless local loops. Although the concept was promising, it did not bring immediate returns to Tellabs. The company's sales rose again in 1996, but its fixed wireless business never got off the ground.

Undeterred, Tellabs also continued to bolster its research and manufacturing capacity. In 1996 the company carried out a $33 million expansion of its plant in Bolingbrook, Illinois. The following year, Tellabs built a new facility in Ireland for the research and development of broadband technologies. Fueled by its growth, Tellabs' revenues topped $1 billion for the first time in 1997.

Despite these successes, some analysts remained downbeat about Tellabs' future prospects. The telecommunications industry was rapidly consolidating in the late 1990s, and the company's major customers increasingly wanted "one-stop shopping" from their suppliers. Tellabs risked becoming a niche player—and a target for acquisition—if it could not bulk up and offer more products. In June 1998, Tellabs announced that it was purchasing Ciena Corp. for about $7.1 billion. Industry pundits applauded the move for many reasons. Not only would Tellabs become a bigger industry player after such a major acquisition, but it also would gain a foothold in the optical technology field. Ciena produced fiber optic transmission gear, which was in high demand as carriers scrambled to convert their networks from traditional copper wires to speedier optical ones. Tellabs itself did not offer optical equipment, and Ciena would help Tellabs to bridge this gap. Despite its potential upside, though, the deal collapsed after Ciena abruptly lost a significant contract with one of its major customers, and its stock price plummeted. Tellabs' shareholders balked at a merger with a company that appeared to be on shaky ground.

Tellabs did not abandon its efforts to expand, however. In August 1998 it purchased Coherent Communications, a leader in the echo canceler field. The following year, Tellabs added Internet backbone specialist Netcore Inc., as well as Salix Technologies, Inc., a producer of switching equipment, and a business unit of the Paris-based Alcatel SA. Also in 1999, the company hired 2,000 new employees and began construction on a new $75 million headquarters.

More impressive was the fact that Tellabs continued its tremendous growth streak. Between 1993 and 1999 Tellabs' revenue increased at a 36.4 percent compound annual rate—with no slowdown in sight. Analysts were surprised that the TITAN equipment kept selling, as they had "anticipated that newer-style networks designed for Internet traffic would make Tellabs' Titan line ... obsolete," *Crain's Chicago Business* explained. But the experts had not counted the fact that carriers were reluctant to abandon their existing networks because of the huge costs involved in building a new optical one. As a result, carriers used the updated TITAN 5500 to manage the transition to new networks. At the same time, Tellabs' research and development arm worked frantically to complete the TITAN 6500, a multiservice transport system that had the data-switching capabilities that were so crucial to handling Internet transmissions. Still further back in the pipeline was the TITAN 6700, an optical switch that could simultaneously carry 80 million Internet calls.

2000 and Beyond

In 2000 Tellabs was sufficiently bullish about its future to announce its "X3 by 03" plan—aimed at tripling the company's annual sales to $9 billion by 2003. To shepherd the company toward this goal, Birck brought in Richard Notebaert to be Tellabs' new president and CEO in 2000. Birck became the chairman of the board of directors, where he hoped to oversee longer-term planning. Tellabs' sales rose to nearly $3.4 billion in 2000, fueled in part by the release of the TITAN 6500 in August of that year. The company introduced five other cutting-edge products in 2000, and planned to release the TITAN 6700 late in 2001.

Tellabs' future prospects looked bright. The company acquired Future Networks Inc. in March 2001, thereby entering more deeply into the data transmission sector. Future Networks made standards-based voice and cable modem technology. The telecommunications industry remained hard to predict, but Tellabs' resilience was impressive. "Tellabs is used to working in chaos. They thrive on it," an analyst told the *Chicago Tribune*.

Principal Competitors

Alcatel; Lucent Technologies Inc.; Cisco Systems, Inc,; Nortel Networks Corporation.

Further Reading

Cahill, Joseph, "Prowling Tech Predators Put Tellabs on the Hunt," *Crain's Chicago Business*, November 17, 1997.

——, "Tellabs Comes Calling in Two New Markets," *Crain's Chicago Business*, October 7, 1996.

Murphy, H. Lee, "Phone Company Competition Dampens Tellabs' Optimism," *Crain's Chicago Business*, May 3, 1980, p. 37.

Osterland, Andrew, "Oh What a Lovely War," *Financial World Partners*, October 10, 1995.

——, "Phone Lines Dial Up Dollars for Tellabs," *Crain's Chicago Business,* May 2, 1988, p. 35.

Rose, Barbara, "Tellabs Bets on Upturn from New Products," *Crain's Chicago Business,* May 6, 1985, p. 56.

——, "Tellabs, Inc.," *Crain's Chicago Business*, June 7, 2000.

Quintanilla, Carl, "As Domestic Growth Eases, Tellabs Sees Europe As Next Site for Expansion," *Wall Street Journal*, February 14, 1994, p. B6.

Slutsker, Gary, "Goliath, Meet Michael Birck," *Forbes,* December 7, 1992, p. 156.

Van, John, "Tellabs' Footing Grows Stronger on Lucent's Turf," *Chicago Tribune,* February 2, 2001.

Yates, Ronald E., "Tellabs Tough on Indifference: Company Makes Its Workers Feel Part of the Action," *Chicago Tribune,* April 17, 1994, p. 1.

—Maura Troester
—update: Rebecca Stanfel

Terex Corporation

500 Post Road East
Suite 320
Westport, Connecticut 06880
U.S.A.
Telephone: (203) 222-7170
Fax: (203) 222-7976
Web site: http://www.terex.com

Public Company
Incorporated: 1925 as Northwest Engineering Co.
Employees: 6,150
Sales: $2.07 billion (2000)
Stock Exchanges: New York
Ticker Symbol: TEX
NAIC: 333120 Construction Machinery Manufacturing;
    333131 Mining Machinery and Equipment
    Manufacturing; 333923 Overhead Traveling Crane,
    Hoist, and Monorail System Manufacturing; 333924
    Industrial Truck, Tractor, Trailer, and Stacker
    Machinery Manufacturing

Terex Corporation designs, manufactures, and markets a broad range of heavy machinery for the construction, infrastructure, and mining industries. It holds one of the top positions in the United States and the world in several product areas, including telescopic mobile cranes, tower cranes, mobile crushing and screening equipment, off-highway trucks, surface mining trucks, and hydraulic mining shovels. Terex also produces light construction equipment, such as floodlighting systems, concrete mixers, and traffic control products. Just over half of the company's revenues are generated domestically, with about 29 percent deriving from Europe and the remaining 21 percent elsewhere. The company has almost 40 manufacturing facilities located in the United States, Canada, Europe, Australia, Malaysia, and Thailand.

Forged from 1980s Acquisitions

Although the company was founded in 1925 (as Northwest Engineering Co.), Terex Corporation evolved mainly from numerous acquisitions made by Randolph W. Lenz, the company's chief executive from 1983 to 1995. Lenz, an ex-Marine with a degree in psychology from the University of Wisconsin, began buying and selling real estate in the late 1960s. He served as president of Milwaukee-based Ranmar Enterprises, Inc. and the Network Investment Real Estate Corporation, in Brookfield, Wisconsin. It was in 1981 that Lenz moved into heavy-equipment manufacturing, buying the assets of the FWD Corporation, a bankrupt manufacturer of snowplows and fire trucks in Clintonville, Wisconsin.

Based on his success with FWD, Lenz began to follow a calculated strategy of buying distressed companies at fire-sale prices when he bought Northwest Engineering Co. for $1,200 in 1983. Northwest Engineering had been manufacturing cranes, power shovels, and draglines for more than 50 years, but the company had declared bankruptcy and was only three months from liquidation. When Lenz stepped in, however, the company's focus was changed from manufacturing and assembling new equipment to spare parts.

Northwest Engineering, in turn, bought the construction-machinery division of the Pennsylvania-based Bucyrus-Erie Company in March 1985. At its peak, Bucyrus-Erie had employed more than 700 people, but the company had shut down its production lines in 1983, and the employees that remained were concentrating on spare parts and service. Less than a month out of bankruptcy, Northwest Engineering paid less than $9 million for a company with $20 million a year in sales. Lenz then revived the company's defunct Dynahoe product line: the new Bucyrus Construction Products (BCP) division of Northwest Engineering produced its first backhoe loader in November 1985. By 1988, *Industry Week* reported that BCP held a 40 percent share of the market in which its products were sold.

Lenz and Terex came together in 1986 when Northwest Engineering purchased Terex USA from General Motors Corporation. GM had acquired Terex, a builder of heavy-duty earthmoving equipment, in 1953. By 1979, Terex had annual sales in excess of $500 million, and employed more than 5,000 people in the United States, Brazil, and the United Kingdom.

In 1980, in an effort to focus on its automotive business, General Motors agreed to sell Terex to IBH Holding AG, a maker of light- and medium-duty construction equipment in the former Federal Republic of Germany. In 1983, however, IBH Holding filed for bankruptcy, and with pressure from the United Auto Workers, ownership of Terex reverted to General Motors. The company was reorganized as Terex Equipment Limited, a manufacturing subsidiary in Scotland, and Terex USA, a distributor for Terex products in the Western Hemisphere. Terex USA also made some equipment and spare parts at a factory in Ohio.

When Northwest Engineering bought Terex USA in 1986, the agreement included an option to purchase Terex Equipment Limited. Northwest Engineering exercised that option in 1987. Then, in a controversial move, Lenz closed the Terex plant in Ohio, and moved all operations to Scotland. Among the items manufactured by Terex Equipment Limited were articulated dump trucks, wheeled loaders, scrapers, and other large construction vehicles.

In 1987 Northwest Engineering paid $21.9 million for Koehring Cranes & Excavators and Benton Engineering, both acquired from Koehring Co., a subsidiary of AMCA International Finance Corporation. A *Financial World* correspondent reported that Koehring had been losing almost $1 million a month for five years, and declared Lenz was able to "get well-respected Koehring excavators and Lorain crane brand names for a song." Five years later the Terex concern sold what had become the Benton Harbor Engineering Division to pay off debt associated with the Koehring purchase.

The next move for Northwest Engineering came in 1988 when it bought Unit Rig and Equipment Company which was also involved in bankruptcy proceedings. Based in Tulsa, Oklahoma, Unit Rig manufactured Lectra Haul trucks and Dart loaders and haulers. That same year, Lenz changed the company's name to Terex Corporation, and Northwest Engineering became a division of Terex.

A *Forbes* reporter described Terex's rise: "Randolph W. Lenz was an obscure Wisconsin businessman in 1983 when he was struck by a simple idea. Some of the best buyout values in the country, Lenz reasoned, could be found among bankrupt and near-bankrupt manufacturers of earth-moving equipment companies with low prices, cleansed assets and a newly pragmatic work force of survivors. From such down-and-outers Lenz, in just six years, has built Terex Corp."

A *Mergers & Acquisitions* correspondent—to whom Lenz described his strategy as one of "pragmatic opportunity"—outlined what happened after a Terex takeover: "A typical Terex acquisition means hard work after the deal is completed. Once in-house, the new business, typically in the lower technology end of the equipment field, will be streamlined to achieve production efficiencies, eliminate marginal product lines, improve marketing

and reorient the work force toward the revamped operating mode." *Forbes* analysts were more blunt in their assessment, however, stating, "Lenz . . . has methodically consolidated factories, slashed payrolls and shrunk product lines to those few profitable niches that his companies still retain."

Late 1980s and Early 1990s: Acquiring Fruehauf, Nearing Bankruptcy

In 1989 Terex nearly tripled its size with the acquisition of yet another famous brand name. Debt-ridden Fruehauf Corp.—arguably the most recognized brand of trailer in the world—sold its trailer and maritime businesses to Terex for $231 million. Fruehauf had dominated the pre-World War II trucking industry with a market penetration estimated at nearly 90 percent. Despite trucking deregulation, an economic downturn, and increased competition in the early 1980s, Fruehauf was still reporting record annual profits. Fruehauf fell victim, however, to the downside of the 1980s' practice of funding massive growth with high debt.

In 1986 corporate raider Asher Edelman purchased 9.5 percent of Fruehauf's stock—then selling for little more than $20 a share—and announced his intention to take over the company. In order to block the move, Fruehauf borrowed nearly $1.4 billion to buy back its own stock and take the company private. Stockholders who sold their stock for cash received almost $50 per share because of the attempted takeover—Edelman reportedly made a profit of almost $100 million. This left Fruehauf heavily in debt, with interest adding up to more than $100 million per year, substantially more than pre-buyout profits. By 1989, five years after posting record profits, Fruehauf was losing nearly $1 million a week, despite having raised $750 million by selling several of its smaller subsidiaries.

Terex completed its purchase of what was named the Fruehauf Trailer Corporation in July 1989. By September, the wholly owned subsidiary was doing well enough for Terex to pre-pay $19 million in debt, and in 1990, Terex opened a new 100,000-square-foot manufacturing facility in Indianola, Iowa, to build foam-insulated refrigerated vans.

In 1991 Fruehauf trailer operations accounted for nearly two-thirds of Terex's $784 million in sales. Terex also took Fruehauf public in 1991 with an initial public offering of four million shares, and began a program to convert its most effective company-owned distribution branches in the United States into independent dealerships. Fruehauf, however, incurred heavy losses in 1991 and 1992, primarily attributed to a worldwide economic slowdown.

Two other Terex acquisitions were completed in the early 1990s. Terex added Mark Industries to its Heavy Equipment Group in 1991. The company, based in Brea, California, manufactured aerial lift equipment, including scissor lifts and boom lifts, used in construction, repair, and maintenance work in many industries. In 1992 Terex added perhaps the best-known brand of forklifts and lift trucks to its Materials Handling Group with the purchase of the material handling division of Clark Equipment Company.

Clark invented the forklift in 1928. When Terex bought the line in 1992, Clark forklifts and lift trucks were the top selling brand in North America. The Clark Material Handling Com-

---

Key Dates:
1925: Northwest Engineering Co., manufacturer of cranes, power shovels, and draglines, is founded.
1983: Randolph W. Lenz buys Northwest Engineering, which had declared bankruptcy.
1986: Northwest buys Terex USA, distributor of heavy-duty earthmoving equipment, from General Motors Corporation.
1987: Northwest buys Terex Equipment Limited, the manufacturing sister of Terex USA, and Koehring Cranes & Excavators, through which the company enters the crane market.
1988: Northwest changes its name to Terex Corporation.
1989: Terex buys the trailer and maritime businesses of Fruehauf Corp., which begins operating as a subsidiary called Fruehauf Trailer Corporation.
1991: Fruehauf is taken public.
1992: Terex acquires Clark Equipment Company's material handling division, maker of forklifts and lift trucks.
1993: Company divests its majority holding in Fruehauf; Ronald M. DeFeo is named president and COO and begins a restructuring effort.
1995: Acquisition of PPM Cranes makes Terex one of the leading makers of hydraulic cranes in the world.
1996: Terex divests Clark Material Handling.
1997: Crane operations are bolstered through acquisitions of Simon Engineering plc's Simon Access division and Baraga Products Inc.
1998: O&K Mining GmbH, a German maker of large hydraulic mining shovels, is acquired.
1999: Terex acquires Powerscreen International plc, a maker of crushing and screening equipment, and Cedarapids, Inc., maker of mobile crushing and screening equipment and asphalt pavers; company enters the light construction equipment sector with the purchase of Amida Industries, Inc.
2000: Company acquires Fermec Manufacturing Limited, a U.K.-based maker of loader backhoes.

pany, with a worldwide network of independent dealers, was also a leading manufacturer and distributor of forklifts in the European market.

Soon after the purchase, Terex moved to solidify its leadership in the North American market by shifting production of its internal combustion forklift trucks from Korea to Lexington, Kentucky. At the same time, Terex announced plans to invest $25 million between 1992 and 1995 to improve its forklifts and lift-trucks with advanced ergonomic features and reduced noise levels. Clark Material Handling continued to build forklifts in Korea—in a partnership formed with Samsung in 1986—to serve the Asian market.

Despite its success in revitalizing financially troubled companies, several financial analysts in the early 1990s were concerned about Terex's ability to cope with the enormous debt it had assumed in amassing its acquisitions. At the end of 1991,

Terex had long-term debt of $189.3 million. With the truck trailer industry experiencing its worst year since 1983, along with stiff price competition among manufacturers, Terex also had a net loss for that year of $33.4 million. Some analysts urged Terex to issue more stock and use the proceeds to pay off some if its long-term debt. As Michael K. Ozanian assessed in *Financial World*, "With its track record, Wall Street would love to buy Terex equity, particularly if the proceeds were used to retire debt." Lenz, however, reportedly did not want to dilute his own holdings and resisted that measure.

Terex posted another loss of $61.1 million on revenues of $1.01 billion in 1992, a year in which the company teetered on the brink of bankruptcy. The following year proved to be a pivotal one, as Terex finally divested itself of its majority control of Fruehauf and installed new management. Ronald M. DeFeo was named president and COO of the company in October of that year and was charged with turning the company around. DeFeo had joined Terex in May 1992 as head of the heavy equipment group. Prior to that he had spent eight years at Tenneco Inc., where he was a senior executive of that firm's J.I. Case Company unit, a maker of farm and construction equipment.

Mid-1990s and Beyond: Sharp Turnaround and Acquisitions-Led Growth Under DeFeo

One of DeFeo's first actions was to turn around the fortunes of Clark Material Handling, which was a bloated operation in 1993 when it lost $30 million on sales of $400 million. Among the cost-cutting initiatives undertaken at Clark were the closure of three of the company's five manufacturing plants and the slashing of 760 jobs from the 1,700-person payroll. By 1996 Clark had been returned to profitability, and Terex was able to offload it to a management-led investment group for $139.5 million, posting a capital gain in the process. Proceeds were used to help pare down the company's still-high debt load.

Under DeFeo, who was named CEO in 1995 (succeeding Lenz), Terex began focusing on two areas: cranes and off-road trucks for the construction and mining industries. Terex Cranes was formed in 1995 following the acquisition of PPM Cranes from Legris Industries S.A. of France. The addition of PPM made Terex one of the leading makers of hydraulic cranes in the world. In 1996 Terex had its first solid year of profitability since the 1980s, reporting net income of $47.7 million on revenues of $678.5 million. Company-wide cost-cutting initiatives and a more focused product line had clearly paid dividends in the form of an impressive financial turnaround.

A revitalized Terex turned aggressively acquisitive in the final years of the 20th century. The company's crane operations were bolstered in 1997 with the purchase of Simon Engineering plc's Simon Access division and Baraga Products Inc. These additions increased Terex's share of the North American crane market to 35 percent, compared to the 9 percent figure of 1993. The broad product line of Terex Cranes now included hydraulic cranes, aerial work platforms, and rough-terrain lift trucks. The purchase of Holland Lift International B.V. in May 1998 added another manufacturer of aerial work platforms, while the July 1998 purchase of the American Crane Corporation brought Terex a maker of lattice boom cranes. Two tower crane manufacturers, Peiner HTS of Germany and Gru Comedi S.p.A. of Italy, were acquired in the final two months of 1998.

Terex's largest acquisitions in the late 1990s, however, were in its earthmoving equipment business. In March 1998 Terex spent about $168 million for O&K Mining GmbH, a German maker of large hydraulic mining shovels with annual revenues of about $265 million. In July 1999 the company acquired Powerscreen International plc, a maker of crushing and screening equipment for the quarrying, construction, and demolition industries based in Dungannon, Northern Ireland. The purchase price was about $294 million for a firm with annual sales of $370 million. One month later, Terex paid $170 million to Raytheon Company for Cedarapids, Inc., whose product line included mobile crushing and screening equipment, asphalt pavers, and asphalt material mixing plants. A smaller earthmoving acquisition was also completed in 1998, that of Payhauler Corp., producer of heavy-duty off-road dump trucks.

The acquisition of Amida Industries, Inc. in April 1999 marked Terex's entrance into the light construction equipment sector. Based in Rock Hill, South Carolina, Amida manufactured light towers, equipment used to create concrete surfaces, and traffic control products, such as directional arrowboards. Terex's acquisition spree—which amounted to the spending of nearly $700 million from 1995 to 1999 to acquire 13 companies—helped increase the company's revenues to $1.86 billion and net income to $172.9 million by 1999. Also aiding in the company's resurgence were a number of major supply contracts received by Terex's earthmoving operations, including deals with three major mining firms: Coal India, U.K.-based Rio Tinto, and Cleveland-Cliffs Inc. of the United States.

During 2000 Terex sold its truck-mounted forklift businesses, most of which had been acquired only the previous year, to Partek Corporation of Finland for $144 million. The proceeds were used to reduce long-term debt, which because of the string of acquisitions had grown to $1.16 billion by the end of 1999. In late 2000 Terex divested its European aerial work platform operations. Acquisitions around the turn of the millennium included Coleman Engineering, Inc., a maker of light towers and power generators for the construction market, which became part of the Terex Light Construction division; and Fermec Manufacturing Limited, a U.K.-based maker of loader backhoes that was purchased from CNH Global N.V. Revenues for 2000 increased to $2.07 billion but net income declined to $95.1 million as an economic slowdown had a negative effect on the mining and construction industries. Despite this setback and the uncertainties surrounding the economic climate of the early 21st century, Terex had made a remarkable comeback from the brink of oblivion in a short span of years and with its lean operating structure seemed well-positioned to weather future economic downturns.

Principal Subsidiaries

The American Crane Corporation; American Crane International B.V. (Netherlands); Amida Industries, Inc.; BCP Construction Products, Inc.; Benford America, Inc.; Benford Limited (U.K.); BL - Pegson (USA), Inc.; BL - Pegson Limited (U.K.); Brimont S.A. (France); Brown Lenox & Co. Limited (U.K.); Bucyrus Construction Products, Inc.; C.P.V. (UK) Ltd.; C.P.V. Refurbishing Ltd. (Ireland); Cedarapids, Inc.; Cliffmere Limited (U.K.); CMP Limited (U.K.); Coleman Engineering Inc.; Comet Coalification Limited (U.K.); Container Design Ltd. (Ireland); Container Engineering Ireland Limited; Containers & Pressure Vessels Limited (Ireland); Crookhall Coal Company Limited (U.K.); EarthKing, Inc.; Energy and Mineral Processing Limited (U.K.); Fermec International Ltd. (U.K.); Fermec Trustee Ltd. (U.K.); Fermec Holding Ltd. (U.K.); Fermec Manufacturing Ltd. (U.K.); Fermec S.A. (France); Fermec North America Ltd. (U.K.); Finlay (Site Handlers) Limited (N. Ireland); Finlay Block Machinery Limited (N. Ireland); Finlay Hydrascreen USA, Inc.; Finlay Hydrascreens (Omagh) Limited (N. Ireland); Finlay Plant (UK) Ltd.; Foray 827 Limited (U.K.); Fyne Limited (U.K.); Fyne Machineries Limited (U.K.); Gatewood Engineers Limited (U.K.); Gru Comedil S.p.A. (Italy); Holland Lift International B.V. (Netherlands); IMACO Blackwood Hodge Group Limited (U.K.); IMACO Blackwood Hodge Limited (U.K.); IMACO Trading Limited (U.K.); Industrial Conveyor's Sdn Bhd (Malaysia); International Machinery Company Limited (U.K.); J.C. Abbott & Co. Ltd. (U.K.); Jaques (Singapore) Pte Ltd; Jaques (Thailand) Limited; Jaques International Limited (Hong Kong); Jaques International Pty. Ltd. (Australia); Jaques International Sdn Bhd (Malaysia); John Finlay (Engineering) Limited (N. Ireland); Keir & Cawder (Engineering) Limited (U.K.); Koehring Cranes, Inc.; Kueken (UK) Ltd.; Matbro (N.I.) Limited (N. Ireland); Moffett Engineering GmbH (Germany); Moffett Iberica S.A. (Spain); New Terex Holdings UK Limited; NGW Supplies Limited (U.K.); O & K Mining GmbH (Germany); O & K Orenstein & Koppel (South Africa) Pty. Ltd.; O & K Orenstein & Koppel Limited (U.K.); O & K Orenstein & Koppel, Inc.; O & K Orenstein & Koppel, Inc. (Canada); Orenstein & Koppel Australia Pty Ltd.; Payhauler Corp.; Pegson Group Limited (U.K.); Pegson Limited (U.K.); Picadilly Maschinenhandels GmbH & Co. KG (Germany); PiCo Real Estate, Inc.; Powerscreen (G.B.) Limited (U.K.); Powerscreen Holdings USA, Inc.; Powerscreen International (Canada) ULC; Powerscreen International (UK) Limited; Powerscreen International Distribution Limited (N. Ireland); Powerscreen International LLC; Powerscreen International plc (U.K.); Powerscreen Limited (Ireland); Powerscreen Manufacturing Limited (N. Ireland); Powerscreen North America Inc.; Powerscreen USA LLC; Powerscreen USC, Inc.; Powersizer Limited (U.K.); PPM Cranes, Inc.; PPM Deutschland GmbH Terex Cranes (Germany); PPM Far East Ltd. (Singapore); PPM S.A.S. (France); Precision Powertrain (UK) Limited; Progressive Components, Inc.; R&R Limited (U.K.); Rhaeader Colliery Co. Limited (U.K.); Royer Industries, Inc.; Sempurna Enterprise (Malaysia) Sdn Bhd; Simon-Tomen Engineering Co., Ltd. (Japan); Sim-Tech Management Limited (Hong Kong); Standard Havens Products, Inc.; Standard Havens, Inc.; Sure Equipment (Sales) Limited (U.K.); Sure Equipment (Scotland) Limited (U.K.); Sure Equipment (Southern) Limited (U.K.); Sure Equipment Group Limited (U.K.); Terex (Mining) Australia Pty. Ltd.; Terex Aerials Limited (Ireland); Terex Aerials, Inc.; Terex Australia Pty. Ltd.; Terex Aviation Ground Equipment, Inc.; Terex Bartell, Inc.; Terex Bartell, Ltd. (Canada); Terex Cranes (Australia) Pty. Ltd.; Terex Cranes, Inc.; Terex Equipment Limited (U.K.); Terex Espana, S.l. (Spain); Terex European Holdings B.V. (Netherlands); Terex Finance, Inc.; Terex International Financial Services Co. (N. Ireland); Terex Italia

S.r.l. (Italy); Terexlift S.r.l. (Italy); Terex Lifting Australia Pty. Ltd. (South Africa); Terex Lifting U.K. Limited; Terex Mining Equipment, Inc.; Terex Netherlands Holdings B.V.; Terex of Western Michigan, Inc.; Terex Peiner GmbH (Germany); Terex Real Property, Inc.; Terex UK Limited; Terex West Coast, Inc.; Terex-RO Corporation; Terex-Telelect, Inc.; Tower Cranes, Inc.; Unit Rig (Canada) Ltd.; Unit Rig (South Africa) Pty. Ltd.

Principal Divisions

Terex Lifting; Terex Earthmoving; Terex Light Construction.

Principal Competitors

Caterpillar Inc.; Ingersoll-Rand Company; Deere & Company; Sumitomo Corp.; CNH Global N.V.; The Manitowoc Company, Inc.; Komatsu Ltd.; Metso Corporation; Allen Engineering Corp.; Allmand Brothers Inc.; Altec Industries Inc.; Astec Industries, Inc.; CMI Corporation; Gencor Corporation; Genie Industries; Grove Worldwide LLC; Hitachi, Ltd.; JCB Service; JLG Industries, Inc.; Kalmar Industries Oy Ab; Legris Industries; Liebherr-International AG; Link-Belt Construction Equipment Co.; Mannesmann AG; Multiquip Inc.; OmniQuip International, Inc.; Potain S.A.; Svedala Industri AB; UpRight Inc.; AB Volvo; Wacker Corp.

Further Reading

Bishop, Phil, ''Growing Pains: The North American Mobile Crane Market Is Going Through Some Interesting Changes,'' *Cranes Today,* November 2000, pp. 14+.

Brezonick, Mike, ''The Quiet Resurrection of Terex Corp.,'' *Diesel Progress North American Edition,* March 2000, p. 34.

Davies, Carole, ''Good-Bye Fruehauf,'' *Ward's Auto World,* January 1990.

Dzikowski, Don, ''Terex to Increase Sales, Expand Manufacturing Operations,'' *Fairfield County Business Journal,* April 21, 1997, p. 14.

Fairclough, Gordon, ''Terex's Fortunes Improve After Tough Cost-Cutting,'' *Wall Street Journal,* September 30, 1997, p. B4.

Mercer, Mike, ''Terex Quietly Continues Its Surge,'' *Diesel Progress North American Edition,* September 1999, pp. 24+.

Ozanian, Michael K., ''Strip Show,'' *Financial World,* March 19, 1991.

Pachuta, Michael J., ''New Contracts, Products Boost Terex in Mining, Construction,'' *Investor's Business Daily,* May 6, 1999.

Reiff, Rick, ''Parlaying the Winnings,'' *Forbes,* July 24, 1989.

''The Rise and Rise of Terex Corporation,'' *Construction Equipment News,* November 1999, pp. 10–12.

Sandler, Larry, ''Lenz, KCS Paid Millions by Terex and Fruehauf,'' *Milwaukee Sentinel,* June 11, 1992, p. 1D.

——, ''Terex Ends Control of Fruehauf,'' *Milwaukee Sentinel,* March 23, 1993, p. 1D.

——, ''Terex to Close Headquarters in Green Bay: Company to Have Base in Tulsa,'' *Milwaukee Sentinel,* March 17, 1993.

''The Terex Prescription,'' *Mergers and Acquisitions,* January/February 1990.

''Terex Rumbles On,'' *Engineering News Review,* August 28, 1986.

Verespej, Michael A., ''From 'Exile' to Profitability,'' *Industry Week,* August 15, 1988.

Wiley, Royallen, ''A Casualty of the Debt-Crazed '80s,'' *Management Accounting,* March 1991.

Yengst, Charles R., ''Once on Shaky Ground, Terex Corp. Now Enjoying Fruits of Well-Managed Turnaround,'' *Diesel Progress North American Edition,* September 1997, p. 4.

—Dean Boyer
—update: David E. Salamie

TOSHIBA

Toshiba Corporation

1-1, Shibaura 1-chome
Minato-ku
Tokyo 105-8001
Japan
Telephone: (03) 3457-2096
Fax: (03) 5444-9202
Web site: http://www.toshiba.co.jp

Public Company
Incorporated: 1939 as Tokyo Shibaura Electric Company, Ltd.
Employees: 190,870
Sales: ¥5.75 trillion ($54.24 billion) (2000)
Stock Exchanges: Tokyo Osaka Nagoya Fukuoka Sapporo Niigata London Luxembourg Amsterdam Frankfurt Düsseldorf Paris Swiss
NAIC: 234930 Industrial Nonbuilding Structure Construction; 333314 Photographic & Photocopying Equipment Mfg.; 333415 Air-Conditioning & Warm Air Heating Equipment & Commercial & Industrial Refrigeration Equipment Mfg.; 333611 Turbine & Turbine Generator Set Unit Mfg.; 333921 Elevator & Moving Stairway Mfg.; 334111 Electronic Computer Mfg.; 334112 Computer Storage Device Mfg.; 334119 Other Computer Peripheral Equipment Mfg.; 334210 Telephone Apparatus Mfg.; 334220 Radio & Television Broadcasting & Wireless Communications Equipment Mfg.; 334290 Other Communications Equipment Mfg.; 334310 Audio & Video Equipment Mfg.; 334411 Electron Tube Mfg.; 334412 Bare Printed Circuit Board Mfg.; 334413 Semiconductor & Related Device Mfg.; 334419 Other Electronic Component Mfg.; 334510 Electromedical & Electrotherapeutic Apparatus Mfg.; 335121 Residential Electric Lighting Fixture Mfg.; 335211 Electric Housewares & Household Fan Mfg.; 335212 Household Vacuum Cleaner Mfg.; 335222 Household Refrigerator & Home Freezer Mfg.; 335224 Household Laundry Equipment Mfg.; 335312 Motor & Generator Mfg.; 335911 Storage Battery Mfg.

Toshiba Corporation is one of Japan's oldest and largest producers of consumer and industrial electric and electronic products. In addition to its position as the world's leading maker of notebook personal computers, Toshiba is among the global leaders in semiconductors and LCDs. More than 60 percent of the company's net sales are derived domestically, with about 16 percent from North America, 11 percent from Asia (not including Japan), and 10 percent from Europe. Toshiba is considered one of Japan's *sogo denki,* or general electric companies, a group that is typically said to also include Fujitsu, Hitachi, Mitsubishi Electric, and NEC Corporation. With a history that dates back to the 19th century and a product line that extends from semiconductors and electromedical devices to consumer electronics, home appliances, and nuclear power plants, Toshiba has played an active role in Japan's rise to the forefront of international business.

Two-Pronged Electric Equipment Roots

Toshiba was formed through the 1939 union of two manufacturers of electrical equipment, Shibaura Seisaku-sho (Shibaura Engineering Works) and Tokyo Electric Company, Ltd. The older of the two, Shibaura, traced its roots to Japan's first telegraph equipment shop, Tanaka Seizo-sho (Tanaka Engineering Works). Hisashige Tanaka, who has been called the "Edison of Japan," established the business in 1875. The business climate in which the company began, however, was far from the atmosphere in which it later operated. During the late 19th century, Japan lagged far behind Britain, France, Germany, and the United States in industrial development. Besieged with economic problems resulting from the overthrow of the Tokugawa government in 1869 and a tremendous influx of imported goods and machinery that threatened her fledgling industries, Japan was vulnerable to colonization. Confronted with the task of strengthening its faltering industries, the new government was quick to respond.

In October 1870 the Ministry of Industry (Kobusho) was formed and subsequently acted as a catalyst for the country's industrial development. In its attempt to integrate contemporary technologies into Japan, the government concentrated on hiring foreign engineers, technicians, and scientists to instruct domes-

---

Company Perspectives:

Basic Commitment of the Toshiba Group: We, the Toshiba Group companies, based on our total commitment to people and to the future, are determined to help create a higher quality of life for all people, and to do our part to help ensure that progress continues within the world community.

Commitment to People: We endeavor to serve the needs of all people, especially our customers, shareholders, and employees, by implementing forward-looking corporate strategies while carrying out responsible and responsive business activities. As good corporate citizens, we actively contribute to further the goals of society.

Commitment to the Future: By continually developing innovative technologies centering on the fields of Electronics and Energy, we strive to create products and services that enhance human life, and which lead to a thriving, healthy society. We constantly seek new approaches that help realize the goals of the world community, including ways to improve the global environment.

---

tic engineers in operating imported machinery; the government also sent its own engineers abroad to inspect manufacturing techniques with the intent of selecting machinery and manufacturing techniques for use in Japanese industries.

The integration of foreign technologies was first put into practice by Tanaka Seizo-sho. The company's 1,300-horsepower steam engine, copied from blueprints of an English counterpart, was successfully constructed in a plant in Kanebo, Japan. This venture convinced Japanese industrialists of their potential for technological advancement through the adoption of foreign technology and its adaptation to domestic skills and resources.

Tanaka Seizo-sho embraced this concept in the 1880s, determining that paying outright for technological knowledge was the most expedient means to upgrade its technological capabilities. This strategy helped the company expand into the manufacture of transformers, electric motors, and other heavy electric equipment in the 1890s.

Tanaka Seizo-sho made its own discoveries as well during this period, originating Japan's first hydroelectric generators in 1894. By 1902 the company's own technological capabilities had produced a 150-kilowatt three-phase-current dynamo for the Yokosuka Bay Arsenal, marking one of the initial transformations from foreign to Japanese-based technology, and the beginning of the company's rise to the forefront of international business. The company, which adopted the name Shibaura Seisaku-sho in 1904, developed Japan's first X-ray tubes in 1915.

While Shibaura and other Japanese corporations were growing in strength and increasing their capabilities, they were deeply debilitated by the advent of World War I. As the war began, Japanese manufacturers were cut off from Germany, England, and the United States, major suppliers of machines, industrial materials, and chemicals, forcing them to turn to one another for necessary materials and machinery to keep their fledgling industries alive. The hardships experienced during this period had long-term advantages, however, for they forced

Japanese industry into self-sufficiency and paved the way for the country's industrial advancement.

Shibaura continued to grow in the interim between world wars, and merged with the Tokyo Electric Company, Ltd. in 1939. Tokyo Electric had also been established before the turn of the 20th century. Originally known as Hakunetsu-sha & Company before adopting the Tokyo Electric name in 1899, the firm was founded in 1890 by Dr. Ichisuke Fujioka and Shoichi Miyoshi. Hakunetsu-sha had distinguished itself as Japan's first manufacturer of incandescent lamps. The newly merged company, named Tokyo Shibaura Electric Company, Ltd., soon became widely known as Toshiba (the company officially adopted the name Toshiba Corporation in 1978). The company's pre-World War II Japanese innovations included fluorescent lamps and radar.

Flourishing Then Faltering in Postwar Period

During the late 1940s, Japan rapidly passed from a period of self-isolation and self-reliance into a period of largely benevolent occupation and advocacy. With the assistance of the Japanese government and its citizens, the American Occupation Authority instituted social and economic reforms, and poured resources into postwar financial markets. Japan's readmittance into the international trading community gave it access to overseas markets for manufactured goods and raw materials. The glut of raw materials available at the time enabled Japan to obtain necessary commodities in large quantities at favorable prices and, consequently, to regain its financial and industrial strength.

In this more favorable climate, Toshiba once again began to flourish. The company's shares were first listed on the Tokyo Stock and Osaka Securities Exchanges in 1949. Backed by the powerful trading house of the Mitsui Group, the company's financial status was well secured. Starting in the 1950s, Toshiba began a program to strengthen its competitiveness in both the domestic and international markets. The company produced Japan's first broadcasting equipment in 1952, launched Japan's first digital computers in 1954, and developed Japan's first microwave ovens in 1959.

Yet it would be some time before modern business policies affected the company in any fundamental way. Toshiba executives were criticized for their rigid adherence to a feudal system of hierarchy and status. Top officials maintained lax working hours and were far removed from any operational business. An indisputable separation between a superior and his subordinates made the exchange of ideas virtually impossible. To reduce the burden of responsibility on any one executive, numerous signatures were needed to approve a document. Thus innovation was easily stymied in a chain of bureaucracy.

In the early 1960s, these internal problems were compounded by an economic recession. In one year Toshiba's pretax profits slid from $36 million to $13 million. To halt any further erosion, a radical change was in order. For only the second time in Toshiba's history the company sought an outsider to aid the ailing business. The company's board hired Toshiwo Doko to take charge of the company. Doko had won acclaim as the architect of the 1960 merger of Ishikawajima

Key Dates:

1875: Hisashige Tanaka establishes Japan's first telegraph equipment shop, Tanaka Seizo-sho.

1890: Hakunetsu-sha & Company is founded as Japan's first manufacturer of incandescent lamps.

1899: Hakunetsu-sha is renamed Tokyo Electric Company, Ltd.

1904: Tanaka Seizo-sho is renamed Shibaura Seisaku-sho.

1939: Tokyo Electric and Shibaura merge to form Tokyo Shibaura Electric Company, Ltd.

1949: Company's shares are first listed on the Tokyo and Osaka exchanges.

1954: Company produces Japan's first digital computers.

1978: Company is renamed Toshiba Corporation.

1985: Toshiba develops the first one-megabyte DRAM memory chip.

1986: Company begins producing laptop personal computers.

1987: The sale of submarine sound-deadening equipment to the then communist Soviet Union by a subsidiary half-owned by Toshiba leads to a U.S. Senate vote banning the import of Toshiba products for three years and the resignation of the company president and chairman.

1995: Toshiba, in partnership with Time Warner, develops the format for DVDs that becomes the industry standard.

1996: Company introduces its first DVD players and DVD drives for computers.

1998: Major restructuring is launched.

1999: Toshiba settles a U.S. class-action lawsuit over an allegedly faulty floppy disc drive in its laptops, agreeing to pay $1.1 billion.

Heavy Industries and Harima Shipbuilding & Engineering Company, which formed the world's largest shipbuilder, IHI.

When he joined Toshiba as president in 1965, Doko retained his title as chairman of IHI. The combined status ranked Doko as Japan's leading industrialist. These two companies had shared interests prior to Doko's appointment at Toshiba; IHI owned over ten million shares in Toshiba and Toshiba controlled over four million shares in IHI. After Doko became president, Toshiba raised its stake in IHI as both companies shared executives on their boards and established trade agreements. This exchange, a *keiretsu* hallmark, strengthened Toshiba's financial standing.

Doko's other corrective measures included the reduction of Toshiba's dependence on borrowed capital. This was aided by the U.S.-based General Electric Company's agreement to purchase all of Toshiba's capital issue. General Electric's interest in Toshiba dated back to before World War II, but had declined in the intervening years. The infusion of capital enabled Toshiba to expand and modernize its operations.

The new company president also initiated a comprehensive campaign to export Toshiba products around the world. By establishing independent departments, the company could better facilitate the export of consumer and industrial goods. Major contracts were finalized with U.S. companies to export generators, transformers, and motors, as well as televisions and home appliances.

Other streamlining efforts took the form of expanding the sales force, hiring new management, and consolidating operations. By 1967 Toshiba controlled 63 subsidiaries and employed more than 100,000 people; the company ranked as the largest electronic manufacturer in Japan and the nation's fourth largest company. But in light of the dramatic expansion of such domestic competitors as Sony Corporation and Hitachi in the 1970s, Toshiba's performance was generally considered mediocre.

Emphasizing Semiconductors, Computers, and Consumer Electronics in the 1980s

In 1980, a new president, Shoichi Saba, brought renewed vigor to the company. Trained as an electrical engineer, Saba funneled vast resources into research and development, especially in the areas of semiconductors, computers, and telecommunications. In October 1984, Toshiba formed an Information and Communications Systems Laboratory to develop and integrate office automation products. That same year, Toshiba was responsible for the world's first direct broadcast satellite. The company's R&D investment paid off handsomely in 1985, when Toshiba won the global race to develop the first one-megabyte DRAM memory chip. By 1987 the company was producing almost half of the world's one-megabyte chips.

Utilized in equipment from stereos to computers, semiconductors soon became an important part of Toshiba's portfolio. In 1986 alone, Toshiba's semiconductor facilities experienced a 55 percent increase due to contracts in France and West Germany, as well as burgeoning domestic demand. For the first time in its history, Toshiba surpassed its closest competitor, Hitachi, to become the second largest semiconductor manufacturer in the world, behind NEC Corporation.

Joint ventures and agreements with both Japanese and foreign corporations facilitated technology exchange. In 1986 Toshiba entered into a joint venture with Motorola for its Japanese production of computer memories and microprocessors. The two companies became involved in the collective development of microcomputer and memory chips based on the exchange of technology, and also developed a manufacturing facility in Japan. Efforts of this type facilitated the development of voice recognition systems and digital private branch exchange systems (PBXs), which transmit telephone calls within private buildings. Through a 1986 agreement with AT&T, Toshiba began marketing these systems throughout Japan, as well as assisting that corporation with technological insight.

In the same year, Toshiba entered into an agreement with IBM-Japan to market their general purpose computers domestically. Through this arrangement, Toshiba marketed its own communications equipment with IBM-Japan's computers, selling to governmental agencies, local governments, and other institutions to which IBM (as a foreign interest) had previously been blocked. An additional marketing contract with IBM introduced the first PC-compatible laptop computer, the TJ3100, to

Japan, and met with great success. By 1991, Toshiba had garnered over one-fifth of the laptop market.

The area for which Toshiba became best known was its consumer products division, which grew at a rapid pace in the 1980s through acquisition and innovation. In April 1984 Toshiba reorganized the production, marketing, and research and development sections of its video and audio products, incorporating them into one centralized location. While sales of standard consumer products such as VCRs, compact disc players, televisions, and personal cassette recorders continued to grow, Toshiba was quick to capitalize on new markets as well. In 1986 the company entered the home video market, creating a wholly owned subsidiary and introducing 110 new video titles to the Japanese market. That same year, it inked an agreement to supply cable equipment to American Television and Communications Corporation.

Although Toshiba was best known in America for its computer-related and consumer products, it had a wide range of additional business ventures. Among Japanese corporations, Toshiba was a leader in the production of advanced medical electronic equipment. In 1986 the corporation initiated the supply of blood chemical analyzers, used to detect liver and kidney disease, to Allied Corporation, a leading U.S. chemical manufacturer. Other accomplishments suggested Toshiba's technological foresight in solving global and domestic problems. Toshiba began production of equipment for uranium fuel enrichment for use in nuclear power plants, marking an important step towards Japan's acquisition of a domestic nuclear fuel supply.

These many successes realized under Shoichi Saba were overshadowed by a 1987 scandal involving Toshiba Machine, a subsidiary half-owned by Toshiba. According to Washington sources, the subsidiary sold submarine sound-deadening equipment to the then communist Soviet Union. The equipment made detection more difficult and forced NATO to modernize its antisubmarine detection equipment. While Toshiba claimed that it was not able to control the subsidiary's daily operations, the sale broke a Western law concerning the sale of technologically advanced equipment to Communist countries. Two executives at the subsidiary under investigation were arrested and four top-ranking officials resigned. The Japanese government prohibited the subsidiary from exporting products to the Soviet Union for one year and repealed its right to sponsor visas for visiting personnel from Eastern-bloc countries. Amid growing protests in both Japan and the United States, Toshiba President Sugichiro Watari issued a public apology to the United States. Then, on July 1, 1987, both Watari and Chairman Shoichi Saba tendered their resignations from the Toshiba Corporation in the wake of a U.S. Senate vote to ban the import of Toshiba products for three years. Joichi Aoi, a former senior executive vice-president, assumed Toshiba's presidency.

Ironically, the anti-Japan mood roused by this episode may have revitalized morale at Toshiba. Perhaps to compensate for the loss of the U.S. market, Chairman Aoi led the company's energetic expansion into global markets. In the latter years of the 1980s, Toshiba began offering its integrated circuit technology to the Chinese Electronics Import and Export Corporation to assist in development of television production. A 1991 joint venture with General Electric furthered this effort, with a special emphasis on large home appliances. The company also won a contract worth ¥12 billion to build a color television assembly plant in Russia, marking Moscow's first agreement of this nature with a Japanese company. Thus, in spite of losing up to ¥5 billion as a result of the U.S. embargo, the company's net income nearly doubled, from ¥61 billion in 1987 to ¥121 billion in 1990. Toshiba's fiscal triumphs were capped with the 1991 naming of chairman Joichi Aoi as Asia's CEO of the Year.

Restructuring in the Difficult 1990s

But with the new decade came new economic imperatives, especially those created by a global recession and the rising value of the yen. While Toshiba's annual revenues remained essentially flat from 1990 to 1994, the electronics giant's profits declined more than 90 percent to ¥12 billion, their lowest level in well over a decade.

Toshiba Chairman Aoi and President Fumio Sato employed a variety of strategies in the hopes of reversing this downward course. A 1993 reorganization focused on fostering interaction between and flexibility among the company's hundreds of operations. In line with industry trends, the leaders worked to shorten product development cycles, lower production expenses, and more closely monitor consumer demands. They also moved to further diversify Toshiba's consumer product line, 50 percent of which was still in color televisions. The company worked to shift its emphasis to such high-potential products as cellular communications, multimedia, and mobile electronics. Amid all these changes, however, the company planned to continue its liberal use of strategic alliances for mutual benefit.

One of the company's key alliances in the early 1990s was with Time Warner Inc. In 1992 Toshiba spent $500 million for a 5.6 percent stake in Time Warner Entertainment, a subsidiary of Time Warner that owned cable television systems, Home Box Office, and Warner Bros. studios. The two companies began developing an industry standard for DVDs, or digital videodisks, CD-like disks capable of holding full-length films for play on television screens via players. By the mid-1990s, the Toshiba/Time Warner format became the industry standard, beating out a rival format developed by Sony and Philips. Toshiba then introduced its first DVD players and DVD drives for computers in 1996, becoming the first company to do so. In another alliance with a U.S. firm, Toshiba and IBM agreed to spend $1.2 billion to build a plant in the United States where 64-megabit DRAM memory chips would be made.

In June 1996 Taizo Nishimuro took over as president of Toshiba. With a background in marketing and multimedia Nishimuro became the first chief not to have an engineering background. The new president already faced the difficulty of contending with a Japanese economy in a prolonged state of stagnation, a situation soon compounded by the fallout from the Asian economic crisis, which erupted in mid-1997. The company's consumer electronics and semiconductor sectors, facing fierce international competition, were buffeted by sharp declines in prices and demand. As a result, for the fiscal year ending in March 1999, Toshiba suffered its first net loss in 23 years, a loss totaling ¥13.9 billion ($112.9 million).

In September 1998, even before these dismal results were released, Toshiba unveiled a multiyear restructuring plan that was radical by Japanese standards. About 6,500 jobs would be trimmed by March 2000 through attrition and hiring cutbacks. The most dramatic changes were a wide-ranging restructuring of operations. The company began placing some of its more peripheral businesses into joint ventures with other firms. In January 1999 its glassmaking subsidiary (a direct descendant of one of the company's founding light bulb businesses) was merged with a subsidiary of Asahi Glass. Another of Toshiba's early business areas, electric motors, was the subject of another tie-up that same month, when the company and Mitsubishi Electric merged their large electric motor divisions into a joint venture called TMA Electric Corporation. In the area of nuclear fuel operations, Toshiba joined with General Electric Company and Hitachi to form Global Nuclear Fuel in January 2000. Yet another joint venture was formed with Carrier Corporation of the United States in the area of air conditioners. Toshiba also sold certain noncore units outright, such as its domestic automated teller machine business, which was bought by Oki Electric Industry Co., Ltd. in April 1999.

Another key move was the reorganization of the company's 15 rambling divisions into eight business groups (or ''in-house companies''), each of which was given more independence and autonomy. The new structure was designed to speed decision-making at what had been a fairly bureaucratic company, and for the same reason the size of the firm's board of directors was reduced from 34 to 12. The number of subsidiaries and affiliates was also drastically reduced from about 1,000 to 300. Aiming to place a greater emphasis on corporate profitability, Toshiba began to link executive pay more closely to performance. In another move to enhance profitability, the company adopted on a wide basis the Six Sigma quality approach made famous by General Electric and its longtime head, Jack Welch, leading to $1.3 billion in cost savings by 2000. Finally, at a company that had traditionally been engineer-focused, and where engineers essentially designed products for themselves, a new emphasis was placed on customer-driven new product development.

In the midst of implementing this sweeping reorganization, Toshiba suffered a potentially major setback when it decided to settle a class-action lawsuit that had been brought against the company in the United States over an allegedly faulty floppy disc drive used in more than five million Toshiba laptop computers. Although Toshiba denied that it was liable for the problem and said that there was no evidence that any data had been lost or corrupted due to the problem, Nishimuro decided to settle the suit, fearing that a jury trial could result in a judgment approaching $10 billion—potentially bankrupting the company. The company therefore agreed to a $1.1 billion settlement in October 1999 and was roundly criticized in some quarters for ''caving in'' too quickly.

The settlement led the company to post another loss for the year ending in March 2000—a net loss of ¥28 billion ($264.2 million). In June 2000 Nishimuro became chairman of Toshiba, while Tadashi Okamura took charge as president and CEO. Okamura, who also had a background in marketing, had been in charge of the sprawling Information and Industrial Systems and Services group, which included everything from telecommunications equipment and control systems to medical systems and elevators and escalators. Under Okamura's leadership, Toshiba continued to place noncore businesses into joint ventures, in-

cluding rechargeable batteries, elevators, and satellites. The troubled and risky semiconductor sector was also targeted for alliances, including a tie-up with arch-rival Fujitsu.

As it was swinging back to profitability in 2000 and 2001, the 125-year-old Toshiba looked to the future with an increased emphasis on information technology and with a focus shifting to several areas within that sector: media cards, mobile applications, networked home appliances, digital broadcasting services, Internet services, and electronic devices for the automobile. By devoting more resources to these emerging areas, Toshiba hoped to place itself on a faster, more profitable growth track in the early 21st century.

Principal Subsidiaries

Kitsuki Toshiba Electronics Corporation; Kyodo Building Corporation; Toshiba Building & Lease Co., Ltd.; Toshiba Chemical Corporation (57%); Toshiba Device Corporation; Toshiba Engineering Corporation; Toshiba Home Technology Corporation; Toshiba Lighting & Technology Corporation; Toshiba Plant Kensetsu Co., Ltd. (56%); Toshiba TEC Corporation (50%); Toshiba America Consumer Products, Inc. (U.S.A.); Toshiba America Electronic Components, Inc. (U.S.A.); Toshiba America Information Systems, Inc. (U.S.A.); Toshiba America, Inc. (U.S.A.); Toshiba Display Devices Inc. (U.S.A.); Toshiba International Corporation (U.S.A.); Toshiba (UK) Ltd.; Toshiba Europe GmbH (Germany); Toshiba Electronics Malaysia Sdn. Bhd.; TEC Singapore Electronics Pte. Ltd.

Principal Competitors

Hewlett-Packard Company; Sony Corporation; International Business Machines Corporation; Hitachi, Ltd.; Fujitsu Limited; Compaq Computer Corporation; Mitsubishi Electric Corporation; NEC Corporation; Matsushita Electric Corporation; Dell Computer Corporation; Samsung Group; Gateway, Inc.; Sun Microsystems, Inc.; Sharp Corporation; SANYO Electric Co., Ltd.; Pioneer Corporation; Daewoo Group; Intel Corporation; Lucent Technologies Inc.; Nokia Corporation; Telefonaktiebolaget LM Ericsson; Koninklijke Philips Electronics N.V.; General Electric Company.

Further Reading

Abrahams, Paul, ''Toshiba Soars As Deep Restructuring Bites,'' *Financial Times,* November 9, 1998, p. 25.

Abrams, Judith, ''Toshiba Eyes New Media Frontier,'' *Dealerscope Merchandising,* July 1994, pp. 24–25.

Brull, Steven V., and Andy Reinhardt, ''Toshiba's Digital Dreams,'' *Business Week,* October 13, 1997, pp. 76+.

Carlton, Jim, ''Toshiba's U.S. Laptop Unit Fights to Regain Lost Turf,'' *Wall Street Journal,* February 8, 1999, p. B4.

Eisenstodt, Gale, '' 'We Are Happy,' '' *Forbes,* May 8, 1995, p. 44.

Fulford, Benjamin, ''Gadget Colossus,'' *Forbes,* January 8, 2001, pp. 238–40.

Guth, Robert A., ''How Japan's Toshiba Got Its Focus Back,'' *Wall Street Journal,* December 28, 2000, pp. A6, A7.

——, ''Toshiba Plans Strategic Shift to Fast Growth,'' *Wall Street Journal,* February 17, 2000, p. A12.

Holyoke, Larry, ''How Toshiba's Laptops Retook the Heights,'' *Business Week,* January 16, 1995, p. 86.

Johnstone, Bob, ''Industry: Quick As a Flash,'' *Far Eastern Economic Review,* January 7, 1993, p. 57.

Keenan, Faith, and Peter Landers, ''Staggering Giants,'' *Far Eastern Economic Review,* April 1, 1999, pp. 10–13.

Kunii, Irene M., ''Toshiba Tries to Reboot,'' *Business Week,* July 24, 2000, p. 26.

Landers, Peter, ''Broken Up: Japan's Biggest Players Get Serious About Restructuring,'' *Far Eastern Economic Review,* February 11, 1999, p. 50.

Meyer, Richard, ''Power Surge,'' *Financial World,* April 3, 1990, pp. 42–46.

——, ''Asia's CEO of the Year: Joichi Aoi of Toshiba—'We Just Stay with It,' '' *Financial World,* October 15, 1991, pp. 50–54.

Pasztor, Andy, and Peter Landers, ''Toshiba Agrees to Settlement on Laptops,'' *Wall Street Journal,* November 1, 1999, p. A3.

Sato, Kazuo, ed., *Industry and Business in Japan,* New York: Croom Helm, 1980.

Schlender, Brenton R., ''How Toshiba Makes Alliances Work,'' *Fortune,* October 4, 1993, pp. 116–20.

Tanzer, Andrew, ''The Man Toshiba Hung Out to Dry,'' *Forbes,* September 7, 1987, pp. 96–98.

Uchida, Michio, ''Toshiba Bounces Back,'' *Tokyo Business Today,* June 1989, pp. 14–19.

Young, Lewis H., ''Why Toshiba Likes the Component Business,'' *Electronic Business Buyer,* December 1994, pp. 52–56.

—April Dougal Gasbarre
—update: David E. Salamie

Trimble Navigation Limited

645 North Mary Avenue
Sunnyvale, California 94088
U.S.A.
Telephone: (408) 481-8000
Fax: (408) 481-2000
Web site: http://www.trimble.com

Public Company
Incorporated: 1978
Employees: 2,306
Sales: $369.79 million (2000)
Stock Exchanges: NASDAQ
Ticker Symbol: TRMB
NAIC: 334511 Search, Detection, Navigation, Guidance, Aeronautical, and Nautical Systems and Instruments

Trimble Navigation Limited develops satellite-based position data products using the Global Positioning System (GPS), a constellation of 24 transmitting satellites that enable instruments to determine precise locations on earth in three dimensions. Trimble designs mapping, marine navigation, and surveying devices capable of measuring latitude, longitude, and altitude. The company also sells components used to aid automobile navigation, machine guidance, and asset tracking.

Origins

In 1978, the year Charles Trimble founded Trimble Navigation, the original NAVSTAR satellite was launched, giving the U.S. government its first reference point for a worldwide radio-navigation system that became known as GPS, or Global Positioning System. Trimble had started his small company to develop marine navigation products, but he was soon intrigued by the business opportunities in GPS technology. Not long after forming his company, Trimble decided to devote Trimble Navigation's resources to the development of products that used the then emerging technology. Although GPS was developed to meet military needs exclusively, Trimble foresaw a wide range of commercial and business applications for a system that could pinpoint locations on every square meter of the planet. Trimble's decision to wed his company to the nascent NAVSTAR system moved his company to the forefront of satellite-based position technology, making Trimble Navigation a GPS pioneer.

The effort to create a revolutionary navigation system had begun in 1973, five years before the first NAVSTAR satellite was launched into orbit. The program was created by the U.S. Department of Defense to aid in the nation's defense against a Soviet attack, specifically to help guard against the attack of a nuclear warhead capable of traveling more than 9,000 miles. The advent of long-range, intercontinental ballistic missiles (ICBMs) had given U.S. and Soviet armed forces the capability to target each other's missile silos from great distances and with great precision. The precision of an ICBM was based on the knowledge of two measurements: the exact location of the target and the exact location of the missile launch site. Meeting these conditions presented a problem to U.S. armed forces, a problem that GPS would help resolve. At any given moment, the U.S. did not know where the majority of its warheads were, at least not as precisely as the targeting calculations for an ICBM required. The majority of the country's nuclear arsenal was at sea, aboard submarines whose exact position could not be quickly pinpointed. GPS, once fully operational, could supply such information by using a constellation of satellites and their ground stations.

The 1978 launch of NAVSTAR represented the first step toward developing a worldwide radio-navigation system. To achieve worldwide coverage, 24 satellites were required, each orbiting roughly 11,000 nautical miles above earth. Once placed in orbit, these satellites and their ground stations would serve as reference points to calculate positions accurate to a matter of meters, enabling GPS receivers to triangulate a position anywhere on earth via radio signals transmitted by the satellites. The U.S. government invested $12 billion in the project, eventually achieving full operational status in 1995, but the NAVSTAR system was partially operational well before the mid-1990s, proving to be an invaluable aid to the U.S. military.

GPS first earned its admirers during the Persian Gulf War, a time when, not coincidentally, Trimble Navigation captured the interest of industry observers. Within a matter of months, the

Company Perspectives:

As the only publicly held company in the world dedicated solely to GPS, Trimble is positioned as the major player in the industry. Every day, all over the world, Trimble GPS solutions go to work. Whether it's locating Caspian oil and gas in Kazakhstan or finding a taxi in Oslo, the variety of applications for Trimble GPS solutions is virtually endless and continues to increase.

company rose out of obscurity and slipped into the ranks of the country's most promising concerns. During Operation Desert Storm, Trimble Navigation provided troops with Trimpacks, devices that enabled soldiers to pinpoint their location. The hand-held receivers performed admirably, earning praise from military commanders and making Trimble Navigation an attractive prospect for investors. The company had completed a $30 million initial public offering of stock several months earlier, in July 1990, which thrust it into the public spotlight at just the right time to capitalize on its well publicized success in the Middle East. When sales in 1990 reached $63.3 million, the announcement fanned investor interest in the company. The figure exceeded Wall Street analysts' expectations by roughly 25 percent, prompting investors to look closer at the Sunnyvale, California-based enterprise. What they saw was a company controlling 60 percent of a market whose revenue volume was more than doubling annually. They saw a company poised to record robust growth in 1991, with industry analysts projecting $110 million in sales by the end of 1991. They saw a company whose orders for Trimpack receivers totaled $40 million between October 1990 and March 1991. Trimble Navigation's stock value soared as a result, but as quickly as the company's stature blossomed within the investment community, its luster began to fade.

Post-Gulf War Decline

A number of factors contributed to Trimble Navigation's anemic performance during the early 1990s. The end of the Persian Gulf War delivered a significant blow to the company's financial vitality. Military sales, which had fueled the company's meteoric rise in 1990 and 1991, plummeted to less than 3 percent of the company's revenue volume by 1992. It was a profound loss, one compounded by slower-than-anticipated growth of other markets. Further, Trimble Navigation's own success during Operation Desert Storm came back to haunt the company. Defense contractors, whose sales were sagging, were eager to find new business opportunities to spark growth. Trimble Navigation's success in developing GPS products for the military had not gone unnoticed, inducing massive concerns such as Honeywell, Hughes, Motorola, and Westinghouse to jump into the GPS market. Consequently, Trimble Navigation, once in firm command of the multibillion-dollar industry, found itself facing intense competition from companies with far greater resources than it possessed. The company also faced stiff competition from foreign concerns, particularly Japanese companies who focused on less expensive consumer products.

In the wake of the Persian Gulf War, Trimble Navigation was reeling from the collapse of its military business and from com-

petitive pressures. The company focused its efforts on the upper end of the market, where it went head to head with defense contractors, but costs ran out of control. Charles Trimble, who served as chairman and chief executive officer, conceded his company's financial performance was "miserable," as quoted in the June 15, 1992 issue of the *Business Journal*. In the first three months of 1992, Trimble Navigation generated $22 million in revenue and posted a net loss of $9.7 million. For the same period in 1991, the company collected $36.8 million and recorded $2.2 million in net income, providing a clear indication of how far the company had fallen in one year. Not surprisingly, the company's reputation on Wall Street suffered, as Trimble Navigation's stock dropped in value from $19.25 per share at the end of 1991 to $8 per share by mid-1992.

Forced to respond to his company's deteriorating condition, Trimble took action shortly after the financial figures for the first quarter of 1992 were announced. In early June, a sweeping restructuring program was begun, which included laying off 100 workers, or 13 percent of Trimble Navigation's workforce. The restructuring effort was expected to lead to a $7 million charge for the company's second quarter in 1992, a sum necessary to cover severance costs, the consolidation of facilities, and other restructuring expenses. At the time the program was announced, analysts questioned whether the company could profit in the harsh competitive environment that existed both domestically and abroad. Survival, some pundits said, depended on Trimble Navigation being acquired by a larger company with greater financial resources and the marketing muscle to compete effectively in the satellite location device market. Trimble flatly refused to consider such an option, insisting that he had an opportunity to turn Trimble Navigation into a *Fortune* 500 company. Instead, he focused on forging strategic alliances with larger companies. By 1992, Trimble Navigation had entered into ventures with Silicon Graphics, Pioneer Electronics, Westinghouse, and others, relying on partnerships to steer its way out of the financial doldrums.

By the mid-1990s, commercial alliances with a variety of companies were propelling Trimble Navigation into new markets. The company was looking beyond supplying GPS devices for the military and nautical navigation markets and diversifying into a number of new areas, including the development of GPS devices for avionics, space, and automobiles. In 1995—the year the NAVSTAR system became fully operational—Trimble Navigation formed a partnership with Adobe Systems Inc., a developer of software that enabled users to create, display, print, and send electronic documents. Adobe and Trimble Navigation planned to create a mapping system for automobiles capable of pinpointing a driver's position and providing directions to particular destinations, such as restaurants, service stations, and airports. Trimble Navigation signed another important agreement in 1995, linking with Honeywell, a competitor in the GPS market. Under the terms of the agreement, the two companies agreed to create GPS-based products for the commercial, space, and military aviation markets.

New Management Sharpening Strategic Focus: Late 1990s

In pursuit of new markets, Trimble Navigation spread its energies far and wide. Commercial alliances enabled the com-

Key Dates:

1978: Company is founded to develop marine navigation products.

1990: Trimble Navigation converts to public ownership in July

1999: Steven Berglund is appointed president and chief executive officer.

2000: Spectra Precision, noted for its expertise in optical and laser technology, is acquired.

2001: Trimble, as part of a new plan to narrow its business focus, sells its commercial avionics segment to Honeywell.

pany to diversify in earnest, but by the late 1990s the time had come for a narrower strategic focus. In 1998, when sales reached $268 million, the company lost a staggering $27 million. Trimble left the company in August; his replacement, Steven W. Berglund, arrived in May 1999, when he took control as Trimble Navigation's president and chief executive officer.

Before joining Trimble Navigation, Berglund had spent the previous 14 years of his professional career at Spectra-Physics AB. Berglund held various senior management positions at the company, whose corporate roots stretched to the 1940s, when a Swedish surveyor patented the principle of precisely measuring distances with a light beam. Later, the company was a pioneer in laser technology, inventing the first rotating construction laser, among other innovations. Berglund rose through the managerial ranks at Spectra-Physics, making his most notable mark on the company's development in the late 1990s. Berglund combined existing Spectra-Physics businesses, which included a GPS survey receiver manufacturer named Geotronics, and several acquisitions to create Spectra Precision, a survey, construction equipment, and machine-control company with $200 million in annual sales, 1,300 employees, and operations in 17 countries. The major restructuring program was completed in 1998, after which Berglund served as president and chief operating officer of Spectra Precision until joining Trimble Navigation.

Under Berglund's stewardship, Trimble Navigation reversed the crippling loss recorded in 1998. Sales in 1999 remained essentially flat, but the company recorded $18.6 million in net income for the year, providing an encouraging start to the Berglund era. The dramatic return to profitability was followed by an acquisition of great significance. In July 2000, Trimble Navigation announced it was acquiring Berglund's former company, Spectra Precision, for $200 million in cash and $80 million in seller debt financing. Spectra, which would be aligned with a new engineering and construction business group headquartered in Dayton, Ohio, gave Trimble Navigation expertise in optical and laser technology.

As Trimble Navigation prepared for the future, it did so with a narrow focus on business areas that were expected to provide

growth and sustained profitability. Toward this end, the company divested its commercial avionics business in March 2001, selling it to Honeywell. The divestiture left the company's business and portfolio of products targeted toward four markets: fleet and asset management, agriculture, component technology, and engineering and construction.

Principal Subsidiaries

Trimble Navigation International Foreign Sales Corporation (Barbados); TR Navigation Corporation; Trimble Export Limited; Tripod Data Systems; TNL Flight Services, Inc.; Trimble Navigation France S.A.; Trimble Navigation Australia Pty Limited; Trimble Mexico S. de R.L.; Trimble Navigation Europe Limited (U.K.); Trimble Navigation Deutschland GmbH (Germany); Trimble Navigation New Zealand Limited; Trimble Navigation Iberica S.L. (Spain); Trimble Navigation Singapore PTE Limited; Datacom Software Limited; Trimble Japan K.K.; Trimble Navigation Italia s.r.l. (Italy); Trimble Navigation International Limited; Trimble International Holdings S.L. (Spain); Trimble Holdings GmbH (Germany); Trimble AB (Sweden); Spectra Precision Inc.; Spectra Precision USA, Inc.; Spectra Precision Software, Inc.; Spectra Precision BVBA (Belgium); Spectra Precision K.K. (Japan); Spectra Precision Pty Ltd. (Australia); Spectra Precision Ltd. (U.K.); SPHM Inc.; SPSE Inc.; Spectra Precision Credit Corp.; Spectra Precision B.V. (Netherlands); Spectra Precision s.r.l (Italy); Spectra Precision of Canada Ltd.; Spectra Precision S.A. (France); Spectra Precision GesmbH (Austria); Spectra Precision Mexicana, SA de CV (Mexico); Spectra Precision Servicios, SA de CV (Mexico); Spectra Precision Mexico, SA de CV; Spectra Precision GmbH (Germany); Spectra Precision Kaiserslautern GmbH (Germany); ZSP Geodetic Systems GmbH (Germany).

Principal Competitors

BAE Systems Canada Inc.; Lowrance Electronics, Inc.; Orbital Sciences Corporation.

Further Reading

Barry, David, "Trimble Signs Sunnyvale Lease," *Business Journal—San Jose,* March 25, 1991, p. 13.

Carlsen, Clifford, "Stirlen Jumps at Chance to Guide Trimble," *San Francisco Business Times,* March 1, 1991, p. 12.

Goldman, James S., "Trimble Searching Markets for Global Location Devices," *Business Journal,* June 15, 1992, p. 4.

Hostetler, Michele, "Trimble Maps Out Deals for Its Global Positioning Systems," *Business Journal,* June 26, 1995, p. 7.

"Trimble," *World Oil,* February 2001, p. 129.

"Trimble Buys Spectra Precision," *Construction Equipment,* January 2001, p. 18.

"Trimble Names CEO," *GPS World,* May 1999, p. 20.

"Trimble Navigation Ltd.," *Insiders' Chronicle,* June 15, 1992, p. 3.

"Trimble to Sell Air Transport Systems Business to Honeywell," *Wireless Satellite and Broadcasting Newsletter,* February 2001, p. 8.

—Jeffrey L. Covell

unibail

Unibail SA

5, boulevard Malesherbes
75008 Paris
France
Telephone: (+33) 1-53-437-437
Fax: (+33) 1-53-437-438
Web site: http://www.unibail.com

Public Company
Incorporated: 1968 as Union du Credit-Bail Immobilier
Employees: 378
Sales: EUR 357.0 million ($350 million) (2000)
Stock Exchanges: Euronext Paris
NAIC: 531 Real Estate; 531390 Other Activities Related to Real Estate; 531312 Nonresidential Property Managers

Unibail SA is France's leading commercial property management company, with a portfolio of office buildings, shopping centers, and convention and exhibition centers valued at EUR 6.4 billion. These sectors make up the three core areas of the company's operations. Office buildings represent the largest part of the company's portfolio, with more than 50 buildings located throughout the Parisian business district valued at nearly EUR 4 billion. The company's office building holdings include such prime Parisian real estate and locations as La Defense, Europe's largest business district, where Unibail's 310,000 square meters of office space make it that center's largest real estate owner. The company's acquisition of the majority share of CNIT SA in 2000 further boosts its presence in La Defense, and also gives it a strong boost into the convention and exhibition centers market. Unibail entered that market in the late 1990s with the acquisition of such important properties as the Paris Expo; the company's holdings in the convention and exhibition centers sector already represent a value of EUR 700 million. The third wing of Unibail's holdings is its extensive array of shopping center complexes, chiefly located around Paris but extending across all of France, with a total value of some EUR 1.9 billion. The company's shopping centers include

Les Halles in Paris, the country's busiest shopping mall. Unibail is quoted on the Paris stock exchange and is led by Chairman and CEO Leon Bressler.

From Leasing Finance to Lease Holder in the 1970s

Unibail was founded as Union du Credit-Bail Immobilier as the real estate leasing division of famed French financial house Worms et Cie in 1968. Formed in 1848 by Hypolite Worms, that company had started business as a coal importer, before it diversified into merchant shipping and then to shipbuilding during World War I. From there Worms grew into one of France's foremost industrial and financial houses, now under the leadership of Hypolite Worms's grandson, also named Hypolite Worms. In the 1920s, the company expanded into banking services, as well as capital investment activities, including financing the launch of France's national airline, Air France. The company's shipbuilding operations led it to enter the long-haul shipping industry, with the creation of Nouvelle Compagnie Havraise Pénninsulaire in 1934.

Following World War II, Worms et Cie branched out into insurance, while also boosting its financial activities, such as construction financing. The company wound down its industrial operations in the 1950s, as its interests turned more and more to banking and financial services. In the mid- and late 1960s, the company shut down its shipbuilding arm and closed its shipping business as well. Taking their place was the Banque de Worms, created in 1965. The company now extended into a new area of business, that of real estate leasing, in 1968, with the creation of a new subsidiary, Union du Credit-Bail Immobilier, known simply as Unibail.

Unibail soon became an independent operation as Worms et Cie turned its concentration more fully on its core banking and insurance operations. Unibail was first introduced to the Paris bourse in 1972, when its shares were on that stock market's spot market. Unibail remained dedicated to its finance leasing operations through the late 1980s. However, the company had already begun to collect its own real estate holdings, beginning with the purchase of 5, rue Royale, in Paris's eighth arrondissement, in 1976.

Unibail moved to a full listing on the Paris main board in 1986, and then began to plan a new era of growth. Shortly thereafter, the company began acquiring other finance leasing firms, including Sliminco, purchased from Credit Lyonnais in 1988, and Pretabail Sicommerce, acquired in 1990. Yet the company, now led by Leon Bressler (who became chairman in 1992) was beginning to plot its transformation for the new decade. In 1987 the company began turning over management of its real estate portfolio to Arc Union.

In 1990 the company backed Arc Union's formation of a new subsidiary, Price, a property company focused on shopping center properties. By the following year, Unibail had decided to abandon lease financing to concentrate its future growth on building a portfolio as a real estate holding company. In 1992, the company disposed of a portion of its lease portfolio, earning FFr 2.2 billion on the sale. In turn the company made its first major real estate purchase, that of a 23 percent stake in the Les Quatre Temps shopping center complex situated in the La Defense business district in Paris.

Unibail's timing might have seemed awkward to observers—the French real estate market was in the midst of a long slump, begun in the late 1980s, that was not to hit bottom until 1995, while the shopping center industry remained crippled by the low consumer spending of the recessionary early 1990s. Unibail, however, remained dedicated to its new strategy, and began building up a new portfolio of property holdings. The company was helped in this quest by the changing French real estate market itself. Until the 1980s, most French property had been held by the country's large banking and other financial institutions, which mostly owned real estate for the tax incentives such holdings offered. At the same time, commercial real estate was largely owned by individual companies. A new breed of real estate investors moved into the market in the 1980s, particularly pension funds and the like. Yet the new property owners, who saw their investments dwindle during the real estate slump late in the decade, began exiting the market in the early 1990s. The recession and real estate slump combined to present banks with large numbers of repossessed properties. Under pressure, the banks were eager to sell off these underperforming properties.

Real Estate Titan for the 21st Century

As an independent real estate company, Unibail was able to focus on its long-term development, building up a portfolio of holdings that was to place it among the industry's leaders by the end of the decade. The company stepped up its purchases of real estate, starting with the acquisition/absorption of Price in 1993 and the purchase of the CFI (Compagnie Foncière Internationale) portfolio held by the Suez Group, for FFr 3 billion, completed in 1994. The following year Unibail took over Arc Union, giving the latter company full active management of Unibail's growing real estate portfolio. In that year, the company also acquired Espace Expansion, one of France's leading developers and managers of shopping centers. At that time, Unibail reorganized its holdings into two main lines, those of office properties and shopping centers.

The company boosted its shopping center portfolio with two important acquisitions at mid-decade. The first raised its share of the Quatre Temps shopping complex to a majority share of 53.3 percent. The company also stepped up its holding in the Forum des Halles shopping center—France's busiest—from 17 percent to a majority control of 64 percent. In 1996, the company shed the Italian wing of its Espace Expansion acquisition, focusing its holdings on the French market. The company acquired two important office buildings that year, the Quai Ouest, in Boulogne sur Seine, with 14,000 square meters of office space, and Le France, in Neuilly, with 27,000 square meters of offices. These properties, located in the so-called Golden Crescent outside of Paris, helped the company expand beyond the Paris city center and attract a strong number of major French and international corporations as clients.

In 1996, also, Unibail took part in the formation of Crossroads Property Investors, a Luxembourg-based partnership created with American and Asian investors. With investment capital of more than FFr 5 billion, Crossroads was to become an important part in building Unibail's market-leading position at decade's end. In 1997, Crossroads began making significant acquisitions in the Parisian market, including a selection of buildings located in the city's 16th and 17th arrondissements that added nearly 50,000 square meters to the Crossroads portfolio.

Meanwhile, Unibail continued making investments under its own name as well. In 1998, the company made a share exchange offer to acquire Frankoparis, the property company that owned the Hotel Meridien located in the Montparnasse business district of Paris. The following year, Unibail hit the big time when it agreed to acquire the FFr 6 billion property portfolio from Vivendi Group, then exiting a real estate strategy begun earlier in the decade. This acquisition not only strengthened the company's park of office buildings—it added some 300,000 square meters of office space, including a share of the Carrousel du Louvre and the CNIT convention center at La Defense—but also gave Unibail the leading share of space in the Paris-La Defense district. With a property portfolio now valued at more than FFr 20 billion (more than EUR 6 billion), Unibail had achieved sufficient size to place it among the top competitors for the European property market.

Later in 1999, Unibail cemented its leadership position with the acquisition of Crossroads Property's portfolio, by then valued at FFr 4.7 billion. At the same time, Unibail moved to extend its operations into a new area of business, that of convention and exhibition centers. As the century drew to a close, opportunities to buy new office building space were shrinking—demand for

Key Dates:

1968: Worms et Cie forms Union du Credit-Bail Immobilier (Unibail).
1972: Unibail lists on Paris bourse spot market.
1976: Company acquires first real estate property.
1986: Unibail lists on Paris main board.
1991: Unibail abandons lease financing and becomes a real estate holding company.
1992: Company acquires 23 percent of Les Quatre Temps.
1994: Company acquires Compagnie Foncière Internationale (CFI) portfolio held by the Suez Group for FFr 3 billion.
1995: Arc Union is taken over; company acquires Espace Expansion.
1998: Company acquires Frankoparis.
1999: Company acquires Vivendi's FFr 6 billion real estate portfolio; acquires Crossroads Property Investors' assets.
2000: Unibail acquires 93 percent of Paris Expo; CNIT merges into Unibail.
2001: Unibail acquires Nice-Etoile shopping center.

space in the Parisian market far exceeded supply—and Unibail's own developments of new building space, including new buildings in La Defense and elsewhere in Paris, were among the last available sites within Paris. The bustling French and European economy, meanwhile, had created a boom in the convention and exhibition market.

Unibail made two significant purchases to give it a strong position in its new core focus area. The first came at the end of 1999, when it made an offer to take over the operation of the Paris Expo. By early 2000, the company had beat out its competitors to take majority control of the Paris Expo and, by October 2000, the company's holding in that site had been raised to 93 percent. In May 2000, the company merged its CNIT holdings into its main portfolio, cementing its position as one of France's leading convention and exhibition center property groups. In January 2001, the company reached an agreement to take over the Nice-Etoile shopping center, adding another 100,000 square meters to its portfolio of retail space.

By early 2001, Unibail's strategy had enabled it to claim France's leading real estate position in its chosen sectors, as well as rising revenues: its 2000 rent levels of EUR 357 represented a 74 percent increase over the previous year. At the same time, the company's strong tenant list of major French and International corporations gave it lease contracts providing it with guaranteed rent levels through the end of the new century's first decade.

Principal Subsidiaries

Omnifinance SA; Uni-Bureaux SAS; Paris expo SA; Tanagra SAS; Doria SAS; Uni-commerces SAS.

Further Reading

Bériot, Frédéric, "Unibail devrait enregistrer une nouvelle progression à deux chiffres," *La Vie Financière*, February 5, 2000.
Besses Boumard, Pascale, "Unibail acquiert l'ex-empire immobilier de Christian Pellerin pour 6 millards de francs," *Les Echos*, March 12, 1999, p. 25.
Chevallard, Lucile, "Nous avons une visibilité de dix ans sur nos revenus," *Les Echos*, July 28, 2000, p. 21.
Tieman, Ross, "Search for Supply," *Financial Times*, March 9, 2001.
"Unibail: très bons resultats," *Le Figaro*, February 15, 2001.

—M. L. Cohen

United Water Resources, Inc.

220 Old Hook Road
Harrington Park, New Jersey
U.S.A.
Telephone: (201) 784-9434
Fax: (201) 767-7018
Web site: http://www.unitedwater.com

Wholly Owned Subsidiary of Suez Lyonnaise des Eaux
Incorporated: 1869 as the Hackensack Water Company
Employees: 1,300
Sales: $362.3 million (1999)
NAIC: 2211310 Water Supply and Irrigation Systems

A subsidiary of French conglomerate Suez Lyonnaise des Eaux since July 2000, New Jersey-based United Water Resources, Inc. is a holding company for a number of entities that together comprise the second largest nonmunicipal water services company in the United States. United Water New Jersey serves customers in northeastern New Jersey, while United Water New York serves customers in Rockland County, New York. United Properties Group is involved in the real estate business, primarily created to take advantage of 1,000 acres of valuable land the company has accumulated over the years in the suburbs outside of New York City, in both New York State and New Jersey. United Waterworks provides water and wastewater services in 11 states. United Water and Suez Lyonnaise have become especially active in the management of municipal-owned water systems, which in recent years cities have been looking to turn over to private firms. United Water and its French parent corporation also have a stake in the British market through United Water UK Limited.

Founding of Original Company in 1869

For more than 100 years, United Water was known as the Hackensack Water Company. Although ensconced in a farming area, the village of Hackensack emerged as a commercial center after the Civil War, and its close proximity to Manhattan proved an attractive place to build homes for many New York businessmen and bankers. Because Hackensack was quickly outgrowing

its wells and cisterns, it became apparent that the community needed a public water system. Two companies headed by rival politicians were formed. Charles H. Voorhis obtained a state charter for the Cherry Hill Water and Gas Company; he was followed by Garret Ackerson, whose Hackensack Water Company was approved by the New Jersey Senate on February 24, 1869. The special Act of the Legislature was signed into law by the governor on March 12, 1869. Voorhis and Ackerson then became preoccupied with the formation of new banks, and both water charters were neglected until 1873, when local citizens and newspapers began to clamor for action. Because Ackerson's charter had more extensive powers than those assigned to Cherry Hill, Voorhis contrived a way to gain a controlling interest in Hackensack Water. It was only then that he began to construct a water system. A large brick reservoir was built on a hill north of Hackensack, pumping facilities were set up to draw water from the Hackensack River, and a network of conduits were laid in the village that would be fed by gravity from the reservoir. On October 21, 1874, the system was complete and service began.

Unfortunately for Voorhis, he began construction on the Hacksensack Water Company in the midst of the Wall Street Panic of 1873 that precipitated a seven-year economic depression. His plans to supply water to a large portion of Bergen County, New Jersey, were never to be realized. By 1879 the Water Company was unable to pay its debts, and all of Voorhis's ventures, the finances of which propped up one another, quickly failed. He lost everything, including his reputation. In the end he was reduced to living in a small Hoboken flat where he killed himself, with nothing but $5 in an envelope to leave his distraught wife.

The Water Company went into receivership, then was acquired and reorganized by Bacot & Ward, the engineers and contractors who built the system. After signing a ten-year deal to supply water to Hoboken, the new owners were unable to command the necessary finances to build the line. In 1881 they sold Hackensack Water to a new group of investors who elected prominent Manhattan lawyer and socialite Robert W. de Forest to run the operation. He would do so for the next 46 years.

In 1886 Hackensack Water issued its first share of common stock, and on January 9, 1889, it was listed on the New York

Stock Exchange. It would remain on the Big Board for the next 111 years continuously, a distinction shared by only a handful of companies. In addition, only one other company among this group could boast a record of paying longer continuous dividends. Under de Forest, Hackensack Water constructed new facilities and moved its headquarters to Weehawken, setting up offices in a massive brick water tower. Steadily, other towns in Bergen County were added to the system. The company was secure enough to withstand the Panic of 1893 with little difficulty.

Hackensack Water had suffered occasional adverse publicity about water quality, much of which was caused by a poor understanding of how to treat organisms, such as algae, that grew in the reservoirs and caused a "fishy taste." During the 1890s, however, the science of water treatment began to make great strides. Microscopic studies of water were able to isolate what caused the poor taste and bad odors that were so prevalent in water supplies, and led to experimentation in filtering systems. These filters occupied patches of land an acre or two in size where water could pass through layers of sand. More than just improving the color and flavor of water, filtration would become critical in reducing water-borne disease. European cities led the way. By the end of the century 11 million people in England would be supplied by filtered water, as would 4.6 million in Germany, 1.4 million in Holland, and approximately three million more in the rest of Europe. In the United States only a handful of communities used some form of filtration, and only two (Poughkeepsie and Albany, New York) had systems comparable in size to Hackensack Water. It was evidence of a forward-thinking company that Hackensack Water would invest in filtration as well as building the additional reservoir that would be required. Moreover, when the Jersey City water supply became the first in the United States to use chlorination to fight bacteria in 1908, Hackensack Water quickly followed suit.

Acquiring Spring Valley Water Company in 1900

In October 1900, Hackensack Water made a minor acquisition that would over the course of time provide a major portion of the company's business. It bought all the outstanding stock of the Spring Valley Water Works and Supply Company located in Rockland County, New York. Incorporated in New York in 1893, the system had but one employee and 91 customers. What de Forest was smart enough to realize, however, was that despite operating in another state, Spring Valley shared the same watershed. Its acquisition would help to protect the integrity of the water supply for the entire region, not just the

territory of one company or another. As a subsidiary of Hackensack Water, Spring Valley would upgrade its facilities and begin to add communities to its system in a manner similar to Hackensack Water.

During the early part of the 20th century, the region surrounding New York City grew at a tremendous pace. Between 1890 and 1910, Bergen County saw its population jump by 300 percent. Hackensack Water continued to expand its operations to meet a rising demand. Even the introduction of a Public Utilities Commission to regulate rates proved to be beneficial to the company. A 1917 Commission study established a uniform system of rates and essentially confirmed to the public that Hackensack Water was not bilking its customers, as newspapers and headline-seeking politicians had been in the habit of claiming.

During World War I the company supplied water to a major embarkation camp that was built in Bergen County. In a matter of months Hackensack Water was able to add to its system an army camp that was the size of a 42,000-person city. Following a short economic depression after the war, the company entered a boom period. After running Hackensack Water for more than four decades, de Forest, almost 80 years old, retired in 1926. His successor, Nicholas S. Hill, was quick to make plans for future expansion; he anticipated a growing need for water supplies for the new housing units that were sure to spring up in Bergen County when the George Washington Bridge, crossing the Hudson River in upper Manhattan, was completed in 1931. Plans were drawn up for a major dam that would raise the level of the Hackensack River, and the process of acquiring thousands of acres of land that would be flooded to make a new reservoir was begun.

The stock market crash of 1929 changed everything. All construction on new housing came to an abrupt stop. Customers cut back on their consumption of water, making a new reservoir unnecessary. Although Hackensack Water remained one of the few stable stocks on the Big Board, it still had trouble raising the necessary funds to pay off the land and other expenses incurred during the heady days of expansion plans. Even the opening of the George Washington Bridge did little to change the economics of Bergen County. Not until the end of World War II would the area begin to feel the true impact of the bridge.

When the company initiated postwar plans to build a major reservoir in New York State, eventually named de Forest Lake Reservoir, it came under heavy fire from critics who claimed that Spring Valley was being used by Hackensack Water to steal New York water. After years of legal wrangling, the new reservoir finally opened in 1957.

In addition to internal growth Hackensack Water continued to bring smaller water companies into its fold. In 1958 it purchased the Montvale Water Company, in 1963 the Bogota Water Company, and in 1965 the water system of the Borough of Franklin Lakes. In 1950 Hackensack Water served 105,000 customers, totaling a population of 500,000, with equipment and facilities worth $40 million. By 1969 its customers had increased 81 percent to about 190,000, and its plant and equipment were worth almost $130 million. Whereas in 1950 Hackensack Water pumped an average of 47 million gallons of water per day, by 1969 it pumped close to 100 million gallons a day.

Key Dates:

1869: Hackensack Water Company is founded.
1874: Following an initial period of inactivity, company begins to offer service.
1889: Company is listed on New York Stock Exchange.
1900: Company acquires Spring Valley Water Works.
1957: Company opens de Forest Lake Reservoir in New York.
1983: Reorganization leads to United Water Resources, Inc.
1994: General Waterworks Corporation is acquired.
2001: Company becomes a subsidiary of Suez Lyonnaise des Eaux in a deal valued at $1.02 billion.

Incorporating United Water Resources in 1983

Hackensack Water continued its steady growth through the 1970s. A severe drought adversely affected earnings in the early 1980s, but the company quickly rebounded. Following the lead of some electric utility companies, Hackensack Water decided to reorganize in 1983 as United Water Resources, Inc., in order to better develop its non-utility assets. The company was now able to move into water-quality testing services, offer management and meter-reading services to municipal water systems, and exploit its large land holdings. United Water owned 290 acres of excess Rockland County land with an assessed value of $1.8 million. In New Jersey it owned an additional 675 acres assessed at $7 million that were not needed for the water system.

Although United Water expanded under its new organization, in the early 1990s it took on a national presence. Under the leadership of Donald L. Correll, who became president in 1991, then a year later was named chief executive officer, United Water completed a major deal in 1994 when it acquired General Waterworks Corporation (GWC) for approximately $200 million in stock and cash. With its revenues doubled, United Water was now the second largest closely held water utility in the United States, boasting more than two million customers in 14 states. Perhaps of more importance, however, was the relationship United Water formed with the principal owner of GWC stock, Lyonnaise des Eaux-Dumez. As part of the transaction, the French water company giant received a 26 percent stake in United Water, becoming the largest outside shareholder.

A French Connection: 1994–2001

After World War II, France nationalized electricity and gas, forcing companies like Lyonnaise des Eaux to sell assets, the proceeds of which they invested in water, the one utility that remained open to them. Because its water industry consolidated rapidly, France produced large companies with considerable cash to spend on research and development—as well as a considerable appetite for growth. The U.S. market became a particularly attractive target. Not only was it highly fragmented, with some 55,000 community companies supplying water, the quality of water was considered poor by European standards. Chlorine had become too easy an answer for aging water systems in the United States. The amount of money that would have to be spent in the country to upgrade the infrastructure alone was staggering, some $330 billion over the course of the next 20 years. Furthermore, local governments were opting to turn over their water operations to private companies. United Water's French partner estimated that the annual revenue for private water management could reach $40 billion by 2015. The way the French chose to enter this enticing market was through forging relationships with U.S. companies such as GWC and United Water.

As drinking water standards became more stringent, and the Internal Revenue Service ruled that a city would not lose the tax-exempt status of its bonds if it placed its waterworks under private management, local governments were even more inclined to turn to outside water companies. United Water had already won large wastewater contracts in Indianapolis and Milwaukee when it teamed with its French partners in 1998 to win the contract to run Atlanta's waterworks, the largest water system in North America. The largest privately run system had been Jersey City, also a United Water contract, with its 80 million-gallons-a-day requirements. Atlanta's system, by contrast, had a capacity of 180 million gallons per day. The arrangement made sense for both parties. Atlanta saved $20 million a year (half of which went to United Water), an amount that it could then leverage into a billion dollars worth of borrowing. In addition, city employees would be taken off Atlanta's rolls and added to the management company. These types of contract operations were equally attractive to United Water. In 1992 they accounted for $10 million in revenues. By 1997 they grew to $50 million, and a year later doubled to approximately $100 million.

In the meantime, there was pressure on United Water's French partners to continue to grow, especially after the 1997 merger of Lyonnaise des Eaux and Compagnie de Suez, whose roots reach back to the building of the Suez Canal in 1858. However large Suez Lyonnaise des Eaux may have been, it was still only the world's second largest water company. Rival French firm Vivendia, with origins that also reached back to the mid-19th century, was even larger. After several years of working together, winning 35 water services contracts in 16 states, Suez Lyonnaise and United Water entered into talks in August 1999 to arrange a French purchase of the remaining shares of United Water stock. This step came on the heels of Suez Lyonnaise buying Calgon Corporation, a water-treatment company, for $425 million, and Nalco Chemical Co., a water-treatment chemicals firm, for $4.1 billion. The offer for United Water was for $35 a share in cash for a total price of $1.36 billion, plus the assumption of about $800 million in debt and other obligations.

A year would pass before the transaction was approved by regulators in New Jersey and New York. United Water, which would continue to operate as a separate entity, agreed to freeze rates for an extended period of time for its different customers, was forbidden from passing transaction costs on to customers, promised to avoid layoffs for at least one year, and signed off on a provision that required the company to give environmental groups and local governments the right of first refusal should it decide to sell any of its real estate holdings in watershed areas that drained into its reservoirs.

The future appeared promising for United Water and Suez Lyonnaise. The U.S. market remained highly fragmented, providing ample opportunities for growth through acquisition. Communities continued to turn to private firms to run their waterworks, although a number were hiring consultants to help them reinvent their operations. Upgrading a decaying U.S. infrastructure was another opportunity for major players including United Water. Indeed, the need for upgrading water facilities around the world was immense. In the end the prosperity of United Water and its French corporate parent could very well depend on the answer to one basic question: Who was going to pay for it all?

Principal Operating Units

United Water New Jersey; United Water New York; United Waterworks; United Properties Group Incorporated.

Principal Competitors

American Water Works Company, Inc.; Philadelphia Suburban; USFilter.

Further Reading

Browning, E.S., "Two Big French Environmental Firms Expand in the U.S. Through Mergers," *Wall Street Journal*, April 6, 1994, p. A8.

Byrne, Harlan S., "Precious Fluids," *Barron's*, August 19, 1996, p. 18.

Campanella, Frank W., "Property Play: There Are More Than Liquid Assets at United Water, A Northeast Utility," *Barron's National Business and Financial Weekly*, September 26, 1983, pp. 70–71.

Dahlburg, John-Thor, "Tap Water Around the World Developing a French Flavor," *Los Angeles Times*, April 30, 2000, p. C1.

Hairston, Julie B., Carlos Campos, and David Pendered, "United Water 'a Safe Selection,'" *Atlanta Journal and Atlanta Constitution*, August 28, 1998, p. D6.

Leiby, Adrian C., *The Hackensack Water Company 1869–1969*, River Edge, N.J.: Bergen County Historical Society, 1969.

Taylor, Andrew, "Water Acquisitions Are Just a Small Drop in the Market," *Financial Times*, June 6, 2000, p. 6.

—Ed Dinger

Wabtec Corporation

1001 Air Brake Avenue
Wilmerding, Pennsylvania 15148
U.S.A.
Telephone: (412) 825-1000
Fax: (412) 825-1019
Web site: http://www.wabtec.com

Public Company
Incorporated: 1869 as Westinghouse Air Brake Company
Employees: 6,500
Sales: $1.02 billion (2000)
Stock Exchanges: New York
Ticker Symbol: WAB
NAIC: 336510 Railroad Rolling Stock Manufacturing

Wabtec Corporation was created as a result of the 1999 merger of Westinghouse Air Brake Company and MotivePower. With annual revenues in excess of $1 billion, it is the largest North American company providing equipment and services to the rail industry (which in addition to freight and passenger trains includes mass transit systems). Wabtec is also the world's largest publicly traded rail equipment supply company. Conducted through its subsidiaries, Wabtec's business covers the gamut of the rail industry. The company manufactures locomotives up to 4,000 horsepower while also offering aftermarket services such as maintenance and logistics support.

Patenting the Air Brake in 1869

Renowned American inventor and manufacturer George Westinghouse established his scientific reputation with the invention of the air brake and built an industrial empire on the foundation laid by the Westinghouse Air Brake Company. In the mid-1800s, before Westinghouse introduced his system, railroads relied on a cumbersome and ineffective method of braking each car individually. First, the brakes of each car had to be set by a brakeman using a pick handle, then in order to coordinate the braking of a train, so that the cars did not slam into one another and possibly cause a derailment, the brakemen had to turn heavy wheels in unison upon hearing the engineer's

whistle signal. Making routine stops was difficult enough, emergency stops almost impossible. Because of poor braking capabilities, trains were unable to travel at high speeds, yet accounts of train wrecks still filled the newspapers of the day.

Growing up in Schenectady, New York, a city rich in railroad tradition and host to a manufacturer of locomotives, George Westinghouse was understandably fascinated by trains. He learned about machinery and business principles in his father's farm equipment factory. Then at the age of 15, in the midst of the Civil War, Westinghouse ran away from home to join the Union Navy, where he became a shipboard engineering officer. After the war he studied engineering at Union College in Schenectady but dropped out after just three months to pursue his life's work. In 1865 he received his first patents, for an improved rotary steam engine and for a device that remounted derailed freight cars.

In 1866, while traveling between Troy and Schenectady, Westinghouse was delayed when two freight trains crashed head-on in the middle of the day on a smooth, level stretch of track. He was told that the engineers saw one another but were still unable to stop the trains in time. Thus the young inventor turned his attention to the development of a unified train braking system that could be controlled from the locomotive. He worked with the concept of running a chain the length of the train to coordinate the brakes of each car, powered by a steam cylinder under the locomotive. He realized that to avoid slack in the chain each car would require an independent brake cylinder, which also would need a continuous supply of steam from the locomotive. As he grappled with the problem of how to pipe steam and create flexible couplings that would be needed between each car, Westinghouse came upon a magazine article on the Mont Cenis tunnel through the Italian Alps. Engineers on the project powered rock drills by the use of compressed air pumped through a 3,000-foot pipeline. When Westinghouse read about the immense energy generated by air compressed to one-sixth its natural volume, he instantly knew how to power his braking system. If engineers could run a pipeline 3,000 feet through a mountain tunnel, he knew he could run one the length of a train.

In April 1869, at the age of 22, Westinghouse received a patent for the air brake. In September, the Westinghouse Air

---
Company Perspectives:

The Wabtec mission is to help its customers achieve higher levels of quality, safety and productivity so they can compete more effectively.

Brake Company was incorporated in Pennsylvania. A year later in Pittsburgh the company began operations. Within five years 2,281 locomotives and 7,254 cars would be equipped with Westinghouse air brakes. Westinghouse continued to improve his system, not only to make the brakes fail-safe but to allow for longer trains carrying heavier loads at greater speeds. The use of air brakes was a major reason why the number of miles of track in the United States doubled between 1870 and 1880, then doubled again the following decade.

While Westinghouse went on to conduct his major work in electricity and would found some 60 companies to market and manufacture his inventions, he never lost touch with his thriving air brake business. Foreign railroads quickly adopted air brakes. Westinghouse's first overseas air brake company was established in France in 1878, followed by England in 1881, Germany in 1884, Russia in 1899, Canada in 1903, Italy in 1906, and Australia in 1907. At home, high demand for air brakes forced the company to move to a larger plant in Allegheny, Pennsylvania, in 1881. When further expansion became impractical, less than ten years later the company purchased farmland in Wilmerding, Pennsylvania, where it built a new factory as well as a company town.

Westinghouse Air Brake was known to be one of the most enlightened employers of its time. In 1871 it became one of the first companies in American industry to adopt the Saturday half-day of work. During the periodic financial panics of the late 1800s, Westinghouse instructed the company to keep the men employed. In the early 1900s it created a pension plan and established group life insurance policies. Later the company offered veteran employees two-week annual vacations, disability payments, and medical services, long before such benefits became standard.

Death of George Westinghouse in 1914

During the financial panic of 1907, Westinghouse lost control of much of his financial empire, but retained control of the air brake company, which was unfettered by debt. By 1911 he severed ties with all of the companies he founded, then died in 1914. For many years Westinghouse Air Brake would be run by men who came up through the ranks: one started in the foundry, another went to work at the company as a 12-year-old office boy. Three of the five men who followed Westinghouse had been with the company for 40 years before becoming president.

For the most part, Westinghouse Air Brake expanded its business by adapting air brakes to other forms of transportation, not only to other rail systems such as street cars, subway trains, and high-speed metropolitan transit lines but to automotive vehicles as well. In 1921 Westinghouse Air Brake introduced pneumatic brakes for cars and buses. The company also made use of its pneumatic technology for other purposes. Westing-

house had used compressed air to develop a signaling system for the railroads, creating Union Switch & Signal Company to handle the business. In 1917 the company was acquired by Westinghouse Air Brake and incorporated into its operations. Westinghouse Air Brake engineers used its compressed air technology for the U.S. Navy during World War II to develop pneumatic controls that allowed a ship to quickly reverse course in an emergency. The company would subsequently apply its pneumatic remote control systems to the commercial marine industry as well as to other uses, such as drilling and pumping operations in oil fields, and earth-moving equipment. During both world wars, Westinghouse Air Brake also produced a great deal of munitions and electronic products.

Despite diversification, Westinghouse Air Brake was still very much dependent on the volume of rail traffic. After World War II the railroad industry lost a great deal of intercity freight traffic to trucks, and passengers to automobiles, buses, and airplanes. When the Interstate Highway System was completed in the 1960s, the decline in rail usage only accelerated. Nevertheless, Westinghouse Air Brake continued to be in the forefront of technology, developing the first true electronically controlled brakes, which would be used on the original Metroliner cars and rapid transit cars. In 1968 Westinghouse Air Brake also lost its independence, when it was acquired by American Standard—a maker of air conditioning and transportation equipment and building products, but better known for its bathroom and kitchen fixtures—and folded into the company's Railway Products Group as a division called WABCO Railway.

In 1984 the management of Westinghouse Air Brake fell to William E. Kassling, an American Standard vice-president in charge of the Railway Products Group. American Standard was taken private in 1988 by an investment group, which then looked to sell off assets to pay down some of the debt incurred from the $2.3 billion leveraged buyout. In 1990 Kassling led a management buyout of the North American operations of the railway braking products group for $160 million, renaming it Westinghouse Air Brake Co. The non-North American railway assets, based mostly in Europe, were sold to Cardo, a Swedish investment and industrial holding company. At the time of the sell-off, the North American operations that comprised the reconstituted Westinghouse Air Brake Company posted annual sales of about $200 million.

Under Kassling, Westinghouse Air Brake set a number of goals: international growth, expanded aftermarket services, and the acquisition of companies with an entrepreneurial culture. Kassling was also quick to incorporate the Japanese technique known as kaizen, or ''continuous improvement,'' to realize as much performance as possible in some of the company's older plants. In theory, kaizen streamlined processes and choreographed workers' every move to boost productivity. In reality, accommodations to American culture were allowed and a hybrid system evolved. More than just establishing efficient movements, kaizen introduced a spirit of collaboration in the company. Shop floor employees, management, and sometimes customers would hold sessions together. Kassling himself not only toured factories but also spent time working on the floor to gain a firsthand view of operations. Management credited the steady rise in productivity to the kaizen approach.

```
┌─────────────────────────────────────────────┐
│                 Key Dates:                    │
│                                               │
│  1869: George Westinghouse establishes        │
│        company after receiving patent on      │
│        the air brake.                         │
│  1878: French plant becomes first overseas    │
│        operation.                             │
│  1914: George Westinghouse dies.              │
│  1917: Company acquires Union Switch &        │
│        Signal Company.                        │
│  1968: Company is sold to American Standard.   │
│  1984: William E. Kassling takes over         │
│        American Standard's Railway            │
│        Products Group.                        │
│  1988: Kassling-led management buyout gains    │
│        control of company.                    │
│  1995: Company goes public.                   │
│  1999: Westinghouse Air Brake and             │
│        MotivePower merge to form Wabtec       │
│        Corporation.                           │
└─────────────────────────────────────────────┘
```

Going Public: 1995

Westinghouse Air Brake went public in 1995 and began trading on the New York Stock Exchange. Its earnings were lower than expected, attributed in large part to a new braking system that proved faulty and required an investment to upgrade reliability; more importantly, the company faced a weak domestic market in some core businesses. Rail freight was dropping, and the number of freight cars and locomotives was expected to decline significantly. Diversification in product offerings and foreign expansion, especially in the developing markets of China, Russia, India, and South Africa, took on even greater importance.

To this point under Kassling, Westinghouse Air Brake had acquired some domestic assets and established an electronics products division. In 1996 it purchased Australian Futuris Industrial Products for $15 million, as well as Vapor Corp. (a leading American maker of subway car doors) for approximately $65 million. The following year, Westinghouse Air Brake purchased Stone Safety Service Corporation and Stone U.K. Limited, which manufactured air conditioning units for passenger transit in both the United States and England. It then acquired the heavy rail air conditioning business of Thermo King Corporation from Westinghouse Electric. Also in 1997, the company acquired an Italian company, H.P.S.r.l., a leading supplier of door controls for transit railcars and buses in the Italian market.

Domestically, business looked to improve as America's largest railways announced plans to invest billions of dollars to improve their systems. Westinghouse Air Brake looked to expand even more aggressively in 1998. To broaden its aftermarket support it acquired three railroad service centers for equipment upgrades from Comet Industries for $13 million. Westinghouse Air Brake now had eight strategically located service centers across the United States, as well as Canada and Mexico. The company acquired Lokring Corporation, makers of technically advanced pipe connectors that were now being used as couplers in air brake lines, and provided Westinghouse Air Brake with a product that could penetrate into other industrial markets. The transit coupler product line of Hadady Corporation also was purchased for $4.5 million in cash. In one of its

largest transactions, the company purchased the railroad electronics division of Rockwell International for $80 million to augment its train brake and communications product lines.

To expand its foreign business, Westinghouse Air Brake in 1998 entered into a joint venture with an Indian company to sell low friction composite brake shoes to the large India railroad market, which included some 7,000 locomotives, 330,000 freight cars, and 70,000 passenger cars. India was converting from cast iron to composition brake shoes. For $10 million and the assumption of debt, Westinghouse Air Brake acquired RFS(E) Limited of England, a 150-year-old provider of vehicle overhaul, conversion, and maintenance services for the English, Welsh, and Scottish railways. Also in 1998, Westinghouse Air Brake established a relationship with MotivePower, a leading maker of components for locomotives, as well as for the power, marine, and industrial markets. The two companies formed a joint venture in Mexico to build locomotive and railcar components, operating out of a facility owned by a MotivePower Mexican subsidiary. Rebuilding brake shoes at first, the joint venture quickly expanded to include the repair and maintenance of railway electronics equipment.

In 1999 Westinghouse Air Brake and MotivePower began to discuss the possibility of merging the two companies. North American railroads had undergone a period of consolidation in which the top ten railroads merged into five, and they were now looking for bigger, and fewer, suppliers. The $25 billion rail-parts industry was highly fragmented, divided among 800 suppliers, with only 13 large enough to generate more than $200 million in annual sales. Westinghouse Air Brake posted $670 million in 1998. Because the businesses of the two companies complemented one another, investors reacted positively when a $557 million stock swap was announced in June 1999. The merger of equals, which was slated to retain the MotivePower name, would create the largest U.S. company in the rail-parts industry. John C. Pope, chairman of MotivePower, would serve as chairman of the new company, and Kassling would become chief executive officer.

In August 1999, however, the deal with MotivePower underwent a reversal of fortune, when the companies announced that combined 1999 earnings would fall short of the forecast made in June. Stocks of both companies fell, Motivepower's more so than Westinghouse's, making the deal less attractive to the latter's shareholders. The merger was renegotiated and under the new terms roles were reversed. The company would now be called Wabtec and Kassling would serve as both chairman and chief executive officer. Pope would leave after the transaction was completed in November.

During 2000, Wabtec consolidated its new operations. Nine facilities were closed and ten product lines were moved to lower-cost plants. Overall, employment was cut by 11 percent. In February 2001, Kassling announced that because the company was well positioned financially and strategically for the future he decided to turn over the job of chief executive to Gregory T.H. Davies, who had led the restructuring program. Kassling would remain as chairman of the board.

Going forward, Wabtec looked to benefit from a rail industry that had undergone something of a revitalization. Railroad traffic increased significantly in the 1990s. A shortage of truck drivers and the cost of trucking freight had caused many shippers to turn to railway intermodal services. Rather than the 1950s' and 1960s' system that used trailers on flatcars, which deserved its poor reputation for damaged goods and tardiness, modern intermodal transport involved specially designed cars hauled by dedicated trains on specific traffic lanes. For long hauls intermodal offered a significant price break over highway transport. Railroad began to make concerted efforts to reintroduce intermodal to many shippers with ingrained misgivings about it. Foreign rail markets, in particular China, Australia, and India, also looked promising. Wabtec, with its variety of products and services, as well as its size, appeared as well suited as any company in the industry to take advantage of future opportunities in rail transport.

Principal Divisions

Electronics; Freight Car; Transit; Locomotive; Friction & Other.

Principal Competitors

ABC-NACO; Adtranz; Alstom; General Electric Company; Knorr-Bremse; Woodward Corp.

Further Reading

Aeppel, Timothy, "More, More, More: Rust-Belt Factory Lifts Productivity, and Staff Finds It's No Picnic," *Wall Street Journal,* May 18, 1999, p. A1.

Gallagher, John, "Reaching Intermodal," *Traffic World,* February 19, 2001, p. 31.

Jacobs, Karen, "Westinghouse Air, MotivePower Alter Terms of Merger," *Wall Street Journal,* September 28, 1999, p. 1.

Prout, Henry G., *A Life of George Westinghouse,* New York: Arno Press, 1921.

75th Anniversary of the Westinghouse Air Brake Company, Wilnerding, Penn.: Westinghouse Air Brake Co., 1944.

Sullivan, Allanna, and Timothy Aeppel, "MotivePower, Westinghouse Air Brake to Merge in a $633.8 Million Accord," *Wall Street Journal,* June 4, 1999, p. B4.

Wicks, Frank, "How George Westinghouse Changed the World," *Mechanical Engineering,* October 1996, pp. 74–79.

—Ed Dinger

WALL DRUG
OF SOUTH DAKOTA

Wall Drug Store, Inc.

---

510 Main Street
Wall, South Dakota 57709
U.S.A.
Telephone: (605) 279-2175
Fax: (605) 279-2699
Web site: http://www.walldrug.com

Private Company
Incorporated: 1931
Employees: 225
Sales: $12 million (2000 est.)
NAIC: 44611 Pharmacies and Drug Stores; 42221 Drugs
and Druggist's Sundries Wholesalers

Wall Drug Store, Inc. is a unique institution in the annals of American business, and its namesake store has become a permanent part of the national landscape. Beginning as a small town pharmacy and sundry outlet, Wall Drug has developed into a 76,000-square-foot western tourist attraction that is visited by up to 20,000 people a day. Visitors flock to Wall Drug from all over the world, due in large part to the unusual advertising methods which the owners have used since the family-run company's inception. Wall Drug specializes in western items, Native American artifacts, fine art, decorative accessories, food and drink, and gifts and collectibles. Other offerings include a restaurant that accommodates over 500 people, a traveler's chapel, and a play area for children. Guests are still treated to free ice water, Wall Drug's original marketing gimmick, and coffee at five cents a cup.

A Small Town with Daily Mass: 1931

Wall Drug began when Ted and Dorothy Hustead, a young married couple looking to settle in a small town somewhere in South Dakota or Nebraska, happened upon Wall, South Dakota. Ted had graduated from pharmacy school in 1929 and had worked steadily for several druggists, ending up in Canova, South Dakota. However, when his father died in 1931, Ted's small inheritance of $3,000 seemed to be the key to realizing the dream he and his wife shared of owning a drugstore.

The couple began searching for available stores. Traveling the countryside in their Ford Model T the Husteads had two particular qualities in mind when it came to selecting a town: they wanted a fairly small town and, being devout Catholics, they wanted to attend mass on a daily basis. The town, therefore, would have to have its own Catholic church. Wall, South Dakota, a town of 326 people at the edge of the Badlands, met the criteria. In December 1931, after prayerful consideration, the Husteads purchased the small local drugstore there.

Business was difficult during the first few years. It was the middle of the Great Depression and money was scarce everywhere, but especially in a place as remote as Wall. The Husteads were not easily discouraged and both agreed to a five-year trial run before moving on. Ted, Dorothy, and their young son, Billy, took up residence in the back of the store where they had made an ''apartment,'' by cordoning off the area with a blanket, and tried their best to make Wall Drug a successful venture.

The family hoped that upon the completion of the Mount Rushmore monument to their west, traffic to the town would increase, and so would their presently meager profits. Depending solely on sales from the impoverished citizens of Wall seemed unrealistic; as the national economy improved, tourists with their ready cash might save Wall's struggling business.

The Husteads' strong religious faith had them believing they were in Wall for a reason; they were making friendships, providing medical care, and feeling a part of community life, but they were beginning to have doubts about their ability to eke out a living in such an unassuming town. With the birth in 1936 of their second child, Mary Elizabeth, the doubts increased. The family was beginning to wonder whether their talents and abilities might be better served in another location.

And Ne'er a Drop to Drink: 1936

The summer of 1936 brought inspiration and renewed faith to Dorothy Hustead and her family. One quiet afternoon Dorothy, tired from caring for her newborn daughter, went to lie down for a nap with Billy and the baby. Dorothy related the story years later recalling that she was having a difficult time falling asleep with all of the noise from traffic on route 16A near the store. She began thinking of how to draw all those travelers into the store and was struck by a revolutionary idea.

People were driving along old rural highways in the tremendously hot prairie sun and were thirsty. Wall Drug would offer these travelers free ice water in order to entice them into the store. The idea was a hit, and the store soon became known for its western small town hospitality, retaining that image throughout its history. The Husteads constructed highway signs and placed them along the busy highway. Dorothy developed the slogan, "Get a soda . . . Get a root beer . . . Turn next corner . . . Just as near . . . To Highway 14 . . . Free Ice Water . . . Wall Drug." The series of signs inspired visitors from the day they were posted to stop at the "ice water store." By the following summer the Husteads employed five additional workers to help run the operation.

Advertising and creative marketing put Wall Drug on the map. Signs were erected in neighboring states to draw traffic to the store and, when those billboards created a sensation, signs were added around the globe. Many signs marked the distance in miles from their location to Wall Drug. The media campaign became so all encompassing that billboards and bumper stickers made Wall Drug a name recognized worldwide. Bill Hustead, Ted and Dorothy's son, joined Wall Drug in 1951 after completing his pharmacy degree. Wall Drug enjoyed moderate success throughout the 1950s, expanding its merchandise and advertising in a grandiose style.

But in 1965, what was to become known as the Lady Bird Johnson Highway Beautification Project, or Highway Beautification Act, threatened the very heart of Wall Drug. Outdoor advertising along the interstate was to be regulated and those billboards that were never awarded permits were to be removed. Wall Drug stood to lose 240 of its 280 road signs under the act. Fortunately for the many small restaurants and hotels that relied on outdoor advertising, funds that were to be used to compensate sign owners ran out in 1983 and the law was never enforced.

In 1974 financial advisors warned Bill Hustead that the future of the drugstore was bleak. The advisors wanted the family to pull their resources out of the company. Instead of taking this recommendation Bill decided to follow the course

his parents had taken before him and he launched a huge expansion. With the store expansion came an equally ambitious advertising campaign. Hustead sunk $280,000 into large highway signs just off I-90 and hoped for success. Wall Drug expanded its operations to the south of the original building in 1975 and the following year the Emporium with its doughnut factory, gift shop, and magazine shop, and a new dining room that could seat up to 520 people, were built. According to President Ted H. Hustead, "The plan was if the drugstore was interesting enough, exciting enough, famous enough, and we could save a few of our signs, we would stay in business."

In 1978 expansion continued to the south of the recently constructed mall. A western wear shop selling hats, boots, and apparel completed the project. Gross sales that year reached an all-time high of $4.4 million and it was looking as if creative marketing and the risk of expansion had paid off.

However, in 1979 there was a dramatic downturn in sales due in large part to the nation's energy crisis, and the subsequent gas shortages, fuel lines, and higher prices. Sales topped off at $3.4 million and the company lost 90 percent of its net income. Fortunately for Wall Drug this slowdown was temporary and by 1980 sales rose to $3.9 million.

In 1991 a notice in the *Federal Register* announced that states would lose significant highway funds if they were not compliant with the Highway Beautification Act by December 1993. States were expected to use a portion of the funds they were given for highway projects to pay for signs that did not meet federal code. According to an article in *Restaurant Business Magazine*, "Overnight the government was talking about spending $428 million to remove an estimated 22,000 illegal and 92,000 non-conforming signs. It was targeting virtually all billboards in rural zones on interstate and federal "primary" highways." Rick Hustead estimated that the removal of billboards could potentially reduce Wall Drug's business by 30 to 50 percent.

Bill's sons Ted and Rick, were the third generation of Husteads to run Wall Drug. The store continued to be a family enterprise. Ted H. Hustead took over as president, with Rick as chairman and the brothers' wives managing the art gallery and soda fountain. Ted Hustead explained their unusual marketing style by saying, "We concentrated on obtaining advertising in strange and different places in hopes of attracting national and international publicity: signs at the canal in Amsterdam, signs on 20 London double-decker buses, in the London underground, in 6,000 Paris bistros, in the railroad stations of Kenya, Africa, ads in the *International Herald Tribune*. We were seeking publicity! Did it come? You bet."

Throughout the 1980s stories of Wall Drug appeared in *Time, Guideposts, USA Today, People,* and other newspapers and magazines; the unusual business was also featured on the *Today Show*. The company continued to do what it did best— promote small-town America, and celebrate the enterprising nature of its owners in the face of adversity. The drugstore became identified as a cultural icon, a pharmaceutical "little engine that could." America was losing its small towns and main streets to big cities, suburbs, and shopping malls. Wall Drug celebrated the small western town to the extreme.

Key Dates:

1931: Ted and Dorothy Hustead buy a small drugstore in Wall, South Dakota.

1936: Dorothy Hustead conceives "Free Ice Water" campaign.

1951: Bill Hustead, son of the founders, joins the family business.

1965: Highway Beautification Act threatens business.

1975: Store additions to "the mall" and the south side of the building almost double Wall Drug's square footage; $280,000 is spent on large signs nearby.

1976: Company adds an Emporium and enlarges the Dining Room.

1981: Rick Hustead, grandson of the founders, joins the Wall Drug staff.

1984: Five-shop addition is completed, including a traveler's chapel.

1991: Federal law allows for construction funds to be used to remove billboard advertising that does not conform to zoning codes.

1995: Cofounder Dorothy Hustead dies.

1996: Expansion continues with the 14,000-square-foot Backyard Mall.

1997: Wall Drug removes old wooden Indian.

1999: Ted Hustead dies at age 97; Bill Hustead dies after two-year battle with Lou Gehrig's disease.

In 1995 Wall Drug partially opened its 14,000-square-foot Backyard Mall, completing the opening the following year. The Backyard Mall included more stores devoted to merchandise, a "skinny" saloon, food shops, and a Wall Drug Outlet store. Some 1,200 photographs dating from 1880–1909 were also put on public display, making it one of the most extensive permanent exhibits of western photographic history.

Facing the Future: 1990s–2001

In the 1990s the store gained the respect of Native Americans when it addressed a store patron's concerns. Wall Drug had always been known for its western atmosphere, and it had displays of all sorts of western-related memorabilia, including Indian encampments and cowboy legends. The owners took pride in paying tribute to the Badlands' rich history of Native American tradition and white settlement in the region, so the Husteads were surprised when one of their displays was criticized as being racist. David Rossetti and Codye Amiotte Jumping Wolf called Wall Drug to say that they were offended by a six-foot tall wooden "cigar store" Indian they had encountered in the Drugstore Mall.

Rossetti and Jumping Wolf viewed the carving as demeaning and suggested that the representation with its red painted face was a distorted racist caricature of an Indian, and that Wall Drug in displaying it was doing a disservice to the Native American community.

To their credit, the Husteads took the issue seriously and went to the store's entrance to look at the statue. The family wondered what the problem could possibly be with a statue they had displayed for over 30 years without complaint. Bill Hustead had always considered himself a friend of the Native American community and was shocked when he looked at the statue with a new awareness. According to an article in *Indian Country Today,* "He (Hustead) really saw the wooden Indian for the first time, it was ugly, he said, and its face was painted red. The family made a unanimous decision to get rid of the statue. Immediately it was hauled away."

The business gradually evolved into a 22-store complex, built to resemble a small western town. Dorothy Hustead passed away in 1996 but founder Ted maintained a managerial presence at Wall Drug well into his 90s, keeping a close eye on his life's work. Ted Hustead died in 1999 at the age of 97. Bill Hustead passed away later that year after battling Lou Gehrig's disease for several years.

In the new millennium, the legacy of Wall Drug continued, drawing people from all over the world to the small and relatively insignificant town of Wall, South Dakota. Except for the idea of Dorothy Hustead, and the enterprising attitude of the rest of the Hustead family, Wall most likely would have continued to go unnoticed. The family's perseverance, however, had created a household word, and a destination for travelers driving down hot, dusty highways looking for ice water and much, much more.

Further Reading

Oleck, Joan, "Roadside Roadblock," *Restaurant Business Magazine,* May 1, 1992, p. 46.

Quinn, Michelle, "From Here to Hell," *Marketing News,* June 19, 2000, p. 10.

Schneider-Levy, Barbara, "The Right Gimmick," *Footwear News,* September 21, 1998, p. 19.

"Wall Drug Store, Wall, S.D., Removes Offensive Wooden Indian," *Knight-Ridder/Tribune Business News,* September 1, 1997 p. 901B0955.

Wascoe, Dan, Jr., "From Wall Drug to InVision: Through the Looking Glass," *Star Tribune* (Minneapolis), April 12, 1992, p. 4D.

"A Watery Success," *Chemist & Druggist,* December 30, 2000, p. 22.

—Susan B. Culligan

Weber-Stephen Products Co.

200 E. Daniels Road
Palatine, Illinois 60067-6266
U.S.A.
Telephone: (847) 934-5700
Fax: (847) 934-0291
Web site: http://www.weberbq.com

Private Company
Incorporated: 1958
Employees: 200
Sales: $145 million (1999 est.)
NAIC: 335221 Household Cooking Appliance
   Manufacturing

Family-owned Weber-Stephen Products Co. manufactures the Weber grill, a brand name that over the years has become all but synonymous with outdoor barbecue grilling. A sales leader in charcoal grills since the company's inception in the 1950s, Weber-Stephen has in more recent years developed a line of gas grills, a market in which the company was late in pursuing. Based in the Chicago area, Weber-Stephen is not only privately held, it is extremely private in general, taking on the personality of publicity-shy George Stephen, who invented the Weber Kettle Grill and ran the company for more than 30 years. Eleven out of his 12 children have been employed by Weber-Stephen. All decline to be interviewed by the press.

Barbecuing—A Developing
American Pastime: 1800s–1940s

Outdoor cooking dates back to the discovery of fire, and many cultures have traditions of great feasts in which wild game was roasted over or under hot coals. Supposedly, grilling came to America by way of the Caribbean island of Hispaniola, where in the 17th century shipwrecked sailors and assorted rogues adapted the native method of cooking over hot coals by suspending meat on a grid of green wood, which the Spanish called a *barbacoa.* They took this method to Mexico and the American Southwest. On the range, cattle ranchers created a metal barbacoa to cook meat in order to feed their ranchhands. The new barbecued meats and outdoor method of cooking became the perfect magnet for social gatherings, drawing crowds for fairs as well as political rallies.

Many houses in the early 1900s featured brick or stone fireplaces in the backyard where outdoor cooking was done. In cases where people were required to burn their own trash, backyard incinerators were modified to accommodate grilling. Many people fashioned barbecue grills and smokers out of wine barrels, oil drums, trash cans, water heater tanks, and metal roofing. Rather than using hot coals, these grills relied on wood and kindling. An unlikely man would develop a more convenient fuel that would greatly increase the popularity of backyard barbecuing. His name was Henry Ford.

Ford, who never cared for waste or passed up a chance to make more money, owned a saw mill that provided the wooden frames for his Model T automobiles. To make use of leftovers he decided to burn wood scrap and sawdust in order to form charcoal, which was then ground into powder, mixed with a starch binder, and compressed into briquettes. The Ford Charcoal Company was located in the Michigan town of Kingsford, which would eventually bear the name of the charcoal business. Ford's method of marketing his briquettes was anything but subtle. With every railcar of automobiles, his dealers also received a railcar of Ford charcoal to sell. At first the briquettes were sold as heating fuel but soon they were discovered to be perfectly suited for outdoor barbecuing. Not only were they easier to use than wood, they provided an evenly distributed source of heat.

Makeshift grills were still the order of the day, but following World War II, when many veterans took advantage of the G.I. Bill to purchase vast numbers of suburban homes complete with backyards and patios, barbecuing became even more widespread and the first manufactured home grills began to appear. Most were of the brazier category: shallow, uncovered grills that tended to burn too hot and, cooking so close to the coals, were prone to flare-ups. Nevertheless, suburbia embraced the backyard grill, whether it be a permanent stone structure, a converted wine barrel, or a cheap tin brazier. Most grills were tended by men, who in the postwar era began to wield the tongs in the family—at least outdoors.

458

Key Dates:

1951: George Stephen invents the kettle grill.
1958: Weber-Stephen Products is established.
1989: Weber Grill Restaurant opens.
1993: George Stephen dies at the age of 71.
1995: Gas grill sales surpass charcoal grill sales.

Invention of the Weber: 1951

One of those weekend chefs was 30-year-old George Stephen, who in 1951 lived in the Chicago suburb of Mount Prospect. He did his barbecuing over an old brick grill. In one of his rare interviews, he told the *New York Times* that ''I was smoking up the neighborhood and burning up half of what I cooked. What was worse, I had to spend all my time away from the bar, standing there with a squirt gun to put out the fire when the grease hit the hot coals.'' Wind and rain also added to the problems of cooking on an open grill. Stephen was part owner of Weber Brothers Metal Works, a Chicago custom order sheet metal shop that produced, among other products, half-spheres that were welded together to make buoys for Lake Michigan. Rather than just dream about the perfect outdoor grill, Stephen decided to create it, utilizing the metal shop at his disposal.

Stephen designed a barbecue grill that featured a ventilated lid to control the smoking and flaming. Using two halves of a buoy, Stephen's prototype stood thigh high with a round fire pan and a matching lid with four closable vents. It worked so well that many of his friends wanted one too. The next year he decided to build 50 of the grills and see if he could sell them. ''George's Barbecue Kettle,'' as the refined product was first called, was priced around $50 at a time when braziers cost just $7, yet it sold so well that by 1958 Stephen bought out Weber Brothers and dropped all other metal working projects in favor of building nothing but his outdoor grill. He renamed the shop Weber-Stephen Products, retaining part of the original name in case he had to return to doing other sheet metal work.

In 1959 Weber-Stephen employed 12 men who turned out 15,000 units. Stephen hired Ed Schaper, a printing salesman, to help sell the kettle grill. Both men not only forged relationships with wholesalers, they visited area supermarkets and shopping centers to show consumers how to cook on the new kettle grill, which unlike open braziers had the ability to circulate heat by an adjustment of the vents. One of their early big breaks came during a Wisconsin bratwurst festival when, because of a sudden rain storm, all of their competitors had to shut down. The kettle grill, protected from the elements by its lid, had the field to itself.

Sales grew steadily, generally between 15 and 30 percent, so that by the late 1960s the Weber grill was a fixture in the Midwest, particularly Chicago and Milwaukee. On either coast, however, Weber grill sales trailed such competing brands as Big Boy and Charbroil. When inexpensive foreign products, including Hibachi grills, entered the U.S. market in the 1970s, many domestic grill manufacturers responded by turning to thinner metal and lightweight designs in order to compete on price. Weber-Stephen took an opposite approach, opting for more solid construction and targeting the high-end market. With many Americans becoming interested in more sophisticated fare than just hamburgers and an occasional chicken breast, the Weber grill became the product of choice for the more upscale market. Clearly well designed and made to last, Weber grills could easily command a premium pricepoint. Weber-Stephen had by this time developed a roster of freelance representatives to sell their grills in the United States and Canada and, to a lesser degree, overseas. Sales increased by 40 percent a year in the mid-1970s. Although the company did not announce its financial results, it was estimated that by the late-1970s Weber-Stephen was shipping between 500,000 and 800,000 units a year, generating gross sales between $15 million and $24 million.

The product was so entrenched by now that ''the Weber'' became almost a generic term for barbecue grill. Stephen continued to run the company, bringing his children into the operation, with 11 out of 12 working for Weber-Stephen at some point. As more and more households purchased grills, the market began to mature and the rapid growth in Weber sales tailed off. In the late 1970s and into the 1980s, Weber-Stephen would make attempts at diversification, turning to such products as lanterns, bird feeders, mailboxes, tablecloths, sail covers, and electronic bug zappers. After suffering poor results in these ventures, the company decided to focus on making its grills even better. They also moved aggressively to protect their kettle design. In 1983, some two dozen foreign competitors exhibited grills that looked like Webers at the National Hardware show, prompting Weber-Stephen to pursue a five-year legal battle to gain trademark status on its kettle design.

Aside from foreign companies, Weber-Stephen faced an additional challenge from the makers of gas grills, which had been around since 1960 when the units were tied to natural gas lines and anchored in place. In the early 1970s propane tanks were introduced, making gas grills portable. George Stephen recognized the potential of gas and as early as 1972 made an attempt to incorporate it into his line of grills, but in the end he decided instead to focus on charcoal grills. By the mid-1980s, however, gas grills were beginning to make significant gains, despite a price that was much higher than charcoal grills. Many consumers were simply won over by the speed and convenience of gas.

Weber-Stephen, well behind in gas grill development to such heavyweight competitors as Sunbeam Products, invested the money and resources necessary to develop gas grills, premiering its Genesis line in 1985. In that year, charcoal grills still outsold gas grills by a wide margin, accounting for 70 of the more than 11 million total units sold, but the momentum was clearly with the gas segment of the market. The sale of charcoal grills peaked in 1988, then began to slide, while the sale of gas grills continued to rise, finally surpassing charcoal in 1995.

Weber-Stephen made another attempt to broaden its business in 1989 by opening The Weber Grill Restaurant in Wheeling, Illinois. With its kitchen using six oversized Weber grills that customers could watch in action through a large window, the restaurant not only offered food that typical outdoor chefs might prepare, it demonstrated the versatility of the Weber grill by featuring such dishes as veal-stuffed pork chops or trout grilled with a bread crumb crust. The Wheeling restaurant was clearly testing the waters for a possible franchising concept, but mixed reviews dampened the enthusiasm for rapid growth. Weber-Stephen maintained that the restaurant was a success and that it would consider opening new outlets if the right situation arose, and in fact the Weber Grill Restaurant was still open a dozen years later, although no new restaurants had been added.

Death of George Stephen: 1993

Although Stephen would remain president and CEO, in the early 1980s he began a transition of power by forming an executive committee, comprised of his heirs and longtime company executives, that would one day run the company. He then spent a good deal of time traveling to such places as Africa and Antarctica. He concentrated on the manufacturing side of the business, leaving marketing to others. Stephen died in 1993 at the age of 71; his son James, the third oldest child, assumed the position of president and CEO. Like his father, James Stephen refused to speak with the press, and the company's financial results were closely guarded. Not having to answer to shareholders on a quarterly basis was an advantage that Weber-Stephen continued to hold over its competitors. The company was able to invest in research and development and not have to show immediate results. No matter how profitable Weber-Stephen may have been when its founder died, some observers questioned how well positioned the company was for the long run.

Weber-Stephen continued to steadily sell its high-end charcoal grills in the 1990s, even after sales of gas grills overtook charcoal. By the end of the century barbecuing was more popular than ever. According to the Barbecue Industry Association, about 75 percent of all U.S. households owned a barbecue grill in 1999, and 40 percent owned more than one. Many owned both a gas and a charcoal grill. Almost 60 percent of grills were used year-round, with men far more likely than women to do the barbecuing. Many consumers buying Weber grills were upgrading to a better-made unit that would not rust out in a season or two. Gas grills, in the meantime, were becoming even more expensive, with new models being introduced each year in a manner similar to luxury cars. With the U.S. economy booming in the late 1990s, deluxe barbecue grills became almost a status purchase. Some of these "outdoor cooking systems," which featured a massive gas grill cooking surface, side burners, and a refrigerator, approached $10,000 in price.

Weber-Stephen, with its reputation for quality and accepted higher pricepoint, was well situated to take advantage of consumers' desire for more expensive gas grills. The company staked its territory below the deluxe market but well above the average-priced grill. While Sunbeam focused on the $150–$200 market, Weber-Stephen's low-end gas grill cost $360 and was never sale priced. In 1997 the top-end Weber gas grill cost $1,000. A year later the company introduced the Summit model costing $3,000, which it launched with a splashy advertising campaign in major magazines.

Entering a new century, Weber-Stephen appeared to have made a successful transition between generations of the Stephen family. Charcoal grills maintained a loyal following, gas grills were highly profitable, and the Weber name continued to be a valuable asset, which along with its grill designs the company was active in protecting. Weber-Stephen sued a Chicago hardware store that had taken the Internet address www.webergrills.com in order to sell Weber grills. When it was clear that it would lose, Weber-Stephen withdrew the suit. The company also sued Sunbeam in 1998 over patent infringement involving the use of a sear grid on gas grills.

Weber-Stephen looked to further expand its distribution channels beyond hardware stores to department stores and other high-end retailers. It also looked to the Internet to sell its high-cost, low volume grills. Discount stores, such as Wal-Mart and Kmart, where most consumers bought grills, was one market that the company needed to shore up. Foreign sales offered potential as well, but presented several ongoing challenges. With little trademark protection in many countries, Weber had to compete with cheaper knock-offs of its designs. Shipping costs of its heavy units also put the Weber grill at a price disadvantage. But perhaps one of the greatest obstacles to increased overseas sales was simply a cultural one: convincing men that there was no shame in doing the cooking.

Principal Subsidiaries

Weber Grill Restaurant.

Principal Competitors

Sunbeam Products; Martin Industries; Salton, Inc.

Further Reading

Drinkard, Lauren, "Weber Still Hot But May Need to Turn Up the Gas," *Advertising Age,* September 11, 1995, p. 4.

Feldman, Amy, "A Second Generation on the Hot Spot," *Forbes,* August 1, 1994, p. 88.

Kelly, Michael, "The Weber Grill: American Classic," *Boston Globe,* May 24, 1989, p. 41.

King, Seth S., "Lighting a Fire in the Barbecue Business," *New York Times,* July 3, 1977, Section 3, p. 3.

"Maker of Weber Grill Fights to Stay on Top," *New York Times,* August 19, 1985, p D1.

Murphy, H. Lee, "Grill Maker Turns Up Gas," *Crain's Chicago Business,* August 14, 1989, p. 3.

Rice, Wandalyn, "The Weber Mystique," *Chicago Tribune,* July 27, 1997, p. 1.

Salmon, Jacqueline, "Summer: The Grill of It All; Many Barbecuers Spare No Expense," *Washington Post,* May 24, 1997, p. B1.

Strauss, Gary, "Holy Smokes! Grill Makers Stake out Tasty Top-End Market," *USA Today,* July 2, 1997, p. B1.

—Ed Dinger

Yamaha Corporation

10-1, Nakazawa-cho
Hamamatsu, Shizuoka 430-8650
Japan
Telephone: (53) 460-2211
Fax: (53) 460-2525
Web site: http://www.yamaha.co.jp

Public Company
Incorporated: 1897 as Nippon Gakki Co., Ltd.
Employees: 21,599
Sales: ¥527.90 billion ($4.97 billion) (2000)
Stock Exchanges: Tokyo Osaka Nagoya
NAIC: 331513 Steel Foundries (Except Investment);
334119 Other Computer Peripheral Equipment
Manufacturing; 334310 Audio and Video
Equipment Manufacturing; 334413 Semiconductor
and Related Device Manufacturing; 339920
Sporting and Athletic Good Manufacturing; 339992
Musical Instrument Manufacturing; 551112 Offices
of Other Holding Companies; 611610 Fine Arts
Schools

Yamaha Corporation, one of Japan's most diversified companies, is the world's largest maker of musical instruments, including pianos and keyboards, wind instruments, string and percussion instruments, and digital musical instruments. Since 1950 the company has also become a major producer of audio products, semiconductors and other electronics products, furniture, sporting goods, and specialty metals. Yamaha also runs music schools in Japan and 40 other countries, owns and operates a string of resorts located throughout Japan, and holds a 33 percent stake in the separately managed Yamaha Motor Company, Ltd., the world's second largest producer of motorcycles, and a producer as well of boats, snowmobiles, golf carts, all-terrain vehicles, engines, and industrial robots. Nearly three-fourths of Yamaha Corporation's net sales are derived from its musical instrument and audio products operations.

19th-Century Origins

Yamaha founder Torakusu Yamaha's venture reflected late 19th-century Japan's enthusiasm for new technologies and the ability of its middle-class entrepreneurs to develop products based on them. Raised in what is now the Wakayama Prefecture, Yamaha received an unusual education for the time from his samurai father, a surveyor with broad interests in astronomy and mechanics and a remarkable library. The Meiji Restoration, a government-subsidized effort to hasten technological development in the late 19th century, put educated people such as Yamaha in a position to capitalize on the new growth.

At age 20 Yamaha studied watch repair in Nagasaki under a British engineer. He formed his own watchmaking company, but he was unable to stay in business because of a lack of money. He then took a job repairing medical equipment in Osaka after completing an apprenticeship at Japan's first school of Western medicine in Nagasaki.

As part of his job, Yamaha repaired surgical equipment in Hamamatsu, a small Pacific coastal fishing town. Because of their area's isolation, a township school there asked him in 1887 to repair their prized U.S.-made Mason & Hamlin reed organ. Seeing the instrument's commercial potential in Japan, Yamaha produced his own functional version of the organ within a year and then set up a new business in Hamamatsu to manufacture organs for Japanese primary schools. In 1889 he established the Yamaha Organ Manufacturing Company, Japan's first maker of Western musical instruments. At the same time, the government granted Hamamatsu township status, which provided it with rail service and made it a regional commerce center.

Western musical traditions interested the Japanese government, which fostered and catered to growing enthusiasm for Western ideas. While Yamaha's technical education enabled him to manufacture a product, government investment in infrastructure made it possible for him to create a business. Yamaha Organ used modern mass-production methods, and by 1889 it employed 100 people and produced 250 organs annually.

During the 1890s the more inexpensive upright piano surpassed the reed organ in popularity in U.S. homes. Yamaha saw

Company Perspectives:

Yamaha is one of the world's leading manufacturers of pianos, digital musical instruments, and wind, string, and percussion instruments. At the same time, the Company has grown through a broad spectrum of business activities, including electronic devices and equipment, professional audio equipment, and audiovisual equipment.

To continue growing in the 21st century, the Yamaha Group will make a concerted effort to become a truly global enterprise that fulfills its corporate mission of contributing to enriching the quality of life of people worldwide.

the potential of this market. In 1897 he renamed his company Nippon Gakki Co., Ltd., which literally means Japan musical instruments. He opened a new plant and headquarters in the Itaya-cho district of Hamamatsu.

In 1899 one of Yamaha's initial investors convinced other investors to pull out of Yamaha in favor of a competitor, a new organ maker that was near failure. Yamaha managed to borrow the money necessary to remain solvent and buy out his partners.

Japan's government not only supported industrialization through heavy manufacturing, but also encouraged upstart businesses to contact overseas markets directly. Expansion into pianos required more research, so the Japanese Ministry of Education sponsored a Yamaha tour of the United States in 1899. He was to study piano making and to establish suppliers for the materials needed to produce pianos in Japan. In one year Nippon Gakki produced its first piano. Governmental and institutional orders were the first filled, including some for the Ministry of Education. In 1902, with U.S. materials and German technology, Nippon Gakki introduced its first grand piano. In 1903 the company produced 21 pianos.

Nippon Gakki demonstrated its new pianos in select international exhibitions. Between 1902 and 1920, the company received awards for its pianos and organs that had never before gone to a Japanese manufacturer, for example a Grand Prix at the St. Louis World Exposition in 1904.

The World Wars

World War I curtailed sales by a German harmonica marker in Japan, so Nippon Gakki took the opportunity to broaden its product base and begin making and exporting harmonicas. Producing new products that required the same raw materials and manufacturing skills became a major operating principle for Nippon Gakki.

Yamaha died suddenly during the war. He had succeeded in introducing Western instruments and assembly techniques, but despite his assembly lines, piano making was still a craftsperson's industry at the time of his death. Vice-President Chiyomaru Amano assumed the presidency in 1917. His political contacts had helped the company expand. He saw the company through repeated labor strife for ten years before being replaced.

World War I produced tremendous growth in Japanese industry, and Nippon Gakki grew with it, supplying Asian markets cut off from traditional sources of supply. By 1920 it employed 1,000 workers and produced 10,000 organs and 1,200 pianos a year. The sales records set during the war continued afterward, despite recession. These gains were largely due to piano sales which doubled to ¥2 million between 1919 and 1921.

The next five years nearly put the company in bankruptcy. Appreciation of the yen, which made Nippon Gakki products less competitive overseas, was part of the problem. In 1922, fire destroyed a new plant in Nakazawa and the main Itayacho plant in Hamamatsu. The next year the Great Kanto earthquake destroyed the Tokyo office and again damaged company plants. Before the company recovered, labor unions went on strike after Amano refused to negotiate. Amano gave in to the union's demands 105 days later, after the company's reserves were depleted.

Board member Kaichi Kawakami, by request of the other directors, took the presidency in 1927. A director of Sumitomo Wire Company, Kawakami made an unexpectedly nontraditional choice in accepting the position at the troubled company. Kawakami cut production costs and reorganized the company. Half of all debts were paid within 18 months of Kawakami taking over.

Between the world wars, Western imports still dominated the Japanese sales of Western instruments. Since Nippon Gakki's advantage was in price alone, Kawakami opened an acoustics lab and research center in 1930 to improve quality. He also hired advisors from C. Bechstein of Germany to improve the quality of the Yamaha piano.

The growth of the public school system of the 1930s expanded the market for Western instruments, and Nippon Gakki introduced lower priced accordions and guitars to capitalize on the expansion.

When World War II began, Nippon Gakki plants produced propellers for Zero fighter planes, fuel tanks, and wing parts. As with expansion during World War I, these items laid the groundwork for broader diversification in the postwar years. In the meantime, Nippon Gakki had to stop making musical instruments altogether in 1945.

Postwar Expansion

Only one Nippon Gakki factory survived the wartime U.S. bombing raids. Postwar financial assistance from the United States made possible the production of harmonicas and xylophones just two months after receipt of the funds. Within six months it produced organs, accordions, tube horns, and guitars. After the Allied powers approved civilian trade in 1947, Nippon Gakki began once again to export harmonicas.

Nippon Gakki already had experience with wooden aircraft parts dating back to 1920, but wartime activity exposed the company to new technologies. By 1947 Nippon Gakki could cast its own metal piano frames and produced its first pianos in three years. The company also produced its first audio component—a phonograph—in 1947.

Postwar growth was rapid. The Japanese government had fostered the growth of Western music in Japan since 1879, but

---

Key Dates:

1887: Company founder Torakusu Yamaha builds his first reed organ.
1889: Yamaha founds Yamaha Organ Manufacturing Company, Japan's first maker of Western musical instruments.
1897: Company's name is changed to Nippon Gakki Co., Ltd.
1900: Company produces its first upright piano.
1902: Production of grand pianos begins.
1930: Company opens an acoustics lab and research center.
1948: Japan's Education Ministry mandates musical education for Japanese children, expanding Yamaha's business.
1954: Yamaha Music Schools debut.
1955: Company produces its first motorcycle through an affiliated company, Yamaha Motor Company, Ltd.
1958: First overseas subsidiary is established in Mexico.
1967: First concert grand piano is produced.
1971: Production of semiconductors begins.
1982: The first Disklavier pianos are produced.
1983: Company introduces the DX-7 digital synthesizer, a top seller.
1987: Company changes its name to Yamaha Corporation to celebrate the 100th anniversary of the firm.
1993: The Silent Piano series debuts.
2000: Yamaha posts a net loss of $384 million for the fiscal year ending in March; newly installed President Shuji Ito initiates a restructuring program.

Nippon Gakki received its biggest boost to date in 1948. That year the Education Ministry mandated musical education for Japanese children—only encouraged before the war—and greatly expanded business.

Kaichi Kawakami's son, Gen'ichi Kawakami, became the company's fourth president in 1950. During his tenure the Japanese rebuilt their economy, and consumer buying power increased. Nippon Gakki became less reliant on institutional purchases. President for 27 years, Kawakami made more progress in popularizing Western music in Japan by beginning the Yamaha Music Schools in 1954 to train young musicians. With the help of the Ministry of Education, Nippon Gakki founded the nonprofit Yamaha Music Foundation in 1966 to sponsor festivals and concerts and run the music schools.

Kawakami's biggest accomplishments were in production, diversification, and the creation of foreign markets, all of which built the framework for the modern Yamaha Corporation. Kawakami toured the United States and Europe in 1953, a trip that inspired diversification into many areas unrelated to the music industry. Like Yamaha's tour of the United States in 1899, G. Kawakami's tour affected the company's product line and reputation for decades to come.

His return sparked research into new uses for materials since capital was scarce. The company researched uses for fiberglass reinforced plastics (FRP). In 1960 the company produced its first sailboat made of FRP. Later Yamaha expanded to produce yachts, patrol boats for Japan's Maritime Safety Agency, and oceangoing fishing vessels. Primarily serving the Asian market, the company eventually became Japan's largest FRP boat producer. FRP capability led to the introduction of other products, such as archery bows, skis, and bathtubs. Through metals research Nippon Gakki developed sophisticated alloys for electronics as well as less complex alloys for structural purposes. Nippon Gakki soon became a major producer of equipment for the household construction industry, such as boilers and central heating systems.

In its traditional line of pianos, Nippon Gakki expanded production, raised its quality standards, and cut production costs, already lower than the industry average, even further. Through a conveyer belt system and an innovative kiln drying technique that facilitated the rapid drying of wood used in pianos, Nippon Gakki decreased the amount of time required to produce a piano from two years to three months.

The first large-scale marketing drive toward the United States was not related to music at all. In 1954 the government returned the company's World War II–era metal working factory, which had been among confiscated assets. Nippon Gakki produced its first motorcycle in 1955 and established the Yamaha Motor Company Ltd., of which it was partial owner. Later it produced smaller motorized vehicles such as snowmobiles, outboard engines, and golf carts. For the next 20 years, however, it was motorcycles for which the West would recognize the Yamaha brand. Following Honda's lead, Yamaha introduced its first motorcycles in the United States in the early 1960s. Along with Suzuki, the three companies made smaller and lower-priced motorcycles and greatly expanded the U.S. market, which had been limited to large cycles for serious enthusiasts. Yamaha also marketed its motorcycles successfully in Asia.

Nippon Gakki began an ambitious drive into electronics in 1959, when it introduced the world's first all-transistor organ to replace electronic organs using vacuum tubes. Nippon Gakki's first electronic instrument represented the company's new competence in product development.

With its new variety of products Nippon Gakki began its first serious export push, establishing an overseas subsidiary in Mexico in 1958. In 1959 the company made a few pianos with a U.S. retailer's name on them, and in 1960 it created its own sales subsidiary in Los Angeles. Within a year Yamaha won a conspicuous contract to supply the Los Angeles Board of Education with 53 grand pianos. For the next seven years, the board annually purchased Yamaha pianos for schools in its jurisdiction. Since Nippon Gakki priced its pianos considerably lower than Western competition, this boost to its reputation for quality allowed it to bid with more success on U.S. institutional contracts.

Having worked well in Japan, Nippon Gakki sponsored overseas musical events and education beginning in 1964, when it opened the first Yamaha school in the United States. Like its Japanese counterpart, it was designed to teach music appreciation to students at an early age and create a long-term market. Financially independent of Yamaha, these nonprofit schools eventually operated throughout Europe and the United States and taught scores of students.

These educational efforts were just beginning to pay off in Japan. During the 1960s Nippon Gakki's domestic market grew tremendously. Annual piano output increased from 24,000 in 1960 to 100,000 in 1966, making the company the world's largest piano maker.

In the mid-1960s, Nippon Gakki began to produce wind instruments on a large scale. In 1968 Nippon Gakki started exporting trumpets, trombones, and xylophones. After five years in development, the company produced is first concert grand piano in 1967.

U.S. instrument makers did not welcome Yamaha's growth. In 1969 U.S. piano manufacturers sought a 30 percent tariff on imported pianos, but the U.S. Tariff Commission ruled in Yamaha's favor. Nonetheless, the hearings delayed for three years a tariff reduction that had already been scheduled and established a hostile precedent for Nippon Gakki expansion in North America. In 1973 Yamaha bought its first U.S. manufacturing facility, but a strike there further delayed Yamaha's U.S. drive.

Electronics Developments in the 1970s

Just as transistors had once replaced tubes in electronics, integrated circuits (ICs) replaced transistors in the 1970s. Because no manufacturer would develop an IC for Nippon Gakki's relatively limited demand, the company built a plant in 1971 to make its own. By developing the technology early, Nippon Gakki established itself as a serious electronics firm, better able to serve the accelerating demand for electronic keyboards and audio components.

Large-scale integrated circuits (LSIs) allowed the company to digitalize its keyboards. Nippon Gakki built an LSI plant in 1976 so it could convert all of its electronic products from analog to digital formats. LSIs also made possible Yamaha's growth as an electronics supplier and the manufacture of advanced electronic systems such as industrial robots. Nippon Gakki developed electronic components more quickly than other types of components. In its traditional line of pianos and organs, by contrast, Nippon Gakki still depended on overseas suppliers for components in the 1970s. While Nippon Gakki's sales in 1979 remained steady, a favorable exchange rate boosted earnings to a record ¥15 billion. Nevertheless, the same exchange rate hurt motorcycle sales.

Overextension in the 1980s

The 1980s were a difficult decade for the company. While there were notable successes, Nippon Gakki was badly mismanaged in a case of imperial overreach. The company's first major blunder actually came from its affiliate, Yamaha Motor, which in 1981 unwisely tried to unseat Honda from its top position in motorcycles. Yamaha introduced new models and increased production. When Honda and other motorcycle manufacturers did the same, the industry faced overproduction. As a result Yamaha Motor posted two consecutive losses totaling $126.1 million. A relatively small motor manufacturer, Yamaha Motor was left with an inventory of one million motorcycles and debts that approached $1 billion. In addition, the price competition among Japanese motorcycle makers caused U.S. manufacturer Harley

Davidson to request tariffs on imports, straining Yamaha's U.S. business, since it did not have any U.S. factories. Nippon Gakki remained profitable since it owned only 39.1 percent of Yamaha Motor (later reduced to 33 percent), but the debacle damaged the company's reputation and position at home.

On the positive side, synthesizers and LSIs brought the company success early in the decade. Electronics research paid off well with the 1983 introduction of the DX-7 digital synthesizer, which went on to become the best-selling synthesizer ever. The development of LSIs allowed Nippon Gakki to produce its first professional sound systems and to keep pace with the consumer audio industry during the early 1980s. In 1983 the company put its LSIs themselves on the market.

Also in the early 1980s, Nippon Gakki divided its research facilities to reflect its electronics emphasis. Research was then carried out by four sections: one on semiconductors and LSIs, a second for research applications to audiovisual equipment, a third on hall and theater acoustic design, and the fourth for products design.

While expanding its product line, Nippon Gakki also initiated a program to spread its manufacturing base overseas, adding to its network of marketing subsidiaries. Hiroshi Kawashima, former president of the U.S. subsidiary, spearheaded the U.S. drive. In 1980 Nippon Gakki opened an electronic keyboard plant in Georgia in the hope that basing this new venture in the United States would ease trade tension.

Further difficulties, however, were in store when Hiroshi, the third generation of Kawakamis, became the company's seventh president in 1983. His father, then chairman, reportedly distrusted Hiroshi and battles between the two helped lead the company astray. Hiroshi brought in outside consultants in end-runs around his father, but this only resulted in such unwise moves as building huge headquarters in London and Buena Park, California, which served simply as symbols of a global powerhouse that was not. The company also became notorious for moving ahead with ambitious projects after doing little, if any, market research. Before there was even the smallest market for it, for example, Nippon Gakki attempted to develop a multimedia computer in the early 1980s and, probably to the company's good fortune, failed. Another marketing miscalculation at the other end of the decade left Yamaha with 200,000 unsold wind instruments in 1990.

Such ventures might have been perceived as noble failures if it were not for the company's increasingly troubled finances. Throughout the 1980s, rising profitability became increasingly elusive. Hiroshi Kawakami's attempt at a reorganization from 1985 to 1987 had failed to turn the company around. Meanwhile, to celebrate the 100th anniversary of the firm, Kawakami changed the corporate name to Yamaha Corporation in 1987.

1990s and Beyond

Kawakami made another attempt to resurrect Yamaha but was thwarted by a demoralized and rebellious workforce. He reportedly had hoped to use early retirement as a means of reducing the company's number of employees, but the workers' labor union refused to go along with the plan and demanded that Kawakami be fired—and he was.

Taking over in 1992 was a 36-year Yamaha veteran with a marketing background, Seisuke Ueshima, who quickly moved to turn the company around. He demoted Kawakami cronies and brokered an agreement with the union that retained all nonmanagerial employees but led to the elimination of 30 percent of the administrative positions in Japan along with overseas employees (notably those in the London and Buena Park headquarters). Ueshima also downsized the noncore resorts and sporting goods operations, both of which were losing money.

For the longer term, Ueshima had to change the way new products were developed and marketed. Specifically, he wanted Yamaha employees to ask "Why are we building this product?," a question rarely raised during previous decades. In the face of the maturation of some markets, Ueshima decided to go after the high end of these markets where larger profits could be made. One example was the Disklavier series of pianos, originally introduced in 1982, with built-in computers for recording and playing back performances; individual Disklavier models could retail for more than $30,000.

Ueshima also pushed the company to develop innovative new products. In 1993 the Silent Piano series was introduced to great success. Costing $7,300 each, more than 17,000 were sold in Japan in their first 12 months on the market, 70 percent above the amount projected. These pianos could either be played as regular acoustic pianos or their sound could be muted and only heard by the pianist through headphones. In 1995, Yamaha introduced a similarly functional electronic trumpet mute and sold 13,000 of them in the first few months. Silent Drums followed in 1996, the Silent Violin in 1997, and the Silent Cello in 1998. Other successful musical introductions of this period included the VL1 and VP1 virtual acoustic synthesizers, which, rather than storing libraries of sounds that could be replayed, stored computer models of the instruments themselves which were then able to reproduce a wider variety of sounds and in a more authentic fashion.

Other innovations during this time included the Yamaha FM sound chip used in many sound boards—an essential feature of multimedia computers—and a karaoke system that received music via phone lines connected to a central computer loaded with laser disks. Such successes returned Yamaha to healthy profitability: ¥6.4 billion in 1994 and ¥28.5 billion in 1995. In June 1997 Kazukiyo Ishimura took over as president of Yamaha, having headed up the company's electronic parts unit, turning it into a ¥100 billion business. Yamaha went on to post solid results for the 1998 fiscal year: net income of ¥13.48 billion ($101.3 million) on revenues of ¥608.99 billion ($4.58 billion).

The end of the 20th century saw Yamaha make another change at the top, as Shuji Ito was named president. By this time, the company had fallen into the red once again as a result of the stagnant Japanese economy, the appreciation in the yen, and a dropoff in results in the company's electronic parts unit. For the fiscal year ending in March 2000, Yamaha posted a net loss of ¥40.78 billion ($384.2 million) on sales of ¥527.9 billion ($4.97 billion). Part of this loss was attributable to restructuring costs, including the company's withdrawal from the manufacturing of storage heads (electronic components that write on and read from hard disks), the sale of a semiconductor plant, an early retirement program that cut the workforce by 11 percent,

and additional restructuring efforts undertaken to turn around several underperforming businesses.

Seeking a quick return to profitability in the early 21st century, Ito aimed to further focus the company's efforts on the core musical instruments and audiovisual groups. Ito also sought to engender more cross-company cooperation by consolidating group management. Another new initiative was the Digital Media Business Strategy, which included a number of components, including an increased emphasis on equipment such as sound chips and digital content designed for mobile phones and other handheld devices; the formation of a new record company called Yamaha Music Communications Co., Ltd., with the eventual goal of offering online downloading of music content; and the development of network-enabled musical instruments and equipment.

Principal Subsidiaries

Yamaha Music Tokyo Co., Ltd.; Yamaha Music Nishitokyo Co., Ltd.; Yamaha Music Yokohama Co., Ltd.; Yamaha Music Kitakanto Co., Ltd.; Yamaha Music Higashikanto Co., Ltd.; Yamaha Music Niigata Co., Ltd.; Yamaha Music Osaka Co., Ltd.; Yamaha Music Kobe Co., Ltd.; Yamaha Music Okayama Co., Ltd.; Yamaha Music Matsuyama Co., Ltd.; Yamaha Music Nagoya Co., Ltd.; Yamaha Music Hamamatsu Co., Ltd.; Yamaha Music Kanazawa Co., Ltd.; Yamaha Music Kyushu Co., Ltd.; Yamaha Music Hokkaido Co., Ltd.; Yamaha Music Tohoku Co., Ltd.; Yamaha Music Hiroshima Co., Ltd.; Yamaha Music Trading Corporation; Yamaha Music Media Corporation; Yamaha Music Communications Co., Ltd.; Yamaha Sound Technologies Inc.; Yamaha Kagoshima Semiconductor Inc.; Yamaha Livingtec Corporation; Yamaha Living Products Corporation; Yamaha Resort Corporation; Kiroro Development Corporation; Haimurubushi Inc.; Yamaha Metanix Corporation; Yamaha Fine Technologies Co., Ltd.; Yamaha Credit Corporation; Yamaha Insurance Service Co., Ltd. THE AMERICAS: Yamaha Corporation of America (U.S.A.); Yamaha Exporting, Inc. (U.S.A.); Yamaha Electronics Corporation, U.S.A.; Yamaha Music Manufacturing, Inc. (U.S.A.); Yamaha Musical Products, Inc. (U.S.A.); Yamaha Canada Music Ltd.; Yamaha de México, S.A. de C.V.; Yamaha de Panamá, S.A. EUROPEAN REGION: Yamaha-Kemble Music (U.K.) Ltd.; Kemble & Company Ltd. (U.K.); Kemble Music Ltd. (U.K.); Yamaha Electronics (U.K.) Ltd.; Yamaha Europa G.m.b.H. (Germany); Yamaha Electronik Europa G.m.b.H. (Germany); Yamaha Musique France S.A.; Yamaha Electronique France S.A.; Yamaha Electronique Alsace S.A. (France); Yamaha Musica Italia s.p.a. (Italy); Yamaha-Hazen Musica S.A. (Spain); Yamaha Scandinavia A.B. (Sweden). ASIA, OCEANIA AND OTHER REGIONS: Tianjin Yamaha Electronic Musical Instruments, Inc. (China); Taiwan Yamaha Musical Instrument Mfg. Co., Ltd.; Yamaha KHS Music Co., Ltd. (Taiwan); Kaohsiung Yamaha Co., Ltd. (Taiwan); P.T. Yamaha Music Indonesia; P.T. Yamaha Indonesia; P.T. Yamaha Music Manufacturing Indonesia; P.T. Yamaha Musical Products Indonesia; P.T. Yamaha Manufacturing Asia; Yamaha Music (Asia) Pte. Ltd. (Singapore); Yamaha Systems Technology Singapore Pte. Ltd.; Yamaha Electronics Manufacturing (M) Sdn. Bhd. (Malaysia); Yamaha Music (Malaysia) Sdn. Bhd.; Yamaha Music Australia Pty., Ltd.

Principal Competitors

Allen Organ Company; Baldwin Piano & Organ Company; C.F. Martin & Company; Casio Computer Co., Ltd.; Fender Musical Instruments Corporation; Gibson Musical Instruments; Kaman Corporation; Kimball International, Inc.; Matsushita Electric Industrial Co., Ltd.; Roland Corporation; Sony Corporation; Steinway Musical Instruments, Inc.

Further Reading

Armstrong, Larry, "Sweet Music with Ominous Undertones for Yamaha," *Business Week,* November 15, 1993, pp. 119–20.

Henry, Lawrence, "Yamaha Stubs Its Imperial Toe," *Industry Week,* April 6, 1992, pp. 29–31.

Lieberman, Richard K., "The Ivory Poachers: Steinway & Sons Was the Incomparable Maker of the Grand Piano—Until Yamaha Came Along," *Financial Times,* August 9, 1997, p. 1.

Morris, Kathleen, "Play It Again, Seisuke," *Financial World,* November 22, 1994, pp. 42–46.

"Perfect Pitch?," *Economist,* February 17, 1996, p. 60.

Schlender, Brenton R., "The Perils of Losing Focus," *Fortune,* May 17, 1993, p. 100.

Yamaha: A Century of Excellence, 1887–1987, Hamamatsu, Japan: Yamaha Corporation, 1987.

"Yamaha's First Century," *Music Trades,* August 1987.

—Ray Walsh
—update: David E. Salamie

Young Broadcasting Inc.

599 Lexington Avenue
New York, New York 10022
U.S.A.
Telephone: (212) 754-7070
Fax: (212) 758-1229

Public Company
Incorporated: 1986
Employees: 2,000
Sales: $280.65 million (1999)
Stock Exchanges: NASDAQ
Ticker Symbol: YBTVA
NAIC: 51312 Television Broadcasting

Young Broadcasting Inc. owns and operates 13 television stations and a television advertising sales firm, Adam Young Inc. Young Broadcasting's station properties include six affiliates of American Broadcasting Companies, Inc. (ABC), four affiliates of CBS Inc., and two affiliates of the National Broadcasting Company, Inc. (NBC). One of the company's stations, KCAL in Los Angeles, operates as an independent station. With the exception of KCAL and San Francisco's KRON, Young Broadcasting's television properties are located in smaller markets. The company's stations include: WTEN in Albany, New York; WRIC in Richmond, Virginia; WATE in Knoxville, Tennessee; WBAY in Green Bay, Wisconsin; KWQC in Davenport, Iowa; WLNS in Lansing, Michigan; KELO in Sioux Falls, South Dakota; KLFY in Lafayette, Louisiana; WKBT in La Crosse, Wisconsin; and WTVO in Rockford, Illinois.

Origins

Father and son Adam and Vincent Young spent 15 years working together in the television industry before starting Young Broadcasting. In 1944, Adam Young formed his own company, Adam Young Inc., and began representing television stations to advertisers, selling airtime on the behalf of broadcasters. His son Vincent joined him in 1971, one year after Vincent had completed his studies at Southhampton College. The pair worked well together, selling airtime primarily for television stations serving the country's smaller markets In 1980, Adam Young appointed his son president, but after several years Vincent began to pine for a more ambitious undertaking. Instead of assisting broadcasters in the operation of their businesses, he wanted to run his own stations. In 1986, he convinced his father to branch out into television station ownership, prompting the formation of a second company, Young Broadcasting.

The Youngs borrowed heavily to acquire their first two television stations, completing the purchases in September 1986. Both stations, WLNS and WKBT, were acquired from Backe Communications Inc., and both were CBS affiliates. WLNS, based in Lansing, Michigan, began operating in 1950. WKBT, located in La Crosse, Wisconsin, began operating in 1954. The Youngs added to their assets two years later with another CBS affiliate, acquiring KLFY, a Lafayette, Louisiana, station in May 1988. Acquired from Texoma Broadcasters, Inc., KLFY was the first television station in the Lafayette area, commencing operations in 1954. In September 1988, Young Broadcasting acquired Winnebago Television Corporation, giving the company an NBC affiliate, WTVO, located in Rockford, Illinois. The Youngs concluded the 1980s by adding to their burgeoning portfolio of properties, completing two more acquisitions in 1989. In June, WKRN, a Nashville, Tennessee, station was acquired from Knight-Ridder Broadcasting, Inc. Knight-Ridder Broadcasting sold Young Broadcasting its sixth station in October 1989, an Albany, New York, station with the call letters WTEN. Both WTEN and WKRN were affiliated with ABC.

Entering the 1990s, Young Broadcasting was supported by six stations, each, with the exception of Nashville-based WKRN, located in small markets. The company had spent approximately $245 million to acquire the six stations, incurring considerable debt to do so, which proved to be a troublesome drag on finances. By 1992, the six stations were generating roughly $30 million a year in cash flow, but were weighed down by $200 million in long-term debt. Vincent Young had paid dearly for his entry into station ownership, purchasing the stations at a time when market prices were high. Consequently, the company found itself facing an uncertain financial future during the early 1990s, unable to demonstrate acceptable profitability because of its substantial

Key Dates:

1986: Young Broadcasting is formed; company acquires two CBS television affiliates, WLNS and WKBT.
1988: CBS affiliate KLFY and NBC affiliate WTVO are acquired.
1989: Two ABC affiliates, WTEN and WKRN, are acquired.
1992: A deal to acquire five television stations is scuttled.
1994: Young Broadcasting debuts as a publicly traded company.
1996: Los Angeles-based independent station KCAL is acquired for $368 million.
2000: KRON, an NBC affiliate based in San Francisco, is acquired for $737 million.

interest payments. To relieve the mounting financial pressures, Young devised a bold plan, one that caused a stir among industry observers. Not for the last time during the 1990s, Young Broadcasting was the object of debate and controversy, as the business press attempted to decipher the ambitious moves made by Vincent Young.

In May 1992, when Young Broadcasting's annual revenues totaled $70 million, the company announced an agreement to pay approximately $400 million in cash for five television stations owned by Houston-based H&C Communications. The stations, each network affiliates, served markets in Houston, Daytona Beach-Orlando, Tucson, Des Moines, and San Antonio, generating combined annual revenues of $130 million. Once completed, Young Broadcasting would rank as the 17th largest television station group owner in the country, covering 6.1 percent of the nation's television audience.

The acquisition, which would nearly triple the size of Young Broadcasting in terms of revenues, represented a mammoth deal for a financially strapped company, prompting analysts to wonder where Young would obtain the money to complete the deal. Young announced he planned to raise $100 million in a private equity placement, obtain $225 million in new bank debt, and gain the remaining $75 million in new junk debt. His plan hinged on borrowing heavily against the new stations, but Young was willing to take on further debt to ease the company's cash flow problems. Compared to the late 1980s, the market prices for stations in the early 1990s were relatively low, enabling Young to dilute the high prices he had paid earlier by combining his six stations with the five owned by H&C Communications. As Young was cobbling together the financial means to complete the acquisition, however, the deal began to unravel. In June 1992, three of the company's subordinated debt holders attempted to force Young Broadcasting into involuntary Chapter 11 bankruptcy. The company had failed to make payment on $7 million in interest and principal, which forced negotiations between Young Broadcasting and H&C Communications to stall. In the end, the deal collapsed, but Young would strike again and draw more national attention to his company.

Young shied away from the acquisition front for two years after the failure of the H&C Communications acquisition. He brokered his next deal the same month he completed an initial public offering of stock in November 1994, when Young Broadcasting debuted at $19 per share. The conversion to public ownership helped raise the capital for Young to add to his stable of television stations, leading to the acquisition of three stations from Nationwide Communications, Inc. WRIC, serving the Richmond, Virginia, market, joined the Young Broadcasting fold, as did another ABC affiliate, WATE, which served the Knoxville, Tennessee, market. The third station, WBAY, was an ABC affiliate as well, serving the Green Bay, Wisconsin, market.

1996 Acquisition of KCAL

With nine stations to its name, Young Broadcasting generated $122 million in revenues in 1995, but the company continued to lose money. A substantial amount of the cash flow generated by the stations was consumed by the company's burdensome debt service, which hamstrung Young's efforts to produce a profit. The massive debt taken on by the company, which totaled roughly $400 million by June 1996, did not spoil Young's appetite for further acquisitions, however. He struck again in April 1996, acquiring NBC affiliate KWQC, located in Davenport, Iowa, from Broad Street Television. The following month, the company acquired the CBS affiliate KELO in Sioux Falls, South Dakota. Both acquisitions paled against Young's third acquisition of the year, a mammoth deal that by far outstripped any acquisition made during the company's first decade of existence. Once the transaction was concluded, Young Broadcasting's annual revenues nearly doubled.

The acquisition prompted *Forbes* to refer to Young as "a crapshooter" in the magazine's July 15, 1996 issue. One broadcasting analyst remarked, "Young is betting the ranch," in the August 19, 1996 issue of *Broadcasting & Cable,* referring to the deal that again drew national attention toward Young. The television station in question was KCAL, owned by Walt Disney Company. Serving the Los Angeles market, KCAL was one of the few viable major-market independent stations in the nation, a valuable prize that attracted a host of suitors after Disney announced it was divesting the property. To the surprise of many industry observers, Young entered into the auction for KCAL, engaging in a bidding war that he ultimately won. Young outbid rivals such as Granite Broadcasting, Argyle Communications, and a group of investors led by basketball star Magic Johnson, agreeing to pay $368 million for the independent station.

The acquisition of KCAL represented a major move on Young's part, adding the largest independent station in the second largest television market in terms of population. In the wake of the acquisition, which was completed in December 1996, Young was forced to restructure KCAL. The station had been used by Disney to display the entertainment company's sports and promotion efforts, which required an extravagant budget. "The way Disney ran the station and the way any of the groups that were bidding would run it are very different," Young explained in a May 20, 1996 interview with *MEDIAWEEK.* "They [Disney] were building their image," he added, "spending so many millions of dollars on things like promotion, that there are significant savings just from cutting costs on a line-by-line basis." Young planned to reduce the station's annual expenses by $21 million and to renegotiate programming contracts for an additional savings of nearly $12 million, but there was no escaping the considerable cost of the acquisition. Much of the money required to complete the purchase was borrowed, lifting the company's debt load to more than $650 million as it entered the late 1990s.

Young's penchant for deal-making took a different twist not long after the purchase of KCAL was completed. In 1998, the company was put up for sale, offered at an estimated price of $1.9 billion. By September 1998, however, the prospect of a sale had been formally quashed. In the aftermath of a downturn suffered by the country's financial markets, the company took itself off the auction block, citing deteriorating market conditions as the reason for withdrawing from the sale. Young Broadcasting's chief financial officer announced that management believed any buyer would face extreme difficulty arranging the financing to complete the deal, but industry analysts offered another reason. Most of the bidders, the pundits claimed, had withdrawn their interest before the market downturn, citing instead the substantial costs required to make KCAL a competitive and profitable station. Although Young Broadcasting had canceled plans for its sale, the company exited 1998 exploring other strategic alternatives, including a possible merger with another television company.

KRON Acquisition: 2000

For Young Broadcasting, the 1990s ended with another spectacular transaction concluded on the acquisition front. In December 1999, Young eclipsed the bravado of the KCAL acquisition by winning the auction for KRON, the NBC affiliate in San Francisco. Young paid $737 million for the station, winning a bidding war against NBC that soon erupted into a contentious battle of wills. After losing the auction, NBC demanded Young Broadcasting pay a $10 million annual fee to maintain its affiliation with the network. Young refused, which meant KRON was scheduled to become an independent station when its contract with NBC expired on December 31, 2001. Young Broadcasting's stock plunged 45 percent after NBC announced it was handing its network affiliation to San Jose-based KNTV, but Young and his management team remained unruffled. Industry observers speculated that Young was interested in selling the company, a supposition that Young himself promoted. "As this industry may continue to consolidate, it's nice having the prettiest girls at the dance," Young said in a February 12, 2001 interview with *Electronic Media,* referring to KCAL and KRON.

As Young Broadcasting entered the 21st century, the fate of the company was a topic of considerable debate. Much of the attention focused on KRON's expected new role as an indepen-

dent and on the station's need to replace the network programming it had relied on for years. There was a possibility that the relationship between KRON and NBC could be restored, a prospect that Young hinted at. The larger question about the company's future centered on Young's repeated claims that he was willing to sell the company. Analysts in early 2001 were expecting such a move, but no one could accurately predict what Young's next deal might be.

Principal Subsidiaries

Young Broadcasting of Louisiana, Inc.; Young Broadcasting of Lansing, Inc.; Young Broadcasting of La Crosse, Inc.; Young Broadcasting of Albany, Inc.; Young Broadcasting of Nashville, Inc.; Young Broadcasting of Green Bay, Inc.; Young Broadcasting of Knoxville, Inc.; Young Broadcasting of Richmond, Inc.; Young Broadcasting of Davenport, Inc.; Young Broadcasting of Sioux Falls, Inc.; Young Broadcasting of Rapid City, Inc.; Young Broadcasting of Los Angeles, Inc.; YBT, Inc.; LAT, Inc.; YBK, Inc.; Fidelity Television, Inc.; WKRN, G.P.; KLFY, L.P.; WATE, G.P.; Adam Young Inc.

Principal Competitors

Sinclair Broadcast Group, Inc.; Hubbard Broadcasting Inc.; Hearst-Argyle Television, Inc.; Granite Broadcasting Corporation.

Further Reading

Chatzky, Jean Sherman, "Betting the Company," *Forbes,* August 3, 1992, p. 82.

Foisie, Geoffrey, "Young Proposes Five-Station Buy," *Broadcasting,* May 25, 1992, p. 5.

Gimein, Mark, "L.A.'s Newest Player," *MEDIAWEEK,* May 20, 1996, p. 12.

Grego, Melissa, "Young Looks at the Bright Side," *Broadcasting & Cable,* February 21, 2000, p. 12.

Lacter, Mark, "The Lone Warrior," *Forbes,* February 19, 2001, p. 109.

McClellan, Steve, "Young Takes Down 'For Sale' Sign," *Broadcasting & Cable,* September 14, 1998, p. 12.

——, "Young's High-Stakes Bid for KCAL; Company Chairman Puts It All on Line to Finance," *Broadcasting & Cable,* August 19, 1996, p. 37.

Mermigas, Diane, "Young Broadcasting Looks Restless to Sell," *Electronic Media,* February 12, 2001, p. 3.

Rudnitsky, Howard, "Pushing the Envelope," *Forbes,* July 15, 1996, p. 74.

"Young Hopes to Raise $165 Million," *Broadcasting & Cable,* September 23, 1996, p. 34.

—Jeffrey L. Covell

Zale Corporation

901 West Walnut Hill Lane
Irving, Texas 75038-1003
U.S.A.
Telephone: (972) 580-4000
Fax: (972) 580-5523
Web site: http://www.zalecorp.com

Public Company
Incorporated: 1924
Employees: 13,000
Sales: $1.79 billion (2000)
Stock Exchanges: New York
Ticker Symbol: ZLC
NAIC: 448310 Jewelry Stores

Zale Corporation is the largest operator of retail jewelry stores in the United States. Zale operates more than 2,300 retail locations—stores and mall kiosks—located in all 50 states, as well as in Puerto Rico and Canada. Covering the full range of consumer markets, Zale stores operate within several distinct divisions: Zales Jewelers, with about 750 stores across the United States and in Puerto Rico, focuses on mainstream, middle-income consumers, specializes heavily in diamonds, and has extensions in the form of two other divisions, Zales Outlet and the online shopping site zales.com; Gordon's Jewelers is positioned as a regional retailer for the upper-middle-income and fashion-conscious consumer, with more than 300 stores operating under the Gordon's name; Bailey Banks & Biddle Fine Jewelers, with about 120 locations, is the company's upscale chain; and Peoples Jewellers, the company's Canadian arm, has about 170 stores, including Peoples Jewellers, the Canadian equivalent of Zales, and Mappins Jewelers, which aims for the upper moderate slice of the market, similar to Gordon's. Piercing Pagoda, another company division, is the largest kiosk-based retailer of gold jewelry in the United States, with more than 940 locations throughout the country offering popular-priced merchandise, mainly for teens. Overall, wedding-related jewelry regularly accounts for between 35 and 40 percent of annual revenues at Zale Corporation.

Early Growth

Morris B. Zale, born in Russia but raised in Texas, opened his first jewelry store in Wichita Falls, Texas, in 1924. Two years later, Zale opened a second Texas store and was joined by childhood friend, and brother-in-law, Ben Lipshy. From the beginning, Zale stores offered credit, with payments typically spread out over 12 months, even to its low-income customers. It leased its first locations, a practice that placed pressure on the company, grown to three stores at the beginning of the 1930s, when the company was stuck with long-term leases fixed at high, pre-Depression rents. Despite the Depression, however, the company continued to expand through the decade, opening a fourth store in Amarillo in 1934, and growing to 12 locations in Texas and Oklahoma by 1941. In that year, the company's revenues had risen to $2.73 million. Zale avoided building long-term debt by paying modest salaries and dividends to himself, Lipshy, and other family members joining the company; instead, earnings were reinvested in the company.

The years of World War II limited Zale's expansion of new locations but not its revenue growth. The devotion of raw materials to the war effort during this period led to a scarcity of most consumer items; jewelry, with limited strategic value, drew consumer interest. By 1944, Zale's revenues had doubled, to over $5 million. In that year, Zale acquired a 13th store, Corrigan's in Houston, which allowed it to move into higher-end jewelry. Two years later, revenues doubled again, passing $10 million for the year. By then, Zale had begun to operate as a big company, rather than as a collection of stores. In 1942, Zale opened a buying office in New York, which allowed the company to purchase diamonds and watches in quantity at wholesale prices. As the company grew to 19 stores in 1946, Zale set up a central design, display, and printing operation in Dallas to service its chain. The company's next step toward centralization of its operations came when it opened its own shops for building store fixtures and constructing store interiors. Company headquarters were also moved to Dallas in 1946.

The postwar boom in consumer spending brought a new period of growth to Zale, which added more than 50 stores between 1947 and 1957, the year in which the company went public. That offering, of 125,000 shares, raised $1.5 million,

470

which, according to *Fortune* magazine, "appear[ed] to have been the only new money put into the company since it was started." Listed on the American Stock Exchange in 1958, the company operated 102 stores, primarily under the Zale trade name. Much of this growth came through the acquisition of existing stores; stores marketing to high-end consumers generally kept their original names. Diamonds formed the largest part of company sales, with diamond rings, other diamond jewelry, and diamond watches providing about 38 percent of revenues; costume jewelry and watches added to sales, while the company also sold electric appliances, silverware, dinnerware, luggage, cameras, eyeglasses, and other items.

With sales topping $37 million in 1958, Zale moved closer to complete vertical integration of the company when it was invited to purchase its diamonds directly from the Central Selling Organization, otherwise known as the diamond syndicate. Based in London and representing a group of diamond producers including De Beers of South Africa, the diamond syndicate represented more than 80 percent of the world's supply of rough diamonds. The syndicate controlled not only the world's diamond output but also the choice of companies allowed to purchase its diamonds, and which diamonds a company was allowed to purchase. Zale, because of its integrated operations, including cutting, polishing, and setting operations in New York, and its ability to market the full scale of diamonds from the smallest to the largest, most expensive diamonds, became the only U.S. jewelry retailer invited to purchase directly from the syndicate.

Branching Out and Buckling Under

By the mid-1960s, Zale operated the nation's—and the world's—largest retail jewelry chain. Its 403 stores produced $81 million in 1963, with a net income of nearly $5 million. Diamonds continued to represent the largest share of Zale's sales, about $27 million. Operating manufacturing plants in New York, Tel Aviv, and Puerto Rico, the company also operated a wholesale division, selling to other jewelry retailers. Zale also made and sold watches under its own Baylor's label, buying mechanisms from Switzerland. The company in 1962 had also bought Bailey Banks & Biddle, a high-end jewelry retailer based in Philadelphia that was founded in 1832.

By 1965, Zale found itself with a surplus of cash. Its business was tied up in its jewelry store operations, and the development of the first synthetic diamonds, at the time viewed as a potential replacement for real diamonds in the retail jewelry trade, frightened the company into diversifying its product base. The company decided to move into the broader retailing field, purchasing the Texas-based Skillern drugstore chain. This acquisition was followed by forays into budget fashion apparel,

sporting goods, shoes, furniture, and a chain of airport-based tobacco and newsstand concessions. By 1974, in addition to 956 retail jewelry stores, Zale had grown to include 351 shoe stores, 83 drugstores, 146 clothing stores, 25 sporting goods stores, 13 home furnishings stores, and 13 tobacco/newsstand concessions. Together, these divisions produced revenues nearing $600 million; half of the company's revenues, however, continued to come from its jewelry operations—with one highlight coming from the 1969 purchase of the Light of Peace diamond for $1.4 million—which also contributed three-quarters of the company's more than $30 million in 1974 profits.

Trouble began to brew for Zale in the mid-1970s. Charges that the company's chief financial officer had been embezzling funds—the CFO was eventually acquitted—led to investigations from the Internal Revenue Service and other government agencies into alleged misappropriation of funds, including avoiding some $27 million in federal tax payments. These investigations would culminate in a $78 million tax charge brought by the IRS against Zale in 1982, and contributed to the replacement of Ben Lipshy, president of the company since 1957 and chairman of the board since 1971, by M.B. Zale's son, Donald Zale, as chairman in 1980. By then, Zale's more than 1,400 stores included international operations in the United Kingdom, Switzerland, France, West Germany, Canada, and South Africa.

At the beginning of the decade, Zale abruptly began selling off its non-jewelry retail operations. Despite raising revenues, which topped $1 billion in 1980, these operations produced little of the company's profits. By then, also, the synthetic diamond scare had passed—these found industrial applications, but could not be successfully developed for retail sales, partly because of consumer insistence on purchasing real diamonds. In the space of a few weeks at the end of 1980, Zale sold off the Skillern chain to Revco, Inc. for $60 million; its 37-store sporting goods chain went to Oshman's Sporting Goods, Inc. for $14 million; and its Butler Shoe division, with 385 stores, went to Sears for $100 million. Except for its newsstand/tobacco concessions, which would grow to 90 stores, and its O.G. Wilson catalog showroom division, the company had come back to its core jewelry business.

Jewelry sales slumped across the industry during the recession of the early 1980s. Worse, gold and diamond values, which had traditionally seen steady appreciation, began to fluctuate wildly. Zale saw revenues fall to $939 million in 1982. Profits slipped more drastically, from $33 million in 1981 to a loss of $6 million in 1982, the result, in part, of a $10.6 million charge brought on by the company's settlement with the IRS for its 1970s tax liabilities. The collapse of the oil industry in the Southwest, where the highest concentration of Zale stores were located, also hurt the company's sales. The company struggled to maintain its share of the jewelry market, while facing increasing competition from department stores. Zale, which had perennially relied on sales of wedding rings for its chief source of revenues, had fallen behind the times—particularly with the decline in marriages since the 1970s. Meanwhile, it saw customers departing for the larger assortments of jewelry, and especially gold jewelry, available elsewhere.

Part of Zale's troubles were blamed on the lingering influence of its old management, which had been manufacturing-oriented,

Key Dates:

1924: Morris B. Zale opens his first jewelry store in Wichita Falls, Texas.

1944: Acquisition of Corrigan's marks move into higher-end jewelry.

1957: Company goes public.

1962: Bailey Banks & Biddle is acquired.

1965: Diversification begins with the purchase of the Skillern drugstore chain.

1974: In addition to jewelry stores, the company is also operating shoe stores, drugstores, clothing stores, sporting goods stores, home furnishings stores, and tobacco newsstands.

1980: Most of the non-jewelry retail operations are divested.

1986: Company disposes of its European retail operations and the remainder of its non-jewelry divisions; business is acquired by Peoples Jewellers of Canada.

1989: Zale acquires Gordon Jewelry Corporation, number two U.S. retail jewelry chain.

1992: Company files for Chapter 11 bankruptcy protection.

1993: Zale emerges from bankruptcy independent, with debt under control and 700 fewer stores.

1994: Robert DiNicola is hired as chairman and CEO and leads a turnaround.

1998: All of Zale's upscale chains are converted to the Bailey Banks & Biddle banner; the first Zales Outlet stores are opened.

1999: Peoples Jewellers, the leading Canadian jewelry chain, is acquired.

2000: Piercing Pagoda, Inc., operator of kiosk-based jewelry outlets, is acquired.

rather than marketing-oriented, allowing further inroads into the jewelry market by retailers more responsive to trends in consumer demands. Breaking the hold of former management, who were still largely loyal to M.B. Zale, would take several years and eventually a relocation of the company's headquarters. Zale struggled to recover from the recession, but sales in its 1,500 stores barely budged, remaining around $1 billion.

The Peoples' Takeover, Mid-to-Late 1980s

In 1986, the company posted a net loss of over $60 million, including a restructuring charge of about $80 million as it disposed of its European retail operations, and the last of its non-jewelry divisions, and a $50 million write-down of old inventory. By that time, Zale had already rejected an attempt at a takeover by Peoples Jewellers of Canada. Peoples, led by Irving Gerstein, was looking to expand beyond its Canadian base. That company already owned 15 percent of Zale's stock, purchased for $70 million in 1980. When Zale's problems rose in the early 1980s, Peoples attempted to sell its stock back to Zale, but Zale refused to buy.

Critical of Zale's efforts to turn the company around, Gerstein became determined to take over the company. Under Texas law, however, Peoples needed approval from at least two-thirds of Zale's stockholders to complete a takeover, and the Zale family controlled more than one-third of the stock.

In early 1986, Peoples, aided by Drexel Burnham Lambert, made offers of $420 million and $470 million to take over the company. The Zale family refused to sell. Gerstein next met with the Swarovski company, makers of crystal and jewelry, which agreed to back Peoples in its next takeover effort. Later in 1986, Gerstein constructed lending arrangements that allowed him to tender an offer of $50 per share of Zale stock—nearly double its trading price. The Zale family, under pressure from its own investment company, at last gave in and agreed to sell the company. By the end of that year, Peoples and Swarovski, each with 50 percent ownership, took Zale private.

Gerstein moved quickly to settle some of the company's debt, selling some $700 million in junk bonds, leaving the company about $900 million in debt. His next step was to close Zale's New York and Puerto Rico manufacturing operations—instead turning to vendors for store stock. He also sold off the company's diamond inventory and reduced the company's large advertising budget. With expenses reduced by $80 million, the company's net earnings rose, allowing Gerstein to declare a $5 million dividend to both Peoples and Swarovski. In 1989 the company acquired Gordon Jewelry Corporation, the nation's second largest retail jewelry chain. Three years later, Zale verged on collapse.

Early to Mid-1990s: Bankruptcy and a Sharp Turnaround

At the beginning of the 1990s, Zale, including the Gordon's chain, had grown to 2,000 stores, with revenues of $1.3 billion. But the international recession of the 1990s, the economic uncertainty produced by the Persian Gulf War, and a new luxury tax on purchases over $10,000 quickly took their toll on jewelry sales. In 1990 Zale posted a $64 million loss. The following year's losses amounted to over $106 million in the first six months alone. By the end of the year, the company was unable to make a $52 million interest payment on its $850 million in debt.

Zale attempted to restructure the company, announcing the closing of 400 stores and a reduction of its headquarters, but its creditors began threatening to force the company into bankruptcy. By the end of January 1992, Zale joined the growing list of failing jewelry companies and petitioned for voluntary bankruptcy.

When Zale emerged from Chapter 11 in 1993 as an independent, publicly traded company (Peoples also went into bankruptcy and lost control of Zale), its debt was settled and it had 700 fewer stores. In April 1994 former Macy's executive Robert DiNicola was hired as chairman and CEO to lead the company back to profitability. The new management team worked to restructure the company, creating separate and independent divisions of the Zales and Gordon's stores. Zales was repositioned as the McDonald's of jewelry retail, with national ads promoting chainwide, standardized merchandise. Gordon's was positioned as more of a regional player, with its product line tailored for the local market; it also aimed for customers slightly more affluent than Zales' middle-class customers, placing Gordon's between Zales and the company's upmarket chains, such as Bailey Banks & Biddle. In all three chains, the merchandising practices were overhauled through a "key item" approach in which each format's bestselling products were given special prominence. The key products were promoted heavily in advertising, and each store began keeping a generous supply of the items to make sure customers could always find them in stock. DiNicola also brought to Zale a newfound focus on tying promotions to the various gift-giving and high-traffic holiday periods that occur throughout the year, rather than depending so heavily on the November-December shopping season, as had been company tradition. At the same time, Zale began spending millions of dollars remodeling stores and also opened new outlets and closed additional underperforming units. During 1995, for example, the company opened 35 units, closed 85, and remodeled 150.

While the overall number of store units was remaining fairly constant in the mid-1990s as the restructuring unfolded, the Zales chain was being steadily expanded. The number of Zales outlets grew from 521 in 1994 to 642 in 1997. The latter year saw Zale initiate additional changes to its lineup of formats. The company's Diamond Park Fine Jewelers division, which at the time operated 186 leased jewelry shops within such department stores as Parisian and Marshall Field's, was sold to Finlay Enterprises, Inc. for about $63 million. Zale also announced late in 1997 that it would convert all of its upscale chains, including Corrigan's, to Bailey Banks & Biddle Jewelers in the spring of 1998. Following this move, Zale had three national jewelry chains positioned in three different segments of the market. It could begin expanding Bailey Banks & Biddle backed by national advertising and promotion.

By 1998 Zale appeared to be fully recovered from its fall into bankruptcy. Revenues that year hit $1.43 billion, a 43 percent increase over the $920 million figure of 1994. Net income during the same period nearly tripled, from $23 million to $63 million. Perhaps even more importantly, for the first time in the company's history Zale posted profits in all four quarters of the 1998 fiscal year; historically, Zale had made all of its profits in the second quarter, which included the November-December shopping season. Another important statistic, sales per store, was also increasing smartly, growing from $770 million in 1994 to $1.17 billion in 1998. At the end of 1998, there were 701 Zales stores, 317 Gordon's, and 107 Bailey Banks & Biddle outlets.

Late 1990s and Beyond: Expanding Aggressively, Then a Setback

Zale's improved financial health provided additional opportunities for expansion beyond the opening of new stores. The company had entered the direct selling business in 1996 when it produced its first sales catalog, then followed up with the launch of zale.com (later relaunched as zales.com) as its Internet shopping site. In 1998 a new division called Zales Outlet was formed, and ten Zales Outlet stores were soon opened throughout the country to pursue sale growth through the burgeoning outlet mall channel. Zale envisioned that there was long-term potential for between 150 and 200 outlet locations nationwide.

The company also felt confident enough about its future to complete two major acquisitions. In June 1999 Zale spent about $75.3 million to acquire Peoples Jewellers Corp., the same firm that had so disastrously acquired Zale in 1986. Peoples had gone through its own period of bankruptcy, and at the time of the acquisition was the leading Canadian jewelry retailer, with 176 stores. Most of these were Peoples Jewellers outlets, which were essentially the Canadian equivalent of the Zales chain, with a couple of dozen or so Mappins Jewelers stores, which were similar to Gordon's. In September 2000 Zale acquired Piercing Pagoda, Inc. for about $260 million. This company's outlets, most of which were mall kiosks operating under the Piercing Pagoda name, catered primarily to teens and offered low-priced gold jewelry—including chains, charms, bracelets, rings, and earrings—and a selection of silver and diamond jewelry. One of the firm's marketing tactics was to offer free ear piercing with the purchase of earrings. Because the typical Piercing Pagoda customer was unlikely to shop at a Zales or any of Zale Corporation's other outlets, Zale saw this acquisition as a way to further expand its presence in malls without cannibalizing existing sales.

In between the two acquisitions, a number of other significant events occurred. In September 1999 Beryl B. Raff was promoted to president and CEO of Zale, with DiNicola remaining chairman. Raff had worked with DiNicola at Macy's and was hired in 1994 by DiNicola from Macy's, where she had been the department store's top jewelry executive. In July 2000 Zale sold its private label credit card operation to Associates First Capital Corporation for about $542 million. By doing so, Zale eliminated its exposure to bad consumer debt, an increasing problem in the late 1990s and into the 21st century as personal bankruptcies were increasing steadily. As part of the deal, Associates agreed to continue to operate Zale's credit card business as a third party. Zale used proceeds from the deal to pay down debt and help fund the acquisition of Piercing Pagoda. Just prior to the completion of the Piercing Pagoda deal, DiNicola retired as chairman of Zale, having shepherded the company to its strong position at the end of the 2000 fiscal year, when the company reported record net income of $112 million on record revenues of $1.79 billion. Zale ended the calendar year 2000 with 2,372 outlets, including 827 Zales, 309 Gordon's, 119 Bailey Banks & Biddle, 171 Peoples Jewellers/Mappins Jewelers, and 946 of the Piercing Pagoda locations. With DiNicola's retirement, Raff became CEO and chairman.

Raff's stay at the top proved short-lived, however, as Zale began suffering from disappointing sales during the 2000 holiday shopping season, when the company reported a 3.1 percent decrease in comparable store sales. Raff resigned in February 2001, and DiNicola, who had remained on the board of directors, became chairman and CEO once again. In the weakening business climate, Zale had $150 million in overstock merchandise and had failed to lower its capital expenditures to match the economic situation. This was particularly true in the company's Internet operation, which generated less than $10 million per year but was the subject of an ambitious expansion under Raff, an expansion halted once DiNicola was back in charge. DiNicola began getting the company's inventory under control, writing off $25 million in the second quarter of fiscal 2001, and took a more conservative approach to the business in keeping with the uncertain state of the economy during the first half of 2001. DiNicola also overhauled the company's team of top managers as part of his effort to return Zale to the strong position of growth and profitability it had enjoyed in the late 1990s.

Principal Subsidiaries

Zale Delaware, Inc.; Zale Puerto Rico, Inc.; Dobbins Jewelers, Inc.; Jewelers Financial Services, Inc.; Zale Life Insurance Company; Zale Indemnity Company; Jewel Re-Insurance Ltd.; Zale Employees Child Care Association, Inc.; Jewelers Credit Corporation; Jewelers National Bank; Jewelry Expansion Corp.; Piercing Pagoda, Inc.; EARS, Inc.; PPIFLA, LLC; Zale International, Inc.; Zale Canada Company; Zale Canada Finance, Inc.

Principal Divisions

Zales Jewelers; Zales Outlet; Gordon's Jewelers; Bailey Banks & Biddle Fine Jewelers; Zale.com; Peoples Jewellers; Piercing Pagoda.

Principal Competitors

Signet Group plc; Wal-Mart Stores, Inc.; Tiffany & Co.; Helzberg Diamonds; J.C. Penney Company, Inc.; Finlay Enterprises, Inc.; Friedman's Inc.; Whitehall Jewellers, Inc.; Fred Meyer, Inc.; QVC Network Inc.; Service Merchandise Company, Inc.; Target Corporation; Kmart Corporation; Mayor's Jewelers, Inc.; Crescent Jewelers; Samuels Jewelers, Inc.; Reeds Jewelers, Inc.

Further Reading

Bancroft, Thomas, "Zale's Woes," *Forbes*, June 22, 1992, p. 46.

Beres, Glen A., "Zale Flexes Its Mall Muscle," *Jewelers Circular Keystone*, December 1997, pp. 60+.

"CEO Interview: Beryl Raff, Zale Corporation," *Wall Street Transcript*, April 10, 2000.

Feldman, Amy, "Shaking Things Up," *Forbes*, October 23, 1995, pp. 260+.

Gubernick, Lisa, "To Catch a Falling Star," *Forbes*, June 2, 1986, p. 71.

Halkias, Maria, "Associates Buys Zale's Credit Cards," *Dallas Morning News*, July 11, 2000, p. 13D.

——, "Former Zale CEO to Return," *Dallas Morning News*, February 13, 2001, p. 1D.

——, "Polishing a Gem in the Rough," *Dallas Morning News*, December 7, 1994, p. 1D.

——, "Zale, FTC Settle Advertising Dispute," *Dallas Morning News*, February 11, 1997, p. 4D.

——, "Zale Promotes President to CEO," *Dallas Morning News*, September 8, 1999, p. 2D.

——, "Zale Reports Lower Profits, Begins 'Rebuilding' Effort," *Dallas Morning News*, March 8, 2001.

——, "Zale to Acquire Peoples Jewellers," *Dallas Morning News*, March 17, 1999, p. 2D.

McDonald, John, "Diamonds for the Masses," *Fortune*, December, 1994, p. 134.

Mehlman, William, "Canadian Admirer Gets Cold Shoulder from Cash-Rich Zale," *Insiders' Chronicle*, February 2, 1981, p. 1.

Moin, David, "DiNicola: Zale Will Shine Again," *Women's Wear Daily*, March 8, 2001, pp. 8+.

——, "Once in Bankruptcy, Zale Outlines Program to Restore the Luster," *Women's Wear Daily*, June 15, 1998, pp. 1+.

——, "Taking Zale Further Down the Growth Trail," *Women's Wear Daily*, August 31, 2000, p. 15.

Reda, Susan, "Turnaround at Zale Highlights Resurgence of Jewelry Business," *Stores*, April 1997, pp. 62, 64.

Shuster, William George, "The New Zale: Focus on 'Basics' Brings Success," *Jewelers Circular Keystone*, March 1996, pp. 80–87.

——, "The Tale of Zale: A 75-Year Retrospective," *Jewelers Circular Keystone*, March 1999, pp. 148+.

——, "Zale Strategy: Return to Fundamentals," *Jewelers Circular Keystone*, September 1994, p. 140.

Weil, Jonathan, "Once-Fading Zale Has Polished Its Act and May Be Ready to Shine," *Wall Street Journal*, September 3, 1997, p. T2.

Wilson, Marianne, "Putting the Sparkle Back in Zale," *Chain Store Age*, January 1999, pp. 48–49.

Zimmerman, Amy, "Zale Chairwoman Raff Resigns; Retired DiNicola to Take Helm," *Wall Street Journal*, February 13, 2001, p. B8.

——, "Zale's Beryl Raff Is Named Chairman As DiNicola Retires amid Record Profit," *Wall Street Journal*, August 31, 2000, p. B2.

—M. L. Cohen
—update: David E. Salamie

INDEX TO COMPANIES

Index to Companies

Listings in this index are arranged in alphabetical order under the company name. Company names beginning with a letter or proper name such as Eli Lilly & Co. will be found under the first letter of the company name. Definite articles (The, Le, La) are ignored for alphabetical purposes as are forms of incorporation that precede the company name (AB, NV). Company names printed in bold type have full, historical essays on the page numbers appearing in bold. Updates to entries that appeared in earlier volumes are signified by the notation (**upd.**). Company names in light type are references within an essay to that company, not full historical essays. This index is cumulative with volume numbers printed in bold type.

Continental Bank Corporation, I 526; II **261–63**, 285, 289, 348; IV 702

Continental Bio-Clinical Laboratories, **26** 391

Continental Blacks Inc., I 403

Continental Cablevision, Inc., **7 98–100**; **17** 148; **19** 201

Continental Can Co., Inc., I 597; II 34, 414; III 471; **10** 130; **13** 255; **15 127–30**; **24** 428; **26** 117, 449; **32** 125

Continental-Caoutchouc und Gutta-Percha Compagnie, V 240

Continental Carbon Co., I 403–05; II 53; IV 401; **36** 146–48

Continental Care Group, **10** 252–53

Continental Casualty Co., III 196, 228–32; **16** 204

Continental Cities Corp., III 344

Continental Corporation, III 230, **239–44**, 273; **10** 561; **12** 318; **15** 30; **38** 142

Continental Cos., III 248

Continental Divide Insurance Co., III 214

Continental Electronics Corporation, **18** 513–14

Continental Emsco, I 490–91; **24** 305

Continental Equipment Company, **13** 225

Continental Express, **11** 299

Continental Fiber Drum, **8** 476

Continental Gas & Electric Corporation, **6** 511

Continental General Tire Corp., **23 140–42**

Continental Grain Company, **10 249–51**; **13 185–87 (upd.)**; **30** 353, 355; **40** 87

Continental Group Co., I **599–600**, 601–02, 604–05, 607–09, 612–13, 615; IV 334; **8** 175, 424; **17** 106

Continental Gummi-Werke Aktiengesellschaft, V 241; **9** 248

Continental Hair Products, Inc. See Conair Corp.

Continental Health Affiliates, **17** 307

Continental Homes, **26** 291

Continental Illinois Corp. See Continental Bank Corporation.

Continental Illinois Venture Co., IV 702

Continental Insurance Co., III 239–42, 372–73, 386

Continental Insurance Cos. of New York, III 230

Continental Investment Corporation, **9** 507; **12** 463; **22** 541; **33** 407

Continental Life Insurance Co., III 225

Continental Medical Systems, Inc., **10 252–54**; **11** 282; **14** 233; **25** 111; **33** 185

Continental Milling Company, **10** 250

Continental Motors Corp., I 199, 524–25; **10** 521–22

Continental Mutual Savings Bank, **17** 529

Continental National American Group, III 230, 404

Continental National Bank, II 261; **11** 119

Continental-National Group, III 230

Continental Oil Co., IV 39, 365, 382, 399–401, 476, 517, 575–76

Continental Packaging Inc., **13** 255

Continental Plastic Containers, Inc., **25** 512

Continental Radio, IV 607

Continental Reinsurance, **11** 533

Continental Research Corporation, **22** 541

Continental Restaurant Systems, **12** 510

Continental Risk Services, III 243

Continental Savouries, II 500

Continental Scale Works, **14** 229–30

Continental Securities Corporation, II 444; **22** 404

Continental Telephone Company, V 296–97; **9** 494–95; **11** 500; **15** 195

Continental Wood Preservers, Inc., **12** 397

Continentale Allgemeine, III 347

ContinueCare Corporation, **25** 41

Contran Corporation, **19** 467

Contrans Acquisitions, Inc., **14** 38

Contred Ltd., **20** 263

Control Data Corporation, **17** 49; **19** 110, 513–15; **25** 496; **30** 338; **38** 58

Control Data Systems, Inc., III 118, **126–28**, 129, 131, 149, 152, 165; **6** 228, 252, 266; **8** 117–18, 467; **10 255–57**, 359, 458–59; **11** 469; **16** 137

Controladora Comercial Mexicana, S.A. de C.V., **36 137–39**

Controladora PROSA, **18** 516, 518

Controlled Materials and Equipment Transportation, **29** 354

Controlonics Corporation, **13** 195

Controls Company of America, **9** 67

Controlware GmbH, **22** 53

Convair, I 82, 121, 123, 126, 131; II 33; **9** 18, 498; **13** 357

Convenient Food Mart Inc., **7** 114; **25** 125

Convergent Technologies, III 166; **6** 283; **11** 519

Converse Inc., III 528–29; V 376; **9 133–36**, 234; **12** 308; **31 134–138 (upd.)**, 211; **39** 170, 172–74

Conway Computer Group, **18** 370

Conwest Exploration Company Ltd., **16** 10, 12

Conycon. See Construcciones y Contratas.

Conzinc Riotinto of Australia. See CRA Limited.

Cook Bates Inc., **40** 347–48

Cook Data Services, Inc., **9** 73

Cook Industrial Coatings, I 307

Cook Standard Tool Co., **13** 369

Cook United, V 172

Cooke Engineering Company, **13** 194

The Cooker Restaurant Corporation, **20 159–61**

Cooking and Crafts Club, **13** 106

Cookson Group plc, III **679–82**; **16** 290

CoolBrands International Inc., **35 119–22**

Coolerator, I 463

Coolidge Mutual Savings Bank, **17** 529

Cooper Cameron Corporation, **20 162–66 (upd.)**

Cooper Canada Ltd., **16** 80

The Cooper Companies, Inc., **39 97–100**

Cooper Industries, Inc., II **14–17**; **14** 564; **19** 43, 45, 140; **30** 266

Cooper Laboratories, I 667, 682

Cooper LaserSonics Inc., IV 100

Cooper McDougall & Robertson Ltd., I 715

Cooper Tire & Rubber Company, **8 126–28**; **23 143–46 (upd.)**

Cooper-Weymouth, **10** 412

Cooper's, Inc., **12** 283

Cooperative Grange League Federation Exchange, **7** 17

Coopers & Lybrand, **9 137–38**; **12** 391; **25** 383. See also PricewaterhouseCoopers.

CooperVision, **7** 46; **25** 55

Coordinated Caribbean Transport. See Crowley Caribbean Transport.

Coors Company. See Adolph Coors Company.

Coorsh and Bittner, **7** 430

Coos Bay Lumber Co., IV 281; **9** 259

Coosa River Newsprint Co., III 40; **16** 303

Coote & Jurgenson, **14** 64

Cooymans, I 281

Copart Inc., **23 147–49**, 285, 287

Copeland Corp., II 20

Copeman Ridley, **13** 103

Copland Brewing Co., I 268; **25** 280

Copley Pharmaceuticals Inc., **13** 264

The Copley Press, Inc., **23 150–52**

Copley Real Estate Advisors, III 313

Copolymer Corporation, **9** 242

Copper Queen Consolidated Mining Co., IV 176–77

Copper Range Company, IV 76; **7** 281–82

Copperweld Steel Co., IV 108–09, 237

The Copps Corporation, **32 120–22**

Copycat Ltd., **8** 383

Cora Verlag, IV 590

Coral Drilling, I 570

Coral Leisure Group, I 248

Coral Petroleum, IV 395

Corange, Ltd., **37** 111–13

Corbett Canyon. See The Wine Group, Inc.

Corbett Enterprises Inc., **13** 270

Corbis Corporation, **31 139–42**

Corby Distilleries Limited, **14 140–42**

Corco. See Commonwealth Oil Refining Company.

Corco, Inc. See Liqui-Box Corporation.

Corcoran & Riggs. See Riggs National Corporation.

Cordiant plc. See Saatchi & Saatchi plc.

Cordis Corp., **19 103–05**; **36** 306

Cordon & Gotch, IV 619

Cordon Bleu, II 609

Cordovan Corp., IV 608

Core Laboratories Inc., I 486; **11** 265

Corel Corporation, **15 131–33**; **33 113–16 (upd.)**

CoreStates Financial Corp, **17 111–15**

CoreTek, Inc., **36** 353

Corfuerte S.A. de C.V., **23** 171

Corimon, **12** 218

Corinthian Broadcast Corporation, IV 605; **10** 4

Corinthian Colleges, Inc., **39 101–04**

Corio Inc., **38** 188, 432

Cormetech, III 685

Corn Exchange Bank, II 316

Corn Exchange Bank Trust Co., II 251; **14** 102

Corn Exchange National Bank, II 261

Corn Products Company. See Bestfoods.

Corn Sweeners Inc., I 421; **11** 23

Cornelia Insurance Agency. See Advantage Insurers, Inc.

Cornell Corrections, **28** 255

Cornerstone Direct Marketing, **8** 385–86

Cornerstone Propane Partners, L.P., **37** 280, 283

Cornerstone Title Company, **8** 461

Cornhill Insurance Co., I 429; III 185, 385

Cornhusker Casualty Co., III 213

Corning Asahi Video Products Co., III 667

Corning Clinical Laboratories, **26** 390–92

Corning Consumer Products Company, **27** 288

M. Polaner Inc., **10** 70; **40** 51–52
M-R Group plc, **31** 312–13
M. Samuel & Co., **II** 208
M. Sobol, Inc., **28** 12
M Stores Inc., **II** 664
M.T.G.I. Textile Manufacturers Group, **25** 121
M.W. Carr, **14** 245
M.W. Kellogg Co., **III** 470; **IV** 408, 534; **34** 81
M-Web Holdings Ltd., **31** 329–30
Ma. Ma-Macaroni Co., **II** 554
Maakauppiaitten Oy, **8** 293–94
Maakuntain Keskus-Pankki, **II** 303
MaasGlas, **III** 667
Maatschappij tot Exploitatie van de Onderneming Krasnapolsky. *See* Grand Hotel Krasnapolsky N.V.
Maatschappij tot Exploitatie van Steenfabrieken Udenhout, voorheen Weyers, **14** 249
MABAG Maschinen- und Apparatebau GmbH, **IV** 198
Mabley & Carew, **10** 282
Mac Frugal's Bargains - Closeouts Inc., 17 297–99
Mac Publications LLC, **25** 240
Mac Tools, **III** 628
MacAndrews & Forbes Holdings Inc., II 679; **III** 56; **9** 129; **11** 334; **28** 246–49; **30** 138; **38** 293–94
MacArthur Foundation. *See* The John D. and Catherine T. MacArthur Foundation.
Macau Telephone, **18** 114
Maccabees Life Insurance Co., **III** 350
MacCall Management, **19** 158
MacDermid Incorporated, 32 318–21
MacDonald Companies, **15** 87
MacDonald Dettwiler and Associates, **32** 436
MacDonald, Halsted, and Laybourne, **10** 127
Macdonald Hamilton & Co., **III** 522–23
Macey Furniture Co., **7** 493
Macfarlane Lang & Co., **II** 592–93
Macfield Inc., **12** 502
MacFrugal's Bargains Close-Outs Inc., **29** 312
MacGregor Sporting Goods Inc., **III** 443; **22** 115, 458; **23** 449
Mach Performance, Inc., **28** 147
Machine Vision International Inc., **10** 232
Macintosh. *See* Apple Computer, Inc.
Mack Trucks, Inc., I 147, **177–79**; **9** 416; **12** 90; **22 329–32 (upd.)**
MacKay-Shields Financial Corp., **III** 316
MacKenzie & Co., **II** 361
Mackenzie Hill, **IV** 724
Mackenzie Mann & Co. Limited, **6** 360
Mackey Airways, **I** 102
Mackie Designs Inc., 30 406; **33 278–81**
Mackinnon Mackenzie & Co., **III** 521–22
Maclaren Power and Paper Co., **IV** 165
Maclean Hunter Limited, III 65; **IV 638–40**, **22** 442; **23** 98
Maclean Hunter Publishing Limited, 26 270–74 (upd.); **30** 388
Maclin Co., **12** 127
The MacManus Group, **32** 140; **40** 140
MacMark Corp., **22** 459
MacMarr Stores, **II** 654
Macmillan & Co. Ltd., **35** 452

MacMillan Bloedel Limited, IV 165, 272, **306–09**, 721; **9** 391; **19** 444, 446; **25** 12; **26** 445
Macmillan, Inc., IV 637, 641–43; **7 284–86**, 311–12, 343; **9** 63; **12** 226; **13** 91, 93; **17** 399; **18** 329; **22** 441–42; **23** 350, 503; **25** 484; **27** 222–23
Macnaughton Blair, **III** 671
The MacNeal-Schwendler Corporation, 25 303–05
Macneill & Co., **III** 522
Macon Gas Company, **6** 447; **23** 28
Macon Kraft Co., **IV** 311; **11** 421; **19** 267
Maconochie Bros., **II** 569
Macrodata, **18** 87
Macwhyte Company, **27** 415
Macy's. *See* R.H. Macy & Co., Inc.
Macy's California, **21** 129
Mad Dog Athletics, **19** 385
Maddingley Brown Coal Pty Ltd., **IV** 249
Maddux Air Lines, **I** 125; **12** 487
Madge Networks N.V., 18 346; **26 275–77**
Madison & Sullivan, Inc., **10** 215
Madison Financial Corp., **16** 145
Madison Foods, **14** 557
Madison Furniture Industries, **14** 436
Madison Gas and Electric Company, 6 605–06; **39 259–62**
Madison Resources, Inc., **13** 502
Madison Square Garden, **I** 452
MAEFORT Hungarian Air Transport Joint Stock Company, **24** 310
Maersk Lines, **22** 167
Maes Group Breweries, **II** 475
Maeva Group, **6** 206
Mafco Holdings, Inc., **28** 248; **38** 293–95
Magasins Armand Thiéry et Sigrand, **V** 11; **19** 308
Magazine and Book Services, **13** 48
Magazins Réal Stores, **II** 651
Magcobar, **III** 472
MagCorp, **28** 198
Magdeburg Insurance Group, **III** 377
Magdeburger Versicherungsgruppe, **III** 377
Magee Company, **31** 435–36
Magellan Corporation, **22** 403
Magic Chef Co., **III** 573; **8** 298; **22** 349
Magic City Food Products Company. *See* Golden Enterprises, Inc.
Magic Marker, **29** 372
Magic Pan, **II** 559–60; **12** 410
Magic Pantry Foods, **10** 382
Magicsilk, Inc., **22** 133
MagicSoft Inc., **10** 557
Magirus, **IV** 126
Maglificio di Ponzano Veneto dei Fratelli Benetton. *See* Benetton.
Magma Copper Company, 7 287–90, 385–87; **22** 107
Magma Power Company, 11 270–72
Magna Computer Corporation, **12** 149; **13** 97
Magnaflux, **III** 519; **22** 282
Magnavox Co., **13** 398; **19** 393
Magne Corp., **IV** 160
Magnesium Metal Co., **IV** 118
Magnet Cove Barium Corp., **III** 472
MagneTek, Inc., 15 287–89
Magnetic Controls Company, **10** 18
Magnetic Peripherals Inc., **19** 513–14
Magnivision, **22** 35
Magnolia Petroleum Co., **III** 497; **IV** 82, 464

Magnus Co., **I** 331; **13** 197
La Magona d'Italia, **IV** 228
Magor Railcar Co., **I** 170
MAGroup Inc., **11** 123
Magyar Viscosa, **37** 428
Mahalo Air, **22** 252; **24** 22
Maharam Fabric, **8** 455
Mahir, **I** 37
Mahou, **II** 474
Mai Nap Rt, **IV** 652; **7** 392
MAI PLC, **28** 504
MAI Systems Corporation, 10 242; **11 273–76**; **26** 497, 499
Maidenform Worldwide Inc., 20 352–55
Mail Boxes Etc., 18 315–17; **25** 500. *See also* U.S. Office Products Company.
Mail.com Inc., **38** 271
Mail-Well, Inc., 25 184; **28 250–52**
Mailson Ferreira da Nobrega, **II** 200
Mailtek, Inc., **18** 518
MAIN. *See* Mid-American Interpool Network.
Main Event Management Corp., **III** 194
Main Plaza Corporation, **25** 115
Main Street Advertising USA, **IV** 597
Maine Central Railroad Company, 16 348–50
Mainline Industrial Distributors, Inc., **13** 79
Mainline Travel, **I** 114
Maison Blanche Department Stores Group, **35** 129
Maison Bouygues, **I** 563
Maison de Schreiber and Aronson, **25** 283
Maison de Valérie, **19** 309
Maison Louis Jadot, 24 307–09
Maizuru Heavy Industries, **III** 514
Majestic Contractors Ltd., **8** 419–20
Majestic Wine Warehouses Ltd., **II** 656
Major League Baseball, **12** 457
Major Video Concepts, **6** 410
Major Video, Inc., **9** 74
MaK Maschinenbau GmbH, **IV** 88
Mak van Waay, **11** 453
Makepeace Preserving Co., **25** 365
Makhteshim Chemical Works Ltd., **II** 47; **25** 266–67
Makita Corporation, III 436; **20** 66; **22 333–35**
Makiyama, **I** 363
Makovsky & Company, **12** 394
Makro Inc., **18** 286
Malama Pacific Corporation, **9** 276
Malapai Resources, **6** 546
Malayan Breweries, **I** 256
Malayan Motor and General Underwriters, **III** 201
Malaysia LNG, **IV** 518–19
Malaysian Airlines System Berhad, 6 71, **100–02**, 117, 415; **29 300–03 (upd.)**
Malaysian International Shipping Co., **IV** 518
Malaysian Sheet Glass, **III** 715
Malbak Ltd., **IV** 92–93
Malcolm's Diary & Time-Table, **III** 256
Malcus Industri, **III** 624
Malden Mills Industries, Inc., 16 351–53
Malév Plc, 24 310–12; **27** 474; **29** 17
Malheur Cooperative Electric Association, **12** 265
Malibu, **25** 141
Mall.com, **38** 271
Mallard Bay Drilling, Inc., **28** 347–48
Malleable Iron Works, **II** 34

McKee Foods Corporation, **7** 320–21; **27** 309–11 (upd.)
McKenna Metals Company, **13** 295–96
McKesson Corporation, **I** 413, **496–98**, 713; **II** 652; **III** 10; **6** 279; **8** 464; **9** 532; **11** 91; **12 331–33** (upd.); **16** 43; **18** 97; **37** 10
McKesson General Medical, **29** 299
McKinsey & Company, Inc., **I** 108, 144, 437, 497; **III** 47, 85, 670; **9 343–45**; **10** 175; **13** 138; **18** 68; **25** 34, 317; **26** 161
McLain Grocery, **II** 625
McLane America, Inc., **29** 481
McLane Company, Inc., **V** 217; **8** 556; **13 332–34**; **36** 269
McLaren Consolidated Cone Corp., **II** 543; **7** 366
McLaughlin Motor Company of Canada, **I** 171; **10** 325
McLean Clinic, **11** 379
McLeodUSA Incorporated, **32 327–30**; **38** 192
McLouth Steel Products, **13** 158
MCM Electronics, **9** 420
McMahan's Furniture Co., **14** 236
McMan Oil and Gas Co., **IV** 369
McManus, John & Adams, Inc., **6** 21
McMoCo, **IV** 82–83; **7** 187
McMoRan, **IV** 81–83; **V** 739; **7** 185, 187
McMullen & Yee Publishing, **22** 442
McMurtry Manufacturing, **8** 553
MCN Corporation, **6 519–22**; **13** 416; **17** 21–23
McNeil Corporation, **26** 363
McNeil Laboratories, **III** 35–36; **8** 282–83
McNellan Resources Inc., **IV** 76
MCO Holdings Inc., **8** 348–49
MCorp, **10** 134; **11** 122
McPaper AG, **29** 152
McQuay International. *See* AAF-McQuay Incorporated.
McRae's, Inc., **19** 324–25
MCS, Inc., **10** 412
MCT Dairies, Inc., **18** 14–16
McTeigue & Co., **14** 502
McVitie & Price, **II** 592–93
McWhorter Inc., **8** 553; **27** 280
MD Distribution Inc., **15** 139
MD Pharmaceuticals, **III** 10
MDC. *See* Mead Data Central, Inc.
MDI Co., Ltd., **IV** 327
MDS/Bankmark, **10** 247
MDU Resources Group, Inc., **7 322–25**
The Mead Corporation, **IV 310–13**, 327, 329, 342–43; **8** 267; **9** 261; **10** 406; **11** 421–22; **17** 399; **19 265–69** (upd.); **20** 18; **33** 263, 265
Mead Cycle Co., **IV** 660
Mead Data Central, Inc., **IV** 312; **7** 581; **10 406–08**; **19** 268. *See also* LEXIS-NEXIS Group.
Mead John & Co., **19** 103
Mead Johnson, **III** 17
Mead Packaging, **12** 151
Meade County Rural Electric Cooperative Corporation, **11** 37
Meadow Gold Dairies, Inc., **II** 473
Meadowcraft, Inc., **29 313–15**
Means Services, Inc., **II** 607
Mears & Phillips, **II** 237
Measurex Corporation, **8** 243; **14** 56; **38** 227
Mebetoys, **25** 312
MEC - Hawaii, UK & USA, **IV** 714

MECA Software, Inc., **18** 363
Mecair, S.p.A., **17** 147
Mecca Leisure PLC, **I** 248; **12** 229; **32** 243
Mechanics Exchange Savings Bank, **9** 173
Mechanics Machine Co., **III** 438; **14** 63
Mecklermedia Corporation, **24 328–30**; **26** 441; **27** 360, 362
Medal Distributing Co., **9** 542
Medallion Pictures Corp., **9** 320
Medar, Inc., **17** 310–11
Medco Containment Services Inc., **9 346–48**; **11** 291; **12** 333
Medcom Inc., **I** 628
Medeco Security Locks, Inc., **10** 350
Medfield Corp., **III** 87
Medford, Inc., **19** 467–68
Medi Mart Drug Store Company. *See* The Stop & Shop Companies, Inc.
Media Exchange International, **25** 509
Media General, Inc., **III** 214; **7 326–28**; **18** 61; **23** 225; **38 306–09** (upd.)
Media Groep West B.V., **23** 271
Media News Corporation, **25** 507
Media Play. *See* Musicland Stores Corporation.
Mediacom Inc., **25** 373
Mediamark Research, **28** 501, 504
Mediamatics, Inc., **26** 329
MediaOne Group Inc. *See* U S West, Inc.
MEDIC Computer Systems, **16** 94
Medical Care America, Inc., **15** 112, 114; **35** 215–17
Medical Development Corp. *See* Cordis Corp.
Medical Development Services, Inc., **25** 307
Medical Economics Data, **23** 211
Medical Expense Fund, **III** 245
Medical Indemnity of America, **10** 160
Medical Innovations Corporation, **21** 46
Medical Marketing Group Inc., **9** 348
Medical Service Assoc. of Pennsylvania, **III** 325–26
Medical Tribune Group, **IV** 591; **20** 53
Medicare-Glaser, **17** 167
Medicine Bow Coal Company, **7** 33–34
Medicine Shoppe International. *See* Cardinal Health, Inc.
Medicor, Inc., **36** 496
Medicus Intercon International, **6** 22
Medifinancial Solutions, Inc., **18** 370
MedImmune, Inc., **35 286–89**
Medinol Ltd., **37** 39
Mediobanca Banca di Credito Finanziario SpA, **II** 191, 271; **III** 208–09; **11** 205
The Mediplex Group, Inc., **III** 16; **11** 282
Medis Health and Pharmaceuticals Services Inc., **II** 653
Medite Corporation, **19** 467–68
Meditrust, **11 281–83**
Medlabs Inc., **III** 73
MedPartners, **36** 367
Medtech, Ltd., **13** 60–62
Medtronic, Inc., **8 351–54**; **11** 459; **18** 421; **19** 103; **22** 359–61; **26** 132; **30** **313–17** (upd.); **37** 39
Medusa Corporation, **8** 135; **24 331–33**; **30** 156
Mees & Hope, **II** 184
The MEGA Life and Health Insurance Co., **33** 418–20
MEGA Natural Gas Company, **11** 28
Megafoods Stores Inc., **13 335–37**; **17** 560

Megasource, Inc., **16** 94
Meggitt PLC, **34 273–76**
MEI Diversified Inc., **18** 455
Mei Foo Investments Ltd., **IV** 718; **38** 319
Meier & Frank Co., **23 345–47**
Meijer Incorporated, **7 329–31**; **15** 449; **17** 302; **27 312–15** (upd.)
Meiji Commerce Bank, **II** 291
Meiji Fire Insurance Co., **III** 384–85
Meiji Milk Products Company, Limited, **II 538–39**
Meiji Mutual Life Insurance Company, **II** 323; **III 288–89**
Meiji Seika Kaisha, Ltd., **I** 676; **II 540–41**
Meikosha Co., **II** 72
Meinecke Muffler Company, **III** 495; **10** 415
Meineke Discount Muffler Shops, **38** 208
Meis of Illiana, **10** 282
Meisei Electric, **III** 742
Meisel. *See* Samuel Meisel & Co.
Meisenzahl Auto Parts, Inc., **24** 205
Meissner, Ackermann & Co., **IV** 463; **7** 351
Meister, Lucious and Company, **13** 262
Meiwa Manufacturing Co., **III** 758
N.V. Mekog, **IV** 531
Mel Farr Automotive Group, **20 368–70**
Mel Klein and Partners, **III** 74
Melaleuca Inc., **31 326–28**
Melamine Chemicals, Inc., **27 316–18**
Melbourne Engineering Co., **23** 83
Melbur China Clay Co., **III** 690
Melco, **II** 58
Meldisco. *See* Footstar, Incorporated.
Melkunie-Holland, **II** 575
Mellbank Security Co., **II** 316
Mello Smello. *See* The Miner Group International.
Mellon Bank Corporation, **I** 67–68, 584; **II 315–17**, 342, 402; **III** 275; **9** 470; **13** 410–11; **18** 112
Mellon Indemnity Corp., **III** 258–59; **24** 177
Mellon-Stuart Co., **I 584–85**; **14** 334
Melmarkets, **24** 462
Mélotte, **III** 418
Meloy Laboratories, Inc., **11** 333
Melroe Company, **8** 115–16; **34** 46
Melville Corporation, **V 136–38**; **9** 192; **13** 82, 329–30; **14** 426; **15** 252–53;, **16** 390; **19** 449; **21** 526; **23** 176; **24** 167, 290; **35** 253
Melvin Simon and Associates, Inc., **8 355–57**; **26** 262
Melwire Group, **III** 673
MEM, **37** 270–71
Memco, **12** 48
Memorex Corp., **III** 110, 166; **6** 282–83
The Men's Wearhouse, Inc., **17 312–15**; **21** 311
Menasco Manufacturing Co., **I** 435; **III** 415
Menasha Corporation, **8 358–61**
Menck, **8** 544
Mendelssohn & Co., **II** 241
Meneven, **IV** 508
Menka Gesellschaft, **IV** 150; **24** 357
The Mennen Company, **I** 19; **6** 26; **14** 122; **18** 69; **35** 113
Mental Health Programs Inc., **15** 122
The Mentholatum Company Inc., **IV** 722; **32 331–33**

INDEX TO INDUSTRIES

Index to Industries

CONGLOMERATES

CONSTRUCTION

CONTAINERS

DRUGS/PHARMACEUTICALS

ELECTRICAL & ELECTRONICS

ENGINEERING & MANAGEMENT SERVICES

ENTERTAINMENT & LEISURE

FINANCIAL SERVICES: BANKS

FINANCIAL SERVICES: NON-BANKS

FOOD PRODUCTS

HEALTH & PERSONAL CARE PRODUCTS

HEALTH CARE SERVICES

HOTELS

INFORMATION TECHNOLOGY

INSURANCE

LEGAL SERVICES

MANUFACTURING

PAPER & FORESTRY

PERSONAL SERVICES

REAL ESTATE

RUBBER & TIRE

TELECOMMUNICATIONS

Cablevision Systems Corporation, 30 (upd.)
The Canadian Broadcasting Corporation
   (CBC), 37
Canal Plus, 10; 34 (upd.)
CanWest Global Communications
   Corporation, 35
Capital Radio plc, 35
Carlton Communications plc, 15
Carolina Telephone and Telegraph
   Company, 10
CBS Corporation, 28 (upd.)
Centel Corporation, 6
Centennial Communications Corporation,
   39
Century Communications Corp., 10
Century Telephone Enterprises, Inc., 9
Chancellor Media Corporation, 24
Charter Communications, Inc., 33
Chris-Craft Industries, Inc., 9
Chrysalis Group plc, 40
Cincinnati Bell, Inc., 6
Citadel Communications Corporation, 35
Clear Channel Communications, Inc., 23
Comcast Corporation, 24 (upd.)
Comdial Corporation, 21
Commonwealth Telephone Enterprises,
   Inc., 25
Comsat Corporation, 23
Comverse Technology, Inc., 15
Cumulus Media Inc., 37
DDI Corporation, 7
Deutsche Bundespost TELEKOM, V
Dialogic Corporation, 18
Directorate General of
   Telecommunications, 7
DIRECTV, Inc., 38
DSC Communications Corporation, 12
EchoStar Communications Corporation, 35
ECI Telecom Ltd., 18
eircom plc, 31 (upd.)
Electric Lightwave, Inc., 37
Electromagnetic Sciences Inc., 21
EXCEL Communications Inc., 18
Executone Information Systems, Inc., 13
Fox Family Worldwide, Inc., 24
France Télécom Group, V; 21 (upd.)
Frontier Corp., 16
Gannett Co., Inc., 30 (upd.)
Gaylord Entertainment Company, 36 (upd.)
General DataComm Industries, Inc., 14
Geotek Communications Inc., 21
Getty Images, Inc., 31
Global Crossing Ltd., 32
Gray Communications Systems, Inc., 24
Groupe Vidéotron Ltée., 20
Grupo Televisa, S.A., 18
GTE Corporation, V; 15 (upd.)
Guthy-Renker Corporation, 32
GWR Group plc, 39
Havas, SA, 10
Hispanic Broadcasting Corporation, 35
Hong Kong Telecommunications Ltd., 6
Hubbard Broadcasting Inc., 24
Hughes Electronics Corporation, 25
IDB Communications Group, Inc., 11
IDT Corporation, 34
Illinois Bell Telephone Company, 14
Indiana Bell Telephone Company,
   Incorporated, 14
Infinity Broadcasting Corporation, 11
IXC Communications, Inc., 29
Jacor Communications, Inc., 23
Jones Intercable, 21
Koninklijke PTT Nederland NV, V
LCI International, Inc., 16
LDDS-Metro Communications, Inc., 8
LIN Broadcasting Corp., 9

Lincoln Telephone & Telegraph Company,
   14
LodgeNet Entertainment Corporation, 28
Mannesmann AG, 38 (upd.)
Martha Stewart Living Omnimedia, L.L.C.,
   24
MasTec, Inc., 19
McCaw Cellular Communications, Inc., 6
MCI Communications Corporation, V
MCI WorldCom, Inc., 27 (upd.)
McLeodUSA Incorporated, 32
Mercury Communications, Ltd., 7
Metromedia Companies, 14
Métropole Télévision, 33
MFS Communications Company, Inc., 11
Michigan Bell Telephone Co., 14
MIH Limited, 31
MITRE Corporation, 26
Mobile Telecommunications Technologies
   Corp., 18
Modern Times Group AB, 36
Multimedia, Inc., 11
National Broadcasting Company, Inc., 28
   (upd.)
NCR Corporation, 30 (upd.)
NetCom Systems AB, 26
Nevada Bell Telephone Company, 14
New Valley Corporation, 17
Nextel Communications, Inc., 27 (upd.)
Nippon Telegraph and Telephone
   Corporation, V
Norstan, Inc., 16
Nortel Networks Corporation, 36 (upd.)
Northern Telecom Limited, V
NYNEX Corporation, V
Octel Communications Corp., 14
Ohio Bell Telephone Company, 14
Olivetti S.p.A., 34 (upd.)
Österreichische Post- und
   Telegraphenverwaltung, V
Pacific Telecom, Inc., 6
Pacific Telesis Group, V
Paging Network Inc., 11
Paxson Communications Corporation, 33
PictureTel Corp., 10; 27 (upd.)
Posti- ja Telelaitos, 6
Qualcomm Inc., 20
QVC Network Inc., 9
Qwest Communications International, Inc.,
   37
Rochester Telephone Corporation, 6
Rogers Communications Inc., 30 (upd.)
Royal KPN N.V., 30
Saga Communications, Inc., 27
SBC Communications Inc., 32 (upd.)
Schweizerische Post-, Telefon- und
   Telegrafen-Betriebe, V
Scientific-Atlanta, Inc., 6
Sinclair Broadcast Group, Inc., 25
Società Finanziaria Telefonica per Azioni,
   V
Southern New England
   Telecommunications Corporation, 6
Southwestern Bell Corporation, V
Spelling Entertainment, 35 (upd.)
Sprint Communications Company, L.P., 9
StrataCom, Inc., 16
Swedish Telecom, V
SynOptics Communications, Inc., 10
Telecom Australia, 6
Telecom Eireann, 7
Telefonaktiebolaget LM Ericsson, V
Telefónica de España, S.A., V
Telefonos de Mexico S.A. de C.V., 14
Telephone and Data Systems, Inc., 9
Télévision Française 1, 23
Tellabs, Inc., 11; 40 (upd.)
The Titan Corporation, 36

TV Azteca, S.A. de C.V., 39
U.S. Satellite Broadcasting Company, Inc.,
   20
U S West, Inc., V; 25 (upd.)
U.S. Cellular Corporation, 31 (upd.)
United States Cellular Corporation, 9
United Telecommunications, Inc., V
United Video Satellite Group, 18
Vodafone Group PLC, 11; 36 (upd.)
The Walt Disney Company, 30 (upd.)
Watkins-Johnson Company, 15
Western Wireless Corporation, 36
Westwood One, Inc., 23
Williams Communications Group, Inc., 34
The Williams Companies, Inc., 31 (upd.)
Wisconsin Bell, Inc., 14
Young Broadcasting Inc., 40

TEXTILES & APPAREL

Abercrombie & Fitch Co., 35 (upd.)
Adidas AG, 14
adidas-Salomon AG, 33 (upd.)
Alba-Waldensian, Inc., 30
Albany International Corp., 8
Algo Group Inc., 24
American Safety Razor Company, 20
Amoskeag Company, 8
Angelica Corporation, 15
AR Accessories Group, Inc., 23
Aris Industries, Inc., 16
Authentic Fitness Corp., 20
Banana Republic, 25
Benetton Group S.p.A., 10
Bill Blass Ltd., 32
Birkenstock Footprint Sandals, Inc., 12
Blair Corporation, 25
Brazos Sportswear, Inc., 23
Brooks Brothers Inc., 22
Brooks Sports Inc., 32
Brown Group, Inc., V; 20 (upd.)
Bugle Boy Industries, Inc., 18
Burberrys Ltd., 17
Burlington Industries, Inc., V; 17 (upd.)
Calcot Ltd., 33
Calvin Klein, Inc., 22
Candie's, Inc., 31
Canstar Sports Inc., 16
Carhartt, Inc., 30
Cato Corporation, 14
Chargeurs International, 21 (upd.)
Charming Shoppes, Inc., 8
Cherokee Inc., 18
Chic by H.I.S, Inc., 20
Chorus Line Corporation, 30
Christian Dior S.A., 19
Claire's Stores, Inc., 17
Coach Leatherware, 10
Coats Viyella Plc, V
Collins & Aikman Corporation, 13
Columbia Sportswear Company, 19
Concord Fabrics, Inc., 16
Cone Mills Corporation, 8
Converse Inc., 31 (upd.)
Courtaulds plc, V; 17 (upd.)
Crown Crafts, Inc., 16
Crystal Brands, Inc., 9
Culp, Inc., 29
Cygne Designs, Inc., 25
Dan River Inc., 35
Danskin, Inc., 12
Deckers Outdoor Corporation, 22
Delta Woodside Industries, Inc., 8; 30
   (upd.)
Designer Holdings Ltd., 20
The Dixie Group, Inc., 20
Dominion Textile Inc., 12
Donna Karan Company, 15

WASTE SERVICES

GEOGRAPHIC INDEX

Geographic Index

NOTES ON CONTRIBUTORS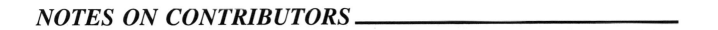

Notes on Contributors

BAXTER, Melissa Rigney. Indiana-based freelance writer.

BISCONTINI, Tracey Vasil. Pennsylvania-based freelance writer, editor, and columnist.

COHEN, M. L. Novelist and freelance writer living in Paris.

COVELL, Jeffrey L. Freelance writer and corporate history contractor.

CULLIGAN, Susan B. Minnesota-based freelance writer.

DINGER, Ed. Freelance writer and editor based in Brooklyn, New York.

HALASZ, Robert. Former editor in chief of *World Progress* and *Funk & Wagnalls New Encyclopedia Yearbook*; author, *The U.S. Marines* (Millbrook Press, 1993).

INGRAM, Frederick C. South Carolina-based business writer who has contributed to *GSA Business, Appalachian Trailway News,* the *Encyclopedia of Business,* the *Encyclopedia of Global Industries,* the *Encyclopedia of Consumer Brands,* and other regional and trade publications.

MEYER, Stephen. Freelance writer living in Missoula, Montana.

MOZZONE, Terri. Minneapolis-based freelance writer specializing in corporate profiles.

ROTHBURD, Carrie. Freelance writer and editor specializing in corporate profiles, academic texts, and academic journal articles.

SALAMIE, David E. Part-owner of InfoWorks Development Group, a reference publication development and editorial services company.

STANFEL, Rebecca. Freelance writer living in Helena, Montana.

UHLE, Frank. Ann Arbor-based freelance writer; movie projectionist, disc jockey, and staff member of *Psychotronic Video* magazine.

WALDEN, David M. Freelance writer and historian in Salt Lake City; adjunct history instructor at Salt Lake City Community College.

WOODWARD, A. Freelance writer.

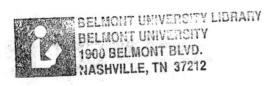